Webster's
Concise Dictionary
& Synonym Guide

Webster's Concise Dictionary & Synonym Guide

Created in Cooperation with the Editors of Merriam-Webster

FEDERAL
STREET
PRESS

A Division of Merriam-Webster, Incorporated
Springfield, Massachusetts

This 2001 edition published by
Federal Street Press
A Division of Merriam-Webster, Incorporated
P.O. Box 281
Springfield, MA 01102

Federal Street Press books are available for bulk purchase for
sales promotion and premium use. For details write the manager
of special sales, Federal Street Press, P.O. Box 281, Springfield,
MA 01102.

ISBN 1-892859-28-9

Printed in the United States of America
12345QPB0504030201

Contents

Contents

DICTIONARY

Preface

Webster's Concise Dictionary & Synonym Guide is a succinct reference to those words which form the very core of the English vocabulary. The Dictionary section is intended to serve as a quick reference, especially for questions of spelling, pronunciation, and hyphenation of the most common words in everyday use.

This dictionary shares many details of presentation with larger dictionaries. However, conciseness of presentation necessarily requires special treatment of entries, and this book has a number of special features uniquely its own. Users need to be familiar with the following major features of this dictionary.

Main entries follow one another in alphabetical order. Centered periods within the entries show points at which a hyphen may be put when the word is broken at the end of a line.

Homographs (words spelled the same but having different meanings) are run into a single main entry when they are closely related. Second and succeeding homographs are represented by a swung dash: ~. Homographs of distinctly different origin (as **¹date** and **²date**) are given separate entries with preceding raised numerals.

Variant spellings that are quite common appear at the main entry following a comma (as **judg·ment, judge·ment**) and following other boldface entry words, such as inflected forms and run-on entries.

Inflected forms of nouns, verbs, adjectives, and adverbs are shown when they are irregular—as when requiring the dropping of a final *e* or changing a final *y* to *i* before the suffix: (as **waged; wag·ing** at **wage**) or when the form of the base word itself changes: (as **rode . . . ; ridden** at **ride**)—or when there might be doubt about their spelling: (as *pl* **egos** at **ego**). They are given either in full (as **better . . . ; best** at **good**) or cut back to a convenient point of division (as **-ut·ed; -ut·ing** at **dis·trib·ute**). Common variants of inflected forms are shown even if they are regular (as **burst** *or* **burst·ed** at **burst**). When the inflected forms of a verb involve no irregularity except the doubling of a final consonant, the double consonant is shown instead of full or cutback inflected forms (as *vb* **-gg-** at **lug**). A variant or inflected form whose alphabetical place is distant from the main entry is entered at its own place with a cross-reference in small capital letters to the main entry (as **hung** *past of* HANG).

Several other kinds of entries are also found in this dictionary. A **run-in entry** is a term related to a main entry that appears within a definition (as **small intestine** at **in·tes·tine**). It is set off by parentheses. Derivative words, made up usually of the main entry and a common word element, such as a suffix, are shown as **undefined run-on entries** following all definitions of a main entry. These are set off by a dash (as —**gar·den·er** at **gar·den**). The meaning of the undefined run-on entry can be inferred from the meaning of the main entry where it appears and that of the added word element, shown elsewhere in the book. A **run-on phrase** is a group of two or more words having the main entry as a major element and having a special meaning of its own (as **in force** at **force** or **look after** at **look**). Run-on phrases are always defined.

Lists of undefined words formed by the addition of a common English prefix to a word entered in the dictionary and having meanings that can be inferred from the meaning of the root word and that of the prefix will be found at entries for the following prefixes: *anti-, bi-, co-, counter-, extra-, hyper-, in-, inter-, mini-, multi-, non-, over-, post-, pre-, re-, self-, sub-, super-, un-,* and *vice-*.

Pronunciation information is either given explicitly or implied for every entry in the dictionary. Pronunciation respellings are placed within reversed slanted lines (as \jē′ämətrē\ at **ge·om·e·try**). Where the pronunciation is not indicated at a particular entry, or is indicated in a cutback form, the full pronunciation is to be inferred from an earlier indicated pronunciation. A full list of the pronunciation symbols used is shown on the page following this Preface.

The grammatical function of entry words is indicated by an italic **functional label** (as *vb, n,* or *prefix*).

Hyphens that are a fixed part of hyphenated compounds (such as *self-conscious*) are converted to a special "double hyphen" when the compound appears in lightface type and that hyphen comes at the end of a line in this dictionary. This indicates to you that the hyphen is to be retained when the word is not at the end of a line. Fixed hyphens in boldface entry words are shown as short boldface dashes, which are a bit larger than ordinary hyphens. These short dashes or long hyphens in bold-face words are retained at the end of a line in this dictionary.

Guide words are used at the top of pages to indicate the range of entries on those pages. In choosing guide words for a page, we select the alphabetically first and last spelled-out bold-face words or phrases on that page. This means that any boldface entry—main entry, variant spelling, inflected form, run-in or run-on entry—can be used as a guide word. Please keep this in mind if the word used as a guide word does not happen to be the first or last main entry on the page. The guide words themselves are in alphabetical order throughout the book, so occasionally it has been necessary to modify this rule. When the alphabeti-cally last entry on one page would come later than the alphabet-ically first entry on the following page, a different word is chosen as guide word. On pages that contain a substantial num-ber of undefined words following a prefix entry, that prefix may be used as the first or last guide word.

All **abbreviations** used in this book are listed, along with a number of other common abbreviations, in a special section immediately following the dictionary proper. This Abbrevia-tions section is followed in turn by a brief **Handbook of Style** discussing and illustrating the chief points of English punctua-tion, italicization, capitalization, and the formation of plurals.

Pronunciation Symbols

ə	banana, collide, abut; raised \ᵊ\ in \ᵊl\, \ᵊn\ as in battle, cotton, in \lᵊ, mᵊ, rᵊ\ as in French table, prisme, titre	œ	French bœuf, German Hölle
ˈə, ˌə	humbug, abut	œ̄	French feu, German Höhle
ər	operation, further	ȯi	toy, sawing
a	map, patch	p	pepper, lip
ā	day, fate	r	rarity
ä	bother, cot, father	s	source, less
ȧ	father as pronounced by those who do not rhyme it with *bother*	sh	shy, mission
		t	tie, attack
		th	thin, ether
		th̲	then, either
aů	now, out	ü	boot, few \ˈfyü\
b	baby, rib	ů	put, pure \ˈpyůr\
ch	chin, catch	ue	German füllen
d	did, adder	ūe	French rue, German fühlen
e	set, red	v	vivid, give
ē	beat, nosebleed, easy	w	we, away
f	fifty, cuff	y	yard, cue \ˈkyü\; raised \ʸ\ indicates that a preceding \l\, \n\, or \w\ is modified by the placing of the tongue tip against the lower front teeth, as in French *digne* \dēnʸ\
g	go, big		
h	hat, ahead		
hw	whale		
i	tip, banish		
ī	site, buy		
j	job, edge	z	zone, raise
k	kin, cook	zh	vision, pleasure
k̲	German ich, Buch	\	slant line used in pairs to mark the beginning and end of a transcription
l	lily, cool		
m	murmur, dim		
n	nine, own; raised \ⁿ\ indicates that a preceding vowel or diphthong is pronounced through both nose and mouth, as in French *bon* \bōⁿ\	ˈ	mark at the beginning of a syllable that has primary (strongest) stress: \ˈpenmən,ship\
		ˌ	mark at the beginning of a syllable that has secondary (next-strongest) stress: \ˈpenmən,ship\
ŋ	sing, singer, finger, ink		
ō	bone, hollow		
ȯ	saw, cork		

A

¹a \'ā\ *n, pl* **a's** *or* **as** \'āz\ : 1st letter of the alphabet

²a \ə, 'ā\ *indefinite article* : one or some—used to indicate an unspecified or unidentified individual

aard·vark \'ärd,värk\ *n* : ant-eating African mammal

aback \ə'bak\ *adv* : by surprise

aba·cus \'abəkəs\ *n, pl* **aba·ci** \'abə,sī, -,kē\ *or* **aba·cus·es** : calculating instrument using rows of beads

abaft \ə'baft\ *adv* : toward or at the stern

ab·a·lo·ne \,abə'lōnē\ *n* : large edible shellfish

¹aban·don \ə'bandən\ *vb* : give up without intent to reclaim —**aban·don·ment** *n*

²abandon *n* : thorough yielding to impulses

aban·doned \ə'bandənd\ *adj* : morally unrestrained

abase \ə'bās\ *vb* **abased; abas·ing** : lower in dignity —**abase·ment** *n*

abash \ə'bash\ *vb* : embarrass —**abash·ment** *n*

abate \ə'bāt\ *vb* **abat·ed; abat·ing** : decrease or lessen

abate·ment \ə'bātmənt\ *n* : tax reduction

ab·at·toir \'abə,twär\ *n* : slaughterhouse

ab·bess \'abəs\ *n* : head of a convent

ab·bey \'abē\ *n, pl* **-beys** : monastery or convent

ab·bot \'abət\ *n* : head of a monastery

ab·bre·vi·ate \ə'brēvē,āt\ *vb* **-at·ed; -at·ing** : shorten —**ab·bre·vi·a·tion** \ə,brēvē'āshən\ *n*

ab·di·cate \'abdi,kāt\ *vb* **-cat·ed; -cat·ing** : renounce —**ab·di·ca·tion** \,abdi-'kāshən\ *n*

ab·do·men \'abdəmən, ab'dōmən\ *n* 1 : body area between chest and pelvis 2 : hindmost part of an insect —**ab·dom·i·nal** \ab'dämənᵊl\ *adj* —**ab·dom·i·nal·ly** *adv*

ab·duct \ab'dəkt\ *vb* : kidnap —**ab·duc·tion** \-'dəkshən\ *n* —**ab·duc·tor** \-tər\ *n*

abed \ə'bed\ *adv or adj* : in bed

ab·er·ra·tion \,abə'rāshən\ *n* : deviation or distortion —**ab·er·rant** \a'berənt\ *adj*

abet \ə'bet\ *vb* **-tt-** : incite or encourage —**abet·tor, abet·ter** \-ər\ *n*

abey·ance \ə'bāəns\ *n* : state of inactivity

ab·hor \əb'hór, ab-\ *vb* **-rr-** : hate —**ab·hor·rence** \-əns\ *n* —**ab·hor·rent** \-ənt\ *adj*

abide \ə'bīd\ *vb* **abode** \-'bōd\ *or* **abid·ed; abid·ing** 1 : endure 2 : remain, last, or reside

ab·ject \'ab,jekt, ab'-\ *adj* : low in spirit or hope —**ab·jec·tion** \ab'jekshən\ *n* —**ab·ject·ly** *adv* —**ab·ject·ness** *n*

ab·jure \ab'júr\ *vb* 1 : renounce 2 : abstain from —**ab·ju·ra·tion** \,abjə'rāshən\ *n*

ablaze \ə'blāz\ *adj or adv* : on fire

able \'ābəl\ *adj* **abler** \-blər\; **ablest** \-bləst\ 1 : having sufficient power, skill, or resources 2 : skilled or efficient —**abil·i·ty** \ə'bilətē\ *n* —**ably** \'āblē\ *adv*

-able, -ible \əbəl\ *adj suffix* 1 : capable of, fit for, or worthy of 2 : tending, given, or liable to

ab·lu·tion \ə'blüshən, a'blü-\ *n* : washing of one's body

ab·ne·gate \'abni,gāt\ *vb* **-gat·ed; -gat·ing** 1 : relinquish 2 : renounce —**ab·ne·ga·tion** \,abni'gāshən\ *n*

ab·nor·mal \ab'nórməl\ *adj* : deviating from the normal or average —**ab·nor·mal·i·ty** \,abnər'malətē, -nór-\ *n* —**ab·nor·mal·ly** *adv*

aboard \ə'bōrd\ *adv* : on, onto, or within a car, ship, or aircraft ~ *prep* : on or within

abode \ə'bōd\ *n* : residence

abol·ish \ə'bälish\ *vb* : do away with —**ab·o·li·tion** \,abə'lishən\ *n*

abom·i·na·ble \ə'bämənəbəl\ *adj* : thoroughly unpleasant or revolting

abom·i·nate \ə'bämə,nāt\ *vb* **-nat·ed;**

-nat•ing : hate —abom•i•na•tion \ə,bämə'nāshən\ n

ab•orig•i•nal \,abə'rijənəl\ adj 1 : original 2 : primitive

ab•orig•i•ne \-'rijənē\ n : original inhabitant

abort \ə'bórt\ vb : terminate prematurely —abor•tive \-'bórtiv\ adj

abor•tion \ə'bórshən\ n : spontaneous or induced termination of pregnancy

abound \ə'baùnd\ vb : be plentiful

about \ə'baùt\ adv : around ~ prep 1 : on every side of 2 : on the verge of 3 : having as a subject

above \ə'bəv\ adv : in or to a higher place ~ prep 1 : in or to a higher place than 2 : more than

above•board adv or adj : without deception

abrade \ə'brād\ vb abrad•ed; abrad•ing : wear away by rubbing —abra•sion \-'brāzhən\ n

abra•sive \ə'brāsiv\ n : substance for grinding, smoothing, or polishing ~ adj 1 : tending to abrade 2 : causing irritation —abra•sive•ly adv —abra•sive•ness n

abreast \ə'brest\ adv or adj 1 : side by side 2 : up to a standard or level

abridge \ə'brij\ vb abridged; abridg•ing : shorten or condense —abridg•ment, abridge•ment n

abroad \ə'bród\ adv or adj 1 : over a wide area 2 : outside one's country

ab•ro•gate \'abrəgāt\ vb -gat•ed; -gat•ing : annul or revoke —ab•ro•ga•tion \,abrə'gāshən\ n

abrupt \ə'brəpt\ adj 1 : sudden 2 : so quick as to seem rude —abrupt•ly adv

ab•scess \'ab,ses\ n : collection of pus surrounded by inflamed tissue —ab•scessed \-,sest\ adj

ab•scond \ab'skänd\ vb : run away and hide

ab•sent \'absənt\ adj : not present —ab•sent \ab'sent\ vb : keep oneself away —ab•sence \'absəns\ n —ab•sen•tee \,absən'tē\ n

ab•sent-mind•ed \,absənt'mīndəd\ adj : unaware of one's surroundings or action —ab•sent-mind•ed•ly adv —ab•sent-mind•ed•ness n

ab•so•lute \'absə,lüt, ,absə'-\ adj 1 : pure 2 : free from restriction 3 : definite —ab•so•lute•ly adv

ab•so•lu•tion \,absə'lüshən\ n : remission of sins

ab•solve \əb'zälv, -'sälv\ vb -solved; -solv•ing : set free of the consequences of guilt

ab•sorb \əb'sórb, -'zórb\ vb 1 : suck up or take in as a sponge does 2 : engage (one's attention) —ab•sor•ben•cy \-'sórbənsē, -'zór-\ n —ab•sor•bent \-bənt\ adj or n —ab•sorb•ing adj —ab•sorb•ing•ly adv

ab•sorp•tion \əb'sórpshən, -'zórp-\ n : process of absorbing —ab•sorp•tive \-tiv\ adj

ab•stain \əb'stān\ vb : refrain from doing something —ab•stain•er n —ab•sten•tion \-'stenchən\ n —ab•sti•nence \'abstənəns\ n

ab•ste•mi•ous \ab'stēmēəs\ adj : sparing in use of food or drink —ab•ste•mi•ous•ly adv —ab•ste•mi•ous•ness n

ab•stract \ab'strakt, 'ab,-\ adj 1 : expressing a quality apart from an object 2 : not representing something specific ~ \'ab,-\ n : summary ~ \ab'-, 'ab,-\ vb 1 : remove or separate 2 : make an abstract of —ab•stract•ly adv —ab•stract•ness n

ab•strac•tion \ab'strakshən\ n 1 : act of abstracting 2 : abstract idea or work of art

ab•struse \əb'strüs, ab-\ adj : hard to understand —ab•struse•ly adv —ab•struse•ness n

ab•surd \əb'sərd, -'zərd\ adj : ridiculous or unreasonable —ab•sur•di•ty \-ətē\ n —ab•surd•ly adv

abun•dant \ə'bəndənt\ adj : more than enough —abun•dance \-dəns\ n —abun•dant•ly adv

abuse \ə'byüz\ vb abused; abus•ing 1 : misuse 2 : mistreat 3 : attack with words ~ \-'byüs\ n 1 : corrupt practice 2 : improper use 3 : mistreatment 4 : coarse and insulting speech —abus•er n —abu•sive \-'byüsiv\ adj —abu•sive•ly adv —abu•sive•ness n

abut \ə'bət\ vb -tt- : touch along a border —abut•ter n

abut•ment \ə'bətmənt\ n : part of a bridge that supports weight

abys•mal \ə'bizməl\ adj 1 : immeasurably deep 2 : wretched —abys•mal•ly adv

abyss \ə'bis\ n : immeasurably deep gulf

-ac \,ak\ n suffix : one affected with

aca•cia \ə'kāshə\ n : leguminous tree or shrub

ac•a•dem•ic \,akə'demik\ adj 1 : relating

to schools or colleges **2** : theoretical —**academic** n —**ac·a·dem·i·cal·ly** \-iklē\ adv

acad·e·my \ə'kadəmē\ n, pl **-mies 1** : private high school **2** : society of scholars or artists

acan·thus \ə'kanthəs\ n, pl **acanthus 1** : prickly Mediterranean herb **2** : ornament representing acanthus leaves

ac·cede \ak'sēd\ vb **-ced·ed; -ced·ing 1** : become a party to an agreement **2** : express approval **3** : enter upon an office

ac·cel·er·ate \ik'selə,rāt, ak-\ vb **-at·ed; -at·ing 1** : bring about earlier **2** : speed up —**ac·cel·er·a·tion** \-,selə'rāshən\ n

ac·cel·er·a·tor \ik'selə,rātər, ak-\ n : pedal for controlling the speed of a motor vehicle

ac·cent \'ak,sent\ n **1** : distinctive manner of pronunciation **2** : prominence given to one syllable of a word **3** : mark (as ´, `, ^) over a vowel in writing or printing to indicate pronunciation — \'ak,-, ak'-\ vb : emphasize — **ac·cen·tu·al** \ak'senchəwəl\ adj

ac·cen·tu·ate \ak'senchə,wāt\ vb **-at·ed; -at·ing** : stress or show off by a contrast —**ac·cen·tu·a·tion** \-,senchə'wāshən\ n

ac·cept \ik'sept, ak-\ vb **1** : receive willingly **2** : agree to —**ac·cept·abil·i·ty** \ik,septə'bilətē, ak-\ n —**ac·cept·able** \-'septəbəl\ adj —**ac·cep·tance** \-'septəns\ n

ac·cess \'ak,ses\ n : capability or way of approaching —**ac·ces·si·bil·i·ty** \ik-,sesə'bilətē, ak-\ n —**ac·ces·si·ble** \-'sesəbəl\ adj

ac·ces·sion \ik'seshən, ak-\ n **1** : something added **2** : act of taking office

ac·ces·so·ry \ik'sesərē, ak-\ n, pl **-ries 1** : nonessential addition **2** : one guilty of aiding a criminal —**accessory** adj

ac·ci·dent \'aksədənt\ n **1** : event occurring by chance or unintentionally **2** : chance —**ac·ci·den·tal** \,aksə'dentᵊl\ adj —**ac·ci·den·tal·ly** adv

ac·claim \ə'klām\ vb or n : praise

ac·cla·ma·tion \,aklə'māshən\ n **1** : eager applause **2** : unanimous vote

ac·cli·mate \'aklə,māt, ə'klīmət\ vb **-mat·ed; -mat·ing** : acclimatize — **ac·cli·ma·tion** \,aklə'māshən, -,klī-\ n

ac·cli·ma·tize \ə'klīmə,tīz\ vb **-tized; -tiz·ing** : accustom to a new climate or situation —**ac·cli·ma·ti·za·tion** \-,klīmətə'zāshən\ n

ac·co·lade \'akə,lād\ n : expression of praise

ac·com·mo·date \ə'kämə,dāt\ vb **-dated; -dat·ing 1** : adapt **2** : provide with something needed **3** : hold without crowding

ac·com·mo·da·tion \ə,kämə'dāshən\ n **1** : quarters —usu. pl. **2** : act of accommodating

ac·com·pa·ny \ə'kəmpənē\ vb **-nied; -ny·ing 1** : go or occur with **2** : play supporting music —**ac·com·pa·ni·ment** \-nəmənt\ n —**ac·com·pa·nist** \-nist\ n

ac·com·plice \ə'kämpləs, -'kəm-\ n : associate in crime

ac·com·plish \ə'kämplish, -'kəm-\ vb : do, fulfill, or bring about —**ac·com·plished** adj —**ac·com·plish·er** n —**ac·com·plish·ment** n

ac·cord \ə'kórd\ vb **1** : grant **2** : agree ~ n **1** : agreement **2** : willingness to act —**ac·cor·dance** \-'kórdᵊns\ n —**ac·cor·dant** \-ᵊnt\ adj

ac·cord·ing·ly \ə'kórdiŋlē\ adv : consequently

according to prep **1** : in conformity with **2** : as stated by

ac·cor·di·on \ə'kórdēən\ n : keyboard instrument with a bellows and reeds ~ adj : folding like an accordion bellows —**ac·cor·di·on·ist** \-nist\ n

ac·cost \ə'kóst\ vb : approach and speak to esp. aggressively

ac·count \ə'kaúnt\ n **1** : statement of business transactions **2** : credit arrangement with a vendor **3** : report **4** : worth **5** : sum deposited in a bank ~ vb : give an explanation

ac·count·able \ə'kaúntəbəl\ adj : responsible —**ac·count·abil·i·ty** \-,kaúntə'bilətē\ n

ac·coun·tant \ə'kaúntᵊnt\ n : one skilled in accounting —**ac·coun·tan·cy** \-ᵊnsē\ n

ac·count·ing \ə'kaúntiŋ\ n : financial record keeping

ac·cou·tre, ac·cou·ter \ə'kütər\ vb **-tred** or **-tered; -tring** or **-ter·ing** \-'kütəriŋ, -'kütriŋ\ : equip

ac·cou·tre·ment, ac·cou·ter·ment \ə'kütrəmənt, -'kütər-\ n **1** : accessory item — usu. pl. **2** : identifying characteristic

ac·cred·it \ə'kredət\ *vb* **1** : approve officially **2** : attribute —**ac·cred·i·ta·tion** \-,kredə'tāshən\ *n*

ac·crue \ə'krü\ *vb* -**crued**; -**cru·ing** : be added by periodic growth —**ac·cru·al** \-əl\ *n*

ac·cu·mu·late \ə'kyümyə,lāt\ *vb* -**lat·ed**; -**lat·ing** : collect or pile up —**ac·cu·mu·la·tion** \-,kyümyə'lāshən\ *n* —**ac·cu·mu·la·tor** \-'kyümyə,lātər\ *n*

ac·cu·rate \'akyərət\ *adj* : free from error —**ac·cu·ra·cy** \-rəsē\ *n* —**ac·cu·rate·ly** *adv* —**ac·cu·rate·ness** *n*

ac·cursed \ə'kərst, -'kərsəd\, **ac·curst** \ə'kərst\ *adj* **1** : being under a curse **2** : damnable

ac·cuse \ə'kyüz\ *vb* -**cused**; -**cus·ing** : charge with an offense —**ac·cu·sa·tion** \,akyə'zāshən\ *n* —**ac·cus·er** *n*

ac·cused \ə'kyüzd\ *n, pl* -**cused** : defendant in a criminal case

ac·cus·tom \ə'kəstəm\ *vb* : make familiar through use or experience

ace \'ās\ *n* : one that excels

acer·bic \ə'sərbik, a-\ *adj* : sour or biting in temper, mood, or tone

acet·amin·o·phen \ə,sētə'minəfən\ *n* : pain reliever

ac·e·tate \'asə,tāt\ *n* : fabric or plastic derived from acetic acid

ace·tic acid \ə'sētik-\ *n* : acid found in vinegar

acet·y·lene \ə'set⁰lən, -⁰l,ēn\ *n* : colorless gas used as a fuel in welding

ache \'āk\ *vb* **ached**; **ach·ing** **1** : suffer a dull persistent pain **2** : yearn —**ache** *n*

achieve \ə'chēv\ *vb* **achieved**; **achiev·ing** : gain by work or effort —**achieve·ment** *n* —**achiev·er** *n*

ac·id \'asəd\ *adj* **1** : sour or biting to the taste **2** : sharp in manner **3** : of or relating to an acid ~ *n* : sour water-soluble chemical compound that reacts with a base to form a salt —**acid·ic** \ə'sidik\ *adj* —**acid·i·fy** \ə'sidə,fī\ *vb* —**acid·i·ty** \-ətē\ *n* —**acid·ly** *adv*

ac·knowl·edge \ik'nälij, ak-\ *vb* -**edged**; -**edg·ing** **1** : admit as true **2** : admit the authority of **3** : express thanks for —**ac·knowl·edg·ment** *n*

ac·me \'akmē\ *n* : highest point

ac·ne \'aknē\ *n* : skin disorder marked esp. by pimples

ac·o·lyte \'akə,līt\ *n* : assistant to a member of clergy in a religious service

acorn \'ā,korn, -kərn\ *n* : nut of the oak

acous·tic \ə'küstik\ *adj* : relating to hearing or sound —**acous·ti·cal** \-stikəl\ *adj* —**acous·ti·cal·ly** \-klē\ *adv*

acous·tics \ə'küstiks\ *n sing or pl* **1** : science of sound **2** : qualities in a room that affect how sound is heard

ac·quaint \ə'kwānt\ *vb* **1** : inform **2** : make familiar

ac·quain·tance \ə'kwānt⁰ns\ *n* **1** : personal knowledge **2** : person with whom one is acquainted —**ac·quain·tance·ship** *n*

ac·qui·esce \,akwē'es\ *vb* -**esced**; -**esc·ing** : consent or submit —**ac·qui·es·cence** \-'es⁰ns\ *n* —**ac·qui·es·cent** \-⁰nt\ *adj* —**ac·qui·es·cent·ly** *adv*

ac·quire \ə'kwīr\ *vb* -**quired**; -**quir·ing** : gain

ac·qui·si·tion \,akwə'zishən\ *n* : a gaining or something gained —**acqui·si·tive** \ə'kwizətiv\ *adj*

ac·quit \ə'kwit\ *vb* -**tt**- **1** : pronounce not guilty **2** : conduct (oneself) usu. well —**ac·quit·tal** \-⁰l\ *n*

acre \'ākər\ *n* **1** *pl* : lands **2** : 4840 square yards

acre·age \'ākərij\ *n* : area in acres

ac·rid \'akrəd\ *adj* : sharp and biting —**acrid·i·ty** \a'kridətē, ə-\ *n* —**ac·rid·ly** *adv* —**ac·rid·ness** *n*

ac·ri·mo·ny \'akrə,mōnē\ *n, pl* -**nies** : harshness of language or feeling —**ac·ri·mo·ni·ous** \,akrə'mōnēəs\ *adj* —**ac·ri·mo·ni·ous·ly** *adv*

ac·ro·bat \'akrə,bat\ *n* : performer of tumbling feats —**ac·ro·bat·ic** \,akrə'batik\ *adj*

across \ə'kros\ *adv* : to or on the opposite side ~ *prep* **1** : to or on the opposite side of **2** : on so as to cross

acryl·ic \ə'krilik\ *n* **1** : plastic used for molded parts or in paints **2** : synthetic textile fiber

act \'akt\ *n* **1** : thing done **2** : law **3** : main division of a play ~ *vb* **1** : perform in a play **2** : conduct oneself **3** : operate **4** : produce an effect

ac·tion \'akshən\ *n* **1** : legal proceeding **2** : manner or method of performing **3** : activity **4** : thing done over a period of time or in stages **5** : combat **6** : events of a literary plot **7** : operating mechanism

ac·ti·vate \'aktə,vāt\ vb -vat·ed; -vat·ing : make active or reactive —**ac·ti·va·tion** \,aktə'vāshən\ n

ac·tive \'aktiv\ adj 1 : causing action or change 2 : lively, vigorous, or energetic 3 : erupting or likely to erupt 4 : now in operation —**active** n —**ac·tive·ly** adv

ac·tiv·i·ty \ak'tivətē\ n, pl -ties 1 : quality or state of being active 2 : what one is actively doing

ac·tor \'aktər\ n : one that acts

ac·tress \'aktrəs\ n : woman who acts in plays

ac·tu·al \'akchəwəl\ adj : really existing —**ac·tu·al·i·ty** \,akchə'walətē\ n —**ac·tu·al·iza·tion** \,akchəwələ'zāshən\ n —**ac·tu·al·ize** \'akchə·wə,līz\ vb —**ac·tu·al·ly** adv

ac·tu·ary \'akchə,werē\ n, pl -ar·ies : one who calculates insurance risks and premiums —**ac·tu·ar·i·al** \,akchə'werēəl\ adj

ac·tu·ate \'akchə,wāt\ vb -at·ed; -at·ing : put into action —**ac·tu·a·tor** \-,wātər\ n

acu·men \ə'kyümən\ n : mental keenness

acu·punc·ture \'akyù,pəŋkchər\ n : treatment by puncturing the body with needles —**acu·punc·tur·ist** \,akyù'pəŋkchərist\ n

acute \ə'kyüt\ adj acut·er; acut·est 1 : sharp 2 : containing less than 90 degrees 3 : mentally alert 4 : severe —**acute·ly** adv —**acute·ness** n

ad \'ad\ n : advertisement

ad·age \'adij\ n : old familiar saying

ad·a·mant \'adəmant, -,mant\ adj : insistent —**ad·a·mant·ly** adv

adapt \ə'dapt\ vb : adjust to be suitable for a new use or condition —**adapt·abil·i·ty** \ə,daptə'bilətē\ n —**adapt·able** adj —**ad·ap·ta·tion** \,ad,ap'tāshən, -əp-\ n —**adap·ter** n —**adap·tive** \ə'daptiv\ adj

add \'ad\ vb 1 : join to something else so as to increase in amount 2 : say further 3 : find a sum —**ad·di·tion** \ə'dishən\ n

ad·der \'adər\ n 1 : poisonous European snake 2 : No. American snake

ad·dict \'adikt\ n : one who is psychologically or physiologically dependent (as on a drug) ~ \ə'dikt\ vb : cause to become an addict —**ad·dic·tion** \ə'dikshən\ n —**ad·dic·tive** \-'diktiv\ adj

ad·di·tion·al \ə'dishənəl\ adj : existing as a result of adding —**ad·di·tion·al·ly** adv

ad·di·tive \'adətiv\ n : substance added to another

ad·dle \'ad^əl\ vb -dled; -dling : confuse

ad·dress \ə'dres\ vb 1 : direct one's remarks to 2 : mark an address on ~ \ə'dres, 'ad,res\ n 1 : formal speech 2 : place where a person may be reached or mail may be delivered

ad·duce \ə'düs, -'dyüs\ vb -duced; -duc·ing : offer as proof

ad·e·noid \'ad,nòid, -^ənòid\ n : enlarged tissue near the opening of the nose into the throat —usu. pl. —**adenoid**, **ad·e·noi·dal** \-əl-\ adj

adept \ə'dept\ adj : highly skilled —**adept·ly** adv —**adept·ness** n

ad·e·quate \'adikwət\ adj : good or plentiful enough —**ad·e·qua·cy** \-kwəsē\ n —**ad·e·quate·ly** adv

ad·here \ad'hir, əd-\ vb -hered; -her·ing 1 : remain loyal 2 : stick fast —**ad·her·ence** \-'hirəns\ n —**ad·her·ent** \-ənt\ adj or n

ad·he·sion \ad'hēzhən, əd-\ n : act of adhering

ad·he·sive \-'hēsiv, -ziv\ adj : tending to adhere ~ n : adhesive substance

adieu \ə'dü, -dyü\ n, pl **adieus** or **adieux** \-'düz,-'dyüz\ : farewell

ad·ja·cent \ə'jās^ənt\ adj : situated near or next

ad·jec·tive \'ajiktiv\ n : word that serves as a modifier of a noun —**ad·jec·ti·val** \,ajik'tīvəl\ adj —**ad·jec·ti·val·ly** adv

ad·join \ə'jòin\ vb : be next to

ad·journ \ə'jərn\ vb : end a meeting —**ad·journ·ment** n

ad·judge \ə'jəj\ vb -judged; -judg·ing 1 : think or pronounce to be 2 : award by judicial decision

ad·ju·di·cate \ə'jüdi,kāt\ vb -cat·ed; -cat·ing : settle judicially —**ad·ju·di·ca·tion** \ə,jüdi'kāshən\ n

ad·junct \'aj,əŋkt\ n : something joined or added but not essential

ad·just \ə'jəst\ vb : fix, adapt, or set right —**ad·just·able** adj —**ad·just·er, ad·jus·tor** \ə'jəstər\ n —**ad·just·ment** \-mənt\ n

ad·ju·tant \'ajətənt\ n : aide esp. to a commanding officer

ad–lib \'ad'lib\ *vb* **-bb-** : speak without preparation —**ad–lib** *n or adj*

ad·min·is·ter \əd'minəstər\ *vb* **1** : manage **2** : give out esp. in doses — **ad·min·is·tra·ble** \-strəbəl\ *adj* —**ad·min·is·trant** \-strənt\ *n*

ad·min·is·tra·tion \əd,minə'strāshən, ad-\ *n* **1** : process of managing **2** : persons responsible for managing — **ad·min·is·tra·tive** \əd'minə,strātiv\ *adj* —**ad·min·is·tra·tive·ly** *adv*

ad·min·is·tra·tor \əd'minə,strātər\ *n* : one that manages

ad·mi·ra·ble \'admərəbəl\ *adj* : worthy of admiration —**ad·mi·ra·bly** \-blē\ *adv*

ad·mi·ral \'admərəl\ *n* : commissioned officer in the navy ranking next below a fleet admiral

ad·mire \əd'mīr\ *vb* **-mired; -mir·ing** : have high regard for —**ad·mi·ra·tion** \,admə'rāshən\ *n* —**ad·mir·er** *n* —**ad·mir·ing·ly** *adv*

ad·mis·si·ble \əd'misəbəl\ *adj* : that can be permitted —**ad·mis·si·bil·i·ty** \-,misə'bilətē\ *n*

ad·mis·sion \əd'mishən\ *n* **1** : act of admitting **2** : admittance or a fee paid for this **3** : acknowledgment of a fact

ad·mit \əd'mit\ *vb* **-tt-** **1** : allow to enter **2** : permit **3** : recognize as genuine — **ad·mit·ted·ly** *adv*

ad·mit·tance \əd'mit⁰ns\ *n* : permission to enter

ad·mix·ture \ad'mikschər\ *n* **1** : thing added in mixing **2** : mixture

ad·mon·ish \ad'mänish\ *vb* : rebuke — **ad·mon·ish·ment** \-mənt\ *n* —**ad·mo·ni·tion** \,admə'nishən\ *n* —**ad·mon·i·to·ry** \ad'mänə,tōrē\ *adj*

ado \ə'dü\ *n* **1** : fuss **2** : trouble

ado·be \ə'dōbē\ *n* : sun-dried building brick

ad·o·les·cence \,ad⁰l'es⁰ns\ *n* : period of growth between childhood and maturity —**ad·o·les·cent** \-⁰nt\ *adj or n*

adopt \ə'däpt\ *vb* **1** : take (a child of other parents) as one's own child **2** : take up and practice as one's own —**adop·tion** \-'däpshən\ *n*

adore \ə'dōr\ *vb* **adored; ador·ing** **1** : worship **2** : be extremely fond of — **ador·able** *adj* —**ador·ably** *adv* — **ad·o·ra·tion** \,adə'rāshən\ *n*

adorn \ə'dórn\ *vb* : decorate with ornaments —**adorn·ment** *n*

adrift \ə'drift\ *adv or adj* **1** : afloat without motive power or moorings **2** : without guidance or purpose

adroit \ə'dróit\ *adj* : dexterous or shrewd —**adroit·ly** *adv* —**adroit·ness** *n*

adult \ə'dəlt, 'ad,əlt\ *adj* : fully developed and mature ~ *n* : grown-up person —**adult·hood** *n*

adul·ter·ate \ə'dəltə,rāt\ *vb* **-at·ed; -at·ing** : make impure by mixture — **adul·ter·a·tion** \-,dəltə'rāshən\ *n*

adul·tery \ə'dəltərē\ *n, pl* **-ter·ies** : sexual unfaithfulness of a married person —**adul·ter·er** \-tərər\ *n* — **adul·ter·ess** \-tərəs\ *n* —**adul·ter·ous** \-tərəs\ *adj*

ad·vance \əd'vans\ *vb* **-vanced; -vanc·ing** **1** : bring or move forward **2** : promote **3** : lend ~ *n* **1** : forward movement **2** : improvement **3** : offer ~ *adj* : being ahead of time —**advance·ment** *n*

ad·van·tage \əd'vantij\ *n* **1** : superiority of position **2** : benefit or gain —**ad·van·ta·geous** \,ad,van'tājəs, -vən-\ *adj* —**ad·van·ta·geous·ly** *adv*

ad·vent \'ad,vent\ *n* **1** *cap* : period before Christmas **2** : a coming into being or use

ad·ven·ti·tious \,advən'tishəs\ *adj* : accidental —**ad·ven·ti·tious·ly** *adv*

ad·ven·ture \əd'venchər\ *n* **1** : risky undertaking **2** : exciting experience — **ad·ven·tur·er** \-chərər\ *n* —**ad·ven·ture·some** \-chərsəm\ *adj* —**ad·ven·tur·ous** \-chərəs\ *adj*

ad·verb \'ad,vərb\ *n* : word that modifies a verb, an adjective, or another adverb —**ad·ver·bi·al** \ad'vərbēəl\ *adj* —**ad·ver·bi·al·ly** *adv*

ad·ver·sary \'advər,serē\ *n, pl* **-sar·ies** : enemy or rival —**adversary** *adj*

ad·verse \ad'vərs, 'ad-,\ *adj* : opposing or unfavorable —**ad·verse·ly** *adv*

ad·ver·si·ty \ad'vərsətē\ *n, pl* **-ties** : hard times

ad·vert \ad'vərt\ *vb* : refer

ad·ver·tise \'advər,tīz\ *vb* **-tised; -tis·ing** : call public attention to —**ad·ver·tise·ment** \,advər'tīzmənt, əd-'vərtəzmənt\ *n* —**ad·ver·tis·er** *n*

ad·ver·tis·ing \'advər,tīziŋ\ *n* : business of preparing advertisements

ad·vice \əd'vīs\ *n* : recommendation with regard to a course of action

ad·vis·able \əd'vīzəbəl\ *adj* : wise or prudent —**ad·vis·abil·i·ty** \-,vīzə'bilətē\ *n*

ad·vise \əd'vīz\ *vb* **-vised; -vis·ing** : give advice to —**ad·vis·er, ad·vis·or** \-'vīzər\ *n*

ad·vise·ment \əd'vīzmənt\ *n* : careful consideration

ad·vi·so·ry \əd'vīzərē\ *adj* : having power to advise

ad·vo·cate \'advəkət, -,kāt\ *n* : one who argues or pleads for a cause or proposal ~ \-,kāt\ *vb* **-cat·ed; -cat·ing** : recommend —**ad·vo·ca·cy** \-vəkə-sē\ *n*

adze \'adz\ *n* : tool for shaping wood

ae·gis \'ējəs\ *n* : protection or sponsorship

ae·on \'ēən, 'ē,än\ *n* : indefinitely long time

aer·ate \'ar,āt\ *vb* **-at·ed; -at·ing** : supply or impregnate with air —**aer·a·tion** \,ar'āshən\ *n* —**aer·a·tor** \'ar,ātər\ *n*

ae·ri·al \'arēəl\ *adj* : inhabiting, occurring in, or done in the air ~ *n* : antenna

ae·rie \'arē, 'irē\ *n* : eagle's nest

aer·o·bic \,ar'ōbik\ *adj* : using or needing oxygen

aer·o·bics \-biks\ *n sing or pl* : exercises that produce a marked increase in respiration and heart rate

aero·dy·nam·ics \,arōdī'namiks\ *n* : science of bodies in motion in a gas —**aero·dy·nam·ic** \-ik\ *adj* —**aero·dy·nam·i·cal·ly** \-iklē\ *adv*

aero·nau·tics \,arə'nótiks\ *n* : science dealing with aircraft —**aero·nau·ti·cal** \-ikəl\ *adj*

aero·sol \'arə,säl, -,sól\ *n* **1** : liquid or solid particles suspended in a gas **2** : substance sprayed as an aerosol

aero·space \'arō,spās\ *n* : earth's atmosphere and the space beyond —**aero·space** *adj*

aes·thet·ic \es'thetik\ *adj* : relating to beauty —**aes·thet·i·cal·ly** \-iklē\ *adv*

aes·thet·ics \-'thetiks\ *n* : branch of philosophy dealing with beauty

afar \ə'fär\ *adv* : from, at, or to a great distance —**afar** *n*

af·fa·ble \'afəbəl\ *adj* : easy to talk to —**af·fa·bil·i·ty** \,afə'bilətē\ *n* —**af·fa·bly** \'afəblē\ *adv*

af·fair \ə'far\ *n* : something that relates to or involves one

¹af·fect \ə'fekt, a-\ *vb* : assume for effect —**af·fec·ta·tion** \,af,ek'tāshən\ *n*

²affect *vb* : produce an effect on

af·fect·ed \ə'fektəd, a-\ *adj* **1** : pretending to some trait **2** : artificially assumed to impress —**af·fect·ed·ly** *adv*

af·fect·ing \ə'fektiŋ, a-\ *adj* : arousing pity or sorrow —**af·fect·ing·ly** *adv*

af·fec·tion \ə'fekshən\ *n* : kind or loving feeling —**af·fec·tion·ate** \-shənət\ *adj* —**af·fec·tion·ate·ly** *adv*

af·fi·da·vit \,afə'dāvət\ *n* : sworn statement

af·fil·i·ate \ə'filē,āt\ *vb* **-at·ed; -at·ing** : become a member or branch —**affil·i·ate** \-ēət\ *n* —**af·fil·i·a·tion** \-,filē'āshən\ *n*

af·fin·i·ty \ə'finətē\ *n, pl* **-ties** : close attraction or relationship

af·firm \ə'fərm\ *vb* : assert positively —**af·fir·ma·tion** \,afər'māshən\ *n*

af·fir·ma·tive \ə'fərmətiv\ *adj* : asserting the truth or existence of something ~ *n* : statement of affirmation or agreement

af·fix \ə'fiks\ *vb* : attach

af·flict \ə'flikt\ *vb* : cause pain and distress to —**af·flic·tion** \-'flikshən\ *n*

af·flu·ence \'af,lüəns; a'flü-, ə-\ *n* : wealth —**af·flu·ent** \-ənt\ *adj*

af·ford \ə'fórd\ *vb* **1** : manage to bear the cost of **2** : provide

af·fray \ə'frā\ *n* : fight

af·front \ə'frənt\ *vb or n* : insult

af·ghan \'af,gan, -gən\ *n* : crocheted or knitted blanket

afire \ə'fīr\ *adj or adv* : being on fire

aflame \ə'flām\ *adj or adv* : flaming

afloat \ə'flōt\ *adj or adv* : floating

afoot \ə'füt\ *adv or adj* **1** : on foot **2** : in progress

afore·said \ə'fōr,sed\ *adj* : said or named before

afraid \ə'frād, South also ə'fred\ *adj* : filled with fear

afresh \ə'fresh\ *adv* : anew

aft \'aft\ *adv* : to or toward the stern or tail

af·ter \'aftər\ *adv* : at a later time ~ *prep* **1** : behind in place or time **2** : in pursuit of ~ *conj* : following the time when ~ *adj* **1** : later **2** : located toward the back

af·ter·life \'aftər,līf\ *n* : existence after death

af·ter·math \-,math\ *n* : results

af·ter·noon \,aftər'nün\ *n* : time between noon and evening

af·ter·thought *n* : later thought

af·ter·ward \'aftərwərd\, **af·ter·wards** \-wərdz\ *adv* : at a later time

again \ə'gen, -'gin\ *adv* 1 : once more 2 : on the other hand 3 : in addition

against \ə'genst\ *prep* 1 : directly opposite to 2 : in opposition to 3 : so as to touch or strike

agape \ə'gāp, -'gap\ *adj or adv* : having the mouth open in astonishment

ag·ate \'agət\ *n* : quartz with bands or masses of various colors

age \'āj\ *n* 1 : length of time of life or existence 2 : particular time in life (as majority or the latter part) 3 : quality of being old 4 : long time 5 : period in history ~ *vb* : become old or mature

-age \ij\ *n suffix* 1 : aggregate 2 : action or process 3 : result of 4 : rate of 5 : place of 6 : state or rank 7 : fee

aged *adj* 1 \'ājəd\ : old 2 \'ājd\ : allowed to mature

age·less \'ājləs\ *adj* : eternal

agen·cy \'ājənsē\ *n, pl* -cies 1 : one through which something is accomplished 2 : office or function of an agent 3 : government administrative division

agen·da \ə'jendə\ *n* : list of things to be done

agent \'ājənt\ *n* 1 : means 2 : person acting or doing business for another

ag·gran·dize \ə'gran,dīz, 'agrən-\ *vb* -dized; -diz·ing : make great or greater —**ag·gran·dize·ment** \ə'grandəzmənt, -,dīz-; ,agrən'dīz-\ *n*

ag·gra·vate \'agrə,vāt\ *vb* -vat·ed; -vat·ing 1 : make more severe 2 : irritate —**ag·gra·va·tion** \,agrə'vāshən\ *n*

ag·gre·gate \'agrigət\ *adj* : formed into a mass ~ \-,gāt\ *vb* -gat·ed; -gat·ing : collect into a mass ~ \-gət\ *n* 1 : mass 2 : whole amount

ag·gres·sion \ə'greshən\ *n* 1 : unprovoked attack 2 : hostile behavior —**ag·gres·sor** \-'gresər\ *n*

ag·gres·sive \ə'gresiv\ *adj* 1 : easily provoked to fight 2 : hard working and enterprising —**ag·gres·sive·ly** *adv* —**ag·gres·sive·ness** *n*

ag·grieve \ə'grēv\ *vb* -grieved; -griev·ing 1 : cause grief to 2 : inflict injury on

aghast \ə'gast\ *adj* : struck with amazement·or horror

ag·ile \'ajəl\ *adj* : able to move quickly and easily —**agil·i·ty** \ə'jilətē\ *n*

ag·i·tate \'aji,tāt\ *vb* -tat·ed; -tat·ing 1 : shake or stir back and forth 2 : excite or trouble the mind of 3 : try to arouse public feeling —**ag·i·ta·tion** \,ajə'tāshən\ *n* —**ag·i·ta·tor** \'ajə-,tātər\ *n*

ag·nos·tic \ag'nästik, əg-\ *n* : one who doubts the existence of God

ago \ə'gō\ *adj or adv* : earlier than the present

agog \ə'gäg\ *adj* : full of excitement

ag·o·nize \'agə,nīz\ *vb* -nized; -niz·ing : suffer mental agony —**ag·o·niz·ing·ly** *adv*

ag·o·ny \'agənē\ *n, pl* -nies : extreme pain or mental distress

agrar·i·an \ə'grerēən\ *adj* : relating to land ownership or farming interests —**agrarian** *n* —**agrar·i·an·ism** *n*

agree \ə'grē\ *vb* agreed; agree·ing 1 : be of the same opinion 2 : express willingness 3 : get along together 4 : be similar 5 : be appropriate, suitable, or healthful

agree·able \-əbəl\ *adj* 1 : pleasing 2 : willing to give approval —**agree·able·ness** *n* —**agree·ably** *adv*

agree·ment \-mənt\ *n* 1 : harmony of opinion or purpose 2 : mutual understanding or arrangement

ag·ri·cul·ture \'agri,kəlchər\ *n* : farming —**ag·ri·cul·tur·al** \,agri'kəlchərəl\ *adj* —**ag·ri·cul·tur·ist** \-rist\, **ag·ri·cul·tur·al·ist** \-rəlist\ *n*

aground \ə'graúnd\ *adv or adj* : on or onto the bottom or shore

ague \'āgyü\ *n* 1 : fever with recurrent chills and sweating 2 : malaria

ahead \ə'hed\ *adv or adj* 1 : in or toward the front 2 : into or for the future 3 : in a more advantageous position

ahead of *prep* 1 : in front or advance of 2 : in excess of

ahoy \ə'hói\ *interj* —used in hailing

aid \'ād\ *vb* : provide help or support ~ *n* : help

aide \'ād\ *n* : helper

AIDS \'ādz\ *n* : serious disease of the human immune system

ail \'āl\ *vb* 1 : trouble 2 : be ill

ai·le·ron \'ālə,rän\ *n* : movable part of an airplane wing

ail·ment \'ālmənt\ *n* : bodily disorder

aim \'ām\ *vb* 1 : point or direct (as a weapon) 2 : direct one's efforts ~ *n* 1 : an aiming or the direction of aiming 2 : object or purpose —**aim·less** *adj* —**aim·less·ly** *adv* —**aim·less·ness** *n*

air \'ar\ *n* 1 : mixture of gases surrounding the earth 2 : melody 3 : outward appearance **4** : artificial manner **5** : compressed air **6** : travel by or use of aircraft **7** : medium of transmission of radio waves ~ *vb* **1** : expose to the air **2** : broadcast —**air·borne** \-,bōrn\ *adj*

air–condition *vb* : equip with an apparatus (**air conditioner**) for filtering and cooling the air

air·craft *n, pl* **aircraft** : craft that flies

Aire·dale terrier \'ar,dāl-\ *n* : large terrier with a hard wiry coat

air·field *n* : airport or its landing field

air force *n* : military organization for conducting warfare by air

air·lift *n* : a transporting of esp. emergency supplies by aircraft —**airlift** *vb*

air·line *n* : air transportation system —**air·lin·er** *n*

air·mail *n* : system of transporting mail by airplane —**airmail** *vb*

air·man \-mən\ *n* **1** : aviator **2** : enlisted man in the air force in one of the 3 ranks below sergeant **3** : enlisted man in the air force ranking just below airman first class

airman basic *n* : enlisted man of the lowest rank in the air force

airman first class *n* : enlisted man in the air force ranking just below sergeant

air·plane *n* : fixed-wing aircraft heavier than air

air·port *n* : place for landing aircraft and usu. for receiving passengers

air·ship *n* : powered lighter-than-air aircraft

air·strip *n* : airfield runway

air·tight *adj* : tightly sealed to prevent flow of air

air·waves \'ar,wāvz\ *n pl* : medium of transmission of radio waves

airy \'arē\ *adj* **air·i·er; -est 1** : delicate **2** : breezy

aisle \'īl\ *n* : passage between sections of seats

ajar \ə'jär\ *adj or adv* : partly open

akim·bo \ə'kimbō\ *adj or adv* : having the hand on the hip and the elbow turned outward

akin \ə'kin\ *adj* **1** : related by blood **2** : similar in kind

-al \əl\ *adj suffix* : of, relating to, or characterized by

al·a·bas·ter \'alə,bastər\ *n* : white or translucent mineral

alac·ri·ty \ə'lakrətē\ *n* : cheerful readiness

alarm \ə'lärm\ *n* **1** : warning signal or device **2** : fear at sudden danger ~ *vb* **1** : warn **2** : frighten

alas \ə'las\ *interj* —used to express unhappiness, pity, or concern

al·ba·tross \'albə,tros, -,träs\ *n, pl* **-tross** *or* **-trosses** : large seabird

al·be·it \ol'bēət, al-\ *conj* : even though

al·bi·no \al'bīnō\ *n, pl* **-nos** : person or animal with abnormally white skin —**al·bi·nism** \'albə,nizəm\ *n*

al·bum \'albəm\ *n* **1** : book for displaying a collection (as of photographs) **2** : collection of recordings

al·bu·men \al'byümən\ *n* **1** : white of an egg **2** : albumin

al·bu·min \-mən\ *n* : protein found in blood, milk, egg white, and tissues

al·che·my \'alkəmē\ *n* : medieval chemistry —**al·che·mist** \'alkəmist\ *n*

al·co·hol \'alkə,hol\ *n* **1** : intoxicating agent in liquor **2** : liquor —**alcoholic** *adj*

al·co·hol·ic \,alkə'holik, -'häl-\ *n* : person affected with alcoholism

al·co·hol·ism \'alkə,hol,izəm\ *n* : addiction to alcoholic beverages

al·cove \'al,kōv\ *n* : recess in a room or wall

al·der·man \'oldərmən\ *n* : city official

ale \'āl\ *n* : beerlike beverage —**ale·house** *n*

alert \ə'lərt\ *adj* **1** : watchful **2** : quick to perceive and act ~ *n* : alarm ~ *vb* : warn —**alert·ly** *adv* —**alert·ness** *n*

ale·wife *n* : fish of the herring family

al·fal·fa \al'falfə\ *n* : cloverlike forage plant

al·ga \'algə\ *n, pl* **-gae** \'al,jē\ : any of a group of lower plants that includes seaweed —**al·gal** \-gəl\ *adj*

al·ge·bra \'aljəbrə\ *n* : branch of mathematics using symbols —**al·ge·bra·ic** \,aljə'brāik\ *adj* —**al·ge·bra·i·cal·ly** \-'brāəklē\ *adv*

alias \'ālēəs, 'ālyəs\ *adv* : otherwise called ~ *n* : assumed name

al·i·bi \'alə,bī\ *n* **1** : defense of having been elsewhere when a crime was committed **2** : justification ~ *vb* **-bied; -bi·ing** : offer an excuse

alien \'ālēən, 'ālyən\ *adj* : foreign ~ *n* **1** : foreign-born resident **2** : extraterrestrial

alien·ate \'ālēə,nāt, 'ālyə-\ *vb* **-at·ed; -at·ing** : cause to be no longer friendly —**alien·ation** \,ālēə'nāshən, ,ālyə-\ *n*

alight \ə'līt\ *vb* : dismount

align \ə'līn\ *vb* : bring into line —**aligner** *n* —**alignment** *n*

alike \ə'līk\ *adj* : identical or very similar ~ *adv* : equally

alimentary \‚alə'mentərē\ *adj* : relating to or functioning in nutrition

alimony \'alə‚mōnē\ *n, pl* **-nies** : money paid to a separated or divorced spouse

alive \ə'līv\ *adj* **1** : having life **2** : lively or animated

alkali \'alkə‚lī\ *n, pl* **-lies** *or* **-lis** : strong chemical base —**alkaline** \-kələn, -‚līn\ *adj* —**alkalinity** \‚alkə'linətē\ *n*

all \'ol\ *adj* **1** : the whole of **2** : greatest possible **3** : every one of ~ *adv* **1** : wholly **2** : so much **3** : for each side ~ *pron* **1** : whole number or amount **2** : everything or everyone

Allah \'älə, 'al-\ *n* : God of Islam

all–around *adj* : versatile

allay \ə'lā\ *vb* **1** : alleviate **2** : calm

allege \ə'lej\ *vb* **-leged; -leging** : assert without proof —**allegation** \‚ali'gāshən\ *n* —**allegedly** \ə'lejədlē\ *adv*

allegiance \ə'lējəns\ *n* : loyalty

allegory \'alə‚gōrē\ *n, pl* **-ries** : story in which figures and actions are symbols of general truths —**allegorical** \‚alə'gorikəl\ *adj*

alleluia \‚alə'lüyə\ *interj* : hallelujah

allergen \'alərjən\ *n* : something that causes allergy —**allergenic** \‚alər'jenik\ *adj*

allergy \'alərjē\ *n, pl* **-gies** : abnormal reaction to a substance —**allergic** \ə'lərjik\ *adj* —**allergist** \'alərjist\ *n*

alleviate \ə'lēvē‚āt\ *vb* **-ated; -ating** : relieve or lessen —**alleviation** \ə‚lēvē'āshən\ *n*

alley \'alē\ *n, pl* **-leys** **1** : place for bowling **2** : narrow passage between buildings

alliance \ə'līəns\ *n* : association

alligator \'alə‚gātər\ *n* : large aquatic reptile related to the crocodiles

alliteration \ə‚litə'rāshən\ *n* : repetition of initial sounds of words —**alliterative** \-'litə‚rātiv\ *adj*

allocate \'alə‚kāt\ *vb* **-cated; -cating** : assign —**allocation** \‚alə'kāshən\ *n*

allot \ə'lät\ *vb* **-tt-** : distribute as a share —**allotment** *n*

allow \ə'laú\ *vb* **1** : admit or concede **2** : permit —**allowable** *adj*

allowance \ə'laúəns\ *n* **1** : allotted share **2** : money given regularly for expenses

alloy \'al‚oí\ *n* : metals melted together —**alloy** \ə'loí\ *vb*

all right *adv or adj* **1** : satisfactorily **2** : yes **3** : certainly

allspice \'olspīs\ *n* : berry of a West Indian tree made into a spice

allude \ə'lüd\ *vb* **-luded; -luding** : refer indirectly —**allusion** \-'lüzhən\ *n* —**allusive** \-'lüsiv\ *adj* —**allusively** *adv* —**allusiveness** *n*

allure \ə'lúr\ *vb* **-lured; -luring** : entice ~ *n* : attractive power

ally \ə'lī, 'al‚ī\ *vb* **-lied; -lying** : enter into an alliance —**ally** \'al‚ī, ə'lī\ *n*

-ally \əlē\ *adv suffix* : -ly

almanac \'olmə‚nak, 'al-\ *n* : annual information book

almighty \ol'mītē\ *adj* : having absolute power

almond \'ämənd , 'am-, 'alm-, 'älm-\ *n* : tree with nutlike fruit kernels

almost \'ol‚mōst, ol-\ *adv* : very nearly

alms \'ämz, 'älmz, 'almz\ *n, pl* **alms** : charitable gift

aloft \ə'loft\ *adv* : high in the air

aloha \ä'lōhä\ *interj* —used to greet or bid farewell

alone \ə'lōn\ *adj* **1** : separated from others **2** : not including anyone or anything else —**alone** *adv*

along \ə'lon\ *prep* **1** : in line with the direction of **2** : at a point on or during ~ *adv* **1** : forward **2** : as a companion **3** : all the time

alongside *adv or prep* : along or by the side

alongside of *prep* : alongside

aloof \ə'lüf\ *adj* : indifferent and reserved —**aloofness** *n*

aloud \ə'laúd\ *adv* : so as to be heard

alpaca \al'pakə\ *n* **1** : So. American mammal related to the llama **2** : alpaca wool or cloth made of this

alphabet \'alfə‚bet, -bət\ *n* : ordered set of letters of a language —**alphabetical** \‚alfə'betikəl\, **alphabetic** \-'betik\ *adj* —**alphabetically** \-iklē\ *adv*

alphabetize \'alfəbə‚tīz\ *vb* **-ized; -izing** : arrange in alphabetical order —**alphabetizer** *n*

already \ol'redē\ *adv* : by a given time

also \'olsō\ *adv* : in addition

al·tar \'óltər\ *n* : structure for rituals

al·ter \'óltər\ *vb* : make different —**al·ter·a·tion** \óltə'rāshən\ *n*

al·ter·ca·tion \óltər'kāshən\ *n* : dispute

al·ter·nate \'óltərnət, 'al-\ *adj* **1** : arranged or succeeding by turns **2** : every other ~ \-ˌnāt\ *vb* -**nat·ed**; -**nat·ing** : occur or cause to occur by turns ~ \-nət\ *n* : substitute —**al·ter·nate·ly** *adv* —**al·ter·na·tion** \ˌóltər'nāshən, ˌal-\ *n*

alternating current *n* : electric current that regularly reverses direction

al·ter·na·tive \ól'tərnətiv, al-\ *adj* : offering a choice —**alternative** *n*

al·ter·na·tor \'óltərˌnātər, 'al-\ *n* : alternating-current generator

al·though \ól'thō\ *conj* : even though

al·tim·e·ter \al'timətər, 'altəˌmētər\ *n* : instrument for measuring altitude

al·ti·tude \'altəˌtüd, -ˌtyüd\ *n* **1** : distance up from the ground **2** : angular distance above the horizon

al·to \'altō\ *n, pl* -**tos** : lower female choral voice

al·to·geth·er \ˌóltə'gethər\ *adv* **1** : wholly **2** : on the whole

al·tru·ism \'altrùˌizəm\ *n* : concern for others —**al·tru·ist** \-ist\ *n* —**al·tru·is·tic** \ˌaltrù'istik\ *adj* —**al·tru·is·ti·cal·ly** \-tiklē\ *adv*

al·um \'aləm\ *n* : crystalline compound containing aluminum

alu·mi·num \ə'lümənəm\ *n* : silver-white malleable ductile light metallic element

alum·na \ə'ləmnə\ *n, pl* -**nae** \-ˌnē\ : woman graduate

alum·nus \ə'ləmnəs\ *n, pl* -**ni** \-ˌnī\ : graduate

al·ways \'ólwēz, -wāz\ *adv* **1** : at all times **2** : forever

am *pres 1st sing of* BE

amal·gam \ə'malgəm\ *n* **1** : mercury alloy **2** : mixture

amal·gam·ate \ə'malgəˌmāt\ *vb* -**at·ed**; -**at·ing** : unite —**amal·ga·ma·tion** \-ˌmalgə'māshən\ *n*

am·a·ryl·lis \ˌamə'riləs\ *n* : bulbous herb with clusters of large colored flowers like lilies

amass \ə'mas\ *vb* : gather

am·a·teur \'aməˌtər, -ˌtür, -ˌtyür, -ˌchür, -chər\ *n* **1** : person who does something for pleasure rather than for pay **2** : person who is not expert —

am·a·teur·ish \ˌamə'tərish, -'tür-, -'tyür-\ *adj* —**ama·teur·ism** \'aməˌtər,izəm, -ˌtür-, -ˌtyür-, -ˌchür-, -chər-\ *n*

am·a·to·ry \'aməˌtōrē\ *adj* : of or expressing sexual love

amaze \ə'māz\ *vb* **amazed; amaz·ing** : fill with wonder —**amaze·ment** *n* —**amaz·ing·ly** *adv*

am·a·zon \'aməˌzän, -zən, -zən\ *n* : tall strong woman —**am·a·zo·ni·an** \ˌamə'zōnēən\ *adj*

am·bas·sa·dor \am'basədər\ *n* : representative esp. of a government — **am·bas·sa·do·ri·al** \-ˌbasə'dōrēəl\ *adj* —**am·bas·sa·dor·ship** *n*

am·ber \'ambər\ *n* : yellowish fossil resin or its color

am·ber·gris \'ambərˌgris, -ˌgrēs\ *n* : waxy substance from certain whales used in making perfumes

am·bi·dex·trous \ˌambi'dekstrəs\ *adj* : equally skilled with both hands — **am·bi·dex·trous·ly** *adv*

am·bi·ence, am·bi·ance \'ambēəns, 'ämbē,äns\ *n* : pervading atmosphere

am·big·u·ous \am'bigyəwəs\ *adj* : having more than one interpretation —**am·bi·gu·i·ty** \ˌambə'gyüətē\ *n*

am·bi·tion \am'bishən\ *n* : eager desire for success or power —**am·bi·tious** \shəs\ *adj* —**am·bi·tious·ly** *adv*

am·biv·a·lence \am'bivələns\ *n* : simultaneous attraction and repulsion —**am·biv·a·lent** \-lənt\ *adj*

am·ble \'ambəl\ *vb* -**bled; -bling** : go at a leisurely gait —**amble** *n*

am·bu·lance \'ambyələns\ *n* : vehicle for carrying injured or sick persons

am·bu·la·to·ry \'ambyələˌtōrē\ *adj* **1** : relating to or adapted to walking **2** : able to walk about

am·bush \'amˌbush\ *n* : trap by which a surprise attack is made from a place of hiding —**ambush** *vb*

ame·lio·rate \ə'mēlyəˌrāt\ *vb* -**rat·ed**; -**rat·ing** : make or grow better— **ame·lio·ra·tion** \-ˌmēlyə'rāshən\ *n*

amen \'ä'men, 'ä-\ *interj* —used for affirmation esp. at the end of prayers

ame·na·ble \ə'mēnəbəl, -'men-\ *adj* : ready to yield or be influenced

amend \ə'mend\ *vb* **1** : improve **2** : alter in writing

amend·ment \-mənt\ *n* : change made in a formal document (as a law)

amends \ə'mendz\ *n sing or pl* : compensation for injury or loss

ame·ni·ty \ə'menətē, -'mē-\ *n, pl* **-ties** 1 : agreeableness 2 *pl* : social conventions 3 : something serving to comfort or accommodate

am·e·thyst \'aməthəst\ *n* : purple gemstone

ami·a·ble \'āmēəbəl\ *adj* : easy to get along with —**ami·a·bil·i·ty** \,āmēə-'bilətē\ *n* —**ami·a·bly** \'āmēəblē\ *adv*

am·i·ca·ble \'amikəbəl\ *adj* : friendly —**am·i·ca·bly** \-blē\ *adv*

amid \ə'mid\, **amidst** \-'midst\ *prep* : in or into the middle of

amino acid \ə'mēnō-\ *n* : nitrogen-containing acid

amiss \ə'mis\ *adv* : in the wrong way ~ *adj* : wrong

am·me·ter \'am,ētər\ *n* : instrument for measuring electric current

am·mo·nia \ə'mōnyə\ *n* 1 : colorless gaseous compound of nitrogen and hydrogen 2 : solution of ammonia in water

am·mu·ni·tion \,amyə'nishən\ *n* 1 : projectiles fired from guns 2 : explosive items used in war

am·ne·sia \am'nēzhə\ *n* : sudden loss of memory —**am·ne·si·ac** \-zē,ak, -zhē-\, **am·ne·sic** \-zik, -sik\ *adj or n*

am·nes·ty \'amnəstē\ *n, pl* **-ties** : a pardon for a group —**amnesty** *vb*

amoe·ba \ə'mēbə\ *n, pl* **-bas** *or* **-bae** \-,bē\ : tiny one-celled animal that occurs esp. in water —**amoe·bic** \-bik\ *adj*

amok \ə'mək, -'mäk\ *adv* : in a violent or uncontrolled way

among \ə'məŋ\ *prep* 1 : in or through 2 : in the number or class of 3 : in shares to each of

am·o·rous \'amərəs\ *adj* 1 : inclined to love 2 : being in love 3 : indicative of love —**am·o·rous·ly** *adv* —**am·o·rous·ness** *n*

amor·phous \ə'morfəs\ *adj* : shapeless

am·or·tize \'amər,tīz, ə'mor-\ *vb* **-tized;** **-tiz·ing** : get rid of (as a debt) gradually with periodic payments —**amor·ti·za·tion** \,amərtə'zāshən, ə,mort-\ *n*

amount \ə'maunt\ *vb* 1 : be equivalent 2 : reach a total ~ *n* : total number or quantity

amour \ə'mùr, ä-, a-\ *n* 1 : love affair 2 : lover

am·pere \'am,pir\ *n* : unit of electric current

am·per·sand \'ampər,sand\ *n* : character & used for the word *and*

am·phib·i·ous \am'fibēəs\ *adj* 1 : able to live both on land and in water 2 : adapted for both land and water —**am·phib·i·an** \-ən\ *n*

am·phi·the·ater \'amfə,thēətər\ *n* : oval or circular structure with rising tiers of seats around an arena

am·ple \'ampəl\ *adj* **-pler** \-plər\; **-plest** \-pləst\ 1 : large 2 : sufficient —**am·ply** \-plē\ *adv*

am·pli·fy \'amplə,fī\ *vb* **-fied;** **-fy·ing** : make louder, stronger, or more thorough —**am·pli·fi·ca·tion** \,ampləfə'kāshən\ *n* —**am·pli·fi·er** \'amplə,fīər\ *n*

am·pli·tude \-,tüd, -,tyüd\ *n* 1 : fullness 2 : extent of a vibratory movement

am·pu·tate \'ampyə,tāt\ *vb* **-tat·ed;** **-tat·ing** : cut off (a body part) —**am·pu·ta·tion** \,ampyə'tāshən\ *n* —**am·pu·tee** \,ampyə'tē\ *n*

amuck \ə'mək\ *var of* AMOK

am·u·let \'amyələt\ *n* : ornament worn as a charm against evil

amuse \ə'myüz\ *vb* **amused; amus·ing** 1 : engage the attention of in an interesting and pleasant way 2 : make laugh —**amuse·ment** *n*

an \ən, 'an\ *indefinite article* : a —used before words beginning with a vowel sound

-an \ən\, **-ian** \ēən\, **-ean** \ēən\ *n suffix* 1 : one that belongs to 2 : one skilled in ~ *adj suffix* 1 : of or belonging to 2 : characteristic of or resembling

anach·ro·nism \ə'nakrə,nizəm\ *n* : one that is chronologically out of place —**anach·ro·nis·tic** \ə,nakrə'nistik\ *adj*

an·a·con·da \,anə'kändə\ *n* : large So. American snake

ana·gram \'anə,gram\ *n* : word or phrase made by transposing the letters of another word or phrase

anal \'ānᵊl\ *adj* : relating to the anus

an·al·ge·sic \,anᵊl'jēzik, -sik\ *n* : pain reliever

anal·o·gy \ə'naləjē\ *n, pl* **-gies** 1 : similarity between unlike things 2 : example of something similar —**an·a·log·i·cal** \,anᵊl'äjikəl\ *adj* —**an·a·log·i·cal·ly** \-iklē\ *adv* —**anal·o·gous** \ə'naləgəs\ *adj*

anal·y·sis \ə'naləsəs\ *n, pl* **-y·ses** \-,sēz\ 1 : examination of a thing to deter-

mine its parts **2** : psychoanalysis —
an·a·lyst \'an°list\ *n* —**an·a·lyt·ic**
\,an°l'itik\, **an·a·lyt·i·cal** \-ikəl\ *adj*
—**an·a·lyt·i·cal·ly** \-iklē\ *adv*

an·a·lyze \'an°l,īz\ *vb* **-lyzed; -lyz·ing**
: make an analysis of

an·ar·chism \'anər,kizəm, -,när-\ *n*
: theory that all government is undesirable —**an·ar·chist** \-kist\ *n or adj*
—**an·ar·chis·tic** \,anər'kistik\ *adj*

an·ar·chy \'anərkē, -,när-\ *n* : lack of
government or order —**an·ar·chic** \a-
'närkik\ *adj* —**an·ar·chi·cal·ly** \-iklē\
adv

anath·e·ma \ə'nathəmə\ *n* **1** : solemn
curse **2** : person or thing accursed or
intensely disliked

anat·o·my \ə'natəmē\ *n, pl* **-mies**
: science dealing with the structure
of organisms —**an·a·tom·ic** \,anə-
'tämik\, **an·a·tom·i·cal** \-ikəl\ *adj*
—**an·a·tom·i·cal·ly** *adv* —**anat-
o·mist** \ə'natəmist\ *n*

-ance \əns\ *n suffix* **1** : action or process
2 : quality or state **3** : amount or degree

an·ces·tor \'an,sestər\ *n* : one from
whom an individual is descended

an·ces·tress \-trəs\ *n* : female ancestor

an·ces·try \-trē\ *n* **1** : line of descent **2**
: ancestors —**an·ces·tral** \an'sestrəl\
adj

an·chor \'aŋkər\ *n* : heavy device that
catches in the sea bottom to hold a
ship in place ~ *vb* : hold or become
held in place by or as if by an anchor
—**an·chor·age** \-kərij\ *n*

an·chor·man \'aŋkər,man\ *n* : news
broadcast coordinator

an·cho·vy \'an,chōvē, an'chō-\ *n, pl*
-vies *or* **-vy** : small herringlike fish

an·cient \'ānshənt\ *adj* **1** : having existed for many years **2** : belonging to
times long past —**ancient** *n*

-ancy \ənsē\ *n suffix* : quality or state

and \ənd, 'and\ *conj* —used to indicate
connection or addition

and·iron \'an,dīərn\ *n* : one of 2 metal
supports for wood in a fireplace

an·drog·y·nous \an'dräjənəs\ *adj* **1**
: having characteristics of both male
and female **2** : suitable for either sex

an·ec·dote \'anik,dōt\ *n* : brief story —
an·ec·dot·al \,anik'dōt°l\ *adj*

ane·mia \ə'nēmēə\ *n* : blood deficiency
—**ane·mic** \ə'nēmik\ *adj*

anem·o·ne \ə'nemənē\ *n* : small herb
with showy usu. white flowers

an·es·the·sia \,anəs'thēzhə\ *n* : loss of
bodily sensation

an·es·thet·ic \,anəs'thetik\ *n* : agent that
produces anesthesia —**anesthetic** *adj*
—**anes·the·tist** \ə'nesthətist\ *n* —
anes·the·tize \-thə,tīz\ *vb*

anew \ə'nü, -'nyü\ *adv* : over again

an·gel \'ānjəl\ *n* : spiritual being superior to humans —**an·gel·ic** \an'jelik\,
an·gel·i·cal \-ikəl\ *adj* —**an·gel·i-
cal·ly** *adv*

an·ger \'aŋgər\ *n* : strong feeling of displeasure ~ *vb* : make angry

an·gi·na \an'jīnə\ *n* : painful disorder of
heart muscles —**an·gi·nal** \an'jīn°l\
adj

¹an·gle \'aŋgəl\ *n* **1** : figure formed by
the meeting of 2 lines in a point **2**
: sharp corner **3** : point of view ~ *vb*
-gled; -gling : turn or direct at an angle

²angle *vb* **an·gled; an·gling** : fish with
a hook and line —**an·gler** \-glər\ *n* —
an·gle·worm *n* —**an·gling** *n*

an·go·ra \aŋ'gōrə, an-\ *n* : yarn or cloth
made from the hair of an Angora goat
or rabbit

an·gry \'aŋgrē\ *adj* **-gri·er; -est** : feeling
or showing anger —**an·gri·ly** \-grəlē\
adv

an·guish \'aŋgwish\ *n* : extreme pain or
distress of mind —**an·guished**
\-gwisht\ *adj*

an·gu·lar \'aŋgyələr\ *adj* **1** : having
many or sharp angles **2** : thin and
bony —**an·gu·lar·i·ty** \,aŋgyə'larətē\
n

an·i·mal \'anəməl\ *n* **1** : living being capable of feeling and voluntary motion
2 : lower animal as distinguished
from humans

an·i·mate \'anəmət\ *adj* : having life ~
\-,māt\ *vb* **-mat·ed; -mat·ing 1** : give
life or vigor to **2** : make appear to
move —**an·i·mat·ed** *adj*

an·i·ma·tion \,anə'māshən\ *n* **1** : liveliness **2** : animated cartoon

an·i·mos·i·ty \,anə'mäsətē\ *n, pl* **-ties**
: resentment

an·i·mus \'anəməs\ *n* : deep-seated hostility

an·ise \'anəs\ *n* : herb related to the carrot with aromatic seeds (**ani·seed**
\-,sēd\) used in flavoring

an·kle \'aŋkəl\ *n* : joint or region between the foot and the leg —**an·kle-
bone** *n*

an·nals \'an⁹lz\ *n pl* : chronological record of history —**an·nal·ist** \-⁹list\ *n*

an·neal \ə'nēl\ *vb* 1 : make less brittle by heating and then cooling 2 : strengthen or toughen

an·nex \ə'neks, 'an,eks\ *vb* : assume political control over (a territory) ~ \'an,eks, -iks\ *n* : added building —**an·nex·a·tion** \,an,ek'sāshən\ *n*

an·ni·hi·late \ə'nīə,lāt\ *vb* -**lat·ed**; -**lat·ing** : destroy —**an·ni·hi·la·tion** \-,nīə'lāshən\ *n*

an·ni·ver·sa·ry \,anə'vərsərē\ *n, pl* -**ries** : annual return of the date of a notable event or its celebration

an·no·tate \'anə,tāt\ *vb* -**tat·ed**; -**tat·ing** : furnish with notes —**an·no·ta·tion** \,anə'tāshən\ *n* —**an·no·ta·tor** \'anə,tātər\ *n*

an·nounce \ə'nauns\ *vb* -**nounced**; -**nounc·ing** : make known publicly —**an·nounce·ment** *n* —**an·nounc·er** *n*

an·noy \ə'nói\ *vb* : disturb or irritate —**an·noy·ance** \-əns\ *n* —**an·noy·ing·ly** \-'nóiiŋlē\ *adv*

an·nu·al \'anyəwəl\ *adj* 1 : occurring once a year 2 : living only one year —**annual** *n* —**an·nu·al·ly** *adv*

an·nu·i·ty \ə'nüətē, -'nyü-\ *n, pl* -**ties** : amount payable annually or the right to such a payment

an·nul \ə'nəl\ *vb* -**ll**- : make legally void —**an·nul·ment** *n*

an·ode \'an,ōd\ *n* 1 : positive electrode 2 : negative battery terminal —**an·od·ic** \a'nädik\

anoint \ə'nóint\ *vb* : apply oil to as a rite —**anoint·ment** *n*

anom·a·ly \ə'näməlē\ *n, pl* -**lies** : something abnormal or unusual —**anom·a·lous** \ə'nämələs\ *adj*

anon·y·mous \ə'nänəməs\ *adj* : of unknown origin —**an·o·nym·i·ty** \,anə'nimətē\ *n* —**anon·y·mous·ly** *adv*

an·oth·er \ə'nəthər\ *adj* 1 : any or some other 2 : one more ~ *pron* 1 : one more 2 : one different

an·swer \'ansər\ *n* 1 : something spoken or written in reply to a question 2 : solution to a problem ~ *vb* 1 : reply to 2 : be responsible 3 : be adequate —**an·swer·er** *n*

an·swer·able \-rəbəl\ *adj* : responsible

ant \'ant\ *n* : small social insect —**ant·hill** *n*

-ant \ənt\ *n suffix* 1 : one that performs or causes an action 2 : thing that is acted upon ~ *adj suffix* 1 : performing an action or being in a condition 2 : causing an action or process

an·tag·o·nism \an'tagə,nizəm\ *n* : active opposition or hostility —**an·tag·o·nist** \-ənist\ *n* —**an·tag·o·nis·tic** \-,tagə'nistik\ *adj*

an·tag·o·nize \an'tagə,nīz\ *vb* -**nized**; -**niz·ing** : cause to be hostile

ant·arc·tic \ant'ärktik, -'ärtik\ *adj* : relating to the region near the south pole

antarctic circle *n* : circle parallel to the equator approximately 23°27' from the south pole

an·te·bel·lum \,anti'beləm\ *adj* : existing before the U.S. Civil War

an·te·ced·ent \,antə'sēd⁹nt\ *n* : one that comes before —**antecedent** *adj*

an·te·lope \'ant⁹l,ōp\ *n, pl* -**lope** *or* -**lopes** : deerlike mammal related to the ox

an·ten·na \an'tenə\ *n, pl* -**nae** \-,nē\ *or* -**nas** 1 : one of the long slender paired sensory organs on the head of an arthropod 2 *pl* -**nas** : metallic device for sending or receiving radio waves

an·te·ri·or \an'tirēər\ *adj* : located before in place or time

an·them \'anthəm\ *n* : song or hymn of praise or gladness

an·ther \'anthər\ *n* : part of a seed plant that contains pollen

an·thol·o·gy \an'thäləjē\ *n, pl* -**gies** : literary collection

an·thra·cite \'anthrə,sīt\ *n* : hard coal

an·thro·poid \'anthrə,póid\ *n* : large ape —**anthropoid** *adj*

an·thro·pol·o·gy \,anthrə'päləjē\ *n* : science dealing with humans —**an·thro·po·log·i·cal** \-pə'läjikəl\ *adj* —**an·thro·pol·o·gist** \-'päləjist\ *n*

anti- \,antē, -,tī\, **ant-**, **anth-** *prefix* 1 : opposite in kind, position, or action 2 : opposing or hostile toward 3 : defending against 4 : curing or treating

antiabortion	antiart
antiacademic	antiauthoritar-
antiadministra-	ian
tion	antiauthority
antiaggression	antibacterial
antiaircraft	antibias
antialien	antiblack
antiapartheid	antibourgeois
antiaristocratic	antiboycott

antibureau-
cratic
antiburglar
antiburglary
antibusiness
anticancer
anticapitalism
anticapitalist
anti-Catholic
anticensorship
anti-Christian
anti-Chris-
tianity
antichurch
anticigarette
anticlerical
anticollision
anticolonial
anticommunism
anticommunist
anticonserva-
tion
anticonserva-
tionist
anticonsumer
anticonven-
tional
anticorrosion
anticorrosive
anticorruption
anticrime
anticruelty
anticult
anticultural
antidandruff
antidemocratic
antidiscrimina-
tion
antidrug
antidumping
antiestablish-
ment
antievolution
antievolutionary
antifamily
antifascism
antifascist
antifatigue
antifemale
antifeminine
antifeminism
antifeminist
antifertility
antiforeign
antiforeigner
antifraud
antigambling
antiglare

antigovernment
antiguerrilla
antigun
antihijack
antihomosexual
antihuman
antihumanism
antihumanistic
antihunting
anti-imperial-
ism
anti-imperialist
anti-inflation
anti-inflationary
anti-institu-
tional
anti-integration
anti-intellectual
anti-intellectual-
ism
antijamming
anti-Jewish
antilabor
antiliberal
antiliberalism
antilitter
antilittering
antilynching
antimale
antimanage-
ment
antimaterialism
antimaterialist
antimicrobial
antimilitarism
antimilitarist
antimilitary
antimiscegena-
tion
antimonopolist
antimonopoly
antimosquito
antinoise
antiobesity
antiobscenity
antipapal
antipersonnel
antipolice
antipollution
antiporno-
graphic
antipornogra-
phy
antipoverty
antiprofiteering
antiprogressive
antiprostitution
antirabies

antiracketeering
antiradical
antirape
antirealism
antirecession
antireform
antireligious
antirevolution-
ary
antiriot
antiromantic
antirust
antisegregation
antisex
antisexist
antisexual
antishoplifting
antislavery
antismoking
antismuggling
antismut
antispending
antistrike
antistudent
antisubmarine
antisubversion
antisubversive
antisuicide
antitank

antitax
antitechnologi-
cal
antitechnology
antiterrorism
antiterrorist
antitheft
antitobacco
antitotalitarian
antitoxin
antitraditional
antitrust
antituberculosis
antitumor
antityphoid
antiulcer
antiunemploy-
ment
antiunion
antiuniversity
antiurban
antiviolence
antiviral
antivivisection
antiwar
anti-West
anti-Western
antiwhite
antiwoman

an·ti·bi·ot·ic \,antēbī'ätik, -bē-\ *n* : substance that inhibits harmful microorganisms —**antibiotic** *adj*

an·ti·body \'anti,bädē\ *n* : bodily substance that counteracts the effects of a foreign substance or organism

an·tic \'antik\ *n* : playful act ~ *adj* : playful

an·tic·i·pate \an'tisə,pāt\ *vb* -**pat·ed**; -**pat·ing** **1** : be prepared for **2** : look forward to —**an·tic·i·pa·tion** \-,tisə-'pāshən\ *n* —**an·tic·i·pa·to·ry** \-'tisəpə,tōrē\ *adj*

an·ti·cli·max \,antē'klī,maks\ *n* : something strikingly less important than what has preceded it —**an·ti·cli·mac·tic** \-klī'maktik\ *adj*

an·ti·dote \'anti,dōt\ *n* : remedy for poison

an·ti·freeze \'anti,frēz\ *n* : substance to prevent a liquid from freezing

an·ti·mo·ny \'antə,mōnē\ *n* : brittle white metallic chemical element

an·tip·a·thy \an'tipəthē\ *n, pl* -**thies** : strong dislike

an·ti·quar·i·an \,antə'kwerēən\ *adj* : relating to antiquities or old books

—**antiquarian** n —**an·ti·quari·an·ism** n

an·ti·quary \'antə,kwerē\ n, pl -**quar·ies** : one who collects or studies antiquities

an·ti·quat·ed \'antə,kwātəd\ adj : out-of-date

an·tique \an'tēk\ adj : very old or out-of-date —**antique** n

an·tiq·ui·ty \an'tikwətē\ n, pl -**ties 1** : ancient times **2** pl : relics of ancient times

an·ti·sep·tic \,antə'septik\ adj : killing or checking the growth of germs —**antiseptic** n —**an·ti·sep·ti·cal·ly** \-tiklē\ adv

an·tith·e·sis \an'tithəsəs\ n, pl -**e·ses** \-,sēz\ : direct opposite

ant·ler \'antlər\ n : solid branched horn of a deer —**ant·lered** \-lərd\ adj

ant·onym \'antə,nim\ n : word of opposite meaning

anus \'ānəs\ n : the rear opening of the alimentary canal

an·vil \'anvəl\ n : heavy iron block on which metal is shaped

anx·i·ety \aŋ'zīətē\ n, pl -**eties** : uneasiness usu. over an expected misfortune

anx·ious \'aŋkshəs\ adj **1** : uneasy **2** : earnestly wishing —**anx·ious·ly** adv

any \'enē\ adj **1** : one chosen at random **2** : of whatever number or quantity ~ pron **1** : any one or ones **2** : any amount ~ adv : to any extent or degree

any·body \-bədē, -,bäd-\ pron : anyone

any·how \-,hau\ adv **1** : in any way **2** : nevertheless

any·more \,enē'mōr\ adv : at the present time

any·one \-'enē,wən\ pron : any person

any·place adv : anywhere

any·thing pron : any thing whatever

any·time adv : at any time whatever

any·way adv : anyhow

any·where adv : in or to any place

aor·ta \ā'ortə\ n, pl -**tas** or -**tae** \-ē\ : main artery from the heart —**aor·tic** \ā'ortik\ adj

apart \ə'pärt\ adv **1** : separately in place or time **2** : aside **3** : to pieces

apart·heid \ə'pär,tāt, -,tīt\ n : racial segregation

apart·ment \ə'pärtmənt\ n : set of usu. rented rooms

ap·a·thy \'apəthē\ n : lack of emotion or interest —**ap·a·thet·ic** \,apə'thetik\ adj —**ap·a·thet·i·cal·ly** \-iklē\ adv

ape \'āp\ n : large tailless primate ~ vb **aped; ap·ing** : imitate

ap·er·ture \'apər,chúr, -chər\ n : opening

apex \'ā,peks\ n, pl **apex·es** or **api·ces** \'āpə,sēz, 'apə-\ : highest point

aphid \'āfid, 'a-\ n : small insect that sucks plant juices

aph·o·rism \'afə,rizəm\ n : short saying stating a general truth —**aph·oris·tic** \,afə'ristik\

aph·ro·di·si·ac \,afrə'dēzē,ak, -'diz-\ : substance that excites sexual desire

api·a·rist \'āpēərist\ n : beekeeper —**api·ary** \-pē,erē\ n

apiece \ə'pēs\ adv : for each one

aplen·ty \ə'plentē\ adj : plentiful or abundant

aplomb \ə'pläm, -'pləm\ n : complete calmness or self-assurance

apoc·a·lypse \ə'päkə,lips\ n : writing prophesying a cataclysm in which evil forces are destroyed —**apoc·alyp·tic** \-,päkə'liptik\ adj

apoc·ry·pha \ə'päkrəfə\ n : writings of dubious authenticity —**apoc·ry·phal** \-fəl\ adj

apol·o·get·ic \ə,pälə'jetik\ adj : expressing apology —**apol·o·get·i·cal·ly** \-iklē\ adv

apol·o·gize \ə'pälə,jīz\ vb -**gized; -giz·ing** : make an apology —**apol·o·gist** \-jist\ n

apol·o·gy \ə'päləjē\ n, pl -**gies 1** : formal justification for a wrong **2** : expression of regret for a wrong

ap·o·plexy \'apə,pleksē\ n : sudden loss of consciousness caused by rupture or obstruction of an artery of the brain —**ap·o·plec·tic** \,apə'plektik\ adj

apos·ta·sy \ə'pästəsē\ n, pl -**sies** : abandonment of a former loyalty —**apos·tate** \ə'päs,tāt\ adj or n

apos·tle \ə'päsəl\ n : disciple or advocate —**apos·tle·ship** n —**ap·os·tolic** \,apə'stälik\ adj

apos·tro·phe \ə'pästrə,fē\ n : punctuation mark ' to indicate the possessive case or the omission of a letter or figure

apoth·e·cary \ə'päthə,kerē\ n, pl -**car·ies** : druggist

ap·pall \ə'pol\ vb : fill with horror or dismay

ap·pa·ra·tus \,apə'ratəs, -'rāt-\ n, pl -**tus·es** or -**tus 1** : equipment **2** : complex machine or device ap·par·el \ə'parəl\ n : clothing

ap·par·ent \ə'parənt\ adj 1 : visible 2 : obvious 3 : seeming —ap·par·ent·ly adv

ap·pa·ri·tion \ˌapə'rishən\ n : ghost

ap·peal \ə'pēl\ vb 1 : try to have a court case reheard 2 : ask earnestly 3 : have an attraction —appeal n

ap·pear \ə'pir\ vb 1 : become visible or evident 2 : come into the presence of someone 3 : seem

ap·pear·ance \ə'pirəns\ n 1 : act of appearing 2 : outward aspect

ap·pease \ə'pēz\ vb -peased; -peas·ing : pacify with concessions —ap·pease·ment n

ap·pel·late \ə'pelət\ adj : having power to review decisions

ap·pend \ə'pend\ vb : attach

ap·pend·age \ə'pendij\ n : something attached

ap·pen·dec·to·my \ˌapən'dektəmē\ n, pl -mies : surgical removal of the appendix

ap·pen·di·ci·tis \ə,pendə'sītəs\ n : inflammation of the appendix

ap·pen·dix \ə'pendiks\ n, pl -dix·es or -di·ces \-də,sēz\ 1 : supplementary matter 2 : narrow closed tube extending from lower right intestine

ap·pe·tite \'apə,tīt\ n 1 : natural desire esp. for food 2 : preference

ap·pe·tiz·er \-,tīzər\ n : food or drink to stimulate the appetite

ap·pe·tiz·ing \-ziŋ\ adj : tempting to the appetite —ap·pe·tiz·ing·ly adv

ap·plaud \ə'plȯd\ vb : show approval esp. by clapping

ap·plause \ə'plȯz\ n : a clapping in approval

ap·ple \'apəl\ n : rounded fruit with firm white flesh

ap·ple·jack \-,jak\ n : brandy made from cider

ap·pli·ance \ə'plīəns\ n : household machine or device

ap·pli·ca·ble \'aplikəbəl, ə'plikə-\ adj : capable of being applied —ap·pli·ca·bil·i·ty \ˌaplikə'bilətē, ə,plikə-\ n

ap·pli·cant \'aplikənt\ n : one who applies

ap·pli·ca·tion \ˌaplə'kāshən\ n 1 : act of applying or thing applied 2 : constant attention 3 : request

ap·pli·ca·tor \'aplə,kātər\ n : device for applying a substance

ap·pli·qué \ˌaplə'kā\ n : cut-out fabric decoration —appliqué vb

ap·ply \ə'plī\ vb -plied; -ply·ing 1 : place in contact 2 : put to practical use 3 : devote (one's) attention or efforts to something 4 : submit a request 5 : have reference or a connection

ap·point \ə'pȯint\ vb 1 : set or assign officially 2 : equip or furnish —ap·point·ee \ə,pȯin'tē, ,a-\ n

ap·point·ment \ə'pȯintmənt\ n 1 : act of appointing 2 : nonelective political job 3 : arrangement for a meeting

ap·por·tion \ə'pōrshən\ vb : distribute proportionately —ap·por·tion·ment n

ap·po·site \'apəzət\ adj : suitable —ap·po·site·ly adv —ap·po·site·ness n

ap·praise \ə'prāz\ vb -praised; -prais·ing : set value on —ap·prais·al \-'prāzəl\ —ap·prais·er n

ap·pre·cia·ble \ə'prēshəbəl\ adj : considerable —ap·pre·cia·bly \-blē\ adv

ap·pre·ci·ate \ə'prēshē,āt\ vb -ated; -at·ing 1 : value justly 2 : be grateful for 3 : increase in value —ap·pre·cia·tion \-,prēshē'āshən\ n

ap·pre·cia·tive \ə'prēshətiv, -shē,āt-\ adj : showing appreciation

ap·pre·hend \ˌapri'hend\ vb 1 : arrest 2 : look forward to in dread 3 : understand —ap·pre·hen·sion \-'henchən\ n

ap·pre·hen·sive \-'hensiv\ adj : fearful —ap·pre·hen·sive·ly adv —ap·pre·hen·sive·ness n

ap·pren·tice \ə'prentəs\ n : person learning a craft ~ vb -ticed; -tic·ing : employ or work as an apprentice —ap·pren·tice·ship n

ap·prise \ə'prīz\ vb -prised; -pris·ing : inform

ap·proach \ə'prōch\ vb 1 : move nearer or be close to 2 : make initial advances or efforts toward —approach n —ap·proach·able adj

ap·pro·ba·tion \ˌaprə'bāshən\ n : approval

ap·pro·pri·ate \ə'prōprē,āt\ vb -at·ed; -at·ing 1 : take possession of 2 : set apart for a particular use ~ \-'prēət\ adj : suitable —ap·pro·pri·ate·ly adv —ap·pro·pri·ate·ness n —ap·pro·pri·a·tion \ə,prōprē'āshən\ n

ap·prov·al \ə'prüvəl\ n : act of approving

ap·prove \ə'prüv\ vb **-proved; -prov·ing** : accept as satisfactory

ap·prox·i·mate \ə'präksəmət\ adj : nearly correct or exact ~ \-,māt\ vb **-mat·ed; -mat·ing** : come near —**ap·prox·i·mate·ly** adv —**ap·prox·i·ma·tion** \-,präksə'māshən\ n

ap·pur·te·nance \ə'pərt⁴nəns\ n : accessory —**ap·pur·te·nant** \-'pərt-⁴nənt\ adj

apri·cot \'aprə,kät, 'ā-\ n : peachlike fruit

April \'āprəl\ n : 4th month of the year having 30 days

apron \'āprən\ n : protective garment

ap·ro·pos \,aprə'pō, 'aprə,pō\ adv : suitably ~ adj : being to the point

apropos of prep : with regard to

apt \'apt\ adj **1** : suitable **2** : likely **3** : quick to learn —**apt·ly** adv —**apt·ness** n

ap·ti·tude \'aptə,tüd, -tyüd\ n **1** : capacity for learning **2** : natural ability

aqua \'akwə, 'äk-\ n : light greenish blue color

aquar·i·um \ə'kwareəm\ n, pl **-i·ums** or **-ia** \-ēə\ : glass container for aquatic animals and plants

aquat·ic \ə'kwätik, -'kwat-\ adj : of or relating to water —**aquatic** n

aq·ue·duct \'akwə,dəkt\ n : conduit for carrying running water

aqui·line \'akwə,līn, -lən\ adj : curved like an eagle's beak

-ar \ər\ adj suffix **1** : of, relating to, or being **2** : resembling

ar·a·besque \,arə'besk\ n : intricate design

ar·a·ble \'arəbəl\ adj : fit for crops

ar·bi·ter \'ärbətər\ n : final authority

ar·bi·trary \'ärbə,trerē\ adj **1** : selected at random **2** : autocratic —**ar·bi·trari·ly** \,ärbə'trerəlē\ adv —**ar·bi·trari·ness** \'ärbə,trerēnəs\ n

ar·bi·trate \'ärbə,trāt\ vb **-trat·ed; -trat·ing** : settle a dispute as arbitrator —**ar·bi·tra·tion** \,ärbə'trāshən\ n

ar·bi·tra·tor \'ärbə,trātər\ n : one chosen to settle a dispute

ar·bor \'ärbər\ n : shelter under branches or vines

ar·bo·re·al \är'bōrēəl\ adj : living in trees

arc \'ärk\ n **1** : part of a circle **2** : bright sustained electrical discharge ~ vb **arced** \'ärkt\; **arc·ing** \'ärkiŋ\ : form an arc

ar·cade \är'kād\ n : arched passageway between shops

ar·cane \är'kān\ adj : mysterious or secret

¹arch \'ärch\ n : curved structure spanning an opening ~ vb : cover with or form into an arch

²arch adj **1** : chief —usu. in combination **2** : mischievous —**arch·ly** adv —**arch·ness** n

ar·chae·ol·o·gy, ar·che·ol·o·gy \,ärkē-'äləjē\ n : study of past human life —**ar·chae·o·log·i·cal** \-kēə'läjikəl\ —**ar·chae·ol·o·gist** \-kē'äləjist\ n

ar·cha·ic \är'kāik\ adj : belonging to an earlier time —**ar·cha·i·cal·ly** \-iklē\ adv

arch·an·gel \'ärk,ānjəl\ n : angel of high rank

arch·bish·op \ärch'bishəp\ n : chief bishop —**arch·bish·op·ric** \-ə,prik\ n

arch·di·o·cese \-'dīəsəs, -,sēz, -,sēs\ n : diocese of an archbishop

ar·chery \'ärchərē\ n : shooting with bow and arrows —**ar·cher** \-chər\ n

ar·che·type \'ärki,tīp\ n : original pattern or model

ar·chi·pel·a·go \,ärkə'pelə,gō, ,ärchə-\ n, pl **-goes** or **-gos** : group of islands

ar·chi·tect \'ärkə,tekt\ n : building designer

ar·chi·tec·ture \'ärkə,tekchər\ n **1** : building design **2** : style of building **3** : manner of organizing elements —**ar·chi·tec·tur·al** \,ärkə'tekchərəl, -'tekshrəl\ adj —**ar·chi·tec·tur·al·ly** adv

ar·chives \'är,kīvz\ n pl : public records or their storage place —**archi·vist** \'ärkəvist, -,kī-\ n

arch·way \'ärch,wā\ n : passageway under an arch

arc·tic \'ärktik, 'ärt-\ adj **1** : relating to the region near the north pole **2** : frigid

arctic circle n : circle parallel to the equator approximately 23°27' from the north pole

-ard \ərd\ n suffix : one that is

ar·dent \'ärd⁴nt\ adj : characterized by warmth of feeling —**ar·dent·ly** adv

ar·dor \'ärdər\ n : warmth of feeling

ar·du·ous \'ärjəwəs\ adj : difficult —**ar·du·ous·ly** adv —**ar·du·ous·ness** n

are pres 2d sing or pres pl of BE

area \'arēə\ n **1** : space for something **2** : amount of surface included **3** : region **4** : range covered by a thing or concept

area code *n* : 3-digit area-identifying telephone number

are·na \ə'rēnə\ *n* 1 : enclosed exhibition area 2 : sphere of activity

ar·gon \'är,gän\ *n* : colorless odorless gaseous chemical element

ar·got \'ärgət, -,gō\ *n* : special language (as of the underworld)

ar·gu·able \'ärgyəwəbəl\ *adj* : open to dispute

ar·gue \'ärgyü\ *vb* **-gued; -gu·ing** 1 : give reasons for or against something 2 : disagree in words

ar·gu·ment \'ärgyəmənt\ *n* 1 : reasons given to persuade 2 : dispute with words

ar·gu·men·ta·tive \,ärgyə'mentətiv\ *adj* : inclined to argue

ar·gyle \'är,gīl\ *n* : colorful diamond pattern in knitting

aria \'ärēə\ *n* : opera solo

ar·id \'arəd\ *adj* : very dry **—arid·i·ty** \ə'ridətē\ *n*

arise \ə'rīz\ *vb* **arose** \-'rōz\; **aris·en** \-'riz°n\; **aris·ing** \-'rīziŋ\ 1 : get up 2 : originate

ar·is·toc·ra·cy \,arə'stäkrəsē\ *n, pl* **-cies** : upper class **—aris·to·crat** \ə'ristə,krat\ *n* **—aris·to·crat·ic** \ə,ristə'kratik\ *adj*

arith·me·tic \ə'rithmə,tik\ *n* : mathematics that deals with numbers **—arith·met·ic** \,arith'metik\, **arith·met·i·cal** \-ikəl\ *adj*

ark \'ärk\ *n* : big boat

¹arm \'ärm\ *n* 1 : upper limb 2 : branch **—armed** \'ärmd\ *adj* **—arm·less** *adj*

²arm *vb* : furnish with weapons ∼ *n* 1 : weapon 2 : branch of the military forces 3 *pl* : family's heraldic designs

ar·ma·da \är'mädə, -'mäd-\ *n* : naval fleet

ar·ma·dil·lo \,ärmə'dilō\ *n, pl* **-los** : burrowing mammal covered with bony plates

ar·ma·ment \'ärməmənt\ *n* : military arms and equipment

ar·ma·ture \'ärmə,chúr, -chər\ *n* : rotating part of an electric generator or motor

armed forces *n pl* : military

ar·mi·stice \'ärməstəs\ *n* : truce

ar·mor \'ärmər\ *n* : protective covering **—ar·mored** \-mərd\ *adj*

ar·mory \'ärmərē\ *n, pl* **-mor·ies** : factory or storehouse for arms

arm·pit *n* : hollow under the junction of the arm and shoulder

ar·my \'ärmē\ *n, pl* **-mies** 1 : body of men organized for war esp. on land 2 : great number

aro·ma \ə'rōmə\ *n* : usu. pleasing odor **—ar·o·mat·ic** \,arə'matik\ *adj*

around \ə'raúnd\ *adv* 1 : in or along a circuit 2 : on all sides 3 : near 4 : in an opposite direction ∼ *prep* 1 : surrounding 2 : along the circuit of 3 : to or on the other side of 4 : near

arouse \ə'raúz\ *vb* **aroused; arous·ing** 1 : awaken from sleep 2 : stir up **—arous·al** \-'raúzəl\ *n*

ar·raign \ə'rān\ *vb* 1 : call before a court to answer to an indictment 2 : accuse **—ar·raign·ment** *n*

ar·range \ə'rānj\ *vb* **-ranged; -rang·ing** 1 : put in order 2 : settle or agree on 3 : adapt (a musical composition) for voices or instruments **—ar·range·ment** *n* **—ar·rang·er** *n*

ar·ray \ə'rā\ *vb* 1 : arrange in order 2 : dress esp. splendidly ∼ *n* 1 : arrangement 2 : rich clothing 3 : imposing group

ar·rears \ə'rirz\ *n pl* : state of being behind in paying debts

ar·rest \ə'rest\ *vb* 1 : stop 2 : take into legal custody **—arrest** *n*

ar·rive \ə'rīv\ *vb* **-rived; -riv·ing** 1 : reach a destination, point, or stage 2 : come near in time **—ar·riv·al** \-əl\ *n*

ar·ro·gant \'arəgənt\ *adj* : showing an offensive sense of superiority **—ar·ro·gance** \-gəns\ *n* **—ar·ro·gant·ly** *adv*

ar·ro·gate \-,gāt\ *vb* **-gat·ed; -gat·ing** : to claim without justification

ar·row \'arō\ *n* : slender missile shot from a bow **—ar·row·head** *n*

ar·royo \ə'róiō, -ə\ *n, pl* **-royos** 1 : watercourse 2 : gully

ar·se·nal \'ärs°nəl\ *n* 1 : place where arms are made or stored 2 : store

ar·se·nic \'ärs°nik\ *n* : solid grayish poisonous chemical element

ar·son \'ärs°n\ *n* : willful or malicious burning of property **—ar·son·ist** \-ist\ *n*

art \'ärt\ *n* 1 : skill 2 : branch of learning 3 : creation of things of beauty or works so produced 4 : ingenuity

ar·te·rio·scle·ro·sis \ar,tirēōsklə'rōsəs\ *n* : hardening of the arteries **—ar·te·rio·scle·rot·ic** \-'rätik\ *adj or n*

ar·tery \'ärtərē\ *n, pl* **-ter·ies** 1 : tubular vessel carrying blood from the heart

2 : thoroughfare —**ar•te•ri•al** \är-'tirēəl\ adj

art•ful \-fəl\ adj 1 : ingenious 2 : crafty —**art•ful•ly** adv —**art•ful•ness** n

ar•thri•tis \är'thrītəs\ n, pl **-ti•des** \-'thritə,dēz\ : inflammation of the joints —**ar•thrit•ic** \,'thritik\ adj or n

ar•thro•pod \'ärthrə,päd\ n : invertebrate animal (as an insect or crab) with segmented body and jointed limbs —**arthropod** adj

ar•ti•choke \'ärtə,chōk\ n : tall thistle-like herb or its edible flower head

ar•ti•cle \'ärtikəl\ n 1 : distinct part of a written document 2 : nonfictional published piece of writing 3 : word (as *an, the*) used to limit a noun 4 : item or piece

ar•tic•u•late \är'tikyələt\ adj : able to speak effectively ~ \-,lāt\ vb **-lated;** **-lat•ing** 1 : utter distinctly 2 : unite by joints —**ar•tic•u•late•ly** adv —**ar•tic•u•late•ness** n —**ar•tic•u•la•tion** \-,tikyə'lāshən\ n

ar•ti•fact \'ärtə,fakt\ n : object of esp. prehistoric human workmanship

ar•ti•fice \'ärtəfəs\ n 1 : trick or trickery 2 : ingenious device or ingenuity

ar•ti•fi•cial \,ärtə'fishəl\ adj 1 : man-made 2 : not genuine —**ar•ti•fi•ci•al•i•ty** \-,fishē'alətē\ n —**ar•ti•fi•cial•ly** adv —**ar•ti•fi•cial•ness** n

ar•til•lery \är'tilərē\ n, pl **-ler•ies** : large caliber firearms

ar•ti•san \'ärtəzən, -sən\ n : skilled craftsman

art•ist \'ärtist\ n : one who creates art —**ar•tis•tic** \är'tistik\ adj —**ar•tis•ti•cal•ly** \-iklē\ adv —**ar•tis•try** \'ärtəstrē\ n

art•less \'ärtləs\ adj : sincere or natural —**art•less•ly** adv —**art•less•ness** n

arty \'ärtē\ adj **art•i•er; -est** : pretentiously artistic —**art•i•ly** \'ärt°lē\ adv —**art•i•ness** n

-ary \,erē\ adj suffix : of, relating to, or connected with

as \əz, ,az\ adv 1 : to the same degree 2 : for example ~ conj 1 : in the same way or degree as 2 : while 3 : because 4 : though ~ pron —used after *same* or *such* ~ prep : in the capacity of

as•bes•tos \as'bestəs, az-\ n : fibrous incombustible mineral

as•cend \ə'send\ vb : move upward —**as•cen•sion** \-'senchən\ n

as•cen•dan•cy \ə'sendənsē\ n : domination

as•cen•dant \ə'sendənt\ n : dominant position ~ adj 1 : moving upward 2 : dominant

as•cent \ə'sent\ n 1 : act of moving upward 2 : degree of upward slope

as•cer•tain \,asər'tān\ vb : determine —**as•cer•tain•able** adj

as•cet•ic \ə'setik\ adj : self-denying —**ascetic** n —**as•cet•i•cism** \-'setə,sizəm\ n

as•cribe \ə'skrīb\ vb **-cribed; -crib•ing** : attribute —**as•crib•able** adj —**as•crip•tion** \-'skripshən\ n

asep•tic \ā'septik\ adj : free of disease germs

¹ash \'ash\ n : tree related to the olives

²ash n : matter left when something is burned —**ash•tray** n

ashamed \ə'shāmd\ adj : feeling shame —**asham•ed•ly** \-'shāmədlē\ adv

ash•en \'ashən\ adj : deadly pale

ashore \ə'shōr\ adv : on or to the shore

aside \ə'sīd\ adv 1 : toward the side 2 : out of the way

aside from prep 1 : besides 2 : except for

as•i•nine \'as°n,īn\ adj : foolish —**asi•nin•i•ty** \,as°n'inətē\ n

ask \'ask\ vb 1 : call on for an answer or help 2 : utter (a question or request) 3 : invite

askance \ə'skans\ adv 1 : with a side glance 2 : with mistrust

askew \ə'skyü\ adv or adj : out of line

asleep \ə'slēp\ adv or adj 1 : sleeping 2 : numbed 3 : inactive

as long as conj 1 : on condition that 2 : because

as of prep : from the time of

as•par•a•gus \ə'sparəgəs\ n : tall herb related to the lilies or its edible stalks

as•pect \'as,pekt\ n 1 : way something looks to the eye or mind 2 : phase

as•pen \'aspən\ n : poplar

as•per•i•ty \a'sperətē, ə-\ n, pl **-ties** 1 : roughness 2 : harshness

as•per•sion \ə'spərzhən\ n : remark that hurts someone's reputation

as•phalt \'as,fòlt\ n : dark tarlike substance used in paving

as•phyx•ia \as'fiksēə\ n : lack of oxygen causing unconsciousness

as•phyx•i•ate \-,se,āt\ vb **-at•ed; -at•ing** : suffocate —**as•phyx•i•a•tion** \-,fiksē'āshən\ n

as·pi·ra·tion \,aspǝ'rāshǝn\ n : strong desire to achieve a goal

as·pire \ǝ'spīr\ vb **-pired; -pir·ing** : have an ambition **—as·pir·ant** \'aspǝrǝnt, ǝ'spīrǝnt\ n

as·pi·rin \'asprǝn\ n, pl **aspirin** or **as·pirins** : pain reliever

ass \'as\ n 1 : long-eared animal related to the horse 2 : stupid person

as·sail \ǝ'sāl\ vb : attack violently **—as·sail·able** adj **—as·sail·ant** n

as·sas·si·nate \ǝ'sas°n,āt\ vb **-nat·ed; -nat·ing** : murder esp. for political reasons **—as·sas·sin** \-'sas°n\ n **—as·sas·si·na·tion** \-,sas°n'āshǝn\ n

as·sault \ǝ'sòlt\ n or vb : attack

as·say \'as,ā, a'sā\ n : analysis (as of an ore) to determine quality or properties **—as·say** \a'sā, 'as,ā\ vb

as·sem·ble \ǝ'sembǝl\ vb **-bled; -bling** 1 : collect into one place 2 : fit together the parts

as·sem·bly \-blē\ n, pl **-blies** 1 : meeting 2 cap : legislative body 3 : a fitting together of parts

as·sem·bly·man \-mǝn\ n : member of a legislative assembly

as·sem·bly·wom·an \-,wù-mǝn\ n : woman who is a member of a legislative assembly

as·sent \ǝ'sent\ vb or n : consent

as·sert \ǝ'sǝrt\ vb 1 : declare 2 : defend **—as·ser·tion** \-'sǝrshǝn\ n **—as·sert·ive** \-'sǝrtiv\ adj **—as·sert·ive·ness** n

as·sess \ǝ'ses\ vb 1 : impose (as a tax) 2 : evaluate for taxation **—as·sess·ment** n **—as·ses·sor** \-ǝr\ n

as·set \'as,et\ n 1 pl : individually owned property 2 : advantage or resource

as·sid·u·ous \ǝ'sijǝwǝs\ adj : diligent **—as·si·du·i·ty** \,asǝ'düǝtē, -'dyü-\ n **—as·sid·u·ous·ly** adv **—as·sid·u·ous·ness** n

as·sign \ǝ'sīn\ vb 1 : transfer to another 2 : appoint to a duty 3 : designate as a task 4 : attribute **—as·sign·able** adj **—as·sign·ment** n

as·sim·i·late \ǝ'simǝ,lāt\ vb **-lat·ed; -lat·ing** 1 : absorb as nourishment 2 : understand **—as·sim·i·la·tion** \-,simǝ'lāshǝn\ n

as·sist \ǝ'sist\ vb : help **—assist** n **—assis·tance** \-'sistǝns\ n **—as·sis·tant** \-tǝnt\ n

as·so·ci·ate \ǝ'sōshē,āt, -sē-\ vb **-at·ed; -at·ing** 1 : join in companionship or

partnership 2 : connect in thought **—as·so·ci·ate** \-shēǝt, -sēǝt\ n **—as·so·ci·a·tion** \-,sōshē'āshǝn, -sē-\ n

as soon as conj : when

as·sort·ed \ǝ'sòrtǝd\ adj : consisting of various kinds

as·sort·ment \-mǝnt\ n : assorted collection

as·suage \ǝ'swāj\ vb **-suaged; -suag·ing** : ease or satisfy

as·sume \ǝ'süm\ vb **-sumed; -sum·ing** 1 : take upon oneself 2 : pretend to have or be 3 : take as true

as·sump·tion \ǝ'sǝmpshǝn\ n : something assumed

as·sure \ǝ'shùr\ vb **-sured; -sur·ing** 1 : give confidence or conviction to 2 : guarantee **—as·sur·ance** \-ǝns\ n

as·ter \'astǝr\ n : herb with daisylike flowers

as·ter·isk \'astǝ,risk\ n : a character * used as a reference mark or as an indication of omission of words

astern \ǝ'stǝrn\ adv or adj 1 : behind 2 : at or toward the stern

as·ter·oid \'astǝ,ròid\ n : small planet between Mars and Jupiter

asth·ma \'azmǝ\ n : disorder marked by difficulty in breathing **—asth·mat·ic** \az'matik\ adj or n

astig·ma·tism \ǝ'stigmǝ,tizǝm\ n : visual defect **—as·tig·mat·ic** \,astig-'matik\ adj

as to prep 1 : concerning 2 : according to

as·ton·ish \ǝ'stänish\ vb : amaze **—aston·ish·ing·ly** adv **—as·ton·ish·ment** n

as·tound \ǝ'staùnd\ vb : fill with confused wonder **—as·tound·ing·ly** adv

astrad·dle \ǝ'strad°l\ adv or prep : so as to straddle

as·tral \'astrǝl\ adj : relating to or coming from the stars

astray \ǝ'strā\ adv or adj : off the right path

astride \ǝ'strīd\ adv : with legs apart or one on each side ~ prep : with one leg on each side of

as·trin·gent \ǝ'strinjǝnt\ adj : causing shrinking or puckering of tissues **—as·trin·gen·cy** \-jǝnsē\ n **—astrin·gent** n

as·trol·o·gy \ǝ'strälǝjē\ n : prediction of events by the stars **—as·trol·o·ger** \-ǝjǝr\ n **—as·tro·log·i·cal** \,astrǝ-'läjikǝl\ adj

as·tro·naut \'astrə,nȯt\ n : space traveler

as·tro·nau·tics \,astrə'nȯtiks\ n : construction and operation of spacecraft —**as·tro·nau·tic** \-ik\, **as·tro·nau·ti·cal** \-ikəl\ adj

as·tro·nom·i·cal \,astrə'nämikəl\ adj 1 : relating to astronomy 2 : extremely large

as·tron·o·my \ə'stränəmē\ n, pl -**mies** : study of the celestial bodies —**as·tron·o·mer** \-əmər\ n

as·tute \ə'stüt, -'styüt\ adj : shrewd —**as·tute·ly** adv —**as·tute·ness** n

asun·der \ə'səndər\ adv or adj 1 : into separate pieces 2 : separated

asy·lum \ə'sīləm\ n 1 : refuge 2 : institution for care esp. of the insane

asym·met·ri·cal \,āsə'metrikəl\, **asym·met·ric** \-trik\ adj : not symmetrical —**asym·me·try** \,ā'simətrē\ n

at \ət, 'at\ prep 1 —used to indicate a point in time or space 2 —used to indicate a goal 3 —used to indicate condition, means, cause, or manner

at all adv : without restriction or under any circumstances

ate past of EAT

-ate \ət, ,āt\ n suffix 1 : office or rank 2 : group of persons holding an office or rank ~ adj suffix 1 : brought into or being in a state 2 : marked by having

athe·ist \'āthēist\ n : one who denies the existence of God —**athe·ism** \-,izəm\ n —**athe·is·tic** \,āthē'istik\ adj

ath·ero·scle·ro·sis \,athərōsklə'rōsəs\ n : arteriosclerosis with deposition of fatty substances in the arteries —**ath·ero·scle·rot·ic** \-'rätik\ adj

ath·lete \'ath,lēt\ n : one trained to compete in athletics

ath·let·ics \ath'letiks\ n sing or pl : exercises and games requiring physical skill —**ath·let·ic** \-ik\ adj

-a·tion \'āshən\ n suffix : action or process

-a·tive \,ātiv, ətiv\ adj suffix 1 : of, relating to, or connected with 2 : tending to

at·las \'atləs\ n : book of maps

at·mo·sphere \'atmə,sfir\ n 1 : mass of air surrounding the earth 2 : surrounding influence —**at·mo·spher·ic** \,atmə'sfirik, -'sfer-\ adj —**at·mo·spher·i·cal·ly** \-iklē\ adv

at·oll \'a,tȯl, 'ā-, -,täl\ n : ring-shaped coral island

at·om \'atəm\ n 1 : tiny bit 2 : smallest particle of a chemical element that can exist alone or in combination

atom·ic \ə'tämik\ adj 1 : relating to atoms 2 : nuclear

atomic bomb n : bomb utilizing the energy released by splitting the atom

at·om·iz·er \'atə,mīzər\ n : device for dispersing a liquid as a very fine spray

atone \ə'tōn\ vb **atoned; aton·ing** : make amends —**atone·ment** n

atop \ə'täp\ prep : on top of ~ adv or adj : on, to, or at the top

atri·um \'ātrēəm\ n, pl **atria** \-trēə\ or **atriums** 1 : open central room or court 2 : heart chamber that receives blood from the veins

atro·cious \ə'trōshəs\ adj : appalling or abominable —**atro·cious·ly** adv —**atro·cious·ness** n

atroc·i·ty \ə'träsətē\ n, pl -**ties** : savage act

at·ro·phy \'atrəfē\ n, pl -**phies** : wasting away of a bodily part or tissue —**at·ro·phy** vb

at·ro·pine \'atrə,pēn\ n : drug used esp. to relieve spasms

at·tach \ə'tach\ vb 1 : seize legally 2 : bind by personalities 3 : join —**at·tach·ment** n

at·ta·ché \,atə'shā, ,a,ta-, ə,ta-\ n : technical expert on a diplomatic staff

at·tack \ə'tak\ vb 1 : try to hurt or destroy with violence or words 2 : set to work on ~ n 1 : act of attacking 2 : fit of sickness

at·tain \ə'tān\ vb 1 : achieve or accomplish 2 : reach —**at·tain·abil·i·ty** \ə,tānə'bilətē\ n —**at·tain·able** adj —**at·tain·ment** n

at·tempt \ə'tempt\ vb : make an effort toward —**attempt** n

at·tend \ə'tend\ vb 1 : handle or provide for the care of something 2 : accompany 3 : be present at 4 : pay attention —**at·ten·dance** \-'tendəns\ n —**at·ten·dant** \-dənt\ adj or n

at·ten·tion \ə'tenchən\ n 1 : concentration of the mind on something 2 : notice or awareness —**at·ten·tive** \-'tentiv\ adj —**at·ten·tive·ly** adv —**at·ten·tive·ness** n

at·ten·u·ate \ə'tenyə,wāt\ vb -**at·ed; -at·ing** 1 : make or become thin 2 : weaken —**at·ten·u·a·tion** \-,tenyə-'wāshən\ n

at·test \ə'test\ vb : certify or bear witness —**at·tes·ta·tion** \,a,tes'tāshən\ n

at·tic \'atik\ n : space just below the roof

at·tire \ə'tīr\ vb -**tired**; -**tir·ing** : dress —**attire** n

at·ti·tude \'atə,tüd, -,tyüd\ n 1 : posture or relative position 2 : feeling, opinion, or mood

at·tor·ney \ə'tərnē\ n, pl -**neys** : legal agent

at·tract \ə'trakt\ vb 1 : draw to oneself 2 : have emotional or aesthetic appeal for —**at·trac·tion** \-'trakshən\ n —**at·trac·tive** \-'traktiv\ adj —**at·trac·tive·ly** adv —**at·trac·tive·ness** n

at·tri·bute \'atrə,byüt\ n : inherent characteristic ~ \ə'tribyət\ vb -**trib·ut·ed**; -**trib·ut·ing** 1 : regard as having a specific cause or origin 2 : regard as a characteristic —**at·trib·ut·able** adj —**at·tri·bu·tion** \,atrə'byüshən\ n

at·tune \ə'tün, -'tyün\ vb : bring into harmony

au·burn \'óbərn\ adj : reddish brown

auc·tion \'ókshən\ n : public sale of property to the highest bidder —**auction** vb —**auc·tion·eer** \,ókshə'nir\ n

au·dac·i·ty \ó'dasətē\ n : boldness or insolence —**au·da·cious** \ó'dāshəs\ adj

au·di·ble \'ódəbəl\ adj : capable of being heard —**au·di·bly** \-blē\ adv

au·di·ence \'ódēəns\ n 1 : formal interview 2 : group of listeners or spectators

au·dio \'ódē,ō\ adj : relating to sound or its reproduction ~ n : television sound

au·dio·vi·su·al \,ódēō'vizhəwəl\ adj : relating to both hearing and sight

au·dit \'ódət\ vb : examine financial accounts —**audit** n —**au·di·tor** \'ódətər\ n

au·di·tion \ó'dishən\ n : tryout performance —**audition** vb

au·di·to·ri·um \,ódə'tōrēəm\ n, pl -**ri·ums** or -**ria** \-'rēə\ : room or building used for public performances

au·di·to·ry \'ódə,tōrē\ adj : relating to hearing

au·ger \'ógər\ n : tool for boring

aug·ment \óg'ment\ vb : enlarge or increase —**aug·men·ta·tion** \,ógmən'tāshən\ n

au·gur \'ógər\ n : prophet ~ vb : predict —**au·gu·ry** \'ógyərē, -gər-\ n

au·gust \ó'gəst\ adj : majestic

Au·gust \'ógəst\ n : 8th month of the year having 31 days

auk \'ók\ n : stocky diving seabird

aunt \'ant, 'ánt\ n 1 : sister of one's father or mother 2 : wife of one's uncle

au·ra \'órə\ n 1 : distinctive atmosphere 2 : luminous radiation

au·ral \'órəl\ adj : relating to the ear or to hearing

au·ri·cle \'órikəl\ n : atrium or ear-shaped pouch in the atrium of the heart

au·ro·ra bo·re·al·is \ə'rōrə,bōrē'aləs\ n : display of light in the night sky of northern latitudes

aus·pic·es \'óspəsəz, -,sēz\ n pl : patronage and protection

aus·pi·cious \ó'spishəs\ adj : favorable

aus·tere \ó'stir\ adj : severe —**aus·tere·ly** adv —**aus·ter·i·ty** \ó'sterətē\ n

au·then·tic \ə'thentik, ó-\ adj : genuine —**au·then·ti·cal·ly** \-iklē\ adv —**au·then·tic·i·ty** \,ó,then'tisətē\ n

au·then·ti·cate \ə'thenti,kāt, ó-\ vb -**cat·ed**; -**cat·ing** : prove genuine —**au·then·ti·ca·tion** \-,thenti'kāshən\ n

au·thor \'óthər\ n 1 : writer 2 : creator —**au·thor·ship** n

au·thor·i·tar·i·an \ó,thärə'terēən, ə-, -,thór-\ adj : marked by blind obedience to authority

au·thor·i·ta·tive \ə'thärə,tātiv, ó-, -'thór-\ adj : being an authority —**au·thor·i·ta·tive·ly** adv —**au·thor·i·ta·tive·ness** n

au·thor·i·ty \ə'thärətē, ó-, -'thór-\ n, pl -**ties** 1 : expert 2 : right, responsibility, or power to influence 3 pl : persons in official positions

au·tho·rize \'óthə,rīz\ vb -**rized**; -**riz·ing** : permit or give official approval for —**au·tho·ri·za·tion** \,óthərə'zāshən\ n

au·to \'ótō\ n, pl **autos** : automobile

au·to·bi·og·ra·phy \,ótəbī'ägrəfē, -bē-\ n : writer's own life story —**au·to·bi·og·ra·pher** \-fər\ n —**au·to·bio·graph·i·cal** \-,bīə'grafikəl\ adj

au·toc·ra·cy \ó'täkrəsē\ n, pl -**cies** : government by one person having unlimited power —**au·to·crat** \'ótə,krat\ n —**au·to·crat·ic** \,ótə'kratik\ adj —**au·to·crat·i·cal·ly** \-iklē\ adv

au·to·graph \'ótə,graf\ n : signature ~ vb : write one's name on

au·to·mate \'ótə,māt\ vb -**mat·ed**; -**mat·ing** : make automatic —**au·to·ma·tion** \,ótə'māshən\ n

au·to·mat·ic \,ȯtə'matik\ *adj* **1** : involuntary **2** : designed to function without human intervention ~ *n* : automatic device (as a firearm) —**au·to·mat·i·cal·ly** \-iklē\ *adv*

au·tom·a·ton \ȯ'tämətən, -,tän\ *n, pl* **-a·tons** *or* **-a·ta** \-tə, -,tä\ : robot

au·to·mo·bile \,ȯtəmō'bēl, -'mō,bēl\ *n* : 4-wheeled passenger vehicle with its own power source

au·to·mo·tive \,ȯtə'mōtiv\ *adj* : relating to automobiles

au·ton·o·mous \ȯ'tänəməs\ *adj* : self-governing —**au·ton·o·mous·ly** *adv* —**au·ton·o·my** \-mē\ *n*

au·top·sy \'ȯ,täpsē, 'ȯtəp-\ *n, pl* **-sies** : medical examination of a corpse

au·tumn \'ȯtəm\ *n* : season between summer and winter —**au·tum·nal** \ȯ-'təmnəl\ *adj*

aux·il·ia·ry \ȯg'zilyərē, -lərē\ *adj* **1** : being a supplement or reserve **2** : accompanying a main verb form to express person, number, mood, or tense —**auxiliary** *n*

avail \ə'vāl\ *vb* : be of use or make use ~ *n* : use

avail·able \ə'vāləbəl\ *adj* **1** : usable **2** : accessible —**avail·abil·i·ty** \-,vālə-'bilətē\ *n*

av·a·lanche \'avə,lanch\ *n* : mass of sliding or falling snow or rock

av·a·rice \'avərəs\ *n* : greed —**av·a·ri·cious** \,avə'rishəs\ *adj*

avenge \ə'venj\ *vb* **avenged**; **aveng·ing** : take vengeance for —**aveng·er** *n*

av·e·nue \'avə,nü, -,nyü\ *n* **1** : way of approach **2** : broad street

av·er·age \'avrij\ *adj* **1** : being about midway between extremes **2** : ordinary ~ *vb* **1** : be usually **2** : find the mean of ~ *n* : mean

averse \ə'vərs\ *adj* : feeling dislike or reluctance —**aver·sion** \-'vərzhən\ *n*

avert \ə'vərt\ *vb* : turn away

avi·ary \'āvē,erē\ *n, pl* **-ar·ies** : place where birds are kept

avi·a·tion \,āvē'āshən, ,av-\ *n* : operation or manufacture of airplanes —**avi·a·tor** \'āvē,ātər, 'av-\ *n*

av·id \'avəd\ *adj* **1** : greedy **2** : enthusiastic —**avid·i·ty** \ə'vidətē, a-\ *n* —**av·id·ly** *adv*

av·o·ca·do \,avə'kädō, ,äv-\ *n, pl* **-dos** : tropical fruit with green pulp

av·o·ca·tion \,avə'kāshən\ *n* : hobby

avoid \ə'vȯid\ *vb* **1** : keep away from **2** : prevent the occurrence of **3** : refrain from —**avoid·able** *adj* —**avoid·ance** \-ᵊns\ *n*

av·oir·du·pois \,avərdə'pȯiz\ *n* : system of weight based on the pound of 16 ounces

avow \ə'vaú\ *vb* : declare openly —**avow·al** \-'vaúəl\ *n*

await \ə'wāt\ *vb* : wait for

awake \ə'wāk\ *vb* **awoke** \-'wōk\; **awok·en** \-'wōkən\ *or* **awaked**; **awak·ing** : wake up —**awake** *adj*

awak·en \ə'wākən\ *vb* **-ened**; **-en·ing** : wake up

award \ə'wȯrd\ *vb* : give (something won or deserved) ~ *n* **1** : judgment **2** : prize

aware \ə'war\ *adj* : having realization or consciousness —**aware·ness** *n*

awash \ə'wȯsh, -'wäsh\ *adv or adj* : flooded

away \ə'wā\ *adv* **1** : from this or that place or time **2** : out of the way **3** : in another direction **4** : from one's possession ~ *adj* **1** : absent **2** : distant

awe \'ȯ\ *n* : respectful fear or reverence ~ *vb* **awed**; **aw·ing** : fill with awe —**awe·some** \-səm\ *adj* —**awe·struck** *adj*

aw·ful \'ȯfəl\ *adj* **1** : inspiring awe **2** : extremely disagreeable **3** : very great —**aw·ful·ly** *adv*

awhile \ə'hwīl\ *adv* : for a while

awk·ward \'ȯkwərd\ *adj* **1** : clumsy **2** : embarrassing —**awk·ward·ly** *adv* —**awk·ward·ness** *n*

awl \'ȯl\ *n* : hole-making tool

aw·ning \'ȯniŋ\ *n* : window cover

awry \ə'rī\ *adv or adj* : wrong

ax, axe \'aks\ *n* : chopping tool

ax·i·om \'aksēəm\ *n* : generally accepted truth —**ax·i·om·at·ic** \,aksēə-'matik\ *adj*

ax·is \'aksəs\ *n, pl* **ax·es** \-,sēz\ : center of rotation —**ax·i·al** \-sēəl\ *adj* —**ax·i·al·ly** *adv*

ax·le \'aksəl\ *n* : shaft on which a wheel revolves

aye \'ī\ *adv* : yes ~ *n* : a vote of yes

aza·lea \ə'zālyə\ *n* : rhododendron with funnel-shaped blossoms

az·i·muth \'azəməth\ *n* : horizontal direction expressed as an angle

azure \'azhər\ *n* : blue of the sky —**azure** *adj*

B

b \'bē\ *n, pl* **b's** *or* **bs** \'bēz\ : 2d letter of the alphabet

bab•ble \'babəl\ *vb* **-bled; -bling 1** : utter meaningless sounds **2** : talk foolishly or too much —**babble** *n* —**bab•bler** *n*

babe \'bāb\ *n* : baby

ba•bel \'bābəl, 'bab-\ *n* : noisy confusion

ba•boon \ba'bün\ *n* : large Asian or African ape with a doglike muzzle

ba•by \'bābē\ *n, pl* **-bies** : very young child ~ *vb* **-bied; -by•ing** : pamper —**baby** *adj* —**ba•by•hood** *n* —**ba•by•ish** *adj*

ba•by-sit *vb* **-sat; -sit•ting** : care for children while parents are away —**baby-sit•ter** *n*

bac•ca•lau•re•ate \,bakə'lórēət\ *n* : bachelor's degree

bac•cha•na•lia \,bakə'nālyə\ *n, pl* **-lia** : drunken orgy —**bac•cha•na•lian** \-yən\ *adj or n*

bach•e•lor \'bachələr\ *n* **1** : holder of lowest 4-year college degree **2** : unmarried man —**bach•e•lor•hood** *n*

ba•cil•lus \bə'siləs\ *n, pl* **-li** \-,lī\ : rod-shaped bacterium —**bac•il•lary** \'basə,lerē\ *adj*

back \'bak\ *n* **1** : part of a human or animal body nearest the spine **2** : part opposite the front **3** : player farthest from the opponent's goal ~ *adv* **1** : to or at the back **2** : ago **3** : to or in a former place or state **4** : in reply ~ *adj* **1** : located at the back **2** : not paid on time **3** : moving or working backward **4** : not current ~ *vb* **1** : support **2** : go or cause to go back **3** : form the back of —**back•ache** *n* —**back•er** *n* —**back•ing** *n* —**back•less** *adj* —**back•rest** *n*

back•bite *vb* **-bit; -bit•ten; -bit•ing** : say spiteful things about someone absent —**back•bit•er** *n*

back•bone *n* **1** : bony column in the back that encloses the spinal cord **2** : firm character

back•drop *n* : painted cloth hung across the rear of a stage

back•fire *n* : loud noise from the wrongly timed explosion of fuel in an engine ~ *vb* **1** : make or undergo a backfire **2** : have a result opposite of that intended

back•gam•mon \'bak,gamən\ *n* : board game

back•ground *n* **1** : scenery behind something **2** : sum of a person's experience or training

back•hand *n* : stroke (as in tennis) made with the back of the hand turned forward —**backhand** *adj or vb* —**back•hand•ed** *adj*

back•lash *n* : adverse reaction

back•log *n* : accumulation of things to be done —**backlog** *vb*

back•pack *n* : camping pack carried on the back ~ *vb* : hike with a backpack —**back•pack•er** *n*

back•slide *vb* **-slid; -slid** *or* **-slid•den** \-,slid³n\; **-slid•ing** : lapse in morals or religious practice —**back•slid•er** *n*

back•stage *adv or adj* : in or to an area behind a stage

back•up *n* : substitute

back•ward \'bakwərd\, **back•wards** *adv* **1** : toward the back **2** : with the back foremost **3** : in a reverse direction **4** : toward an earlier or worse state ~ *adj* **1** : directed, turned, or done backward **2** : retarded in development —**back•ward•ness** *n*

back•woods *n pl* : remote or isolated place

ba•con \'bākən\ *n* : salted and smoked meat from a pig

bac•te•ri•um \bak'tirēəm\ *n, pl* **-ria** \-ēə\ : microscopic plant —**bac•te•ri•al** \-ēəl\ *adj* —**bac•te•ri•o•log•ic** \-,tir-ēə'läjik\, **bac•te•ri•o•log•i•cal** \-əl\ *adj* —**bac•te•ri•ol•o•gist** \-ē'älə-jist\ *n* —**bac•te•ri•ol•o•gy** \-jē\ *n*

bad \'bad\ *adj* **worse** \'wərs\; **worst** \'wərst\ **1** : not good **2** : naughty **3** : faulty **4** : spoiled —**bad** *n or adv* —**bad•ly** *adv* —**bad•ness** *n*

bade *past of* BID

badge \'baj\ *n* : symbol of status

bad·ger \'bajər\ *n* : burrowing mammal ~ *vb* : harass

bad·min·ton \'bad,mint⁰n\ *n* : tennis-like game played with a shuttlecock

baf·fle \'bafəl\ *vb* **-fled; -fling** : perplex ~ *n* : device to alter flow (as of liquid or sound) —**baf·fle·ment** *n*

bag \'bag\ *n* : flexible usu. closable container ~ *vb* **-gg-** 1 : bulge out 2 : put in a bag 3 : catch in hunting

bag·a·telle \,bagə'tel\ *n* : trifle

ba·gel \'bāgəl\ *n* : hard doughnut-shaped roll

bag·gage \'bagij\ *n* : traveler's bags and belongings

bag·gy \'bagē\ *adj* **-gi·er; -est** : puffed out like a bag —**bag·gi·ly** *adv* —**bag·gi·ness** *n*

bag·pipe *n* : musical instrument with a bag, a tube with valves, and sounding pipes —often pl.

¹bail \'bāl\ *n* : container for scooping water out of a boat —**bail** *vb* —**bail·er** *n*

²bail *n* 1 : security given to guarantee a prisoner's appearance in court 2 : release secured by bail ~ *vb* : bring about the release of by giving bail

bai·liff \'bāləf\ *n* 1 : British sheriff's aide 2 : minor officer of a U.S. court

bai·li·wick \'bāli,wik\ *n* : one's special field or domain

bail·out \'bā,laut\ *n* : rescue from financial distress

bait \'bāt\ *vb* 1 : harass with dogs usu. for sport 2 : furnish (a hook or trap) with bait ~ *n* : lure esp. for catching animals

bake \'bāk\ *vb* **baked; bak·ing** : cook in dry heat esp. in an oven ~ *n* : party featuring baked food —**baker** *n* —**bak·ery** \'bākərē\ *n* —**bake·shop** *n*

bal·ance \'baləns\ *n* 1 : weighing device 2 : counteracting weight, force, or influence 3 : equilibrium 4 : that which remains ~ *vb* **-anced; -anc·ing** 1 : compute the balance 2 : equalize 3 : bring into harmony or proportion —**bal·anced** *adj*

bal·co·ny \'balkənē\ *n, pl* **-nies** : platform projecting from a wall

bald \'bόld\ *adj* 1 : lacking a natural or usual covering (as of hair) 2 : plain —**bald·ing** *adj* —**bald·ly** *adv* —**bald·ness** *n*

bal·der·dash \'bόldər,dash\ *n* : nonsense

bale \'bāl\ *n* : large bundle ~ *vb* **baled; bal·ing** : pack in a bale —**bal·er** *n*

bale·ful \'bālfəl\ *adj* 1 : deadly 2 : ominous

balk \'bόk\ *n* : hindrance ~ *vb* 1 : thwart 2 : stop short and refuse to go on —**balky** *adj*

¹ball \'bόl\ *n* 1 : rounded mass 2 : game played with a ball ~ *vb* : form into a ball

²ball *n* : large formal dance —**ballroom** *n*

bal·lad \'baləd\ *n* 1 : narrative poem 2 : slow romantic song —**bal·lad·eer** \,balə'diər\ *n*

bal·last \'baləst\ *n* : heavy material to steady a ship or balloon ~ *vb* : provide with ballast

bal·le·ri·na \,balə'rēnə\ *n* : female ballet dancer

bal·let \'ba,lā, ba'lā\ *n* : theatrical dancing

bal·lis·tics \bə'listiks\ *n sing or pl* : science of projectile motion —**ballistic** *adj*

bal·loon \bə'lün\ *n* : inflated bag ~ *vb* 1 : travel in a balloon 2 : swell out —**bal·loon·ist** *n*

bal·lot \'balət\ *n* 1 : paper used to cast a vote 2 : system of voting ~ *vb* : vote

bal·ly·hoo \'balē,hü\ *n* : publicity —**ballyhoo** *vb*

balm \'bäm, 'bälm\ *n* 1 : fragrant healing or soothing preparation 2 : spicy fragrant herb

balmy \'bämē, 'bälmē\ *adj* **balm·i·er; -est** : gently soothing —**balm·i·ness** *n*

ba·lo·ney \bə'lōnē\ *n* : nonsense

bal·sa \'bόlsə\ *n* : very light wood of a tropical tree

bal·sam \-səm\ *n* 1 : aromatic resinous plant substance 2 : balsam-yielding plant —**bal·sam·ic** \bόl'samik\ *adj*

bal·us·ter \'baləstər\ *n* : upright support for a rail

bal·us·trade \-,strād\ *n* : row of balusters topped by a rail

bam·boo \bam'bü\ *n* : tall tropical grass with strong hollow stems

bam·boo·zle \bam'büzəl\ *vb* **-zled; -zling** : deceive

ban \'ban\ *vb* **-nn-** : prohibit ~ *n* : legal prohibition

ba·nal \bə'näl, -'nal; 'bān⁰l\ *adj*

: ordinary and uninteresting —**ba-nal·ity** \bə'nalətē\ n

ba·nana \bə'nanə\ n : elongated fruit of a treelike tropical plant

¹**band** \'band\ n 1 : something that ties or binds 2 : strip or stripe different (as in color) from nearby matter 3 : range of radio wavelengths ~ vb 1 : enclose with a band 2 : unite for a common end —**band·ed** adj —**band·er** n

²**band** n 1 : group 2 : musicians playing together

ban·dage \'bandij\ n : material used esp. in dressing wounds ~ vb : dress or cover with a bandage

ban·dan·na, ban·dana \ban'danə\ n : large colored figured handkerchief

ban·dit \'bandət\ n : outlaw or robber —**ban·dit·ry** \-dətrē\ n

band·stand n : stage for band concerts

band·wag·on n : candidate, side, or movement gaining support

¹**ban·dy** \'bandē\ vb -**died; -dy·ing** : exchange in rapid succession

²**bandy** adj : curved outward

bane \'bān\ n 1 : poison 2 : cause of woe —**bane·ful** adj

¹**bang** \'baŋ\ vb : strike, thrust, or move usu. with a loud noise ~ n 1 : blow 2 : sudden loud noise ~ adv : directly

²**bang** n : fringe of short hair over the forehead —usu. pl. ~ vb : cut in bangs

ban·gle \'baŋgəl\ n : bracelet

ban·ish \'banish\ vb 1 : force by authority to leave a country 2 : expel —**ban·ish·ment** n

ban·is·ter \-əstər\ n 1 : baluster 2 : handrail

ban·jo \'banjō\ n, pl -**jos** : stringed instrument with a drumlike body —**banjo·ist** n

¹**bank** \'baŋk\ n 1 : piled-up mass 2 : rising ground along a body of water 3 : sideways slope along a curve ~ vb 1 : form a bank 2 : cover (as a fire) to keep inactive 3 : incline (an airplane) laterally

²**bank** n : tier of objects

³**bank** n 1 : money institution 2 : reserve supply ~ vb : conduct business in a bank —**bank·book** n —**bank·er** n —**bank·ing** n

bank·rupt \'baŋ,krəpt\ n : one required by law to forfeit assets to pay off debts ~ adj 1 : legally a bankrupt 2 : lacking something essential —

bankrupt vb —**bank·rupt·cy** \-,krəp-sē\ n

ban·ner \'banər\ n : flag ~ adj : excellent

banns \'banz\ n pl : announcement in church of a proposed marriage

ban·quet \'baŋkwət\ n : ceremonial dinner —**banquet** vb

ban·shee \'banshē\ n : wailing female spirit that foretells death

ban·tam \'bantəm\ n : miniature domestic fowl

ban·ter \'bantər\ n : good-natured joking —**banter** vb

ban·yan \'banyən\ n : large tree that grows new trunks from the limbs

bap·tism \'bap,tizəm\ n : Christian rite signifying spiritual cleansing —**bap·tis·mal** \bap'tizməl\ adj

bap·tize \bap'tīz, 'bap,tīz\ vb -**tized; -tiz·ing** : administer baptism to

bar \'bär\ n 1 : long narrow object used esp. as a lever, fastening, or support 2 : barrier 3 : body of practicing lawyers 4 : wide stripe 5 : food counter 6 : place where liquor is served 7 : vertical line across the musical staff ~ vb -**rr**- 1 : obstruct with a bar 2 : shut out 3 : prohibit ~ prep : excluding —**barred** adj —**bar·room** n —**bar·tend·er** n

barb \'bärb\ n : sharp projection pointing backward —**barbed** adj

bar·bar·ian \bär'barēən\ adj 1 : relating to people considered backward 2 : not refined —**barbarian** n

bar·bar·ic \'barik\ adj : barbarian

bar·ba·rous \'bärbərəs\ adj 1 : lacking refinement 2 : mercilessly cruel —**bar·bar·ism** \-bə,rizəm\ n —**bar·bar·i·ty** \bär'barətē\ n —**bar·ba·rous·ly** adv

bar·be·cue \'bärbi,kyü\ n : gathering at which barbecued food is served ~ vb -**cued; -cu·ing** : cook over hot coals or on a spit often with a highly seasoned sauce

bar·ber \'bärbər\ n : one who cuts hair

bar·bi·tu·rate \bär'bichərət\ n : sedative or hypnotic drug

bard \'bärd\ n : poet

bare \'bar\ adj **barer; barest** 1 : naked 2 : not concealed 3 : empty 4 : leaving nothing to spare 5 : plain ~ vb **bared; bar·ing** : make or lay bare —**bare·foot, bare·foot·ed** adv or adj —**bare·hand·ed** adv or adj —

bare·head·ed adv or adj —**bare·ly** adv —**bare·ness** n

bare·back, bare·backed adv or adj : without a saddle

bare·faced adj : open and esp. brazen

bar·gain \'bärgən\ n 1 : agreement 2 : something bought for less than its value ~ vb 1 : negotiate 2 : barter

barge \'bärj\ n : broad flat-bottomed boat ~ vb **barged; barg·ing** : move rudely or clumsily —**barge·man** n

bari·tone \'barə,tōn\ n : male voice between bass and tenor

bar·i·um \'bareəm\ n : silver-white metallic chemical element

¹bark \'bärk\ vb 1 : make the sound of a dog 2 : speak in a loud curt tone ~ n : sound of a barking dog

²bark n : tough corky outer covering of a woody stem or root ~ vb : remove bark or skin from

³bark n : sailing ship with a fore-and-aft rear sail

bark·er \'bärkər\ n : one who calls out to attract people to a show

bar·ley \'bärlē\ n : cereal grass or its seeds

barn \'bärn\ n : building for keeping hay or livestock —**barn·yard** n

bar·na·cle \'bärnikəl\ n : marine crustacean

barn·storm vb : tour through rural districts giving performances

ba·rom·e·ter \bə'rämətər\ n : instrument for measuring atmospheric pressure —**baro·met·ric** \,barə'metrik\ adj

bar·on \'barən\ n : British peer —**bar·on·age** \-ij\ n —**ba·ro·ni·al** \bə'rōnēəl\ adj —**bar·ony** \'barənē\ n

bar·on·ess \-ənəs\ n 1 : baron's wife 2 : woman holding a baronial title

bar·on·et \-ənət\ n : man holding a rank between a baron and a knight —**bar·on·et·cy** \-sē\ n

ba·roque \bə'rōk, -'räk\ adj : elaborately ornamented

bar·racks \'barəks\ n sing or pl : soldiers' housing

bar·ra·cu·da \,barə'küdə\ n, pl **-da** or **-das** : large predatory sea fish

bar·rage \bə'räzh, -'räj\ n : heavy artillery fire

bar·rel \'barəl\ n 1 : closed cylindrical container 2 : amount held by a barrel 3 : cylindrical part ~ vb **-reled** or **-relled; -rel·ing** or **-rel·ling** 1 : pack in a barrel 2 : move at high speed —**bar·reled** adj

bar·ren \'barən\ adj 1 : unproductive of life 2 : uninteresting —**bar·ren·ness** n

bar·rette \bä'ret, bə-\ n : clasp for a woman's hair

bar·ri·cade \'barə,kād, ,barə'-\ n : barrier —**barricade** vb

bar·ri·er \'barēər\ n : something that separates or obstructs

bar·ring \'bäriŋ\ prep : omitting

bar·ris·ter \'barəstər\ n : British trial lawyer

bar·row \'barō\ n : wheelbarrow

bar·ter \'bärtər\ vb : trade by exchange of goods —**barter** n

ba·salt \bə'sölt, 'bä,-\ n : dark fine-grained igneous rock —**ba·sal·tic** \bə'söltik\ adj

¹base \'bās\ n, pl **bas·es** 1 : bottom 2 : fundamental part 3 : beginning point 4 : supply source of a force 5 : compound that reacts with an acid to form a salt ~ vb **based; bas·ing** : establish —**base·less** adj

²base adj **bas·er; bas·est** 1 : inferior 2 : contemptible —**base·ly** adv —**base·ness** n

base·ball n : game played with a bat and ball by 2 teams

base·ment \-mənt\ n : part of a building below ground level

bash \'bash\ vb : strike violently ~ n : heavy blow

bash·ful \-fəl\ adj : self-conscious —**bash·ful·ness** n

ba·sic \'bāsik\ adj 1 : relating to or forming the base or essence 2 : relating to a chemical base —**ba·si·cally** adv —**ba·sic·i·ty** \bā'sisətē\ n

ba·sil \'bazəl, 'bās-, 'bāz-\ n : aromatic mint

ba·sil·i·ca \bə'silikə\ n : important church or cathedral

ba·sin \'bāsᵊn\ n 1 : large bowl or pan 2 : region drained by a river

ba·sis \'bāsəs\ n, pl **ba·ses** \-,sēz\ 1 : something that supports 2 : fundamental principle

bask \'bask\ vb : enjoy pleasant warmth

bas·ket \'baskət\ n : woven container —**bas·ket·ful** n

bas·ket·ball n : game played with a ball on a court by 2 teams

bas-re·lief \,bäri'lēf\ n : flat sculpture with slightly raised design

¹bass \'bas\ n, pl **bass** or **bass·es** : spiny-finned sport and food fish

²**bass** \'bās\ *n* 1 : deep tone 2 : lowest choral voice

bas·set hound \'basət-\ *n* : short-legged dog with long ears

bas·si·net \,basə'net\ *n* : baby's bed

bas·soon \bə'sün, ba-\ *n* : low-pitched wind instrument

bas·tard \'bastərd\ *n* 1 : illegitimate child 2 : offensive person ~ *adj* 1 : illegitimate 2 : inferior —**bas·tard·ize** *vb* —**bas·tardy** *n*

¹**baste** \'bāst\ *vb* **bast·ed; bast·ing** : sew temporarily with long stitches

²**baste** *vb* **bast·ed; bast·ing** : moisten at intervals while cooking

bas·tion \'baschən\ *n* : fortified position

¹**bat** \'bat\ *n* 1 : stick or club 2 : sharp blow ~ *vb* **-tt-** : hit with a bat

²**bat** *n* : small flying mammal

³**bat** *vb* **-tt-** : wink or blink

batch \'bach\ *n* : quantity used or produced at one time

bate \'bāt\ *vb* **bat·ed; bat·ing** : moderate or reduce

bath \'bath, 'bath\ *n, pl* **baths** \'bathz, 'baths, 'bathz, 'baths\ 1 : a washing of the body 2 : water for washing the body 3 : liquid in which something is immersed 4 : bathroom 5 : large financial loss —**bath·tub** *n*

bathe \'bāth\ *vb* **bathed; bath·ing** 1 : wash in liquid 2 : flow against so as to wet 3 : shine light over 4 : take a bath or a swim —**bath·er** *n*

bath·robe *n* : robe worn around the house

bath·room *n* : room with a bathtub or shower and usu. a sink and toilet

ba·tiste \bə'tēst\ *n* : fine sheer fabric

ba·ton \bə'tän\ *n* : musical conductor's stick

bat·tal·ion \bə'talyən\ *n* : military unit composed of a headquarters and two or more companies

bat·ten \'bat³n\ *n* : strip of wood used to seal or reinforce ~ *vb* : furnish or fasten with battens

¹**bat·ter** \'batər\ *vb* : beat or damage with repeated blows

²**batter** *n* : mixture of flour and liquid

³**batter** *n* : player who bats

bat·tery \'batərē\ *n, pl* **-ter·ies** 1 : illegal beating of a person 2 : group of artillery guns 3 : group of electric cells

bat·ting \'batiŋ\ *n* : layers of cotton or wool for stuffing

bat·tle \'bat³l\ *n* : military fighting ~ *vb* **-tled; -tling** : engage in battle —**bat·tle·field** *n*

bat·tle-ax *n* : long-handled ax formerly used as a weapon

bat·tle·ment \-mənt\ *n* : parapet on top of a wall

bat·tle·ship *n* : heavily armed warship

bat·ty \'batē\ *adj* **-ti·er; -est** : crazy

bau·ble \'bóbəl\ *n* : trinket

bawdy \'bódē\ *adj* **bawd·i·er; -est** : obscene or lewd —**bawd·i·ly** *adv* —**bawd·i·ness** *n*

bawl \'ból\ *vb* : cry loudly ~ *n* : long loud cry

¹**bay** \'bā\ *adj* : reddish brown ~ *n* : bay-colored animal

²**bay** *n* : European laurel

³**bay** *n* 1 : compartment 2 : area projecting out from a building and containing a window (**bay window**)

⁴**bay** *vb* : bark with deep long tones ~ *n* 1 : position of one unable to escape danger 2 : baying of dogs

⁵**bay** *n* : body of water smaller than a gulf and nearly surrounded by land

bay·ber·ry \-,berē\ *n* : shrub bearing small waxy berries

bay·o·net \'bāənət, ,bāə'net\ *n* : dagger that fits on the end of a rifle ~ *vb* **-net·ed; -net·ing** : stab with a bayonet

bay·ou \'bīü, -ō\ *n* : creek flowing through marshy land

ba·zaar \bə'zär\ *n* 1 : market 2 : fair for charity

ba·zoo·ka \-'zükə\ *n* : weapon that shoots armor-piercing rockets

BB *n* : small shot pellet

be \'bē\ *vb* **was** \'wəz, 'wäz\, **were** \'wər\; **been** \'bin\; **be·ing** \'bēiŋ\; **am** \əm, 'am\, **is** \'iz, əz\, **are** \ər, 'är\ 1 : equal 2 : exist 3 : occupy a certain place 4 : occur ~ *verbal auxiliary* — used to show continuous action or to form the passive voice

beach \'bēch\ *n* : sandy shore of a sea, lake, or river ~ *vb* : drive ashore

beach·comb·er \-,kōmər\ *n* : one who searches the shore for useful objects

beach·head *n* : shore area held by an attacking force in an invasion

bea·con \'bēkən\ *n* : guiding or warning light or signal

bead \'bēd\ *n* : small round body esp. strung on a thread ~ *vb* : form into a bead —**bead·ing** *n* —**beady** *adj*

bea·gle \'bēgəl\ *n* : small short-legged hound

beak \'bēk\ *n* : bill of a bird —**beaked** *adj*

bea·ker \'bēkər\ *n* 1 : large drinking cup 2 : laboratory vessel

beam \'bēm\ *n* 1 : large long piece of timber or metal 2 : ray of light 3 : directed radio signals for the guidance of pilots ~ *vb* 1 : send out light 2: smile 3 : aim a radio broadcast

bean \'bēn\ *n* : edible plant seed borne in pods

¹bear \'bar\ *n*, *pl* **bears** 1 *or pl* **bear** : large heavy mammal with shaggy hair 2 : gruff or sullen person —**bear·ish** *adj*

²bear *vb* **bore** \'bōr\; **borne** \'bōrn\; **bear·ing** 1 : carry 2 : give birth to or produce 3 : endure 4 : press 5 : go in an indicated direction —**bear·able** *adj* —**bear·er** *n*

beard \'bird\ *n* 1 : facial hair on a man 2 : tuft like a beard ~ *vb* : confront boldly —**beard·ed** *adj* —**beard·less** *adj*

bear·ing *n* 1 : way of carrying oneself 2 : supporting object or purpose 3 : significance 4 : machine part in which another part turns 5 : direction with respect esp. to compass points

beast \'bēst\ *n* 1 : animal 2 : brutal person —**beast·li·ness** *n* —**beast·ly** *adj*

beat \'bēt\ *vb* **beat**; **beat·en** \'bēt⁰n\ *or* **beat**; **beat·ing** 1 : strike repeatedly 2 : defeat 3 : act or arrive before 4 : throb ~ *n* 1 : single stroke or pulsation 2 : rhythmic stress in poetry or music ~ *adj* : exhausted —**beat·er** *n*

be·atif·ic \,bēə'tifik\ *adj* : blissful

be·at·i·fy \bē'atə,fī\ *vb* **-fied; -fy·ing** : make happy or blessed —**be·at·i·fi·ca·tion** \,atəfə'kāshən\ *n*

be·at·i·tude \-'atə,tüd, -,tyüd\ *n* : saying in the Sermon on the Mount (Matthew 5:3-12) beginning "Blessed are"

beau \'bō\ *n*, *pl* **beaux** \'bōz\ *or* **beaus** : suitor

beau·ty \'byütē\ *n*, *pl* **-ties** : qualities that please the senses or mind —**beau·te·ous** \-ēəs\ *adj* —**beau·te·ous·ly** *adv* —**beau·ti·fi·ca·tion** \,byütəfə'kāshən\ *n* —**beau·ti·fi·er** \'byütə,fīər\ *n* —**beau·ti·ful** \-ifəl\ *adj* —**beau·ti·ful·ly** *adv* —**beau·ti·fy** \-ə,fī\ *vb*

bea·ver \'bēvər\ *n* : large fur-bearing rodent

be·cause \bi'kóz, -'kəz\ *conj* : for the reason that

because of *prep* : by reason of

beck \'bek\ *n* : summons

beck·on \'bekən\ *vb* : summon esp. by a nod or gesture

be·come \bi'kəm\ *vb* **-came** \-'kām\; **-come; -com·ing** 1 : come to be 2 : be suitable —**be·com·ing** *adj* —**be·com·ing·ly** *adv*

bed \'bed\ *n* 1 : piece of furniture to sleep on 2 : flat or level surface ~ *vb* **-dd-** : put or go to bed —**bed·spread** *n*

bed·bug *n* : wingless bloodsucking insect

bed·clothes *n pl* : bedding

bed·ding *n* 1 : sheets and blankets for a bed 2 : soft material (as hay) for an animal's bed

be·deck \bi'dek\ *vb* : adorn

be·dev·il \-'devəl\ *vb* : harass

bed·lam \'bedləm\ *n* : uproar and confusion

be·drag·gled \bi'dragəld\ *adj* : dirty and disordered

bed·rid·den \'bed,rid⁰n\ *adj* : kept in bed by illness

bed·rock *n* : solid subsurface rock —**bedrock** *adj*

¹bee \'bē\ *n* : 4-winged honey-producing insect —**bee·hive** *n* —**bee·keep·er** *n* —**bees·wax** *n*

²bee *n* : neighborly work session

beech \'bēch\ *n*, *pl* **beech·es** *or* **beech** : tree with smooth gray bark and edible nuts (**beech·nuts**) —**beech·en** \-ən\ *adj*

beef \'bēf\ *n*, *pl* **beefs** \'bēfs\ *or* **beeves** \'bēvz\ : flesh of a steer, cow, or bull ~ *vb* : strengthen —used with *up* —**beef·steak** *n*

bee·line *n* : straight course

been *past part of* BE

beep \'bēp\ *n* : short usu. high-pitched warning sound —**beep** *vb* —**beep·er** *n*

beer \'bir\ *n* : alcoholic drink brewed from malt and hops —**beery** *adj*

beet \'bēt\ *n* : garden root vegetable

bee·tle \'bētəl\ *n* : 4-winged insect

be·fall \bi'fól\ *vb* **-fell; -fall·en** : happen to

be·fit \bi'fit\ *vb* : be suitable to

be·fore \bi'fōr\ *adv* 1 : in front 2 : earlier ~ *prep* 1 : in front of 2 : earlier than ~ *conj* : earlier than

be·fore·hand *adv or adj* : in advance

be·friend \bi'frend\ *vb* : act as friend to

be·fud·dle \-'fəd^əl\ *vb* : confuse

beg \'beg\ *vb* **-gg-** : ask earnestly

be·get \bi'get\ *vb* **-got; -got·ten** *or* **-got; -get·ting** : become the father of

beg·gar \'begər\ *n* : one that begs ~ *vb* : make poor —**beg·gar·ly** *adj* —**beg·gary** *n*

be·gin \bi'gin\ *vb* **-gan** \-'gan\; **-gun** \-'gən\, **-gin·ning** 1 : start 2 : come into being —**be·gin·ner** *n*

be·gone \bi'gòn\ *vb* : go away

be·go·nia \-'gōnyə\ *n* : tropical herb with waxy flowers

be·grudge \-'grəj\ *vb* 1 : concede reluctantly 2 : look upon disapprovingly

be·guile \-'gīl\ *vb* **-guiled; -guil·ing** 1 : deceive 2 : amuse

be·half \-'haf, -'hàf\ *n* : benefit

be·have \-'hāv\ *vb* **-haved; -hav·ing** : act in a certain way

be·hav·ior \-'hāvyər\ *n* : way of behaving —**be·hav·ior·al** \-əl\ *adj*

be·head \-'hed\ *vb* : cut off the head of

be·hest \-'hest\ *n* : command

be·hind \bi'hīnd\ *adv* : at the back ~ *prep* 1 : in back of 2 : less than 3 : supporting

be·hold \-'hōld\ *vb* **-held; -hold·ing** : see —**be·hold·er** *n*

be·hold·en \-'hōldən\ *adj* : indebted

be·hoove \-'hüv\ *vb* **-hooved; -hoov·ing** : be necessary for

beige \'bāzh\ *n* : yellowish brown —**beige** *adj*

be·ing \'bēiŋ\ *n* 1 : existence 2 : living thing

be·la·bor \bi'lābər\ *vb* : carry on to absurd lengths

be·lat·ed \-'lātəd\ *adj* : delayed

belch \'belch\ *vb* 1 : expel stomach gas orally 2 : emit forcefully —**belch** *n*

be·lea·guer \bi'lēgər\ *vb* 1 : besiege 2 : harass

bel·fry \'belfrē\ *n, pl* **-fries** : bell tower

be·lie \bi'lī\ *vb* **-lied; -ly·ing** 1 : misrepresent 2 : prove false

be·lief \bə'lēf\ *n* 1 : trust 2 : something believed

be·lieve \-'lēv\ *vb* **-lieved; -liev·ing** 1 : trust in 2 : accept as true 3 : hold as an opinion —**be·liev·able** *adj* —**be·liev·ably** *adv* —**be·liev·er** *n*

be·lit·tle \bi'lit^əl\ *vb* **-lit·tled; -lit·tling** 1 : disparage 2 : make seem less

bell \'bel\ *n* : hollow metallic device that rings when struck ~ *vb* : provide with a bell

bel·la·don·na \,belə'dänə\ *n* : poisonous herb yielding a drug

belle \'bel\ *n* : beautiful woman

bel·li·cose \'beli,kōs\ *adj* : pugnacious —**bel·li·cos·i·ty** \,beli'käsətē\ *n*

bel·lig·er·ent \bə'lijərənt\ *adj* 1 : waging war 2 : truculent —**bel·lig·er·ence** \-rəns\ *n* —**bel·lig·er·en·cy** \-rənsē\ *n* —**belligerent** *n*

bel·low \'belō\ *vb* : make a loud deep roar or shout —**bellow** *n*

bel·lows \-ōz, -əz\ *n sing or pl* : device with sides that can be compressed to expel air

bell·weth·er \'bel'wethər, -,weth-\ *n* : leader

bel·ly \'belē\ *n, pl* **-lies** : abdomen ~ *vb* **-lied; -ly·ing** : bulge

be·long \bi'lòŋ\ *vb* 1 : be suitable 2 : be owned 3 : be a part of

be·long·ings \-iŋz\ *n pl* : possessions

be·loved \bi'ləvəd, -'ləvd\ *adj* : dearly loved —**beloved** *n*

be·low \-'lō\ *adv* : in or to a lower place ~ *prep* : lower than

belt \'belt\ *n* 1 : strip (as of leather) worn about the waist 2 : endless band to impart motion 3 : distinct region ~ *vb* 1 : put a belt around 2 : thrash

be·moan \bi'mōn\ *vb* : lament

be·muse \-'myüz\ *vb* : confuse

bench \'bench\ *n* 1 : long seat 2 : judge's seat 3 : court

bend \'bend\ *vb* **bent** \'bent\; **bending** 1 : curve or cause a change of shape in 2 : turn in a certain direction ~ *n* 1 : act of bending 2 : curve

be·neath \bi'nēth\ *adv or prep* : below

bene·dic·tion \,benə'dikshən\ *n* : closing blessing

bene·fac·tor \'benə,faktər\ *n* : one who gives esp. charitable aid

be·nef·i·cence \bə'nefəsəns\ *n* : quality of doing good —**be·nef·i·cent** \-sənt\ *adj*

ben·e·fi·cial \,benə'fishəl\ *adj* : being of benefit —**ben·e·fi·cial·ly** *adv*

ben·e·fi·cia·ry \-'fishē,erē, -'fishərē\ *n, pl* **-ries** : one who receives benefits

ben·e·fit \'benə,fit\ *n* 1 : something that does good 2 : help 3 : fund-raising event —**benefit** *vb*

be·nev·o·lence \bə'nevələns\ *n* 1 : charitable nature 2 : act of kindness —**be·nev·o·lent** \-lənt\ *adj* —**be·nev·o·lent·ly** *adv*

be·night·ed \bi'nītəd\ *adj* : ignorant

be·nign \bi'nīn\ *adj* 1 : gentle or kindly 2 : not malignant —**be·nig·ni·ty** \-'nignətē\ *n*

be·nig·nant \-'nignənt\ *adj* : benign

bent \'bent\ *n* : aptitude or interest

be·numb \bi'nəm\ *vb* : make numb esp. by cold

ben·zene \'ben,zēn\ *n* : colorless flammable liquid

be·queath \bi'kwēth, -'kwēth\ *vb* 1 : give by will 2 : hand down

be·quest \bi'kwest\ *n* : something bequeathed

be·rate \-'rāt\ *vb* : scold harshly

be·reaved \-'rēvd\ *adj* : suffering the death of a loved one ~ *n, pl* bereaved : one who is bereaved —**be·reave·ment** *n*

be·reft \-'reft\ *adj* : deprived of or lacking something

be·ret \bə'rā\ *n* : round soft visorless cap

beri·beri \,berē'berē\ *n* : thiamine-deficiency disease

berm \'bərm\ *n* : bank of earth

ber·ry \'berē\ *n, pl* **-ries** : small pulpy fruit

ber·serk \bər'sərk, -'zərk\ *adj* : crazed —**berserk** *adv*

berth \'bərth\ *n* 1 : place where a ship is anchored 2 : place to sit or sleep esp. on a ship 3 : job ~ *vb* : to bring or come into a berth

ber·yl \'berəl\ *n* : light-colored silicate mineral

be·seech \bi'sēch\ *vb* **-sought** \-'sót\ *or* **-seeched; -seech·ing** : entreat

be·set \-'set\ *vb* 1 : harass 2 : hem in

be·side \-'sīd\ *prep* 1 : by the side of 2 : besides

be·sides \-'sīdz\ *adv* 1 : in addition 2 : moreover ~ *prep* 1 : other than 2 : in addition to

be·siege \-'sēj\ *vb* : lay siege to —**be·sieg·er** *n*

be·smirch \-'smərch\ *vb* : soil

be·sot \-'sät\ *vb* **-tt-** : become drunk

be·speak \bi'spēk\ *vb* **-spoke; -spo·ken; -speak·ing** 1 : address 2 : indicate

best \'best\ *adj, superlative of* GOOD 1 : excelling all others 2 : most productive 3 : largest ~ *adv, superlative of* WELL 1 : in the best way 2 : most ~ *n* : one that is best ~ *vb* : outdo

bes·tial \'beschəl, 'bēs-\ *adj* 1 : relating to beasts 2 : brutish —**bes·ti·al·i·ty** \,beschē'alətē, ,bēs-\ *n*

be·stir \bi'stər\ *vb* : rouse to action

best man *n* : chief male attendant at a wedding

be·stow \bi'stō\ *vb* : give —**be·stow·al** \-əl\ *n*

bet \'bet\ *n* 1 : something risked or pledged on the outcome of a contest 2 : the making of a bet ~ *vb* bet; bet·ting 1 : risk (as money) on an outcome 2 : make a bet with

be·tide \bi'tīd\ *vb* : happen to

be·to·ken \bi'tōkən\ *vb* : give an indication of

be·tray \bi'trā\ *vb* 1 : seduce 2 : report or reveal to an enemy by treachery 3 : abandon 4 : prove unfaithful to 5 : reveal unintentionally —**be·tray·al** *n* —**be·tray·er** *n*

be·troth \-'träth, -'tróth, -'trōth, *or with* th\ *vb* : promise to marry —**be·troth·al** *n* —**be·trothed** *n*

bet·ter \'betər\ *adj, comparative of* GOOD 1 : more than half 2 : improved in health 3 : of higher quality ~ *adv, comparative of* WELL 1 : in a superior manner 2 : more ~ *n* 1 : one that is better 2 : advantage ~ *vb* 1 : improve 2 : surpass —**bet·ter·ment** \-mənt\ *n*

bet·tor, bet·ter \'betər\ *n* : one who bets

be·tween \bi'twēn\ *prep* 1 —used to show two things considered together 2 : in the space separating 3 —used to indicate a comparison or choice ~ *adv* : in an intervening space or interval

bev·el \'bevəl\ *n* : slant on an edge ~ *vb* **-eled** *or* **-elled; -el·ing** *or* **-el·ling** 1 : cut or shape to a bevel 2 : incline

bev·er·age \'bevrij\ *n* : drink

bevy \'bevē\ *n, pl* **bev·ies** : large group

be·wail \bi'wāl\ *vb* : lament

be·ware \-'war\ *vb* : be cautious

be·wil·der \-'wildər\ *vb* : confuse —**be·wil·der·ment** *n*

be·witch \-'wich\ *vb* 1 : affect by witchcraft 2 : charm —**be·witch·ment** *n*

be·yond \bē'yänd\ *adv* 1 : farther 2 : besides ~ *prep* 1 : on or to the farther side of 2 : out of the reach of 3 : besides

bi- \'bī, ,bī\ *prefix* 1 : two 2 : coming or occurring every two 3 : twice, doubly, or on both sides

bicolored	bicultural
biconcave	bidirectional
biconcavity	bifunctional
biconvex	bimetal
biconvexity	bimetallic

binational   bipolar
biparental   biracial

bi·an·nu·al \bī'anyəwəl\ adj : occurring twice a year —**bi·an·nu·al·ly** adv

bi·as \'bīəs\ n 1 : line diagonal to the grain of a fabric 2 : prejudice ~ vb -ased or -assed; -as·ing or -as·sing : prejudice

bib \'bib\ n : shield tied under the chin to protect the clothes while eating

Bi·ble \'bībəl\ n 1 : sacred scriptures of Christians 2 : sacred scriptures of Judaism or of some other religion —**bib·li·cal** \'biblikəl\ adj

bib·li·og·ra·phy \,biblē'ägrəfē\ n, pl -phies : list of writings on a subject or of an author —**bib·li·og·ra·pher** \-fər\ n —**bib·li·o·graph·ic** \-lēə'grafik\ adj

bi·cam·er·al \'bī'kamərəl\ adj : having 2 legislative chambers

bi·car·bon·ate \-'kärbə,nāt, -nət\ n : acid carbonate

bi·cen·ten·ni·al \,bīsen'tenēəl\ n : 200th anniversary —**bicentennial** adj

bi·ceps \'bī,seps\ n : large muscle of the upper arm

bick·er \'bikər\ vb or n : squabble

bi·cus·pid \bī'kəspəd\ n : double-pointed tooth

bi·cy·cle \'bī,sikəl\ n : 2-wheeled vehicle moved by pedaling ~ vb -cled; -cling : ride a bicycle —**bi·cy·cler** \-klər\ n **bi·cy·clist** \-list\ n

bid \'bid\ vb **bade** \'bad, 'bād\ or **bid**; **bid·den** \'bidⁿn\ or **bid**; **bid·ding** 1 : order 2 : invite 3 : express 4 : make a bid ~ n 1 : act of bidding 2 : buyer's proposed price —**bid·da·ble** \-əbəl\ adj —**bid·der** n

bide \'bīd\ vb **bode** \'bōd\ or **bid·ed**; **bided**; **bid·ing** 1 : wait 2 : dwell

bi·en·ni·al \bī'enēəl\ adj 1 : occurring once in 2 years 2 : lasting 2 years —**biennial** n —**bi·en·ni·al·ly** adv

bier \'bir\ n : stand for a coffin

bi·fo·cals \'bī,fōkəlz\ n pl : eyeglasses that correct for near and distant vision

big \'big\ adj -gg- : large in size, amount, or scope —**big·ness** n

big·a·my \'bigəmē\ n : marrying one person while still married to another —**big·a·mist** \-mist\ n —**big·a·mous** \-məs\ adj

big·horn n, pl -horn or -horns : wild mountain sheep

bight \'bīt\ n 1 : loop of a rope 2 : bay

big·ot \'bigət\ n : one who is intolerant of others —**big·ot·ed** \-ətəd\ adj —**big·ot·ry** \-ətrē\ n

big shot n : important person

big·wig n : big shot

bike \'bīk\ n : bicycle or motorcycle

bi·ki·ni \bə'kēnē\ n : woman's brief 2-piece bathing suit

bi·lat·er·al \bī'latərəl\ adj : involving 2 sides —**bi·lat·er·al·ly** adv

bile \'bīl\ n 1 : greenish liver secretion that aids digestion 2 : bad temper

bi·lin·gual \bī'liŋgwəl\ adj : using 2 languages

bil·ious \'bilyəs\ adj : irritable —**bil·ious·ness** n

bilk \'bilk\ n : cheat

¹**bill** \'bil\ n : jaws of a bird together with their horny covering ~ vb : caress fondly —**billed** adj

²**bill** n 1 : draft of a law 2 : list of things to be paid for 3 : printed advertisement 4 : piece of paper money ~ vb : submit a bill or account to

bill·board n : surface for displaying advertising bills

bil·let \'bilət\ n : soldiers' quarters ~ vb : lodge in a billet

bill·fold n : wallet

bil·liards \'bilyərdz\ n : game of driving balls into one another or into pockets on a table

bil·lion \'bilyən\ n, pl **billions** or **billion** : 1000 millions —**billion** adj —**bil·lionth** \-yənth\ adj or n

bil·low \'bilō\ n 1 : great wave 2 : rolling mass ~ vb : swell out —**bil·lowy** \'biləwē\ adj

billy goat n : male goat

bin \'bin\ n : storage box

bi·na·ry \'bīnərē\ adj : consisting of 2 things —**binary** n

bind \'bīnd\ vb **bound** \'baúnd\; **bind·ing** 1 : tie 2 : obligate 3 : unite into a mass 4 : bandage —**bind·er** n —**binding** n

binge \'binj\ n : spree

bin·go \'biŋgō\ n, pl -gos : game of covering numbers on a card

bin·oc·u·lar \bī'näkyələr, bə-\ adj : of or relating to both eyes ~ n : binocular optical instrument —usu. pl.

bio·chem·is·try \,bīō'keməstrē\ n : chemistry dealing with organisms —**bio·chem·i·cal** adj or n —**bio·chem·ist** n

bio·de·grad·able \ˌbīodiˈgrādəbəl\ adj : able to be reduced to harmless products by organisms —**bio·de·grad·abil·i·ty** n —**bio·deg·ra·da·tion** n —**bio·de·grade** vb

bi·og·ra·phy \bīˈägrəfē, bē-\ n, pl -phies : written history of a person's life —**bi·og·ra·pher** \-fər\ n —**bio·graph·i·cal** \ˌbīəˈgrafikəl\ adj

bi·ol·o·gy \bīˈäləjē\ n : science of living beings and life processes —**bi·o·log·ic** \ˌbīəˈläjik\, **bi·o·log·i·cal** \-əl\ adj —**bi·ol·o·gist** \bīˈäləjist\ n

bio·phys·ics \ˌbīōˈfiziks\ n : application of physics to biological problems —**bio·phys·i·cal** adj —**bio·phys·i·cist** n

bi·op·sy \ˈbīˌäpsē\ n, pl -sies : removal of live bodily tissue for examination

bio·tech·nol·o·gy \ˌbīōtekˈnäləjē\ n : manufacture of products using techniques involving the manipulation of DNA

bi·par·ti·san \bīˈpärtəzən, -sən\ adj : involving members of 2 parties

bi·ped \ˈbīˌped\ n : 2-footed animal

birch \ˈbərch\ n : deciduous tree with close-grained wood —**birch, birch·en** \-ən\ adj

bird \ˈbərd\ n : warm-blooded egg-laying vertebrate with wings and feathers —**bird·bath** n —**bird·house** n —**bird·seed** n

bird's–eye \ˈbərdzˌī\ adj 1 : seen from above 2 : cursory

birth \ˈbərth\ n 1 : act or fact of being born or of producing young 2 : origin —**birth·day** n —**birth·place** n —**birth·rate** n

birth·mark n : unusual blemish on the skin at birth

birth·right n : something one is entitled to by birth

bis·cuit \ˈbiskət\ n : small bread made with leavening other than yeast

bi·sect \ˈbīˌsekt\ vb : divide into 2 parts —**bi·sec·tion** \ˈbīˌsekshən\ n —**bi·sec·tor** \-tər\ n

bish·op \ˈbishəp\ n : clergy member higher than a priest

bish·op·ric \-shəˌprik\ n 1 : diocese 2 : office of bishop

bis·muth \ˈbizməth\ n : heavy brittle metallic chemical element

bi·son \ˈbīsᵊn, ˈbīz-\ n, pl -son : large shaggy wild ox of central U.S.

bis·tro \ˈbēstrō, ˈbis-\ n, pl -tros : small restaurant or bar

¹bit \ˈbit\ n 1 : part of a bridle that goes in a horse's mouth 2 : drilling tool

²bit n 1 : small piece or quantity 2 : small degree

bitch \ˈbich\ n : female dog ~ vb : complain

bite \ˈbīt\ vb **bit** \ˈbit\; **bit·ten** \ˈbitᵊn\; **bit·ing** \ˈbītiŋ\ 1 : to grip or cut with teeth or jaws 2 : dig in or grab and hold 3 : sting 4 : take bait ~ n 1 : act of biting 2 : bit of food 3 : wound made by biting —**bit·ing** adj

bit·ter \ˈbitər\ adj 1 : having an acrid lingering taste 2 : intense or severe 3 : extremely harsh or resentful —**bit·ter·ly** adv —**bit·ter·ness** n

bit·tern \ˈbitərn\ n : small heron

bi·tu·mi·nous coal \bəˈtümənəs-, -ˈtyü-\ n : coal that yields volatile waste matter when heated

bi·valve \ˈbīˌvalv\ n : animal (as a clam) with a shell of 2 parts —**bivalve** adj

biv·ouac \ˈbivəˌwak\ n : temporary camp ~ vb -**ouacked**; -**ouack·ing** : camp

bi·zarre \bəˈzär\ adj : very strange —**bi·zarre·ly** adv

blab \ˈblab\ vb -**bb-** : talk too much

black \ˈblak\ adj 1 : of the color black 2 : Negro 3 : soiled 4 : lacking light 5 : wicked or evil 6 : gloomy ~ n 1 : black pigment or dye 2 : something black 3 : color of least lightness 4 : person of a dark-skinned race ~ vb : blacken —**black·ing** n —**black·ish** adj —**black·ly** adv —**black·ness** n

black–and–blue adj : darkly discolored from bruising

black·ball \ˈblakˌból\ vb 1 : ostracize 2 : boycott —**blackball** n

black·ber·ry \ˈblakˌberē\ n : black or purple fruit of a bramble

black·bird n : bird of which the male is largely or wholly black

black·board n : dark surface for writing on with chalk

black·en \ˈblakən\ vb 1 : make or become black 2 : defame

black·guard \ˈblagərd, -ˌärd\ n : scoundrel

black·head n : small dark oily mass plugging the outlet of a skin gland

black hole n : invisible extremely massive celestial object

black·jack n 1 : flexible leather-covered club 2 : card game ~ vb : hit with a blackjack

black·list n : list of persons to be punished or boycotted —**blacklist** vb

black·mail n 1 : extortion by threat of exposure 2 : something extorted by blackmail —**blackmail** vb —**black·mail·er** n

black·out n 1 : darkness due to electrical failure 2 : brief fainting spell — **black out** vb

black·smith n : one who forges iron

black·top n : dark tarry material for surfacing roads —**blacktop** vb

blad·der \'bladər\ n : sac into which urine passes from the kidneys

blade \'blād\ n 1 : leaf esp. of grass 2 : something resembling the flat part of a leaf 3 : cutting part of an instrument or tool —**blad·ed** \'blādəd\ adj

blame \'blām\ vb **blamed; blam·ing** 1 : find fault with 2 : hold responsible or responsible for —**blam·able** adj — **blame** n —**blame·less** adj —**blame·less·ly** adv —**blame·worthi·ness** n —**blame·worthy** adj

blanch \'blanch\ vb : make or become white or pale

bland \'bland\ adj 1 : smooth in manner 2 : soothing 3 : tasteless —**bland·ly** adv —**bland·ness** n

blan·dish·ment \'blandishmənt\ n : flattering or coaxing speech or act

blank \'blaŋk\ adj 1 : showing or causing a dazed look 2 : lacking expression 3 : empty 4 : free from writing 5 : downright ~ n 1 : an empty space 2 : form with spaces to write in 3 : unfinished form (as of a key) 4 : cartridge with no bullet ~ vb : cover or close up —**blank·ly** adv —**blank·ness** n

blan·ket \'blaŋkət\ n 1 : heavy covering for a bed 2 : covering layer ~ vb : cover ~ adj : applying to a group

blare \'blar\ vb **blared; blar·ing** : make a loud harsh sound —**blare** n

blar·ney \'blärnē\ n : skillful flattery

bla·sé \blä'zā\ adj : indifferent to pleasure or excitement

blas·pheme \blas'fēm\ vb **-phemed; -phem·ing** : speak blasphemy — **blas·phem·er** n

blas·phe·my \'blasfəmē\ n, pl **-mies** : irreverence toward God or anything sacred —**blas·phe·mous** adj

blast \'blast\ n 1 : violent gust of wind 2 : explosion ~ vb : shatter by or as if by explosive —**blast off** vb : take off esp. in a rocket

bla·tant \'blāt³nt\ adj : offensively showy —**bla·tan·cy** \-³nsē\ n —**bla·tant·ly** adv

¹blaze \'blāz\ n 1 : fire 2 : intense direct light 3 : strong display ~ vb **blazed; blaz·ing** : burn or shine brightly

²blaze n 1 : white stripe on an animal's face 2 : trail marker esp. on a tree ~ vb **blazed; blaz·ing** : mark with blazes

blaz·er \-ər\ n : sports jacket

bleach \'blēch\ vb : whiten —**bleach** n

bleach·ers \-ərz\ n sing or pl : uncovered stand for spectators

bleak \'blēk\ adj 1 : desolately barren 2 : lacking cheering qualities — **bleak·ish** adj —**bleak·ly** adv — **bleak·ness** n

blear \'blir\ adj : dim with water or tears

bleary \'blirē\ adj : dull or dimmed esp. from fatigue

bleat \'blēt\ n : cry of a sheep or goat or a sound like it —**bleat** vb

bleed \'blēd\ vb **bled** \'bled\; **bleed·ing** 1 : lose or shed blood 2 : feel distress 3 : flow from a wound 4 : draw fluid from 5 : extort money from — **bleed·er** n

blem·ish \'blemish\ vb : spoil by a flaw ~ n : noticeable flaw

¹blench \'blench\ vb : flinch

²blench vb : grow or make pale

blend \'blend\ vb 1 : mix thoroughly 2 : combine into an integrated whole — **blend** n —**blend·er** n

bless \'bles\ vb **blessed** \'blest\; **bless·ing** 1 : consecrate by religious rite 2 : invoke divine care for 3 : make happy —**blessed** \'blesəd\, **blest** \'blest\ adj —**bless·ed·ly** \'blesədlē\ adv —**bless·ed·ness** \'blesədnəs\ n — **bless·ing** n

blew past of BLOW

blight \'blīt\ n 1 : plant disorder marked by withering or an organism causing it 2 : harmful influence 3 : deteriorated condition ~ vb : affect with or suffer from blight

blimp \'blimp\ n : airship holding form by pressure of contained gas

blind \'blīnd\ adj 1 : lacking or quite deficient in ability to see 2 : not intelligently controlled 3 : having no way out ~ vb 1 : to make blind 2 : dazzle ~ n 1 : something to conceal or darken 2 : place of concealment — **blind·ly** adv —**blind·ness** n

blind·fold *vb* : cover the eyes of — **blindfold** *n*

blink \'bliŋk\ *vb* 1 : wink 2 : shine intermittently ~ *n* : wink

blink·er *n* : a blinking light

bliss \'blis\ *n* 1 : complete happiness 2 : heaven or paradise — **bliss·ful** *adj* — **bliss·ful·ly** *adv*

blis·ter \'blistər\ *n* 1 : raised area of skin containing watery fluid 2 : raised or swollen spot ~ *vb* : develop or cause blisters

blithe \'blīth, 'blīth\ *adj* **blith·er; blith·est** :- cheerful — **blithe·ly** *adv* — **blithe·some** \-səm\ *adj*

blitz \'blits\ *n* 1 : series of air raids 2 : fast intensive campaign — **blitz** *vb*

bliz·zard \'blizərd\ *n* : severe snowstorm

bloat \'blōt\ *vb* : swell

blob \'bläb\ *n* : small lump or drop

bloc \'bläk\ *n* : group working together

block \'bläk\ *n* 1 : solid piece 2 : frame enclosing a pulley 3 : quantity considered together 4 : large building divided into separate units 5 : a city square or the distance along one of its sides 6 : obstruction 7 : interruption of a bodily or mental function ~ *vb* : obstruct or hinder

block·ade \blä'kād\ *n* : isolation of a place usu. by troops or ships — **block·ade** *vb* — **block·ad·er** *n*

block·head *n* : stupid person

blond, blonde \'bländ\ *adj* 1 : fair in complexion 2 : of a light color — **blond, blonde** *n*

blood \'bləd\ *n* 1 : red liquid that circulates in the heart, arteries, and veins of animals 2 : lifeblood 3 : lineage — **blood·ed** *adj* — **blood·less** *adj* — **blood·stain** *n* — **blood·stained** *adj* — **blood·suck·er** *n* — **blood·suck·ing** *n* — **bloody** *adj*

blood·cur·dling *adj* : terrifying

blood·hound *n* : large hound with a keen sense of smell

blood·mo·bile \-mō,bēl\ *n* : truck for collecting blood from donors

blood·shed *n* : slaughter

blood·shot *adj* : inflamed to redness

blood·stream *n* : blood in a circulatory system

blood·thirsty *adj* : eager to shed blood — **blood·thirst·i·ly** *adv* — **blood·thirst·i·ness** *n*

bloom \'blüm\ *n* 1 : flower 2 : period of

flowering 3 : fresh or healthy look ~ *vb* 1 : yield flowers 2 : mature — **bloomy** *adj*

bloo·mers \'blümərz\ *n pl* : woman's underwear of short loose trousers

bloop·er \'blüpər\ *n* : public blunder

blos·som \'bläsəm\ *n or vb* : flower

blot \'blät\ *n* 1 : stain 2 : blemish ~ *vb* -tt- 1 : spot 2 : dry with absorbent paper — **blot·ter** *n*

blotch \'bläch\ *n* : large spot — **blotch** *vb* — **blotchy** *adj*

blouse \'blaus, 'blauz\ *n* : loose garment reaching from the neck to the waist

¹blow \'blō\ *vb* **blew** \'blü\; **blown** \'blōn\; **blow·ing** 1 : move forcibly 2 : send forth a current of air 3 : sound 4 : shape by blowing 5 : explode 6 : bungle ~ *n* 1 : gale 2 : act of blowing — **blow·er** *n* — **blowy** *adj*

²blow *n* 1 : forcible stroke 2 *pl* : fighting 3 : calamity

blow·out *n* : bursting of a tire

blow·torch *n* : small torch that uses a blast of air

¹blub·ber \'bləbər\ *n* : fat of whales

²blubber *vb* : cry noisily

blud·geon \'bləjən\ *n* : short club ~ *vb* : hit with a bludgeon

blue \'blü\ *adj* **blu·er; blu·est** 1 : of the color blue 2 : melancholy ~ *n* : color of the clear sky — **blu·ish** \-ish\ *adj*

blue·bell *n* : plant with blue bell-shaped flowers

blue·ber·ry \-,berē\ *n* : edible blue or blackish berry

blue·bird *n* : small bluish songbird

blue·fish *n* : bluish marine food fish

blue jay *n* : American crested jay

blue·print *n* 1 : photographic print in white on blue of a mechanical drawing 2 : plan of action — **blueprint** *vb*

blues \'blüz\ *n pl* 1 : depression 2 : music in a melancholy style

¹bluff \'bləf\ *adj* 1 : rising steeply with a broad flat front 2 : frank ~ *n* : cliff

²bluff *vb* : deceive by pretense ~ *n* : act of bluffing — **bluff·er** \-ər\ *n*

blu·ing, blue·ing \'blüiŋ\ *n* : laundry preparation to keep fabrics white

blun·der \'bləndər\ *vb* 1 : move clumsily 2 : make a stupid mistake ~ *n* : bad mistake

blun·der·buss \-,bəs\ *n* : obsolete short-barreled firearm

blunt \'blənt\ *adj* 1 : not sharp 2

: tactless ~ *vb* : make dull —**blunt-ly** *adv* —**blunt·ness** *n*

blur \'blǝr\ *n* 1 : smear 2 : something perceived indistinctly ~ *vb* -**rr**- : cloud or obscure —**blur·ry** \-ē\ *adj*

blurb \'blǝrb\ *n* : short publicity notice

blurt \'blǝrt\ *vb* : utter suddenly

blush \'blǝsh\ *n* : reddening of the face —**blush** *vb* —**blush·ful** *adj*

blus·ter \'blǝstǝr\ *vb* 1 : blow violently 2 : talk or act with boasts or threats —**blus·ter** *n* —**blus·tery** *adj*

boa \'bōǝ\ *n* 1 : a large snake (as the **boa con·stric·tor** \-kǝn'striktǝr\ that crushes its prey 2 : fluffy scarf

boar \'bōr\ *n* : male swine

board \'bōrd\ *n* 1 : long thin piece of sawed lumber 2 : flat thin sheet esp. for games 3 : daily meals furnished for pay 4 : official body ~ *vb* 1 : go aboard 2 : cover with boards 3 : supply meals to —**board·er** *n*

board·walk *n* : wooden walk along a beach

boast \'bōst\ *vb* : praise oneself or one's possessions —**boast** *n* —**boast·er** *n*—**boast·ful** *adj* —**boast·ful·ly** *adv*

boat \'bōt\ *n* : small vessel for traveling on water —**boat** *vb* —**boat·man** \-mǝn\ *n*

boat·swain \'bōsᵊn\ *n* : ship's officer in charge of the hull

¹**bob** \'bäb\ *vb* -**bb**- 1 : move up and down 2 : appear suddenly

²**bob** *n* 1 : float 2 : woman's short haircut ~ *vb* : cut hair in a bob

bob·bin \'bäbǝn\ *n* : spindle for holding thread

bob·ble \'bäbǝl\ *vb* -**bled**; -**bling** : fumble —**bobble** *n*

bob·cat *n* : small American lynx

bob·o·link \'bäbǝ,liŋk\ *n* : American songbird

bob·sled \'bäb,sled\ *n* : racing sled —**bobsled** *vb*

bob·white \bäb'hwīt\ *n* : quail

bock \'bäk\ *n* : dark beer

¹**bode** \'bōd\ *vb* **bod·ed**; **bod·ing** : indicate by signs

²**bode** *past of* BIDE

bod·ice \'bädǝs\ *n* : close-fitting top of dress

bod·i·ly \'bädᵊlē\ *adj* : relating to the body ~ *adv* 1 : in the flesh 2 : as a whole

body \'bädē\ *n, pl* **bod·ies** 1 : the physical whole of an organism 2 : human being 3 : main part 4 : mass of matter 5 : group —**bod·ied** *adj* —**bodi·less** \-iläs, -ᵊlǝs\ *adj* —**body·guard** *n*

bog \'bäg, 'bȯg\ *n* : swamp ~ *vb* -**gg**- : sink in or as if in a bog —**bog·gy** *adj*

bo·gey \'bugē, 'bō-\ *n, pl* -**geys** : someone or something frightening

bog·gle \'bägǝl\ *vb* -**gled**; -**gling** : overwhelm with amazement

bo·gus \'bōgǝs\ *adj* : fake

bo·he·mi·an \bō'hēmēǝn\ *n* : one living unconventionally —**bohemian** *adj*

¹**boil** \'bȯil\ *n* : inflamed swelling

²**boil** *vb* 1 : heat to a temperature (**boil·ing point**) at which vapor forms 2 : cook in boiling liquid 3 : be agitated —**boil** *n*

boil·er \'bȯilǝr\ *n* : tank holding hot water or steam

bois·ter·ous \'bȯistǝrǝs\ *adj* : noisily turbulent —**bois·ter·ous·ly** *adv*

bold \'bōld\ *adj* 1 : courageous 2 : insolent 3 : daring —**bold·ly** *adv* —**bold·ness** *n*

bo·le·ro \bǝ'lerō\ *n, pl* -**ros** 1 : Spanish dance 2 : short open jacket

boll \'bōl\ *n* : seed pod

boll weevil *n* : small grayish weevil that infests the cotton plant

bo·lo·gna \bǝ'lōnē\ *n* : large smoked sausage

bol·ster \'bōlstǝr\ *n* : long pillow ~ *vb* -**stered**; -**ster·ing** : support

bolt \'bōlt\ *n* 1 : flash of lightning 2 : sliding bar used to fasten a door 3 : roll of cloth 4 : threaded pin used with a nut ~ *vb* 1 : move suddenly 2 : fasten with a bolt 3 : swallow hastily

bomb \'bäm\ *n* : explosive device ~ *vb* : attack with bombs —**bomb·proof** *adj*

bom·bard \bäm'bärd, bǝm-\ *vb* : attack with or as if with artillery —**bom·bard·ment** *n*

bom·bar·dier \,bämbǝ'dir\ *n* : one who releases the bombs from a bomber

bom·bast \'bäm,bast\ *n* : pretentious language —**bom·bas·tic** \bäm'bastik\ *adj*

bomb·er *n* 1 : one that bombs 2 : airplane for dropping bombs

bomb·shell *n* 1 : bomb 2 : great surprise

bona fide \'bōnǝ,fīd, 'bän-; ,bōnǝ'fīdē\ *adj* 1 : made in good faith 2 : genuine

bo·nan·za \bǝ'nanzǝ\ *n* : something yielding a rich return

bon·bon \'bän,bän\ *n* : piece of candy

bond \'bänd\ *n* 1 *pl* : fetters 2 : uniting

force **3** : obligation made binding by money **4** : interest-bearing certificate ~ vb **1** : insure **2** : cause to adhere —**bond·hold·er** n

bond·age \'bändij\ n : slavery —**bond·man** \-mən\ n —**bond·wom·an** n

¹**bonds·man** \'bändzmən\ n : slave

²**bondsman** n : surety

bone \'bōn\ n : skeletal material ~ vb **boned; bon·ing** : to free from bones —**bone·less** adj —**bony** \'bōnē\ adj

bon·er \'bōnər\ n : blunder

bon·fire \'bän,fīr\ n : outdoor fire

bo·ni·to \bə'nētō\ n, pl **-tos** or **-to** : medium-sized tuna

bon·net \'bänət\ n : hat for a woman or infant

bo·nus \'bōnəs\ n : extra payment

boo \'bü\ n, pl **boos** : shout of disapproval —**boo** vb

boo·by \'bübē\ n, pl **-bies** : dunce

book \'bük\ n **1** : paper sheets bound into a volume **2** : long literary work or a subdivision of one ~ vb : reserve —**book·case** n —**book·let** \-lət\ n —**book·mark** n —**book·sell·er** n —**book·shelf** n

book·end n : support to hold up a row of books

book·ie \-ē\ n : bookmaker

book·ish \-ish\ adj : fond of books and reading

book·keep·er n : one who keeps business accounts —**book·keep·ing** n

book·mak·er n : one who takes bets —**book·mak·ing** n

book·worm n : one devoted to reading

¹**boom** \'büm\ n **1** : long spar to extend the bottom of a sail **2** : beam projecting from the pole of a derrick

²**boom** vb **1** : make a deep hollow sound **2** : grow rapidly esp. in value ~ n **1** : booming sound **2** : rapid growth

boo·mer·ang \'bümə,raŋ\ n : angular club that returns to the thrower

¹**boon** \'bün\ n : benefit

²**boon** adj : congenial

boon·docks \'bün,däks\ n pl : rural area

boor \'bùr\ n : rude person —**boor·ish** adj

boost \'büst\ vb **1** : raise **2** : promote —**boost** n —**boost·er** n

boot \'büt\ n **1** : covering for the foot and leg **2** : kick ~ vb : kick

boo·tee, boo·tie \'bütē\ n : infant's knitted sock

booth \'büth\ n, pl **booths** \'büthz\

'büths\ : small enclosed stall or seating area

boot·leg \'büt,leg\ vb : make or sell liquor illegally —**bootleg** adj or n —**boot·leg·ger** n

boo·ty \'bütē\ n, pl **-ties** : plunder

booze \'büz\ vb **boozed; booz·ing** : drink liquor to excess ~ n : liquor —**booz·er** n —**boozy** adj

bo·rax \'bōr,aks\ n : crystalline compound of boron

bor·der \'bórdər\ n **1** : edge **2** : boundary ~ vb **1** : put a border on **2** : be close

¹**bore** \'bōr\ vb **bored; bor·ing 1** : pierce **2** : make by piercing ~ n : cylindrical hole or its diameter —**bor·er** n

²**bore** past of BEAR

³**bore** n : one that is dull ~ vb **bored; bor·ing** : tire with dullness —**bore·dom** \'bōrdəm\ n

born \'bórn\ adj **1** : brought into life **2** : being such by birth

borne past part of BEAR

bo·ron \'bōr,än\ n : dark-colored chemical element

bor·ough \'bərō\ n : incorporated town or village

bor·row \'bärō\ vb **1** : take as a loan **2** : take into use

bo·som \'büzəm, 'bü-\ n : breast ~ adj : intimate —**bo·somed** adj

boss \'bós\ n : employer or supervisor ~ vb : supervise —**bossy** adj

bot·a·ny \'bätᵊnē\ n : plant biology —**bo·tan·i·cal** \bə'tanikəl\ adj —**bot·a·nist** \'bätᵊnist\ n —**bot·a·nize** \-ᵊn,īz\ vb

botch \'bäch\ vb : do clumsily —**botch** n

both \'bōth\ adj or pron : the one and the other ~ conj —used to show each of two is included

both·er \'bäthər\ vb **1** : annoy or worry **2** : take the trouble —**bother** n —**both·er·some** \-səm\ adj

bot·tle \'bätᵊl\ n : container with a narrow neck and no handles ~ vb **bot·tled; bot·tling** : put into a bottle

bot·tle·neck n : place or cause of congestion

bot·tom \'bätəm\ n **1** : supporting surface **2** : lowest part or place —**bottom** adj —**bot·tomed** adj —**bot·tom·less** adj

bot·u·lism \'bächə,lizəm\ n : acute food poisoning

bou·doir \'bü,dwär, 'bù-, ,bü'-, ,bù'-\ *n* : woman's private room

bough \'baù\ *n* : large tree branch

bought *past of* BUY

bouil·lon \'bù,yän; 'bùl,yän, -yən\ *n* : clear soup

boul·der \'bōldər\ *n* : large rounded rock —**boul·dered** *adj*

bou·le·vard \'bùlə,värd, 'bü-\ *n* : broad thoroughfare

bounce \'baùns\ *vb* **bounced; bounc·ing** 1 : spring back 2 : make bounce —**bounce** *n* —**bouncy** \'baùnsē\ *adj*

¹bound \'baùnd\ *adj* : intending to go

²bound *n* : limit or boundary ~ *vb* : be a boundary of —**bound·less** *adj* —**bound·less·ness** *n*

³bound *adj* 1 : obliged 2 : having a binding 3 : determined 4 : incapable of failing

⁴bound *n* : leap ~ *vb* : move by springing

bound·ary \'baùndrē\ *n, pl* **-aries** : line marking extent or separation

boun·ty \'baùntē\ *n, pl* **-ties** 1 : generosity 2 : reward —**boun·te·ous** \-ēəs\ *adj* —**boun·te·ous·ly** *adv* —**boun·ti·ful** \-ifəl\ *adj* —**boun·ti·ful·ly** *adv*

bou·quet \bō'kā, bü-\ *n* 1 : bunch of flowers 2 : fragrance

bour·bon \'bərbən\ *n* : corn whiskey

bour·geoi·sie \,bùrzh,wä'zē\ *n* : middle class of society —**bour·geois** \'bùrzh-,wä, bùrzh'wä\ *n or adj*

bout \'baùt\ *n* 1 : contest 2 : outbreak

bou·tique \bü'tēk\ *n* : specialty shop

bo·vine \'bō,vīn, -, vēn\ *adj* : relating to cattle —**bovine** *n*

¹bow \'baù\ *vb* 1 : submit 2 : bend the head or body ~ *n* : act of bowing

²bow \'bō\ *n* 1 : bend or arch 2 : weapon for shooting arrows 3 : knot with loops 4 : rod with stretched horsehairs for playing a stringed instrument ~ *vb* : curve or bend —**bow·man** \-mən\ *n* —**bow·string** *n*

³bow \'baù\ *n* : forward part of a ship —**bow** *adj*

bow·els \'baùəls\ *n pl* 1 : intestines 2 : inmost parts

bow·er \'baùər\ *n* : arbor

¹bowl \'bōl\ *n* : concave vessel or part —**bowl·ful** \-,fùl\ *n*

²bowl *n* : round ball for bowling ~ *vb* : roll a ball in bowling —**bowl·er** *n*

bowl·ing *n* : game in which balls are rolled to knock down pins

¹box \'bäks\ *n, pl* **box** *or* **box·es** : evergreen shrub —**box·wood** \-,wùd\ *n*

²box *n* 1 : container usu. with 4 sides and a cover 2 : small compartment ~ *vb* : put in a box

³box *n* : slap ~ *vb* 1 : slap 2 : fight with the fists —**box·er** *n* —**box·ing** *n*

box·car *n* : roofed freight car

box office *n* : theater ticket office

boy \'bói\ *n* : male child —**boy·hood** *n* —**boy·ish** *adj* —**boy·ish·ly** *adv* —**boy·ish·ness** *n*

boy·cott \-,kät\ *vb* : refrain from dealing with —**boycott** *n*

boy·friend \'bói,frend\ *n* 1 : male friend 2 : woman's regular male companion

brace \'brās\ *n* 1 : crank for turning a bit 2 : something that resists weight or supports 3 : punctuation mark {or} ~ *vb* **braced; brac·ing** 1 : make taut or steady 2 : invigorate 3 : strengthen

brace·let \'brāslət\ *n* : ornamental band for the wrist or arm

brack·et \'brakət\ *n* 1 : projecting support 2 : punctuation mark [or] 3 : class ~ *vb* 1 : furnish or fasten with brackets 2 : place within brackets 3 : group

brack·ish \-ish\ *adj* : salty

brad \'brad\ *n* : nail with a small head

brag \'brag\ *vb* **-gg-** : boast —**brag** *n*

brag·gart \'bragərt\ *n* : boaster

braid \'brād\ *vb* : interweave ~ *n* : something braided

braille \'brāl\ *n* : system of writing for the blind using raised dots

brain \'brān\ *n* 1 : organ of thought and nervous coordination enclosed in the skull 2 : intelligence ~ *vb* : smash the skull of —**brained** *adj* —**brain·less** *adj* —**brainy** *adj*

braise \'brāz\ *vb* **braised; brais·ing** : cook (meat) slowly in a covered dish

brake \'brāk\ *n* : device for slowing or stopping ~ *vb* **braked; brak·ing** : slow or stop by a brake

bram·ble \'brambəl\ *n* : prickly shrub

bran \'bran\ *n* : edible cracked grain husks

branch \'branch\ *n* 1 : division of a plant stem 2 : part ~ *vb* 1 : develop branches 2 : diverge —**branched** *adj*

brand \'brand\ *n* 1 : identifying mark made by burning 2 : stigma 3 : distinctive kind (as of goods from one firm) ~ *vb* : mark with a brand

bran·dish \'brandish\ *vb* : wave

brand–new *adj* : unused

bran·dy \'brandē\ *n, pl* **-dies** : liquor distilled from wine

brash \'brash\ *adj* **1** : impulsive **2** : aggressively self-assertive

brass \'bras\ *n* **1** : alloy of copper and zinc **2** : brazen self-assurance **3** : high-ranking military officers — **brassy** *adj*

bras·siere \brə'zir\ *n* : woman's undergarment to support the breasts

brat \'brat\ *n* : ill-behaved child — **brat·ti·ness** *n* —**brat·ty** *adj*

bra·va·do \brə'vädō\ *n, pl* **-does** *or* **-dos** : false bravery

¹brave \'brāv\ *adj* **brav·er; brav·est** : showing courage ~ *vb* **braved; brav·ing** : face with courage — **brave·ly** *adv* —**brav·ery** \-ərē\ *n*

²brave *n* : American Indian warrior

bra·vo \'brävō\ *n, pl* **-vos** : shout of approval

brawl \'brȯl\ *n* : noisy quarrel or violent fight —**brawl** *vb* —**brawl·er** *n*

brawn \'brȯn\ *n* : muscular strength — **brawny** \-ē\ *adj* —**brawn·i·ness** *n*

bray \'brā\ *n* : harsh cry of a donkey — **bray** *vb*

bra·zen \'brāz°n\ *adj* **1** : made of brass **2** : bold —**bra·zen·ly** *adv* —**bra·zen·ness** *n*

bra·zier \'brāzhər\ *n* : charcoal grill

breach \'brēch\ *n* **1** : breaking of a law, obligation, or standard **2** : gap ~ *vb* : make a breach in

bread \'bred\ *n* : baked food made of flour ~ *vb* : cover with bread crumbs

breadth \'bredth\ *n* : width

bread·win·ner *n* : wage earner

break \'brāk\ *vb* **broke** \'brōk\; **bro·ken** \'brōkən\; **break·ing** **1** : knock into pieces **2** : transgress **3** : force a way into or out of **4** : exceed **5** : interrupt **6** : fail ~ *n* **1** : act or result of breaking **2** : stroke of good luck —**break·able** *adj or n* —**break·age** \'brākij\ *n* — **break·er** *n* —**break in** *vb* **1** : enter by force **2** : interrupt **3** : train — **break out** *vb* **1** : erupt with force **2** : develop a rash

break·down *n* : physical or mental failure —**break down** *vb*

break·fast \'brekfəst\ *n* : first meal of the day —**breakfast** *vb*

breast \'brest\ *n* **1** : milk-producing gland esp. of a woman **2** : front part of the chest

breast·bone *n* : sternum

breath \'breth\ *n* **1** : slight breeze **2** : air breathed in or out —**breath·less** *adj* —**breath·less·ly** *adv* —**breath·less·ness** *n* —**breathy** \'brethē\ *adj*

breathe \'brēth\ *vb* **breathed; breath·ing** **1** : draw air into the lungs and expel it **2** : live **3** : utter

breath·tak·ing *adj* : exciting

breech·es \'brichəz\ *n pl* : trousers ending near the knee

breed \'brēd\ *vb* **bred** \'bred\; **breed·ing** **1** : give birth to **2** : propagate **3** : raise ~ *n* **1** : kind of plant or animal usu. developed by humans **2** : class — **breed·er** *n*

breeze \'brēz\ *n* : light wind ~ *vb* **breezed; breez·ing** : move fast — **breezy** *adj*

breth·ren \'brethrən, -ərn\ *pl of* BROTHER

bre·via·ry \'brēvərē, 'bre-, -vyərē, -vē-, erē\ *n, pl* **-ries** : prayer book used by Roman Catholic priests

brev·i·ty \'brevətē\ *n, pl* **-ties** : shortness or conciseness

brew \'brü\ *vb* : make by fermenting or steeping —**brew** *n* —**brew·er** *n* — **brew·ery** \'brüərē, 'brúrē\ *n*

bri·ar *var of* BRIER

bribe \'brīb\ *vb* **bribed; brib·ing** : corrupt or influence by gifts ~ *n* : something offered or given in bribing —**brib·able** *adj* —**brib·ery** \-ərē\ *n*

bric-a-brac \'brikə,brak\ *n pl* : small ornamental articles

brick \'brik\ *n* : building block of baked clay —**brick** *vb* —**brick·lay·er** *n* — **brick·lay·ing** *n*

bride \'brīd\ *n* : woman just married or about to be married —**brid·al** \-°l\ *adj*

bride·groom *n* : man just married or about to be married

brides·maid *n* : woman who attends a bride at her wedding

¹bridge \'brij\ *n* **1** : structure built for passage over a depression or obstacle **2** : upper part of the nose **3** : compartment from which a ship is navigated **4** : artificial replacement for missing teeth ~ *vb* : build a bridge over —**bridge·able** *adj*

²bridge *n* : card game for 4 players

bri·dle \'brīd°l\ *n* : headgear to control a horse ~ *vb* **-dled; -dling** **1** : put a bridle on 2 : restrain 3 : show hostility or scorn

brief \'brēf\ adj : short or concise ~ n : concise summary (as of a legal case) ~ vb : give final instructions or essential information to —**brief·ly** adv —**brief·ness** n

brief·case n : case for papers

¹bri·er \'brīər\ n : thorny plant

²brier n : heath of southern Europe

¹brig \'brig\ n : 2-masted ship

²brig n : jail on a naval ship

bri·gade \brig'ād\ n 1 : large military unit 2 : group organized for a special activity

brig·a·dier general \,brigə'dir-\ n : officer ranking next below a major general

brig·and \'brigənd\ n : bandit —**brig·and·age** \-ij\ n

bright \'brīt\ adj 1 : radiating or reflecting light 2 : cheerful 3 : intelligent —**bright·en** \-ᵊn\ vb —**bright·en·er** \'brītᵊnər\ n —**bright·ly** adv —**bright·ness** n

bril·liant \'brilyənt\ adj 1 : very bright 2 : splendid 3 : very intelligent —**bril·liance** \-yəns\ n —**bril·lian·cy** \-yənsē\ n —**bril·liant·ly** adv

brim \'brim\ n : edge or rim ~ vb : be or become full —**brim·less** adj —**brimmed** adj

brim·ful \-'fül\ adj : full to the brim

brim·stone n : sulfur

brin·dled \'brindᵊld\ adj : gray or tawny with dark streaks or flecks

brine \'brīn\ n 1 : salt water 2 : ocean —**brin·i·ness** n —**briny** adj

bring \'briŋ\ vb **brought** \'brȯt\; **bring·ing** 1 : cause to come with one 2 : persuade 3 : produce 4 : sell for —**bring·er** n —**bring about** vb : make happen —**bring up** vb 1 : care for and educate 2 : cause to be noticed

brink \'briŋk\ n : edge

bri·quette, bri·quet \bri'ket\ n : pressed mass (as of charcoal)

brisk \'brisk\ adj 1 : lively 2 : invigorating —**brisk·ly** adv —**brisk·ness** n

bris·ket \'briskət\ n : breast or lower chest of a quadruped

bris·tle \'brisəl\ n : short stiff hair ~ vb **-tled**; **-tling** 1 : stand erect 2 : show angry defiance 3 : appear as if covered with bristles —**bris·tly** adj

brit·tle \'britᵊl\ adj **-tler**; **-tlest** : easily broken —**brit·tle·ness** n

broach \'brōch\ n : pointed tool (as for opening casks) ~ vb 1 : pierce (as a cask) to open 2 : introduce for discussion

broad \'brȯd\ adj 1 : wide 2 : spacious 3 : clear or open 4 : obvious 5 : tolerant in outlook 6 : widely applicable 7 : dealing with essential points —**broad·en** \-ᵊn\ vb —**broad·ly** adv —**broad·ness** n

broad·cast n 1 : transmission by radio waves 2 : radio or television program ~ vb **-cast**; **-cast·ing** 1 : scatter or sow in all directions 2 : make widely known 3 : send out on a broadcast —**broad·cast·er** n

broad·cloth n : fine cloth

broad·loom adj : woven on a wide loom esp. in solid color

broad–mind·ed adj : tolerant of varied opinions —**broad–mind·ed·ly** adv —**broad–mind·ed·ness** n

broad·side n 1 : simultaneous firing of all guns on one side of a ship 2 : verbal attack

bro·cade \brō'kād\ n : usu. silk fabric with a raised design

broc·co·li \'bräkəlē\ n : green vegetable akin to cauliflower

bro·chure \brō'shùr\ n : pamphlet

brogue \'brōg\ n : Irish accent

broil \'brȯil\ vb : cook by radiant heat —**broil** n

broil·er n 1 : utensil for broiling 2 : chicken fit for broiling

¹broke \'brōk\ past of BREAK

²broke adj : out of money

bro·ken \'brōkən\ adj : imperfectly spoken —**bro·ken·ly** adv

bro·ken·heart·ed \-'härtəd\ adj : overcome by grief or despair

bro·ker \'brōkər\ n : agent who buys and sells for a fee —**broker** vb —**bro·ker·age** \-kərij\ n

bro·mine \'brō,mēn\ n : deep red liquid corrosive chemical element

bron·chi·tis \brän'kītəs, bräŋ-\ n : inflammation of the bronchi

bron·chus \'bräŋkəs\ n, pl **-chi** \-,kī, -,kē\ : division of the windpipe leading to a lung —**bron·chi·al** \-kēəl\ adj

bronze \'bränz\ vb **bronzed**; **bronz·ing** : make bronze in color ~ n 1 : alloy of copper and tin 2 : yellowish brown —**bronzy** \-ē\ adj

brooch \'brōch, 'brüch\ n : ornamental clasp or pin

brood \'brüd\ n : family of young ~ vb

1 : sit on eggs to hatch them 2 : ponder ~ *adj* : kept for breeding —**brood·er** *n* —**brood·ing·ly** *adv*

¹**brook** \'brůk\ *vb* : tolerate

²**brook** *n* : small stream

broom \'brüm, 'brům\ *n* 1 : flowering shrub 2 : implement for sweeping —**broom·stick** *n*

broth \'bróth\ *n, pl* **broths** \'bróths, 'bró̄th z\ : liquid in which meat has been cooked

broth·el \'bräthəl, 'bróth-\ *n* : house of prostitutes

broth·er \'brəthər\ *n, pl* **brothers** *also* **breth·ren** \'brethrən, -ərn\ 1 : male sharing one or both parents with another person 2 : kinsman —**broth·er·hood** *n* —**broth·er·li·ness** *n* —**broth·er·ly** *adj*

broth·er–in–law *n, pl* **brothers–in–law** : brother of one's spouse or husband or husband of one's sister or of one's spouse's sister

brought *past of* BRING

brow \'braů\ *n* 1 : eyebrow 2 : forehead 3 : edge of a steep place

brow·beat *vb* -**beat;** -**beat·en** *or* -**beat;** -**beat·ing** : intimidate

brown \'braůn\ *adj* 1 : of the color brown 2 : of dark or tanned complexion ~ *n* : a color like that of coffee ~ *vb* : make or become brown —**brown·ish** *adj*

browse \'braůz\ *vb* **browsed; brows·ing** 1 : graze 2 : look over casually —**brows·er** *n*

bru·in \'brüən\ *n* : bear

bruise \'brüz\ *vb* **bruised; bruis·ing** 1 : make a bruise on 2 : become bruised ~ *n* : surface injury to flesh

brunch \'brənch\ *n* : late breakfast, early lunch, or combination of both

bru·net, bru·nette \brü'net\ *adj* : having dark hair and usu. dark skin —**brunet, brunette** *n*

brunt \'brənt\ *n* : main impact

¹**brush** \'brəsh\ *n* 1 : small cut branches 2 : coarse shrubby vegetation

²**brush** *n* 1 : bristles set in a handle used esp. for cleaning or painting 2 : light touch ~ *vb* 1 : apply a brush to 2 : remove with or as if with a brush 3 : dismiss in an offhand way 4 : touch lightly —**brush up** *vb* : renew one's skill

³**brush** *n* : skirmish

brush–off *n* : curt dismissal

brusque \'brəsk\ *adj* : curt or blunt in manner —**brusque·ly** *adv*

bru·tal \'brüt°l\ *adj* : like a brute and esp. cruel —**bru·tal·i·ty** \brü'talətē\ *n* —**bru·tal·ize** \'brüt°l,īz\ *vb* —**bru·tal·ly** \-°lē\ *adv*

brute \'brüt\ *adj* 1 : relating to beasts 2 : unreasoning 3 : purely physical ~ *n* 1 : beast 2 : brutal person —**brut·ish** \-ish\ *adj*

bub·ble \'bəbəl\ *vb* -**bled;** -**bling** : form, rise in, or give off bubbles ~ *n* : globule of gas in or covered with a liquid —**bub·bly** \-əlē\ *adj*

bu·bo \'bübō, 'byü-\ *n, pl* **buboes** : inflammatory swelling of a lymph gland —**bu·bon·ic** \bü'bänik, 'byü-\ *adj*

buc·ca·neer \,bəkə'nir\ *n* : pirate

buck \'bək\ *n, pl* **buck** *or* **bucks** 1 : male animal (as a deer) 2 : dollar ~ *vb* 1 : jerk forward 2 : oppose

buck·et \'bəkət\ *n* : pail —**buck·et·ful** *n*

buck·le \'bəkəl\ *n* 1 : clasp (as on a belt) for two loose ends 2 : bend or fold ~ *vb* -**led;** -**ling** 1 : fasten with a buckle 2 : apply oneself 3 : bend or crumple

buck·ler \'bəklər\ *n* : shield

buck·shot *n* : coarse lead shot

buck·skin *n* : soft leather (as from the skin of a buck) —**buckskin** *adj*

buck·tooth *n* : large projecting front tooth —**buck–toothed** *adj*

buck·wheat *n* : herb whose seeds are used as a cereal grain or the seeds themselves

bu·col·ic \byü'kälik\ *adj* : pastoral

bud \'bəd\ *n* 1 : undeveloped plant shoot 2 : partly opened flower ~ *vb* -**dd-** 1 : form or put forth buds 2 : be or develop like a bud

Bud·dhism \'bü,dizəm, 'bů-\ *n* : religion of eastern and central Asia —**Bud·dhist** \'büdist, 'bůd-\ *n or adj*

bud·dy \'bədē\ *n, pl* -**dies** : friend

budge \'bəj\ *vb* **budged; budg·ing** : move from a place

bud·get \'bəjət\ *n* 1 : estimate of income and expenses 2 : plan for coordinating income and expenses 3 : money available for a particular use —**budget** *vb or adj* —**bud·get·ary** \-ə,terē\ *adj*

buff \'bəf\ *n* 1 : yellow to orange yellow color 2 : enthusiast ~ *adj* : of the color buff ~ *vb* : polish

buf·fa·lo \'bəfə,lō\ *n, pl* -**lo** *or* -**loes** : wild ox (as a bison)

¹**buffer** \'bəfər\ *n* : shield or protector

²**buffer** *n* : one that buffs

¹buf·fet \'bəfət\ *n* : blow or slap ~ *vb* : hit esp. repeatedly

²buf·fet \ˌbə'fā, bü-\ *n* **1** : sideboard **2** : meal at which people serve themselves

buf·foon \ˌbə'fün\ *n* : clown —**buf·foon·ery** \-ərē\ *n*

bug \'bəg\ *n* **1** : small usu. obnoxious crawling creature **2** : 4-winged sucking insect **3** : unexpected imperfection **4** : disease-producing germ **5** : hidden microphone ~ *vb* -**gg- 1** : pester **2** : conceal a microphone in

bug·a·boo \'bəgəˌbü\ *n, pl* -**boos** : bogey

bug·bear *n* : source of dread

bug·gy \'bəgē\ *n, pl* -**gies** : light carriage

bu·gle \'byügəl\ *n* : trumpetlike brass instrument —**bu·gler** \-glər\ *n*

build \'bild\ *vb* **built** \'bilt\; **build·ing 1** : put together **2** : establish **3** : increase ~ *n* : physique —**build·er** *n*

build·ing \'bildiŋ\ *n* **1** : roofed and walled structure **2** : art or business of constructing buildings

bulb \'bəlb\ *n* **1** : large underground plant bud **2** : rounded or pear-shaped object —**bul·bous** \-əs\ *adj*

bulge \'bəlj\ *n* : swelling projecting part ~ *vb* **bulged; bulg·ing** : swell out

bulk \'bəlk\ *n* **1** : magnitude **2** : indigestible food material **3** : large mass **4** : major portion ~ *vb* : cause to swell or bulge —**bulky** \-ē\ *adj*

bulk·head *n* : ship's partition

¹bull \'bùl\ *n* : large adult male animal (as of cattle) ~ *adj* : male

²bull *n* **1** : papal letter **2** : decree

bull·dog *n* : compact short-haired dog

bull·doze \-ˌdōz\ *vb* **1** : move or level with a tractor (**bull·doz·er**) having a broad blade **2** : force

bul·let \'bùlət\ *n* : missile to be shot from a gun —**bul·let·proof** *adj*

bul·le·tin \'bùlətən\ *n* **1** : brief public report **2** : periodical

bull·fight *n* : sport of taunting and killing bulls —**bull·fight·er** *n*

bull·frog *n* : large deep-voiced frog

bull·head·ed *adj* : stupidly stubborn

bul·lion \'bùlyən\ *n* : gold or silver esp. in bars

bull·ock \'bùlək\ *n* **1** : young bull **2** : steer

bull's-eye *n, pl* **bull's-eyes** : center of a target

bul·ly \'bùlē\ *n, pl* -**lies** : one who hurts

or intimidates others ~ *vb* -**lied; -ly·ing** : act like a bully toward

bul·rush \'bùlˌrəsh\ *n* : tall coarse rush or sedge

bul·wark \'bùlˌwərk, -, wòrk; 'bəlˌwərk\ *n* **1** : wall-like defense **2** : strong support or protection

bum \'bəm\ *vb* -**mm- 1** : wander as a tramp **2** : get by begging ~ *n* : idle worthless person ~ *adj* : bad

bum·ble·bee \'bəmbəlˌbē\ *n* : large hairy bee

bump \'bəmp\ *vb* : strike or knock forcibly ~ *n* **1** : sudden blow **2** : small bulge or swelling —**bumpy** *adj*

¹bump·er \'bəmpər\ *adj* : unusually large

²bump·er \'bəmpər\ *n* : shock-absorbing bar at either end of a car

bump·kin \'bəmpkən\ *n* : awkward country person

bun \'bən\ *n* : sweet biscuit or roll

bunch \'bənch\ *n* : group ~ *vb* : form into a group —**bunchy** *adj*

bun·dle \'bəndəl\ *n* **1** : several items bunched together **2** : something wrapped for carrying **3** : large amount ~ *vb* -**dled; -dling** : gather into a bundle

bun·ga·low \'bəŋgəˌlō\ *n* : one-story house

bun·gle \'bəŋgəl\ *vb* -**gled; -gling** : do badly —**bungle** *n* —**bun·gler** *n*

bun·ion \'bənyən\ *n* : inflamed swelling of the first joint of the big toe

¹bunk \'bəŋk\ *n* : built-in bed that is often one of a tier ~ *vb* : sleep

²bunk *n* : nonsense

bun·ker \-ər\ *n* **1** : storage compartment **2** : protective embankment

bun·kum, bun·combe \'bəŋkəm\ *n* : nonsense

bun·ny \'bənē\ *n, pl* -**nies** : rabbit

¹bun·ting \'bəntiŋ\ *n* : small finch

²bunting *n* : flag material

buoy \'büē, 'bòi\ *n* : floating marker anchored in water ~ *vb* **1** : keep afloat **2** : raise the spirits of —**buoy·an·cy** \'bòiənsē, 'büyən-\ *n* —**buoy·ant** \-yənt\ *adj*

bur, burr \'bər\ *n* : rough or prickly covering of a fruit —**bur·ry** *adj*

bur·den \'bərdən\ *n* **1** : something carried **2** : something oppressive **3** : cargo ~ *vb* : load or oppress —**bur·den·some** \-səm\ *adj*

bur·dock \'bərˌdäk\ *n* : tall coarse herb with prickly flower heads

bu·reau \'byu̇rō\ n 1 : chest of drawers 2 : administrative unit 3 : business office

bu·reau·cra·cy \byu̇'räkrəsē\ n, pl -cies 1 : body of government officials 2 : unwieldy administrative system —**bu·reau·crat** \'byu̇rə,krat\ n —**bu·reau·crat·ic** \,byu̇rə'kratik\ adj

bur·geon \'bərjən\ vb : grow

bur·glary \'bərglərē\ n, pl -glar·ies : forcible entry into a building to steal —**bur·glar** \-glər\ n —**bur·glar·ize** \'bərglə,rīz\ vb

bur·gle \'bərgəl\ vb -gled; -gling : commit burglary on or in

Bur·gun·dy \'bərgəndē\ n, pl -dies : kind of table wine

buri·al \'berēəl\ n : act of burying

bur·lap \'bər,lap\ n : coarse fabric usu. of jute or hemp

bur·lesque \bər'lesk\ n 1 : witty or derisive imitation 2 : broadly humorous variety show ~ vb -lesqued; -lesqu·ing : mock

bur·ly \'bərlē\ adj -li·er; -est : strongly and heavily built

burn \'bərn\ vb burned \'bərnd, 'bərnt\ or burnt \'bərnt\; burn·ing 1 : be on fire 2 : feel or look as if on fire 3 : alter or become altered by or as if by fire or heat 4 : cause or make by fire ~ n : injury or effect produced by burning —**burn·er** n

bur·nish \'bərnish\ vb : polish

burp \'bərp\ n or vb : belch

bur·ro \'bərō, 'bu̇r-\ n, pl -os : small donkey

bur·row \'bərō\ n : hole in the ground made by an animal ~ vb : make a burrow —**bur·row·er** n

bur·sar \'bərsər\ n : treasurer esp. of a college

bur·si·tis \bər'sītəs\ n : inflammation of a sac (**bur·sa** \'bərsə\) in a joint

burst \'bərst\ vb burst or burst·ed; burst·ing 1 : fly apart or into pieces 2 : enter or emerge suddenly ~ n : sudden outbreak or effort

bury \'berē\ vb bur·ied; bury·ing 1 : deposit in the earth 2 : hide

bus \'bəs\ n, pl bus·es or bus·ses : large motor-driven passenger vehicle ~ vb bused or bussed; bus·ing or bus·sing : travel or transport by bus

bus·boy n : waiter's helper

bush \'bu̇sh\ n 1 : shrub 2 : rough uncleared country 3 : a thick tuft or mat —**bushy** adj

bush·el \'bu̇shəl\ n : 4 pecks

bush·ing \'bu̇shiŋ\ n : metal lining used as a guide or bearing

busi·ness \'biznəs, -nəz\ n 1 : vocation 2 : commercial or industrial enterprise 3 : personal concerns —**busi·ness·man** \-,man\ n —**busi·ness·wom·an** \-,wu̇mən\ n

¹bust \'bəst\ n 1 : sculpture of the head and upper torso 2 : breasts of a woman

²bust vb 1 : burst or break 2 : tame ~ n 1 : punch 2 : failure

¹bus·tle \'bəsəl\ vb -tled; -tling : move or work briskly ~ n : energetic activity

²bustle n : pad or frame formerly worn under a woman's skirt

busy \'bizē\ adj busi·er; -est 1 : engaged in action 2 : being in use 3 : full of activity ~ vb bus·ied; busy·ing : make or keep busy —**busi·ly** adv

busy·body n : meddler

but \'bət\ conj 1 : if not for the fact 2 : that 3 : without the certainty that 4 : rather 5 : yet ~ prep : other than

butch·er \'bu̇chər\ n 1 : one who slaughters animals or dresses their flesh 2 : brutal killer 3 : bungler —**butcher** vb —**butch·ery** \-ərē\ n

but·ler \'bətlər\ n : chief male household servant

¹butt \'bət\ vb : strike with a butt ~ n : blow with the head or horns

²butt n 1 : target 2 : victim

³butt vb : join edge to edge

⁴butt n : large end or bottom

⁵butt n : large cask

butte \'byüt\ n : isolated steep hill

but·ter \'bətər\ n : solid edible fat churned from cream ~ vb : spread with butter —**but·tery** adj

but·ter·cup n : yellow-flowered herb

but·ter·fat n : natural fat of milk and of butter

but·ter·fly n : insect with 4 broad wings

but·ter·milk n : liquid remaining after butter is churned

but·ter·nut n : edible nut of a tree related to the walnut or this tree

but·ter·scotch \-,skäch\ n : candy made from sugar, corn syrup, and water

but·tocks \'bətəks\ n pl : rear part of the hips

but·ton \'bət^ən\ n 1 : small knob for fastening clothing 2 : buttonlike object ~ vb : fasten with buttons

but·ton·hole n : hole or slit for a button ~ vb : hold in talk

but·tress \'bətrəs\ n 1 : projecting structure to support a wall 2 : support —**buttress** vb

bux·om \'bəksəm\ adj : full-bosomed

buy \'bī\ vb **bought** \'bȯt\; **buy·ing** : purchase ~ n : bargain —**buy·er** n

buzz \'bəz\ vb : make a low humming sound ~ n : act or sound of buzzing

buz·zard \'bəzərd\ n : large bird of prey

buzz·er n : signaling device that buzzes

buzz·word \'bəz,wərd\ n : word or phrase in vogue

by \'bī\ prep 1 : near 2 : through 3 : beyond 4 : throughout 5 : no later than ~ adv 1 : near 2 : farther

by·gone \'bī,gȯn\ adj : past —**bygone** n

by·law, bye·law n : organization's rule

by–line n : writer's name on an article

by·pass n : alternate route ~ vb : go around

by–prod·uct n : product in addition to the main product

by·stand·er n : spectator

by·way \'bī,wā\ n : side road

by·word n : proverb

C

c \'sē\ n, pl **c's** or **cs** \'sēz\ : 3d letter of the alphabet

cab \'kab\ n 1 : light closed horse-drawn carriage 2 : taxicab 3 : compartment for a driver —**cab·bie, cabby** n —**cab·stand** n

ca·bal \kə'bal\ n : group of conspirators

ca·bana \kə'banə, -nyə\ n : shelter at a beach or pool

cab·a·ret \,kabə'rā\ n : nightclub

cab·bage \'kabij\ n : vegetable with a dense head of leaves

cab·in \-ən\ n 1 : private room on a ship 2 : small house 3 : airplane compartment

cab·i·net \'kabnət\ n 1 : display case or cupboard 2 : advisory council of a head of state —**cab·i·net·mak·er** n —**cab·i·net·mak·ing** n —**cab·i·net·work** n

ca·ble \'kābəl\ n 1 : strong rope, wire, or chain 2 : cablegram 3 : bundle of electrical wires ~ vb **-bled; -bling** : send a cablegram to

ca·ble·gram \-,gram\ n : message sent by a submarine telegraph cable

ca·boose \kə'büs\ n : crew car on a train

ca·cao \kə'kaü, -'kāō\ n, pl **cacaos** : So. American tree whose seeds (**cacao beans**) yield cocoa and chocolate

cache \'kash\ n 1 : hiding place 2 : something hidden —**cache** vb

ca·chet \ka'shā\ n : prestige or a feature conferring this

cack·le \'kakəl\ vb **-led; -ling** : make a cry or laugh like the sound of a hen —**cackle** n —**cack·ler** n

ca·coph·o·ny \ka'käfənē\ n, pl **-nies** : harsh noise —**ca·coph·o·nous** \-nəs\ adj

cac·tus \'kaktəs\ n, pl **cac·ti** \-,tī\ or **-tus·es** : drought-resistant flowering plant with scales or prickles

cad \'kad\ n : ungentlemanly person —**cad·dish** \-ish\ adj —**cad·dish·ly** adv —**cad·dish·ness** n

ca·dav·er \kə'davər\ n : dead body —**ca·dav·er·ous** \-ərəs\ adj

cad·die, cad·dy \'kadē\ n, pl **-dies** : golfer's helper —**caddie, caddy** vb

cad·dy \'kadē\ n, pl **-dies** : small tea chest

ca·dence \'kād^əns\ n : measure of a rhythmical flow —**ca·denced** \-^ənst\ adj

ca·det \kə'det\ n : student in a military academy

cadge \'kaj\ vb **cadged; cadg·ing** : beg —**cadg·er** n

cad·mi·um \'kadmēəm\ n : grayish metallic chemical element

cad·re \-rē\ n : nucleus of highly trained people

ca·fé \ka'fā, kə-\ n : restaurant

caf·e·te·ria \,kafə'tirēə\ n : self-service restaurant

caf·feine \ka'fēn, 'ka,fēn\ n : stimulating alkaloid in coffee and tea

cage \'kāj\ *n* : box of wire or bars for confining an animal ~ *vb* **caged; caging** : put or keep in a cage

ca·gey \-ē\ *adj* **-gi·er; -est** : shrewd —**ca·gi·ly** *adv* —**ca·gi·ness** *n*

cais·son \'kā,sän, -sən\ *n* **1** : ammunition carriage **2** : watertight chamber for underwater construction

ca·jole \kə'jōl\ *vb* **-joled; -jol·ing** : persuade or coax —**ca·jol·ery** \-ərē\ *n*

cake \'kāk\ *n* **1** : food of baked or fried usu. sweet batter **2** : compacted mass ~ *vb* **caked; cak·ing 1** : form into a cake **2** : encrust

cal·a·bash \'kalə,bash\ *n* : gourd

cal·a·mine \'kalə,mīn\ *n* : lotion of oxides of zinc and iron

ca·lam·i·ty \kə'lamətē\ *n, pl* **-ties** : disaster —**ca·lam·i·tous** \-ətəs\ *adj* —**ca·lam·i·tous·ly** *adv* —**ca·lam·i·tous·ness** *n*

cal·ci·fy \'kalsə,fī\ *vb* **-fied; -fy·ing** : harden —**cal·ci·fi·ca·tion** \,ka lsəfə'kāshən\ *n*

cal·ci·um \'kalsēəm\ *n* : silver-white soft metallic chemical element

cal·cu·late \'kalkyə,lāt\ *vb* **-lat·ed; -lat·ing 1** : determine by mathematical processes **2** : judge —**cal·cu·la·ble** \-ləbəl\ *adj* —**cal·cu·la·tion** \,kalkyə-'lāshən\ *n* —**cal·cu·la·tor** \'kalkyə,lātər\ *n*

cal·cu·lat·ing *adj* : shrewd

cal·cu·lus \'kalkyələs\ *n, pl* **-li** \-,lī\ : higher mathematics dealing with rates of change

cal·dron *var of* CAULDRON

cal·en·dar \'kaləndər\ *n* : list of days, weeks, and months

¹calf \'kaf, 'káf\ *n, pl* **calves** \'kavz, 'kávz\ : young cow or related mammal —**calf·skin** *n*

²calf *n, pl* **calves** : back part of the leg below the knee

cal·i·ber, cal·i·bre \'kaləbər\ *n* **1** : diameter of a bullet or shell or of a gun bore **2** : degree of mental or moral excellence

cal·i·brate \'kalə,brāt\ *vb* **-brat·ed; -brating** : adjust precisely —**cal·i·bra·tion** \,kalə'brāshən\ *n*

cal·i·co \'kali,kō\ *n, pl* **-coes** *or* **-cos 1** : printed cotton fabric **2** : animal with fur having patches of different colors

cal·i·pers \'kaləpərz\ *n* : measuring instrument with two adjustable legs

ca·liph \'kāləf, 'kal-\ *n* : title of head of Islam —**ca·liph·ate** \-,āt, -ət\ *n*

cal·is·then·ics \,kaləs'theniks\ *n sing or pl* : stretching and jumping exercises —**cal·is·then·ic** *adj*

calk \'kók\ *var of* CAULK

call \'kól\ *vb* **1** : shout **2** : summon **3** : demand **4** : telephone **5** : make a visit **6** : name —**call** *n* —**call·er** *n* —**call down** *vb* : reprimand —**call off** *vb* : cancel

call·ing *n* : vocation

cal·li·ope \kə'līə,pē, 'kalē,ōp\ : musical instrument of steam whistles

cal·lous \'kaləs\ *adj* **1** : thickened and hardened **2** : unfeeling ~ *vb* : make callous —**cal·los·i·ty** \ka'läsətē\ *n* —**cal·lous·ly** *adv* —**cal·lous·ness** *n*

cal·low \'kalō\ *adj* : inexperienced or innocent —**cal·low·ness** *n*

cal·lus \'kaləs\ *n* : callous area on skin or bark ~ *vb* : form a callus

calm \'käm, 'kälm\ *n* **1** : period or condition of peacefulness or stillness ~ *adj* : still or tranquil ~ *vb* : make calm —**calm·ly** *adv* —**calm·ness** *n*

ca·lor·ic \kə'lórik\ *adj* : relating to heat or calories

cal·o·rie \'kalərē\ *n* : unit for measuring heat and energy value of food

ca·lum·ni·ate \kə'ləmnē,āt\ *vb* **-at·ed; -at·ing** : slander —**ca·lum·ni·a·tion** \-,ləmnē'āshən\ *n*

cal·um·ny \'kaləmnē\ *n, pl* **-nies** : false and malicious charge —**ca·lum·ni·ous** \kə'ləmnēəs\ *adj*

calve \'kav, 'káv\ *vb* **calved; calv·ing** : give birth to a calf

calves *pl of* CALF

ca·lyp·so \kə'lipsō\ *n, pl* **-sos** : West Indian style of music

ca·lyx \'kāliks, 'kal-\ *n, pl* **-lyx·es** *or* **-ly·ces** \-lə,sēz\ : sepals of a flower

cam \'kam\ *n* : machine part that slides or rotates irregularly to transmit linear motion

ca·ma·ra·de·rie \,käm'rädərē, ,kam-, -mə'-, -'rad-\ *n* : fellowship

cam·bric \'kāmbrik\ *n* : fine thin linen or cotton fabric

came *past of* COME

cam·el \'kaməl\ *n* : large hoofed mammal of desert areas

ca·mel·lia \kə'mēlyə\ *n* : shrub or tree grown for its showy roselike flowers or the flower itself

cam·eo \'kamē,ō\ *n, pl* **-eos** : gem carved in relief

cam·era \'kamrə\ *n* : box with a lens for taking pictures —**cam·era·man** \-,man, -mən\ *n*

cam·ou·flage \'kamə,fläzh, -,fläj\ *vb* : hide by disguising —**camouflage** *n*

camp \'kamp\ *n* 1 : place to stay temporarily esp. in a tent 2 : group living in a camp ~ *vb* : make or live in a camp —**camp·er** *n* —**camp·ground** *n* —**camp·site** *n*

cam·paign \kam'pān\ *n* : series of military operations or of activities meant to gain a result —**campaign** *vb*

cam·pa·ni·le \,kampə'nēlē, -'nēl\ *n, pl* **-ni·les** *or* **-ni·li** \-'nēlē\ : bell tower

cam·phor \'kamfər\ *n* : gummy volatile aromatic compound from an evergreen tree (**cam·phor tree**)

cam·pus \'kampəs\ *n* : grounds and buildings of a college or school

¹can \kən, 'kan\ *vb, past* **could** \kəd, 'kud\; *pres sing & pl* **can** 1 : be able to 2 : be permitted to by conscience or feeling 3 : have permission or liberty to

²can \'kan\ *n* : metal container ~ *vb* **-nn-** : preserve by sealing in airtight cans or jars —**can·ner** *n* —**can·nery** \-ərē\ *n*

ca·nal \kə'nal\ *n* 1 : tubular passage in the body 2 : channel filled with water

can·a·pé \'kanəpē, -,pā\ *n* : appetizer

ca·nard \kə'närd\ *n* : false report

ca·nary \kə'nerē\ *n, pl* **-nar·ies** : yellow or greenish finch often kept as a pet

can·cel \'kansəl\ *vb* **-celed** *or* **-celled**; **-cel·ing** *or* **-cel·ling** 1 : cross out 2 : destroy, neutralize, or match the force or effect of —**cancel** *n* —**can·cel·la·tion** \,kansə'lāshən\ *n* —**can·cel·er, can·cel·ler** *n*

can·cer \'kansər\ *n* 1 : malignant tumor that tends to spread 2 : slowly destructive evil —**can·cer·ous** \-ərəs\ *adj* —**can·cer·ous·ly** *adv*

can·de·la·bra \,kandə'läbrə, -'lab-\ *n* : candelabrum

can·de·la·brum \-rəm\ *n, pl* **-bra** \-rə\ : ornamental branched candlestick

can·did \'kandəd\ *adj* 1 : frank 2 : unposed —**can·did·ly** *adv* —**can·did·ness** *n*

can·di·date \'kandə,dāt, -dət\ *n* : one who seeks an office or membership —**can·di·da·cy** \-dəsē\ *n*

can·dle \'kand⁰l\ *n* : tallow or wax

molded around a wick and burned to give light —**can·dle·light** *n* —**can·dle·stick** *n*

can·dor \'kandər\ *n* : frankness

can·dy \'kandē\ *n, pl* **-dies** : food made from sugar ~ *vb* **-died; -dy·ing** : encrust with sugar

cane \'kān\ *n* 1 : slender plant stem 2 : a tall woody grass or reed 3 : stick for walking or beating ~ *vb* **caned**; **can·ing** 1 : beat with a cane 2 : weave or make with cane —**can·er** *n*

ca·nine \'kā,nīn\ *adj* : relating to dogs ~ *n* 1 : pointed tooth next to the incisors 2 : dog

can·is·ter \'kanəstər\ *n* : cylindrical container

can·ker \'kaŋkər\ *n* : mouth ulcer —**can·ker·ous** \-kərəs\ *adj*

can·na·bis \'kanəbəs\ *n* : preparation derived from hemp

can·ni·bal \'kanəbəl\ *n* : human or animal that eats its own kind —**can·ni·bal·ism** \-bə,lizəm\ *n* —**can·ni·bal·is·tic** \,kanəbə'listik\ *adj*

can·ni·bal·ize \'kanəbə,līz\ *vb* **-ized; -iz·ing** 1 : take usable parts from 2 : practice cannibalism

can·non \'kanən\ *n, pl* **-nons** *or* **-non** : large heavy gun —**can·non·ball** *n* —**can·non·eer** \,kanə'nir\ *n*

can·non·ade \,kanə'nād\ *n* : heavy artillery fire ~ *vb* **-ad·ed; -ad·ing** : bombard

can·not \'kan,ät; kə'nät\ : can not —**cannot but** : be bound to

can·ny \'kanē\ *adj* **-ni·er, -est** : shrewd —**can·ni·ly** *adv* —**can·ni·ness** *n*

ca·noe \kə'nü\ *n* : narrow sharp-ended boat propelled by paddles —**canoe** *vb* —**ca·noe·ist** *n*

¹can·on \'kanən\ *n* 1 : regulation governing a church 2 : authoritative list 3 : an accepted principle

²canon *n* : clergy member in a cathedral

ca·non·i·cal \kə'nänikəl\ *adj* 1 : relating to or conforming to a canon 2 : orthodox —**ca·non·i·cal·ly** *adv*

can·on·ize \'kanə,nīz\ *vb* **-ized** \-,nīzd\, **-iz·ing** : recognize as a saint —**can·on·iza·tion** \,kanənə'zāshən\ *n*

can·o·py \'kanəpē\ *n, pl* **-pies** : overhanging cover —**canopy** *vb*

¹cant \'kant\ *n* 1 : slanting surface 2 : slant ~ *vb* 1 : tip up 2 : lean to one side

²cant *vb* : talk hypocritically ~ *n* 1 : jargon 2 : insincere talk

can't \'kant, 'kȧnt\ : can not

can·ta·loupe \'kant³l,ōp\ n : muskmelon with orange flesh

can·tan·ker·ous \kan'taŋkərəs\ adj : hard to deal with —**can·tan·ker·ous·ly** adv —**can·tan·ker·ous·ness** n

can·ta·ta \kən'tätə\ n : choral work

can·teen \kan'tēn\ n 1 : place of recreation for service personnel 2 : water container

can·ter \'kantər\ n : slow gallop —**can·ter** vb

can·ti·cle \'kantikəl\ n : liturgical song

can·ti·le·ver \'kant³l,ēvər, -,ev-\ : beam or structure supported only at one end

can·to \'kan,tō\ n, pl **-tos** : major division of a long poem

can·tor \'kantər\ n : synagogue official who sings liturgical music

can·vas \'kanvəs\ n 1 : strong cloth orig. used for making tents and sails 2 : set of sails 3 : oil painting

can·vass \-vəs\ vb : solicit votes, orders, or opinions from ~ n : act of canvassing —**can·vass·er** n

can·yon \'kanyən\ n : deep valley with steep sides

cap \'kap\ n 1 : covering for the head 2 : top or cover like a cap 3 : upper limit ~ vb **-pp-** 1 : provide or protect with a cap 2 : climax —**cap·ful** \-,fûl\ n

ca·pa·ble \'kāpəbəl\ adj : able to do something —**ca·pa·bil·i·ty** \,kāpə'bilə-tē\ n —**ca·pa·bly** \'kāpəblē\ adv

ca·pa·cious \kə'pāshəs\ adj : able to contain much

ca·pac·i·tance \kə'pasətəns\ n : ability to store electrical energy

ca·pac·i·tor \-ətər\ n : device for storing electrical energy

ca·pac·i·ty \-ətē\ n, pl **-ties** 1 : ability to contain 2 : volume 3 : ability 4 : role or job ~ adj : equaling maximum capacity

¹**cape** \'kāp\ n : point of land jutting out into water

²**cape** n : garment that drapes over the shoulders

¹**ca·per** \'kāpər\ n : flower bud of a shrub pickled for use as a relish

²**caper** vb : leap or prance about ~ n 1 : frolicsome leap 2 : escapade

cap·il·lary \'kapə,lerē\ adj 1 : resembling a hair 2 : having a very small bore ~ n, pl **-lar·ies** : tiny thin-walled blood vessel

¹**cap·i·tal** \'kapət³l\ adj 1 : punishable by death 2 : being in the series A, B, C rather than a, b, c 3 : relating to capital 4 : excellent ~ n 1 : capital letter 2 : seat of government 3 : wealth 4 : total face value of a company's stock 5 : investors as a group

²**capital** n : top part of a column

cap·i·tal·ism \-,izəm\ n : economic system of private ownership of capital

cap·i·tal·ist \-ist\ n 1 : person with capital invested in business 2 : believer in capitalism ~ adj : owning capital 2 : practicing, advocating, or marked by capitalism —**cap·i·tal·is·tic** \,kapət³l'istik\ adj —**cap·i·tal·is·ti·cal·ly** \-klē\ adv

cap·i·tal·ize \-,īz\ vb **-ized; -iz·ing** 1 : write or print with a capital letter 2 : use as capital 3 : supply capital for 4 : turn something to advantage —**cap·i·tal·i·za·tion** \,kapət³lə-'zāshən\ n

cap·i·tol \'kapət³l\ n : building in which a legislature sits

ca·pit·u·late \kə'pichə,lāt\ vb **-lat·ed; -lat·ing** : surrender —**ca·pit·u·la·tion** \-,pichə'lāshən\ n

ca·pon \'kā,pän, -pən\ n : castrated male chicken

ca·price \kə'prēs\ n : whim —**ca·pri·cious** \-'prishəs\ adj —**ca·pri·cious·ly** adv —**ca·pri·cious·ness** n

cap·size \'kap,sīz, kap'sīz\ vb **-sized; -siz·ing** : overturn

cap·stan \'kapstən, -,stan\ n : upright winch

cap·sule \'kapsəl, -sül\ n 1 : enveloping cover (as for medicine) 2 : small pressurized compartment for astronauts ~ adj : very brief or compact —**cap·su·lar** \-sələr\ adj —**cap·su·lat·ed** \-sə,lātəd\ adj

cap·tain \'kaptən\ n 1 : commander of a body of troops 2 : officer in charge of a ship 3 : commissioned officer in the navy ranking next below a rear admiral or a commodore 4 : commissioned officer (as in the army) ranking next below a major 5 : leader ~ vb : be captain of —**cap·tain·cy** n

cap·tion \'kapshən\ n 1 : title 2 : explanation with an illustration —**caption** vb

cap·tious \'kapshəs\ *adj* : tending to find fault —**cap·tious·ly** *adv*

cap·ti·vate \'kaptə,vāt\ *vb* **-vat·ed; -vat·ing** : attract and charm —**cap·ti·va·tion** \,kaptə'vāshən\ *n* —**cap·ti·va·tor** \'kaptə,vātər\ *n*

cap·tive \-tiv\ *adj* **1** : made prisoner **2** : confined or under control —**captive** *n* —**cap·tiv·i·ty** \kap'tivətē\ *n*

cap·tor \'kaptər\ *n* : one that captures

cap·ture \-chər\ *n* : seizure by force or trickery ~ *vb* **-tured; -tur·ing** : take captive

car \'kär\ *n* **1** : vehicle moved on wheels **2** : cage of an elevator

ca·rafe \kə'raf, -'räf\ *n* : decanter

car·a·mel \'karəməl, 'kärməl\ *n* **1** : burnt sugar used for flavoring and coloring **2** : firm chewy candy

¹carat *var of* KARAT

²car·at \'karət\ *n* : unit of weight for precious stones

car·a·van \'karə,van\ *n* : travelers journeying together (as in a line)

car·a·way \'karə,wā\ *n* : aromatic herb with seeds used in seasoning

car·bine \'kär,bēn, -,bīn\ *n* : short-barreled rifle

car·bo·hy·drate \,kärbō'hī,drāt, -drət\ *n* : compound of carbon, hydrogen, and oxygen

car·bon \'kärbən\ *n* **1** : chemical element occurring in nature esp. as diamond and graphite **2** : piece of carbon paper or a copy made with it

¹car·bon·ate \'kärbə,nāt, -nət\ *n* : salt or ester of a carbon-containing acid

²car·bon·ate \-,nāt\ *vb* **-at·ed; -at·ing** : impregnate with carbon dioxide —**car·bon·ation** \,kärbə'nāshən\ *n*

carbon paper *n* : thin paper coated with a pigment for making copies

car·bun·cle \'kär,bəŋkəl\ *n* : painful inflammation of the skin and underlying tissue

car·bu·re·tor \'kärbə,rātər, -byə-\ *n* : device for mixing fuel and air

car·cass \'kärkəs\ *n* : dead body

car·cin·o·gen \kär'sinəjən\ *n* : agent causing cancer —**car·ci·no·gen·ic** \,kärs,nō'jenik\ *adj*

car·ci·no·ma \,kärs'n'ōmə\ *n, pl* **-mas** *or* **-ma·ta** \-mətə\ : malignant tumor —**car·ci·no·ma·tous** \-mətəs\ *adj*

¹card \'kärd\ *vb* : comb (fibers) before spinning ~ *n* : device for carding fibers —**card·er** *n*

²card *n* **1** : playing card **2** *pl* : game played with playing cards **3** : small flat piece of paper

card·board *n* : stiff material like paper

car·di·ac \'kärdē,ak\ *adj* : relating to the heart

car·di·gan \'kärdigən\ *n* : sweater with an opening in the front

¹car·di·nal \'kärd°nəl\ *n* **1** : official of the Roman Catholic Church **2** : bright red songbird

²cardinal *adj* : of basic importance

cardinal number *n* : number (as 1, 82, 357) used in counting

car·di·ol·o·gy \,kärdē'äləjē\ *n* : study of the heart —**car·di·ol·o·gist** \-jist\ *n*

car·dio·vas·cu·lar \-ō'vaskyələr\ *adj* : relating to the heart and blood vessels

care \'ker\ *n* **1** : anxiety **2** : watchful attention **3** : supervision ~ *vb* **cared; car·ing 1** : feel anxiety or concern **2** : like **3** : provide care —**care·free** —**care·ful** \-fəl\ *adj* —**care·ful·ly** *adv* —**care·ful·ness** *n* —**care·giv·er** \-,givər\ *n* —**care·less** *adj* —**care·less·ly** *adv* —**care·less·ness** *n*

ca·reen \kə'rēn\ *vb* **1** : sway from side to side **2** : career

ca·reer \kə'rir\ *n* : vocation ~ *vb* : go at top speed

ca·ress \kə'res\ *n* : tender touch ~ *vb* : touch lovingly or tenderly

car·et \'karət\ *n* : mark showing where something is to be inserted

care·tak·er *n* : one in charge for another or temporarily

car·go \'kärgō\ *n, pl* **-goes** *or* **-gos** : transported goods

car·i·bou \'karə,bü\ *n, pl* **-bou** *or* **-bous** : large No. American deer

car·i·ca·ture \'karikə,chùr\ *n* : distorted representation for humor or ridicule —**caricature** *vb* —**car·i·ca·tur·ist** \-ist\ *n*

car·ies \'karēz\ *n, pl* **caries** : tooth decay

car·il·lon \'karə,län\ *n* : set of tuned bells

car·mine \'kärmən, -,mīn\ *n* : vivid red

car·nage \'kärnij\ *n* : slaughter

car·nal \'kärn°l\ *adj* : sensual —**car·nal·i·ty** \kär'nalətē\ *n* —**car·nal·ly** *adv*

car·na·tion \kär'nāshən\ *n* : showy flower

car·ni·val \'kärnəvəl\ *n* **1** : festival **2** : traveling enterprise offering amusements

car·ni·vore \-,vȯr\ *n* : flesh-eating animal —car·niv·o·rous \kär'nivərəs\ adj —car·niv·o·rous·ly adv —car·niv·o·rous·ness n

car·ol \'karəl\ n : song of joy —carol vb —car·ol·er, car·ol·ler \-ələr\ n

car·om \-əm\ or n : rebound

ca·rouse \kə'rauz\ vb -roused; -rous·ing : drink and be boisterous —carouse n —ca·rous·er n

car·ou·sel, car·rou·sel \,karə'sel, 'karə,-\ n : merry-go-round

¹carp \'kärp\ vb : find fault

²carp n, pl carp or carps : freshwater fish

car·pel \'kärpəl\ n : modified leaf forming part of the ovary of a flower

car·pen·ter \'kärpəntər\ n : one who builds with wood —carpenter vb —car·pen·try \-trē\ n

car·pet \'kärpət\ n : fabric floor covering ~ vb : cover with a carpet —car·pet·ing \-iŋ\ n

car·port n : open-sided automobile shelter

car·riage \'karij\ n 1 : conveyance 2 : manner of holding oneself 3 : wheeled vehicle

car·ri·on \'karēən\ n : dead and decaying flesh

car·rot \'karət\ n : orange root vegetable

car·ry \'karē\ vb -ried; -ry·ing 1 : move while supporting 2 : hold (oneself) in a specified way 3 : support 4 : keep in stock 5 : reach to a distance 6 : win —car·ri·er \-ēər\ n —carry on vb 1 : conduct 2 : behave excitedly —carry out vb : put into effect

cart \'kärt\ n : wheeled vehicle ~ vb : carry in a cart —cart·age \-ij\ n —cart·er n

car·tel \kär'tel\ n : business combination designed to limit competition

car·ti·lage \'kärtᵊlij\ n : elastic skeletal tissue —car·ti·lag·i·nous \,kärtᵊl'a-jənəs\ adj

car·tog·ra·phy \kär'tägrəfē\ n : making of maps —car·tog·ra·pher \-fər\ n

car·ton \'kärtᵊn\ n : cardboard box

car·toon \kär'tün\ n 1 : humorous drawing 2 : comic strip —cartoon vb —car·toon·ist n

car·tridge \'kärtrij\ n 1 : tube containing powder and a bullet or shot for a firearm 2 : container of material for insertion into an apparatus

carve \'kärv\ vb carved; carv·ing 1 : cut with care 2 : cut into pieces or slices —carv·er n

cas·cade \kas'kād\ n : small steep waterfall ~ vb -cad·ed; -cad·ing : fall in a cascade

¹case \'kās\ n 1 : particular instance 2 : convincing argument 3 : inflectional form esp. of a noun or pronoun 4 : fact 5 : lawsuit 6 : instance of disease —in case : as a precaution —in case of : in the event of

²case n : box 2 : outer covering ~ vb cased; cas·ing 1 : enclose 2 : inspect

case·ment \-mənt\ n : window that opens like a door

cash \'kash\ n 1 : ready money 2 : money paid at the time of purchase ~ vb : give or get cash for

ca·shew \'kashü, kə'shü\ n : tropical American tree or its nut

¹ca·shier \ka'shir\ vb : dismiss in disgrace

²cash·ier n : person who receives and records payments

cash·mere \'kazh,mir, 'kash-\ n : fine goat's wool or a fabric of this

ca·si·no \kə'sēnō\ n, pl -nos : place for gambling

cask \'kask\ n : barrel-shaped container for liquids

cas·ket \'kaskət\ n : coffin

cas·se·role \'kasə,rōl\ n : baking dish or the food cooked in this

cas·sette \kə'set, ka-\ n : case containing magnetic tape

cas·sock \'kasək\ n : long clerical garment

cast \'kast\ vb cast; cast·ing 1 : throw 2 : deposit (a ballot) 3 : assign parts in a play 4 : mold ~ n 1 : throw 2 : appearance 3 : rigid surgical dressing 4 : actors in a play

cas·ta·nets \,kastə'nets\ n pl : shells clicked together in the hand

cast·away \'kastə,wā\ n : survivor of a shipwreck —castaway adj

caste \'kast\ n : social class or rank

cast·er \'kastər\ n : small wheel on furniture

cas·ti·gate \'kastə,gāt\ vb -gat·ed; -gat·ing : chastise severely —cas·ti·ga·tion \,kastə'gāshən\ n —cas·ti·ga·tor \'kastə,gātər\ n

cast iron n : hard brittle alloy of iron

cas·tle \'kasəl\ n : fortified building

cast-off adj : thrown away —cast·off n

cas·trate \'kas,trāt\ vb -trat·ed; -trat·ing : remove the testes of —cas·tra·tion \ka'strāshən\ n

ca·su·al \'kazhəwəl\ adj 1 : happening

by chance 2 : showing little concern
3 : informal —**ca·su·al·ly** \-ē\ *adv* —
ca·su·al·ness *n*

ca·su·al·ty \-tē\ *n, pl* **-ties 1** : serious or
fatal accident 2 : one injured, lost, or
destroyed

ca·su·ist·ry \'kazhəwəstrē\ *n, pl* **-ries**
: rationalization —**ca·su·ist** \-wist\ *n*

cat \'kat\ *n* 1 : small domestic mammal
2 : related animal (as a lion) —
cat·like *adj*

cat·a·clysm \'katə,klizəm\ *n* : violent
change —**cat·a·clys·mal** \,katə'kliz-
məl\, **cat·a·clys·mic** \-'klizmik\ *adj*

cat·a·comb \'katə,kōm\ *n* : underground
burial place

cat·a·log, cat·a·logue \'katəl,óg\ *n*
1 : list 2 : book containing a description
of items ~ *vb* **-loged** *or* **-logued;**
-log·ing *or* **-logu·ing** 1 : make a catalog of 2 : enter in a catalog —**cat·a·**
log·er, cat·a·logu·er *n*

ca·tal·pa \kə'talpə\ *n* : tree with broad
leaves and long pods

ca·tal·y·sis \kə'taləsəs\ *n, pl* **-y·ses**
\-,sēz\ : increase in the rate of chemical reaction caused by a substance
(**cat·a·lyst** \'katəl,ist\) that is itself unchanged —**cat·a·lyt·ic** \,katəl'itik\
adj

cat·a·ma·ran \katəmə'ran\ *n* : boat with
twin hulls

cat·a·mount \'katə,maúnt\ *n* : cougar

cat·a·pult \'katə,pəlt, -,púlt\ *n* : device
for hurling or launching —**catapult**
vb

cat·a·ract \'katə,rakt\ *n* 1 : large waterfall 2 : cloudiness of the lens of the
eye

ca·tarrh \kə'tär\ *n* : inflammation of the
nose and throat

ca·tas·tro·phe \kə'tastrə,fē\ *n* 1 : great
disaster or misfortune 2 : utter failure
—**cat·a·stroph·ic** \,katə'sträfik\ *adj*
—**cat·a·stroph·i·cal·ly** \-iklē\ *adv*

cat·bird *n* : American songbird

cat·call *n* : noise of disapproval

catch \'kach, 'kech\ *vb* **caught** \'kót\;
catch·ing 1 : capture esp. after pursuit
2 : trap 3 : detect esp. by surprise 4
: grasp 5 : get entangled 6 : become
affected with or by 7 : seize and hold
firmly ~ *n* 1 : act of catching 2
: something caught 3 : something that
fastens 4 : hidden difficulty —
catch·er *n*

catch·ing \-iŋ\ *adj* : infectious

catch·up \'kechəp, 'kach-; 'katsəp\ *var*
of KETCHUP

catch·word *n* : slogan

catchy \-ē\ *adj* **catch·i·er; -est** : likely
to catch interest

cat·e·chism \'katə,kizəm\ *n* : set of
questions and answers esp. to teach
religious doctrine

cat·e·gor·i·cal \,katə'górikəl\ *adj* : absolute —**cat·e·gor·i·cal·ly** \-klē\ *adv*

cat·e·go·ry \'katə,gōrē\ *n, pl* **-ries**
: group or class —**cat·e·go·ri·za·tion**
\,katigərə'zāshən\ *n* —**cat·e·go·rize**
\'katigə,rīz\ *vb*

ca·ter \'kātər\ *vb* 1 : provide food for 2
: supply what is wanted —**ca·ter·er**
n

cat·er·cor·ner \,katē'kórnər, ,katə-,
,kitē-\, **cat·er·cor·nered** *adv or adj*
: in a diagonal position

cat·er·pil·lar \'katər,pilər\ *n* : butterfly
or moth larva

cat·er·waul \'katər,wól\ *vb* : make the
harsh cry of a cat —**caterwaul** *n*

cat·fish *n* : big-headed fish with feelers
about the mouth

cat·gut *n* : tough cord made usu. from
sheep intestines

ca·thar·sis \kə'thärsəs\ *n, pl* **ca·thar·ses**
\-,sēz\ : a purging —**ca·thar·tic** \kə-
'thärtik\ *adj or n*

ca·the·dral \-'thēdrəl\ *n* : principal
church of a diocese

cath·e·ter \'kathətər\ *n* : tube for insertion into a body cavity

cath·ode \'kath,ōd\ *n* 1 : negative electrode 2 : positive battery terminal —
ca·thod·ic \ka'thädik\ *adj*

cath·o·lic \'kathəlik\ *adj* 1 : universal 2
cap : relating to Roman Catholics

Cath·o·lic *n* : member of the Roman
Catholic Church —**Ca·thol·i·cism**
\kə'thälə,sizəm\ *n*

cat·kin \'katkən\ *n* : long dense flower
cluster

cat·nap *n* : short light nap —**catnap** *vb*

cat·nip \-,nip\ *n* : aromatic mint relished by cats

cat's-paw *n, pl* **cat's-paws** : person
used as if a tool

cat·sup \'kechəp, 'kach-; 'katsəp\ *var of*
KETCHUP

cat·tail *n* : marsh herb with furry brown
spikes

cat·tle \'katəl\ *n pl* : domestic bovines
—**cat·tle·man** \-mən, -,man\ *n*

cat·ty \'katē\ *adj* **-ti·er; -est** : mean or
spiteful —**cat·ti·ly** *adv* —**cat·ti·ness**
n

cat·walk *n* : high narrow walk

Cau·ca·sian \kȯ'kāzhən, 'kä-\ *adj* : relating to the white race —**Caucasian** *n*

cau·cus \'kȯkəs\ *n* : political meeting —**caucus** *vb*

caught *past of* CATCH

caul·dron \'kȯldrən\ *n* : large kettle

cau·li·flow·er \'kȯli,flaủər, 'käl-\ *n* : vegetable having a compact head of usu. white undeveloped flowers

caulk \'kȯk\ *vb* : make seams watertight —**caulk** *n* —**caulk·er** *n*

caus·al \'kȯzəl\ *adj* : relating to or being a cause —**cau·sal·i·ty** \kȯ'zalətē\ *n* —**caus·al·ly** \'kȯzəlē\ *adv*

cause \'kȯz\ *n* 1 : something that brings about a result 2 : reason 3 : lawsuit 4 : principle or movement to support ~ *vb* **caused; caus·ing** : be the cause of —**cau·sa·tion** \kȯ'zāshən\ *n* —**caus·ative** \'kȯzətiv\ *adj* —**cause·less** *adj* —**caus·er** *n*

cause·way *n* : raised road esp. over water

caus·tic \'kȯstik\ *adj* 1 : corrosive 2 : sharp or biting —**caustic** *n*

cau·ter·ize \'kȯtə,rīz\ *vb* **-ized; -iz·ing** : burn to prevent infection or bleeding —**cau·ter·i·za·tion** \,kȯtərə'zāshən\ *n*

cau·tion \'kȯshən\ *n* 1 : warning 2 : care or prudence ~ *vb* : warn —**cau·tion·ary** \-shə,nerē\ *adj*

cau·tious \'kȯshəs\ *adj* : taking caution —**cau·tious·ly** *adv* —**cau·tious·ness** *n*

cav·al·cade \,kavəl'kād, 'kavəl,-\ *n* 1 : procession on horseback 2 : series

cav·a·lier \,kavə'lir\ *n* : mounted soldier ~ *adj* : disdainful or arrogant —**cav·a·lier·ly** *adv*

cav·al·ry \'kavəlrē\ *n, pl* **-ries** : troops on horseback or in vehicles —**cav·al·ry·man** \-mən, -,man\ *n*

cave \'kāv\ *n* : natural underground chamber —**cave in** *vb* : collapse

cav·ern \'kavərn\ *n* : large cave —**cav·ern·ous** *adj* —**cav·ern·ous·ly** *adv*

cav·i·ar, cav·i·are \'kavē,är, 'käv-\ *n* : salted fish roe

cav·il \'kavəl\ *vb* **-iled** *or* **-illed; -il·ing** *or* **-il·ling** : raise trivial objections —**cavil** *n* —**cav·il·er, cav·il·ler** *n*

cav·i·ty \'kavətē\ *n, pl* **-ties** 1 : unfilled place within a mass 2 : decay in a tooth

ca·vort \kə'vȯrt\ *vb* : prance or caper

caw \'kȯ\ *vb* : utter the harsh call of the crow —**caw** *n*

cay·enne pepper \,kī'en-, ,kā-\ *n* : ground dried fruits of a hot pepper

CD \,sē'dē\ *n* : compact disc

cease \'sēs\ *vb* **ceased; ceas·ing** : stop

cease·less \-ləs\ *adj* : continuous

ce·dar \'sēdər\ *n* : cone-bearing tree with fragrant durable wood

cede \'sēd\ *vb* **ced·ed; ced·ing** : surrender —**ced·er** *n*

ceil·ing \'sēliŋ\ *n* 1 : overhead surface of a room 2 : upper limit

cel·e·brate \'selə,brāt\ *vb* **-brat·ed; -brat·ing** 1 : perform with appropriate rites 2 : honor with ceremonies 3 : extol —**cel·e·brant** \-brənt\ *n* —**cel·e·bra·tion** \,selə'brāshən\ *n* —**cel·e·bra·tor** \'selə,brātər\ *n*

cel·e·brat·ed \-əd\ *adj* : renowned

ce·leb·ri·ty \sə'lebrətē\ *n, pl* **-ties** 1 : renown 2 : well-known person

ce·ler·i·ty \sə'lerətē\ *n* : speed

cel·ery \'selərē\ *n, pl* **-er·ies** : herb grown for crisp edible stalks

ce·les·ta \sə'lestə\, **ce·leste** \sə'lest\ *n* : keyboard musical instrument

ce·les·tial \sə'leschəl\ *adj* 1 : relating to the sky 2 : heavenly

cel·i·ba·cy \'seləbəsē\ *n* 1 : state of being unmarried 2 : abstention from sexual intercourse —**cel·i·bate** \'seləbət\ *n or adj*

cell \'sel\ *n* 1 : small room 2 : tiny mass of protoplasm that forms the fundamental unit of living matter 3 : container holding an electrolyte for generating electricity —**celled** *adj*

cel·lar \'selər\ *n* : room or area below ground

cel·lo \'chelō\ *n, pl* **-los** : bass member of the violin family —**cel·list** \-ist\ *n*

cel·lo·phane \'selə,fān\ *n* : thin transparent cellulose wrapping

cel·lu·lar \'selyələr\ *adj* : relating to or consisting of cells

cel·lu·lose \'selyə,lōs\ *n* : complex plant carbohydrate

Cel·sius \'selsēəs\ *adj* : relating to a thermometer scale on which the freezing point of water is 0° and the boiling point is 100°

ce·ment \si'ment\ *n* 1 : powdery mixture of clay and limestone that hardens when wetted 2 : binding agent ~ *vb* : unite or cover with cement —**ce·ment·er** *n*

cem·e·tery \'semə,terē\ *n, pl* **-ter·ies** : burial ground

cen·ser \'sensər\ *n* : vessel for burning incense

cen·sor \'sensər\ *n* : one with power to suppress anything objectionable (as in printed matter) ~ *vb* : be a censor of —**cen·so·ri·al** \sen'sōrēəl\ *adj* —**cen·sor·ship** \-,ship\ *n*

cen·so·ri·ous \sen'sōrēəs\ *adj* : critical —**cen·so·ri·ous·ly** *adv* —**cen·so·ri·ous·ness** *n*

cen·sure \'senchər\ *n* : official reprimand ~ *vb* **-sured; -sur·ing** : find blameworthy —**cen·sur·able** *adj*

cen·sus \'sensəs\ *n* : periodic population count —**census** *vb*

cent \'sent\ *n* : monetary unit equal to 1/100 of a basic unit of value

cen·taur \'sen,tòr\ *n* : mythological creature that is half man and half horse

cen·ten·ni·al \sen'tenēəl\ *n* : 100th anniversary —**centennial** *adj*

cen·ter \'sentər\ *n* 1 : middle point 2 : point of origin or greatest concentration 3 : region of concentrated population 4 : player near the middle of the team ~ *vb* 1 : place, fix, or concentrate at or around a center 2 : have a center —**cen·ter·piece** *n*

cen·ti·grade \'sentə,grād, 'sänt-\ *adj* : Celsius

cen·ti·me·ter \'sentə,mētər, 'sänt-\ *n* : 1/100 meter

cen·ti·pede \'sentə,pēd\ *n* : long flat many-legged arthropod

cen·tral \'sentrəl\ *adj* 1 : constituting or being near a center 2 : essential or principal —**cen·tral·ly** *adv*

cen·tral·ize \-trə,līz\ *vb* **-ized; -iz·ing** : bring to a central point or under central control —**cen·tral·i·za·tion** \,sentrələ'zāshən\ *n* —**cen·tral·iz·er** *n*

cen·tre *chiefly Brit var of* CENTER

cen·trif·u·gal \sen'trifyəgəl, -'trifigəl\ *adj* : acting in a direction away from a center or axis

cen·tri·fuge \'sentrə,fyüj\ *n* : machine that separates substances by spinning

cen·trip·e·tal \sen'tripətᵊl\ *adj* : acting in a direction toward a center or axis

cen·tu·ri·on \sen'chùrēən, -'tùr-\ *n* : Roman military officer

cen·tu·ry \'senchərē\ *n, pl* **-ries** : 100 years

ce·ram·ic \sə'ramik\ *n* 1 *pl* : art or pro-

cess of shaping and hardening articles from clay 2 : product of ceramics —**ceramic** *adj*

ce·re·al \'sirēəl\ *adj* : made of or relating to grain or to the plants that produce it ~ *n* 1 : grass yielding edible grain 2 : food prepared from a cereal grain

ce·re·bel·lum \,serə'beləm\ *n, pl* **-bellums** *or* **-bel·la** \-'belə\ : part of the brain controlling muscular coordination —**ce·re·bel·lar** \-ər\ *adj*

ce·re·bral \sə'rēbrəl, 'serə-\ *adj* 1 : relating to the brain, intellect, or cerebrum 2 : appealing to the intellect

cerebral palsy *n* : disorder caused by brain damage and marked esp. by defective muscle control

ce·re·brate \'serə,brāt\ *vb* **-brat·ed; -brat·ing** : think —**ce·re·bra·tion** \,serə'brāshən\ *n*

ce·re·brum \sə'rēbrəm, 'serə-\ *n, pl* **-brums** *or* **-bra** \-brə\ : part of the brain that contains the higher nervous centers

cer·e·mo·ny \'serə,mōnē\ *n, pl* **-nies** 1 : formal act prescribed by law, ritual, or convention 2 : prescribed procedures —**cer·e·mo·ni·al** \,serə'mōnēəl\ *adj or n* —**cer·e·mo·ni·ous** \-nēəs\ *adj*

ce·rise \sə'rēs\ *n* : moderate red

cer·tain \'sərtᵊn\ *adj* 1 : settled 2 : true 3 : specific but not named 4 : bound 5 : assured ~ *pron* : certain ones —**cer·tain·ly** *adv* —**cer·tain·ty** \-tē\ *n*

cer·tif·i·cate \sər'tifikət\ *n* : document establishing truth or fulfillment

cer·ti·fy \'sərtə,fī\ *vb* **-fied; -fy·ing** 1 : verify 2 : endorse —**cer·ti·fi·able** \-,fīəbəl\ *adj* —**cer·ti·fi·ably** \-blē\ *adv* —**cer·ti·fi·ca·tion** \,sərtəfə'kāshən\ *n* —**cer·ti·fi·er** *n*

cer·ti·tude \'sərtə,tüd, -,tyüd\ *n* : state of being certain

cer·vix \'sərviks\ *n, pl* **-vi·ces** \-və-,sēz\ *or* **-vix·es** 1 : neck 2 : narrow end of the uterus —**cer·vi·cal** \-vikəl\ *adj*

ce·sar·e·an \si'zarēən\ *n* : surgical operation to deliver a baby —**cesarean** *adj*

ce·si·um \'sēzēəm\ *n* : silver-white soft ductile chemical element

ces·sa·tion \se'sāshən\ *n* : a halting

ces·sion \'seshən\ *n* : a yielding

cess·pool \'ses,pül\ *n* : underground sewage pit

Cha·blis \'shab,lē; sha'blē\ *n, pl* **Chablis** \-,lēz, -'blēz\ : dry white wine

chafe \'chāf\ vb **chafed; chaf·ing 1** : fret **2** : make sore by rubbing

chaff \'chaf\ n **1** : debris separated from grain **2** : something worthless

chaf·ing dish \'chāfiŋ-\ n : utensil for cooking at the table

cha·grin \shə'grin\ n : embarrassment or humiliation ~ vb : cause to feel chagrin

chain \'chān\ n **1** : flexible series of connected links **2** pl : fetters **3** : linked series ~ vb : bind or connect with a chain

chair \'cher\ n **1** : seat with a back **2** : position of authority or dignity **3** : chairman ~ vb : act as chairman of

chair·man \-mən\ n : presiding officer —**chair·man·ship** n

chair·wom·an \-,wùmən\ n : woman who acts as a presiding officer

chaise longue \'shāz'lôŋ\ n, pl **chaise longues** \-lôŋ, -'lôŋz\ : long chair for reclining

cha·let \sha'lā\ n : Swiss mountain cottage with overhanging roof

chal·ice \'chaləs\ n : eucharistic cup

chalk \'chôk\ n **1** : soft limestone **2** : chalky material used as a crayon ~ vb : mark with chalk —**chalky** adj —**chalk up** vb **1** : credit **2** : achieve

chalk·board n : blackboard

chal·lenge \'chalənj\ vb **-lenged; -leng·ing 1** : dispute **2** : invite or dare to act or compete —**challenge** n —**chal·leng·er** n

cham·ber \'chāmbər\ n **1** : room **2** : enclosed space **3** : legislative meeting place or body **4** pl : judge's consultation room —**cham·bered** adj

cham·ber·maid n : bedroom maid

chamber music n : music by a small group for a small audience

cha·me·leon \kə'mēlyən\ n : small lizard whose skin changes color

cham·ois \'shamē\ n, pl **cham·ois** \-ē, -ēz\ **1** : goatlike antelope **2** : soft leather

¹champ \'champ, 'chämp\ vb : chew noisily

²champ \'champ\ n : champion

cham·pagne \sham'pān\ n : sparkling white wine

cham·pi·on \'champēən\ n **1** : advocate or defender **2** : winning contestant ~ vb : protect or fight for

cham·pi·on·ship \-,ship\ n **1** : title of a champion **2** : contest to pick a champion

chance \'chans\ n **1** : unpredictable element of existence **2** : opportunity **3** : probability **4** : risk **5** : raffle ticket ~ vb **chanced; chanc·ing 1** : happen **2** : encounter unexpectedly **3** : risk —**chance** adj

chan·cel \'chansəl\ n : part of a church around the altar

chan·cel·lery, chan·cel·lory \'chansələrē\ n, pl **-leries** or **-lories 1** : position of a chancellor **2** : chancellor's office

chan·cel·lor \-sələr\ n **1** : chief or high state official **2** : head of a university —**chan·cel·lor·ship** n

chan·cre \'shaŋkər\ n : skin ulcer esp. from syphilis

chancy \'chansē\ adj **chanc·i·er; -est** : risky

chan·de·lier \,shandə'lir\ n : hanging lighting fixture

chan·dler \'chandlər\ n : provisions dealer —**chan·dlery** n

change \'chānj\ vb **changed; chang·ing 1** : make or become different **2** : exchange **3** : give or receive change for ~ n **1** : a changing **2** : excess from a payment **3** : money in smaller denominations **4** : coins —**change·able** adj —**change·less** adj —**chang·er** n

chan·nel \'chanᵊl\ n **1** : deeper part of a waterway **2** : means of passage or communication **3** : strait **4** : broadcast frequency ~ vb **-neled** or **-nelled; -nel·ing** or **-nel·ling** : make or direct through a channel

chant \'chant\ vb : sing or speak in one tone —**chant** n —**chant·er** n

chan·tey, chan·ty \'shantē, 'chant-\ n, pl **-teys** or **-ties** : sailors' work song

Cha·nu·kah \'känəkə, 'hän-\ var of HANUKKAH

cha·os \'kā,äs\ n : complete disorder —**cha·ot·ic** \kā'ätik\ adj —**cha·ot·i·cal·ly** \-iklē\ adv

¹chap \'chap\ n : fellow

²chap vb **-pp-** : dry and crack open usu. from wind and cold

cha·pel \'chapəl\ n : private or small place of worship

chap·er·on, chap·er·one \'shapə,rōn\ n : older person who accompanies young people at a social gathering ~ vb --nied; -on·ing : act as chaperon at or for —**chap·er·on·age** \-ij\ n

chap·lain \'chaplən\ n : clergy member in a military unit or a prison —**chap·lain·cy** \-sē\ n

chap·ter \'chaptər\ *n* 1 : main book division 2 : branch of a society

char \'chär\ *vb* -rr- 1 : burn to charcoal 2 : scorch

char·ac·ter \'kariktər\ *n* 1 : letter or graphic mark 2 : trait or distinctive combination of traits 3 : peculiar person 4 : fictional person —**char·ac·ter·i·za·tion** \,kariktərə'zāshən\ *n* —**char·ac·ter·ize** \'kariktə,rīz\ *vb*

char·ac·ter·is·tic \,kariktə'ristik\ *adj* : typical ~ *n* : distinguishing quality —**char·ac·ter·is·ti·cal·ly** \-tiklē\ *adv*

cha·rades \shə'rādz\ *n sing or pl* : pantomime guessing game

char·coal \'chär,kōl\ *n* : porous carbon prepared by partial combustion

chard \'chärd\ *n* : leafy vegetable

charge \'chärj\ *vb* **charged; charg·ing** 1 : give an electric charge to 2 : impose a task or responsibility on 3 : command 4 : accuse 5 : rush forward in assault 6 : assume a debt for 7 : fix as a price ~ *n* 1 : excess or deficiency of electrons in a body 2 : tax 3 : responsibility 4 : accusation 5 : cost 6 : attack —**charge·able** *adj*

charg·er \-ər\ *n* : horse ridden in battle

char·i·ot \'charēət\ *n* : ancient 2-wheeled vehicle —**char·i·o·teer** \,charēə'tir\ *n*

cha·ris·ma \kə'rizmə\ *n* : special ability to lead —**char·is·mat·ic** \,karəz'matik\ *adj*

char·i·ty \'charətē\ *n, pl* **-ties** 1 : love for mankind 2 : generosity or leniency 3 : alms 4 : institution for relief of the needy —**char·i·ta·ble** \-əbəl\ *adj* —**char·i·ta·ble·ness** *n* —**char·i·ta·bly** \-blē\ *adv*

char·la·tan \'shärlətən\ *n* : impostor

charm \'chärm\ *n* 1 : something with magic power 2 : appealing trait 3 : small ornament ~ *vb* : fascinate —**charm·er** *n* —**charm·ing** *adj* —**charm·ing·ly** *adv*

char·nel house \'chärn³l-\ *n* : place for dead bodies

chart \'chärt\ *n* 1 : map 2 : diagram ~ *vb* 1 : make a chart of 2 : plan

char·ter \-ər\ *n* 1 : document granting rights 2 : constitution ~ *vb* 1 : establish by charter 2 : rent —**char·ter·er** *n*

char·treuse \shär'trüz, -'trüs\ *n* : brilliant yellow green

char·wom·an \'chär,wùmən\ *n* : cleaning woman

chary \'charē\ *adj* **chari·er; -est** : cautious —**char·i·ly** \'charəlē\ *adv*

¹chase \'chās\ *vb* **chased; chas·ing** 1 : follow trying to catch 2 : drive away —**chase** *n* —**chas·er** *n*

²chase *vb* **chased; chas·ing** : decorate (metal) by embossing or engraving

chasm \'kazəm\ *n* : gorge

chas·sis \'chasē, 'shasē\ *n, pl* **chas·sis** \-ēz\ : supporting structural frame

chaste \'chāst\ *adj* **chast·er; chast·est** 1 : abstaining from all or unlawful sexual relations 2 : modest or decent 3 : severely simple —**chaste·ly** *adv* —**chaste·ness** *n* —**chas·ti·ty** \'chastətē\ *n*

chas·ten \'chās³n\ *vb* : discipline

chas·tise \chas'tīz\ *vb* **-tised; -tis·ing** 1 : punish 2 : censure —**chas·tise·ment** \-mənt, 'chastəz-\ *n*

chat \'chat\ *n* : informal talk —**chat** *vb* —**chat·ty** \-ē\ *adj*

châ·teau \sha'tō\ *n, pl* **-teaus** \-'tōz\ *or* **-teaux** \-'tō, -'tōz\ 1 : large country house 2 : French vineyard estate

chat·tel \'chat³l\ *n* : item of tangible property other than real estate

chat·ter \'chatər\ *vb* 1 : utter rapidly succeeding sounds 2 : talk fast or too much —**chatter** *n* —**chat·ter·er** *n*

chat·ter·box *n* : incessant talker

chauf·feur \'shōfər, shō'fər\ *n* : hired car driver ~ *vb* : work as a chauffeur

chau·vin·ism \'shōvə,nizəm\ *n* : excessive patriotism —**chau·vin·ist** \-vənist\ *n* —**chau·vin·is·tic** \,shōvə'nistik\ *adj*

cheap \'chēp\ *adj* 1 : inexpensive 2 : shoddy —**cheap** *adv* —**cheap·en** \'chēpən\ *vb* —**cheap·ly** *adv* —**cheap·ness** *n*

cheap·skate *n* : stingy person

cheat \'chēt\ *n* 1 : act of deceiving 2 : one that cheats ~ *vb* 1 : deprive through fraud or deceit 2 : violate rules dishonestly —**cheat·er** *n*

check \'chek\ *n* 1 : sudden stoppage 2 : restraint 3 : test or standard for testing 4 : written order to a bank to pay money 5 : ticket showing ownership 6 : slip showing an amount due 7 : pattern in squares or fabric in such a pattern 8 : mark placed beside an item noted ~ *vb* 1 : slow down or stop 2 : restrain 3 : compare or correspond with a source or original 4 : inspect or test for condition **5** : mark with a check **6** : leave or accept for safekeeping or shipment **7** : checker — **check in** vb : report one's arrival — **check out** vb : settle one's account and leave

1check·er \-ər\ n : piece in checkers — vb : mark with different colors or into squares

2checker n : one that checks

check·er·board \-ˌbȯrd\ n : board of 64 squares of alternate colors

check·ers \'chekərz\ n : game for 2 played on a checkerboard

check·mate vb : thwart completely — **checkmate** n

check·point n : place where traffic is checked

check·up n : physical examination

ched·dar \'chedər\ n : hard smooth cheese

cheek \'chēk\ n **1** : fleshy side part of the face **2** : impudence —**cheeked** \'chēkt\ adj —**cheeky** adj

cheep \'chēp\ vb : utter faint shrill sounds —**cheep** n

cheer \'chir\ n **1** : good spirits **2** : food and drink for a feast **3** : shout of applause or encouragement ~ vb **1** : give hope or courage to **2** : make or become glad **3** : urge on or applaud with shouts —**cheer·er** n —**cheer·ful** \-fəl\ adj —**cheer·ful·ly** adv —**cheer·ful·ness** n —**cheer·lead·er** n — **cheer·less** adj —**cheer·less·ly** adv — **cheer·less·ness** n

cheery \'chirē\ adj **cheer·i·er**; **-est** : cheerful —**cheer·i·ly** adv —**cheer·i·ness** n

cheese \'chēz\ n : curd of milk usu. pressed and cured —**cheesy** adj

cheese·cloth n : lightweight coarse cotton gauze

chee·tah \'chētə\ n : spotted swift-moving African cat

chef \'shef\ n : chief cook

chem·i·cal \'kemikəl\ adj **1** : relating to chemistry **2** : working or produced by chemicals ~ n : substance obtained by chemistry —**chem·i·cal·ly** \-klē\ adv

che·mise \shə'mēz\ n **1** : woman's one-piece undergarment **2** : loose dress

chem·ist \'kemist\ n **1** : one trained in chemistry **2** Brit : pharmacist

chem·is·try \-istrē\ n, pl **-tries** : science that deals with the composition and properties of substances

che·mo·ther·a·py \ˌkēmō'therəpē, ˌkemō-\ n : use of chemicals in the treatment of disease —**che·mo·ther·a·peu·tic** adj

che·nille \shə'nēl\ n : yarn with protruding pile or fabric of such yarn

cheque \'chek\ chiefly Brit var of CHECK 4

cher·ish \'cherish\ vb : hold dear

cher·ry \'cherē\ n, pl **-ries** : small fleshy fruit of a tree related to the roses or the tree or its wood

cher·ub \'cherəb\ n **1** pl **-u·bim** \-ˌbim, -yə-\ : angel **2** pl **-ubs** : chubby child —**che·ru·bic** \chə'rübik\ adj

chess \'ches\ n : game for 2 played on a checkerboard —**chess·board** n — **chess·man** n

chest \'chest\ n **1** : boxlike container **2** : part of the body enclosed by the ribs and breastbone —**chest·ed** adj

chest·nut \'ches,nət\ n : nut of a tree related to the beech or the tree

chev·i·ot \'shevēət\ n **1** : heavy rough wool fabric **2** : soft-finished cotton fabric

chev·ron \'shevrən\ n : V-shaped insignia

chew \'chü\ vb : crush or grind with the teeth ~ n : something to chew — **chew·able** adj —**chew·er** n —**chewy** adj

chic \'shēk\ n : smart elegance of dress or manner ~ adj **1** : stylish **2** : currently fashionable

chi·ca·nery \shik'ānərē\ n, pl **-ner·ies** : trickery

chick \'chik\ n : young chicken or bird

chick·a·dee \-ə,dē\ n : small grayish American bird

chick·en \'chikən\ n **1** : common domestic fowl or its flesh used as food **2** : coward

chicken pox n : acute contagious virus disease esp. of children

chi·cle \'chikəl\ n : gum from a tropical evergreen tree

chic·o·ry \'chikərē\ n, pl **-ries** : herb used in salad or its dried ground root used to adulterate coffee

chide \'chīd\ vb **chid** \'chid\ or **chid·ed** \'chīdəd\; **chid** or **chid·den** \'chidᵊn\ or **chided**; **chid·ing** \'chīdiŋ\ : scold

chief \'chēf\ n : leader ~ adj **1** : highest in rank **2** : most important —**chief·dom** n —**chief·ly** adv

chief·tain \'chēftən\ n : chief

chif·fon \shif'än, 'shif,-\ n : sheer fabric

chig·ger \'chigər\ *n* : bloodsucking mite

chi·gnon \'shēn,yän\ *n* : knot of hair

chil·blain \'chil,blān\ *n* : sore or inflamed swelling caused by cold

child \'chīld\ *n, pl* **chil·dren** \'childrən\ **1** : unborn or recently born person **2** : son or daughter —**child·bear·ing** *n or adj* —**child·birth** *n* —**child·hood** *n* —**child·ish** *adj* —**child·ish·ly** *adv* —**child·ish·ness** *n* —**child·less** *adj* —**child·less·ness** *n* —**child·like** *adj* —**child·proof** \-,prüf\ *adj*

chili, chile, chil·li \'chilē\ *n, pl* **chil·ies** *or* **chil·es** *or* **chil·lies** **1** : hot pepper **2** : spicy stew of ground beef, chilies, and beans

chill \'chil\ *vb* : make or become cold or chilly ~ *adj* : moderately cold ~ *n* **1** : feeling of coldness with shivering **2** : moderate coldness

chilly \-ē\ *adj* **chill·i·er; -est** : noticeably cold —**chill·i·ness** *n*

chime \'chīm\ *n* : set of tuned bells or their sound ~ *vb* : make bell-like sounds —**chime in** *vb* : break into or join in a conversation

chi·me·ra, chi·mae·ra \kī'mirə, kə-\ *n* **1** : imaginary monster **2** : illusion —**chi·me·ri·cal** \-'merikəl\ *adj*

chim·ney \'chimnē\ *n, pl* **-neys 1** : passage for smoke **2** : glass tube around a lamp flame

chimp \'chimp, 'shimp\ *n* : chimpanzee

chim·pan·zee \,chim,pan'zē, ,shim-; chim'panzē, shim-\ *n* : small ape

chin \'chin\ *n* : part of the face below the mouth —**chin·less** *adj*

chi·na \'chīnə\ *n* **1** : porcelain ware **2** : domestic pottery

chin·chil·la \chin'chilə\ *n* : small So. American rodent with soft pearl-gray fur or this fur

chink \'chiŋk\ *n* : small crack ~ *vb* : fill chinks of

chintz \'chints\ *n* : printed cotton cloth

chip \'chip\ *n* **1** : small thin flat piece cut or broken off **2** : thin crisp morsel of food **3** : counter used in games **4** : flaw where a chip came off **5** : small slice of semiconductor containing electronic circuits ~ *vb* **-pp-** : cut or break chips from —**chip in** *vb* : contribute

chip·munk \'chip,məŋk\ *n* : small striped ground-dwelling rodent

chip·per \-ər\ *adj* : lively and cheerful

chi·rop·o·dy \kə'räpədē, shə-\ *n* : podiatry —**chi·rop·o·dist** \-ədist\ *n*

chi·ro·prac·tic \'kīrə,praktik\ *n* : system of healing based esp. on manipulation of body structures —**chi·ro·prac·tor** \-tər\ *n*

chirp \'chərp\ *n* : short sharp sound like that of a bird or cricket —**chirp** *vb*

chis·el \'chizəl\ *n* : sharp-edged metal tool ~ *vb* **-eled** *or* **-elled; -el·ing** *or* **-el·ling 1** : work with a chisel **2** : cheat —**chis·el·er** \-ələr\ *n*

chit \'chit\ *n* : signed voucher for a small debt

chit·chat \-,chat\ *n* : casual conversation —**chitchat** *vb*

chiv·al·rous \'shivəlrəs\ *adj* **1** : relating to chivalry **2** : honest, courteous, or generous —**chiv·al·rous·ly** *adv* —**chiv·al·rous·ness** *n*

chiv·al·ry \-rē\ *n, pl* **-ries 1** : system or practices of knighthood **2** : spirit or character of the ideal knight —**chi·val·ric** \shə'valrik\ *adj*

chive \'chīv\ *n* : herb related to the onion

chlo·ride \'klōr,īd\ *n* : compound of chlorine

chlo·ri·nate \-ə,nāt\ *vb* **-nat·ed; -nat·ing** : treat or combine with chlorine —**chlo·ri·na·tion** \,klōrə'nāshən\ *n*

chlo·rine \'klōr,ēn\ *n* : chemical element that is a heavy strong-smelling greenish yellow irritating gas

chlo·ro·form \'klōrə,fȯrm\ *n* : etherlike colorless heavy fluid ~ *vb* : anesthetize or kill with chloroform

chlo·ro·phyll \'klōr-ə,fil\ *n* : green coloring matter of plants

chock \'chäk\ *n* : wedge for blocking the movement of a wheel —**chock** *vb*

chock-full \'chək'ful, 'chäk-\ *adj* : full to the limit

choc·o·late \'chäkələt, 'chȯk-\ *n* **1** : ground roasted cacao beans or a beverage made from them **2** : candy made of or with chocolate **3** : dark brown

choice \'chȯis\ *n* **1** : act or power of choosing **2** : one selected **3** : variety offered for selection ~ *adj* **choic·er; choic·est 1** : worthy of being chosen **2** : selected with care **3** : of high quality

choir \'kwīr\ *n* : group of singers esp. in church —**choir·boy** *n* —**choir·mas·ter** *n*

choke \'chōk\ *vb* **choked; chok·ing 1** : hinder breathing **2** : clog or obstruct ~ *n* **1** : a choking or sound of choking **2** : valve for controlling air intake in a gasoline engine

chok·er \-ər\ *n* : tight necklace

cho·ler \'kälər, 'kō-\ *n* : bad temper — **cho·ler·ic** \'kälərik, kə'ler-\ *adj*

chol·era \'kälərə\ *n* : disease marked by severe vomiting and dysentery

cho·les·ter·ol \kə'lestə,ról, -,rōl\ *n* : waxy substance in animal tissues

choose \'chüz\ *vb* **chose** \'chōz\; **cho·sen** \'chōzᵊn\; **choos·ing** **1** : select after consideration **2** : decide **3** : prefer — **choos·er** *n*

choosy, **choos·ey** \'chüzē\ *adj* **choos·i·er**; **-est** : fussy in making choices

chop \'chäp\ *vb* **-pp- 1** : cut by repeated blows **2** : cut into small pieces ~ *n* **1** : sharp downward blow **2** : small cut of meat often with part of a rib

chop·per \-ər\ *n* **1** : one that chops **2** : helicopter

chop·py \-ē\ *adj* **-pi·er; -est 1** : rough with small waves **2** : jerky or disconnected — **chop·pi·ly** *adv* — **chop·pi·ness** *n*

chops \'chäps\ *n pl* : fleshy covering of the jaws

chop·sticks *n pl* : pair of sticks used in eating in oriental countries

cho·ral \'kórəl\ *adj* : relating to or sung by a choir or chorus or in chorus — **cho·ral·ly** *adv*

cho·rale \kə'ral, -'räl\ *n* **1** : hymn tune or harmonization of a traditional melody **2** : chorus or choir

¹chord \'kórd\ *n* : harmonious tones sounded together

²chord *n* **1** : cordlike anatomical structure **2** : straight line joining 2 points on a curve

chore \'chōr\ *n* **1** *pl* : daily household or farm work **2** : routine or disagreeable task

cho·re·og·ra·phy \,kōrē'ägrəfē\ *n, pl* **-phies** : art of composing and arranging dances — **cho·reo·graph** \'kōrēə,graf\ *vb* — **cho·re·og·ra·pher** \,kō·rē'ägrəfər\ *n* — **cho·reo·graph·ic** \-ēə'grafik\ *adj*

cho·ris·ter \'kórəstər\ *n* : choir singer

chor·tle \'chórtᵊl\ *vb* **-tled; -tling** : laugh or chuckle — **chortle** *n*

cho·rus \'kórəs\ *n* **1** : group of singers or dancers **2** : part of a song repeated at intervals **3** : composition for a chorus ~ *vb* : sing or utter together

chose *past of* CHOOSE

cho·sen \'chōzᵊn\ *adj* : favored

¹chow \'chaú\ *n* : food

²chow *n* : thick-coated muscular dog

chow·der \'chaúdər\ *n* : thick soup usu. of seafood and milk

chow mein \'chaú'mān\ *n* : thick stew of shredded vegetables and meat

chris·ten \'krisᵊn\ *vb* **1** : baptize **2** : name — **chris·ten·ing** *n*

Chris·ten·dom \-dəm\ *n* : areas where Christianity prevails

Chris·tian \'krischən\ *n* : adherent of Christianity ~ *adj* : relating to or professing a belief in Christianity or Jesus Christ — **Chris·tian·ize** \'krischə,nīz\ *vb*

Chris·ti·an·i·ty \,krischē'anətē\ *n* : religion derived from the teachings of Jesus Christ

Christian name *n* : first name

Christ·mas \'krisməs\ *n* : December 25 celebrated as the birthday of Christ

chro·mat·ic \krō'matik\ *adj* **1** : relating to color **2** : proceeding by half steps of the musical scale

chrome \'krōm\ *n* : chromium or something plated with it

chro·mi·um \-ēəm\ *n* : a bluish white metallic element used esp. in alloys

chro·mo·some \'krōmə,sōm, -,zōm\ *n* : part of a cell nucleus that contains the genes — **chro·mo·som·al** \,krōmə'sōməl, -'zō-\ *adj*

chron·ic \'kränik\ *adj* : frequent or persistent — **chron·i·cal·ly** \-iklē\ *adv*

chron·i·cle \'kränikəl\ *n* : history ~ *vb* **-cled; -cling** : record — **chron·i·cler** \-iklər\ *n*

chro·nol·o·gy \krə'näləjē\ *n, pl* **-gies** : list of events in order of their occurrence — **chron·o·log·i·cal** \,krän·ᵊl'äjikəl\ *adj* — **chron·o·log·i·cal·ly** \-iklē\ *adv*

chro·nom·e·ter \krə'nämətər\ *n* : very accurate timepiece

chrys·a·lis \'krisələs\ *n, pl* **chrys·al·i·des** \kris'alə,dēz\ *or* **chrys·a·lis·es** : insect pupa enclosed in a shell

chrys·an·the·mum \kris'anthəməm\ *n* : plant with showy flowers

chub·by \'chəbē\ *adj* **-bi·er; -est** : fat — **chub·bi·ness** *n*

¹chuck \'chək\ *vb* **1** : tap **2** : toss ~ *n* **1** : light pat under the chin **2** : toss

²chuck *n* **1** : cut of beef **2** : machine part that holds work or another part

chuck·le \'chəkəl\ *vb* **-led; -ling** : laugh quietly — **chuckle** *n*

chug \'chəg\ *n* : sound of a laboring engine ~ *vb* **-gg-** : work or move with chugs

chum \'chəm\ *n* : close friend ~ *vb* **-mm-** : be chums —**chum·my** \-ē\ *adj*

chump \'chəmp\ *n* : fool

chunk \'chəŋk\ *n* 1 : short thick piece 2 : sizable amount

chunky \-ē\ *adj* **chunk·i·er; -est** 1 : stocky 2 : containing chunks

church \'chərch\ *n* 1 : building esp. for Christian public worship 2 : whole body of Christians 3 : denomination 4 : congregation —**church·go·er** *n* — **church·go·ing** *adj or n*

church·yard *n* : cemetery beside a church

churl \'chərl\ *n* : rude ill-bred person — **churl·ish** *adj*

churn \'chərn\ *n* : container in which butter is made ~ *vb* 1 : agitate in a churn 2 : shake violently

chute \'shüt\ *n* : trough or passage

chut·ney \'chətnē\ *n, pl* **-neys** : sweet and sour relish

chutz·pah \'hutspə, 'kut-, -,spä\ *n* : nerve or insolence

ci·ca·da \sə'kādə\ *n* : stout-bodied insect with transparent wings

ci·der \'sīdər\ *n* : apple juice

ci·gar \sig'är\ *n* : roll of leaf tobacco for smoking

cig·a·rette \,sigə'ret, 'sigə,ret\ *n* : cut tobacco rolled in paper for smoking

cinch \'sinch\ *n* 1 : strap holding a saddle or pack in place 2 : sure thing — **cinch** *vb*

cin·cho·na \siŋ'kōnə\ *n* : So. American tree that yields quinine

cinc·ture \'siŋkchər\ *n* : belt or sash

cin·der \'sindər\ *n* 1 *pl* : ashes 2 : piece of partly burned wood or coal

cin·e·ma \'sinəmə\ *n* : movies or a movie theater —**cin·e·mat·ic** \,sinə'matik\ *adj*

cin·na·mon \'sinəmən\ *n* : spice from an aromatic tree bark

ci·pher \'sīfər\ *n* 1 : zero 2 : code

cir·ca \'sərkə\ *prep* : about

cir·cle \'sərkəl\ *n* 1 : closed symmetrical curve 2 : cycle 3 : group with a common tie ~ *vb* **-cled; -cling** 1 : enclose in a circle 2 : move or revolve around

cir·cuit \'sərkət\ *n* 1 : boundary 2 : regular tour of a territory 3 : complete path of an electric current 4 : group of electronic components

cir·cu·itous \,sər'kyüətəs\ *adj* : circular or winding

cir·cuit·ry \'sərkətrē\ *n, pl* **-ries** : arrangement of an electric circuit

cir·cu·lar \'sərkyələr\ *adj* 1 : round 2 : moving in a circle ~ *n* : advertising leaflet —**cir·cu·lar·i·ty** \,sərkyə-'larətē\ *n*

cir·cu·late \'sərkyə,lāt\ *vb* **-lat·ed; -lat·ing** : move or cause to move in a circle or from place to place or person to person —**cir·cu·la·tion** \,sərkyə'lā-shən\ *n* —**cir·cu·la·to·ry** \'sərkyələ-,tōrē\ *adj*

cir·cum·cise \'sərkəm,sīz\ *vb* **-cised; -cis·ing** : cut off the foreskin of —**cir·cum·ci·sion** \,sərkəm'sizhən\ *n*

cir·cum·fer·ence \sər'kəmfrəns\ *n* : perimeter of a circle

cir·cum·flex \'sərkəm,fleks\ *n* : phonetic mark (as ^)

cir·cum·lo·cu·tion \,sərkəmlō'kyüshən\ *n* : excessive use of words

cir·cum·nav·i·gate \,sərkəm'navə,gāt\ *vb* : sail completely around —**cir·cum·nav·i·ga·tion** *n*

cir·cum·scribe \'sərkəm,skrīb\ *vb* 1 : draw a line around 2 : limit

cir·cum·spect \'sərkəm,spekt\ *adj* : careful —**cir·cum·spec·tion** \,sər-kəm'spekshən\ *n*

cir·cum·stance \'sərkəm,stans\ *n* 1 : fact or event 2 *pl* : surrounding conditions 3 *pl* : financial situation —**cir·cum·stan·tial** \,sərkəm- 'stanchəl\ *adj*

cir·cum·vent \,sərkəm'vent\ *vb* : get around esp. by trickery —**cir·cum·ven·tion** \-'venchən\ *n*

cir·cus \'sərkəs\ *n* : show with feats of skill, animal acts, and clowns

cir·rho·sis \sə'rōsəs\ *n, pl* **-rho·ses** \-,sēz\ : fibrosis of the liver —**cir·rhot·ic** \-'rätik\ *adj or n*

cir·rus \'sirəs\ *n, pl* **-ri** \-,ī\ : wispy white cloud

cis·tern \'sistərn\ *n* : underground water tank

cit·a·del \'sitəd³l, -ə,del\ *n* : fortress

cite \'sīt\ *vb* **cit·ed; cit·ing** 1 : summon before a court 2 : quote 3 : refer to esp. in commendation —**ci·ta·tion** \sī'tāshən\ *n*

cit·i·zen \'sitəzən\ *n* : member of a country —**cit·i·zen·ry** \-rē\ *n* —**cit·i·zen·ship** *n*

cit·ron \'sitrən\ *n* : lemonlike fruit

cit·rus \'sitrəs\ *n, pl* **-rus** *or* **-rus·es** : evergreen tree or shrub grown for its fruit (as the orange or lemon)

city \'sitē\ n, pl **cit·ies** : place larger or more important than a town

civ·ic \'sivik\ adj : relating to citizenship or civil affairs

civ·ics \-iks\ n : study of citizenship

civ·il \'sivəl\ adj 1 : relating to citizens 2 : polite 3 : relating to or being a lawsuit —**civ·il·ly** adv

ci·vil·ian \sə'vilyən\ n : person not in a military, police, or fire-fighting force

ci·vil·i·ty \sə'vilətē\ n, pl **-ties** : courtesy

civ·i·li·za·tion \,sivələ'zāshən\ n 1 : high level of cultural development 2 : culture of a time or place

civ·i·lize \'sivə,līz\ vb **-lized; -liz·ing** : raise from a primitive stage of cultural development —**civ·i·lized** adj

civil liberty n : freedom from arbitrary governmental interference —usu. pl.

civil rights n pl : nonpolitical rights of a citizen

civil service n : government service

civil war n : war among citizens of one country

clack \'klak\ vb : make or cause a clatter —**clack** n

clad \'klad\ adj : covered

claim \'klām\ vb 1 : demand or take as the rightful owner 2 : maintain ~ n 1 : demand of right or ownership 2 : declaration 3 : something claimed —**claim·ant** \-ənt\ n

clair·voy·ant \klar'vóiənt\ adj : able to perceive things beyond the senses —**clair·voy·ance** \-əns\ n —**clairvoy·ant** n

clam \'klam\ n : bivalve mollusk

clam·ber \'klambər\ vb : climb awkwardly

clam·my \'klamē\ adj **-mi·er; -est** : being damp, soft, and usu. cool —**clam·mi·ness** n

clam·or \-ər\ n 1 : uproar 2 : protest —**clamor** vb —**clam·or·ous** adj

clamp \'klamp\ n : device for holding things together —**clamp** vb

clan \'klan\ n : group of related families —**clan·nish** adj —**clan·nish·ness** n

clan·des·tine \klan'destən\ adj : secret

clang \'klaŋ\ n : loud metallic ringing —**clang** vb

clan·gor \-ər, -gər\ n : jumble of clangs

clank \'klaŋk\ n : brief sound of struck metal —**clank** vb

clap \'klap\ vb **-pp-** 1 : strike noisily 2 : applaud ~ n 1 : loud crash 2 : noise made by clapping the hands

clap·board \'klabərd, 'klap-, -,bōrd\ n : narrow tapered board used for siding

clap·per \'klapər\ n : tongue of a bell

claque \'klak\ n 1 : group hired to applaud at a performance 2 : group of sycophants

clar·et \'klarət\ n : dry red wine

clar·i·fy \'klarə,fī\ vb **-fied; -fy·ing** : make or become clear —**clar·i·fi·ca·tion** \,klarəfə'kāshən\ n

clar·i·net \,klarə'net\ n : woodwind instrument shaped like a tube —**clar·i·net·ist, clar·i·net·tist** \-ist\ n

clar·i·on \'klarēən\ adj : loud and clear

clar·i·ty \'klarətē\ n : clearness

clash \'klash\ vb 1 : make or cause a clash 2 : be in opposition or disharmony ~ n 1 : crashing sound 2 : hostile encounter

clasp \'klasp\ n 1 : device for holding things together 2 : embrace or grasp ~ vb 1 : fasten 2 : embrace or grasp

class \'klas\ n 1 : group of the same status or nature 2 : social rank 3 : course of instruction 4 : group of students ~ vb : classify —**class·less** adj —**class·mate** n —**class·room** n

clas·sic \'klasik\ adj 1 : serving as a standard of excellence 2 : classical ~ n : work of enduring excellence and esp. of ancient Greece or Rome —**clas·si·cal** \-ikəl\ adj —**clas·si·cal·ly** \-klē\ adv —**clas·si·cism** \'klasə,sizəm\ n —**clas·si·cist** \-sist\ n

clas·si·fied \'klasə,fīd\ adj : restricted for security reasons

clas·si·fy \-,fī\ vb **-fied; -fy·ing** : arrange in or assign to classes —**clas·si·fi·ca·tion** \,klasəfə'kāshən\ n —**clas·si·fi·er** \'klasə,fīər\ n

clat·ter \'klatər\ n : rattling sound —**clatter** vb

clause \'klóz\ n 1 : separate part of a document 2 : part of a sentence with a subject and predicate

claus·tro·pho·bia \,klóstrə'fōbēə\ n : fear of closed or narrow spaces —**claus·tro·pho·bic** \-bik\ adj

clav·i·chord \'klavə,kórd\ n : early keyboard instrument

clav·i·cle \'klavikəl\ n : collarbone

claw \'kló\ n : sharp curved nail or process (as on the toe of an animal) ~ vb : scratch or dig —**clawed** adj

clay \'klā\ n : plastic earthy material —**clay·ey** \-ē\ adj

clean \'klēn\ adj 1 : free from dirt or disease 2 : pure or honorable 3

: thorough ~ *vb* : make or become clean —**clean** *adv* —**clean·er** *n* —**clean·ly** \-lē\ *adv* —**clean·ness** *n*

clean·ly \'klenlē\ *adj* -li·er; -est : clean —**clean·li·ness** *n*

cleanse \'klenz\ *vb* **cleansed; cleans·ing** : make clean —**cleans·er** *n*

clear \'klir\ *adj* 1 : bright 2 : free from clouds 3 : transparent 4 : easily heard, seen or understood 5 : free from doubt 6 : free from restriction or obstruction ~ *vb* 1 : make or become clear 2 : go away 3 : free from accusation or blame 4 : explain or settle 5 : net 6 : jump or pass without touching ~ *n* : clear space or part —**clear** *adv* —**clear·ance** \'klirəns\ *n*

clear·ing \'kliriŋ\ *n* : land cleared of wood

clear·ly *adv* 1 : in a clear manner 2 : it is obvious that

cleat \'klēt\ *n* : projection that strengthens or prevents slipping

cleav·age \'klēvij\ *n* 1 : a splitting apart 2 : depression between a woman's breasts

¹**cleave** \'klēv\ *vb* **cleaved** \'klēvd\ *or* **clove** \'klōv\; **cleav·ing** : adhere

²**cleave** *vb* **cleaved** \'klēvd\; **cleav·ing** : split apart

cleav·er \'klēvər\ *n* : heavy chopping knife

clef \'klef\ *n* : sign on the staff in music to show pitch

cleft \'kleft\ *n* : crack

clem·ent \'klemənt\ *adj* 1 : merciful 2 : temperate or mild —**clem·en·cy** \-ənsē\ *n*

clench \'klench\ *vb* 1 : hold fast 2 : close tightly

cler·gy \'klərjē\ *n* : body of religious officials —**cler·gy·man** \-jimən\ *n*

cler·ic \'klerik\ *n* : member of the clergy

cler·i·cal \-ikəl\ *adj* 1 : relating to the clergy 2 : relating to a clerk or office worker

clerk \'klərk, *Brit* 'klärk\ *n* 1 : official responsible for record-keeping 2 : person doing general office work 3 : salesperson in a store —**clerk** *vb* —**clerk·ship** *n*

clev·er \'klevər\ *adj* 1 : resourceful 2 : marked by wit or ingenuity —**clev·er·ly** *adv* —**clev·er·ness** *n*

clew *var of* CLUE

cli·ché \kli'shā\ *n* : trite phrase —**cli·chéd** \-'shād\ *adj*

click \'klik\ *n* : slight sharp noise ~ *vb* : make or cause to make a click

cli·ent \'klīənt\ *n* 1 : person who engages professional services 2 : customer

cli·en·tele \,klīən'tel, ,klē-\ *n* : body of customers

cliff \'klif\ *n* : high steep face of rock

cli·mate \'klīmət\ *n* : average weather conditions over a period of years —**cli·mat·ic** \klī'matik\ *adj*

cli·max \'klī,maks\ *n* : the highest point ~ *vb* : come to a climax —**cli·mac·tic** \klī'maktik\ *adj*

climb \'klīm\ *vb* 1 : go up or down by use of hands and feet 2 : rise ~ *n* : a climbing —**climb·er** *n*

clinch \'klinch\ *vb* 1 : fasten securely 2 : settle 3 : hold fast or firmly —**clinch** *n* —**clinch·er** *n*

cling \'kliŋ\ *vb* **clung** \'kləŋ\; **cling·ing** 1 : adhere firmly 2 : hold on tightly

clin·ic \'klinik\ *n* : facility for diagnosis and treatment of outpatients —**clin·i·cal** \-əl\ *adj* —**clin·i·cal·ly** \-klē\ *adv*

clink \'kliŋk\ *vb* : make a slight metallic sound —**clink** *n*

clin·ker \'kliŋkər\ *n* : fused stony matter esp. in a furnace

¹**clip** \'klip\ *vb* **-pp-** : fasten with a clip ~ *n* : device to hold things together

²**clip** *vb* **-pp-** 1 : cut or cut off 2 : hit ~ *n* 1 : clippers 2 : sharp blow 3 : rapid pace

clip·per \'klipər\ *n* 1 *pl* : implement for clipping 2 : fast sailing ship

clique \'klēk, 'klik\ *n* : small exclusive group of people

cli·to·ris \'klitərəs, kli'tōrəs\ *n, pl* **cli·to·ri·des** \-'tōrə,dēz\ : small organ at the front of the vulva

cloak \'klōk\ *n* 1 : loose outer garment 2 : something that conceals ~ *vb* : cover or hide with a cloak

clob·ber \'kläbər\ *vb* : hit hard

clock \'kläk\ *n* : timepiece not carried on the person ~ *vb* : record the time of

clock·wise \-,wīz\ *adv or adj* : in the same direction as a clock's hands move

clod \'kläd\ *n* 1 : lump esp. of earth 2 : dull insensitive person

clog \'kläg\ *n* 1 : restraining weight 2 : thick-soled shoe ~ *vb* **-gg-** 1 : impede with a clog 2 : obstruct passage through 3 : become plugged up

clois·ter \'klȯistər\ *n* 1 : monastic estab-

lishment **2** : covered passage ~ *vb*
: shut away from the world

clone \'klōn\ *n* **1** : offspring produced
from a single organism **2** : copy

1close \'klōz\ *vb* **closed; clos·ing 1**
: shut **2** : cease operation **3** : terminate
4 : bring or come together ~ *n*
: conclusion or end

2close \'klōs\ *adj* **clos·er; clos·est 1**
: confining **2** : secretive **3** : strict **4**
: stuffy **5** : having little space between
items **6** : fitting tightly **7** : near **8**
: intimate **9** : accurate **10** : nearly
even —**close** *adv* —**close·ly** *adv* —
close·ness *n*

clos·et \'kläzət, 'klóz-\ *n* : small compartment for household utensils or
clothing ~ *vb* : take into a private
room for a talk

clo·sure \'klōzhər\ *n* **1** : act of closing **2**
: something that closes

clot \'klät\ *n* : dried mass of a liquid —
clot *vb*

cloth \'klóth\ *n, pl* **cloths** \'klóthz,
'klóths\ **1** : fabric **2** : tablecloth

clothe \'klōth\ *vb* **clothed** *or* **clad**
\'klad\; **cloth·ing** : dress

clothes \'klōthz, 'klóz\ *n pl* **1** : clothing
2 : bedclothes

cloth·ier \'klōthyər, -thēər\ *n* : maker or
seller of clothing

cloth·ing \'klōthiŋ\ *n* : covering for the
human body

cloud \'klaud\ *n* **1** : visible mass of particles in the air **2** : something that
darkens, hides, or threatens ~ *vb*
: darken or hide —**cloud·i·ness** *n* —
cloud·less *adj* —**cloudy** *adj*

cloud·burst *n* : sudden heavy rain

clout \'klaut\ *n* **1** : blow **2** : influence ~
vb : hit forcefully

1clove \'klōv\ *n* : section of a bulb

2clove *past of* CLEAVE

3clove *n* : dried flower bud of an East
Indian tree used as a spice

clo·ver \'klōvər\ *n* : leguminous herb
with usu. 3-part leaves

clo·ver·leaf *n, pl* **-leafs** *or* **-leaves**
: highway interchange

clown \'klaun\ *n* : funny costumed entertainer esp. in a circus ~ *vb* : act
like a clown —**clown·ish** *adj* —
clown·ish·ly *adv* —**clown·ish·ness** *n*

cloy \'klói\ *vb* : disgust with excess —
cloy·ing·ly \-iŋlē\ *adv*

club \'kləb\ *n* **1** : heavy wooden stick **2**
: playing card of a suit marked with a
black figure like a clover leaf **3**

: group associated for a common purpose ~ *vb* **-bb-** : hit with a club

club·foot *n* : misshapen foot twisted out
of position from birth —**club·foot·ed**
\-,fútəd\ *adj*

cluck \'klək\ *n* : sound made by a hen
—**cluck** *vb*

clue \'klü\ *n* : piece of evidence that
helps solve a problem ~ *vb* **clued;
clue·ing** *or* **clu·ing** : provide with a
clue

clump \'kləmp\ *n* **1** : cluster **2** : heavy
tramping sound ~ *vb* : tread heavily

clum·sy \'kləmzē\ *adj* **-si·er; -est 1**
: lacking dexterity, nimbleness, or
grace **2** : tactless —**clum·si·ly** *adv* —
clum·si·ness *n*

clung *past of* CLING

clunk·er \'kləŋkər\ *n* : old automobile

clus·ter \'kləstər\ *n* : group ~ *vb* : grow
or gather in a cluster

clutch \'kləch\ *vb* : grasp ~ *n* **1**
: grasping hand or claws **2** : control
or power **3** : coupling for connecting
two working parts in machinery

clut·ter \'klətər\ *vb* : fill with things that
get in the way —**clutter** *n*

co- *prefix* : with, together, joint, or
jointly

coact	cofounder
coactor	coheir
coauthor	coheiress
coauthorship	cohost
cocaptain	cohostess
cochairman	coinvent
cochampion	coinventor
cocomposer	coinvestigator
coconspirator	coleader
cocreator	comanagement
codefendant	comanager
codesign	co-organizer
codevelop	co-own
codeveloper	co-owner
codirect	copartner
codirector	copartnership
codiscoverer	copresident
codrive	coprincipal
codriver	coprisoner
coedit	coproduce
coeditor	coproducer
coexecutor	coproduction
coexist	copromoter
coexistence	coproprietor
coexistent	copublish
cofeature	copublisher
cofinance	corecipient
cofound	coresident

cosignatory
cosigner
cosponsor
costar

cowinner
coworker
cowrite

coach \'kōch\ *n* **1** : closed 2-door 4-wheeled carriage **2** : railroad passenger car **3** : bus **4** : 2d-class air travel **5** : one who instructs or trains performers ~ *vb* : instruct or direct as a coach

co·ag·u·late \kō'agyə,lāt\ *vb* **-lat·ed; -lat·ing** : clot —**co·ag·u·lant** \-lənt\ *n* —**co·ag·u·la·tion** \-,agyə'lāshən\ *n*

coal \'kōl\ *n* **1** : ember **2** : black solid mineral used as fuel —**coal·field** *n*

co·alesce \,kōə'les\ *vb* **-alesced; -alesc·ing** : grow together —**co·ales·cence** \-'lesᵊns\ *n*

co·ali·tion \-'lishən\ *n* : temporary alliance

coarse \'kōrs\ *adj* **coars·er; coars·est 1** : composed of large particles **2** : rough or crude —**coarse·ly** *adv* —**coars·en** \-ᵊn\ *vb* —**coarse·ness** *n*

coast \'kōst\ *n* : seashore ~ *vb* : move without effort —**coast·al** \-ᵊl\ *adj*

coast·er \-ər\ *n* **1** : one that coasts **2** : plate or mat to protect a surface

coast guard *n* : military force that guards or patrols a coast —**coast·guards·man** \'kōst,gärdzmən\ *n*

coast·line *n* : shape of a coast

coat \'kōt\ *n* **1** : outer garment for the upper body **2** : external growth of fur or feathers **3** : covering layer ~ *vb* : cover with a coat —**coat·ed** *adj* —**coat·ing** *n*

coax \'kōks\ *vb* : move to action or achieve by gentle urging or flattery

cob \'käb\ *n* : corncob

co·balt \'kō,bȯlt\ *n* : shiny silver-white magnetic metallic chemical element

cob·ble \'käbəl\ *vb* **cob·bled; cob·bling** : make or put together hastily

cob·bler \'käblər\ *n* **1** : shoemaker **2** : deep-dish fruit pie

cob·ble·stone *n* : small round paving stone

co·bra \'kōbrə\ *n* : venomous snake

cob·web \'käb,web\ *n* : network spun by a spider or a similar filament

co·caine \kō'kān, 'kō,kān\ *n* : drug obtained from the leaves of a So. American shrub (**co·ca** \'kōkə\)

co·chlea \'kōklēə, 'käk-\ *n, pl* **-chle·as** *or* **-chle·ae** \-lē,ē, -,ī\ : the usu. spiral

part of the inner ear —**coch·le·ar** \-lēər\ *adj*

cock \'käk\ *n* **1** : male fowl **2** : valve or faucet ~ *vb* **1** : draw back the hammer of a firearm **2** : tilt to one side —**cock·fight** *n*

cock·ade \kä'kād\ *n* : badge on a hat

cock·a·too \'käkə,tü\ *n, pl* **-toos** : large Australian crested parrot

cock·eyed \'käk'īd\ *adj* **1** : tilted to one side **2** : slightly crazy

cock·le \'käkəl\ *n* : edible shellfish

cock·pit \'käk,pit\ *n* : place for a pilot, driver, or helmsman

cock·roach *n* : nocturnal insect often infesting houses

cock·tail \'käk,tāl\ *n* **1** : iced drink of liquor and flavorings **2** : appetizer

cocky \'käkē\ *adj* **cock·i·er; -est** : overconfident —**cock·i·ly** \-əlē\ *adv* —**cock·i·ness** *n*

co·coa \'kōkō\ *n* **1** : cacao **2** : powdered chocolate or a drink made from this

co·co·nut \'kōkə,nət\ *n* : large nutlike fruit of a tropical palm (**coconut palm**)

co·coon \kə'kün\ *n* : case protecting an insect pupa

cod \'käd\ *n, pl* **cod** : food fish of the No. Atlantic

cod·dle \'kädᵊl\ *vb* **-dled; -dling** : pamper

code \'kōd\ *n* **1** : system of laws or rules **2** : system of signals

co·deine \'kō,dēn\ *n* : narcotic drug used in cough remedies

cod·ger \'käjər\ *n* : odd fellow

cod·i·cil \'kädəsəl, -,sil\ *n* : postscript to a will

cod·i·fy \'kädə,fī, 'kōd-\ *vb* **-fied; -fy·ing** : arrange systematically —**cod·i·fi·ca·tion** \,kädəfə'kāshən, ,kōd-\ *n*

co·ed \'kō,ed\ *n* : female student in a coeducational institution —**coed** *adj*

co·ed·u·ca·tion \,kō-\ *n* : education of the sexes together —**co·ed·u·ca·tion·al** *adj*

co·ef·fi·cient \,kōə'fishənt\ *n* **1** : number that is a multiplier of another **2** : number that serves as a measure of some property

co·erce \kō'ərs\ *vb* **-erced; -erc·ing** : force —**co·er·cion** \-'ərzhən, -shən\ *n* —**co·er·cive** \-'ərsiv\ *adj*

cof·fee \'kȯfē\ *n* : drink made from the roasted and ground seeds (**coffee**

beans) of a tropical shrub —**cof·fee·house** n —**cof·fee·pot** n

cof·fer \'kȯfər\ n : box for valuables

cof·fin \-fən\ n : box for burial

cog \'käg\ n : tooth on the rim of a gear —**cogged** \'kägd\ adj —**cog·wheel** n

co·gent \'kōjənt\ adj : compelling or convincing —**co·gen·cy** \-jənsē\ n

cog·i·tate \'käjə,tāt\ vb -**tat·ed**; -**tat·ing** : think over —**cog·i·ta·tion** \,käjə'tā-shən\ n —**cog·i·ta·tive** \'käjə,tātiv\ adj

co·gnac \'kōn,yak\ n : French brandy

cog·nate \'käg,nāt\ adj : related —**cog·nate** n

cog·ni·tion \käg'nishən\ n : act or process of knowing —**cog·ni·tive** \'kägnətiv\ adj

cog·ni·zance \'kägnəzəns\ n : notice or awareness —**cog·ni·zant** \'kägnəzənt\ adj

co·hab·it \kō'habət\ vb : live together as husband and wife —**co·hab·i·ta·tion** \-,habə'tāshən\ n

co·here \kō'hir\ vb -**hered**; -**her·ing** : stick together

co·her·ent \-'hirənt\ adj 1 : able to stick together 2 : logically consistent —**co·her·ence** \-əns\ n —**co·her·ent·ly** adv

co·he·sion \-'hēzhən\ n : a sticking together —**co·he·sive** \-siv\ adj —**co·he·sive·ly** adv —**co·he·sive·ness** n

co·hort \'kō,hȯrt\ n 1 : group of soldiers 2 : companion

coif·fure \kwä'fyu̇r\ n : hair style

coil \'kȯil\ vb : wind in a spiral ~ n : series of loops (as of rope)

coin \'kȯin\ n : piece of metal used as money ~ vb 1 : make (a coin) by stamping 2 : create —**coin·age** \-ij\ n —**coin·er** n

co·in·cide \,kōən'sīd, 'kōən,sīd\ vb -**cid·ed**; -**cid·ing** 1 : be in the same place 2 : happen at the same time 3 : be alike —**co·in·ci·dence** \kō-'insədəns\ n —**co·in·ci·dent** \-ənt\ adj —**co·in·ci·den·tal** \-,insə'dentᵊl\ adj

co·itus \'kōətəs\ n : sexual intercourse —**co·ital** \-ətᵊl\ adj

coke \'kōk\ n : fuel made by heating soft coal

co·la \'kōlə\ n : carbonated soft drink

col·an·der \'kələndər, 'käl-\ n : perforated utensil for draining food

cold \'kōld\ adj 1 : having a low or below normal temperature 2 : lacking warmth of feeling 3 : suffering from lack of warmth ~ n 1 : low temperature 2 : minor respiratory illness —**cold·ly** adv —**cold·ness** n —**in cold blood** : with premeditation

cold–blood·ed adj 1 : cruel or merciless 2 : having a body temperature that varies with the temperature of the environment

cole·slaw \'kōl,slȯ\ n : cabbage salad

col·ic \'kälik\ n : sharp abdominal pain —**col·icky** adj

col·i·se·um \,kälə'sēəm\ n : arena

col·lab·o·rate \kə'labə,rāt\ vb -**rat·ed**; -**rat·ing** 1 : work jointly with others 2 : help the enemy —**col·lab·o·ra·tion** \-,labə'rāshən\ n —**col·lab·o·ra·tor** \-'labə,rātər\ n

col·lapse \kə'laps\ vb -**lapsed**; -**laps·ing** 1 : fall in 2 : break down physically or mentally 3 : fold down ~ n : breakdown —**col·laps·ible** adj

col·lar \'kälər\ n : part of a garment around the neck ~ vb 1 : seize by the collar 2 : grab —**col·lar·less** adj

col·lar·bone n : bone joining the breastbone and the shoulder blade

col·lards \'kälərdz\ n pl : kale

col·late \kə'lāt; 'käl,āt, 'kōl-\ vb -**lat·ed**; -**lat·ing** 1 : compare carefully 2 : assemble in order

col·lat·er·al \kə'latərəl\ adj 1 : secondary 2 : descended from the same ancestors but not in the same line 3 : similar ~ n : property used as security for a loan

col·league \'käl,ēg\ n : associate

col·lect \kə'lekt\ vb 1 : bring, come, or gather together 2 : receive payment of ~ adv or adj : to be paid for by the receiver —**col·lect·ible, col·lect·able** adj —**col·lec·tion** \-'lekshən\ n —**col·lec·tor** \-'lektər\ n

col·lec·tive \-tiv\ adj : denoting or shared by a group ~ n : a cooperative unit —**col·lec·tive·ly** adv

col·lege \'kälij\ n : institution of higher learning granting a bachelor's degree —**col·le·gian** \kə'lējən\ n —**col·le·giate** \kə'lējət\ adj

col·lide \kə'līd\ vb -**lid·ed**; -**lid·ing** : strike together —**col·li·sion** \-'lizhən\ n

col·lie \'kälē\ n : large long-haired dog

col·loid \'käl,ȯid\ n : tiny particles in suspension in a fluid —**col·loi·dal** \kə'lȯidᵊl\ adj

col·lo·qui·al \kə'lōkwēəl\ adj : used in

informal conversation —**col·lo·qui·al·ism** \-ə,lizəm\ *n*

col·lo·quy \'käləkwē\ *n, pl* **-quies** : formal conversation or conference

col·lu·sion \kə'lüzhən\ *n* : secret cooperation for deceit —**col·lu·sive** \-'lüsiv\ *adj*

co·logne \kə'lōn\ *n* : perfumed liquid

¹co·lon \'kōlən\ *n, pl* **colons** *or* **co·la** \-lə\ : lower part of the large intestine —**co·lon·ic** \kō'länik\ *adj*

²colon *n, pl* **colons** : punctuation mark : used esp. to direct attention to following matter

col·o·nel \'kərnᵊl\ *n* : commissioned officer (as in the army) ranking next below a brigadier general

col·o·nize \'kälə,nīz\ *vb* **-nized; -niz·ing 1** : establish a colony in **2** : settle —**col·o·ni·za·tion** \,kälənə'zāshən\ *n* —**col·o·niz·er** *n*

col·on·nade \,kälə'nād\ *n* : row of supporting columns

col·o·ny \'kälənē\ *n, pl* **-nies 1** : people who inhabit a new territory or the territory itself **2** : animals of one kind (as bees) living together —**co·lo·nial** \kə'lōnēəl\ *adj or n* —**col·o·nist** \'kälənist\ *n*

col·or \'kələr\ *n* **1** : quality of visible things distinct from shape that results from light reflection **2** *pl* : flag **3** : liveliness ~ *vb* **1** : give color to **2** : blush —**col·or·fast** *adj* —**col·or·ful** *adj* —**col·or·less** *adj*

col·or–blind *adj* : unable to distinguish colors —**color blindness** *n*

col·ored \'kələrd\ *adj* **1** : having color **2** : of a race other than the white ~ *n, pl* **colored** *or* **coloreds** : colored person

co·los·sal \kə'läsəl\ *adj* : very large or great

co·los·sus \-əs\ *n, pl* **-si** \-'läs,ī\ : something of great size or scope

colt \'kōlt\ *n* : young male horse —**colt·ish** *adj*

col·umn \'käləm\ *n* **1** : vertical section of a printed page **2** : regular feature article (as in a newspaper) **3** : pillar **4** : row (as of soldiers) —**co·lum·nar** \kə'ləmnər\ *adj* —**col·um·nist** \'käləmnist\ *n*

co·ma \'kōmə\ *n* : deep prolonged unconsciousness —**co·ma·tose** \-,tōs, 'kämə-\ *adj*

comb \'kōm\ *n* **1** : toothed instrument for arranging the hair **2** : crest on a fowl's head —**comb** *vb* —**combed** \'kōmd\ *adj*

com·bat \kəm'bat, 'käm,bat\ *vb* **-bat·ed** *or* **-bat·ted; -bat·ing** *or* **-bat·ting** : fight —**com·bat** \'käm,bat\ *n* —**com·bat·ant** \kəm'batᵊnt *n* —**com·bat·ive** \kəm'bativ\ *adj*

com·bi·na·tion \,kämbə'nāshən\ *n* **1** : process or result of combining **2** : code for opening a lock

com·bine \kəm'bīn\ *vb* **-bined; -bin·ing** : join together ~ \'käm,bīn\ *n* **1** : association for business or political advantage **2** : harvesting machine

com·bus·ti·ble \kəm'bəstəbəl\ *adj* : apt to catch fire —**com·bus·ti·bil·i·ty** \-,bəstə'bilətē\ *n* —**combustible** *n*

com·bus·tion \-'bəschən\ *n* : process of burning

come \'kəm\ *vb* **came** \'kām\; **come; com·ing 1** : move toward or arrive at something **2** : reach a state **3** : originate or exist **4** : amount —**come clean** *vb* : confess —**come into** *vb* : acquire, achieve —**come off** *vb* : succeed —**come to** *vb* : regain consciousness —**come to pass** : happen —**come to terms** : reach an agreement

come·back *n* **1** : retort **2** : return to a former position —**come back** *vb*

co·me·di·an \kə'mēdēən\ *n* **1** : comic actor **2** : funny person **3** : entertainer specializing in comedy

co·me·di·enne \-,mēdē'en\ *n* : a woman who is a comedian

com·e·dy \'kämədē\ *n, pl* **-dies 1** : an amusing play **2** : humorous entertainment

come·ly \'kəmlē\ *adj* **-li·er; -est** : attractive —**come·li·ness** *n*

com·et \'kämət\ *n* : small bright celestial body having a tail

com·fort \'kəmfərt\ *n* **1** : consolation **2** : well-being or something that gives it ~ *vb* **1** : give hope to **2** : console —**com·fort·able** \'kəmftəbəl, 'kəmfərt-\ *adj* —**com·fort·ably** \-blē\ *adv* —**com·fort·less** *adj*

com·fort·er \'kəmfərtər\ *n* **1** : one that comforts **2** : quilt

com·ic \'kämik\ *adj* **1** : relating to comedy **2** : funny ~ *n* **1** : comedian **2** : sequence of cartoons —**com·i·cal** *adj*

com·ing \'kəmiŋ\ *adj* : next

com·ma \'kämə\ *n* : punctuation mark , used esp. to separate sentence parts

com·mand \kə'mand\ vb 1 : order 2 : control ~ n 1 : act of commanding 2 : an order given 3 : mastery 4 : troops under a commander —**com·man·dant** \'kämən,dant, -,dänt\ n

com·man·deer \,kämən'dir\ vb : seize by force

com·mand·er \kə'mandər\ n 1 : officer commanding an army or subdivision of an army 2 : commissioned officer in the navy ranking next below a captain

com·mand·ment \-'mandmənt\ n : order

command sergeant major n : non-commissioned officer in the army ranking above a first sergeant

com·mem·o·rate \kə'memə,rāt\ vb -rat·ed; -rat·ing : celebrate or honor —**com·mem·o·ra·tion** \-,memə-'rāshən\ n —**com·mem·o·ra·tive** \-'memrətiv, -'memə,rāt-\ adj

com·mence \kə'mens\ vb -menced; -menc·ing : start

com·mence·ment \-mənt\ n 1 : beginning 2 : graduation ceremony

com·mend \kə'mend\ vb 1 : entrust 2 : recommend 3 : praise —**commend·able** \-əbəl\ adj —**com·men·da·tion** \,kämən'dāshən, -,en-\ n

com·men·su·rate \kə'mensərət, -'mench-\ adj : equal in measure or extent

com·ment \'käm,ent\ n : statement of opinion or remark —**comment** vb

com·men·tary \-ən,terē\ n, pl -tar·ies : series of comments

com·men·ta·tor \-ən,tātər\ n : one who discusses news

com·merce \'kämərs\ n : business

com·mer·cial \kə'mərshəl\ adj : designed for profit or for mass appeal ~ n : broadcast advertisement —**com·mer·cial·ize** \-,īz\ vb —**com·mer·cial·ly** \-ē\ adv

com·min·gle \kə'miŋgəl\ vb : mix

com·mis·er·ate \kə'mizə,rāt\ vb -at·ed; -at·ing : sympathize —**com·mis·er·a·tion** \-,mizə'rāshən\ n

com·mis·sary \'kämə,serē\ n, pl -sar·ies : store esp. for military personnel

com·mis·sion \kə'mishən\ n 1 : order granting power or rank 2 : panel to judge, approve, or act 3 : the doing of an act 4 : agent's fee ~ vb 1 : confer rank or authority to or for 2 : request something be done

com·mis·sion·er \-shənər\ n 1 : member of a commission 2 : head of a government department

com·mit \kə'mit\ vb -tt- 1 : turn over to someone for safekeeping or confinement 2 : perform or do 3 : pledge —**com·mit·ment** n

com·mit·tee \kə'mitē\ n : panel that examines or acts on something

com·mo·di·ous \kə'mōdēəs\ adj : spacious

com·mod·i·ty \kə'mädətē\ n, pl -ties : article for sale

com·mo·dore \'kämə,dōr\ n 1 : former commissioned officer in the navy ranking next below a rear admiral 2 : officer commanding a group of merchant ships

com·mon \'kämən\ adj 1 : public 2 : shared by several 3 : widely known, found, or observed 4 : ordinary ~ n : community land —**com·mon·ly** adv —**in common** : shared together

com·mon·place \'kämən,plās\ n : cliché ~ adj : ordinary

common sense n : good judgment

com·mon·weal \-,wēl\ n : general welfare

com·mon·wealth \-,welth\ n : state

com·mo·tion \kə'mōshən\ n : disturbance

¹**com·mune** \kə'myün\ vb -muned; -mun·ing : communicate intimately

²**com·mune** \'käm,yün\ n : community that shares all ownership and duties —**com·mu·nal** \-ᵊl\ adj

com·mu·ni·cate \kə'myünə,kāt\ vb -cat·ed; -cat·ing 1 : make known 2 : transmit 3 : exchange information or opinions —**com·mu·ni·ca·ble** \-'myünikəbəl\ adj —**com·mu·ni·ca·tion** \-,myünə'kāshən\ n —**com·mu·ni·ca·tive** \-'myüni,kātiv, -kət-\ adj

Com·mu·nion \kə'myünyən\ n : Christian sacrament of partaking of bread and wine

com·mu·ni·qué \kə'myünə,kā, -,myünə'kā\ n : official bulletin

com·mu·nism \'kämyə,nizəm\ n 1 : social organization in which goods are held in common 2 cap : political doctrine based on revolutionary Marxist socialism —**com·mu·nist** \-nist\ n or adj, often cap —**com·mu·nis·tic** \,kämyə'nistik\ adj, often cap

com·mu·ni·ty \kə'myünətē\ n, pl -ties

: body of people living in the same place under the same laws

com·mute \kə'myüt\ *vb* **-mut·ed; -mut·ing 1** : reduce (a punishment) **2** : travel back and forth regularly ~ *n* : trip made in commuting —**com·mu·ta·tion** \,kämyə'tāshən\ *n* —**com·mut·er** *n*

¹**com·pact** \kəm'pakt, 'käm,pakt\ *adj* **1** : hard **2** : small or brief ~ *vb* : pack together ~ \'käm,pakt\ *n* **1** : cosmetics case **2** : small car —**com·pact·ly** *adv* —**com·pact·ness** *n*

²**com·pact** \'käm,pakt\ *n* : agreement

compact disc *n* : plastic-coated disc with laser-readable recorded music

com·pan·ion \kəm'panyən\ *n* **1** : close friend **2** : one of a pair —**com·pan·ion·able** *adj* —**com·pan·ion·ship** *n*

com·pa·ny \'kəmpənē\ *n, pl* **-nies 1** : business organization **2** : group of performers **3** : guests **4** : infantry unit

com·par·a·tive \kəm'parətiv\ *adj* **1** : relating to or being an adjective or adverb form that denotes increase **2** : relative —**comparative** *n* —**com·par·a·tive·ly** *adv*

com·pare \kəm'par\ *vb* **-pared; -par·ing 1** : represent as similar **2** : check for likenesses or differences ~ *n* : comparison —**com·pa·ra·ble** \'kämprəbəl\ *adj*

com·par·i·son \kəm'parəsən\ *n* **1** : act of comparing **2** : change in the form and meaning of an adjective or adverb to show different levels of quality, quantity, or relation

com·part·ment \kəm'pärtmənt\ *n* : section or room

com·pass \'kəmpəs, 'käm-\ *n* **1** : scope **2** : device for drawing circles **3** : device for determining direction

com·pas·sion \kəm'pashən\ *n* : pity —**com·pas·sion·ate** \-ənət\ *adj*

com·pat·i·ble \-'patəbəl\ *adj* : harmonious —**com·pat·i·bil·i·ty** \-,patə-'bilətē\ *n*

com·pa·tri·ot \kəm'pātrēət, -trē,ät\ *n* : fellow countryman

com·pel \kəm'pel\ *vb* **-ll-** : cause through necessity

com·pen·di·ous \kəm'pendēəs\ *adj* **1** : concise and comprehensive **2** : comprehensive

com·pen·di·um \-'pendēəm\ *n, pl* **-di·ums** *or* **-dia** \-dēə\ : summary

com·pen·sate \'kämpən,sāt\ *vb* **-sat·ed;**

-sat·ing 1 : offset or balance **2** : repay —**com·pen·sa·tion** \,kämpən'sāshən\ *n* —**com·pen·sa·to·ry** \kəm'pensə-,tōrē\ *adj*

com·pete \kəm'pēt\ *vb* **-pet·ed; -pet·ing** : strive to win —**com·pe·ti·tion** \,kämpə'tishən\ *n* —**com·pet·i·tive** \kəm'petətiv\ *adj* —**com·pet·i·tive·ness** *n* —**com·pet·i·tor** \kəm'petətər\ *n*

com·pe·tent \'kämpətənt\ *adj* : capable —**com·pe·tence** \-əns\ *n* —**com·pe·ten·cy** \-ənsē\ *n*

com·pile \kəm'pīl\ *vb* **-piled; -pil·ing** : collect or compose from several sources —**com·pi·la·tion** \,kämpə-'lāshən\ *n* —**com·pil·er** \kəm'pīlər\ *n*

com·pla·cen·cy \kəm'plāsənsē\ *n* : self-satisfaction —**com·pla·cent** \-ənt\ *adj*

com·plain \kəm'plān\ *vb* **1** : express grief, pain, or discontent **2** : make an accusation —**com·plain·ant** *n* —**com·plain·er** *n*

com·plaint \-'plānt\ *n* **1** : expression of grief or discontent **2** : ailment **3** : formal accusation

com·ple·ment \'kämpləmənt\ *n* **1** : something that completes **2** : full number or amount ~ \-,ment\ *vb* : complete —**com·ple·men·ta·ry** \,kämplə'mentərē\ *adj*

com·plete \kəm'plēt\ *adj* **-plet·er; -est 1** : having all parts **2** : finished **3** : total ~ *vb* **-plet·ed; -plet·ing 1** : make whole **2** : finish —**com·plete·ly** *adv* —**com·plete·ness** *n* —**com·ple·tion** \-'plēshən\ *n*

com·plex \käm'pleks, kəm-; 'käm-,pleks\ *adj* **1** : having many parts **2** : intricate ~ \'käm,pleks\ *n* : psychological problem —**com·plex·i·ty** \kəm'pleksətē, käm-\ *n*

com·plex·ion \kəm'plekshən\ *n* : hue or appearance of the skin esp. of the face —**com·plex·ioned** *adj*

com·pli·cate \'kämplə,kāt\ *vb* **-cat·ed; -cat·ing** : make complex or hard to understand —**com·pli·cat·ed** \-əd\ *adj* —**com·pli·ca·tion** \,kämplə-'kāshən\ *n*

com·plic·i·ty \kəm'plisətē\ *n, pl* **-ties** : participation in guilt

com·pli·ment \'kämpləmənt\ *n* **1** : flattering remark **2** *pl* : greeting ~ \-,ment-əs\ *vb* : pay a compliment to

com·pli·men·ta·ry \,kämplə'mentərē\ adj 1 : praising 2 : free

com·ply \kəm'plī\ vb **-plied; -ply·ing** : conform or yield **—com·pli·ance** \-əns\ n **—com·pli·ant** \-ənt\ n

com·po·nent \kəm'pōnənt, 'käm,pō-\ n : part of something larger ~ adj : serving as a component

com·port \kəm'pōrt\ vb 1 : agree 2 : behave **—com·port·ment** \-mənt\ n

com·pose \kəm'pōz\ vb **-posed; -pos·ing** 1 : create (as by writing) or put together 2 : calm 3 : set type **—com·pos·er** n **—com·po·si·tion** \,kämpə'zishən\ n

com·pos·ite \käm'päzət, kəm-\ adj : made up of diverse parts **—composite** n

com·post \'käm,pōst\ n : decayed organic fertilizing material

com·po·sure \kəm'pōzhər\ n : calmness

com·pote \'käm,pōt\ n : fruits cooked in syrup

¹**com·pound** \'käm,paúnd, kəm'paúnd\ vb 1 : combine or add 2 : pay (interest) on principal and accrued interest ~ \'käm,paúnd\ adj : made up of 2 or more parts ~ \'käm,paúnd\ n : something that is compound

²**com·pound** \'käm,paúnd\ n : enclosure

com·pre·hend \,kämpri'hend\ vb 1 : understand 2 : include **—com·pre·hen·si·ble** \-'hensəbəl\ adj**—com·pre·hen·sion** \-'henchən\ n **—com·pre·hen·sive** \-siv\ adj

com·press \kəm'pres\ vb : squeeze together ~ \'käm,pres\ n : pad for pressing on a wound **—com·pres·sion** \-'preshən\ n **—com·pres·sor** \-'presər\ n

compressed air n : air under pressure greater than that of the atmosphere

com·prise \kəm'prīz\ vb **-prised; -pris·ing** 1 : contain or cover 2 : be made up of

com·pro·mise \'kämprə,mīz\ vb **-mised; -mis·ing** : settle differences by mutual concessions **—compromise** n

comp·trol·ler \kən'trōlər, 'kämp,trō-\ n : financial officer

com·pul·sion \kəm'pəlshən\ n 1 : coercion 2 : irresistible impulse **—com·pul·sive** \-siv\ adj **—com·pul·so·ry** \-'pəlsərē\ adj

com·punc·tion \-'pənkshən\ n : remorse

com·pute \-'pyüt\ vb **-put·ed; -put·ing** : calculate **—com·pu·ta·tion** \,kämpyú'tāshən\ n

com·put·er \kəm'pyütər\ n : electronic data processing machine **—com·put·er·i·za·tion** \-,pyütərə'zāshən\ n **—com·put·er·ize** \-'pyütə,rīz\ vb

com·rade \'käm,rad, -rəd\ n : companion **—com·rade·ship** n

¹**con** \'kän\ adv : against ~ n : opposing side or person

²**con** vb **-nn-** : swindle

con·cave \kän'kāv, 'kän,kāv\ adj : curved like the inside of a sphere **—con·cav·i·ty** \kän'kavətē\ n

con·ceal \kən'sēl\ vb : hide **—con·ceal·ment** n

con·cede \-'sēd\ vb **-ced·ed; -ced·ing** : grant

con·ceit \-'sēt\ n : excessively high opinion of oneself **—con·ceit·ed** \-əd\ adj

con·ceive \-'sēv\ vb **-ceived; -ceiv·ing** 1 : become pregnant 2 : think of **—con·ceiv·able** \-'sēvəbəl\ adj **—con·ceiv·ably** \-blē\ adv

con·cen·trate \'känsən,trāt\ vb **-trat·ed; -trat·ing** 1 : gather together 2 : make stronger 3 : fix one's attention ~ n : something concentrated **—con·cen·tra·tion** \,känsən'trāshən\ n

con·cen·tric \kən'sentrik\ adj : having a common center

con·cept \'kän,sept\ n : thought or idea

con·cep·tion \kən'sepshən\ n 1 : act of conceiving 2 : idea

con·cern \kən'sərn\ vb 1 : relate to 2 : involve ~ n 1 : affair 2 : worry 3 : business **—con·cerned** \-'sərnd\ adj **—con·cern·ing** \-'sərniŋ\ prep

con·cert \'kän,sərt\ n 1 : agreement or joint action 2 : public performance of music **—con·cert·ed** \kən'sərtəd\ adj

con·cer·ti·na \,känsər'tēnə\ n : accordionlike instrument

con·cer·to \kən'chertō\ n, pl **-ti** \-tē\ or **-tos** : orchestral work with solo instruments

con·ces·sion \-'seshən\ n 1 : act of conceding 2 : something conceded 3 : right to do business on a property

conch \'käŋk, 'känch\ n, pl **conchs** \'käŋks\ or **conch·es** \'känchəz\ : large spiral-shelled marine mollusk

con·cil·ia·to·ry \kən'silēə,tōrē\ adj : mollifying

con·cise \kən'sīs\ adj : said in few words **—con·cise·ly** adv **—con·cise·ness** n **—con·ci·sion** \kən'sizhən\ n

con·clave \'kän,klāv\ n : private meeting

con·clude \kən'klüd\ vb -clud·ed; -clud·ing 1 : end 2 : decide —con·clu·sion \-'klüzhən\ n —con·clu·sive \-siv\ adj —con·clu·sive·ly adv

con·coct \kən'käkt, kän-\ vb : prepare or devise —con·coc·tion \-'käkshən\ n

con·com·i·tant \-'kämətənt\ adj : accompanying —concomitant n

con·cord \'kän,kord, 'käŋ-\ n : agreement

con·cor·dance \kən'kord³ns\ n 1 : agreement 2 : index of words —con·cor·dant \-³nt\ adj

con·course \'kän,kōrs\ n : open space where crowds gather

con·crete \kän'krēt, 'kän,krēt\ adj 1 : naming something real 2 : actual or substantial 3 : made of concrete ~ \'kän,krēt, kän'krēt\ n : hard building material made of cement, sand, gravel, and water

con·cre·tion \kän'krēshən\ n : hard mass

con·cu·bine \'käŋkyù,bīn\ n : mistress

con·cur \kən'kər\ vb -rr- : agree —con·cur·rence \-'kərəns\ n

con·cur·rent \-ənt\ adj : happening at the same time

con·cus·sion \kən'kəshən\ n 1 : shock 2 : brain injury from a blow

con·demn \-'dem\ vb 1 : declare to be wrong, guilty, or unfit for use 2 : sentence —con·dem·na·tion \,kän,dem'nāshən\ n

con·dense \kən'dens\ vb -densed; -dens·ing 1 : make or become more compact 2 : change from vapor to liquid —con·den·sa·tion \,kän,den-'sāshən, -dən-\ n —con·dens·er n

con·de·scend \,kändi'send\ vb 1 : lower oneself 2 : act haughtily —con·de·scen·sion \-'senchən\ n

con·di·ment \'kändəmənt\ n : pungent seasoning

con·di·tion \kən'dishən\ n 1 : necessary situation or stipulation 2 pl : state of affairs 3 : state of being ~ vb : put into proper condition —con·di·tion·al \kən'dishənəl\ adj —con·di·tion·al·ly \-ē\ adv

con·do·lence \kən'dōləns\ n : expression of sympathy—usu. pl.

con·do·min·i·um \,kändə'minēəm\ n, pl -ums : individually owned apartment

con·done \kən'dōn\ vb -doned; -don·ing : overlook or forgive

con·dor \'kändər, -,dor\ n : large western American vulture

con·du·cive \kən'düsiv, -'dyü-\ adj : tending to help or promote

con·duct \'kän,dəkt\ n 1 : management 2 : behavior ~ \kən'dəkt\ vb 1 : guide 2 : manage or direct 3 : be a channel for 4 : behave —con·duc·tion \-'dəkshən\ n —con·duc·tive \-'dək-tiv\ adj —con·duc·tiv·i·ty \,kän,dək-'tivətē\ n —con·duc·tor \-'dəktər\ n

con·duit \'kän,düət, -,dyü-\ n : channel (as for conveying fluid)

cone \'kōn\ n 1 : scaly fruit of pine and related trees 2 : solid figure having a circular base and tapering sides

con·fec·tion \kən'fekshən\ n : sweet dish or candy —con·fec·tion·er \-shənər\ n

con·fed·er·a·cy \kən'fedərəsē\ n, pl -cies 1 : league 2 cap : 11 southern states that seceded from the U.S. in 1860 and 1861

con·fed·er·ate \-rət\ adj 1 : united in a league 2 cap : relating to the Confederacy ~ n 1 : ally 2 cap : adherent of the Confederacy ~ \-'fedə,rāt\ vb -at·ed; -at·ing : unite —con·fed·er·a·tion \-,fedə'rāshən\ n

con·fer \kən'fər\ vb -rr- : give 2 : meet to exchange views —con·fer·ee \,känfə'rē\ n —con·fer·ence \'känfərəns\ n

con·fess \kən'fes\ vb 1 : acknowledge or disclose one's misdeed, fault, or sin 2 : declare faith in —con·fes·sion \-'feshən\ n —con·fes·sion·al \-'feshənəl\ n or adj

con·fes·sor \kən'fesər, 2 also 'kän,fes-\ n 1 : one who confesses 2 : priest who hears confessions

con·fet·ti \kən'fetē\ n : bits of paper or ribbon thrown in celebration

con·fi·dant \'känfə,dant, -,dänt\ n : one to whom secrets are confided

con·fide \kən'fīd\ vb -fid·ed; -fid·ing 1 : share private thoughts 2 : reveal in confidence

con·fi·dence \'känfədəns\ n 1 : trust 2 : self-assurance 3 : something confided —con·fi·dent \-ənt\ adj —con·fi·den·tial \,känfə'denchəl\ adj —con·fi·den·tial·ly \-ē\ adv —con·fi·dent·ly adv

con·fig·u·ra·tion \kən,figyə'rāshən\ n : arrangement

con·fine \kən'fīn\ vb -fined; -fin·ing 1 : restrain or restrict to a limited area 2 : imprison —con·fine·ment n —con·fin·er n

confines \'kän,fīnz\ n pl : bounds

con·firm \kən'fərm\ vb 1 : ratify 2 : verify 3 : admit as a full member of a church or synagogue —con·fir·ma·tion \,känfər'māshən\ n

con·fis·cate \'känfə,skāt\ vb -cat·ed; -cat·ing : take by authority —con·fis·ca·tion \,känfə'skāshən\ n —con·fis·ca·to·ry \kən'fiskə,tōrē\ adj

con·fla·gra·tion \,känflə'grāshən\ n : great fire

con·flict \'kän,flikt\ n 1 : war 2 : clash of ideas ~ \kən'flikt\ vb : clash

con·form \kən'fórm\ vb 1 : make or be like 2 : obey —con·for·mi·ty \kən'fórmətē\ n

con·found \kən'faúnd, kän-\ vb : confuse

con·front \kən'frənt\ vb : oppose or face —con·fron·ta·tion \,känfrən-'tā-shən\ n

con·fuse \kən'fyüz\ vb -fused; -fus·ing 1 : make mentally uncertain 2 : jumble —con·fu·sion \-'fyüzhən\ n

con·fute \-'fyüt\ vb -fut·ed; -fut·ing : overwhelm by argument

con·geal \kən'jēl\ vb 1 : freeze 2 : become thick and solid

con·ge·nial \kən'jēnēəl\ adj : kindred or agreeable —con·ge·ni·al·i·ty n

con·gen·i·tal \kən'jenət°l\ adj : existing from birth

con·gest \kən'jest\ vb : overcrowd or overfill —con·ges·tion \-'jeschən\ n —con·ges·tive \-'jestiv\ adj

con·glom·er·ate \kən'glämərət\ adj : made up of diverse parts ~ \-ə,rāt\ vb -at·ed; -at·ing : form into a mass ~ \-ərət\ n : diversified corporation —con·glom·er·a·tion \-,glämə'rā-shən\ n

con·grat·u·late \kən'gracha,lāt, -'graj-\ vb -lat·ed; -lat·ing : express pleasure to for good fortune —con·grat·u·la·tion \-,gracha'lāshən, -,graj-\ n —con·grat·u·la·to·ry \-'grachələ,tōrē-'graj-\ adj

con·gre·gate \'käŋgri,gāt\ vb -gat·ed; -gat·ing : assemble

con·gre·ga·tion \,käŋgri'gāshən\ n 1 : assembly of people at worship 2 : religious group —con·gre·ga·tion·al \-shənəl\ adj

con·gress \'käŋgrəs\ n : assembly of delegates or of senators and representatives —con·gres·sio·nal \kən-'greshənəl, kän-\ adj —con·gress·man \'käŋgrəsmən\ n —con·gress·wom·an \ n

con·gru·ence \kən'grüəns, 'käŋgrə-wəns\ n : likeness —con·gru·ent \-ənt\ adj

con·gru·ity \kən'grüətē, kän-\ n : correspondence between things —con·gru·ous \'käŋgrəwəs\ adj

con·ic \'känik\ adj : relating to or like a cone —con·i·cal \-ikəl\ adj

co·ni·fer \'känəfər, 'kōn-\ n : cone-bearing tree —co·nif·er·ous \kə'nifərəs\ adj

con·jec·ture \kən'jekchər\ n or vb : guess —con·jec·tur·al \-əl\ adj

con·join \kən'jóin\ vb : join together —con·joint \-'jóint\ adj

con·ju·gal \'känjigəl, kən'jü-\ adj : relating to marriage

con·ju·gate \'känjə,gāt\ vb -gat·ed; -gat·ing : give the inflected forms of (a verb) —con·ju·ga·tion \,känjə-'gāshən\ n

con·junc·tion \kən'jəŋkshən\ n 1 : combination 2 : occurrence at the same time 3 : a word that joins other words together —con·junc·tive \-tiv\ adj

con·jure \'känjər, 'kən-\ vb -jured; -jur·ing 1 : summon by sorcery 2 : practice sleight of hand 3 : entreat —con·jur·er, con·ju·ror \'känjərər, 'kən-\ n

con·nect \kə'nekt\ vb : join or associate —con·nect·able adj —con·nec·tion \-'nekshən\ n —con·nec·tive \-tiv\ n or adj —con·nec·tor n

con·nive \kə'nīv\ vb -nived; -niv·ing 1 : pretend ignorance of wrongdoing 2 : cooperate secretly —con·niv·ance n

con·nois·seur \,känə'sər, -'súr\ n : expert judge esp. of art

con·note \kə'nōt\ vb -not·ed; -not·ing : suggest additional meaning —con·no·ta·tion \,känə'tāshən\ n

con·nu·bi·al \kə'nübēəl, -'nyü-\ adj : relating to marriage

con·quer \'käŋkər\ vb : defeat or overcome —con·quer·or \-kərər\ n

con·quest \'kän,kwest, 'käŋ-\ n 1 : act of conquering 2 : something conquered

con·science \'känchəns\ n : awareness of right and wrong

con·sci·en·tious \,känchē'enchəs\ adj

: honest and hard-working —**con·sci·en·tious·ly** adv

con·scious \'känchəs\ adj 1 : aware 2 : mentally awake or alert 3 : intentional —**con·scious·ly** adv —**con·scious·ness** n

con·script \kən'skript\ vb : draft for military service —**con·script** \'kän-ˌskript\ n —**con·scrip·tion** \kən-'skripshən\ n

con·se·crate \'känsəˌkrāt\ vb -**crat·ed**; -**crat·ing** 1 : declare sacred 2 : devote to a solemn purpose —**con·se·cra·tion** \ˌkänsə'krāshən\ n

con·sec·u·tive \kən'sekyətiv\ adj : following in order —**con·sec·u·tive·ly** adv

con·sen·sus \-'sensəs\ n 1 : agreement in opinion 2 : collective opinion

con·sent \-'sent\ vb : give permission or approval —**consent** n

con·se·quence \'känsəˌkwens\ n 1 : result or effect 2 : importance —**con·se·quent** \-kwənt, -ˌkwent\ adj —**con·se·quent·ly** adv

con·se·quen·tial \ˌkänsə'kwenchəl\ adj : important

con·ser·va·tion \ˌkänsər'vāshən\ n : planned management of natural resources —**con·ser·va·tion·ist** \-shə-nist\ n

con·ser·va·tive \kən'sərvətiv\ adj 1 : disposed to maintain the status quo 2 : cautious —**con·ser·va·tism** \-vəˌtizəm\ n —**conservative** n —**con·ser·va·tive·ly** adv

con·ser·va·to·ry \kən'sərvəˌtōrē\ n, pl -**ries** : school for art or music

con·serve \-'sərv\ vb -**served**; -**serv·ing** : keep from wasting ~ \'kän,sərv\ n : candied fruit or fruit preserves

con·sid·er \kən'sidər\ vb 1 : think about 2 : give thoughtful attention to 3 : think that —**con·sid·er·ate** \-'sidər-ət\ adj —**con·sid·er·a·tion** \-,sidə-'rāshən\ n

con·sid·er·able \-'sidərəbəl\ adj 1 : significant 2 : noticeably large —**con·sid·er·a·bly** \-blē\ adv

con·sid·er·ing prep : taking notice of

con·sign \kən'sīn\ vb 1 : transfer 2 : send to an agent for sale —**con·sign·ee** \ˌkänsə'nē, -ˌsī-; kənˌsī-\ n —**con·sign·ment** \kən'sīnmənt\ n —**con·sign·or** \ˌkänsə'nȯr, -ˌsī-; kənˌsī-\ n

con·sist \kən'sist\ vb 1 : be inherent —

used with in 2 : be made up —used with of

con·sis·ten·cy \-'sistənsē\ n, pl -**cies** 1 : degree of thickness or firmness 2 : quality of being consistent

con·sis·tent \-tənt\ adj : being steady and regular —**con·sis·tent·ly** adv

¹**con·sole** \kən'sōl\ vb -**soled**; -**sol·ing** : soothe the grief of —**con·so·la·tion** \ˌkänsə'lāshən\ n

²**con·sole** \'känˌsōl\ n : cabinet or part with controls

con·sol·i·date \kən'sälə,dāt\ vb -**dat·ed**; -**dat·ing** : unite or compact —**con·sol·i·da·tion** \-ˌsälə'dāshən\ n

con·som·mé \ˌkänsə'mā\ n : clear soup

con·so·nance \'känsənəns\ n : agreement or harmony —**con·so·nant** \-nənt\ adj —**con·so·nant·ly** adv

con·so·nant \-nənt\ n 1 : speech sound marked by constriction or closure in the breath channel 2 : letter other than a, e, i, o, and u —**con·so·nan·tal** \ˌkänsə'nantəl\ adj

con·sort \'känˌsȯrt\ n : spouse ~ \kən'sȯrt\ vb : keep company

con·spic·u·ous \kən'spikyəwəs\ adj : very noticeable —**con·spic·u·ous·ly** adv

con·spire \kən'spīr\ vb -**spired**; -**spir·ing** : secretly plan an unlawful act —**con·spir·a·cy** \-'spirəsē\ n —**con·spir·a·tor** \-'spirətər\ n —**con·spir·a·to·ri·al** \-ˌspirə'tōrēəl\ adj

con·sta·ble \'känstəbəl, 'kän-\ n : police officer

con·stab·u·lary \kən'stabyəˌlerē\ n, pl -**lar·ies** : police force

con·stant \'känstənt\ adj 1 : steadfast or faithful 2 : not varying 3 : continually recurring ~ n : something unchanging —**con·stan·cy** \-stənsē\ n —**con·stant·ly** adv

con·stel·la·tion \ˌkänstə'lāshən\ n : group of stars

con·ster·na·tion \-stər'nāshən\ n : amazed dismay

con·sti·pa·tion \-stə'pāshən\ n : difficulty of defecation —**con·sti·pate** \'känstəˌpāt\ vb

con·stit·u·ent \kən'stichəwənt\ adj 1 : component 2 : having power to elect ~ n 1 : component part 2 : one who may vote for a representative —**con·stit·u·en·cy** \-wənsē\ n

con·sti·tute \'känstəˌtüt, -ˌtyüt\ vb

-tut·ed; -tut·ing 1 : establish 2 : be all or a basic part of

con·sti·tu·tion \,känstə'tüshən, -'tyü-\ n 1 : physical composition or structure 2 : the basic law of an organized body or the document containing it —con·sti·tu·tion·al \-əl\ adj —con·sti·tu·tion·al·i·ty \-,tüshə'nalətē, -,tyü-\ n

con·strain \kən'strān\ vb 1 : compel 2 : confine 3 : restrain —con·straint \-'strānt\ n

con·strict \-'strikt\ vb : draw or squeeze together —con·stric·tion \-'strik-shən\ n —con·stric·tive \-'striktiv\ adj

con·struct \kən'strəkt\ vb : build or make —con·struc·tion \-'strəkshən\ n —con·struc·tive \-tiv\ adj

con·strue \kən'strü\ vb -strued; -stru·ing : explain or interpret

con·sul \'känsəl\ n 1 : Roman magistrate 2 : government commercial official in a foreign country —con·sul·ar \-sələr\ adj —con·sul·ate \-lət\ n

con·sult \kən'səlt\ vb 1 : ask the advice or opinion of 2 : confer —con·sul·tant \-ənt\ n —con·sul·ta·tion \,kän-səl'tāshən\ n

con·sume \kən'süm\ vb -sumed; -sum·ing : eat or use up —con·sum·able adj —con·sum·er n

con·sum·mate \kən'səmət\ adj : complete or perfect ~ \'känsə,māt\ vb -mat·ed; -mat·ing : make complete —con·sum·ma·tion \,känsə'māshən\ n

con·sump·tion \kən'səmpshən\ n 1 : act of consuming 2 : use of goods 3 : tuberculosis —con·sump·tive \-tiv\ adj or n

con·tact \'kän,takt\ n 1 : a touching 2 : association or relationship 3 : connection or communication ~ vb 1 : come or bring into contact 2 : communicate with

con·ta·gion \kən'tājən\ n 1 : spread of disease by contact 2 : disease spread by contact —con·ta·gious \-jəs\ adj

con·tain \-'tān\ vb 1 : enclose or include 2 : have or hold within 3 : restrain —con·tain·er n —con·tain·ment n

con·tam·i·nate \kən'tamə,nāt\ vb -nat·ed; -nat·ing : soil or infect by contact or association —con·tam·i·na·tion \-,tamə'nāshən\ n

con·tem·plate \'käntəm,plāt\ vb -pla·ted; -plat·ing : view or consider thoughtfully —con·tem·pla·tion \,käntəm'plāshən\ n —con·tem·pla·tive \kən'templətiv; 'käntəm,plāt-\ adj

con·tem·po·ra·ne·ous \kən,tempə-'rānēəs\ adj : contemporary

con·tem·po·rary \-'tempə,rerē\ adj 1 : occurring or existing at the same time 2 : of the same age —contemporary n

con·tempt \kən'tempt\ n 1 : feeling of scorn 2 : state of being despised 3 : disobedience to a court or legislature —con·tempt·ible \-'temptəbəl\ adj

con·temp·tu·ous \-'tempchəwəs\ adj : feeling or expressing contempt —con·temp·tu·ous·ly adv

con·tend \-'tend\ vb 1 : strive against rivals or difficulties 2 : argue 3 : maintain or claim —con·tend·er n

¹con·tent \kən'tent\ adj : satisfied ~ vb : satisfy ~ n : ease of mind —con·tent·ed adj —con·tent·ed·ly adv —con·tent·ed·ness n —con·tent·ment n

²con·tent \'kän,tent\ n 1 pl : something contained 2 pl : subject matter (as of a book) 3 : essential meaning 4 : proportion contained

con·ten·tion \kən'tenchən\ n : state of contending —con·ten·tious \-chəs\ adj —con·ten·tious·ly adv

con·test \kən'test\ vb : dispute or challenge ~ \'kän,test\ n 1 : struggle 2 : game —con·test·able \kən'testəbəl\ adj —con·tes·tant \-'testənt\ n

con·text \'kän,tekst\ n : words surrounding a word or phrase

con·tig·u·ous \kən'tigyəwəs\ adj : connected to or adjoining —con·ti·gu·i·ty \,käntə'gyüətē\ n

con·ti·nence \'känt°nəns\ n : self-restraint —con·ti·nent \-ənt\ adj

con·ti·nent \'känt°nənt\ n : great division of land on the globe —con·ti·nen·tal \,känt°n'ent°l\ adj

con·tin·gen·cy \kən'tinjənsē\ n, pl -cies : possible event

con·tin·gent \-jənt\ adj : dependent on something else ~ n : a quota from an area or group

con·tin·u·al \kən'tinyəwəl\ adj 1 : continuous 2 : steadily recurring —con·tin·u·al·ly \-ē\ adv

con·tin·ue \kən'tinyü\ vb -tin·ued; -tinu·ing 1 : remain in a place or condition 2 : endure 3 : resume after an intermission 4 : extend —

con·tin·u·ance \-yəwəns\ n —con·tin·u·a·tion \-,tinyə'wāshən\ n

con·tin·u·ous \-'tinyəwəs\ adj : continuing without interruption —con·ti·nu·ity \,käntᵊn'üətē, -'yü-\ n —con·tin·u·ous·ly adv

con·tort \kən'tórt\ vb : twist out of shape —con·tor·tion \-'tórshən\ n

con·tour \'kän,tùr\ n 1 : outline 2 pl : shape

con·tra·band \'käntrə,band\ n : illegal goods

con·tra·cep·tion \,käntrə'sepshən\ n : prevention of conception —con·tra·cep·tive \-'septiv\ adj or n

con·tract \'kän,trakt\ n : binding agreement ~ \kən'trakt, 1 usu 'kän,trakt\ vb 1 : establish or undertake by contract 2 : become ill with 3 : make shorter —con·trac·tion \kən'trakshən\ n —con·trac·tor \'kän,traktər, kən'trak-\ n —con·trac·tu·al \kən'trakchəwəl\ adj —con·trac·tu·al·ly adv

con·tra·dict \,käntrə'dikt\ vb : state the contrary of —con·tra·dic·tion \-'dikshən\ n —con·tra·dic·to·ry \-'diktərē\ adj

con·tral·to \kən'traltō\ n, pl -tos : lowest female singing voice

con·trap·tion \kən'trapshən\ n : device or contrivance

con·trary \'kän,trerē, 4 often kən'trerē\ adj 1 : opposite in character, nature, or position 2 : mutually opposed 3 : unfavorable 4 : uncooperative or stubborn —con·trar·i·ly \-,trerəlē, -'trer-\ adv —con·trari·wise \-,wīz\ adv —contrary \'kän,trerē\ n

con·trast \'kän,trast\ n 1 : unlikeness shown by comparing 2 : unlike color or tone of adjacent parts ~ \kən'trast\ vb 1 : show differences 2 : compare so as to show differences

con·tra·vene \,käntrə'vēn\ vb -vened; -ven·ing : go or act contrary to

con·trib·ute \kən'tribyət\ vb -ut·ed; -ut·ing : give or help along with others —con·tri·bu·tion \,käntrə'byüshən\ n —con·trib·u·tor \kən'tribyətər\ n —con·trib·u·to·ry \-yə,tōrē\ adj

con·trite \'kän,trīt, kən'trīt\ adj : repentant —con·tri·tion \kən'trishən\ n

con·trive \kən'trīv\ vb -trived; -triv·ing 1 : devise or make with ingenuity 2

: bring about —con·triv·ance \-'trīvəns\ n —con·triv·er n

con·trol \-'trōl\ vb -ll- 1 : exercise power over 2 : dominate or rule ~ n 1 : power to direct or regulate 2 : restraint 3 : regulating device —con·trol·la·ble adj —con·trol·ler \-'trōlər, 'kän,-\ n

con·tro·ver·sy \'käntrə,vərsē\ n, pl -sies : clash of opposing views —con·tro·ver·sial \,käntrə'vərshəl, -sēəl\ adj

con·tro·vert \'käntrə,vərt, ,käntrə'-\ vb : contradict —con·tro·vert·ible adj

con·tu·ma·cious \,käntə'māshəs, -tyə-\ adj : rebellious

con·tu·me·ly \kən'tümələ, 'käntü,mēlē, -tyü-\ n : rudeness

con·tu·sion \kən'tüzhən, -tyü-\ n : bruise —con·tuse \-'tüz, -'tyüz\ vb

co·nun·drum \kə'nəndrəm\ n : riddle

con·va·lesce \,känvə'les\ vb -lesced; -lesc·ing : gradually recover health —con·va·les·cence \-ᵊns\ n —con·va·les·cent \-ᵊnt\ adj or n

con·vec·tion \kən'vekshən\ n : circulation in fluids due to warmer portions rising and colder ones sinking —con·vec·tion·al \-'vekshənəl\ adj —con·vec·tive \-'vektiv\ adj

con·vene \kən'vēn\ vb -vened; -ven·ing : assemble or meet

con·ve·nience \-'vēnyəns\ n 1 : personal comfort or ease 2 : device that saves work

con·ve·nient \-nyənt\ adj 1 : suited to one's convenience 2 : near at hand —con·ve·nient·ly adv

con·vent \'känvənt, -,vent\ n : community of nuns

con·ven·tion \kən'venchən\ n 1 : agreement esp. between nations 2 : large meeting 3 : body of delegates 4 : accepted usage or way of behaving —con·ven·tion·al \-'venchənəl\ adj —con·ven·tion·al·ly adv

con·verge \kən'vərj\ vb -verged; -verg·ing : approach a single point —con·ver·gence \-'vərjəns\ n —con·ver·gent \-jənt\ adj

con·ver·sant \-'vərsᵊnt\ adj : having knowledge and experience

con·ver·sa·tion \,känvər'sāshən\ n : an informal talking together —con·ver·sa·tion·al \-shənəl\ adj

¹con·verse \kən'vərs\ vb -versed; -vers·ing : engage in conversation —con·verse \'kän,vərs\ n

²con·verse \kən'vərs, 'kän,vers\ *adj*
: opposite —**con·verse** \'kän,vərs\ *n*
—**con·verse·ly** *adv*

con·ver·sion \kən'vərzhən\ *n* **1** : change
2 : adoption of religion

con·vert \kən'vərt\ *vb* **1** : turn from one
belief or party to another **2** : change
~ \'kän,vərt\ *n* : one who has undergone religious conversion —**con·**
vert·er, con·ver·tor \kən'vərtər\ *n* —
con·vert·ible *adj*

con·vert·ible \kən'vərtəbəl\ *n* : automobile with a removable top

con·vex \kän'veks, 'kän,-, kən'-\ *adj*
: curved or rounded like the outside
of a sphere —**con·vex·i·ty** \kən-
'veksətē, kän-\ *n*

con·vey \kən'vā\ *vb* -**veyed; -vey·ing**
: transport or transmit —**con·vey-**
ance \-'vāəns\ *n* —**con·vey·or** \-ər\
n

con·vict \kən'vikt\ *vb* : find guilty ~
\'kän,vikt\ *n* : person in prison

con·vic·tion \kən'vikshən\ *n* **1** : act of
convicting **2** : strong belief

con·vince \-'vins\ *vb* -**vinced; -vinc·ing**
: cause to believe —**con·vinc·ing·ly**
adv

con·viv·ial \-'vivyəl, -'vivēəl\ *adj*
: cheerful or festive —**con·viv·i·al·i-**
ty \-,vivē'alətē\ *n*

con·voke \kən'vōk\ *vb* -**voked; -vok·ing**
: call together to a meeting —**con·vo-**
ca·tion \,känvə'kāshən\ *n*

con·vo·lut·ed \'känvə,lütəd\ *adj* **1**
: intricately folded **2** : intricate

con·vo·lu·tion \,känvə'lüshən\ *n* : con-
voluted structure

con·voy \'kän,vói, kən'vói\ *vb*
: accompany for protection ~ \'kän-
,vói\ *n* : group of vehicles or ships
moving together

con·vul·sion \kən'vəlshən\ *n* : violent
involuntary muscle contraction —
con·vulse \-'vəls\ *vb* —**con·vul·sive**
\-'vəlsiv\ *adj*

coo \'kü\ *n* : sound of a pigeon —**coo**
vb

cook \'kük\ *n* : one who prepares food
~ *vb* : prepare food —**cook·book** \-
—**cook·er** *n* —**cook·ery** \-ərē\ *n* —
cook·ware *n*

cook·ie, cooky \'kúkē\ *n, pl* -**ies** : small
sweet flat cake

cool \'kül\ *adj* **1** : moderately cold **2**
: not excited **3** : unfriendly ~ *vb*
: make or become cool ~ *n* **1** : cool
time or place **2** : composure —**cool-**

ant \-ənt\ *n* —**cool·er** *n* —
cool·ly *adv* —**cool·ness** *n*

coo·lie \'külē\ *n* : unskilled Oriental laborer

coop \'küp, 'kúp\ *n* : enclosure usu. for
poultry ~ *vb* : confine in or as if in a
coop

co–op \'kō,äp\ *n* : cooperative

coo·per \'küpər, 'kúp-\ *n* : barrel maker
—**cooper** *vb*

co·op·er·ate \kō'äpə,rāt\ *vb* : act jointly
—**co·op·er·a·tion** \-,äpə'rāshən\ *n*

co·op·er·a·tive \kō'äpərətiv, -'äpə,rāt-\
adj : willing to work with others ~ *n*
: enterprise owned and run by those
using its services

co–opt \kō'äpt\ *vb* **1** : elect as a colleague **2** : take over

co·or·di·nate \-'órdᵊnət\ *adj* : equal esp.
in rank ~ *n* : any of a set of numbers
used in specifying the location of a
point on a surface or in space ~ \-ᵊn-
,āt\ *vb* -**nat·ed; -nat·ing** **1** : make or
become coordinate **2** : work or act together harmoniously —**co·or-**
di·nate·ly *adv* —**co·or·di·na·tion**
\-,órdᵊn'āshən\ *n* —**co·or·di·na·tor**
\-ᵊn,ātər\ *n*

coot \'küt\ *n* **1** : dark-colored ducklike
bird **2** : harmless simple person

cop \'käp\ *n* : police officer

¹cope \'kōp\ *n* : cloaklike ecclesiastical
vestment

²cope *vb* **coped; cop·ing** : deal with difficulties

co·pi·lot \'kō,pīlət\ *n* : assistant airplane
pilot

cop·ing \'kōpiŋ\ *n* : top layer of a wall

co·pi·ous \'kōpēəs\ *adj* : very abundant
—**co·pi·ous·ly** *adv* —**co·pi·ous·ness**
n

cop·per \'käpər\ *n* **1** : malleable reddish
metallic chemical element **2** : penny
—**cop·pery** *adj*

cop·per·head *n* : largely coppery brown
venomous snake

co·pra \'kōprə\ *n* : dried coconut meat

copse \'käps\ *n* : thicket

cop·u·la \'käpyələ\ *n* : verb linking subject and predicate —**cop·u·la·tive**
\-,lātiv\ *adj*

cop·u·late \'käpyə,lāt\ *vb* -**lat·ed; -lat-**
ing : engage in sexual intercourse —
cop·u·la·tion \,käpyə'lāshən\ *n*

copy \'käpē\ *n, pl* **cop·ies** **1** : imitation
or reproduction of an original **2**
: writing to be set for printing ~ *vb*
cop·ied; copy·ing **1** : make a copy of

2 : imitate —**copi·er** \-ər\ *n* —**copyist** *n*

copy·right *n* : sole right to a literary or artistic work ~ *vb* : get a copyright on

co·quette \kō'ket\ *n* : flirt

cor·al \'kȯrəl\ *n* 1 : skeletal material of colonies of tiny sea polyps 2 : deep pink —**coral** *adj*

cord \'kȯrd\ *n* 1 : usu. heavy string 2 : long slender anatomical structure 3 : measure of firewood equal to 128 cu. ft. 4 : small electrical cable ~ *vb* 1 : tie or furnish with a cord 2 : pile (wood) in cords

cor·dial \'kȯrjəl\ *adj* : warmly welcoming — *n* : liqueur —**cor·di·al·i·ty** \ˌkȯrjē'alətē, kȯrd'yal-\ *n* —**cor·dial·ly** \'kȯrjəlē\ *adv*

cor·don \'kȯrd⁰n\ *n* : encircling line of troops or police —**cordon** *vb*

cor·do·van \'kȯrdəvən\ *n* : soft fine-grained leather

cor·du·roy \'kȯrdəˌrȯi\ *n* 1 : heavy ribbed fabric 2 *pl* : trousers of corduroy

core \'kȯr\ *n* 1 : central part of some fruits 2 : inmost part ~ *vb* **cored; cor·ing** : take out the core of —**cor·er** *n*

cork \'kȯrk\ *n* 1 : tough elastic bark of a European oak (**cork oak**) 2 : stopper of cork ~ *vb* : stop up with a cork —**corky** *adj*

cork·screw *n* : device for drawing corks from bottles

cor·mo·rant \'kȯrmərənt, -ˌrant\ *n* : dark seabird

¹**corn** \'kȯrn\ *n* : cereal grass or its seeds ~ *vb* : cure or preserve in brine —**corn·meal** *n* —**corn·stalk** *n* —**corn·starch** *n*

²**corn** *n* : local hardening and thickening of skin

corn·cob *n* : axis on which the kernels of Indian corn are arranged

cor·nea \'kȯrnēə\ *n* : transparent part of the coat of the eyeball —**cor·ne·al** *adj*

cor·ner \'kȯrnər\ *n* 1 : point or angle formed by the meeting of lines or sides 2 : place where two streets meet 3 : inescapable position 4 : control of the supply of something ~ *vb* 1 : drive into a corner 2 : get a corner on 3 : turn a corner

cor·ner·stone *n* 1 : stone at a corner of a wall 2 : something basic

cor·net \kȯr'net\ *n* : trumpetlike instrument

cor·nice \'kȯrnəs\ *n* : horizontal wall projection

cor·nu·co·pia \ˌkȯrnə'kōpēə, -nyə-\ *n* : goat's horn filled with fruits and grain emblematic of abundance

co·rol·la \kə'rälə\ *n* : petals of a flower

co·rol·lary \'kȯrəˌlerē\ *n, pl* **-lar·ies** 1 : logical deduction 2 : consequence or result

co·ro·na \kə'rōnə\ *n* : shining ring around the sun seen during eclipses

cor·o·nary \'kȯrəˌnerē\ *adj* : relating to the heart or its blood vessels ~ *n* 1 : thrombosis of an artery supplying the heart 2 : heart attack

cor·o·na·tion \ˌkȯrə'nāshən\ *n* : crowning of a monarch

cor·o·ner \'kȯrənər\ *n* : public official who investigates causes of suspicious deaths

¹**cor·po·ral** \'kȯrpərəl\ *adj* : bodily

²**corporal** *n* : noncommissioned officer ranking next below a sergeant

cor·po·ra·tion \ˌkȯrpə'rāshən\ *n* : legal creation with the rights and liabilities of a person —**cor·po·rate** \'kȯrpərət\ *adj*

cor·po·re·al \kȯr'pōrēəl\ *adj* : physical or material —**cor·po·re·al·ly** *adv*

corps \'kōr\ *n, pl* **corps** \'kȯrz\ 1 : subdivision of a military force 2 : working group

corpse \'kȯrps\ *n* : dead body

cor·pu·lence \'kȯrpyələns\ *n* : obesity —**cor·pu·lent** \-lənt\ *adj*

cor·pus \'kȯrpəs\ *n, pl* **-po·ra** \-pərə\ 1 : corpse 2 : body of writings

cor·pus·cle \'kȯr,pəsəl\ *n* : blood cell

cor·ral \kə'ral\ *n* : enclosure for animals —**corral** *vb*

cor·rect \kə'rekt\ *vb* 1 : make right 2 : chastise ~ *adj* 1 : true or factual 2 : conforming to a standard —**cor·rec·tion** \-'rekshən\ *n* —**cor·rec·tive** \-'rektiv\ *adj* —**cor·rect·ly** *adv* —**cor·rect·ness** *n*

cor·re·late \'kȯrəˌlāt\ *vb* **-lat·ed; -lat·ing** : show a connection between —**cor·re·late** \-lət, -ˌlāt\ *n* —**cor·re·la·tion** \ˌkȯrə'lāshən\ *n*

cor·rel·a·tive \kə'relətiv\ *adj* : regularly used together —**correlative** *n*

cor·re·spond \ˌkȯrə'spänd\ *vb* 1 : match 2 : communicate by letter —**cor·re·spon·dence** \-'spändəns\ *n* —**cor·re·spond·ing·ly** \-'spändiŋlē\ *adv*

cor·re·spon·dent \-'spändənt\ n 1 : person one writes to 2 : reporter

cor·ri·dor \'kórədər, -,dór\ n : passageway connecting rooms

cor·rob·o·rate \kə'räbə,rāt\ vb -rat·ed; -rat·ing : support with evidence — **cor·rob·o·ra·tion** \-,räbə'rāshən\ n

cor·rode \kə'rōd\ vb -rod·ed; -rod·ing : wear away by chemical action — **cor·ro·sion** \-'rōzhən\ n — **cor·ro·sive** \-'rōsiv\ adj or n

cor·ru·gate \'kórə,gāt\ vb -gat·ed; -gat·ing : form into ridges and grooves — **cor·ru·gat·ed** adj — **cor·ru·ga·tion** \,kórə'gāshən\ n

cor·rupt \kə'rəpt\ vb 1 : change from good to bad 2 : bribe ~ adj : morally debased — **cor·rupt·ible** adj — **cor·rup·tion** \-'rəpshən\ n

cor·sage \kór'säzh, -'säj\ n : bouquet worn by a woman

cor·set \'kórsət\ n : woman's stiffened undergarment

cor·tege \kór'tezh, 'kór-\ n : funeral procession

cor·tex \'kór,teks\ n, pl -ti·ces \'kórtə,sēz\ or -tex·es : outer or covering layer of an organism or part (as the brain) — **cor·ti·cal** \'kórtikəl\ adj

cor·ti·sone \'kórtə,sōn, -,zōn\ n : adrenal hormone

cos·met·ic \käz'metik\ n : beautifying preparation ~ adj : relating to beautifying

cos·mic \'käzmik\ adj 1 : relating to the universe 2 : vast or grand

cos·mo·naut \'käzmə,nót\ n : Soviet or Russian astronaut

cos·mo·pol·i·tan \,käzmə'pälət³n\ adj : belonging to all the world — **cosmopolitan** n

cos·mos \'käzməs, -,mōs, -,mäs\ n : universe

cos·sack \'käs,ak, -ək\ n : Russian czarist cavalryman

cost \'kóst\ n 1 : amount paid for something 2 : loss or penalty ~ vb cost; cost·ing 1 : require so much in payment 2 : cause to pay, suffer, or lose — **cost·li·ness** \-lēnəs\ n — **cost·ly** \-lē\ adj

cos·tume \'käs,tüm, -,tyüm\ n : clothing

co·sy \'kōzē\ var of COZY

cot \'kät\ n : small bed

cote \'kōt, 'kät\ n : small shed or coop

co·te·rie \'kōtə,rē, ,kōtə'-\ n : exclusive group of persons

co·til·lion \kō'tilyən\ n : formal ball

cot·tage \'kätij\ n : small house

cot·ton \'kät³n\ n : soft fibrous plant substance or thread or cloth made of it — **cot·ton·seed** n — **cot·tony** adj

cot·ton·mouth \'kät³n,mauth\ n : poisonous snake

couch \'kauch\ vb 1 : lie or place on a couch 2 : phrase ~ n : bed or sofa

cou·gar \'kügər, -,gär\ n : large tawny wild American cat

cough \'kóf\ vb : force air from the lungs with short sharp noises — **cough** n

could \'kud\ past of CAN

coun·cil \'kaunsəl\ n 1 : assembly or meeting 2 : body of lawmakers — **coun·cil·lor, coun·cil·or** \-sələr\ n — **coun·cil·man** \-mən\ n — **coun·cil·wom·an** n

coun·sel \'kaunsəl\ n 1 : advice 2 : deliberation together 3 pl -sel : lawyer ~ vb -seled or -selled; -sel·ing or -sel·ling 1 : advise 2 : consult together — **coun·sel·or, coun·sel·lor** \-sələr\ n

¹**count** \'kaunt\ vb 1 : name or indicate one by one to find the total number 2 : recite numbers in order 3 : rely 4 : be of value or account ~ n 1 : act of counting or the total obtained by counting 2 : charge in an indictment — **count·able** adj

²**count** n : European nobleman

coun·te·nance \'kaunt³nəns\ n : face or facial expression ~ vb -nanced; -nanc·ing : allow or encourage

¹**count·er** \'kaunter\ n 1 : piece for reckoning or games 2 : surface over which business is transacted

²**count·er** n : one that counts

³**coun·ter** vb : oppose ~ adv : in an opposite direction ~ n : offsetting force or move ~ adj : contrary

counter- prefix 1 : contrary or opposite 2 : opposing 3 : retaliatory

counteraccusation	countercharge
counteraggression	counterclaim
counterargue	countercomplaint
counterassault	countercoup
counterattack	countercriticism
counterbid	counterdemand
counterblockade	counterdemonstration
counterblow	counterdemonstrator
countercampaign	countereffort
	counterevidence

counterguerrilla
counterinflationary
counterinfluence
countermeasure
countermove
countermovement
counteroffer
counterpetition
counterploy
counterpower
counterpressure
counterpropaganda
counterproposal
counterprotest
counterquestion
counterraid
counterrally
counterreform

counterresponse
counterretaliation
counterrevolution
counterrevolutionary
counterstrategy
counterstyle
countersue
countersuggestion
countersuit
countertendency
counterterror
counterterrorism
counterterrorist
counterthreat
counterthrust
countertrend

coun·ter·act *vb* : lessen the force of — **coun·ter·ac·tive** *adj*

coun·ter·bal·ance *n* : balancing influence or weight ~ *vb* : oppose or balance

coun·ter·clock·wise *adv or adj* : opposite to the way a clock's hands move

coun·ter·feit \'kaúntər,fit\ *vb* 1 : copy in order to deceive 2 : pretend ~ *adj* : spurious ~ *n* : fraudulent copy — **coun·ter·feit·er** *n*

coun·ter·mand \-,mand\ *vb* : supersede with a contrary order

coun·ter·pane \-,pān\ *n* : bedspread

coun·ter·part *n* : one that is similar or corresponds

coun·ter·point *n* : music with interwoven melodies

coun·ter·sign *n* : secret signal ~ *vb* : add a confirming signature to

count·ess \'kaúntəs\ *n* : wife or widow of a count or an earl or a woman holding that rank in her own right

count·less \-ləs\ *adj* : too many to be numbered

coun·try \'kəntrē\ *n, pl* **-tries** 1 : nation 2 : rural area ~ *adj* : rural —**coun·try·man** \-mən\ *n*

coun·try·side *n* : rural area or its people

coun·ty \'kaúntē\ *n, pl* **-ties** : local government division esp. of a state

coup \'kü\ *n, pl* **coups** \'küz\ 1 : brilliant sudden action or plan 2 : sudden overthrow of a government

coupe \'küp\ *n* : 2-door automobile with an enclosed body

cou·ple \'kəpəl\ *vb* **-pled; -pling** : link together ~ *n* 1 : pair 2 : two persons closely associated or married

cou·pling \'kəpliŋ\ *n* : connecting device

cou·pon \'kü,pän, 'kyü-\ *n* : certificate redeemable for goods or a cash discount

cour·age \'kərij\ *n* : ability to conquer fear or despair —**cou·ra·geous** \kə'rājəs\ *adj*

cou·ri·er \'kúrēər, 'kərē-\ *n* : messenger

course \'kōrs\ *n* 1 : progress 2 : ground over which something moves 3 : part of a meal served at one time 4 : method of procedure 5 : subject taught in a series of classes ~ *vb* coursed; cours·ing 1 : hunt with dogs 2 : run speedily —**of course** : as might be expected

court \'kōrt\ *n* 1 : residence of a sovereign 2 : sovereign and his or her officials and advisers 3 : area enclosed by a building 4 : space marked for playing a game 5 : place where justice is administered ~ *vb* : woo —**court·house** *n* —**court·room** *n* —**court·ship** \-,ship\ *n*

cour·te·ous \'kərtēəs\ *adj* : showing politeness and respect for others — **cour·te·ous·ly** *adv*

cour·te·san \'kōrtəzən, 'kərt-\ *n* : prostitute

cour·te·sy \'kərtəsē\ *n, pl* **-sies** : courteous behavior

cour·tier \'kōrtēər, 'kōrtyər\ *n* : person in attendance at a royal court

court·ly \'kōrtlē\ *adj* **-li·er; -est** : polite or elegant —**court·li·ness** *n*

court-mar·tial *n, pl* **courts-martial** : military trial court —**court-martial** *vb*

court·yard *n* : enclosure open to the sky that is attached to a house

cous·in \'kəz°n\ *n* : child of one's uncle or aunt

cove \'kōv\ *n* : sheltered inlet or bay

co·ven \'kəvən\ *n* : group of witches

cov·e·nant \'kəvənənt\ *n* : binding agreement —**cov·e·nant** \-nənt. -,nant\ *vb*

cov·er \'kəvər\ *vb* 1 : place something over or upon 2 : protect or hide 3 : include or deal with ~ *n* : something that covers —**cov·er·age** \-ərij\ *n*

cov·er·let \-lət\ *n* : bedspread

co·vert \'kō,vərt, 'kəvərt\ *adj* : secret ~ \'kəvərt, 'kō-\ *n* : thicket that shelters animals

cov·et \'kəvət\ *vb* : desire enviously — **cov·et·ous** *adj*

cov·ey \'kəvē\ *n, pl* **-eys 1** : bird with her young **2** : small flock (as of quail)

¹cow \'kaů\ *n* : large adult female animal (as of cattle) —**cow·hide** *n*

²cow *vb* : intimidate

cow·ard \'kaůərd\ *n* : one who lacks courage —**cow·ard·ice** \-əs\ *n* — **cow·ard·ly** *adv or adj*

cow·boy *n* : a mounted ranch hand who tends cattle

cow·er \'kaůər\ *vb* : shrink from fear or cold

cow·girl *n* : woman ranch hand who tends cattle

cowl \'kaůl\ *n* : monk's hood

cow·lick \'kaů,lik\ *n* : turned-up tuft of hair that resists control

cow·slip \-,slip\ *n* : yellow flower

cox·swain \'käksən, -,swān\ *n* : person who steers a boat

coy \'kói\ *adj* : shy or pretending shyness

coy·ote \'kī,ōt, kī'ōtē\ *n, pl* **coy·otes** *or* **coyote** : small No. American wolf

coz·en \'kəzən\ *vb* : cheat

co·zy \'kōzē\ *adj* **-zi·er; -est** : snug

crab \'krab\ *n* : short broad shellfish with pincers

crab·by \'krabē\ *adj* **-bi·er; -est** : cross

¹crack \'krak\ *vb* **1** : break with a sharp sound **2** : fail in tone **3** : break without completely separating ~ *n* **1** : sudden sharp noise **2** : witty remark **3** : narrow break **4** : sharp blow **5** : try

²crack *adj* : extremely proficient

crack·down *n* : disciplinary action — **crack down** *vb*

crack·er \-ər\ *n* : thin crisp bakery product

crack·le \'krakəl\ *vb* **-led; -ling 1** : make snapping noises **2** : develop fine cracks in a surface —**crackle** *n*

crack·pot \'krak,pät\ *n* : eccentric

crack-up *n* : crash

cra·dle \'krād³l\ *n* : baby's bed ~ *vb* **-dled; -dling 1** : place in a cradle **2** : hold securely

craft \'kraft\ *n* **1** : occupation requiring special skill **2** : craftiness **3** *pl usu* **craft** : structure designed to provide transportation **4** *pl usu* **craft** : small boat —**crafts·man** \'kraftsmən\ *n* — **crafts·man·ship** \-,ship\ *n*

crafty \'kraftē\ *adj* **craft·i·er; -est** : sly —**craft·i·ness** *n*

crag \'krag\ *n* : steep cliff —**crag·gy** \-ē\ *adj*

cram \'kram\ *vb* **-mm- 1** : eat greedily **2** : pack in tight **3** : study intensely for a test

cramp \'kramp\ *n* **1** : sudden painful contraction of muscle **2** *pl* : sharp abdominal pains ~ *vb* **1** : affect with cramp **2** : restrain

cran·ber·ry \'kran,berē\ *n* : red acid berry of a trailing plant

crane \'krān\ *n* **1** : tall wading bird **2** : machine for lifting heavy objects ~ *vb* **craned; cran·ing** : stretch one's neck to see

cra·ni·um \'krānēəm\ *n, pl* **-ni·ums** *or* **-nia** \-nēə\ : skull —**cra·ni·al** \-əl\ *adj*

crank \'krank\ *n* **1** : bent lever turned to operate a machine **2** : eccentric ~ *vb* : start or operate by turning a crank

cranky \'krankē\ *adj* **crank·i·er; -est** : irritable

cran·ny \'kranē\ *n, pl* **-nies** : crevice

craps \'kraps\ *n* : dice game

crash \'krash\ *vb* **1** : break noisily **2** : fall and hit something with noise and damage ~ *n* **1** : loud sound **2** : action of crashing **3** : failure

crass \'kras\ *adj* : crude or unfeeling

crate \'krāt\ *n* : wooden shipping container —**crate** *vb*

cra·ter \'krātər\ *n* : volcanic depression

cra·vat \krə'vat\ *n* : necktie

crave \'krāv\ *vb* **craved; crav·ing** : long for —**crav·ing** *n*

cra·ven \'krāvən\ *adj* : cowardly —**craven** *n*

craw·fish \'kró,fish\ *n* : crayfish

crawl \'król\ *vb* **1** : move slowly (as by drawing the body along the ground) **2** : swarm with creeping things ~ *n* : very slow pace

cray·fish \'krā,fish\ *n* : lobsterlike freshwater crustacean

cray·on \'krā,än. -ən\ *n* : stick of chalk or wax used for drawing or coloring —**crayon** *vb*

craze \'krāz\ *vb* **crazed; craz·ing** : make or become insane ~ *n* : fad

cra·zy \'krāzē\ *adj* **cra·zi·er; -est 1** : mentally disordered **2** : wildly impractical —**cra·zi·ly** *adv* —**cra·zi·ness** *n*

creak \'krēk\ *vb or n* : squeak —**creaky** *adj*

cream \'krēm\ *n* **1** : yellowish fat-rich part of milk **2** : thick smooth sauce.

confection, or cosmetic **3** : choicest part ~ *vb* : beat into creamy consistency —**creamy** *adj*

cream·ery \-ərē\ *n, pl* **-er·ies** : place where butter and cheese are made

crease \'krēs\ *n* : line made by folding —**crease** *vb*

cre·ate \krē'āt\ *vb* **-at·ed; -at·ing** : bring into being —**cre·ation** \krē'āshən\ *n* —**cre·ative** \-'ātiv\ *adj* —**cre·ativ·i·ty** \krēā'tivətē\ *n* —**cre·ator** \krē-'ātər\ *n*

crea·ture \'krēchər\ *n* : lower animal or human being

cre·dence \'krēd°ns\ *n* : belief

cre·den·tials \kri'denchəlz\ *n* : evidence of qualifications or authority

cred·i·ble \'kredəbəl\ *adj* : believable —**cred·i·bil·i·ty** \,kredə'bilətē\ *n*

cred·it \'kredət\ *n* **1** : balance in a person's favor **2** : time given to pay for goods **3** : belief **4** : esteem **5** : source of honor ~ *vb* **1** : believe **2** : give credit to

cred·it·able \-əbəl\ *adj* : worthy of esteem or praise —**cred·it·ably** \-əblē\ *adv*

cred·i·tor \-ər\ *n* : person to whom money is owed

cred·u·lous \'krejələs\ *adj* : easily convinced —**cre·du·li·ty** \kri'dülətē, -'dyü-\ *n*

creed \'krēd\ *n* : statement of essential beliefs

creek \'krēk, 'krik\ *n* : small stream

creel \'krēl\ *n* : basket for carrying fish

creep \'krēp\ *vb* **crept** \'krept\; **creeping 1** : crawl **2** : grow over a surface like ivy —**creep** *n* —**creep·er** *n*

cre·mate \'krē,māt\ *vb* **-mat·ed; -mat·ing** : burn up (a corpse) —**cre·mation** \kri'māshən\ *n* —**cre·ma·to·ry** \'krēmə,tōrē, 'krem-\ *n*

cre·o·sote \'krēə,sōt\ *n* : oily wood preservative

crepe, crêpe \'krāp\ *n* : light crinkled fabric

cres·cen·do \krə'shendō\ *adv or adj* : growing louder —**crescendo** *n*

cres·cent \'kres°nt\ *n* : shape of the moon between new moon and first quarter

crest \'krest\ *n* **1** : tuft on a bird's head **2** : top of a hill or wave **3** : part of a coat of arms ~ *vb* : rise to a crest —**crest·ed** \-əd\ *adj*

crest·fall·en *adj* : sad

cre·tin \'krēt°n\ *n* : stupid person

cre·vasse \kri'vas\ *n* : deep fissure esp. in a glacier

crev·ice \'krevəs\ *n* : narrow fissure

crew \'krü\ *n* : body of workers (as on a ship) —**crew·man** \-mən\ *n*

crib \'krib\ *n* **1** : manger **2** : grain storage bin **3** : baby's bed ~ *vb* **-bb-** : put in a crib

crib·bage \'kribij\ *n* : card game scored by moving pegs on a board (**cribbage board**)

crick \'krik\ *n* : muscle spasm

¹crick·et \'krikət\ *n* : insect noted for the chirping of the male

²cricket *n* : bat and ball game played on a field with wickets

cri·er \'krīər\ *n* : one who calls out announcements

crime \'krīm\ *n* : serious violation of law

crim·i·nal \'krimən°l\ *adj* : relating to or being a crime or its punishment ~ *n* : one who commits a crime

crimp \'krimp\ *vb* : cause to become crinkled, wavy, or bent —**crimp** *n*

crim·son \'krimzən\ *n* : deep red —**crimson** *adj*

cringe \'krinj\ *vb* **cringed; cring·ing** : shrink in fear

crin·kle \'kriŋkəl\ *vb* **-kled; -kling** : wrinkle —**crinkle** *n* —**crin·kly** \-klē\ *adj*

crin·o·line \'krin°lən\ *n* **1** : stiff cloth **2** : full stiff skirt or petticoat

crip·ple \'kripəl\ *n* : disabled person ~ *vb* **-pled; -pling** : disable

cri·sis \'krīsəs\ *n, pl* **cri·ses** \-,sēz\ : decisive or critical moment

crisp \'krisp\ *adj* **1** : easily crumbled **2** : firm and fresh **3** : lively **4** : invigorating —**crisp** *vb* —**crisp·ly** *adv* —**crisp·ness** *n* —**crispy** *adj*

criss·cross \'kris,krós\ *n* : pattern of crossed lines ~ *vb* : mark with or follow a crisscross

cri·te·ri·on \krī'tirēən\ *n, pl* **-ria** \-ēə\ : standard

crit·ic \'kritik\ *n* : judge of literary or artistic works

crit·i·cal \-ikəl\ *adj* **1** : inclined to criticize **2** : being a crisis **3** : relating to criticism or critics —**crit·i·cal·ly** \-iklē\ *adv*

crit·i·cize \'kritə,sīz\ *vb* **-cized; -cizing 1** : judge as a critic **2** : find fault —**crit·i·cism** \-ə,sizəm\ *n*

cri·tique \krə'tēk\ *n* : critical estimate

croak \'krōk\ *n* : hoarse harsh cry (as of a frog) —**croak** *vb*

cro·chet \krō'shā\ *n* : needlework done with a hooked needle —**crochet** *vb*

crock \'kräk\ *n* : thick earthenware pot or jar —**crock·ery** \-ərē\ *n*

croc·o·dile \'kräkə,dīl\ *n* : large reptile of tropical waters

cro·cus \'krōkəs\ *n*, *pl* **-cus·es** : herb with spring flowers

crone \'krōn\ *n* : ugly old woman

cro·ny \'krōnē\ *n*, *pl* **-nies** : chum

crook \'krúk\ *n* **1** : bent or curved tool or part **2** : thief ~ *vb* : curve sharply

crook·ed \'krúkəd\ *adj* **1** : bent **2** : dishonest —**crook·ed·ness** *n*

croon \'krün\ *vb* : sing softly —**croon·er** *n*

crop \'kräp\ *n* **1** : pouch in the throat of a bird or insect **2** : short riding whip **3** : something that can be harvested ~ *vb* **-pp-** **1** : trim **2** : appear unexpectedly : —used with *up*

cro·quet \krō'kā\ *n* : lawn game of driving balls through wickets

cro·quette \-'ket\ *n* : mass of minced food deep-fried

cro·sier \'krōzhər\ *n* : bishop's staff

cross \'krós\ *n* **1** : figure or structure consisting of an upright and a cross piece **2** : interbreeding of unlike strains ~ *vb* **1** : intersect **2** : cancel **3** : go or extend across **4** : interbreed ~ *adj* **1** : going across **2** : contrary **3** : marked by bad temper —**cross·ing** *n* —**cross·ly** *adv*

cross·bow \-,bō\ *n* : short bow mounted on a rifle stock

cross·breed *vb* **-bred; -breed·ing** : hybridize

cross-ex·am·ine *vb* : question about earlier testimony —**cross-ex·am·i·na·tion** *n*

cross-eyed *adj* : having the eye turned toward the nose

cross-re·fer *vb* : refer to another place (as in a book) —**cross-ref·er·ence** *n*

cross·roads *n* : place where 2 roads cross

cross section *n* : representative portion

cross·walk *n* : path for pedestrians crossing a street

cross·ways *adv* : crosswise

cross·wise \-,wīz\ *adv* : so as to cross something —**crosswise** *adj*

crotch \'kräch\ *n* : angle formed by the parting of 2 legs or branches

crotch·ety \'krächətē\ *adj* : cranky, ill-natured

crouch \'kraúch\ *vb* : stoop over —**crouch** *n*

croup \'krüp\ *n* : laryngitis of infants

crou·ton \'krü,tän\ *n* : bit of toast

¹crow \'krō\ *n* : large glossy black bird

²crow *vb* **1** : make the loud sound of the cock **2** : gloat ~ *n* : cry of the cock

crow·bar *n* : metal bar used as a pry or lever

crowd \'kraúd\ *vb* : collect or cram together ~ *n* : large number of people

crown \'kraún\ *n* **1** : wreath of honor or victory **2** : royal headdress **3** : top or highest part ~ *vb* **1** : place a crown on **2** : honor —**crowned** \'kraúnd\ *adj*

cru·cial \'krüshəl\ *adj* : vitally important

cru·ci·ble \'krüsəbəl\ *n* : heat-resisting container

cru·ci·fix \'krüsə,fiks\ *n* : representation of Christ on the cross

cru·ci·fix·ion \,krüsə'fikshən\ *n* : act of crucifying

cru·ci·fy \'krüsə,fī\ *vb* **-fied; -fy·ing** **1** : put to death on a cross **2** : persecute

crude \'krüd\ *adj* **crud·er; -est** **1** : not refined **2** : lacking grace or elegance ~ *n* : unrefined petroleum —**crude·ly** *adv* —**cru·di·ty** \-ətē\ *n*

cru·el \'krüəl\ *adj* **-el·er** *or* **-el·ler; -el·est** *or* **-el·lest** : causing suffering to others —**cru·el·ly** \-ē\ *adv* —**cru·el·ty** \tē\ *n*

cru·et \'krüət\ *n* : bottle for salad dressings

cruise \'krüz\ *vb* **cruised; cruis·ing** **1** : sail to several ports **2** : travel at the most efficient speed —**cruise** *n*

cruis·er \'krüzər\ *n* **1** : warship **2** : police car

crumb \'krəm\ *n* : small fragment

crum·ble \'krəmbəl\ *vb* **-bled; -bling** : break into small pieces —**crum·bly** \-blē\ *adj*

crum·ple \'krəmpəl\ *vb* **-pled; -pling** **1** : crush together **2** : collapse

crunch \'krənch\ *vb* : chew or press with a crushing noise ~ *n* : crunching sound —**crunchy** *adj*

cru·sade \krü'sād\ *n* **1** *cap* : medieval Christian expedition to the Holy Land **2** : reform movement —**crusade** *vb* —**cru·sad·er** *n*

crush \'krəsh\ *vb* **1** : squeeze out of shape **2** : grind or pound to bits **3** : suppress ~ *n* **1** : severe crowding **2** : infatuation

crust \'krəst\ n **1** : hard outer part of bread or a pie **2** : hard surface layer —**crust·al** adj —**crusty** adj

crus·ta·cean \,krəs'tāshən\ n : aquatic arthropod having a firm shell

crutch \'krəch\ n : support for use by the disabled in walking

crux \'krəks, 'krúks\ n, pl **crux·es 1** : hard problem **2** : crucial point

cry \'krī\ vb **cried; cry·ing 1** : call out **2** : weep ~ n, pl **cries 1** : shout **2** : fit of weeping **3** : characteristic sound of an animal

crypt \'kript\ n : underground chamber

cryp·tic \'kriptik\ adj : enigmatic

cryp·tog·ra·phy \krip'tägrəfē\ n : coding and decoding of messages —**cryp·tog·ra·pher** \-fər\ n

crys·tal \'krist°l\ n **1** : transparent quartz **2** : something (as glass) like crystal **3** : body formed by solidification that has a regular repeating atomic arrangement —**crys·tal·line** \-tələn\ adj

crys·tal·lize \-tə,līz\ vb **-lized; -liz·ing** : form crystals or a definite shape —**crys·tal·li·za·tion** \,kristələ'zāshən\ n

cub \'kəb\ n : young animal

cub·by·hole \'kəbē,hōl\ n : small confined space

cube \'kyüb\ n **1** : solid having 6 equal square sides **2** : product obtained by taking a number 3 times as a factor ~ vb **cubed; cub·ing 1** : raise to the 3d power **2** : form into a cube **3** : cut into cubes —**cu·bic** \'kyübik\ adj

cu·bi·cle \-bikəl\ n : small room

cu·bit \'kyübət\ n : ancient unit of length equal to about 18 inches

cuck·old \'kəkəld, 'kúk-\ n : man whose wife is unfaithful —**cuckold** vb

cuck·oo \'kükü, 'kúk-\ n, pl **-oos** : brown European bird ~ adj : silly

cu·cum·ber \'kyü,kəmbər\ n : fleshy fruit related to the gourds

cud \'kəd\ n : food chewed again by ruminating animals

cud·dle \'kəd°l\ vb **-dled; -dling** : lie close

cud·gel \'kəjəl\ n or vb : club

¹cue \'kyü\ n : signal —**cue** vb

²cue n : stick used in pool

¹cuff \'kəf\ n **1** : part of a sleeve encircling the wrist **2** : folded trouser hem

²cuff vb or n : slap

cui·sine \kwi'zēn\ n : manner of cooking

cu·li·nary \'kələ,nerē, 'kyülə-\ adj : of or relating to cookery

cull \'kəl\ vb : select

cul·mi·nate \'kəlmə,nāt\ vb **-nat·ed; -nat·ing** : rise to the highest point —**cul·mi·na·tion** \,kəlmə'nāshən\ n

cul·pa·ble \'kəlpəbəl\ adj : deserving blame

cul·prit \'kəlprət\ n : guilty person

cult \'kəlt\ n **1** : religious system **2** : faddish devotion —**cult·ist** n

cul·ti·vate \'kəltə,vāt\ vb **-vat·ed; -vat·ing 1** : prepare for crops **2** : foster the growth of **3** : refine —**cul·ti·va·tion** \,kəltə'vāshən\ n

cul·ture \'kəlchər\ n **1** : cultivation **2** : refinement of intellectual and artistic taste **3** : particular form or stage of civilization —**cul·tur·al** \'kəlchərəl\ adj —**cul·tured** \'kəlchərd\ adj

cul·vert \'kəlvərt\ n : drain crossing under a road or railroad

cum·ber·some \'kəmbərsəm\ adj : awkward to handle due to bulk

cu·mu·la·tive \'kyümyələtiv, -,lāt-\ adj : increasing by additions

cu·mu·lus \'kyümyələs\ n, pl **-li** \-,lī, -,lē\ : massive rounded cloud

cun·ning \'kəniŋ\ adj **1** : crafty **2** : clever **3** : appealing ~ n **1** : skill **2** : craftiness

cup \'kəp\ n **1** : small drinking vessel **2** : contents of a cup **3** : a half pint ~ vb **-pp-** : shape like a cup —**cup·ful** n

cup·board \'kəbərd\ n : small storage closet

cup·cake n : small cake

cu·pid·i·ty \kyu'pidətē\ n, pl **-ties** : excessive desire for money

cu·po·la \'kyüpələ, -,lō\ n : small rooftop structure

cur \'kər\ n : mongrel dog

cu·rate \'kyürət\ n : member of the clergy —**cu·ra·cy** \-əsē\ n

cu·ra·tor \kyü'rātər\ n : one in charge of a museum or zoo

curb \'kərb\ n **1** : restraint **2** : raised edging along a street ~ vb : hold back

curd \'kərd\ n : coagulated milk

cur·dle \'kərd°l\ vb **-dled; -dling 1** : form curds **2** : sour

cure \'kyúr\ n **1** : recovery from disease **2** : remedy ~ vb **cured; cur·ing 1** : restore to health **2** : process for storage or use —**cur·able** adj

cur·few \'kər,fyü\ n : requirement to be off the streets at a set hour

cu·rio \'kyúrē,ō\ n, pl **-ri·os** : rare or unusual article

cu·ri·ous \'kyurēəs\ *adj* **1** : eager to learn **2** : strange —**cu·ri·os·i·ty** \,kyurē'äsətē\ *n* —**cu·ri·ous·ness** *n*

curl \'kərl\ *vb* **1** : form into ringlets **2** : curve ~ *n* **1** : ringlet of hair **2** : something with a spiral form —**curl·er** *n* —**curly** *adj*

cur·lew \'kərlü, -lyü\ *n, pl* **-lews** *or* **-lew** : long-legged brownish bird

curli·cue \'kərli,kyü\ *n* : fanciful curve

cur·rant \'kərənt\ *n* **1** : small seedless raisin **2** : berry of a shrub

cur·ren·cy \'kərənsē\ *n, pl* **-cies 1** : general use or acceptance **2** : money

cur·rent \'kərənt\ *adj* : occurring in or belonging to the present ~ *n* **1** : swiftest part of a stream **2** : flow of electricity

cur·ric·u·lum \kə'rikyələm\ *n, pl* **-la** \-lə\ : course of study

¹**cur·ry** \'kərē\ *vb* **-ried; -ry·ing** : brush (a horse) with a wire brush (**cur·ry·comb** \-,kōm\) —**curry fa·vor** : seek favor by flattery

²**curry** *n, pl* **-ries** : blend of pungent spices or a food seasoned with this

curse \'kərs\ *n* **1** : a calling down of evil or harm upon one **2** : affliction ~ *vb* **cursed; curs·ing 1** : call down injury upon **2** : swear at **3** : afflict

cur·sor \'kərsər\ *n* : indicator on a computer screen

cur·so·ry \'kərsərē\ *adj* : hastily done

curt \'kərt\ *adj* : rudely abrupt —**curt·ly** *adv* —**curt·ness** *n*

cur·tail \kər'tāl\ *vb* : shorten —**cur·tail·ment** *n*

cur·tain \'kərtᵊn\ *n* : hanging screen that can be drawn back or raised —**curtain** *vb*

curt·sy, curt·sey \'kərtsē\ *n, pl* **-sies** *or* **-seys** : courteous bow made by bending the knees —**curtsy, curtsey** *vb*

cur·va·ture \'kərvə,chúr\ *n* : amount or state of curving

curve \'kərv\ *vb* **curved; curv·ing** : bend from a straight line or course ~ *n* **1** : a bending without angles **2** : something curved

cush·ion \'kúshən\ *n* **1** : soft pillow **2** : something that eases or protects ~ *vb* **1** : provide with a cushion **2** : soften the force of

cusp \'kəsp\ *n* : pointed end

cus·pid \'kəspəd\ *n* : a canine tooth

cus·pi·dor \'kəspə,dòr\ *n* : spittoon

cus·tard \'kəstərd\ *n* : sweetened cooked mixture of milk and eggs

cus·to·dy \'kəstədē\ *n, pl* **-dies** : immediate care or charge —**cus·to·di·al** \,kəs'tōdēəl\ *adj* —**cus·to·di·an** \-ēən\ *n*

cus·tom \'kəstəm\ *n* **1** : habitual course of action **2** *pl* : import taxes ~ *adj* : made to personal order —**cus·tom·ar·i·ly** \,kəstə'merəlē\ *adv* —**cus·tom·ary** \'kəstə,merē\ *adj* —**custom–built** *adj* —**cus·tom–made** *adj*

cus·tom·er \'kəstəmər\ *n* : buyer

cut \'kət\ *vb* **cut; cut·ting 1** : penetrate or divide with a sharp edge **2** : experience the growth of (a tooth) through the gum **3** : shorten **4** : remove by severing **5** : intersect ~ *n* **1** : something separated by cutting **2** : reduction —**cut in** *vb* : thrust oneself between others

cu·ta·ne·ous \kyú'tānēəs\ *adj* : relating to the skin

cute \'kyüt\ *adj* **cut·er; -est** : pretty

cu·ti·cle \'kyütikəl\ *n* : outer layer (as of skin)

cut·lass \'kətləs\ *n* : short heavy curved sword

cut·lery \-lərē\ *n* : cutting utensils

cut·let \-lət\ *n* : slice of meat

cut·ter \'kətər\ *n* **1** : tool or machine for cutting **2** : small armed motorboat **3** : light sleigh

cut·throat *n* : murderer ~ *adj* : ruthless

-cy \sē\ *n suffix* **1** : action or practice **2** : rank or office **3** : body **4** : state or quality

cy·a·nide \'sīə,nīd, -nəd\ *n* : poisonous chemical salt

cy·cle \'sīkəl, *4 also* 'sikəl\ *n* **1** : period of time for a series of repeated events **2** : recurring round of events **3** : long period of time **4** : bicycle or motorcycle ~ *vb* **-cled; -cling** : ride a cycle —**cy·clic** \'sīklik, 'sik-\, **cy·cli·cal** \-əl\ *adj* —**cy·clist** \'sīklist, 'sik-\ *n*

cy·clone \'sī,klōn\ *n* : tornado —**cy·clon·ic** \sī'klänik\ *adj*

cy·clo·pe·dia, cy·clo·pae·dia \,sīklə'pēdēə\ *n* : encyclopedia

cyl·in·der \'siləndər\ *n* **1** : long round body or figure **2** : rotating chamber in a revolver **3** : piston chamber in an engine —**cy·lin·dri·cal** \sə'lindrikəl\ *adj*

cym·bal \'simbəl\ *n* : one of 2 concave brass plates clashed together

cyn·ic \'sinik\ *n* : one who attributes all actions to selfish motives —**cyn·i·cal** \-ikəl\ *adj* —**cyn·i·cism** \-ə,sizəm\ *n*

cy·no·sure \'sīnə,shúr. 'sin-\ n : center of attraction

cy·press \'sīprəs\ n : evergreen tree related to the pines

cyst \'sist\ n : abnormal bodily sac — **cys·tic** \'sistik\ adj

czar \'zär\ n : ruler of Russia until 1917 —**czar·ist** n or adj

D

d \'dē\ n, pl **d's** or **ds** \'dēz\ : 4th letter of the alphabet

¹dab \'dab\ n : gentle touch or stroke ~ vb **-bb-** : touch or apply lightly

²dab n : small amount

dab·ble \'dabəl\ vb **-bled; -bling** 1 : splash 2 : work without serious effort —**dab·bler** \-blər\ n

dachs·hund \'däks,hūnt\ n : small dog with a long body and short legs

dad \'dad\ n : father

dad·dy \'dadē\ n, pl **-dies** : father

daf·fo·dil \'dafə,dil\ n : narcissus with trumpetlike flowers

daft \'daft\ adj : foolish —**daft·ness** n

dag·ger \'dagər\ n : knife for stabbing

dahl·ia \'dalyə. 'däl-\ n : tuberous herb with showy flowers

dai·ly \'dālē\ adj 1 : occurring. done. or used every day or every weekday 2 : computed in terms of one day ~ n. pl **-lies** : daily newspaper —**daily** adv

dain·ty \'dāntē\ n, pl **-ties** : something delicious ~ adj **-ti·er; -est** : delicately pretty —**dain·ti·ly** adv —**dain·ti·ness** n

dairy \'darē\ n, pl **-ies** : farm that produces or company that processes milk —**dairy·maid** n —**dairy·man** \-mən. -,man\ n

da·is \'dāəs\ n : raised platform (as for a speaker)

dai·sy \'dāzē\ n, pl **-sies** : tall leafy-stemmed plant bearing showy flowers

dale \'dāl\ n : valley

dal·ly \'dalē\ vb **-lied; -ly·ing** 1 : flirt 2 : dawdle —**dal·li·ance** \-əns\ n

dal·ma·tian \dal'māshən\ n : large dog having a spotted white coat

¹dam \'dam\ n : female parent of a domestic animal

²dam n : barrier to hold back water — **dam** vb

dam·age \'damij\ n 1 : loss or harm due to injury 2 pl : compensation for loss or injury ~ vb **-aged; -ag·ing** : do damage to

dam·ask \'daməsk\ n : firm lustrous figured fabric

dame \'dām\ n : woman of rank or authority

damn \'dam\ vb 1 : condemn to hell 2 : curse —**dam·na·ble** \-nəbəl\ adj — **dam·na·tion** \dam'nāshən\ n — **damned** adj

damp \'damp\ n : moisture ~ vb 1 : reduce the draft in 2 : restrain 3 : moisten ~ adj : moist —**damp·ness** n

damp·en \'dampən\ vb 1 : diminish in activity or vigor 2 : make or become damp

damp·er \'dampər\ n : movable plate to regulate a flue draft

dam·sel \'damzəl\ n : young woman

dance \'dans\ vb **danced; danc·ing** : move rhythmically to music ~ n : act of dancing or a gathering for dancing —**danc·er** n

dan·de·li·on \'dand³l,īən\ n : common yellow-flowered herb

dan·der \'dandər\ n : temper

dan·druff \'dandrəf\ n : whitish thin dry scales of skin on the scalp

dan·dy \'dandē\ n, pl **-dies** 1 : man too concerned with clothes 2 : something excellent ~ adj **-di·er; -est** : very good

dan·ger \'dānjər\ n 1 : exposure to injury or evil 2 : something that may cause injury —**dan·ger·ous** \'dānjə-rəs\ adj

dan·gle \'dangəl\ vb **-gled; -gling** 1 : hang and swing freely 2 : be left without support or connection 3 : allow or cause to hang 4 : offer as an inducement

dank \'dank\ adj : unpleasantly damp

dap·per \'dapər\ adj : neat and stylishly dressed

dap·ple \'dapəl\ vb -pled; -pling : mark with colored spots

dare \'dar\ vb dared; dar·ing 1 : have sufficient courage 2 : urge or provoke to contend —dare n —dar·ing \'dariŋ\ n or adj

dare·dev·il n : recklessly bold person

dark \'därk\ adj 1 : having little or no light 2 : not light in color 3 : gloomy ~ n : absence of light —dark·en \-ən\ vb —dark·ly adv —dark·ness n

dar·ling \'därliŋ\ n 1 : beloved 2 : favorite ~ adj 1 : dearly loved 2 : very pleasing

darn \'därn\ vb : mend with interlacing stitches —darn·er n

dart \'därt\ n 1 : small pointed missile 2 pl : game of throwing darts at a target 3 : tapering fold in a garment 4 : quick movement ~ vb : move suddenly or rapidly

dash \'dash\ vb 1 : smash 2 : knock or hurl violently 3 : ruin 4 : perform or finish hastily 5 : move quickly ~ n 1 : sudden burst, splash, or stroke 2 : punctuation mark — 3 : tiny amount 4 : showiness or liveliness 5 : sudden rush 6 : short race 7 : dashboard

dash·board n : instrument panel

dash·ing \'dashiŋ\ adj : dapper and charming

das·tard \'dastərd\ n : one who sneakingly commits malicious acts

das·tard·ly \-lē\ adj : base or malicious

da·ta \'dātə, 'dat-, 'dät-\ n sing or pl : factual information

da·ta·base \-,bās\ n : data organized for computer search

¹date \'dāt\ n : edible fruit of a palm

²date n 1 : day, month, or year when something is done or made 2 : historical time period 3 : social engagement or the person one goes out with ~ vb dat·ed; dat·ing 1 : determine or record the date of 2 : have a date with 3 : originate —to date : up to now

dat·ed \-əd\ adj : old-fashioned

da·tum \'dātəm, 'dat-, 'dät-\ n, pl -ta \-ə\ or -tums : piece of data

daub \'dób\ vb : smear ~ n : something daubed on —daub·er n

daugh·ter \'dótər\ n : human female offspring

daugh·ter–in–law n, pl daughters–in–law : wife of one's son

daunt \'dónt\ vb : lessen the courage of

daunt·less \-ləs\ adj : fearless

dav·en·port \'davən,pórt\ n : sofa

daw·dle \'dódᵊl\ vb -dled; -dling 1 : waste time 2 : loiter

dawn \'dón\ vb 1 : grow light as the sun rises 2 : begin to appear, develop, or be understood ~ n : first appearance (as of daylight)

day \'dā\ n 1 : period of light between one night and the next 2 : 24 hours 3 : specified date 4 : particular time or age 5 : period of work for a day —day·light n —day·time n

day·break n : dawn

day·dream n : fantasy of wish fulfillment —daydream vb

daylight saving time n : time one hour ahead of standard time

daze \'dāz\ vb dazed; daz·ing 1 : stun by a blow 2 : dazzle —daze n

daz·zle \'dazəl\ vb -zled; -zling 1 : overpower with light 2 : impress greatly —dazzle n

DDT \,dē,dē'tē\ n : long-lasting insecticide

dea·con \'dēkən\ n : subordinate church officer

dea·con·ess \'dēkənəs\ n : woman who assists in church ministry

dead \'ded\ adj 1 : lifeless 2 : unresponsive or inactive 3 : exhausted 4 : obsolete 5 : precise ~ n, pl dead 1 : one that is dead —usu. with the 2 : most lifeless time ~ adv 1 : completely 2 : directly —dead·en \'dedᵊn\ vb

dead·beat n : one who will not pay debts

dead end n : end of a street with no exit —dead–end adj

dead heat n : tie in a contest

dead·line n : time by which something must be finished

dead·lock n : struggle that neither side can win —deadlock vb

dead·ly \'dedlē\ adj -li·er; -est 1 : capable of causing death 2 : very accurate 3 : fatal to spiritual progress 4 : suggestive of death 5 : very great ~ adv : extremely —dead·li·ness n

dead·pan adj : expressionless —deadpan n or vb or adv

dead·wood n : something useless

deaf \'def\ adj : unable or unwilling to hear —deaf·en \-ən\ vb —deaf·ness n

deaf–mute n : deaf person unable to speak

deal \'dēl\ *n* **1** : indefinite quantity **2** : distribution of playing cards **3** : negotiation or agreement **4** : treatment received **5** : bargain ~ *vb* **dealt** \'delt\; **deal·ing** \'dēliŋ\ **1** : distribute playing cards **2** : be concerned with **3** : administer or deliver **4** : take action **5** : sell **6** : reach a state of acceptance —**deal·er** *n* —**deal·ing** *n*

dean \'dēn\ *n* **1** : head of a group of clergy members **2** : university or school administrator **3** : senior member

dear \'dir\ *adj* **1** : highly valued or loved **2** : expensive ~ *n* : loved one — **dear·ly** *adv* —**dear·ness** *n*

dearth \'dərth\ *n* : scarcity

death \'deth\ *n* **1** : end of life **2** : cause of loss of life **3** : state of being dead **4** : destruction or extinction —**death·less** *adj* —**death·ly** *adj or adv*

de·ba·cle \di'bäkəl, -'bakəl\ *n* : disaster or fiasco

de·bar \di'bär\ *vb* : bar from something

de·bark \-'bärk\ *vb* : disembark —**de·bar·ka·tion** \,dē,bär'kāshən\ *n*

de·base \di'bās\ *vb* : disparage —**de·base·ment** *n*

de·bate \-'bāt\ *vb* -**bat·ed**; -**bat·ing** : discuss a question by argument — **de·bat·able** *adj* —**debate** *n* —**de·bat·er** *n*

de·bauch \-'bóch\ *vb* : seduce or corrupt —**de·bauch·ery** \-ərē\ *n*

de·bil·i·tate \di'bilə,tāt\ *vb* -**tat·ed**; -**tat·ing** : make ill or weak

de·bil·i·ty \-'bilətē\ *n, pl* -**ties** : physical weakness

deb·it \'debət\ *n* : account entry of a payment or debt ~ *vb* : record as a debit

deb·o·nair \,debə'nar\ *adj* : suave

de·bris \də'brē, dā-; 'dā,brē\ *n, pl* -**bris** \-'brēz, -,brēz\ : remains of something destroyed

debt \'det\ *n* **1** : sin **2** : something owed **3** : state of owing —**debt·or** \-ər\ *n*

de·bunk \dē'bəŋk\ *vb* : expose as false

de·but \'dā,byü, dā'byü\ *n* **1** : first public appearance **2** : formal entrance into society —**debut** *vb* —**deb·u·tante** \'debyù,tänt\ *n*

de·cade \'dek,ād, -əd; de'kād\ *n* : 10 years

dec·a·dence \'dekədəns, di'kād⁰ns\ *n* : deterioration —**dec·a·dent** \-ənt, -⁰nt\ *adj or n*

de·cal \'dē,kal, di'kal, 'dekəl\ *n* : picture or design for transfer from prepared paper

de·camp \di'kamp\ *vb* : depart suddenly

de·cant \di'kant\ *vb* : pour gently

de·cant·er \-ər\ *n* : ornamental bottle

de·cap·i·tate \di'kapə,tāt\ *vb* -**tat·ed**; -**tat·ing** : behead —**de·cap·i·ta·tion** \-,kapə'tāshən\ *n*

de·cay \di'kā\ *vb* **1** : decline in condition **2** : decompose —**decay** *n*

de·cease \-'sēs\ *n* : death —**decease** *vb*

de·ceit \-'sēt\ *n* **1** : deception **2** : dishonesty —**de·ceit·ful** \-fəl\ *adj* —**de·ceit·ful·ly** *adv* —**de·ceit·ful·ness** *n*

de·ceive \-'sēv\ *vb* -**ceived**; -**ceiv·ing** : trick or mislead —**de·ceiv·er** *n*

de·cel·er·ate \dē'selə,rāt\ *vb* -**at·ed**; -**at·ing** : slow down

De·cem·ber \di'sembər\ *n* : 12th month of the year having 31 days

de·cent \'dēs⁰nt\ *adj* **1** : good, right, or just **2** : clothed **3** : not obscene **4** : fairly good —**de·cen·cy** \-⁰nsē\ *n* —**de·cent·ly** *adv*

de·cep·tion \di'sepshən\ *n* **1** : act or fact of deceiving **2** : fraud —**de·cep·tive** \-'septiv\ *adj* —**de·cep·tive·ly** *adv* —**de·cep·tive·ness** *n*

de·cide \di'sīd\ *vb* -**cid·ed**; -**cid·ing** **1** : make a choice or judgment **2** : bring to a conclusion **3** : cause to decide

de·cid·ed *adj* **1** : unquestionable **2** : resolute —**de·cid·ed·ly** *adv*

de·cid·u·ous \di'sijəwəs\ *adj* : having leaves that fall annually

dec·i·mal \'desəməl\ *n* : fraction in which the denominator is a power of 10 expressed by a point (**decimal point**) placed at the left of the numerator —**decimal** *adj*

de·ci·pher \di'sīfər\ *vb* : make out the meaning of —**de·ci·pher·able** *adj*

de·ci·sion \-'sizhən\ *n* **1** : act or result of deciding **2** : determination

de·ci·sive \-'sīsiv\ *adj* **1** : having the power to decide **2** : conclusive **3** : showing determination —**de·ci·sive·ly** *adv* —**de·ci·sive·ness** *n*

deck \'dek\ *n* **1** : floor of a ship **2** : pack of playing cards ~ *vb* **1** : array or dress up **2** : knock down

de·claim \di'klām\ *vb* : speak loudly or impressively —**dec·la·ma·tion** \,deklə'māshən\ *n*

de·clare \di'klar\ *vb* -**clared**; -**clar·ing** **1** : make known formally **2** : state emphatically —**dec·la·ra·tion** \,deklə-

'rāshən\ *n* —**de·clar·a·tive** \di'klarə-tiv\ *adj* —**de·clar·a·to·ry** \di'kla-rə,tōrē\ *adj* —**de·clar·er** *n*

de·clen·sion \di'klenchən\ *n* : inflectional forms of a noun, pronoun, or adjective

de·cline \di'klīn\ *vb* **-clined; -clin·ing** 1 : turn or slope downward 2 : wane 3 : refuse to accept 4 : inflect ~ *n* 1 : gradual wasting away 2 : change to a lower state or level 3 : a descending slope —**dec·li·na·tion** \,deklə-'nā-shən\ *n*

de·code \dē'kōd\ *vb* : decipher (a coded message) —**de·cod·er** *n*

de·com·mis·sion \,dēkə'mishən\ *vb* : remove from service

de·com·pose \,dēkəm'pōz\ *vb* 1 : separate into parts 2 : decay —**de·com·po·si·tion** \dē,kämpə'zishən\ *n*

de·con·ges·tant \,dēkən'jestənt\ *n* : agent that relieves congestion

de·cor, dé·cor \dā'kór, 'dā,kór\ *n* : room design or decoration

dec·o·rate \'dekə,rāt\ *vb* **-rat·ed; -rat·ing** 1 : add something attractive to 2 : honor with a medal —**dec·o·ra·tion** \,dekə'rāshən\ *n* —**dec·o·ra·tive** \'dekərətiv\ *adj* —**dec·o·ra·tor** \'dekə,rātər\ *n*

de·co·rum \di'kōrəm\ *n* : proper behavior —**dec·o·rous** \'dekərəs, di'kōrəs\ *adj*

de·coy \'dē,kói, di'-\ *n* : something that tempts or draws attention from another ~ *vb* : tempt

de·crease \di'krēs\ *vb* **-creased; -creas·ing** : grow or cause to grow less —**decrease** \'dē,krēs\ *n*

de·cree \di'krē\ *n* : official order —**decree** *vb*

de·crep·it \di'krepət\ *adj* : impaired by age

de·cre·scen·do \,dākrə'shendō\ *adv or adj* : with a decrease in volume

de·cry \di'krī\ *vb* : express strong disapproval of

ded·i·cate \'dedi,kāt\ *vb* **-cat·ed; -cat·ing** 1 : set apart for a purpose (as honor or worship) 2 : address to someone as a compliment —**ded·i·ca·tion** \,dedi'kāshən\ *n* —**ded·i·ca·to·ry** \'dedikə,tōrē\ *adj*

de·duce \di'düs, -'dyüs\ *vb* **-duced; -duc·ing** : derive by reasoning —**de·duc·ible** *adj*

de·duct \-'dəkt\ *vb* : subtract —**deduct·ible** *adj*

de·duc·tion \-'dəkshən\ *n* 1 : subtraction 2 : reasoned conclusion —**de·duc·tive** \-'dəktiv\ *adj*

deed \'dēd\ *n* 1 : exploit 2 : document showing ownership ~ *vb* : convey by deed

deem \'dēm\ *vb* : think

deep \'dēp\ *adj* 1 : extending far or a specified distance down, back, within, or outward 2 : occupied 3 : dark and rich in color 4 : low in tone ~ *adv* 1 : deeply 2 : far along in time ~ *n* : deep place —**deep·en** \'dēpən\ *vb* —**deep·ly** *adv*

deep-seat·ed \-'sētəd\ *adj* : firmly established

deer \'dir\ *n, pl* **deer** : ruminant mammal with antlers in the male —**deer·skin** *n*

de·face \di'fās\ *vb* : mar the surface of —**de·face·ment** *n* —**de·fac·er** *n*

de·fame \di'fām\ *vb* **-famed; -fam·ing** : injure the reputation of —**def·a·ma·tion** \,defə'māshən\ *n* —**de·fam·a·to·ry** \di'famə,tōrē\ *adj*

de·fault \di'fólt\ *n* : failure in a duty —**default** *vb* —**de·fault·er** *n*

de·feat \di'fēt\ *vb* 1 : frustrate 2 : win victory over ~ *n* : loss of a battle or contest

def·e·cate \'defi,kāt\ *vb* **-cat·ed; -cat·ing** : discharge feces from the bowels —**def·e·ca·tion** \,defi'kāshən\ *n*

de·fect \'dē,fekt, di'fekt\ *n* : imperfection ~ \di'-\ *vb* : desert —**de·fection** \-'fekshən\ *n* —**de·fec·tor** \-'fektər\ *n*

de·fec·tive \di'fektiv\ *adj* : faulty or deficient —**defective** *n*

de·fend \-'fend\ *vb* 1 : protect from danger or harm 2 : take the side of —**de·fend·er** *n*

de·fen·dant \-'fendənt\ *n* : person charged or sued in a court

de·fense \-'fens\ *n* 1 : act of defending 2 : something that defends 3 : party, group, or team that opposes another —**de·fense·less** *adj* —**de·fen·si·ble** *adj* —**de·fen·sive** *adj or n*

¹**de·fer** \di'fər\ *vb* **-rr-** : postpone —**de·fer·ment** \di'fərmənt\ *n* —**de·fer·ra·ble** \-əbəl\ *adj*

²**defer** *vb* **-rr-** : yield to the opinion or wishes of another —**def·er·ence** \'defrəns\ *n* —**def·er·en·tial** \,defə-'renchəl\ *adj*

de·fi·ance \di'fīəns\ n : disposition to resist —**de·fi·ant** \-ənt\ adj

de·fi·cient \di'fishənt\ adj 1 : lacking something necessary 2 : not up to standard —**de·fi·cien·cy** \-'fishənsē\ n

def·i·cit \'defəsət\ n : shortage esp. in money

de·file \di'fīl\ vb -filed; -fil·ing 1 : make filthy or corrupt 2 : profane or dishonor —**de·file·ment** n

de·fine \di'fīn\ vb -fined; -fin·ing 1 : fix or mark the limits of 2 : clarify in outline 3 : set forth the meaning of —**de·fin·able** adj —**de·fin·ably** adv —**de·fin·er** n —**def·i·ni·tion** \,defə'nishən\ n

def·i·nite \'defənət\ adj 1 : having distinct limits 2 : clear in meaning, intent, or identity 3 : typically designating an identified or immediately identifiable person or thing —**def·i·nite·ly** adv

de·fin·i·tive \di'finətiv\ adj 1 : conclusive 2 : authoritative

de·flate \di'flāt\ vb -flat·ed; -flat·ing 1 : release air or gas from 2 : reduce —**de·fla·tion** \-'flāshən\ n

de·flect \di-'flekt\ vb : turn aside —**de·flec·tion** \-'flekshən\ n

de·fog \-'fóg, -'fäg\ vb : remove condensed moisture from —**de·fog·ger** n

de·fo·li·ate \dē'fōlē,āt\ vb -at·ed; -at·ing : deprive of leaves esp. prematurely —**de·fo·li·ant** \-lēənt\ n —**de·fo·li·a·tion** \-,fōlē'āshən\ n

de·form \di'fórm\ vb 1 : distort 2 : disfigure —**de·for·ma·tion** \,dē,fór'māshən, ,defər-\ n —**de·for·mi·ty** \di'fórmətē\ n

de·fraud \di'fród\ vb : cheat

de·fray \-'frā\ vb : pay

de·frost \-'fróst\ vb 1 : thaw out 2 : free from ice —**de·frost·er** n

deft \'deft\ adj : quick and skillful —**deft·ly** adv —**deft·ness** n

de·funct \di'fəŋkt\ adj : dead

de·fy \-'fī\ vb -fied; -fy·ing 1 : challenge 2 : boldly refuse to obey

de·gen·er·ate \di'jenərət\ adj : degraded or corrupt ~ n : degenerate person ~ \-ə,rāt\ vb : become degenerate —**de·gen·er·a·cy** \-ərəsē\ n —**de·gen·er·a·tion** \-,jenə'rāshən\ n —**de·gen·er·a·tive** \-'jenə,rātiv\ adj

de·grade \di'grād\ vb 1 : reduce from a higher to a lower rank or degree 2 : debase 3 : decompose —**de·grad·able** \-əbəl\ adj —**deg·ra·da·tion** \,degrə'dāshən\ n

de·gree \di'grē\ n 1 : step in a series 2 : extent, intensity, or scope 3 : title given to a college graduate 4 : a 360th part of the circumference of a circle 5 : unit for measuring temperature

de·hy·drate \dē'hī,drāt\ vb 1 : remove water from 2 : lose liquid —**de·hy·dra·tion** \,dēhī'drāshən\ n

de·i·fy \'dēə,fī, 'dā-\ vb -fied; -fy·ing : make a god of —**de·i·fi·ca·tion** \,dēəfə'kāshən, ,dā-\ n

deign \'dān\ vb : condescend

de·i·ty \'dēətē, 'dā-\ n, pl -ties 1 cap : God 2 : a god or goddess

de·ject·ed \di'jektəd\ adj : sad —**de·jec·tion** \-shən\ n

de·lay \di'lā\ n : a putting off of something ~ vb 1 : postpone 2 : stop or hinder for a time

de·lec·ta·ble \di'lektəbəl\ adj : delicious

del·e·gate \'deligət, -,gāt\ n : representative ~ \-,gāt\ vb -gat·ed; -gat·ing 1 : entrust to another 2 : appoint as one's delegate —**del·e·ga·tion** \,deli'gāshən\ n

de·lete \di'lēt\ vb -let·ed; -let·ing : eliminate something written —**de·le·tion** \-'lēshən\ n

del·e·te·ri·ous \,delə'tirēəs\ adj : harmful

de·lib·er·ate \di'libərət\ adj 1 : determined after careful thought 2 : intentional 3 : not hurried ~ \-ə,rāt\ vb -at·ed; -at·ing : consider carefully —**de·lib·er·ate·ly** adv —**de·lib·er·ate·ness** n —**de·lib·er·a·tion** \-,libə'rāshən\ n —**de·lib·er·a·tive** \-'libə,rātiv, -rət-\ adj

del·i·ca·cy \'delikəsē\ n, pl -cies 1 : something special and pleasing to eat 2 : fineness 3 : frailty

del·i·cate \'delikət\ adj 1 : subtly pleasing to the senses 2 : dainty and charming 3 : sensitive and fragile 4 : requiring fine skill or tact —**del·i·cate·ly** adv

del·i·ca·tes·sen \,delikə'tesᵊn\ n : store that sells ready-to-eat food

de·li·cious \di'lishəs\ adj : very pleasing esp. in taste or aroma —**de·li·cious·ly** adv —**de·li·cious·ness** n

de·light \di'līt\ n 1 : great pleasure 2 : source of great pleasure ~ vb 1 : take great pleasure 2 : satisfy greatly —**de·light·ful** \-fəl\ adj —**de·light·ful·ly** adv

de·lin·eate \di'linē,āt\ vb -eat·ed; -eat·ing : sketch or portray —de·lin·ea·tion \-,linē'āshən\ n

de·lin·quent \-'liŋkwənt\ n : delinquent person ~ adj 1 : violating duty or law 2 : overdue in payment —de·lin·quen·cy \-kwənsē\ n

de·lir·i·um \di'lirēəm\ n : mental disturbance —de·lir·i·ous \-ēəs\ adj

de·liv·er \di'livər\ vb 1 : set free 2 : hand over 3 : assist in birth 4 : say or speak 5 : send to an intended destination —de·liv·er·ance \-ərəns\ n —de·liv·er·er n —de·liv·ery \-ərē\ n

dell \'del\ n : small secluded valley

del·ta \'deltə\ n : triangle of land at the mouth of a river

de·lude \di'lüd\ vb -lud·ed; -lud·ing : mislead or deceive

del·uge \'delyüj\ n 1 : flood 2 : drenching rain ~ vb -uged; -ug·ing 1 : flood 2 : overwhelm

de·lu·sion \di'lüzhən\ n : false belief

de·luxe \di'lùks, -'ləks, -'lüks\ adj : very luxurious or elegant

delve \'delv\ vb delved; delv·ing 1 : dig 2 : seek information in records

dem·a·gogue, dem·a·gog \'demə,gäg\ n : politician who appeals to emotion and prejudice —dem·a·gogu·ery \-,gägərē\ n —dem·a·gogy \-,gägē, -,gäjē\ n

de·mand \di'mand\ n 1 : act of demanding 2 : something claimed as due 3 : ability and desire to buy 4 : urgent need ~ vb 1 : ask for with authority 2 : require

de·mar·cate \di'mär,kāt, 'dē,mär-\ vb -cat·ed; -cat·ing : mark the limits of —de·mar·ca·tion \,dē,mär'kāshən\ n

de·mean \di'mēn\ vb : degrade

de·mean·or \-'mēnər\ n : behavior

de·ment·ed \-'mentəd\ adj : crazy

de·mer·it \-'merət\ n : mark given an offender

demi·god \'demi,gäd\ n : mythological being less powerful than a god

de·mise \di'mīz\ n 1 : death 2 : loss of status

demi·tasse \'demi,tas\ n : small cup of coffee

de·mo·bi·lize \di'mōbə,līz, dē-\ vb : disband from military service —de·mo·bi·li·za·tion \-,mōbələ'zāshən\ n

de·moc·ra·cy \di'mäkrəsē\ n, pl -cies 1 : government in which the supreme power is held by the people 2

: political unit with democratic government

dem·o·crat \'demə,krat\ n : adherent of democracy

dem·o·crat·ic \,demə'kratik\ adj : relating to or favoring democracy —dem·o·crat·i·cal·ly \-tiklē\ adv —de·moc·ra·tize \di'mäkrə,tīz\ vb

de·mol·ish \di'mälish\ vb 1 : tear down or smash 2 : put an end to —de·mo·li·tion \,demə'lishən, ,dē-\ n

de·mon \'dēmən\ n : evil spirit —de·mon·ic \di'mänik\ adj

dem·on·strate \'demən,strāt\ vb -strat·ed; -strat·ing 1 : show clearly or publicly 2 : prove 3 : explain —de·mon·stra·ble \di'mänstrəbəl\ adj —de·mon·stra·bly \-blē\ adv —dem·on·stra·tion \,demən'strāshən\ n —de·mon·stra·tive \di'mänstrətiv\ adj or n —dem·on·stra·tor \'demən,strātər\ n

de·mor·al·ize \di'mórə,līz\ vb : destroy the enthusiasm of

de·mote \di'mōt\ vb -mot·ed; -mot·ing : reduce to a lower rank —de·mo·tion \-'mōshən\ n

de·mur \di'mər\ vb -rr- : object —de·mur n

de·mure \di'myùr\ adj : modest —de·mure·ly adv

den \'den\ n 1 : animal's shelter 2 : hiding place 3 : cozy private little room

de·na·ture \dē'nāchər\ vb -tured; -tur·ing : make (alcohol) unfit for drinking

de·ni·al \di'nīəl\ n : rejection of a request or of the validity of a statement

den·i·grate \'deni,grāt\ vb -grat·ed; -grat·ing : speak ill of

den·im \'denəm\ n 1 : durable twilled cotton fabric 2 pl : pants of denim

den·i·zen \'denəzən\ n : inhabitant

de·nom·i·na·tion \di,nämə'nāshən\ n 1 : religious body 2 : value or size in a series —de·nom·i·na·tion·al \-shə-nəl\ adj

de·nom·i·na·tor \-'nämə,nātər\ n : part of a fraction below the line

de·note \di'nōt\ vb 1 : mark out plainly 2 : mean —de·no·ta·tion \,dēnō'tāshən\ n —de·no·ta·tive \'dēnō-,tātiv, di'nōtətiv\ adj

de·noue·ment \,dā,nü'mäⁿ\ n : final outcome (as of a drama)

de·nounce \di'naùns\ vb -nounced; -nounc·ing 1 : pronounce blameworthy or evil 2 : inform against

dense \'dens\ *adj* **dens·er; -est 1** : thick, compact, or crowded **2** : stupid — **dense·ly** *adv* — **dense·ness** *n* — **den·si·ty** \'densətē\ *n*

dent \'dent\ *n* : small depression — **dent** *vb*

den·tal \'dentᵊl\ *adj* : relating to teeth or dentistry

den·ti·frice \'dentəfrəs\ *n* : preparation for cleaning teeth

den·tin \'dentᵊn\, **den·tine** \'den,tēn, ,den'-\ *n* : bonelike component of teeth

den·tist \'dentist\ *n* : one who cares for and replaces teeth — **den·tist·ry** *n*

den·ture \'denchər\ *n* : artificial teeth

de·nude \di'nüd, -'nyüd\ *vb* **-nud·ed; -nud·ing** : strip of covering

de·nun·ci·a·tion \di,nənsē'āshən\ *n* : act of denouncing

de·ny \-'nī\ *vb* **-nied; -ny·ing 1** : declare untrue **2** : disavow **3** : refuse to grant

de·odor·ant \dē'ōdərənt\ *n* : preparation to prevent unpleasant odors — **de·odor·ize** \-,rīz\ *vb*

de·part \di'pärt\ *vb* **1** : go away or away from **2** : die — **de·par·ture** \-'pärchər\ *n*

de·part·ment \di'pärtmənt\ *n* **1** : area of responsibility or interest **2** : functional division — **de·part·men·tal** \di,pärt'mentᵊl, ,dē-\ *adj*

de·pend \di'pend\ *vb* **1** : rely for support **2** : be determined by or based on something else — **de·pend·abil·i·ty** \-,pendə'bilətē\ *n* — **de·pend·able** *adj* — **de·pen·dence** \di'pendəns\ *n* — **de·pen·den·cy** \-dənsē\ *n* — **de·pen·dent** \-ənt\ *adj or n*

de·pict \di'pikt\ *vb* : show by or as if by a picture — **de·pic·tion** \-'pikshən\ *n*

de·plete \di'plēt\ *vb* **-plet·ed; -plet·ing** : use up resources of — **de·ple·tion** \-'plēshən\ *n*

de·plore \-'plōr\ *vb* **-plored; -plor·ing** : regret strongly — **de·plor·able** \-əbəl\ *adj*

de·ploy \-'ploi\ *vb* : spread out for battle — **de·ploy·ment** \-mənt\ *n*

de·port \di'pōrt\ *vb* **1** : behave **2** : send out of the country — **de·por·ta·tion** \,dē,pōr'tāshən\ *n* — **de·port·ment** \di'pōrtmənt\ *n*

de·pose \-'pōz\ *vb* **-posed; -pos·ing 1** : remove (a ruler) from office **2** : testify — **de·po·si·tion** \,depə'zishən, ,dē-\ *n*

de·pos·it \di'päzət\ *vb* **-it·ed; -it·ing** : place esp. for safekeeping ~ *n* **1** : state of being deposited **2** : something deposited **3** : act of depositing **4** : natural accumulation — **de·pos·i·tor** \-'päzətər\ *n*

de·pos·i·to·ry \di'päzə,tōrē\ *n, pl* **-ries** : place for deposit

de·pot \/ *usu* 'depō, 2 *usu* 'dēp-\ *n* **1** : place for storage **2** : bus or railroad station

de·prave \di'prāv\ *vb* **-praved; -prav·ing** : corrupt morally — **de·praved** *adj* — **de·prav·i·ty** \-'pravətē\ *n*

dep·re·cate \'depri,kāt\ *vb* **-cat·ed; -cat·ing 1** : express disapproval of **2** : belittle — **dep·re·ca·tion** \,depri'kāshən\ *n* — **dep·re·ca·tory** \'deprikə,tōrē\ *adj*

de·pre·ci·ate \di'prēshē,āt\ *vb* **-at·ed; -at·ing 1** : lessen in value **2** : belittle — **de·pre·ci·a·tion** \-,prēshē'āshən\ *n*

dep·re·da·tion \,deprə'dāshən\ *n* : a laying waste or plundering — **dep·re·date** \'deprə,dāt\ *vb*

de·press \di'pres\ *vb* **1** : press down **2** : lessen the activity or force of **3** : discourage **4** : decrease the market value of — **de·pres·sant** \-ᵊnt\ *n or adj* — **de·pressed** *adj* — **de·pres·sive** \-iv\ *adj or n* — **de·pres·sor** \-ər\ *n*

de·pres·sion \di'preshən\ *n* **1** : act of depressing or state of being depressed **2** : depressed place **3** : period of low economic activity

de·prive \-'prīv\ *vb* **-prived; -priv·ing** : take or keep something away from — **de·pri·va·tion** \,deprə'vāshən\ *n*

depth \'depth\ *n, pl* **depths 1** : something that is deep **2** : distance down from a surface **3** : distance from front to back **4** : quality of being deep

dep·u·ta·tion \,depyə'tāshən\ *n* : delegation

dep·u·ty \'depyətē\ *n, pl* **-ties** : person appointed to act for another — **dep·u·tize** \-yə,tīz\ *vb*

de·rail \di'rāl\ *vb* : leave the rails — **de·rail·ment** *n*

de·range \-'rānj\ *vb* **-ranged; -rang·ing 1** : disarrange or upset **2** : make insane — **de·range·ment** *n*

der·by \'dərbē, *Brit* 'där-\ *n, pl* **-bies 1** : horse race **2** : stiff felt hat with dome-shaped crown

de·reg·u·late \dē'regyù,lāt\ *vb* : remove restrictions on — **de·reg·u·la·tion** \-,regyù'lāshən\ *n*

der·e·lict \'derə,likt\ *adj* **1** : abandoned

2 : negligent ~ *n* 1 : something abandoned 2 : bum —**der·e·lic·tion** \,derə'likshən\ *n*

de·ride \di'rīd\ *vb* -rid·ed; -rid·ing : make fun of —**de·ri·sion** \-'rizhən\ *n* —**de·ri·sive** \-'rīsiv\ *adj* —**de·ri·sive·ly** *adv* —**de·ri·sive·ness** *n*

de·rive \di'rīv\ *vb* -rived; -riv·ing 1 : obtain from a source or parent 2 : come from a certain source 3 : infer or deduce —**der·i·va·tion** \,derə'vāshən\ *n* —**de·riv·a·tive** \di'rivətiv\ *adj or n*

der·ma·tol·o·gy \,dərmə'täləjē\ *n* : study of the skin and its disorders —**der·ma·tol·o·gist** \-jist\ *n*

de·rog·a·tive \di'rägətiv\ *adj* : derogatory

de·rog·a·to·ry \di'rägə,tōrē\ *adj* : intended to lower the reputation

der·rick \'derik\ *n* 1 : hoisting apparatus 2 : framework over an oil well

de·scend \di'send\ *vb* 1 : move or climb down 2 : derive 3 : extend downward 4 : appear suddenly (as in an attack) —**de·scen·dant, de·scen·dent** \-ənt\ *adj or n* —**de·scent** \di'sent\ *n*

de·scribe \di'skrīb\ *vb* -scribed; -scrib·ing : represent in words —**de·scrib·able** *adj* —**de·scrip·tion** \-'skripshən\ *n* —**de·scrip·tive** \-'skriptiv\ *adj*

de·scry \di'skrī\ *vb* -scried; -scry·ing : catch sight of

des·e·crate \'desi,krāt\ *vb* -crat·ed; -crat·ing : treat (something sacred) with disrespect —**des·e·cra·tion** \,desi'krāshən\ *n*

de·seg·re·gate \dē'segrə,gāt\ *vb* : eliminate esp. racial segregation in —**de·seg·re·ga·tion** *n*

¹**des·ert** \'dezərt\ *n* : dry barren region —**desert** *adj*

²**de·sert** \di'zərt\ *n* : what one deserves

³**de·sert** \di'zərt\ *vb* : abandon —**de·sert·er** *n* —**de·ser·tion** \-'zərshən\ *n*

de·serve \-'zərv\ *vb* -served; -serv·ing : be worthy of

des·ic·cate \'desi,kāt\ *vb* -cat·ed; -cat·ing : dehydrate —**des·ic·ca·tion** \,desi'kāshən\ *n*

de·sign \di'zīn\ *vb* 1 : create and work out the details of 2 : make a pattern or sketch of ~ *n* 1 : mental project or plan 2 : purpose 3 : preliminary sketch 4 : underlying arrangement of elements 5 : decorative pattern —**de·sign·er** *n*

des·ig·nate \'dezig,nāt\ *vb* -nat·ed; -nat·ing 1 : indicate, specify, or name 2 : appoint —**des·ig·na·tion** \,dezig-'nāshən\ *n*

de·sire \di'zīr\ *vb* -sired; -sir·ing 1 : feel desire for 2 : request ~ *n* 1 : strong conscious impulse to have, be, or do something 2 : something desired —**de·sir·abil·i·ty** \-,zīrə'bilətē\ *n* —**de·sir·able** \-'zīrəbəl\ *adj* —**de·sir·able·ness** *n* —**de·sir·ous** \-'zīrəs\ *adj*

de·sist \di'zist, -'sist\ *vb* : stop

desk \'desk\ *n* : table esp. for writing and reading

des·o·late \'desələt, 'dez-\ *adj* 1 : lifeless 2 : disconsolate ~ \-,lāt\ *vb* -lat·ed; -lat·ing : lay waste —**des·o·la·tion** \,desə'lāshən, ,dez-\ *n*

de·spair \di'spar\ *vb* : lose all hope ~ *n* : loss of hope

des·per·a·do \,despə'rädō, -'rād-\ *n*, *pl* -does *or* -dos : desperate criminal

des·per·ate \'desprət\ *adj* 1 : hopeless 2 : rash 3 : extremely intense —**des·per·ate·ly** *adv* —**des·per·a·tion** \,despə'rāshən\ *n*

de·spi·ca·ble \di'spikəbəl, 'despik-\ *adj* : deserving scorn

de·spise \di'spīz\ *vb* -spised; -spis·ing : feel contempt for

de·spite \-'spīt\ *prep* : in spite of

de·spoil \-'spóil\ *vb* : strip of possessions or value

de·spon·den·cy \-'spändənsē\ *n* : dejection —**de·spon·dent** \-dənt\ *adj*

des·pot \'despət, -,pät\ *n* : tyrant —**des·pot·ic** \des'pätik\ *adj* —**des·po·tism** \'despə,tizəm\ *n*

des·sert \di'zərt\ *n* : sweet food, fruit, or cheese ending a meal

des·ti·na·tion \,destə'nāshən\ *n* : place where something or someone is going

des·tine \'destən\ *vb* -tined; -tin·ing 1 : designate, assign, or determine in advance 2 : direct

des·ti·ny \'destənē\ *n*, *pl* -nies : that which is to happen in the future

des·ti·tute \'destə,tüt, -,tyüt\ *adj* 1 : lacking something 2 : very poor —**des·ti·tu·tion** \,destə'tüshən, -'tyü-\ *n*

de·stroy \di'strói\ *vb* : kill or put an end to

de·stroy·er \-'stróiər\ *n* 1 : one that destroys 2 : small speedy warship

de·struc·tion \-'strəkshən\ *n* 1 : action of destroying 2 : ruin —

de·struc·ti·bil·i·ty \-,strəktə'bilətē\ n —de·struc·ti·ble \-'strəktəbəl\ adj —de·struc·tive \-'strəktiv\ adj

des·ul·to·ry \'desəl,tōrē\ adj : aimless

de·tach \di'tach\ vb : separate

de·tached \-'tacht\ adj 1 : separate 2 : aloof or impartial

de·tach·ment \-'tachmənt\ n 1 : separation 2 : troops or ships on special service 3 : aloofness 4 : impartiality

de·tail \di'tāl, 'dē,tāl\ n : small item or part ~ vb : give details of

de·tain \di'tān\ vb 1 : hold in custody 2 : delay

de·tect \di'tekt\ vb : discover —de·tect·able adj —de·tec·tion \-'tekshən\ n —de·tec·tor \-tər\ n

de·tec·tive \di'tektiv\ n : one who investigates crime

dé·tente \dā'tä⁴t\ n : relaxation of tensions between nations

de·ten·tion \di'tenchən\ n : confinement

de·ter \-'tər\ vb -rr- : discourage or prevent —de·ter·rence \-əns\ n —de·ter·rent \-ənt\ adj or n

de·ter·gent \di'tərjənt\ n : cleansing agent

de·te·ri·o·rate \-'tirēə,rāt\ vb -rat·ed; -rat·ing : make or become worse —de·te·ri·o·ra·tion \-,tirēə'rāshən\ n

de·ter·mi·na·tion \di,tərmə'nāshən\ n 1 : act of deciding or fixing 2 : firm purpose

de·ter·mine \-'tərmən\ vb -mined; -min·ing 1 : decide on, establish, or settle 2 : find out 3 : bring about as a result

de·test \-'test\ vb : hate —de·test·able adj —de·tes·ta·tion \,dē,tes'tāshən\ n

det·o·nate \'det⁴n,āt\ vb -nat·ed; -nat·ing : explode —det·o·na·tion \,det⁴n'āshən\ n —det·o·na·tor \'det⁴n,ātər\ n

de·tour \'dē,tùr\ n : temporary indirect route —detour vb

de·tract \di'trakt\ vb : take away —de·trac·tion \-'trakshən\ n —de·trac·tor \-'traktər\ n

det·ri·ment \'detrəmənt\ n : damage —det·ri·men·tal \,detrə'ment⁴l\ adj —det·ri·men·tal·ly adv

deuce \'düs, 'dyüs\ n 1 : 2 in cards or dice 2 : tie in tennis 3 : devil —used as an oath

deut·sche mark \'dóichə-\ n : monetary unit of Germany

de·val·ue \dē'val,yü\ vb : reduce the value of —de·val·u·a·tion n

dev·as·tate \'devə,stāt\ vb -tat·ed; -tat·ing : ruin —dev·as·ta·tion \,devə'stāshən\ n

de·vel·op \di'veləp\ vb 1 : grow, increase, or evolve gradually 2 : cause to grow, increase, or reach full potential —de·vel·op·er n —de·vel·op·ment n —de·vel·op·men·tal \-,veləp'ment⁴l\ adj

de·vi·ate \'dēvē,āt\ vb -at·ed; -at·ing : change esp. from a course or standard —de·vi·ant \-vēənt\ adj or n —de·vi·ate \-vēət, -vē,āt\ n —de·vi·a·tion \,dēvē'āshən\ n

de·vice \di'vīs\ n 1 : specialized piece of equipment or tool 2 : design

dev·il \'devəl\ n 1 : personified supreme spirit of evil 2 : demon 3 : wicked person ~ vb -iled or -illed; -il·ing or -il·ling 1 : season highly 2 : pester —dev·il·ish \'devəlish\ adj —dev·il·ry \'devəlrē\, dev·il·try \-trē\ n

de·vi·ous \'dēvēəs\ adj : tricky

de·vise \di'vīz\ vb -vised; -vis·ing 1 : invent 2 : plot 3 : give by will

de·void \-'vóid\ adj : entirely lacking

de·vote \di'vōt\ vb -vot·ed; -vot·ing : set apart for a special purpose

de·vot·ed adj : faithful

dev·o·tee \,devə'tē, -'tā\ n : ardent follower

de·vo·tion \di'vōshən\ n 1 : prayer —usu. pl. 2 : loyalty and dedication —de·vo·tion·al \-shənəl\ adj

de·vour \di'vaùər\ vb : consume ravenously —de·vour·er n

de·vout \-'vaùt\ adj 1 : devoted to religion 2 : serious —de·vout·ly adv —de·vout·ness n

dew \'dü, 'dyü\ n : moisture condensed at night —dew·drop n —dewy adj

dex·ter·ous \'dekstrəs\ adj : skillful with the hands —dex·ter·i·ty \dek'sterətē\ n —dex·ter·ous·ly adv

dex·trose \'dek,strōs\ n : plant or blood sugar

di·a·be·tes \,dīə'bētēz, -'bētəs\ n : disorder in which the body has too little insulin or too much sugar —di·a·bet·ic \-'betik\ adj or n

di·a·bol·ic \-'bälik\, di·a·bol·i·cal \-ikəl\ adj : fiendish

di·a·crit·ic \-'kritik\ n : mark accompanying a letter and indicating a specific sound value —di·a·crit·i·cal \-'kritikəl\ adj

di·a·dem \'dīə,dem\ n : crown

di·ag·no·sis \,dīig'nōsəs, -əg-\ n, pl **-no·ses** \-,sēz\ : identifying of a disease from its symptoms —**di·ag·nose** \'dīig,nōs, -əg-\ vb —**di·ag·nos·tic** \,dīig'nästik, -əg-\ adj

di·ag·o·nal \dī'agənəl\ adj : extending from one corner to the opposite corner ~ n : diagonal line, direction, or arrangement —**di·ag·o·nal·ly** adv

di·a·gram \'dīə,gram\ n : explanatory drawing or plan ~ vb **-gramed** or **-grammed**; **-gram·ing** or **gram·ming** : represent by a diagram —**di·a·gram·mat·ic** \,dīəgrə'matik\ adj

di·al \'dīəl\ n 1 : face of a clock, meter, or gauge 2 : control knob or wheel ~ vb **-aled** or **-ailed**; **-al·ing** or **-al·ling** : turn a dial to call, operate, or select

di·a·lect \'dīə,lekt\ n : variety of language confined to a region or group

di·a·logue \-,lȯg\ n : conversation

di·am·e·ter \dī'amətər\ n 1 : straight line through the center of a circle 2 : thickness

di·a·met·ric \,dīə'metrik\, **di·a·met·ri·cal** \-trikəl\ adj : completely opposite —**di·a·met·ri·cal·ly** \-iklē\ adv

di·a·mond \'dīmənd, 'dīə-\ n 1 : hard brilliant mineral that consists of crystalline carbon 2 : flat figure having 4 equal sides, 2 acute angles, and 2 obtuse angles 3 : playing card of a suit marked with a red diamond 4 : baseball field

di·a·per \'dīpər\ n : baby's garment for receiving bodily wastes ~ vb : put a diaper on

di·a·phragm \'dīə,fram\ n 1 : sheet of muscle between the chest and abdominal cavity 2 : contraceptive device

di·ar·rhea \,dīə'rēə\ n : abnormally watery discharge from bowels

di·a·ry \'dīərē\ n, pl **-ries** : daily record of personal experiences —**di·a·rist** \'dīərist\ n

di·a·tribe \'dīə,trīb\ n : biting or abusive denunciation

dice \'dīs\ n, pl **dice** : die or a game played with dice ~ vb **diced**; **dic·ing** : cut into small cubes

dick·er \'dikər\ vb : bargain

dic·tate \'dik,tāt\ vb **-tat·ed**; **-tat·ing** 1 : speak for a person or a machine to record 2 : command ~ n : order —**dic·ta·tion** \dik'tāshən\ n

dic·ta·tor \'dik,tātər\ n : person ruling absolutely and often brutally —**dic·ta·to·ri·al** \,diktətōrēəl\ adj —**dic·ta·tor·ship** \dik'tātər,ship, 'dik,-\ n

dic·tion \'dikshən\ n 1 : choice of the best word 2 : precise pronunciation

dic·tio·nary \-shə,nerē\ n, pl **-nar·ies** : reference book of words with information about their meanings

dic·tum \'diktəm\ n, pl **-ta** \-tə\ : authoritative or formal statement

did past of DO

di·dac·tic \dī'daktik\ adj : intended to teach a moral lesson

¹die \'dī\ vb **died**; **dy·ing** \'dīiŋ\ 1 : stop living 2 : pass out of existence 3 : stop or subside 4 : long

²die \'dī\ n 1 pl **dice** \'dīs\ : small marked cube used in gambling 2 pl **dies** \'dīz\ : form for stamping or cutting

die·sel \'dēzəl, -səl\ n : engine in which high compression causes ignition of the fuel

di·et \'dīət\ n : food and drink regularly consumed (as by a person) ~ vb : eat less or according to certain rules —**di·etary** \'dīə,terē\ adj or n —**di·et·er** n

di·etet·ics \,dīə'tetiks\ n sing or pl : science of nutrition —**di·etet·ic** adj —**di·eti·tian, di·eti·cian** \-'tishən\ n

dif·fer \'difər\ vb 1 : be unlike 2 : vary 3 : disagree —**dif·fer·ence** \'difrəns\ n

dif·fer·ent \-rənt\ adj : not the same —**dif·fer·ent·ly** adv

dif·fer·en·ti·ate \,difə'renchē,āt\ vb **-at·ed**; **-at·ing** 1 : make or become different 2 : distinguish —**dif·fer·en·ti·a·tion** \-,renchē'āshən\ n

dif·fi·cult \'difikəlt\ adj : hard to do, understand, or deal with

dif·fi·cul·ty \-kəltē\ n, pl **-ties** 1 : difficult nature 2 : great effort 3 : something hard to do, understand, or deal with

dif·fi·dent \'difədənt\ adj : reserved —**dif·fi·dence** \-əns\ n

dif·fuse \dif'yüs\ adj 1 : wordy 2 : not concentrated ~ \-'yüz\ vb **-fused**; **-fus·ing** : pour out or spread widely —**dif·fu·sion** \-'yüzhən\ n

dig \'dig\ vb **dug** \'dəg\; **dig·ging** 1 : turn up soil 2 : hollow out or form by removing earth 3 : uncover by turning up earth ~ n 1 : thrust 2

: cutting remark —**dig in** vb 1
: establish a defensive position 2
: begin working or eating —**dig up**
vb : discover

¹**di·gest** \'dī,jest\ n : body of information in shortened form

²**di·gest** \dī'jest, də-\ vb 1 : think over 2
: convert (food) into a form that can
be absorbed 3 : summarize —**di·gest-
ible** adj —**di·ges·tion** \-'jeschən\ n —
di·ges·tive \-'jestiv\ adj

dig·it \'dijət\ n 1 : any of the figures 1
to 9 inclusive and usu. the symbol 0
2 : finger or toe

dig·i·tal \-ᵊl\ adj : providing information in numerical digits —**dig·i·tal·ly**
adv

dig·ni·fy \'dignə,fī\ vb **-fied; -fy·ing**
: give dignity or attention to

dig·ni·tary \-,terē\ n, pl **-taries** : person
of high position

dig·ni·ty \'dignətē\ n, pl **-ties** 1 : quality
or state of being worthy or honored 2
: formal reserve (as of manner)

di·gress \dī'gres, də-\ vb : wander from
the main subject —**di·gres·sion**
\-'greshən\ n

dike \'dīk\ n : earth bank or dam

di·lap·i·dat·ed \də'lapə,dātəd\ adj
: fallen into partial ruin —**di·lap·i·da-
tion** \-,lapə'dāshən\ n

di·late \dī'lāt, 'dī,lāt\ vb **-lat·ed; -lat·ing**
: swell or expand —**di·la·ta·tion**
\,dilə'tāshən\ n —**di·la·tion** \dī-
'lāshən\ n

di·la·to·ry \'dilə,tōrē\ adj 1 : delaying 2
: tardy or slow

di·lem·ma \də'lemə\ n 1 : undesirable
choice 2 : predicament

dil·et·tante \'dilə,tänt, -,tant; ,dilə'tänt,
-'tant\ n, pl **-tantes** or **-tan·ti** \-'täntē,
-'tantē\ : one who dabbles in a field
of interest

dil·i·gent \'diləjənt\ adj : attentive and
busy —**dil·i·gence** \-jəns\ n —**dil·i·
gent·ly** adv

dill \'dil\ n : herb with aromatic leaves
and seeds

dil·ly·dal·ly \'dilē,dalē\ vb : waste time
by delay

di·lute \dī'lüt, də-\ vb **-lut·ed; -lut·ing**
: lessen the consistency or strength
of by mixing with something else
~ adj : weak —**di·lu·tion** \-'lüshən\
n

dim \'dim\ adj **-mm-** 1 : not bright or
distinct 2 : having no luster 3 : not
seeing or understanding clearly —

dim vb —**dim·ly** adv —**dim·mer** n
—**dim·ness** n

dime \'dīm\ n : U.S. coin worth 1/10
dollar

di·men·sion \də'menchən, dī-\ n 1
: measurement of extension (as in
length, height, or breadth) 2 : extent
—**di·men·sion·al** \-'menchənəl\ adj

di·min·ish \də'minish\ vb 1 : make less
or cause to appear less 2 : dwindle

di·min·u·tive \də'minyətiv\ adj : extremely small

dim·ple \'dimpəl\ n : small depression
esp. in the cheek or chin

din \'din\ n : loud noise

dine \'dīn\ vb **dined; din·ing** : eat dinner

din·er \'dīnər\ n 1 : person eating dinner
2 : railroad dining car or restaurant
resembling one

din·ghy \'diŋē, -gē, -kē\ n, pl **-ghies**
: small boat

din·gy \'dinjē\ adj **-gi·er; -est** 1 : dirty
2 : shabby —**din·gi·ness** n

din·ner \'dinər\ n : main daily meal

di·no·saur \'dīnə,sȯr\ n : extinct often
huge reptile

dint \'dint\ n : force—in the phrase by
dint of

di·o·cese \'dīəsəs, -,sēz, -,sēs\ n, pl
-ces·es \-əz, 'dīə,sēz\ : territorial jurisdiction of a bishop —**di·oc·e·san**
\dī'äsəsən, ,dīə'sēzᵊn\ adj or n

dip \'dip\ vb **-pp-** 1 : plunge into a liquid
2 : take out with a ladle 3 : lower and
quickly raise again 4 : sink or slope
downward suddenly ~ n 1 : plunge
into water for sport 2 : sudden downward movement or incline —**dip·per**
n

diph·the·ria \dif'thirēə\ n : acute contagious disease

diph·thong \'dif,thȯŋ\ n : two vowel
sounds joined to form one speech
sound (as ou in out)

di·plo·ma \də'plōmə\ n, pl **-mas**
: record of graduation from a school

di·plo·ma·cy \-məsē\ n 1 : business of
conducting negotiations between
nations 2 : tact —**dip·lo·mat** \'dip-
lə,mat\ n —**dip·lo·mat·ic** \,dip-
lə'matik\ adj

dire \'dīr\ adj **dir·er; -est** 1 : very horr-
rible 2 : extreme

di·rect \də'rekt, dī-\ vb 1 : address 2
: cause to move or to follow a certain
course 3 : show (someone) the way 4
: regulate the activities or course of 5
: request with authority ~ adj 1

: leading to or coming from a point without deviation or interruption **2** : frank —**direct** adv —**di·rect·ly** adv —**di·rect·ness** n —**di·rec·tor** \-tər\ n

direct current n : electric current flowing in one direction only

di·rec·tion \də'rekshən, dī-\ n **1** : supervision **2** : order **3** : course along which something moves —**di·rec·tion·al** \-shənəl\ adj

di·rec·tive \-tiv\ n : order

di·rec·to·ry \-tərē\ n, pl **-ries** : alphabetical list of names and addresses

dirge \'dərj\ n : funeral hymn

di·ri·gi·ble \'dirəjəbəl, də'rijə-\ n : airship

dirt \'dərt\ n **1** : mud, dust, or grime that makes something unclean **2** : soil

dirty \-ē\ adj **dirt·i·er; -est 1** : not clean **2** : unfair **3** : indecent ~ vb **dirt·ied; dirty·ing** : make or become dirty —**dirt·i·ness** n

dis·able \dis'ābəl\ vb **-abled; -abling** : make unable to function —**dis·abil·i·ty** \,disə'bilətē\ n

dis·abuse \,disə'byüz\ vb : free from error or misconception

dis·ad·van·tage \,disəd'vantij\ n : something that hinders success —**dis·ad·van·ta·geous** adj

dis·af·fect \,disə'fekt\ vb : cause discontent in —**dis·af·fec·tion** n

dis·agree \,disə'grē\ vb **1** : fail to agree **2** : differ in opinion —**dis·agree·ment** n

dis·agree·able \-əbəl\ adj : unpleasant

dis·al·low \,disə'laü\ vb : refuse to admit or recognize

dis·ap·pear \,disə'pir\ vb **1** : pass out of sight **2** : cease to be —**dis·ap·pear·ance** n

dis·ap·point \,disə'póint\ vb : fail to fulfill the expectation or hope of —**dis·ap·point·ment** n

dis·ap·prove \-ə'prüv\ vb **1** : condemn or reject **2** : feel or express dislike or rejection —**dis·ap·prov·al** n —**dis·ap·prov·ing·ly** adv

dis·arm \dis'ärm\ vb **1** : take weapons from **2** : reduce armed forces **3** : make harmless or friendly —**dis·ar·ma·ment** \-'ärməmənt\ n

dis·ar·range \,disə'rānj\ vb : throw into disorder —**dis·ar·range·ment** n

dis·ar·ray \,disə'rā\ n : disorder

di·sas·ter \diz'astər, dis-\ n : sudden great misfortune —**di·sas·trous** \-'astrəs\ adj

dis·avow \,disə'vaü\ vb : deny responsibility for —**dis·avow·al** \-'vaüəl\ n

dis·band \dis'band\ vb : break up the organization of

dis·bar \dis'bär\ vb : expel from the legal profession —**dis·bar·ment** n

dis·be·lieve \,disbi'lēv\ vb : hold not worthy of belief —**dis·be·lief** n

dis·burse \dis'bərs\ vb **-bursed; -bursing** : pay out —**dis·burse·ment** n

disc var of DISK

dis·card \dis'kärd, 'dis,kärd\ vb : get rid of as unwanted —**dis·card** \'dis,kärd\ n

dis·cern \dis'ərn, diz-\ vb : discover with the eyes or the mind —**dis·cern·ible** adj —**dis·cern·ment** n

dis·charge \dis'chärj, 'dis,chärj\ vb **1** : unload **2** : shoot **3** : set free **4** : dismiss from service **5** : let go or let off **6** : give forth fluid ~ \'dis,-, dis'-\ n **1** : act of discharging **2** : a flowing out (as of blood) **3** : dismissal

dis·ci·ple \di'sīpəl\ n : one who helps spread another's teachings

dis·ci·pli·nar·i·an \,disəplə'nerēən\ n : one who enforces order

dis·ci·pline \'disəplən\ n **1** : field of study **2** : training that corrects, molds, or perfects **3** : punishment **4** : control gained by obedience or training ~ vb **-plined; -plin·ing 1** : punish **2** : train in self-control —**dis·ci·plin·ary** \'disəplə,nerē\ adj

dis·claim \dis'klām\ vb : disavow

dis·close \-'klōz\ vb : reveal —**dis·clo·sure** \-'klōzhər\ n

dis·col·or \dis'kələr\ vb : change the color of esp. for the worse —**dis·col·or·ation** \dis,kələ'rāshən\ n

dis·com·fit \dis'kəmfət\ vb : upset —**dis·com·fi·ture** \dis'kəmfə,chür\ n

dis·com·fort \dis'kəmfərt\ n : uneasiness

dis·con·cert \,diskən'sərt\ vb : upset

dis·con·nect \,diskə'nekt\ vb : undo the connection of

dis·con·so·late \dis'känsələt\ adj : hopelessly sad

dis·con·tent \,diskən'tent\ n : uneasiness of mind —**dis·con·tent·ed** adj

dis·con·tin·ue \,diskən'tinyü\ vb : end —**dis·con·tin·u·ance** n —**dis·con·ti·nu·i·ty** \dis,käntə'nüətē, -'nyü-\ n

—**dis·con·tin·u·ous** \,diskən'tin-yəwəs\ adj

dis·cord \'dis,kórd\ n : lack of harmony —**dis·cor·dant** \dis'kórd³nt\ adj —**dis·cor·dant·ly** adv

dis·count \'dis,kaúnt\ n : reduction from a regular price ~ \'dis,-, dis'-\ vb 1 : reduce the amount of 2 : disregard —**discount** adj —**dis·count·er** n

dis·cour·age \dis'kərij\ vb -aged; -ag·ing 1 : deprive of courage, confidence, or enthusiasm 2 : dissuade —**dis·cour·age·ment** n

dis·course \'dis,kórs\ n 1 : conversation 2 : formal treatment of a subject ~ \dis'-\ vb -coursed; -cours·ing : talk at length

dis·cour·te·ous \dis'kərtēəs\ adj : lacking courtesy —**dis·cour·te·ous·ly** adv —**dis·cour·te·sy** n

dis·cov·er \dis'kəvər\ vb 1 : make known 2 : obtain the first sight or knowledge of 3 : find out —**dis·cov·er·er** n —**dis·cov·ery** \-ərē\ n

dis·cred·it \dis'kredət\ vb 1 : disbelieve 2 : destroy confidence in ~ n 1 : loss of reputation 2 : disbelief —**dis·cred·it·able** adj

dis·creet \dis'krēt\ adj : capable of keeping a secret —**dis·creet·ly** adv

dis·crep·an·cy \dis'krepənsē\ n, pl -cies : difference or disagreement

dis·crete \dis'krēt, 'dis,-\ adj : individually distinct

dis·cre·tion \dis'kreshən\ n 1 : discreet quality 2 : power of decision or choice —**dis·cre·tion·ary** adj

dis·crim·i·nate \dis'krimə,nāt\ vb -nat·ed; -nat·ing 1 : distinguish 2 : show favor or disfavor unjustly —**dis·crim·i·na·tion** \-,krimə'nāshən\ n —**dis·crim·i·na·to·ry** \-'krimənə,tōrē\ adj

dis·cur·sive \dis'kərsiv\ adj : passing from one topic to another —**dis·cur·sive·ly** adv —**dis·cur·sive·ness** n

dis·cus \'diskəs\ n, pl -cus·es : disk hurled for distance in a contest

dis·cuss \dis'kəs\ vb : talk about or present —**dis·cus·sion** \-'kəshən\ n

dis·dain \dis'dān\ n : feeling of contempt ~ vb : look upon or reject with disdain —**dis·dain·ful** \-fəl\ adj —**dis·dain·ful·ly** adv

dis·ease \di'zēz\ n : condition of a body that impairs its functioning —**dis·eased** \-'zēzd\ adj

dis·em·bark \,disəm'bärk\ vb : get off a ship —**dis·em·bar·ka·tion** \dis,em,bär'kāshən\ n

dis·em·bod·ied \,disəm'bädēd\ adj : having no substance or reality

dis·en·chant \,dis³n'chant\ vb : to free from illusion —**dis·en·chant·ment** n

dis·en·chant·ed \-'chantəd\ adj : disappointed

dis·en·gage \-³n'gāj\ vb : release —**dis·en·gage·ment** n

dis·en·tan·gle \-³n'taŋgəl\ vb : free from entanglement

dis·fa·vor \dis'fāvər\ n : disapproval

dis·fig·ure \dis'figyər\ vb : spoil the appearance of —**dis·fig·ure·ment** n

dis·fran·chise \dis'fran,chīz\ vb : deprive of the right to vote —**dis·fran·chise·ment** n

dis·gorge \dis'górj\ vb : spew forth

dis·grace \dis'grās\ vb : bring disgrace to ~ n 1 : shame 2 : cause of shame —**dis·grace·ful** \-fəl\ adj —**dis·grace·ful·ly** adv

dis·grun·tle \dis'grənt³l\ vb -tled; -tling : put in bad humor

dis·guise \dis'gīz\ vb -guised; -guis·ing : hide the true identity or nature of ~ n : something that conceals

dis·gust \dis'gəst\ n : strong aversion ~ vb : provoke disgust in —**dis·gust·ed·ly** adv —**dis·gust·ing·ly** adv

dish \'dish\ n 1 : vessel for serving food or the food it holds 2 : food prepared in a particular way ~ vb : put in a dish —**dish·cloth** n —**dish·rag** n —**dish·wash·er** n —**dish·wa·ter** n

dis·har·mo·ny \dis'härmənē\ n : lack of harmony —**dis·har·mo·ni·ous** \,dishär'mōnēəs\ adj

dis·heart·en \dis'härt³n\ vb : discourage

di·shev·el \di'shevəl\ vb -eled or -elled; -el·ing or -el·ling : throw into disorder —**di·shev·eled, di·shev·elled** adj

dis·hon·est \dis'änəst\ adj : not honest —**dis·hon·est·ly** adv —**dis·hon·es·ty** n

dis·hon·or \dis'änər\ n or vb : disgrace —**dis·hon·or·able** adj —**dis·hon·or·ably** adv

dis·il·lu·sion \,disə'lüzhən\ vb : to free from illusion —**dis·il·lu·sion·ment** n

dis·in·cli·na·tion \dis,inklə'nāshən\ n : slight aversion —**dis·in·cline** \,dis³n'klīn\ vb

dis·in·fect \,dis³n'fekt\ vb : destroy disease germs in or on —**dis·in·fec·tant**

\-'fektənt\ *adj or n* —**dis·in·fec·tion** \-'fekshən\ *n*

dis·in·gen·u·ous \‚disᵊn'jenyəwəs\ *adj* : lacking in candor

dis·in·her·it \-ᵊn'herət\ *vb* : prevent from inheriting property

dis·in·te·grate \dis'intə‚grāt\ *vb* : break into parts or small bits —**dis·in·te·gra·tion** \dis‚intə'grāshən\ *n*

dis·in·ter·est·ed \dis'intərəstəd, -‚res-\ *adj* 1 : not interested 2 : not prejudiced —**dis·in·ter·est·ed·ness** *n*

dis·joint·ed \dis'jóintəd\ *adj* 1 : separated at the joint 2 : incoherent

disk \'disk\ *n* : something round and flat

dis·like \dis'līk\ *vb* : regard with dislike ~ *n* : feeling that something is unpleasant and to be avoided

dis·lo·cate \'dislō‚kāt, dis'-\ *vb* : move out of the usual or proper place —**dis·lo·ca·tion** \‚dislō'kāshən\ *n*

dis·lodge \dis'läj\ *vb* : force out of a place

dis·loy·al \dis'lóiəl\ *adj* : not loyal —**dis·loy·al·ty** *n*

dis·mal \'dizməl\ *adj* : showing or causing gloom —**dis·mal·ly** *adv*

dis·man·tle \dis'mantᵊl\ *vb* -**tled; -tling** : take apart

dis·may \dis'mā\ *vb* -**mayed; -may·ing** : discourage —**dismay** *n*

dis·mem·ber \dis'membər\ *vb* : cut into pieces —**dis·mem·ber·ment** *n*

dis·miss \dis'mis\ *vb* 1 : send away 2 : remove from service 3 : put aside or out of mind —**dis·miss·al** *n*

dis·mount \dis'maúnt\ *vb* 1 : get down from something 2 : take apart

dis·obey \‚disə'bā\ *vb* : refuse to obey —**dis·obe·di·ence** \-'bēdēəns\ *n* —**dis·obe·di·ent** \-ənt\ *adj*

dis·or·der \dis'órdər\ *n* 1 : lack of order 2 : breach of public order 3 : abnormal state of body or mind —**disorder** *vb* —**dis·or·der·li·ness** *n* —**dis·or·der·ly** *adj*

dis·or·ga·nize \dis'órgə‚nīz\ *vb* : throw into disorder —**dis·or·ga·ni·za·tion** *n*

dis·own \dis'ōn\ *vb* : repudiate

dis·par·age \-'parij\ *vb* -**aged; -ag·ing** : say bad things about —**dis·par·age·ment** *n*

dis·pa·rate \dis'parət, 'dispərət\ *adj* : different in quality or character —**dis·par·i·ty** \dis'parətē\ *n*

dis·pas·sion·ate \dis'pashənət\ *adj* : not influenced by strong feeling —**dis·pas·sion·ate·ly** *adv*

dis·patch \dis'pach\ *vb* 1 : send 2 : kill 3 : attend to rapidly 4 : defeat ~ *n* 1 : message 2 : news item from a correspondent 3 : promptness and efficiency —**dis·patch·er** *n*

dis·pel \dis'pel\ *vb* -**ll-** : clear away

dis·pen·sa·ry \-'pensərē\ *n, pl* -**ries** : place where medical or dental aid is provided

dis·pen·sa·tion \‚dispən'sāshən\ *n* 1 : system of principles or rules 2 : exemption from a rule 3 : act of dispensing

dis·pense \dis'pens\ *vb* -**pensed; -pens·ing** 1 : portion out 2 : make up and give out (remedies) —**dis·pens·er** *n* —**dispense with** : do without

dis·perse \-'pərs\ *vb* -**persed; -pers·ing** : scatter —**dis·per·sal** \-'pərsəl\ *n* —**dis·per·sion** \-'perzhən\ *n*

dis·place \-'plās\ *vb* 1 : expel or force to flee from home or native land 2 : take the place of —**dis·place·ment** \-mənt\ *n*

dis·play \-'plā\ *vb* : present to view —**display** *n*

dis·please \-'plēz\ *vb* : arouse the dislike of —**dis·plea·sure** \-'plezhər\ *n*

dis·port \dis'pórt\ *vb* 1 : amuse 2 : frolic

dis·pose \dis'pōz\ *vb* -**posed; -pos·ing** 1 : give a tendency to 2 : settle —**dis·pos·able** \-'pōzəbəl\ *adj* —**dis·pos·al** \-'pōzəl\ *n* —**dis·pos·er** *n* —**dispose of** 1 : determine the fate, condition, or use of 2 : get rid of

dis·po·si·tion \‚dispə'zishən\ *n* 1 : act or power of disposing of 2 : arrangement 3 : natural attitude

dis·pos·sess \‚dispə'zes\ *vb* : deprive of possession or occupancy —**dis·pos·ses·sion** \-'zeshən\ *n*

dis·pro·por·tion \‚disprə'pórshən\ *n* : lack of proportion —**dis·pro·por·tion·ate** \-shənət\ *adj*

dis·prove \dis'prüv\ *vb* : prove false —**dis·proof** *n*

dis·pute \dis'pyüt\ *vb* -**put·ed; -put·ing** 1 : argue 2 : deny the truth or rightness of 3 : struggle against or over ~ *n* : debate or quarrel —**dis·put·able** \-əbəl, 'dispyət-\ *adj* —**dis·pu·ta·tion** \‚dispyə'tāshən\ *n*

dis·qual·i·fy \dis'kwälə‚fī\ *vb* : make ineligible —**dis·qual·i·fi·ca·tion** *n*

dis·qui·et \dis'kwīət\ *vb* : make uneasy or restless ~ *n* : anxiety

dis·re·gard \‚disri'gärd\ *vb* : pay no attention to ~ *n* : neglect

dis·re·pair \,disri'par\ *n* : need of repair

dis·rep·u·ta·ble \dis'repyətəbəl\ *adj* : having a bad reputation

dis·re·pute \,disri'pyüt\ *n* : low regard

dis·re·spect \,disri'spekt\ *n* : lack of respect —**dis·re·spect·ful** *adj*

dis·robe \dis'rōb\ *vb* : undress

dis·rupt \dis'rəpt\ *vb* : throw into disorder —**dis·rup·tion** \-'rəpshən\ *n* — **dis·rup·tive** \-'rəptiv\ *adj*

dis·sat·is·fac·tion \dis,satəs'fakshən\ *n* : lack of satisfaction

dis·sat·is·fy \dis'satəs,fī\ *vb* : fail to satisfy

dis·sect \di'sekt\ *vb* : cut into parts esp. to examine —**dis·sec·tion** \-'sekshən\ *n*

dis·sem·ble \di'sembəl\ *vb* -**bled; -bling** : disguise feelings or intention —**dis·sem·bler** *n*

dis·sem·i·nate \di'semə,nāt\ *vb* -**nat·ed; -nat·ing** : spread around —**dis·sem·i·na·tion** \-,semə'nāshən\ *n*

dis·sen·sion \di'senchən\ *n* : discord

dis·sent \di'sent\ *vb* : object or disagree ~ *n* : difference of opinion — **dis·sent·er** *n* —**dis·sen·tient** \-'senchənt\ *adj or n*

dis·ser·ta·tion \,disər'tāshən\ *n* : long written study of a subject

dis·ser·vice \dis'sərvəs\ *n* : injury

dis·si·dent \'disədənt\ *n* : one who differs openly with an establishment — **dis·si·dence** \-əns\ *n* —**dissident** *adj*

dis·sim·i·lar \di'simələr\ *adj* : different —**dis·sim·i·lar·i·ty** \di,simə'larətē\ *n*

dis·si·pate \'disə,pāt\ *vb* -**pat·ed; -pat·ing 1** : break up and drive off **2** : squander —**dis·si·pa·tion** \,disə'pāshən\ *n*

dis·so·ci·ate \dis'ōsē,āt, -shē-\ *vb* -**at·ed; -at·ing** : separate from association — **dis·so·ci·a·tion** \dis,ōsē'āshən, -shē-\ *n*

dis·so·lute \'disə,lüt\ *adj* : loose in morals or conduct

dis·so·lu·tion \,disə'lüshən\ *n* : act or process of dissolving

dis·solve \di'zälv\ *vb* **1** : break up or bring to an end **2** : pass or cause to pass into solution

dis·so·nance \'disənəns\ *n* : discord — **dis·so·nant** \-nənt\ *adj*

dis·suade \di'swād\ *vb* -**suad·ed; -suad·ing** : persuade not to do something — **dis·sua·sion** \-'swāzhən\ *n*

dis·tance \'distəns\ *n* **1** : measure of separation in space or time **2** : reserve

dis·tant \-tənt\ *adj* **1** : separate in space **2** : remote in time, space, or relationship **3** : reserved —**dis·tant·ly** *adv*

dis·taste \dis'tāst\ *n* : dislike —**dis·taste·ful** *adj*

dis·tem·per \dis'tempər\ *n* : serious virus disease of dogs

dis·tend \dis'tend\ *vb* : swell out —**dis·ten·sion, dis·ten·tion** \-'tenchən\ *n*

dis·till \di'stil\ *vb* : obtain by distillation —**dis·til·late** \'distə,lāt, -lət\ *n* —**dis·till·er** *n* —**dis·till·ery** \di'stilərē\ *n*

dis·til·la·tion \,distə'lāshən\ *n* : purification of liquid by evaporating then condensing

dis·tinct \dis'tiŋkt\ *adj* **1** : distinguishable from others **2** : readily discerned —**dis·tinc·tive** \-tiv\ *adj* —**dis·tinc·tive·ly** *adv* —**dis·tinc·tive·ness** *n* — **dis·tinct·ly** *adv* —**dis·tinct·ness** *n*

dis·tinc·tion \-'tiŋkshən\ *n* **1** : act of distinguishing **2** : difference **3** : special recognition

dis·tin·guish \-'tiŋgwish\ *vb* **1** : perceive as different **2** : set apart **3** : discern **4** : make outstanding —**dis·tin·guish·able** *adj* —**dis·tin·guished** \-gwisht\ *adj*

dis·tort \dis'tort\ *vb* : twist out of shape, condition, or true meaning — **dis·tor·tion** \-'tórshən\ *n*

dis·tract \di'strakt\ *vb* : divert the mind or attention of —**dis·trac·tion** \-'strakshən\ *n*

dis·traught \dis'trót\ *adj* : agitated with mental conflict

dis·tress \-'tres\ *n* **1** : suffering **2** : misfortune **3** : state of danger or great need ~ *vb* : subject to strain or distress —**dis·tress·ful** *adj*

dis·trib·ute \-'tribyət\ *vb* -**ut·ed; -ut·ing 1** : divide among many **2** : spread or hand out —**dis·tri·bu·tion** \,distrə'byüshən\ *n* —**dis·trib·u·tive** \dis'tribyətiv\ *adj* —**dis·trib·u·tor** \-ər\ *n*

dis·trict \'dis,trikt\ *n* : territorial division

dis·trust \dis'trəst\ *vb or n* : mistrust — **dis·trust·ful** \-fəl\ *adj*

dis·turb \dis'tərb\ *vb* **1** : interfere with **2** : destroy the peace, composure, or order of —**dis·tur·bance** \-'tərbəns\ *n* —**dis·turb·er** *n*

dis·use \dis'yüs\ *n* : lack of use

ditch \'dich\ *n* : trench ~ *vb* **1** : dig a ditch in **2** : get rid of

dith·er \'dithǝr\ n : highly nervous or excited state

dit·to \'ditō\ n, pl **-tos** : more of the same

dit·ty \'ditē\ n, pl **-ties** : short simple song

di·uret·ic \,dīyù'retik\ adj : tending to increase urine flow —**diuretic** n

di·ur·nal \dī'ǝrnᵊl\ adj 1 : daily 2 : of or occurring in the daytime

di·van \'dī,van, di'-\ n : couch

dive \'dīv\ vb **dived** \'dīvd\ or **dove** \'dōv\; **dived; div·ing** 1 : plunge into water headfirst 2 : submerge 3 : descend quickly ~ n 1 : act of diving 2 : sharp decline —**div·er** n

di·verge \dǝ'vǝrj, dī-\ vb **-verged; -verg·ing** 1 : move in different directions 2 : differ —**di·ver·gence** \-'vǝrjǝns\ n —**di·ver·gent** \-jǝnt\ adj

di·vers \'dīvǝrz\ adj : various

di·verse \dī'vǝrs, dǝ-, 'dī,vǝrs\ adj : involving different forms —**di·ver·si·fi·ca·tion** \dǝ,vǝrsǝfǝ'kāshǝn, dī-\ n —**di·ver·si·fy** \-'vǝrsǝ,fī\ vb —**di·ver·si·ty** \-sǝtē\ n

di·vert \dǝ'vǝrt, dī-\ vb 1 : turn from a course or purpose 2 : distract 3 : amuse —**di·ver·sion** \-'vǝrzhǝn\ n

di·vest \dī'vest, dǝ-\ vb : strip of clothing, possessions, or rights

di·vide \dǝ'vīd\ vb **-vid·ed; -vid·ing** 1 : separate 2 : distribute 3 : share 4 : subject to mathematical division ~ n : watershed —**di·vid·er** n

div·i·dend \'divǝ,dend\ n 1 : individual share 2 : bonus 3 : number to be divided

div·i·na·tion \,divǝ'nāshǝn\ n : practice of trying to foretell future events

di·vine \dǝ'vīn\ adj **-vin·er; -est** 1 : relating to or being God or a god 2 : supremely good ~ n : clergy member ~ vb **-vined; -vin·ing** 1 : infer 2 : prophesy —**di·vine·ly** adv —**di·vin·er** n —**di·vin·i·ty** \dǝ'vinǝtē\ n

di·vis·i·ble \-'vizǝbǝl\ adj : capable of being divided —**di·vis·i·bil·i·ty** \-,vizǝ'bilǝtē\ n

di·vi·sion \-'vizhǝn\ n 1 : distribution 2 : part of a whole 3 : disagreement 4 : process of finding out how many times one number is contained in another

di·vi·sive \dǝ'vīsiv, -'vi-, -ziv\ adj : creating dissension

di·vi·sor \-'vīzǝr\ n : number by which a dividend is divided

di·vorce \dǝ'vōrs\ n : legal breaking up of a marriage —**divorce** vb

di·vor·cée \-,vōr'sā, -'sē\ n : divorced woman

di·vulge \dǝ'vǝlj, dī-\ vb **-vulged; -vulg·ing** : reveal

diz·zy \'dizē\ adj **-zi·er; -est** 1 : having a sensation of whirling 2 : causing or caused by giddiness —**diz·zi·ly** adv —**diz·zi·ness** n

DNA \,dē,en'ā\ n : compound in cell nuclei that is the basis of heredity

do \'dü\ vb **did** \'did\; **done** \'dǝn\; **do·ing** \'düiŋ\; **does** \'dǝz\ 1 : work to accomplish (an action or task) 2 : behave 3 : prepare or fix up 4 : fare 5 : finish 6 : serve the needs or purpose of 7 —used as an auxiliary verb —**do away with** 1 : get rid of 2 : destroy —**do by** : deal with —**do·er** \'düǝr\ n —**do in** vb 1 : ruin 2 : kill

doc·ile \'däsǝl\ adj : easily managed —**do·cil·i·ty** \dä'silǝtē\ n

¹dock \'däk\ vb 1 : shorten 2 : reduce

²dock n 1 : berth between 2 piers to receive ships 2 : loading wharf or platform ~ vb : bring or come into dock —**dock·work·er** n

³dock n : place in a court for a prisoner

dock·et \'däkǝt\ n 1 : record of the proceedings in a legal action 2 : list of legal causes to be tried —**docket** vb

doc·tor \'däktǝr\ n 1 : person holding one of the highest academic degrees 2 : one (as a surgeon) skilled in healing arts ~ vb 1 : give medical treatment to 2 : repair or alter —**doc·tor·al** \-tǝrǝl\ adj

doc·trine \'däktrǝn\ n : something taught —**doc·tri·nal** \-trǝnᵊl\ adj

doc·u·ment \'däkyǝmǝnt\ n : paper that furnishes information or legal proof —**doc·u·ment** \-,ment\ vb —**doc·u·men·ta·tion** \,däkyǝmǝn-'tāshǝn\ n —**doc·u·ment·er** n

doc·u·men·ta·ry \,däkyǝ'mentǝrē\ adj 1 : of or relating to documents 2 : giving a factual presentation —**doc·umentary** n

dod·der \'dädǝr\ vb : become feeble usu. from age

dodge \'däj\ vb **dodged; dodg·ing** 1 : move quickly aside or out of the way of 2 : evade —**dodge** n

do·do \'dōdō\ n, pl **-does** or **-dos** 1 : heavy flightless extinct bird 2 : stupid person

doe \'dō\ *n, pl* **does** *or* **doe** : adult female deer —**doe·skin** \-ˌskin\ *n*

does *pres 3d sing of* DO

doff \'däf\ *vb* : remove

dog \'dóg\ *n* 1 : flesh-eating domestic mammal ~ *vb* 1 : hunt down or track like a hound 2 : harass —**dog·catch·er** *n* —**dog·gy** \-ē\ *n or adj* —**dog·house** *n*

dog-ear \'dóg,ir\ *n* : turned-down corner of a page —**dog-ear** *vb* —**dog-eared** \-,ird\ *adj*

dog·ged \'dógəd\ *adj* : stubbornly determined

dog·ma \'dógmə\ *n* : tenet or code of tenets

dog·ma·tism \-,tizəm\ *n* : unwarranted stubbornness of opinion —**dog·ma·tic** \dóg'matik\ *adj*

dog·wood *n* : flowering tree

doi·ly \'dóilē\ *n, pl* **-lies** : small decorative mat

¹**do·ings** \'düiŋz\ *n pl* : events

dol·drums \'dōldrəmz,'däl-\ *n pl* : spell of listlessness, despondency, or stagnation

dole \'dōl\ *n* : distribution esp. of money to the needy or unemployed —**dole out** *vb* : give out esp. in small portions

dole·ful \'dōlfəl\ *adj* : sad —**dole·ful·ly** *adv*

doll \'däll, 'dól\ *n* : small figure of a person used esp. as a child's toy

dol·lar \'dälər\ *n* : any of various basic monetary units (as in the U.S. and Canada)

dol·ly \'dälē\ *n, pl* **-lies** : small cart or wheeled platform

dol·phin \'dälfən\ *n* 1 : sea mammal related to the whales 2 : saltwater food fish

dolt \'dōlt\ *n* : stupid person —**dolt·ish** *adj*

-dom \dəm\ *n suffix* 1 : office or realm 2 : state or fact of being 3 : those belonging to a group

do·main \dō'mān, də-\ *n* 1 : territory over which someone reigns 2 : sphere of activity or knowledge

dome \'dōm\ *n* 1 : large hemispherical roof 2 : roofed stadium

do·mes·tic \də'mestik\ *adj* 1 : relating to the household or family 2 : relating and limited to one's own country 3 : tame ~ *n* : household servant —**do·mes·ti·cal·ly** \-tiklē\ *adv*

do·mes·ti·cate \-ti,kāt\ *vb* **-cat·ed;**

-cat·ing : tame —**do·mes·ti·ca·tion** \-,mesti'kāshən\ *n*

do·mi·cile \'dämə,sīl, 'dō-; 'däməsəl\ *n* : home —**domicile** *vb*

dom·i·nance \'dämənəns\ *n* : control —**dom·i·nant** \-nənt\ *adj*

dom·i·nate \-,nāt\ *vb* **-nat·ed; -nat·ing** 1 : have control over 2 : rise high above —**dom·i·na·tion** \,dämə-'nāshən\ *n*

dom·i·neer \,dämə'nir\ *vb* : exercise arbitrary control

do·min·ion \də'minyən\ *n* 1 : supreme authority 2 : governed territory

dom·i·no \'dämə,nō\ *n, pl* **-noes** *or* **-nos** : flat rectangular block used as a piece in a game (**dominoes**)

don \'dän\ *vb* **-nn-** : put on (clothes)

do·nate \'dō,nāt\ *vb* **-nat·ed; -nat·ing** : make a gift of —**do·na·tion** \dō-'nāshən\ *n*

¹**done** \'dən\ *past part of* DO

²**done** *adj* 1 : finished or ended 2 : cooked sufficiently

don·key \'däŋkē, 'dəŋ-\ *n, pl* **-keys** : sturdy domestic ass

do·nor \'dōnər\ *n* : one that gives

doo·dle \'düd³l\ *vb* **-dled; -dling** : draw or scribble aimlessly —**doodle** *n*

doom \'düm\ *n* 1 : judgment 2 : fate 3 : ruin —**doom** *vb*

door \'dōr\ *n* : passage for entrance or a movable barrier that can open or close such a passage —**door·jamb** *n* —**door·knob** *n* —**door·mat** *n* —**door·step** *n* —**door·way** *n*

dope \'dōp\ 1 : narcotic preparation 2 : stupid person 3 : information ~ *vb* **doped; dop·ing** : drug

dor·mant \'dórmənt\ *adj* : not actively growing or functioning —**dor·man·cy** \-mənsē\ *n*

dor·mer \'dórmər\ *n* : window built upright in a sloping roof

dor·mi·to·ry \'dórmə,tōrē\ *n, pl* **-ries** : residence hall (as at a college)

dor·mouse \'dór,maus\ *n* : squirrellike rodent

dor·sal \'dórsəl\ *adj* : relating to or on the back —**dor·sal·ly** *adv*

do·ry \'dōrē\ *n, pl* **-ries** : flat-bottomed boat

dose \'dōs\ *n* 1 : quantity (as of medicine) taken at one time ~ *vb* **dosed; dos·ing** : give medicine to —**dos·age** \'dōsij\ *n*

dot \'dät\ *n* 1 : small spot 2 : small round

mark made with or as if with a pen ~ *vb* -tt- : mark with dots

dot•age \'dōtij\ *n* : senility

dote \'dōt\ *vb* **dot•ed; dot•ing 1** : act feeblemindedly **2** : be foolishly fond

dou•ble \'dəbəl\ *adj* **1** : consisting of 2 members or parts **2** : being twice as great or as many **3** : folded in two ~ *n* **1** : something twice another **2** : one that resembles another ~ *adv* : doubly ~ *vb* **-bled; -bling 1** : make or become twice as great **2** : fold or bend **3** : clench

dou•ble–cross *vb* : deceive by trickery —**dou•ble–cross•er** *n*

dou•bly \'dəblē\ *adv* : to twice the degree

doubt \'daút\ *vb* **1** : be uncertain about **2** : mistrust **3** : consider unlikely ~ *n* **1** : uncertainty **2** : mistrust **3** : inclination not to believe —**doubt•ful** \-fəl\ *adj* —**doubt•ful•ly** *adv* —**doubt•less** \-ləs\ *adv*

douche \'düsh\ *n* : jet of fluid for cleaning a body part

dough \'dō\ *n* : stiff mixture of flour and liquid —**doughy** \'dōē\ *adj*

dough•nut \-,nət\ *n* : small fried ringshaped cake

dough•ty \'daútē\ *adj* **-ti•er; -est** : able, strong, or valiant

dour \'daúər, 'dúr\ *adj* **1** : severe **2** : gloomy or sullen —**dour•ly** *adv*

douse \'daús, 'daúz\ *vb* **doused; dous•ing 1** : plunge into or drench with water **2** : extinguish

1dove \'dəv\ *n* : small wild pigeon

2dove \'dōv\ *past of* DIVE

dove•tail \'dəv,tāl\ *vb* : fit together neatly

dow•a•ger \'daúijər\ *n* **1** : widow with wealth or a title **2** : dignified elderly woman

dowdy \'daúdē\ *adj* **dowd•i•er; -est** : lacking neatness and charm

dow•el \'daúəl\ *n* **1** : peg used for fastening two pieces **2** : wooden rod

dow•er \'daúər\ *n* : property given a widow for life ~ *vb* : supply with a dower

1down \'daún\ *adv* **1** : toward or in a lower position or state **2** : to a lying or sitting position **3** : as a cash deposit **4** : on paper ~ *adj* **1** : lying on the ground **2** : directed or going downward **3** : being at a low level~ *prep* : toward the bottom of ~ *vb* **1** : cause to go down **2** : defeat

2down *n* : fluffy feathers

down•cast *adj* **1** : sad **2** : directed down

down•fall *n* : ruin or cause of ruin

down•grade *n* : downward slope ~ *vb* : lower in grade or position

down•heart•ed *adj* : sad

down•pour *n* : heavy rain

down•right *adv* : thoroughly ~ *adj* : absolute or thorough

downs \'daúnz\ *n pl* : rolling treeless uplands

down•size \'daún,sīz\ *vb* : reduce in size

down•stairs *adv* : on or to a lower floor and esp. the main floor —**downstairs** *adj or n*

down–to–earth *adj* : practical

down•town *adv* : to, toward, or in the business center of a town —**downtown** *n or adj*

down•trod•den \'daún,träd³n\ *adj* : suffering oppression

down•ward \'daúnwərd\, **down•wards** \-wərdz\ *adv* : to a lower place or condition —**downward** *adj*

down•wind *adv or adj* : in the direction the wind is blowing

downy \'daúnē\ *adj* **-i•er; -est** : resembling or covered with down

dow•ry \'daúrē\ *n, pl* **-ries** : property a woman gives her husband in marriage

dox•ol•o•gy \'däk'säləjē\ *n, pl* **-gies** : hymn of praise to God

doze \'dōz\ *vb* **dozed; doz•ing** : sleep lightly —**doze** *n*

doz•en \'dəz³n\ *n, pl* **-ens** *or* **-en** : group of 12 —**doz•enth** \-³nth\ *adj*

drab \'drab\ *adj* **-bb- 1** : dull —**drab•ly** *adv* —**drab•ness** *n*

dra•co•ni•an \drā'kōnēən, dra-\ *adj, often cap* : harsh, cruel

draft \'draft, 'dráft\ *n* **1** : act of drawing or hauling **2** : act of drinking **3** : amount drunk at once **4** : preliminary outline or rough sketch **5** : selection from a pool or the selection process **6** : order for the payment of money **7** : air current ~ *vb* **1** : select usu. on a compulsory basis **2** : make a preliminary sketch, version, or plan of ~ *adj* : drawn from a container —**draft•ee** \draf'tē, dráf-\ *n* —**drafty** \'draftē\ *adj*

drafts•man \'draftsmən, 'dráft-\ *n* : person who draws plans

drag \'drag\ *n* **1** : something dragged over a surface or through water **2** : something that hinders progress or is boring **3** : act or an instance of dragging ~ *vb* **-gg- 1** : haul **2** : move or work with difficulty **3** : pass slowly **4** : search or fish with a drag — **drag·ger** *n*

drag·net \-ˌnet\ *n* **1** : trawl **2** : planned actions for finding a criminal

dra·gon \'dragən\ *n* : fabled winged serpent

drag·on·fly *n* : large 4-winged insect

drain \'drān\ *vb* **1** : draw off or flow off gradually or completely **2** : exhaust ~ *n* : means or act of draining — **drain·age** \-ij\ *n* — **drain·er** *n* — **drain·pipe** *n*

drake \'drāk\ *n* : male duck

dra·ma \'dramə, 'dram-\ *n* **1** : composition for theatrical presentation esp. on a serious subject **2** : series of events involving conflicting forces — **dra·mat·ic** \drə'matik\ *adj* —**dra·mat·i·cal·ly** \-iklē\ *adv* —**dram·a·tist** \'dramətist, 'dräm-\ *n* —**dram·a·ti·za·tion** \ˌdramətə'zāshən, ˌdräm-\ *n* —**dra·ma·tize** \'dramə̩tīz, 'dräm-\ *vb*

drank *past of* DRINK

drape \'drāp\ *vb* **draped; drap·ing 1** : cover or adorn with folds of cloth **2** : cause to hang in flowing lines or folds ~ *n* : curtain

drap·ery \'drāpərē\ *n, pl* **-er·ies** : decorative fabric hung esp. as a heavy curtain

dras·tic \'drastik\ *adj* : extreme or harsh —**dras·ti·cal·ly** \-tiklē\ *adv*

draught \'draft\, **draughty** \'draftē\ *chiefly Brit var of* DRAFT, DRAFTY

draw \'drȯ\ *vb* **drew** \'drü\; **drawn** \'drȯn\; **draw·ing 1** : move or cause to move (as by pulling) **2** : attract or provoke **3** : extract **4** : take or receive (as money) **5** : bend a bow in preparation for shooting **6** : leave a contest undecided **7** : sketch **8** : write out **9** : deduce ~ *n* **1** : act, process, or result of drawing **2** : tie —**draw out** : cause to speak candidly —**draw up 1** : write out **2** : pull oneself erect **3** : bring or come to a stop

draw·back *n* : disadvantage

draw·bridge *n* : bridge that can be raised

draw·er \'drȯr, 'drȯər\ *n* **1** : one that draws **2** : sliding boxlike compartment **3** *pl* : underpants

draw·ing \'drȯiŋ\ *n* **1** : occasion of choosing by lot **2** : act or art of mak-

ing a figure, plan, or sketch with lines **3** : something drawn

drawl \'drȯl\ *vb* : speak slowly —**drawl** *n*

dread \'dred\ *vb* : feel extreme fear or reluctance ~ *n* : great fear ~ *adj* : causing dread —**dread·ful** \-fəl\ *adj* —**dread·ful·ly** *adv*

dream \'drēm\ *n* **1** : series of thoughts or visions during sleep **2** : dreamlike vision **3** : something notable **4** : ideal ~ *vb* **dreamed** \'dremt, 'drēmd\ *or* **dreamt** \'dremt\ **dream·ing 1** : have a dream **2** : imagine —**dream·er** *n* —**dream·like** *adj* —**dreamy** *adj*

drea·ry \'drirē\ *adj* **-ri·er; -est** : dismal —**drea·ri·ly** \'drirəlē\ *adv*

¹dredge \'drej\ *n* : machine for removing earth esp. from under water ~ *vb* **dredged; dredg·ing** : dig up or search with a dredge —**dredg·er** *n*

²dredge *vb* **dredged; dredg·ing** : coat (food) with flour

dregs \'dregz\ *n pl* **1** : sediment **2** : most worthless part

drench \'drench\ *vb* : wet thoroughly

dress \'dres\ *vb* **1** : put clothes on **2** : decorate **3** : prepare (as a carcass) for use **4** : apply dressings, remedies, or fertilizer to ~ *n* **1** : apparel **2** : single garment of bodice and skirt ~ *adj* : suitable for a formal event —**dress·mak·er** *n* —**dress·mak·ing** *n*

dress·er \'dresər\ *n* : bureau with a mirror

dress·ing *n* **1** : act or process of dressing **2** : sauce or a seasoned mixture **3** : material to cover an injury

dressy \'dresē\ *adj* **dress·i·er; -est 1** : showy in dress **2** : stylish

drew *past of* DRAW

drib·ble \'dribəl\ *vb* **-bled; -bling 1** : fall or flow in drops **2** : drool —**dribble** *n*

drier *comparative of* DRY

driest *superlative of* DRY

drift \'drift\ *n* **1** : motion or course of something drifting **2** : mass piled up by wind **3** : general intention or meaning ~ *vb* **1** : float or be driven along (as by a current) **2** : wander without purpose **3** : pile up under force — **drift·er** *n* —**drift·wood** *n*

¹drill \'dril\ *vb* **1** : bore with a drill **2** : instruct by repetition ~ *n* **1** : tool for boring holes **2** : regularly practiced exercise —**drill·er** *n*

²drill *n* : seed-planting implement

³drill n : twill-weave cotton fabric

dri·ly var of DRYLY

drink \'driŋk\ vb **drank** \'draŋk\; **drunk** \'drəŋk\ or **drank**; **drink·ing** 1 : swallow liquid 2 : absorb 3 : drink alcoholic beverages esp. to excess ~ n 1 : beverage 2 : alcoholic liquor — **drink·able** adj —**drink·er** n

drip \'drip\ vb **-pp-** : fall or let fall in drops ~ n 1 : a dripping 2 : sound of falling drops

drive \'drīv\ vb **drove** \'drōv\; **driv·en** \'drivən\; **driv·ing** 1 : urge or force onward 2 : direct the movement or course of 3 : compel 4 : cause to become 5 : propel forcefully ~ n 1 : trip in a vehicle 2 : intensive campaign 3 : aggressive or dynamic quality 4 : basic need —**driv·er** n

drive–in adj : accommodating patrons in cars —**drive–in** n

driv·el \'drivəl\ vb **-eled** or **-elled**; **-el·ing** or **el·ling** 1 : drool 2 : talk stupidly ~ n : nonsense

drive·way n : usu. short private road from the street to a house

driz·zle \'drizəl\ n : fine misty rain — **drizzle** vb

droll \'drōl\ adj : humorous or whimsical —**droll·ery** n —**drol·ly** adv

drom·e·dary \'drämə,derē\ n, pl **-dar·ies** : speedy one-humped camel

drone \'drōn\ n 1 : male honeybee 2 : deep hum or buzz ~ vb **droned**; **dron·ing** : make a dull monotonous sound

drool \'drül\ vb : let liquid run from the mouth

droop \'drüp\ vb 1 : hang or incline downward 2 : lose strength or spirit —**droop** n —**droopy** \-ē\ adj

drop \'dräp\ n 1 : quantity of fluid in one spherical mass 2 pl : medicine used by drops 3 : decline or fall 4 : distance something drops ~ vb **-pp-** 1 : fall in drops 2 : let fall 3 : convey 4 : go lower or become less strong or less active —**drop·let** \-lət\ n —**drop back** vb : move toward the rear — **drop behind** : fail to keep up —**drop in** vb : pay an unexpected visit

drop·per n : device that dispenses liquid by drops

drop·sy \'dräpsē\ n : edema

dross \'dräs\ n : waste matter

drought \'draut\ n : long dry spell

¹drove \'drōv\ n : crowd of moving people or animals

²drove past of DRIVE

drown \'draun\ vb 1 : suffocate in water 2 : overpower or become overpowered

drowse \'drauz\ vb **drowsed**; **drows·ing** : doze —**drowse** n

drowsy \'drauzē\ adj **drows·i·er**; **-est** : sleepy —**drows·i·ly** adv —**drows·i·ness** n

drub \'drəb\ vb **-bb-** : beat severely

drudge \'drəj\ vb **drudged**; **drudg·ing** : do hard or boring work —**drudge** n —**drudg·ery** \-ərē\ n

drug \'drəg\ n 1 : substance used as or in medicine 2 : narcotic ~ vb **-gg-** : affect with drugs —**drug·gist** \-ist\ n —**drug·store** n

dru·id \'drüəd\ n : ancient Celtic priest

drum \'drəm\ n 1 : musical instrument that is a skin-covered cylinder beaten usu. with sticks 2 : drum-shaped object (as a container) ~ vb **-mm-** 1 : beat a drum 2 : drive, force, or bring about by steady effort —**drum·beat** n —**drum·mer** n

drum·stick n 1 : stick for beating a drum 2 : lower part of a fowl's leg

drunk \'drəŋk\ adj : having the faculties impaired by alcohol ~ n : one who is drunk —**drunk·ard** \'drəŋkərd\ n —**drunk·en** \-kən\ adj —**drunk·en·ly** adv —**drunk·en·ness** n

dry \'drī\ adj **dri·er** \'drīər\; **dri·est** \'drīəst\ 1 : lacking water or moisture 2 : thirsty 3 : marked by the absence of alcoholic beverages 4 : uninteresting 5 : not sweet ~ vb **dried**; **dry·ing** : make or become dry —**dry·ly** adv —**dry·ness** n

dry–clean vb : clean (fabrics) chiefly with solvents other than water —**dry cleaning** n

dry·er \'drīər\ n : device for drying

dry goods n pl : textiles, clothing, and notions

dry ice n : solid carbon dioxide

du·al \'düəl, 'dyü-\ adj : twofold — **du·al·ism** \-ə,lizəm\ n —**du·al·i·ty** \dü'alətē, dyü-\ n

dub \'dəb\ vb **-bb-** : name

du·bi·ous \'dübēəs, 'dyü-\ adj 1 : uncertain 2 : questionable —**du·bi·ous·ly** adv —**du·bi·ous·ness** n

du·cal \'dükəl, 'dyü-\ adj : relating to a duke or dukedom

duch·ess \'dəchəs\ n 1 : wife of a duke 2 : woman holding a ducal title

duchy \-ē\ *n, pl* -ies : territory of a duke or duchess

1duck \'dək\ *n, pl* : swimming bird related to the goose and swan ~ *vb* 1 : thrust or plunge under water 2 : lower the head or body suddenly 3 : evade —**duck·ling** \-liŋ\ *n*

2duck *n* : cotton fabric

duct \'dəkt\ *n* : canal for conveying a fluid —**duct·less** \-ləs\ *adj*

duc·tile \'dəktᵊl\ *adj* : able to be drawn out or shaped —**duc·til·i·ty** \,dək-'tilətē\ *n*

dude \'düd, 'dyüd\ *n* 1 : dandy 2 : guy

dud·geon \'dəjən\ *n* : ill humor

due \'dü, 'dyü\ *adj* 1 : owed 2 : appropriate 3 : attributable 4 : scheduled ~ *n* 1 : something due 2 *pl* : fee ~ *adv* : directly

du·el \'düəl, 'dyü-\ *n* : combat between 2 persons —**duel** *vb* —**du·el·ist** *n*

du·et \dü'et, dyü-\ *n* : musical composition for 2 performers

due to *prep* : because of

dug *past of* DIG

dug·out \'dəg,aút\ *n* 1 : boat made by hollowing out a log 2 : shelter made by digging

duke \'dük, 'dyük\ *n* : nobleman of the highest rank —**duke·dom** *n*

dull \'dəl\ *adj* 1 : mentally slow 2 : blunt 3 : not brilliant or interesting —**dull** *vb* —**dul·lard** \'dələrd\ *n* —**dull·ness** *n* —**dul·ly** *adv*

du·ly \'dülē, 'dyü-\ *adv* : in a due manner or time

dumb \'dəm\ *adj* 1 : mute 2 : stupid —**dumb·ly** *adv*

dumb·bell \'dəm,bel\ *n* 1 : short bar with weights on the ends used for exercise 2 : stupid person

dumb·found, dum·found \,dəm'faúnd\ *vb* : amaze

dum·my \'dəmē\ *n, pl* -mies 1 : stupid person 2 : imitative substitute

dump \'dəmp\ *vb* : let fall in a pile ~ *n* : place for dumping something (as refuse) —**in the dumps** : sad

dump·ling \'dəmpliŋ\ *n* : small mass of boiled or steamed dough

dumpy \'dəmpē\ *adj* **dump·i·er; -est** : short and thick in build

1dun \'dən\ *adj* : brownish gray

2dun *vb* **-nn-** : hound for payment of a debt

dunce \'dəns\ *n* : stupid person

dune \'dün, 'dyün\ *n* : hill of sand

dung \'dəŋ\ *n* : manure

dun·ga·ree \,dəŋgə'rē\ *n* 1 : blue denim 2 *pl* : work clothes made of dungaree

dun·geon \'dənjən\ *n* : underground prison

dunk \'dəŋk\ *vb* : dip or submerge temporarily in liquid

duo \'düō, 'dyüō\ *n, pl* **du·os** : pair

du·o·de·num \,düə'dēnəm, ,dyü-; du-'äd²nəm, dyü-\ *n, pl* **-na** \-'dēnə, -²nə\ *or* **-nums** : part of the small intestine nearest the stomach —**du·o·de·nal** \-'dēn²l, -²nəl\ *adj*

dupe \'düp, dyüp\ *n* : one easily deceived or cheated —**dupe** *vb*

du·plex \'dü,pleks, 'dyü-\ *adj* : double ~ *n* : 2-family house

du·pli·cate \'düplikət, 'dyü-\ *adj* 1 : consisting of 2 identical items 2 : being just like another ~ *n* : exact copy ~ \-,kāt\ *vb* **-cat·ed; -cat·ing** 1 : make an exact copy of 2 : repeat or equal —**du·pli·ca·tion** \,düpli-'kāshən, ,dyü-\ *n* —**du·pli·ca·tor** \'düpli,kātər, dyü-\ *n*

du·plic·i·ty \dü'plisətē, ,dyü-\ *n, pl* -ties : deception

du·ra·ble \'dùrəbəl, 'dyúr-\ *adj* : lasting a long time —**du·ra·bil·i·ty** \,dùrə'bilətē, ,dyùr-\ *n*

du·ra·tion \dù'rāshən, dyü-\ *n* : length of time something lasts

du·ress \dù'res, dyü-\ *n* : coercion

dur·ing \'dùriŋ, 'dyúr-\ *prep* 1 : throughout 2 : at some point in

dusk \'dəsk\ *n* : twilight —**dusky** *adj*

dust \'dəst\ *n* : powdered matter ~ *vb* 1 : remove dust from 2 : sprinkle with fine particles —**dust·er** *n* —**dust·pan** *n* —**dusty** *adj*

du·ty \'dütē, 'dyü-\ *n, pl* -ties 1 : action required by one's occupation or position 2 : moral or legal obligation 3 : tax —**du·te·ous** \-əs\ *adj* —**du·ti·able** \-əbəl\ *adj* —**du·ti·ful** \'dütifəl, 'dyü-\ *adj*

dwarf \'dwórf\ *n, pl* **dwarfs** \'dwórfs\ *or* **dwarves** \'dwórvz\ : one that is much below normal size ~ *vb* 1 : stunt 2 : cause to seem smaller —**dwarf·ish** *adj*

dwell \'dwel\ *vb* **dwelt** \'dwelt\ *or* **dwelled** \'dweld, 'dwelt\; **dwell·ing** 1 : reside 2 : keep the attention directed —**dwell·er** *n* —**dwell·ing** *n*

dwin·dle \'dwind²l\ *vb* **-dled; -dling** : become steadily less

dye \'dī\ *n* : coloring material ~ *vb* **dyed; dye·ing** : give a new color to

dying *pres part of* DIE

dyke *var of* DIKE

dy·nam·ic \dī'namik\ *adj* **1** : relating to physical force producing motion **2** : energetic or forceful

dy·na·mite \'dīnə,mīt\ *n* : explosive made of nitroglycerin —**dynamite** *vb*

dy·na·mo \-,mō\ *n, pl* **-mos** : electrical generator

dy·nas·ty \'dīnəstē, -,nas-\ *n, pl* **-ties** : succession of rulers of the same family —**dy·nas·tic** \dī'nastik\ *adj*

dys·en·tery \'disⁿn,terē\ *n, pl* **-ter·ies** : disease marked by diarrhea

dys·lex·ia \dis'leksēə\ *n* : disturbance of the ability to read —**dys·lex·ic** \-sik\ *adj*

dys·pep·sia \-'pepshə, -sēə\ *n* : indigestion —**dys·pep·tic** \-'peptik\ *adj or n*

dys·tro·phy \'distrəfē\ *n, pl* **-phies** : disorder involving nervous and muscular tissue

E

e \'ē\ *n, pl* **e's** *or* **es** \'ēz\ : 5th letter of the alphabet

each \'ēch\ *adj* : being one of the class named ~ *pron* : every individual one ~ *adv* : apiece

ea·ger \'ēgər\ *adj* : enthusiastic or anxious —**ea·ger·ly** *adv* —**ea·ger·ness** *n*

ea·gle \'ēgəl\ *n* : large bird of prey

-ean —see -AN

¹ear \'ir\ *n* : organ of hearing or the outer part of this —**ear·ache** *n* —**eared** *adj* —**ear·lobe** \-,lōb\ *n*

²ear *n* : fruiting head of a cereal

ear·drum *n* : thin membrane that receives and transmits sound waves in the ear

earl \'ərl\ *n* : British nobleman —**earl·dom** \-dəm\ *n*

ear·ly \'ərlē\ *adj* **-li·er; -est** **1** : relating to or occurring near the beginning or before the usual time **2** : ancient —**early** *adv*

ear·mark *vb* : designate for a specific purpose

earn \'ərn\ *vb* **1** : receive as a return for service **2** : deserve

ear·nest \'ərnəst\ *n* : serious state of mind —**earnest** *adj* —**ear·nest·ly** *adv* —**ear·nest·ness** *n*

earn·ings \'ərniŋz\ *n pl* : something earned

ear·phone *n* : device that reproduces sound and is worn over or in the ear

ear·ring *n* : earlobe ornament

ear·shot *n* : range of hearing

earth \'ərth\ *n* **1** : soil or land **2** : planet inhabited by man —**earth·li·ness** *n*

—**earth·ly** *adj* —**earth·ward** \-wərd\ *adv*

earth·en \'ərthən\ *adj* : made of earth or baked clay —**earth·en·ware** \-,war\ *n*

earth·quake *n* : shaking or trembling of the earth

earth·worm *n* : long segmented worm

earthy \'ərthē\ *adj* **earth·i·er; -est** **1** : relating to or consisting of earth **2** : practical **3** : coarse —**earth·i·ness** *n*

ease \'ēz\ *n* **1** : comfort **2** : naturalness of manner **3** : freedom from difficulty ~ *vb* **eased; eas·ing** **1** : relieve from distress **2** : lessen the tension of **3** : make easier

ea·sel \'ēzəl\ *n* : frame to hold a painter's canvas

east \'ēst\ *adv* : to or toward the east ~ *adj* : situated toward or at or coming from the east ~ *n* **1** : direction of sunrise **2** *cap* : regions to the east —**east·er·ly** \'ēstərlē\ *adv or adj* —**east·ward** *adv or adj* —**east·wards** *adv*

Eas·ter \'ēstər\ *n* : church feast celebrating Christ's resurrection

east·ern \'ēstərn\ *adj* **1** *cap* : relating to a region designated East **2** : lying toward or coming from the east —**East·ern·er** *n*

easy \'ēzē\ *adj* **eas·i·er; -est** **1** : marked by ease **2** : lenient —**eas·i·ly** \'ēzəlē\ *adv* —**eas·i·ness** \-ēnəs\ *n*

easy·go·ing *adj* : relaxed and casual

eat \'ēt\ *vb* **ate** \'āt\; **eat·en** \'ētⁿn\; **eat·ing** **1** : take in as food **2** : use up or corrode —**eat·able** *adj or n* —**eat·er** *n*

eaves \'ēvz\ *n pl* : overhanging edge of a roof

eaves·drop *vb* : listen secretly —**eaves·drop·per** *n*

ebb \'eb\ *n* **1** : outward flow of the tide **2** : decline ~ *vb* **1** : recede from the flood state **2** : wane

eb·o·ny \'ebənē\ *n, pl* -**nies** : hard heavy wood of tropical trees ~ *adj* **1** : made of ebony **2** : black

ebul·lient \i'bulyənt, -'bəl-\ *adj* : exuberant —**ebul·lience** \-yəns\ *n*

ec·cen·tric \ik'sentrik\ *adj* **1** : odd in behavior **2** : being off center —**eccentric** *n* —**ec·cen·tri·cal·ly** \-triklē\ *adv* —**ec·cen·tric·i·ty** \,ek,sen'trisətē\ *n*

ec·cle·si·as·tic \ik,lēzē'astik\ *n* : clergyman

ec·cle·si·as·ti·cal \-tikəl\, **ecclesiastic** *adj* : relating to a church —**ec·cle·si·as·ti·cal·ly** \-tiklē\ *adv*

ech·e·lon \'eshə,län\ *n* **1** : steplike arrangement **2** : level of authority

echo \'ekō\ *n, pl* **ech·oes** : repetition of a sound caused by a reflection of the sound waves —**echo** *vb*

éclair \ā'klar\ *n* : custard-filled pastry

eclec·tic \e'klektik, i-\ *adj* : drawing or drawn from varied sources

eclipse \i'klips\ *n* : total or partial obscuring of one celestial body by another —**eclipse** *vb*

ecol·o·gy \i'käləjē, e-\ *n, pl* -**gies** : science concerned with the interaction of organisms and their environment —**eco·log·i·cal** \,ēkə'läjikəl, ,ek-\ *adj* —**eco·log·i·cal·ly** *adv* —**ecol·o·gist** \i'käləjist, e-\ *n*

eco·nom·ic \,ekə'nämik, ,ēkə-\ *adj* : relating to the producing and the buying and selling of goods and services

eco·nom·ics \-'nämiks\ *n* : branch of knowledge dealing with goods and services —**econ·o·mist** \i'känəmist\ *n*

econ·o·mize \i'känə,mīz\ *vb* -**mized**; -**miz·ing** : be thrifty —**econ·o·miz·er** *n*

econ·o·my \-əmē\ *n, pl* -**mies** **1** : thrifty use of resources **2** : economic system —**eco·nom·i·cal** \,ekə'nämikəl, ,ēkə-\ *adj* —**eco·nom·i·cal·ly** *adv* —**economy** *adj*

ecru \'ekrü, 'ākrü\ *n* : beige

ec·sta·sy \'ekstəsē\ *n, pl* -**sies** : extreme emotional excitement —**ec·stat·ic** \ek'statik, ik-\ *adj* —**ec·stat·i·cal·ly** \-iklē\ *adv*

ec·u·men·i·cal \,ekyə'menikəl\ *adj* : promoting worldwide Christian unity

ec·ze·ma \ig'zēmə, 'egzəmə, 'eksə-\ *n* : itching skin inflammation

¹**-ed** \d *after a vowel or* b, g, j, l, m, n, ŋ, r, th, v, z, zh; əd, id *after* d, t; *after other sounds*\ *vb suffix or adj suffix* **1** —used to form the past participle of regular verbs **2** : having or having the characteristics of

²**-ed** *vb suffix* —used to form the past tense of regular verbs

ed·dy \'edē\ *n, pl* -**dies** : whirlpool —**eddy** *vb*

ede·ma \i'dēmə\ *n* : abnormal accumulation of fluid in the body tissues —**edem·a·tous** \-'demətəs\ *adj*

Eden \'ēd⁰n\ *n* : paradise

edge \'ej\ *n* **1** : cutting side of a blade **2** : line where something begins or ends ~ *vb* **edged**; **edg·ing** **1** : give or form an edge **2** : move gradually **3** : narrowly defeat —**edg·er** *n*

edge·wise \-,wīz\ *adv* : sideways

edgy \'ejē\ *adj* **edg·i·er**; -**est** : nervous —**edg·i·ness** *n*

ed·i·ble \'edəbəl\ *adj* : fit or safe to be eaten —**ed·i·bil·i·ty** \,edə'bilətē\ *n* —**edible** *n*

edict \'ē,dikt\ *n* : order or decree

ed·i·fi·ca·tion \,edəfə'kāshən\ *n* : instruction or information —**ed·i·fy** \'edə,fī\ *vb*

ed·i·fice \'edəfəs\ *n* : large building

ed·it \'edət\ *vb* **1** : revise and prepare for publication **2** : delete —**ed·i·tor** \-ər\ *n* —**ed·i·tor·ship** *n*

edi·tion \i'dishən\ *n* **1** : form in which a text is published **2** : total number published at one time

ed·i·to·ri·al \,edə'tōrēəl\ *adj* **1** : relating to an editor or editing **2** : expressing opinion ~ *n* : article (as in a newspaper) expressing the views of an editor —**ed·i·to·ri·al·ize** \-ē∂,līz\ *vb* —**ed·i·to·ri·al·ly** *adv*

ed·u·cate \'ejə,kāt\ *vb* -**cat·ed**; -**cat·ing** **1** : give instruction to **2** : develop mentally and morally **3** : provide with information —**ed·u·ca·ble** \'ejəkəbəl\ *adj* —**ed·u·ca·tion** \,ejə'kāshən\ *n* —**ed·u·ca·tion·al** \-shənəl\ *adj* —**ed·u·ca·tor** \-ər\ *n*

eel \'ēl\ *n* : snakelike fish

ee·rie \'irē\ *adj* -**ri·er**; -**est** : weird —**ee·ri·ly** \'irəlē\ *adv*

ef·face \i'fās, e-\ *vb* -**faced**; -**fac·ing**

: obliterate by rubbing out —**ef·face·ment** *n*

ef·fect \i'fekt\ *n* **1** : result **2** : meaning **3** : influence **4** *pl* : goods or possessions ~ *vb* : cause to happen —**in effect** : in substance

ef·fec·tive \i'fektiv\ *adj* **1** : producing a strong or desired effect **2** : being in operation —**ef·fec·tive·ly** *adv* —**ef·fec·tive·ness** *n*

ef·fec·tu·al \i'fekchəwəl\ *adj* : producing an intended effect —**ef·fec·tu·al·ly** *adv* —**ef·fec·tu·al·ness** *n*

ef·fem·i·nate \ə'femənət\ *adj* : unsuitably womanish —**ef·fem·i·na·cy** \-nəsē\ *n*

ef·fer·vesce \efər'ves\ *vb* -**vesced**; -**vescing** **1** : bubble and hiss as gas escapes **2** : show exhilaration —**ef·fer·ves·cence** \-'vesᵊns\ *n* —**ef·fer·ves·cent** \-ᵊnt\ *adj* —**ef·fer·ves·cent·ly** *adv*

ef·fete \e'fēt\ *adj* **1** : worn out **2** : weak or decadent **3** : effeminate

ef·fi·ca·cious \efə'kāshəs\ *adj* : effective —**ef·fi·ca·cy** \'efikəsē\ *n*

ef·fi·cient \i'fishənt\ *adj* : working well with little waste —**ef·fi·cien·cy** \-ənsē\ *n* —**ef·fi·cient·ly** *adv*

ef·fi·gy \'efəjē\ *n, pl* -**gies** : usu. crude image of a person

ef·flu·ent \'e,flüənt, e'flü-\ *n* : something that flows out —**effluent** *adj*

ef·fort \'efərt\ *n* **1** : a putting forth of strength **2** : use of resources toward a goal **3** : product of effort —**ef·fort·less** *adj* —**ef·fort·less·ly** *adv*

ef·fron·tery \i'frəntərē\ *n, pl* -**ter·ies** : insolence

ef·fu·sion \i'fyüzhən, e-\ *n* : a gushing forth —**ef·fu·sive** \-'fyüsiv\ *adj* —**ef·fu·sive·ly** *adv*

¹**egg** \'eg, 'āg\ *vb* : urge to action

²**egg** *n* **1** : rounded usu. hard-shelled reproductive body esp. of birds and reptiles from which the young hatches **2** : ovum —**egg·shell** *n*

egg·nog \-,näg\ *n* : rich drink of eggs and cream

egg·plant *n* : edible purplish fruit of a plant related to the potato

ego \'ēgō\ *n, pl* **egos** : self-esteem

ego·cen·tric \,ēgō'sentrik\ *adj* : self-centered

ego·tism \'ēgə,tizəm\ *n* : exaggerated sense of self-importance —**ego·tist**

\-tist\ *n* —**ego·tis·tic** \,ēgə'tistik\, **ego·tis·ti·cal** \-tikəl\ *adj* —**ego·tis·ti·cal·ly** *adv*

egre·gious \i'grējəs\ *adj* : notably bad —**egre·gious·ly** *adv*

egress \'ē,gres\ *n* : a way out

egret \'ēgrət, i'gret, 'egrət\ *n* : long-plumed heron

ei·der·down \'īdər,daun\ *n* : soft down obtained from a northern sea duck (**ei·der**)

eight \'āt\ *n* **1** : one more than 7 **2** : 8th in a set or series **3** : something having 8 units —**eight** *adj or pron* —**eighth** \'ātth\ *adj or adv or n*

eigh·teen \āt'tēn\ *n* : one more than 17 —**eigh·teen** *adj or pron* —**eigh·teenth** \-'tēnth\ *adj or n*

eighty \'ātē\ *n, pl* **eight·ies** : 8 times 10 —**eight·i·eth** \'ātēəth\ *adj or n* —**eighty** *adj or pron*

ei·ther \'ēthər, 'ī-\ *adj* **1** : both **2** : being the one or the other of two ~ *pron* : one of two or more ~ *conj* : one or the other

ejac·u·late \i'jakyə,lāt\ *vb* -**lat·ed**; -**lat·ing 1** : say suddenly **2** : eject a fluid (as semen) —**ejac·u·la·tion** \-,jak-yə'lāshən\ *n*

eject \i'jekt\ *vb* : drive or throw out —**ejec·tion** \-'jekshən\ *n*

eke \'ēk\ *vb* **eked**; **ek·ing** : barely gain with effort —usu. with *out*

elab·o·rate \i'labərət\ *adj* **1** : planned in detail **2** : complex and ornate ~ \-ə,rāt\ *vb* -**rat·ed**; -**rat·ing** : work out in detail —**elab·o·rate·ly** *adv* —**elab·o·rate·ness** *n* —**elab·o·ra·tion** \-,labə'rāshən\ *n*

elapse \i'laps\ *vb* **elapsed**; **elaps·ing** : slip by

elas·tic \i'lastik\ *adj* **1** : springy **2** : flexible ~ *n* **1** : elastic material **2** : rubber band —**elas·tic·i·ty** \-,las-'tisətē, ,ē,las-\ *n*

elate \i'lāt\ *vb* **elat·ed**; **elat·ing** : fill with joy —**ela·tion** \-'lāshən\ *n*

el·bow \'el,bō\ *n* **1** : joint of the arm **2** : elbow-shaped bend or joint ~ *vb* : push aside with the elbow

el·der \'eldər\ *adj* : older ~ *n* **1** : one who is older **2** : church officer

el·der·ber·ry \'eldər,berē\ *n* : edible black or red fruit or a tree or shrub bearing these

el·der·ly \'eldərlē\ *adj* : past middle age

el·dest \'eldəst\ *adj* : oldest

elect \i'lekt\ *adj* : elected but not yet in

office ~ *n* **elect** *pl* : exclusive group ~ *vb* : choose esp. by vote —**election** \i'lekshən\ *n* —**elective** \i'lektiv\ *n or adj* —**elector** \i'lektər\ *n* —**electoral** \-tərəl\ *adj*

elec·tor·ate \i'lektərət\ *n* : body of persons entitled to vote

elec·tric \i'lektrik\ *adj* 1 : *or* **electrical** \-trikəl\ : relating to or run by electricity 2 : thrilling —**electrically** *adv*

elec·tri·cian \i,lek'trishən\ *n* : person who installs or repairs electrical equipment

elec·tric·i·ty \-'trisətē\ *n, pl* -**ties** 1 : fundamental form of energy occurring naturally (as in lightning) or produced artificially 2 : electric current

elec·tri·fy \i'lektrə,fī\ *vb* -**fied**; -**fy·ing** 1 : charge with electricity 2 : equip for use of electric power 3 : thrill —**elec·tri·fi·ca·tion** \-,lektrəfə'kāshən\ *n*

elec·tro·car·dio·gram \i,lektrō'kärdē-ə,gram\ *n* : tracing made by an electrocardiograph

elec·tro·car·dio·graph \-,graf\ *n* : instrument for monitoring heart function

elec·tro·cute \i'lektrə,kyüt\ *vb* -**cut·ed**; -**cut·ing** : kill by an electric shock —**elec·tro·cu·tion** \-,lektrə'kyüshən\ *n*

elec·trode \i'lek,trōd\ *n* : conductor at a nonmetallic part of a circuit

elec·trol·y·sis \i,lek'träləsəs\ *n* 1 : production of chemical changes by passage of an electric current through a substance 2 : destruction of hair roots with an electric current —**elec·tro·lyt·ic** \-trə'litik\ *adj*

elec·tro·lyte \i'lektrə,līt\ *n* : nonmetallic electric conductor

elec·tro·mag·net \i,lektrō'magnət\ *n* : magnet made using electric current

elec·tro·mag·net·ism \-nə,tizəm\ *n* : natural force responsible for interactions between charged particles —**elec·tro·mag·net·ic** \-mag'netik\ *adj* —**elec·tro·mag·net·i·cal·ly** \-iklē\ *adv*

elec·tron \i'lek,trän\ *n* : negatively charged particle within the atom

elec·tron·ic \i,lek'tränik\ *adj* : relating to electrons or electronics —**electron·i·cal·ly** \-iklē\ *adv*

elec·tron·ics \-iks\ *n* : physics of electrons and their use esp. in devices

elec·tro·plate \i'lektrə,plāt\ *vb* : coat (as with metal) by electrolysis

el·e·gance \'eligəns\ *n* : refined gracefulness —**el·e·gant** \-gənt\ *adj* —**el·e·gant·ly** *adv*

el·e·gy \'eləjē\ *n, pl* -**gies** : poem expressing grief for one who is dead—**ele·gi·ac** \,elə'jīak, -,ak\ *adj*

el·e·ment \'eləmənt\ *n* 1 *pl* : weather conditions 2 : natural environment 3 : constituent part 4 *pl* : simplest principles 5 : substance that has atoms of only one kind —**el·e·men·tal** \,elə'mentᵊl\ *adj*

el·e·men·ta·ry \,elə'mentrē\ *adj* 1 : simple 2 : relating to the basic subjects of education

el·e·phant \'eləfənt\ *n* : huge mammal with a trunk and 2 ivory tusks

el·e·vate \'elə,vāt\ *vb* -**vat·ed**; -**vat·ing** 1 : lift up 2 : exalt

el·e·va·tion \,elə'vāshən\ *n* : height or a high place

el·e·va·tor \'elə,vātər\ *n* 1 : cage or platform for raising or lowering something 2 : grain storehouse

elev·en \i'levən\ *n* 1 : one more than 10 2 : 11th in a set or series 3 : something having 11 units —**eleven** *adj or pron* —**elev·enth** \-ənth\ *adj or n*

elf \'elf\ *n, pl* **elves** \'elvz\ : mischievous fairy —**elf·in** \'elfən\ *adj* —**elf·ish** \'elfish\ *adj*

elic·it \i'lisət\ *vb* : draw forth

el·i·gi·ble \'eləjəbəl\ *adj* : qualified to participate or to be chosen —**el·i·gi·bil·i·ty** \,eləjə'bilətē\ *n* —**eligible** *n*

elim·i·nate \i'limə,nāt\ *vb* -**nat·ed**; -**nat·ing** : get rid of —**elim·i·na·tion** \i,limə'nāshən\ *n*

elite \ā'lēt\ *n* : choice or select group

elix·ir \i'liksər\ *n* : medicinal solution

elk \'elk\ *n* : large deer

el·lipse \i'lips, e-\ *n* : oval

el·lip·sis \-'lipsəs\ *n, pl* -**lip·ses** \-,sēz\ 1 : omission of a word or words 2 : marks (as . . .) to show omission

el·lip·ti·cal \-tikəl\, **el·lip·tic** \-tik\ *adj* 1 : relating to or shaped like an ellipse 2 : relating to or marked by ellipsis

elm \'elm\ *n* : tall shade tree

el·o·cu·tion \,elə'kyüshən\ *n* : art of public speaking

elon·gate \i'lóŋ,gāt\ *vb* -**gat·ed**; -**gat·ing** : make or grow longer —**elon·ga·tion** \,ē,lóŋ'gāshən\ *n*

elope \i'lōp\ *vb* **eloped**; **elop·ing** : run

away esp. to be married —**elope**-**ment** *n* —**elop·er** *n*

el·o·quent \\'eləkwənt\\ *adj* : forceful and persuasive in speech —**el·o·quence** \\-kwəns\\ *n* —**el·o·quent·ly** *adv*

else \\'els\\ *adv* 1 : in a different way, time, or place 2 : otherwise ~ *adj* 1 : other 2 : more

else·where *adv* : in or to another place

elu·ci·date \\i'lüsə,dāt\\ *vb* -**dat**-**ed**; -**dat·ing** : explain —**elu·ci·da·tion** \\i,lüsə'dāshən\\ *n*

elude \\ē'lüd\\ *vb* **elud·ed**; **elud·ing** : evade —**elu·sive** \\ē'lüsiv\\ *adj* —**elu·sive·ly** *adv* —**elu·sive·ness** *n*

elves *pl of* ELF

ema·ci·ate \\i'māshē,āt\\ *vb* -**at·ed**; -**at·ing** : become or make very thin —**ema·ci·a·tion** \\i,māsē'āshən, -shē-\\ *n*

em·a·nate \\'emə,nāt\\ *vb* -**nat·ed**; -**nat·ing** : come forth —**em·a·na·tion** \\,emə'nāshən\\ *n*

eman·ci·pate \\i'mansə,pāt\\ *vb* -**pat·ed**; -**pat·ing** : set free —**eman·ci·pa·tion** \\i,mansə'pāshən\\ *n* —**eman·ci·pa·tor** \\i'mansə,pātər\\ *n*

emas·cu·late \\i'maskyə,lāt\\ *vb* -**lat·ed**; -**lat·ing** 1 : castrate 2 : weaken —**emas·cu·la·tion** \\i,maskyə'lāshən\\ *n*

em·balm \\im'bäm, -'bälm\\ *vb* : preserve (a corpse) —**em·balm·er** *n*

em·bank·ment \\im'baŋkmənt\\ *n* : protective barrier of earth

em·bar·go \\im'bärgō\\ *n, pl* -**goes** : ban on trade —**embargo** *vb*

em·bark \\-'bärk\\ *vb* 1 : go on board a ship or airplane 2 : make a start —**em·bar·ka·tion** \\,em,bär'kāshən\\ *n*

em·bar·rass \\im'barəs\\ *vb* : cause distress and self-consciousness —**em·bar·rass·ment** *n*

em·bas·sy \\'embəsē\\ *n, pl* -**sies** : residence and offices of an ambassador

em·bed \\im'bed\\ *vb* -**dd**- : fix firmly

em·bel·lish \\-'belish\\ *vb* : decorate —**em·bel·lish·ment** *n*

em·ber \\'embər\\ *n* : smoldering fragment from a fire

em·bez·zle \\im'bezəl\\ *vb* -**zled**; -**zling** : steal (money) by falsifying records —**em·bez·zle·ment** *n* —**em·bez·zler** \\-ələr\\ *n*

em·bit·ter \\im'bitər\\ *vb* : make bitter

em·bla·zon \\-'blāzᵊn\\ *vb* : display conspicuously

em·blem \\'embləm\\ *n* : symbol —**em·blem·at·ic** \\,emblə'matik\\ *adj*

em·body \\im'bädē\\ *vb* -**bod·ied**; -**body·ing** : give definite form or expression to —**em·bodi·ment** \\-'bädimənt\\ *n*

em·boss \\-'bäs, -'bȯs\\ *vb* : ornament with raised work

em·brace \\-'brās\\ *vb* -**braced**; -**brac·ing** 1 : clasp in the arms 2 : welcome 3 : include —**embrace** *n*

em·broi·der \\-'brȯidər\\ *vb* : ornament with or do needlework —**em·broi·dery** \\-ərē\\ *n*

em·broil \\im'brȯil\\ *vb* : involve in conflict or difficulties

em·bryo \\'embrē,ō\\ *n* : living being in its earliest stages of development —**em·bry·on·ic** \\,embrē'änik\\ *adj*

emend \\ē'mend\\ *vb* : correct —**emen·da·tion** \\,ē,men'dāshən\\ *n*

em·er·ald \\'emrəld, 'emə-\\ *n* : green gem ~ *adj* : bright green

emerge \\i'mərj\\ *vb* **emerged**; **emerg·ing** : rise, come forth, or appear —**emer·gence** \\-'mərjəns\\ *n* —**emer·gent** \\-jənt\\ *adj*

emer·gen·cy \\i'mərjənsē\\ *n, pl* -**cies** : condition requiring prompt action

em·ery \\'emərē\\ *n, pl* -**er·ies** : dark granular mineral used for grinding

emet·ic \\i'metik\\ *n* : agent that induces vomiting —**emetic** *adj*

em·i·grate \\'emə,grāt\\ *vb* -**grat·ed**; -**grat·ing** : leave a country to settle elsewhere —**em·i·grant** \\-igrənt\\ *n* —**em·i·gra·tion** \\,emə'grāshən\\ *n*

em·i·nence \\'emənəns\\ *n* 1 : prominence or superiority 2 : person of high rank

em·i·nent \\-nənt\\ *adj* : prominent —**em·i·nent·ly** *adv*

em·is·sary \\'emə,serē\\ *n, pl* -**sar·ies** : agent

emis·sion \\ē'mishən\\ *n* : substance discharged into the air

emit \\ē'mit\\ *vb* -**tt**- : give off or out

emol·u·ment \\i'mälyəmənt\\ *n* : salary or fee

emote \\i'mōt\\ *vb* **emot·ed**; **emot·ing** : express emotion

emo·tion \\i'mōshən\\ *n* : intense feeling —**emo·tion·al** \\-shənəl\\ *adj* —**emo·tion·al·ly** *adv*

em·per·or \\'empərər\\ *n* : ruler of an empire

em·pha·sis \\'emfəsəs\\ *n, pl* -**pha·ses** \\-,sēz\\ : stress

em·pha·size \\-,sīz\\ *vb* -**sized**; -**siz·ing** : stress

em·phat·ic \\im'fatik, em-\\ *adj* : uttered

with emphasis —**em·phat·i·cal·ly** \-iklē\ adv

em·pire \'em,pīr\ n : large state or a group of states

em·pir·i·cal \im'pirikəl\ adj : based on observation —**em·pir·i·cal·ly** \-iklē\ adv

em·ploy \im'plòi\ vb 1 : use 2 : occupy ~ n : paid occupation —**em·ploy·ee**, **em·ploye** \im,plòi'ē, -'plòi,ē\ n —**em·ploy·er** n —**em·ploy·ment** \-mənt\ n

em·pow·er \im'pauòr\ vb : give power to —**em·pow·er·ment** n

em·press \'emprəs\ n 1 : wife of an emperor 2 : woman emperor

emp·ty \'emptē\ adj 1 : containing nothing 2 : not occupied 3 : lacking value, sense, or purpose ~ vb -**tied**; -**ty·ing** : make or become empty —**emp·ti·ness** \-tēnəs\ n

emu \'ēmyü\ n : Australian bird related to the ostrich

em·u·late \'emyə,lāt\ vb -**lated**; -**lat·ing** : try to equal or excel —**em·u·la·tion** \,emyə'lāshən\ n

emul·si·fy \i'məlsə,fī\ vb -**fied**; -**fy·ing** : convert into an emulsion —**emul·si·fi·ca·tion** \i,məlsəfə'kāshən\ n —**emul·si·fi·er** \-'məlsə,fīər\ n

emul·sion \i'məlshən\ n 1 : mixture of mutually insoluble liquids 2 : light-sensitive coating on photographic film

-**en** \ən, ³n\ vb suffix 1 : become or cause to be 2 : cause or come to have

en·able \in'ābəl\ vb -**abled**; -**abling** : give power, capacity, or ability to

en·act \in'akt\ vb 1 : make into law 2 : act out —**en·act·ment** n

enam·el \in'aməl\ n 1 : glasslike substance used to coat metal or pottery 2 : hard outer layer of a tooth 3 : glossy paint —**enamel** vb

en·am·or \in'amər\ vb : excite with love

en·camp \in'kamp\ vb : make camp —**en·camp·ment** n

en·case \in'kās\ vb : enclose in or as if in a case

-**ence** \əns, ³ns\ n suffix 1 : action or process 2 : quality or state

en·ceph·a·li·tis \in,sefə'lītəs\ n, pl -**lit·i·des** \-'litə,dēz\ : inflammation of the brain

en·chant \in'chant\ vb 1 : bewitch 2 : fascinate —**en·chant·er** n —**en·chant·ment** n —**en·chant·ress** \-'chantrəs\ n

en·cir·cle \in'sərkəl\ vb : surround

en·close \in'klōz\ vb 1 : shut up or surround 2 : include —**en·clo·sure** \in-'klōzhər\ n

en·co·mi·um \en'kōmēəm\ n, pl -**mi·ums** or -**mia** \-mēə\ : high praise

en·com·pass \in'kəmpəs, -'käm-\ vb : surround or include

en·core \'än,kòr\ n : further performance

en·coun·ter \in'kauntər\ vb 1 : fight 2 : meet unexpectedly —**encounter** n

en·cour·age \in'kərij\ vb -**aged**; -**ag·ing** 1 : inspire with courage and hope 2 : foster —**en·cour·age·ment** n

en·croach \in'krōch\ vb : enter upon another's property or rights —**en·croach·ment** n

en·crust \in'krəst\ vb : form a crust on

en·cum·ber \in'kəmbər\ vb : burden —**en·cum·brance** \-brəns\ n

-**en·cy** \ənsē, ³n-\ n suffix : -ence

en·cyc·li·cal \in'siklikəl, en-\ n : papal letter to bishops

en·cy·clo·pe·dia \in,sīklə'pēdēə\ n : reference work on many subjects —**en·cy·clo·pe·dic** \-'pēdik\ adj

end \'end\ n 1 : point at which something stops or no longer exists 2 : cessation 3 : purpose ~ vb 1 : stop or finish 2 : be at the end of —**end·ed** adj —**end·less** adj —**end·less·ly** adv

en·dan·ger \in'dānjər\ vb : bring into danger

en·dear \in'dir\ vb 1 : make dear —**en·dear·ment** \-mənt\ n

en·deav·or \in'devər\ vb or n : attempt

end·ing \'endiŋ\ n : end

en·dive \'en,dīv\ n : salad plant

en·do·crine \'endəkrən, -,krīn, -,krēn\ adj : producing secretions distributed by the bloodstream

en·dorse \in'dòrs\ vb -**dorsed**; -**dors·ing** 1 : sign one's name to 2 : approve —**en·dorse·ment** n

en·dow \in'dau\ vb 1 : furnish with funds 2 : furnish naturally —**en·dow·ment** n

en·dure \in'dùr, -'dyùr\ vb -**dured**; -**dur·ing** 1 : last 2 : suffer patiently 3 : tolerate —**en·dur·able** adj —**en·dur·ance** \-əns\ n

en·e·ma \'enəmə\ n : injection of liquid into the rectum

en·e·my \-mē\ n, pl -**mies** : one that attacks or tries to harm another

en·er·get·ic \,enər'jetik\ adj : full of energy or activity —**en·er·get·i·cal·ly** \-iklē\ adv

en·er·gize \'enər,jīz\ vb -**gized**; -**giz·ing** : give energy to

en·er·gy \'enərjē\ n, pl -**gies** 1 : capacity for action 2 : vigorous action 3 : capacity for doing work

en·er·vate \'enər,vāt\ vb -**vat·ed**; -**vat·ing** : make weak or listless —**en·er·va·tion** \,enər'vāshən\ n

en·fold \in'fōld\ vb : surround or embrace

en·force \-'fōrs\ vb 1 : compel 2 : carry out —**en·force·able** \-əbəl\ adj —**en·force·ment** n

en·fran·chise \-'fran,chīz\ vb -**chised**; -**chis·ing** : grant voting rights to —**en·fran·chise·ment** \-,chīzmənt, -chəz-\ n

en·gage \in'gāj\ vb -**gaged**; -**gag·ing** 1 : participate or cause to participate 2 : bring or come into working contact 3 : bind by a pledge to marry 4 : hire 5 : bring or enter into conflict —**en·gage·ment** \-mənt\ n

en·gag·ing adj : attractive

en·gen·der \in'jendər\ vb -**dered**; -**der·ing** : create

en·gine \'enjən\ n 1 : machine that converts energy into mechanical motion 2 : locomotive

en·gi·neer \,enjə'nir\ n 1 : one trained in engineering 2 : engine operator ~ vb : lay out or manage as an engineer

en·gi·neer·ing \-iŋ\ n : practical application of science and mathematics

en·grave \in'grāv\ vb -**graved**; -**grav·ing** : cut into a surface —**en·grav·er** n —**en·grav·ing** n

en·gross \-'grōs\ vb : occupy fully

en·gulf \-'gəlf\ vb : swallow up

en·hance \-'hans\ vb -**hanced**; -**hanc·ing** : improve in value —**en·hance·ment** n

enig·ma \i'nigmə\ n : puzzle or mystery —**enig·mat·ic** \,enig'matik, ,ē-\ adj —**enig·mat·i·cal·ly** adv

en·join \in'jóin\ vb 1 : command 2 : forbid

en·joy \-'jói\ vb : take pleasure in —**en·joy·able** adj —**en·joy·ment** n

en·large \-'lärj\ vb -**larged**; -**larg·ing** : make or grow larger —**en·large·ment** n —**en·larg·er** n

en·light·en \-'līt°n\ vb : give knowledge or spiritual insight to —**en·light·en·ment** n

en·list \-'list\ vb 1 : join the armed forces 2 : get the aid of —**en·list·ee** \-,lis'tē\ n —**en·list·ment** \-'listmənt\ n

en·liv·en \in'līvən\ vb : give life or spirit to

en·mi·ty \'enmətē\ n, pl -**ties** : mutual hatred

en·no·ble \in'ōbəl\ vb -**bled**; -**bling** : make noble

en·nui \,än'wē\ n : boredom

enor·mi·ty \i'nórmətē\ n, pl -**ties** 1 : great wickedness 2 : huge size

enor·mous \i'nórməs\ adj : great in size, number, or degree —**enor·mous·ly** adv —**enor·mous·ness** n

enough \i'nəf\ adj : adequate ~ adv 1 : in an adequate manner 2 : in a tolerable degree ~ pron : adequate number, quantity, or amount

en·quire \in'kwīr\, **en·qui·ry** \in,kwīrē, in'-; 'inkwərē, 'in-\ var of INQUIRE, INQUIRY

en·rage \in'rāj\ vb : fill with rage

en·rich \-'rich\ vb : make rich —**en·rich·ment** n

en·roll, **en·rol** \-'rōl\ vb -**rolled**; -**roll·ing** 1 : enter on a list 2 : become enrolled —**en·roll·ment** n

en route \än'rüt, en-, in-\ adv or adj : on or along the way

en·sconce \in'skäns\ vb -**sconced**; -**sconc·ing** : settle snugly

en·sem·ble \än'sämbəl\ n 1 : small group 2 : complete costume

en·shrine \in'shrīn\ vb 1 : put in a shrine 2 : cherish

en·sign \'ensən, 1 also 'en,sīn\ n 1 : flag 2 : lowest ranking commissioned officer in the navy

en·slave \in'slāv\ vb : make a slave of —**en·slave·ment** n

en·snare \-'snar\ vb : trap

en·sue \-'sü\ vb -**sued**; -**su·ing** : follow as a consequence

en·sure \-'shùr\ vb -**sured**; -**sur·ing** : guarantee

en·tail \-'tāl\ vb : involve as a necessary result

en·tan·gle \-'taŋgəl\ vb : tangle —**en·tan·gle·ment** n

en·ter \'entər\ vb 1 : go or come in or into 2 : start 3 : set down (as in a list)

en·ter·prise \'entər,prīz\ n 1 : an undertaking 2 : business organization 3 : initiative

en·ter·pris·ing \-,prīziŋ\ adj : showing initiative

en·ter·tain \,entər'tān\ vb 1 : treat or receive as a guest 2 : hold in mind 3 : amuse —**en·ter·tain·er** n —**en·ter·tain·ment** n

en·thrall, en·thral \in'thròl\ vb -thralled; -thrall·ing : hold spellbound

en·thu·si·asm \-'thüzē,azəm, -'thyü-\ n : strong excitement of feeling or its cause —**en·thu·si·ast** \-,ast, -əst\ n — **en·thu·si·as·tic** \-,thüzē'astik, -,thyü-\ adj —**en·thu·si·as·ti·cal·ly** \-tiklē\ adv

en·tice \-'tīs\ vb -ticed; -tic·ing : tempt —**en·tice·ment** n

en·tire \in'tīr\ adj : complete or whole —**en·tire·ly** adv —**en·tire·ty** \-'tīrətē, -'tīrtē\ n

en·ti·tle \-'tīt⁹l\ vb -tled; -tling 1 : name 2 : give a right to

en·ti·ty \'entətē\ n, pl -ties : something with separate existence

en·to·mol·o·gy \,entə'mäləjē\ n : study of insects —**en·to·mo·log·i·cal** \-mə'läjikəl\ adj —**en·to·mol·o·gist** \-'mäləjist\ n

en·tou·rage \,äntü'räzh\ n : retinue

en·trails \'entrəlz, -,trālz\ n pl : intestines

¹en·trance \'entrəns\ n 1 : act of entering 2 : means or place of entering — **en·trant** \'entrənt\ n

²en·trance \in'trans\ vb -tranced; -tranc·ing : fascinate or delight

en·trap \in'trap\ vb : trap —**en·trap·ment** n

en·treat \-'trēt\ vb : ask urgently — **en·treaty** \-'trētē\ n

en·trée, en·tree \'än,trā\ n : principal dish of the meal

en·trench \in'trench\ vb : establish in a strong position —**en·trench·ment** n

en·tre·pre·neur \,äntrəprə'nər\ n : organizer or promoter of an enterprise

en·trust \in'trəst\ vb : commit to another with confidence

en·try \'entrē\ n, pl -tries 1 : entrance 2 : an entering in a record or an item so entered

en·twine \in'twīn\ vb : twine together or around

enu·mer·ate \i'nümə,rāt, -'nyü-\ vb -at·ed; -at·ing 1 : count 2 : list —**enu·mer·a·tion** \i,nümə'rāshən, -,nyü-\ n

enun·ci·ate \ē'nənsē,āt\ vb -at·ed; -at·ing 1 : announce 2 : pronounce — **enun·ci·a·tion** \-,nənsē'āshən\ n

en·vel·op \in'veləp\ vb : surround — **en·vel·op·ment** n

en·ve·lope \'envə,lōp, 'än-\ n : paper container for a letter

en·vi·ron·ment \in'vīrənmənt\ n : surroundings —**en·vi·ron·men·tal** \-,vīrən'ment⁹l\ adj

en·vi·ron·men·tal·ist \-⁹list\ n : person concerned about the environment

en·vi·rons \in'vīrənz\ n pl : vicinity

en·vis·age \in'vizij\ vb -aged; -ag·ing : have a mental picture of

en·vi·sion \-'vizhən\ vb : picture to oneself

en·voy \'en,vòi, 'än-\ n : diplomat

en·vy \'envē\ n 1 : resentful awareness of another's advantage 2 : object of envy ~ vb -vied; -vy·ing : feel envy toward or on account of —**en·vi·able** \-vēəbəl\ adj —**en·vi·ous** \-vēəs\ adj —**en·vi·ous·ly** adv

en·zyme \'en,zīm\ n : biological catalyst

eon \'ēən, ē,än\ var of AEON

ep·au·let \,epə'let\ n : shoulder ornament on a uniform

ephem·er·al \i'femərəl\ adj : short-lived

ep·ic \'epik\ n : long poem about a hero —**epic** adj

ep·i·cure \'epi,kyúr\ n : person with fastidious taste esp. in food and wine — **ep·i·cu·re·an** \,epikyú'rēən, -'kyúrē-\ n or adj

ep·i·dem·ic \,epə'demik\ adj : affecting many persons at one time —**epidemic** n

epi·der·mis \,epə'dərməs\ n : outer layer of skin

ep·i·gram \'epə,gram\ n : short witty poem or saying —**ep·i·gram·mat·ic** \,epəgrə'matik\ adj

ep·i·lep·sy \'epə,lepsē\ n, pl -sies : nervous disorder marked by convulsive attacks —**ep·i·lep·tic** \,epə'leptik\ adj or n

epis·co·pal \i'piskəpəl\ adj : governed by bishops

ep·i·sode \'epə,sōd, -,zōd\ n : occurrence —**ep·i·sod·ic** \,epə'sädik, -'zäd-\ adj

epis·tle \i'pisəl\ n : letter

ep·i·taph \'epə,taf\ n : inscription in memory of a dead person

ep·i·thet \'epə,thet, -thət\ n : characterizing often abusive word or phrase

epit·o·me \i'pitəmē\ n 1 : summary 2 : ideal example —**epit·o·mize** \-,mīz\ vb

ep·och \'epək, 'ep,äk\ n : extended period —**ep·och·al** \'epəkəl, 'ep,äkəl\ adj

ep·oxy \'ep,äksē, ep'äksē\ n : synthetic resin used esp. in adhesives ~ vb -**ox·ied** or **-oxyed**; **-oxy·ing** : glue with epoxy

equa·ble \'ekwəbəl, 'ēkwə-\ adj : free from unpleasant extremes —**eq·ua·bil·i·ty** \,ekwə'bilətē, ,ē-\ n —**equa·bly** \-blē\ adv

equal \'ēkwəl\ adj : of the same quantity, value, quality, number, or status as another ~ n : one that is equal ~ vb equaled or equalled; equal·ing or equal·ling : be or become equal to —**equal·i·ty** \i'kwälətē\ n —**equal·ize** \'ēkwə,līz\ vb —**equal·ly** \'ēkwəlē\ adv

equa·nim·i·ty \,ēkwə'nimətē, ,ek-\ n, pl -ties : calmness

equate \i'kwāt\ vb equat·ed; equat·ing : treat or regard as equal

equa·tion \i'kwāzhən, -shən\ n : mathematical statement that two things are equal

equa·tor \i'kwātər\ n : imaginary circle that separates the northern and southern hemispheres —**equa·to·ri·al** \,ēkwə'tōrēəl, ,ek-\ adj

eques·tri·an \i'kwestrēən\ adj : relating to horseback riding ~ n : horseback rider

equi·lat·er·al \,ēkwə'latərəl\ adj : having equal sides

equi·lib·ri·um \-'librēəm\ n, pl -ri·ums or -ria \-rēə\ : state of balance

equine \'ē,kwīn, 'ek,wīn\ adj : relating to the horse —**equine** n

equi·nox \'ēkwə,näks, 'ek-\ n : time when day and night are everywhere of equal length

equip \i'kwip\ vb -pp- : furnish with needed resources —**equip·ment** \-mənt\ n

equi·ta·ble \'ekwətəbəl\ adj : fair

eq·ui·ty \'ekwətē\ n, pl -ties 1 : justice 2 : value of a property less debt

equiv·a·lent \i'kwivələnt\ adj : equal —**equiv·a·lence** \-ləns\ n —**equivalent** n

equiv·o·cal \i'kwivəkəl\ adj : ambiguous or uncertain

equiv·o·cate \i'kwivə,kāt\ vb -cat·ed; -cat·ing 1 : use misleading language 2 : avoid answering definitely —**equiv·o·ca·tion** \-,kwivə'kāshən\ n

1-er \ər\ adj suffix or adv suffix —used to form the comparative degree of ad-

jectives and adverbs and esp. those of one or two syllables

2-er \ər\, **-ier** \ēər, yər\, **-yer** \yər\ n suffix 1 : one that is associated with 2 : one that performs or is the object of an action 3 : one that is

era \'irə, 'erə, 'ērə\ n : period of time associated with something

erad·i·cate \i'radə,kāt\ vb -cat·ed; -cat·ing : do away with

erase \i'rās\ vb erased; eras·ing : rub or scratch out —**eras·er** n —**era·sure** \i'rāshər\ n

ere \'er\ prep or conj : before

erect \i'rekt\ adj : not leaning or lying down ~ vb 1 : build 2 : bring to an upright position —**erec·tion** \i'rekshən\ n

er·mine \'ərmən\ n : weasel with white winter fur or its fur

erode \i'rōd\ vb erod·ed; erod·ing : wear away gradually

ero·sion \i'rōzhən\ n : process of eroding

erot·ic \i'rätik\ adj : sexually arousing —**erot·i·cal·ly** \-iklē\ adv —**erot·i·cism** \i'rätə,sizəm\ n

err \'er, 'ər\ vb : be or do wrong

er·rand \'erənd\ n : short trip taken to do something often for another

er·rant \-ənt\ adj 1 : traveling about 2 : going astray

er·rat·ic \ir'atik\ adj 1 : eccentric 2 : inconsistent —**er·rat·i·cal·ly** \-iklē\ adv

er·ro·ne·ous \ir'ōnēəs, e'rō-\ adj : wrong —**er·ro·ne·ous·ly** adv

er·ror \'erər\ n 1 : something that is not accurate 2 : state of being wrong

er·satz \'er,säts\ adj : phony

erst·while \'ərst,hwīl\ adv : in the past ~ adj : former

eru·di·tion \,erə'dishən, ,eryə-\ n : great learning —**er·u·dite** \'erə,dīt, 'eryə-\ adj

erupt \i'rəpt\ vb : burst forth esp. suddenly and violently —**erup·tion** \i'rəpshən\ n —**erup·tive** \-tiv\ adj

-ery \ərē\ n suffix 1 : character or condition 2 : practice 3 : place of doing

1-es \əz, iz after s, z, sh, ch; z after v or a vowel\ n pl suffix —used to form the plural of some nouns

2-es vb suffix —used to form the 3d person singular present of some verbs

es·ca·late \'eskə,lāt\ vb -lat·ed; -lat·ing : become quickly larger or greater —**es·ca·la·tion** \,eskə'lāshən\ n es·ca·la·tor \'eskə,lātər\ n : moving stairs

es·ca·pade \'eskə,pād\ n : mischievous adventure

es·cape \is'kāp\ vb -caped; -cap·ing : get away or get away from ~ n 1 : flight from or avoidance of something unpleasant 2 : leakage 3 : means of escape ~ adj : providing means of escape —es·cap·ee \is,kā'pē, ,es-\ n

es·ca·role \'eskə,rōl\ n : salad green

es·carp·ment \is'kärpmənt\ n : cliff

es·chew \is'chü\ vb : shun

es·cort \'es,kórt\ n : one accompanying another —es·cort \is'kórt, es-\ vb

es·crow \'es,krō\ n : deposit to be delivered upon fulfillment of a condition

esoph·a·gus \i'säfəgəs\ n, pl -gi \-,gī, -,jī\ : muscular tube connecting the mouth and stomach

es·o·ter·ic \,esə'terik\ adj : mysterious or secret

es·pe·cial·ly \is'peshəlē\ adv : particularly or notably

es·pi·o·nage \'espēə,näzh, -nij\ n : practice of spying

es·pous·al \is'pauzəl\ n 1 : betrothal 2 : wedding 3 : a taking up as a supporter —es·pouse \-'pauz\ vb

es·pres·so \e'spresō\ n, pl -sos : strong steam-brewed coffee

es·py \is'pī\ vb -pied; -py·ing : catch sight of

es·quire \'es,kwīr\ n —used as a title of courtesy

-ess \əs, ,es\ n suffix : female

es·say \'es,ā\ n : literary composition ~ vb \e'sā, 'es,ā\ : attempt —es·say·ist \'es,āist\ n

es·sence \'es⁰ns\ n 1 : fundamental nature or quality 2 : extract 3 : perfume

es·sen·tial \is'senchəl\ adj : basic or necessary —essential n —es·sen·tial·ly adv

-est \əst, ist\ adj suffix or adv suffix —used to form the superlative degree of adjectives and adverbs and esp. those of 1 or 2 syllables

es·tab·lish \is'tablish\ vb 1 : bring into existence 2 : put on a firm basis 3 : cause to be recognized

es·tab·lish·ment \-mənt\ n 1 : business or a place of business 2 : an establishing or being established 3 : controlling group

es·tate \is'tāt\ n 1 : one's possessions 2 : large piece of land with a house

es·teem \is'tēm\ n or vb : regard

es·ter \'estər\ n : organic chemical compound

es·thet·ic var of AESTHETIC

es·ti·ma·ble \'estəməbəl\ adj : worthy of esteem

es·ti·mate \'estə,māt\ vb -mat·ed; -mat·ing : judge the approximate value, size, or cost ~ \-mət\ n 1 : rough or approximate calculation 2 : statement of the cost of a job —es·ti·ma·tion \,estə'māshən\ n —es·ti·ma·tor \'estə,mātər\ n

es·trange \is'tränj\ vb -tranged; -trang·ing : make hostile —es·trange·ment n

es·tro·gen \'estrəjən\ n : hormone that produces female characteristics

es·tu·ary \'eschə,werē\ n, pl -ar·ies : arm of the sea at a river's mouth

et cet·era \et'setərə, -'setrə\ : and others esp. of the same kind

etch \'ech\ vb : produce by corroding parts of a surface with acid —etch·er n —etch·ing n

eter·nal \i'tərn⁰l\ adj : lasting forever —eter·nal·ly adv

eter·ni·ty \-nətē\ n, pl -ties : infinite duration

eth·ane \'eth,ān\ n : gaseous hydrocarbon

eth·a·nol \'ethə,nól, -,nōl\ n : alcohol

ether \'ēthər\ n : light flammable liquid used as an anesthetic

ethe·re·al \i'thirēəl\ adj 1 : celestial 2 : exceptionally delicate

eth·i·cal \'ethikəl\ adj 1 : relating to ethics 2 : honorable —eth·i·cal·ly adv

eth·ics \-iks\ n sing or pl 1 : study of good and evil and moral duty 2 : moral principles or practice

eth·nic \'ethnik\ adj : relating to races or groups of people with common customs ~ n : member of a minority ethnic group

eth·nol·o·gy \eth'näləjē\ n : study of the races of human beings —eth·no·log·i·cal \,ethnə'läjikəl\ adj —eth·nol·o·gist \eth'näləjist\ n

et·i·quette \'etikət, -,ket\ n : good manners

et·y·mol·o·gy \,etə'mäləjē\ n, pl -gies 1 : history of a word 2 : study of etymologies —et·y·mo·log·i·cal \-mə'läjikəl\ adj —et·y·mol·o·gist \-'mäləjist\ n

eu·ca·lyp·tus \,yükə'liptəs\ n, pl -ti \-,tī\ or -tus·es : Australian evergreen tree

Eu·cha·rist \'yükərəst\ n : Communion —eu·cha·ris·tic \,yükə'ristik\ adj

eu·lo·gy \'yüləjē\ n, pl -gies : speech in praise —eu·lo·gis·tic \,yülə'jistik\ adj —eu·lo·gize \'yülə,jīz\ vb

eu·nuch \'yünək\ n : castrated man

eu·phe·mism \'yüfə,mizəm\ n : substitution of a pleasant expression for an unpleasant or offensive one —eu·phe·mis·tic \,yüfə'mistik\ adj

eu·pho·ni·ous \yù'fōnēəs\ adj : pleasing to the ear —eu·pho·ny \'yüfənē\ n

eu·pho·ria \yù'fōrēə\ n : elation —eu·phor·ic \-'fòrik\ adj

eu·tha·na·sia \,yüthə'nāzhə, -zhēə\ n : mercy killing

evac·u·ate \i'vakyə,wāt\ vb -at·ed; -at·ing 1 : discharge wastes from the body 2 : remove or withdraw from —evac·u·a·tion \i,vakyə'wāshən\ n

evade \i'vād\ vb evad·ed; evad·ing : manage to avoid

eval·u·ate \i'valyə,wāt\ vb -at·ed; -at·ing : appraise —eval·u·a·tion \i,valyə'wāshən\ n

evan·gel·i·cal \,ē,van'jelikəl, ,evən-\ adj : relating to the Christian gospel

evan·ge·lism \i'vanjə,lizəm\ n : the winning or revival of personal commitments to Christ —evan·ge·list \i'vanjəlist\ n —evan·ge·lis·tic \i,vanjə'listik\ adj

evap·o·rate \i'vapə,rāt\ vb -rat·ed; -rat·ing 1 : pass off in or convert into vapor 2 : disappear quickly —evap·o·ra·tion \i,vapə'rāshən\ n —evap·o·ra·tor \i'vapə,rātər\ n

eva·sion \i'vāzhən\ n : act or instance of evading —eva·sive \i'vāsiv\ adj —eva·sive·ness n

eve \'ēv\ n : evening

even \'ēvən\ adj 1 : smooth 2 : equal or fair 3 : fully revenged 4 : divisible by 2 ~ adv 1 : already 2 —used for emphasis ~ vb : make or become even —even·ly adv —even·ness n

eve·ning \'ēvniŋ\ n : early part of the night

event \i'vent\ n 1 : occurrence 2 : noteworthy happening 3 : eventuality —event·ful adj

even·tu·al \i'venchəwəl\ adj : later —even·tu·al·ly adv

even·tu·al·i·ty \i,venchə'walətē\ n, pl -ties : possible occurrence or outcome

ev·er \'evər\ adv 1 : always 2 : at any time 3 : in any case

ev·er·green adj : having foliage that remains green —evergreen n

ev·er·last·ing \,evər'lastiŋ\ adj : lasting forever

ev·ery \'evrē\ adj 1 : being each one of a group 2 : all possible

ev·ery·body \'evri,bädē, -bəd-\ pron : every person

ev·ery·day adj : ordinary

ev·ery·one \-,wən\ pron : every person

ev·ery·thing pron : all that exists

ev·ery·where adv : in every place or part

evict \i'vikt\ vb : force (a person) to move from a property —evic·tion \i-'vikshən\ n

ev·i·dence \'evədəns\ n 1 : outward sign 2 : proof or testimony

ev·i·dent \-ənt\ adj : clear or obvious —ev·i·dent·ly \-ədəntlē, -ə,dent-\ adv

evil \'ēvəl\ adj evil·er or evil·ler; evil·est or evil·lest : wicked ~ n 1 : sin 2 : source of sorrow or distress —evil·do·er \,ēvəl'düər\ n —evil·ly adv

evince \i'vins\ vb evinced; evinc·ing : show

evis·cer·ate \i'visə,rāt\ vb -at·ed; -at·ing : remove the viscera of —evis·cer·a·tion \i,visə'rāshən\ n

evoke \i'vōk\ vb evoked; evok·ing : call forth or up —evo·ca·tion \,ēvō-'kāshən, ,evə-\ n —evoc·a·tive \i-'väkətiv\ adj

evo·lu·tion \,evə'lüshən\ n : process of change by degrees —evo·lu·tion·ary \-shə,nerē\ adj

evolve \i'välv\ vb evolved; evolv·ing : develop or change by degrees

ewe \'yü\ n : female sheep

ew·er \'yüər\ n : water pitcher

ex·act \ig'zakt\ vb : compel to furnish ~ adj : precisely correct —ex·act·ing adj —ex·ac·tion \-'zakshən\ n —ex·ac·ti·tude \-'zaktə,tüd, -,tyüd\ n —ex·act·ly adv —ex·act·ness n

ex·ag·ger·ate \ig'zajə,rāt\ vb -at·ed; -at·ing : say more than is true —ex·ag·ger·at·ed·ly adv —ex·ag·ger·a·tion \-,zajə'rāshən\ n —ex·ag·ger·a·tor \-'zajərātər\ n

ex·alt \ig'zòlt\ vb : glorify —ex·al·ta·tion \,eg,zòl'tāshən, ,ek,sòl-\ n

ex·am \ig'zam\ n : examination

ex·am·ine \-ən\ vb -ined; -in·ing 1 : inspect closely 2 : test by questioning —ex·am·i·na·tion \-,zamə'nā·shən\ n

example 115 **exerciser**

ex·am·ple \ig'zampəl\ *n* **1** : representative sample **2** : model **3** : problem to be solved for teaching purposes

ex·as·per·ate \ig'zaspə,rāt\ *vb* **-at·ed; -at·ing** : thoroughly annoy —**ex·as·per·a·tion** \-,zaspə'rāshən\ *n*

ex·ca·vate \'ekskə,vāt\ *vb* **-vat·ed; -vat·ing** : dig or hollow out —**ex·ca·va·tion** \,ekskə'vāshən\ *n* —**ex·ca·va·tor** \'ekskə,vātər\ *n*

ex·ceed \ik'sēd\ *vb* **1** : go or be beyond the limit of **2** : do better than

ex·ceed·ing·ly *adv* : extremely

ex·cel \ik'sel\ *vb* **-ll-** : do extremely well or far better than

ex·cel·lence \'eksələns\ *n* : quality of being excellent

ex·cel·len·cy \lənsē\ *n, pl* **-cies** —used as a title of honor

ex·cel·lent \'eksələnt\ *adj* : very good —**ex·cel·lent·ly** *adv*

ex·cept \ik'sept\ *vb* : omit ~ *prep* : excluding ~ *conj* : but —**ex·cep·tion** \-'sepshən\ *n*

ex·cep·tion·al \-'sepshənəl\ *adj* : superior —**ex·cep·tion·al·ly** *adv*

ex·cerpt \'ek,sərpt, 'eg,zərpt\ *n* : brief passage ~ \ek'-, eg'-, 'ek,-, 'eg,-\ *vb* : select an excerpt

ex·cess \ik'ses, 'ek,ses\ *n* : amount left over —**excess** *adj* —**ex·ces·sive** \ik'sesiv\ *adj* —**ex·ces·sive·ly** *adv*

ex·change \iks'chānj, 'eks,chānj\ *n* **1** : the giving or taking of one thing in return for another **2** : marketplace esp. for securities ~ *vb* **-changed; -chang·ing** : transfer in return for some equivalent —**ex·change·able** \iks'chānjəbəl\ *adj*

¹**ex·cise** \'ek,sīz, -,sīs\ *n* : tax

²**ex·cise** \ik'sīz\ *vb* **-cised; -cis·ing** : cut out —**ex·ci·sion** \-'sizhən\ *n*

ex·cite \ik'sīt\ *vb* **-cit·ed; -cit·ing** **1** : stir up **2** : kindle the emotions of —**ex·cit·abil·i·ty** \-,sītə'bilətē\ *n* —**ex·cit·able** \-'sītəbəl\ *adj* —**ex·ci·ta·tion** \,ek,sī'tāshən, -sə-\ *n* —**ex·cit·ed·ly** *adv* —**ex·cite·ment** \ik'sītmənt\ *n*

ex·claim \iks'klām\ *vb* : cry out esp. in delight —**ex·cla·ma·tion** \,eksklə'māshən\ *n* —**ex·clam·a·to·ry** \iks'klamə,tōrē\ *adj*

exclamation point *n* : punctuation mark ! used esp. after an interjection or exclamation

ex·clude \iks'klüd\ *vb* **-clud·ed; -clud·ing** : leave out —**ex·clu·sion** \-'klüzhən\ *n*

ex·clu·sive \-'klüsiv\ *adj* **1** : reserved for particular persons **2** : stylish **3** : sole —**exclusive** *n* —**ex·clu·sive·ly** *adv* —**ex·clu·sive·ness** *n*

ex·com·mu·ni·cate \,eksə'myünə,kāt\ *vb* : expel from a church —**ex·com·mu·ni·ca·tion** \-,myünə'kāshən\ *n*

ex·cre·ment \'ekskrəmənt\ *n* : bodily waste —**ex·cre·men·tal** \,ekskrə'mentᵊl\ *adj*

ex·crete \ik'skrēt\ *vb* **-cret·ed; -cret·ing** : eliminate wastes from the body —**ex·cre·tion** \-'skrēshən\ *n* —**ex·cre·to·ry** \'ekskrə,tōrē\ *adj*

ex·cru·ci·at·ing \ik'skrüshē,ātiŋ\ *adj* : intensely painful —**ex·cru·ci·at·ing·ly** *adv*

ex·cul·pate \'ekskəl,pāt\ *vb* **-pat·ed; -pat·ing** : clear from alleged fault

ex·cur·sion \ik'skərzhən\ *n* : pleasure trip

ex·cuse \ik'skyüz\ *vb* **-cused; -cus·ing** **1** : pardon **2** : release from an obligation **3** : justify ~ \-'skyüs\ *n* **1** : justification **2** : apology

ex·e·cute \'eksi,kyüt\ *vb* **-cut·ed; -cut·ing** **1** : carry out fully **2** : enforce **3** : put to death —**ex·e·cu·tion** \,eksi'kyüshən\ *n* —**ex·e·cu·tion·er** \-shənər\ *n*

ex·ec·u·tive \ig'zekyətiv\ *adj* : relating to the carrying out of decisions, plans, or laws ~ *n* **1** : branch of government with executive duties **2** : administrator

ex·ec·u·tor \-yətər\ *n* : person named in a will to execute it

ex·ec·u·trix \ig'zekyə,triks\ *n, pl* **ex·ec·u·tri·ces** \-,zekyə'trī-,sēz\ *or* **ex·ec·u·trix·es** : woman executor

ex·em·pla·ry \ig'zemplərē\ *adj* : so commendable as to serve as a model

ex·em·pli·fy \-plə,fī\ *vb* **-fied; -fy·ing** : serve as an example of —**ex·em·pli·fi·ca·tion** \-,zempləfə'kāshən\ *n*

ex·empt \ig'zempt\ *adj* : being free from some liability ~ *vb* : make exempt —**ex·emp·tion** \-'zempshən\ *n*

ex·er·cise \'eksər,sīz\ *n* **1** : a putting into action **2** : exertion to develop endurance or a skill **3** *pl* : public ceremony ~ *vb* **-cised; -cis·ing** **1** : exert **2** : engage in exercise —**ex·er·cis·er** *n*

ex•ert \ig'zərt\ *vb* : put into action —**ex•er•tion** \-'zərshən\ *n*

ex•hale \eks'hāl\ *vb* -**haled; -hal•ing** : breathe out —**ex•ha•la•tion** \ekshə'lāshən\ *n*

ex•haust \ig'zóst\ *vb* **1** : draw out or develop completely **2** : use up **3** : tire or wear out ~ *n* : waste steam or gas from an engine or a system for removing it —**ex•haus•tion** \-'zóschən\ *n* —**ex•haus•tive** \-'zóstiv\ *adj*

ex•hib•it \ig'zibət\ *vb* : display esp. publicly ~ *n* **1** : act of exhibiting **2** : something exhibited —**ex•hi•bi•tion** \eksə'bishən\ *n* —**ex•hib•i•tor** \ig-'zibətər\ *n*

ex•hil•a•rate \ig'zilə,rāt\ *vb* -**rat•ed; -rat•ing** : thrill —**ex•hil•a•ra•tion** \-,zilə'rāshən\ *n*

ex•hort \-'zórt\ *vb* : urge earnestly —**ex•hor•ta•tion** \,eks,ór'tāshən, ,egz-, -ər-\ *n*

ex•hume \igz'üm, -'yüm; iks'yüm, -'hyüm\ *vb* -**humed; -hum•ing** : dig up (a buried corpse) —**ex•hu•ma•tion** \,eksyü'māshən, -hyü-; ,egzü-, -zyü-\ *n*

ex•i•gen•cies \'eksəjənsēz, ig-'zijən-\ *pl* : requirements (as of a situation)

ex•ile \'eg,zīl, 'ek,sīl\ *n* **1** : banishment **2** : person banished from his or her country —**exile** *vb*

ex•ist \ig'zist\ *vb* **1** : have real or actual being **2** : live —**ex•is•tence** \-əns\ *n* —**ex•is•tent** \-ənt\ *adj*

ex•it \'egzət, 'eksət\ *n* **1** : departure **2** : way out of an enclosed space **3** : way off an expressway —**exit** *vb*

ex•o•dus \'eksədəs\ *n* : mass departure

ex•on•er•ate \ig'zänə,rāt\ *vb* -**at•ed; -at•ing** : free from blame —**ex•on•er•a•tion** \-,zänə'rāshən\ *n*

ex•or•bi•tant \ig'zórbətənt\ *adj* : exceeding what is usual or proper

ex•or•cise \'ek,sór,sīz, -sər-\ *vb* -**cised; -cis•ing** : drive out (as an evil spirit) —**ex•or•cism** \-,sizəm\ *n* —**ex•or•cist** \-,sist\ *n*

ex•ot•ic \ig'zätik\ *adj* : foreign or strange —**exotic** *n* —**ex•ot•i•cal•ly** \-iklē\ *adv*

ex•pand \ik'spand\ *vb* : enlarge

ex•panse \-'spans\ *n* : very large area

ex•pan•sion \-'spanchən\ *n* **1** : act or process of expanding **2** : expanded part

ex•pan•sive \-'spansiv\ *adj* **1** : tending to expand **2** : warmly benevolent **3** : of large extent —**ex•pan•sive•ly** *adv* —**ex•pan•sive•ness** *n*

ex•pa•tri•ate \ek'spātrē,āt, -ət\ *n* : exile —**expatriate** \-,āt\ *adj or vb*

ex•pect \ik'spekt\ *vb* **1** : look forward to **2** : consider probable or one's due —**ex•pec•tan•cy** \-ənsē\ *n* —**ex•pec•tant** \-ənt\ *adj* —**ex•pec•tant•ly** *adv* —**ex•pec•ta•tion** \,ek,spek'tāshən\ *n*

ex•pe•di•ent \ik'spēdēənt\ *adj* : convenient or advantageous rather than right or just ~ *n* : convenient often makeshift means to an end

ex•pe•dite \'ekspə,dīt\ *vb* -**dit•ed; -dit•ing** : carry out or handle promptly —**ex•pe•dit•er** *n*

ex•pe•di•tion \,ekspə'dishən\ *n* : long journey for work or research or the people making this

ex•pe•di•tious \-əs\ *adj* : prompt and efficient

ex•pel \ik'spel\ *vb* -**ll-** : force out

ex•pend \-'spend\ *vb* **1** : pay out **2** : use up —**ex•pend•able** *adj*

ex•pen•di•ture \-'spendichər, -də,chùr\ *n* : act of using or spending

ex•pense \ik'spens\ *n* : cost —**ex•pen•sive** \-'spensiv\ *adj* —**ex•pen•sive•ly** *adv*

ex•pe•ri•ence \ik'spirēəns\ *n* **1** : a participating in or living through an event **2** : an event that affects one **3** : knowledge from doing ~ *vb* -**enced; -enc•ing** : undergo

ex•per•i•ment \ik'sperəmənt\ *n* : test to discover something ~ *vb* : make experiments —**ex•per•i•men•tal** \-,sperə'mentʰl\ *adj* —**ex•per•i•men•ta•tion** \-mən'tāshən\ *n* —**ex•per•i•men•ter** \-'sperə,mentər\ *n*

ex•pert \'ek,spərt\ *adj* : thoroughly skilled ~ *n* : person with special skill —**ex•pert•ly** *adv* —**ex•pert•ness** *n*

ex•per•tise \,ekspər'tēz\ *n* : skill

ex•pi•ate \'ekspē,āt\ *vb* : make amends for —**ex•pi•a•tion** \,ekspē'āshən\ *n*

ex•pire \ik'spīr, ek-\ *vb* -**pired; -pir•ing** **1** : breathe out **2** : die **3** : end —**ex•pi•ra•tion** \,ekspə'rāshən\ *n*

ex•plain \ik'splān\ *vb* **1** : make clear **2** : give the reason for —**ex•plain•able** \-əbəl\ *adj* —**ex•pla•na•tion** \,eksplə-'nāshən\ *n* —**ex•plan•a•to•ry** \ik-'splanə,tōrē\ *adj*

ex•ple•tive \'eksplətiv\ *n* : usu. profane exclamation

ex•pli•ca•ble \ek'splikəbəl, 'eksplik-\ *adj* : capable of being explained

ex·plic·it \ik'splisət\ adj : absolutely clear or precise —**ex·plic·it·ly** adv —**ex·plic·it·ness** n

ex·plode \ik'splōd\ vb -**plod·ed; -plod·ing** 1 : discredit 2 : burst or cause to burst violently 3 : increase rapidly

ex·ploit \'ek,sploit\ n : heroic act ~ \ik-'sploit\ vb 1 : utilize 2 : use unfairly —**ex·ploi·ta·tion** \,ek,sploi'tāshən\ n

ex·plore \ik'splōr\ vb -**plored; -plor·ing** : examine or range over thoroughly —**ex·plo·ra·tion** \,eksplə'rāshən\ n —**ex·plor·a·to·ry** \ik'splōrə,tōrē\ adj —**ex·plor·er** n

ex·plo·sion \ik'splōzhən\ n : process or instance of exploding

ex·plo·sive \-siv\ adj 1 : able to cause explosion 2 : likely to explode —**explosive** n —**ex·plo·sive·ly** adv

ex·po·nent \ik'spōnənt, 'ek,spō-\ n 1 : mathematical symbol showing how many times a number is to be repeated as a factor 2 : advocate —**ex·po·nen·tial** \,ekspə'nenchəl\ adj —**ex·po·nen·tial·ly** adv

ex·port \ek'spōrt, 'ek,spōrt\ vb : send to foreign countries —**export** \'ek,-\ n —**ex·por·ta·tion** \,ek,spōr'tāshən\ n —**ex·port·er** \ek'spōrtər, 'ek,spōrt-\ n

ex·pose \ik'spōz\ vb -**posed; -pos·ing** 1 : deprive of shelter or protection 2 : subject (film) to light 3 : make known —**ex·po·sure** \-'spōzhər\ n

ex·po·sé, ex·pose \,ekspō'zā\ n : exposure of something discreditable

ex·po·si·tion \,ekspə'zishən\ n : public exhibition

ex·pound \ik'spaünd\ vb : set forth or explain in detail

1**ex·press** \-'spres\ adj 1 : clear 2 : specific 3 : traveling at high speed with few stops —**express** adv or n —**ex·press·ly** adv

2**express** vb 1 : make known in words or appearance 2 : press out (as juice)

ex·pres·sion \-'spreshən\ n 1 : utterance 2 : mathematical symbol 3 : significant word or phrase 4 : look on one's face —**ex·pres·sion·less** adj —**ex·pres·sive** \-'spresiv\ adj —**ex·pres·sive·ness** n

ex·press·way \ik'spres,wā\ n : high-speed divided highway with limited access

ex·pul·sion \ik'spəlshən\ n : an expelling or being expelled

ex·pur·gate \'ekspər,gāt\ vb -**gat·ed; -gat·ing** : censor —**ex·pur·ga·tion** \,ekspər'gāshən\ n

ex·qui·site \ek'skwizət, 'ekskwiz-\ adj 1 : flawlessly beautiful and delicate 2 : keenly discriminating

ex·tant \'ekstənt, ek'stant\ adj : existing

ex·tem·po·ra·ne·ous \ek,stempə'rā-nēəs\ adj : impromptu —**ex·tem·po·ra·ne·ous·ly** adv

ex·tend \ik'stend\ vb 1 : stretch forth or out 2 : prolong 3 : enlarge —**ex·tend·able, -**'stendəbəl\ adj

ex·ten·sion \-'stenchən\ n 1 : an extending or being extended 2 : additional part 3 : extra telephone line

ex·ten·siv \-'stensiv\ adj : of considerable extent —**ex·ten·sive·ly** adv

ex·tent \-'stent\ n : range, space, or degree to which something extends

ex·ten·u·ate \ik'stenyə,wāt\ vb -**at·ed; -at·ing** : lessen the seriousness of —**ex·ten·u·a·tion** \-,stenyə'wāshən\ n

ex·te·ri·or \ek'stirēər\ adj : external ~ n : external part or surface

ex·ter·mi·nate \ik'stərmə,nāt\ vb -**nat·ed; -nat·ing** : destroy utterly —**ex·ter·mi·na·tion** \-,stərmə'nāshən\ n —**ex·ter·mi·na·tor** \-'stərmə,nātər\ n

ex·ter·nal \ek'stərnᵊl\ adj : relating to or on the outside —**ex·ter·nal·ly** adv

ex·tinct \ik'stiŋkt\ adj : no longer existing —**ex·tinc·tion** \-'stiŋkshən\ n

ex·tin·guish \-'stiŋgwish\ vb : cause to stop burning —**ex·tin·guish·able** adj —**ex·tin·guish·er** n

ex·tir·pate \'ekstər,pāt\ vb -**pat·ed; -pat·ing** : destroy

ex·tol \ik'stōl\ vb -**ll-** : praise highly

ex·tort \-'stort\ vb : obtain by force or improper pressure —**ex·tor·tion** \-'stórshən\ n —**ex·tor·tion·er** n —**ex·tor·tion·ist** n

ex·tra \'ekstrə\ adj 1 : additional 2 : superior —**extra** n or adv

extra- prefix : outside or beyond

ex·tract \ik'strakt\ vb 1 : pull out forcibly 2 : withdraw (as a juice) ~ \'ek,-\ n 1 : excerpt 2 : product (as a juice) obtained by extracting —**ex·tract·able** adj —**ex·trac·tion** \ik-'strakshən\ n —**ex·trac·tor** \-tər\ n

ex·tra·cur·ric·u·lar \,ekstrəkə'rikyələr\ adj : lying outside the regular curriculum

ex·tra·dite \'ekstrə,dīt\ vb -**dit·ed; -dit·ing** : bring or deliver a suspect to a different jurisdiction for trial —**ex·tra·di·tion** \,ekstrə'dishən\ n

ex·tra·mar·i·tal \,ekstrə'marət∂l\ *adj* : relating to sexual relations of a married person outside of the marriage

ex·tra·ne·ous \ek'strānēəs\ *adj* : not essential or relevant —**ex·tra·ne·ous·ly** *adv*

ex·traor·di·nary \ik'strȯrd∂n,erē, ,ekstrə'ȯrd-\ *adj* : notably unusual or exceptional —**ex·traor·di·nari·ly** \ik-,strȯrd∂n'erəlē, ,ekstrə'ȯrd-\ *adv*

ex·tra·sen·so·ry \,ekstrə'sensərē\ *adj* : outside the ordinary senses

ex·tra·ter·res·tri·al \,ekstrətə'restrēəl\ *n* : one existing or coming from outside the earth ~ *adj* : relating to an extraterrestrial

ex·trav·a·gant \ik'stravigənt\ *adj* : wildly excessive, lavish, or costly — **ex·trav·a·gance** \-gəns\ *n* —**ex·trav·a·gant·ly** *adv*

ex·trav·a·gan·za \-,stravə'ganzə\ *n* : spectacular event

ex·tra·ve·hic·u·lar \,ekstrəvē'hikyələr\ *adj* : occurring outside a spacecraft

ex·treme \ik'strēm\ *adj* **1** : very great or intense **2** : very severe **3** : not moderate **4** : most remote ~ *n* **1** : extreme state **2** : something located at one end or the other of a range —**ex·treme·ly** *adv*

ex·trem·i·ty \-'stremətē\ *n, pl* **-ties 1** : most remote part **2** : human hand or foot **3** : extreme degree or state (as of need)

ex·tri·cate \'ekstrə,kāt\ *vb* **-cat·ed; -cat·ing** : set or get free from an entanglement or difficulty —**ex·tri·ca·ble** \ik-'strikəbəl, ek-; 'ekstrik-\ *adj* **ex·tri·ca·tion** \,ekstrə'kāshən\ *n*

ex·tro·vert \'ekstrə,vərt\ *n* : gregarious person —**ex·tro·ver·sion** \,ekstrə-'vərzhən\ *n* —**ex·tro·vert·ed** \'ekstrə-,vərtəd\ *adj*

ex·trude \ik'strüd\ *vb* **-trud·ed; -trud·ing** : to force or push out

ex·u·ber·ant \ig'zübərənt\ *adj* : joyously unrestrained —**ex·u·ber·ance** \-rəns\ *n* —**ex·u·ber·ant·ly** *adv*

ex·ude \ig'züd\ *vb* **-ud·ed; -ud·ing 1** : discharge slowly through pores **2** : display conspicuously

ex·ult \ig'zəlt\ *vb* : rejoice —**ex·ul·tant** \-'zəlt∂nt\ *adj* —**ex·ul·tant·ly** *adv* — **ex·ul·ta·tion** \,eksəl'tāshən, ,egzəl-\ *n*

-ey —see -Y

eye \'ī\ *n* **1** : organ of sight consisting of a globular structure (**eye·ball**) in a socket of the skull with thin movable covers (**eye·lids**) bordered with hairs (**eye·lash·es**) **2** : vision **3** : judgment **4** : something suggesting an eye ~ *vb* **eyed; eye·ing** *or* **ey·ing** : look at — **eye·brow** \-,braú\ *n* —**eyed** \'īd\ *adj* —**eye·strain** *n*

eye·drop·per *n* : dropper

eye·glass·es *n pl* : glasses

eye·let \'īlət\ *n* : hole (as in cloth) for a lacing or rope

eye–open·er *n* : something startling — **eye–open·ing** *adj*

eye·piece *n* : lens at the eye end of an optical instrument

eye·sight *n* : sight

eye·sore *n* : unpleasant sight

eye·tooth *n* : upper canine tooth

eye·wit·ness *n* : person who actually sees something happen

ey·rie \'īrē, *or like* AERIE\ *var of* AERIE

F

f \'ef\ *n, pl* **f's** *or* **fs** \'efs\ : 6th letter of the alphabet

fa·ble \'fābəl\ *n* **1** : legendary story **2** : story that teaches a lesson —**fa·bled** \-bəld\ *adj*

fab·ric \'fabrik\ *n* **1** : structure **2** : material made usu. by weaving or knitting fibers

fab·ri·cate \'fabri,kāt\ *vb* **-cat·ed; -cat·ing 1** : construct **2** : invent —**fab·ri·ca·tion** \,fabri'kāshən\ *n*

fab·u·lous \'fabyələs\ *adj* **1** : like, told in, or based on fable **2** : incredible or marvelous —**fab·u·lous·ly** *adv*

fa·cade \fə'säd\ *n* **1** : principal face of a building **2** : false or superficial appearance

face \'fās\ *n* **1** : front or principal surface (as of the head) **2** : presence **3** : facial expression **4** : grimace **5** : outward

appearance ~ *vb* **faced; fac·ing 1**
: challenge or resist firmly or brazenly
2 : cover with different material **3** : sit
or stand with the face toward **4** : have
the front oriented toward —**faced**
\'fāst\ *adj* —**face·less** *adj n* —**fa·cial**
\'fāshəl\ *adj or n*

face·down *adv* : with the face downward

face–lift \'fās,lift\ *n* **1** : cosmetic surgery
on the face **2** : modernization

fac·et \'fasət\ *n* **1** : surface of a cut gem
2 : phase —**fac·et·ed** *adj*

fa·ce·tious \fə'sēshəs\ *adj* : jocular —
fa·ce·tious·ly *adv* —**fa·ce·tious·ness**
n

fac·ile \'fasəl\ *adj* **1** : easy **2** : fluent

fa·cil·i·tate \fə'silə,tāt\ *vb* **-tat·ed; -tat·**
ing : make easier

fa·cil·i·ty \fə'silətē\ *n, pl* **-ties 1** : ease
in doing or using **2** : something built
or installed to serve a purpose or facilitate an activity

fac·ing \'fāsiŋ\ *n* : lining or covering or
material for this

fac·sim·i·le \fak'siməlē\ *n* : exact copy

fact \'fakt\ *n* **1** : act or action **2**
: something that exists or is real **3**
: piece of information —**fac·tu·al**
\'fakchəwəl\ *adj* —**fac·tu·al·ly** *adv*

fac·tion \'fakshən\ *n* : part of a larger
group —**fac·tion·al·ism** \-shənə-
,lizəm\ *n*

fac·tious \'fakshəs\ *adj* : causing discord

fac·ti·tious \fak'tishəs\ *adj* : artificial

fac·tor \'faktər\ *n* **1** : something that has
an effect **2** : gene **3** : number used in
multiplying

fac·to·ry \'faktərē\ *n, pl* **-ries** : place for
manufacturing

fac·to·tum \fak'tōtəm\ *n* : person (as a
servant) with varied duties

fac·ul·ty \'fakəltē\ *n, pl* **-ties 1** : ability
to act **2** : power of the mind or body
3 : body of teachers or department of
instruction

fad \'fad\ *n* : briefly popular practice
or interest —**fad·dish** *adj* —**fad·dist**
n

fade \'fād\ *vb* **fad·ed; fad·ing 1** : wither
2 : lose or cause to lose freshness or
brilliance **3** : grow dim **4** : vanish

fag \'fag\ *vb* **-gg- 1** : drudge **2** : tire or
exhaust

fag·ot, fag·got \'fagət\ *n* : bundle of
twigs

Fah·ren·heit \'farən,hīt\ *adj* : relating to
a thermometer scale with the boiling

point at 212 degrees and the freezing
point at 32 degrees

fail \'fāl\ *vb* **1** : decline in health **2** : die
away **3** : stop functioning **4** : be unsuccessful **5** : become bankrupt **6**
: disappoint **7** : neglect ~ *n* : act of
failing

fail·ing *n* : slight defect in character or
conduct ~ *prep* : in the absence or
lack of

faille \'fīl\ *n* : closely woven ribbed fabric

fail·ure \'fālyər\ *n* **1** : absence of expected action or performance **2**
: bankruptcy **3** : deficiency **4** : one
that has failed

faint \'fānt\ *adj* **1** : cowardly or spiritless
2 : weak and dizzy **3** : lacking vigor
4 : indistinct ~ *vb* : lose consciousness ~ *n* : act or condition of fainting
—**faint·heart·ed** *adj* —**faint·ly** *adv*
—**faint·ness** *n*

¹fair \'far\ *adj* **1** : pleasing in appearance **2** : not stormy or cloudy **3** : just
or honest **4** : conforming with the
rules **5** : open to legitimate pursuit or
attack **6** : light in color **7** : adequate
—**fair·ness** *n*

²fair *adv, chiefly Brit* : FAIRLY

³fair *n* : exhibition for judging or selling
—**fair·ground** *n*

fair·ly \'farlē\ *adv* **1** : in a manner of
speaking **2** : without bias **3**
: somewhat

fairy \'farē\ *n, pl* **fair·ies** : usu. small
imaginary being —**fairy tale** *n*

fairy·land \-,land\ *n* **1** : land of fairies **2**
: beautiful or charming place

faith \'fāth\ *n, pl* **faiths** \'fāths, 'fāthz\ **1**
: allegiance **2** : belief and trust in God
3 : confidence **4** : system of religious
beliefs —**faith·ful** \-fəl\ *adj* —
faith·ful·ly *adv* —**faith·ful·ness** *n* —
faith·less *adj* —**faith·less·ly** *adv* —
faith·less·ness *n*

fake \'fāk\ *vb* **faked; fak·ing 1** : falsify
2 : counterfeit ~ *n* : copy, fraud, or
impostor ~ *adj* : not genuine —
fak·er *n*

fa·kir \fə'kir\ *n* : wandering beggar of
India

fal·con \'falkən, 'fól-\ *n* : small long-
winged hawk used esp. for hunting —
fal·con·ry \-rē\ *n*

fall \'fól\ *vb* **fell** \'fel\; **fall·en** \'fólən\;
fall·ing 1 : go down by gravity **2**
: hang freely **3** : go lower **4** : be defeated or ruined **5** : commit a sin **6**

: happen at a certain time **7** : become gradually ~ *n* **1** : act of falling **2** : autumn **3** : downfall **4** *pl* : waterfall **5** : distance something falls

fal·la·cy \'faləsē\ *n, pl* **-cies 1** : false idea **2** : false reasoning —**fal·la·cious** \fə'lāshəs\ *adj*

fal·li·ble \'faləbəl\ *adj* : capable of making a mistake —**fal·li·bly** \-blē\ *adv*

fall·out *n* **1** : radioactive particles from a nuclear explosion **2** : secondary effects

fal·low \'falō\ *adj* **1** : plowed but not planted **2** : dormant —**fallow** *n or vb*

false \'fóls\ *adj* **fals·er; fals·est 1** : not genuine, true, faithful, or permanent **2** : misleading —**false·ly** *adv* —**false·ness** *n* —**fal·si·fi·ca·tion** \,fólsəfə'kāshən\ *n* —**fal·si·fy** \'fólsə,fī\ *vb* —**fal·si·ty** \'fólsətē\ *n*

false·hood \'fóls,hùd\ *n* : lie

fal·set·to \fól'setō\ *n, pl* **-tos** : artificially high singing voice

fal·ter \'fóltər\ *vb* **-tered; -ter·ing 1** : move unsteadily **2** : hesitate —**fal·ter·ing·ly** *adv*

fame \'fām\ *n* : public reputation —**famed** \'fāmd\ *adj*

fa·mil·ial \fə'milyəl\ *adj* : relating to a family

¹**fa·mil·iar** \fə'milyər\ *n* **1** : companion **2** : guardian spirit

²**familiar** *adj* **1** : closely acquainted **2** : forward **3** : frequently seen or experienced —**fa·mil·iar·i·ty** \fə,mil'yarətē, -,milē'yar-\ *n* —**fa·mil·iar·ize** \fə'milyə,rīz\ *vb* —**fa·mil·iar·ly** *adv*

fam·i·ly \'famlē\ *n, pl* **-lies 1** : persons of common ancestry **2** : group living together **3** : parents and children **4** : group of related individuals

fam·ine \'famən\ *n* : extreme scarcity of food

fam·ish \'famish\ *vb* : starve

fa·mous \'fāməs\ *adj* : widely known or celebrated

fa·mous·ly *adv* : very well

¹**fan** \'fan\ *n* : device for producing a current of air ~ *vb* **-nn- 1** : move air with a fan **2** : direct a current of air upon **3** : stir to activity

²**fan** *n* : enthusiastic follower or admirer

fa·nat·ic \fə'natik\, **fa·nat·i·cal** \-ikəl\ *adj* : excessively enthusiastic or devoted —**fanatic** *n* —**fa·nat·i·cism** \-'natə,sizəm\ *n*

fan·ci·er \'fansēər\ *n* : one devoted to raising a particular plant or animal

fan·cy \'fansē\ *n, pl* **-cies 1** : liking **2** : whim **3** : imagination ~ *vb* **-cied; -cy·ing 1** : like **2** : imagine ~ *adj* **-cier; -est 1** : not plain **2** : of superior quality —**fan·ci·ful** \-sifəl\ *adj* —**fan·ci·ful·ly** \-fəlē\ *adv* —**fan·ci·ly** *adv*

fan·dan·go \fan'dangō\ *n, pl* **-gos** : lively Spanish dance

fan·fare \'fan,far\ *n* **1** : a sounding of trumpets **2** : showy display

fang \'faŋ\ *n* : long sharp tooth

fan·light *n* : semicircular window

fan·ta·sia \fan'tāzhə, -zēə; ,fantə'zēə\ *n* : music written to fancy rather than to form

fan·tas·tic \fan'tastik\ *adj* **1** : imaginary or unrealistic **2** : exceedingly or unbelievably great —**fan·tas·ti·cal·ly** \-tiklē\ *adv*

fan·ta·sy \'fantəsē\ *n* **1** : imagination **2** : product (as a daydream) of the imagination **3** : fantasia —**fan·ta·size** \'fantə,sīz\ *vb*

far \'fär\ *adv* **far·ther** \-thər\ *or* **fur·ther** \'fər-\; **far·thest** *or* **fur·thest** \-thəst\ **1** : at or to a distance **2** : much **3** : to a degree **4** : to an advanced point or extent ~ *adj* **farther** *or* **further; farthest** *or* **furthest 1** : remote **2** : long **3** : being more distant

far·away *adj* : distant

farce \'färs\ *n* **1** : satirical comedy with an improbable plot **2** : ridiculous display —**far·ci·cal** \-sikəl\ *adj*

¹**fare** \'far\ *vb* **fared; far·ing** : get along

²**fare** *n* **1** : price of transportation **2** : range of food

fare·well \far'wel\ *n* **1** : wish of welfare at parting **2** : departure —**farewell** *adj*

far-fetched \'fär'fecht\ *adj* : improbable

fa·ri·na \fə'rēnə\ *n* : fine meal made from cereal grains

farm \'färm\ *n* : place where something is raised for food ~ *vb* **1** : use (land) as a farm **2** : raise plants or animals for food —**farm·er** *n* —**farm·hand** \-,hand\ *n* —**farm·house** *n* —**farm·ing** *n* —**farm·land** \-,land\ *n* —**farm·yard** *n*

far-off *adj* : remote in time or space

far·ri·er \'färēər\ *n* : blacksmith who shoes horses

far·row \'färō\ *vb* : give birth to a litter of pigs —**farrow** *n*

far·sight·ed *adj* **1** : better able to see distant things than near **2** : judicious or shrewd —**far·sight·ed·ness** *n*

far·ther \'färthər\ *adv* **1** : at or to a greater distance or more advanced point **2** : to a greater degree or extent ~ *adj* : more distant

far·ther·most *adj* : most distant

far·thest \'färthəst\ *adj* : most distant ~ *adv* **1** : to or at the greatest distance **2** : to the most advanced point **3** : by the greatest extent

fas·ci·cle \'fasikəl\ *n* **1** : small bundle **2** : division of a book published in parts —**fas·ci·cled** \-kəld\ *adj*

fas·ci·nate \'fas²n,āt\ *vb* **-nat·ed; -nat·ing** : transfix and hold spellbound —**fas·ci·na·tion** \,fas²n'āshən\ *n*

fas·cism \'fash,izəm\ *n* : dictatorship that exalts nation and race —**fas·cist** \-ist\ *n or adj* —**fas·cis·tic** \fa'shistik\ *adj*

fash·ion \'fashən\ *n* **1** : manner **2** : prevailing custom or style ~ *vb* : form or construct —**fash·ion·able** \-ənəbəl\ *adj* —**fash·ion·ably** \-blē\ *adv*

¹fast \'fast\ *adj* **1** : firmly fixed, bound, or shut **2** : faithful **3** : moving or acting quickly **4** : indicating ahead of the correct time **5** : deep and undisturbed **6** : permanently dyed **7** : wild or promiscuous ~ *adv* **1** : so as to be secure or bound **2** : soundly or deeply **3** : swiftly

²fast *vb* : abstain from food or eat sparingly ~ *n* : act or time of fasting

fas·ten \'fas²n\ *vb* : attach esp. by pinning or tying —**fas·ten·er** *n* —**fas·ten·ing** *n*

fas·tid·i·ous \fas'tidēəs\ *adj* : hard to please —**fas·tid·i·ous·ly** *adv* —**fas·tid·i·ous·ness** *n*

fat \'fat\ *adj* **-tt-** **1** : having much fat **2** : thick ~ *n* : animal tissue rich in greasy or oily matter —**fat·ness** *n* —**fat·ten** \'fat²n\ *vb* —**fat·ty** *adj or n*

fa·tal \'fāt²l\ *adj* : causing death or ruin —**fa·tal·i·ty** \fā'talətē, fə-\ *n* —**fa·tal·ly** *adv*

fa·tal·ism \'fāt²l,izəm\ *n* : belief that fate determines events —**fa·tal·ist** \-ist\ *n* —**fa·tal·is·tic** \,fāt²l'istik\ *adj* —**fa·tal·is·ti·cal·ly** \-tiklē\ *adv*

fate \'fāt\ *n* **1** : principle, cause, or will held to determine events **2** : end or outcome —**fat·ed** *adj* —**fate·ful** \-fəl\ *adj* —**fate·ful·ly** *adv*

fa·ther \'fäthər, 'fath-\ *n* **1** : male parent **2** *cap* : God **3** : originator —**father** *vb* —**fa·ther·hood** \-,hud\ *n* —

fa·ther·land \-,land\ *n* —**fa·ther·less** *adj* —**fa·ther·ly** *adj*

father-in-law *n, pl* **fa·thers-in-law** : father of one's spouse

fath·om \'fathəm\ *n* : nautical unit of length equal to 6 feet ~ *vb* : understand —**fath·om·able** *adj* —**fath·om·less** *adj*

fa·tigue \fə'tēg\ *n* **1** : weariness from labor or use **2** : tendency to break under repeated stress ~ *vb* **-tigued; -tigu·ing** : tire out

fat·u·ous \'fachəwəs\ *adj* : foolish or stupid —**fat·u·ous·ly** *adv* —**fat·u·ous·ness** *n*

fau·cet \'fȯsət, 'fäs-\ *n* : fixture for drawing off a liquid

fault \'fȯlt\ *n* **1** : weakness in character **2** : something wrong or imperfect **3** : responsibility for something wrong **4** : fracture in the earth's crust ~ *vb* : find fault in or with —**fault·find·er** *n* —**fault·find·ing** *n* —**fault·i·ly** \'fȯltəlē\ *adv* —**fault·less** *adj* —**fault·less·ly** *adv* —**faulty** *adj*

fau·na \'fȯnə\ *n* : animals or animal life esp. of a region —**fau·nal** \-²l\ *adj*

faux pas \'fō'pä\ *n, pl* **faux pas** *same or* -'päz\ : social blunder

fa·vor \'fāvər\ *n* **1** : approval **2** : partiality **3** : act of kindness ~ *vb* : regard or treat with favor —**fa·vor·able** \'fāvərəbəl\ *adj* —**fa·vor·ably** \-blē\ *adv*

fa·vor·ite \'fāvərət\ *n* : one favored —**favorite** *adj* —**fa·vor·it·ism** \-,izəm\ *n*

¹fawn \'fȯn\ *vb* : seek favor by groveling

²fawn *n* : young deer

faze \'fāz\ *vb* **fazed; faz·ing** : disturb the composure of

fear \'fir\ *n* : unpleasant emotion caused by expectation or awareness of danger ~ *vb* : be afraid of —**fear·ful** \-fəl\ *adj* —**fear·ful·ly** *adv* —**fear·less** *adj* —**fear·less·ly** *adv* —**fear·less·ness** *n* —**fear·some** \-səm\ *adj*

fea·si·ble \'fēzəbəl\ *adj* : capable of being done —**fea·si·bil·i·ty** \,fēzə'bilətē\ *n* —**fea·si·bly** \'fēzəblē\ *adv*

feast \'fēst\ *n* **1** : large or fancy meal **2** : religious festival ~ *vb* : eat plentifully

feat \'fēt\ *n* : notable deed

feath·er \'fethər\ *n* : one of the light horny outgrowths that form the external covering of a bird's body —

feather *vb* —**feath·ered** \-ərd\ *adj* —**feath·er·less** *adj* —**feath·ery** *adj*

fea·ture \'fēchər\ *n* 1 : shape or appearance of the face 2 : part of the face 3 : prominent characteristic 4 : special attraction ~ *vb* : give prominence to —**fea·ture·less** *adj*

Feb·ru·ary \'febyə,werē, 'febə-, 'febrə-\ *n* : 2d month of the year having 28 and in leap years 29 days

fe·ces \'fē,sēz\ *n pl* : intestinal body waste —**fe·cal** \-kəl\ *adj*

feck·less \'fekləs\ *adj* : irresponsible

fe·cund \'fekənd, 'fē-\ *adj* : prolific —**fe·cun·di·ty** \fi'kəndətē, fe-\ *n*

fed·er·al \'fedrəl, -dərəl\ *adj* : of or constituting a government with power distributed between a central authority and constituent units —**fed·er·al·ism** \-rə,lizəm\ *n* —**fed·er·al·ist** \-list\ *n or adj* —**fed·er·al·ly** *adv*

fed·er·ate \'fedə,rāt\ *vb* -**at·ed; -at·ing** : join in a federation

fed·er·a·tion \,fedə'rāshən\ *n* : union of organizations

fe·do·ra \fi'dōrə\ *n* : soft felt hat

fed up *adj* : out of patience

fee \'fē\ *n* : fixed charge

fee·ble \'fēbəl\ *adj* -**bler; -blest** : weak or ineffective —**fee·ble·mind·ed** \,fēbəl'mīndəd\ *adj* —**fee·ble·mind·ed·ness** *n* —**fee·ble·ness** *n* —**fee·bly** \-blē\ *adv*

feed \'fēd\ *vb* **fed** \'fed\; **feed·ing** 1 : give food to 2 : eat 3 : furnish ~ *n* : food for livestock—**feed·er** *n*

feel \'fēl\ *vb* **felt** \'felt\; **feel·ing** 1 : perceive or examine through physical contact 2 : think or believe 3 : be conscious of 4 : seem 5 : have sympathy ~ *n* 1 : sense of touch 2 : quality of a thing imparted through touch —**feel·er** *n*

feel·ing \'fēliŋ\ *n* 1 : sense of touch 2 : state of mind 3 *pl* : sensibilities 4 : opinion

feet *pl of* FOOT

feign \'fān\ *vb* : pretend

feint \'fānt\ *n* : mock attack intended to distract attention —**feint** *vb*

fe·lic·i·tate \fi'lisə,tāt\ *vb* -**tat·ed; -tat·ing** : congratulate —**fe·lic·i·ta·tion** \-,lisə'tāshən\ *n*

fe·lic·i·tous \fi'lisətəs\ *adj* : aptly expressed —**fe·lic·i·tous·ly** *adv*

fe·lic·i·ty \-'lisətē\ *n, pl* -**ties** 1 : great

happiness 2 : pleasing faculty esp. in art or language

fe·line \'fē,līn\ *adj* : relating to cats —**feline** *n*

¹**fell** \'fel\ *vb* : cut or knock down

²**fell** *past of* FALL

fel·low \'felō\ *n* 1 : companion or associate 2 : man or boy —**fel·low·ship** \-,ship\ *n*

fel·low·man \,felō'man\ *n* : kindred human being

fel·on \'felən\ *n* : one who has committed a felony

fel·o·ny \'felənē\ *n, pl* -**nies** : serious crime —**fe·lo·ni·ous** \fə'lōnēəs\ *adj*

¹**felt** \'felt\ *n* : cloth made of pressed wool and fur

²**felt** *past of* FEEL

fe·male \'fē,māl\ *adj* : relating to or being the sex that bears young —**female** *n*

fem·i·nine \'femənən\ *adj* : relating to the female sex —**fem·i·nin·i·ty** \,femə'ninətē\ *n*

fem·i·nism \'femə,nizəm\ *n* : organized activity on behalf of women's rights —**fem·i·nist** \-nist\ *n or adj*

fe·mur \'fēmər\ *n, pl* **fe·murs** *or* **fem·o·ra** \'femərə\ : long bone of the thigh —**fem·o·ral** \'femərəl\ *adj*

fence \'fens\ *n* : enclosing barrier esp. of wood or wire ~ *vb* **fenced; fenc·ing** 1 : enclose with a fence 2 : practice fencing —**fenc·er** *n*

fenc·ing \'fensiŋ\ *n* 1 : combat with swords for sport 2 : material for building fences

fend \'fend\ *vb* : ward off

fend·er \'fendər\ *n* : guard over an automobile wheel

fen·nel \'fenᵊl\ *n* : herb related to the carrot

fer·ment \fər'ment\ *vb* : cause or undergo fermentation ~ \'fər,ment\ *n* : agitation

fer·men·ta·tion \,fərmən'tāshən, -,men-\ *n* : chemical decomposition of an organic substance in the absence of oxygen

fern \'fərn\ *n* : flowerless seedless green plant

fe·ro·cious \fə'rōshəs\ *adj* : fierce or savage —**fe·ro·cious·ly** *adv* —**fe·ro·cious·ness** *n* —**fe·roc·i·ty** \-'räsətē\ *n*

fer·ret \'ferət\ *n* : white European polecat ~ *vb* : find out by searching

fer·ric \'ferik\, **fer·rous** \'ferəs\ adj : relating to or containing iron

fer·rule \'ferəl\ n : metal band or ring

fer·ry \'ferē\ vb **-ried; -ry·ing** : carry by boat over water ~ n, pl **-ries** : boat used in ferrying —**fer·ry·boat** n

fer·tile \'fərtᵊl\ adj 1 : producing plentifully 2 : capable of developing or reproducing —**fer·til·i·ty** \fər'tilətē\ n

fer·til·ize \'fərtᵊl,īz\ vb **-ized; -iz·ing** : make fertile —**fer·til·iza·tion** \,fərtᵊlə'zāshən\ n —**fer·til·iz·er** n

fer·vid \'fərvəd\ adj : ardent or zealous —**fer·vid·ly** adv

fer·vor \'fərvər\ n : passion —**fer·ven·cy** \-vənsē\ n —**fer·vent** \-vənt\ adj —**fer·vent·ly** adv

fes·ter \'festər\ vb 1 : form pus 2 : become more bitter or malignant

fes·ti·val \'festəvəl\ n : time of celebration

fes·tive \-tiv\ adj : joyous or happy —**fes·tive·ly** adv —**fes·tiv·i·ty** \fes'tivətē\ n

fes·toon \fes'tün\ n : decorative chain or strip hanging in a curve —**festoon** vb

fe·tal \'fētᵊl\ adj : of, relating to, or being a fetus

fetch \'fech\ vb 1 : go or come after and bring or take back 2 : sell for

fetch·ing \'fechiŋ\ adj : attractive —**fetch·ing·ly** adv

fête \'fāt, 'fet\ n : lavish party ~ vb **fêt·ed; fêt·ing** : honor or commemorate with a fête

fet·id \'fetəd\ adj : having an offensive smell

fe·tish \'fetish\ n 1 : object believed to have magical powers 2 : object of unreasoning devotion or concern

fet·lock \'fet,läk\ n : projection on the back of a horse's leg above the hoof

fet·ter \'fetər\ n : chain or shackle for the feet —**fetter** vb

fet·tle \'fetᵊl\ n : state of fitness

fe·tus \'fētəs\ n : vertebrate not yet born or hatched

feud \'fyüd\ n : prolonged quarrel —**feud** vb

feu·dal \'fyüdᵊl\ adj : of or relating to feudalism

feu·dal·ism \-,izəm\ n : medieval political order in which land is granted in return for service —**feu·dal·is·tic** \,fyüdᵊl'istik\ adj

fe·ver \'fēvər\ n 1 : abnormal rise in body temperature 2 : state of heightened emotion —**fe·ver·ish** adj —**fe·ver·ish·ly** adv

few \'fyü\ pron : not many ~ adj : some but not many —often with a ~ n : small number —often with a

few·er \-ər\ pron : smaller number of things

fez \'fez\ n, pl **fez·zes** : round flat-crowned hat

fi·an·cé \,fē,än'sā\ n : man one is engaged to

fi·an·cée \,fē,än'sā\ n : woman one is engaged to

fi·as·co \fē'askō\ n, pl **-coes** : ridiculous failure

fi·at \'fēət, -,at, -,ät; 'fīət, -,at\ n : decree

fib \'fib\ n : trivial lie —**fib** vb —**fib·ber** n

fi·ber, fi·bre \'fībər\ n 1 : threadlike substance or structure (as a muscle cell or fine root) 2 : indigestible material in food 3 : element that gives texture or substance —**fi·brous** \-brəs\ adj

fi·ber·board n : construction material made of compressed fibers

fi·ber·glass n : glass in fibrous form in various products (as insulation)

fi·bril·la·tion \,fibrə'lāshən, ,fīb-\ n : rapid irregular contractions of heart muscle —**fib·ril·late** \'fibrə,lāt, 'fīb-\ vb

fib·u·la \'fibyələ\ n, pl **-lae** \-lē, -,lī\ or **-las** : outer of the two leg bones below the knee —**fib·u·lar** \-lər\ adj

fick·le \'fikəl\ adj : unpredictably changeable —**fick·le·ness** n

fic·tion \'fikshən\ n : a made-up story or literature consisting of these —**fic·tion·al** \-shənəl\ adj

fic·ti·tious \fik'tishəs\ adj : made up or pretended

fid·dle \'fidᵊl\ n : violin ~ vb **-dled; -dling** 1 : play on the fiddle 2 : move the hands restlessly —**fid·dler** \'fidlər, -ᵊlər\ n

fid·dle·sticks n : nonsense —used as an interjection

fi·del·i·ty \fə'delətē, fī-\ n, pl **-ties** 1 : quality or state of being faithful 2 : quality of reproduction

fid·get \'fijət\ n 1 pl : restlessness 2 : one that fidgets ~ vb : move restlessly —**fid·gety** adj

fi·du·cia·ry \fə'düshē,erē, -'dyü-, -shərē\ adj : held or holding in trust —**fiduciary** n

field \'fēld\ n 1 : open country 2

: cleared land **3** : land yielding some special product **4** : sphere of activity **5** : area for sports **6** : region or space in which a given effect (as magnetism) exists ~ *vb* : put into the field —**field**·*ed* —**field**·*er n*

fiend \'fēnd\ *n* **1** : devil **2** : extremely wicked person —**fiend**·*ish adj* —**fiend**·*ish*·*ly adv*

fierce \'firs\ *adj* **fierc**·*er*; -*est* **1** : violently hostile or aggressive **2** : intense **3** : menacing looking —**fierce**·*ly adv* —**fierce**·*ness n*

fiery \'fīǝrē\ *adj* **fier**·*i*·*er*; -*est* **1** : burning **2** : hot or passionate —**fi**·*eri*·*ness* \'fīrēnǝs\ *n*

fiesta \fē'estǝ\ *n* : festival

fife \'fīf\ *n* : small flute

fifteen \fif'tēn\ *n* : one more than 14 — **fifteen** *adj or pron* —**fif**·*teenth* \-'tēnth\ *adj or n*

fifth \'fifth\ *n* **1** : one that is number 5 in a countable series **2** : one of 5 equal parts of something —**fifth** *adj or adv*

fifty \'fiftē\ *n, pl* -**ties** : 5 times 10 — **fif**·*ti*·*eth* \-tēǝth\ *adj or n* —**fifty** *adj or pron*

fifty-fifty *adv or adj* : shared equally

fig \'fig\ *n* : pear-shaped edible fruit

fight \'fīt\ *vb* **fought** \'fot\; **fight**·*ing* **1** : contend against another in battle **2** : box **3** : struggle ~ *n* **1** : hostile encounter **2** : boxing match **3** : verbal disagreement —**fight**·*er n*

figment \'figmǝnt\ *n* : something imagined or made up

fig·*u*·*ra*·*tive* \'figyǝrǝtiv, -gǝ-\ *adj* : metaphorical —**fig**·*u*·*ra*·*tive*·*ly adv*

fig·*ure* \'figyǝr, -gǝr\ *n* **1** : symbol representing a number **2** *pl* : arithmetical calculations **3** : price **4** : shape or outline **5** : illustration **6** : pattern or design **7** : prominent person ~ *vb* -**ured**; -**ur**·*ing* **1** : be important **2** : calculate —**fig**·*ured adj*

fig·*u*·*rine* \,figyǝ'rēn\ *n* : small statue

fil·*a*·*ment* \'filǝmǝnt\ *n* : fine thread or threadlike part —**fil**·*a*·*men*·*tous* \,filǝ'mentǝs\ *adj*

fil·*bert* \'filbǝrt\ *n* : edible nut of a European hazel

filch \'filch\ *vb* : steal furtively

¹file \'fīl\ *n* : tool for smoothing or sharpening ~ *vb* **filed**; **fil**·*ing* : rub or smooth with a file

²file *vb* **filed**; **fil**·*ing* **1** : arrange in order **2** : enter or record officially ~ *n* : device for keeping papers in order

³file *n* : row of persons or things one behind the other ~ *vb* **filed**; **fil**·*ing* : march in file

fil·ial \'filēǝl, 'filyǝl\ *adj* : relating to a son or daughter

fil·i·bus·ter \'filǝ,bǝstǝr\ *n* : long speeches to delay a legislative vote — **filibuster** *vb* —**fil**·*i*·*bus*·*ter*·*er n*

fil·i·gree \'filǝ,grē\ *n* : ornamental designs of fine wire —**fil**·*i*·*greed* \-,grēd\ *adj*

fill \'fil\ *vb* **1** : make or become full **2** : stop up **3** : feed **4** : satisfy **5** : occupy fully **6** : spread through ~ *n* **1** : full supply **2** : material for filling —**fill**·*er n* —**fill in** *vb* **1** : provide information to or for **2** : substitute

fil·let \'filǝt, fi'lā, 'fil,ā\ *n* : piece of boneless meat or fish ~ *vb* : cut into fillets

fill·ing *n* : material used to fill something

fil·ly \'filē\ *n, pl* -**lies** : young female horse

film \'film\ *n* **1** : thin skin or membrane **2** : thin coating or layer **3** : strip of material used in taking pictures **4** : movie ~ *vb* : make a movie of — **filmy** *adj*

film·strip *n* : strip of film with photographs for still projection

fil·ter \'filtǝr\ *n* **1** : device for separating matter from a fluid **2** : device (as on a camera lens) that absorbs light ~ *vb* **1** : pass through a filter **2** : remove by means of a filter —**fil**·*ter*·*able adj* —**fil**·*tra*·*tion* \fil'trāshǝn\ *n*

filth \'filth\ *n* : repulsive dirt or refuse —**filth**·*i*·*ness n* —**filthy** \'filthē\ *adj*

fin \'fin\ *n* **1** : thin external process controlling movement in an aquatic animal **2** : fin-shaped part (as on an airplane) **3** : flipper —**finned** \'find\ *adj*

fi·na·gle \fǝ'nāgǝl\ *vb* -**gled**; -**gling** : get by clever or tricky means —**fi**·*na*·*gler n*

fi·nal \'fīnᵊl\ *adj* **1** : not to be changed **2** : ultimate **3** : coming at the end — **final** *n* —**fi**·*nal*·*ist* \'fīnᵊlist\ *n* —**fi**·*nal*·*i*·*ty* \fī'nalǝtē, fǝ-\ *n* —**fi**·*nal*·*ize* \-,īz\ *vb* —**fi**·*nal*·*ly adv*

fi·na·le \fǝ'nalē, fi'näl-\ *n* : last or climactic part

fi·nance \fǝ'nans, 'fī,nans\ *n* **1** *pl* : money resources **2** : management of money affairs ~ *vb* -**nanced**; -**nanc**·*ing* **1** : raise funds for **2** : give necessary funds to **3** : sell on credit

fi·nan·cial \fə'nanchəl, fī-\ *adj* : relating to finance —**fi·nan·cial·ly** *adv*

fi·nan·cier \,finən'sir, ,fī,nan-\ *n* : person who invests large sums of money

finch \'finch\ *n* : songbird (as a sparrow or linnet) with a strong bill

find \'fīnd\ *vb* **found** \'faùnd\; **find·ing** **1** : discover or encounter **2** : obtain by effort **3** : experience or feel **4** : gain or regain the use of **5** : decide on (a verdict) ~ *n* **1** : act or instance of finding **2** : something found —**find·er** *n* —**find·ing** *n* —**find out** *vb* : learn, discover, or verify something

fine \'fīn\ *n* : money paid as a penalty ~ *vb* **fined; fin·ing** : impose a fine on ~ *adj* **fin·er; -est 1** : free from impurity **2** : small or thin **3** : not coarse **4** : superior in quality or appearance ~ *adv* : finely —**fine·ly** *adv* —**fine·ness** *n*

fin·ery \'fīnərē\ *n, pl* -er·ies : showy clothing and jewels

fi·nesse \fə'nes\ *n* **1** : delicate skill **2** : craftiness —**finesse** *vb*

fin·ger \'fiŋgər\ *n* **1** : one of the 5 divisions at the end of the hand and esp. one other than the thumb **2** : something like a finger **3** : part of a glove for a finger ~ *vb* **1** : touch with the fingers **2** : identify as if by pointing —**fin·gered** *adj* —**fin·ger·nail** *n* —**fin·ger·tip** *n*

fin·ger·ling \-gərliŋ\ *n* : small fish

fin·ger·print *n* : impression of the pattern of marks on the tip of a finger —**fingerprint** *vb*

fin·icky \'finikē\ *adj* : excessively particular in taste or standards

fin·ish \'finish\ *vb* **1** : come or bring to an end **2** : use or dispose of entirely **3** : put a final coat or surface on ~ *n* **1** : end **2** : final treatment given a surface —**fin·ish·er** *n*

fi·nite \'fī,nīt\ *adj* : having definite limits

fink \'fiŋk\ *n* : contemptible person

fiord *var of* FJORD

fir \'fər\ *n* : erect evergreen tree or its wood

fire \'fīr\ *n* **1** : light or heat and esp. the flame of something burning **2** : destructive burning (as of a house) **3** : enthusiasm **4** : the shooting of weapons ~ *vb* **fired; fir·ing 1** : kindle **2** : stir up or enliven **3** : dismiss from employment **4** : shoot **5** : bake —

fire·bomb *n or vb* —**fire·fight·er** *n* —**fire·less** *adj* —**fire·proof** *adj or vb* —**fire·wood** *n*

fire·arm *n* : weapon (as a rifle) that works by an explosion of gunpowder

fire·ball *n* **1** : ball of fire **2** : brilliant meteor

fire·boat *n* : boat equipped for fighting fire

fire·box *n* **1** : chamber (as of a furnace) that contains a fire **2** : fire-alarm box

fire·break *n* : cleared land for checking a forest fire

fire·bug *n* : person who deliberately sets destructive fires

fire·crack·er *n* : small firework that makes noise

fire·fly *n* : night-flying beetle that produces a soft light

fire·man \'fīrmən\ *n* **1** : person trained to put out fires **2** : stoker

fire·place *n* : opening made in a chimney to hold an open fire

fire·plug *n* : hydrant

fire·side *n* **1** : place near the fire or hearth **2** : home ~ *adj* : having an informal quality

fire·trap *n* : place apt to catch on fire

fire·work *n* : device that explodes to produce noise or a display of light

¹firm \'fərm\ *adj* **1** : securely fixed in place **2** : strong or vigorous **3** : not subject to change **4** : resolute ~ *vb* : make or become firm —**firm·ly** *adv* —**firm·ness** *n*

²firm *n* : business enterprise

fir·ma·ment \'fərməmənt\ *n* : sky

first \'fərst\ *adj* **1** : being number one **2** : foremost ~ *adv* **1** : before any other **2** : for the first time ~ *n* **1** : number one **2** : one that is first —**first class** *n* —**first-class** *adj or adv* —**first·ly** *adv* —**first-rate** *adj or adv*

first aid *n* : emergency care

first lieutenant *n* : commissioned officer ranking next below a captain

first sergeant *n* **1** : noncommissioned officer serving as the chief assistant to the commander of a military unit **2** : rank in the army below a command sergeant major and in the marine corps below a sergeant major

firth \'fərth\ *n* : estuary

fis·cal \'fiskəl\ *adj* : relating to money —**fis·cal·ly** *adv*

fish \'fish\ *n, pl* **fish** *or* **fish·es** : water animal with fins, gills, and usu. scales

~ *vb* **1** : try to catch fish **2** : grope — **fish·er** *n* —**fish·hook** *n* —**fish·ing** *n*

fish·er·man \-mən\ *n* : one who fishes

fish·ery \'fishərē\ *n, pl* -er·ies : fishing business or a place for this

fishy \'fishē\ *adj* **fish·i·er; -est 1** : relating to or like fish **2** : questionable

fis·sion \'fishən, 'fizh-\ *n* : splitting of an atomic nucleus —**fis·sion·able** \-ənəbəl\ *adj*

fis·sure \'fishər\ *n* : crack

fist \'fist\ *n* : hand doubled up —**fist·ed** \'fistəd\ *adj* —**fist·ful** \-ˌfu̇l\ *n*

fist·i·cuffs \'fisti,kəfs\ *n pl* : fist fight

¹fit \'fit\ *n* : sudden attack of illness or emotion

²fit *adj* **-tt- 1** : suitable **2** : qualified **3** : sound in body ~ *vb* **-tt- 1** : be suitable to **2** : insert or adjust correctly **3** : make room for **4** : supply or equip **5** : belong ~ *n* **1** : state of fitting or being fitted —**fit·ly** *adv* —**fit·ness** *n* —**fit·ter** *n*

fit·ful \'fitfəl\ *adj* : restless —**fit·ful·ly** *adv*

fit·ting *adj* : suitable ~ *n* : a small part

five \'fiv\ *n* **1** : one more than 4 **2** : 5th in a set or series **3** : something having 5 units —**five** *adj or pron*

fix \'fiks\ *vb* **1** : attach **2** : establish **3** : make right **4** : prepare **5** : improperly influence ~ *n* **1** : predicament **2** : determination of location —**fix·er** *n*

fix·a·tion \fik'sāshən\ *n* : obsessive attachment —**fix·ate** \'fik,sāt\ *vb*

fixed \'fikst\ *adj* **1** : stationary **2** : settled —**fixed·ly** \'fiksədlē\ *adv* —**fixed·ness** \-nəs\ *n*

fix·ture \'fikschər\ *n* : permanent part of something

fizz \'fiz\ *vb* : make a hissing sound ~ *n* : effervescence

fiz·zle \'fizəl\ *vb* **-zled; -zling 1** : fizz **2** : fail ~ *n* : failure

fjord \fē'ȯrd\ *n* : inlet of the sea between cliffs

flab \'flab\ *n* : flabby flesh

flab·ber·gast \'flabər,gast\ *vb* : astound

flab·by \'flabē\ *adj* **-bi·er; -est** : not firm —**flab·bi·ness** *n*

flac·cid \'flaksəd, 'flasəd\ *adj* : not firm

¹flag \'flag\ *n* : flat stone

²flag *n* **1** : fabric that is a symbol (as of a country) **2** : something used to signal ~ *vb* **-gg-** : signal with a flag —**flag·pole** *n* —**flag·staff** *n*

³flag *vb* **-gg-** : lose strength or spirit

flag·el·late \'flajə,lāt\ *vb* **-lat·ed; -lat·ing** : whip —**flag·el·la·tion** \,flajə-'lāshən\ *n*

flag·on \'flagən\ *n* : container for liquids

fla·grant \'flāgrənt\ *adj* : conspicuously bad —**fla·grant·ly** *adv*

flag·ship *n* : ship carrying a commander

flag·stone *n* : flag

flail \'flāl\ *n* : tool for threshing grain ~ *vb* : beat with or as if with a flail

flair \'flar\ *n* : natural aptitude

flak \'flak\ *n, pl* **flak 1** : antiaircraft fire **2** : criticism

flake \'flāk\ *n* : small flat piece ~ *vb* **flaked; flak·ing** : separate or form into flakes

flam·boy·ant \flam'bȯiənt\ *adj* : showy —**flam·boy·ance** \-əns\ *n* —**flam·boy·ant·ly** *adv*

flame \'flām\ *n* **1** : glowing part of a fire **2** : state of combustion **3** : burning passion —**flame** *vb* —**flam·ing** *adj*

fla·min·go \flə'miŋgō\ *n, pl* **-gos** : long-legged long-necked tropical water bird

flam·ma·ble \'flaməbəl\ *adj* : easily ignited

flange \'flanj\ *n* : rim

flank \'flaŋk\ *n* : side of something ~ *vb* **1** : attack or go around the side of **2** : be at the side of

flan·nel \'flanªl\ *n* : soft napped fabric

flap \'flap\ *n* **1** : slap **2** : something flat that hangs loose ~ *vb* **-pp- 1** : move (wings) up and down **2** : swing back and forth noisily

flap·jack \-,jak\ *n* : pancake

flare \'flar\ *vb* **flared; flar·ing** : become suddenly bright or excited ~ *n* : blaze of light

flash \'flash\ *vb* **1** : give off a sudden flame or burst of light **2** : appear or pass suddenly ~ *n* **1** : sudden burst of light or inspiration **2** : instant ~ *adj* : coming suddenly

flash·light *n* : small battery-operated light

flashy \'flashē\ *adj* **flash·i·er; -est** : showy —**flash·i·ly** *adv* —**flash·i·ness** *n*

flask \'flask\ *n* : flattened bottle

flat \'flat\ *adj* **-tt- 1** : smooth **2** : broad and thin **3** : definite **4** : uninteresting **5** : deflated **6** : below the true pitch ~ *n* **1** : level surface of land **2** : flat note in music **3** : apartment **4** : deflated tire ~ *adv* **-tt- 1** : exactly **2** : below the true pitch ~ *vb* **-tt-** : make

flat —**flat·ly** adv —**flat·ness** n —
flat·ten \-ᵊn\ vb

flat·car n : railroad car without sides

flat·fish n : flattened fish with both eyes
on the upper side

flat·foot n, pl **flat·feet** : foot condition
in which the arch is flattened —**flat·
foot·ed** adj

flat–out adj 1 : being maximum effort
or speed 2 : downright

flat·ter \'flatər\ vb 1 : praise insincerely
2 : judge or represent too favorably
—**flat·ter·er** n —**flat·tery** \'flatərē\ n

flat·u·lent \'flachələnt\ adj : full of gas
—**flat·u·lence** \-ləns\ n

flat·ware n : eating utensils

flaunt \'flȯnt\ vb : display ostentatiously
—**flaunt** n

fla·vor \'flāvər\ n 1 : quality that affects
the sense of taste 2 : something that
adds flavor ~ vb : give flavor to —
fla·vor·ful adj —**fla·vor·ing** n —
fla·vor·less adj

flaw \'flȯ\ n : fault —**flaw·less** adj —
flaw·less·ly adv —**flaw·less·ness** n

flax \'flaks\ n : plant from which linen
is made

flax·en \'flaksən\ adj : made of or like
flax

flay \'flā\ vb 1 : strip off the skin of 2
: criticize harshly

flea \'flē\ n : leaping bloodsucking insect

fleck \'flek\ vb or n : streak or spot

fledg·ling \'flejliŋ\ : young bird

flee \'flē\ vb **fled** \'fled\; **flee·ing** : run
away

fleece \'flēs\ n : sheep's wool ~ vb
fleeced; fleec·ing 1 : shear 2 : get
money from dishonestly —**fleecy** adj

¹**fleet** \'flēt\ vb : pass rapidly ~ adj
: swift —**fleet·ing** adj —**fleet·ness** n

²**fleet** n : group of ships

fleet admiral n : commissioned officer
of the highest rank in the navy

flesh \'flesh\ n 1 : soft parts of an animal's body 2 : soft plant tissue (as
fruit pulp) —**fleshed** \'flesht\ adj —
flesh out vb : make fuller —**fleshy**
adj

flesh·ly \'fleshlē\ adj : sensual

flew past of FLY

flex \'fleks\ vb : bend

flex·i·ble \'fleksəbəl\ adj 1 : capable of
being flexed 2 : adaptable —**flex·i·
bil·i·ty** \,fleksə'bilətē\ n —**flex·i·bly**
\-əblē\ adv

flick \'flik\ n : light jerky stroke ~ vb 1
: strike lightly 2 : flutter

flick·er \'flikər\ vb 1 : waver 2 : burn
unsteadily ~ n 1 : sudden movement
2 : wavering light

fli·er \'flīər\ n 1 : aviator 2 : advertising
circular

¹**flight** \'flīt\ n 1 : act or instance of flying 2 : ability to fly 3 : a passing
through air or space 4 : series of stairs
—**flight·less** adj

²**flight** n : act or instance of running
away

flighty \-ē\ adj **flight·i·er; -est**
: capricious or silly —**flight·i·ness** n

flim·flam \'flim,flam\ n : trickery

flim·sy \-zē\ adj **-si·er; -est** 1 : not
strong or well made 2 : not believable
—**flim·si·ly** adv —**flim·si·ness** n

flinch \'flinch\ vb : shrink from pain

fling \'fliŋ\ vb **flung** \'fləŋ\; **fling·ing** 1
: move brusquely 2 : throw ~ n 1 : act
or instance of flinging 2 : attempt 3
: period of self-indulgence

flint \'flint\ n : hard quartz that gives off
sparks when struck with steel —**flinty**
adj

flip \'flip\ vb **-pp-** 1 : cause to turn over
quickly or many times 2 : move with
a quick push ~ adj : insolent —**flip**
n

flip·pant \'flipənt\ adj : not serious
enough —**flip·pan·cy** \-ənsē\ n

flip·per \'flipər\ n : paddlelike limb (as
of a seal) for swimming

flirt \'flərt\ vb 1 : be playfully romantic
2 : show casual interest ~ n : one who
flirts —**flir·ta·tion** \,flər'tāshən\ n —
flir·ta·tious \-shəs\ adj

flit \'flit\ vb **-tt-** : dart

float \'flōt\ n 1 : something that floats 2
: vehicle carrying an exhibit ~ vb 1
: rest on or in a fluid without sinking
2 : wander 3 : finance by issuing
stock or bonds —**float·er** n

flock \'fläk\ n : group of animals (as
birds) or people ~ vb : gather or
move as a group

floe \'flō\ n : mass of floating ice

flog \'fläg\ vb **-gg-** : beat with a rod or
whip —**flog·ger** n

flood \'fləd\ n 1 : great flow of water
over the land 2 : overwhelming volume ~ vb : cover or fill esp. with water —**flood·wa·ter** n

floor \'flōr\ n 1 : bottom of a room on
which one stands 2 : story of a building 3 : lower limit ~ vb 1 : furnish

with a floor 2 : knock down 3 : amaze —**floor•board** n —**floor•ing** \-iŋ\ n

floo•zy, floo•zie \'flüzē\ n, pl **-zies** : promiscuous young woman

flop \'fläp\ vb **-pp-** 1 : flap 2 : slump heavily 3 : fail —**flop** n

flop•py \'fläpē\ adj **-pi•er; -est** : soft and flexible

flo•ra \'flōrə\ n : plants or plant life of a region

flo•ral \'flōrəl\ adj : relating to flowers

flor•id \'flȯrəd\ adj 1 : very flowery in style 2 : reddish

flo•rist \'flōrist\ n : flower dealer

floss \'fläs\ n 1 : soft thread for embroidery 2 : thread used to clean between teeth —**floss** vb

flo•ta•tion \flō'tāshən\ n : process or instance of floating

flo•til•la \flō'tilə\ n : small fleet

flot•sam \'flätsəm\ n : floating wreckage

¹flounce \'flau̇ns\ vb **flounced; flounc•ing** : move with exaggerated jerky motions —**flounce** n

²flounce n : fabric border or wide ruffle

¹floun•der \'flau̇ndər\ n, pl **flounder** or **flounders** : flatfish

²flounder vb 1 : struggle for footing 2 : proceed clumsily

flour \'flau̇ər\ n : finely ground meal ~ vb : coat with flour —**floury** adj

flour•ish \'flərish\ vb 1 : thrive 2 : wave threateningly ~ n 1 : embellishment 2 : fanfare 3 : wave 4 : showiness of action

flout \'flau̇t\ vb : treat with disdain

flow \'flō\ vb 1 : move in a stream 2 : proceed smoothly and readily ~ n : uninterrupted stream

flow•er \'flau̇ər\ n 1 : showy plant shoot that bears seeds 2 : state of flourishing ~ vb 1 : produce flowers 2 : flourish —**flow•ered** adj —**flow•er•i•ness** n —**flow•er•less** adj —**flow•er•pot** n —**flow•ery** \-ē\ adj

flown past part of FLY

flu \'flü\ n 1 : influenza 2 : minor virus ailment

flub \'fləb\ vb **-bb-** : bungle —**flub** n

fluc•tu•ate \'fləkchə‚wāt\ vb **-at•ed; -at•ing** : change rapidly esp. up and down —**fluc•tu•a•tion** \‚fləkchə'wāshən\ n

flue \'flü\ n : smoke duct

flu•ent \'flüənt\ adj : speaking with ease —**flu•en•cy** \-ənsē\ n —**flu•ent•ly** adv

fluff \'fləf\ n 1 : something soft and light 2 : blunder ~ vb 1 : make fluffy 2 : make a mistake —**fluffy** \-ē\ adj

flu•id \'flüəd\ adj : flowing ~ n : substance that can flow —**flu•id•i•ty** \flü'idətē\ n —**flu•id•ly** adv

fluid ounce n : unit of liquid measure equal to ¹⁄₁₆ pint

fluke \'flük\ n : stroke of luck

flume \'flüm\ n : channel for water

flung past of FLING

flunk \'fləŋk\ vb : fail in school work

flun•ky, flun•key \'fləŋkē\ n, pl **-kies** or **keys** : lackey

flu•o•res•cence \‚flu̇r'esⁿns, ‚flȯr-\ n : emission of light after initial absorption —**flu•o•resce** \-'es\ vb —**flu•o•res•cent** \-'esⁿnt\ adj

flu•o•ri•date \'flȯrə‚dāt, 'flu̇r-\ vb **-dat•ed; -dat•ing** : add fluoride to —**flu•o•ri•da•tion** \‚flȯrə'dāshən, ‚flu̇r-\ n

flu•o•ride \'flȯr‚īd, 'flu̇r-\ n : compound of fluorine

flu•o•rine \'flu̇r‚ēn, -ən\ n : toxic gaseous chemical element

flu•o•ro•car•bon \‚flȯrō'kärbən, ‚flu̇r-\ n : compound containing fluorine and carbon

flu•o•ro•scope \'flu̇rə‚skōp\ n : instrument for internal examination —**flu•o•ro•scop•ic** \‚flu̇rə'skäpik\ adj —**flu•o•ros•co•py** \‚flu̇r'äskəpē\ n

flur•ry \'flərē\ n, pl **-ries** 1 : light snowfall 2 : bustle 3 : brief burst of activity —**flurry** vb

¹flush \'fləsh\ vb : cause (a bird) to fly from cover

²flush n 1 : sudden flow (as of water) 2 : surge of emotion 3 : blush ~ vb 1 : blush 2 : wash out with a rush of liquid ~ adj 1 : filled to overflowing 2 : of a reddish healthy color 3 : smooth or level 4 : abutting —**flush** adv

³flush n : cards of the same suit

flus•ter \'fləstər\ vb : upset —**fluster** n

flute \'flüt\ n 1 : pipelike musical instrument 2 : groove —**flut•ed** adj —**flut•ing** n —**flut•ist** \-ist\ n

flut•ter \'flətər\ vb 1 : flap the wings rapidly 2 : move with quick wavering or flapping motions 3 : behave in an agitated manner ~ n 1 : a fluttering 2 : state of confusion —**flut•tery** \-ərē\ adj

flux \'fləks\ n : state of continuous change

¹fly \'flī\ vb **flew** \'flü\; **flown** \'flōn\; **fly•ing** 1 : move through the air with wings 2 : float or soar 3 : flee 4

: move or pass swiftly **5** : operate an airplane

²fly *n, pl* **flies** : garment closure

³fly *n, pl* **flies** : winged insect

fly·er *var of* FLIER

fly·pa·per *n* : sticky paper for catching flies

fly·speck *n* **1** : speck of fly dung **2** : something tiny

fly·wheel *n* : rotating wheel that regulates the speed of machinery

foal \'fōl\ *n* : young horse —**foal** *vb*

foam \'fōm\ *n* **1** : mass of bubbles on top of a liquid **2** : material of cellular form ~ *vb* : form foam —**foamy** *adj*

fob \'fäb\ *n* : short chain for a pocket watch

fo·'c·'sle *var of* FORECASTLE

fo·cus \'fōkəs\ *n, pl* **-ci** \-ˌsī\ **1** : point at which reflected or refracted rays meet **2** : adjustment (as of eyeglasses) for clear vision **3** : central point ~ *vb* : bring to a focus —**fo·cal** \-kəl\ *adj* —**fo·cal·ly** *adv*

fod·der \'fädər\ *n* : food for livestock

foe \'fō\ *n* : enemy

fog \'fog, 'fäg\ *n* **1** : fine particles of water suspended near the ground **2** : mental confusion ~ *vb* **-gg-** : obscure or be obscured with fog — **fog·gy** *adj*

fog·horn *n* : warning horn sounded in a fog

fo·gy \'fōgē\ *n, pl* **-gies** : person with old-fashioned ideas

foi·ble \'fóibəl\ *n* : minor character fault

¹foil \'fóil\ *vb* : defeat ~ *n* : light fencing sword

²foil *n* **1** : thin sheet of metal **2** : one that sets off another by contrast

foist \'fóist\ *vb* : force another to accept

¹fold \'fōld\ *n* **1** : enclosure for sheep **2** : group with a common interest

²fold *vb* **1** : lay one part over another **2** : embrace ~ *n* : part folded

fold·er \'fōldər\ *n* **1** : one that folds **2** : circular **3** : folded cover or envelope for papers

fol·de·rol \'fäldəˌräl\ *n* : nonsense

fo·liage \'fōlēij, -lij\ *n* : plant leaves

fo·lio \'fōlēˌō\ *n, pl* **-li·os** : sheet of paper folded once

folk \'fōk\ *n, pl* **folk** *or* **folks** **1** : people in general **2** *folks pl* : one's family ~ *adj* : relating to the common people

folk·lore *n* : customs and traditions of a people —**folk·lor·ist** *n*

folksy \'fōksē\ *adj* **folks·i·er; -est** : friendly and informal

fol·li·cle \'fälikəl\ *n* : small anatomical cavity or gland

fol·low \'fälō\ *vb* **1** : go or come after **2** : pursue **3** : obey **4** : proceed along **5** : keep one's attention fixed on **6** : result from —**fol·low·er** *n*

fol·low·ing \'fäləwiŋ\ *adj* : next ~ *n* : group of followers ~ *prep* : after

fol·ly \'fälē\ *n, pl* **-lies** : foolishness

fo·ment \fō'ment\ *vb* : incite

fond \'fänd\ *adj* **1** : strongly attracted **2** : affectionate **3** : dear —**fond·ly** *adv* —**fond·ness** *n*

fon·dle \'fändᵊl\ *vb* **-dled; -dling** : touch lovingly

fon·due \fän'dü, -'dyü\ *n* : preparation of melted cheese

font \'fänt\ *n* **1** : baptismal basin **2** : fountain

food \'füd\ *n* : material eaten to sustain life

fool \'fül\ *n* **1** : stupid person **2** : jester ~ *vb* **1** : waste time **2** : meddle **3** : deceive —**fool·ery** \'fülərē\ *n*

fool·ish \'fülish\ *adj* —**fool·ish·ly** *adv* —**fool·ish·ness** *n* —**fool·proof** *adj*

fool·har·dy \'fül,härdē\ *adj* : rash — **fool·har·di·ness** *n*

foot \'fút\ *n, pl* **feet** \'fēt\ **1** : end part of a leg **2** : unit of length equal to ⅓ yard **3** : unit of verse meter **4** : bottom — **foot·age** \-ij\ *n* —**foot·ed** *adj* —**foot·path** *n* —**foot·print** *n* —**foot·race** *n* —**foot·rest** *n* —**foot·wear** *n*

foot·ball *n* : ball game played by 2 teams on a rectangular field

foot·bridge *n* : bridge for pedestrians

foot·hill *n* : hill at the foot of higher hills

foot·hold *n* : support for the feet

foot·ing *n* **1** : foothold **2** : basis

foot·lights *n pl* : stage lights along the floor

foot·lock·er *n* : small trunk

foot·loose *adj* : having no ties

foot·man \'fútmən\ *n* : male servant

foot·note *n* : note at the bottom of a page

foot·step *n* **1** : step **2** : distance covered by a step **3** : footprint

foot·stool *n* : stool to support the feet

foot·work *n* : skillful movement of the feet (as in boxing)

fop \'fäp\ *n* : dandy —**fop·pery** \-ərē\ *n* —**fop·pish** *adj*

for \'fór\ *prep* **1** —used to show preparation or purpose **2** : because of **3** —

used to show a recipient **4** : in support of **5** : so as to support or help cure **6** : so as to be equal to **7** : concerning **8** : through the period of ~ *conj* : because

for·age \'fŏrij\ *n* : food for animals ~ *vb* -**aged; -ag·ing 1** : hunt food **2** : search for provisions

for·ay \'fŏr‚ā\ *n or vb* : raid

¹for·bear \fŏr'bar\ *vb* -**bore** \-'bōr\; -**borne** \-'bōrn\; -**bear·ing 1** : refrain from **2** : be patient —**for·bear·ance** \-'barəns\ *n*

²forbear *var of* FOREBEAR

for·bid \fər'bid\ *vb* -**bade** \-'bad, -'bād\ *or* -**bad** \-'bad\; -**bid·den** \-'bid³n\; -**bid·ding 1** : prohibit **2** : order not to do something

for·bid·ding *adj* : tending to discourage

force \'fŏrs\ *n* **1** : exceptional strength or energy **2** : military strength **3** : body (as of persons) available for a purpose **4** : violence **5** : influence (as a push or pull) that causes motion ~ *vb* **forced; forc·ing 1** : compel **2** : gain against resistance **3** : break open —**force·ful** \-fəl\ *adj* —**force·ful·ly** *adv* —**in force 1** : in great numbers **2** : valid

for·ceps \'fŏrsəps\ *n, pl* **forceps** : surgical instrument for grasping objects

forc·ible \'fŏrsəbəl\ *adj* **1** : done by force **2** : showing force —**forc·i·bly** \-blē\ *adv*

ford \'fŏrd\ *n* : place to wade across a stream ~ *vb* : wade across

fore \'fŏr\ *adv* : in or toward the front ~ *adj* : being or coming before in time, place, or order ~ *n* : front

fore–and–aft *adj* : lengthwise

fore·arm \'fŏr‚ärm\ *n* : part of the arm between the elbow and the wrist

fore·bear \'fŏr‚bar\ *n* : ancestor

fore·bod·ing \fŏr'bōdiŋ\ *n* : premonition of disaster —**fore·bod·ing** *adj*

fore·cast \'fŏr‚kast\ *vb* -**cast; -cast·ing** : predict —**forecast** *n* —**fore·cast·er** *n*

fore·cas·tle \'fŏksəl\ *n* : forward part of a ship

fore·close \fŏr'klōz\ *vb* : take legal measures to terminate a mortgage —**fore·clo·sure** \-'klōzhər\ *n*

fore·fa·ther \'fŏr‚fäthər\ *n* : ancestor

fore·fin·ger \'fŏr‚fiŋgər\ *n* : finger next to the thumb

fore·foot \'fŏr‚fût\ *n* : front foot of a quadruped

fore·front \'fŏr‚frənt\ *n* : foremost position or place

¹fore·go \fŏr'gō\ *vb* -**went; -gone; -go·ing** : precede

²forego *var of* FORGO

fore·go·ing *adj* : preceding

fore·gone *adj* : determined in advance

fore·ground \'fŏr‚graúnd\ *n* : part of a scene nearest the viewer

fore·hand \'fŏr‚hand\ *n* : stroke (as in tennis) made with the palm of the hand turned forward —**forehand** *adj*

fore·head \'fŏrəd, 'fŏr‚hed\ *n* : part of the face above the eyes

for·eign \'fŏrən\ *adj* **1** : situated outside a place or country and esp. one's own country **2** : belonging to a different place or country **3** : not pertinent **4** : related to or dealing with other nations —**for·eign·er** \-ər\ *n*

fore·know \fŏr'nō\ *vb* -**knew; -known; -know·ing** : know beforehand —**fore·knowl·edge** *n*

fore·leg \'fŏr‚leg\ *n* : front leg

fore·lock \'fŏr‚läk\ *n* : front lock of hair

fore·man \'fŏrmən\ *n* **1** : spokesman of a jury **2** : workman in charge

fore·most \'fŏr‚mōst\ *adj* : first in time, place, or order —**foremost** *adv*

fore·noon \'fŏr‚nün\ *n* : morning

fo·ren·sic \fə'rensik\ *adj* : relating to courts or public speaking or debate

fo·ren·sics \-siks\ *n pl* : art or study of speaking or debating

fore·or·dain \‚fŏrŏr'dān\ *vb* : decree beforehand

fore·quar·ter \'fŏr‚kwŏrtər\ *n* : front half on one side of the body of a quadruped

fore·run·ner \'fŏr‚rənər\ *n* : one that goes before

fore·see \fŏr'sē\ *vb* -**saw; -seen; -see·ing** : see or realize beforehand —**fore·see·able** *adj*

fore·shad·ow \'fŏr‚shadō\ *vb* : hint or suggest beforehand

fore·sight \'fŏr‚sīt\ *n* : care or provision for the future —**fore·sight·ed** *adj* —**fore·sight·ed·ness** *n*

for·est \'fŏrəst\ *n* : large thick growth of trees and underbrush —**for·est·ed** \'fŏrəstəd\ *adj* —**for·est·er** \-əstər\ *n* —**for·est·land** \-‚land\ *n* —**for·est·ry** \-əstrē\ *n*

fore·stall \fŏr'stŏl, fŏr-\ *vb* : prevent by acting in advance

foreswear *var of* FORSWEAR

fore·taste \'fōr,tāst\ *n* : advance indication or notion ~ *vb* : anticipate

fore·tell \fōr'tel\ *vb* **-told; -tell·ing** : predict

fore·thought \'fōr,thȯt\ *n* : foresight

for·ev·er \fōr'evər\ *adv* 1 : for a limitless time 2 : always

for·ev·er·more \-,evər'mōr\ *adv* : forever

fore·warn \fōr'wȯrn\ *vb* : warn beforehand

fore·word \'fōrwərd\ *n* : preface

for·feit \'fōrfət\ *n* : something forfeited ~ *vb* : lose or lose the right to by an error or crime —**for·fei·ture** \-fə,chu̇r\ *n*

¹**forge** \'fȯrj\ *n* : smithy ~ *vb* **forged; forg·ing** 1 : form (metal) by heating and hammering 2 : imitate falsely esp. to defraud —**forg·er** *n* —**forg·ery** \-ərē\ *n*

²**forge** *vb* **forged; forg·ing** : move ahead steadily

for·get \fər'get\ *vb* **-got** \-'gät\; **-got·ten** \-'gätᵊn\ *or* **-got; -get·ting** 1 : be unable to think of or recall 2 : fail to think of at the proper time —**for·get·ta·ble** *adj* —**for·get·ful** \-fəl\ *adj* —**for·get·ful·ly** *adv*

forget-me-not *n* : small herb with blue or white flowers

for·give \fər'giv\ *vb* **-gave** \-'gāv\; **-giv·en** \-'givən\; **-giv·ing** : pardon —**for·giv·able** *adj* —**for·give·ness** *n*

for·giv·ing *adj* 1 : able to forgive 2 : allowing room for error or weakness

for·go, fore·go \fōr'gō\ *vb* **-went; -gone; -go·ing** : do without

fork \'fȯrk\ *n* 1 : implement with prongs for lifting, holding, or digging 2 : forked part 3 : a dividing into branches or a place where something branches ~ *vb* 1 : divide into branches 2 : move with a fork —**forked** \'fȯrkt, 'fȯrkəd\ *adj*

fork·lift *n* : machine for lifting with steel fingers

for·lorn \fər'lȯrn\ *adj* 1 : deserted 2 : wretched —**for·lorn·ly** *adv*

form \'fȯrm\ *n* 1 : shape 2 : set way of doing or saying something 3 : document with blanks to be filled in 4 : manner of performing with respect to what is expected 5 : mold 6 : kind or variety 7 : one of the ways in which a word is changed to show difference in use ~ *vb* 1 : give form or shape to

2 : train 3 : develop 4 : constitute —**for·ma·tive** \'fȯrmətiv\ *adj* —**form·less** \-ləs\ *adj*

for·mal \'fȯrməl\ *adj* : following established custom ~ *n* : formal social event —**for·mal·i·ty** \fȯr'malətē\ *n* —**for·mal·ize** \'fȯrmə,līz\ *vb* —**for·mal·ly** *adv*

form·al·de·hyde \fȯr'maldə,hīd\ *n* : colorless pungent gas used as a preservative and disinfectant

for·mat \'fȯr,mat\ *n* : general style or arrangement of something —**format** *vb*

for·ma·tion \fȯr'māshən\ *n* 1 : a giving form to something 2 : something formed 3 : arrangement

for·mer \'fȯrmər\ *adj* : coming before in time —**for·mer·ly** *adv*

for·mi·da·ble \'fȯrmədəbəl, fȯr'mid-\ *adj* 1 : causing fear or dread 2 : very difficult —**for·mi·da·bly** \-blē\ *adv*

for·mu·la \'fȯrmyələ\ *n, pl* **-las** *or* **-lae** \-,lē, -,lī\ 1 : set form of words for ceremonial use 2 : recipe 3 : milk mixture for a baby 4 : group of symbols or figures briefly expressing information 5 : set form or method

for·mu·late \-,lāt\ *vb* **-lat·ed; -lat·ing** : design, devise —**for·mu·la·tion** \,fȯrmyə'lāshən\ *n*

for·ni·ca·tion \,fȯrnə'kāshən\ *n* : illicit sexual intercourse —**for·ni·cate** \'fȯrnə,kāt\ *vb* —**for·ni·ca·tor** \-,kātər\ *n*

for·sake \fər'sāk\ *vb* **-sook** \-'su̇k\; **-sak·en** \-'sākən\; **-sak·ing** : renounce completely

for·swear \fȯr'swar\ *vb* **-swore; -sworn; -swear·ing** 1 : renounce under oath 2 : perjure

for·syth·ia \fər'sithēə\ *n* : shrub grown for its yellow flowers

fort \'fȯrt\ *n* 1 : fortified place 2 : permanent army post

forte \'fȯrt, 'fȯr,tā\ *n* : something at which a person excels

forth \'fȯrth\ *adv* : forward

forth·com·ing *adj* 1 : coming or available soon 2 : open and direct

forth·right *adj* : direct —**forth·right·ly** *adv* —**forth·right·ness** *n*

forth·with *adv* : immediately

for·ti·fy \'fȯrtə,fī\ *vb* **-fied; -fy·ing** : make strong —**for·ti·fi·ca·tion** \,fȯrtəfə'kāshən\ *n*

for·ti·tude \'fȯrtə,tüd, -,tyüd\ *n* : ability to endure

fort·night \'fort,nīt\ n : 2 weeks —**fort·night·ly** adj or adv

fort·ress \'fortrəs\ n : strong fort

for·tu·itous \for'tüətəs, -'tyü-\ adj : accidental

for·tu·nate \'forchənət\ adj 1 : coming by good luck 2 : lucky —**for·tu·nate·ly** adv

for·tune \'forchən\ n 1 : prosperity attained partly through luck 2 : good or bad luck 3 : destiny 4 : wealth

fortune–tell·er \-,telər\ n : one who foretells a person's future —**for·tune–tell·ing** \-iŋ\ n or adj

for·ty \'fortē\ n, pl **forties** : 4 times 10 —**for·ti·eth** \-ēəth\ adj or n —**forty** adj or pron

fo·rum \'forəm\ n, pl **-rums** 1 : Roman marketplace 2 : medium for open discussion

for·ward \'forwərd\ adj 1 : being near or at or belonging to the front 2 : brash ~ adv : toward what is in front ~ n : player near the front of his team ~ vb 1 : help onward 2 : send on —**for·ward·er** \-wərdər\ n —**for·ward·ness** n

for·wards \'forwərdz\ adv : forward

fos·sil \'fäsəl\ n : preserved trace of an ancient plant or animal ~ adj : being or originating from a fossil —**fos·sil·ize** vb

fos·ter \'fostər\ adj : being, having, or relating to substitute parents ~ vb : help to grow or develop

fought past of FIGHT

foul \'faul\ adj 1 : offensive 2 : clogged with dirt 3 : abusive 4 : wet and stormy 5 : unfair ~ n 1 : a breaking of the rules in a game ~ adv : foully ~ vb 1 : make or become foul or filthy 2 : tangle —**foul·ly** adv —**foul-mouthed** \-'mauthd, -'mautht\ adj —**foul·ness** n

fou·lard \fu'lärd\ n : lightweight silk

foul-up n : error or state of confusion —**foul up** vb : bungle

¹found \'faund\ past of FIND

²found vb : establish —**found·er** n

foun·da·tion \faun'dāshən\ n 1 : act of founding 2 : basis for something 3 : endowed institution 4 : supporting structure —**foun·da·tion·al** \-shənəl\ adj

foun·der \'faundər\ vb : sink

found·ling \'faundliŋ\ n : abandoned infant that is found

found·ry \'faundrē\ n, pl **-dries** : place where metal is cast

fount \'faunt\ n : fountain

foun·tain \'fauntᵊn\ n 1 : spring of water 2 : source 3 : artificial jet of water

four \'for\ n 1 : one more than 3 2 : 4th in a set or series 3 : something having 4 units —**four** adj or pron

four·fold adj : quadruple —**four·fold** adv

four·score adj : 80

four·some \'forsəm\ n : group of 4

four·teen \for'tēn\ n : one more than 13 —**fourteen** adj or pron —**four·teenth** \-'tēnth\ adj or n

fourth \'forth\ n 1 : one that is 4th 2 : one of 4 equal parts of something —**fourth** adj or adv

fowl \'faul\ n, pl **fowl** or **fowls** 1 : bird 2 : chicken

fox \'fäks\ n, pl **fox·es** 1 : small mammal related to wolves 2 : clever person ~ vb : trick —**foxy** \'fäksē\ adj

fox·glove n : flowering plant that provides digitalis

fox·hole \'fäks,hōl\ n : pit for protection against enemy fire

foy·er \'foiər, 'foi,yā\ n : entrance hallway

fra·cas \'frākəs, 'frak-\ n, pl **-cas·es** \-əsəz\ : brawl

frac·tion \'frakshən\ n 1 : number indicating one or more equal parts of a whole 2 : portion —**frac·tion·al** \-shənəl\ adj —**frac·tion·al·ly** adv

frac·tious \'frakshəs\ adj : hard to control

frac·ture \'frakchər\ n : a breaking of something —**fracture** vb

frag·ile \'frajəl, -,īl\ adj : easily broken —**fra·gil·i·ty** \frə'jilətē\ n

frag·ment \'fragmənt\ n : part broken off ~ \-,ment\ vb : break into parts —**frag·men·tary** \'fragmən,terē\ adj —**frag·men·ta·tion** \,fragmən'tāshən, -,men-\ n

fra·grant \'frāgrənt\ adj : sweet-smelling —**fra·grance** \-grəns\ n —**fra·grant·ly** adv

frail \'frāl\ adj : weak or delicate —**frail·ty** \-tē\ n

frame \'frām\ vb **framed; fram·ing** 1 : plan 2 : formulate 3 : construct or arrange 4 : enclose in a frame 5 : make appear guilty ~ n 1 : makeup of the body 2 : supporting or enclosing structure 3 : state or disposition (as of mind) —**frame·work** n

franc \'fraŋk\ *n* : monetary unit (as of France)

fran·chise \'fran,chīz\ *n* 1 : special privilege 2 : the right to vote —**fran·chi·see** \,fran,chī'zē, -chə-\ *n*

fran·gi·ble \'franjəbəl\ *adj* : breakable —**fran·gi·bil·i·ty** \,franjə'bilətē\ *n*

¹frank \'fraŋk\ *adj* : direct and sincere —**frank·ly** *adv* —**frank·ness** *n*

²frank *vb* : mark (mail) with a sign showing it can be mailed free ~ *n* : sign on franked mail

frank·furt·er \'fraŋkfərtər, -,fərt-\, **frank·furt** \-fərt\ *n* : cooked sausage

frank·in·cense \'fraŋkən,sens\ *n* : incense resin

fran·tic \'frantik\ *adj* : wildly excited —**fran·ti·cal·ly** \-iklē\ *adv*

fra·ter·nal \frə'tərn³l\ *adj* 1 : brotherly 2 : of a fraternity —**fra·ter·nal·ly** *adv*

fra·ter·ni·ty \frə'tərnətē\ *n, pl* **-ties** : men's student social group

frat·er·nize \'fratər,nīz\ *vb* **-nized; -niz·ing** 1 : mingle as friends 2 : associate with members of a hostile group —**frat·er·ni·za·tion** \,fratərnə'zāshən\ *n*

frat·ri·cide \'fratrə,sīd\ *n* : killing of a sibling —**frat·ri·cid·al** \,fratrə'sīd³l\ *adj*

fraud \'frȯd\ *n* : trickery —**fraud·u·lent** \'frȯjələnt\ *adj* —**fraud·u·lent·ly** *adv*

fraught \'frȯt\ *adj* : full of or accompanied by something specified

¹fray \'frā\ *n* : fight

²fray *vb* 1 : wear by rubbing 2 : separate the threads of 3 : irritate

fraz·zle \'frazəl\ *vb* **-zled; -zling** : wear out ~ *n* : exhaustion

freak \'frēk\ *n* 1 : something abnormal or unusual 2 : enthusiast —**freak·ish** *adj* —**freak out** *vb* 1 : experience nightmarish hallucinations from drugs 2 : distress or become distressed

freck·le \'frekəl\ *n* : brown spot on the skin —**freckle** *vb*

free \'frē\ *adj* **fre·er; fre·est** 1 : having liberty or independence 2 : not taxed 3 : given without charge 4 : voluntary 5 : not in use 6 : not fastened ~ *adv* : without charge ~ *vb* **freed; free·ing** : set free —**free** *adv* —**free·born** *adj* —**free·dom** \'frēdəm\ *n* —**free·ly** *adv*

free·boot·er \-,bütər\ *n* : pirate

free-for-all *n* : fight with no rules

free·load *vb* : live off another's generosity —**free·load·er** *n*

free·stand·ing *adj* : standing without support

free·way \'frē,wā\ *n* : expressway

free will *n* : independent power to choose —**free·will** *adj*

freeze \'frēz\ *vb* **froze** \'frōz\; **fro·zen** \'frōz³n\; **freez·ing** 1 : harden into ice 2 : become chilled 3 : damage by frost 4 : stick fast 5 : become motionless 6 : fix at one stage or level ~ *n* 1 : very cold weather 2 : state of being frozen —**freez·er** *n*

freeze-dry *vb* : preserve by freezing then drying —**freeze-dried** *adj*

freight \'frāt\ *n* 1 : carrying of goods or payment for this 2 : shipped goods ~ *vb* : load or ship goods —**freight·er** *n*

french fry *vb* : fry in deep fat —**french fry** *n*

fre·net·ic \fri'netik\ *adj* : frantic —**fre·net·i·cal·ly** \-iklē\ *adv*

fren·zy \'frenzē\ *n, pl* **-zies** : violent agitation —**fren·zied** \-zēd\ *adj*

fre·quen·cy \'frēkwənsē\ *n, pl* **-cies** 1 : frequent or regular occurrence 2 : number of cycles or sound waves per second

fre·quent \'frēkwənt\ *adj* : happening often ~ \frē'kwent, 'frēkwənt\ *vb* : go to habitually —**fre·quent·er** *n* —**fre·quent·ly** *adv*

fres·co \'freskō\ *n, pl* **-coes** : painting on fresh plaster

fresh \'fresh\ *adj* 1 : not salt 2 : pure 3 : not preserved 4 : not stale 5 : like new 6 : insolent —**fresh·en** \-ən\ *vb* —**fresh·ly** *adv* —**fresh·ness** *n*

fresh·et \-ət\ *n* : overflowing stream

fresh·man \-mən\ *n* : first-year student

fresh·wa·ter *n* : water that is not salty

fret \'fret\ *vb* **-tt-** 1 : worry or become irritated 2 : fray 3 : agitate ~ *n* 1 : worn spot 2 : irritation —**fret·ful** \-fəl\ *adj* —**fret·ful·ly** *adv* —**fret·ful·ness** *n*

fri·a·ble \'frīəbəl\ *adj* : easily pulverized

fri·ar \'frīər\ *n* : member of a religious order

fri·ary \-ē\ *n, pl* **-ar·ies** : monastery of friars

fric·as·see \'frikə,sē, ,frikə'-\ *n* : meat stewed in a gravy ~ *vb* **-seed; -see·ing** : stew in gravy

fric·tion \'frikshən\ *n* 1 : a rubbing between 2 surfaces 2 : clash of opinions —**fric·tion·al** *adj*

Fri·day \'frīdā\ *n* : 6th day of the week

friend \'frend\ *n* : person one likes —

friend·less \-ləs\ adj —**friend·li·ness** \-lēnəs\ n —**friend·ly** adj —**friend·ship** \-,ship\ n

frieze \'frēz\ n : ornamental band around a room

frig·ate \'frigət\ n : warship smaller than a destroyer

fright \'frīt\ n : sudden fear —**frigh·ten** \-ᵊn\ vb —**fright·ful** \-fəl\ adj —**fright·ful·ly** adv —**fright·ful·ness** n

frig·id \'frijəd\ adj : intensely cold —**fri·gid·i·ty** \frij'idətē\ n

frill \'fril\ n 1 : ruffle 2 : pleasing but nonessential addition —**frilly** adj

fringe \'frinj\ n 1 : ornamental border of short hanging threads or strips 2 : edge —**fringe** vb

frisk \'frisk\ vb 1 : leap about 2 : search (a person) esp. for weapons

frisky \'friskē\ adj **frisk·i·er; -est** : playful —**frisk·i·ly** adv —**frisk·i·ness** n

¹frit·ter \'fritər\ n : fried batter containing fruit or meat

²fritter vb : waste little by little

friv·o·lous \'frivələs\ adj : not important or serious —**fri·vol·i·ty** \friv'älətē\ n —**friv·o·lous·ly** adv

frizz \'friz\ vb : curl tightly —**frizz** n —**frizzy** adj

fro \'frō\ adv : away

frock \'fräk\ n 1 : loose outer garment 2 : dress

frog \'frog, 'fräg\ n 1 : leaping amphibian 2 : hoarseness 3 : ornamental braid fastener 4 : small holder for flowers

frog·man \-,man, -mən\ n : underwater swimmer

frol·ic \'frälik\ vb **-icked; -ick·ing** : romp ~ n : fun —**frol·ic·some** \-səm\ adj

from \'frəm, 'främ\ prep —used to show a starting point

frond \'fränd\ n : fern or palm leaf

front \'frənt\ n 1 : face 2 : behavior 3 : main side of a building 4 : forward part 5 : boundary between air masses ~ vb 1 : have the main side adjacent to something 2 : serve as a front —**fron·tal** \-ᵊl\ adj

front·age \'frəntij\ n : length of boundary line on a street

fron·tier \,frən'tir\ n : outer edge of settled territory —**fron·tiers·man** \-'tirzmən\ n

fron·tis·piece \'frəntə,spēs\ n : illustration facing a title page

frost \'frost\ n 1 : freezing temperature 2 : ice crystals on a surface ~ vb 1 : cover with frost 2 : put icing on (a cake) —**frosty** adj

frost·bite \-,bīt\ n : partial freezing of part of the body —**frost·bit·ten** \-,bitᵊn\ adj

frost·ing n : icing

froth \'froth\ n, pl **froths** \'froths, 'frothz\ : bubbles on a liquid —**frothy** adj

fro·ward \'frōwərd\ adj : willful

frown \'fraun\ vb or n : scowl

frow·sy, frow·zy \'frauzē\ adj **-si·er** or **-zi·er, -est** : untidy

froze past of FREEZE

frozen past part of FREEZE

fru·gal \'frügəl\ adj : thrifty —**fru·gal·i·ty** \frü'galətē\ n —**fru·gal·ly** adv

fruit \'früt\ n 1 : usu. edible and sweet part of a seed plant 2 : result ~ vb : bear fruit —**fruit·cake** n —**fruit·ed** \-əd\ adj —**fruit·ful** adj —**fruit·ful·ness** n —**fruit·less** adj —**fruit·less·ly** adv —**fruity** adj

fru·ition \frü'ishən\ n : completion

frum·py \'frəmpē\ adj **frump·i·er; -est** : dowdy

frus·trate \'frəs,trāt\ vb **-trat·ed; -trat·ing** 1 : block 2 : cause to fail —**frus·trat·ing·ly** adv —**frus·tra·tion** \,frəs'trāshən\ n

¹fry \'frī\ vb **fried; fry·ing** 1 : cook esp. with fat or oil 2 : be cooked by frying ~ n, pl **fries** 1 : something fried 2 : social gathering with fried food

²fry n, pl **fry** : recently hatched fish

fud·dle \'fədᵊl\ vb **-dled; -dling** : muddle

fud·dy-dud·dy \'fədē,dədē\ n, pl **-dies** : one who is old-fashioned or unimaginative

fudge \'fəj\ vb **fudged; fudg·ing** : cheat or exaggerate ~ n : creamy candy

fu·el \'fyüəl\ n : material burned to produce heat or power ~ vb **-eled** or **-elled; -el·ing** or **-el·ling** : provide with or take in fuel

fu·gi·tive \'fyüjətiv\ adj 1 : running away or trying to escape 2 : not lasting —**fugitive** n

-ful \'fəl\ adj suffix 1 : full of 2 : having the qualities of 3 : -able ~ n suffix : quantity that fills

ful·crum \'fulkrəm, 'fəl-\ n, pl **-crums** or **-cra** \-krə\ : support on which a lever turns

ful·fill, ful·fil \fùl'fil\ *vb* **-filled; -fill·ing** 1 : perform 2 : satisfy —**ful·fill·ment** *n*

¹full \'fùl\ *adj* 1 : filled 2 : complete 3 : rounded 4 : having an abundance of something ~ *adv* : entirely .~ *n* : utmost degree —**full·ness** *n* —**ful·ly** *adv*

²full *vb* : shrink and thicken woolen cloth —**full·er** *n*

full–fledged \'fùl'flejd\ *adj* : fully developed

ful·some \'fùlsəm\ *adj* : copious verging on excessive

fum·ble \'fəmbəl\ *vb* **-bled; -bling** : fail to hold something properly —**fumble** *n*

fume \'fyüm\ *n* : irritating gas ~ *vb* **fumed; fum·ing** 1 : give off fumes 2 : show annoyance

fu·mi·gate \'fyümə,gāt\ *vb* **-gat·ed; -gat·ing** : treat with pest-killing fumes —**fu·mi·gant** \'fyümigənt\ *n* —**fu·mi·ga·tion** \,fyümə'gāshən\ *n*

fun \'fən\ *n* 1 : something providing amusement or enjoyment 2 : enjoyment ~ *adj* : full of fun

func·tion \'fəŋkshən\ *n* 1 : special purpose 2 : formal ceremony or social affair ~ *vb* : have or carry on a function —**func·tion·al** \-shənəl\ *adj* —**func·tion·al·ly** *adv*

func·tion·ary \-shə,nerē\ *n, pl* **-ar·ies** : official

fund \'fənd\ *n* 1 : store 2 : sum of money intended for a special purpose 3 *pl* : available money ~ *vb* : provide funds for

fun·da·men·tal \,fəndə'mentᵊl\ *adj* 1 : basic 2 : of central importance or necessity —**fundamental** *n* —**fun·da·men·tal·ly** *adv*

fu·ner·al \'fyünərəl\ *n* : ceremony for a dead person —**funeral** *adj* —**fu·ne·re·al** \fyü'nirēəl\ *adj*

fun·gi·cide \'fənjə,sīd, 'fəŋgə-\ *n* : agent that kills fungi —**fun·gi·cid·al** \,fənjə'sīdᵊl, ,fəŋgə-\ *adj*

fun·gus \'fəŋgəs\ *n, pl* **fun·gi** \'fən,jī, 'fəŋ,gī\ : lower plant that lacks chlorophyll —**fun·gal** \'fəŋgəl\ *adj* —**fun·gous** \-gəs\ *adj*

funk \'fəŋk\ *n* : state of depression

funky \'fəŋkē\ *adj* **funk·i·er; -est** : unconventional and unsophisticated

fun·nel \'fənᵊl\ *n* 1 : cone-shaped utensil with a tube for directing the flow of a liquid 2 : ship's smokestack ~

vb **-neled; -nel·ing** : move to a central point or into a central channel

fun·nies \'fənēz\ *n pl* : section of comic strips

fun·ny \'fənē\ *adj* **-ni·er; -est** 1 : amusing 2 : strange

fur \'fər\ *n* 1 : hairy coat of a mammal 2 : article of clothing made with fur —**fur** *adj* —**furred** \'fərd\ *adj* —**fur·ry** \-ē\ *adj*

fur·bish \'fərbish\ *vb* : make lustrous or new looking

fu·ri·ous \'fyùrēəs\ *adj* : fierce or angry —**fu·ri·ous·ly** *adv*

fur·long \'fər,lóŋ\ *n* : a unit of distance equal to 220 yards

fur·lough \'fərlō\ *n* : authorized absence from duty —**furlough** *vb*

fur·nace \'fərnəs\ *n* : enclosed structure in which heat is produced

fur·nish \'fərnish\ *vb* 1 : provide with what is needed 2 : make available for use

fur·nish·ings \-iŋs\ *n pl* 1 : articles or accessories of dress 2 : furniture

fur·ni·ture \'fərnichər\ *n* : movable articles for a room

fu·ror \'fyùr,ór\ *n* 1 : anger 2 : sensational craze

fur·ri·er \'fərēər\ *n* : dealer in furs

fur·row \'fərō\ *n* 1 : trench made by a plow 2 : wrinkle or groove —**furrow** *vb*

fur·ther \'fər<u>th</u>ər\ *adv* 1 : at or to a more advanced point 2 : more ~ *adj* : additional ~ *vb* : promote —**fur·ther·ance** \-ərəns\ *n*

fur·ther·more \'fər<u>th</u>ər,mōr\ *adv* : in addition

fur·ther·most \-,mōst\ *adj* : most distant

fur·thest \'fər<u>th</u>əst\ *adv or adj* : farthest

fur·tive \'fərtiv\ *adj* : slyly or secretly done —**fur·tive·ly** *adv* —**fur·tive·ness** *n*

fu·ry \'fyùrē\ *n, pl* **-ries** 1 : intense rage 2 : violence

¹fuse \'fyüz\ *n* 1 : cord lighted to transmit fire to an explosive 2 *usu* **fuze** : device for exploding a charge ~, **fuse** *vb* **fused** *or* **fuzed**; **fus·ing** *or* **fuz·ing** : equip with a fuse

²fuse *vb* **fused; fus·ing** 1 : melt and run together 2 : unite ~ *n* : electrical safety device —**fus·ible** *adj*

fu·se·lage \'fyüsə,läzh, -zə-\ *n* : main body of an aircraft

fu·sil·lade \'fyüsə,läd, -,lād, ,fyüsə'-, -zə-\ *n* : volley of fire

fu·sion \'fyüzhən\ *n* 1 : process of merging by melting 2 : union of atomic nuclei

fuss \'fəs\ *n* 1 : needless bustle or excitement 2 : show of attention 3 : objection or protest ~ *vb* : make a fuss

fuss·bud·get \-ˌbəjət\ *n* : one who fusses or is fussy about trifles

fussy \'fəsē\ *adj* **fuss·i·er; -est** 1 : irritable 2 : paying very close attention to details —**fuss·i·ly** *adv* — **fuss·i·ness** *n*

fu·tile \'fyütᵊl, 'fyüˌtīl\ *adj* : useless or vain —**fu·til·i·ty** \fyü'tilətē\ *n*

fu·ture \'fyüchər\ *adj* : coming after the present ~ *n* 1 : time yet to come 2 : what will happen —**fu·tur·is·tic** \ˌfyüchə'ristik\ *adj*

fuze *var of* FUSE

fuzz \'fəz\ *n* : fine particles or fluff

fuzzy \-ē\ *adj* **fuzz·i·er; -est** 1 : covered with or like fuzz 2 : indistinct —**fuzz·i·ness** *n*

-fy \ˌfī\ *vb suffix* : make —**-fi·er** \ˌfīər\ *n suffix*

G

g \'jē\ *n, pl* **g's** *or* **gs** \'jēz\ 1 : 7th letter of the alphabet 2 : unit of gravitational force

gab \'gab\ *vb* **-bb-** : chatter —**gab** *n* — **gab·by** \'gabē\ *adj*

gab·ar·dine \'gabərˌdēn\ *n* : durable twilled fabric

ga·ble \'gābəl\ *n* : triangular part of the end of a building —**ga·bled** \-bəld\ *adj*

gad \'gad\ *vb* **-dd-** : roam about —**gad·der** *n*

gad·fly *n* : persistently critical person

gad·get \'gajət\ *n* : device —**gad·get·ry** \'gajətrē\ *n*

gaff \'gaf\ *n* : metal hook for lifting fish —**gaff** *vb*

gaffe \'gaf\ *n* : social blunder

gag \'gag\ *vb* **-gg-** 1 : prevent from speaking or crying out by stopping up the mouth 2 : retch or cause to retch ~ *n* 1 : something that stops up the mouth 2 : laugh-provoking remark or act

gage *var of* GAUGE

gag·gle \'gagəl\ *n* : flock of geese

gai·ety \'gāətē\ *n, pl* **-eties** : high spirits

gai·ly \'gālē\ *adv* : in a gay manner

gain \'gān\ *n* 1 : profit 2 : obtaining of profit or possessions 3 : increase ~ *vb* 1 : get possession of 2 : win 3 : arrive at 4 : increase or increase in 5 : profit —**gain·er** *n* —**gain·ful** *adj* —**gain·ful·ly** *adv*

gain·say \gān'sā\ *vb* **-said** \-'sād, -'sed\; **-say·ing; -says** \-'sāz, -'sez\ : deny or dispute —**gain·say·er** *n*

gait \'gāt\ *n* : manner of walking or running —**gait·ed** *adj*

gal \'gal\ *n* : girl

ga·la \'gālə, 'galə, 'gälə\ *n* : festive celebration —**gala** *adj*

gal·axy \'galəksē\ *n, pl* **-ax·ies** : very large group of stars —**ga·lac·tic** \gə'laktik\ *adj*

gale \'gāl\ *n* 1 : strong wind 2 : outburst

¹gall \'gȯl\ *n* 1 : bile 2 : insolence

²gall *n* 1 : skin sore caused by chafing 2 : swelling of plant tissue caused by parasites ~ *vb* 1 : chafe 2 : irritate or vex

gal·lant \gə'lant, -'länt; 'galənt\ *n* : man very attentive to women ~ \'galənt; gə'lant, -'länt\ *adj* 1 : splendid 2 : brave 3 : polite and attentive to women —**gal·lant·ly** *adv* —**gal·lant·ry** \'galəntrē\ *n*

gall·blad·der *n* : pouch attached to the liver in which bile is stored

gal·le·on \'galyən\ *n* : large sailing ship formerly used esp. by the Spanish

gal·lery \'galərē\ *n, pl* **-ler·ies** 1 : outdoor balcony 2 : long narrow passage or hall 3 : room or building for exhibiting art 4 : spectators —**gal·ler·ied** \-rēd\ *adj*

gal·ley \'galē\ *n, pl* **-leys** 1 : old ship propelled by oars 2 : kitchen of a ship or airplane

gal·li·um \'galēəm\ *n* : bluish white metallic chemical element

gal·li·vant \'galəˌvant\ *vb* : travel or roam about for pleasure

gal·lon \'galən\ *n* : unit of liquid measure equal to 4 quarts

gal·lop \'galəp\ *n* : fast 3-beat gait of a horse —**gallop** *vb* —**gal·lop·er** *n*

gal·lows \'galōz\ *n, pl* -**lows** *or* -**lows·es** : upright frame for hanging criminals

gall·stone *n* : abnormal concretion in the gallbladder or bile passages

ga·lore \gə'lōr\ *adj* : in abundance

ga·losh \gə'läsh\ *n* : overshoe —usu. pl.

gal·va·nize \'galvə,nīz\ *vb* -**nized**; -**niz·ing** 1 : shock into action 2 : coat (iron or steel) with zinc —**gal·va·ni·za·tion** \,galvənə'zāshən\ *n* —**gal·va·niz·er** *n*

gam·bit \'gambit\ *n* 1 : opening tactic in chess 2 : stratagem

gam·ble \'gambəl\ *vb* -**bled**; -**bling** 1 : play a game for stakes 2 : bet 3 : take a chance ~ *n* : risky undertaking —**gam·bler** \-blər\ *n*

gam·bol \'gambəl\ *vb* -**boled** *or* -**bolled**; -**bol·ing** *or* -**bol·ling** : skip about in play —**gambol** *n*

game \'gām\ *n* 1 : playing activity 2 : competition according to rules 3 : animals hunted for sport or food ~ *vb* gamed; gam·ing : gamble ~ *adj* 1 : plucky 2 : lame —**game·ly** *adv* —**game·ness** *n*

game·cock *n* : fighting cock

game·keep·er *n* : person in charge of game animals or birds

gam·ete \gə'mēt, 'gam,ēt\ *n* : mature germ cell —**ga·met·ic** \gə'metik\ *adj*

ga·mine \ga'mēn\ *n* : charming tomboy

gam·ut \'gamət\ *n* : entire range or series

gamy *or* **gam·ey** \'gāmē\ *adj* **gam·i·er**; -**est** : having the flavor of game esp. when slightly tainted —**gam·i·ness** *n*

¹**gan·der** \'gandər\ *n* : male goose

²**gander** *n* : glance

gang \'gaŋ\ *n* 1 : group of persons working together 2 : group of criminals ~ *vb* : attack in a gang —**with** *up*

gan·gling \'gaŋgliŋ\ *adj* : lanky

gan·gli·on \'gaŋglēən\ *n, pl* -**glia** \-glēə\ : mass of nerve cells

gang·plank *n* : platform used in boarding or leaving a ship

gan·grene \'gaŋ,grēn, gaŋ-; 'gan-, gan-\ *n* : local death of body tissue —**gangrene** *vb* —**gan·gre·nous** \'gaŋgrənəs\ *adj*

gang·ster \'gaŋstər\ *n* : member of criminal gang

gang·way \-,wā\ *n* : passage in or out

gan·net \'ganət\ *n* : large fish-eating marine bird

gan·try \'gantrē\ *n, pl* -**tries** : frame structure supported over or around something

gap \'gap\ *n* 1 : break in a barrier 2 : mountain pass 3 : empty space

gape \'gāp\ *vb* gaped; gap·ing 1 : open widely 2 : stare with mouth open —**gape** *n*

ga·rage \gə'räzh, -'räj\ *n* : shelter or repair shop for automobiles ~ *vb* -**raged**; -**rag·ing** : put or keep in a garage

garb \'gärb\ *n* : clothing ~ *vb* : dress

gar·bage \'gärbij\ *n* 1 : food waste 2 : trash —**gar·bage·man** *n*

gar·ble \'gärbəl\ *vb* -**bled**; -**bling** : distort the meaning of

gar·den \'gärdᵊn\ *n* 1 : plot for growing fruits, flowers, or vegetables 2 : public recreation area ~ *vb* : work in a garden —**gar·den·er** \'gärdᵊnər\ *n*

gar·de·nia \gär'dēnyə\ *n* : tree or shrub with fragrant white or yellow flowers or the flower

gar·gan·tuan \gär'ganchəwən\ *adj* : having tremendous size or volume

gar·gle \'gärgəl\ *vb* -**gled**; -**gling** : rinse the throat with liquid —**gargle** *n*

gar·goyle \'gär,goil\ *n* : waterspout in the form of a grotesque human or animal

gar·ish \'garish\ *adj* : offensively bright or gaudy

gar·land \'gärlənd\ *n* : wreath ~ *vb* : form into or deck with a garland

gar·lic \'gärlik\ *n* : herb with pungent bulbs used in cooking —**gar·licky** \-likē\ *adj*

gar·ment \'gärmənt\ *n* : article of clothing

gar·ner \'gärnər\ *vb* : acquire by effort

gar·net \'gärnət\ *n* : deep red mineral

gar·nish \'gärnish\ *vb* : add decoration to (as food) —**garnish** *n*

gar·nish·ee \,gärnə'shē\ *vb* -**eed**; -**ee·ing** : take (as a debtor's wages) by legal authority

gar·nish·ment \'gärnishmənt\ *n* : attachment of property to satisfy a creditor

gar·ret \'garət\ *n* : attic

gar·ri·son \'garəsən\ *n* : military post or the troops stationed there —**garrison** *vb*

gar·ru·lous \'garələs\ *adj* : talkative —

gar·ru·li·ty \gə'rülətē\ n —**gar·ru·lous·ly** adv —**gar·ru·lous·ness** n

gar·ter \'gärtər\ n : band to hold up a stocking or sock

gas \'gas\ n, pl **gas·es** 1 : fluid (as hydrogen or air) that tends to expand indefinitely 2 : gasoline ~ vb **gassed; gas·sing** 1 : treat with gas 2 : fill with gasoline —**gas·eous** \'gasēəs, 'gashəs\ adj

gash \'gash\ n : deep long cut —**gash** vb

gas·ket \'gaskət\ n : material or a part used to seal a joint

gas·light n : light of burning illuminating gas

gas·o·line \'gasə,lēn, ,gasə'-\ n : flammable liquid from petroleum

gasp \'gasp\ vb 1 : catch the breath audibly 2 : breathe laboriously —**gasp** n

gas·tric \'gastrik\ adj : relating to or located near the stomach

gas·tron·o·my \gas'tränəmē\ n : art of good eating —**gas·tro·nom·ic** \,gastrə'nämik\ adj

gate \'gāt\ n : an opening for passage in a wall or fence —**gate·keep·er** n —**gate·post** n

gate·way n : way in or out

gath·er \'gathər\ vb 1 : bring or come together 2 : harvest 3 : pick up little by little 4 : deduce —**gath·er·er** n —**gath·er·ing** n

gauche \'gōsh\ adj : crude or tactless

gaudy \'gódē\ adj **gaud·i·er; -est** : tastelessly showy —**gaud·i·ly** \'gódəlē\ adv —**gaud·i·ness** n

gauge \'gāj\ n : instrument for measuring ~ vb **gauged; gaug·ing** : measure

gaunt \'gónt\ adj : thin or emaciated —**gaunt·ness** n

¹gaunt·let \-lət\ n 1 : protective glove 2 : challenge to combat

²gauntlet n : ordeal

gauze \'góz\ n : thin often transparent fabric —**gauzy** adj

gave past of GIVE

gav·el \'gavəl\ n : mallet of a presiding officer, auctioneer, or judge

gawk \'gók\ vb : stare stupidly

gawky \-ē\ adj **gawk·i·er; -est** : clumsy

gay \'gā\ adj 1 : merry 2 : bright and lively 3 : homosexual —**gay** n

gaze \'gāz\ vb **gazed; gaz·ing** : fix the eyes in a steady intent look —**gaze** n —**gaz·er** n

ga·zelle \gə'zel\ n : small swift antelope

ga·zette \-'zet\ n : newspaper

gaz·et·teer \,gazə'tir\ n : geographical dictionary

gear \'gir\ n 1 : clothing 2 : equipment 3 : toothed wheel —**gear** vb

gear·shift n : mechanism by which automobile gears are shifted

geek \'gēk\ n : socially inept person

geese pl of GOOSE

gei·sha \'gāshə, 'gē-\ n, pl **-sha** or **-shas** : Japanese girl or woman trained to entertain men

gel·a·tin \'jelət°n\ n : sticky substance obtained from animal tissues by boiling —**ge·lat·i·nous** \jə'lat°nəs\ adj

geld \'geld\ vb : castrate

geld·ing \-iŋ\ n : castrated horse

gem \'jem\ n : cut and polished valuable stone —**gem·stone** n

gen·der \'jendər\ n 1 : sex 2 : division of a class of words (as nouns) that determines agreement of other words

gene \'jēn\ n : segment of DNA that controls inheritance of a trait

ge·ne·al·o·gy \,jēnē'äləjē, ,jen-, -'al-\ n, pl **-gies** : study of family pedigrees —**ge·ne·a·log·i·cal** \-ē-'läjikəl\ adj —**ge·ne·a·log·i·cal·ly** adv —**ge·ne·al·o·gist** \-ē'äləjist, -'al-\ n

genera pl of GENUS

gen·er·al \'jenrəl, 'jenə-\ adj 1 : relating to the whole 2 : applicable to all of a group 3 : common or widespread ~ n 1 : something that involves or is applicable to the whole 2 : commissioned officer in the army, air force, or marine corps ranking above a lieutenant general —**gen·er·al·ly** adv —**in general** : for the most part

gen·er·al·i·ty \,jenə'ralətē\ n, pl **-ties** : general statement

gen·er·al·ize \'jenrə,līz, 'jenə-\ vb **-ized; -iz·ing** : reach a general conclusion esp. on the basis of particular instances —**gen·er·al·iza·tion** \,jenrələ'zāshən, ,jenə-\ n

general of the air force : commissioned officer of the highest rank in the air force

general of the army : commissioned officer of the highest rank in the army

gen·er·ate \'jenə,rāt\ vb **-at·ed; -at·ing** : create or produce

gen·er·a·tion \,jenə'rāshən\ n 1 : living beings constituting a single step in a line of descent 2 : production —**gen·er·a·tive** \'jenə,rātiv, -rət-\ adj

gen·er·a·tor \'jenə,rātər\ n 1 : one that generates 2 : machine that turns mechanical into electrical energy

ge·ner·ic \jə'nerik\ adj 1 : general 2 : not protected by a trademark 3 : relating to a genus —**generic** n

gen·er·ous \'jenərəs\ adj : freely giving or sharing —**gen·er·os·i·ty** \,jenə'räsətē\ n —**gen·er·ous·ly** adv —**gen·er·ous·ness** n

ge·net·ics \jə'netiks\ n : biology dealing with heredity and variation —**ge·net·ic** \-ik\ adj —**ge·net·i·cal·ly** adv —**ge·net·i·cist** \-'netəsist\ n

ge·nial \'jēnēəl\ adj : cheerful —**ge·nial·i·ty** \,jēnē'alətē\ n —**ge·nial·ly** adv

ge·nie \'jēnē\ n : supernatural spirit that often takes human form

gen·i·tal \'jenətᵊl\ adj : concerned with reproduction —**gen·i·tal·ly** \-tᵊlē\ adv

gen·i·ta·lia \,jenə'tālyə\ n pl : external genital organs

gen·i·tals \'jenətᵊlz\ n pl : genitalia

ge·nius \'jēnyəs\ n 1 : single strongly marked capacity 2 : extraordinary intellectual power or a person having such power

geno·cide \'jenə,sīd\ n : systematic destruction of a racial or cultural group

genre \'zhänrə, 'zhäⁿrə\ n : category esp. of literary composition

gen·teel \jen'tēl\ adj : polite or refined

gen·tile \'jen,tīl\ n : person who is not Jewish —**gentile** adj

gen·til·i·ty \jen'tilətē\ n, pl -ties 1 : good birth and family 2 : good manners

gen·tle \'jentᵊl\ adj -tler; -tlest 1 : of a family of high social station 2 : not harsh, stern, or violent 3 : soft or delicate ~ vb -tled; -tling : make gentle —**gen·tle·ness** n —**gen·tly** adv

gen·tle·man \-mən\ n : man of good family or manners —**gen·tle·man·ly** adv

gen·tle·wom·an \-,wŭmən\ n : woman of good family or breeding

gen·try \'jentrē\ n, pl -tries : people of good birth or breeding

gen·u·flect \'jenyə,flekt\ vb : bend the knee in worship —**gen·u·flec·tion** \,jenyə'flekshən\ n

gen·u·ine \'jenyəwən\ adj : being the same in fact as in appearance —**gen·u·ine·ly** adv —**gen·u·ine·ness** n

ge·nus \'jēnəs\ n, pl **gen·era** \'jenərə\ : category of biological classification

ge·ode \'jē,ōd\ n : stone having a mineral-lined cavity

geo·de·sic \,jēə'desik, -'dēs-\ adj : made of a framework of linked polygons

ge·og·ra·phy \jē'ägrəfē\ n 1 : study of the earth and its climate, products, and inhabitants 2 : natural features of a region —**ge·og·ra·pher** \-fər\ n —**geo·graph·ic** \,jēə'grafik\, **geo·graph·i·cal** \-ikəl\ adj —**geo·graph·i·cal·ly** adv

ge·ol·o·gy \jē'äləjē\ n : study of the history of the earth and its life esp. as recorded in rocks —**geo·log·ic** \,jēə'läjik\, **geo·log·i·cal** \-ikəl\ adj —**geo·log·i·cal·ly** adv —**ge·ol·o·gist** \jē-'äləjist\ n

ge·om·e·try \jē'ämətrē\ n, pl -tries : mathematics of the relations, properties, and measurements of solids, surfaces, lines, and angles —**geo·met·ric** \,jēə-'metrik\, **geo·met·ri·cal** \-rikəl\ adj

geo·ther·mal \,jēo'thərməl\ adj : relating to or derived from the heat of the earth's interior

ge·ra·ni·um \jə'rānēəm\ n : garden plant with clusters of white, pink, or scarlet flowers

ger·bil \'jərbəl\ n : burrowing desert rodent

ge·ri·at·ric \,jerē'atrik\ adj 1 : relating to aging or the aged 2 : old

ge·ri·at·rics \-triks\ n : medicine dealing with the aged and aging

germ \'jərm\ n 1 : microorganism 2 : source or rudiment

ger·mane \jər'mān\ adj : relevant

ger·ma·ni·um \-'mānēəm\ n : grayish white hard chemical element

ger·mi·cide \'jərmə,sīd\ n : agent that destroys germs —**ger·mi·cid·al** \,jərmə'sīdᵊl\ adj

ger·mi·nate \'jərmə,nāt\ vb -nat·ed; -nat·ing : begin to develop —**ger·mi·na·tion** \,jərmə'nāshən\ n

ger·ry·man·der \,jerē'mandər, 'jerē,-, ,gerē'-, 'gerē,-\ vb : divide into election districts so as to give one political party an advantage —**gerrymander** n

ger·und \'jerənd\ n : word having the characteristics of both verb and noun

ge·sta·po \gə'stäpō\ n, pl -pos : secret police

ges·ta·tion \je'stāshən\ n : pregnancy or incubation —**ges·tate** \'jes,tāt\ vb

ges·ture \'jeschər\ *n* 1 : movement of the body or limbs that expresses something 2 : something said or done for its effect on the attitudes of others —**ges·tur·al** \-chərəl\ *adj* —**gesture** *vb*

ge·sund·heit \gə'zúnt,hīt\ *interj* —used to wish good health to one who has just sneezed

get \'get\ *vb* **got** \'gät\; **got** *or* **got·ten** \'gät°n\; **get·ting** 1 : gain or be in possession of 2 : succeed in coming or going 3 : cause to come or go or to be in a certain condition or position 4 : become 5 : be subjected to 6 : understand 7 : be obliged —**get along** *vb* 1 : get by 2 : be on friendly terms —**get by** *vb* : meet one's needs

get·away \'getə,wā\ *n* 1 : escape 2 : a starting or getting under way

gey·ser \'gīzər\ *n* : spring that intermittently shoots up hot water and steam

ghast·ly \'gastlē\ *adj* **-li·er; -est** : horrible or shocking

gher·kin \'gərkən\ *n* : small pickle

ghet·to \'getō\ *n, pl* **-tos** *or* **-toes** : part of a city in which members of a minority group live

ghost \'gōst\ *n* : disembodied soul — **ghost·ly** *adv*

ghost·write *vb* **-wrote; -writ·ten** : write for and in the name of another — **ghost·writ·er** *n*

ghoul \'gül\ *n* : legendary evil being that feeds on corpses —**ghoul·ish** *adj*

GI \jē'ī\ *n, pl* **GI's** *or* **GIs** : member of the U.S. armed forces

gi·ant \'jīənt\ *n* 1 : huge legendary being 2 : something very large or very powerful —**giant** *adj*

gib·ber \'jibər\ *vb* **-bered; -ber·ing** : speak rapidly and foolishly

gib·ber·ish \'jibərish\ *n* : unintelligible speech or language

gib·bon \'gibən\ *n* : manlike ape

gibe \'jīb\ *vb* **gibed; gib·ing** : jeer at — **gibe** *n*

gib·lets \'jibləts\ *n pl* : edible fowl viscera

gid·dy \'gidē\ *adj* **-di·er; -est** 1 : silly 2 : dizzy —**gid·di·ness** *n*

gift \'gift\ *n* 1 : something given 2 : talent —**gift·ed** *adj*

gi·gan·tic \jī'gantik\ *adj* : very big

gig·gle \'gigəl\ *vb* **-gled; -gling** : laugh in a silly manner —**giggle** *n* —**gig·gly** \-əlē\ *adj*

gig·o·lo \'jigə,lō\ *n, pl* **-los** : man living on the earnings of a woman

Gi·la monster \'hēlə-\ *n* : large venomous lizard

gild \'gild\ *vb* **gild·ed** \'gildəd\ *or* **gilt** \'gilt\; **gild·ing** : cover with or as if with gold

gill \'gil\ *n* : organ of a fish for obtaining oxygen from water

gilt \'gilt\ *adj* : gold-colored ~ *n* : gold or goldlike substance on the surface of an object

gim·bal \'gimbəl, 'jim-\ *n* : device that allows something to incline freely

gim·let \'gimlət\ *n* : small tool for boring holes

gim·mick \'gimik\ *n* : new and ingenious scheme, feature, or device — **gim·mick·ry** *n* —**gim·micky** \-ikē\ *adj*

gimpy \'gimpē\ *adj* : lame

¹**gin** \'jin\ *n* : machine to separate seeds from cotton —**gin** *vb*

²**gin** *n* : clear liquor flavored with juniper berries

gin·ger \'jinjər\ *n* : pungent aromatic spice from a tropical plant —**gin·ger·bread** *n*

gin·ger·ly *adj* : very cautious or careful —**gingerly** *adv*

ging·ham \'giņəm\ *n* : cotton clothing fabric

gin·gi·vi·tis \,jinjə'vītəs\ *n* : inflammation of the gums

gink·go \'giņkō\ *n, pl* **-goes** *or* **-gos** : tree of eastern China

gin·seng \'jin,siņ, -,seņ, -saņ\ *n* : aromatic root of a Chinese herb

gi·raffe \jə'raf\ *n* : African mammal with a very long neck

gird \'gərd\ *vb* **gird·ed** \'gərdəd\ *or* **girt** \'gərt\; **gird·ing** 1 : encircle or fasten with or as if with a belt 2 : prepare

gird·er \'gərdər\ *n* : horizontal supporting beam

gir·dle \'gərdᵊl\ *n* : woman's supporting undergarment ~ *vb* : surround

girl \'gərl\ *n* 1 : female child 2 : young woman 3 : sweetheart —**girl·hood** \-,hùd\ *n* —**girl·ish** *adj*

girlfriend *n* : frequent or regular female companion of a boy or man

girth \'gərth\ *n* : measure around something

gist \'jist\ *n* : main point or part

give \'giv\ *vb* **gave** \'gāv\; **giv·en** \'givən\; **giv·ing** 1 : put into the possession or keeping of another 2 : pay

3 : perform 4 : contribute or donate 5 : produce 6 : utter 7 : yield to force, strain, or pressure — ~ n : capacity or tendency to yield to force or strain — **give in** vb : surrender — **give out** vb : become used up or exhausted — **give up** vb 1 : let out of one's control 2 : cease from trying, doing, or hoping

give·away \'givən\ n 1 : unintentional betrayal 2 : something given free

giv·en \'givən\ adj 1 : prone or disposed 2 : having been specified

giz·zard \'gizərd\ n : muscular usu. horny-lined enlargement following the crop of a bird

gla·cial \'glāshəl\ adj 1 : relating to glaciers 2 : very slow — **gla·cial·ly** adv

gla·cier \'glāshər\ n : large body of ice moving slowly

glad \'glad\ adj -dd- 1 : experiencing or causing pleasure, joy, or delight 2 : very willing — **glad·den** \-ᵊn\ vb — **glad·ly** adv — **glad·ness** n

glade \'glād\ n : grassy open space in a forest

glad·i·a·tor \'gladē,ātər\ n : one who fought to the death for the entertainment of ancient Romans — **glad·i·a·to·ri·al** \,gladē'tōrēəl\ adj

glad·i·o·lus \,gladē'ōləs\ n, pl -li \-lē, -,lī\ : plant related to the irises

glam·our, **glam·or** \'glamər\ n : romantic or exciting attractiveness — **glam·or·ize** \-ə,rīz\ vb — **glam·or·ous** \-ərəs\ adj

glance \'glans\ vb glanced; glanc·ing 1 : strike and fly off to one side 2 : give a quick look — ~ n : quick look

gland \'gland\ n : group of cells that secretes a substance — **glan·du·lar** \'glanjələr\ adj

glans \'glanz\ n, pl glan·des \'glan,dēz\ : conical vascular body forming the end of the penis or clitoris

glare \'glar\ vb glared; glar·ing 1 : shine with a harsh dazzling light 2 : stare angrily — ~ n 1 : harsh dazzling light 2 : angry stare

glar·ing \'glariŋ\ adj : painfully obvious — **glar·ing·ly** adv

glass \'glas\ n 1 : hard usu. transparent material made by melting sand and other materials 2 : something made of glass 3 pl : lenses used to correct defects of vision — **glass** adj — **glass·ful** \-,fùl\ n — **glass·ware** \-,war\ n — **glassy** adj

glass·blow·ing n : art of shaping a mass of molten glass by blowing air into it — **glass·blow·er** n

glau·co·ma \glaú'kōmə, glò-\ n : state of increased pressure within the eyeball

glaze \'glāz\ vb glazed; glaz·ing 1 : furnish with glass 2 : apply glaze to — ~ n : glassy surface or coating

gla·zier \'glāzhər\ n : one who sets glass in window frames

gleam \'glēm\ n 1 : transient or partly obscured light 2 : faint trace — ~ vb : send out gleams

glean \'glēn\ vb : collect little by little — **glean·able** adj — **glean·er** n

glee \'glē\ n : joy — **glee·ful** adj

glen \'glen\ n : narrow hidden valley

glib \'glib\ adj -bb- : speaking or spoken with ease — **glib·ly** adv

glide \'glīd\ vb glid·ed; glid·ing : move or descend smoothly and effortlessly — **glide** n

glid·er \'glīdər\ n 1 : winged aircraft having no engine 2 : swinging porch seat

glim·mer \'glimər\ vb : shine faintly or unsteadily — ~ n 1 : faint light 2 : small amount

glimpse \'glimps\ vb glimpsed; glimps·ing : take a brief look at — **glimpse** n

glint \'glint\ vb : gleam or sparkle — **glint** n

glis·ten \'glisᵊn\ vb : shine or sparkle by reflection — **glisten** n

glit·ter \'glitər\ vb : shine with brilliant or metallic luster — ~ n : small glittering ornaments — **glit·tery** adj

gloat \'glōt\ vb : think of something with triumphant delight

glob \'gläb\ n : large rounded lump

glob·al \'glōbəl\ adj : worldwide — **glob·al·ly** adv

globe \'glōb\ n 1 : sphere 2 : the earth or a model of it

glob·u·lar \'gläbyələr\ adj 1 : round 2 : made up of globules

glob·ule \'gläbyül\ n : tiny ball

glock·en·spiel \'gläkən,shpēl\ n : portable musical instrument consisting of tuned metal bars

gloom \'glüm\ n 1 : darkness 2 : sadness — **gloom·i·ly** adv — **gloom·i·ness** n — **gloomy** adj

glop \'gläp\ n : messy mass or mixture

glo·ri·fy \'glōrə,fī\ vb -fied; -fy·ing 1 : make to seem glorious 2 : worship — **glo·ri·fi·ca·tion** \,glōrəfə'kāshən\ n

glo·ry \'glōrē\ *n, pl* **-ries 1** : praise or honor offered in worship **2** : cause for praise or renown **3** : magnificence **4** : heavenly bliss ~ *vb* **-ried; -ry·ing** : rejoice proudly —**glo·ri·ous** \'glōrēəs\ *adj* —**glo·ri·ous·ly** *adv*

¹gloss \'gläs, 'glós\ *n* : luster —**gloss·i·ly** \-əlē\ *adv* —**gloss·i·ness** \-ēnəs\ *n* —**gloss over** *vb* **1** : mask the true nature of **2** : deal with only superficially —**glossy** \-ē\ *adj*

²gloss *n* : brief explanation or translation ~ *vb* : translate or explain

glos·sa·ry \'gläsərē, 'glós-\ *n, pl* **-ries** : dictionary —**glos·sar·i·al** \glä'sarēəl, glő-\ *adj*

glove \'gləv\ *n* : hand covering with sections for each finger

glow \'glō\ *vb* **1** : shine with or as if with intense heat **2** : show exuberance ~ *n* : brightness or warmth of color or feeling

glow·er \'glaúər\ *vb* : stare angrily —**glower** *n*

glow·worm *n* : insect or insect larva that emits light

glu·cose \'glü,kōs\ *n* : sugar found esp. in blood, plant sap, and fruits

glue \'glü\ *n* : substance used for sticking things together —**glue** *vb* —**glu·ey** \'glüē\ *adj*

glum \'gləm\ *adj* **-mm- 1** : sullen **2** : dismal

glut \'glət\ *vb* **-tt-** : fill to excess —**glut** *n*

glu·ten \'glüt³n\ *n* : gluey protein substance in flour

glu·ti·nous \'glüt³nəs\ *adj* : sticky

glut·ton \'glət³n\ *n* : one who eats to excess —**glut·ton·ous** \'glət³nəs\ *adj* —**glut·tony** \'glət³nē\ *n*

gnarled \'närld\ *adj* **1** : knotty **2** : gloomy or sullen

gnash \'nash\ *vb* : grind (as teeth) together

gnat \'nat\ *n* : small biting fly

gnaw \'nó\ *vb* : bite or chew on —**gnaw·er** *n*

gnome \'nōm\ *n* : dwarf of folklore —**gnom·ish** *adj*

gnu \'nü, 'nyü\ *n, pl* **gnu** *or* **gnus** : large African antelope

go \'gō\ *vb* **went** \'went\, **gone** \'gón, 'gän\, **go·ing** \'goiŋ\, **goes** \'gōz\ **1** : move, proceed, run, or pass **2** : leave **3** : extend or lead **4** : sell or amount —with *for* **5** : happen **6** —used in present participle to show intent or imminent action **7** : become **8** : fit or harmonize **9** : belong ~ *n, pl* **goes 1** : act or manner of going **2** : vigor **3** : attempt —**go back on** : betray —**go by the board** : be discarded —**go for** : favor —**go off** : explode —**go one better** : outdo —**go over 1** : examine **2** : study —**go to town** : be very successful —**on the go** : constantly active

goad \'gōd\ *n* : something that urges —**goad** *vb*

goal \'gōl\ *n* **1** : mark to reach in a race **2** : purpose **3** : object in a game through which a ball is propelled

goal·ie \'gōlē\ *n* : player who defends the goal

goal·keep·er *n* : goalie

goat \'gōt\ *n* : horned ruminant mammal related to the sheep —**goat·skin** *n*

goa·tee \gō'tē\ *n* : small pointed beard

gob \'gäb\ *n* : lump

¹gob·ble \'gäbəl\ *vb* **-bled; -bling** : eat greedily

²gobble *vb* **-bled; -bling** : make the noise of a turkey (**gobbler**)

gob·ble·dy·gook \'gäbəldē,gúk, -'gük\ *n* : nonsense

gob·let \'gäblət\ *n* : large stemmed drinking glass

gob·lin \'gäblən\ *n* : ugly mischievous sprite

god \'gäd, 'gód\ *n* **1** *cap* : supreme being **2** : being with supernatural powers —**god·like** *adj* —**god·ly** *adj*

god·child *n* : person one sponsors at baptism —**god·daugh·ter** *n* —**god·son** *n*

god·dess \'gädəs, 'gód-\ *n* : female god

god·less \-ləs\ *adj* : not believing in God —**god·less·ness** *n*

god·parent *n* : sponsor at baptism —**god·fa·ther** *n* —**god·moth·er** *n*

god·send \-,send\ *n* : something needed that comes unexpectedly

goes *pres 3d sing of* GO

go·get·ter \'gō,getər\ *n* : enterprising person —**go-get·ting** \-iŋ\ *adj or n*

gog·gle \'gägəl\ *vb* **-gled; -gling** : stare wide-eyed

gog·gles \-əlz\ *n pl* : protective glasses

go·ings-on \,gōiŋz'ón, -'än\ *n pl* : events

goi·ter \'góitər\ *n* : abnormally enlarged thyroid gland

gold \'gōld\ *n* : malleable yellow metallic chemical element —**gold·smith** \-,smith\ *n*

gold·brick \-,brik\ n : person who shirks duty —**goldbrick** vb

gold·en \'gōldən\ adj 1 : made of, containing, or relating to gold 2 : having the color of gold 3 : precious or favorable

gold·en·rod \'gōldən,räd\ n : herb having tall stalks with tiny yellow flowers

gold·finch \'gōld,finch\ n : yellow American finch

gold·fish \-,fish\ n : small usu. orange or golden carp

golf \'gälf, 'golf\ n : game played by hitting a small ball (**golf ball**) with clubs (**golf clubs**) into holes placed in a field (**golf course**) —**golf** vb —**golf·er** n

go·nad \'gō,nad\ n : sex gland

gon·do·la \'gändələ (usual for 1), gän-'dō-\ n 1 : long narrow boat used on the canals of Venice 2 : car suspended from a cable

gon·do·lier \,gändə'lir\ n : person who propels a gondola

gone \'gón\ adj 1 : past 2 : involved

gon·er \'gónər\ n : hopeless case

gong \'gäŋ, 'góŋ\ n : metallic disk that makes a deep sound when struck

gon·or·rhea \,gänə'rēə\ n : bacterial inflammatory venereal disease of the genital tract —**gon·or·rhe·al** \-'rēəl\ adj

goo \'gü\ n : thick or sticky substance —**goo·ey** \-ē\ adj

good \'gúd\ adj **bet·ter** \'betər\; **best** \'best\ 1 : satisfactory 2 : salutary 3 : considerable 4 : desirable 5 : well-behaved, kind, or virtuous ~ n 1 : something good 2 : benefit 3 pl : personal property 4 pl : wares ~ adv : well —**good-heart·ed** \-'härtəd\ adj —**good-look·ing** adj —**good-na·tured** adj —**good·ness** n —**good-tem·pered** \-'tempərd\ adj —**for good** : forever

good-bye, good-by \gúd'bī\ n : parting remark

good-for-noth·ing n : idle worthless person

Good Friday n : Friday before Easter observed as the anniversary of the crucifixion of Christ

good·ly adj -li·er; -est : considerable

good·will n 1 : good intention 2 : kindly feeling

goody \'gúdē\ n, pl **good·ies** : something that is good esp. to eat

goody-goody adj : affectedly or annoy-ingly sweet or self-righteous —**goody-goody** n

goof \'gúf\ vb 1 : blunder 2 : waste time —usu. with off or around —**goof** n —**goof-off** n

goofy \'gúfē\ adj **goof·i·er; -est** : crazy —**goof·i·ness** n

goose \'güs\ n, pl **geese** \'gēs\ : large bird with webbed feet

goose·ber·ry \'güs,berē, 'güz-\ n : berry of a shrub related to the currant

goose bumps n pl : roughening of the skin caused by fear, excitement, or cold

goose·flesh n : goose bumps

goose pimples n pl : goose bumps

go·pher \'gōfər\ n : burrowing rodent

¹**gore** \'gōr\ n : blood

²**gore** vb **gored; gor·ing** : pierce or wound with a horn or tusk

¹**gorge** \'górj\ n : narrow ravine

²**gorge** vb **gorged; gorg·ing** : eat greedily

gor·geous \'górjəs\ adj : supremely beautiful

go·ril·la \gə'rilə\ n : African manlike ape

gory \'gōrē\ adj **gor·i·er; -est** : bloody

gos·hawk \'gäs,hók\ n : long-tailed hawk with short rounded wings

gos·ling \'gäzliŋ, 'góz-\ n : young goose

gos·pel \'gäspəl\ n 1 : teachings of Christ and the apostles 2 : something accepted as infallible truth —**gospel** adj

gos·sa·mer \'gäsəmər, gäz-\ n 1 : film of cobweb 2 : light filmy substance

gos·sip \'gäsəp\ n 1 : person who reveals personal information 2 : rumor or report of an intimate nature ~ vb : spread gossip —**gos·sipy** \-ē\ adj

got past of GET

Goth·ic \'gäthik\ adj : relating to a medieval style of architecture

gotten past part of GET

gouge \'gaúj\ n 1 : rounded chisel 2 : cavity or groove scooped out ~ vb **gouged; goug·ing** 1 : cut or scratch a groove in 2 : overcharge

gou·lash \'gü,läsh, -,lash\ n : beef stew with vegetables and paprika

gourd \'gōrd, 'gúrd\ n 1 : any of a group of vines including the cucumber, squash, and melon 2 : inedible hard-shelled fruit of a gourd

gour·mand \'gúr,mänd\ n : person who loves good food and drink

gour·met \'gùr,mā, gùr'mā\ n : connoisseur of food and drink

gout \'gaùt\ n : disease marked by painful inflammation and swelling of the joints —**gouty** adj

gov·ern \'gəvərn\ vb 1 : control and direct policy in 2 : guide or influence strongly 3 : restrain —**gov·ern·ment** \-ərmənt\ n —**gov·ern·men·tal** \,gəvər'mentⁿl\ adj

gov·ern·ess \'gəvərnəs\ n : female teacher in a private home

gov·er·nor \'gəvənər, 'gəvər-\ n 1 : head of a political unit 2 : automatic speed-control device —**gov·er·nor·ship** n

gown \'gaùn\ n 1 : loose flowing outer garment 2 : woman's formal evening dress —**gown** vb

grab \'grab\ vb -bb- : take by sudden grasp —**grab** n

grace \'grās\ n 1 : unmerited divine assistance 2 : short prayer before or after a meal 3 : respite 4 : ease of movement or bearing ~ vb **graced; grac·ing** 1 : honor 2 : adorn —**grace·ful** \-fəl\ adj —**grace·ful·ly** adv —**grace·ful·ness** n —**grace·less** adj

gra·cious \'grāshəs\ adj : marked by kindness and courtesy or charm and taste —**gra·cious·ly** adv —**gra·cious·ness** n

grack·le \'grakəl\ n : American blackbird

gra·da·tion \grā'dāshən, grə-\ n : step, degree, or stage in a series

grade \'grād\ n 1 : stage in a series, order, or ranking 2 : division of school representing one year's work 3 : mark of accomplishment in school 4 : degree of slope ~ vb **grad·ed; grad·ing** 1 : arrange in grades 2 : make level or evenly sloping 3 : give a grade to —**grad·er** n

grade school n : school including the first 4 or 8 grades

gra·di·ent \'grādēənt\ n : slope

grad·u·al \'grajəwəl\ adj : going by steps or degrees —**grad·u·al·ly** adv

grad·u·ate \'grajəwət\ n : holder of a diploma ~ adj : of or relating to studies beyond the bachelor's degree ~ \-ə,wāt\ vb -**at·ed; -at·ing** 1 : grant or receive a diploma 2 : mark with degrees of measurement —**grad·u·a·tion** \,grajə'wāshən\ n

graf·fi·to \grə'fētō, grä-\ n, pl -**ti** \-ē\ : inscription on a wall

graft \'graft\ vb : join one thing to another so that they grow together ~ n 1 : grafted plant 2 : the getting of money dishonestly or the money so gained —**graft·er** n

grain \'grān\ n 1 : seeds or fruits of cereal grasses 2 : small hard particle 3 : arrangement of fibers in wood —**grained** \'grānd\ adj —**grainy** adj

gram \'gram\ n : metric unit of weight equal to 1/1000 kilogram

gram·mar \'gramər\ n : study of words and their functions and relations in the sentence —**gram·mar·i·an** \grə'mareēən\ n —**gram·mat·i·cal** \-'matikəl\ adj —**gram·mat·i·cal·ly** adv

grammar school n : grade school

gra·na·ry \'grānərē, 'gran-\ n, pl -**ries** : storehouse for grain

grand \'grand\ adj 1 : large or striking in size or scope 2 : fine and imposing 3 : very good —**grand·ly** adv —**grand·ness** n

grand·child \-,chīld\ n : child of one's son or daughter —**grand·daugh·ter** n —**grand·son** n

gran·deur \'granjər\ n : quality or state of being grand

gran·dil·o·quence \gran'diləkwəns\ n : pompous speaking —**gran·dil·o·quent** \-kwənt\ adj

gran·di·ose \'grandē,ōs, ,grandē'-\ adj 1 : impressive 2 : affectedly splendid —**gran·di·ose·ly** adv

grand·par·ent \'grand,parənt\ n : parent of one's father or mother —**grand·fa·ther** \-,fäthər, -,fàth-\ n —**grand·moth·er** \-,məthər\ n

grand·stand \-,stand\ n : usu. roofed stand for spectators

grange \'grānj\ n : farmers association

gran·ite \'granət\ n : hard igneous rock

grant \'grant\ vb 1 : consent to 2 : give 3 : admit as true ~ n 1 : act of granting 2 : something granted —**grant·ee** \grant'ē\ n —**grant·er** \'grantər\ n —**grant·or** \-ər, -,ór\ n

gran·u·late \'granyə,lāt\ vb -**lat·ed; -lat·ing** : form into grains or crystals —**gran·u·la·tion** \,granyə'lāshən\ n

gran·ule \'granyül\ n : small particle —**gran·u·lar** \-yələr\ adj —**gran·u·lar·i·ty** \,granyə'larətē\ n

grape \'grāp\ n : smooth juicy edible berry of a woody vine (**grape·vine**)

grape·fruit \'grāp,früt\ n : large edible yellow-skinned citrus fruit

graph 145 grid

graph \'graf\ *n* : diagram that shows relationships between things —**graph** *vb*

graph·ic \'grafik\ *adj* 1 : vividly described 2 : relating to the arts (**graphic arts**) of representation and printing on flat surfaces ~ *n* 1 : picture used for illustration 2 *pl* : computer screen display —**graph·i·cal·ly** \-iklē\ *adv*

graph·ite \'graf,īt\ *n* : soft carbon used for lead pencils and lubricants

grap·nel \'grapnəl\ *n* : small anchor with several claws

grap·ple \'grapəl\ *vb* -**pled**; -**pling** 1 : seize or hold with or as if with a hooked implement 2 : wrestle

grasp \'grasp\ *vb* 1 : take or seize firmly 2 : understand ~ *n* 1 : one's hold or control 2 : one's reach 3 : comprehension

grass \'gras\ *n* : plant with jointed stem and narrow leaves —**grassy** *adj*

grass·hop·per \-,häpər\ *n* : leaping plant-eating insect

grass·land *n* : land covered with grasses

¹grate \'grāt\ *n* 1 : grating 2 : frame of iron bars to hold burning fuel

²grate *vb* **grat·ed**; -**ing** 1 : pulverize by rubbing against something rough 2 : irritate —**grat·er** *n* —**grat·ing·ly** *adv*

grate·ful \'grātfəl\ *adj* : thankful or appreciative —**grate·ful·ly** *adv* —**grate·ful·ness** *n*

grat·i·fy \'gratə,fī\ *vb* -**fied**; -**fy·ing** : give pleasure to —**grat·i·fi·ca·tion** \,gratəfə'kāshən\ *n*

grat·ing \'grātiŋ\ *n* : framework with bars across it

gra·tis \'gratəs, 'grāt-\ *adv or adj* : free

grat·i·tude \'gratə,tüd, -,tyüd\ *n* : state of being grateful

gra·tu·i·tous \grə'tüətəs, -'tyü-\ *adj* 1 : free 2 : uncalled-for

gra·tu·i·ty \-ətē\ *n*, *pl* -**ities** : tip

¹grave \'grāv\ *n* : place of burial —**grave·stone** *n* —**grave·yard** *n*

²grave *adj* **grav·er**; **grav·est** 1 : threatening great harm or danger 2 : solemn —**grave·ly** *adv* —**grave·ness** *n*

grav·el \'gravəl\ *n* : loose rounded fragments of rock —**grav·el·ly** *adj*

grav·i·tate \'gravə,tāt\ *vb* -**tat·ed**; -**tat·ing** : move toward something

grav·i·ta·tion \,gravə'tāshən\ *n* : natural force of attraction that tends to draw bodies together —**grav·i·ta·tion·al** \-shənəl\ *adj* —**grav·i·ta·tion·al·ly** *adv*

grav·i·ty \'gravətē\ *n*, *pl* -**ties** 1 : serious importance 2 : gravitation

gra·vy \'grāvē\ *n*, *pl* -**vies** : sauce made from thickened juices of cooked meat

gray \'grā\ *adj* 1 : of the color gray 2 : having gray hair ~ *n* : neutral color between black and white ~ *vb* : make or become gray —**gray·ish** \-ish\ *adj* —**gray·ness** *n*

¹graze \'grāz\ *vb* **grazed**; **graz·ing** : feed on herbage or pasture —**graz·er** *n*

²graze *vb* **grazed**; **graz·ing** : touch lightly in passing

grease \'grēs\ *n* : thick oily material or fat ~ \'grēs, 'grēz\ *vb* **greased**; **greas·ing** : smear or lubricate with grease —**greasy** \'grēsē, -zē\ *adj*

great \'grāt\ *adj* 1 : large in size or number 2 : larger than usual —**great·ly** *adv* —**great·ness** *n*

grebe \'grēb\ *n* : diving bird related to the loon

greed \'grēd\ *n* : selfish desire beyond reason —**greed·i·ly** \-³lē\ *adv* —**greed·i·ness** \-ēnəs\ *n* —**greedy** \'grēdē\ *adj*

green \'grēn\ *adj* 1 : of the color green 2 : unripe 3 : inexperienced ~ *vb* : become green ~ *n* 1 : color between blue and yellow 2 *pl* : leafy parts of plants —**green·ish** *adj* —**green·ness** *n*

green·ery \'grēnərē\ *n*, *pl* -**er·ies** : green foliage or plants

green·horn *n* : inexperienced person

green·house *n* : glass structure for the growing of plants

greet \'grēt\ *vb* 1 : address with expressions of kind wishes 2 : react to —**greet·er** *n*

greet·ing *n* 1 : friendly address on meeting 2 *pl* : best wishes

gre·gar·i·ous \gri'gareəs\ *adj* : social or companionable —**gre·gar·i·ous·ly** *adv* —**gre·gar·i·ous·ness** *n*

grem·lin \'gremlən\ *n* : small mischievous gnome

gre·nade \grə'nād\ *n* : small missile filled with explosive or chemicals

grew *past of* GROW

grey *var of* GRAY

grey·hound \'grā,haund\ *n* : tall slender dog noted for speed

grid \'grid\ *n* 1 : grating 2 : evenly

spaced horizontal and vertical lines (as on a map)

grid·dle \'grid°l\ n : flat metal surface for cooking

grid·iron \'grid,īərn\ n 1 : grate for broiling 2 : football field

grief \'grēf\ n 1 : emotional suffering caused by or as if by bereavement 2 : disaster

griev·ance \'grēvəns\ n : complaint

grieve \'grēv\ vb **grieved; griev·ing** : feel or cause to feel grief or sorrow

griev·ous \'grēvəs\ adj 1 : oppressive 2 : causing grief or sorrow —**griev·ous·ly** adv

grill \'gril\ vb 1 : cook on a grill 2 : question intensely ~ n 1 : griddle 2 : informal restaurant

grille, grill \'gril\ n : grating forming a barrier or screen —**grill·work** n

grim \'grim\ adj -**mm**- 1 : harsh and forbidding in appearance 2 : relentless —**grim·ly** adv —**grim·ness** n

gri·mace \'griməs, grim'ās\ n : facial expression of disgust —**grimace** vb

grime \'grīm\ n : embedded or accumulated dirt —**grimy** adj

grin \'grin\ vb -**nn**- : smile so as to show the teeth —**grin** n

grind \'grīnd\ vb **ground** \'graùnd\; **grind·ing** 1 : reduce to powder 2 : wear down or sharpen by friction 3 : operate or produce by turning a crank ~ n : monotonous labor or routine —**grind·er** n —**grind·stone** \'grīn,stōn\ n

grip \'grip\ vb -**pp**- : seize or hold firmly ~ n 1 : grasp 2 : control 3 : device for holding

gripe \'grīp\ vb **griped; grip·ing** 1 : cause pains in the bowels 2 : complain —**gripe** n

grippe \'grip\ n : influenza

gris·ly \'grizlē\ adj -**li·er; -est** : horrible or gruesome

grist \'grist\ n : grain to be ground or already ground —**grist·mill** n

gris·tle \'grisəl\ n : cartilage —**gris·tly** \-lē\ adj

grit \'grit\ n 1 : hard sharp granule 2 : material composed of granules 3 : unyielding courage ~ vb -**tt**- : press with a grating noise —**grit·ty** adj

grits \'grits\ n pl : coarsely ground hulled grain

griz·zled \'grizəld\ adj : streaked with gray

groan \'grōn\ vb 1 : moan 2 : creak under a strain —**groan** n

gro·cer \'grōsər\ n : food dealer —**gro·cery** \'grōsrē, 'grōsh-, -ərē\ n

grog \'gräg\ n : rum diluted with water

grog·gy \-ē\ adj -**gi·er; -est** : dazed and unsteady on the feet —**grog·gi·ly** adv —**grog·gi·ness** n

groin \'gròin\ n : juncture of the lower abdomen and inner thigh

grom·met \'grämət, 'gram-\ n : eyelet

groom \'grüm, 'grùm\ n 1 : one who cares for horses 2 : bridegroom ~ vb 1 : clean and care for (as a horse) 2 : make neat or attractive 3 : prepare

groove \'grüv\ n 1 : long narrow channel 2 : fixed routine —**groove** vb

grope \'grōp\ vb **groped; grop·ing** : search for by feeling

gros·beak \'grōs,bēk\ n : finch with large conical bill

¹**gross** \'grōs\ adj 1 : glaringly noticeable 2 : bulky 3 : consisting of an overall total exclusive of deductions 4 : vulgar ~ n : the whole before any deductions ~ vb : earn as a total —**gross·ly** adv —**gross·ness** n

²**gross** n, pl **gross** : 12 dozen

gro·tesque \grō'tesk\ adj 1 : absurdly distorted or repulsive 2 : ridiculous —**gro·tesque·ly** adv

grot·to \'grätō\ n, pl -**toes** : cave

grouch \'graùch\ n : complaining person —**grouch** vb —**grouchy** adj

¹**ground** \'graùnd\ n 1 : bottom of a body of water 2 pl : sediment 3 : basis for something 4 : surface of the earth 5 : conductor that makes electrical connection with the earth or a framework ~ vb 1 : force or bring down to the ground 2 : give basic knowledge to 3 : connect with an electrical ground —**ground·less** adj

²**ground** past of GRIND

ground·hog n : woodchuck

ground·wa·ter n : underground water

ground·work n : foundation

group \'grüp\ n : number of associated individuals ~ vb : gather or collect into groups

grou·per \'grüpər\ n : large fish of warm seas

grouse \'graùs\ n, pl **grouse** or **grouses** : ground-dwelling game bird

grout \'graùt\ n : mortar for filling cracks —**grout** vb

grove \'grōv\ n : small group of trees

grov·el \'grävəl, 'grav-\ vb -**eled** or

-elled; -el·ing *or* -el·ling : abase one-self

grow \'grō\ *vb* grew \'grü\; grown \'grōn\; grow·ing 1 : come into existence and develop to maturity 2 : be able to grow 3 : advance or increase 4 : become 5 : cultivate —grow·er *n*

growl \'graul\ *vb* : utter a deep threatening sound —growl *n*

grown-up \'grōn,əp\ *n* : adult — grown-up *adj*

growth \'grōth\ *n* 1 : stage in growing 2 : process of growing 3 : result of something growing

grub \'grəb\ *vb* -bb- 1 : root out by digging 2 : search about ~ *n* 1 : thick wormlike larva 2 : food

grub·by \'grəbē\ *adj* -bi·er; -est : dirty —grub·bi·ness *n*

grub·stake *n* : supplies for a prospector

grudge \'grəj\ *vb* grudged; grudg·ing : be reluctant to give ~ *n* : feeling of ill will

gru·el \'grüəl\ *n* : thin porridge

gru·el·ing, gru·el·ling \-əliŋ\ *adj* : requiring extreme effort

grue·some \'grüsəm\ *adj* : horribly repulsive

gruff \'grəf\ *adj* : rough in speech or manner —gruff·ly *adv*

grum·ble \'grəmbəl\ *vb* -bled; -bling : mutter in discontent —grum·bler \-blər\ *n*

grumpy \-pē\ *adj* grump·i·er; -est : cross —grump·i·ly *adv* —grump·i·ness *n*

grun·ion \'grənyən\ *n* : fish of the California coast

grunt \'grənt\ *n* : deep guttural sound —grunt *vb*

gua·no \'gwänō\ *n* : excrement of seabirds used as fertilizer

guar·an·tee \,garən'tē\ *n* 1 : assurance of the fulfillment of a condition 2 : something given or held as a security ~ *vb* -teed; -tee·ing 1 : promise to be responsible for 2 : state with certainty —guar·an·tor \,garən'tór\ *n*

guar·an·ty \'garəntē\ *n, pl* -ties 1 : promise to answer for another's failure to pay a debt 2 : guarantee 3 : pledge ~ *vb* -tied; -ty·ing : guarantee

guard \'gärd\ *n* 1 : defensive position 2 : act of protecting 3 : an individual or group that guards against danger 4 : protective or safety device ~ *vb* 1 : protect or watch over 2 : take precautions —guard·house *n* — guard·room *n*

guard·ian \'gärdēən\ *n* : one who has responsibility for the care of the person or property of another — guard·ian·ship *n*

gua·va \'gwävə\ *n* : shrubby tropical tree or its mildly acid fruit

gu·ber·na·to·ri·al \,gübənə'tōrēəl, ,gyü-\ *adj* : relating to a governor

guer·ril·la, guer·ril·la \gə'rilə\ *n* : soldier engaged in small-scale harassing tactics

guess \'ges\ *vb* 1 : form an opinion from little evidence 2 : state correctly solely by chance 3 : think or believe —guess *n*

guest \'gest\ *n* 1 : person to whom hospitality (as of a house) is extended 2 : patron of a commercial establishment (as a hotel) 3 : person not a regular cast member who appears on a program

guf·faw \gə'fó, 'gəf,ó\ *n* : loud burst of laughter —guf·faw \gə'fó\ *vb*

guide \'gīd\ *n* 1 : one that leads or gives direction to another 2 : device on a machine to direct motion ~ *vb* guid·ed; guid·ing 1 : show the way to 2 : direct —guid·able *adj* —guid·ance \'gīdᵊns\ *n* —guide·book *n*

guide·line \-,līn\ *n* : summary of procedures regarding policy or conduct

guild \'gild\ *n* : association

guile \'gīl\ *n* : craftiness —guile·ful *adj* —guile·less *adj* —guile·less·ness *n*

guil·lo·tine \'gilə,tēn, ,gēyə'tēn, 'gēyə,-\ *n* : machine for beheading persons —guillotine *vb*

guilt \'gilt\ *n* 1 : fact of having committed an offense 2 : feeling of responsibility for offenses —guilt·i·ly *adv* —guilt·i·ness *n* —guilty \giltē\ *adj*

guin·ea \'ginē\ *n* 1 : old gold coin of United Kingdom 2 : 21 shillings

guinea pig *n* : small So. American rodent

guise \'gīz\ *n* : external appearance

gui·tar \gə'tär, gi-\ *n* : 6-stringed musical instrument played by plucking

gulch \'gəlch\ *n* : ravine

gulf \'gəlf\ *n* 1 : extension of an ocean or a sea into the land 2 : wide gap

¹gull \'gəl\ *n* : seabird with webbed feet

²gull *vb* : make a dupe of ~ *n* : dupe —gull·ible *adj*

gul·let \'gələt\ *n* : throat

gul·ly \'gəlē\ *n, pl* -lies : trench worn by running water

gulp \'gəlp\ *vb* : swallow hurriedly or greedily —**gulp** *n*

¹gum \'gəm\ *n* : tissue along the jaw at the base of the teeth

²gum *n* **1** : sticky plant substance **2** : gum usu. of sweetened chicle prepared for chewing —**gum·my** *adj*

gum·bo \'gəmbō\ *n* : thick soup

gum·drop *n* : gumlike candy

gump·tion \'gəmpshən\ *n* : initiative

gun \'gən\ *n* **1** : cannon **2** : portable firearm **3** : discharge of a gun **4** : something like a gun ~ *vb* **-nn-** : hunt with a gun —**gun·fight** *n* —**gun·fight·er** *n* —**gun·fire** *n* —**gun·man** \-mən\ *n* —**gun·pow·der** *n* —**gun·shot** *n* —**gun·smith** *n*

gun·boat *n* : small armed ship

gun·ner \'gənər\ *n* : person who uses a gun

gun·nery sergeant \'gənərē-\ *n* : noncommissioned officer in the marine corps ranking next below a first sergeant

gun·ny·sack \'gənē,sak\ *n* : burlap sack

gun·slinger \'gən,sliŋər\ *n* : skilled gunman in the old West

gun·wale \'gənᵊl\ *n* : upper edge of a boat's side

gup·py \'gəpē\ *n*, *pl* **-pies** : tiny tropical fish

gur·gle \'gərgəl\ *vb* **-gled; -gling** : make a sound like that of a flowing and gently splashing liquid —**gurgle** *n*

gu·ru \'gü,rü\ *n*, *pl* **-rus** **1** : personal religious teacher in Hinduism **2** : expert

gush \'gəsh\ *vb* : pour forth violently or enthusiastically —**gush·er** \'gəshər\ *n*

gushy \-ē\ *adj* **gush·i·er; -est** : effusively sentimental

gust \'gəst\ *n* **1** : sudden brief rush of wind **2** : sudden outburst —**gust** *vb* —**gusty** *adj*

gus·ta·to·ry \'gəstə,tōrē\ *adj* : relating to the sense of taste

gus·to \'gəstō\ *n* : zest

gut \'gət\ *n* **1** *pl* : intestines **2** : digestive canal **3** *pl* : courage ~ *vb* **-tt-** : eviscerate

gut·ter \'gətər\ *n* : channel for carrying off rainwater

gut·tur·al \'gətərəl\ *adj* : sounded in the throat —**guttural** *n*

¹guy \'gī\ *n* : rope, chain, or rod attached to something to steady it —**guy** *vb*

²guy *n* : person

guz·zle \'gəzəl\ *vb* **-zled; -zling** : drink greedily

gym \'jim\ *n* : gymnasium

gym·na·si·um \jim'nāzēəm, -zhəm\ *n*, *pl* **-si·ums** *or* **-sia** \-zēə, -zhə\ : place for indoor sports

gym·nas·tics \jim'nastiks\ *n* : physical exercises performed in a gymnasium —**gym·nast** \'jim,nast\ *n* —**gym·nas·tic** *adj*

gy·ne·col·o·gy \gīnə'käləjē, jin-\ *n* : branch of medicine dealing with the diseases of women —**gy·ne·co·log·ic** \-ikə'läjik\, **gy·ne·co·log·i·cal** \-ikəl\ *adj* —**gy·ne·col·o·gist** \-ə'käləjist\ *n*

gyp \'jip\ *n* **1** : cheat **2** : trickery —**gyp** *vb*

gyp·sum \'jipsəm\ *n* : calcium-containing mineral

gy·rate \'jī,rāt\ *vb* **-rat·ed; -rat·ing** : revolve around a center —**gy·ra·tion** \jī'rāshən\ *n*

gy·ro·scope \'jīrō,skōp\ *n* : wheel mounted to spin rapidly about an axis that is free to turn in various directions

H

h \'āch\ *n*, *pl* **h's** *or* **hs** \'āchəz\ : **1** : 8th letter of the alphabet

hab·er·dash·er \'habər,dashər\ *n* : men's clothier —**hab·er·dash·ery** \-ərē\ *n*

hab·it \'habət\ *n* **1** : monk's or nun's clothing **2** : usual behavior **3** : addiction —**hab·it-form·ing** *adj*

hab·it·able \-əbəl\ *adj* : capable of being lived in

hab·i·tat \'habə,tat\ *n* : place where a plant or animal naturally occurs

hab·i·ta·tion \,habə'tāshən\ *n* **1** : occupancy **2** : dwelling place

ha·bit·u·al \hə'bichəwəl\ *adj* **1** : commonly practiced or observed **2** : doing, practicing, or acting by habit —**ha·bit·u·al·ly** *adv* —**ha·bit·u·al·ness** *n*

ha·bit·u·ate \hə'bichə‚wāt\ vb **-at·ed;
-at·ing** : accustom

ha·ci·en·da \‚häsē'endə\ n : ranch house

¹hack \'hak\ vb **1** : cut with repeated
irregular blows **2** : cough in a short
dry manner **3** : manage successfully
—**hack** n —**hack·er** n

²hack n **1** : horse or vehicle for hire **2**
: saddle horse **3** : writer for hire —
hack adj —**hack·man** \-mən\ n

hack·le \'hakəl\ n **1** : long feather on the
neck or back of a bird **2** pl : hairs that
can be erected **3** pl : temper

hack·ney \-nē\ n, pl **-neys 1** : horse for
riding or driving **2** : carriage for hire

hack·neyed \-nēd\ adj : trite

hack·saw n : saw for metal

had past of HAVE

had·dock \'hadək\ n, pl **haddock** : Atlantic food fish

Ha·des \'hādēz\ n **1** : mythological
abode of the dead **2** : often not cap
: hell

haft \'haft\ n : handle of a weapon or
tool

hag \'hag\ n **1** : witch **2** : ugly old
woman

hag·gard \'hagərd\ adj : worn or emaciated —**hag·gard·ly** adv

hag·gle \'hagəl\ vb **-gled; -gling** : argue
in bargaining —**hag·gler** n

¹hail \'hāl\ n **1** : precipitation in small
lumps of ice **2** : something like a rain
of hail ~ vb : rain hail —**hail·stone**
n —**hail·storm** n

²hail vb **1** : greet or salute **2** : summon
~ n : expression of greeting or praise
—often used as an interjection

hair \'har\ n : threadlike growth from
the skin —**hair·brush** n —**hair·cut** n
—**hair·dress·er** n —**haired** adj —
hair·i·ness n —**hair·less** adj —**hair·
pin** n —**hair·style** n —**hair·styl·ing**
n —**hair·styl·ist** n —**hairy** adj

hair·breadth \-‚bredth\, **hairs·breadth**
\'harz-\ n : tiny distance or margin

hair·do \-‚dü\ n, pl **-dos** : style of wearing hair

hair·line n **1** : thin line **2** : outline of the
hair on the head

hair·piece n : toupee

hair-rais·ing adj : causing terror or
astonishment

hake \'hāk\ n : marine food fish

hal·cy·on \'halsēən\ adj : prosperous or
most pleasant

¹hale \'hāl\ adj : healthy or robust

²hale vb **haled; hal·ing 1** : haul **2** : compel to go

half \'haf, 'háf\ n, pl **halves** \'havz,
'hávz\ : either of 2 equal parts ~ adj
1 : being a half or nearly a half **2**
: partial —**half** adv

half brother n : brother related through
one parent only

half-heart·ed \-'härtəd\ adj : without
enthusiasm —**half·heart·ed·ly** adv
—**half·heart·ed·ness** n

half-life n : time for half of something
to undergo a process

half sister n : sister related through one
parent only

half·way adj : midway between 2 points
—**half·way** adv

half-wit \-‚wit\ n : foolish person —
half-wit·ted \-‚witəd\ adj

hal·i·but \'haləbət\ n, pl **halibut** : large
edible marine flatfish

hal·i·to·sis \‚halə'tōsəs\ n : bad breath

hall \'hól\ n **1** : large public or college
or university building **2** : lobby **3**
: auditorium

hal·le·lu·jah \‚halə'lüyə\ interj —used
to express praise, joy, or thanks

hall·mark \'hól‚märk\ n : distinguishing
characteristic

hal·low \'halō\ vb : consecrate —**hallowed** \-ōd, -əwəd\ adj

Hal·low·een \‚halə'wēn, ‚häl-\ n : evening of October 31 observed esp. by
children in merrymaking and mas-
querading

hal·lu·ci·na·tion \hə‚lüsⁿ'āshən\ n
: perception of objects that are not
real —**hal·lu·ci·nate** \ha'lusⁿ‚āt\ vb
—**hal·lu·ci·na·to·ry** \-'lüsⁿə‚tōrē\
adj

hal·lu·ci·no·gen \hə'lüsⁿəjən\ n : substance that induces hallucinations —
hal·lu·ci·no·gen·ic \-‚lüsⁿə'jenik\
adj

hall·way n : entrance hall

ha·lo \'hālō\ n, pl **-los** or **-loes** : circle of
light appearing to surround a shining
body

¹halt \'hólt\ adj : lame

²halt vb : stop or cause to stop —**halt**
n

hal·ter \'hóltər\ n **1** : rope or strap for
leading or tying an animal **2** : brief
blouse held up by straps ~ vb : catch
(an animal) with a halter

halt·ing \'hóltiŋ\ adj : uncertain —
halt·ing·ly adv

halve \'hav, 'háv\ vb **halved; halv·ing 1** : divide into halves **2** : reduce to half

halves pl of HALF

ham \'ham\ n **1** : thigh—usu. pl. **2** : cut esp. of pork from the thigh **3** : showy actor **4** : amateur radio operator ~ vb **-mm-** : overplay a part —**ham** adj

ham·burg·er \'ham,bərgər\, **ham·burg** \-,bərg\ n : ground beef or a sandwich made with this

ham·let \'hamlət\ n : small village

ham·mer \'hamər\ n **1** : hand tool for pounding **2** : gun part whose striking explodes the charge ~ vb : beat, drive, or shape with a hammer — **hammer out** vb : produce with effort

ham·mer·head n **1** : striking part of a hammer **2** : shark with a hammerlike head

ham·mock \'hamək\ n : swinging bed hung by cords at each end

¹ham·per \'hampər\ vb : impede

²hamper n : large covered basket

ham·ster \'hamstər\ n : stocky short-tailed rodent

ham·string \'ham,striŋ\ vb **-strung** \-,strəŋ\; **-string·ing** \-,striŋiŋ\ **1** : cripple by cutting the leg tendons **2** : make ineffective or powerless

hand \'hand\ n **1** : end of a front limb adapted for grasping **2** : side **3** : promise of marriage **4** : handwriting **5** : assistance or participation **6** : applause **7** : cards held by a player **8** : worker ~ vb : lead, assist, give, or pass with the hand —**hand·clasp** n —**hand·craft** vb —**hand·ful** n —**hand·gun** n —**hand·less** adj —**hand·made** adj —**hand·rail** n —**hand·saw** n —**hand·wo·ven** adj —**hand·writ·ing** n —**hand·writ·ten** adj

hand·bag n : woman's purse

hand·ball n : game played by striking a ball with the hand

hand·bill n : printed advertisement or notice distributed by hand

hand·book n : concise reference book

hand·cuffs n pl : locking bracelets that bind the wrists together —**handcuff** vb

hand·i·cap \'handē,kap\ n **1** : advantage given or disadvantage imposed to equalize a competition **2** : disadvantage —**handicap** vb —**hand·i·capped** adj —**hand·i·cap·per** n

hand·i·craft \'handē,kraft\ n **1** : manual skill **2** : article made by hand —

hand·i·craft·er n —**hand·i·crafts·man** \-,kraftsmən\ n

hand·i·work \-,wərk\ n : work done personally or by the hands

hand·ker·chief \'haŋkərchəf, -,chēf\ n, pl **-chiefs** \-chəfs, -,chēfs\ : small piece of cloth carried for personal use

han·dle \'hand²l\ n : part to be grasped ~ vb **-dled; -dling 1** : touch, hold, or manage with the hands **2** : deal with **3** : deal or trade in —**han·dle·bar** n —**han·dled** \-d²ld\ adj —**han·dler** \'handlər\ n

hand·maid·en n : female attendant

hand·out n : something given out

hand·pick vb : select personally

hand·shake n : clasping of hands (as in greeting)

hand·some \'hansəm\ adj **-som·er; -est 1** : sizable **2** : generous **3** : nice-looking —**hand·some·ly** adv —**hand·some·ness** n

hand·spring n : somersault on the hands

hand·stand n : a balancing upside down on the hands

handy \'handē\ adj **hand·i·er; -est 1** : conveniently near **2** : easily used **3** : dexterous —**hand·i·ly** adv —**hand·i·ness** n

handy·man \-,man\ n : one who does odd jobs

hang \'haŋ\ vb **hung** \'həŋ\ **hang·ing 1** : fasten or remain fastened to an elevated point without support from below **2** : suspend by the neck until dead—past tense often **hanged 3** : droop ~ n **1** : way a thing hangs **2** : an understanding of something — **hang·er** n —**hang·ing** n

han·gar \'haŋər\ n : airplane shelter

hang·dog \'haŋ,dóg\ adj : ashamed or guilty

hang·man \-mən\ n : public executioner

hang·nail n : loose skin near a fingernail

hang·out n : place where one likes to spend time

hang·over n : sick feeling following heavy drinking

hank \'haŋk\ n : coil or loop

han·ker \'haŋkər\ vb : desire strongly —**han·ker·ing** n

han·ky-pan·ky \,haŋkē'paŋkē\ n : questionable or underhanded activity

han·som \'hansəm\ n : 2-wheeled covered carriage

Ha·nuk·kah \'känəkə, 'hän-\ n : 8-day Jewish holiday commemorating the rededication of the Temple of Jerusalem after its defilement by Antiochus of Syria

hap·haz·ard \hap'hazərd\ adj : having no plan or order —**hap·haz·ard·ly** adv

hap·less \'hapləs\ adj : unfortunate —**hap·less·ly** adv —**hap·less·ness** n

hap·pen \'hapən\ vb 1 : take place 2 : be fortunate to encounter something unexpectedly —often used with infinitive

hap·pen·ing \-əniŋ\ n : occurrence

hap·py \'hapē\ adj -pi·er; -est 1 : fortunate 2 : content, pleased, or joyous —**hap·pi·ly** \'hapəlē\ adv —**hap·pi·ness** n

ha·rangue \hə'raŋ\ n : ranting or scolding speech —**harangue** vb —**ha·rangu·er** \-'raŋər\ n

ha·rass \hə'ras, 'harəs\ vb 1 : disturb and impede by repeated raids 2 : annoy continually —**ha·rass·ment** n

har·bin·ger \'härbənjər\ n : one that announces or foreshadows what is coming

har·bor \-bər\ n : protected body of water suitable for anchorage ~ vb 1 : give refuge to 2 : hold as a thought or feeling

hard \'härd\ adj 1 : not easily penetrated 2 : firm or definite 3 : close or searching 4 : severe or unfeeling 5 : strenuous or difficult 6 : physically strong or intense —**hard** adv —**hard·ness** n

hard·en \'härdᵊn\ vb : make or become hard or harder —**hard·en·er** n

hard·head·ed \,härd'hedəd\ adj 1 : stubborn 2 : realistic —**hard·head·ed·ly** adv —**hard·head·ed·ness** n

hard-heart·ed \-'härtəd\ adj : lacking sympathy —**hard-heart·ed·ly** adv —**hard-heart·ed·ness** n

hard·ly \'härdlē\ adv 1 : only just 2 : certainly not

hard-nosed \-,nōzd\ adj : tough or uncompromising

hard·ship \-,ship\ n : suffering or privation

hard·tack \-,tak\ n : hard biscuit

hard·ware n 1 : cutlery or tools made of metal 2 : physical components of a vehicle or apparatus

hard·wood n : wood of a broad-leaved usu. deciduous tree —**hardwood** adj

har·dy \'härdē\ adj -di·er; -est : able to withstand adverse conditions —**har·di·ly** adv —**har·di·ness** n

hare \'har\ n, pl **hare** or **hares** : long-eared mammal related to the rabbit

hare-brained \-,brānd\ adj : foolish

hare·lip n : deformity in which the upper lip is vertically split —**hare·lipped** \-,lipt\ adj

ha·rem \'harəm\ n : house or part of a house allotted to women in a Muslim household or the women and servants occupying it

hark \'härk\ vb : listen

har·le·quin \'härlikən, -kwən\ n : clown

har·lot \'härlət\ n : prostitute

harm \'härm\ n 1 : physical or mental damage 2 : mischief ~ vb : cause harm —**harm·ful** \-fəl\ adj —**harm·ful·ly** adv —**harm·ful·ness** n —**harm·less** adj —**harm·less·ly** adv —**harm·less·ness** n

har·mon·ic \här'mänik\ adj 1 : of or relating to musical harmony 2 : pleasing to hear —**har·mon·i·cal·ly** \-iklē\ adv

har·mon·i·ca \här'mänikə\ n : small wind instrument with metallic reeds

har·mo·ny \'härmənē\ n, pl -nies 1 : musical combination of sounds 2 : pleasing arrangement of parts 3 : lack of conflict 4 : internal calm —**har·mo·ni·ous** \här'mōnēəs\ adj —**har·mo·ni·ous·ly** adv —**har·mo·ni·ous·ness** n —**har·mo·ni·za·tion** \,härmənə'zāshən\ n —**har·mo·nize** \'härmə,nīz\ vb

har·ness \'härnəs\ n : gear of a draft animal ~ vb 1 : put a harness on 2 : put to use

harp \'härp\ n : musical instrument with many strings plucked by the fingers ~ vb 1 : play on a harp 2 : dwell on a subject tiresomely —**harp·er** n —**harp·ist** n

har·poon \här'pün\ n : barbed spear used in hunting whales —**harpoon** vb —**har·poon·er** n

harp·si·chord \'härpsi,kord\ n : keyboard instrument with strings that are plucked

har·py \'härpē\ n, pl -pies : shrewish woman

har·row \'harō\ n : implement used to break up soil ~ vb 1 : cultivate with a harrow 2 : distress

har·ry \'harē\ vb -ried; -ry·ing : torment by or as if by constant attack

harsh \'härsh\ adj 1 : disagreeably

rough **2** : severe —**harsh·ly** adv —
harsh·ness n

har·um–scar·um \,harəm'skarəm\ adv
: recklessly

har·vest \'härvəst\ n **1** : act or time of
gathering in a crop **2** : mature crop
—**harvest** vb —**har·vest·er** n

has pres 3d sing of HAVE

hash \'hash\ vb : chop into small pieces
~ n : chopped meat mixed with po-
tatoes and browned

hasp \'hasp\ n : hinged strap fastener
esp. for a door

has·sle \'hasəl\ n **1** : quarrel **2** : struggle
3 : cause of annoyance —**hassle** vb

has·sock \'hasək\ n : cushion used as a
seat or leg rest

haste \'hāst\ n **1** : rapidity of motion **2**
: rash action **3** : excessive eagerness
—**hast·i·ly** \'hāstəlē\ adv —**hast·
i·ness** \-stēnəs\ n —**hasty** \-stē\ adj

has·ten \'hās³n\ vb : hurry

hat \'hat\ n : covering for the head

¹hatch \'hach\ n : small door or opening
—**hatch·way** n

²hatch vb : emerge from an egg —
hatch·ery \-ərē\ n

hatch·et \'hachət\ n : short-handled ax

hate \'hāt\ n : intense hostility and aversion ~ vb **hat·ed; hat·ing 1** : express
or feel hate **2** : dislike —**hate·ful**
\-fəl\ adj —**hate·ful·ly** adv —**hate·
ful·ness** n —**hat·er** n

ha·tred \'hātrəd\ n : hate

hat·ter \'hatər\ n : one that makes or
sells hats

haugh·ty \'hótē\ adj **-ti·er; -est** : disdainfully proud —**haugh·ti·ly** adv —
haugh·ti·ness n

haul \'hól\ vb **1** : draw or pull **2** : transport or carry ~ n **1** : amount collected
2 : load or the distance it is transported —**haul·er** n

haunch \'hónch\ n : hip or hindquarter
—usu. pl.

haunt \'hónt\ vb **1** : visit often **2** : visit
or inhabit as a ghost ~ n : place
frequented —**haunt·er** n —**haunt·
ing·ly** adv

have \'hav, in sense 2 before "to" usu
'haf\ vb **had** \'had\; **hav·ing** \'havin\;
has \'haz, in sense 2 before "to" usu
'has\ **1** : hold in possession, service,
or affection **2** : be compelled or
forced to **3** —used as an auxiliary
with the past participle to form the
present perfect, past perfect, or future
perfect **4** : obtain or receive **5** : un-

dergo **6** : cause to **7** : bear —**have to
do with** : have in the way of connection or relation with or effect on

ha·ven \'hāvən\ n : place of safety

hav·oc \'havək\ n **1** : wide destruction **2**
: great confusion

¹hawk \'hók\ n : bird of prey with a
strong hooked bill and sharp talons

²hawk vb : offer for sale by calling out
in the street —**hawk·er** n

haw·ser \'hózər\ n : large rope

haw·thorn \'hó,thórn\ n : spiny shrub or
tree with pink or white fragrant flowers

hay \'hā\ n : herbs (as grass) cut and
dried for use as fodder —**hay** vb —
hay·loft n —**hay·mow** \-,maú\ n —
hay·stack n

hay·cock \'hā,käk\ n : small pile of hay

hay·rick \-,rik\ n : large outdoor stack
of hay

hay·seed \'hā,sēd\ n : bumpkin

hay·wire adj : being out of order

haz·ard \'hazərd\ n **1** : source of danger
2 : chance ~ vb: venture or risk —
haz·ard·ous adj

¹haze \'hāz\ n : fine dust, smoke, or
light vapor in the air that reduces vis-
ibility

²haze vb **hazed; haz·ing** : harass by
abusive and humiliating tricks

ha·zel \'hāzəl\ n **1** : shrub or small tree
bearing edible nuts (**ha·zel·nuts**) **2**
: light brown color

hazy \'hāzē\ adj **haz·i·er; -est 1** : obscured by haze **2** : vague or indefinite
—**haz·i·ly** adv —**haz·i·ness** n

he \'hē\ pron **1** : that male one **2** : a or
the person

head \'hed\ n **1** : front or upper part of
the body **2** : mind **3** : upper or higher
end **4** : director or leader **5** : place of
leadership or honor ~ adj : principal
or chief ~ vb **1** : provide with or form
a head **2** : put, stand, or be at the head
3 : point or proceed in a certain direction —**head·ache** n —**head·band**
n —**head·dress** n —**head·ed** adj —
head·first adv or adj —**head·gear** n
—**head·less** adj —**head·rest** n —
head·ship n —**head·wait·er** n

head·ing \-in\ n **1** : direction in which a
plane or ship heads **2** : something (as
a title) standing at the top or beginning

head·land \'hedlənd, -,land\ n : prom-
ontory

head·light *n* : light on the front of a vehicle

head·line *n* : introductory line of a newspaper story printed in large type

head·long \-ˈlȯŋ\ *adv* 1 : head foremost 2 : in a rash or reckless manner — **head·long** \-ˌlȯŋ\ *adj*

head·mas·ter *n* : man who is head of a private school

head·mis·tress *n* : woman who is head of a private school

head–on *adj* : having the front facing in the direction of initial contact — **head–on** *adv*

head·phone *n* : an earphone held on by a band over the head—usu. pl.

head·quar·ters *n sing or pl* : command or administrative center

head·stone *n* : stone at the head of a grave

head·strong *adj* : stubborn or willful

head·wa·ters *n pl* : source of a stream

head·way *n* : forward motion

heady \ˈhedē\ *adj* **head·i·er; -est** 1 : intoxicating 2 : shrewd

heal \ˈhēl\ *vb* : make or become sound or whole — **heal·er** *n*

health \ˈhelth\ *n* : sound physical or mental condition

health·ful \-fəl\ *adj* : beneficial to health — **health·ful·ly** *adv* — **health·ful·ness** *n*

healthy \ˈhelthē\ *adj* **health·i·er; -est** : enjoying or typical of good health — **health·i·ly** *adv* — **health·i·ness** *n*

heap \ˈhēp\ *n* : pile ~ *vb* : throw or lay in a heap

hear \ˈhir\ *vb* **heard** \ˈhərd\; **hear·ing** \ˈhiriŋ\ 1 : perceive by the ear 2 : heed 3 : learn

hear·ing *n* 1 : process or power of perceiving sound 2 : earshot 3 : session in which witnesses are heard

heark·en \ˈhärkən\ *vb* : give attention

hear·say *n* : rumor

hearse \ˈhərs\ *n* : vehicle for carrying the dead to the grave

heart \ˈhärt\ *n* 1 : hollow muscular organ that keeps up the circulation of the blood 2 : playing card of a suit marked with a red heart 3 : whole personality or the emotional or moral part of it 4 : courage 5 : essential part — **heart·beat** *n* — **heart·ed** *adj*

heart·ache *n* : anguish of mind

heart·break *n* : crushing grief — **heart·break·er** *n* — **heart·break·ing** *adj* — **heart·bro·ken** *adj*

heart·burn *n* : burning distress in the heart area after eating

heart·en \ˈhärtᵊn\ *vb* : encourage

hearth \ˈhärth\ *n* 1 : area in front of a fireplace 2 : home — **hearth·stone** *n*

heart·less \ˈhärtləs\ *adj* : cruel

heart·rend·ing \-ˌrendiŋ\ *adj* : causing intense grief or anguish

heart·sick *adj* : very despondent — **heart·sick·ness** *n*

heart·strings *n pl* : deepest emotions

heart·throb *n* : sweetheart

heart·warm·ing *adj* : inspiring sympathetic feeling

heart·wood *n* : central portion of wood

hearty \ˈhärtē\ *adj* **heart·i·er; -est** 1 : vigorously healthy 2 : nourishing — **heart·i·ly** *adv* — **heart·i·ness** *n*

heat \ˈhēt\ *vb* : make or become warm or hot ~ *n* 1 : condition of being hot 2 : form of energy that causes a body to rise in temperature 3 : intensity of feeling — **heat·ed·ly** *adv* — **heat·er** *n*

heath \ˈhēth\ *n* 1 : often evergreen shrubby plant of wet acid soils 2 : tract of wasteland — **heathy** *adj*

hea·then \ˈhēthən\ *n, pl* **-thens** *or* **-then** : uncivilized or godless person — **heathen** *adj*

heath·er \ˈhethər\ *n* : evergreen heath with lavender flowers — **heath·ery** *adj*

heat·stroke *n* : disorder that follows prolonged exposure to excessive heat

heave \ˈhēv\ *vb* **heaved** *or* **hove** \ˈhōv\; **heav·ing** 1 : rise or lift upward 2 : throw 3 : rise and fall ~ *n* 1 : an effort to lift or raise 2 : throw

heav·en \ˈhevən\ *n* 1 : sky 2 : abode of the Deity and of the blessed dead 3 : place of supreme happiness **heav·en·ly** *adj* — **heav·en·ward** *adv or adj*

heavy \ˈhevē\ *adj* **heavi·er, -est** 1 : having great weight 2 : hard to bear 3 : greater than the average — **heav·i·ly** *adv* — **heavi·ness** *n* — **heavy·weight** *n*

heavy–du·ty *adj* : able to withstand unusual strain

heavy·set *adj* : stocky and compact in build

heck·le \ˈhekəl\ *vb* **-led; -ling** : harass with gibes — **heck·ler** \-ˈheklər\ *n*

hec·tic \ˈhektik\ *adj* : filled with excitement, activity, or confusion — **hec·ti·cal·ly** \-tiklē\ *adv*

hedge \ˈhej\ *n* 1 : fence or boundary of

shrubs or small trees 2 : means of protection ~ *vb* hedged; hedg·ing 1 : protect oneself against loss 2 : evade the risk of commitment —hedg·er *n*

hedge·hog *n* : spiny mammal (as a porcupine)

he·do·nism \'hēd³n,izəm\ *n* : way of life devoted to pleasure —he·do·nist \-³nist\ *n* —he·do·nis·tic \,hēd-³n'istik\ *adj*

heed \'hēd\ *vb* : pay attention ~ *n* : attention —heed·ful \-fəl\ *adj* —heed·ful·ly *adv* —heed·ful·ness *n* —heed·less *adj* —heed·less·ly *adv* —heed·less·ness *n*

¹heel \'hēl\ *n* 1 : back of the foot 2 : crusty end of a loaf of bread 3 : solid piece forming the back of the sole of a shoe —heel·less \'hēlləs\ *adj*

²heel *vb* : tilt to one side

heft \'heft\ *n* : weight ~ *vb* : judge the weight of by lifting

hefty \'heftē\ *adj* heft·i·er; -est : big and bulky

he·ge·mo·ny \hi'jemənē\ *n* : preponderant influence over others

heif·er \'hefər\ *n* : young cow

height \'hīt, 'hītth\ *n* 1 : highest part or point 2 : distance from bottom to top 3 : altitude

height·en \'hīt³n\ *vb* : increase in amount or degree

hei·nous \'hānəs\ *adj* : shockingly evil —hei·nous·ly *adv* —hei·nous·ness *n*

heir \'ar\ *n* : one who inherits or is entitled to inherit property

heir·ess \'arəs\ *n* : female heir esp. to great wealth

heir·loom \'ar,lüm\ *n* : something handed on from one generation to another

held *past of* HOLD

he·li·cal \'helikəl, 'hē-\ *adj* : spiral

he·li·cop·ter \'helə,käptər, 'hē-\ *n* : aircraft supported in the air by rotors

he·lio·trope \'hēlyə,trōp\ *n* : garden herb with small fragrant white or purple flowers

he·li·um \'hēlēəm\ *n* : very light nonflammable gaseous chemical element

he·lix \'hēliks\ *n, pl* -li·ces \'helə,sēz, 'hē-\ : something spiral

hell \'hel\ *n* 1 : nether world in which the dead continue to exist 2 : realm of the devil 3 : place or state of torment or destruction —hell·ish *adj*

hell·gram·mite \'helgrə,mīt\ *n* : aquatic insect larva

hel·lion \'helyən\ *n* : troublesome person

hel·lo \hə'lō, he-\ *n, pl* -los : expression of greeting

helm \'helm\ *n* : lever or wheel for steering a ship —helms·man \'helmzmən\ *n*

hel·met \'helmət\ *n* : protective covering for the head

help \'help\ *vb* 1 : supply what is needed 2 : be of use 3 : refrain from or prevent ~ *n* 1 : something that helps or a source of help 2 : one who helps another —help·er *n* —help·ful \-fəl\ *adj* —help·ful·ly *adv* —help·ful·ness *n* —help·less *adj* —help·less·ly *adv* —help·less·ness *n*

help·ing \'helpiŋ\ *n* : portion of food

help·mate *n* 1 : helper 2 : wife

help·meet \-,mēt\ *n* : helpmate

hel·ter-skel·ter \,heltər'skeltər\ *adv* : in total disorder

hem \'hem\ *n* : border of an article of cloth doubled back and stitched down ~ *vb* -mm- 1 : sew a hem 2 : surround restrictively —hem·line *n*

he·ma·tol·o·gy \,hēmə'täləjē\ *n* : study of the blood and blood-forming organs —hema·to·log·ic \-tə'läjik\ *adj* —he·ma·tol·o·gist \-'täləjist\ *n*

hemi·sphere \'hemə,sfir\ *n* : one of the halves of the earth divided by the equator into northern and southern parts (northern hemisphere, southern hemisphere) or by a meridian into eastern and western parts (eastern hemisphere, western hemisphere) —hemi·spher·ic \,hemə-'sfirik, -'sfer-\, hemi·spher·i·cal \-'sfirikəl, -'sfer-\ *adj*

hem·lock \'hem,läk\ *n* 1 : poisonous herb related to the carrot 2 : evergreen tree related to the pines

he·mo·glo·bin \'hēmə,glōbən\ *n* : iron-containing compound found in red blood cells

he·mo·phil·ia \,hēmə'filēə\ *n* : hereditary tendency to severe prolonged bleeding —he·mo·phil·i·ac \-ē,ak\ *adj or n*

hem·or·rhage \'hemərij\ *n* : large discharge of blood —hemorrhage *vb* —hem·or·rhag·ic \,hemə'rajik\ *adj*

hem·or·rhoids \'hemə,róidz\ *n pl* : swollen mass of dilated veins at or just within the anus

hemp \'hemp\ *n* : tall Asian herb grown

for its tough fiber —**hemp•en**
\'hempən\ adj

hen \'hen\ n : female domestic fowl

hence \'hens\ adv 1 : away 2 : therefore
3 : from this source or origin

hence•forth adv : from this point on

hence•for•ward adv : henceforth

hench•man \'henchmən\ n : trusted follower

hen•na \'henə\ n : reddish brown dye
from a tropical shrub used esp. on hair

hen•peck \'hen,pek\ vb : subject (one's
husband) to persistent nagging

he•pat•ic \hi'patik\ adj : relating to or
resembling the liver

hep•a•ti•tis \,hepə'tītəs\ n, pl -**tit•i•des**
\-'titə,dēz\ : disease in which the liver
becomes inflamed

her \'hər\ adj : of or relating to her or
herself ~ \ər, (')hər\ pron, objective
case of SHE

her•ald \'herəld\ n 1 : official crier or
messenger 2 : harbinger ~ vb : give
notice

her•ald•ry \'herəldrē\ n, pl -**ries** : practice
of devising and granting stylized
emblems (as for a family) —**he•ral•dic** \he'raldik, hə-\ adj

herb \'ərb, 'hərb\ n 1 : seed plant that
lacks woody tissue 2 : plant or plant
part valued for medicinal or savory
qualities —**her•ba•ceous** \,ər'bāshəs,
,hər-\ adj —**herb•age** \'ərbij, 'hər-\ n
—**herb•al** \-bəl\ n or adj —**herb•al•ist** \-bəlist\ n

her•bi•cide \'ərbə,sīd, 'hər-\ n : agent
that destroys plants —**her•bi•cid•al**
\,ərbə'sīdəl, ,hər-\ adj

her•biv•o•rous \,ər'bivərəs, ,hər-\ adj
: feeding on plants —**her•bi•vore**
\'ərbə,vōr, 'hər-\ n

her•cu•le•an \,hərkyə'lēən, ,hər'kyū-
lēən\ adj : of extraordinary power,
size, or difficulty

herd \'hərd\ n : group of animals of one
kind ~ vb : assemble or move in a
herd —**herd•er** n —**herds•man**
\'hərdzmən\ n

here \'hir\ adv 1 : in, at, or to this place
2 : now 3 : at or in this point or particular
4 : in the present life or state
~ n : this place —**here•abouts**
\'hirə,baúts\, **here•about** \-,baút\ adv

here•af•ter adv : in some future time or
state ~ n : existence beyond earthly
life

here•by adv : by means of this

he•red•i•tary \hə'redə,terē\ adj 1 : genetically
passed or passable from parent
to offspring 2 : passing by inheritance

he•red•i•ty \-ətē\ n : the passing of characteristics
from parent to offspring

here•in adv : in this

here•of adv : of this

here•on adv : on this

her•e•sy \'herəsē\ n, pl -**sies** : opinion or
doctrine contrary to church dogma —
her•e•tic \-,tik\ n —**he•re•ti•cal**
\hə'retikəl\ adj

here•to adv : to this document

here•to•fore \'hirtü,fōr\ adv : up to this
time

here•un•der adv : under this

here•un•to adv : to this

here•upon adv : on this

here•with adv 1 : with this 2 : hereby

her•i•tage \'herətij\ n 1 : inheritance 2
: birthright

her•maph•ro•dite \hər'mafrə,dīt\ n : animal
or plant having both male and
female reproductive organs —**her•maphrodite**
adj —**her•maph•ro•dit•ic** \-,mafrə'ditik\ adj

her•met•ic \hər'metik\ adj : sealed airtight
—**her•met•i•cal•ly** \-iklē\ adv

her•mit \'hərmət\ n : one who lives in
solitude

her•nia \'hərnēə\ n, pl -**ni•as** or -**ni•ae**
\-nē,ē, -nē,ī\ : protrusion of a bodily
part through the weakened wall of its
enclosure —**her•ni•ate** \-nē,āt\ vb

he•ro \'hērō, 'hirō\ n, pl -**roes** : one that
is much admired or shows great courage
—**he•ro•ic** \hi'rōik\ adj —**he•ro•i•cal•ly**
\-iklē\ adv —**he•ro•ics** \-iks\ n
pl —**her•o•ism** \'herə,wizəm\ n

her•o•in \'herəwən\ n : strongly addictive
narcotic

her•o•ine \'herəwən\ n : woman of heroic
achievements or qualities

her•on \'herən\ n : long-legged longbilled
wading bird

her•pes \'hərpēz\ n : virus disease characterized
by the formation of blisters

her•pe•tol•o•gy \,hərpə'täləjē\ n : study
of reptiles and amphibians —**her•pe•tol•o•gist**
\-pə'täləjist\ n

her•ring \'heriŋ\ n, pl -**ring** or -**rings**
: narrow-bodied Atlantic food fish

hers \'hərz\ pron : one or the ones belonging
to her

her•self \hər'self\ pron : she, her —used
reflexively or for emphasis

hertz \'herts, 'hərts\ n, pl **hertz** : unit of

frequency equal to one cycle per second

hes•i•tant \'hezətənt\ *adj* : tending to hesitate —**hes•i•tance** \-təns\ *n* —**hes•i•tan•cy** \-tənsē\ *n* —**hes•i•tant•ly** *adv*

hes•i•tate \'hezə,tāt\ *vb* **-tat•ed; -tat•ing** 1 : hold back esp. in doubt 2 : pause —**hes•i•ta•tion** \,hezə'tāshən\ *n*

het•er•o•ge•neous \,hetərə'jēnēəs, -nyəs\ *adj* : consisting of dissimilar ingredients or constituents —**het•er•o•ge•ne•ity** \-jə'nēətē\ *n* —**het•ero•ge•neous•ly** *adv*

het•ero•sex•u•al \,hetərō'sekshəwəl\ *adj* : oriented toward the opposite sex —**heterosexual** *n* —**het•ero•sex•u•al•i•ty** \-,sekshə'walətē\ *n*

hew \'hyü\ *vb* **hewed; hewed** *or* **hewn** \'hyün\; **hew•ing** 1 : cut or shape with or as if with an ax 2 : conform strictly —**hew•er** *n*

hex \'heks\ *vb* : put an evil spell on —**hex** *n*

hexa•gon \'heksə,gän\ *n* : 6-sided polygon —**hex•ag•o•nal** \hek'sagənᵊl\ *adj*

hey•day \'hā,dā\ *n* : time of flourishing

hi•a•tus \hī'ātəs\ *n* : lapse in continuity

hi•ba•chi \hi'bächē\ *n* : brazier

hi•ber•nate \'hībər,nāt\ *vb* **-nat•ed; -nat•ing** : pass the winter in a torpid or resting state —**hi•ber•na•tion** \,hībər'nāshən\ *n* —**hi•ber•na•tor** \'hībər,nātər\ *n*

hic•cup \'hikəp\ *vb* : **-cuped; -cup•ing** : to inhale spasmodically and make a peculiar sound ~ *n pl* : attack of hiccuping

hick \'hik\ *n* : awkward provincial person —**hick** *adj*

hick•o•ry \'hikərē\ *n, pl* **-ries** : No. American hardwood tree —**hickory** *adj*

1**hide** \'hīd\ *vb* **hid** \'hid\; **hid•den** \'hidᵊn\ *or* **hid; hid•ing** : put or remain out of sight —**hid•er** *n*

2**hide** *n* : animal skin

hide•bound \'hīd,baůnd\ *adj* : inflexible or conservative

hid•eous \'hidēəs\ *adj* : very ugly —**hid•eous•ly** *adv* —**hid•eous•ness** *n*

hie \'hī\ *vb* **hied; hy•ing** *or* **hie•ing** : hurry

hi•er•ar•chy \'hīə,rärkē\ *n, pl* **-chies** : persons or things arranged in a graded series —**hi•er•ar•chi•cal** \,hīə'rärkikəl\ *adj*

hi•er•o•glyph•ic \,hīərə'glifik\ *n* : character in the picture writing of the ancient Egyptians

high \'hī\ *adj* 1 : having large extension upward 2 : elevated in pitch 3 : exalted in character 4 : of greater degree or amount than average 5 : expensive 6 : excited or stupefied by alcohol or a drug ~ *adv* : at or to a high place or degree ~ *n* 1 : elevated point or level 2 : automobile gear giving the highest speed —**highly** *adv*

high•boy *n* : high chest of drawers on legs

high•brow \-,braů\ *n* : person of superior learning or culture —**highbrow** *adj*

high–flown *adj* : pretentious

high–hand•ed *adj* : willful and arrogant —**high–hand•ed•ly** *adv* —**high–hand•ed•ness** *n*

high•land \'hīlənd\ *n* : hilly country —**high•land•er** \-ləndər\ *n*

high•light *n* : event or detail of major importance ~ *vb* 1 : emphasize 2 : be a highlight of

high•ness \-nəs\ *n* 1 : quality or degree of being high 2 —used as a title (as for kings)

high–rise *adj* : having several stories

high school *n* : school usu. including grades 9 to 12 or 10 to 12

high–spir•it•ed *adj* : lively

high–strung \,hī'strəŋ\ *adj* : very nervous or sensitive

high•way *n* : public road

high•way•man \-mən\ *n* : one who robs travelers on a road

hi•jack \'hī,jak\ *vb* : steal esp. by commandeering a vehicle —**hijack** *n* —**hi•jack•er** *n*

hike \'hīk\ *vb* **hiked; hik•ing** 1 : raise quickly 2 : take a long walk ~ *n* 1 : long walk 2 : increase —**hik•er** *n*

hi•lar•i•ous \hi'larēəs, hī'-\ *adj* : extremely funny —**hi•lar•i•ous•ly** *adv* —**hi•lar•i•ty** \-ətē\ *n*

hill \'hil\ *n* : place where the land rises —**hill•side** *n* —**hill•top** *n* —**hilly** *adj*

hill•bil•ly \'hil,bilē\ *n, pl* **-lies** : person from a backwoods area

hill•ock \'hilək\ *n* : small hill

hilt \'hilt\ *n* : handle of a sword

him \'him\ *pron, objective case of* HE

him•self \him'self\ *pron* : he, him —used reflexively or for emphasis

1**hind** \'hīnd\ *n* : female deer

2**hind** *adj* : back

hin·der \'hindər\ *vb* : obstruct or hold back

hind·most *adj* : farthest to the rear

hind·quar·ter *n* : back half of a complete side of a carcass

hin·drance \'hindrəns\ *n* : something that hinders

hind·sight *n* : understanding of an event after it has happened

Hin·du·ism \'hindü,izəm\ *n* : body of religious beliefs and practices native to India —**Hin·du** *n or adj*

hinge \'hinj\ *n* : jointed piece on which a swinging part (as a door) turns ~ *vb* **hinged; hing·ing** 1 : attach by or furnish with hinges 2 : depend

hint \'hint\ *n* 1 : indirect suggestion 2 : clue 3 : very small amount —**hint** *vb*

hin·ter·land \'hintər,land\ *n* : remote region

hip \'hip\ *n* : part of the body on either side just below the waist —**hip·bone** *n*

hip·po·pot·a·mus \,hipə'pätəməs\ *n, pl* **-mus·es** *or* **-mi** \-,mī\ : large thick-skinned African river animal

hire \'hīr\ *n* 1 : payment for labor 2 : employment 3 : one who is hired ~ *vb* **hired; hir·ing** : employ for pay

hire·ling \-liŋ\ *n* : one who serves another only for gain

hir·sute \'hər,süt, 'hir-\ *adj* : hairy

his \'hiz\ *adj* : of or belonging to him ~ *pron* : ones belonging to him

hiss \'his\ *vb* 1 : make a sibilant sound 2 : show dislike by hissing —**hiss** *n*

his·to·ri·an \his'tōrēən\ *n* : writer of history

his·to·ry \'histərē\ *n, pl* **-ries** 1 : chronological record of significant events 2 : study of past events 3 : an established record —**his·tor·ic** \his-'tôrik\, **his·tor·i·cal** \-ikəl\ *adj* —**his·tor·i·cal·ly** \-klē\ *adv*

his·tri·on·ics \,histrē'äniks\ *n pl* : exaggerated display of emotion

hit \'hit\ *vb* **hit; hit·ting** 1 : reach with a blow 2 : come or cause to come in contact 3 : affect detrimentally ~ *n* 1 : blow 2 : great success —**hit·ter** *n*

hitch \'hich\ *vb* 1 : move by jerks 2 : catch by a hook 3 : hitchhike ~ *n* 1 : jerk 2 : sudden halt

hitch·hike \'hich,hīk\ *vb* : travel by securing free rides from passing vehicles —**hitch·hik·er** *n*

hith·er \'hithər\ *adv* : to this place

hith·er·to \-,tü\ *adv* : up to this time

hive \'hīv\ *n* 1 : container housing honeybees 2 : colony of bees —**hive** *vb*

hives \'hīvz\ *n sing or pl* : allergic disorder with itchy skin patches

HMO \,āch,em'ō\ *n* : comprehensive health-care organization financed by clients

hoard \'hōrd\ *n* : hidden accumulation —**hoard** *vb* —**hoard·er** *n*

hoar·frost \'hōr,frȯst\ *n* : frost

hoarse \'hōrs\ *adj* **hoars·er; -est** 1 : harsh in sound 2 : speaking in a harsh strained voice —**hoarse·ly** *adv* —**hoarse·ness** *n*

hoary \'hōrē\ *adj* **hoar·i·er; -est** : gray or white with age —**hoar·i·ness** *n*

hoax \'hōks\ *n* : act intended to trick or dupe —**hoax** *vb* —**hoax·er** *n*

hob·ble \'häbəl\ *vb* **-bled; -bling** : limp along ~ *n* : hobbling movement

hob·by \'häbē\ *n, pl* **-bies** : interest engaged in for relaxation —**hob·by·ist** \-ēist\ *n*

hob·gob·lin \'häb,gäblən\ *n* 1 : mischievous goblin 2 : bogey

hob·nail \-,nāl\ *n* : short nail for studding shoe soles —**hob·nailed** \-,nāld\ *adj*

hob·nob \-,näb\ *vb* **-bb-** : associate socially

ho·bo \'hōbō\ *n, pl* **-boes** : tramp

¹**hock** \'häk\ *n* : joint or region in the hind limb of a quadruped corresponding to the human ankle

²**hock** *n or vb* : pawn

hock·ey \'häkē\ *n* : game played on ice or a field by 2 teams

hod \'häd\ *n* : carrier for bricks or mortar

hodge·podge \'häj,päj\ *n* : heterogeneous mixture

hoe \'hō\ *n* : long-handled tool for cultivating or weeding —**hoe** *vb*

hog \'hȯg, 'häg\ *n* 1 : domestic adult swine 2 : glutton ~ *vb* : take selfishly —**hog·gish** *adj*

hogs·head \'hȯgz,hed, 'hägz-\ *n* : large cask or barrel

hog·wash *n* : nonsense

hoist \'hȯist\ *vb* : lift ~ *n* 1 : lift 2 : apparatus for hoisting

hok·ey \'hōkē\ *adj* **hok·i·er; -est** 1 : tiresomely simple or sentimental 2 : phony

¹**hold** \'hōld\ *vb* **held** \'held\; **hold·ing** 1 : possess 2 : restrain 3 : have a grasp on 4 : remain or keep in a particular

situation or position **5** : contain **6** : regard **7** : cause to occur **8** : occupy esp. by appointment or election ~ *n* **1** : act or manner of holding **2** : restraining or controlling influence —**hold·er** *n* —**hold forth** : speak at length —**hold to** : adhere to —**hold with** : agree with

²hold *n* : cargo area of a ship

hold·ing \'hōldiŋ\ *n* : property owned — usu. pl.

hold·up *n* **1** : robbery at the point of a gun **2** : delay

hole \'hōl\ *n* **1** : opening into or through something **2** : hollow place (as a pit) **3** : den —**hole** *vb*

hol·i·day \'hälə,dā\ *n* **1** : day of freedom from work **2** : vacation —**holiday** *vb*

ho·li·ness \'hōlēnəs\ *n* : quality or state of being holy—used as a title for a high religious official

ho·lis·tic \hō'listik\ *adj* : relating to a whole (as the body)

hol·ler \'hälər\ *vb* : cry out —**holler** *n*

hol·low \'hälō\ *adj* -**low·er** \-əwər\; -**est** **1** : sunken **2** : having a cavity within **3** : sounding like a noise made in an empty place **4** : empty of value or meaning ~ *vb* : make or become hollow ~ *n* **1** : surface depression **2** : cavity —**hol·low·ness** *n*

hol·ly \'hälē\ *n*, *pl* -**lies** : evergreen tree or shrub with glossy leaves

hol·ly·hock \-,häk, -,hók\ *n* : tall perennial herb with showy flowers

ho·lo·caust \'hälə,kóst, 'hō-, 'hó-\ *n* : thorough destruction esp. by fire

hol·stein \'hōl,stēn, -,stīn\ *n* : large black-and-white dairy cow

hol·ster \'hōlstər\ *n* : case for a pistol

ho·ly \'hōlē\ *adj* -**li·er**; -**est 1** : sacred **2** : spiritually pure

hom·age \'ämij, 'hä-\ *n* : reverent regard

home \'hōm\ *n* **1** : residence **2** : congenial environment **3** : place of origin or refuge ~ *vb* homed; **hom·ing** : go or return home —**home·bred** *adj* —**home·com·ing** *n* —**home·grown** *adj* —**home·land** \-,land\ *n* —**home·less** *adj* —**home·made** \-'mād\ *adj*

home·ly \-lē\ *adj* -**li·er**; -**est** : plain or unattractive —**home·li·ness** *n*

home·mak·er *n* : one who manages a household —**home·mak·ing** *n*

home·sick *adj* : longing for home — **home·sick·ness** *n*

home·spun \-,spən\ *adj* : simple

home·stead \-,sted\ *n* : home and land

occupied and worked by a family — **home·stead·er** \-ər\ *n*

home·stretch *n* **1** : last part of a race-track **2** : final stage

home·ward \-wərd\, **home·wards** \-wərdz\ *adv* : toward home —**home·ward** *adj*

home·work *n* : school lessons to be done outside the classroom

hom·ey \'hōmē\ *adj* **hom·i·er**; -**est** : characteristic of home

ho·mi·cide \'hämə,sīd, 'hō-\ *n* : the killing of one human being by another— **hom·i·cid·al** \,hämə'sīdᵊl, ,hō-\ *adj*

hom·i·ly \'häməlē\ *n*, *pl* -**lies** : sermon

hom·i·ny \'hämənē\ *n* : type of processed hulled corn

ho·mo·ge·neous \,hōmə'jēnēəs, -nyəs\ *adj* : of the same or a similar kind — **ho·mo·ge·ne·i·ty** \-jə'nēətē\ *n* —**ho·mo·ge·neous·ly** *adv*

ho·mog·e·nize \hō'mäjə,nīz, hə-\ *vb* -**nized**; -**niz·ing** : make the particles in (as milk) of uniform size and even distribution —**ho·mog·e·ni·za·tion** \-,mäjənə'zāshən\ *n* —**ho·mog·e·niz·er** *n*

ho·mo·graph \'hämə,graf, 'hō-\ *n* : one of 2 or more words (as the noun *conduct* and the verb *conduct*) spelled alike but different in origin or meaning or pronunciation

hom·onym \'hämə,nim, 'hō-\ *n* **1** : homophone **2** : homograph **3** : one of 2 or more words (as *pool* of water and *pool* the game) spelled and pronounced alike but different in meaning

ho·mo·phone \'hämə,fōn, 'hō-\ *n* : one of 2 or more words (as *to*, *too*, and *two*) pronounced alike but different in origin or meaning or spelling

Ho·mo sa·pi·ens \,hōmō'sapēənz, -'sā-\ *n* : humankind

ho·mo·sex·u·al \,hōmə'sekshəwəl\ *adj* : oriented toward one's own sex — **homosexual** *n* —**ho·mo·sex·u·al·i·ty** \-,seksha'walətē\ *n*

hone \'hōn\ *vb* : sharpen with or as if with an abrasive stone

hon·est \'änəst\ *adj* **1** : free from deception **2** : trustworthy **3** : frank —**hon·est·ly** *adv* —**hon·esty** \-əstē\ *n*

hon·ey \'hənē\ *n*, *pl* -**eys** : sweet sticky substance made by bees (**hon·ey·bees**) from the nectar of flowers

hon·ey·comb *n* : mass of 6-sided wax

cells built by honeybees or something like it ~ *vb* : make or become full of holes like a honeycomb

hon·ey·moon *n* : holiday taken by a newly married couple —**honeymoon** *vb*

hon·ey·suck·le \-ˌsəkəl\ *n* : shrub or vine·with flowers rich in nectar

honk \'haŋk, 'hoŋk\ *n* : cry of a goose or a similar sound —**honk** *vb* — **honk·er** *n*

hon·or \'änər\ *n* **1** : good name **2** : outward respect or symbol of this **3** : privilege **4** : person of superior rank or position —used esp. as a title **5** : something or someone worthy of respect **6** : integrity ~ *vb* **1** : regard with honor **2** : confer honor on **3** : fulfill the terms of —**hon·or·able** \'änərəbəl\ *adj* —**hon·or·ably** \-blē\ *adv* —**hon·or·ari·ly** \ˌänəˈrerəlē\ *adv* —**hon·or·ary** \'änəˌrerē\ *adj* —**hon·or·ee** \ˌänəˈrē\ *n*

hood \'húd\ *n* **1** : part of a garment that covers the head **2** : covering over an automobile engine compartment — **hood·ed** *adj*

-hood \ˌhúd\ *n suffix* **1** : state, condition, or quality **2** : individuals sharing a state or character

hood·lum \'húdləm, 'húd-\ *n* : thug

hood·wink \'húdˌwiŋk\ *vb* : deceive

hoof \'húf, 'húf\ *n, pl* **hooves** \'húvz, 'húvz\ *or* **hoofs** : horny covering of the toes of some mammals (as horses or cattle) —**hoofed** \'húft, 'húft\ *adj*

hook \'húk\ *n* : curved or bent device for catching, holding, or pulling ~ *vb* : seize or make fast with a hook — **hook·er** *n*

hook·worm *n* : parasitic intestinal worm

hoo·li·gan \'húligən\ *n* : thug

hoop \'húp\ *n* : circular strip, figure, or object

hoot \'hút\ *vb* **1** : shout in contempt **2** : make the cry of an owl —**hoot** *n* — **hoot·er** *n*

¹hop \'häp\ *vb* **-pp-** : move by quick springy leaps —**hop** *n*

²hop *n* : vine whose ripe dried flowers are used to flavor malt liquors

hope \'hōp\ *vb* **hoped; hop·ing** : desire with expectation of fulfillment ~ *n* **1** : act of hoping **2** : something hoped for —**hope·ful** \-fəl\ *adj* —**hope·fully** *adv* —**hope·ful·ness** *n* —**hope·less** *adj* —**hope·less·ly** *adv* —**hope·less·ness** *n*

hop·per \'häpər\ *n* : container that releases its contents through the bottom

horde \'hórd\ *n* : throng or swarm

ho·ri·zon \hə'rīzən\ *n* : apparent junction of earth and sky

hor·i·zon·tal \ˌhórə'zäntəl\ *adj* : parallel to the horizon —**hor·i·zon·tal·ly** *adv*

hor·mone \'hórˌmōn\ *n* : cell product in body fluids that has a specific effect on other cells —**hor·mon·al** \hór-'mōnəl\ *adj*

horn \'hórn\ *n* **1** : hard bony projection on the head of a hoofed animal **2** : brass wind instrument —**horned** *adj* —**horn·less** *adj*

hor·net \'hórnət\ *n* : large social wasp

horny \'hórnē\ *adj* **horn·i·er; -est 1** : made of horn **2** : hard or callous **3** : sexually aroused

horo·scope \'hórəˌskōp\ *n* : astrological forecast

hor·ren·dous \hó'rendəs\ *adj* : horrible

hor·ri·ble \'hórəbəl\ *adj* **1** : having or causing horror **2** : highly disagreeable —**hor·ri·ble·ness** *n* —**hor·ri·bly** \-blē\ *adv*

hor·rid \'hórəd\ *adj* : horrible —**hor·rid·ly** *adv*

hor·ri·fy \'hórəˌfī\ *vb* **-fied; -fy·ing** : cause to feel horror

hor·ror \'hórər\ *n* **1** : intense fear, dread, or dismay **2** : intense repugnance **3** : something horrible

hors d'oeuvre \ór'dərv\ *n, pl* **hors d'oeuvres** \-'dərvz\ : appetizer

horse \'hórs\ *n* : large solid-hoofed domesticated mammal —**horse·back** *n or adv* —**horse·hair** *n* —**horse·hide** *n* —**horse·less** *adj* —**horse·man** \-mən\ *n* —**horse·man·ship** *n* — **horse·wom·an** *n* —**hors·ey, horsy** *adj*

horse·fly *n* : large fly with bloodsucking female

horse·play *n* : rough boisterous play

horse·pow·er *n* : unit of mechanical power

horse·rad·ish *n* : herb with a pungent root used as a condiment

horse·shoe *n* : U-shaped protective metal plate fitted to the rim of a horse's hoof

hor·ti·cul·ture \'hórtəˌkəlchər\ *n* : science of growing fruits, vegetables, and flowers —**hor·ti·cul·tur·al** \ˌhórtə'kəlchərəl\ *adj* —**hor·ti·cul·tur·ist** \-rist\ *n*

ho·san·na \hō'zanə, -'zän-\ *interj* —

used as a cry of acclamation and adoration —**hosanna** n

hose \'hōz\ n 1 pl **hose** : stocking or sock 2 pl **hos·es** : flexible tube for conveying fluids ~ vb **hosed; hos·ing** : spray, water, or wash with a hose

ho·siery \'hōzhərē, 'hōzə-\ n : stockings or socks

hos·pice \'häspəs\ n 1 : lodging (as for travelers) maintained by a religious order 2 : facility or program for caring for dying persons

hos·pi·ta·ble \hä'spitəbəl, 'häs,pit-\ adj : given to generous and cordial reception of guests —**hos·pi·ta·bly** \-blē\ adv

hos·pi·tal \'häs,pit°l\ n : institution where the sick or injured receive medical care —**hos·pi·tal·i·za·tion** \,häs-,pit°lə'zāshən\ n —**hos·pi·tal·ize** \'häs,pit°l,īz\ vb

hos·pi·tal·i·ty \,häspə'talətē\ n, pl -ties : hospitable treatment, reception, or disposition

¹host \'hōst\ n 1 : army 2 : multitude

²host n : one who receives or entertains guests —**host** vb

³host n : eucharistic bread

hos·tage \'hästij\ n : person held to guarantee that promises be kept or demands met

hos·tel \'häst°l\ n : lodging for youth —**hos·tel·er** n

hos·tel·ry \-rē\ n, pl -ries : hotel

host·ess \'hōstəs\ n : woman who is host

hos·tile \'häst°l, -,tīl\ adj : openly or actively unfriendly or opposed to someone or something —**hostile** n —**hos·tile·ly** adv —**hos·til·i·ty** \häs'tilətē\ n

hot \'hät\ adj -tt- 1 : having a high temperature 2 : giving a sensation of heat or burning 3 : ardent 4 : pungent —**hot** adv —**hot·ly** adv —**hot·ness** n

hot·bed n : environment that favors rapid growth

hot dog n : frankfurter

ho·tel \hō'tel\ n : building where lodging and personal services are provided

hot·head·ed adj : impetuous —**hot·head** n —**hot·head·ed·ly** adv —**hot·head·ed·ness** n

hot·house n : greenhouse

hound \'haund\ n : long-eared hunting dog ~ vb : pursue relentlessly

hour \'aur\ n 1 : 24th part of a day 2 : time of day —**hour·ly** adv or adj

hour·glass n : glass vessel for measuring time

house \'haus\ n, pl **hous·es** \'hauzəz\ 1 : building to live in 2 : household 3 : legislative body 4 : business firm ~ \'hauz\ vb **housed; hous·ing** : provide with or take shelter —**house·boat** \'haus,bōt\ n —**house·clean** \'haus,klēn\ vb —**house·clean·ing** n —**house·ful** \-,fúl\ n —**house·maid** n —**house·wares** n pl —**house·work** n

house·bro·ken \-,brōkən\ adj : trained in excretory habits acceptable in indoor living

house·fly n : two-winged fly common about human habitations

house·hold \-,hōld\ n : those who dwell as a family under the same roof ~ adj 1 : domestic 2 : common or familiar —**house·hold·er** n

house·keep·ing \-,kēpiŋ\ n : care and management of a house or institution —**house·keep·er** n

house·warm·ing n : party to celebrate moving into a house

house·wife \'haus,wīf\ n : married woman in charge of a household —**house·wife·ly** adj —**house·wif·ery** \-,wīfərē\ n

hous·ing \'hauziŋ\ n 1 : dwellings for people 2 : protective covering

hove past of HEAVE

hov·el \'həvəl, 'häv-\ n : small wretched house

hov·er \'həvər, 'häv-\ vb 1 : remain suspended in the air 2 : move about in the vicinity

how \'hau\ adv 1 : in what way or condition 2 : for what reason 3 : to what extent ~ conj : the way or manner in which

how·ev·er \hau'evər\ conj : in whatever manner ~ adv 1 : to whatever degree or in whatever manner 2 : in spite of that

how·it·zer \'hauətsər\ n : short cannon

howl \'haul\ vb : emit a loud long doleful sound like a dog —**howl** n —**howl·er** n

hoy·den \'hoid°n\ n : girl or woman of saucy or carefree behavior

hub \'həb\ n : central part of a circular object (as of a wheel) —**hub·cap** n

hub·bub \'həb,əb\ n : uproar

hu·bris \'hyübrəs\ n : excessive pride

huck·le·ber·ry \'həkəl,berē\ n 1 : shrub

related to the blueberry or its berry **2** : blueberry

huck·ster \'həkstər\ *n* : peddler

hud·dle \'hədᵊl\ *vb* **-dled; -dling 1** : crowd together **2** : confer —**huddle** *n*

hue \'hyü\ *n* : color or gradation of color —**hued** \'hyüd\ *adj*

huff \'həf\ *n* : fit of pique —**huffy** *adj*

hug \'həg\ *vb* **-gg- 1** : press tightly in the arms **2** : stay close to —**hug** *n*

huge \'hyüj\ *adj* **hug·er; hug·est** : very large or extensive —**huge·ly** *adv* —**huge·ness** *n*

hu·la \'hülä\ *n* : Polynesian dance

hulk \'həlk\ *n* **1** : bulky or unwieldy person or thing **2** : old ship unfit for service —**hulk·ing** *adj*

hull \'həl\ *n* **1** : outer covering of a fruit or seed **2** : frame or body of a ship or boat ~ *vb* : remove the hulls of —**hull·er** *n*

hul·la·ba·loo \'hələbə,lü\ *n, pl* **-loos** : uproar

hum \'həm\ *vb* **-mm- 1** : make a prolonged sound like that of the speech sound \m\ **2** : be busily active **3** : run smoothly **4** : sing with closed lips —**hum** *n* —**hum·mer** *n*

hu·man \'hyümən, 'yü-\ *adj* **1** : of or relating to the species people belong to **2** : by, for, or like people —**human** *n* —**hu·man·kind** *n* —**hu·man·ly** *adv* —**hu·man·ness** *n*

hu·mane \hyü'mān, ,yü-\ *adj* : showing compassion or consideration for others —**hu·mane·ly** *adv* —**hu·mane·ness** *n*

hu·man·ism \'hyümə,nizəm, 'yü-\ *n* : doctrine or way of life centered on human interests or values —**hu·man·ist** \-nist\ *n or adj* —**hu·man·is·tic** \,hyümə'nistik, ,yü-\ *adj*

hu·man·i·tar·i·an \hyü,manə'terēən, yü-\ *n* : person promoting human welfare —**humanitarian** *adj* —**hu·man·i·tar·i·an·ism** *n*

hu·man·i·ty \hyü'manətē, yü-\ *n, pl* **-ties 1** : human or humane quality or state **2** : the human race

hu·man·ize \'hyümə,nīz, 'yü-\ *vb* **-ized; -iz·ing** : make human or humane —**hu·man·iza·tion** \,hyümənə'zāshən, ,yü-\ *n* —**hu·man·iz·er** *n*

hu·man·oid \'hyümə,nóid, 'yü-\ *adj* : having human form —**humanoid** *n*

hum·ble \'həmbəl\ *adj* **-bler; -blest 1**

: not proud or haughty **2** : not pretentious ~ *vb* **-bled; -bling** : make humble —**hum·ble·ness** *n* —**hum·bler** *n* —**hum·bly** \-blē\ *adv*

hum·bug \'həm,bəg\ *n* : nonsense

hum·drum \-,drəm\ *adj* : monotonous

hu·mid \'hyüməd, 'yü-\ *adj* : containing or characterized by moisture —**hu·mid·i·fi·ca·tion** \hyü,midəfə'kāshən\ *n* —**hu·mid·i·fi·er** \-'midə,fīər\ *n* —**hu·mid·i·fy** \-,fī\ *vb* —**hu·mid·ly** *adv*

hu·mid·i·ty \hyü'midətē, yü-\ *n, pl* **-ties** : atmospheric moisture

hu·mi·dor \'hyümə,dòr, 'yü-\ *n* : humidified storage case (as for cigars)

hu·mil·i·ate \hyü'milē,āt, yü-\ *vb* **-at·ed; -at·ing** : injure the self-respect of —**hu·mil·i·at·ing·ly** *adv* —**hu·mil·i·ation** \-,milē'āshən\ *n*

hu·mil·i·ty \hyü'milətē, yü-\ *n* : humble quality or state

hum·ming·bird \'həmiŋ,bərd\ *n* : tiny American bird that can hover

hum·mock \'həmək\ *n* : mound or knoll —**hum·mocky** \-mək\ē\ *adj*

hu·mor \'hyümər, 'yü-\ *n* **1** : mood **2** : quality of being laughably ludicrous or incongruous **3** : appreciation of what is ludicrous or incongruous **4** : something intended to be funny ~ *vb* : comply with the wishes or mood of —**hu·mor·ist** \-ərist\ *n* —**hu·mor·less** *adj* —**hu·mor·less·ly** *adv* —**hu·mor·less·ness** *n* —**hu·mor·ous** \'hyümərəs, 'yü-\ *adj* —**hu·mor·ous·ly** *adv* —**hu·mor·ous·ness** *n*

hump \'həmp\ *n* : rounded protuberance —**humped** *adj*

hump·back *n* : hunchback —**hump·backed** *adj*

hu·mus \'hyüməs, 'yü-\ *n* : dark organic part of soil

hunch \'hənch\ *vb* : assume or cause to assume a bent or crooked posture ~ *n* : strong intuitive feeling

hunch·back *n* **1** : back with a hump **2** : person with a crooked back —**hunch·backed** *adj*

hun·dred \'həndrəd\ *n, pl* **-dreds** *or* **-dred** : 10 times 10 —**hundred** *adj* —**hun·dredth** \-drədth\ *adj or n*

¹hung *past of* HANG

²hung *adj* : unable to reach a verdict

hun·ger \'həŋgər\ *n* **1** : craving or urgent need for food **2** : strong desire —**hunger** *vb* —**hun·gri·ly** \-grəlē\ *adv* —**hun·gry** *adj*

hunk \'həŋk\ *n* : large piece

hun·ker \'həŋkər\ *vb* : settle in for a sustained period—used with *down*

hunt \'hənt\ *vb* **1** : pursue for food or sport **2** : try to find ~ *n* **1** : act or instance of hunting —**hunt·er** *n*

hur·dle \'hərdᵊl\ *n* **1** : barrier to leap over in a race **2** : obstacle —**hurdle** *vb* —**hur·dler** *n*

hurl \'hərl\ *vb* : throw with violence —**hurl** *n* —**hurl·er** *n*

hur·rah \hu̇'rä, -'ró\ *interj* —used to express joy or approval

hur·ri·cane \'hərə,kān\ *n* : tropical storm with winds of 74 miles per hour or greater

hur·ry \'hərē\ *vb* **-ried; -ry·ing** : go or cause to go with haste ~ *n* : extreme haste —**hur·ried·ly** *adv* —**hur·ried·ness** *n*

hurt \'hərt\ *vb* **hurt; hurt·ing 1** : feel or cause pain **2** : do harm to ~ *n* **1** : bodily injury **2** : harm —**hurt·ful** \-fəl\ *adj* —**hurt·ful·ness** *n*

hur·tle \'hərtᵊl\ *vb* **-tled; -tling** : move rapidly or forcefully

hus·band \'həzbənd\ *n* : married man ~ *vb* : manage prudently

hus·band·ry \-bəndrē\ *n* **1** : careful use **2** : agriculture

hush \'həsh\ *vb* : make or become quiet ~ *n* : silence

husk \'həsk\ *n* : outer covering of a seed or fruit ~ *vb* : strip the husk from —**husk·er** *n*

1hus·ky \'həskē\ *adj* **-ki·er; -est** : hoarse —**hus·ki·ly** *adv* —**hus·ki·ness** *n*

2husky *adj* **-ki·er; -est** : burly —**husk·i·ness** *n*

3husky *n, pl* **-kies** : working dog of the arctic

hus·sy \'həsē, -zē\ *n, pl* **-sies 1** : brazen woman **2** : mischievous girl

hus·tle \'həsəl\ *vb* **-tled; -tling 1** : hurry **2** : work energetically —**hustle** *n* —**hus·tler** \'həslər\ *n*

hut \'hət\ *n* : small often temporary dwelling

hutch \'həch\ *n* **1** : cupboard with open shelves **2** : pen for an animal

hy·a·cinth \'hīə,sinth\ *n* : bulbous herb grown for bell-shaped flowers

hy·brid \'hībrəd\ *n* : offspring of genetically differing parents —**hybrid** *adj* —**hy·brid·iza·tion** \,hībrədə-'zāshən\ *n* —**hy·brid·ize** \'hībrəd-,īz\ *vb* —**hy·brid·iz·er** *n*

hy·drant \'hīdrənt\ *n* : pipe from which water may be drawn to fight fires

hy·drau·lic \hī'dròlik\ *adj* : operated by liquid forced through a small hole —**hy·drau·lics** \-liks\ *n*

hy·dro·car·bon \,hīdrə'kärbən\ *n* : organic compound of carbon and hydrogen

hy·dro·elec·tric \,hīdrōi'lektrik\ *adj* : producing electricity by waterpower —**hy·dro·elec·tric·i·ty** \-,lek'trisətē\ *n*

hy·dro·gen \'hīdrəjən\ *n* : very light gaseous colorless odorless flammable chemical element

hydrogen bomb *n* : powerful bomb that derives its energy from the union of atomic nuclei

hy·dro·pho·bia \,hīdrə'fōbēə\ *n* : rabies

hy·dro·plane \'hīdrə,plān\ *n* : speedboat that skims the water

hy·drous \'hīdrəs\ *adj* : containing water

hy·e·na \hī'ēnə\ *n* : nocturnal carnivorous mammal of Asia and Africa

hy·giene \'hī,jēn\ *n* : conditions or practices conducive to health —**hy·gien·ic** \hī'jenik, -'jēn-; ,hījē'enik\ *adj* —**hy·gien·i·cal·ly** \-iklē\ *adv* —**hy·gien·ist** \hī'jēnist, -'jen-; 'hī,jēn-\ *n*

hy·grom·e·ter \hī'grämətər\ *n* : instrument for measuring atmospheric humidity

hying *pres part of* HIE

hymn \'him\ *n* : song of praise esp. to God —**hymn** *vb*

hym·nal \'himnəl\ *n* : book of hymns

hype \'hīp\ *vb* **hyped; hyp·ing** : publicize extravagantly—**hype** *n*

hyper- *prefix* **1** : above or beyond **2** : excessively or excessive

hyperacid	hypernationalis-
hyperacidity	tic
hyperactive	hyperreactive
hyperacute	hyperrealistic
hyperaggressive	hyperromantic
hypercautious	hypersensitive
hypercorrect	hypersensitive-
hypercritical	ness
hyperemotional	hypersensitivity
hyperenergetic	hypersexual
hyperexcitable	hypersusceptible
hyperfastidious	hypertense
hyperintense	hypervigilant
hypermasculine	

hy·per·bo·le \hī'pərbəlē\ *n* : extravagant exaggeration

hy·per·ten·sion \'hīpər,tenchən\ *n*

: high blood pressure —**hy•per•ten•sive** \,hīpər'tensiv\ adj or n

hy•phen \'hīfən\ n : punctuation mark - used to divide or compound words — **hyphen** vb

hy•phen•ate \'hīfə,nāt\ vb -at•ed; -at•ing : connect or divide with a hyphen —**hy•phen•ation** \,hīfə'nāshən\ n

hyp•no•sis \hip'nōsəs\ n, pl -no•ses \-,sēz\ : induced state like sleep in which the subject is responsive to suggestions of the inducer (**hyp•no•tist** \'hipnətist\) —**hyp•no•tism** \'hipnə,tizəm\ n —**hyp•no•tiz•able** \,hipnə'tīzəbəl\ adj —**hyp•no•tize** \'hipnə,tīz\ vb

hyp•not•ic \hip'nätik\ adj : relating to hypnosis —**hypnotic** n —**hyp•not•i•cal•ly** \-iklē\ adv

hy•po•chon•dria \,hīpə'kändrēə\ n : morbid concern for one's health —**hy•po•chon•dri•ac** \-drē,ak\ adj or n

hy•poc•ri•sy \hip'äkrəsē\ n, pl -sies : a feigning to be what one is not —**hyp•o•crite** \'hipə,krit\ n —**hyp•o•crit•i•cal** \,hipə'kritikəl\ adj —**hyp•o•crit•i•cal•ly** adv

hy•po•der•mic \,hīpə'dərmik\ adj : administered or used in making an injection beneath the skin ~ n : hypodermic syringe

hy•pot•e•nuse \hī'pätə,nüs, -,nüz, -,nyüs, -,nyüz\ n : side of a right-angled triangle opposite the right angle

hy•poth•e•sis \hī'päthəsəs\ n, pl -e•ses \-,sēz\ : assumption made in order to test its consequences —**hy•poth•e•size** \-,sīz\ vb —**hy•po•thet•i•cal** \,hīpə'thetikəl\ adj —**hy•po•thet•i•cal•ly** adv

hys•ter•ec•to•my \,histə'rektəmē\ n, pl -mies : surgical removal of the uterus

hys•te•ria \his'terēə, -tir-\ n : uncontrollable fear or outburst of emotion —**hys•ter•i•cal** \-'terikəl\ adj —**hys•ter•i•cal•ly** adv

hys•ter•ics \-'teriks\ n pl : uncontrollable laughter or crying

I

i \'ī\ n, pl **i's** or **is** \'īz\ : 9th letter of the alphabet

I \'ī\ pron : the speaker

-ial adj suffix : of, relating to, or characterized by

-ian —see -AN

ibis \'ībəs\ n, pl **ibis** or **ibis•es** : wading bird with a down-curved bill

-ible —see -ABLE

ibu•pro•fen \,ībyù'prōfən\ n : drug used to relieve inflammation, pain, and fever

-ic \ik\ adj suffix 1 : of, relating to, or being 2 : containing 3 : characteristic of 4 : marked by 5 : caused by

-i•cal \ikəl\ adj suffix : -ic — **-i•cal•ly** \iklē, -kəlē\ adv suffix

ice \'īs\ n 1 : frozen water 2 : flavored frozen dessert ~ vb **iced; ic•ing** 1 : freeze 2 : chill 3 : cover with icing

ice•berg \'īs,bərg\ n : large floating mass of ice

ice•box n : refrigerator

ice•break•er n : ship equipped to cut through ice

ice cream n : sweet frozen food

ice-skate vb : skate on ice —**ice skater** n

ich•thy•ol•o•gy \,ikthē'äləjē\ n : study of fishes —**ich•thy•ol•o•gist** \-jist\ n

ici•cle \'ī,sikəl\ n : hanging mass of ice

ic•ing \'īsiŋ\ n : sweet usu. creamy coating for baked goods

icon \'ī,kän\ n 1 : religious image 2 : small picture on a computer screen identified with an available function

icon•o•clast \ī'känə,klast\ n : attacker of cherished beliefs or institutions —**icon•o•clasm** \-,klazəm\ n

icy \'īsē\ adj **ic•i•er; -est** 1 : covered with or consisting of ice 2 : very cold —**ic•i•ly** adv —**ic•i•ness** n

id \'id\ n : unconscious instinctual part of the mind

idea \ī'dēə\ n 1 : something imagined in the mind 2 : purpose or plan

ide•al \ī'dēəl\ adj 1 : imaginary 2 : perfect ~ n 1 : standard of excellence 2 : model 3 : aim —**ide•al•ly** adv

ide•al•ism \ī'dēə,lizəm\ n : adherence to ideals —**ide•al•ist** \-list\ n —**ide-**

al·is·tic \ī,dēə'listik\ adj —ide·al·is·ti·cal·ly \-tiklē\ adv

ide·al·ize \ī'dēə,līz\ vb -ized; -iz·ing : think of or represent as ideal —ide·al·i·za·tion \-,dēələ'zāshən\ n

iden·ti·cal \ī'dentikəl\ adj 1 : being the same 2 : exactly or essentially alike

iden·ti·fi·ca·tion \ī,dentəfə'kāshən\ n 1 : act of identifying 2 : evidence of identity

iden·ti·fy \ī'dentə,fī\ vb -fied; -fy·ing 1 : associate 2 : establish the identity of —iden·ti·fi·able \ī,dentə'fīəbəl\ adj —iden·ti·fi·er \ī'dentə,fīər\ n

iden·ti·ty \ī'dentətē\ n, pl -ties 1 : sameness of essential character 2 : individuality 3 : fact of being what is supposed

ide·ol·o·gy \,īdē'äləjē, ,id-\ n, pl -gies : body of beliefs —ide·o·log·i·cal \,īdēə'läjikəl, ,id-\ adj

id·i·om \'idēəm\ n 1 : language peculiar to a person or group 2 : expression with a special meaning —id·i·om·at·ic \,idēə'matik\ adj —id·i·om·at·i·cal·ly \-iklē\ adv

id·io·syn·cra·sy \,idēō'siŋkrəsē\ n, pl -sies : personal peculiarity —id·io·syn·crat·ic \-sin'kratik\ adj —id·io·syn·crat·i·cal·ly \-'kratiklē\ adv

id·i·ot \'idēət\ n : mentally retarded or foolish person —id·i·o·cy \-əsē\ n —id·i·ot·ic \,idē'ätik\ adj —id·i·ot·i·cal·ly \-iklē\ adv

idle \'īd³l\ adj idler; idlest 1 : worthless 2 : inactive 3 : lazy ~ vb idled; idling : spend time doing nothing —idle·ness \-n\ —idler n —idly \'īdlē\ adv

idol \'īd³l\ n 1 : image of a god 2 : object of devotion —idol·iza·tion \,īd³lə'zāshən\ n —idol·ize \'īd³l,īz\ vb

idol·a·ter, idol·a·tor \ī'dälətər\ n : worshiper of idols —idol·a·trous \-trəs\ adj —idol·a·try \-trē\ n

idyll \'īd³l\ n : period of peace and contentment —idyl·lic \ī'dilik\ adj

-ier —see -ER

if \'if\ conj 1 : in the event that 2 : whether 3 : even though

-i·fy \ə,fī\ vb suffix : -fy

ig·loo \'iglü\ n, pl -loos : hut made of snow blocks

ig·nite \ig'nīt\ vb -nit·ed; -nit·ing : set afire or catch fire —ig·nit·able \-'nītəbəl\ adj

ig·ni·tion \ig'nishən\ n 1 : a setting on fire 2 : process or means of igniting fuel

ig·no·ble \ig'nōbəl\ adj : not honorable —ig·no·bly \-blē\ adv

ig·no·min·i·ous \,ignə'minēəs\ adj 1 : dishonorable 2 : humiliating —ig·no·min·i·ous·ly adv —ig·no·mi·ny \'ignə,minē, ig'nämənē\ n

ig·no·ra·mus \,ignə'rāməs\ n : ignorant person

ig·no·rant \'ignərənt\ adj 1 : lacking knowledge 2 : showing a lack of knowledge or intelligence 3 : unaware —ig·no·rance \-rəns\ n —ig·no·rant·ly adv

ig·nore \ig'nōr\ vb -nored; -nor·ing : refuse to notice

igua·na \i'gwänə\ n : large tropical American lizard

ilk \'ilk\ n : kind

ill \'il\ adj worse \'wərs\; worst \'wərst\ 1 : sick 2 : bad 3 : rude or unacceptable 4 : hostile ~ adv worse; worst 1 : with displeasure 2 : harshly 3 : scarcely 4 : badly ~ n 1 : evil 2 : misfortune 3 : sickness

il·le·gal \il'lēgəl\ adj : not lawful —il·le·gal·i·ty \ili'galətē\ n —il·le·gal·ly \il'lēgəlē\ adv

il·leg·i·ble \il'lejəbəl\ adj : not legible —il·leg·i·bil·i·ty \il,lejə'bilətē\ n —il·leg·i·bly \il'lejəblē\ adv

il·le·git·i·mate \,ili'jitəmət\ adj 1 : born of unmarried parents 2 : illegal —il·le·git·i·ma·cy \-əməsē\ n —il·le·git·i·mate·ly adv

il·lic·it \il'lisət\ adj : not lawful —il·lic·it·ly adv

il·lim·it·able \il'limətəbəl\ adj : boundless —il·lim·it·ably \-blē\ adv

il·lit·er·ate \il'litərət\ adj : unable to read or write —il·lit·er·a·cy \-ərəsē\ n —illiterate n

ill-na·tured \-'nāchərd\ adj : cross —ill-na·tured·ly adv

ill·ness \'ilnəs\ n : sickness

il·log·i·cal \il'läjikəl\ adj : contrary to sound reasoning —il·log·i·cal·ly adv

ill-starred \'il'stärd\ adj : unlucky

il·lu·mi·nate \il'ümə,nāt\ vb -nat·ed; -nat·ing 1 : light up 2 : make clear —il·lu·mi·nat·ing·ly \-,nātiŋlē\ adv —il·lu·mi·na·tion \-,ümə'nāshən\ n

ill-use \-'yüz\ vb : abuse —ill-use \-'yüs\ n

il·lu·sion \il'üzhən\ n 1 : mistaken idea 2 : misleading visual image il·lu·so·ry \il'üsərē, -'üz-\ adj : based on or producing illusion

il·lus·trate \'iləs,trāt\ vb -trated; -trating 1 : explain by example 2 : provide with pictures or figures —il·lus·tra·tor \-ər\ n

il·lus·tra·tion \,iləs'trāshən\ n 1 : example that explains 2 : pictorial explanation

il·lus·tra·tive \il'əstrativ\ adj : designed to illustrate —il·lus·tra·tive·ly adv

il·lus·tri·ous \-trēəs\ adj : notably or brilliantly outstanding —il·lus·tri·ous·ness n

ill will n : unfriendly feeling

im·age \'imij\ n 1 : likeness 2 : visual counterpart of an object formed by a lens or mirror 3 : mental picture ~ vb -aged; -ag·ing : create a representation of

im·ag·ery \'imijrē\ n 1 : images 2 : figurative language

imag·i·nary \im'aja,nerē\ adj : existing only in the imagination

imag·i·na·tion \im,aja'nāshən\ n 1 : act or power of forming a mental image 2 : creative ability —imag·i·na·tive \im'ajənətiv, -ə,nātiv\ adj —imag·i·na·tive·ly adv

imag·ine \im'ajən\ vb -ined; -in·ing : form a mental picture of something not present —imag·in·able \-'ajənəbəl\ adj —imag·in·ably \-blē\ adv

im·bal·ance \im'baləns\ n : lack of balance

im·be·cile \'imbəsəl, -,sil\ n : idiot —imbecile, im·be·cil·ic \,imbə'silik\ adj —im·be·cil·i·ty \-'silətē\ n

im·bibe \im'bīb\ vb -bibed; -bib·ing : drink —im·bib·er n

im·bro·glio \im'brōlyō\ n, pl -glios : complicated situation

im·bue \-'byü\ vb -bued; -bu·ing : fill (as with color or a feeling)

im·i·tate \'imə,tāt\ vb -tat·ed; -tat·ing 1 : follow as a model 2 : mimic —im·i·ta·tive \-,tātiv\ adj —im·i·ta·tor \-ər\ n

im·i·ta·tion \,imə'tāshən\ n 1 : act of imitating 2 : copy —imitation adj

im·mac·u·late \im'akyələt\ adj : without stain or blemish —im·mac·u·late·ly adv

im·ma·te·ri·al \,imə'tirēəl\ adj 1 : spiritual 2 : not relevant —im·ma·te·ri·al·i·ty \-,tirē'alətē\ n

im·ma·ture \,imə'túr, -'tyúr\ adj : not yet mature —im·ma·tu·ri·ty \-ətē\ n

im·mea·sur·able \im'ezhərəbəl\ adj : indefinitely extensive —immea·sur·ably \-blē\ adv

im·me·di·a·cy \im'ēdēəsē\ n, pl -cies : quality or state of being urgent

im·me·di·ate \-ēət\ adj 1 : direct 2 : being next in line 3 : made or done at once 4 : not distant —im·me·di·ate·ly adv

im·me·mo·ri·al \,imə'mōrēəl\ adj : old beyond memory

im·mense \im'ens\ adj : vast —immense·ly adv —im·men·si·ty \-'ensətē\ n

im·merse \im'ərs\ vb -mersed; -mers·ing 1 : plunge or dip esp. into liquid 2 : engross —im·mer·sion \-'ərzhən\ n

im·mi·grant \'imigrənt\ n : one that immigrates

im·mi·grate \'imə,grāt\ vb -grat·ed; -grat·ing : come into a place and take up residence —im·mi·gra·tion \,imə'grāshən\ n

im·mi·nent \'imənənt\ adj : ready to take place —im·mi·nence \-nəns\ n —im·mi·nent·ly adv

im·mo·bile \im'ōbəl\ adj : incapable of being moved —im·mo·bil·i·ty \,imō'bilətē\ n —im·mo·bi·lize \im'ōbəlīz\ vb

im·mod·er·ate \im'ädərət\ adj : not moderate —im·mod·er·a·cy \-ərəsē\ n —im·mod·er·ate·ly adv

im·mod·est \im'ädəst\ adj : not modest —im·mod·est·ly adv —im·mod·es·ty \-əstē\ n

im·mo·late \'imə,lāt\ vb -lat·ed; -lat·ing : offer in sacrifice —im·mo·la·tion \,imə'lāshən\ n

im·mor·al \im'órəl\ adj : not moral —im·mo·ral·i·ty \,imó'ralətē, ,imə-\ n —im·mor·al·ly adv

im·mor·tal \im'órtᵊl\ adj 1 : not mortal 2 : having lasting fame ~ n : one exempt from death or oblivion —im·mor·tal·i·ty \,im,ór'talətē\ n —im·mor·tal·ize \im'órtᵊl,īz\ vb

im·mov·able \im'üvəbəl\ adj 1 : stationary 2 : unyielding —im·mov·abil·i·ty \,im,üvə'bilətē\ n —im·mov·ably adv

im·mune \im'yün\ adj : not liable esp. to disease —im·mu·ni·ty \im'yünətē\ n —im·mu·ni·za·tion \,imyənə-

'zāshən\ *n* —im•mu•nize \'imyə-
,nīz\ *vb*

im•mu•nol•o•gy \,imyə'näləjē\ *n* : science of immunity to disease —im-
mu•no•log•ic \-yən^əl'äjik\, im-
mu•no•log•i•cal \-ikəl\ *adj* —im•mu-
nol•o•gist \,imyə'näləjist\ *n*

im•mu•ta•ble \im'yütəbəl\ *adj* : un-
changeable —im•mu•ta•bil•i•ty \im,-
yütə'bilətē\ *n* —im•mu•ta•bly *adv*

imp \'imp\ *n* 1 : demon 2 : mischievous
child

im•pact \im'pakt\ *vb* 1 : press close 2
: have an effect on ~ \'im,pakt\ *n* 1
: forceful contact 2 : influence

im•pact•ed \im'paktəd\ *adj* : wedged
between the jawbone and another
tooth

im•pair \im'par\ *vb* : diminish in quantity, value, or ability —im•pair•ment
n

im•pa•la \im'palə\ *n, pl* impalas *or* im-
pala : large African antelope

im•pale \im'pāl\ *vb* -paled; -pal•ing
: pierce with something pointed

im•pal•pa•ble \im'palpəbəl\ *adj* : incapable of being felt —im•pal•pa•bly
adv

im•pan•el \im'pan^əl\ *vb* : enter in or on
a panel

im•part \-'pärt\ *vb* : give from or as if
from a store

im•par•tial \im'pärshəl\ *adj* : not partial
—im•par•tial•i•ty \im,pärshē'alətē\ *n*
—im•par•tial•ly *adv*

im•pass•able \im'pasəbəl\ *adj* : not
passable —im•pass•ably \-'pasəblē\
adv

im•passe \'im,pas\ *n* : inescapable predicament

im•pas•sioned \im'pashənd\ *adj* : filled
with passion

im•pas•sive \im'pasiv\ *adj* : showing no
feeling or interest —im•pas•sive•ly
adv —im•pas•siv•i•ty \,im,pas'ivətē\
n

im•pa•tiens \im'pāshənz, -shəns\ *n*
: annual herb with showy flowers

im•pa•tient \im'pāshənt\ *adj* : not patient —im•pa•tience \-shəns\ *n* —
im•pa•tient•ly *adv*

im•peach \im'pēch\ *vb* 1 : charge (an official) with misconduct 2 : cast doubt
on 3 : remove from office for misconduct —im•peach•ment *n*

im•pec•ca•ble \im'pekəbəl\ *adj* : faultless —im•pec•ca•bly *adv*

im•pe•cu•nious \,impi'kyünēəs\ *adj*
: broke —im•pe•cu•nious•ness *n*

im•pede \im'pēd\ *vb* -ped•ed; -ped•ing
: interfere with

im•ped•i•ment \-'pedəmənt\ *n* 1 : hindrance 2 : speech defect

im•pel \-'pel\ *vb* -pelled; -pel•ling : urge
forward

im•pend \-'pend\ *vb* : be about to occur

im•pen•e•tra•ble \im'penətrəbəl\ *adj*
: incapable of being penetrated or understood —im•pen•e•tra•bil•i•ty \im,-
,penətrə'bilətē\ *n* —im•pen•e•tra•bly
adv

im•pen•i•tent \im'penətənt\ *adj* : not
penitent —im•pen•i•tence \-təns\ *n*

im•per•a•tive \im'perətiv\ *adj* 1
: expressing a command 2 : urgent ~
n 1 : imperative mood or verb form 2
: unavoidable fact, need, or obligation
—im•per•a•tive•ly *adv*

im•per•cep•ti•ble \,impər'septəbəl\ *adj*
: not perceptible —im•per•cep•ti•bly
adv

im•per•fect \im'pərfikt\ *adj* : not perfect
—im•per•fec•tion *n* —im•per•fect•ly
adv

im•pe•ri•al \im'pirēəl\ *adj* 1 : relating to
an empire or an emperor 2 : royal

im•pe•ri•al•ism \im'pirēə,lizəm\ *n*
: policy of controlling other nations
—im•pe•ri•al•ist \-list\ *n or adj* —
im•pe•ri•al•is•tic \-,pirēə'listik\ *adj* —
im•pe•ri•al•is•ti•cal•ly \-tiklē\ *adv*

im•per•il \im'perəl\ *vb* -iled *or* -illed;
-il•ing *or* -il•ling : endanger

im•pe•ri•ous \im'pirēəs\ *adj* : arrogant
or domineering —im•pe•ri•ous•ly
adv

im•per•ish•able \im'perishəbəl\ *adj*
: not perishable

im•per•ma•nent \-'pərmənənt\ *adj* : not
permanent —im•per•ma•nent•ly *adv*

im•per•me•able \-'pərmēəbəl\ *adj* : not
permeable

im•per•mis•si•ble \,impər'misəbəl\ *adj*
: not permissible

im•per•son•al \im'pərs^ənəl\ *adj* : not involving human personality or emo-
tion —im•per•son•al•i•ty \im,pər-
s^ən'alətē\ *n* —im•per•son•al•ly *adv*

im•per•son•ate \im'pərs^ən,āt\ *vb* -at•ed;
-at•ing : assume the character of —
im•per•son•ation \-,pərs^ən'āshən\ *n*
—im•per•son•ator \-'pərs^ən,ātər\ *n*

im•per•ti•nent \im'pərt^ənənt\ *adj* 1
: irrelevant 2 : insolent —im•per-

ti·nence \-ᵊnəns\ n —im·per·ti·
nent·ly adv

im·per·turb·able \,impər'tərbəbəl\ adj
: calm and steady

im·per·vi·ous \im'pərvēəs\ adj : incapable of being penetrated or affected

im·pet·u·ous \im'pechəwəs\ adj : impulsive —im·pet·u·os·i·ty \im-
,pechə'wäsətē\ n —im·pet·u·ous·ly
adv

im·pe·tus \impətəs\ n : driving force

im·pi·ety \im'pīətē\ n : quality or state
of being impious

im·pinge \im'pinj\ vb -pinged; -pinging : encroach —im·pinge·ment
\-mənt\ n

im·pi·ous \'impēəs, im'pī-\ adj : not pious

imp·ish \'impish\ adj : mischievous —
imp·ish·ly adv —imp·ish·ness n

im·pla·ca·ble \im'plakəbəl, -'plā-\ adj
: not capable of being appeased or
changed —im·pla·ca·bil·i·ty \im-
,plakə'bilətē, -,plā-\ n —im·pla·
ca·bly \im'plakəblē\ adv

im·plant \im'plant\ vb 1 : set firmly or
deeply 2 : fix in the mind or spirit ~
\'im,plant\ n : something implanted
in tissue —im·plan·ta·tion \,im-
,plan'tāshən\ n

im·plau·si·ble \im'plózəbəl\ adj : not
plausible —im·plau·si·bil·i·ty \im-
,plózə'bilətē\ n

im·ple·ment \'impləmənt\ n : tool, utensil ~ \-,ment\ vb : put into practice —
im·ple·men·ta·tion \,impləmən'tā-
shən\ n

im·pli·cate \'implə,kāt\ vb -cat·ed; -cating : involve

im·pli·ca·tion \,implə'kāshən\ n 1 : an
implying 2 : something implied

im·plic·it \im'plisət\ adj 1 : understood
though only implied 2 : complete and
unquestioning —im·plic·it·ly adv

im·plode \im'plōd\ vb -plod·ed; -ploding : burst inward —im·plo·sion
\-'plōzhən\ n —im·plo·sive \-'plōsiv\
adj

im·plore \im'plōr\ vb -plored; -plor·ing
: entreat

im·ply \-'plī\ vb -plied; -ply·ing
: express indirectly

im·po·lite \,impə'līt\ adj : not polite

im·pol·i·tic \im'pälə,tik\ adj : not politic

im·pon·der·a·ble \im'pändərəbəl\ adj
: incapable of being precisely evaluated —imponderable n

im·port \im'pōrt\ vb 1 : mean 2 : bring
in from an external source ~ \'im-
,pōrt\ n 1 : meaning 2 : importance 3
: something imported —im·por·ta·
tion \,im,pōr'tāshən\ n —im·port·er
n

im·por·tant \im'pōrtənt\ adj : having
great worth, significance, or influence
—im·por·tance \-ᵊns\ n —important·ly adv

im·por·tu·nate \im'pórchənət\ adj
: troublesomely persistent or urgent

im·por·tune \,impər'tün, -'tyün; im-
'pórchən\ vb -tuned; -tun·ing : urge
or beg persistently —im·por·tu·ni·ty
\,impər'tünətē, -'tyü-\ n

im·pose \im'pōz\ vb -posed; -pos·ing 1
: establish as compulsory 2 : take unwarranted advantage of —im·po·
si·tion \,impə'zishən\ n

im·pos·ing \im'pōziŋ\ adj : impressive
—im·pos·ing·ly adv

im·pos·si·ble \im'päsəbəl\ adj 1 : incapable of occurring 2 : enormously difficult —im·pos·si·bil·i·ty \im,päsə-
'bilətē\ n —im·pos·si·bly \im'päs-
əblē\ adv

im·post \'im,pōst\ n : tax

im·pos·tor, im·pos·ter \im'pästər\ n
: one who assumes an identity or title
to deceive —im·pos·ture \-'päschər\
n

im·po·tent \'impətənt\ adj 1 : lacking
power 2 : sterile —im·po·tence
\-pətəns\ n —im·po·ten·cy \-ənsē\ n
—im·po·tent·ly adv

im·pound \im'paùnd\ vb : seize and
hold in legal custody —im·pound·
ment n

im·pov·er·ish \im'pävərish\ vb : make
poor —im·pov·er·ish·ment n

im·prac·ti·ca·ble \im'praktikəbəl\ adj
: not practicable

im·prac·ti·cal \-'praktikəl\ adj : not
practical

im·pre·cise \,impri'sīs\ adj : not precise
—im·pre·cise·ly adv —im·pre·
cise·ness n —im·pre·ci·sion \-'si-
zhən\ n

im·preg·na·ble \im'pregnəbəl\ adj
: able to resist attack —im·preg·na·
bil·i·ty \im,pregnə'bilətē\ n

im·preg·nate \im'preg,nāt\ vb -nat·ed;
-nat·ing 1 : make pregnant 2 : cause
to be filled, permeated, or saturated
—im·preg·na·tion \,im,preg'nāshən\
n

im·pre·sa·rio \,imprə'särē,ō\ *n, pl* **-ri·os** : one who sponsors an entertainment

¹im·press \im'pres\ *vb* **1** : apply with or produce by pressure **2** : press, stamp, or print in or upon **3** : produce a vivid impression of **4** : affect (as the mind) forcibly

²im·press \im'pres\ *vb* : force into naval service —**im·press·ment** *n*

im·pres·sion \im'preshən\ *n* **1** : mark made by impressing **2** : marked influence or effect **3** : printed copy **4** : vague notion or recollection —**im·pres·sion·able** \-'preshənəbəl\ *adj*

im·pres·sive \im'presiv\ *adj* : making a marked impression —**im·pres·sive·ly** *adv* —**im·pres·sive·ness** *n*

im·pri·ma·tur \,imprə'mä,tùr\ *n* : official approval (as of a publication by a censor)

im·print \im'print, 'im,-\ *vb* : stamp or mark by or as if by pressure ~ \'im,-\ *n* : something imprinted or printed

im·pris·on \im'priz³n\ *vb* : put in prison —**im·pris·on·ment** \-mənt\ *n*

im·prob·a·ble \im'präbəbəl\ *adj* : unlikely to be true or to occur —**im·prob·a·bil·i·ty** \im,präbə'bilətē\ *n* — **im·prob·a·bly** *adv*

im·promp·tu \im'prämptü, -tyü\ *adj* : not planned beforehand —**im·promptu** *adv or n*

im·prop·er \im'präpər\ *adj* : not proper —**im·prop·er·ly** *adv*

im·pro·pri·ety \,imprə'prīətē\ *n, pl* **-eties** : state or instance of being improper

im·prove \im'prüv\ *vb* **-proved; -proving** : grow or make better —**im·prov·able** \-'prüvəbəl\ *adj* —**im·prove·ment** *n*

im·prov·i·dent \im'prävədənt\ *adj* : not providing for the future —**improv·i·dence** \-əns\ *n*

im·pro·vise \'imprə,vīz\ *vb* **-vised; -vis·ing** : make, invent, or arrange offhand —**im·pro·vi·sa·tion** \im,prävə'zäshən, ,imprəvə-\ *n* —**im·pro·vis·er, im·pro·vi·sor** \'imprə-,vīzər\ *n*

im·pru·dent \im'prüd³nt\ *adj* : not prudent —**im·pru·dence** \-³ns\ *n*

im·pu·dent \'impyədənt\ *adj* : insolent —**im·pu·dence** \-əns\ *n* —**im·pu·dent·ly** *adv*

im·pugn \im'pyün\ *vb* : attack as false

im·pulse \'im,pəls\ *n* **1** : moving force **2** : sudden inclination

im·pul·sive \im'pəlsiv\ *adj* : acting on impulse —**im·pul·sive·ly** *adv* —**im·pul·sive·ness** *n*

im·pu·ni·ty \im'pyünətē\ *n* : exemption from punishment or harm

im·pure \im'pyùr\ *adj* : not pure —**im·pu·ri·ty** \-'pyùrətē\ *n*

im·pute \im'pyüt\ *vb* **-put·ed; -put·ing** : credit to or blame on a person or cause —**im·pu·ta·tion** \,impyə-'tāshən\ *n*

in \'in\ *prep* **1** —used to indicate location, inclusion, situation, or manner **2** : into **3** : during ~ *adv* : to or toward the inside ~ *adj* : located inside

in- \in\ *prefix* **1** : not **2** : lack of

inability	incoherently
inaccessibility	incombustible
inaccessible	incommensurate
inaccuracy	incommodious
inaccurate	incommunicable
inaction	incompatibility
inactive	incompatible
inactivity	incomplete
inadequacy	incompletely
inadequate	incompleteness
inadequately	incomprehensible
inadmissibility	inconclusive
inadmissible	incongruent
inadvisability	inconsecutive
inadvisable	inconsiderate
inapparent	inconsiderately
inapplicable	inconsiderateness
inapposite	inconsistency
inappositely	inconsistent
inappositeness	inconsistently
inappreciative	inconspicuous
inapproachable	inconspicuously
inappropriate	inconstancy
inappropriately	inconstant
inappropriateness	inconstantly
inapt	inconsumable
inarguable	incontestable
inartistic	incontestably
inartistically	incorporeal
inattentive	incorporeally
inattentively	incorrect
inattentiveness	incorrectly
inaudible	incorrectness
inaudibly	incorruptible
inauspicious	inculpable
inauthentic	incurable
incapability	incurious
incapable	indecency
incautious	indecent
incoherence	indecently
incoherent	indecipherable

indecisive	inextricable
indecisively	infeasibility
indecisiveness	infeasible
indecorous	infelicitous
indecorously	infelicity
indecorousness	infertile
indefensible	infertility
indefinable	inflexibility
indefinably	inflexible
indescribable	inflexibly
indescribably	infrequent
indestructibility	infrequently
indestructible	inglorious
indigestible	ingloriously
indiscernible	ingratitude
indiscreet	inhumane
indiscreetly	inhumanely
indiscretion	injudicious
indisputable	injudiciously
indisputably	injudiciousness
indistinct	inoffensive
indistinctly	inoperable
indistinctness	inoperative
indivisibility	insalubrious
indivisible	insensitive
ineducable	insensitivity
ineffective	inseparable
ineffectively	insignificant
ineffectiveness	insincere
ineffectual	insincerely
ineffectually	insincerity
ineffectualness	insolubility
inefficiency	insoluble
inefficient	instability
inefficiently	insubstantial
inelastic	insufficiency
inelasticity	insufficient
inelegance	insufficiently
inelegant	insupportable
ineligibility	intangibility
ineligible	intangible
ineradicable	intangibly
inessential	intolerable
inexact	intolerably
inexactly	intolerance
inexpedient	intolerant
inexpensive	intractable
inexperience	invariable
inexperienced	invariably
inexpert	inviable
inexpertly	invisibility
inexpertness	invisible
inexplicable	invisibly
inexplicably	involuntarily
inexplicit	involuntary
inexpressible	invulnerability
inexpressibly	invulnerable
inextinguishable	invulnerably

in·ad·ver·tent \,inəd'vərt³nt\ *adj* : unintentional —**in·ad·ver·tence** \-³ns\ *n* —**in·ad·ver·ten·cy** \-³nsē\ *n* —**in·ad·ver·tent·ly** *adv*

in·alien·able \in'ālyənəbəl, -'ālēənə-\ *adj* : incapable of being transferred or given up —**in·alien·abil·i·ty** \in-,ālyənə'bilətē, -'ālēənə-\ *n* —**in·alien·ably** *adv*

inane \in'ān\ *adj* **inan·er; -est** : silly or stupid —**inan·i·ty** \in'anətē\ *n*

in·an·i·mate \in'anəmət\ *adj* : not animate or animated —**in·an·i·mate·ly** *adv* —**in·an·i·mate·ness** *n*

in·ap·pre·cia·ble \,inə'prēshəbəl\ *adj* : too small to be perceived —**in·ap·pre·cia·bly** *adv*

in·ar·tic·u·late \,inär'tikyələt\ *adj* : without the power of speech or effective expression —**in·ar·tic·u·lately** *adv*

in·as·much as \,inaz'məchaz\ *conj* : because

in·at·ten·tion \,inə'tenchən\ *n* : failure to pay attention

in·au·gu·ral \in'ógyərəl, -gərəl\ *adj* : relating to an inauguration ~ *n* **1** : inaugural speech **2** : inauguration

in·au·gu·rate \in'ógyə,rāt, -gə-\ *vb* **-rated; -rat·ing** **1** : install in office **2** : start —**in·au·gu·ra·tion** \-,ógyə-'rāshən, -gə-\ *n*

in·board \,in,bōrd\ *adv* : inside a vehicle or craft —**inboard** *adj*

in·born \'in,bórn\ *adj* : present from birth

in·bred \'in,bred\ *adj* : deeply ingrained in one's nature

in·breed·ing \'in,brēdiŋ\ *n* : interbreeding of closely related individuals —**in·breed** \-,brēd\ *vb*

in·cal·cu·la·ble \in'kalkyələbəl\ *adj* : too large to be calculated —**in·cal·cu·la·bly** *adv*

in·can·des·cent \,inkən'des³nt\ *adj* **1** : glowing with heat **2** : brilliant —**in·can·des·cence** \-³ns\ *n*

in·can·ta·tion \,in,kan'tāshən\ *n* : use of spoken or sung charms or spells as a magic ritual

in·ca·pac·i·tate \,inkə'pasə,tāt\ *vb* **-tated; -tat·ing** : disable

in·ca·pac·i·ty \,inkə'pasətē\ *n, pl* **-ties** : quality or state of being incapable

in·car·cer·ate \in'kärsə,rāt\ *vb* **-at·ed; -at·ing** : imprison —**in·car·cer·a·tion** \in,kärsə'rāshən\ *n*

in·car·nate \in'kärnət, -,nāt\ *adj* : having bodily form and substance —**in·car·nate** \-,nāt\ *vb* —**in·car·na·tion** \-,kär'näshən\ *n*

in·cen·di·ary \in'sendē,erē\ *adj* **1** : pertaining to or used to ignite fire **2** : tending to excite —**incendiary** *n*

in·cense \'in,sens\ *n* : material burned to produce a fragrant odor or its smoke ~ \in'sens\ *vb* -censed; -cens·ing : make very angry

in·cen·tive \in'sentiv\ *n* : inducement to do something

in·cep·tion \in'sepshən\ *n* : beginning

in·ces·sant \in'ses³nt\ *adj* : continuing without interruption —**in·ces·sant·ly** *adv*

in·cest \'in,sest\ *n* : sexual intercourse between close relatives —**in·ces·tu·ous** \in'seschəwəs\ *adj*

inch \'inch\ *n* : unit of length equal to 1/12 foot ~ *vb* : move by small degrees

in·cho·ate \in'kōət, 'inkə,wāt\ *adj* : new and not fully formed or ordered

in·ci·dent \'insədənt\ *n* : occurrence —**in·ci·dence** \-əns\ *n* —**incident** *adj*

in·ci·den·tal \,insə'dent³l\ *adj* **1** : subordinate, nonessential, or attendant **2** : met by chance ~ *n* **1** : something incidental **2** *pl* : minor expenses that are not itemized —**in·ci·den·tal·ly** *adv*

in·cin·er·ate \in'sinə,rāt\ *vb* -at·ed; -at·ing : burn to ashes —**in·cin·er·a·tor** \-,rātər\ *n*

in·cip·i·ent \in'sipēənt\ *adj* : beginning to be or appear

in·cise \in'sīz\ *vb* -cised; -cis·ing : carve into

in·ci·sion \in'sizhən\ *n* : surgical cut

in·ci·sive \in'sīsiv\ *adj* : keen and discerning —**in·ci·sive·ly** *adv*

in·ci·sor \in'sīzər\ *n* : tooth for cutting

in·cite \in'sīt\ *vb* -cit·ed; -cit·ing : arouse to action —**in·cite·ment** *n*

in·ci·vil·i·ty \,insə'vilətē\ *n* : rudeness

in·clem·ent \in'klemənt\ *adj* : stormy —**in·clem·en·cy** \-ənsē\ *n*

in·cline \in'klīn\ *vb* -clined; -clin·ing **1** : bow **2** : tend toward an opinion **3** : slope ~ *n* **1** : slope —**in·cli·na·tion** \,inklə'nāshən\ *n* —**in·clin·er** *n*

inclose, inclosure *var of* ENCLOSE, ENCLOSURE

in·clude \in'klüd\ *vb* -clud·ed; -clud·ing : take in or comprise —**in·clu·sion** \in'klüzhən\ *n* —**in·clu·sive** \-'klüsiv\ *adj*

in·cog·ni·to \,in,käg'nētō, in'kägnə,tō\

adv or adj : with one's identity concealed

in·come \'in,kəm\ *n* : money gained (as from work or investment)

in·com·ing \'in,kəmiŋ\ *adj* : coming in

in·com·mu·ni·ca·do \,inkə,myünə'kädō\ *adv or adj* : without means of communication

in·com·pa·ra·ble \in'kämpərəbəl\ *adj* : eminent beyond comparison

in·com·pe·tent \in'kämpətənt\ *adj* : lacking sufficient knowledge or skill —**in·com·pe·tence** \-pətəns\ *n* —**in·com·pe·ten·cy** \-ənsē\ *n* —**incompetent** *n*

in·con·ceiv·able \,inkən'sēvəbəl\ *adj* **1** : impossible to comprehend **2** : unbelievable —**in·con·ceiv·ably** \-blē\ *adv*

in·con·gru·ous \in'käŋgrəwəs\ *adj* : inappropriate or out of place —**incongru·i·ty** \,inkən'grüətē, -,kän-\ *n* —**in·con·gru·ous·ly** *adv*

in·con·se·quen·tial \,in,känsə'kwenchəl\ *adj* : unimportant —**incon·se·quence** \in'känsə,kwens\ *n* —**in·con·se·quen·tial·ly** *adv*

in·con·sid·er·able \,inkən'sidərəbəl\ *adj* : trivial

in·con·sol·able \,inkən'sōləbəl\ *adj* : incapable of being consoled —**in·con·sol·ably** *adv*

in·con·ve·nience \,inkən'vēnyəns\ *n* **1** : discomfort **2** : something that causes trouble or annoyance ~ *vb* : cause inconvenience to —**in·con·ve·nient** \,inkən'vēnyənt\ *adj* —**in·con·ve·nient·ly** *adv*

in·cor·po·rate \in'kórpə,rāt\ *vb* -rat·ed; -rat·ing **1** : blend **2** : form into a legal body —**in·cor·po·rat·ed** *adj* —**in·cor·po·ra·tion** \-,kórpə'rāshən\ *n*

in·cor·ri·gi·ble \in'kórəjəbəl\ *adj* : incapable of being corrected or reformed —**in·cor·ri·gi·bil·i·ty** \in-,kórəjə'bilətē\ *n*

in·crease \in'krēs, 'in,krēs\ *vb* -creased; -creas·ing : make or become greater ~ \'in,-, in'-\ *n* **1** : enlargement in size **2** : something added —**in·creas·ing·ly** \-'krēsiŋlē\ *adv*

in·cred·i·ble \in'kredəbəl\ *adj* : too extraordinary to be believed —**incred·ibil·i·ty** \in,kredə'bilətē\ *n* —**incred·i·bly** \in'kredəblē\ *adv*

in·cred·u·lous \in'krejələs\ *adj* : skeptical —**in·cre·du·li·ty** \,inkri'dülətē, -'dyü-\ *n* —**in·cred·u·lous·ly** *adv*

in·cre·ment \'iŋkrəmənt, 'in-\ *n* : increase or amount of increase —**incre·men·tal** \,iŋkrə'mentᵊl, ,in-\ *adj*

in·crim·i·nate \in'krimə,nāt\ *vb* -**nat·ed; -nat·ing** : show to be guilty of a crime —**in·crim·i·na·tion** \-,krimə·'nāshən\ *n* —**in·crim·i·na·to·ry** \-'krimənə,tōrē\ *adj*

in·cu·bate \'iŋkyə,bāt, 'in-\ *vb* -**bat·ed; -bat·ing** : keep (as eggs) under conditions favorable for development —**in·cu·ba·tion** \,iŋkyə'bāshən, ,in-\ *n* —**in·cu·ba·tor** \'iŋkyə,bātər, 'in-\ *n*

in·cul·cate \in'kəl,kāt, 'in,kəl-\ *vb* -**cat·ed; -cat·ing** : instill by repeated teaching —**in·cul·ca·tion** \,in,kəl·'kāshən\ *n*

in·cum·bent \in'kəmbənt\ *n* : holder of an office ~ *adj* : obligatory —**incum·ben·cy** \-bənsē\ *n*

in·cur \in'kər\ *vb* -**rr**- : become liable or subject to

in·cur·sion \in'kərzhən\ *n* : invasion

in·debt·ed \in'detəd\ *adj* : owing something —**in·debt·ed·ness** *n*

in·de·ci·sion \,indi'sizhən\ *n* : inability to decide

in·deed \in'dēd\ *adv* : without question

in·de·fat·i·ga·ble \indi'fatigəbəl\ *adj* : not tiring —**in·de·fat·i·ga·bly** \-blē\ *adv*

in·def·i·nite \in'defənət\ *adj* **1** : not defining or identifying **2** : not precise **3** : having no fixed limit —**in·def·i·nite·ly** *adv*

in·del·i·ble \in'deləbəl\ *adj* : not capable of being removed or erased —**in·del·i·bly** *adv*

in·del·i·cate \in'delikət\ *adj* : improper —**in·del·i·ca·cy** \in'deləkəsē\ *n*

in·dem·ni·fy \in'demnə,fī\ *vb* -**fied; -fy·ing** : repay for a loss —**in·dem·ni·fi·ca·tion** \-,demnəfə'kāshən\ *n*

in·dem·ni·ty \in'demnətē\ *n, pl* -**ties** : security against loss or damage

¹in·dent \in'dent\ *vb* : leave a space at the beginning of a paragraph

²indent *vb* : force inward so as to form a depression or dent

in·den·ta·tion \,in,den'tashən\ *n* **1** : notch, recess, or dent **2** : action of indenting **3** : space at the beginning of a paragraph

in·den·ture \in'denchər\ *n* : contract binding one person to work for another for a given period —usu. in pl. ~ *vb* -**tured; -tur·ing** : bind by indentures

Independence Day *n* : July 4 observed as a legal holiday in commemoration of the adoption of the Declaration of Independence in 1776

in·de·pen·dent \,ində'pendənt\ *adj* **1** : not governed by another **2** : not requiring or relying on something or somebody else **3** : not easily influenced —**in·de·pen·dence** \-dəns\ *n* —**independent** *n* —**in·de·pen·dent·ly** *adv*

in·de·ter·mi·nate \,indi'tərmənət\ *adj* : not definitely determined —**in·de·ter·mi·na·cy** \-nəsē\ *n* —**inde·ter·mi·nate·ly** *adv*

in·dex \'in,deks\ *n, pl* -**dex·es** *or* -**di·ces** \-də,sēz\ **1** : alphabetical list of items (as topics in a book) **2** : a number that serves as a measure or indicator of something ~ *vb* **1** : provide with an index **2** : serve as an index of

index finger *n* : forefinger

in·di·cate \'ində,kāt\ *vb* -**cat·ed; -cat·ing 1** : point out or to **2** : show indirectly **3** : state briefly —**in·di·ca·tion** \,ində'kāshən\ *n* —**in·di·ca·tor** \'ində,kātər\ *n*

in·dic·a·tive \in'dikətiv\ *adj* : serving to indicate

in·dict \in'dīt\ *vb* : charge with a crime —**in·dict·able** *adj* —**in·dict·ment** *n*

in·dif·fer·ent \in'difrənt\ *adj* **1** : having no preference **2** : showing neither interest nor dislike **3** : mediocre —**in·dif·fer·ence** \-'difrəns\ *n* —**in·dif·fer·ent·ly** *adv*

in·dig·e·nous \in'dijənəs\ *adj* : native to a particular region

in·di·gent \'indijənt\ *adj* : needy —**in·di·gence** \-jəns\ *n*

in·di·ges·tion \,indī'jeschən, -də-\ *n* : discomfort from inability to digest food

in·dig·na·tion \,indig'nāshən\ *n* : anger aroused by something unjust or unworthy —**in·dig·nant** \in'dignənt\ *adj* —**in·dig·nant·ly** *adv*

in·dig·ni·ty \in'dignətē\ *n, pl* -**ties 1** : offense against self-respect **2** : humiliating treatment

in·di·go \'indi,gō\ *n, pl* -**gos** *or* -**goes 1** : blue dye **2** : deep reddish blue color

in·di·rect \,ində'rekt, -dī-\ *adj* : not straight or straightforward —**in·di·rec·tion** \-'rekshən\ *n* —**in·di·rect·ly** *adv* —**in·di·rect·ness** *n*

in·dis·crim·i·nate \,indis'krimənət\ *adj* **1** : not careful or discriminating **2**

: haphazard —**in·dis·crim·i·nate·ly** *adv*

in·dis·pens·able \,indis'pensəbəl\ *adj* : absolutely essential —**in·dis·pens·abil·i·ty** \-,pensə'bilətē\ *n* —**indispensable** *n* —**in·dis·pens·ably** \-'pensəblē\ *adv*

in·dis·posed \-'pōzd\ *adj* : slightly ill —**in·dis·po·si·tion** \in,dispə'zishən\ *n*

in·dis·sol·u·ble \,indis'älyəbəl\ *adj* : not capable of being dissolved or broken

in·di·vid·u·al \,ində'vijəwəl\ *adj* 1 : single member of a category 2 : person —**individual** *adj* —**in·di·vid·u·al·ly** *adv*

in·di·vid·u·al·ist \-əwəlist\ *n* : person who is markedly independent in thought or action

in·di·vid·u·al·i·ty \-,vijə'walətē\ *n* : special quality that distinguishes an individual

in·di·vid·u·al·ize \-'vijəwə,līz\ *vb* -**ized**; -**iz·ing** 1 : make individual 2 : treat individually

in·doc·tri·nate \in'däktrə,nāt\ *vb* -**nated**; -**nat·ing** : instruct in fundamentals (as of a doctrine) —**in·doc·tri·na·tion** \in,däktrə'nāshən\ *n*

in·do·lent \'indələnt\ *adj* : lazy —**in·do·lence** \-ləns\ *n*

in·dom·i·ta·ble \in'dämətəbəl\ *adj* : invincible —**in·dom·i·ta·bly** \-blē\ *adv*

in·door \'in'dōr\ *adj* : relating to the inside of a building

in·doors \in'dōrz\ *adv* : in or into a building

in·du·bi·ta·ble \in'dübətəbəl, -'dyü-\ *adj* : being beyond question —**in·du·bi·ta·bly** \-blē\ *adv*

in·duce \in'düs, -'dyüs\ *vb* -**duced**; -**duc·ing** 1 : persuade 2 : bring about —**in·duce·ment** *n* —**in·duc·er** *n*

in·duct \in'dəkt\ *vb* 1 : put in office 2 : admit as a member 3 : enroll (as for military service) —**in·duct·ee** \in-,dək'tē\ *n*

in·duc·tion \in'dəkshən\ *n* 1 : act or instance of inducting 2 : reasoning from particular instances to a general conclusion

in·duc·tive \in'dəktiv\ *adj* : reasoning by induction

in·dulge \in'dəlj\ *vb* -**dulged**; -**dulg·ing** : yield to the desire of or for —**indulgence** \-'dəljəns\ *n* —**in·dul·gent** \-jənt\ *adj* —**in·dul·gent·ly** *adv*

in·dus·tri·al \in'dəstrēəl\ *adj* 1 : relating to industry 2 : heavy-duty —**in·dus·tri·al·ist** \-əlist\ *n* —**in·dus·tri·al·iza·tion** \-,dəstrēələ'zāshən\ *n* —**in·dus·tri·al·ize** \-'dəstrēə,līz\ *vb* —**in·dus·tri·al·ly** *adv*

in·dus·tri·ous \in'dəstrēəs\ *adj* : diligent or busy —**in·dus·tri·ous·ly** *adv* —**in·dus·tri·ous·ness** *n*

in·dus·try \'indəstrē\ *n*, *pl* -**tries** 1 : diligence 2 : manufacturing enterprises or activity

in·e·bri·at·ed \i'nēbrē,ātəd\ *adj* : drunk —**ine·bri·a·tion** \-,ēbrē'āshən\ *n*

in·ef·fa·ble \in'efəbəl\ *adj* : incapable of being expressed in words —**in·ef·fa·bly** \-blē\ *adv*

in·ept \in'ept\ *adj* 1 : inappropriate or foolish 2 : generally incompetent —**in·ep·ti·tude** \in'eptə,tüd, -,tyüd\ *n* —**in·ept·ly** *adv* —**in·ept·ness** *n*

in·equal·i·ty \,ini'kwälətē\ *n* : quality of being unequal or uneven

in·ert \in'ərt\ *adj* 1 : powerless to move or act 2 : sluggish —**in·ert·ly** *adv* —**in·ert·ness** *n*

in·er·tia \in'ərshə\ *n* : tendency of matter to remain at rest or in motion —**in·er·tial** \-shəl\ *adj*

in·es·cap·able \,inə'skāpəbəl\ *adj* : inevitable —**in·es·cap·ably** \-blē\ *adv*

in·es·ti·ma·ble \in'estəməbəl\ *adj* : incapable of being estimated —**in·es·ti·ma·bly** \-blē\ *adv*

in·ev·i·ta·ble \in'evətəbəl\ *adj* : incapable of being avoided or escaped —**in·ev·i·ta·bil·i·ty** \in,evətə'bilətē\ *n* —**in·ev·i·ta·bly** \in'evətəblē\ *adv*

in·ex·cus·able \,inik'skyüzəbəl\ *adj* : being without excuse or justification —**in·ex·cus·ably** \-blē\ *adv*

in·ex·haust·ible \,inig'zóstəbəl\ *adj* : incapable of being used up or tired out —**in·ex·haust·ibly** \-blē\ *adv*

in·ex·o·ra·ble \in'eksərəbəl\ *adj* : unyielding or relentless —**in·ex·o·ra·bly** *adv*

in·fal·li·ble \in'faləbəl\ *adj* : incapable of error —**in·fal·li·bil·i·ty** \in,falə'bilətē\ *n* —**in·fal·li·bly** *adv*

in·fa·mous \'infəməs\ *adj* : having the worst kind of reputation —**in·fa·mous·ly** *adv*

in·fa·my \-mē\ *n*, *pl* -**mies** : evil reputation

in·fan·cy \'infənsē\ *n*, *pl* -**cies** 1 : early childhood 2 : early period of existence

in·fant \'infənt\ *n* : baby

in·fan·tile \'infən,tīl, -t^əl, -,tēl\ *adj* 1 : relating to infants 2 : childish

in·fan·try \'infəntrē\ *n, pl* **-tries** : soldiers that fight on foot

in·fat·u·ate \in'fachə,wāt\ *vb* **-at·ed; -at·ing** : inspire with foolish love or admiration —**in·fat·u·a·tion** \-,fachə-'wāshən\ *n*

in·fect \in'fekt\ *vb* : contaminate with disease-producing matter —**in·fec·tion** \-'fekshən\ *n* —**in·fec·tious** \-shəs\ *adj* —**in·fec·tive** \-'fektiv\ *adj*

in·fer \in'fər\ *vb* **-rr-** : deduce —**in·fer·ence** \'infərəns\ *n* —**in·fer·en·tial** \,infə'renchəl\ *adj*

in·fe·ri·or \in'firēər\ *adj* 1 : being lower in position, degree, rank, or merit 2 : of lesser quality —**inferior** *n* —**in·fe·ri·or·i·ty** \in,firē'órətē\ *n*

in·fer·nal \in'fərn^əl\ *adj* : of or like hell—often used as a general expression of disapproval —**in·fer·nal·ly** *adv*

in·fer·no \in'fərnō\ *n, pl* **-nos** : place or condition suggesting hell

in·fest \in'fest\ *vb* : swarm or grow in or over —**in·fes·ta·tion** \,in,fes'tāshən\ *n*

in·fi·del \'infəd^əl, -fə,del\ *n* : one who does not believe in a particular religion

in·fi·del·i·ty \,infə'delətē, -fī-\ *n, pl* **-ties** : lack of faithfulness

in·field \'in,fēld\ *n* : baseball field inside the base lines —**in·field·er** *n*

in·fil·trate \in'fil,trāt, 'infil-\ *vb* **-trat·ed; -trat·ing** : enter or become established in without being noticed —**in·fil·tra·tion** \,infil'trāshən\ *n*

in·fi·nite \'infənət\ *adj* 1 : having no limit or extending indefinitely 2 : vast —**infinite** *n* —**in·fi·nite·ly** *adv* —**in·fin·i·tude** \in'finə,tüd, -tyüd\ *n*

in·fin·i·tes·i·mal \,in,finə'tesəməl\ *adj* : immeasurably small —**in·fin·i·tes·i·mal·ly** *adv*

in·fin·i·tive \in'finətiv\ *n* : verb form in English usu. used with *to*

in·fin·i·ty \in'finətē\ *n, pl* **-ties** 1 : quality or state of being infinite 2 : indefinitely great number or amount

in·firm \in'fərm\ *adj* : feeble from age —**in·fir·mi·ty** \-'fərmətē\ *n*

in·fir·ma·ry \in'fərmərē\ *n, pl* **-ries** : place for the care of the sick

in·flame \in'flām\ *vb* **-flamed;**

-flam·ing 1 : excite to intense action or feeling 2 : affect or become affected with redden and inflammation —**in·flam·ma·to·ry** \-'flamə,tōrē\ *adj*

in·flam·ma·ble \in'flaməbəl\ *adj* : flammable

in·flam·ma·tion \,inflə'māshən\ *n* : response to injury in which an affected area becomes red and painful and congested with blood

in·flate \in'flāt\ *vb* **-flat·ed; -flat·ing** 1 : swell or puff up (as with gas) 2 : expand or increase abnormally —**in·flat·able** *adj*

in·fla·tion \in'flāshən\ *n* 1 : act of inflating 2 : continual rise in prices —**in·fla·tion·ary** \-shə,nerē\ *adj*

in·flec·tion \in'flekshən\ *n* 1 : change in pitch or loudness of the voice 2 : change in form of a word —**in·flect** \-'flekt\ *vb* —**in·flec·tion·al** \-'flek-shənəl\ *adj*

in·flict \in'flikt\ *vb* : give by or as if by hitting —**in·flic·tion** \-'flikshən\ *n*

in·flu·ence \'in,flüəns\ *n* 1 : power or capacity of causing an effect in indirect or intangible ways 2 : one that exerts influence — *vb* **-enced; -enc·ing** : affect or alter by influence —**in·flu·en·tial** \,inflü'enchəl\ *adj*

in·flu·en·za \,inflü'enzə\ *n* : acute very contagious virus disease

in·flux \'in,fləks\ *n* : a flowing in

in·form \in'fórm\ *vb* : give information or knowledge to —**in·for·mant** \-ənt\ *n* —**in·form·er** *n*

in·for·mal \in'fórməl\ *adj* 1 : without formality or ceremony 2 : for ordinary or familiar use —**in·for·mal·i·ty** \,infór'malətē, -fər-\ *n* —**in·for·mal·ly** *adv*

in·for·ma·tion \,infər'māshən\ *n* : knowledge obtained from investigation, study, or instruction —**infor·ma·tion·al** \-shənəl\ *adj*

in·for·ma·tive \in'fórmətiv\ *adj* : giving knowledge

in·frac·tion \in'frakshən\ *n* : violation

in·fra·red \,infrə'red\ *adj* : being, relating to, or using radiation of wavelengths longer than those of red light —**infrared** *n*

in·fra·struc·ture \'infrə,strəkchər\ *n* : foundation of a system or organization

in·fringe \in'frinj\ *vb* **-fringed; -fring-**

ing : violate another's right or privilege —**in·fringe·ment** n

in·fu·ri·ate \in'fyùrē,āt\ vb -**at·ed**; -**at·ing** : make furious —**in·fu·ri·at·ing·ly** \-,ātiŋlē\ adv

in·fuse \in'fyüz\ vb -**fused**; -**fus·ing** 1 : instill a principle or quality in 2 : steep in liquid without boiling —**in·fu·sion** \-'fyüzhən\ n

¹**-ing** \iŋ\ vb suffix or adj suffix —used to form the present participle and sometimes an adjective resembling a present participle

²**-ing** n suffix 1 : action or process 2 : something connected with or resulting from an action or process

in·ge·nious \in'jēnyəs\ adj : very clever —**in·ge·nious·ly** adv —**in·ge·nious·ness** n

in·ge·nue, **in·gé·nue** \'anjə,nü, 'än-; 'aⁿzhə-, 'äⁿ-\ n : naive young woman

in·ge·nu·i·ty \,injə'nüətē, -'nyü-\ n, pl -**ities** : skill or cleverness in planning or inventing

in·gen·u·ous \in'jenyəwəs\ adj : innocent and candid —**in·gen·u·ous·ly** adv —**in·gen·u·ous·ness** n

in·gest \in'jest\ vb : eat —**in·ges·tion** \-'jeschən\ n

in·gle·nook \'iŋgəl,nùk\ n : corner by the fireplace

in·got \'iŋgət\ n : block of metal

in·grained \in'grānd\ adj : deep-seated

in·grate \'in,grāt\ n : ungrateful person

in·gra·ti·ate \in'grāshē,āt\ vb -**at·ed**; -**at·ing** : gain favor for (oneself) —**in·gra·ti·at·ing** adj

in·gre·di·ent \in'grēdēənt\ n : one of the substances that make up a mixture

in·grown \'in,grōn\ adj : grown in and esp. into the flesh

in·hab·it \in'habət\ vb : live or dwell in —**in·hab·it·able** adj —**in·hab·it·ant** \-ətənt\ n

in·hale \in'hāl\ vb -**haled**; -**hal·ing** : breathe in —**in·hal·ant** \-ənt\ n —**in·ha·la·tion** \,inhə'lāshən, ,inə-\ n —**in·hal·er** n

in·here \in'hir\ vb -**hered**; -**her·ing** : be inherent

in·her·ent \in'hirənt, -'her-\ adj : being an essential part of something —**in·her·ent·ly** adv

in·her·it \in'herət\ vb : receive from one's ancestors —**in·her·it·able** \-əbəl\ adj —**in·her·i·tance** \-ətəns\ n —**in·her·i·tor** \-ətər\ n

in·hib·it \in'hibət\ vb : hold in check —**in·hi·bi·tion** \,inhə'bishən, ,inə-\ n

in·hu·man \in'hyümən, -'yü-\ adj : cruel or impersonal —**in·hu·man·i·ty** \-hyü'manətē, -yü-\ n —**in·hu·man·ly** adv —**in·hu·man·ness** n

in·im·i·cal \in'imikəl\ adj : hostile or harmful —**in·im·i·cal·ly** adv

in·im·i·ta·ble \in'imətəbəl\ adj : not capable of being imitated

in·iq·ui·ty \in'ikwətē\ n, pl -**ties** : wickedness —**in·iq·ui·tous** \-wətəs\ adj

ini·tial \in'ishəl\ adj 1 : of or relating to the beginning 2 : first ~ n : 1st letter of a word or name ~ vb -**tialed** or -**tialled**; -**tial·ing** or -**tial·ling** : put initials on —**ini·tial·ly** adv

ini·ti·ate \in'ishē,āt\ vb -**at·ed**; -**at·ing** 1 : start 2 : induct into membership 3 : instruct in the rudiments of something —**initiate** \-'ishēət\ n —**ini·ti·a·tion** \-,ishē'āshən\ n —**ini·tia·to·ry** \-'ishēə,tōrē\ adj

ini·tia·tive \in'ishətiv\ n 1 : first step 2 : readiness to undertake something on one's own

in·ject \in'jekt\ vb : force or introduce into something —**in·jec·tion** \-'jekshən\ n

in·junc·tion \in'jəŋkshən\ n : court writ requiring one to do or to refrain from doing a specified act

in·jure \'injər\ vb -**jured**; -**jur·ing** : do damage, hurt, or a wrong to

in·ju·ry \'injərē\ n, pl -**ries** 1 : act that injures 2 : hurt, damage, or loss sustained —**in·ju·ri·ous** \in'jùrēəs\ adj

in·jus·tice \in'jəstəs\ n : unjust act

ink \'iŋk\ n : usu. liquid and colored material for writing and printing ~ vb : put ink on —**ink·well** \-,wel\ n —**inky** adj

in·kling \'iŋkliŋ\ n : hint or idea

in·land \'in,land, -lənd\ n : interior of a country —**inland** adj or adv

in-law \'in,lò\ n : relative by marriage

in·lay \in'lā, 'in,lā\ vb -**laid** \-'lād\; -**lay·ing** : set into a surface for decoration ~ \'in,lā\ n 1 : inlaid work 2 : shaped filling cemented into a tooth

in·let \'in,let, -lət\ n : small bay

in·mate \'in,māt\ n : person confined to an asylum or prison

in me·mo·ri·am \,inmə'mōrēəm\ prep : in memory of

in·most \'in,mōst\ adj : deepest within

inn \'in\ *n* : hotel

in·nards \'inərdz\ *n pl* : internal parts

in·nate \in'āt\ *adj* 1 : inborn 2 : inherent —**in·nate·ly** *adv*

in·ner \'inər\ *adj* : being on the inside

in·ner·most \'inər‚mōst\ *adj* : farthest inward

in·ner·sole \‚inər'sōl\ *n* : insole

in·ning \'iniŋ\ *n* : baseball team's turn at bat

inn·keep·er \'in‚kēpər\ *n* : owner of an inn

in·no·cent \'inəsənt\ *adj* 1 : free from guilt 2 : harmless 3 : not sophisticated —**in·no·cence** \-səns\ *n* —**innocent** *n* —**in·no·cent·ly** *adv*

in·noc·u·ous \in'äkyəwəs\ *adj* 1 : harmless 2 : inoffensive

in·no·va·tion \‚inə'vāshən\ *n* : new idea or method —**in·no·vate** \'inə‚vāt\ *vb* —**in·no·va·tive** \'inə‚vātiv\ *adj* —**in·no·va·tor** \-‚vātər\ *n*

in·nu·en·do \‚inyə'wendō\ *n, pl* -dos *or* -does : insinuation

in·nu·mer·a·ble \in'ümərəbəl, -'yüm-\ *adj* : countless

in·oc·u·late \in'äkyə‚lāt\ *vb* -lat·ed; -lat·ing : treat with something esp. to establish immunity —**in·oc·u·la·tion** \-‚äkyə'lāshən\ *n*

in·op·por·tune \in‚äpər'tün, -'tyün\ *adj* : inconvenient —**in·op·por·tune·ly** *adv*

in·or·di·nate \in'ördªnət\ *adj* : unusual or excessive —**in·or·di·nate·ly** *adv*

in·or·gan·ic \‚in‚ör'ganik\ *adj* : made of mineral matter

in·pa·tient \'in‚pāshənt\ *n* : patient who stays in a hospital

in·put \'in‚pút\ *n* : something put in —**input** *vb*

in·quest \'in‚kwest\ *n* : inquiry esp. before a jury

in·quire \in'kwīr\ *vb* -quired; -quir·ing 1 : ask 2 : investigate —**in·quir·er** *n* —**in·quir·ing·ly** *adv* —**in·qui·ry** \in-‚kwīrē, in'kwīrē; 'inkwərē, 'iŋ-\ *n*

in·qui·si·tion \‚inkwə'zishən, ‚iŋ-\ *n* 1 : official inquiry 2 : severe questioning —**in·quis·i·tor** \in'kwizətər\ *n* —**in·quis·i·to·ri·al** \-‚kwizə'tōrēəl\ *adj*

in·quis·i·tive \in'kwizətiv\ *adj* : curious —**in·quis·i·tive·ly** *adv* —**in·quis·i·tive·ness** *n*

in·road \'in‚rōd\ *n* : encroachment

in·rush \'in‚rəsh\ *n* : influx

in·sane \in'sān\ *adj* 1 : not sane 2 : ab-surd —**in·sane·ly** *adv* —**in·san·i·ty** \in'sanətē\ *n*

in·sa·tia·ble \in'sāshəbəl\ *adj* : in-capable of being satisfied —**in·sa·tia·bil·i·ty** \in‚sāshə'bilətē\ *n* —**in·sa·tia·bly** *adv*

in·scribe \in'skrīb\ *vb* 1 : write 2 : engrave 3 : dedicate (a book) to someone —**in·scrip·tion** \-'skrip-shən\ *n*

in·scru·ta·ble \in'skrütəbəl\ *adj* : mys-terious —**in·scru·ta·bly** *adv*

in·seam \'in‚sēm\ *n* : inner seam (of a garment)

in·sect \'in‚sekt\ *n* : small usu. winged animal with 6 legs

in·sec·ti·cide \in'sektə‚sīd\ *n* : insect poison —**in·sec·ti·cid·al** \in‚sektə-'sīdªl\ *adj*

in·se·cure \‚insi'kyúr\ *adj* 1 : uncertain 2 : unsafe 3 : fearful —**in·se·cure·ly** *adv* —**in·se·cu·ri·ty** \-'kyúrətē\ *n*

in·sem·i·nate \in'semə‚nāt\ *vb* -nat·ed; -nat·ing : introduce semen into —**in·sem·i·na·tion** \-‚semə'nāshən\ *n*

in·sen·si·ble \in'sensəbəl\ *adj* 1 : uncon-scious 2 : unable to feel 3 : unaware —**in·sen·si·bil·i·ty** \in‚sensə'bilətē\ *n* —**in·sen·si·bly** *adv*

in·sen·tient \in'senchənt\ *adj* : lacking feeling —**in·sen·tience** \-chəns\ *n*

in·sert \in'sərt\ *vb* : put in —**insert** \'in-‚sərt\ *n* —**in·ser·tion** \in'sərshən\ *n*

in·set \'in‚set\ *vb* inset *or* **in·set·ted**; in·set·ting : set in —**inset** *n*

in·shore \'in‚shōr\ *adj* 1 : situated near shore 2 : moving toward shore ~ *adv* : toward shore

in·side \in'sīd, 'in‚sīd\ *n* 1 : inner side 2 *pl* : innards ~ *prep* 1 : in or into the inside of 2 : within ~ *adv* 1 : on the inner side 2 : into the interior —**inside** *adj* —**in·sid·er** \in'sīdər\ *n*

inside of *prep* : inside

in·sid·i·ous \in'sidēəs\ *adj* 1 : treacher-ous 2 : seductive —**in·sid·i·ous·ly** *adv* —**in·sid·i·ous·ness** *n*

in·sight \'in‚sīt\ *n* : understanding —**in·sight·ful** \in'sītfəl-\ *adj*

in·sig·nia \in'signēə\, **in·sig·ne** \-‚nē\ *n, pl* -nia *or* -ni·as : badge of authority or office

in·sin·u·ate \in'sinyə‚wāt\ *vb* -at·ed; -at·ing 1 : imply 2 : bring in artfully —**in·sin·u·a·tion** \in‚sinyə'wāshən\ *n*

in·sip·id \in'sipəd\ *adj* 1 : tasteless 2

: not stimulating —**in·si·pid·i·ty** \ˌinsəˈpidətē\ n

in·sist \inˈsist\ vb : be firmly demanding —**in·sis·tence** \inˈsistəns\ n —**insis·tent** \-tənt\ adj —**in·sis·tent·ly** adv

insofar as \ˌinsōˈfärəz\ conj : to the extent that

in·sole \ˈinˌsōl\ n : inside sole of a shoe

in·so·lent \ˈinsələnt\ adj : contemptuously rude —**in·so·lence** \-ləns\ n

in·sol·vent \inˈsälvənt\ adj : unable or insufficient to pay debts —**in·sol·ven·cy** \-vənsē\ n

in·som·nia \inˈsämnēə\ n : inability to sleep

in·so·much as \ˌinsōˈməchaz\ conj : inasmuch as

insomuch that conj : to such a degree that

in·sou·ci·ance \inˈsüsēəns, aⁿsüˈsyäⁿs\ n : lighthearted indifference —**insou·ci·ant** \inˈsüsēənt, aⁿsüˈsyäⁿ\ adj

in·spect \inˈspekt\ vb : view closely and critically —**in·spec·tion** \-ˈspekshən\ n —**in·spec·tor** \-tər\ n

in·spire \inˈspīr\ vb -**spired**; -**spir·ing** 1 : inhale 2 : influence by example 3 : bring about 4 : stir to action —**in·spi·ra·tion** \ˌinspəˈrāshən\ n —**in·spi·ra·tion·al** \-ˈrāshənəl\ adj —**in·spir·er** n

in·stall, in·stal \inˈstȯl\ vb -**stalled**; -**stall·ing** 1 : induct into office 2 : set up for use —**in·stal·la·tion** \ˌinstəˈlāshən\ n

in·stall·ment \inˈstȯlmənt\ n : partial payment

in·stance \ˈinstəns\ n 1 : request or instigation 2 : example

in·stant \ˈinstənt\ n : moment ~ adj 1 : immediate 2 : ready to mix —**in·stan·ta·neous** \ˌinstənˈtānēəs\ adj —**in·stan·ta·neous·ly** adv —**in·stant·ly** adv

in·stead \inˈsted\ adv : as a substitute or alternative

instead of prep : as a substitute for or alternative to

in·step \ˈinˌstep\ n : part of the foot in front of the ankle

in·sti·gate \ˈinstəˌgāt\ vb -**gat·ed**; -**gat·ing** : incite —**in·sti·ga·tion** \ˌinstəˈgā·shən\ n —**in·sti·ga·tor** \ˈinstəˌgātər\ n

in·still \inˈstil\ vb -**stilled**; -**still·ing** : impart gradually

in·stinct \ˈinˌstiŋkt\ n 1 : natural talent

2 : natural inherited or subconsciously motivated behavior —**in·stinc·tive** \inˈstiŋktiv\ adj —**in·stinc·tive·ly** adv —**in·stinc·tu·al** \inˈstiŋkchəwəl\ adj

in·sti·tute \ˈinstəˌtüt, -ˌtyüt\ vb -**tut·ed**; -**tut·ing** : establish, start, or organize ~ n 1 : organization promoting a cause 2 : school

in·sti·tu·tion \ˌinstəˈtüshən, -ˈtyü-\ n 1 : act of instituting 2 : custom 3 : corporation or society of a public character —**in·sti·tu·tion·al** \-shənəl\ adj —**in·sti·tu·tion·al·ize** \-ˌīz\ vb —**in·sti·tu·tion·al·ly** adv

in·struct \inˈstrəkt\ vb 1 : teach 2 : give an order to —**in·struc·tion** \-ˈstrəkshən\ n —**in·struc·tion·al** \-shənəl\ adj —**in·struc·tive** \inˈstrəktiv\ adj —**in·struc·tor** \inˈstrəktər\ n —**in·struc·tor·ship** n

in·stru·ment \ˈinstrəmənt\ n 1 : something that produces music 2 : means 3 : device for doing work and esp. precision work 4 : legal document —**in·stru·men·tal** \ˌinstrəˈmentᵊl\ adj —**in·stru·men·tal·ist** \-ist\ n —**in·stru·men·tal·i·ty** \ˌinstrəmənˈtalətē, -ˌmen-\ n —**in·stru·men·ta·tion** \ˌinstrəmənˈtäshən, -ˌmen-\ n

in·sub·or·di·nate \ˌinsəˈbȯrdᵊnət\ adj : not obeying —**in·sub·or·di·na·tion** \-ˌbȯrdᵊnˈāshən\ n

in·suf·fer·able \inˈsəfərəbəl\ adj : unbearable —**in·suf·fer·ably** \-blē\ adv

in·su·lar \ˈinsülər, -syü-\ adj 1 : relating to or residing on an island 2 : narrow-minded —**in·su·lar·i·ty** \ˌinsüˈlarətē, -syü-\ n

in·su·late \ˈinsəˌlāt\ vb -**lat·ed**; -**lat·ing** : protect from heat loss or electricity —**in·su·la·tion** \ˌinsəˈlāshən\ n —**in·su·la·tor** \ˈinsəˌlātər\ n

in·su·lin \ˈinsələn\ n : hormone used by diabetics

in·sult \inˈsəlt\ vb : treat with contempt ~ \ˈinˌsəlt\ n : insulting act or remark —**in·sult·ing·ly** \-iŋlē\ adv

in·su·per·a·ble \inˈsüpərəbəl\ adj : too difficult —**in·su·per·a·bly** \-blē\ adv

in·sure \inˈshu̇r\ vb -**sured**; -**sur·ing** 1 : guarantee against loss 2 : make certain —**in·sur·able** \-əbəl\ adj —**in·sur·ance** \-əns\ n —**in·sured** \inˈshu̇rd\ —**in·sur·er** n

in·sur·gent \in'sərjənt\ n : rebel —**in·sur·gence** \-jəns\ n —**in·sur·gen·cy** \-jənsē\ n —**in·sur·gent** adj

in·sur·mount·able \,insər'maůntəbəl\ adj : too great to be overcome —**in·sur·mount·ably** \-blē\ adv

in·sur·rec·tion \,insə'rekshən\ n : revolution —**in·sur·rec·tion·ist** n

in·tact \in'takt\ adj : undamaged

in·take \'in,tāk\ n 1 : opening through which something enters 2 : act of taking in 3 : amount taken in

in·te·ger \'intijər\ n : number that is not a fraction and does not include a fraction

in·te·gral \'intigrəl\ adj : essential

in·te·grate \'intə,grāt\ vb -grat·ed; -grat·ing 1 : unite 2 : end segregation of or at —**in·te·gra·tion** \,intə-'grāshən\ n

in·teg·ri·ty \in'tegrətē\ n 1 : soundness 2 : adherence to a code of values 3 : completeness

in·tel·lect \'int⁹l,ekt\ n : power of knowing or thinking —**in·tel·lec·tu·al** \,int⁹l'ekchəwəl\ adj or n —**in·tel·lec·tu·al·ism** \-chəwə,lizəm\ n —**in·tel·lec·tu·al·ly** adv

in·tel·li·gence \in'teləjəns\ n 1 : ability to learn and understand 2 : mental acuteness 3 : information

in·tel·li·gent \in'teləjənt\ adj : having or showing intelligence —**in·tel·li·gent·ly** adv

in·tel·li·gi·ble \in'teləjəbəl\ adj : understandable —**in·tel·li·gi·bil·i·ty** \-,teləjə'bilətē\ n —**in·tel·li·gi·bly** adv

in·tem·per·ance \in'tempərəns\ n : lack of moderation —**in·tem·per·ate** \-pərət\ adj —**in·tem·per·ate·ness** n

in·tend \in'tend\ vb : have as a purpose

in·tend·ed \-'tendəd\ n : engaged person —**intended** adj

in·tense \in'tens\ adj 1 : extreme 2 : deeply felt —**in·tense·ly** adv —**in·ten·si·fi·ca·tion** \-,tensəfə'kāshən\ n —**in·ten·si·fy** \-'tensə,fī\ vb —**in·ten·si·ty** \-'tensətē\ n —**in·ten·sive** \in-'tensiv\ adj —**in·ten·sive·ly** adv

¹**in·tent** \in'tent\ n : purpose —**in·ten·tion** \-'tenchən\ n —**in·ten·tion·al** \-'tenchənəl\ adj —**in·ten·tion·al·ly** adv

²**intent** adj : concentrated —**in·tent·ly** adv —**in·tent·ness** n

in·ter \in'tər\ vb -rr- : bury

inter- prefix : between or among

interagency
interatomic
interbank
interborough
intercampus
interchurch
intercity
interclass
intercoastal
intercollegiate
intercolonial
intercommunal
intercommunity
intercompany
intercontinental
intercounty
intercultural
interdenomina-
  tional
interdepartmen-
  tal
interdivisional
interelectronic
interethnic
interfaculty
interfamily
interfiber
interfraternity
intergalactic
intergang
intergovern-
  mental
intergroup
interhemi-
  spheric

interindustry
interinstitu-
  tional
interisland
interlibrary
intermolecular
intermountain
interoceanic
interoffice
interparticle
interparty
interpersonal
interplanetary
interpopulation
interprovincial
interracial
interregional
interreligious
interscholastic
intersectional
interstate
interstellar
intersystem
interterm
interterminal
intertribal
intertroop
intertropical
interuniversity
interurban
intervalley
intervillage
interwar
interzonal
interzone

in·ter·ac·tion \,intər'akshən\ n : mutual influence —**in·ter·act** \-'akt\ vb —**in·ter·ac·tive** adj

in·ter·breed \,intər'brēd\ vb -bred \-'bred\; -breed·ing : breed together

in·ter·ca·late \in'tərkə,lāt\ vb -lat·ed; -lat·ing : insert —**in·ter·ca·la·tion** \-,tərkə'lāshən\ n

in·ter·cede \,intər'sēd\ vb -ced·ed; -ced·ing : act to reconcile —**in·ter·ces·sion** \-'seshən\ n —**in·ter·ces·sor** \-'sesər\ n

in·ter·cept \,intər'sept\ vb : interrupt the progress of —**intercept** \'intər,sept\ n —**in·ter·cep·tion** \,intər'sepshən\ n —**in·ter·cep·tor** \-'septər\ n

in·ter·change \,intər'chānj\ vb 1 : exchange 2 : change places ~ \'intər,chānj\ n 1 : exchange 2 : junction of highways —**in·ter·change·able** \,intər'chānjəbəl\ adj

in·ter·course \'intər,kōrs\ n 1 : relations

between persons or nations **2** : copulation

in·ter·de·pen·dent \,intərdi'pendənt\ adj : mutually dependent —**in·ter·de·pen·dence** \-dəns\ n

in·ter·dict \,intər'dikt\ vb **1** : prohibit **2** : destroy or cut (an enemy supply line) —**in·ter·dic·tion** \-'dikshən\ n

in·ter·est \'intrəst, -tə,rest\ n **1** : right **2** : benefit **3** : charge for borrowed money **4** : readiness to pay special attention **5** : quality that causes interest ~ vb **1** : concern **2** : get the attention of —**in·ter·est·ing** adj —**in·ter·est·ing·ly** adv

in·ter·face \'intər,fās\ n : common boundary —**in·ter·fa·cial** \,intər'fāshəl\ adj

in·ter·fere \,intər'fir\ vb **-fered; -fer·ing** **1** : collide or be in opposition **2** : try to run the affairs of others —**in·ter·fer·ence** \-'firəns\ n

in·ter·im \'intərəm\ n : time between —**interim** adj

in·te·ri·or \in'tirēər\ adj : being on the inside ~ n **1** : inside **2** : inland area

in·ter·ject \,intər'jekt\ vb : stick in between

in·ter·jec·tion \-'jekshən\ n : an exclamatory word —**in·ter·jec·tion·al·ly** \-shənəlē\ adv

in·ter·lace \,intər'lās\ vb : cross or cause to cross one over another

in·ter·lin·ear \,intər'linēər\ adj : between written or printed lines

in·ter·lock \,intər'läk\ vb **1** : interlace **2** : connect for mutual effect —**interlock** \'intər,läk\ n

in·ter·lop·er \,intər'lōpər\ n : intruder or meddler

in·ter·lude \'intər,lüd\ n : intervening period

in·ter·mar·ry \,intər'marē\ vb **1** : marry each other **2** : marry within a group —**in·ter·mar·riage** \-'marij\ n

in·ter·me·di·ary \,intər'mēdē,erē\ n, pl **-ar·ies** : agent between individuals or groups —**intermediary** adj

in·ter·me·di·ate \,intər'mēdēət\ adj : between extremes —**intermediate** n

in·ter·ment \in'tərmənt\ n : burial

in·ter·mi·na·ble \in'tərmənəbəl\ adj : endless —**in·ter·mi·na·bly** adv

in·ter·min·gle \,intər'miŋgəl\ vb : mingle

in·ter·mis·sion \,intər'mishən\ n : break in a performance

in·ter·mit·tent \-'mit^ənt\ adj : coming at intervals —**in·ter·mit·tent·ly** adv

in·ter·mix \,intər'miks\ vb : mix together —**in·ter·mix·ture** \-'mikschər\ n

¹in·tern \'in,tərn, in'tərn\ vb : confine esp. during a war —**in·tern·ee** \,in,tər'nē\ n —**in·tern·ment** n

²in·tern \'in,tərn\ n : advanced student (as in medicine) gaining supervised experience ~ vb : act as an intern —**in·tern·ship** n

in·ter·nal \in'tərn^əl\ adj **1** : inward **2** : inside of the body **3** : relating to or existing in the mind —**in·ter·nal·ly** adv

in·ter·na·tion·al \,intər'nashənəl\ adj : affecting 2 or more nations ~ n : something having international scope —**in·ter·na·tion·al·ism** \-,izəm\ n —**in·ter·na·tion·al·ize** \-,īz\ vb —**in·ter·na·tion·al·ly** adv

in·tern·ist \'in,tərnist\ n : specialist in nonsurgical medicine

in·ter·play \'intər,plā\ n : interaction

in·ter·po·late \in'tərpə,lāt\ vb **-lat·ed; -lat·ing** : insert —**in·ter·po·la·tion** \-,tərpə'lāshən\ n

in·ter·pose \,intər'pōz\ vb **-posed; -pos·ing** **1** : place between **2** : intrude —**in·ter·po·si·tion** \-pə'zishən\ n

in·ter·pret \in'tərprət\ vb : explain the meaning of —**in·ter·pre·ta·tion** \in,tərprə'tāshən\ n —**in·ter·pre·ta·tive** \-'tərprə,tātiv\ adj —**in·ter·pret·er** n —**in·ter·pre·tive** \-'tərprətiv\ adj

in·ter·re·late \,intəri'lāt\ vb : have a mutual relationship —**in·ter·re·lat·ed·ness** \-'lātədnəs\ n —**in·ter·re·la·tion** \-'lāshən\ n —**in·ter·re·la·tion·ship** n

in·ter·ro·gate \in'terə,gāt\ vb **-gat·ed; -gat·ing** : question —**in·ter·ro·ga·tion** \-,terə'gāshən\ n —**in·ter·rog·a·tive** \,intə'rägətiv\ adj or n —**in·ter·ro·ga·tor** \-'terə,gātər\ n —**in·ter·rog·a·to·ry** \,intə'rägə,tōrē\ adj

in·ter·rupt \,intə'rəpt\ vb : intrude so as to hinder or end continuity —**in·ter·rupt·er** n —**in·ter·rup·tion** \-'rəpshən\ n —**in·ter·rup·tive** \-'rəptiv\ adv

in·ter·sect \,intər'sekt\ vb **1** : cut across or divide **2** : cross —**in·ter·sec·tion** \-'sekshən\ n

in·ter·sperse \,intər'spərs\ vb **-spersed;**

-spers·ing : insert at intervals —**in·ter·sper·sion** \-'spərzhən\ n

in·ter·stice \in'tərstəs\ n, pl **-stic·es** \-stə,sēz, -stəsəz\ : space between —**in·ter·sti·tial** \,intər'stishəl\ adj

in·ter·twine \,intər'twīn\ vb : twist together —**in·ter·twine·ment** n

in·ter·val \'intərvəl\ n 1 : time between 2 : space between

in·ter·vene \,intər'vēn\ vb **-vened; -ven·ing** 1 : happen between events 2 : intercede —**in·ter·ven·tion** \-'venchən\ n

in·ter·view \'intər,vyü\ n : a meeting to get information —**interview** vb —**in·ter·view·er** n

in·ter·weave \,intər'wēv\ vb **-wove** \-'wōv\; **-wo·ven** \-'wōvən\; **-weav·ing** : weave together —**in·ter·wo·ven** \-'wōvən\ adj

in·tes·tate \in'tes,tāt, -tət\ adj : not leaving a will

in·tes·tine \in'testən\ n : tubular part of the digestive system after the stomach including a long narrow upper part (**small intestine**) followed by a broader shorter lower part (**large intestine**) —**in·tes·ti·nal** \-tən⁹l\ adj

in·ti·mate \'intə,māt\ vb **-mat·ed; -mat·ing** : hint ~ \'intəmət\ adj 1 : very friendly 2 : suggesting privacy 3 : very personal ~ n : close friend —**in·ti·ma·cy** \'intəməsē\ n —**in·ti·mate·ly** adv —**in·ti·ma·tion** \,intə'māshən\ n

in·tim·i·date \in'timə,dāt\ vb **-dat·ed; -dat·ing** : make fearful —**in·tim·i·da·tion** \-,timə'dāshən\ n

in·to \'intü\ prep 1 : to the inside of 2 : to the condition of 3 : against

in·to·na·tion \,intō'nāshən\ n : way of singing or speaking

in·tone \in'tōn\ vb **-toned; -ton·ing** : chant

in·tox·i·cate \in'täksə,kāt\ vb **-cat·ed; -cat·ing** : make drunk —**in·tox·i·cant** \-sikənt\ n or adj —**in·tox·i·ca·tion** \-,täksə'kāshən\ n

in·tra·mu·ral \,intrə'myürəl\ adj : within a school

in·tran·si·gent \in'transəjənt\ adj : uncompromising —**in·tran·si·gence** \-jəns\ n —**intransigent** n

in·tra·ve·nous \,intrə'vēnəs\ adj : by way of the veins —**in·tra·ve·nous·ly** adv

in·trep·id \in'trepəd\ adj : fearless —**in·tre·pid·i·ty** \,intrə'pidətē\ n

in·tri·cate \'intrikət\ adj : very complex and delicate —**in·tri·ca·cy** \-trikəsē\ n —**in·tri·cate·ly** adv

in·trigue \in'trēg\ vb **-trigued; -tri·gu·ing** 1 : scheme 2 : arouse curiosity of ~ n : secret scheme —**in·tri·gu·ing·ly** \-iŋlē\ adv

in·trin·sic \in'trinzik, -sik\ adj : essential —**in·trin·si·cal·ly** \-ziklē, -si-\ adv

in·tro·duce \,intrə'düs, -'dyüs\ vb **-duced; -duc·ing** 1 : bring in esp. for the 1st time 2 : cause to be acquainted 3 : bring to notice 4 : put in —**in·tro·duc·tion** \'dəkshən\ n —**in·tro·duc·to·ry** \-'dəktərē\ adj

in·tro·spec·tion \,intrə'spekshən\ n : examination of one's own thoughts or feelings —**in·tro·spec·tive** \-'spektiv\ adj —**in·tro·spec·tive·ly** adv

in·tro·vert \'intrə,vərt\ n : shy or reserved person —**in·tro·ver·sion** \,intrə'vərzhən\ n —**introvert** adj —**in·tro·vert·ed** \'intrə,vərtəd\ adj

in·trude \in'trüd\ vb **-trud·ed; -trud·ing** 1 : thrust in 2 : encroach —**in·trud·er** n —**in·tru·sion** \-'trüzhən\ n —**in·tru·sive** \-'trüsiv\ adj —**in·tru·sive·ness** n

in·tu·ition \,intü'ishən, -tyü-\ n : quick and ready insight —**in·tu·it** \in'tüət, -'tyü-\ vb —**in·tu·i·tive** \-ətiv\ adj —**in·tu·i·tive·ly** adv

in·un·date \'inən,dāt\ vb **-dat·ed; -dat·ing** : flood —**in·un·da·tion** \,inən-'dāshən\ n

in·ure \in'ùr, -'yùr\ vb **-ured; -ur·ing** : accustom to accept something undesirable

in·vade \in'vād\ vb **-vad·ed; -vad·ing** : enter for conquest —**in·vad·er** n —**in·va·sion** \-'vāzhən\ n

¹in·val·id \in'valəd\ adj : not true or legal —**in·va·lid·i·ty** \,invə'lidətē\ n —**in·val·id·ly** adv

²in·va·lid \'invələd\ adj : sickly ~ n : one chronically ill

in·val·i·date \in'valə,dāt\ vb : make invalid —**in·val·i·da·tion** \in,valə'dā-shən\

in·valu·able \in'valyəwəbəl\ adj : extremely valuable

in·va·sive \in'vāsiv\ adj : involving entry into the body

in·vec·tive \in'vektiv\ n : abusive language —**invective** adj

in·veigh \in'vā\ *vb* : protest or complain forcefully

in·vei·gle \in'vāgəl, -'vē-\ *vb* **-gled; -gling** : win over or get by flattery

in·vent \in'vent\ *vb* **1** : think up **2** : create for the 1st time **—in·ven·tion** \-'venchən\ *n* **—in·ven·tive** \-'ventiv\ *adj* **—in·ven·tive·ness** *n* **—in·ven·tor** \-'ventər\ *n*

in·ven·to·ry \'invən,tōrē\ *n, pl* **-ries 1** : list of goods **2** : stock **—inventory** *vb*

in·verse \in'vərs, 'in,vərs\ *adj or n* : opposite **—in·verse·ly** *adv*

in·vert \in'vərt\ *vb* **1** : turn upside down or inside out **2** : reverse **—in·ver·sion** \-'verzhən\ *n*

in·ver·te·brate \in'vərtəbrət, -,brāt\ *adj* : lacking a backbone ~ *n* : invertebrate animal

in·vest \in'vest\ *vb* **1** : give power or authority to **2** : endow with a quality **3** : commit money to someone else's use in hope of profit **—in·vest·ment** \-mənt\ *n* **—in·ves·tor** \-'vestər\ *n*

in·ves·ti·gate \in'vestə,gāt\ *vb* **-gat·ed; -gat·ing** : study closely and systematically **—in·ves·ti·ga·tion** \-,vestə'gāshən\ *n* **—in·ves·ti·ga·tive** \-'vestə,gātiv\ *adj* **—in·ves·ti·ga·tor** \-'vestə,gātər\ *n*

in·ves·ti·ture \in'vestə,chúr, -chər\ *n* : act of establishing in office

in·vet·er·ate \in'vetərət\ *adj* : acting out of habit

in·vid·i·ous \in'vidēəs\ *adj* : harmful or obnoxious **—in·vid·i·ous·ly** *adv*

in·vig·o·rate \in'vigə,rāt\ *vb* **-rat·ed; -rat·ing** : give life and energy to **—in·vig·o·ra·tion** \-,vigə'rāshən\ *n*

in·vin·ci·ble \in'vinsəbəl\ *adj* : incapable of being conquered **—in·vin·ci·bil·i·ty** \in,vinsə'bilətē\ *n* **—in·vin·ci·bly** \in'vinsəblē\ *adv*

in·vi·o·la·ble \in'vīələbəl\ *adj* : safe from violation or desecration **—in·vi·o·la·bil·i·ty** \in,vīələ'bilətē\ *n*

in·vi·o·late \in'vīələt\ *adj* : not violated or profaned

in·vite \in'vīt\ *vb* **-vit·ed; -vit·ing 1** : entice **2** : increase the likelihood of **3** : request the presence or participation of **4** : encourage **—in·vi·ta·tion** \,invə'tāshən\ *n* **—in·vit·ing** \in'vītiŋ\ *adj*

in·vo·ca·tion \,invə'kāshən\ *n* **1** : prayer **2** : incantation

in·voice \'in,vóis\ *n* : itemized bill for goods shipped ~ *vb* **-voiced; -voic·ing** : bill

in·voke \in'vōk\ *vb* **-voked; -vok·ing 1** : call on for help **2** : cite as authority **3** : conjure **4** : carry out

in·volve \in'välv\ *vb* **-volved; -volv·ing 1** : draw in as a participant **2** : relate closely **3** : require as a necessary part **4** : occupy fully **—in·volve·ment** *n*

in·volved \-'välvd\ *adj* : intricate

¹in·ward \'inwərd\ *adj* : inside

²inward, in·wards \-wərdz\ *adv* : toward the inside, center, or inner being

in·ward·ly *adv* **1** : mentally or spiritually **2** : internally **3** : to oneself

io·dide \'īə,dīd\ *n* : compound of iodine

io·dine \'īə,dīn, -əd³n\ *n* **1** : nonmetallic chemical element **2** : solution of iodine used as an antiseptic

io·dize \'īə,dīz\ *vb* **-dized; -diz·ing** : treat with iodine or an iodide

ion \'īən, 'ī,än\ *n* : electrically charged particle **—ion·ic** \ī'änik\ *adj* **—ion·iz·able** \'īə,nīzəbəl\ *adj* **—ion·iza·tion** \,īənə'zāshən\ *n* **—ion·ize** \'īə,nīz\ *vb* **—ion·iz·er** \'īə,nīzər\ *n*

-ion *n suffix* **1** : act or process **2** : state or condition

ion·o·sphere \ī'änə,sfir\ *n* : layer of the upper atmosphere containing ionized gases **—ion·o·spher·ic** \ī,änə'sfirik, -'sfer-\ *adj*

io·ta \ī'ōtə\ *n* : small quantity

IOU \,ī,ō'yü\ *n* : acknowledgment of a debt

iras·ci·ble \ir'asəbəl, ī'ras-\ *adj* : marked by hot temper **—iras·ci·bil·i·ty** \-,asə'bilətē, -,ras-\ *n*

irate \ī'rāt\ *adj* : roused to intense anger **—irate·ly** *adv*

ire \'īr\ *n* : anger

ir·i·des·cence \,irə'des³ns\ *n* : rainbow-like play of colors **—ir·i·des·cent** \-³nt\ *adj*

iris \'īrəs\ *n, pl* **iris·es** *or* **iri·des** \'īrə,dēz, 'ir-\ **1** : colored part around the pupil of the eye **2** : plant with long leaves and large showy flowers

irk \'ərk\ *vb* : annoy **—irk·some** \-səm\ *adj* **—irk·some·ly** *adv*

iron \'īərn\ *n* **1** : heavy metallic chemical element **2** : something made of iron **3** : heated device for pressing clothes **4** : hardness, determination ~

vb : press or smooth out with an iron
—**iron•ware** *n* —**iron•work** *n* —
iron•work•er *n* —**iron•works** *n pl*
iron•clad \-'klad\ *adj* **1** : sheathed in
iron armor **2** : strict or exacting
iron•ing \'īərniŋ\ *n* : clothes to be ironed
iron•wood \-,wùd\ *n* : tree or shrub with
very hard wood or this wood
iro•ny \'īrənē\ *n, pl* **-nies** **1** : use of
words to express the opposite of the
literal meaning **2** : incongruity between the actual and expected result
of events —**iron•ic** \ī'ränik\, **iron•i-
cal** \-ikəl\ *adj* —**iron•i•cal•ly** \-iklē\
adv
ir•ra•di•ate \ir'ādē,āt\ *vb* **-at•ed**; **-at•ing**
: treat with radiation —**ir•ra•di•a•tion**
\-,ādē'āshən\ *n*
ir•ra•tio•nal \ir'ashənəl\ *adj* **1**
: incapable of reasoning **2** : not based
on reason —**ir•ra•tio•nal•i•ty** \ir-
,ashə'nalətē\ *n* —**ir•ra•tio•nal•ly** *adv*
ir•rec•on•cil•able \ir,ekən'sīləbəl\ *adj*
: impossible to reconcile —**ir•rec•on-
cil•abil•i•ty** \-,sīlə'bilətē\ *n*
ir•re•cov•er•able \,iri'kəvərəbəl\ *adj*
: not capable of being recovered —
ir•re•cov•er•ably \-blē\ *adv*
ir•re•deem•able \,iri'dēməbəl\ *adj* : not
redeemable
ir•re•duc•ible \,iri'düsəbəl, -'dyü-\ *adj*
: not reducible —**ir•re•duc•ibly** \-blē\
adv
ir•re•fut•able \,iri'fyütəbəl, ir'refyət-\
adj : impossible to refute
ir•reg•u•lar \ir'egyələr\ *adj* : not regular
or normal —**irregular** *n* —**irreg•u-
lar•i•ty** \ir,egyə'larətē\ *n* —**ir•reg•u-
lar•ly** *adv*
ir•rel•e•vant \ir'eləvənt\ *adj* : not relevant —**ir•rel•e•vance** \-vəns\ *n*
ir•re•li•gious \,iri'lijəs\ *adj* : not following religious practices
ir•rep•a•ra•ble \ir'epərəbəl\ *adj* : impossible to make good, undo, or remedy
ir•re•place•able \,iri'plāsəbəl\ *adj* : not
replaceable
ir•re•press•ible \-'presəbəl\ *adj* : impossible to repress or control
ir•re•proach•able \,iri'prōchəbəl\ *adj*
: blameless
ir•re•sist•ible \-'zistəbəl\ *adj* : impossible to successfully resist —**ir•re-
sist•ibly** \-blē\ *adv*
ir•res•o•lute \ir'ezəlüt\ *adj* : uncertain
—**ir•res•o•lute•ly** *adv* —**ir•res•o-
lu•tion** \-,ezə'lüshən\ *n*

ir•re•spec•tive of \,iri'spektiv-\ *prep*
: without regard to
ir•re•spon•si•ble \,iri'spänsəbəl\ *adj*
: not responsible —**ir•re•spon•si•bil-
i•ty** \-,spänsə'bilətē\ *n* —**ir•re•spon-
si•bly** *adv*
ir•re•triev•able \,iri'trēvəbəl\ *adj* : not
retrievable
ir•rev•er•ence \ir'evərəns\ *n* **1** : lack of
reverence **2** : irreverent act or utterance —**ir•rev•er•ent** \-rənt\ *adj*
ir•re•vers•ible \,iri'vərsəbəl\ *adj* : incapable of being reversed
ir•re•vo•ca•ble \ir'evəkəbəl\ *adj* : incapable of being revoked —**ir•rev•o-
ca•bly** \-blē\ *adv*
ir•ri•gate \'irə,gāt\ *vb* **-gat•ed**; **-gat•ing**
: supply with water by artificial
means —**ir•ri•ga•tion** \,irə'gāshən\ *n*
ir•ri•tate \'irə,tāt\ *vb* **-tat•ed**; **-tat•ing**
: excite to anger **2** : make sore or inflamed —**ir•ri•ta•bil•i•ty** \,irətə-
'bilətē\ *n* —**ir•ri•ta•ble** \'irətəbəl\ *adj*
—**ir•ri•ta•bly** \'irətəblē\ *adv* —**ir•ri-
tant** \'irətənt\ *adj or n* —**ir•ri-
tat•ing•ly** *adv* —**ir•ri•ta•tion** \,irə-
'tāshən\ *n*
is *pres 3d sing of* BE
-ish \ish\ *adj suffix* **1** : characteristic of
2 : somewhat
Is•lam \is'läm, iz-, -'lam\ *n* : religious
faith of Muslims —**Is•lam•ic** \-ik\ *adj*
is•land \'īlənd\ *n* : body of land surrounded by water —**is•land•er**
\'īləndər\ *n*
isle \'īl\ *n* : small island
is•let \'īlət\ *n* : small island
-ism \,izəm\ *n suffix* **1** : act or practice
2 : characteristic manner **3** : condition
4 : doctrine
iso•late \'īsə,lāt\ *vb* **-lat•ed**; **-lat•ing**
: place or keep by itself —**iso•la•tion**
\,īsə'lāshən\ *n*
iso•met•rics \,īsə'metriks\ *n sing or pl*
: exercise against unmoving resistance —**isometric** *adj*
isos•ce•les \ī'säsə,lēz\ *adj* : having 2
equal sides
iso•tope \'īsə,tōp\ *n* : species of atom of
a chemical element —**iso•to•pic**
\,īsə'täpik, -'tō-\ *adj*
is•sue \'ishü\ *vb* **-sued**; **-su•ing** **1** : go,
come, or flow out **2** : descend from a
specified ancestor **3** : emanate or result **4** : put forth or distribute officially ~ *n* **1** : action of issuing **2**

: offspring **3** : result **4** : point of controversy **5** : act of giving out or printing **6** : quantity given out or printed —**is·su·ance** \'ishəwəns\ *n* —**is·su·er** *n*

-ist \ist\ *n suffix* **1** : one that does **2** : one that plays **3** : one that specializes in **4** : follower of a doctrine

isth·mus \'isməs\ *n* : narrow strip of land connecting 2 larger portions

it \'it\ *pron* **1** : that one —used of a lifeless thing or an abstract entity **2** — used as an anticipatory subject or object ~ *n* : player who tries to catch others (as in a game of tag)

ital·ic \ə'talik, i-, ī-\ *n* : style of type with slanting letters —**italic** *adj* —**ital·i·ci·za·tion** \ə,taləsə'zāshən, i-, ī-\ *n* —**ital·i·cize** \ə'talə,sīz, i-, ī-\ *vb*

itch \'ich\ *n* **1** : uneasy irritating skin sensation **2** : skin disorder **3** : persistent desire —**itch** *vb* —**itchy** *adj*

item \'ītəm\ *n* **1** : particular in a list, account, or series **2** : piece of news —**item·iza·tion** \,ītəmə'zāshən\ *n* —**item·ize** \'ītə,mīz\ *vb*

itin·er·ant \ī'tinərənt, ə-\ *adj* : traveling from place to place

itin·er·ary \ī'tinə,rerē, ə-\ *n, pl* **-ar·ies** : route or outline of a journey

its \'its\ *adj* : relating to it

it·self \it'self\ *pron* : it—used reflexively or for emphasis

-ity \ətē\ *n suffix* : quality, state, or degree

-ive \iv\ *adj suffix* : that performs or tends toward an action

ivo·ry \'īvərē\ *n, pl* **-ries** **1** : hard creamy-white material of elephants' tusks **2** : pale yellow color

ivy \'īvē\ *n, pl* **ivies** : trailing woody vine with evergreen leaves

-ize \,īz\ *vb suffix* **1** : cause to be, become, or resemble **2** : subject to an action **3** : treat or combine with **4** : engage in an activity

J

j \'jā\ *n, pl* **j's** *or* **js** \'jāz\ : 10th letter of the alphabet

jab \'jab\ *vb* **-bb-** : thrust quickly or abruptly ~ *n* : short straight punch

jab·ber \'jabər\ *vb* : talk rapidly or unintelligibly —**jabber** *n*

jack \'jak\ *n* **1** : mechanical device to raise a heavy body **2** : small flag **3** : small 6-pointed metal object used in a game (**jacks**) **4** : electrical socket ~ *vb* **1** : raise with a jack **2** : increase

jack·al \'jakəl, -,ȯl\ *n* : wild dog

jack·ass *n* **1** : male ass **2** : stupid person

jack·et \'jakət\ *n* : garment for the upper body

jack·ham·mer \'jak,hamər\ *n* : pneumatic tool for drilling

jack·knife \'jak,nīf\ *n* : pocketknife ~ *vb* : fold like a jackknife

jack-o'-lan·tern \'jakə,lantərn\ *n* : lantern made of a carved pumpkin

jack·pot \'jak,pät\ *n* : sum of money won

jack·rab·bit \-,rabət\ *n* : large hare of western No. America

jade \'jād\ *n* : usu. green gemstone

jad·ed \'jādəd\ *adj* : dulled or bored by having too much

jag·ged \'jagəd\ *adj* : sharply notched

jag·uar \'jag,wär, 'jagyə-\ *n* : black-spotted tropical American cat

jai alai \'hī,līʌ *n* : game with a ball propelled by a basket on the hand

jail \'jāl\ *n* : prison —**jail** *vb* —**jail·break** *n* —**jail·er, jail·or** *n*

ja·la·pe·ño \,hälə'pān,yō, -,pēnō\ *n* : Mexican hot pepper

ja·lopy \jə'läpē\ *n, pl* **-lop·ies** : dilapidated vehicle

jal·ou·sie \'jaləsē\ *n* : door or window with louvers

jam \'jam\ *vb* **-mm-** **1** : press into a tight position **2** : cause to become wedged and unworkable ~ *n* **1** : crowded mass that blocks or impedes **2** : difficult situation **3** : thick sweet food made of cooked fruit

jamb \'jam\ *n* : upright framing piece of a door

jam·bo·ree \,jambə'rē\ *n* : large festive gathering

jan·gle \'jaŋgəl\ *vb* -gled; -gling : make a harsh ringing sound —**jangle** *n*

jan·i·tor \'janətər\ *n* : person who has the care of a building —**jan·i·to·ri·al** \,janə'tōrēəl\ *adj*

Jan·u·ary \'janyə,werē\ *n* : 1st month of the year having 31 days

¹jar \'jär\ *vb* -rr- 1 : have a harsh or disagreeable effect 2 : vibrate or shake ~ *n* 1 : jolt 2 : painful effect

²jar *n* : wide-mouthed container

jar·gon \'järgən, -,gän\ *n* : special vocabulary of a group

jas·mine \'jazmən\ *n* : climbing shrub with fragrant flowers

jas·per \'jaspər\ *n* : red, yellow, or brown opaque quartz

jaun·dice \'jóndəs\ *n* : yellowish discoloration of skin, tissues, and body fluids

jaun·diced \-dəst\ *adj* : exhibiting envy or hostility

jaunt \'jónt\ *n* : short pleasure trip

jaun·ty \'jóntē\ *adj* -ti·er; -est : lively in manner or appearance —**jaun·ti·ly** \'jónt°lē\ *adv* —**jaun·ti·ness** *n*

jave·lin \'javələn\ *n* : light spear

jaw \'jó\ *n* 1 : either of the bony or cartilaginous structures that support the mouth 2 : one of 2 movable parts for holding or crushing ~ *vb* : talk indignantly or at length —**jaw·bone** \-,bōn\ *n* —**jawed** \'jód\ *adj*

jay \'jā\ *n* : noisy brightly colored bird

jay·bird *n* : jay

jay·walk *vb* : cross a street carelessly —**jay·walk·er** *n*

jazz \'jaz\ *vb* : enliven ~ *n* 1 : kind of American music involving improvisation 2 : empty talk —**jazzy** *adj*

jeal·ous \'jeləs\ *adj* : suspicious of a rival or of one believed to enjoy an advantage —**jeal·ous·ly** *adv* —**jeal·ou·sy** \-əsē\ *n*

jeans \'jēnz\ *n pl* : pants made of durable twilled cotton cloth

jeep \'jēp\ *n* : 4-wheel army vehicle

jeer \'jir\ *vb* 1 : speak or cry out in derision 2 : ridicule ~ *n* : taunt

Je·ho·vah \ji'hōvə\ *n* : God

je·june \ji'jün\ *adj* : dull or childish

jell \'jel\ *vb* 1 : come to the consistency of jelly 2 : take shape

jel·ly \'jelē\ *n, pl* -lies : a substance (as food) with a soft somewhat elastic consistency —**jelly** *vb*

jel·ly·fish *n* : sea animal with a saucer-shaped jellylike body

jen·ny \'jenē\ *n, pl* -nies : female bird or donkey

jeop·ar·dy \'jepərdē\ *n* : exposure to death, loss, or injury —**jeop·ar·dize** \-ər,dīz\ *vb*

jerk \'jərk\ *vb* 1 : give a sharp quick push, pull, or twist 2 : move in short abrupt motions ~ *n* 1 : short quick pull or twist 2 : stupid or foolish person —**jerk·i·ly** *adv* —**jerky** *adj*

jer·kin \'jərkən\ *n* : close-fitting sleeveless jacket

jer·ry–built \'jerē,bilt\ *adj* : built cheaply and flimsily

jer·sey \'jərzē\ *n, pl* -seys 1 : plain knit fabric 2 : knitted shirt

jest \'jest\ *n* : witty remark —**jest** *vb*

jest·er \'jestər\ *n* : one employed to entertain a court

¹jet \'jet\ *n* : velvet-black coal used for jewelry

²jet *vb* -tt- 1 : spout or emit in a stream 2 : travel by jet ~ *n* 1 : forceful rush of fluid through a narrow opening 2 : jet-propelled airplane

jet–propelled *adj* : driven by an engine (**jet engine**) that produces propulsion (**jet propulsion**) by the rearward discharge of a jet of fluid

jet·sam \'jetsəm\ *n* : jettisoned goods

jet·ti·son \'jetəsən\ *vb* 1 : throw (goods) overboard 2 : discard —**jettison** *n*

jet·ty \'jetē\ *n, pl* -ties : pier or wharf

Jew \'jü\ *n* : one whose religion is Judaism —**Jew·ish** *adj*

jew·el \'jüəl\ *n* 1 : ornament of precious metal 2 : gem ~ *vb* -eled *or* -elled; -el·ing *or* -el·ling : adorn with jewels —**jew·el·er, jew·el·ler** \-ər\ *n* —**jew·el·ry** \-rē\ *n*

jib \'jib\ *n* : triangular sail

jibe \'jīb\ *vb* jibed; jib·ing : be in agreement

jif·fy \'jifē\ *n, pl* -fies : short time

jig \'jig\ *n* 1 : lively dance ~ *vb* -gg- : dance a jig

jig·ger \'jigər\ *n* : measure used in mixing drinks

jig·gle \'jigəl\ *vb* -gled; -gling : move with quick little jerks —**jiggle** *n*

jig·saw *n* : machine saw with a narrow blade that moves up and down

jilt \'jilt\ *vb* : drop (a lover) unfeelingly

jim·my \'jimē\ *n, pl* -mies : small crowbar ~ *vb* -mied; -my·ing : pry open

jim·son·weed \'jimsən,wēd\ *n* : coarse poisonous weed

jin·gle \'jiŋgəl\ *vb* -gled; -gling : make

a light tinkling sound ~ *n* **1** : light tinkling sound **2** : short verse or song

jin·go·ism \'jiŋgō,izəm\ *n* : extreme chauvinism or nationalism —**jin·go·ist** \-ist\ *n* —**jin·go·is·tic** \,jiŋgō'istik\ *adj*

jinx \'jiŋks\ *n* : one that brings bad luck —**jinx** *vb*

jit·ney \'jitnē\ *n, pl* -**neys** : small bus

jit·ters \'jitərz\ *n pl* : extreme nervousness —**jit·tery** \-ərē\ *adj*

job \'jäb\ *n* **1** : something that has to be done **2** : regular employment —**job·hold·er** *n* —**job·less** *adj*

job·ber \'jäbər\ *n* : middleman

jock·ey \'jäkē\ *n, pl* -**eys** : one who rides a horse in a race ~ *vb* -**eyed**; -**ey·ing** : manipulate or maneuver adroitly

jo·cose \jō'kōs\ *adj* : jocular

joc·u·lar \'jäkyələr\ *adj* : marked by jesting —**joc·u·lar·i·ty** \jäkyə'larətē\ *n* —**joc·u·lar·ly** *adv*

jo·cund \'jäkənd\ *adj* : full of mirth or gaiety

jodh·purs \'jädpərz\ *n pl* : riding breeches

¹jog \'jäg\ *vb* -**gg-** **1** : give a slight shake or push to **2** : run or ride at a slow pace ~ *n* **1** : slight shake **2** : slow pace —**jog·ger** *n*

²jog *n* : brief abrupt change in direction or line

join \'jóin\ *vb* **1** : come or bring together **2** : become a member of —**join·er** *n*

joint \'jóint\ *n* **1** : point of contact between bones **2** : place where 2 parts connect **3** : often disreputable place ~ *adj* : common to 2 or more —**joint·ed** *adj* —**joint·ly** *adv*

joist \'jóist\ *n* : beam supporting a floor or ceiling

joke \'jōk\ *n* : something said or done to provoke laughter ~ *vb* **joked**; **jok·ing** : make jokes —**jok·er** *n* —**jok·ing·ly** \'jōkiŋlē\ *adv*

jol·li·ty \'jälətē\ *n, pl* -**ties** : gaiety or merriment

jol·ly \'jälē\ *adj* -**li·er**; -**est** : full of high spirits

jolt \'jōlt\ *vb* **1** : move with a sudden jerky motion **2** : give a jolt to ~ *n* **1** : abrupt jerky blow or movement **2** : sudden shock —**jolt·er** *n*

jon·quil \'jänkwəl\ *n* : narcissus with white or yellow flowers

josh \'jäsh\ *vb* : tease or joke

jos·tle \'jäsəl\ *vb* -**tled**; -**tling** : push or shove

jot \'jät\ *n* : least bit ~ *vb* -**tt-** : write briefly and hurriedly

jounce \'jaùns\ *vb* **jounced**; **jounc·ing** : jolt —**jounce** *n*

jour·nal \'jərnᵊl\ *n* **1** : brief account of daily events **2** : periodical (as a newspaper)

jour·nal·ism \'jərnᵊl,izəm\ *n* : business of reporting or printing news —**jour·nal·ist** \-ist\ *n* —**jour·nal·is·tic** \,jərnᵊl'istik\ *adj*

jour·ney \'jərnē\ *n, pl* -**neys** : a going from one place to another ~ *vb* -**neyed**; -**ney·ing** : make a journey

jour·ney·man \-mən\ *n* : worker who has learned a trade and works for another person

joust \'jaùst\ *n* : combat on horseback between 2 knights with lances —**joust** *vb*

jo·vial \'jōvēəl\ *adj* : marked by good humor —**jo·vi·al·i·ty** \,jōvē'alətē\ —**jo·vi·al·ly** \'jōvēəlē\ *adv*

¹jowl \'jaùl\ *n* : loose flesh about the lower jaw or throat

²jowl *n* **1** : lower jaw **2** : cheek

joy \'jói\ *n* **1** : feeling of happiness **2** : source of happiness —**joy** *vb* —**joy·ful** *adj* —**joy·ful·ly** *adv* —**joy·less** *adj* —**joy·ous** \'jóiəs\ *adj* —**joy·ous·ly** *adv* —**joy·ous·ness** *n*

joy·ride *n* : reckless ride for pleasure —**joy·rid·er** *n* —**joy·rid·ing** *n*

ju·bi·lant \'jübələnt\ *adj* : expressing great joy —**ju·bi·lant·ly** *adv* —**ju·bi·la·tion** \jübə'lāshən\ *n*

ju·bi·lee \'jübə,lē\ *n* **1** : 50th anniversary **2** : season or occasion of celebration

Ju·da·ism \'jüdə,izəm\ *n* : religion developed among the ancient Hebrews —**Ju·da·ic** \jù'dāik\ *adj*

judge \'jəj\ *vb* **judged**; **judg·ing** **1** : form an opinion **2** : decide as a judge ~ *n* **1** : public official authorized to decide questions brought before a court **2** : one who gives an authoritative opinion —**judge·ship** *n*

judg·ment, judge·ment \'jəjmənt\ *n* **1** : decision or opinion given after judging **2** : capacity for judging —**judg·men·tal** \,jəj'mentəl\ *adj* —**judg·men·tal·ly** *adv*

ju·di·ca·ture \'jüdikə,chùr\ *n* : administration of justice

ju·di·cial \jù'dishəl\ *adj* : relating to judicature or the judiciary —**ju·di·cial·ly** *adv*

ju·di·cia·ry \jù'dishē,erē, -'dishərē\

: system of courts of law or the judges of them —**judiciary** adj

ju·di·cious \ju'dishəs\ adj : having or characterized by sound judgment — **ju·di·cious·ly** adv

ju·do \'judo\ n : form of wrestling — **judo·ist** n

jug \'jəg\ n : large deep container with a narrow mouth and a handle

jug·ger·naut \'jəgər,not\ n : massive inexorable force or object

jug·gle \'jəgəl\ vb -**gled; -gling** 1 : keep several objects in motion in the air at the same time 2 : manipulate for an often tricky purpose —**jug·gler** \'jəglər\ n

jug·u·lar \'jəgyələr\ adj : in or on the throat or neck

juice \'jüs\ n 1 : extractable fluid contents of cells or tissues 2 : electricity —**juic·er** n —**juic·i·ly** \'jüsəlē\ adv —**juic·i·ness** \-sēnəs\ n —**juicy** \'jüsē\ adj

ju·jube \'jü,jüb, 'jüjú,bē\ n : gummy candy

juke·box \'jük,bäks\ n : coin-operated machine for playing music recordings

ju·lep \'jüləp\ n : mint-flavored bourbon drink

Ju·ly \jú'lī\ n : 7th month of the year having 31 days

jum·ble \'jəmbəl\ vb -**bled; -bling** : mix in a confused mass —**jumble** n

jum·bo \'jəmbō\ n, pl -**bos** : very large version —**jumbo** adj

jump \'jəmp\ vb 1 : rise into or through the air esp. by muscular effort 2 : pass over 3 : give a start 4 : rise or increase sharply ~ n 1 : a jumping 2 : sharp sudden increase 3 : initial advantage

¹jump·er \'jəmpər\ n : one that jumps

²jumper n : sleeveless one-piece dress

jumpy \'jəmpē\ adj **jump·i·er; -est** : nervous or jittery

junc·tion \'jəŋkshən\ n 1 : a joining 2 : place or point of meeting

junc·ture \'jəŋkchər\ n 1 : joint or connection 2 : critical time or state of affairs

June \'jün\ n : 6th month of the year having 30 days

jun·gle \'jəŋgəl\ n : thick tangled mass of tropical vegetation

ju·nior \'jünyər\ n 1 : person who is younger or of lower rank than another 2 : student in the next-to-last year ~ adj : younger or lower in rank

ju·ni·per \'jünəpər\ n : evergreen shrub or tree

¹junk \'jəŋk\ n 1 : discarded articles 2 : shoddy product ~ vb : discard or scrap —**junky** adj

²junk n : flat-bottomed ship of Chinese waters

jun·ket \'jəŋkət\ n : trip made by an official at public expense

jun·ta \'húntə, 'jəntə, 'həntə\ n : group of persons controlling a government

ju·ris·dic·tion \,jùrəs'dikshən\ n 1 : right or authority to interpret and apply the law 2 : limits within which authority may be exercised —**ju·ris·dic·tion·al** \-shənəl\ adj

ju·ris·pru·dence \-'prüd²ns\ n 1 : system of laws 2 : science or philosophy of law

ju·rist \'júrist\ n : judge

ju·ror \'júrər\ n : member of a jury

ju·ry \'júrē\ n, pl -**ries** : body of persons sworn to give a verdict on a matter

just \'jəst\ adj 1 : reasonable 2 : correct or proper 3 : morally or legally right 4 : deserved ~ adv 1 : exactly 2 : very recently 3 : barely 4 : only 5 : quite 6 : possibly —**just·ly** adv —**just·ness** n

jus·tice \'jəstəs\ n 1 : administration of what is just 2 : judge 3 : administration of law 4 : fairness

jus·ti·fy \'jəstə,fī\ vb -**fied; -fy·ing** : prove to be just, right, or reasonable —**jus·ti·fi·able** adj —**jus·ti·fi·ca·tion** \,jəstəfə'kāshən\ n

jut \'jət\ vb -**tt-** : stick out

jute \'jüt\ n : strong glossy fiber from a tropical plant

ju·ve·nile \'jüvə,nīl, -vən²l\ adj : relating to children or young people ~ n : young person

jux·ta·pose \'jəkstə,pōz\ vb -**posed; -pos·ing** : place side by side —**jux·ta·po·si·tion** \,jəkstəpə'zishən\ n

K

k \'kā\ *n, pl* **k's** *or* **ks** \'kāz\ : 11th letter of the alphabet

kai·ser \'kīzər\ *n* : German ruler

kale \'kāl\ *n* : curly cabbage

ka·lei·do·scope \kə'līdə,skōp\ *n* : device containing loose bits of colored material reflecting in many patterns —**ka·lei·do·scop·ic** \-,līdə'skäpik\ *adj* —**ka·lei·do·scop·i·cal·ly** \-iklē\ *adv*

kan·ga·roo \,kaŋgə'rü\ *n, pl* **-roos** : large leaping Australian mammal

ka·o·lin \'kāələn\ *n* : fine white clay

kar·at \'karət\ *n* : unit of gold content

ka·ra·te \kə'rätē\ *n* : art of self-defense by crippling kicks and punches

ka·ty·did \'kātē,did\ *n* : large American grasshopper

kay·ak \'kī,ak\ *n* : Eskimo canoe

ka·zoo \kə'zü\ *n, pl* **-zoos** : toy musical instrument

keel \'kēl\ *n* : central lengthwise strip on the bottom of a ship —**keeled** \'kēld\ *adj*

keen \'kēn\ *adj* 1 : sharp 2 : severe 3 : enthusiastic 4 : mentally alert —**keen·ly** *adv* —**keen·ness** *n*

keep \'kēp\ *vb* **kept** \'kept\; **keep·ing** 1 : perform 2 : guard 3 : maintain 4 : retain in one's possession 5 : detain 6 : continue in good condition 7 : refrain ~ *n* 1 : fortress 2 : means by which one is kept —**keep·er** *n*

keep·ing \'kēpiŋ\ *n* : conformity

keep·sake \'kēp,sāk\ *n* : souvenir

keg \'keg\ *n* : small cask or barrel

kelp \'kelp\ *n* : coarse brown seaweed

ken \'ken\ *n* : range of sight or understanding

ken·nel \'kenᵊl\ *n* : dog shelter —**kennel** *vb*

ker·chief \'kərchəf, -,chēf\ *n* : square of cloth worn as a head covering

ker·nel \'kərnᵊl\ *n* 1 : inner softer part of a seed or nut 2 : whole seed of a cereal 3 : central part

ker·o·sene, ker·o·sine \'kerə,sēn, ,kerə'-\ *n* : thin flammable oil from petroleum

ketch·up \'kechəp, 'ka-\ *n* : spicy tomato sauce

ket·tle \'ketᵊl\ *n* : vessel for boiling liquids

ket·tle·drum \-,drum\ *n* : brass or copper kettle-shaped drum

¹key \'kē\ *n* 1 : usu. metal piece to open a lock 2 : explanation 3 : lever pressed by a finger in playing an instrument or operating a machine 4 : leading individual or principle 5 : system of musical tones or pitch ~ *vb* : attune ~ *adj* : basic —**key·hole** *n* —**key up** *vb* : make nervous

²key *n* : low island or reef

key·board *n* : arrangement of keys

key·note \-,nōt\ *n* 1 : 1st note of a scale 2 : central fact, idea, or mood ~ *vb* 1 : set the keynote of 2 : deliver the major speech

key·stone *n* : wedge-shaped piece at the crown of an arch

kha·ki \'kakē, 'käk-\ *n* : light yellowish brown color

khan \'kän, 'kan\ *n* : Mongol leader

kib·butz \kib'üts, -'üts\ *n, pl* **-but·zim** \-,üt'sēm, -,üt-\ : Israeli communal farm or settlement

kib·itz·er \'kibətsər, kə'bit-\ *n* : one who offers unwanted advice —**kib·itz** \'kibəts\ *vb*

kick \'kik\ *vb* 1 : strike out or hit with the foot 2 : object strongly 3 : recoil ~ *n* 1 : thrust with the foot 2 : recoil of a gun 3 : stimulating effect —**kick·er** *n*

kid \'kid\ *n* 1 : young goat 2 : child ~ *vb* **-dd-** 1 : deceive as a joke 2 : tease —**kid·der** *n* —**kid·ding·ly** *adv*

kid·nap \'kid,nap\ *vb* **-napped** *or* **-naped** \-,napt\; **-nap·ping** *or* **-nap·ing** : carry a person away by illegal force —**kid·nap·per, kid·nap·er** *n*

kid·ney \'kidnē\ *n, pl* **-neys** : either of a pair of organs that excrete urine

kill \'kil\ *vb* 1 : deprive of life 2 : finish 3 : use up (time) ~ *n* : act of killing —**kill·er** *n*

kiln \'kil, 'kiln\ *n* : heated enclosure for burning, firing, or drying —**kiln** *vb*

ki·lo \'kēlō\ *n, pl* **-los** : kilogram

ki·lo·cy·cle \'kilə,sīkəl\ n : kilohertz

ki·lo·gram \'kēlə,gram, 'kilə-\ n : basic metric mass unit nearly equal to the mass of 1000 cubic centimeters of water at its maximum density

ki·lo·hertz \'kilə,hərts, 'kēlə-, -,herts\ n : 1000 hertz

ki·lo·me·ter \kil'ämətər, 'kilə,mēt-\ n : 1000 meters

ki·lo·volt \'kilə,vōlt\ n : 1000 volts

kilo·watt \'kilə,wät\ n : 1000 watts

kilt \'kilt\ n : knee-length pleated skirt

kil·ter \'kiltər\ n : proper condition

ki·mo·no \kə'mōnō\ n, pl -nos : loose robe

kin \'kin\ n 1 : one's relatives 2 : kinsman

kind \'kīnd\ n 1 : essential quality 2 : group with common traits 3 : variety ~ adj 1 : of a sympathetic nature 2 : arising from sympathy — **kind·heart·ed** adj —**kind·ness** n

kin·der·gar·ten \'kindər,gärtᵊn\ n : class for young children —**kin·der·gart·ner** \-,gärtnər\ n

kin·dle \'kind°l\ vb -dled; -dling 1 : set on fire or start burning 2 : stir up

kin·dling \'kindlinȷ, 'kinlən\ n : material for starting a fire

kind·ly \'kīndlē\ adj -li·er; -est : of a sympathetic nature ~ adv 1 : sympathetically 2 : courteously —**kind·li·ness** n

kin·dred \'kindrəd\ n 1 : related individuals 2 : kin ~ adj : of a like nature

kin·folk \'kin,fōk\, **kinfolks** n pl : kin

king \'kinȷ\ n : male sovereign —**king·dom** \-dəm\ n —**king·less** adj —**king·ly** adj —**king·ship** n

king·fish·er \-,fishər\ n : bright-colored crested bird

kink \'kinȷk\ n 1 : short tight twist or curl 2 : cramp —**kinky** adj

kin·ship n : relationship

kins·man \'kinzmən\ n : male relative

kins·wom·an \-,wùmən\ n : female relative

kip·per \'kipər\ n : dried or smoked fish —**kipper** vb

kiss \'kis\ vb : touch with the lips as a mark of affection —**kiss** n

kit \'kit\ n : set of articles (as tools or parts)

kitch·en \'kichən\ n : room with cooking facilities

kite \'kīt\ n 1 : small hawk 2 : covered framework flown at the end of a string

kith \'kith\ n : familiar friends

kit·ten \'kitᵊn\ n : young cat —**kit·ten·ish** adj

¹kit·ty \'kitē\ n, pl -ties : kitten

²kitty n, pl -ties : fund or pool (as in a card game)

kit·ty-cor·ner, kit·ty-cor·nered var of CATERCORNER

ki·wi \'kē,wē\ n : small flightless New Zealand bird

klep·to·ma·nia \,kleptə'mānēə\ n : neurotic impulse to steal —**klep·to·ma·ni·ac** \-nē,ak\ n

knack \'nak\ n 1 : clever way of doing something 2 : natural aptitude

knap·sack \'nap,sak\ n : bag for carrying supplies on one's back

knave \'nāv\ n : rogue —**knav·ery** \'nāvərē\ n —**knav·ish** \'nāvish\ adj

knead \'nēd\ vb 1 : work and press with the hands 2 : massage —**knead·er** n

knee \'nē\ n : joint in the middle part of the leg —**kneed** \'nēd\ adj

knee·cap \'nē,kap\ n : bone forming the front of the knee

kneel \'nēl\ vb **knelt** \'nelt\ or **kneeled**; **kneel·ing** : rest on one's knees

knell \'nel\ n : stroke of a bell

knew past of KNOW

knick·ers \'nikərz\ n pl : pants gathered at the knee

knick·knack \'nik,nak\ n : small decorative object

knife \'nīf\ n, pl **knives** \'nīvz\ : sharp blade with a handle ~ vb **knifed**; **knif·ing** : stab or cut with a knife

knight \'nīt\ n 1 : mounted warrior of feudal times 2 : man honored by a sovereign ~ vb : make a knight of —**knight·hood** n —**knight·ly** adv

knit \'nit\ vb **knit** or **knit·ted**; **knit·ting** 1 : link firmly or closely 2 : form a fabric by interlacing yarn or thread ~ n : knitted garment —**knit·ter** n

knob \'näb\ n : rounded protuberance or handle —**knobbed** \'näbd\ adj —**knob·by** \'näbē\ adj

knock \'näk\ vb 1 : strike with a sharp blow 2 : collide 3 : find fault with ~ n : sharp blow —**knock out** vb : make unconscious

knock·er n : device hinged to a door to knock with

knoll \'nōl\ n : small round hill

knot \'nät\ n 1 : interlacing (as of string) that forms a lump 2 : base of a woody branch in the stem 3 : group 4 : one nautical mile per hour ~ vb **-tt-** : tie in or with a knot —**knot·ty** adj

know \'nō\ vb **knew** \'nü, 'nyü\; **known** \'nōn\; **know·ing 1** : perceive directly or understand **2** : be familiar with —**know·able** adj —**know·er** n

know·ing \'nōiŋ\ adj : shrewdly and keenly alert —**know·ing·ly** adv

knowl·edge \'nälij\ n **1** : understanding gained by experience **2** : range of information —**knowl·edge·able** adj

knuck·le \'nəkəl\ n : rounded knob at a finger joint

ko·ala \kō'älə\ n : gray furry Australian animal

kohl·ra·bi \kōl'rabē, -'räb-\ n, pl **-bies** : cabbage that forms no head

Ko·ran \kə'ran, -'rän\ n : book of Islam containing revelations made to Muhammad by Allah

ko·sher \'kōshər\ adj : ritually fit for use according to Jewish law

kow·tow \kaü'taü, 'kaü,taü\ vb : show excessive deference

kryp·ton \'krip,tän\ n : gaseous chemical element used in lamps

ku·dos \'kyü,däs, 'kü-, -,dōz\ n : fame and renown

kum·quat \'kəm,kwät\ n : small citrus fruit

L

l \'el\ n, pl **l's** or **ls** \'elz\ : 12th letter of the alphabet

lab \'lab\ n : laboratory

la·bel \'lābəl\ n **1** : identification slip **2** : identifying word or phrase ~ vb **-beled** or **-belled**; **-bel·ing** or **-bel·ling** : put a label on

la·bi·al \'lābēəl\ adj : of or relating to the lips

la·bor \'lābər\ n **1** : physical or mental effort **2** : physical efforts of childbirth **3** : task **4** : people who work manually ~ vb : work esp. with great effort —**la·bor·er** n

lab·o·ra·to·ry \'labrə,tōrē\ n, pl **-ries** : place for experimental testing

Labor Day n : 1st Monday in September observed as a legal holiday in recognition of working people

la·bo·ri·ous \lə'bōrēəs\ adj : requiring great effort —**la·bo·ri·ous·ly** adv

lab·y·rinth \'labə,rinth\ n : maze —**lab·y·rin·thine** \,labə'rinthən\ adj

lace \'lās\ n **1** : cord or string for tying **2** : fine net usu. figured fabric ~ vb **laced**; **lac·ing 1** : tie **2** : adorn with lace —**lacy** \'lāsē\ adj

lac·er·ate \'lasə,rāt\ vb **-at·ed**; **-at·ing** : tear roughly —**lac·er·a·tion** \,lasə'rāshən\ n

lach·ry·mose \'lakrə,mōs\ adj : tearful

lack \'lak\ vb : be missing or deficient in ~ n : deficiency

lack·a·dai·si·cal \,lakə'dāzikəl\ adj : lacking spirit —**lack·a·dai·si·cal·ly** \-klē\ adv

lack·ey \'lakē\ n, pl **-eys 1** : footman or servant **2** : toady

lack·lus·ter \'lak,ləstər\ adj : dull

la·con·ic \lə'känik\ adj : sparing of words —**la·con·i·cal·ly** \-iklē\ adv

lac·quer \'lakər\ n : glossy surface coating —**lacquer** vb

la·crosse \lə'krós\ n : ball game played with long-handled rackets

lac·tate \'lak,tāt\ vb **-tat·ed**; **-tat·ing** : secrete milk —**lac·ta·tion** \lak'tāshən\ n

lac·tic \'laktik\ adj : relating to milk

la·cu·na \lə'künə, -'kyü-\ n, pl **-nae** \-,nē\ or **-nas** : blank space or missing part

lad \'lad\ n : boy

lad·der \'ladər\ n : device with steps or rungs for climbing

lad·en \'lād³n\ adj : loaded

la·dle \'lād³l\ n : spoon with a deep bowl —**ladle** vb

la·dy \'lādē\ n, pl **-dies 1** : woman of rank or authority **2** : woman

la·dy·bird \'lādē,bərd\ n : ladybug

la·dy·bug \-,bəg\ n : brightly colored beetle

lag \'lag\ vb **-gg-** : fail to keep up ~ n **1** : a falling behind **2** : interval

la·ger \'lägər\ n : beer

lag·gard \'lagərd\ adj : slow ~ n : one that lags —**lag·gard·ly** adv or adj —**lag·gard·ness** n la•gniappe \'lan,yap\ n : bonus

la•goon \lə'gün\ n : shallow sound, channel, or pond near or connecting with a larger body of water

laid past of LAY

lain past part of LIE

lair \'lar\ n : den

lais•sez-faire \,les,ā'far\ n : doctrine opposing government interference in business

la•ity \'lāətē\ n : people of a religious faith who are not clergy members

lake \'lāk\ n : inland body of water

la•ma \'lämə\ n : Buddhist monk

lamb \'lam\ n : young sheep or its flesh used as food

lam•baste \lam'bāst, -'bast\ vb 1 : beat 2 : censure

lam•bent \'lambənt\ adj : light or bright —lam•ben•cy \-bənsē\ n —lam•bent•ly adv

lame \'lām\ adj lam•er; lam•est 1 : having a limb disabled 2 : weak ~ vb lamed; lam•ing : make lame —lame•ly adv —lame•ness n

la•mé \lä'mā, la-\ n : cloth with tinsel threads

lame•brain \'lām,brān\ n : fool

la•ment \lə'ment\ vb 1 : mourn 2 : express sorrow for ~ n 1 : mourning 2 : complaint —lam•en•ta•ble \'laməntəbəl, lə'mentə-\ adj —lam•en•ta•bly \-blē\ adv —lam•en•ta•tion \,lamən'tāshən\ n

lam•i•nat•ed \'lamə,nātəd\ adj : made of thin layers of material —lam•i•nate \-,nāt\ vb —lam•i•nate \-nət\ n or adj —lam•i•na•tion \,lamə'nāshən\ n

lamp \'lamp\ n : device for producing light or heat

lam•poon \lam'pün\ n : satire —lam•poon vb

lam•prey \'lamprē\ n, pl -preys : sucking eellike fish

lance \'lans\ n : spear ~ vb lanced; lanc•ing : pierce or open with a lancet

lance corporal n : enlisted man in the marine corps ranking above a private first class and below a corporal

lan•cet \'lansət\ n : pointed surgical instrument

land \'land\ n 1 : solid part of the surface of the earth 2 : country ~ vb 1 : go ashore 2 : catch or gain 3 : touch the ground or a surface —land•less adj —land•own•er n

land•fill n : dump

land•ing \'landiŋ\ n 1 : action of one that

lands 2 : place for loading passengers and cargo 3 : level part of a staircase

land•la•dy \'land,lādē\ n : woman landlord

land•locked adj : enclosed by land

land•lord n : owner of property

land•lub•ber \-,ləbər\ n : one with little sea experience

land•mark \-,märk\ n 1 : object that marks a boundary or serves as a guide 2 : event that marks a turning point

land•scape \-,skāp\ n : view of natural scenery ~ vb -scaped; -scap•ing : beautify a piece of land (as by decorative planting)

land•slide n 1 : slipping down of a mass of earth 2 : overwhelming victory

land•ward \'landwərd\ adj : toward the land —landward adv

lane \'lān\ n : narrow way

lan•guage \'laŋgwij\ n : words and the methods of combining them for communication

lan•guid \'laŋgwəd\ adj 1 : weak 2 : sluggish —lan•guid•ly adv —lan•guid•ness n

lan•guish \'laŋgwish\ vb : become languid or discouraged

lan•guor \'laŋgər\ n : listless indolence —lan•guor•ous adj —lan•guor•ous•ly adv

lank \'laŋk\ adj 1 : thin 2 : limp

lanky adj lank•i•er; -est : tall and thin

lan•o•lin \'lan∂lən\ n : fatty wax from sheep's wool used in ointments

lan•tern \'lantərn\ n : enclosed portable light

¹lap \'lap\ n 1 : front part of the lower trunk and thighs of a seated person 2 : overlapping part 3 : one complete circuit completing a course (as around a track or pool) ~ vb : fold over

²lap vb -pp- 1 : scoop up with the tongue 2 : splash gently

lap•dog n : small dog

la•pel \lə'pel\ n : fold of the front of a coat

lap•i•dary \'lapə,derē\ n : one who cuts and polishes gems ~ adj : relating to gems

lapse \'laps\ n 1 : slight error 2 : termination of a right or privilege 3 : interval ~ vb lapsed; laps•ing 1 : slip 2 : subside 3 : cease

lap•top \'lap,täp\ adj : of a size that may be used on one's lap

lar•board \'iärbərd\ n : port side

lar·ce·ny \'lärsᵊnē\ n, pl **-nies** : theft — **lar·ce·nous** \'lärsᵊnəs\ adj

larch \'lärch\ n : tree like a pine that loses its needles

lard \'lärd\ n : pork fat

lard·er \'lärdər\ n : pantry

large \'lärj\ adj **larg·er; larg·est** : greater than average — **large·ly** adv — **large·ness** n

lar·gesse, lar·gess \lär'zhes, -'jes; 'lär,-\ n : liberal giving

lar·i·at \'larēət\ n : lasso

¹**lark** \'lärk\ n : small songbird

²**lark** vb or n : romp

lar·va \'lärvə\ n, pl **-vae** \-,vē\ : wormlike form of an insect — **lar·val** \-vəl\ adj

lar·yn·gi·tis \,larən'jītəs\ n : inflammation of the larynx

lar·ynx \'lariŋks\ n, pl **-ryn·ges** \lə'rin,jēz\ or **-ynx·es** : upper part of the trachea — **la·ryn·ge·al** \,larən-'jēəl, lə'rinjēəl\ adj

la·sa·gna \lə'zänyə\ n : flat noodles baked usu. with tomato sauce, meat, and cheese

las·civ·i·ous \lə'sivēəs\ adj : lewd — **las·civ·i·ous·ness** n

la·ser \'lāzər\ n : device that produces an intense light beam

¹**lash** \'lash\ vb : whip ~ n 1 : stroke esp. of a whip 2 : eyelash

²**lash** vb : bind with a rope or cord

lass \'las\ n : girl

lass·ie \'lasē\ n : girl

las·si·tude \'lasə,tüd, -,tyüd\ n 1 : fatigue 2 : listlessness

las·so \'lasō, la'sü\ n, pl **-sos** or **-soes** : rope with a noose for catching livestock — **lasso** vb

¹**last** \'last\ vb : continue in existence or operation

²**last** adj 1 : final 2 : previous 3 : least likely ~ adv 1 : at the end 2 : most recently 3 : in conclusion ~ n : something that is last — **last·ly** adv — **at last** : finally

³**last** n : form on which a shoe is shaped

latch \'lach\ vb : catch or get hold ~ n : catch that holds a door closed

late \'lāt\ adj **lat·er; lat·est** 1 : coming or staying after the proper time 2 : advanced toward the end 3 : recently deceased 4 : recent — **late** adv — **late·com·er** \-,kəmər\ n — **late·ly** adv — **late·ness** n

la·tent \'lātᵊnt\ adj : present but not visible or expressed — **la·ten·cy** \-ᵊnsē\ n

lat·er·al \'latərəl\ adj : on or toward the side — **lat·er·al·ly** adv

la·tex \'lā,teks\ n, pl **-ti·ces** \'lātə,sēz, 'lat-\ or **-tex·es** : emulsion of synthetic rubber or plastic

lath \'lath, 'lath\ n, pl **laths** or **lath** : building material (as a thin strip of wood) used as a base for plaster — **lath** vb — **lath·ing** \-iŋ\ n

lathe \'lāth\ n : machine that rotates material for shaping

lath·er \'lathər\ n : foam ~ vb : form or spread lather

lat·i·tude \'latə,tüd, -,tyüd\ n 1 : distance north or south from the earth's equator 2 : freedom of action

la·trine \lə'trēn\ n : toilet

lat·ter \'latər\ adj 1 : more recent 2 : being the second of 2 — **lat·ter·ly** adv

lat·tice \'latəs\ n : framework of crossed strips

laud vb or n : praise — **laud·able** adj — **laud·ably** adv

laugh \'laf, 'laf\ vb : show mirth, joy, or scorn with a smile and explosive sound — **laugh** n — **laugh·able** adj — **laugh·ing·ly** \-iŋlē\ adv

laugh·ing·stock \'lafiŋ,stäk, 'laf-\ n : object of ridicule

laugh·ter \'laftər, 'laf-\ n : action or sound of laughing

¹**launch** \'lonch\ vb 1 : hurl or send off 2 : set afloat 3 : start — **launch** n — **launch·er** n

²**launch** n : small open boat

laun·der \'londər\ vb : wash or iron fabrics — **laun·der·er** n — **laun·dress** \-drəs\ n — **laun·dry** \-drē\ n

lau·re·ate \'lorēət\ n : recipient of honors — **laureate** adj

lau·rel \'lorəl\ n 1 : small evergreen tree 2 : honor

la·va \'lävə, 'lav-\ n : volcanic molten rock

lav·a·to·ry \'lavə,torē\ n, pl **-ries** : bathroom

lav·en·der \'lavəndər\ n 1 : aromatic plant used for perfume 2 : pale purple color

lav·ish \'lavish\ adj : expended profusely ~ vb : expend or give freely — **lav·ish·ly** adv — **lav·ish·ness** n

law \'lo\ n 1 : established rule of conduct 2 : body of such rules 3 : principle of construction or procedure 4 : rule stating uniform behavior under uniform conditions 5 : lawyer's profession —

law·break·er n —**law·giv·er** n —**law·less** adj —**law·less·ly** adv —**law·less·ness** n —**law·mak·er** n —**law·man** \-mən\ n —**law·suit** n

law·ful \'lófəl\ adj : permitted by law —**law·ful·ly** adv

lawn \'lón\ n : grass-covered yard

law·yer \'lóyər\ n : legal practitioner

lax \'laks\ adj : not strict or tense —**lax·i·ty** \'laksətē\ n —**lax·ly** adv

lax·a·tive \'laksətiv\ n : drug relieving constipation

¹lay \'lā\ vb **laid** \'lād\; **lay·ing 1** : put or set down **2** : produce eggs **3** : bet **4** : impose as a duty or burden **5** : put forward ~ n : way something lies or is laid

²lay past of LIE

³lay n : song

⁴lay adj : of the laity —**lay·man** \-mən\ n —**lay·wom·an** \-,wumən\ n

lay·er \'lāər\ n **1** : one that lays **2** : one thickness over or under another

lay·off \'lā,óf\ n : temporary dismissal of a worker

lay·out \'lā,aút\ n : arrangement

la·zy \'lāzē\ adj **-zi·er; -est** : disliking activity or exertion —**la·zi·ly** \'lāzəlē\ adv —**la·zi·ness** n

lea \'lē, 'lā\ n : meadow

leach \'lēch\ vb : remove (a soluble part) with a solvent

¹lead \'lēd\ vb **led** \'led\; **lead·ing 1** : guide on a way **2** : direct the activity of **3** : go at the head of **4** : tend to a definite result ~ n : position in front —**lead·er** n —**lead·er·less** adj —**lead·er·ship** n

²lead \'led\ n **1** : heavy bluish white chemical element **2** : marking substance in a pencil —**lead·en** \'ledᵊn\ adj

leaf \'lēf\ n, pl **leaves** \'lēvz\ **1** : green outgrowth of a plant stem **2** : leaflike thing ~ vb **1** : produce leaves **2** : turn book pages —**leaf·age** \'lēfij\ n —**leafed** \'lēft\ adj —**leaf·less** adj —**leafy** adj —**leaved** \'lēfd\ adj

leaf·let \'lēflət\ n : pamphlet

¹league \'lēg\ n : unit of distance equal to about 3 miles

²league n : association for a common purpose —**league** vb —**leagu·er** n

leak \'lēk\ vb **1** : enter or escape through a leak **2** : become or make known ~ n : opening that accidentally admits or lets out a substance —**leak·age** \'lēkij\ n —**leaky** adj

¹lean \'lēn\ vb **1** : bend from a vertical position **2** : rely on for support **3** : incline in opinion —**lean** n

²lean adj **1** : lacking in flesh **2** : lacking richness —**lean·ness** \'lēnnəs\ n

leap \'lēp\ vb **leapt** or **leaped** \'lēpt, 'lept\; **leap·ing** : jump —**leap** n

leap year n : 366-day year

learn \'lərn\ vb **1** : gain understanding or skill by study or experience **2** : memorize **3** : find out —**learn·er** n

learn·ed \-əd\ adj : having great learning —**learn·ed·ness** n

learn·ing \-iŋ\ n : knowledge

lease \'lēs\ n : contract transferring real estate for a term and usu. for rent ~ vb **leased; leas·ing** : grant by or hold under a lease

leash \'lēsh\ n : line to hold an animal —**leash** vb

least \'lēst\ adj **1** : lowest in importance or position **2** : smallest **3** : scantiest ~ n : one that is least ~ adv : in the smallest or lowest degree

leath·er \'lethər\ n : dressed animal skin —**leath·ern** \-ərn\ adj —**leath·ery** adj

¹leave \'lēv\ vb **left** \'left\; **leav·ing 1** : bequeath **2** : allow or cause to remain **3** : have as a remainder **4** : go away ~ n **1** : permission **2** : authorized absence **3** : departure

²leave vb **leaved; leav·ing** : leaf

leav·en \'levən\ n : substance for producing fermentation ~ vb : raise dough with a leaven

leaves pl of LEAF

lech·ery \'lechərē\ n : inordinate indulgence in sex —**lech·er** \'lechər\ n —**lech·er·ous** \-chərəs\ adj —**lech·er·ous·ly** adv —**lech·er·ous·ness** n

lec·ture \'lekchər\ n **1** : instructive talk **2** : reprimand —**lecture** vb —**lec·tur·er** n —**lec·ture·ship** n

led past of LEAD

ledge \'lej\ n : shelflike projection

led·ger \'lejər\ n : account book

lee \'lē\ n : side sheltered from the wind —**lee** adj

leech \'lēch\ n : segmented freshwater worm that feeds on blood

leek \'lēk\ n : onionlike herb

leer \'lir\ n : suggestive or malicious look —**leer** vb

leery \'lirē\ adj : suspicious or wary

lees \'lēz\ n pl : dregs

lee·ward \'lēwərd, 'lüərd\ adj : situated away from the wind ~ n : the lee side

lee·way \'lē,wā\ *n* : allowable margin

¹left \'left\ *adj* : on the same side of the body as the heart ~ *n* : left hand — **left** *adv*

²left *past of* LEAVE

leg \'leg\ *n* 1 : limb of an animal that supports the body 2 : something like a leg 3 : clothing to cover the leg ~ *vb* **-gg-** : walk or run — **legged** \'legəd\ *adj* — **leg·less** *adj*

leg·a·cy \'legəsē\ *n, pl* **-cies** : inheritance

le·gal \'lēgəl\ *adj* 1 : relating to law or lawyers 2 : lawful — **le·gal·is·tic** \,lēgə'listik\ *adj* — **le·gal·i·ty** \li-'galətē\ *n* — **le·gal·ize** \'lēgə,līz\ *vb* — **le·gal·ly** \-gəlē\ *adv*

leg·ate \'legət\ *n* : official representative

le·ga·tion \li'gāshən\ *n* 1 : diplomatic mission 2 : official residence and office of a diplomat

leg·end \'lejənd\ *n* 1 : story handed down from the past 2 : inscription 3 : explanation of map symbols — **leg·end·ary** \-ən,derē\ *adj*

leg·er·de·main \,lejərdə'mān\ *n* : sleight of hand

leg·ging, leg·gin \'legən, -iŋ\ *n* : leg covering

leg·i·ble \'lejəbəl\ *adj* : capable of being read — **leg·i·bil·i·ty** \,lejə'bilətē\ *n* — **leg·i·bly** \'lejəblē\ *adv*

le·gion \'lējən\ *n* 1 : large army unit 2 : multitude 3 : association of former servicemen — **le·gion·ary** \-,erē\ *n* — **le·gion·naire** \,lējən'ar\ *n*

leg·is·late \'lejə,slāt\ *vb* **-lat·ed; -lat·ing** : enact or bring about with laws — **leg·is·la·tion** \,lejə'slāshən\ *n* — **leg·is·la·tive** \'lejə,slātiv\ *adj* — **leg·is·la·tor** \-ər\ *n*

leg·is·la·ture \'lejə,slāchər\ *n* : organization with authority to make laws

le·git·i·mate \li'jitəmət\ *adj* 1 : lawfully begotten 2 : genuine 3 : conforming with law or accepted standards — **le·git·i·ma·cy** \-məsē\ *n* — **le·git·i·mate·ly** *adv* — **le·git·i·mize** \-,mīz\ *vb*

le·gume \'leg,yüm, li'gyüm\ *n* : plant bearing pods — **le·gu·mi·nous** \li-'gyümənəs\ *adj*

lei \'lā\ *n* : necklace of flowers

lei·sure \'lēzhər, 'lezh-, 'lāzh-\ *n* 1 : free time 2 : ease 3 : convenience — **lei·sure·ly** *adj or adv*

lem·ming \'lemiŋ\ *n* : short-tailed rodent

lem·on \'lemən\ *n* : yellow citrus fruit — **lem·ony** *adj*

lem·on·ade \,lemə'nād\ *n* : sweetened lemon beverage

lend \'lend\ *vb* **lent** \'lent\; **lend·ing** 1 : give for temporary use 2 : furnish — **lend·er** *n*

length \'leŋth\ *n* 1 : longest dimension 2 : duration in time 3 : piece to be joined to others — **length·en** \'leŋthən\ *vb* — **length·wise** *adv or adj* — **lengthy** *adj*

le·nient \'lēnēənt, -nyənt\ *adj* : of mild and tolerant disposition or effect — **le·ni·en·cy** \'lēnēənsē -nyənsē\ *n* — **le·ni·ent·ly** *adv*

len·i·ty \'lenətē\ *n* : leniency

lens \'lenz\ *n* 1 : curved piece for forming an image in an optical instrument 2 : transparent body in the eye that focuses light rays

Lent \'lent\ *n* : 40-day period of penitence and fasting from Ash Wednesday to Easter — **Lent·en** \-ᵊn\ *adj*

len·til \'lentᵊl\ *n* : legume with flat edible seeds

le·o·nine \'lēə,nīn\ *adj* : like a lion

leop·ard \'lepərd\ *n* : large tawny black-spotted cat

le·o·tard \'lēə,tärd\ *n* : close-fitting garment

lep·er \'lepər\ *n* : person with leprosy

lep·re·chaun \'leprə,kän\ *n* : mischievous Irish elf

lep·ro·sy \'leprəsē\ *n* : chronic bacterial disease — **lep·rous** \-rəs\ *adj*

les·bi·an \'lezbēən\ *n* : female homosexual — **lesbian** *adj* — **les·bi·an·ism** \-,izəm\ *n*

le·sion \'lēzhən\ *n* : abnormal area in the body due to injury or disease

less \'les\ *adj* 1 : fewer 2 : of lower rank, degree, or importance 3 : smaller ~ *adv* : to a lesser degree ~ *n, pl* **less** : smaller portion ~ *prep* : minus — **less·en** \-ᵊn\ *vb*

-less \ləs\ *adj suffix* 1 : not having 2 : unable to act or be acted on

les·see \le'sē\ *n* : tenant under a lease

less·er \'lesər\ *adj* : of less size, quality, or significance

les·son \'lesᵊn\ *n* 1 : reading or exercise to be studied by a pupil 2 : something learned

les·sor \'les,ór, le'sór\ *n* : one who transfers property by a lease

lest \'lest\ *conj* : for fear that

¹let \'let\ *n* : hindrance or obstacle

²**let** vb **let; let·ting 1** : cause to **2** : rent **3** : permit

-let \lət\ n suffix : small one

le·thal \'lēthəl\ adj : deadly —**le·thal·ly** adv

leth·ar·gy \'lethərjē\ n **1** : drowsiness **2** : state of being lazy or indifferent —**le·thar·gic** \li'thärjik\ adj

let·ter \'letər\ n **1** : unit of an alphabet **2** : written or printed communication **3** pl : literature or learning **4** : literal meaning ~ vb : mark with letters —**let·ter·er** n

let·tuce \'letəs\ n : garden plant with crisp leaves

leu·ke·mia \lü'kēmēə\ n : cancerous blood disease —**leu·ke·mic** \-mik\ adj or n

lev·ee \'levē\ n : embankment to prevent flooding

lev·el \'levəl\ n **1** : device for establishing a flat surface **2** : horizontal surface **3** : position in a scale ~ vb **-eled** or **-elled; -el·ing** or **-el·ling 1** : make flat or level **2** : aim **3** : raze ~ adj **1** : having an even surface **2** : of the same height or rank —**lev·el·er** n —**lev·el·ly** adv —**lev·el·ness** n

le·ver \'levər, 'lē-\ n : bar for prying or dislodging something —**le·ver·age** \'levərij, 'lēv-\ n

le·vi·a·than \li'vīəthən\ n **1** : large sea animal **2** : enormous thing

lev·i·ty \'levətē\ n : unseemly frivolity

levy \'levē\ n, pl **lev·ies** : imposition or collection of a tax ~ vb **lev·ied; levy·ing 1** : impose or collect legally **2** : enlist for military service **3** : wage

lewd \'lüd\ adj **1** : sexually unchaste **2** : vulgar —**lewd·ly** adv —**lewd·ness** n

lex·i·cog·ra·phy \,leksə'kägrəfē\ n : dictionary making —**lex·i·cog·rapher** \-fər\ n —**lex·i·co·graph·i·cal** \-kō'grafikəl\ or **lex·i·co·graph·ic** \-ik\ adj

lex·i·con \'leksə,kän\ n, pl **-i·ca** \-sikə\ or **-icons** : dictionary

li·a·ble \'līəbəl\ adj **1** : legally obligated **2** : probable **3** : susceptible —**li·a·bil·i·ty** \,līə'bilətē\ n

li·ai·son \'lēə,zän, lē'ā-\ n **1** : close bond **2** : communication between groups

li·ar \'līər\ n : one who lies

li·bel \'lībəl\ n : action, crime, or an instance of injuring a person's reputation esp. by something written ~ vb **-beled** or **-belled; -bel·ing** or **-bel-** ling : make or publish a libel —**li·bel·er** n —**li·bel·ist** n —**li·bel·ous, li·bel·lous** \-bələs\ adj

lib·er·al \'librəl, 'libə-\ adj : not stingy, narrow, or conservative —**liberal** n —**lib·er·al·ism** \-,izəm\ n —**lib·er·al·i·ty** \,libə'ralətē\ n —**lib·er·al·ize** \'librə,līz, 'libə-\ vb —**lib·er·al·ly** \-rəlē\ adv

lib·er·ate \'libə,rāt\ vb **-at·ed; -at·ing** : set free —**lib·er·a·tion** \,libə'rāshən\ n —**lib·er·a·tor** \'libə,rātər\ n

lib·er·tine \'libər,tēn\ n : one who leads a dissolute life

lib·er·ty \'libərtē\ n, pl **-ties 1** : quality or state of being free **2** : action going beyond normal limits

li·bi·do \lə'bēdō, -'bīd-\ n, pl **-dos** : sexual drive —**li·bid·i·nal** \lə'bidᵊnəl\ adj —**li·bid·i·nous** \-əs\ adj

li·brary \'lī,brerē\ n, pl **-brar·ies 1** : place where books are kept for use **2** : collection of books —**li·brar·i·an** \lī'brerēən\ n

li·bret·to \lə'bretō\ n, pl **-tos** or **-ti** \-ē\ : text of an opera —**li·bret·tist** \-ist\ n

lice pl of LOUSE

li·cense, li·cence \'līsᵊns\ n **1** : legal permission to engage in some activity **2** : document or tag providing proof of a license **3** : irresponsible use of freedom —**license** vb —**li·cens·ee** \,līsᵊn'sē\ n

li·cen·tious \lī'senchəs\ adj : disregarding sexual restraints —**li·cen·tious·ly** adv —**li·cen·tious·ness** n

li·chen \'līkən\ n : complex lower plant made up of an alga and a fungus

lic·it \'lisət\ adj : lawful

lick \'lik\ vb **1** : draw the tongue over **2** : beat ~ n **1** : stroke of the tongue **2** : small amount

lic·o·rice \'likərish, -rəs\ n : dried root of a European legume or candy flavored by it

lid \'lid\ n **1** : movable cover **2** : eyelid

¹**lie** \'lī\ vb **lay** \'lā\; **lain** \'lān\; **ly·ing** \'līiŋ\ **1** : be in, rest in, or assume a horizontal position **2** : occupy a certain relative position ~ n : position in which something lies

²**lie** vb **lied; ly·ing** \'līiŋ\ : tell a lie ~ n : untrue statement

liege \'lēj\ n : feudal superior or vassal

lien \'lēn, 'lēən\ *n* : legal claim on the property of another

lieu·ten·ant \lü'tenənt\ *n* **1** : representative **2** : first lieutenant or second lieutenant **3** : commissioned officer in the navy ranking next below a lieutenant commander —**lieu·ten·an·cy** \-ənsē\ *n*

lieutenant colonel *n* : commissioned officer (as in the army) ranking next below a colonel

lieutenant commander *n* : commissioned officer in the navy ranking next below a commander

lieutenant general *n* : commissioned officer (as in the army) ranking next below a general

lieutenant junior grade *n, pl* **lieutenants junior grade** : commissioned officer in the navy ranking next below a lieutenant

life \'līf\ *n, pl* **lives** \'līvz\ **1** : quality that distinguishes a vital and functional being from a dead body or inanimate matter **2** : physical and mental experiences of an individual **3** : biography **4** : period of existence **5** : way of living **6** : liveliness —**life·less** *adj* —**life·like** *adj*

life·blood *n* : basic source of strength and vitality

life·boat *n* : boat for saving lives at sea

life·guard *n* : one employed to safeguard bathers

life·long *adj* : continuing through life

life·sav·ing *n* : art or practice of saving lives —**life·sav·er** \-,sāvər\ *n*

life·style \'līf,stīl\ *n* : a way of life

life·time *n* : duration of an individual's existence

lift \'lift\ *vb* **1** : move upward or cause to move upward **2** : put an end to —**lift** *n* —**lift·er** *n*

lift-off \'lift,óf\ *n* : vertical takeoff by a rocket

lig·a·ment \'ligəmənt\ *n* : band of tough tissue that holds bones together

lig·a·ture \'ligə,chùr, -chər\ *n* : something that binds or ties

¹light \'līt\ *n* **1** : radiation that makes vision possible **2** : daylight **3** : source of light **4** : public knowledge **5** : aspect **6** : celebrity **7** : flame for lighting —*adj* **1** : bright **2** : weak in color ~ *vb* **lit** \'lit\ *or* **light·ed; light·ing 1** : make or become light **2** : cause to burn —**light·er** *n* —**light·ness** *n* —**light·proof** *adj*

²light *adj* : not heavy, serious, or abundant —**light** *adv* —**light·ly** *adv* —**light·ness** *n* —**light·weight** *adj*

³light *vb* **light·ed** *or* **lit** \'lit\; **light·ing** : settle or dismount

¹light·en \'lītⁿn\ *vb* **1** : make light or bright **2** : give out flashes of lightning

²lighten *vb* **1** : relieve of a burden **2** : become lighter

light·heart·ed \-'härtəd\ *adj* : free from worry —**light·heart·ed·ly** *adv* —**light·heart·ed·ness** *n*

light·house *n* : structure with a powerful light for guiding sailors

light·ning \'lītniŋ\ *n* : flashing discharge of atmospheric electricity

light-year \'līt,yir\ *n* : distance traveled by light in one year equal to about 5.88 trillion miles

lig·nite \'lig,nīt\ *n* : brownish black soft coal

¹like \'līk\ *vb* **liked; lik·ing 1** : enjoy **2** : desire ~ *n* : preference —**lik·able, like·able** \'līkəbəl\ *adj*

²like *adj* : similar ~ *prep* **1** : similar or similarly to **2** : typical of **3** : such as ~ *n* : counterpart ~ *conj* : as or as if —**like·ness** *n* —**like·wise** *adv*

-like \,līk\ *adj comb form* : resembling or characteristic of

like·li·hood \'līklē,hùd\ *n* : probability

like·ly \'līklē\ *adj* **-li·er; -est 1** : probable **2** : believable ~ *adv* : in all probability

lik·en \'līkən\ *vb* : compare

lik·ing \'līkiŋ\ *n* : favorable regard

li·lac \'līlək, -,lak, -,läk\ *n* : shrub with clusters of fragrant pink, purple, or white flowers

lilt \'lilt\ *n* : rhythmical swing or flow

lily \'lilē\ *n, pl* **lil·ies** : tall bulbous herb with funnel-shaped flowers

lima bean \'līmə-\ *n* : flat edible seed of a plant or the plant itself

limb \'lim\ *n* **1** : projecting appendage used in moving or grasping **2** : tree branch —**limb·less** *adj*

lim·ber \'limbər\ *adj* : supple or agile ~ *vb* : make or become limber

lim·bo \'limbō\ *n, pl* **-bos** : place or state of confinement or oblivion

¹lime \'līm\ *n* : caustic white oxide of calcium

²lime *n* : small green lemonlike citrus fruit —**lime·ade** \-,ād\ *n*

lime·light *n* : center of public attention

lim·er·ick \'limərik\ *n* : light poem of 5 lines

lime·stone *n* : rock that yields lime when burned

lim·it \'limət\ *n* **1** : boundary **2** : something that restrains or confines ~ *vb* : set limits on **—lim·i·ta·tion** \,limə'tāshən\ *n* **—lim·it·less** *adj*

lim·ou·sine \'limə,zēn, ,limə'-\ *n* : large luxurious sedan

limp \'limp\ *vb* : walk lamely ~ *n* : limping movement or gait ~ *adj* : lacking firmness and body **—limp·ly** *adv* **—limp·ness** *n*

lim·pid \'limpəd\ *adj* : clear or transparent

lin·den \'lindən\ *n* : tree with large heart-shaped leaves

¹line \'līn\ *vb* **lined; lin·ing** : cover the inner surface of **—lin·ing** *n*

²line *n* **1** : cord, rope, or wire **2** : row or something like a row **3** : note **4** : course of action or thought **5** : state of agreement **6** : occupation **7** : limit **8** : transportation system **9** : long narrow mark ~ *vb* **lined; lin·ing 1** : mark with a line **2** : place in a line **3** : form a line

lin·eage \'linēij\ *n* : descent from a common ancestor

lin·eal \'linēəl\ *adj* **1** : linear **2** : in a direct line of ancestry

lin·ea·ments \'linēəmənts\ *n pl* : features or contours esp. of a face

lin·ear \'linēər\ *adj* **1** : straight **2** : long and narrow

lin·en \'linən\ *n* **1** : cloth or thread made of flax **2** : household articles made of linen cloth

lin·er \'linər\ *n* **1** : one that lines **2** : ship or airplane belonging to a line

line·up \'līn,əp\ *n* **1** : line of persons for inspection or identification **2** : list of players in a game

-ling \liŋ\ *n suffix* **1** : one linked with **2** : young, small, or minor one

lin·ger \'liŋgər\ *vb* : be slow to leave or act **—lin·ger·er** *n*

lin·ge·rie \,länjə'rā, ,laⁿzhə-, -'rē\ *n* : women's underwear

lin·go \'liŋgō\ *n, pl* **-goes** : usu. strange language

lin·guist \'liŋgwist\ *n* **1** : person skilled in speech or languages **2** : student of language **—lin·guis·tic** \liŋ'gwistik\ *adj* **—lin·guis·tics** *n pl*

lin·i·ment \'linəmənt\ *n* : liquid medication rubbed on the skin

link \'liŋk\ *n* **1** : connecting structure (as a ring of a chain) **2** : bond **—link** *vb* **—link·age** \-ij\ *n* **—link·er** *n*

li·no·leum \lə'nōlēəm\ *n* : floor covering with hard surface

lin·seed \'lin,sēd\ *n* : seeds of flax yielding an oil (**linseed oil**)

lint \'lint\ *n* : fine fluff or loose short fibers from fabric

lin·tel \'lintᵊl\ *n* : horizontal piece over a door or window

li·on \'līən\ *n* : large cat of Africa and Asia **—li·on·ess** \'līənəs\ *n*

li·on·ize \'līə,nīz\ *vb* **-ized; -iz·ing** : treat as very important **—li·on·iza·tion** \,līənə'zāshən\ *n*

lip \'lip\ *n* **1** : either of the 2 fleshy folds surrounding the mouth **2** : edge of something hollow **—lipped** \'lipt\ *adj* **—lip·read·ing** *n*

li·po·suc·tion \'lipə,səkshən, 'lī-\ *n* : surgical removal of fat deposits (as from the thighs)

lip·stick \'lip,stik\ *n* : stick of cosmetic to color lips

liq·ue·fy \'likwə,fī\ *vb* **-fied; -fy·ing** : make or become liquid **—liq·ue·fi·er** \'likwə,fīər\ *n*

li·queur \li'kər\ *n* : sweet or aromatic alcoholic liquor

liq·uid \'likwəd\ *adj* **1** : flowing freely like water **2** : neither solid nor gaseous **3** : of or convertible to cash **—liquid** *n* **—li·quid·i·ty** \lik'widətē\ *n*

liq·ui·date \'likwə,dāt\ *vb* **-dat·ed; -dat·ing 1** : pay off **2** : dispose of **—liq·ui·da·tion** \,likwə'dāshən\ *n*

li·quor \'likər\ *n* : liquid substance and esp. a distilled alcoholic beverage

lisp \'lisp\ *vb* : pronounce *s* and *z* imperfectly **—lisp** *n*

lis·some \'lisəm\ *adj* : supple or agile

¹list \'list\ *n* **1** : series of names or items ~ *vb* **1** : make a list of **2** : put on a list

²list *vb* : tilt or lean over ~ *n* : slant

lis·ten \'lisᵊn\ *vb* **1** : pay attention in order to hear **2** : heed **—lis·ten·er** \'lisᵊnər\ *n*

list·less \'listləs\ *adj* : having no desire to act **—list·less·ly** *adv* **—list·less·ness** *n*

lit \'lit\ *past of* LIGHT

lit·a·ny \'litᵊnē\ *n, pl* **-nies 1** : prayer said as a series of responses to a leader **2** : long recitation

li·ter \'lētər\ *n* : unit of liquid measure equal to about 1.06 quarts

lit·er·al \'litərəl\ *adj* : being exactly as stated —**lit·er·al·ly** *adv*

lit·er·ary \'litə,rerē\ *adj* : relating to literature

lit·er·ate \'litərət\ *adj* : able to read and write —**lit·er·a·cy** \'litərəsē\ *n*

lit·er·a·ture \'litərə,chur, -chər\ *n* : writings of enduring interest

lithe \'lῑth, 'lῑth\ *adj* 1 : supple 2 : graceful —**lithe·some** \-səm\ *adj*

lith·o·graph \'lithə,graf\ *n* : print from a drawing on metal or stone —**li·thog·ra·pher** \lith'ägrəfər, 'lithə,grafər\ *n* —**lith·o·graph·ic** \,lithə'grafik\ *adj* —**li·thog·ra·phy** \lith'ägrəfē\ *n*

lit·i·gate \'litə,gāt\ *vb* -gat·ed; -gat·ing : carry on a lawsuit —**lit·i·gant** \'litigənt\ *n* —**lit·i·ga·tion** \,litə'gāshən\ *n* —**li·ti·gious** \lə'tijəs, li-\ *adj* —**li·ti·gious·ness** *n*

lit·mus \'litməs\ *n* : coloring matter that turns red in acid solutions and blue in alkaline

lit·ter \'litər\ *n* 1 : animal offspring of one birth 2 : stretcher 3 : rubbish 4 : material to absorb animal waste ~ *vb* 1 : give birth to young 2 : strew with litter

lit·tle \'litᵊl\ *adj* **lit·tler** *or* **less** \'les\ *or* **less·er** \'lesər\; **lit·tlest** *or* **least** \'lēst\ 1 : not big 2 : not much 3 : not important — *adv* **less** \'les\; **least** \'lēst\ 1 : slightly 2 : not often — *n* : small amount —**lit·tle·ness** *n*

lit·ur·gy \'litərjē\ *n*, *pl* -gies : rite of worship —**li·tur·gi·cal** \lə'tərjikəl\ *adj* —**li·tur·gi·cal·ly** \-klē\ *adv* —**lit·ur·gist** \'litərjist\ *n*

liv·able \'livəbəl\ *adj* : suitable for living in or with —**liv·a·bil·i·ty** \,livə'bilətē\ *n*

¹live \'liv\ *vb* **lived; liv·ing** 1 : be alive 2 : conduct one's life 3 : subsist 4 : reside

²live \'līv\ *adj* 1 : having life 2 : burning 3 : connected to electric power 4 : not exploded 5 : of continuing interest 6 : involving the actual presence of real people

live·li·hood \'līvlē,hud\ *n* : means of subsistence

live·long \'liv'loŋ\ *adj* : whole

live·ly \'līvlē\ *adj* **-li·er; -est** : full of life and vigor —**live·li·ness** *n*

liv·en \'līvən\ *vb* : enliven

liv·er \'livər\ *n* : organ that secretes bile

liv·ery \'livərē\ *n*, *pl* -er·ies 1 : servant's uniform 2 : care of horses for pay —**liv·er·ied** \-rēd\ *adj* —**liv·ery·man** \-mən\ *n*

lives *pl of* LIFE

live·stock \'līv,stäk\ *n* : farm animals

liv·id \'livəd\ *adj* 1 : discolored by bruising 2 : pale 3 : enraged

liv·ing \'liviŋ\ *adj* : having life ~ *n* : livelihood

liz·ard \'lizərd\ *n* : reptile with 4 legs and a long tapering tail

lla·ma \'lämə\ *n* : So. American mammal related to the camel

load \'lōd\ *n* 1 : cargo 2 : supported weight 3 : burden 4 : a large quantity—usu. pl. ~ *vb* 1 : put a load on 2 : burden 3 : put ammunition in

¹loaf \'lōf\ *n*, *pl* **loaves** \'lōvz\ : mass of bread

²loaf *vb* : waste time —**loaf·er** *n*

loam \'lōm, 'lüm\ *n* : soil —**loamy** *adj*

loan \'lōn\ *n* 1 : money borrowed at interest 2 : something lent temporarily 3 : grant of use ~ *vb* : lend

loath \'lōth, 'lōth\ *adj* : very reluctant

loathe \'lōth\ *vb* **loathed; loath·ing** : hate

loath·ing \'lōthiŋ\ *n* : extreme disgust

loath·some \'lōthsəm, 'lōth-\ *adj* : repulsive

lob \'läb\ *vb* -bb- : throw or hit in a high arc —**lob** *n*

lob·by \'läbē\ *n*, *pl* -bies 1 : public waiting room at the entrance of a building 2 : persons lobbying ~ *vb* -bied; -by·ing : try to influence legislators —**lob·by·ist** *n*

lobe \'lōb\ *n* : rounded part —**lo·bar** \'lōbər\ *adj* —**lobed** \'lōbd\ *adj*

lo·bot·o·my \lō'bätəmē\ *n*, *pl* -mies : surgical severance of nerve fibers in the brain

lob·ster \'läbstər\ *n* : marine crustacean with 2 large pincerlike claws

lo·cal \'lōkəl\ *adj* : confined to or serving a limited area —**local** *n* —**lo·cal·ly** *adv*

lo·cale \lō'kal\ *n* : setting for an event

lo·cal·i·ty \lō'kalətē\ *n*, *pl* -ties : particular place

lo·cal·ize \'lōkə,līz\ *vb* -ized; -iz·ing : confine to a definite place —**lo·cal·i·za·tion** \,lōkələ'zāshən\ *n*

lo·cate \'lō,kāt, lō'kāt\ *vb* -cat·ed; -cat·ing 1 : settle 2 : find a site for 3

: discover the place of —**lo·ca·tion**
\lō'kāshən\ *n*

¹lock \'läk\ *n* : tuft or strand of hair

²lock *n* **1** : fastener using a bolt **2**
: enclosure in a canal to raise or lower
boats ~ *vb* **1** : make fast with a lock
2 : confine **3** : interlock

lock·er \'läkər\ *n* : storage compartment

lock·et \'läkət\ *n* : small case worn on a
necklace

lock·jaw *n* : tetanus

lock·out *n* : closing of a plant by an employer during a labor dispute

lock·smith \-,smith\ *n* : one who makes
or repairs locks

lo·co·mo·tion \,lōkə'mōshən\ *n* : power
of moving —**lo·co·mo·tive** \-'mōtiv\
adj

lo·co·mo·tive \-'mōtiv\ *n* : vehicle that
moves railroad cars

lo·co·weed \'lōkō,wēd\ *n* : western plant
poisonous to livestock

lo·cust \'lōkəst\ *n* **1** : migratory grasshopper **2** : cicada **3** : tree with hard
wood or this wood

lo·cu·tion \lō'kyüshən\ *n* : way of saying something

lode \'lōd\ *n* : ore deposit

lode·stone *n* : magnetic rock

lodge \'läj\ *vb* **lodged; lodg·ing 1**
: provide quarters for **2** : come to rest
3 : file ~ *n* **1** : special house (as for
hunters) **2** : animal's den **3** : branch
of a fraternal organization —**lodg·er**
\'läjər\ *n* —**lodg·ing** *n* —**lodg·ment,
lodge·ment** \-mənt\ *n*

loft \'lòft\ *n* **1** : attic **2** : upper floor (as
of a warehouse)

lofty \'lòftē\ *adj* **loft·i·er; -est 1** : noble
2 : proud **3** : tall or high —**loft·i·ly**
adv —**loft·i·ness** *n*

log \'lòg, 'läg\ *n* **1** : unshaped timber **2**
: daily record of a ship's or plane's
progress ~ *vb* **-gg- 1** : cut (trees) for
lumber **2** : enter in a log —**log·ger**
\-ər\ *n*

log·a·rithm \'lògə,rithəm, 'läg-\ *n*
: exponent to which a base number is
raised to produce a given number

loge \'lōzh\ *n* : box in a theater

log·ger·head \'lògər,hed, 'läg-\ *n* : large
Atlantic sea turtle —**at loggerheads**
: in disagreement

log·ic \'läjik\ *n* **1** : science of reasoning
2 : sound reasoning —**log·i·cal** \-ikəl\
adj —**log·i·cal·ly** *adv* —**lo·gi·cian**
\lō'jishən\ *n*

lo·gis·tics \lō'jistiks\ *n sing or pl*
: procurement and movement of people and supplies —**lo·gis·tic** *adj*

logo \'lōgō, 'lòg-, 'läg-\ *n, pl* **log·os** \-ōz\
: advertising symbol

loin \'lòin\ *n* **1** : part of the body on each
side of the spine between the hip and
lower ribs **2** *pl* : pubic regions

loi·ter \'lòitər\ *vb* : remain around a
place idly —**loi·ter·er** *n*

loll \'läl\ *vb* : lounge

lol·li·pop, lol·ly·pop \'läli,päp\ *n* : hard
candy on a stick

lone \'lōn\ *adj* **1** : alone or isolated **2**
: only —**lone·li·ness** —**lone·ly** *adj*
—**lon·er** \'lōnər\ *n*

lone·some \-səm\ *adj* : sad from lack of
company —**lone·some·ly** *adv* —
lone·some·ness *n*

long \'lòŋ\ *adj* **lon·ger** \'lòŋgər\; **longest**
\'lòŋgəst\ **1** : extending far or for a
considerable time **2** : having a specified length **3** : tedious **4** : well supplied—used with *on* ~ *adv* : for a
long time ~ *n* : long period ~ *vb*
: feel a strong desire —**long·ing**
\'lòŋiŋ\ *n* —**long·ing·ly** *adv*

lon·gev·i·ty \län'jevətē\ *n* : long life

long·hand *n* : handwriting

long·horn *n* : cattle with long horns

lon·gi·tude \'länjə,tüd, -,tyüd\ *n*
: angular distance east or west from a
meridian

lon·gi·tu·di·nal \,länjə'tüd°nəl, -'tyüd-\
adj : lengthwise —**lon·gi·tu·di·nal·ly**
adv

long·shore·man \'lòŋ'shōrmən\ *n* : one
who loads and unloads ships

look \'lùk\ *vb* **1** : see **2** : seem **3** : direct
one's attention **4** : face ~ *n* **1** : action
of looking **2** : appearance of the face
3 : aspect —**look after** : take care of
—**look for 1** : expect **2** : search for

look·out *n* **1** : one who watches **2**
: careful watch

¹loom \'lüm\ *n* : frame or machine for
weaving

²loom *vb* : appear large and indistinct
or impressive

loon \'lün\ *n* : black-and-white diving
bird

loo·ny, loo·ney \'lünē\ *adj* **-ni·er-**
: crazy

loop \'lüp\ *n* **1** : dou[b...]
leaves an opening [...]
a loop —**loop** *vb*

loop·hole \'lüp,hōl\ *n* : means of evading

loose \'lüs\ *adj* **loos·er; -est 1** : not fixed tight **2** : not restrained **3** : not dense **4** : slack **5** : not exact ~ *vb* **loosed; loos·ing 1** : release **2** : untie or relax —**loose** *adv* —**loose·ly** *adv* —**loos·en** \'lüs⁰n\ *vb* —**loose·ness** *n*

loot \'lüt\ *n or vb* : plunder —**loot·er** *n*

lop \'läp\ *vb* **-pp-** : cut off

lope \'lōp\ *n* : bounding gait —**lope** *vb*

lop·sid·ed \'läp'sīdəd\ *adj* **1** : leaning to one side **2** : not symmetrical —**lop·sid·ed·ly** *adv* —**lop·sid·ed·ness** *n*

lo·qua·cious \lō'kwāshəs\ *adj* : very talkative —**lo·quac·i·ty** \-'kwasətē\ *n*

lord \'lȯrd\ *n* **1** : one with authority over others **2** : British nobleman

lord·ly \-lē\ *adj* **-li·er; -est** : haughty

lord·ship \-,ship\ *n* : rank of a lord

Lord's Supper *n* : Communion

lore \'lȯr\ *n* : traditional knowledge

lose \'lüz\ *vb* **lost** \'lȯst\; **los·ing** \'lüziŋ\ **1** : have pass from one's possession **2** : be deprived of **3** : waste **4** : be defeated in **5** : fail to keep to or hold **6** : get rid of —**los·er** *n*

loss \'lȯs\ *n* **1** : something lost **2** *pl* : killed, wounded, or captured soldiers **3** : failure to win

lost \'lȯst\ *adj* **1** : not used, won, or claimed **2** : unable to find the way

lot \'lät\ *n* **1** : object used in deciding something by chance **2** : share **3** : fate **4** : plot of land **5** : much

loth \'lōth, 'lōth\ *var of* LOATH

lo·tion \'lōshən\ *n* : liquid to rub on the skin

lot·tery \'lätərē\ *n, pl* **-ter·ies** : drawing of lots with prizes going to winners

lo·tus \'lōtəs\ *n* **1** : legendary fruit that causes forgetfulness **2** : water lily

loud \'laúd\ *adj* **1** : high in volume of sound **2** : noisy **3** : obtrusive in color or pattern —**loud** *adv* —**loud·ly** *adv* —**loud·ness** *n*

loud·speak·er *n* : device that amplifies sound

lounge \'laúnj\ *vb* **lounged; loung·ing** : act or move lazily ~ *n* : room with comfortable furniture

lour \'laúər\ *var of* LOWER

louse \'laús\ *n, pl* **lice** \'līs\ : parasitic wingless usu. flat insect

lousy \'laúzē\ *adj* **lous·i·er; -est 1** : infested with lice **2** : not good —**lous·i·ly** *adv* —**lous·i·ness** *n*

lout \'laút\ *n* : stupid awkward person —**lout·ish** *adj* —**lout·ish·ly** *adv*

lou·ver, lou·vre \'lüvər\ *n* : opening having parallel slanted slats for ventilation or such a slat

love \'ləv\ *n* **1** : strong affection **2** : warm attachment **3** : beloved person ~ *vb* **loved; lov·ing 1** : feel affection for **2** : enjoy greatly —**lov·able** \-əbəl\ *adj* —**love·less** *adj* —**lov·er** *n* —**lov·ing·ly** *adv*

love·lorn \-,lȯrn\ *adj* : deprived of love or of a lover

love·ly \'ləvlē\ *adj* **-li·er; -est** : beautiful —**love·li·ness** *n* —**lovely** *adv*

¹low \'lō\ *vb or n* : moo

²low *adj* **low·er; low·est 1** : not high or tall **2** : below normal level **3** : not loud **4** : humble **5** : sad **6** : less than usual **7** : falling short of a standard **8** : unfavorable ~ *n* **1** : something low **2** : automobile gear giving the slowest speed —**low** *adv* —**low·ness** *n*

low·brow \'lō,braú\ *n* : person with little taste or intellectual interest

¹low·er \'laúər\ *vb* **1** : scowl **2** : become dark and threatening

²low·er \'lōər\ *adj* : relatively low (as in rank)

³low·er \'lōər\ *vb* **1** : drop **2** : let descend **3** : reduce in amount

low·land \'lōlənd, -,land\ *n* : low flat country

low·ly \'lōlē\ *adj* **-li·er; -est 1** : humble **2** : low in rank —**low·li·ness** *n*

loy·al \'lȯiəl\ *adj* : faithful to a country, cause, or friend —**loy·al·ist** *n* —**loy·al·ly** *adv* —**loy·al·ty** \'lȯiəltē\ *n*

loz·enge \'läzənj\ *n* : small medicated candy

lu·bri·cant \'lübrikənt\ *n* : material (as grease) to reduce friction

lu·bri·cate \-,kāt\ *vb* **-cat·ed; -cat·ing** : apply a lubricant to —**lu·bri·ca·tion** \,lübrə'kāshən\ *n* —**lu·bri·ca·tor** \'lübrə,kātər\ *n*

lu·cid \'lüsəd\ *adj* **1** : mentally sound **2** : easily understood —**lu·cid·i·ty** \lü-'sidətē\ *n* —**lu·cid·ly** *adv* —**lu·cid·ness** *n*

luck \'lək\ *n* **1** : chance **2** : good fortune —**luck·i·ly** *adv* —**luck·i·ness** *n* —**luck·less** *adj* —**lucky** *adj*

lu·cra·tive \'lükrətiv\ *adj* : profitable —**lu·cra·tive·ly** *adv* —**lu·cra·tive·ness** *n*

lu·di·crous \'lüdəkrəs\ *adj* : comically

ridiculous —lu·di·crous·ly adv —lu·di·crous·ness n

lug \'ləg\ vb -gg- : drag or carry laboriously

lug·gage \'ləgij\ n : baggage

lu·gu·bri·ous \lu̇'gübrēəs\ adj : mournful often to an exaggerated degree —lu·gu·bri·ous·ly adv —lu·gu·bri·ous·ness n

luke·warm \'lük'wȯrm\ adj 1 : moderately warm 2 : not enthusiastic

lull \'ləl\ vb : make or become quiet or relaxed ~ vb : temporary calm

lul·la·by \'lələ,bī\ n, pl -bies : song to lull children to sleep

lum·ba·go \,ləm'bāgō\ n : rheumatic back pain

lum·ber \'ləmbər\ n : timber dressed for use ~ vb : cut logs —lum·ber·man n —lum·ber·yard n

lum·ber·jack \-,jak\ n : logger

lu·mi·nary \'lümə,nerē\ n, pl -nar·ies : very famous person

lu·mi·nes·cence \,lümə'nes³ns\ n : low-temperature emission of light —lu·mi·nes·cent \-³nt\ adj

lu·mi·nous \'lümənəs\ adj : emitting light —lu·mi·nance \-nəns\ n —lu·mi·nos·i·ty \,lümə'näsətē\ n —lu·mi·nous·ly adv

lump \'ləmp\ n 1 : mass of irregular shape 2 : abnormal swelling ~ vb : heap together —lump·ish adj —lumpy adj

lu·na·cy \'lünəsē\ n, pl -cies : state of insanity

lu·nar \'lünər\ adj : of the moon

lu·na·tic \'lünə,tik\ adj : insane —lunatic n

lunch \'lənch\ n : noon meal ~ vb : eat lunch

lun·cheon \'lənchən\ n : usu. formal lunch

lung \'ləŋ\ n : breathing organ in the chest —lunged \'ləŋd\ adj

lunge \'lənj\ n 1 : sudden thrust 2 : sudden move forward —lunge vb

lurch \'lərch\ n : sudden swaying —lurch vb

lure \'lu̇r\ n 1 : something that attracts 2 : artificial fish bait ~ vb lured; lur·ing : attract

lu·rid \'lu̇rəd\ adj 1 : gruesome 2 : sensational —lu·rid·ly adv

lurk \'lərk\ vb : lie in wait

lus·cious \'ləshəs\ adj 1 : pleasingly sweet in taste or smell 2 : sensually appealing —lus·cious·ly adv —lus·cious·ness n

lush \'ləsh\ adj : covered with abundant growth

lust \'ləst\ n 1 : intense sexual desire 2 : intense longing —lust vb —lust·ful adj

lus·ter, lus·tre \'ləstər\ n 1 : brightness from reflected light 2 : magnificence —lus·ter·less adj —lus·trous \-trəs\ adj

lusty \'ləstē\ adj lust·i·er; -est : full of vitality —lust·i·ly adv —lust·i·ness n

lute \'lüt\ n : pear-shaped stringed instrument —lute·nist, lu·ta·nist \'lüt³nist\ n

lux·u·ri·ant \,ləg'zhu̇rēənt, ,lək'shu̇r-\ adj 1 : growing plentifully 2 : rich and varied —lux·u·ri·ance \-ēəns\ n —lux·u·ri·ant·ly adv

lux·u·ri·ate \-ē,āt\ vb -at·ed; -at·ing : revel

lux·u·ry \'ləkshərē, 'ləgzh-\ n, pl -ries 1 : great comfort 2 : something adding to pleasure or comfort —lux·u·ri·ous \,ləg'zhu̇rēəs, ,lək'shu̇r-\ adj —lux·u·ri·ous·ly adv

-ly \lē\ adv suffix 1 : in a specified way 2 : from a specified point of view

ly·ce·um \lī'sēəm, 'līsē-\ n : hall for public lectures

lye \'lī\ n : caustic alkaline substance

lying pres part of LIE

lymph \'limf\ n : bodily liquid consisting chiefly of blood plasma and white blood cells —lym·phat·ic \lim'fatik\ adj

lynch \'linch\ vb : put to death by mob action —lynch·er n

lynx \'links\ n, pl lynx or lynx·es : wildcat

lyre \'līr\ n : ancient Greek stringed instrument

lyr·ic \'lirik\ adj 1 : suitable for singing 2 : expressing direct personal emotion ~ n 1 : lyric poem 2 pl : words of a song —lyr·i·cal \-ikəl\ adj

M

m \\'em\\ *n*, *pl* **m's** *or* **ms** \\'emz\\ : 13th letter of the alphabet

ma'am \\'mam\\ *n* : madam

ma·ca·bre \\mə'käb, -'käbər, -'käbrə\\ *adj* : gruesome

mac·ad·am \\mə'kadəm\\ *n* : pavement of cemented broken stone —**mac·ad·am·ize** \\-,īz\\ *vb*

mac·a·ro·ni \\,makə'rōnē\\ *n* : tube-shaped pasta

mac·a·roon \\,makə'rün\\ *n* : cookie of ground almonds or coconut

ma·caw \\mə'kó\\ *n* : large long-tailed parrot

¹mace \\'mās\\ *n* **1** : heavy spiked club **2** : ornamental staff as a symbol of authority

²mace *n* : spice from the fibrous coating of the nutmeg

ma·chete \\mə'shetē\\ *n* : large heavy knife

mach·i·na·tion \\,makə'nāshən, ,mashə-\\ *n* : plot or scheme —**mach·i·nate** \\'makə,nāt, 'mash-\\ *vb*

ma·chine \\mə'shēn\\ *n* : combination of mechanical or electrical parts ~ *vb* **-chined; -chin·ing** : modify by machine-operated tools —**ma·chin·able** *adj* —**ma·chin·ery** \\-ərē\\ *n* —**ma·chin·ist** *n*

mack·er·el \\'makərəl\\ *n*, *pl* **-el** *or* **-els** : No. Atlantic food fish

mack·i·naw \\'makə,nó\\ *n* : short heavy plaid coat

mac·ra·mé \\,makrə'mā\\ *n* : coarse lace or fringe made by knotting

mac·ro \\'makrō\\ *adj* : very large

mac·ro·cosm \\'makrə,käzəm\\ *n* : universe

mad \\'mad\\ *adj* **-dd-** **1** : insane or rabid **2** : rash and foolish **3** : angry **4** : carried away by enthusiasm —**mad·den** \\'mad°n\\ *vb* —**mad·den·ing·ly** \\'mad°niŋlē\\ *adv* —**mad·ly** *adv* —**mad·ness** *n*

mad·am \\'madəm\\ *n*, *pl* **mes·dames** \\mā'däm\\ —used in polite address to a woman

~dame \\mə'dam, *before a surname* ~o 'madəm\\ *n*, *pl* **mes·dames** \\mā-'däm\\ —used as a title for a woman not of English-speaking nationality

mad·cap \\'mad,kap\\ *adj* : wild or zany —**madcap** *n*

made *past of* MAKE

Ma·dei·ra \\mə'dirə\\ *n* : amber-colored dessert wine

ma·de·moi·selle \\,madmwə'zel, -mə-'zel\\ *n*, *pl* **ma·de·moi·selles** \\-'zelz\\ *or* **mes·de·moi·selles** \\,mādmwə'zel\\ : an unmarried girl or woman —used as a title for a woman esp. of French nationality

mad·house *n* **1** : insane asylum **2** : place of great uproar or confusion

mad·man \\-,man, -mən\\ *n* : lunatic

mad·ri·gal \\'madrigəl\\ *n* : elaborate song for several voice parts

mad·wom·an \\'mad,wùmən\\ *n* : woman who is insane

mael·strom \\'mälstrəm\\ *n* **1** : whirlpool **2** : tumult

mae·stro \\'mīstrō\\ *n*, *pl* **-stros** *or* **-stri** \\-,strē\\ : eminent composer or conductor

Ma·fia \\'mäfēə\\ *n* : secret criminal organization

ma·fi·o·so \\,mäfē'ōsō\\ *n*, *pl* **-si** \\-sē\\ : member of the Mafia

mag·a·zine \\'magə,zēn\\ *n* **1** : storehouse **2** : publication issued at regular intervals **3** : cartridge container in a gun

ma·gen·ta \\mə'jentə\\ *n* : deep purplish red color

mag·got \\'magət\\ *n* : wormlike fly larva —**mag·goty** *adj*

mag·ic \\'majik\\ *n* **1** : art of using supernatural powers **2** : extraordinary power or influence **3** : sleight of hand —**magic, mag·i·cal** \\-ikəl\\ *adj* —**mag·i·cal·ly** *adv* —**ma·gi·cian** \\mə-'jishən\\ *n*

mag·is·te·ri·al \\,majə'stirēəl\\ *adj* **1** : authoritative **2** : relating to a magistrate

mag·is·trate \\'majə,strāt\\ *n* : judge —**mag·is·tra·cy** \\-strəsē\\ *n*

mag·ma \\'magmə\\ *n* : molten rock

mag·nan·i·mous \\mag'nanəməs\\ *adj* : noble or generous —**mag·na·nim-**

i•ty \,magnə′nimətē\ n —**mag•nan•i•mous•ly** adv —**mag•nan•i•mous•ness** n

mag•ne•sia \mag′nēzhə, -shə\ n : oxide of magnesium used as a laxative

mag•ne•sium \mag′nēzēəm, -zhəm\ n : silver-white metallic chemical element

mag•net \′magnət\ n 1 : body that attracts iron 2 : something that attracts —**mag•net•ic** \mag′netik\ adj —**mag•net•i•cal•ly** \-iklē\ adv —**mag•ne•tism** \′magnə,tizəm\ n

mag•ne•tite \′magnə,tīt\ n : black iron ore

mag•ne•tize \′magnə,tīz\ vb -**tized; -tiz•ing** 1 : attract like a magnet 2 : give magnetic properties to —**mag•ne•tiz•able** adj —**mag•ne•ti•za•tion** \,magnətə′zāshən\ n —**mag•ne•tiz•er** n

mag•nif•i•cent \mag′nifəsənt\ adj : splendid —**mag•nif•i•cence** \-səns\ n —**mag•nif•i•cent•ly** adv

mag•ni•fy \′magnə,fī\ vb -**fied; -fy•ing** 1 : intensify 2 : enlarge —**mag•ni•fi•ca•tion** \,magnəfə′kāshən\ n —**mag•ni•fi•er** \′magnə,fīər\ n

mag•ni•tude \′magnə,tüd, -,tyüd\ n 1 : greatness of size or extent 2 : quantity

mag•no•lia \mag′nōlyə\ n : shrub with large fragrant flowers

mag•pie \′mag,pī\ n : long-tailed black-and-white bird

ma•hog•a•ny \mə′hägənē\ n, pl -**nies** : tropical evergreen tree or its reddish brown wood

maid \′mād\ n 1 : unmarried young woman 2 : female servant

maid•en \′mādᵊn\ n : unmarried young woman ~ adj 1 : unmarried 2 : first —**maid•en•hood** \-,hůd\ n —**maid•en•ly** adj

maid•en•hair \-,har\ n : fern with delicate feathery fronds

¹**mail** \′māl\ n 1 : something sent or carried in the postal system 2 : postal system ~ vb : send by mail —**mail•box** n —**mail•man** \-,man, -mən\ n

²**mail** n : armor of metal links or plates

maim \′mām\ vb : seriously wound or disfigure

main \′mān\ n 1 : force 2 : ocean 3 : principal pipe, duct, or circuit of a utility system ~ adj : chief —**main•ly** adv

main•frame \′mān,frām\ n : large fast computer

main•land \′mān,land, -lənd\ n : part of a country on a continent

main•stay n : chief support

main•stream n : prevailing current or direction of activity or influence —**mainstream** adj

main•tain \mān′tān\ vb 1 : keep in an existing state (as of repair) 2 : sustain 3 : declare —**main•tain•abil•i•ty** \-,tānə′bilətē\ n —**main•tain•able** \-′tānəbəl\ adj —**main•te•nance** \′māntᵊnəns\ n

mai•tre d'hô•tel \,mātrədō′tel, ,me-\ n : head of a dining room staff

maize \′māz\ n : corn

maj•es•ty \′majəstē\ n, pl -**ties** 1 : sovereign power or dignity —used as a title 2 : grandeur or splendor —**ma•jes•tic** \mə′jestik\ adj —**ma•jes•ti•cal•ly** \-tiklē\ adv

ma•jor \′mājər\ adj 1 : larger or greater 2 : noteworthy or conspicuous ~ n 1 : commissioned officer (as in the army) ranking next below a lieutenant colonel 2 : main field of study ~ vb -**jored; -jor•ing** : pursue an academic major

ma•jor•do•mo \,mājər′dōmō\ n, pl -**mos** : head steward

major general n : commissioned officer (as in the army) ranking next below a lieutenant general

ma•jor•i•ty \mə′jórətē\ n, pl -**ties** 1 : age of full civil rights 2 : quantity more than half

make \′māk\ vb **made** \′mād\; **mak•ing** 1 : cause to exist, occur, or appear 2 : fashion or manufacture 3 : formulate in the mind 4 : constitute 5 : prepare 6 : cause to be or become 7 : carry out or perform 8 : compel 9 : gain 10 : have an effect —used with for ~ n : brand —**mak•er** n —**make do** vb : get along with what is available —**make good** vb 1 : repay 2 : succeed —**make out** vb 1 : draw up or write 2 : discern or understand 3 : fare —**make up** vb 1 : invent 2 : become reconciled 3 : compensate for

make-be•lieve n : a pretending to believe ~ adj : imagined or pretended

make•shift n : temporary substitute —**makeshift** adj

make•up \-,əp\ n 1 : way in which something is constituted 2 : cosmetics

mal·ad·just·ed \,malə'jəstəd\ *adj* : poorly adjusted (as to one's environment) —**mal·ad·just·ment** \-'jəstmənt\ *n*

mal·adroit \,malə'droit\ *adj* : clumsy or inept

mal·a·dy \'malədē\ *n, pl* **-dies** : disease or disorder

mal·aise \mə'lāz, ma-\ *n* : sense of being unwell

mal·a·mute \'malə,myüt\ *n* : powerful heavy-coated dog

mal·a·prop·ism \'malə,präp,izəm\ *n* : humorous misuse of a word

ma·lar·ia \mə'lerēə\ *n* : disease transmitted by a mosquito —**ma·lar·i·al** \-əl\ *adj*

ma·lar·key \mə'lärkē\ *n* : foolishness

mal·con·tent \,malkən'tent\ *n* : discontented person —**malcontent** *adj*

male \'māl\ *adj* **1** : relating to the sex that performs a fertilizing function **2** : masculine ~ *n* : male individual —**male·ness** *n*

male·dic·tion \,malə'dikshən\ *n* : curse

male·fac·tor \'malə,faktər\ *n* : one who commits an offense esp. against the law

ma·lef·i·cent \mə'lefəsənt\ *adj* : harmful

ma·lev·o·lent \mə'levələnt\ *adj* : malicious or spiteful —**ma·lev·o·lence** \-ləns\ *n*

mal·fea·sance \mal'fēzⁿns\ *n* : misconduct by a public official

mal·for·ma·tion \,malfór'māshən\ *n* : distortion or faulty formation —**mal·formed** \mal'fórmd\ *adj*

mal·func·tion \mal'fəŋkshən\ *vb* : fail to operate properly —**malfunction** *n*

mal·ice \'maləs\ *n* : desire to cause pain or injury to another —**ma·li·cious** \mə'lishəs\ *adj* —**ma·li·cious·ly** *adv*

ma·lign \mə'līn\ *adj* **1** : wicked **2** : malignant ~ *vb* : speak evil of

ma·lig·nant \mə'lignənt\ *adj* **1** : harmful **2** : likely to cause death —**ma·lig·nan·cy** \-nənsē\ *n* —**ma·lig·nant·ly** *adv* —**ma·lig·ni·ty** \-nətē\ *n*

ma·lin·ger \mə'liŋgər\ *vb* : pretend illness to avoid duty —**ma·lin·ger·er** *n*

mall \'mól\ *n* **1** : shaded promenade **2** : concourse providing access to rows of shops

mal·lard \'malərd\ *n, pl* **-lard** *or* **-lards** : common wild duck

mal·lea·ble \'malēəbəl\ *adj* **1** : easily shaped **2** : adaptable —**mal·le·a·bil·i·ty** \,malēə'bilətē\ *n*

mal·let \'malət\ *n* : hammerlike tool

mal·nour·ished \mal'nərisht\ *adj* : poorly nourished

mal·nu·tri·tion \,malnú'trishən, -nyü-\ *n* : inadequate nutrition

mal·odor·ous \mal'ōdərəs\ *adj* : foulsmelling —**mal·odor·ous·ly** *adv* —**mal·odor·ous·ness** *n*

mal·prac·tice \-'praktəs\ *n* : failure of professional duty

malt \'mólt\ *n* : sprouted grain used in brewing

mal·treat \mal'trēt\ *vb* : treat badly —**mal·treat·ment** *n*

ma·ma, mam·ma \'mämə\ *n* : mother

mam·mal \'maməl\ *n* : warm-blooded vertebrate animal that nourishes its young with milk —**mam·ma·li·an** \mə'mālēən, ma-\ *adj or n*

mam·ma·ry \'mamərē\ *adj* : relating to the milk-secreting glands (**mammary glands**) of mammals

mam·mo·gram \'mamə,gram\ *n* : X-ray photograph of the breasts

mam·moth \'maməth\ *n* : large hairy extinct elephant ~ *adj* : enormous

man \'man\ *n, pl* **men** \'men\ **1** : human being **2** : adult male **3** : mankind ~ *vb* **-nn-** : supply with people for working —**man·hood** *n* —**man·hunt** *n* —**man·like** *adj* —**man·li·ness** *n* —**man·ly** *adj or adv* —**man·made** *adj* —**man·nish** *adj* —**man·nish·ly** *adv* —**man·nish·ness** *n* —**man-size,** **man-sized** *adj*

man·a·cle \'manikəl\ *n* : shackle for the hands or wrists —**manacle** *vb*

man·age \'manij\ *vb* **-aged; -ag·ing** **1** : control **2** : direct or carry on business or affairs **3** : cope —**man·age·abil·i·ty** \,manijə'bilətē\ *n* — **man·age·able** \'manijəbəl\ *adj* —**man·age·able·ness** *n* —**man·age·ably** \-blē\ *adv* —**man·age·ment** \'manijmənt\ *n* —**man·ag·er** \'manijər\ *n* —**man·a·ge·ri·al** \,manə'jirēəl\ *adj*

man·da·rin \'mandərən\ *n* : Chinese imperial official

man·date \'man,dāt\ *n* : authoritative command

man·da·to·ry \'mandə,tórē\ *adj* : obligatory

man·di·ble \'mandəbəl\ *n* : lower jaw —**man·dib·u·lar** \man'dibyələr\ *adj*

man·do·lin \,mandə'lin, 'mand°lən\ *n* : stringed musical instrument

man·drake \'man,drāk\ *n* : herb with a large forked root

mane \'mān\ *n* : animal's neck hair — **maned** \'mānd\ *adj*

ma·neu·ver \mə'nüvər, -'nyü-\ *n* **1** : planned movement of troops or ships **2** : military training exercise **3** : clever or skillful move or action — **maneuver** *vb* — **ma·neu·ver·abil·i·ty** \-,nüvərə'bilətē, -,nyü-\ *n*

man·ful \'manfəl\ *adj* : courageous — **man·ful·ly** *adv*

man·ga·nese \'maŋgə,nēz, -,nēs\ *n* : gray metallic chemical element

mange \'mānj\ *n* : skin disease of domestic animals — **mangy** \'mānjē\ *adj*

man·ger \'mānjər\ *n* : feeding trough for livestock

man·gle \'maŋgəl\ *vb* **-gled; -gling 1** : mutilate **2** : bungle — **man·gler** *n*

man·go \'maŋgō\ *n, pl* **-goes** : juicy yellowish red tropical fruit

man·grove \'man,grōv, 'maŋ-\ *n* : tropical tree growing in salt water

man·han·dle *vb* : handle roughly

man·hole *n* : entry to a sewer

ma·nia \'mānēə, -nyə\ *n* **1** : insanity marked by uncontrollable emotion or excitement **2** : excessive enthusiasm — **ma·ni·ac** \-nē,ak\ *n* — **ma·ni·a·cal** \mə'nīəkəl\ *adj* — **man·ic** \'manik\ *adj or n*

man·i·cure \'manə,kyùr\ *n* : treatment for the fingernails ~ *vb* **-cured; -curing 1** : do manicure work on **2** : trim precisely — **man·i·cur·ist** \-,kyùrist\ *n*

¹man·i·fest \'manə,fest\ *adj* : clear to the senses or to the mind ~ *vb* : make evident — **man·i·fes·ta·tion** \,manəfə'stāshən\ *n* — **man·i·fest·ly** *adv*

²manifest *n* : invoice of cargo or list of passengers

man·i·fes·to \,manə'festō\ *n, pl* **-tos** or **-toes** : public declaration of policy or views

man·i·fold \'manə,fōld\ *adj* : marked by diversity or variety ~ *n* : pipe fitting with several outlets for connections

ma·nila paper \mə'nilə-\ *n* : durable brownish paper

ma·nip·u·late \mə'nipyə,lāt\ *vb* **-lat·ed; -lat·ing 1** : treat or operate manually or mechanically **2** : influence esp. by cunning — **ma·nip·u·la·tion** \mə,nipyə'lāshən\ *n* — **ma·nip·u·la·tive** \-'nipyə,lātiv, -lətiv\ *adj* — **ma·nip·u·la·tor** \-,lātər\ *n*

man·kind \'man'kīnd\ *n* : human race

man·na \'manə\ *n* : something valuable that comes unexpectedly

manned \'mand\ *adj* : carrying or performed by a man

man·ne·quin \'manikən\ *n* : dummy used to display clothes

man·ner \'manər\ *n* **1** : kind **2** : usual way of acting **3** : artistic method **4** *pl* : social conduct

man·nered \-ərd\ *adj* **1** : having manners of a specified kind **2** : artificial

man·ner·ism \'manə,rizəm\ *n* : individual peculiarity of action

man·ner·ly \-lē\ *adj* : polite — **man·ner·li·ness** *n* — **mannerly** *adv*

man–of–war \,manə'wȯr, -əv'wȯr\ *n, pl* **men–of–war** \,men-\ : warship

man·or \'manər\ *n* : country estate — **ma·no·ri·al** \mə'nōrēəl\ *adj*

man·pow·er *n* : supply of people available for service

man·sard \'man,särd\ *n* : roof with two slopes on all sides and the lower slope the steeper

manse \'mans\ *n* : parsonage

man·ser·vant *n, pl* **men·ser·vants** : a male servant

man·sion \'manchən\ *n* : very big house

man·slaugh·ter *n* : unintentional killing of a person

man·tel \'mantəl\ *n* : shelf above a fireplace

man·tis \'mantəs\ *n, pl* **-tis·es** or **-tes** \'man,tēz\ : large green insect-eating insect with stout forelegs

man·tle \'mantəl\ *n* **1** : sleeveless cloak **2** : something that covers, enfolds, or envelops — **mantle** *vb*

man·tra \'mantrə\ *n* : mystical chant

man·u·al \'manyəwəl\ *adj* : involving the hands or physical force ~ *n* : handbook — **man·u·al·ly** *adv*

man·u·fac·ture \,manyə'fakchər, ,manə-\ *n* : process of making wares by hand or by machinery ~ *vb* **-tured; -tur·ing** : make from raw materials — **man·u·fac·tur·er** *n*

ma·nure \mə'nùr, -'nyùr\ *n* : animal excrement used as fertilizer

manu·script \'manyə,skript\ *n* **1** : something written or typed **2** : document submitted for publication

many \'menē\ *adj* **more** \'mȯr\; **most** \'mōst\ : consisting of a large number — **many** *n or pron*

map \'map\ *n* : representation of a geographical area ~ *vb* **-pp- 1** : make a map of 2 : plan in detail —**map·pa·ble** \-əbəl\ *adj* —**map·per** *n*

ma·ple \'māpəl\ *n* : tree with hard light-colored wood

mar \'mär\ *vb* -**rr**- : damage

mar·a·schi·no \,marə'skēnō, -'shē-\ *n, pl* -**nos** : preserved cherry

mar·a·thon \'marə,thän\ *n* 1 : long-distance race 2 : test of endurance —**mar·a·thon·er** \-,thänər\ *n*

ma·raud \mə'ród\ *vb* : roam about in search of plunder —**ma·raud·er** *n*

mar·ble \'märbəl\ *n* 1 : crystallized limestone 2 : small glass ball used in a children's game (**marbles**)

mar·bling \-bəliŋ\ *n* : intermixture of fat and lean in meat

march \'märch\ *vb* : move with regular steps or in a purposeful manner ~ *n* 1 : distance covered in a march 2 : measured stride 3 : forward movement 4 : music for marching —**march·er** *n*

March *n* : 3d month of the year having 31 days

mar·chio·ness \'märshənəs\ *n* : woman holding the rank of a marquess

Mar·di Gras \'märdē,grä\ *n* : Tuesday before the beginning of Lent often observed with parades and merrymaking

mare \'mar\ *n* : female horse

mar·ga·rine \'märjərən\ *n* : butter substitute made usu. from vegetable oils

mar·gin \'märjən\ *n* 1 : edge 2 : spare amount, measure, or degree

mar·gin·al \-jənəl\ *adj* 1 : relating to or situated at a border or margin 2 : close to the lower limit of acceptability —**mar·gin·al·ly** *adv*

mari·gold \'marə,gōld\ *n* : garden plant with showy flower heads

mari·jua·na \,marə'wänə, -'hwä-\ *n* : intoxicating drug obtained from the hemp plant

ma·ri·na \mə'rēnə\ *n* : place for mooring pleasure boats

mari·nate \'marə,nāt\ *vb* -**nat·ed**; -**nat·ing** : soak in a savory sauce

ma·rine \mə'rēn\ *adj* 1 : relating to the sea 2 : relating to marines ~ *n* : infantry soldier associated with a navy

mar·i·ner \'marənər\ *n* : sailor

mari·o·nette \,marē∂'net\ *n* : puppet

mar·i·tal \'marət∂l\ *adj* : relating to marriage

mar·i·time \'marə,tīm\ *adj* : relating to the sea or commerce on the sea

mar·jo·ram \'märjərəm\ *n* : aromatic mint used as a seasoning

mark \'märk\ *n* 1 : something aimed at 2 : something (as a line) designed to record position 3 : visible sign 4 : written symbol 5 : grade 6 : lasting impression 7 : blemish ~ *vb* 1 : designate or set apart by a mark or make a mark on 2 : characterize 3 : remark —**mark·er** *n*

marked \'märkt\ *adj* : noticeable —**mark·ed·ly** \'märkədlē\ *adv*

mar·ket \'märkət\ *n* 1 : buying and selling of goods or the place this happens 2 : demand for commodities 3 : store ~ *vb* : sell —**mar·ket·able** *adj*

mar·ket·place *n* 1 : market 2 : world of trade or economic activity

marks·man \'märksmən\ *n* : good shooter —**marks·man·ship** *n*

mar·lin \'märlən\ *n* : large oceanic fish

mar·ma·lade \'märmə,lād\ *n* : jam with pieces of fruit and rind

mar·mo·set \'märmə,set\ *n* : small bushy-tailed monkey

mar·mot \'märmət\ *n* : burrowing rodent

¹**ma·roon** \mə'rün\ *vb* : isolate without hope of escape

²**maroon** *n* : dark red color

mar·quee \mär'kē\ *n* : canopy over an entrance

mar·quess \'märkwəs\, **mar·quis** \'märkwəs, mär'kē\ *n, pl* -**quess·es** *or* -**quis·es** *or* -**quis** : British noble ranking next below a duke

mar·quise \mär'kēz\ *n, pl* **mar·quises** \-'kēz, -'kēzəz\ : marchioness

mar·riage \'marij\ *n* 1 : state of being married 2 : wedding ceremony —**mar·riage·able** *adj*

mar·row \'marō\ *n* : soft tissue in the cavity of bone

mar·ry \'marē\ *vb* -**ried**; -**ry·ing** 1 : join as husband and wife 2 : take or give in marriage —**mar·ried** *adj or n*

marsh \'märsh\ *n* : soft wet land —**marshy** *adj*

mar·shal \'märshəl\ *n* 1 : leader of ceremony 2 : usu. high military or administrative officer ~ *vb* -**shaled** *or* -**shalled**; -**shal·ing** *or* -**shal·ling** 1 : arrange in order, rank, or position 2 : lead with ceremony

marsh·mal·low \'märsh,melō, -,malō\ *n* : spongy candy

mar·su·pi·al \mär'süpēəl\ *n* : mammal

that nourishes young in an abdominal pouch —**marsupial** *adj*

mart \'märt\ *n* : market

mar·ten \'märt³n\ *n, pl* **-ten** *or* **-tens** : weasellike mammal with soft fur

mar·tial \'märshəl\ *adj* **1** : relating to war or an army **2** : warlike

mar·tin \'märt³n\ *n* : small swallow

mar·ti·net \,märt³n'et\ *n* : strict disciplinarian

mar·tyr \'märtər\ *n* : one who dies or makes a great sacrifice for a cause ~ *vb* : make a martyr of —**mar·tyr·dom** \-dəm\ *n*

mar·vel \'märvəl\ *vb* **-veled** *or* **-velled**; **-vel·ing** *or* **-vel·ling** : feel surprise or wonder ~ *n* : something amazing —**mar·vel·ous, mar·vel·lous** \'märvələs\ *adj* —**mar·vel·ous·ly** *adv* —**mar·vel·ous·ness** *n*

Marx·ism \'märk,sizəm\ *n* : political and social principles of Karl Marx —**Marx·ist** \-sist\ *n or adj*

mas·ca·ra \mas'karə\ *n* : eye cosmetic

mas·cot \'mas,kät, -kət\ *n* : one believed to bring good luck

mas·cu·line \'maskyələn\ *adj* : relating to the male sex —**mas·cu·lin·i·ty** \,maskyə'linətē\ *n*

mash \'mash\ *n* **1** : crushed steeped grain for fermenting **2** : soft pulpy mass ~ *vb* **1** : reduce to a pulpy mass **2** : smash —**mash·er** *n*

mask \'mask\ *n* : disguise for the face ~ *vb* **1** : disguise **2** : cover to protect —**mask·er** *n*

mas·och·ism \'masə,kizəm, 'maz-\ *n* : pleasure in being abused —**mas·och·ist** \-kist\ *n* —**mas·och·is·tic** \,ma-sə'kistik, ,maz-\ *adj*

ma·son \'mās³n\ *n* : workman who builds with stone or brick —**ma·son·ry** \-rē\ *n*

mas·quer·ade \,maskə'rād\ *n* **1** : costume party **2** : disguise ~ *vb* **-ad·ed**; **-ad·ing 1** : disguise oneself **2** : take part in a costume party —**mas·quer·ad·er** *n*

mass \'mas\ *n* **1** : large amount of matter or number of things **2** : expanse or magnitude **3** : great body of people — usu. pl. ~ *vb* : form into a mass — **mass·less** \-ləs\ *adj* —**massy** *adj*

Mass *n* : worship service of the Roman Catholic Church

mas·sa·cre \'masikər\ *n* : wholesale slaughter —**massacre** *vb*

mas·sage \mə'säzh, -'säj\ *n* : a rubbing of the body —**massage** *vb*

mas·seur \ma'sər\ *n* : man who massages

mas·seuse \-'sœz, -'süz\ *n* : woman who massages

mas·sive \'masiv\ *adj* **1** : being a large mass **2** : large in scope —**mas·sive·ly** *adv* —**mas·sive·ness** *n*

mast \'mast\ *n* : tall pole esp. for supporting sails —**mast·ed** *adj*

mas·ter \'mastər\ *n* **1** : male teacher **2** : holder of an academic degree between a bachelor's and a doctor's **3** : one highly skilled **4** : one in authority ~ *vb* **1** : subdue **2** : become proficient in —**mas·ter·ful** \-fəl\ *adj* —**mas·ter·ful·ly** *adv* —**mas·ter·ly** *adj* —**mas·tery** \'mastərē\ *n*

master chief petty officer *n* : petty officer of the highest rank in the navy

master gunnery sergeant *n* : noncommissioned officer in the marine corps ranking above a master sergeant

mas·ter·piece \'mastər,pēs\ *n* : great piece of work

master sergeant *n* **1** : noncommissioned officer in the army ranking next below a sergeant major **2** : noncommissioned officer in the air force ranking next below a senior master sergeant **3** : noncommissioned officer in the marine corps ranking next below a master gunnery sergeant

mas·ter·work *n* : masterpiece

mas·tic \'mastik\ *n* : pasty glue

mas·ti·cate \'mastə,kāt\ *vb* **-cat·ed**; **-cat·ing** : chew —**mas·ti·ca·tion** \,mastə'kāshən\ *n*

mas·tiff \'mastəf\ *n* : large dog

mast·odon \'mastə,dän\ *n* : extinct elephantlike animal

mas·toid \'mas,tóid\ *n* : bone behind the ear —**mastoid** *adj*

mas·tur·ba·tion \,mastər'bāshən\ *n* : stimulation of sex organs by hand —**mas·tur·bate** \'mastər,bāt\ *vb*

¹mat \'mat\ *n* **1** : coarse woven or plaited fabric **2** : mass of tangled strands **3** : thick pad ~ *vb* **-tt-** : form into a mat

²mat *vb* **-tt- 1** : make matte **2** : provide (a picture) with a mat ~ *or* **matt** *or* **matte** *n* : border around a picture

³mat *var of* MATTE

mat·a·dor \'matə,dór\ *n* : bullfighter

¹match \'mach\ *n* **1** : one equal to an-

other 2 : one able to cope with another
3 : suitable pairing 4 : game 5
: marriage ~ *vb* 1 : set in competition
2 : marry 3 : be or provide the equal
of 4 : fit or go together —**match·less**
adj —**match·mak·er** *n*

²**match** *n* : piece of wood or paper material with a combustible tip

mate \'māt\ *n* 1 : companion 2
: subordinate officer on a ship 3 : one
of a pair ~ *vb* **mat·ed; mat·ing** 1 : fit
together 2 : come together as a pair 3
: copulate

ma·te·ri·al \mə'tirēəl\ *adj* 1 : natural 2
: relating to matter 3 : important 4 : of
a physical or worldly nature ~ *n*
: stuff something is made of —**ma·te·ri·al·ly** *adv*

ma·te·ri·al·ism \mə'tirēə,lizəm\ *n* 1
: theory that matter is the only reality
2 : preoccupation with material and
not spiritual things —**ma·te·ri·al·ist**
\-list\ *n or adj* —**ma·te·ri·al·is·tic**
\-,tirēə'listik\ *adj*

ma·te·ri·al·ize \mə'tirēə,līz\ *vb* **-ized;
-iz·ing** : take or cause to take bodily
form —**ma·te·ri·al·i·za·tion** \mə-
,tirēələ'zāshən\ *n*

ma·té·ri·el, ma·te·ri·el \mə,tirē'el\ *n*
: military supplies

ma·ter·nal \mə'tərnᵊl\ *adj* : motherly
—**ma·ter·nal·ly** *adv*

ma·ter·ni·ty \mə'tərnətē\ *n, pl* **-ties** 1
: state of being a mother 2 : hospital's
childbirth facility ~ *adj* 1 : worn during pregnancy 2 : relating to the period close to childbirth

math \'math\ *n* : mathematics

math·e·mat·ics \,mathə'matiks\ *n pl*
: science of numbers and of shapes in
space —**math·e·mat·i·cal** \-ikəl\ *adj*
—**math·e·mat·i·cal·ly** *adv* —**math·e·ma·ti·cian** \,mathəmə'tishən\ *n*

mat·i·nee, mat·i·née \,matᵊn'ā\ *n*
: afternoon performance

mat·ins \'matᵊnz\ *n* : morning prayers

ma·tri·arch \'mātrē,ärk\ *n* : woman who
rules a family —**ma·tri·ar·chal**
\,mātrē'ärkəl\ *adj* —**ma·tri·ar·chy**
\'mātrē,ärkē\ *n*

ma·tri·cide \'matrə,sīd, 'mā-\ *n* : murder
of one's mother —**ma·tri·cid·al**
\,matrə'sīdᵊl\, ,mā-\ *adj*

ma·tric·u·late \mə'trikyə,lāt\ *vb* **-lat·ed; -lat·ing** : enroll in school —**ma·tric·u·la·tion** \-,trikyə'lāshən\ *n*

mat·ri·mo·ny \'matrə,mōnē\ *n* : marriage —**mat·ri·mo·ni·al** \,matrə-

'mōnēəl\ *adj* —**mat·ri·mo·ni·al·ly**
adv

ma·trix \'mātriks\ *n, pl* **-tri·ces** \'mā-
trə,sēz, 'ma-\ *or* **-trix·es** \'mātriksəz\
: something (as a mold) that gives
form, foundation, or origin to something else enclosed in it

ma·tron \'mātrən\ *n* 1 : dignified mature
woman 2 : woman supervisor —**ma·tron·ly** *adj*

matte \'mat\ *adj* : not shiny

mat·ter \'matər\ *n* 1 : subject of interest
2 *pl* : circumstances 3 : trouble 4
: physical substance ~ *vb* : be important

mat·tock \'matək\ *n* : a digging tool

mat·tress \'matrəs\ *n* : pad to sleep on

ma·ture \mə'tùr, -'tyùr, -'chùr\ *adj*
-tur·er; -est 1 : carefully considered
2 : fully grown or developed 3 : due
for payment ~ *vb* **-tured; -tur·ing**
: become mature —**mat·u·ra·tion**
\,machə'rāshən\ *n* —**ma·ture·ly** *adv*
—**ma·tu·ri·ty** \-ətē\ *n*

maud·lin \'mòdlən\ *adj* : excessively
sentimental

maul \'mòl\ *n* : heavy hammer ~ *vb* 1
: beat 2 : handle roughly

mau·so·le·um \,mòsə'lēəm, ,mòzə-\ *n,
pl* **-leums** *or* **-lea** \-'lēə\ : large aboveground tomb

mauve \'mōv, 'mòv\ *n* : lilac color

ma·ven, ma·vin \'māvən\ *n* : expert

mav·er·ick \'mavrik\ *n* 1 : unbranded
range animal 2 : nonconformist

maw \'mò\ *n* 1 : stomach 2 : throat,
esophagus, or jaws

mawk·ish \'mòkish\ *adj* : sickly sentimental —**mawk·ish·ly** *adv* —**mawk·ish·ness** *n*

max·im \'maksəm\ *n* : proverb

max·i·mum \'maksəməm\ *n, pl* **-ma**
\-səmə\ *or* **-mums** 1 : greatest quantity 2 : upper limit 3 : largest amount
—**maximum** *adj* —**max·i·mize** \-sə-
,mīz\ *vb*

may \'mā\ *verbal auxiliary, past* **might**
\'mīt\; *pres sing & pl* **may** 1 : have
permission 2 : be likely to 3 —used
to express desire, purpose, or contingency

May \'mā\ *n* : 5th month of the year having 31 days

may·ap·ple *n* : woodland herb having
edible fruit

may·be \'mābē\ *adv* : perhaps

may·flow·er *n* : spring-blooming herb

may·fly *n* : fly with an aquatic larva

may·hem \'mā,hem, 'māəm\ n 1 : crippling or mutilation of a person 2 : needless damage

may·on·naise \'māə,nāz\ n : creamy white sandwich spread

may·or \'māər, 'mer\ n : chief city official —**may·or·al** \-əl\ adj —**may·or·al·ty** \-əltē\ n

maze \'māz\ n : confusing network of passages —**mazy** adj

ma·zur·ka \mə'zərkə\ n : Polish dance

me \'mē\ pron, objective case of I

mead \'mēd\ n : alcoholic beverage brewed from honey

mead·ow \'medō\ n : low-lying usu. level grassland —**mead·ow·land** \-,land\ n

mead·ow·lark n : songbird with a yellow breast

mea·ger, mea·gre \'mēgər\ adj 1 : thin 2 : lacking richness or strength —**mea·ger·ly** adv —**mea·ger·ness** n

¹meal \'mēl\ n 1 : food to be eaten at one time 2 : act of eating —**meal·time** n

²meal n : ground grain —**mealy** adj

¹mean \'mēn\ adj 1 : humble 2 : worthy of or showing little regard 3 : stingy 4 : malicious —**mean·ly** adv —**mean·ness** n

²mean \'mēn\ vb **meant** \'ment\; **mean·ing** \'mēniŋ\ 1 : intend 2 : serve to convey, show, or indicate 3 : be important

³mean n 1 : middle point 2 pl : something that helps gain an end 3 pl : material resources 4 : sum of several quantities divided by the number of quantities ~ adj : being a mean

me·an·der \mē'andər\ vb -**dered**; -**der·ing** 1 : follow a winding course 2 : wander aimlessly —**meander** n

mean·ing \'mēniŋ\ n 1 : idea conveyed or intended to be conveyed 2 : aim —**mean·ing·ful** \-fəl\ adj —**mean·ing·ful·ly** adv —**mean·ing·less** adj

mean·time \'mēn,tīm\ n : intervening time —**meantime** adv

mean·while \-,hwīl\ n : meantime ~ adv 1 : meantime 2 : at the same time

mea·sles \'mēzəlz\ n pl : disease that is marked by red spots on the skin

mea·sly \'mēzlē\ adj -**sli·er**; -**est** : contemptibly small in amount

mea·sure \'mezhər, 'māzh-\ n 1 : moderate amount 2 : dimensions or amount 3 : something to show amount 4 : unit or system of measurement 5 : act of measuring 6 : means to an end ~ vb -**sured**; -**sur·ing** 1 : find out or mark off size or amount of 2 : have a specified measurement —**mea·sur·able** \'mezhərəbəl, 'māzh-\ adj —**mea·sur·ably** \-blē\ adv —**mea·sure·less** adj —**mea·sure·ment** n —**mea·sur·er** n

meat \'mēt\ n 1 : food 2 : animal flesh used as food —**meat·ball** n —**meaty** adj

me·chan·ic \mi'kanik\ n : worker who repairs cars

me·chan·i·cal \mi'kanikəl\ adj 1 : relating to machines or mechanics 2 : involuntary —**me·chan·i·cal·ly** adv

me·chan·ics \-iks\ n sing or pl 1 : branch of physics dealing with energy and forces in relation to bodies 2 : mechanical details

mech·a·nism \'mekə,nizəm\ n 1 : piece of machinery 2 : technique for gaining a result 3 : basic processes producing a phenomenon —**mech·a·nis·tic** \,mekə'nistik\ adj —**mech·a·ni·za·tion** \,mekənə'zāshən\ n —**mech·a·nize** \'mekə,nīz\ vb —**mech·a·niz·er** n

med·al \'medᵊl\ n 1 : religious pin or pendant 2 : coinlike commemorative metal piece

med·al·ist, med·al·list \'medᵊlist\ n : person awarded a medal

me·dal·lion \mə'dalyən\ n : large medal

med·dle \'medᵊl\ vb -**dled**; -**dling** : interfere —**med·dler** \'medᵊlər\ n —**med·dle·some** \'medᵊlsəm\ adj

me·dia \'mēdēə\ n pl : communications organizations

me·di·an \'mēdēən\ n : middle value in a range —**median** adj

me·di·ate \'mēdē,āt\ vb -**at·ed**; -**at·ing** : help settle a dispute —**me·di·a·tion** \,mēdē'āshən\ n —**me·di·a·tor** \'mēdē,ātər\ n

med·ic \'medik\ n : medical worker esp. in the military

med·i·ca·ble \'medikəbəl\ adj : curable

med·ic·aid \'medi,kād\ n : government program of medical aid for the poor

med·i·cal \'medikəl\ adj : relating to medicine —**med·i·cal·ly** \-klē\ adv

medi·care \'medi,ker\ n : government program of medical care for the aged

med·i·cate \'medə,kāt\ vb -**cat·ed**; -**cat·ing** : treat with medicine

med·i·ca·tion \,medə'kāshən\ n 1 : act of medicating 2 : medicine

med·i·cine \'medəsən\ *n* 1 : preparation used to treat disease 2 : science dealing with the cure of disease —**me·dic·i·nal** \mə'dis³nəl\ *adj* —**me·dic·i·nal·ly** *adv*

me·di·eval, me·di·ae·val \,mēdē'ēvəl, ,med-, ,mid-; ,mē'dē-, ,me-, ,mi-\ *adj* : of or relating to the Middle Ages —**me·di·eval·ist** \-ist\ *n*

me·di·o·cre \,mēdē'ōkər\ *adj* : not very good —**me·di·oc·ri·ty** \-'äkrətē\ *n*

med·i·tate \'medə,tāt\ *vb* -**tat·ed; -tat·ing** : contemplate —**med·i·ta·tion** \,medə'tāshən\ *n* —**med·i·ta·tive** \'medə,tātiv\ *adj* —**med·i·ta·tive·ly** *adv*

me·di·um \'mēdēəm\ *n, pl* -**diums** or -**dia** \-ēə\ 1 : middle position or degree 2 : means of effecting or conveying something 3 : surrounding substance 4 : means of communication 5 : mode of artistic expression —**medium** *adj*

med·ley \'medlē\ *n, pl* -**leys** : series of songs performed as one

meek \'mēk\ *adj* 1 : mild-mannered 2 : lacking spirit —**meek·ly** *adv* —**meek·ness** *n*

meer·schaum \'mirshəm, -,shóm\ *n* : claylike tobacco pipe

¹**meet** \'mēt\ *vb* met \'met\; **meet·ing** 1 : run into 2 : join 3 : oppose 4 : assemble 5 : satisfy 6 : be introduced to ~ *n* : sports team competition

²**meet** *adj* : proper

meet·ing \'mētiŋ\ *n* : a getting together —**meet·ing·house** *n*

mega·byte \'megəbīt\ *n* : unit of computer storage capacity

mega·hertz \-,hərts, -,herts\ *n* : one million hertz

mega·phone \'megə,fōn\ *n* : coneshaped device to intensify or direct the voice

mel·an·choly \'melən,kälē\ *n* : depression —**mel·an·chol·ic** \,melən'kälik\ *adj* —**melancholy** *adj*

mel·a·no·ma \,melə'nōmə\ *n, pl* -**mas** : usu. malignant skin tumor

me·lee \'mā,lā, mā'lā\ *n* : brawl

me·lio·rate \'mēlyə,rāt, 'mēlēə-\ *vb* -**rat·ed; -rat·ing** : improve —**me·lio·ra·tion** \,mēlyə'rāshən, ,mēlēə-\ *n* —**me·lio·ra·tive** \'mēlyə,rātiv, 'mēlēə-\ *adj*

mel·lif·lu·ous \me'lifləwəs, mə-\ *adj* : sweetly flowing —**mel·lif·lu·ous·ly** *adv* —**mel·lif·lu·ous·ness** *n*

mel·low \'melō\ *adj* 1 : grown gentle or mild 2 : rich and full —**mellow** *vb* —**mel·low·ness** *n*

melo·dra·ma \'melə,drämə, -,dram-\ *n* : overly theatrical play —**melo·dra·mat·ic** \,melədrə'matik\ *adj* —**melo·dra·mat·i·cal·ly** \-tiklē\ *adv*

mel·o·dy \'melədē\ *n, pl* -**dies** 1 : agreeable sound 2 : succession of musical notes —**me·lod·ic** \mə'lädik\ *adj* —**me·lod·i·cal·ly** \-iklē\ *adv* —**me·lo·di·ous** \mə'lōdēəs\ *adj* —**me·lo·di·ous·ly** *adv* —**me·lo·di·ous·ness** *n*

mel·on \'melən\ *n* : gourdlike fruit

melt \'melt\ *vb* 1 : change from solid to liquid usu. by heat 2 : dissolve or disappear gradually 3 : move or be moved emotionally

mem·ber \'membər\ *n* 1 : part of a person, animal, or plant 2 : one of a group 3 : part of a whole —**mem·ber·ship** \-,ship\ *n*

mem·brane \'mem,brān\ *n* : thin layer esp. in an organism —**mem·bra·nous** \-brənəs\ *adj*

me·men·to \mi'mentō\ *n, pl* -**tos** or -**toes** : souvenir

memo \'memō\ *n, pl* **mem·os** : memorandum

mem·oirs \'mem,wärz\ *n pl* : autobiography

mem·o·ra·bil·ia \,memərə'bilēə, -'bilyə\ *n pl* 1 : memorable things 2 : mementos

mem·o·ra·ble \'memərəbəl\ *adj* : worth remembering —**mem·o·ra·bil·i·ty** \,memərə'bilətē\ *n* —**mem·o·ra·ble·ness** *n* —**mem·o·ra·bly** \-blē\ *adv*

mem·o·ran·dum \,memə'randəm\ *n, pl* -**dums** or -**da** \-də\ : informal note

me·mo·ri·al \mə'mōrēəl\ *n* : something (as a monument) meant to keep remembrance alive —**memorial** *adj* —**me·mo·ri·al·ize** *vb*

Memorial Day *n* : last Monday in May or formerly May 30 observed as a legal holiday in commemoration of dead servicemen

mem·o·ry \'memrē, 'memə-\ *n, pl* -**ries** 1 : power of remembering 2 : something remembered 3 : commemoration 4 : time within which past events are remembered —**mem·o·ri·za·tion** \,memərə'zāshən\ *n* —**mem·o·rize** \'memə,rīz\ *vb* —**mem·o·riz·er** *n*

men *pl of* MAN

men·ace \'menəs\ *n* : threat of danger ~

vb **-aced; -ac·ing 1** : threaten **2** : endanger —**men·ac·ing·ly** *adv*

me·nag·er·ie \mə'najərē\ *n* : collection of wild animals

mend \'mend\ *vb* **1** : improve **2** : repair **3** : heal —**mend** *n* —**mend·er** *n*

men·da·cious \men'dāshəs\ *adj* : dishonest —**men·da·cious·ly** *adv* —**men·dac·i·ty** \-'dasətē\ *n*

men·di·cant \'mendikənt\ *n* : beggar —**men·di·can·cy** \-kənsē\ *n* —**mendicant** *adj*

men·ha·den \men'hād³n, mən-\ *n, pl* **-den** : fish related to the herring

me·nial \'mēnēəl, -nyəl\ *adj* **1** : relating to servants **2** : humble ~ *n* : domestic servant —**me·ni·al·ly** *adv*

men·in·gi·tis \,menən'jītəs\ *n, pl* **-git·i·des** \-'jitə,dēz\ : disease of the brain and spinal cord

meno·pause \'menə,póz\ *n* : time when menstruation ends —**meno·paus·al** \,menə'pózəl\ *adj*

me·no·rah \mə'nōrə\ *n* : candelabrum used in Jewish worship

men·stru·a·tion \,menstrə'wāshən, men'strā-\ *n* : monthly discharge of blood from the uterus —**men·stru·al** \'menstrəwəl\ *adj* —**men·stru·ate** \'menstrə,wāt, -,strāt\ *vb*

-ment \mənt\ *n suffix* **1** : result or means of an action **2** : action or process **3** : place of an action **4** : state or condition

men·tal \'ment³l\ *adj* : relating to the mind or its disorders —**men·tal·i·ty** \men'talətē\ *n* —**men·tal·ly** *adv*

men·thol \'men,thól, -,thōl\ *n* : soothing substance from oil of peppermint —**men·tho·lat·ed** \-thə,lātəd\ *adj*

men·tion \'menchən\ *vb* : refer to —**mention** *n*

men·tor \'men,tòr, 'mentər\ *n* : instructor

menu \'menyü\ *n* **1** : restaurant's list of food **2** : list of offerings

me·ow \mē'aú\ *n* : characteristic cry of a cat —**meow** *vb*

mer·can·tile \'mərkən,tēl, -,tīl\ *adj* : relating to merchants or trade

mer·ce·nary \'mərs³n,erē\ *n, pl* **-nar·ies** : hired soldier ~ *adj* : serving only for money

mer·chan·dise \'mərchən,dīz, -,dīs\ *n* : goods bought and sold ~ *vb* **-dised; -dis·ing** : buy and sell —**mer·chan·dis·er** *n*

mer·chant \'mərchənt\ *n* : one who buys and sells

merchant marine *n* : commercial ships

mer·cu·ri·al \,mər'kyúrēəl\ *adj* : unpredictable —**mer·cu·ri·al·ly** *adv* —**mer·cu·ri·al·ness** *n*

mer·cu·ry \'mərkyərē\ *n* : heavy liquid metallic chemical element

mer·cy \'mərsē\ *n, pl* **-cies 1** : show of pity or leniency **2** : divine blessing —**mer·ci·ful** \-sifəl\ *adj* —**mer·ci·ful·ly** *adv* —**mer·ci·less** \-siləs\ *adj* —**mer·ci·less·ly** *adv* —**mercy** *adj*

mere \'mir\ *adj, superlative* **mer·est** : nothing more than —**mere·ly** *adv*

merge \'mərj\ *vb* **merged; merg·ing 1** : unite **2** : blend —**merg·er** \'mərjər\ *n*

me·rid·i·an \mə'ridēən\ *n* : imaginary circle on the earth's surface passing through the poles —**meridian** *adj*

me·ringue \mə'raŋ\ *n* : baked dessert topping of beaten egg whites

me·ri·no \mə'rēnō\ *n, pl* **-nos 1** : kind of sheep **2** : fine soft woolen yarn

mer·it \'merət\ *n* **1** : praiseworthy quality **2** *pl* : rights and wrongs of a legal case ~ *vb* : deserve —**mer·i·to·ri·ous** \,merə'tōrēəs\ *adj* —**mer·i·to·ri·ous·ly** *adv* —**mer·i·to·ri·ous·ness** *n*

mer·maid \'mər,mād\ *n* : legendary female sea creature

mer·ry \'merē\ *adj* **-ri·er; -est** : full of high spirits —**mer·ri·ly** *adv* —**mer·riment** \'merimənt\ *n* —**mer·ry·mak·er** \'merē,mākər\ *n* —**mer·ry·mak·ing** \'merē,mākiŋ\ *n*

merry-go-round *n* : revolving amusement ride

me·sa \'māsə\ *n* : steep flat-topped hill

mesdames *pl of* MADAM *or of* MADAME *or of* MRS.

mesdemoiselles *pl of* MADEMOISELLE

mesh \'mesh\ *n* **1** : one of the openings in a net **2** : net fabric **3** : working contact ~ *vb* : fit together properly —**meshed** \'mesht\ *adj*

mes·mer·ize \'mezmə,rīz\ *vb* **-ized; -iz·ing** : hypnotize

mess \'mes\ *n* **1** : meal eaten by a group **2** : confused, dirty, or offensive state ~ *vb* **1** : make dirty or untidy **2** : putter **3** : interfere —**messy** *adj*

mes·sage \'mesij\ *n* : news, information, or a command sent by one person to another

mes·sen·ger \'mes³njər\ *n* : one who carries a message or does an errand

Mes·si·ah \mə'sīə\ n 1 : expected deliverer of the Jews 2 : Jesus Christ 3 not cap : great leader

messieurs pl of MONSIEUR

Messrs. pl of MR.

mes·ti·zo \me'stēzō\ n, pl -zos : person of mixed blood

met past of MEET

me·tab·o·lism \mə'tabə,lizəm\ n : biochemical processes necessary to life —**met·a·bol·ic** \,metə'bälik\ adj —**me·tab·o·lize** \mə'tabə,līz\ vb

met·al \'met⁸l\ n : shiny substance that can be melted and shaped and conducts heat and electricity —**me·tal·lic** \mə'talik\ adj —**met·al·ware** n —**met·al·work** n —**met·al·work·er** n —**met·al·work·ing** n

met·al·lur·gy \'met⁸l,ərjē\ n : science of metals —**met·al·lur·gi·cal** \,met⁸l'ərjikəl\ adj —**met·al·lur·gist** \'met⁸l,ərjist\ n

meta·mor·pho·sis \,metə'mórfəsəs\ n, pl -pho·ses \-,sēz\ : sudden and drastic change (as of form) —**metamor·phose** \-,fōz, -,fōs\ vb

met·a·phor \'metə,fór, -fər\ n : use of a word denoting one kind of object or idea in place of another to suggest a likeness between them —**met·a·phor·i·cal** \,metə'fórikəl\ adj

meta·phys·ics \,metə'fiziks\ n : study of the causes and nature of things —**meta·phys·i·cal** \-'fizikəl\ adj

mete \'mēt\ vb **met·ed; met·ing** : allot

me·te·or \'mētēər, -ē,ór\ n : small body that produces a streak of light as it burns up in the atmosphere

me·te·or·ic \,mētē'órik\ adj 1 : relating to a meteor 2 : sudden and spectacular —**me·te·or·i·cal·ly** \-i,klē\ adv

me·te·or·ite \'mētēə,rīt\ n : meteor that reaches the earth

me·te·o·rol·o·gy \,mētēə'räləjē\ n : science of weather —**me·te·o·ro·log·ic** \,mētē,órə'läjik\, **me·te·o·ro·log·i·cal** \-'läjikəl\ adj —**me·te·o·rol·o·gist** \-ēə'räləjist\ n

¹me·ter \'mētər\ n : rhythm in verse or music

²meter n : unit of length equal to 39.37 inches

³meter n : measuring instrument

meth·a·done \'methə,dōn\ n : synthetic addictive narcotic

meth·ane \'meth,ān\ n : colorless odorless flammable gas

meth·a·nol \'methə,nól, -,nōl\ n : volatile flammable poisonous liquid

meth·od \'methəd\ n 1 : procedure for achieving an end 2 : orderly arrangement or plan —**me·thod·i·cal** \mə'thädikəl\ adj —**me·thod·i·cal·ly** \-klē\ adv —**me·thod·i·cal·ness** n

me·tic·u·lous \mə'tikyələs\ adj : extremely careful in attending to details —**me·tic·u·lous·ly** adv —**me·tic·u·lous·ness** n

met·ric \'metrik\, **met·ri·cal** \-trikəl\ adj : relating to meter or the metric system —**met·ri·cal·ly** adv

metric system n : system of weights and measures using the meter and kilogram

met·ro·nome \'metrə,nōm\ n : instrument that ticks regularly to mark a beat in music

me·trop·o·lis \mə'träpələs\ n : major city —**met·ro·pol·i·tan** \,metrə'pälət⁸n\ adj

met·tle \'met⁸l\ n : spirit or courage —**met·tle·some** \-səm\ adj

mez·za·nine \'mez⁸n,ēn, ,mez⁸n'ēn\ n 1 : intermediate level between 2 main floors 2 : lowest balcony

mez·zo·so·pra·no \,metsōsə'pranō, ,medz-\ n : voice between soprano and contralto

mi·as·ma \mī'azmə\ n 1 : noxious vapor 2 : harmful influence —**mi·as·mic** \-mik\ adj

mi·ca \'mīkə\ n : mineral separable into thin transparent sheets

mice pl of MOUSE

mi·cro \'mīkrō\ adj : very small

mi·crobe \'mī,krōb\ n : disease-causing microorganism —**mi·cro·bi·al** \mī'krōbēəl\ adj

mi·cro·bi·ol·o·gy \,mīkrōbī'äləjē\ n : biology dealing with microscopic life —**mi·cro·bi·o·log·i·cal** \'mīkrō,bīə'läjikəl\ adj —**mi·cro·bi·ol·o·gist** \,mīkrōbī'äləjist\ n

mi·cro·com·put·er \'mīkrōkəm,pyütər\ n : small computer that uses a microprocessor

mi·cro·cosm \'mīkrə,käzəm\ n : one thought of as a miniature universe

mi·cro·film \-,film\ n : small film recording printed matter —**microfilm** vb

mi·crom·e·ter \mī'krämətər\ n : instrument for measuring minute distances

mi·cro·min·ia·tur·ized \,mīkrō'minēəchə,rīzd, -'minichə-\ *adj* : reduced to a very small size —**mi·cro·min·ia·tur·iza·tion** \-,minēə,chùrə'zāshən, -,mini,chùr-, -chər-\ *n*

mi·cron \'mī,krän\ *n* : one millionth of a meter

mi·cro·or·gan·ism \,mīkrō'órgə,nizəm\ *n* : very tiny living thing

mi·cro·phone \'mīkrə,fōn\ *n* : instrument for changing sound waves into variations of an electric current

mi·cro·pro·ces·sor \'mīkrō,präsesər\ *n* : miniaturized computer processing unit on a single chip

mi·cro·scope \-,skōp\ *n* : optical device for magnifying tiny objects —**mi·cro·scop·ic** \,mīkrə'skäpik\ *adj* —**mi·cro·scop·i·cal·ly** *adv* —**mi·cros·copy** \mī'kräskəpē\ *n*

mi·cro·wave \'mīkrə,wāv\ *n* 1 : short radio wave 2 : oven that cooks food using microwaves ~ *vb* : heat or cook in a microwave oven —**mi·cro·wav·able, mi·cro·wave·able** \,mīkrə'wā-vəbəl\ *adj*

mid \'mid\ *adj* : middle —**mid·point** *n* —**mid·stream** *n* —**mid·sum·mer** *n* —**mid·town** *n or adj* —**mid·week** *n* —**mid·win·ter** *n* —**mid·year** *n*

mid·air *n* : a point in the air well above the ground

mid·day *n* : noon

mid·dle \'midᵊl\ *adj* 1 : equally distant from the extremes 2 : being at neither extreme ~ *n* : middle part or point

Middle Ages *n pl* : period from about A.D. 500 to about 1500

mid·dle·man \-,man\ *n* : dealer or agent between the producer and consumer

mid·dling \'midliŋ, -lən\ *adj* 1 : of middle or medium size, degree, or quality 2 : mediocre

midge \'mij\ *n* : very tiny fly

midg·et \'mijət\ *n* : very small person or thing

mid·land \'midlənd, -,land\ *n* : interior of a country

mid·most *adj* : being nearest the middle —**midmost** *adv*

mid·night *n* : 12 o'clock at night

mid·riff \'mid,rif\ *n* : mid-region of the torso

mid·ship·man \'mid,shipmən, ,mid-'ship-\ *n* : student naval officer

midst \'midst\ *n* : position close to or surrounded by others —**midst** *prep*

mid·way \'mid,wā\ *n* : concessions and

amusements at a carnival ~ *adv* : in the middle

mid·wife \'mid,wīf\ *n* : person who aids at childbirth —**mid·wife·ry** \mid-'wīfərē, -'wīf-\ *n*

mien \'mēn\ *n* : appearance

miff \'mif\ *vb* : upset or peeve

¹**might** \'mīt\ *past of* MAY —used to express permission or possibility or as a polite alternative to *may*

²**might** *n* : power or resources

mighty \'mītē\ *adj* **might·i·er; -est** 1 : very strong 2 : great —**might·i·ly** *adv* —**might·i·ness** *n* —**mighty** *adv*

mi·graine \'mī,grān\ *n* : severe headache often with nausea

mi·grant \'mīgrənt\ *n* : one who moves frequently to find work

mi·grate \'mī,grāt\ *vb* **-grat·ed; -grat·ing** 1 : move from one place to another 2 : pass periodically from one region or climate to another —**mi·gra·tion** \mī'grāshən\ *n* —**mi·gra·to·ry** \'mīgrə,tōrē\ *adj*

mild \'mīld\ *adj* 1 : gentle in nature or behavior 2 : moderate in action or effect —**mild·ly** *adv* —**mild·ness** *n*

mil·dew \'mil,dü, -,dyü\ *n* : whitish fungal growth —**mildew** *vb*

mile \'mīl\ *n* : unit of length equal to 5280 feet

mile·age \'mīlij\ *n* 1 : allowance per mile for traveling expenses 2 : amount or rate of use expressed in miles

mile·stone *n* : significant point in development

mi·lieu \mēl'yü, -'yœ̄\ *n, pl* **-lieus** *or* **-lieux** \-'yüz, -'yœ̄\ : surroundings or setting

mil·i·tant \'milətənt\ *adj* : aggressively active or hostile —**mil·i·tan·cy** \-tənsē\ *n* —**militant** *n* —**mil·i·tant·ly** *adv*

mil·i·ta·rism \'milətə,rizəm\ *n* : dominance of military ideals or of a policy of aggressive readiness for war —**mil·i·ta·rist** \-rist\ *n* —**mil·i·tar·is·tic** \,milətə'ristik\ *adj*

mil·i·tary \'milə,terē\ *adj* 1 : relating to soldiers, arms, or war 2 : relating to or performed by armed forces ~ *n* : armed forces or the people in them —**mil·i·tar·i·ly** \,milə'terəlē\ *adv*

mil·i·tate \-,tāt\ *vb* **-tat·ed; -tat·ing** : have an effect

mi·li·tia \mə'lishə\ *n* : civilian soldiers —**mi·li·tia·man** \-mən\ *n*

milk \'milk\ n : white nutritive fluid secreted by female mammals for feeding their young ~ vb 1 : draw off the milk of 2 : draw something from as if by milking —**milk·er** n —**milk·i·ness** \-ēnəs\ n —**milky** adj

milk·man \-,man, -mən\ n : man who sells or delivers milk

milk·weed n : herb with milky juice

¹**mill** \'mil\ n 1 : building in which grain is ground into flour 2 : manufacturing plant 3 : machine used esp. for forming or processing ~ vb 1 : subject to a process in a mill 2 : move in a circle —**mill·er** n

²**mill** n : 1/10 cent

mil·len·ni·um \mə'lenēəm\ n, pl **-nia** \-ēə\ or **-niums** : a period of 1000 years

mil·let \'milət\ n : cereal and forage grass with small seeds

mil·li·gram \'milə,gram\ n : 1/1000 gram

mil·li·li·ter \-,lētər\ n : 1/1000 liter

mil·li·me·ter \-,mētər\ n : 1/1000 meter

mil·li·ner \'milənər\ n : person who makes or sells women's hats —**mil·li·nery** \'milə,nerē\ n

mil·lion \'milyən\ n, pl **millions** or **million** : 1000 thousands —**million** adj —**mil·lionth** \-yənth\ adj or n

mil·lion·aire \,milyə'nar, 'milyə,nar\ n : person worth a million or more (as of dollars)

mil·li·pede \'milə,pēd\ n : longbodied arthropod with 2 pairs of legs on most segments

mill·stone n : either of 2 round flat stones used for grinding grain

mime \'mīm\ n 1 : mimic 2 : pantomime —**mime** vb

mim·eo·graph \'mimēə,graf\ n : machine for making many stencil copies —**mimeograph** vb

mim·ic \'mimik\ n : one that mimics ~ vb **-icked; -ick·ing** 1 : imitate closely 2 : ridicule by imitation —**mim·ic·ry** \'mimikrē\ n

min·a·ret \,minə'ret\ n : tower attached to a mosque

mince \'mins\ vb **minced; minc·ing** 1 : cut into small pieces 2 : choose (one's words) carefully 3 : walk in a prim affected manner

mind \'mīnd\ n 1 : memory 2 : the part of an individual that feels, perceives, and esp. reasons 3 : intention 4 : normal mental condition 5 : opinion 6

: intellectual ability ~ vb 1 : attend to 2 : obey 3 : be concerned about 4 : be careful —**mind·ed** adj —**mind·less** \'mīndləs\ adj —**mind·less·ly** adv —**mind·less·ness** n

mind·ful \-fəl\ adj : aware or attentive —**mind·ful·ly** adv —**mind·ful·ness** n

¹**mine** \'mīn\ pron : that which belongs to me

²**mine** \'mīn\ n 1 : excavation from which minerals are taken 2 : explosive device placed in the ground or water for destroying enemy vehicles or vessels that later pass ~ vb **mined; min·ing** 1 : get ore from 2 : place military mines in —**mine·field** n —**min·er** n

min·er·al \'minərəl\ n 1 : crystalline substance not of organic origin 2 : useful natural substance (as coal) obtained from the ground —**mineral** adj

min·er·al·o·gy \,minə'räləjē, -'ral-\ n : science dealing with minerals —**min·er·al·og·i·cal** \,minərə'läjikəl\ adj —**min·er·al·o·gist** \,minə'räləjist, -'ral-\ n

min·gle \'mingəl\ vb **-gled; -gling** : bring together or mix

mini- comb form : miniature or of small dimensions

min·ia·ture \'minēə,chúr, 'mini,chúr, -chər\ n : tiny copy or very small version —**miniature** adj —**min·ia·tur·ist** \-,chúrist, -chər-\ n —**min·ia·tur·ize** \-ēəchə,rīz, -ichə-\ vb

mini·bike \'minē,bīk\ n : small motorcycle

mini·bus \-,bəs\ n : small bus

mini·com·put·er \-kəm,pyütər\ n : computer intermediate between a mainframe and a microcomputer in size and speed

mini·course \-,kórs\ n : short course of study

min·i·mal \'minəməl\ adj : relating to or being a minimum —**min·i·mal·ly** adv

min·i·mize \'minə,mīz\ vb **-mized; -miz·ing** 1 : reduce to a minimum 2 : underestimate intentionally

min·i·mum \'minəməm\ n, pl **-ma** \-mə\ or **-mums** : lowest quantity or amount —**minimum** adj

min·ion \'minyən\ n 1 : servile dependent 2 : subordinate official

mini·se·ries \'minē,sirēz\ n : television story in several parts

mini·skirt \-,skərt\ *n* : very short skirt

min·is·ter \'minəstər\ *n* **1** : Protestant member of the clergy **2** : high officer of state **3** : diplomatic representative ~ *vb* : give aid or service —**min·is·te·ri·al** \,minə'stirēəl\ *adj* —**min·is·tra·tion** *n*

min·is·try \'minəstrē\ *n, pl* **-tries 1** : office or duties of a minister **2** : body of ministers **3** : government department headed by a minister

mini·van \'minē,van\ *n* : small van

mink \'miŋk\ *n, pl* **mink** *or* **minks** : weasellike mammal or its soft brown fur

min·now \'minō\ *n, pl* **-nows** : small freshwater fish

mi·nor \'mīnər\ *adj* **1** : less in size, importance, or value **2** : not serious ~ *n* **1** : person not yet of legal age **2** : secondary field of academic specialization

mi·nor·i·ty \mə'nórətē, mī-\ *n, pl* **-ties 1** : time or state of being a minor **2** : smaller number (as of votes) **3** : part of a population differing from others (as in race or religion)

min·strel \'minstrəl\ *n* **1** : medieval singer of verses **2** : performer in a program usu. of black American songs and jokes —**min·strel·sy** \-sē\ *n*

¹mint \'mint\ *n* **1** : fragrant herb that yields a flavoring oil **2** : mint-flavored piece of candy —**minty** *adj*

²mint *n* **1** : place where coins are made **2** : vast sum ~ *adj* : unused —**mint** *vb* —**mint·er** *n*

min·u·et \,minyə'wet\ *n* : slow graceful dance

mi·nus \'mīnəs\ *prep* **1** : diminished by **2** : lacking ~ *n* : negative quantity or quality

mi·nus·cule \'minəs,kyül, min'əs-\, **min·is·cule** \'minəs-\ *adj* : very small

¹min·ute \'minət\ *n* **1** : 60th part of an hour or of a degree **2** : short time **3** *pl* : official record of a meeting

²mi·nute \mī'nüt, mə-, -'nyüt\ *adj* **-nut·er; -est 1** : very small **2** : marked by close attention to details —**mi·nute·ly** *adv* —**mi·nute·ness** *n*

mir·a·cle \'mirikəl\ *n* **1** : extraordinary event taken as a sign of divine intervention in human affairs **2** : marvel —**mi·rac·u·lous** \mə'rakyələs\ *adj* —**mi·rac·u·lous·ly** *adv*

mi·rage \mə'räzh\ *n* : distant illusion caused by atmospheric conditions (as in the desert)

mire \'mīr\ *n* : heavy deep mud ~ *vb* **mired; mir·ing** : stick or sink in mire —**miry** *adj*

mir·ror \'mirər\ *n* : smooth surface (as of glass) that reflects images ~ *vb* : reflect in or as if in a mirror

mirth \'mərth\ *n* : gladness and laughter —**mirth·ful** \-fəl\ *adj* —**mirth·ful·ly** *adv* —**mirth·ful·ness** *n* —**mirth·less** *adj*

mis·an·thrope \'mis°n,thrōp\ *n* : one who hates mankind —**mis·an·throp·ic** \,mis°n'thräpik\ *adj* —**mis·an·thro·py** \mis'anthrəpē\ *n*

mis·ap·pre·hend \,mis,aprə'hend\ *vb* : misunderstand —**mis·ap·pre·hen·sion** *n*

mis·ap·pro·pri·ate \,misə'prōprē,āt\ *vb* : take dishonestly for one's own use —**mis·ap·pro·pri·a·tion** *n*

mis·be·got·ten \-bi'gät°n\ *adj* **1** : illegitimate **2** : ill-conceived

mis·be·have \,misbi'hāv\ *vb* : behave improperly —**mis·be·hav·er** *n* —**mis·be·hav·ior** *n*

mis·cal·cu·late \mis'kalkyə,lāt\ *vb* : calculate wrongly —**mis·cal·cu·la·tion**

mis·car·ry \,mis'karē, 'mis,karē\ *vb* **1** : give birth prematurely before the fetus can survive **2** : go wrong or be unsuccessful —**mis·car·riage** \-rij\ *n*

mis·ce·ge·na·tion \mis,ejə'nāshən, ,misijə'nā-\ *n* : marriage between persons of different races

mis·cel·la·neous \,misə'lānēəs\ *adj* : consisting of many things of different kinds —**mis·cel·la·neous·ly** *adv* —**mis·cel·la·neous·ness** *n*

mis·cel·la·ny \'misə,lānē\ *n, pl* **-nies** : collection of various things

mis·chance \mis'chans\ *n* : bad luck

mis·chief \'mischəf\ *n* : conduct esp. of a child that annoys or causes minor damage

mis·chie·vous \'mischəvəs\ *adj* **1** : causing annoyance or minor injury **2** : irresponsibly playful —**mis·chie·vous·ly** *adv* —**mis·chie·vous·ness** *n*

mis·con·ceive \,miskən'sēv\ *vb* : interpret incorrectly —**mis·con·cep·tion** *n*

mis·con·duct \mis'kändəkt\ *n* **1** : mismanagement **2** : bad behavior

mis·con·strue \,miskən'strü\ *vb* : misinterpret —**mis·con·struc·tion** *n*

mis·cre·ant \'miskrēənt\ n : one who behaves criminally or viciously —**miscreant** adj

mis·deed \mis'dēd\ n : wrong deed

mis·de·mean·or \,misdi'mēnər\ n : crime less serious than a felony

mi·ser \'mīzər\ n : person who hoards and is stingy with money —**mi·ser·li·ness** \-lēnəs\ n —**mi·ser·ly** adj

mis·er·a·ble \'mizərəbəl\ adj 1 : wretchedly deficient 2 : causing extreme discomfort 3 : shameful —**mis·er·a·ble·ness** n —**mis·er·a·bly** \-blē\ adv

mis·ery \'mizərē\ n, pl -er·ies : suffering and want caused by distress or poverty

mis·fire \mis'fīr\ vb 1 : fail to fire 2 : miss an intended effect —**mis·fire** \'mis,fīr\ n

mis·fit \'mis,fit, mis'fit\ n : person poorly adjusted to his environment

mis·for·tune \mis'fórchən\ n 1 : bad luck 2 : unfortunate condition or event

mis·giv·ing \mis'givin\ n : doubt or concern

mis·guid·ed \mis'gīdəd\ adj : mistaken, uninformed, or deceived

mis·hap \'mis,hap\ n : accident

mis·in·form \,misᵊn'fórm\ vb : give wrong information to —**mis·in·for·ma·tion** \,mis,infər'māshən\ n

mis·in·ter·pret \,misᵊn'tərprət\ vb : understand or explain wrongly —**mis·in·ter·pre·ta·tion** \-,tərprə-'tāshən\ n

mis·judge \mis'jəj\ vb : judge incorrectly or unjustly —**mis·judg·ment** n

mis·lay \mis'lā\ vb -laid; -lay·ing : misplace

mis·lead \mis'lēd\ vb -led; -lead·ing : lead in a wrong direction or into error —**mis·lead·ing·ly** adv

mis·man·age \mis'manij\ vb : manage badly —**mis·man·age·ment** n

mis·no·mer \mis'nōmər\ n : wrong name

mi·sog·y·nist \mə'säjənist\ n : one who hates or distrusts women —**mi·sog·y·nis·tic** \mə,säjə'nistik\ adj —**mi·sog·y·ny** \-nē\ n

mis·place \mis'plās\ vb : put in a wrong or unremembered place

mis·print \'mis,print, mis'-\ n : error in printed matter

mis·pro·nounce \,misprə'naúns\ vb : pronounce incorrectly —**mis·pro·nun·ci·a·tion** n

mis·quote \mis'kwōt\ vb : quote incorrectly —**mis·quo·ta·tion** \,miskwō-'tāshən\ n

mis·read \mis'rēd\ vb -read; -read·ing : read or interpret incorrectly

mis·rep·re·sent \,mis,repri'zent\ vb : represent falsely or unfairly —**mis·rep·re·sen·ta·tion** n

mis·rule \mis'rül\ vb : govern badly ~ n 1 : bad or corrupt government 2 : disorder

¹miss \'mis\ vb 1 : fail to hit, reach, or contact 2 : notice the absence of 3 : fail to obtain 4 : avoid 5 : omit —**miss** n

²miss n : young unmarried woman or girl —often used as a title

mis·sal \'misəl\ n : book containing what is said at mass during the year

mis·shap·en \mis'shāpən\ adj : distorted

mis·sile \'misəl\ n : object (as a stone or rocket) thrown or shot

miss·ing \'misin\ adj : absent or lost

mis·sion \'mishən\ n 1 : ministry sent by a church to spread its teaching 2 : group of diplomats sent to a foreign country 3 : task

mis·sion·ary \'mishə,nerē\ adj : relating to religious missions ~ n, pl -ar·ies : person sent to spread religious faith

mis·sive \'misiv\ n : letter

mis·spell \mis'spel\ vb : spell incorrectly —**mis·spell·ing** n

mis·state \mis'stāt\ vb : state incorrectly —**mis·state·ment** n

mis·step \'mis,step\ n 1 : wrong step 2 : mistake

mist \'mist\ n : particles of water falling as fine rain

mis·take \mə'stāk\ n 1 : misunderstanding or wrong belief 2 : wrong action or statement —**mistake** vb

mis·tak·en \-'stākən\ adj : having a wrong opinion or incorrect information —**mis·tak·en·ly** adv

mis·ter \'mistər\ n : sir —used without a name in addressing a man

mis·tle·toe \'misəl,tō\ n : parasitic green shrub with waxy white berries

mis·treat \mis'trēt\ vb : treat badly —**mis·treat·ment** n

mis·tress \'mistrəs\ n 1 : woman in control 2 : a woman not his wife with whom a married man has recurrent sexual relations

mis·tri·al \mis'trīəl\ n : trial that has no legal effect

mis·trust \-'trəst\ n : lack of confidence ~ vb : have no confidence in —**mis·trust·ful** \-fəl\ adj —**mis·trust·ful·ly** adv —**mis·trust·ful·ness** n

misty \'mistē\ adj **mist·i·er; -est** 1 : obscured by mist 2 : tearful—**mist·i·ly** adv —**mist·i·ness** n

mis·un·der·stand \,mis,əndər'stand\ vb 1 : fail to understand 2 : interpret incorrectly

mis·un·der·stand·ing \-'standiŋ\ n 1 : wrong interpretation 2 : disagreement

mis·use \mis'yüz\ vb 1 : use incorrectly 2 : mistreat —**mis·use** \-'yüs\ n

mite \'mīt\ n 1 : tiny spiderlike animal 2 : small amount

mi·ter, mi·tre \'mītər\ n 1 : bishop's headdress 2 : angular joint in wood ~ vb **-tered** or **-tred; -ter·ing** or **-tring** \'mītəriŋ\ : bevel the ends of for a miter joint

mit·i·gate \'mitə,gāt\ vb **-gat·ed; -gat·ing** : make less severe —**mit·i·ga·tion** \,mitə'gāshən\ n —**mit·i·ga·tive** \'mitə,gātiv\ adj

mi·to·sis \mī'tōsəs\ n, pl **-to·ses** \-,sēz\ : process of forming 2 cell nuclei from one —**mi·tot·ic** \-'tätik\ adj

mitt \'mit\ n : mittenlike baseball glove

mit·ten \'mit²n\ n : hand covering without finger sections

mix \'miks\ vb : combine or join into one mass or group ~ n : commercially prepared food mixture —**mix·able** adj —**mix·er** n —**mix up** vb : confuse

mix·ture \'mikschər\ n : act or product of mixing

mix–up n : instance of confusion

mne·mon·ic \ni'mänik\ adj : relating to or assisting memory

moan \'mōn\ n : low prolonged sound of pain or grief —**moan** vb

moat \'mōt\ n : deep wide trench around a castle

mob \'mäb\ n 1 : large disorderly crowd 2 : criminal gang ~ vb **-bb-** : crowd around and attack or annoy

mo·bile \'mōbəl, -,bēl, -,bīl\ adj : capable of moving or being moved ~ \'mō,bēl\ n : suspended art construction with freely moving parts —**mo·bil·i·ty** \mō'bilətē\ n

mo·bi·lize \'mōbə,līz\ vb **-lized; -liz·ing** : assemble and make ready for war

duty —**mo·bi·li·za·tion** \,mōbələ'zāshən\ n

moc·ca·sin \'mäkəsən\ n 1 : heelless shoe 2 : venomous U.S. snake

mo·cha \'mōkə\ n 1 : mixture of coffee and chocolate 2 : dark brown color

mock \'mäk, 'mók\ vb 1 : ridicule 2 : mimic in derision ~ adj 1 : simulated 2 : phony —**mock·er** n —**mock·ery** \-ərē\ n —**mock·ing·ly** adv

mock·ing·bird \'mäkiŋ,bərd, 'mók-\ n : songbird that mimics other birds

mode \'mōd\ n 1 : particular form or variety 2 : style —**mod·al** \-²l\ adj —**mod·ish** \'mōdish\ adj

mod·el \'mäd²l\ n 1 : structural design 2 : miniature representation 3 : something worthy of copying 4 : one who poses for an artist or displays clothes 5 : type or design ~ vb **-eled** or **-elled; -el·ing** or **-el·ling** 1 : shape 2 : work as a model ~ adj 1 : serving as a pattern 2 : being a miniature representation of

mo·dem \'mōdəm, -,dem\ n : device by which a computer communicates with another computer over telephone lines

mod·er·ate \'mädərət\ adj : avoiding extremes ~ \'mädə,rāt\ vb **-at·ed; -at·ing** 1 : lessen the intensity of 2 : act as a moderator —**moderate** n —**mod·er·ate·ly** adv —**mod·er·ate·ness** n —**mod·er·a·tion** \,mädə'rāshən\ n

mod·er·a·tor \'mädə,rātər\ n : one who presides

mod·ern \'mädərn\ adj : relating to or characteristic of the present —**modern** n —**mo·der·ni·ty** \mə'dərnətē\ n —**mod·ern·iza·tion** \,mädərnə'zāshən\ n —**mod·ern·ize** \'mädər,nīz\ vb —**mod·ern·iz·er** \'mädər,nīzər\ n —**mod·ern·ly** adv —**modern·ness** n

mod·est \'mädəst\ adj 1 : having a moderate estimate of oneself 2 : reserved or decent in thoughts or actions 3 : limited in size, amount, or aim —**mod·est·ly** adv —**mod·es·ty** \-əstē\ n

mod·i·cum \'mädikəm\ n : small amount

mod·i·fy \'mädə,fī\ vb **-fied; -fy·ing** 1 : limit the meaning of 2 : change —**mod·i·fi·ca·tion** \,mädəfə'kāshən\ n —**mod·i·fi·er** \'mädə,fīər\ n

mod·u·lar \'mäjələr\ adj : built with

standardized units —mod·u·lar·ized \-lə,rīzd\ adj

mod·u·late \'mäjə,lāt\ vb -lat·ed; -lat·ing 1 : keep in proper measure or proportion 2 : vary a radio wave —mod·u·la·tion \,mäjə'lāshən\ n —mod·u·la·tor \'mäjə,lātər\ n —mod·u·la·to·ry \-lə,tōrē\ adj

mod·ule \'mäjül\ n : standardized unit

mo·gul \'mōgəl\ n : important person

mo·hair \'mō,har\ n : fabric made from the hair of the Angora goat

moist \'moist\ adj : slightly or moderately wet —moist·en \'mois⁹n\ vb —moist·en·er \'mois⁹nər\ n —moist·ly adv —moist·ness n

mois·ture \'moischər\ n : small amount of liquid that causes dampness —mois·tur·ize \-chə,rīz\ vb —mois·tur·iz·er n

mo·lar \'mōlər\ n : grinding tooth —molar adj

mo·las·ses \mə'lasəz\ n : thick brown syrup from raw sugar

¹mold \'mōld\ n : crumbly organic soil

²mold n : frame or cavity for forming ~ vb : shape in or as if in a mold —mold·er n

³mold n : surface growth of fungus ~ vb : become moldy —mold·i·ness \'mōldēnəs\ n —moldy adj

mold·er \'mōldər\ vb : crumble

mold·ing \'mōldiŋ\ n : decorative surface, plane, or strip

¹mole \'mōl\ n : spot on the skin

²mole n : small burrowing mammal —mole·hill n

mol·e·cule \'mäli,kyül\ n : small particle of matter —mo·lec·u·lar \mə'lekyələr\ adj

mole·skin \-,skin\ n : heavy cotton fabric

mo·lest \mə'lest\ vb 1 : annoy or disturb 2 : force physical and usu. sexual contact on —mo·les·ta·tion \,mōl,es'tāshən, mäl-\ n —mo·lest·er n

mol·li·fy \'mälə,fī\ vb -fied; -fy·ing : soothe in temper —mol·li·fi·ca·tion \,mäləfə'kāshən\ n

mol·lusk, mol·lusc \'mäləsk\ n : shelled aquatic invertebrate — mol·lus·can \mə'ləskən\ adj

mol·ly·cod·dle \'mälē,kädⁿl\ vb -dled; -dling : pamper

molt \'mōlt\ vb : shed hair, feathers, outer skin, or horns periodically —molt n —molt·er n

mol·ten \'mōlt⁹n\ adj : fused or liquefied by heat

mom \'mäm, 'mǝm\ n : mother

mo·ment \'mōmənt\ n 1 : tiny portion of time 2 : time of excellence 3 : importance

mo·men·tar·i·ly \,mōmən'terəlē\ adv 1 : for a moment 2 : at any moment

mo·men·tary \'mōmən,terē\ adj : continuing only a moment —mo·men·tar·i·ness n

mo·men·tous \mō'mentəs\ adj : very important —mo·men·tous·ly adv —mo·men·tous·ness n

mo·men·tum \-əm\ n, pl -ta \-ə\ or -tums : force of a moving body

mon·arch \'mänərk, -,ärk\ n : ruler of a kingdom or empire —mo·nar·chi·cal \mə'närkikəl\ adj

mon·ar·chist \'mänərkist\ n : believer in monarchical government —mon·ar·chism \-,kizəm\ n

mon·ar·chy \'mänərkē\ n, pl -chies : realm of a monarch

mon·as·tery \'mänə,sterē\ n, pl -ter·ies : house for monks

mo·nas·tic \mə'nastik\ adj : relating to monasteries, monks, or nuns —monastic n —mo·nas·ti·cal·ly \-tiklē\ adv —mo·nas·ti·cism \-tə,sizəm\ n

Mon·day \'məndā, -dē\ n : 2d day of the week

mon·e·tary \'mänə,terē, 'mən-\ adj : relating to money

mon·ey \'mənē\ n, pl -eys or -ies \'mənēz\ 1 : something (as coins or paper currency) used in buying 2 : wealth —mon·eyed \-ēd\ adj —mon·ey·lend·er n

mon·ger \'məŋgər, 'mäŋ-\ n : dealer

mon·gol·ism \'mäŋgə,lizəm\ n : congenital mental retardation —Mon·gol·oid \-gə,lòid\ adj or n

mon·goose \'män,güs, 'mäŋ-\ n, pl -goos·es : small agile mammal esp. of India

mon·grel \'mäŋgrəl, 'məŋ-\ n : offspring of mixed breed

mon·i·tor \'mänətər\ n 1 : student assistant 2 : television screen ~ vb : watch or observe esp. for quality

monk \'məŋk\ n : member of a religious order living in a monastery —monk·ish adj

mon·key \'məŋkē\ n, pl -keys : small long-tailed arboreal primate ~ vb 1 : fool 2 : tamper

mon·key·shines \-,shīnz\ n pl : pranks

monks·hood \'məŋks,hůd\ *n* : poisonous herb with showy flowers

mon·o·cle \'mänikəl\ *n* : eyeglass for one eye

mo·nog·a·my \mə'nägəmē\ *n* **1** : marriage with one person at a time **2** : practice of having a single mate for a period of time —**mo·nog·a·mist** \mə'nägəmist\ *n* —**mo·nog·a·mous** \-məs\ *adj*

mono·gram \'mänə,gram\ *n* : sign of identity made of initials —**monogram** *vb*

mono·graph \-,graf\ *n* : learned treatise

mono·lin·gual \,mänə'liŋgwəl\ *adj* : using only one language

mono·lith \'män⁽ᵊ⁾l,ith\ *n* **1** : single great stone **2** : single uniform massive whole —**mono·lith·ic** \,män⁽ᵊ⁾l'ithik\ *adj*

mono·logue \'män⁽ᵊ⁾l,óg\ *n* : long speech —**mono·logu·ist** \-,ógist\, **mo·no·lo·gist** \mə'näləjist, 'män⁽ᵊ⁾l,ógist\ *n*

mono·nu·cle·o·sis \,mänō,nůklē'ōsəs, -,nyü-\ *n* : acute infectious disease

mo·nop·o·ly \mə'näpəlē\ *n, pl* **-lies 1** : exclusive ownership or control of a commodity **2** : one controlling a monopoly —**mo·nop·o·list** \-list\ *n* —**mo·nop·o·lis·tic** \mə,näpə'listik\ *adj* —**mo·nop·o·li·za·tion** \-lə'zāshən\ *n* —**mo·nop·o·lize** \mə'näpə,līz\ *vb*

mono·rail \'mänə,rāl\ *n* : single rail for a vehicle or a vehicle or system using it

mono·syl·lab·ic \,mänəsə'labik\ *adj* : consisting of or using words of only one syllable —**mono·syl·la·ble** \'mänə,siləbəl\ *n*

mono·the·ism \'mänōthē,izəm\ *n* : doctrine or belief that there is only one deity —**mono·the·ist** \-,thēist\ *n* —**mono·the·is·tic** \,mänōthē'istik\ *adj*

mono·tone \'mänə,tōn\ *n* : succession of words in one unvarying tone

mo·not·o·nous \mə'nät⁵nəs\ *adj* **1** : sounded in one unvarying tone **2** : tediously uniform —**mo·not·o·nous·ly** *adv* —**mo·not·o·nous·ness** *n* —**mo·not·o·ny** \-⁽ᵊ⁾nē\ *n*

mon·ox·ide \mə'näk,sīd\ *n* : oxide containing one atom of oxygen in a molecule

mon·sieur \məs'yər, məsh-\ *n, pl* **mes·sieurs** \-yərz, mā'syərz\ : man of high rank or station —used as a title for a man esp. of French nationality

mon·si·gnor \män'sēnyər\ *n, pl* **monsi-**

gnors *or* **mon·si·gno·ri** \,män,sēn'yōrē\ : Roman Catholic prelate —used as a title

mon·soon \män'sün\ *n* : periodic rainy season

mon·ster \'mänstər\ *n* **1** : abnormal or terrifying animal **2** : ugly, wicked, or cruel person —**mon·stros·i·ty** \män·'sträsətē\ *n* —**mon·strous** \'mänstrəs\ *adj* —**mon·strous·ly** *adv*

mon·tage \män'täzh\ *n* : artistic composition of several different elements

month \'mənth\ *n* : 12th part of a year —**month·ly** *adv or adj or n*

mon·u·ment \'mänyəmənt\ *n* : structure erected in remembrance

mon·u·men·tal \,mänyə'ment⁽ᵊ⁾l\ *adj* **1** : serving as a monument **2** : outstanding **3** : very great —**mon·u·men·tal·ly** *adv*

moo \'mü\ *vb* : make the noise of a cow —**moo** *n*

mood \'müd\ *n* : state of mind or emotion

moody \'müdē\ *adj* **mood·i·er; -est 1** : sad **2** : subject to changing moods and esp. to bad moods — **mood·i·ly** \'müd⁽ᵊ⁾lē\ *adv* —**mood·i·ness** \-ēnəs\ *n*

moon \'mün\ *n* : natural satellite (as of earth) —**moon·beam** *n* —**moon·light** *n* —**moon·lit** *adj*

moon·light \-,līt\ *vb* **-ed; -ing** : hold a 2d job —**moon·light·er** *n*

moon·shine *n* **1** : moonlight **2** : meaningless talk **3** : illegally distilled liquor

¹**moor** \'mür\ *n* : open usu. swampy wasteland —**moor·land** \-lənd, -,land\ *n*

²**moor** *vb* : fasten with line or anchor

moor·ing \-iŋ\ *n* : place where boat can be moored

moose \'müs\ *n, pl* **moose** : large heavy-antlered deer

moot \'müt\ *adj* : open to question

mop \'mäp\ *n* : floor-cleaning implement ~ *vb* **-pp-** : use a mop on

mope \'mōp\ *vb* **moped; mop·ing** : be sad or listless

mo·ped \'mō,ped\ *n* : low-powered motorbike

mo·raine \mə'rān\ *n* : glacial deposit of earth and stones

mor·al \'mórəl\ *adj* **1** : relating to principles of right and wrong **2** : conforming to a standard of right behavior **3** : relating to or acting on the mind, character, or will ~ *n* 1 : point of a story 2 *pl* : moral practices or teachings —**mor·al·ist** \'mórəlist\ *n* —**mor·al·is·tic** \,mórə'listík\ *adj* —**mor·al·i·ty** \mə'ralətē\ *n* —**mor·al·ize** \'mórə,līz\ *vb* —**mor·al·ly** *adv*

mo·rale \mə'ral\ *n* : emotional attitude

mo·rass \mə'ras\ *n* : swamp

mor·a·to·ri·um \,mórə'tōrēəm\ *n, pl* -**ri·ums** *or* -**ria** \-ēə\ : suspension of activity

mo·ray \'mór,ā, mə'rā\ *n* : savage eel

mor·bid \'mórbid\ *adj* 1 : relating to disease 2 : gruesome —**mor·bid·i·ty** \mór'bidətē\ *n* —**mor·bid·ly** *adv* —**mor·bid·ness** *n*

mor·dant \'mórd^ənt\ *adj* : sarcastic —**mor·dant·ly** *adv*

more \'mōr\ *adj* 1 : greater 2 : additional ~ *adv* 1 : in addition 2 : to a greater degree ~ *n* 1 : greater quantity 2 : additional amount ~ *pron* : additional ones

mo·rel \mə'rel\ *n* : pitted edible mushroom

more·over \mōr'ōvər\ *adv* : in addition

mo·res \'mór,āz, -ēz\ *n, pl* : customs

morgue \'mórg\ *n* : temporary holding place for dead bodies

mor·i·bund \'mórə,bənd\ *adj* : dying

morn \'mórn\ *n* : morning

morn·ing \'mórniŋ\ *n* : time from sunrise to noon

mo·ron \'mór,än\ *n* 1 : mentally retarded person 2 : very stupid person —**mo·ron·ic** \mə'ränik\ *adj* —**mo·ron·i·cal·ly** *adv*

mo·rose \mə'rōs\ *adj* : sullen —**mo·rose·ly** *adv* —**mo·rose·ness** *n*

mor·phine \'mór,fēn\ *n* : addictive pain-killing drug

mor·row \'märō\ *n* : next day

Morse code \'mórs-\ *n* : code of dots and dashes or long and short sounds used for transmitting messages

mor·sel \'mórsəl\ *n* : small piece or quantity

mor·tal \'mórt^əl\ *adj* 1 : causing or subject to death 2 : extreme —**mortal** *n* —**mor·tal·i·ty** \mór'talətē\ *n* —**mor·tal·ly** \'mórt^əlē\ *adv*

mor·tar \'mórtər\ *n* 1 : strong bowl 2 : short-barreled cannon 3 : masonry material used to cement bricks or stones in place —**mortar** *vb*

mort·gage \'mórgij\ *n* : transfer of property rights as security for a loan —**mortgage** *vb* —**mort·gag·ee** \,mór-gi'jē\ *n* —**mort·ga·gor** \,mórgi'jór\ *n*

mor·ti·fy \'mórtə,fī\ *vb* -**fied**; -**fy·ing** 1 : subdue by abstinence or self-inflicted pain 2 : humiliate —**mor·ti·fi·ca·tion** \,mórtəfə'kāshən\ *n*

mor·tu·ary \'mórchə,werē\ *n, pl* -**ar·ies** : place where dead bodies are kept until burial

mo·sa·ic \mō'zāik\ *n* : inlaid stone decoration —**mosaic** *adj*

Mos·lem \'mäzləm\ *var of* MUSLIM

mosque \'mäsk\ *n* : building where Muslims worship

mos·qui·to \mə'skētō\ *n, pl* -**toes** : biting bloodsucking insect

moss \'mós\ *n* : green seedless plant —**mossy** *adj*

most \'mōst\ *adj* 1 : majority of 2 : greatest ~ *adv* : to the greatest or a very great degree ~ *n* : greatest amount ~ *pron* : greatest number or part

-most \,mōst\ *adj suffix* : most : most toward

most·ly \'mōstlē\ *adv* : mainly

mote \'mōt\ *n* : small particle

mo·tel \mō'tel\ *n* : hotel with rooms accessible from the parking lot

moth \'móth\ *n* : small pale insect related to the butterflies

moth·er \'məthər\ *n* 1 : female parent 2 : source ~ *vb* 1 : give birth to 2 : cherish or protect —**moth·er·hood** \-,húd\ *n* —**moth·er·land** \-,land\ *n* —**moth·er·less** *adj* —**moth·er·ly** *adj*

moth·er-in-law *n, pl* **mothers-in-law** : spouse's mother

mo·tif \mō'tēf\ *n* : dominant theme

mo·tion \'mōshən\ *n* 1 : act or instance of moving 2 : proposal for action ~ *vb* : direct by a movement —**mo·tion·less** *adj* —**mo·tion·less·ly** *adv* —**mo·tion·less·ness** *n*

motion picture *n* : movie

mo·ti·vate \'mōtə,vāt\ *vb* -**vat·ed**; -**vat·ing** : provide with a motive —**mo·ti·va·tion** \,mōtə'vāshən\ *n* —**mo·ti·va·tor** \'mōtə,vātər\ *n*

mo·tive \'mōtiv\ *n* : cause of a person's action ~ *adj* 1 : moving to action 2 : relating to motion —**mo·tive·less** *adj*

mot·ley \'mätlē\ *adj* : of diverse colors or elements

mo·tor \'mōtər\ *n* : unit that supplies power or motion ~ *vb* : travel by automobile —**mo·tor·ist** \-ist\ *n* —**mo·tor·ize** \'mōtə,rīz\ *vb*

mo·tor·bike *n* : lightweight motorcycle

mo·tor·boat *n* : engine-driven boat

mo·tor·car *n* : automobile

mo·tor·cy·cle *n* : 2-wheeled automotive vehicle —**mo·tor·cy·clist** *n*

mo·tor·truck *n* : automotive truck

mot·tle \'mät³l\ *vb* -**tled; -tling** : mark with spots of different color

mot·to \'mätō\ *n, pl* -**toes** : brief guiding rule

mould \'mōld\ *var of* MOLD

mound \'maund\ *n* : pile (as of earth)

¹**mount** \'maunt\ *n* : mountain

²**mount** *vb* 1 : increase in amount 2 : get up on 3 : put in position ~ *n* 1 : frame or support 2 : horse to ride —**mount·able** *adj* —**mount·er** *n*

moun·tain \'maunt³n\ *n* : elevated land higher than a hill —**moun·tain·ous** \'maunt³nəs\ *adj* —**moun·tain·top** *n*

moun·tain·eer \,maunt³n'ir\ *n* : mountain resident or climber

moun·te·bank \'maunti,baŋk\ *n* : impostor

mourn \'mōrn\ *vb* : feel or express grief —**mourn·er** *n* —**mourn·ful** \-fəl\ *adj* —**mourn·ful·ly** *adv* —**mourn·ful·ness** *n* —**mourn·ing** *n*

mouse \'maus\ *n, pl* **mice** \'mīs\ 1 : small rodent 2 : device for controlling cursor movement on a computer display —**mouse·trap** *n or vb* —**mousy, mous·ey** \'mausē, -zē\ *adj*

mousse \'müs\ *n* 1 : light chilled dessert 2 : foamy hair-styling preparation

mous·tache \'məs,tash, məs'tash\ *var of* MUSTACHE

mouth \'mauth\ *n* : opening through which an animal takes in food ~ \'mauth\ *vb* 1 : speak 2 : repeat without comprehension or sincerity 3 : form soundlessly with the lips —**mouthed** \'mauthd, 'mautht\ *adj* —**mouth·ful** \-,fùl\ *n*

mouth·piece *n* 1 : part (as of a musical instrument) held in or to the mouth 2 : spokesman

mou·ton \'mü,tän\ *n* : processed sheepskin

move \'müv\ *vb* **moved; mov·ing** 1 : go or cause to go to another point 2 : change residence 3 : change or cause to change position 4 : take or cause to take action 5 : make a formal request 6 : stir the emotions ~ *n* 1 : act or instance of moving 2 : step taken

to achieve a goal—**mov·able, move·able** \-əbəl\ *adj* —**move·ment** *n* —**mov·er** *n*

-**mov·ie** \'müvē\ *n* : projected picture in which persons and objects seem to move

¹**mow** \'mau\ *n* : part of a barn where hay or straw is stored

²**mow** \'mō\ *vb* **mowed; mowed** *or* **mown** \'mōn\; **mow·ing** : cut with a machine —**mow·er** *n*

Mr. \'mistər\ *n, pl* **Messrs.** \'mesərz\ —conventional title for a man

Mrs. \'misəz, -əs, *esp South* 'mizəz. -əs\ *n, pl* **Mes·dames** \mā'dām, -'dam\ —conventional title for a married woman

Ms. \'miz\ *n* —conventional title for a woman

much \'məch\ *adj* **more** \'mōr\: **most** \'mōst\ : great in quantity, extent, or degree ~ *adv* **more; most** : to a great degree or extent ~ *n* : great quantity, extent, or degree

mu·ci·lage \'myüsəlij\ *n* : weak glue

muck \'mək\ *n* : manure, dirt, or mud —**mucky** *adj*

mu·cus \'myükəs\ *n* : slippery protective secretion of membranes (**mucous membranes**) lining body cavities —**mu·cous** \-kəs\ *adj*

mud \'məd\ *n* : soft wet earth —**mud·di·ly** \'məd³lē\ *adv* —**mud·di·ness** \-ēnəs\ *n* —**mud·dy** *adj or vb*

mud·dle \'məd³l\ *vb* -**dled; -dling** 1 : make, be, or act confused 2 : make a mess of —**muddle** *n* —**mud·dle·head·ed** \,məd³l'hedəd\ *adj*

mu·ez·zin \mü'ez³n, myü-\ *n* : Muslim who calls the hour of daily prayer

¹**muff** \'məf\ *n* : tubular hand covering

²**muff** *vb* : bungle —**muff** *n*

muf·fin \'məfən\ *n* : soft cake baked in a cup-shaped container

muf·fle \'məfəl\ *vb* -**fled; -fling** 1 : wrap up 2 : dull the sound of —**muf·fler** \'məflər\ *n*

muf·ti \'məftē\ *n* : civilian clothes

¹**mug** \'məg\ *n* : drinking cup ~ *vb* -**gg**- : make faces

²**mug** *vb* -**gg**- : assault with intent to rob —**mug·ger** *n*

mug·gy \'məgē\ *adj* -**gi·er; -est** : hot and humid —**mug·gi·ness** *n*

Mu·ham·mad·an \mō'hamədən, -'häm-; mü-\ *n* : Muslim —**Mu·ham·mad·an·ism** \-,izəm\ *n*

mu·lat·to \mù'lätō, -'lat-\ *n, pl* -**toes** *or*

-tos : person of mixed black and white ancestry

mul·ber·ry \'məl,berē\ n : tree with small edible fruit

mulch \'məlch\ n : protective ground covering —**mulch** vb

mulct \'məlkt\ n or vb : fine

¹mule \'myül\ n 1 : offspring of a male ass and a female horse 2 : stubborn person —**mul·ish** \'myülish\ adj —**mul·ish·ly** adv —**mul·ish·ness** n

²mule n : backless shoe

mull \'məl\ vb : ponder

mul·let \'məlat\ n, pl **-let** or **-lets** : marine food fish

multi- comb form 1 : many or multiple 2 : many times over

multiarmed	multimember
multibarreled	multimillion
multibillion	multimillionaire
multibranched	multipart
multibuilding	multipartite
multicenter	multiparty
multichambered	multiplant
multichannel	multipolar
multicolored	multiproblem
multicounty	multiproduct
multicultural	multipurpose
multidimen-	multiracial
sional	multiroom
multidirectional	multisense
multidisciplin-	multiservice
ary	multisided
multidiscipline	multispeed
multidivisional	multistage
multifaceted	multistep
multifamily	multistory
multifilament	multisyllabic
multifunction	multitalented
multifunctional	multitrack
multigrade	multiunion
multiheaded	multiunit
multihospital	multiuse
multihued	multivitamin
multilane	multiwarhead
multilevel	multiyear
multimedia	

mul·ti·far·i·ous \,məltə'farēəs\ adj : diverse

mul·ti·lat·er·al \,məlti'latərəl, -,tī-\ adj : having many sides or participants

mul·ti·lin·gual \-'liŋgwəl\ adj : knowing or using several languages —**mul·ti·lin·gual·ism** \-gwə,lizəm\ n

mul·ti·na·tion·al \-'nashənəl\ adj 1 : re-

lating to several nations or nationalities 2 : having divisions in several countries —**multinational** n

mul·ti·ple \'məltəpəl\ adj 1 : several or many 2 : various ~ n : product of one number by another

multiple sclerosis \-sklə'rōsəs\ n : brain or spinal disease affecting muscle control

mul·ti·pli·ca·tion \,məltəplə'kāshən\ n 1 : increase 2 : short method of repeated addition

mul·ti·plic·i·ty \,məltə'plisətē\ n, pl **-ties** : great number or variety

mul·ti·ply \'məltə,plī\ vb **-plied; -plying** 1 : increase in number 2 : perform multiplication —**mul·ti·pli·er** \-,plīər\ n

mul·ti·tude \'məltə,tüd, -,tyüd\ n : great number —**mul·ti·tu·di·nous** \,məltə'tüd²nəs, -,tyü-\ adj

¹mum \'məm\ adj : silent

²mum n : chrysanthemum

mum·ble \'məmbəl\ vb **-bled; -bling** : speak indistinctly —**mumble** n —**mum·bler** n

mum·mer \'məmər\ n 1 : actor esp. in a pantomime 2 : disguised merrymaker —**mum·mery** n

mum·my \'məmē\ n, pl **-mies** : embalmed body —**mum·mi·fi·ca·tion** \,məmifə'kāshən\ n —**mum·mi·fy** \'məmi,fī\ vb

mumps \'məmps\ n sing or pl : virus disease with swelling esp. of the salivary glands

munch \'mənch\ vb : chew

mun·dane \,mən'dān, 'mən,-\ adj 1 : relating to the world 2 : lacking concern for the ideal or spiritual — **mun·dane·ly** adv

mu·nic·i·pal \myü'nisəpəl\ adj : of or relating to a town or city —**mu·nic·i·pal·i·ty** \myü,nisə'palətē\ n

mu·nif·i·cent \myü'nifəsənt\ adj : generous —**mu·nif·i·cence** \-səns\ n

mu·ni·tion \myü'nishən\ n : armaments

mu·ral \'myürəl\ adj : relating to a wall ~ n : wall painting —**mu·ra·list** n

mur·der \'mərdər\ n : unlawful killing of a person ~ vb : commit a murder —**mur·der·er** n —**mur·der·ess** \-əs\ n —**mur·der·ous** \-əs\ adj —**mur·der·ous·ly** adv

murk \'mərk\ n : darkness —**murk·i·ly** \'mərkəlē\ adv —**murk·i·ness** \-kēnəs\ n —**murky** adj

mur·mur \'mərmər\ n 1 : muttered

complaint **2** : low indistinct sound —
murmur vb —**mur·mur·er** n —
mur·mur·ous adj

mus·ca·tel \,məskə'tel\ n : sweet wine

mus·cle \'məsəl\ n **1** : body tissue capable of contracting to produce mo-
tion **2** : strength ~ vb -**cled**; -**cling**
: force one's way —**mus·cled** adj —
mus·cu·lar \'məskyələr\ adj —
mus·cu·lar·i·ty \,məskyə'larətē\ n

muscular dystrophy n : disease marked
by progressive wasting of muscles

mus·cu·la·ture \'məskyələ,chúr\ n
: bodily muscles

¹muse \'myüz\ vb **mused**; **mus·ing**
: ponder —**mus·ing·ly** adv

²muse n : source of inspiration

mu·se·um \myu'zēəm\ n : institution
displaying objects of interest

mush \'məsh\ n **1** : corn meal boiled in
water or something of similar consistency **2** : sentimental nonsense —
mushy adj

mush·room \'məsh,rüm, -,rûm\ n : cap-
like organ of a fungus ~ vb : grow
rapidly

mu·sic \'myüzik\ n : vocal or instrumental sounds —**mu·si·cal** \-zikəl\ adj or
n —**mu·si·cal·ly** adv

mu·si·cian \myu'zishən\ n : composer
or performer of music —**mu·si·cian·**
ly adj —**mu·si·cian·ship** n

musk \'məsk\ n : strong-smelling substance from an Asiatic deer used in
perfume —**musk·i·ness** \'məskēnəs\
n —**musky** adj

mus·kel·lunge \'məskə,lənj\ n, pl
-**lunge** : large No. American pike

mus·ket \'məskət\ n : former shoulder
firearm —**mus·ke·teer** \,məskə'tir\ n

musk·mel·on \'məsk,melən\ n : small
edible melon

musk-ox \'məsk,äks\ n : shaggy-coated
wild ox of the arctic

musk·rat \-,rat\ n, pl -**rat** or -**rats** : No.
American aquatic rodent

Mus·lim \'məzləm, 'mús-, 'mûz-\ n : adherent of Islam —**Muslim** adj

mus·lin \'məzlən\ n : cotton fabric

muss \'məs\ n : untidy state ~ vb : disarrange —**muss·i·ly** \'məsəlē\ adv —
muss·i·ness \-ēnəs\ n —**mussy** adj

mus·sel \'məsəl\ n : edible mollusk

must \'məst\ vb —used as an auxiliary
esp. to express a command, obligation, or necessity ~ \'məst\ n
: something necessary

mus·tache \'məs,tash, məs'-\ n : hair of
the human upper lip

mus·tang \'məs,taŋ\ n : wild horse of
Western America

mus·tard \'məstərd\ n : pungent yellow
seasoning

mus·ter \'məstər\ vb **1** : assemble **2**
: rouse ~ n : assembled group

musty \'məstē\ adj **mus·ti·er**; -**est** : stale
—**must·i·ly** adv —**must·i·ness** n

mu·ta·ble \'myütəbəl\ adj : changeable
—**mu·ta·bil·i·ty** \,myütə'bilətē\ n

mu·tant \'myüt°nt\ adj : relating to or
produced by mutation —**mutant** n

mu·tate \'myü,tāt\ vb -**tat·ed**; -**tat·ing**
: undergo mutation —**mu·ta·tive**
\'myü,tātiv, 'myütət-\ adj

mu·ta·tion \myu'tāshən\ n : change in a
hereditary character —**mu·ta·tion·al**
adj

mute \'myüt\ adj **mut·er**; **mut·est 1**
: unable to speak **2** : silent ~ n : one
who is mute **2** : muffling device ~ vb
mut·ed; **mut·ing** : muffle —**mute·ly**
adv —**mute·ness** n

mu·ti·late \'myüt°l,āt\ vb -**lat·ed**; -**lat·**
ing : damage seriously (as by cutting
off or altering an essential part) —
mu·ti·la·tion \,myüt°l'āshən\ n —
mu·ti·la·tor \'myüt°l,ātər\ n

mu·ti·ny \'myüt°nē\ n, pl -**nies**
: rebellion —**mu·ti·neer** \,myüt°n'ir\
n —**mu·ti·nous** \'myüt°nəs\ adj —
mu·ti·nous·ly adv —**mutiny** vb

mutt \'mət\ n : mongrel

mut·ter \'mətər\ vb **1** : speak indistinctly or softly **2** : grumble —**mutter**
n

mut·ton \'mət°n\ n : flesh of a mature
sheep —**mut·tony** adj

mu·tu·al \'myüchəwəl\ adj **1** : given or
felt by one another in equal amount **2**
: common —**mu·tu·al·ly** adv

muz·zle \'məzəl\ n **1** : nose and jaws of
an animal **2** : muzzle covering to im-
mobilize an animal's jaws **3** : discharge end of a gun ~ vb -**zled**; -**zling**
: restrain with or as if with a muzzle

my \'mī\ adj **1** : relating to me or myself
2 —used interjectionally esp. to express surprise

my·nah, my·na \'mīnə\ n : dark crested
Asian bird

my·o·pia \mī'ōpēə\ n : nearsightedness
—**my·o·pic** \-'ōpik, -'äpik\ adj —
my·o·pi·cal·ly adv

myr·i·ad \'mirēəd\ n : indefinitely large
number —**myriad** adj

myrrh \'mər\ *n* : aromatic plant gum

myr·tle \'mərt⁹l\ *n* : shiny evergreen

my·self \mī'self\ *pron* : I, me —used reflexively or for emphasis

mys·tery \'mistərē\ *n, pl* **-ter·ies** 1 : religious truth 2 : something not understood 3 : puzzling or secret quality or state —**mys·te·ri·ous** \mis'tirēəs\ *adj* —**mys·te·ri·ous·ly** *adv* —**mys·te·ri·ous·ness** *n*

mys·tic \'mistik\ *adj* : mystical or mysterious ~ *n* : one who has mystical experiences —**mys·ti·cism** \-tə-,sizəm\ *n*

mys·ti·cal \'mistikəl\ *adj* 1 : spiritual 2 : relating to direct communion with God —**mys·ti·cal·ly** *adj*

mys·ti·fy \'mistə,fī\ *vb* **-fied; -fy·ing** : perplex —**mys·ti·fi·ca·tion** \,mistəfə'kāshən\ *n*

mys·tique \mis'tēk\ *n* : aura of mystery surrounding something

myth \'mith\ *n* 1 : legendary narrative explaining a belief or phenomenon 2 : imaginary person or thing —**myth·i·cal** \-ikəl\ *adj*

my·thol·o·gy \mith'äləjē\ *n, pl* **-gies** : body of myths —**myth·o·log·i·cal** \,mithə'läjikəl\ *adj* —**my·thol·o·gist** \mith'äləjist\ *n*

N

n \'en\ *n, pl* **n's** *or* **ns** \'enz\ : 14th letter of the alphabet

nab \'nab\ *vb* **-bb-** : seize or arrest

na·dir \'nā,dir, 'nādər\ *n* : lowest point

¹**nag** \'nag\ *n* : old or decrepit horse

²**nag** *vb* **-gg-** 1 : complain 2 : scold or urge continually 3 : be persistently annoying ~ *n* : one who nags habitually

na·iad \'nāəd, 'nī-, -,ad\ *n, pl* **-iads** *or* **-ia·des** \-ə,dēz\ : mythological water nymph

nail \'nāl\ *n* 1 : horny sheath at the end of each finger and toe 2 : pointed metal fastener ~ *vb* : fasten with a nail —**nail·er** *n*

na·ive, na·ïve \nä'ēv\ *adj* **-iv·er; -est** 1 : innocent and unsophisticated 2 : easily deceived —**na·ive·ly** *adv* —**na·ive·ness** *n*

na·ive·té \,näēvə'tā, nä'ēvə,-\ *n* : quality or state of being naive

na·ked \'nākəd, 'nekəd\ *adj* 1 : having no clothes on 2 : uncovered 3 : plain or obvious 4 : unaided —**na·ked·ly** *adv* —**na·ked·ness** *n*

nam·by-pam·by \,nambē'pambē\ *adj* : weak or indecisive

name \'nām\ *n* 1 : word by which a person or thing is known 2 : disparaging word for someone 3 : distinguished reputation ~ *vb* **named; nam·ing** 1 : give a name to 2 : mention or identify by name 3 : nominate or appoint ~ *adj* 1 : relating to a name 2 : prominent —**name·able** *adj* —**name·less** *adj* —**name·less·ly** *adv*

name·ly \'nāmlē\ *adv* : that is to say

name·sake \-,sāk\ *n* : one named after another

¹**nap** \'nap\ *vb* **-pp-** 1 : sleep briefly 2 : be off guard ~ *n* : short sleep

²**nap** *n* : soft downy surface —**nap·less** *adj* —**napped** \'napt\ *adj*

na·palm \'nā,pälm, -,päm\ *n* : gasoline in the form of a jelly

nape \'nāp, 'nap\ *n* : back of the neck

naph·tha \'nafthə\ *n* : flammable solvent

nap·kin \'napkən\ *n* : small cloth for use at the table

nar·cis·sism \'närsə,sizəm\ *n* : self-love —**nar·cis·sist** \-sist\ *n or adj* —**nar·cis·sis·tic** \,närsə'sistik\ *adj*

nar·cis·sus \när'sisəs\ *n, pl* **-cis·sus** *or* **-cis·sus·es** *or* **-cis·si** \-'sis,ī, -,ē\ : plant with flowers usu. borne separately

nar·cot·ic \när'kätik\ *n* : painkilling addictive drug —**narcotic** *adj*

nar·rate \'nar,āt\ *vb* **nar·rat·ed; nar·rat·ing** : tell (a story) —**nar·ra·tion** \na'rāshən\ *n* —**nar·ra·tive** \'narətiv\ *n or adj* —**nar·ra·tor** \'nar,ātər\ *n*

nar·row \'narō\ *adj* 1 : of less than standard width 2 : limited 3 : not liberal 4 : barely successful ~ *vb* : make narrow—**nar·row·ly** *adv* —**nar·row·ness** *n*

nar·row–mind·ed \,narō'mīndəd\ *adj* : shallow, provincial, or bigoted

nar·rows \'naröz\ *n pl* : narrow passage

nar·whal \'när,hwäl, 'närwəl\ *n* : sea mammal with a tusk

nasal \'nāzəl\ *adj* : relating to or uttered through the nose —**na·sal·ly** *adv*

nas·tur·tium \nə'stərshəm, na-\ *n* : herb with showy flowers

nas·ty \'nastē\ *adj* **nas·ti·er; -est** 1 : filthy 2 : indecent 3 : malicious or spiteful 4 : difficult or disagreeable 5 : unfair —**nas·ti·ly** \'nastəlē\ *adv* —**nas·ti·ness** \-tēnəs\ *n*

na·tal \'nāt³l\ *adj* : relating to birth

na·tion \'nāshən\ *n* 1 : people of similar characteristics 2 : community with its own territory and government —**na·tion·al** \'nashənəl\ *adj or n* —**na·tion·al·ly** *adv* —**na·tion·hood** *n* —**na·tion·wide** *adj*

na·tion·al·ism \'nashənəl,izəm\ *n* : devotion to national interests, unity, and independence —**na·tion·al·ist** \-ist\ *n or adj* —**na·tion·al·is·tic** \,nashənəl'istik\ *adj*

na·tion·al·i·ty \,nashə'nalətē\ *n, pl* **-ties** 1 : national character 2 : membership in a nation 3 : political independence 4 : ethnic group

na·tion·al·ize \'nashənəl,īz\ *vb* **-ized; -iz·ing** 1 : make national 2 : place under government control —**na·tion·al·i·za·tion** \,nashənələ'zāshən\ *n*

na·tive \'nātiv\ *adj* 1 : belonging to a person at or by way of birth 2 : born or produced in a particular place ~ *n* : one who belongs to a country by birth

Na·tiv·i·ty \nə'tivətē, nā-\ *n, pl* **-ties** 1 : birth of Christ 2 *not cap* : birth

nat·ty \'natē\ *adj* **-ti·er; -est** : smartly dressed —**nat·ti·ly** \'nat³lē\ *adv* —**nat·ti·ness** \-ēnəs\ *n*

nat·u·ral \'nachərəl\ *adj* 1 : relating to or determined by nature 2 : not artificial 3 : simple and sincere 4 : lifelike ~ *n* : one having an innate talent —**nat·u·ral·ness** *n*

nat·u·ral·ism \'nachərə,lizəm\ *n* : realism in art and literature —**nat·u·ral·is·tic** \,nachərə'listik\ *adj*

nat·u·ral·ist \-list\ *n* 1 : one who practices naturalism 2 : student of animals or plants

nat·u·ral·ize \-,līz\ *vb* **-ized; -iz·ing** 1 : become or cause to become established 2 : confer citizenship on —**nat·u·ral·i·za·tion** \,nachərələ'-zāshən\ *n*

nat·u·ral·ly \'nachərəlē\ *adv* 1 : in a natural way 2 : as might be expected

na·ture \'nāchər\ *n* 1 : basic quality of something 2 : kind 3 : disposition 4 : physical universe 5 : natural environment

naught \'nòt, 'nät\ *n* 1 : nothing 2 : zero

naugh·ty \'nòtē, 'nät-\ *adj* **-ti·er; -est** 1 : disobedient or misbehaving 2 : improper —**naught·i·ly** \'nòt³lē, 'nät-\ *adv* —**naught·i·ness** \-ēnəs\ *n*

nau·sea \'nòzēə, -shə\ *n* 1 : sickness of the stomach with a desire to vomit 2 : extreme disgust —**nau·seous** \-shəs, -zēəs\ *adj*

nau·se·ate \'nòzē,āt, -zhē-, -sē-, -shē-\ *vb* **-ated; -at·ing** : affect or become affected with nausea —**nau·se·at·ing·ly** \-,ātiŋlē\ *adv*

nau·ti·cal \'nòtikəl\ *adj* : relating to ships and sailing —**nau·ti·cal·ly** *adv*

nau·ti·lus \'nòt³ləs\ *n, pl* **-lus·es** *or* **-li** \-³l,ī, -,ē\ : sea mollusk with a spiral shell

na·val \'nāvəl\ *adj* : relating to a navy

nave \'nāv\ *n* : central part of a church

na·vel \'nāvəl\ *n* : depression in the abdomen

nav·i·ga·ble \'navigəbəl\ *adj* : capable of being navigated —**nav·i·ga·bil·i·ty** \,navigə'bilətē\ *n*

nav·i·gate \'navə,gāt\ *vb* **-gat·ed; -gat·ing** 1 : sail on or through 2 : direct the course of —**nav·i·ga·tion** \,navə'gāshən\ *n* —**nav·i·ga·tor** \'navə-,gātər\ *n*

na·vy \'nāvē\ *n, pl* **-vies** 1 : fleet 2 : nation's organization for sea warfare

nay \'nā\ *adv* : no—used in oral voting ~ *n* : negative vote

Na·zi \'nätsē, 'nat-\ *n* : member of a German fascist party from 1933 to 1945 —**Nazi** *adj* —**Na·zism** \'nät,sizəm, 'nat-\, **Na·zi·ism** \-sē,izəm\ *n*

near \'nir\ *adv* : at or close to ~ *prep* : close to ~ *adj* 1 : not far away 2 : very much like ~ *vb* : approach —**near·ly** *adv* —**near·ness** *n*

near·by \nir'bī, 'nir,bī\ *adv or adj* : near

near·sight·ed \'nir'sītəd\ *adj* : seeing well at short distances only —**near·sight·ed·ly** *adv* —**near·sight·ed·ness** *n*

neat \'nēt\ *adj* 1 : not diluted 2 : tastefully simple 3 : orderly and clean —**neat** *adv* —**neat·ly** *adv* —**neat·ness** *n*

neb·u·la \'nebyələ\ *n, pl* **-lae** \-,lē, -,lī\

: large cloud of interstellar gas —
neb·u·lar \-lər\ *adj*

neb·u·lous \-ləs\ *adj* : indistinct

nec·es·sary \'nesə,serē\ *n, pl* **-saries**
: indispensable item ~ *adj* 1
: inevitable 2 : compulsory 3
: positively needed —**nec·es·sar·i·ly**
\,nesə'serəlē\ *adv*

ne·ces·si·tate \ni'sesə,tāt\ *vb* **-tat·ed;**
-tat·ing : make necessary

ne·ces·si·ty \ni'sesətē\ *n, pl* **-ties** 1 : very
great need 2 : something that is nec-
essary 3 : poverty 4 : circumstances
that cannot be changed

neck \'nek\ *n* 1 : body part connecting
the head and trunk 2 : part of a garment at the neck 3 : narrow part ~ *vb*
: kiss and caress —**necked** \'nekt\ *adj*

neck·er·chief \'nekərchəf, -,chēf\ *n, pl*
-chiefs \-chəfs, -,chēfs\ : cloth worn
tied about the neck

neck·lace \'nekləs\ *n* : ornament worn
around the neck

neck·tie *n* : ornamental cloth tied under
a collar

nec·ro·man·cy \'nekrə,mansē\ *n* : art of
conjuring up the spirits of the dead —
nec·ro·man·cer \-sər\ *n*

ne·cro·sis \nə'krōsəs, ne-\ *n, pl* **-cro·ses**
\-,sēz\ : death of body tissue

nec·tar \'nektər\ *n* : sweet plant secretion

nec·tar·ine \,nektə'rēn\ *n* : smooth-
skinned peach

née, nee \'nā\ *adj*—used to identify a
married woman by maiden name

need \'nēd\ *n* 1 : obligation 2 : lack of
something or what is lacking 3
: poverty ~ *vb* 1 : be in want 2 : have
cause for 3 : be under obligation —
need·ful \-fəl\ *adj* —**need·less** *adj* —
need·less·ly *adv* —**needy** *adj*

nee·dle \'nēdᵊl\ *n* 1 : pointed sewing implement or something like it 2
: movable bar in a compass 3 : hollow
instrument for injecting or withdrawing material ~ *vb* **-dled; -dling**
: incite to action by repeated gibes —
nee·dle·work \-,wərk\ *n*

nee·dle·point \'nēdᵊl,point\ *n* 1 : lace
fabric 2 : embroidery on canvas —
needlepoint *adj*

ne·far·i·ous \ni'farēəs\ *adj* : very
wicked —**ne·far·i·ous·ly** *adv*

ne·gate \ni'gāt\ *vb* **-gat·ed; -gat·ing** 1
: deny 2 : nullify —**ne·ga·tion**
\-'gāshən\ *n*

neg·a·tive \'negətiv\ *adj* 1 : marked by

denial or refusal 2 : showing a lack of
something suspected or desirable 3
: less than zero 4 : having more electrons than protons 5 : having light and
shadow images reversed ~ *n* 1
: negative word or vote 2 : a negative
number 3 : negative photographic
image —**neg·a·tive·ly** *adv* —**neg·**
a·tive·ness *n* —**neg·a·tiv·i·ty** \,negə-
'tivətē\ *n*

ne·glect \ni'glekt\ *vb* 1 : disregard 2
: leave unattended to ~ *n* 1 : act of
neglecting 2 : condition of being neglected —**ne·glect·ful** *adj*

neg·li·gee \,neglə'zhā\ *n* : woman's
loose robe

neg·li·gent \'neglijənt\ *adj* : marked by
neglect —**neg·li·gence** \-jəns\ *n* —
neg·li·gent·ly *adv*

neg·li·gi·ble \'neglijəbəl\ *adj* : insignificant

ne·go·ti·ate \ni'gōshē,āt\ *vb* **-at·ed; -at·**
ing 1 : confer with another to settle a
matter 2 : obtain cash for 3 : get
through successfully —**ne·go·tia·ble**
\-shəbəl, -shēə-\ *adj* —**ne·go·ti·a·tion**
\-,gōshē'āshən, -shē'ā-\ *n* —**ne·go·**
ti·a·tor \-'gōshē,ātər\ *n*

Ne·gro \'nēgrō\ *n, pl* **-groes** : member
of the black race —**Negro** *adj* —**Ne·**
groid \'nē,groid\ *n or adj, often not*
cap

neigh \'nā\ *n* : cry of a horse —**neigh** *vb*

neigh·bor \'nābər\ *n* 1 : one living
nearby 2 : fellowman ~ *vb* : be near
or next to —**neigh·bor·hood** \-,hud\
n —**neigh·bor·li·ness** *n* —**neigh·**
bor·ly *adv*

nei·ther \'nēthər, 'nī-\ *pron or adj* : not
the one or the other ~ *conj* 1 : not
either 2 : nor

nem·e·sis \'neməsəs\ *n, pl* **-e·ses** \-ə,sēz\
1 : old and usu. frustrating rival 2
: retaliation

ne·ol·o·gism \nē'älə,jizəm\ *n* : new
word

ne·on \'nē,än\ *n* : gaseous colorless
chemical element that emits a reddish
glow in electric lamps —**neon** *adj*

neo·phyte \'nēə,fīt\ *n* : beginner

neph·ew \'nefyü, *chiefly Brit* 'nev-\ *n* : a
son of one's brother, sister, brother-
in-law, or sister-in-law

nep·o·tism \'nepə,tizəm\ *n* : favoritism
shown in hiring a relative

nerd \'nərd\ *n* : one who is not stylish
or socially at ease —**nerdy** *adj*

nerve \'nərv\ *n* 1 : strand of body tissue

that connects the brain with other parts of the body **2** : self-control **3** : daring **4** *pl* : nervousness —**nerved** \\'nərvd\ *adj* —**nerve·less** *adj*

ner·vous \\'nərvəs\ *adj* **1** : relating to or made up of nerves **2** : easily excited **3** : timid or fearful —**nerv·ous·ly** *adv* —**nerv·ous·ness** *n*

nervy \\'nərvē\ *adj* **nerv·i·er; -est** : insolent or presumptuous

-ness \nəs\ *n suffix* : condition or quality

nest \\'nest\ *n* **1** : shelter prepared by a bird for its eggs **2** : place where eggs (as of insects or fish) are laid and hatched **3** : snug retreat **4** : set of objects fitting one inside or under another ~ *vb* : build or occupy a nest

nes·tle \\'nesəl\ *vb* **-tled; -tling** : settle snugly (as in a nest)

¹net \\'net\ *n* : fabric with spaces between strands or something made of this ~ *vb* **-tt-** : cover with or catch in a net

²net *adj* : remaining after deductions ~ *vb* **-tt-** : have as profit

neth·er \\'nethər\ *adj* : situated below

net·tle \\'net'l\ *n* : coarse herb with stinging hairs ~ *vb* **-tled; -tling** : provoke or vex —**net·tle·some** *adj*

net·work *n* : system of crossing or connected elements

neu·ral \\'nurəl, 'nyur-\ *adj* : relating to a nerve

neu·ral·gia \nu'raljə, nyu-\ *n* : pain along a nerve —**neu·ral·gic** \-jik\ *adj*

neu·ri·tis \nu'rītəs, nyu-\ *n, pl* **-rit·i·des** \-'ritə,dēz\ *or* **-ri·tis·es** : inflammation of a nerve

neu·rol·o·gy \nu'räləjē, nyu-\ *n* : study of the nervous system —**neu·ro·log·i·cal** \,nürə'läjikəl, ,nyur-\, **neu·ro·log·ic** \-ik\ *adj* —**neu·rol·o·gist** \nu'räləjist, nyu-\ *n*

neu·ro·sis \nu'rōsəs, nyu-\ *n, pl* **-ro·ses** \-,sēz\ : nervous disorder

neu·rot·ic \nu'rätik, nyu-\ *adj* : relating to neurosis ~ *n* : unstable person —**neu·rot·i·cal·ly** *adv*

neu·ter \\'nütər, 'nyü-\ *adj* : neither masculine nor feminine ~ *vb* : castrate or spay

neu·tral \-trəl\ *adj* **1** : not favoring either side **2** : being neither one thing nor the other **3** : not decided in color **4** : not electrically charged ~ *n* **1** : one that is neutral **2** : position of gears that are not engaged —**neu-**

tral·i·za·tion \,nütrələ'zāshən, ,nyü-\ *n* —**neu·tral·ize** \'nütrə,līz, 'nyü-\ *vb*

neu·tral·i·ty \nü'tralətē, nyü-\ *n* : state of being neutral

neu·tron \\'nü,trän, 'nyü-\ *n* : uncharged atomic particle

nev·er \\'nevər\ *adv* **1** : not ever **2** : not in any degree, way, or condition

nev·er·more *adv* : never again

nev·er·the·less *adv* : in spite of that

new \\'nü, 'nyü\ *adj* **1** : not old or familiar **2** : different from the former **3** : recently discovered or learned **4** : not accustomed **5** : refreshed or regenerated **6** : being such for the first time ~ *adv* : newly —**new·ish** *adj* —**new·ness** *n*

new·born *adj* **1** : recently born **2** : born anew ~ *n, pl* **-born** *or* **-borns** : newborn individual

new·ly \-lē\ *adv* : recently

news \\'nüz, 'nyüz\ *n* : report of recent events —**news·let·ter** *n* —**news·mag·a·zine** *n* —**news·man** \-mən, -,man\ *n* —**news·pa·per** *n* —**news·pa·per·man** \-,man\ *n* —**news·stand** *n* —**news·wom·an** \-,wùmən\ *n* —**news·wor·thy** *adj*

news·cast \-,kast\ *n* : broadcast of news —**news·cast·er** \-,kastər\ *n*

news·print *n* : paper made from wood pulp

newsy \\'nüzē, 'nyü-\ *adj* **news·i·er; -est** : filled with news

newt \\'nüt, 'nyüt\ *n* : small salamander

New Year *n* : New Year's Day

New Year's Day *n* : January 1 observed as a legal holiday

next \\'nekst\ *adj* : immediately preceding or following ~ *adv* **1** : in the time or place nearest **2** : at the first time yet to come ~ *prep* : nearest to

nex·us \\'neksəs\ *n, pl* **-us·es** \-səsəz\ *or* **-us** \-səs, -,süs\ : connection

nib \\'nib\ *n* : pen point

nib·ble \\'nibəl\ *vb* **-bled; -bling** : bite gently or bit by bit ~ *n* : small bite

nice \\'nīs\ *adj* **nic·er; nic·est** **1** : fastidious **2** : very precise or delicate **3** : pleasing **4** : respectable —**nice·ly** *adv* —**nice·ness** *n*

nice·ty \\'nīsətē\ *n, pl* **-ties** **1** : dainty or elegant thing **2** : fine detail **3** : exactness

niche \\'nich\ *n* **1** : recess in a wall **2** : fitting place, work, or use

nick \\'nik\ *n* **1** : small broken area or

chip **2** : critical moment ~ *vb* : make a nick in

nick·el \'nikəl\ *n* **1** : hard silver-white metallic chemical element used in alloys **2** : U.S. 5-cent piece

nick·name \'nik,nām\ *n* : informal substitute name —**nickname** *vb*

nic·o·tine \'nikə,tēn\ *n* : poisonous and addictive substance in tobacco

niece \'nēs\ *n* : a daughter of one's brother, sister, brother-in-law, or sister-in-law

nig·gard·ly \'nigərdlē\ *adj* : stingy — **nig·gard** *n* —**nig·gard·li·ness** *n*

nig·gling \'nigəliŋ\ *adj* : petty and annoying

nigh \'nī\ *adv or adj or prep* : near

night \'nīt\ *n* **1** : period between dusk and dawn **2** : the coming of night — **night** *adj* —**night·ly** *adj or adv* — **night·time** *n*

night·clothes *n pl* : garments worn in bed

night·club \-,kləb\ *n* : place for drinking and entertainment open at night

night crawler *n* : earthworm

night·fall *n* : the coming of night

night·gown *n* : gown worn for sleeping

night·in·gale \'nīt°n,gāl, -iŋ-\ *n* : Old World thrush that sings at night

night·mare \'nīt,mar\ *n* : frightening dream —**nightmare** *adj* —**night·mar·ish** \-,marish\ *adj*

night·shade \'nīt,shād\ *n* : group of plants that include poisonous forms and food plants (as the potato and eggplant)

nil \'nil\ *n* : nothing

nim·ble \'nimbəl\ *adj* **-bler; -blest** **1** : agile **2** : clever —**nim·ble·ness** *n* — **nim·bly** \-blē\ *adv*

nine \'nīn\ *n* **1** : one more than 8 **2** : 9th in a set or series —**nine** *adj or pron* —**ninth** \'nīnth\ *adj or adv or n*

nine·pins *n* : bowling game using 9 pins

nine·teen \nīn'tēn\ *n* : one more than 18 —**nineteen** *adj or pron* —**nine·teenth** \-'tēnth\ *adj or n*

nine·ty \'nīntē\ *n, pl* **-ties** : 9 times 10 —**nine·ti·eth** \-ēəth\ *adj or n* — **ninety** *adj or pron*

nin·ny \'ninē\ *n, pl* **nin·nies** : fool

¹nip \'nip\ *vb* **-pp-** **1** : catch hold of and squeeze tightly **2** : pinch or bite off **3** : destroy the growth or fulfillment of ~ *n* **1** : biting cold **2** : tang **3** : pinch or bite

²nip *n* : small quantity of liquor ~ *vb* **-pp-** : take liquor in nips

nip·per \'nipər\ *n* **1** : one that nips **2** *pl* : pincers **3** : small boy

nip·ple \'nipəl\ *n* : tip of the breast or something resembling it

nip·py \'nipē\ *adj* **-pi·er; -est** **1** : pungent **2** : chilly

nir·va·na \nir'vänə\ *n* : state of blissful oblivion

nit \'nit\ *n* : egg of a parasitic insect

ni·ter \'nītər\ *n* : potassium nitrate used in gunpowder or fertilizer or in curing meat

ni·trate \'nī,trāt, -trət\ *n* : chemical salt used esp. in curing meat

ni·tric acid \'nītrik-\ *n* : liquid acid used in making dyes, explosives, and fertilizers

ni·trite \-,trīt\ *n* : chemical salt used in curing meat

ni·tro·gen \'nītrəjən\ *n* : tasteless odorless gaseous chemical element

ni·tro·glyc·er·in, ni·tro·glyc·er·ine \,nītrō'glisərən\ *n* : heavy oily liquid used as an explosive and as a blood-vessel relaxer

nit·wit \'nit,wit\ *n* : stupid person

no \'nō\ *adv* **1** —used to express the negative **2** : in no respect or degree **3** : not so **4** —used as an interjection of surprise or doubt ~ *adj* **1** : not any **2** : not a ~ *n, pl* **noes** *or* **nos** \'nōz\ **1** : refusal **2** : negative vote

no·bil·i·ty \nō'bilətē\ *n* **1** : quality or state of being noble **2** : class of people of noble rank

no·ble \'nōbəl\ *adj* **-bler; -blest** **1** : illustrious **2** : aristocratic **3** : stately **4** : of outstanding character ~ *n* : nobleman —**no·ble·ness** *n* —**no·bly** *adv*

no·ble·man \-mən\ *n* : member of the nobility

no·ble·wom·an \-,wùmən\ *n* : a woman of noble rank

no·body \'nōbədē, -,bädē\ *pron* : no person ~ *n, pl* **-bod·ies** : person of no influence or importance

noc·tur·nal \näk'tərn°l\ *adj* : relating to, occurring at, or active at night

noc·turne \'näk,tərn\ *n* : dreamy musical composition

nod \'näd\ *vb* **-dd-** **1** : bend the head downward or forward (as in bowing or going to sleep or as a sign of assent) **2** : move up and down **3** : show by a nod of the head —**nod** *n*

node \'nōd\ *n* : stem part from which a leaf arises —**nod•al** \-ᵊl\ *adj*

nod•ule \'näjül\ *n* : small lump or swelling —**nod•u•lar** \'näjələr\ *adj*

no•el \nō'el\ *n* **1** : Christmas carol **2** *cap* : Christmas season

noes *pl of* NO

nog•gin \'nägən\ *n* **1** : small mug **2** : person's head

no•how \'nō,hau̇\ *adv* : in no manner

noise \'nȯiz\ *n* : loud or unpleasant sound ~ *vb* noised; nois•ing : spread by rumor —noise•less *adj* —noise•less•ly *adv* —noise•mak•er *n* —nois•i•ly \'nȯizəlē\ *adv* —nois•i•ness \-zēnəs\ *n* —noisy \'nȯizē\ *adj*

noi•some \'nȯisəm\ *adj* : harmful or offensive

no•mad \'nō,mad\ *n* : one who has no permanent home —nomad *adj* —no•mad•ic \nō'madik\ *adj*

no•men•cla•ture \'nōmən,klāchər\ *n* : system of names

nom•i•nal \'nämənᵊl\ *adj* **1** : being something in name only **2** : small or negligible —**nom•i•nal•ly** *adv*

nom•i•nate \'nämə,nāt\ *vb* -nat•ed; -nat•ing : propose or choose as a candidate —**nom•i•na•tion** \,nämə-'nāshən\ *n*

nom•i•na•tive \'nämənətiv\ *adj* : relating to or being a grammatical case marking typically the subject of a verb —**nominative** *n*

nom•i•nee \,nämə'nē\ *n* : person nominated

non- \'nän, ,nän\ *prefix* **1** : not, reverse of, or absence of **2** : not important

nonabrasive
nonabsorbent
nonacademic
nonaccredited
nonacid
nonaddictive
nonadhesive
nonadjacent
nonadjustable
nonaffiliated
nonaggression
nonalcoholic
nonaligned
nonappearance
nonautomatic
nonbeliever
nonbinding
nonbreakable
noncancerous

noncandidate
non-Catholic
non-Christian
nonchurchgoer
noncitizen
nonclassical
nonclassified
noncombat
noncombatant
noncombustible
noncommercial
noncommunist
noncompliance
nonconflicting
nonconforming
nonconsecutive
nonconstructive
noncontagious
noncontrollable

noncontroversial
noncorrosive
noncriminal
noncritical
noncumulative
noncurrent
nondeductible
nondeferrable
nondegradable
nondelivery
nondemocratic
nondenominational
nondestructive
nondiscrimination
nondiscriminatory
noneducational
nonelastic
nonelected
nonelective
nonelectric
nonelectronic
nonemotional
nonenforcement
nonessential
nonexclusive
nonexistence
nonexistent
nonexplosive
nonfat
nonfatal
nonfattening
nonfictional
nonflammable
nonflowering
nonfunctional
nongovernmental
nongraded
nonhazardous
nonhereditary
nonindustrial
nonindustrialized
noninfectious
noninflationary
nonintegrated
nonintellectual
noninterference
nonintoxicating
noninvasive
non-Jewish
nonlegal
nonlethal
nonliterary

nonliving
nonmagnetic
nonmalignant
nonmedical
nonmember
nonmetal
nonmetallic
nonmilitary
nonmusical
nonnative
nonnegotiable
nonobjective
nonobservance
nonorthodox
nonparallel
nonparticipant
nonparticipating
nonpaying
nonpayment
nonperformance
nonperishable
nonphysical
nonpoisonous
nonpolitical
nonpolluting
nonporous
nonpregnant
nonproductive
nonprofessional
nonprofit
nonracial
nonradioactive
nonrated
nonrealistic
nonrecurring
nonrefillable
nonrefundable
nonreligious
nonrenewable
nonrepresentative
nonresident
nonresponsive
nonrestricted
nonreversible
nonsalable
nonscientific
nonscientist
nonsegregated
non-self-governing
nonsexist
nonsexual
nonsignificant
nonskier
nonsmoker

nonsmoking
nonspeaking
nonspecialist
nonspecific
nonstandard
nonstick
nonstop
nonstrategic
nonstudent
nonsugar
nonsurgical
nonswimmer
nontaxable
nonteaching

nontechnical
nontoxic
nontraditional
nontransferable
nontropical
nontypical
nonunion
nonuser
nonvenomous
nonverbal
nonvoter
nonwhite
nonworker

non·age \\'nänij, 'nōnij\\ n : period of youth and esp. legal minority

nonce \\'näns\\ n : present occasion ~ adj : occurring, used, or made only once

non·cha·lant \\,nänshə'länt\\ adj : showing indifference —**non·cha·lance** \\-'läns\\ n —**non·cha·lant·ly** adv

non·com·mis·sioned officer \\,nänkə-'mishənd-\\ n : subordinate officer in the armed forces appointed from enlisted personnel

non·com·mit·tal \\,nänkə'mit^əl\\ adj : indicating neither consent nor dissent

non·con·duc·tor n : substance that is a very poor conductor

non·con·form·ist n : one who does not conform to an established belief or mode of behavior —**non·con·for·mi·ty** n

non·de·script \\,nändi'skript\\ adj : lacking distinctive qualities

none \\'nən\\ pron : not any ~ adv : not at all

non·en·ti·ty n : one of no consequence

none·the·less \\,nənthə'les\\ adv : nevertheless

non·pa·reil \\,nänpə'rel\\ adj : having no equal ~ n 1 : one who has no equal 2 : chocolate candy disk

non·par·ti·san adj : not influenced by political party bias

non·per·son n : person without social or legal status

non·plus \\,nän'pləs\\ vb -ss- : perplex

non·pre·scrip·tion adj : available without a doctor's prescription

non·pro·lif·er·a·tion adj : aimed at ending increased use of nuclear arms

non·sched·uled adj : licensed to carry by air without a regular schedule

non·sense \\'nän,sens, -səns\\ n : foolish or meaningless words or actions —

non·sen·si·cal \\nän'sensikəl\\ adj —**non·sen·si·cal·ly** adv

non·sup·port n : failure in a legal obligation to provide for someone's needs

non·vi·o·lence n : avoidance of violence esp. in political demonstrations —**non·vi·o·lent** adj

noo·dle \\'nüd^əl\\ n : ribbon-shaped food paste

nook \\'nùk\\ n 1 : inside corner 2 : private place

noon \\'nün\\ n : middle of the day —**noon** adj

noon·day \\-,dā\\ n : noon

no one pron : no person

noon·time n : noon

noose \\'nüs\\ n : rope loop that slips down tight

nor \\nòr\\ conj : and not—used esp. after *neither* to introduce and negate the 2d member of a series

norm \\'nòrm\\ n 1 : standard usu. derived from an average 2 : typical widespread practice or custom

nor·mal \\'nòrməl\\ adj : average, regular, or standard —**nor·mal·cy** \\-sē\\ n —**nor·mal·i·ty** \\nòr'malətē\\ n —**nor·mal·i·za·tion** \\,nòrmələ'zāshən\\ n —**nor·mal·ize** \\'nòrmə,līz\\ vb —**nor·mal·ly** adv

north \\'nòrth\\ adv : to or toward the north ~ adj : situated toward, at, or coming from the north ~ n 1 : direction to the left of one facing east 2 cap : regions to the north —**north·er·ly** \\'nòrthərlē\\ adv or adj —**north·ern** \\-ərn\\ adj —**North·ern·er** n —**north·ern·most** \\-,mōst\\ adj —**north·ward** \\-wərd\\ adv or adj —**north·wards** \\-wərdz\\ adv

north·east \\nòrth'ēst\\ n 1 : direction between north and east 2 cap : regions to the northeast —**northeast** adj or adv —**north·east·er·ly** \\-ərlē\\ adv or adj —**north·east·ern** \\-ərn\\ adj

northern lights n pl : aurora borealis

north pole n : northernmost point of the earth

north·west \\-'west\\ n 1 : direction between north and west 2 cap : regions to the northwest —**northwest** adj or adv —**north·west·er·ly** \\-ərlē\\ adv or adj —**north·west·ern** \\-ərn\\ adj

nose \\'nōz\\ n 1 : part of the face containing the nostrils 2 : sense of smell 3 : front part ~ vb nosed; nos·ing 1 : detect by smell 2 : push aside with the nose 3 : pry 4 : inch ahead —

nose·bleed n —**nosed** \'nōzd\ adj —
nose out vb : narrowly defeat

nose·gay \-,gā\ n : small bunch of flowers

nos·tal·gia \nä'staljə, nə-\ n : wistful
yearning for something past —**nos-
tal·gic** \-jik\ adj

nos·tril \'nästrəl\ n : opening of the nose

nos·trum \-trəm\ n : questionable remedy

nosy, nos·ey \'nōzē\ adj **nos·i·er; -est**
: tending to pry

not \'nät\ adv —used to make a statement negative

no·ta·ble \'nōtəbəl\ adj 1 : noteworthy
2 : distinguished ~ n : notable person
—**no·ta·bil·i·ty** \nōtə'bilətē\ n —
no·ta·bly \'nōtəblē\ adv

no·ta·rize \'nōtə,rīz\ vb -**rized; -riz·ing**
: attest as a notary public

no·ta·ry public \'nōtərē-\ n, pl -**ries
public** or -**ry publics** : public official
who attests writings to make them legally authentic

no·ta·tion \nō'tāshən\ n 1 : note 2 : act,
process, or method of marking things
down

notch \'näch\ n : V-shaped hollow —
notch vb

note \'nōt\ vb **not·ed; not·ing** 1 : notice
2 : write down ~ n 1 : musical tone
2 : written comment or record 3
: short informal letter 4 : notice or
heed —**note·book** n

not·ed \'nōtəd\ adj : famous

note·wor·thy \-,wərthē\ adj : worthy of
special mention

noth·ing \'nəthiŋ\ pron 1 : no thing 2
: no part 3 : one of no value or importance ~ adv : not at all ~ n 1
: something that does not exist 2
: zero 3 : one of little or no importance —**noth·ing·ness** n

no·tice \'nōtəs\ n 1 : warning or announcement 2 : attention ~ vb -**ticed;
-tic·ing** : take notice of —**no·tice-
able** adj —**no·tice·ably** adv

no·ti·fy \'nōtə,fī\ vb -**fied; -fy·ing** : give
notice of or to —**no·ti·fi·ca·tion**
\,nōtəfə'kāshən\ n

no·tion \'nōshən\ n 1 : idea or opinion
2 : whim

no·to·ri·ous \nō'tōrēəs\ adj : widely and
unfavorably known —**no·to·ri·ety**
\,nōtə'rīətē\ n —**no·to·ri·ous·ly** adv

not·with·stand·ing \,nätwith'standiŋ,
-with-\ prep : in spite of ~ adv
: nevertheless ~ conj : although

nou·gat \'nügət\ n : nuts or fruit pieces
in a sugar paste

nought \'nȯt, 'nät\ var of NAUGHT

noun \'naún\ n : word that is the name
of a person, place, or thing

nour·ish \'nərish\ vb : promote the
growth of —**nour·ish·ing** adj —
nour·ish·ment n

no·va \'nōvə\ n, pl -**vas** or -**vae** \-,vē,
-,vī\ : star that suddenly brightens and
then fades gradually

nov·el \'nävəl\ adj : new or strange ~ n
: long invented prose story —**nov-
el·ist** \-əlist\ n

nov·el·ty \'nävəltē\ n, pl -**ties** 1
: something new or unusual 2
: newness 3 : small manufactured article—usu. pl.

No·vem·ber \nō'vembər\ n : 11th month
of the year having 30 days

nov·ice \'nävəs\ n 1 : one preparing to
take vows in a religious order 2 : one
who is inexperienced or untrained

no·vi·tiate \nō'vishət, nə-\ n : period or
state of being a novice

now \'naú\ adv 1 : at the present time or
moment 2 : forthwith 3 : under these
circumstances ~ conj : in view of the
fact ~ n : present time

now·a·days \'naúə,dāz\ adv : now

no·where \-,hwer\ adv : not anywhere
—**no·where** n

nox·ious \'näkshəs\ adj : harmful

noz·zle \'näzəl\ n : device to direct or
control a flow of fluid

nu·ance \'nü,äns, 'nyü-\ n : subtle distinction or variation

nub \'nəb\ n 1 : knob or lump 2 : gist

nu·bile \'nü,bīl, 'nyü-, -bəl\ adj 1 : of
marriageable condition or age 2
: sexually attractive

nu·cle·ar \'nüklēər, 'nyü-\ adj 1
: relating to the atomic nucleus or
atomic energy 2 : relating to a weapon
whose power is from a nuclear reaction

nu·cle·us \'nüklēəs, 'nyü-\ n, pl -**clei**
\-klē,ī\ : central mass or part (as of a
cell or an atom)

nude \'nüd, 'nyüd\ adj **nud·er; nud·est**
: naked ~ n : nude human figure —
nu·di·ty \'nüdətē, 'nyü-\ n

nudge \'nəj\ vb **nudged; nudg·ing**
: touch or push gently —**nudge** n

nud·ism \'nüd,izəm, 'nyü-\ n : practice
of going nude —**nud·ist** \'nüdist-
'nyü-\ n

nug·get \'nəgət\ n : lump of gold

nui·sance \'nüsᵊns, 'nyü-\ n : something annoying

null \'nəl\ adj : having no legal or binding force —**nul·li·ty** \'nələtē\ n

nul·li·fy \'nələ,fī\ vb -**fied**; -**fy·ing** : make null or valueless —**nul·li·fi·ca·tion** \,nələfə'kāshən\ n

numb \'nəm\ adj : lacking feeling —**numb** vb —**numb·ly** adv —**numb·ness** n

num·ber \'nəmbər\ n 1 : total of individuals taken together 2 : indefinite total 3 : unit of a mathematical system 4 : numeral 5 : one in a sequence ~ vb 1 : count 2 : assign a number to 3 : comprise in number —**num·ber·less** adj

nu·mer·al \'nümərəl, 'nyü-\ n : conventional symbol representing a number

nu·mer·a·tor \'nümə,rātər, 'nyü-\ n : part of a fraction above the line

nu·mer·i·cal \nù'merikəl, nyü-\, **nu·meric** \-'merik\ adj 1 : relating to numbers 2 : expressed in or involving numbers —**nu·mer·i·cal·ly** adv

nu·mer·ol·o·gy \,nümə'räləjē, ,nyü-\ n : occult study of numbers —**nu·mer·ol·o·gist** \-jist\ n

nu·mer·ous \'nümərəs, 'nyü-\ adj : consisting of a great number

nu·mis·mat·ics \,nüməz'matiks, ,nyü-\ n : study or collection of monetary objects —**nu·mis·mat·ic** \-ik\ adj —**nu·mis·ma·tist** \nü'mizmətist, nyü-\ n

num·skull \'nəm,skəl\ n : stupid person

nun \'nən\ n : woman belonging to a religious order —**nun·nery** \-ərē\ n

nup·tial \'nəpshəl\ adj : relating to marriage or a wedding ~ n : marriage or wedding—usu. pl.

nurse \'nərs\ n 1 : one hired to care for children 2 : person trained to care for sick people ~ vb **nursed**; **nurs·ing** 1 : suckle 2 : care for

nurs·ery \'nərsərē\ n, pl -**er·ies** 1 : place where children are cared for 2 : place where young plants are grown

nursing home n : private establishment providing care for persons who are unable to care for themselves

nur·ture \'nərchər\ n 1 : training or upbringing 2 : food or nourishment ~ vb -**tured**; -**tur·ing** 1 : care for or feed 2 : educate

nut \'nət\ n 1 : dry hard-shelled fruit or seed with a firm inner kernel 2 : metal block with a screw hole through it 3 : foolish, eccentric, or crazy person 4 : enthusiast —**nut·crack·er** n —**nut·shell** n —**nut·ty** adj

nut·hatch \'nət,hach\ n : small bird

nut·meg \'nət,meg, -,māg\ n : nutlike aromatic seed of a tropical tree

nu·tri·ent \'nütrēənt, 'nyü-\ n : something giving nourishment —**nutrient** adj

nu·tri·ment \-trəmənt\ n : nutrient

nu·tri·tion \nù'trishən, nyü-\ n : act or process of nourishing esp. with food —**nu·tri·tion·al** \-'trishənəl\ adj —**nu·tri·tious** \-'trishəs\ adj —**nu·tri·tive** \'nütrətiv, 'nyü-\ adj

nuts \'nəts\ adj 1 : enthusiastic 2 : crazy

nuz·zle \'nəzəl\ vb -**zled**; -**zling** 1 : touch with or as if with the nose 2 : snuggle

ny·lon \'nī,län\ n 1 : tough synthetic material used esp. in textiles 2 pl : stockings made of nylon

nymph \'nimf\ n 1 : lesser goddess in ancient mythology 2 : girl 3 : immature insect

O

o \'ō\ n, pl **o's** or **os** \'ōz\ 1 : 15th letter of the alphabet 2 : zero

O var of OH

oaf \'ōf\ n : stupid or awkward person —**oaf·ish** \'ōfish\ adj

oak \'ōk\ n, pl **oaks** or **oak** : tree bearing a thin-shelled nut or its wood —**oak·en** \'ōkən\ adj

oar \'ōr\ n : pole with a blade at the end used to propel a boat

oar·lock \-,läk\ n : u-shaped device for holding an oar

oa·sis \ō'āsəs\ *n, pl* **oa·ses** \-,sēz\ : fertile area in a desert

oat \'ōt\ *n* : cereal grass or its edible seed —**oat·cake** *n* —**oat·en** \-∍n\ *adj* —**oat·meal** *n*

oath \'ōth\ *n, pl* **oaths** \'ōthz, 'ōths\ **1** : solemn appeal to God as a pledge of sincerity **2** : profane utterance

ob·du·rate \'äbdúrət, -dyù-\ *adj* : stubbornly resistant —**ob·du·ra·cy** \-rəsē\ *n*

obe·di·ent \ō'bēdēənt\ *adj* : willing to obey —**obe·di·ence** \-əns\ *n* —**obe·di·ent·ly** *adv*

obei·sance \ō'bēsəns, -'bās-\ *n* : bow of respect or submission

obe·lisk \'äbə,lisk\ *n* : 4-sided tapering pillar

obese \ō'bēs\ *adj* : extremely fat —**obe·si·ty** \-'bēsətē\ *n*

obey \ō'bā\ *vb* **obeyed; obey·ing 1** : follow the commands or guidance of **2** : behave in accordance with

ob·fus·cate \'äbfə,skāt\ *vb* **-cat·ed; -cat·ing** : confuse —**ob·fus·ca·tion** \,äbfəs'kāshən\ *n*

obit·u·ary \ō'bichə,werē\ *n, pl* **-ar·ies** : death notice

¹ob·ject \'äbjikt\ *n* **1** : something that may be seen or felt **2** : purpose **3** : noun or equivalent toward which the action of a verb is directed or which follows a preposition

²ob·ject \əb'jekt\ *vb* : offer opposition or disapproval —**ob·jec·tion** \-'jek-shən\ *n* —**ob·jec·tion·able** \-shə-nəbəl\ *adj* —**ob·jec·tion·ably** \-blē\ *adv* —**ob·jec·tor** \-'jektər\ *n*

ob·jec·tive \əb'jektiv\ *adj* **1** : relating to an object or end **2** : existing outside an individual's thoughts or feelings **3** : treating facts without distortion **4** : relating to or being a grammatical case marking objects ~ *n* : aim or end of action —**ob·jec·tive·ly** *adv* —**ob·jec·tive·ness** *n* —**ob·jec·tiv·i·ty** \,äbjek'tivətē\ *n*

ob·li·gate \'äblə,gāt\ *vb* **-gat·ed; -gat·ing** : bind legally or morally —**ob·li·ga·tion** \,äblə'gāshən\ *n* —**oblig·a·to·ry** \ə'bligə,tōrē, 'äbligə-\ *adj*

oblige \ə'blīj\ *vb* **obliged; oblig·ing 1** : compel **2** : do a favor for —**oblig·ing** *adj* —**oblig·ing·ly** *adv*

oblique \ō'blēk, -'blīk\ *adj* **1** : lying at a slanting angle **2** : indirect —**oblique·ly** *adv* —**oblique·ness** *n* — **obliq·ui·ty** \-'blikwətē\ *n*

oblit·er·ate \ə'blitə,rāt\ *vb* **-at·ed; -at·ing** : completely remove or destroy —**oblit·er·a·tion** \-,blitə'rāshən\ *n*

obliv·i·on \ə'blivēən\ *n* **1** : state of having lost conscious awareness **2** : state of being forgotten

obliv·i·ous \-ēəs\ *adj* : not aware or mindful—with *to* or *of* —**obliv·i·ous·ly** *adv* —**obliv·i·ous·ness** *n*

ob·long \'äb,lòŋ\ *adj* : longer in one direction than in the other with opposite sides parallel —**oblong** *n*

ob·lo·quy \'äbləkwē\ *n, pl* **-quies 1** : strongly condemning utterance **2** : bad repute

ob·nox·ious \äb'näkshəs, əb-\ *adj* : repugnant —**ob·nox·ious·ly** *adv* —**ob·nox·ious·ness** *n*

oboe \'ōbō\ *n* : slender woodwind instrument with a reed mouthpiece —**obo·ist** \'ō,bōist\ *n*

ob·scene \äb'sēn, əb-\ *adj* : repugnantly indecent —**ob·scene·ly** *adv* —**ob·scen·i·ty** \-'senətē\ *n*

ob·scure \äb'skyùr, əb-\ *adj* **1** : dim or hazy **2** : not well known **3** : vague ~ *vb* : make indistinct or unclear —**ob·scure·ly** *adv* —**ob·scu·ri·ty** \-'skyù-rətē\ *n*

ob·se·quies \'äbsəkwēz\ *n pl* : funeral or burial rite

ob·se·qui·ous \əb'sēkwēəs\ *adj* : excessively attentive or flattering —**ob·se·qui·ous·ly** *adv* —**ob·se·qui·ous·ness** *n*

ob·ser·va·to·ry \əb'zərvə,tōrē\ *n, pl* **-ries** : place for observing astronomical phenomena

ob·serve \əb'zərv\ *vb* **-served; -serv·ing 1** : conform to **2** : celebrate **3** : see, watch, or notice **4** : remark —**ob·serv·able** *adj* —**ob·ser·vance** \-'zərvəns\ *n* —**ob·ser·vant** \-vənt\ *adj* —**ob·ser·va·tion** \,äbsər'vāshən, -zər-\ *n*

ob·sess \əb'ses\ *vb* : preoccupy intensely or abnormally —**ob·ses·sion** \äb-'seshən, əb-\ *n* —**ob·ses·sive** \-'sesiv\ *adj* —**ob·ses·sive·ly** *adv*

ob·so·les·cent \,äbsə'les∍nt\ *adj* : going out of use —**ob·so·les·cence** \-∍ns\ *n*

ob·so·lete \,äbsə'lēt, 'äbsə,-\ *adj* : no longer in use

ob·sta·cle \'äbstikəl\ *n* : something that stands in the way or opposes

ob·stet·rics \əb'stetriks\ *n sing or pl* : branch of medicine that deals with childbirth —**ob·stet·ric** \-rik\, **ob·stet·ri·cal** \-rikəl\ *adj* —**ob·ste·tri·cian** \ˌäbstə'trishən\ *n*

ob·sti·nate \'äbstənət\ *adj* : stubborn —**ob·sti·na·cy** \-nəsē\ *n* —**ob·sti·nate·ly** *adv*

ob·strep·er·ous \əb'strepərəs\ *adj* : uncontrollably noisy or defiant —**ob·strep·er·ous·ness** *n*

ob·struct \əb'strəkt\ *vb* : block or impede —**ob·struc·tion** \-'strəkshən\ *n* —**ob·struc·tive** \-'strəktiv\ *adj* —**ob·struc·tor** \-tər\ *n*

ob·tain \əb'tān\ *vb* 1 : gain by effort 2 : be generally recognized —**ob·tain·able** *adj*

ob·trude \əb'trüd\ *vb* -**trud·ed; -trud·ing** 1 : thrust out 2 : intrude —**ob·tru·sion** \-'trüzhən\ *n* —**ob·tru·sive** \-'trüsiv\ *adj* —**ob·tru·sive·ly** *adv* —**ob·tru·sive·ness** *n*

ob·tuse \äb'tüs, əb-, -'tyüs\ *adj* 1 : slow-witted 2 : exceeding 90 but less than 180 degrees —**ob·tuse·ly** *adv* —**obtuse·ness** *n*

ob·verse \'äb,vərs, äb'-\ *n* : principal side (as of a coin)

ob·vi·ate \'äbvē,āt\ *vb* -**at·ed; -at·ing** : make unnecessary —**ob·vi·a·tion** \ˌäbvē'āshən\ *n*

ob·vi·ous \'äbvēəs\ *adj* : plain or unmistakable —**ob·vi·ous·ly** *adv* —**obvi·ous·ness** *n*

oc·ca·sion \ə'kāzhən\ *n* 1 : favorable opportunity 2 : cause 3 : time of an event 4 : special event ~ *vb* : cause —**oc·ca·sion·al** \-'kāzhənəl\ *adj* —**oc·ca·sion·al·ly** *adv*

oc·ci·den·tal \ˌäksə'dentⁿl\ *adj* : western —**Occidental** *n*

oc·cult \ə'kəlt, 'äk,əlt\ *adj* 1 : secret or mysterious 2 : relating to supernatural agencies —**oc·cult·ism** \-'kəl,tizəm\ *n* —**oc·cult·ist** \-tist\ *n*

oc·cu·pan·cy \'äkyəpənsē\ *n, pl* -**cies** : an occupying

oc·cu·pant \-pənt\ *n* : one who occupies

oc·cu·pa·tion \ˌäkyə'pāshən\ *n* 1 : vocation 2 : action or state of occupying —**oc·cu·pa·tion·al** \-shənəl\ *adj* —**oc·cu·pa·tion·al·ly** *adv*

oc·cu·py \'äkyə,pī\ *vb* -**pied; -py·ing** 1 : engage the attention of 2 : fill up 3 : take or hold possession of 4 : reside in —**oc·cu·pi·er** \-,pīər\ *n*

oc·cur \ə'kər\ *vb* -**rr**- 1 : be found or

met with 2 : take place 3 : come to mind

oc·cur·rence \ə'kərəns\ *n* : something that takes place

ocean \'ōshən\ *n* 1 : whole body of salt water 2 : very large body of water —**ocean·front** *n* —**ocean·go·ing** *adj* —**oce·an·ic** \ˌōshē'anik\ *adj*

ocean·og·ra·phy \ˌōshə'nägrəfē\ *n* : science dealing with the ocean —**ocean·og·ra·pher** \-fər\ *n* —**ocean·o·graph·ic** \-nə'grafik\ *adj*

oce·lot \'äsə,lät, 'ōsə-\ *n* : medium-sized American wildcat

ocher, ochre \'ōkər\ *n* : red or yellow pigment

o'·clock \ə'kläk\ *adv* : according to the clock

oc·ta·gon \'äktə,gän\ *n* : 8-sided polygon —**oc·tag·o·nal** \äk'tagənⁿl\ *adj*

oc·tave \'äktiv\ *n* : musical interval of 8 steps or the notes within this interval

Oc·to·ber \äk'tōbər\ *n* : 10th month of the year having 31 days

oc·to·pus \'äktəpəs\ *n, pl* -**pus·es** *or* -**pi** \-,pī\ : sea mollusk with 8 arms

oc·u·lar \'äkyələr\ *adj* : relating to the eye

oc·u·list \'äkyəlist\ *n* 1 : ophthalmologist 2 : optometrist

odd \'äd\ *adj* 1 : being only one of a pair or set 2 : not divisible by two without a remainder 3 : additional to what is usual or to the number mentioned 4 : queer —**odd·ly** *adv* —**odd·ness** *n*

odd·i·ty \'ädətē\ *n, pl* -**ties** : something odd

odds \'ädz\ *n pl* 1 : difference by which one thing is favored 2 : disagreement 3 : ratio between winnings and the amount of the bet

ode \'ōd\ *n* : solemn lyric poem

odi·ous \'ōdēəs\ *adj* : hated —**odi·ous·ly** *adv* —**odi·ous·ness** *n*

odi·um \'ōdēəm\ *n* 1 : merited loathing 2 : disgrace

odor \'ōdər\ *n* : quality that affects the sense of smell —**odor·less** *adj* —**odor·ous** *adj*

od·ys·sey \'ädəsē\ *n, pl* -**seys** : long wandering

o'er \'ōr\ *adv or prep* : OVER

of \'əv, 'äv\ *prep* 1 : from 2 : distinguished by 3 : because of 4 : made or written by 5 : made with, being, or containing 6 : belonging to or connected with 7 : about 8 : that is 9 : concerning 10 : before

off \'òf\ *adv* 1 : from a place 2 : unattached or removed 3 : to a state of being no longer in use 4 : away from work 5 : at a distance in time or space ~ *prep* 1 : away from 2 : at the expense of 3 : not engaged in or abstaining from 4 : below the usual level of ~ *adj* 1 : not operating, up to standard, or correct 2 : remote 3 : provided for

of·fal \'òfəl\ *n* 1 : waste 2 : viscera and trimmings of a butchered animal

of·fend \ə'fend\ *vb* 1 : sin or act in violation 2 : hurt, annoy, or insult —**of·fend·er** *n*

of·fense, of·fence \ə'fens, 'äf,ens\ *n* : attack, misdeed, or insult

of·fen·sive \ə'fensiv, 'äf,en-\ *adj* : causing offense ~ *n* : attack —**of·fen·sive·ly** *adv* —**of·fen·sive·ness** *n*

of·fer \'òfər\ *vb* 1 : present for acceptance 2 : propose 3 : put up (an effort) ~ *n* 1 : proposal 2 : bid —**of·fer·ing** *n*

of·fer·to·ry \'òfər,tōrē\ *n, pl* -**ries** : presentation of offerings or its musical accompaniment

off·hand *adv or adj* : without previous thought or preparation

of·fice \'òfəs\ *n* 1 : position of authority (as in government) 2 : rite 3 : place where a business is transacted —**of·fice·hold·er** *n*

of·fi·cer \'òfəsər\ *n* 1 : one charged with law enforcement 2 : one who holds an office of trust or authority 3 : one who holds a commission in the armed forces

of·fi·cial \ə'fishəl\ *n* : one in office ~ *adj* : authorized or authoritative —**of·fi·cial·dom** \-dəm\ *n* —**of·fi·cial·ly** *adv*

of·fi·ci·ant \ə'fishēənt\ *n* : clergy member who officiates at a religious rite

of·fi·ci·ate \ə'fishē,āt\ *vb* -**at·ed;** -**at·ing** : perform a ceremony or function

of·fi·cious \ə'fishəs\ *adj* : volunteering one's services unnecessarily —**of·fi·cious·ly** *adv* —**of·fi·cious·ness** *n*

off·ing \'òfiŋ\ *n* : future

off·set \'òf,set\ *vb* -**set;** -**set·ting** : provide an opposite or equaling effect to

off·shoot \'òf,shüt\ *n* : outgrowth

off·shore *adv* : at a distance from the shore ~ *adj* : moving away from or situated off the shore

off·spring \'òf,spriŋ\ *n, pl* **offspring** : one coming into being through animal or plant reproduction

of·ten \'òfən, 'òft-\ *adv* : many times —**of·ten·times, oft·times** *adv*

ogle \'ōgəl\ *vb* **ogled; ogling** : stare at lustily —**ogle** *n* —**ogler** \-ələr\ *n*

ogre \'ōgər\ *n* 1 : monster 2 : dreaded person

oh \'ō\ *interj* 1—used to express an emotion 2—used in direct address

ohm \'ōm\ *n* : unit of electrical resistance —**ohm·ic** \'ōmik\ *adj* —**ohm·me·ter** \'ōm,mētər\ *n*

oil \'òil\ *n* 1 : greasy liquid substance 2 : petroleum ~ *vb* : put oil in or on —**oil·er** *n* —**oil·i·ness** \'òilēnəs\ *n* —**oily** \'òilē\ *adj*

oil·cloth *n* : cloth treated with oil or paint and used for coverings

oil·skin *n* : oiled waterproof cloth

oink \'òiŋk\ *n* : natural noise of a hog —**oink** *vb*

oint·ment \'òintmənt\ *n* : oily medicinal preparation

OK *or* **okay** \ō'kā\ *adv or adj* : all right ~ *vb* **OK'd** *or* **okayed; OK'ing** *or* **okay·ing** : approve ~ *n* : approval

okra \'ōkrə, *South also* -krē\ *n* : leafy vegetable with edible green pods

old \'ōld\ *adj* 1 : of long standing 2 : of a specified age 3 : relating to a past era 4 : having existed a long time —**old·ish** \'ōldish\ *adj*

old·en \'ōldən\ *adj* : of or relating to a bygone era

old–fash·ioned \-'fashənd\ *adj* 1 : out-of-date 2 : conservative

old maid *n* : spinster

old–tim·er \'ōld'tīmər\ *n* 1 : veteran 2 : one who is old

ole·an·der \'ōlē,andər\ *n* : poisonous evergreen shrub

oleo·mar·ga·rine \,ōlēō'märjərən\ *n* : margarine

ol·fac·to·ry \äl'faktərē, ōl-\ *adj* : relating to the sense of smell

oli·gar·chy \'älə,gärkē, 'ōlə-\ *n, pl* -**chies** 1 : government by a few people 2 : those holding power in an oligarchy —**oli·garch** \-,gärk\ *n* —**oli·gar·chic** \,älə'gärkik, ,ōlə-\, **oli·gar·chi·cal** \-kikəl\ *adj*

ol·ive \'äliv, -əv\ *n* 1 : evergreen tree bearing small edible fruit or the fruit 2 : dull yellowish green color

om·buds·man \'äm,bùdzmən, äm'bùdz-\ *n, pl* -**men** \-mən\ : complaint investigator

om·e·let, om·e·lette \'ämələt\ *n* : beaten eggs lightly fried and folded

omen \'ōmən\ *n* : sign or warning of the future

om·i·nous \'ämənəs\ *adj* : presaging evil —**om·i·nous·ly** *adv* —**om·i·nous·ness** *n*

omit \ō'mit\ *vb* **-tt-** 1 : leave out 2 : fail to perform —**omis·si·ble** \ō'misəbəl\ *adj* —**omis·sion** \-'mishən\ *n*

om·nip·o·tent \äm'nipətənt\ *adj* : almighty —**om·nip·o·tence** \-əns\ *n* —**om·nip·o·tent·ly** *adv*

om·ni·pres·ent \,ämni'prez²nt\ *adj* : ever-present —**om·ni·pres·ence** \-²ns\ *n*

om·ni·scient \äm'nishənt\ *adj* : all-knowing —**om·ni·science** \-əns\ *n* —**om·ni·scient·ly** *adv*

om·niv·o·rous \äm'nivərəs\ *adj* 1 : eating both meat and vegetables 2 : avid —**om·niv·o·rous·ly** *adv*

on \'ȯn, 'än\ *prep* 1 : in or to a position over and in contact with 2 : at or to 3 : about 4 : from 5 : with regard to 6 : in a state or process 7 : during the time of ~ *adv* 1 : in or into contact with 2 : forward 3 : into operation

once \'wəns\ *adv* 1 : one time only 2 : at any one time 3 : formerly ~ *n* : one time ~ *conj* : as soon as ~ *adj* : former —**at once** 1 : simultaneously 2 : immediately

once—over *n* : swift examination

on·com·ing *adj* : approaching

one \'wən\ *adj* 1 : being a single thing 2 : being one in particular 3 : being the same in kind ~ *pron* 1 : certain indefinitely indicated person or thing 2 : a person in general ~ *n* 1 : 1st in a series 2 : single person or thing —**one·ness** *n*

oner·ous \'änərəs, 'ōn-\ *adj* : imposing a burden

one·self \,wən'self\ *pron* : one's own self—usu. used reflexively or for emphasis

one-sid·ed \-'sīdəd\ *adj* 1 : occurring on one side only 2 : partial

one-time *adj* : former

one—way *adj* : made or for use in only one direction

on·go·ing *adj* : continuing

on·ion \'ənyən\ *n* : plant grown for its pungent edible bulb or this bulb

on·ly \'ōnlē\ *adj* : alone in its class ~ *adv* 1 : merely or exactly 2 : solely 3

: at the very least 4 : as a result ~ *conj* : but

on·set *n* : start

on·shore *adj* 1 : moving toward shore 2 : lying on or near the shore —**on·shore** *adv*

on·slaught \'än,slȯt, 'ȯn-\ *n* : attack

on·to \'ȯntü, 'än-\ *prep* : to a position or point on

onus \'ōnəs\ *n* : burden (as of obligation or blame)

on·ward \'ȯnwərd, 'än-\ *adv or adj* : forward

on·yx \'äniks\ *n* : quartz used as a gem

¹ooze \'üz\ *n* : soft mud ~ *vb* **oozed; ooz·ing** : flow or leak out slowly —**oozy** \'üzē\ *adj*

opac·i·ty \ō'pasətē\ *n* : quality or state of being opaque or an opaque spot

opal \'ōpəl\ *n* : gem with delicate colors

opaque \ō'pāk\ *adj* 1 : blocking light 2 : not easily understood 3 : dull-witted —**opaque·ly** *adv*

open \'ōpən\ *adj* 1 : not shut or shut up 2 : not secret or hidden 3 : frank or generous 4 : extended 5 : free from controls 6 : not decided ~ *vb* 1 : make or become open 2 : make or become functional 3 : start ~ *n* : outdoors —**open·er** \-ər\ *n* —**open·ly** *adv* —**open·ness** *n*

open·hand·ed \-'handəd\ *adj* : generous —**open·hand·ed·ly** *adv*

open·ing \'ōpəniŋ\ *n* 1 : act or instance of making open 2 : something that is open 3 : opportunity

op·era \'äpərə, 'äprə\ *n* : drama set to music —**op·er·at·ic** \,äpə'ratik\ *adj*

op·er·a·ble \'äpərəbəl\ *adj* 1 : usable or in working condition 2 : suitable for surgical treatment

op·er·ate \'äpə,rāt\ *vb* **-at·ed; -at·ing** 1 : perform work 2 : perform an operation 3 : manage —**op·er·a·tor** \-,rātər\ *n*

op·er·a·tion \,äpə'rāshən\ *n* 1 : act or process of operating 2 : surgical work on a living body 3 : military action or mission —**op·er·a·tion·al** \-shənəl\ *adj*

op·er·a·tive \'äpərətiv, -,rāt-\ *adj* : working or having an effect

op·er·et·ta \,äpə'retə\ *n* : light opera

oph·thal·mol·o·gy \,äf,thal'mäləjē\ *n* : branch of medicine dealing with the eye —**oph·thal·mol·o·gist** \-jist\ *n*

opi·ate \'ōpēət, -pē,āt\ *n* : preparation or derivative of opium

opine \ō'pīn\ *vb* **opined; opin·ing**
: express an opinion

opin·ion \ə'pinyən\ *n* **1** : belief **2**
: judgment **3** : formal statement by an
expert

opin·ion·at·ed \-yə,nātəd\ *adj* : stubborn in one's opinions

opi·um \'ōpēəm\ *n* : addictive narcotic
drug that is the dried juice of a poppy

opos·sum \ə'päsəm\ *n* : common tree-
dwelling nocturnal mammal

op·po·nent \ə'pōnənt\ *n* : one that opposes

op·por·tune \,äpər'tün, -'tyün\ *adj*
: suitable or timely —**op·por·tune·ly**
adv

op·por·tun·ism \-'tü,nizəm, -'tyü-\ *n* : a
taking advantage of opportunities —
op·por·tun·ist \-nist\ *n* —**op·por·
tu·nis·tic** \-tü'nistik, -tyü-\ *adj*

op·por·tu·ni·ty \-'tünətē, -'tyü-\ *n, pl*
-ties : favorable time

op·pose \ə'pōz\ *vb* **-posed; -pos·ing 1**
: place opposite or against something
2 : resist —**op·po·si·tion** \,äpə-
'zishən\ *n*

op·po·site \'äpəzət\ *n* : one that is opposed ~ *adj* **1** : set facing something
that is at the other side or end **2**
: opposed or contrary ~ *adv* : on opposite sides ~ *prep* : across from —
op·po·site·ly *adv*

op·press \ə'pres\ *vb* **1** : persecute **2**
: weigh down —**op·pres·sion** \ə-
'preshən\ *n* —**op·pres·sive** \-'presiv\
adj —**op·pres·sive·ly** *adv* —**op·pres·
sor** \-'presər\ *n*

op·pro·bri·ous \ə'prōbrēəs\ *adj* : expressing or deserving opprobrium —
op·pro·bri·ous·ly *adv*

op·pro·bri·um \-brēəm\ *n* **1** : something
that brings disgrace **2** : infamy

opt \'äpt\ *vb* : choose

op·tic \'äptik\ *adj* : relating to vision or
the eye

op·ti·cal \'äptikəl\ *adj* : relating to op-
tics, vision, or the eye

op·ti·cian \äp'tishən\ *n* : maker of or
dealer in eyeglasses

op·tics \'äptiks\ *n pl* : science of light
and vision

op·ti·mal \'äptəməl\ *adj* : most favorable —**op·ti·mal·ly** *adv*

op·ti·mism \'äptə,mizəm\ *n* : tendency
to hope for the best —**op·ti·mist**
\-mist\ *n* —**op·ti·mis·tic** \,äptə'mistik\
adj —**op·ti·mis·ti·cal·ly** *adv*

op·ti·mum \'äptəməm\ *n, pl* **-ma** \-mə\

: amount or degree of something
most favorable to an end —**optimum**
adj

op·tion \'äpshən\ *n* **1** : ability to choose
2 : right to buy or sell a stock **3**
: alternative —**op·tion·al** \-shənəl\
adj

op·tom·e·try \äp'tämətrē\ *n* : profession
of examining the eyes —**op·tom·e·
trist** \-trist\ *n*

op·u·lent \'äpyələnt\ *adj* : lavish —**op·
u·lence** \-ləns\ *n* —**op·u·lent·ly** *adv*

opus \'ōpəs\ *n, pl* **opera** \'ōpərə, 'äpə-\
: work esp. of music

or \'ȯr\ *conj* —used to indicate an alternative

-or \ər\ *n suffix* : one that performs an
action

or·a·cle \'ȯrəkəl\ *n* **1** : one held to give
divinely inspired answers or revela-
tions **2** : wise person or an utterance
of such a person —**orac·u·lar** \ȯ-
'rakyələr\ *adj*

oral \'ȯrəl\ *adj* **1** : spoken **2** : relating to
the mouth —**oral·ly** *adv*

or·ange \'ȯrinj\ *n* **1** : reddish yellow citrus fruit **2** : color between red and yellow —**or·ange·ade** \,ȯrinj'ād\ *n*

orang·u·tan \ə'raŋə,taŋ, -,taŋ\ *n* : large
reddish brown ape

ora·tion \ə'rāshən\ *n* : elaborate formal
speech

or·a·tor \'ȯrətər\ *n* : one noted as a public speaker

or·a·to·rio \,ȯrə'tōrē,ō\ *n, pl* **-ri·os**
: major choral work

or·a·to·ry \'ȯrə,tōrē\ *n* : art of public
speaking —**or·a·tor·i·cal** \,ȯrə'tō-
rikəl\ *adj*

orb \'ȯrb\ *n* : spherical body

or·bit \'ȯrbət\ *n* : path made by one
body revolving around another ~ *vb*
: revolve around —**or·bit·al** \-ᵊl\ *adj*
—**or·bit·er** *n*

or·chard \'ȯrchərd\ *n* : place where fruit
or nut trees are grown —**or·chard·ist**
\-ist\ *n*

or·ches·tra \'ȯrkəstrə\ *n* **1** : group of
musicians **2** : front seats of a theater's
main floor —**or·ches·tral** \ȯr'kestrəl\
adj —**or·ches·tral·ly** *adv*

or·ches·trate \'ȯrkə,strāt\ *vb* **-trat·ed;
-trat·ing 1** : compose or arrange for
an orchestra **2** : arrange or combine
for best effect —**or·ches·tra·tion**
\,ȯrkə'strāshən\ *n*

or·chid \'ȯrkəd\ *n* : plant with showy 3-
petal flowers or its flower

or·dain \ȯr'dān\ vb 1 : admit to the clergy 2 : decree

or·deal \ȯr'dēl, 'ȯr,dēl\ n : severely trying experience

or·der \'ȯrdər\ n 1 : rank, class, or special group 2 : arrangement 3 : rule of law 4 : authoritative regulation or instruction 5 : working condition 6 : special request for a purchase or what is purchased ~ vb 1 : arrange 2 : give an order to 3 : place an order for

or·der·ly \-lē\ adj 1 : being in order or tidy 2 : well behaved ~ n, pl -lies 1 : officer's attendant 2 : hospital attendant —**or·der·li·ness** n

or·di·nal \'ȯrdᵊnəl\ n : number indicating order in a series

or·di·nance \-ᵊnəns\ n : municipal law

or·di·nary \'ȯrdᵊn,erē\ adj : of common occurrence, quality, or ability —**or·di·nar·i·ly** \,ȯrdᵊn'erəlē\ adv

or·di·na·tion \,ȯrdᵊn'āshən\ n : act of ordaining

ord·nance \'ȯrdnəns\ n : military supplies

ore \'ȯr\ n : mineral containing a valuable constituent

oreg·a·no \ə'regə,nō\ n : mint used as a seasoning and source of oil

or·gan \'ȯrgən\ n 1 : air-powered or electronic keyboard instrument 2 : animal or plant structure with special function 3 : periodical

or·gan·ic \ȯr'ganik\ adj 1 : relating to a bodily organ 2 : relating to living things 3 : relating to or containing carbon or its compounds 4 : relating to foods produced without the use of laboratory-made products —**or·gan·i·cal·ly** adv

or·gan·ism \'ȯrgə,nizəm\ n : a living thing

or·gan·ist \'ȯrgənist\ n : organ player

or·ga·nize \'ȯrgə,nīz\ vb -nized; -niz·ing : form parts into a functioning whole —**or·ga·ni·za·tion** \,ȯrgə·nə'zāshən\ n —**or·ga·ni·za·tion·al** \-shənəl\ adj —**or·ga·niz·er** n

or·gasm \'ȯr,gazəm\ n : climax of sexual excitement —**or·gas·mic** \ȯr'gazmik\ adj

or·gy \'ȯrjē\ n, pl -gies : unrestrained indulgence (as in sexual activity)

ori·ent \'ȯrē,ent\ vb 1 : set in a definite position 2 : acquaint with a situation —**ori·en·ta·tion** \,ȯrēən'tāshən\ n

ori·en·tal \,ȯrē'entᵊl\ adj : Eastern —**Oriental** n

or·i·fice \'ȯrəfəs\ n : opening

or·i·gin \'ȯrəjən\ n 1 : ancestry 2 : rise, beginning, or derivation from a source —**orig·i·nate** \ə'rijə,nāt\ vb —**orig·i·na·tor** \-ər\ n

orig·i·nal \ə'rijənəl\ n : something from which a copy is made ~ adj 1 : first 2 : not copied from something else 3 : inventive —**orig·i·nal·i·ty** n —**orig·i·nal·ly** adv

ori·ole \'ȯrē,ōl, -ēəl\ n : American songbird

or·na·ment \'ȯrnəmənt\ n : something that adorns ~ vb : provide with ornament —**or·na·men·tal** \,ȯrnə'mentᵊl\ adj —**or·na·men·ta·tion** \-mən'tāshən\ n

or·nate \ȯr'nāt\ adj : elaborately decorated —**or·nate·ly** adv —**or·nate·ness** n

or·nery \'ȯrnərē, 'än-\ adj : irritable

or·ni·thol·o·gy \,ȯrnə'thäləjē\ n, pl -gies : study of birds —**or·ni·tho·log·i·cal** \-thə'läjikəl\ adj —**or·ni·thol·o·gist** \-'thäləjist\ n

or·phan \'ȯrfən\ n : child whose parents are dead —**orphan** vb —**or·phan·age** \-ənij\ n

or·tho·don·tics \,ȯrthə'däntiks\ n : dentistry dealing with straightening teeth —**or·tho·don·tist** \-'däntist\ n

or·tho·dox \'ȯrthə,däks\ adj 1 : conforming to established doctrine 2 cap : of or relating to a Christian church originating in the Eastern Roman Empire —**or·tho·doxy** \-,däksē\ n

or·thog·ra·phy \ȯr'thägrəfē\ n : spelling —**or·tho·graph·ic** \,ȯrthə'grafik\ adj

or·tho·pe·dics \,ȯrthə'pēdiks\ n sing or pl : correction or prevention of skeletal deformities —**or·tho·pe·dic** \-ik\ adj —**or·tho·pe·dist** \-'pēdist\ n

-o·ry \,ȯrē, ,ȯrē, ərē\ adj suffix 1 : of, relating to, or characterized by 2 : serving for, producing, or maintaining

os·cil·late \'äsə,lāt\ vb -lat·ed; -lat·ing : swing back and forth —**os·cil·la·tion** \,äsə'lāshən\ n

os·mo·sis \äz'mōsəs, äs-\ n : diffusion esp. of water through a membrane —**os·mot·ic** \-'mätik\ adj

os·prey \'äsprē, -,prā\ n, pl -preys : large fish-eating hawk os·si·fy \'äsə,fī\ vb -fied; -fy·ing : make or become hardened or set in one's ways

os·ten·si·ble \ä'stensəbəl\ adj : seeming ——os·ten·si·bly \-blē\ adv

os·ten·ta·tion \,ästən'tāshən\ n : pretentious display ——os·ten·ta·tious \-shəs\ adj ——os·ten·ta·tious·ly adv

os·te·op·a·thy \,ästē'äpəthē\ n : system of healing that emphasizes manipulation (as of joints) ——os·te·o·path \'ästēə,path\ n ——os·te·o·path·ic \,ästē'pathik\ adj

os·te·o·po·ro·sis \,ästēōpə'rōsəs\ n, pl -ro·ses \-,sēz\ : condition characterized by fragile and porous bones

os·tra·cize \'ästrə,sīz\ vb -cized; -ciz·ing : exclude by common consent —— ostra·cism \-,sizəm\ n

os·trich \'ästrich, 'ós-\ n : very large flightless bird

oth·er \'əthər\ adj 1 : being the one left 2 : alternate 3 : additional ~ pron 1 : remaining one 2 : different one

oth·er·wise adv 1 : in a different way 2 : in different circumstances 3 : in other respects ——otherwise adj

ot·ter \'ätər\ n : fish-eating mammal with webbed feet

ot·to·man \'ätəmən\ n : upholstered footstool

ought \'ót\ verbal auxiliary—used to express obligation, advisability, or expectation

ounce \'aúns\ n 1 : unit of weight equal to about 28.3 grams 2 : unit of capacity equal to about 29.6 milliliters

our \'är, 'aúr\ adj : of or relating to us

ours \'aúrz, 'ärz\ pron : that which belongs to us

our·selves \är'selvz, aúr-\ pron : we, us—used reflexively or for emphasis

-ous \əs\ adj suffix : having or having the qualities of

oust \'aúst\ vb : expel or eject

oust·er \'aústər\ n : expulsion

out \'aút\ adv 1 : away from the inside or center 2 : beyond control 3 : to extinction, exhaustion, or completion 4 : in or into the open ~ vb : become known ~ adj 1 : situated outside 2 : absent ~ prep 1 : out through 2 : outward on or along ——out·bound adj ——out·build·ing n

out·age \'aútij\ n : period of no electricity

out·board \'aút,bōrd\ adv : outside a boat or ship ——outboard adj

out·break \'aút,brāk\ n : sudden occurrence

out·burst \-,bərst\ n : violent expression of feeling

out·cast \-,kast\ n : person cast out by society

out·come \-,kəm\ n : result

out·crop \'aút,kräp\ n : part of a rock stratum that appears above the ground ——outcrop vb

out·cry \-,krī\ n : loud cry

out·dat·ed \aút'dātəd\ adj : out-of-date

out·dis·tance vb : go far ahead of

out·do \aút'dü\ vb -did \-'did\; -done \-'dən\; -do·ing \-'düiŋ\; -does \-'dəz\ : do better than

out·doors \aút'dōrz\ adv : in or into the open air ~ n : open air ——out·door adj

out·er \'aútər\ adj 1 : external 2 : farther out ——out·er·most adj

out·field \'aút,fēld\ n : baseball field beyond the infield ——out·field·er \-,fēldər\ n

out·fit \'aút,fit\ n 1 : equipment for a special purpose 2 : group ~ vb -tt- : equip ——out·fit·ter n

out·go \'aút,gō\ n, pl outgoes : expenditure

out·go·ing \'aút,gōiŋ\ adj 1 : retiring from a position 2 : friendly

out·grow \aút'grō\ vb -grew \-'grü\; -grown \-'grōn\; -grow·ing 1 : grow faster than 2 : grow too large for

out·growth \'aút,grōth\ n 1 : product of growing out 2 : consequence

out·ing \'aútiŋ\ n : excursion

out·land·ish \aút'landish\ adj : very strange ——out·land·ish·ly adv

outlast vb : last longer than

out·law \'aút,ló\ n : lawless person ~ vb : make illegal

out·lay \'aút,lā\ n : expenditure

out·let \'aút,let, -lət\ n 1 : exit 2 : means of release 3 : market for goods 4 : electrical device that gives access to wiring

out·line \'aút,līn\ n 1 : line marking the outer limits 2 : summary ~ vb 1 : draw the outline of 2 : indicate the chief parts of

out·live \aút'liv\ vb : live longer than

out·look \'aút,lúk\ n 1 : viewpoint 2 : prospect for the future

out·ly·ing \'aút,līiŋ\ adj : far from a central point

out·ma·neu·ver \,aútmə'nüvər, -'nyü-\

vb : defeat by more skillful maneuvering

out·mod·ed \aut'mōdəd\ *adj* : out-of-date

out·num·ber \-'nəmbər\ *vb* : exceed in number

out of *prep* **1** : out from within **2** : beyond the limits of **3** : among **4** — used to indicate absence or loss **5** : because of **6** : from or with

out-of-date *adj* : no longer in fashion or in use

out·pa·tient *n* : person treated at a hospital who does not stay overnight

out·post *n* : remote military post

out·put *n* : amount produced ~ *vb* **-put·ted** *or* **-put**; **-put·ting** : produce

out·rage \'aut,rāj\ *n* **1** : violent or shameful act **2** : injury or insult **3** : extreme anger ~ *vb* **-raged**; **-rag·ing** **1** : subject to violent injury **2** : make very angry

out·ra·geous \aut'rājəs\ *adj* : extremely offensive or shameful —**out·ra·geous·ly** *adv* —**out·ra·geous·ness** *n*

out·right *adv* **1** : completely **2** : instantly ~ *adj* **1** : complete **2** : given without reservation

out·set *n* : beginning

out·side \aut'sīd, 'aut,-\ *n* **1** : place beyond a boundary **2** : exterior **3** : utmost limit ~ *adj* **1** : outer **2** : coming from without **3** : remote ~ *adv* : on or to the outside ~ *prep* **1** : on or to the outside of **2** : beyond the limits of

outside of *prep* **1** : outside **2** : besides

out·sid·er \-'sīdər\ *n* : one who does not belong to a group

out·skirts *n pl* : outlying parts (as of a city)

out·smart \aut'smärt\ *vb* : outwit

out·spo·ken *adj* : direct and open in speech —**out·spo·ken·ness** *n*

out·stand·ing *adj* **1** : unpaid **2** : very good —**out·stand·ing·ly** *adv*

out·strip \aut'strip\ *vb* **1** : go faster than **2** : surpass

¹**out·ward** \'autwərd\ *adj* **1** : being toward the outside **2** : showing outwardly

²**outward, out·wards** \-wərdz\ *adv* : toward the outside —**out·ward·ly** *adv*

out·wit \aut'wit\ *vb* : get the better of by superior cleverness

ova *pl of* OVUM

oval \'ōvəl\ *adj* : egg-shaped —**oval** *n*

ova·ry \'ōvərē\ *n, pl* **-ries 1** : egg-producing organ **2** : seed-producing part of a flower —**ovar·i·an** \ō'varēən\ *adj*

ova·tion \ō'vāshən\ *n* : enthusiastic applause

ov·en \'əvən\ *n* : chamber (as in a stove) for baking

over \'ōvər\ *adv* **1** : across **2** : upside down **3** : in excess or addition **4** : above **5** : at an end **6** : again ~ *prep* **1** : above in position or authority **2** : more than **3** : along, through, or across **4** : because of ~ *adj* **1** : upper **2** : remaining **3** : ended

over- *prefix* **1** : so as to exceed or surpass **2** : excessive or excessively

overabundance	overcontrol
overabundant	overcook
overachiever	overcorrect
overactive	overcritical
overaggressive	overcrowd
overambitious	overdecorate
overanalyze	overdependence
overanxiety	overdependent
overanxious	overdevelop
overarousal	overdose
overassertive	overdramatic
overbake	overdramatize
overbid	overdress
overbill	overdrink
overbold	overdue
overborrow	overeager
overbright	overeat
overbroad	overeducated
overbuild	overelaborate
overburden	overemotional
overbusy	overemphasis
overbuy	overemphasize
overcapacity	overenergetic
overcapitalize	overenthusiastic
overcareful	overestimate
overcautious	overexaggerate
overcharge	overexaggera-
overcivilized	tion
overclean	overexcite
overcommit	overexcited
overcompensate	overexercise
overcomplicate	overexert
overconcern	overexertion
overconfidence	overexpand
overconfident	overexpansion
overconscien-	overexplain
tious	overexploit
overconsume	overexpose
overconsump-	overextend
tion	overextension

overexuberant
overfamiliar
overfatigued
overfeed
overfertilize
overfill
overfond
overgeneraliza-
   tion
overgeneralize
overgenerous
overglamorize
overgraze
overharvest
overhasty
overheat
overidealize
overimaginative
overimpress
overindebted-
   ness
overindulge
overindulgence
overindulgent
overinflate
overinsistent
overintense
overintensity
overinvestment
overladen
overlarge
overlend
overload
overlong
overloud
overmedicate
overmodest
overmuch
overobvious
overoptimistic
overorganize
overparticular
overpay
overpayment
overplay
overpopulated
overpraise
overprescribe
overpressure
overprice

overprivileged
overproduce
overproduction
overpromise
overprotect
overprotective
overqualified
overrate
overreact
overreaction
overrefined
overregulate
overregulation
overreliance
overrepresented
overrespond
overripe
oversaturate
oversell
oversensitive
overserious
oversexed
oversimple
oversimplify
oversolicitous
overspecialize
overspend
overstaff
overstimula-
   tion
overstock
overstrain
overstress
overstretch
oversubtle
oversupply
oversuspicious
oversweeten
overtax
overtighten
overtip
overtired
overtrain
overtreat
overuse
overutilize
overvalue
overweight
overwork
overzealous

over·awe vb : subdue by awe
over·bear·ing \-'barin\ adj : arrogant
over·blown \-'blōn\ adj : pretentious
over·board adv : over the side into the water
over·cast adj : clouded over ~ n : cloud covering
over·coat n : outer coat
over·come vb **-came** \-'kām\; **-come**; **-com·ing 1** : defeat **2** : make helpless or exhausted
over·do vb **-did**; **-done**; **-do·ing**; **-does** : do too much
over·draft n : overdrawn sum
over·draw vb **-drew**; **-drawn**; **-draw·ing** : write checks for more than one's bank balance
over·flow \,ōvər'flō\ vb **1** : flood **2** : flow over —**overflow** \'ōvər,flō\ n
over·grow vb **-grew**; **-grown**; **-grow·ing** : grow over
over·hand adj : made with the hand brought down from above —**overhand** adv —**over·hand·ed** \-,handəd\ adv or adj
over·hang vb **-hung**; **-hang·ing** : jut out over ~ n : something that overhangs
over·haul vb **1** : repair **2** : overtake
over·head \,ōvər'hed\ adv : aloft ~ \'ōvər,-\ adj : situated above ~ \'ōvər,-\ n : general business expenses
over·hear vb **-heard**; **-hear·ing** : hear without the speaker's knowledge
over·joyed adj : filled with joy
over·kill \'ōvər,kil\ n : large excess
over·land \-,land, -lənd\ adv or adj : by, on, or across land
over·lap vb : lap over —**over·lap** \'ōvər,lap\ n
over·lay \,ōvər'lā\ vb **-laid**; **-lay·ing** : lay over or across —**over·lay** \'ōvər,lā\ n
over·look \,ōvər'lúk\ vb **1** : look down on **2** : fail to see **3** : ignore **4** : pardon **5** : supervise ~ \'ōvər,-\ n : observation point
over·ly \'ōvərlē\ adv : excessively
over·night adv **1** : through the night **2** : suddenly —**overnight** adj
over·pass n : bridge over a road
over·pow·er vb : conquer
over·reach \,ōvər'rēch\ vb : try or seek too much
over·ride vb **-rode**; **-rid·den**; **-rid·ing** : neutralize action of
over·rule vb : rule against or set aside
over·run vb **-ran**; **-run·ning 1** : swarm

¹**over·age** \,ōvər'āj\ adj : too old
²**over·age** \'ōvərij\ n : surplus
over·all \,ōvər'ól\ adj : including everything
over·alls \'ōvər,ólz\ n pl : pants with an extra piece covering the chest

or flow over **2** : go beyond ~ *n* : an exceeding of estimated costs

over·seas *adv or adj* : beyond or across the sea

over·see \,ōvər'sē\ *vb* -**saw**; -**seen**; -**see·ing** : supervise —**over·seer** \'ōvər-,siər\ *n*

over·shad·ow *vb* : exceed in importance

over·shoe *n* : protective outer shoe

over·shoot *vb* -**shot**; -**shoot·ing** : shoot or pass beyond

over·sight *n* : inadvertent omission or error

over·sleep *vb* -**slept**; -**sleep·ing** : sleep longer than intended

over·spread *vb* -**spread**; -**spread·ing** : spread over or above

over·state *vb* : exaggerate —**over·state·ment** *n*

over·stay *vb* : stay too long

over·step *vb* : exceed

overt \ō'vərt, 'ō,vərt\ *adj* : not secret —**overt·ly** *adv*

over·take *vb* -**took**; -**tak·en**; -**tak·ing** : catch up with

over·throw \,ōvər'thrō\ *vb* -**threw**; -**thrown**; -**throw·ing** **1** : upset **2** : defeat —**over·throw** \'ōvər,-\ *n*

over·time *n* : extra working time —**overtime** *adv*

over·tone *n* **1** : higher tone in a complex musical tone **2** : suggestion

over·ture \'ōvər,chur, -chər\ *n* **1** : opening offer **2** : musical introduction

over·turn *vb* **1** : turn over **2** : nullify

over·view *n* : brief survey

over·ween·ing \,ōvər'wēniŋ\ *adj* **1** : arrogant **2** : excessive

over·whelm \,ōvər'hwelm\ *vb* : overcome completely —**over·whelm·ing·ly** \-'hwelmiŋlē\ *adv*

over·wrought \,ōvər'rót\ *adj* : extremely excited

ovoid \'ō,vóid\, **ovoi·dal** \ō'vóidᵊl\ *adj* : egg-shaped

ovu·late \'ävyə,lāt, 'ōv-\ *vb* -**lat·ed**; -**lat·ing** : produce eggs from an ovary —**ovu·la·tion** \,ävyə'lāshən, ,ōv-\ *n*

ovum \'ōvəm\ *n, pl* **ova** \-və\ : female germ cell

owe \'ō\ *vb* **owed**; **ow·ing 1** : have an obligation to pay **2** : be indebted to or for

owing to *prep* : because of

owl \'aúl\ *n* : nocturnal bird of prey —**owl·ish** *adj* —**owl·ish·ly** *adv*

own \'ōn\ *adj* : belonging to oneself ~ *vb* **1** : have as property **2** : acknowledge ~ *pron* : one or ones belonging to oneself —**own·er** *n* —**own·er·ship** *n*

ox \'äks\ *n, pl* **ox·en** \'äksən\ : bovine mammal and esp. a castrated bull

ox·ide \'äk,sīd\ *n* : compound of oxygen

ox·i·dize \'äksə,dīz\ *vb* -**dized**; -**diz·ing** : combine with oxygen —**ox·i·da·tion** \,äksə'dāshən\ *n* —**ox·i·diz·er** *n*

ox·y·gen \'äksijən\ *n* : gaseous chemical element essential for life

oys·ter \'óistər\ *n* : bivalve mollusk —**oys·ter·ing** \-riŋ\ *n*

ozone \'ō,zōn\ *n* : very reactive bluish form of oxygen

P

p \'pē\ *n, pl* **p's** *or* **ps** \'pēz\ : 16th letter of the alphabet

pace \'pās\ *n* **1** : walking step **2** : rate of progress ~ *vb* **paced**; **pac·ing 1** : go at a pace **2** : cover with slow steps **3** : set the pace of

pace·mak·er *n* : electrical device to regulate heartbeat

pachy·derm \'paki,dərm\ *n* : elephant

pa·cif·ic \pə'sifik\ *adj* : calm or peaceful

pac·i·fism \'pasə,fizəm\ *n* : opposition to war or violence —**pac·i·fist** \-fist\

n or adj —**pac·i·fis·tic** \,pasə'fistik\ *adj*

pac·i·fy \'pasə,fī\ *vb* -**fied**; -**fy·ing** : make calm —**pac·i·fi·ca·tion** \,pasə-fə'kāshən\ *n* —**pac·i·fi·er** \'pasə,-fīər\ *n*

pack \'pak\ *n* **1** : compact bundle **2** : group of animals ~ *vb* **1** : put into a container **2** : fill tightly or completely **3** : send without ceremony —**pack·er** *n*

pack·age \'pakij\ *n* : items bundled together ~ *vb* **-aged; -ag·ing** : enclose in a package

pack·et \'pakət\ *n* : small package

pact \'pakt\ *n* : agreement

pad \'pad\ *n* 1 : cushioning part or thing 2 : floating leaf of a water plant 3 : tablet of paper ~ *vb* **-dd-** 1 : furnish with a pad 2 : expand with needless matter —**pad·ding** *n*

pad·dle \'pad³l\ *n* : implement with a flat blade ~ *vb* **-dled; -dling** : move, beat, or stir with a paddle

pad·dock \'padək\ *n* : enclosed area for racehorses

pad·dy \'padē\ *n, pl* **-dies** : wet land where rice is grown

pad·lock *n* : lock with a U-shaped catch —**padlock** *vb*

pae·an \'pēən\ *n* : song of praise

pa·gan \'pāgən\ *n or adj* : heathen —**pa·gan·ism** \-,izəm\ *n*

¹**page** \'pāj\ *n* : messenger ~ *vb* **paged; pag·ing** : summon by repeated calls —**pag·er** *n*

²**page** *n* : single leaf (as of a book) or one side of the leaf

pag·eant \'pajənt\ *n* : elaborate spectacle or procession —**pag·eant·ry** \-əntrē\ *n*

pa·go·da \pə'gōdə\ *n* : tower with roofs curving upward

paid *past of* PAY

pail \'pāl\ *n* : cylindrical container with a handle —**pail·ful** \-,fùl\ *n*

pain \'pān\ *n* 1 : punishment or penalty 2 : suffering of body or mind 3 *pl* : great care ~ *vb* : cause or experience pain —**pain·ful** \-fəl\ *adj* —**pain·ful·ly** *adv* —**pain·kill·er** *n* —**pain·kill·ing** *adj* —**pain·less** *adj* —**pain·less·ly** *adv*

pains·tak·ing \'pān,stākiŋ\ *adj* : taking pains —**painstaking** *n* —**pains·tak·ing·ly** *adv*

paint \'pānt\ *vb* 1 : apply color or paint to 2 : portray esp. in color ~ *n* : mixture of pigment and liquid —**paint·brush** *n* —**paint·er** *n* —**paint·ing** *n*

pair \'par\ *n* : a set of two ~ *vb* : put or go together as a pair

pa·ja·mas \pə'jäməz, -'jam-\ *n pl* : loose suit for sleeping

pal \'pal\ *n* : close friend

pal·ace \'paləs\ *n* 1 : residence of a chief of state 2 : mansion —**pa·la·tial** \pə'lāshəl\ *adj*

pal·at·able \'palətəbəl\ *adj* : agreeable to the taste

pal·ate \'palət\ *n* 1 : roof of the mouth 2 : taste —**pal·a·tal** \-ət³l\ *adj*

pa·la·ver \pə'lavər, -'läv-\ *n* : talk —**palaver** *vb*

¹**pale** \'pāl\ *adj* **pal·er; pal·est** 1 : lacking in color or brightness 2 : light in color or shade ~ *vb* **paled; pal·ing** : make or become pale —**pale·ness** *n*

²**pale** *n* 1 : fence stake 2 : enclosed place

pa·le·on·tol·o·gy \,pālē,än'täləjē\ *n* : branch of biology dealing with ancient forms of life known from fossils —**pa·le·on·tol·o·gist** \-,än'täləjist, -ən-\ *n*

pal·ette \'palət\ *n* : board on which paints are laid and mixed

pal·i·sade \,palə'sād\ *n* 1 : high fence 2 : line of cliffs

¹**pall** \'pòl\ *n* 1 : cloth draped over a coffin 2 : something that produces gloom

²**pall** *vb* : lose in interest or attraction

pall·bear·er *n* : one who attends the coffin at a funeral

¹**pal·let** \'palət\ *n* : makeshift bed

²**pallet** *n* : portable storage platform

pal·li·ate \'palē,āt\ *vb* **-at·ed; -at·ing** 1 : ease without curing 2 : cover or conceal by excusing —**pal·li·a·tion** \,palē'āshən\ *n* —**pal·li·a·tive** \'palē,ātiv\ *adj or n*

pal·lid \'paləd\ *adj* : pale

pal·lor \'palər\ *n* : paleness

¹**palm** \'päm, 'pälm\ *n* 1 : tall tropical tree crowned with large leaves 2 : symbol of victory

²**palm** *n* : underside of the hand ~ *vb* 1 : conceal in the hand 2 : impose by fraud

palm·ist·ry \'päməstrē, 'pälmə-\ *n* : reading a person's character or future in his palms —**palm·ist** \'pämist, 'pälm-\ *n*

palmy \'pämē, 'pälmē\ *adj* **palm·i·er; -est** : flourishing

pal·o·mi·no \,palə'mēnō\ *n, pl* **-nos** : light-colored horse

pal·pa·ble \'palpəbəl\ *adj* 1 : capable of being touched 2 : obvious —**pal·pa·bly** \-blē\ *adv*

pal·pi·tate \'palpə,tāt\ *vb* **-tat·ed; -tat·ing** : beat rapidly —**pal·pi·ta·tion** \,palpə'tāshən\ *n*

pal·sy \'pôlzē\ *n, pl* **-sies** 1 : paralysis 2

: condition marked by tremor —**pal-sied** \-zēd\ adj

pal-try \'póltrē\ adj **-tri-er; -est** : trivial

pam-per \'pampər\ vb : spoil or indulge-

pam-phlet \'pamflət\ n : unbound publication —**pam-phle-teer** \,pamflə-'tir\ n

pan \'pan\ n : broad, shallow, and open container ~ vb 1 : wash gravel in a pan to search for gold 2 : criticize severely

pan-a-cea \,panə'sēə\ n : remedy for all ills or difficulties

pan-cake n : fried flat cake

pan-cre-as \'paŋkrēəs, 'pan-\ n : gland that produces insulin —**pan-cre-at-ic** \,paŋkrē'atik, ,pan-\ adj

pan-da \'pandə\ n : black-and-white bearlike animal

pan-de-mo-ni-um \,pandə'mōnēəm\ n : wild uproar

pan-der \'pandər\ n 1 : pimp 2 : one who caters to others' desires or weaknesses ~ vb : act as a pander

pane \'pān\ n : sheet of glass

pan-e-gyr-ic \,panə'jirik\ n : eulogistic oration —**pan-e-gyr-ist** \-'jirist\ n

pan-el \'panəl\ n 1 : list of persons (as jurors) 2 : discussion group 3 : flat piece of construction material 4 : board with instruments or controls ~ vb **-eled** or **-elled; -el-ing** or **-el-ling** : decorate with panels —**pan-el-ing** n —**pan-el-ist** \-ist\ n

pang \'paŋ\ n : sudden sharp pain

pan-han-dle \'pan,handᵊl\ vb **-dled; -dling** : ask for money on the street —**pan-han-dler** \-ər\ n

pan-ic \'panik\ n : sudden overpowering fright ~ vb **-icked; -ick-ing** : affect or be affected with panic —**pan-icky** \-ikē\ adj

pan-o-ply \'panəplē\ n, pl **-plies** 1 : full suit of armor 2 : impressive array

pan-o-ra-ma \,panə'ramə, -'räm-\ n : view in every direction —**pan-o-ram-ic** \-'ramik\ adj

pan-sy \'panzē\ n, pl **-sies** : low-growing garden herb with showy flowers

pant \'pant\ vb 1 : breathe with great effort 2 : yearn ~ n : panting sound

pan-ta-loons \,pantᵊl'ünz\ n pl : pants

pan-the-on \'panthē,än, -ən\ n 1 : the gods of a people 2 : group of famous people

pan-ther \'panthər\ n : large wild cat

pant-ies \'pantēz\ n pl : woman's or child's short underpants

pan-to-mime \'pantə,mīm\ n 1 : play without words 2 : expression by bodily or facial movements ~ vb : represent by pantomime

pan-try \'pantrē\ n, pl **-tries** : storage room for food and dishes

pants \'pants\ n pl 1 : 2-legged outer garment 2 : panties

pap \'pap\ n : soft food

pa-pa-cy \'pāpəsē\ n, pl **-cies** 1 : office of pope 2 : reign of pope

pa-pal \'pāpəl\ adj : relating to the pope

pa-pa-ya \pə'pīə\ n : tropical tree with large yellow edible fruit

pa-per \'pāpər\ n 1 : pliable substance used to write or print on, to wrap things in, or to cover walls 2 : printed or written document 3 : newspaper —paper adj or vb —**pa-per-hang-er** n —**pa-per-weight** n —**pa-pery** \'pā-pərē\ adj

pa-per-board n : cardboard

pa-pier–mâ-ché \,pāpərmə'shā, ,pap-,yämə-, -ma-\ n : molding material of waste paper

pa-poose \pa'püs, pə-\ n : young child of American Indian parents

pa-pri-ka \pə'prēkə, pa-\ n : mild red spice from sweet peppers

pa-py-rus \pə'pīrəs\ n, pl **-rus-es** or **-ri** \-,rē, -,rī\ 1 : tall grasslike plant 2 : paper from papyrus

par \'pär\ n 1 : stated value 2 : common level 3 : accepted standard or normal condition —par adj

par-a-ble \'parəbəl\ n : simple story illustrating a moral truth

para-chute \'parə,shüt\ n : large umbrella-shaped device for making a descent through air —parachute vb —**para-chut-ist** \-,shütist\ n

pa-rade \pə'rād\ n 1 : pompous display 2 : ceremonial formation and march ~ vb **-rad-ed; -rad-ing** 1 : march in a parade 2 : show off

par-a-digm \'parə,dīm, -,dim\ n : model

par-a-dise \'parə,dīs, -,dīz\ n : place of bliss

par-a-dox \'parə,däks\ n : statement that seems contrary to common sense yet is perhaps true —**par-a-dox-i-cal** \,parə'däksikəl\ adj —**par-a-dox-i-cal-ly** adv

par-af-fin \'parəfən\ n : white waxy substance used esp. for making candles and sealing foods

par-a-gon \'parə,gän, -gən\ n : model of perfection

para·graph \'parə,graf\ *n* : unified division of a piece of writing ~ *vb* : divide into paragraphs

par·a·keet \'parə,kēt\ *n* : small slender parrot

par·al·lel \'parə,lel\ *adj* **1** : lying or moving in the same direction but always the same distance apart **2** : similar ~ *n* **1** : parallel line, curve, or surface **2** : line of latitude **3** : similarity ~ *vb* **1** : compare **2** : correspond to —**par·al·lel·ism** \-,izəm\ *n*

par·al·lel·o·gram \,parə'lelə,gram\ *n* : 4-sided polygon with opposite sides equal and parallel

pa·ral·y·sis \pə'raləsəs\ *n, pl* **-y·ses** \-,sēz\ : loss of function and esp. of voluntary motion —**par·a·lyt·ic** \,parə'litik\ *adj or n*

par·a·lyze \'parə,līz\ *vb* **-lyzed; -lyz·ing** : affect with paralysis —**par·a·lyz·ing·ly** *adv*

para·med·ic \,parə'medik\ *n* : person trained to provide initial emergency medical treatment

pa·ram·e·ter \pə'ramətər\ *n* : characteristic element —**para·met·ric** \,parə'metrik\ *adj*

par·a·mount \'parə,maúnt\ *adj* : superior to all others

par·amour \'parə,múr\ *n* : illicit lover

para·noia \,parə'nóiə\ *n* : mental disorder marked by irrational suspicion —**para·noid** \'parə,nóid\ *adj or n*

par·a·pet \'parəpət, -,pet\ *n* : protecting rampart in a fort

par·a·pher·na·lia \,parəfə'nālyə, -fər-\ *n sing or pl* : equipment

para·phrase \'parə,frāz\ *n* : restatement of a text giving the meaning in different words —**paraphrase** *vb*

para·ple·gia \,parə'plējə, -jēə\ *n* : paralysis of the lower trunk and legs —**para·ple·gic** \-jik\ *adj or n*

par·a·site \'parə,sīt\ *n* : organism living on another —**par·a·sit·ic** \,parə'sitik\ *adj* —**par·a·sit·ism** \'parəse,tizəm, -,sīt,iz-\ *n*

para·sol \'parə,sol\ *n* : umbrella used to keep off the sun

para·troops \-,trüps\ *n pl* : troops trained to parachute from an airplane —**para·troop·er** \-,trüpər\ *n*

par·boil \'pär,bóil\ *vb* : boil briefly

par·cel \'pärsəl\ *n* **1** : lot **2** : package ~ *vb* **-celed** *or* **-celled; -cel·ing** *or* **-cel·ling** : divide into portions

parch \'pärch\ *vb* : toast or shrivel with dry heat

parch·ment \'pärchmənt\ *n* : animal skin prepared to write on

par·don \'pärd⁰n\ *n* : excusing of an offense ~ *vb* : free from penalty —**par·don·able** \'pärd⁰nəbəl\ *adj* —**par·don·er** \-⁰nər\

pare \'par\ *vb* **pared; par·ing 1** : trim off an outside part **2** : reduce as if by paring —**par·er** *n*

par·e·gor·ic \,parə'górik\ *n* : tincture of opium and camphor

par·ent \'parənt\ *n* : one that begets or brings up offspring —**par·ent·age** \-ij\ *n* —**pa·ren·tal** \pə'rent⁰l\ *adj* —**par·ent·hood** *n*

pa·ren·the·sis \pə'renthəsəs\ *n, pl* **-the·ses** \-,sēz\ **1** : word or phrase inserted in a passage **2** : one of a pair of punctuation marks ( ) —**par·en·thet·ic** \,parən'thetik\, **par·en·thet·i·cal** \-ikəl\ *adj* —**par·en·thet·i·cal·ly** *adv*

par·fait \pär'fā\ *n* : layered cold dessert

pa·ri·ah \pə'rīə\ *n* : outcast

par·ish \'parish\ *n* : local church community

pa·rish·io·ner \pə'rishənər\ *n* : member of a parish

par·i·ty \'parətē\ *n, pl* **-ties** : equality

park \'pärk\ *n* : land set aside for recreation or for its beauty ~ *vb* : leave a vehicle standing

par·ka \'pärkə\ *n* : usu. hooded heavy jacket

park·way \'pärk,wā\ *n* : broad landscaped thoroughfare

par·lance \'pärləns\ *n* : manner of speaking

par·lay \'pär,lā\ *n* : the risking of a stake plus its winnings —**parlay** *vb*

par·ley \'pärlē\ *n, pl* **-leys** : conference about a dispute —**parley** *vb*

par·lia·ment \'pärləmənt\ *n* : legislative assembly —**par·lia·men·tar·i·an** \-,parlia·men·ta·ry**, \,pärlə'mentərē\ *adj*

par·lor \'pärlər\ *n* **1** : reception room **2** : place of business

pa·ro·chi·al \pə'rōkēəl\ *adj* **1** : relating to a church parish **2** : provincial —**pa·ro·chi·al·ism** \-ə,lizəm\ *n*

par·o·dy \'parədē\ *n, pl* **-dies** : humorous or satirical imitation —**parody** *vb*

pa·role \pə'rōl\ *n* : conditional release of a prisoner —**parole** *vb* —**pa·rol·ee** \-,rō'lē, -'rō,lē\ *n*

par·ox·ysm \'parək,sizəm, pə'räk-\ *n* : convulsion

par·quet \'pär,kā, pär'kā\ *n* : flooring of patterned wood inlay

par·ra·keet *var of* PARAKEET

par·rot \'parət\ *n* : bright-colored tropical bird

par·ry \'parē\ *vb* **-ried; -ry·ing 1** : ward off a blow **2** : evade adroitly —**parry** *n*

parse \'pärs\ *vb* **parsed; pars·ing** : analyze grammatically

par·si·mo·ny \'pärsə,mōnē\ *n* : extreme frugality —**par·si·mo·ni·ous** \,pärsə-'mōnēəs\ *adj* —**par·si·mo·ni·ous·ly** *adv*

pars·ley \'pärslē\ *n* : garden plant used as a seasoning or garnish

pars·nip \'pärsnəp\ *n* : carrotlike vegetable with a white edible root

par·son \'pärsᵊn\ *n* : minister

par·son·age \'pärsᵊnij\ *n* : parson's house

part \'pärt\ *n* **1** : one of the units into which a larger whole is divided **2** : function or role ~ *vb* **1** : take leave **2** : separate **3** : go away **4** : give up

par·take \pär'tāk, pər-\ *vb* **-took; -tak·en; -tak·ing** : have or take a share —**par·tak·er** *n*

par·tial \'pärshəl\ *adj* **1** : favoring one over another **2** : affecting a part only —**par·tial·i·ty** \,pärshē'alətē\ *n* —**par·tial·ly** \'pärshəlē\ *adv*

par·tic·i·pate \pər'tisə,pāt, pär-\ *vb* **-pat·ed; -pat·ing** : take part in something —**par·tic·i·pant** \-pənt\ *adj or n* —**par·tic·i·pa·tion** \-,tisə'pāshən\ *n* —**par·tic·i·pa·to·ry** \-'tisəpə,tōrē\ *adj*

par·ti·ci·ple \'pärtə,sipəl\ *n* : verb form with functions of both verb and adjective —**par·ti·cip·i·al** \,pärtə'si-pēəl\ *adj*

par·ti·cle \'pärtikəl\ *n* : small bit

par·tic·u·lar \pär'tikyələr\ *adj* **1** : relating to a specific person or thing **2** : individual **3** : hard to please ~ *n* : detail —**par·tic·u·lar·ly** *adv*

par·ti·san \'pärtəzen, -sən\ *n* **1** : adherent **2** : guerrilla —**partisan** *adj* —**par·ti·san·ship** *n*

par·tite \'pär,tīt\ *adj* : divided into parts

par·ti·tion \pər'tishən, pär-\ *n* **1** : distribution **2** : something that divides —**partition** *vb*

part·ly \'pärtlē\ *adv* : in some degree

part·ner \'pärtnər\ *n* **1** : associate **2** : companion **3** : business associate —**part·ner·ship** *n*

part of speech : class of words distinguished esp. according to function

par·tridge \'pärtrij\ *n, pl* **-tridge** *or* **-tridg·es** : stout-bodied game bird

par·ty \'pärtē\ *n, pl* **-ties 1** : political organization **2** : participant **3** : company of persons esp. with a purpose **4** : social gathering

par·ve·nu \'pärvə,nü, -,nyü\ *n* : social upstart

pass \'pas\ *vb* **1** : move past, over, or through **2** : go away or die **3** : allow to elapse **4** : go unchallenged **5** : transfer or undergo transfer **6** : render a judgment **7** : occur **8** : enact **9** : undergo testing successfully **10** : be regarded **11** : decline ~ *n* **1** : low place in a mountain range **2** : act of passing **3** : accomplishment **4** : permission to leave, enter, or move about —**pass·able** *adj* —**pass·ably** *adv* —**pass·er** *n* —**pass·er·by** *n*

pas·sage \'pasij\ *n* **1** : process of passing **2** : means of passing **3** : voyage **4** : right to pass **5** : literary selection —**pas·sage·way** *n*

pass·book *n* : bankbook

pas·sé \pa'sā\ *adj* : out-of-date

pas·sen·ger \'pasᵊnjər\ *n* : traveler in a conveyance

pass·ing \'pasiŋ\ *n* : death

pas·sion \'pashən\ *n* **1** : strong feeling esp. of anger, love, or desire **2** : object of affection or enthusiasm —**pas·sion·ate** \'pashənət\ *adj* —**pas·sion·ate·ly** *adv* —**pas·sion·less** *adj*

pas·sive \'pasiv\ *adj* **1** : not active but acted upon **2** : submissive —**passive** *n* —**pas·sive·ly** *adv* —**pas·siv·i·ty** \pa'sivətē\ *n*

Pass·over \'pas,ōvər\ *n* : Jewish holiday celebrated in March or April in commemoration of the Hebrews' liberation from slavery in Egypt

pass·port \'pas,pōrt\ *n* : government document needed for travel abroad

pass·word *n* **1** : word or phrase spoken to pass a guard **2** : sequence of characters needed to get into a computer system

past \'past\ *adj* **1** : ago **2** : just gone by **3** : having existed before the present **4** : expressing past time ~ *prep or adv* : beyond ~ *n* **1** : time gone by **2** : verb tense expressing time gone by **3** : past life

pas·ta \\'pästə\ *n* : fresh or dried shaped dough

paste \\'pāst\ *n* 1 : smooth ground food 2 : moist adhesive ~ *vb* **past·ed**; **past·ing** : attach with paste —**pasty** *adj*

paste·board *n* : cardboard

pas·tel \pas'tel\ *n* : light color —**pastel** *adj*

pas·teur·ize \\'paschə,rīz, 'pästə-\ *vb* **-ized**; **-iz·ing** : heat (as milk) so as to kill germs —**pas·teur·i·za·tion** \,paschərə'zäshən, ,pästə-\ *n*

pas·time \\'pas,tīm\ *n* : amusement

pas·tor \\'pastər\ *n* : priest or minister serving a church or parish —**pas·tor·ate** \-tərət\ *n*

pas·to·ral \\'pastərəl\ *adj* 1 : relating to rural life 2 : of or relating to spiritual guidance or a pastor ~ *n* : literary work dealing with rural life

past·ry \\'pāstrē\ *n, pl* **-ries** : sweet baked goods

pas·ture \\'paschər\ *n* : land used for grazing ~ *vb* **-tured**; **-tur·ing** : graze

pat \\'pat\ *n* 1 : light tap 2 : small mass ~ *vb* **-tt-** : tap gently ~ *adj or adv* 1 : apt or glib 2 : unyielding

patch \\'pach\ *n* 1 : piece used for mending 2 : small area distinct from surrounding area ~ *vb* 1 : mend with a patch 2 : make of fragments 3 : repair hastily —**patchy** \-ē\ *adj*

patch·work *n* : something made of pieces of different materials, shapes, or colors

pate \\'pāt\ *n* : crown of the head

pa·tel·la \pə'telə\ *n, pl* **-lae** \-'tel,ē, -,ī\ *or* **-las** : kneecap

pa·tent *adj* 1 \\'pat°nt, 'pāt-\ : obvious 2 \\'pat-\ : protected by a patent ~ \\'pat-\ *n* : document conferring or securing a right ~ \\'pat-\ *vb* : secure by patent —**pat·ent·ly** *adv*

pa·ter·nal \pə'tərn°l\ *adj* 1 : fatherly 2 : related through or inherited from a father —**pa·ter·nal·ly** *adv*

pa·ter·ni·ty \pə'tərnətē\ *n* : fatherhood

path \\'path, 'påth\ *n* 1 : trodden way 2 : route or course —**path·find·er** *n* —**path·way** *n* —**path·less** *adj*

pa·thet·ic \pə'thetik\ *adj* : pitiful —**pa·thet·i·cal·ly** *adv*

pa·thol·o·gy \pə'thäləjē\ *n, pl* **-gies** 1 : study of disease 2 : physical abnormality —**path·o·log·i·cal** \,pathə-'läjikəl\ *adj* —**pa·thol·o·gist** \pə-'thäləjist\ *n*

pa·thos \\'pā,thäs\ *n* : element evoking pity

pa·tience \\'pāshəns\ *n* : habit or fact of being patient

pa·tient \\'pāshənt\ *adj* : bearing pain or trials without complaint ~ *n* : one under medical care —**pa·tient·ly** *adv*

pa·ti·na \pə'tēnə, 'patənə\ *n, pl* **-nas** \-nəz\ *or* **-nae** \-,nē, -,nī\ : green film formed on copper and bronze

pa·tio \\'patē,ō, 'pät-\ *n, pl* **-ti·os** 1 : courtyard 2 : paved recreation area near a house

pa·tri·arch \\'pātrē,ärk\ *n* 1 : man revered as father or founder 2 : venerable old man —**pa·tri·ar·chal** \,pātrē'ärkəl\ *adj* —**pa·tri·ar·chy** \-,ärkē\ *n*

pa·tri·cian \pə'trishən\ *n* : person of high birth —**patrician** *adj*

pat·ri·mo·ny \\'patrə,mōnē\ *n* : something inherited —**pat·ri·mo·ni·al** \,patrə'mōnēəl\ *adj*

pa·tri·ot \\'pātrēət, -,ät\ *n* : one who loves his or her country —**pa·tri·ot·ic** \,pātrē'ätik\ *adj* —**pa·tri·ot·i·cal·ly** *adv* —**pa·tri·o·tism** \\'pātrēə,tizəm\ *n*

pa·trol \pə'trōl\ *n* 1 : a going around for observation or security 2 : group on patrol ~ *vb* **-ll-** : carry out a patrol

pa·trol·man \-mən\ *n* : police officer

pa·tron \\'pātrən\ *n* 1 : special protector 2 : wealthy supporter 3 : customer

pa·tron·age \\'patrənij, 'pā-\ *n* 1 : support or influence of a patron 2 : trade of customers 3 : control of government appointments

pa·tron·ess \\'pātrənəs\ *n* : woman who is a patron

pa·tron·ize \\'pātrə,nīz, 'pa-\ *vb* **-ized**; **-iz·ing** 1 : be a customer of 2 : treat with condescension

¹**pat·ter** \\'patər\ *vb* : talk glibly or mechanically ~ *n* : rapid talk

²**patter** *vb* : pat or tap rapidly ~ *n* : quick succession of pats or taps

pat·tern \\'patərn\ *n* 1 : model for imitation or for making things 2 : artistic design 3 : noticeable formation or set of characteristics ~ *vb* : form according to a pattern

pat·ty \\'patē\ *n, pl* **-ties** : small flat cake

pau·ci·ty \\'pósətē\ *n* : shortage

paunch \\'pónch\ *n* : large belly —**paunchy** *adj*

pau·per \\'pópər\ *n* : poor person —**pau·per·ism** \-pə,rizəm\ *n* —**pau·per·ize** \-pə,rīz\ *vb*

pause \'póz\ *n* : temporary stop ~ *vb* **paused; paus·ing** : stop briefly

pave \'pāv\ *vb* **paved; pav·ing** : cover to smooth or firm the surface —**pave·ment** \-mənt\ *n* —**pav·ing** *n*

pa·vil·ion \pə'vilyən\ *n* 1 : large tent 2 : light structure used for entertainment or shelter

paw \'pó\ *n* : foot of a 4-legged clawed animal ~ *vb* 1 : handle clumsily or rudely 2 : touch or strike with a paw

pawn \'pón\ *n* 1 : goods deposited as security for a loan 2 : state of being pledged ~ *vb* : deposit as a pledge —**pawn·bro·ker** *n* —**pawn·shop** *n*

pay \'pā\ *vb* **paid** \'pād\; **pay·ing** 1 : make due return for goods or services 2 : discharge indebtedness for 3 : requite 4 : give freely or as fitting 5 : be profitable ~ *n* 1 : status of being paid 2 : something paid —**pay·able** *adj* —**pay·check** *n* —**pay·ee** \pā'ē\ *n* —**pay·er** *n* —**pay·ment** *n*

PC \,pē'sē\ *n, pl* **PCs** *or* **PC's** : microcomputer

pea \'pē\ *n* : round edible seed of a leguminous vine

peace \'pēs\ *n* 1 : state of calm and quiet 2 : absence of war or strife —**peace·able** \-əbəl\ *adj* —**peace·ably** \-blē\ *adv* —**peace·ful** \-fəl\ *adj* —**peace·ful·ly** *adv* —**peace·keep·er** *n* —**peace·keep·ing** *n* —**peace·mak·er** *n* —**peace·time** *n*

peach \'pēch\ *n* : sweet juicy fruit of a flowering tree or this tree

pea·cock \'pē,käk\ *n* : brilliantly colored male pheasant

peak \'pēk\ *n* 1 : pointed or projecting part 2 : top of a hill 3 : highest level ~ *vb* : reach a maximum —**peak** *adj*

peak·ed \'pēkəd\ *adj* : sickly

peal \'pēl\ *n* : loud sound (as of ringing bells) ~ *vb* : give out peals

pea·nut \'pē,nət\ *n* : annual herb that bears underground pods or the pod or the edible seed inside

pear \'par\ *n* : fleshy fruit of a tree related to the apple

pearl \'pərl\ *n* : gem formed within an oyster —**pearly** \'pərlē\ *adj*

peas·ant \'pez²nt\ *n* : tiller of the soil —**peas·ant·ry** \-²ntrē\ *n*

peat \'pēt\ *n* : decayed organic deposit often dried for fuel —**peaty** *adj*

peb·ble \'pebəl\ *n* : small stone —**peb·bly** *adj*

pe·can \pi'kän, -'kan\ *n* : hickory tree bearing a smooth-shelled nut or the nut

pec·ca·dil·lo \,pekə'dilō\ *n, pl* **-loes** *or* **-los** : slight offense

¹**peck** \'pek\ *n* : unit of dry measure equal to 8 quarts

²**peck** *vb* : strike or pick up with the bill ~ *n* : quick sharp stroke

pec·tin \'pektən\ *n* : water-soluble plant substance that causes fruit jellies to set —**pec·tic** \-tik\ *adj*

pec·to·ral \'pektərəl\ *adj* : relating to the breast or chest

pe·cu·liar \pi'kyülyər\ *adj* 1 : characteristic of only one 2 : strange —**pe·cu·liar·i·ty** \-,kyül'yaretē, -ē'ar-\ *n* —**pe·cu·liar·ly** *adv*

pe·cu·ni·ary \pi'kyünē,erē\ *adj* : relating to money

ped·a·go·gy \'pedə,gōjē, -,gäj-\ *n* : art or profession of teaching —**ped·a·gog·ic** \,pedə'gäjik, -'gōj-\, **ped·a·gog·i·cal** \-ikəl\ *adj* —**ped·a·gogue** \'pedə,gäg\ *n*

ped·al \'ped²l\ *n* : lever worked by the foot ~ *adj* : relating to the foot ~ *vb* : use a pedal

ped·ant \'ped²nt\ *n* : learned bore —**pe·dan·tic** \pi'dantik\ *adj* —**ped·ant·ry** \'ped²ntrē\ *n*

ped·dle \'ped²l\ *vb* **-dled; -dling** : offer for sale —**ped·dler** \'pedlər\ *n*

ped·es·tal \'pedəst²l\ *n* : support or foot of something upright

pe·des·tri·an \pə'destrēən\ *adj* 1 : ordinary 2 : walking ~ *n* : person who walks

pe·di·at·rics \,pēdē'atriks\ *n* : branch of medicine dealing with children —**pe·di·at·ric** \-trik\ *adj* —**pe·di·a·tri·cian** \,pēdēə'trishən\ *n*

ped·i·gree \'pedə,grē\ *n* : line of ancestors or a record of it

ped·i·ment \'pedəmənt\ *n* : triangular gablelike decoration on a building

peek \'pēk\ *vb* 1 : look furtively 2 : glance —**peek** *n*

peel \'pēl\ *vb* 1 : strip the skin or rind from 2 : lose the outer layer ~ *n* : skin or rind —**peel·ing** *n*

¹**peep** \'pēp\ *vb or n* : cheep

²**peep** *vb* 1 : look slyly 2 : begin to emerge ~ *n* : brief look —**peep·er** *n* —**peep·hole** *n*

¹**peer** \'pir\ *n* 1 : one's equal 2 : nobleman —**peer·age** \-ij\ *n*

²**peer** *vb* : look intently or curiously

peer·less \-ləs\ *adj* : having no equal

peeve \'pēv\ vb **peeved; peev·ing** : make resentful ~ n : complaint — **peev·ish** \-ish\ adj —**peev·ish·ly** adv —**peev·ish·ness** n

peg \'peg\ n : small pinlike piece ~ vb **-gg- 1** : put a peg into **2** : fix or mark with or as if with pegs

peignoir \pān'wär, pen-\ n : negligee

pe·jo·ra·tive \pi'jórətiv\ adj : having a negative or degrading effect ~ n : a degrading word or phrase —**pe·jo·ra·tive·ly** adv

pel·i·can \'pelikən\ n : large-billed seabird

pel·la·gra \pə'lagrə, -'lāg-\ n : protein-deficiency disease

pel·let \'pelət\ n : little ball —**pel·let·al** \-ᵊl\ adj —**pel·let·ize** \-,īz\ vb

pell-mell \'pel'mel\ adv : in confusion or haste

pel·lu·cid \pə'lüsəd\ adj : very clear

¹**pelt** \'pelt\ n : skin of a fur-bearing animal

²**pelt** vb : strike with blows or missiles

pel·vis \'pelvəs\ n, pl **-vis·es** \-vəsəz\ or **-ves** \-,vēz\ : cavity formed by the hip bones —**pel·vic** \-vik\ adj

¹**pen** \'pen\ n : enclosure for animals ~ vb **-nn-** : shut in a pen

²**pen** n : tool for writing with ink ~ vb **-nn-** : write

pe·nal \'pēnᵊl\ adj : relating to punishment

pe·nal·ize \'pēnᵊl,īz, 'pen-\ vb **-ized; -iz·ing** : put a penalty on

pen·al·ty \'penᵊltē\ n, pl **-ties 1** : punishment for crime **2** : disadvantage, loss, or hardship due to an action

pen·ance \'penəns\ n : act performed to show repentance

pence \'pens\ pl of PENNY

pen·chant \'penchənt\ n : strong inclination

pen·cil \'pensəl\ n : writing or drawing tool with a solid marking substance (as graphite) as its core ~ vb **-ciled** or **-cilled; -cil·ing** or **-cil·ling** : draw or write with a pencil

pen·dant \'pendənt\ n : hanging ornament

pen·dent, pen·dant \'pendənt\ adj : hanging

pend·ing \'pendiŋ\ prep : while awaiting ~ adj : not yet decided

pen·du·lous \'penjələs, -dyùləs\ adj : hanging loosely

pen·du·lum \-ləm\ n : a hanging weight that is free to swing

pen·e·trate \'penə,trāt\ vb **-trat·ed; -trat·ing 1** : enter into **2** : permeate **3** : see into —**pen·e·tra·ble** \-trəbəl\ adj —**pen·e·tra·tion** \,penə'trāshən\ n —**pen·e·tra·tive** \'penə,trātiv\ adj

pen·guin \'pengwən, 'peŋ-\ n : short-legged flightless seabird

pen·i·cil·lin \,penə'silən\ n : antibiotic usu. produced by a mold

pen·in·su·la \pə'ninsələ, -'ninchə-\ n : land extending out into the water —**pen·in·su·lar** \-lər\ adj

pe·nis \'pēnəs\ n, pl **-nes** \-,nēz\ or **-nis·es** : male organ of copulation

pen·i·tent \'penətənt\ adj : feeling sorrow for sins or offenses ~ n : penitent person —**pen·i·tence** \-təns\ n —**pen·i·ten·tial** \,penə'tenchəl\ adj

pen·i·ten·tia·ry \,penə'tenchərē\ n, pl **-ries** : state or federal prison

pen·man·ship \'penmən,ship\ n : art or practice of writing

pen·nant \'penənt\ n : nautical or championship flag

pen·ny \'penē\ n, pl **-nies** \-ēz\ or **pence** \'pens\ **1** : monetary unit equal to 1/100 pound **2** pl **-nies** : cent —**pen·ni·less** \'peniləs\ adj

pen·sion \'penchən\ n : retirement income ~ vb : pay a pension to —**pen·sion·er** n

pen·sive \'pensiv\ adj : thoughtful —**pen·sive·ly** adv

pent \'pent\ adj : confined

pent·a·gon \'pentə,gän\ n : 5-sided polygon —**pen·tag·o·nal** \pen'tagənᵊl\ adj

pen·tam·e·ter \pen'tamətər\ n : line of verse containing 5 metrical feet

pent·house \'pent,haùs\ n : rooftop apartment

pen·u·ry \'penyərē\ n **1** : poverty **2** : thrifty or stingy manner —**pe·nu·ri·ous** \pə'nùreəs, -'nyùr-\ adj

pe·on \'pē,än, -ən\ n, pl **-ons** or **-ones** \pā'ōnēz\ : landless laborer in Spanish America —**pe·on·age** \-ənij\ n

pe·o·ny \'pēənē\ n, pl **-nies** : garden plant having large flowers

peo·ple \'pēpəl\ n, pl **people 1** pl : human beings in general **2** pl : human beings in a certain group (as a family) or community **3** pl **peoples** : tribe, nation, or race ~ vb **-pled; -pling** : constitute the population of

pep \'pep\ n : brisk energy ~ vb

pepped; pep·ping : put pep into — **pep·py** adj

pep·per \'pepər\ n 1 : pungent seasoning from the berry (**peppercorn**) of a shrub 2 : vegetable grown for its hot or sweet fruit ~ vb : season with pepper —**pep·pery** \-ərē\ adj

pep·per·mint \-ˌmint, -mənt\ n : pungent aromatic mint

pep·per·o·ni \ˌpepəˈrōnē\ n : spicy beef and pork sausage

pep·tic \'peptik\ adj : relating to digestion or the effect of digestive juices

per \'pər\ prep 1 : by means of 2 : for each 3 : according to

per·am·bu·late \pəˈrambyəˌlāt\ vb -lated; -lat·ing : walk —**per·am·bu·la·tion** \-ˌrambyəˈlāshən\ n

per·cale \ˌpərˈkāl, 'pər-ˌ; ˌpərˈkal\ n : fine woven cotton cloth

per·ceive \pərˈsēv\ vb -ceived; -ceiv·ing 1 : realize 2 : become aware of through the senses —**per·ceiv·able** adj

per·cent \pərˈsent\ adv : in each hundred ~ n, pl -cent or -cents 1 : one part in a hundred 2 : percentage

per·cent·age \pərˈsentij\ n : part expressed in hundredths

per·cen·tile \pərˈsenˌtīl\ n : a standing on a scale of 0–100

per·cep·ti·ble \pərˈseptəbəl\ adj : capable of being perceived —**per·cep·ti·bly** \-blē\ adv

per·cep·tion \pərˈsepshən\ n 1 : act or result of perceiving 2 : ability to understand

per·cep·tive \pərˈseptiv\ adj : showing keen perception —**per·cep·tive·ly** adv

¹**perch** \'pərch\ n : roost for birds ~ vb : roost

²**perch** n, pl **perch** or **perch·es** : freshwater spiny-finned food fish

per·co·late \'pərkəˌlāt\ vb -lat·ed; -lat·ing : trickle or filter down through a substance —**per·co·la·tor** \-ˌlātər\ n

per·cus·sion \pərˈkəshən\ n 1 : sharp blow 2 : musical instrument sounded by striking

pe·remp·to·ry \pəˈremptərē\ adj 1 : imperative 2 : domineering — **pe·remp·to·ri·ly** \-tərəlē\ adv

pe·ren·ni·al \pəˈrenēəl\ adj 1 : present at all seasons 2 : continuing from year to year 3 : recurring regularly ~ n : perennial plant —**pe·ren·ni·al·ly** adv

per·fect \'pərfikt\ adj 1 : being without fault or defect 2 : exact 3 : complete ~ \pərˈfekt\ vb : make perfect —**per·fect·ibil·i·ty** \pərˌfektəˈbilətē\ n — **per·fect·ible** \pərˈfektəbəl\ adj — **per·fect·ly** adv —**per·fect·ness** n

per·fec·tion \pərˈfekshən\ n 1 : quality or state of being perfect 2 : highest degree of excellence —**per·fec·tion·ist** \-shənist\ n

per·fid·i·ous \pərˈfidēəs\ adj : treacherous —**per·fid·i·ous·ly** adv

per·fo·rate \'pərfəˌrāt\ vb -rat·ed; -rat·ing : make a hole in —**per·fo·ra·tion** \ˌpərfəˈrāshən\ n

per·force \pərˈfōrs\ adv : of necessity

per·form \pərˈfōrm\ vb 1 : carry out 2 : do in a set manner 3 : give a performance —**per·form·er** n

per·for·mance \pərˈfōrməns\ n 1 : act or process of performing 2 : public presentation

per·fume \'pərˌfyüm, pərˈ-\ n 1 : pleasant odor 2 : something that gives a scent ~ \pərˈ-, 'pərˌ-\ vb -fumed; -fum·ing : add scent to

per·func·to·ry \pərˈfəŋktərē\ adj : done merely as a duty —**per·func·to·ri·ly** \-tərəlē\ adv

per·haps \pərˈhaps\ adv : possibly but not certainly

per·il \'perəl\ n : danger —**per·il·ous** adj —**per·il·ous·ly** adv

pe·rim·e·ter \pəˈrimətər\ n : outer boundary of a body or figure

pe·ri·od \'pirēəd\ n 1 : punctuation mark . used esp. to mark the end of a declarative sentence or an abbreviation 2 : division of time 3 : stage in a process or development

pe·ri·od·ic \ˌpirēˈädik\ adj : occurring at regular intervals —**pe·ri·od·i·cal·ly** adv

pe·ri·od·i·cal \ˌpirēˈädikəl\ n : newspaper or magazine

pe·riph·ery \pəˈrifərē\ n, pl -er·ies : outer boundary —**pe·riph·er·al** \-ərəl\ adj

peri·scope \'perəˌskōp\ n : optical instrument for viewing from a submarine

per·ish \'perish\ vb : die or spoil —**per·ish·able** \-əbəl\ adj or n

per·ju·ry \'pərjərē\ n : lying under oath —**per·jure** \'pərjər\ vb —**per·jur·er** n

¹**perk** \'pərk\ vb 1 : thrust (as the head)

up jauntily 2 : freshen 3 : gain vigor or spirit —**perky** adj

²perk vb : percolate

³perk n : privilege or benefit in addition to regular pay

per·ma·nent \'pərmənənt\ adj : lasting ~ n : hair wave —**per·ma·nence** \-nəns\ n —**per·ma·nent·ly** adv

per·me·able \'pərmēəbəl\ adj : permitting fluids to seep through —**per·me·a·bil·i·ty** \,pərmēə'bilətē\ n

per·me·ate \'pərmē,āt\ vb -at·ed; -at·ing 1 : seep through 2 : pervade —**per·me·ation** \,pərmē'āshən\ n

per·mis·si·ble \pər'misəbəl\ adj : that may be permitted

per·mis·sion \pər'mishən\ n : formal consent

per·mis·sive \pər'misiv\ adj : granting freedom esp. to excess —**per·miss·ive·ly** adv —**per·mis·sive·ness** n

per·mit \pər'mit\ vb -tt- 1 : approve 2 : make possible ~ \'pər,-, pər'-\ n : license

per·ni·cious \pər'nishəs\ adj : very harmful —**per·ni·cious·ly** adv

per·ox·ide \pə'räk,sīd\ n : compound (as hydrogen peroxide) in which oxygen is joined to oxygen

per·pen·dic·u·lar \,pərpən'dikyələr\ adj 1 : vertical 2 : meeting at a right angle —**perpendicular** n —**per·pen·dic·u·lar·i·ty** \-,dikyə'larətē\ n —**per·pen·dic·u·lar·ly** adv

per·pe·trate \'pərpə,trāt\ vb -trat·ed; -trat·ing : be guilty of doing —**per·pe·tra·tion** \,pərpə'trāshən\ n —**per·pe·tra·tor** \'pərpə,trātər\ n

per·pet·u·al \pər'pechəwəl\ adj 1 : continuing forever 2 : occurring continually —**per·pet·u·al·ly** adv —**per·pe·tu·ity** \,pərpə'tüətē, -'tyü-\ n

per·pet·u·ate \pər'pechə,wāt\ vb -at·ed; -at·ing : make perpetual —**per·pet·u·a·tion** \-,pechə'wāshən\ n

per·plex \pər'pleks\ vb : confuse —**per·plex·i·ty** \-ətē\ n

per·se·cute \'pərsi,kyüt\ vb -cut·ed; -cut·ing : harass, afflict —**per·se·cu·tion** \,pərsi'kyüshən\ n —**per·se·cu·tor** \'pərsi,kyütər\ n

per·se·vere \,pərsə'vir\ vb -vered; -ver·ing : persist —**per·se·ver·ance** \-'virəns\ n

per·sist \pər'sist, -'zist\ vb 1 : go on resolutely in spite of difficulties 2 : continue to exist —**per·sis·tence** \-'sistəns, -'zis-\ n —**per·sis·ten·cy**

\-tənsē\ n —**per·sis·tent** \-tənt\ adj —**per·sis·tent·ly** adv

per·son \'pərsᵊn\ n 1 : human being 2 : human being's body or individuality 3 : reference to the speaker, one spoken to, or one spoken of

per·son·able \'pərsᵊnəbəl\ adj : having a pleasing personality

per·son·age \'pərsᵊnij\ n : person of rank or distinction

per·son·al \'pərsᵊnəl\ adj 1 : relating to a particular person 2 : done in person 3 : affecting one's body 4 : offensive to a certain individual —**per·son·al·ly** adv

per·son·al·i·ty \,pərsᵊn'alətē\ n, pl -ties 1 : manner and disposition of an individual 2 : distinctive or well-known person

per·son·al·ize \'pərsᵊnə,līz\ vb -ized; -iz·ing : mark as belonging to a particular person

per·son·i·fy \pər'sänə,fī\ vb -fied; -fy·ing 1 : represent as a human being 2 : be the embodiment of —**per·son·i·fi·ca·tion** \-,sänəfə'kāshən\ n

per·son·nel \,pərsᵊn'el\ n : body of persons employed

per·spec·tive \pər'spektiv\ n 1 : apparent depth and distance in painting 2 : view of things in their true relationship or importance

per·spi·ca·cious \,pərspə'kāshəs\ adj : showing keen understanding or discernment —**per·spi·cac·i·ty** \-'kasətē\ n

per·spire \pər'spīr\ vb -spired; -spir·ing : sweat —**per·spi·ra·tion** \,pərspə'rāshən\ n

per·suade \pər'swād\ vb -suad·ed; -suad·ing : win over to a belief or course of action by argument or entreaty —**per·sua·sion** \pər'swāzhən\ n —**per·sua·sive** \-'swāsiv, -ziv\ adj —**per·sua·sive·ly** adv —**per·sua·sive·ness** n

pert \'pərt\ adj : flippant or irreverent

per·tain \pər'tān\ vb 1 : belong 2 : relate

per·ti·nent \'pərtᵊnənt\ adj : relevant —**per·ti·nence** \-əns\ n

per·turb \pər'tərb\ vb : make uneasy —**per·tur·ba·tion** \,pərtər'bāshən\ n

pe·ruse \pə'rüz\ vb -rused; -rus·ing : read attentively —**pe·rus·al** \-'rüzəl\ n

per·vade \pər'vād\ vb -vad·ed; -vad·ing : spread through every part of —**per·va·sive** \-'vāsiv, -ziv\ adj

per·verse \pər'vərs\ *adj* 1 : corrupt 2 : unreasonably contrary —**per·verse·ly** *adv* —**per·verse·ness** *n* — **per·ver·sion** \-'vərzhən\ *n* — **per·ver·si·ty** \-'vərsətē\ *n*

per·vert \pər'vərt\ *vb* : corrupt or distort ~ \'pər,-\ *n* : one that is perverted

pe·so \'pāsō\ *n, pl* -sos : monetary unit (as of Mexico)

pes·si·mism \'pesə,mizəm\ *n* : inclination to expect the worst —**pes·si·mist** \-mist\ *n* —**pes·si·mis·tic** \,pesə'mistik\ *adj*

pest \'pest\ *n* 1 : nuisance 2 : plant or animal detrimental to humans or their crops —**pes·ti·cide** \'pestə,sīd\ *n*

pes·ter \'pestər\ *vb* -tered; -ter·ing : harass with petty matters

pes·ti·lence \'pestələns\ *n* : plague —**pes·ti·lent** \-lənt\ *adj*

pes·tle \'pesəl, 'pestᵊl\ *n* : implement for grinding substances in a mortar

pet \'pet\ *n* 1 : domesticated animal kept for pleasure 2 : favorite ~ *vb* -tt- : stroke gently or lovingly

pet·al \'petᵊl\ *n* : modified leaf of a flower head

pe·tite \pə'tēt\ *adj* : having a small trim figure

pe·ti·tion \pə'tishən\ *n* : formal written request ~ *vb* : make a request —**pe·ti·tion·er** *n*

pet·ri·fy \'petrə,fī\ *vb* -fied; -fy·ing 1 : change into stony material 2 : make rigid or inactive (as from fear) —**pet·ri·fac·tion** \,petrə'fakshən\ *n*

pe·tro·leum \pə'trōlēəm\ *n* : raw oil obtained from the ground

pet·ti·coat \'petē,kōt\ *n* : skirt worn under a dress

pet·ty \'petē\ *adj* -ti·er; -est 1 : minor 2 : of no importance 3 : narrow-minded or mean —**pet·ti·ly** \'petᵊlē\ *adv* —**pet·ti·ness** *n*

petty officer *n* : subordinate officer in the navy or coast guard

pet·u·lant \'pechələnt\ *adj* : irritable —**pet·u·lance** \-ləns\ *n* —**pet·u·lant·ly** *adv*

pe·tu·nia \pi'tünyə, -'tyü-\ *n* : tropical herb with bright flowers

pew \'pyü\ *n* : bench with a back used in a church

pew·ter \'pyütər\ *n* : alloy of tin used for household utensils

pH \,pē'āch\ *n* : number expressing relative acidity and alkalinity

pha·lanx \'fā,laŋks\ *n, pl* -lanx·es or

-lan·ges \fə'lan,jēz\ 1 : body (as of troops) in compact formation 2 *pl* *phalanges* : digital bone of the hand or foot

phal·lus \'faləs\ *n, pl* -li \'fal,ī\ or -lus·es : penis —**phal·lic** *adj*

phantasy *var of* FANTASY

phan·tom \'fantəm\ *n* : something that only appears to be real —**phantom** *adj*

pha·raoh \'ferō, 'fārō\ *n* : ruler of ancient Egypt

phar·ma·ceu·ti·cal \,färmə'sütikəl\ *adj* : relating to pharmacy or the making and selling of medicinal drugs — **pharmaceutical** *n*

phar·ma·col·o·gy \,färmə'käləjē\ *n* : science of drugs esp. as related to medicinal uses —**phar·ma·co·log·i·cal** \-ikəl\ *adj* —**phar·ma·col·o·gist** \-'käləjist\ *n*

phar·ma·cy \'färməsē\ *n, pl* -cies 1 : art or practice of preparing and dispensing medical drugs 2 : drugstore — **phar·ma·cist** \-sist\ *n*

phar·ynx \'fariŋks\ *n, pl* **pha·ryn·ges** \fə'rin,jēz\ : space behind the mouth into which the nostrils, esophagus, and windpipe open —**pha·ryn·ge·al** \fə'rinjəl, ,farən'jēəl\ *adj*

phase \'fāz\ *n* 1 : particular appearance or stage in a recurring series of changes 2 : stage in a process — **phase in** *vb* : introduce in stages — **phase out** *vb* : discontinue gradually

pheas·ant \'fezᵊnt\ *n, pl* -ant or -ants : long-tailed brilliantly colored game bird

phe·nom·e·non \fi'nämə,nän, -nən\ *n, pl* -na \-nə\ or -nons 1 : observable fact or event 2 *pl* -nons : prodigy — **phe·nom·e·nal** \-'nämənᵊl\ *adj*

phi·lan·der·er \fə'landərər\ *n* : one who makes love without serious intent

phi·lan·thro·py \fə'lanthrəpē\ *n, pl* -pies : charitable act or gift or an organization that distributes such gifts —**phil·an·throp·ic** \,filən'thräpik\ *adj* —**phi·lan·thro·pist** \fə'lanthrə·pist\ *n*

phi·lat·e·ly \fə'latᵊlē\ *n* : collection and study of postage stamps —**phi·lat·e·list** \-ᵊlist\ *n*

phi·lis·tine \'filə,stēn, fə'listən\ *n* : one who is smugly indifferent to intellectual or artistic values —**philistine** *adj*

philo·den·dron \,filə'dendrən\ *n, pl*

-drons or **-dra** \-drə\ : plant grown for its showy leaves

phi·los·o·pher \fə'läsəfər\ n 1 : reflective thinker 2 : student of philosophy

phi·los·o·phy \fə'läsəfē\ n. pl **-phies** 1 : critical study of fundamental beliefs 2 : sciences and liberal arts exclusive of medicine, law, and theology 3 : system of ideas 4 : sum of personal convictions —**phil·o·soph·ic** \filə-'säfik\, **phil·o·soph·i·cal** \-ikəl\ adj —**phil·o·soph·i·cal·ly** \-klē\ adv —**phi·los·o·phize** \fə'läsə,fīz\ vb

phle·bi·tis \fli'bītəs\ n : inflammation of a vein

phlegm \'flem\ n : thick mucus in the nose and throat

phlox \'fläks\ n, pl **phlox** or **phlox·es** : herb grown for its flower clusters

pho·bia \'fōbēə\ n : irrational persistent fear

phoe·nix \'fēniks\ n : legendary bird held to burn itself to death and rise fresh and young from its ashes

phone \'fōn\ n : telephone ~ vb **phoned; phon·ing** : call on a telephone

pho·neme \'fō,nēm\ n : basic distinguishable unit of speech —**pho·ne·mic** \fō'nēmik\ adj

pho·net·ics \fə'netiks\ n : study of speech sounds —**pho·net·ic** \-ik\ adj —**pho·ne·ti·cian** \,fōnə'tishən\ n

pho·nics \'fäniks\ n : method of teaching reading by stressing sound values of syllables and words

pho·no·graph \'fōnə,graf\ n : instrument that reproduces sounds from a grooved disc

pho·ny, pho·ney \'fōnē\ adj **-ni·er; -est** : not sincere or genuine —**phony** n

phos·phate \'fäs,fāt\ n : chemical salt used in fertilizers —**phos·phat·ic** \fäs'fatik\ adj

phos·phor \'fäsfər\ n : phosphorescent substance

phos·pho·res·cence \,fäsfə'res^ns\ n : luminescence from absorbed radiation —**phos·pho·res·cent** \-^nt\ adj —**phos·pho·res·cent·ly** adv

phos·pho·rus \'fäsfərəs\ n : poisonous waxy chemical element —**phos·phor·ic** \fäs'fòrik, -'fär-\ adj —**phos·pho·rous** \'fäsfərəs, fäs'fōrəs\ adj

pho·to \'fōtō\ n, pl **-tos** : photograph —**photo** vb or adj

pho·to·copy \'fōtə,käpē\ n : photographic copy (as of a printed page) —**photocopy** vb

pho·to·elec·tric \,fōtōi'lektrik\ adj : relating to an electrical effect due to the interaction of light with matter

pho·to·ge·nic \,fōtə'jenik\ adj : suitable for being photographed

pho·to·graph \'fōtə,graf\ n : picture taken by photography —**photograph** vb —**pho·tog·ra·pher** \fə'tägrəfər\ n

pho·tog·ra·phy \fə'tägrəfē\ n : process of using light to produce images on a sensitized surface —**pho·to·graph·ic** \,fōtə'grafik\ adj —**pho·to·graph·i·cal·ly** adv

pho·to·syn·the·sis \,fōtō'sinthəsəs\ n : formation of carbohydrates by chlorophyll-containing plants exposed to sunlight —**pho·to·syn·the·size** \-,sīz\ vb —**pho·to·syn·thet·ic** \-sin'thetik\ adj

phrase \'frāz\ n 1 : brief expression 2 : group of related words that express a thought ~ vb **phrased; phras·ing** : express in a particular manner

phrase·ol·o·gy \frāzē'äləjē\ n, pl **-gies** : manner of phrasing

phy·lum \'fīləm\ n, pl **-la** \-lə\ : major division of the plant or animal kingdom

phys·i·cal \'fizikəl\ adj 1 : relating to nature 2 : material as opposed to mental or spiritual 3 : relating to the body ~ n : medical examination —**phys·i·cal·ly** \-klē\ adv

phy·si·cian \fə'zishən\ n : doctor of medicine

physician's assistant n : person certified to provide basic medical care under a physician's supervision

phys·i·cist \'fizəsist\ n : specialist in physics

phys·ics \'fiziks\ n : science that deals with matter and motion

phys·i·og·no·my \,fizē'ägnəmē\ n, pl **-mies** : facial appearance esp. as a reflection of inner character

phys·i·ol·o·gy \,fizē'äləjē\ n : functional processes in an organism —**phys·i·o·log·i·cal** \-ēə'läjikəl\, **phys·i·o·log·ic** \-ik\ adj —**phys·i·ol·o·gist** \-ē'äləjist\ n

phy·sique \fə'zēk\ n : build of a person's body

pi \'pī\ n, pl **pis** \'pīz\ : symbol π denoting the ratio of the circumference of a circle to its diameter or the ratio itself

pi·a·nist \pē'anist, 'pēənist\ n : one who plays the piano

pi·ano \pē'anō\ n, pl **-anos** : musical instrument with strings sounded by hammers operated from a keyboard

pi·az·za \pē'azə, -'äz-, -tsə\ n, pl **-zas** or **-ze** \-tsä\ : public square in a town

pic·a·yune \,pikē'yün\ adj : trivial or petty

pic·co·lo \'pikə,lō\ n, pl **-los** : small shrill flute

1pick \'pik\ vb 1 : break up with a pointed instrument 2 : remove bit by bit 3 : gather by plucking 4 : select 5 : rob 6 : provoke 7 : unlock with a wire 8 : eat sparingly ~ n 1 : act of choosing 2 : choicest one —**pick·er** n —**pick up** vb 1 : improve 2 : put in order

2pick n : pointed digging tool

pick·ax n : pick

pick·er·el \'pikərəl\ n, pl **-el** or **-els** : small pike

pick·et \'pikət\ n 1 : pointed stake (as for a fence) 2 : worker demonstrating on strike ~ vb : demonstrate as a picket

pick·le \'pikəl\ n 1 : brine or vinegar solution for preserving foods or a food preserved in a pickle 2 : bad state —**pickle** vb

pick·pock·et n : one who steals from pockets

pick·up \'pik,əp\ n 1 : revival or acceleration 2 : light truck with an open body

pic·nic \'pik,nik\ n : outing with food usu. eaten in the open ~ vb **-nicked**; **-nick·ing** : go on a picnic

pic·to·ri·al \pik'tōrēəl\ adj : relating to pictures

pic·ture \'pikchər\ n 1 : representation by painting, drawing, or photography 2 : vivid description 3 : copy 4 : movie ~ vb **-tured**; **-tur·ing** : form a mental image of

pic·tur·esque \,pikchə'resk\ adj : attractive or charming enough for a picture —**pic·tur·esque·ness** n

pie \'pī\ n : pastry crust and a filling

pie·bald \'pī,bȯld\ adj : blotched with white and black

piece \'pēs\ n 1 : part of a whole 2 : one of a group or set 3 : single item 4 : product of creative work ~ vb **pieced**; **piec·ing** : join into a whole

piece·meal \'pēs,mēl\ adv or adj : gradually

pied \'pīd\ adj : colored in blotches

pier \'pir\ n 1 : support for a bridge span 2 : deck or wharf built out over water 3 : pillar

pierce \'pirs\ vb **pierced**; **pierc·ing** 1 : enter or thrust into or through 2 : penetrate 3 : see through

pi·ety \'pīətē\ n, pl **-eties** : devotion to religion

pig \'pig\ n 1 : young swine 2 : dirty or greedy individual 3 : iron casting —**pig·gish** \-ish\ adj —**pig·let** \-lət\ n —**pig·pen** n —**pig·sty** n

pi·geon \'pijən\ n : stout-bodied short-legged bird

pi·geon·hole n : small open compartment for letters or documents ~ vb 1 : place in a pigeonhole 2 : classify

pig·gy·back \'pigē,bak\ adv or adj : up on the back and shoulders

pig·head·ed \-'hedəd\ adj : stubborn

pig·ment \'pigmənt\ n : coloring matter —**pig·men·ta·tion** n

pigmy var of PYGMY

pig·tail n : tight braid of hair

1pike \'pīk\ n, pl **pike** or **pikes** : large freshwater fish

2pike n : former weapon consisting of a long wooden staff with a steel point

3pike n : turnpike

pi·laf, pi·laff \pi'läf, 'pē,läf\, **pi·lau** \pi-'lȯ, -'lȯ; 'pēlȯ, -lȯ\ n : dish of seasoned rice

1pile \'pīl\ n : supporting pillar driven into the ground

2pile n : quantity of things thrown on one another ~ vb **piled**; **pil·ing** : heap up, accumulate

3pile n : surface of fine hairs or threads —**piled** adj

piles \'pīlz\ n pl : hemorrhoids

pil·fer \'pilfər\ vb : steal in small quantities

pil·grim \'pilgrəm\ n 1 : one who travels to a shrine or holy place in devotion 2 cap : one of the English settlers in America in 1620

pil·grim·age \-grəmij\ n : pilgrim's journey

pill \'pil\ n : small rounded mass of medicine —**pill·box** n

pil·lage \'pilij\ vb **-laged**; **-lag·ing** : loot and plunder —**pillage** n

pil·lar \'pilər\ n : upright usu. supporting column —**pil·lared** adj

pil·lo·ry \'pilərē\ n, pl **-ries** : wooden frame for public punishment with holes for the head and hands ~ vb

-ried; -ry·ing 1 : set in a pillory **2** : expose to public scorn

pil·low \'pilō\ *n* : soft cushion for the head —**pil·low·case** *n*

pi·lot \'pīlət\ *n* **1** : helmsman **2** : person licensed to take ships into and out of a port **3** : guide **4** : one that flies an aircraft or spacecraft ~ *vb* : act as pilot of —**pi·lot·less** *adj*

pi·men·to \pə'mentō\ *n, pl* **-tos** *or* **-to 1** : allspice **2** : pimiento

pi·mien·to \pə'mentō, -'myen-\ *n, pl* **-tos** : mild red sweet pepper

pimp \'pimp\ *n* : man who solicits clients for a prostitute —**pimp** *vb*

pim·ple \'pimpəl\ *n* : small inflamed swelling on the skin —**pim·ply** \-pəlē\ *adj*

pin \'pin\ *n* **1** : fastener made of a small pointed piece of wire **2** : ornament or emblem fastened to clothing with a pin **3** : wooden object used as a target in bowling ~ *vb* **-nn- 1** : fasten with a pin **2** : hold fast or immobile —**pin·hole** *n*

pin·a·fore \'pinə,fōr\ *n* : sleeveless dress or apron fastened at the back

pin·cer \'pinsər\ *n* **1** *pl* : gripping tool with 2 jaws **2** : pincerlike claw

pinch \'pinch\ *vb* **1** : squeeze between the finger and thumb or between the jaws of a tool **2** : compress painfully **3** : restrict **4** : steal ~ *n* **1** : emergency **2** : painful effect **3** : act of pinching **4** : very small quantity

pin·cush·ion *n* : cushion for storing pins

¹pine \'pīn\ *n* : evergreen cone-bearing tree or its wood

²pine *vb* **pined; pin·ing 1** : lose health through distress **2** : yearn for intensely

pine·ap·ple *n* : tropical plant bearing an edible juicy fruit

pin·feath·er *n* : new feather just coming through the skin

¹pin·ion \'pinyən\ *vb* : restrain by binding the arms

²pinion *n* : small gear

¹pink \'piŋk\ *n* **1** : plant with narrow leaves and showy flowers **2** : highest degree

²pink *n* : light red color —**pink** *adj* —**pink·ish** *adj*

pink·eye *n* : contagious eye inflammation

pin·na·cle \'pinikəl\ *n* : highest point

pi·noch·le \'pē,nəkəl\ *n* : card game played with a 48-card deck

pin·point *vb* : locate, hit, or aim with great precision

pint \'pīnt\ *n* : 1/2 quart

pin·to \'pin,tō\ *n, pl* **pintos** : spotted horse or pony

pin·worm *n* : small parasitic intestinal worm

pi·o·neer \,pīə'nir\ *n* **1** : one that originates or helps open up a new line of thought or activity **2** : early settler ~ *vb* : act as a pioneer

pi·ous \'pīəs\ *adj* **1** : conscientious in religious practices **2** : affectedly religious —**pi·ous·ly** *adv*

pipe \'pīp\ *n* **1** : tube that produces music when air is forced through **2** : bagpipe **3** : long tube for conducting a fluid **4** : smoking tool ~ *vb* **piped; pip·ing 1** : play on a pipe **2** : speak in a high voice **3** : convey by pipes —**pip·er** *n*

pipe·line *n* **1** : line of pipe **2** : channel for information

pip·ing \'pīpiŋ\ *n* **1** : music of pipes **2** : narrow fold of material used to decorate edges or seams

pi·quant \'pēkənt\ *adj* **1** : tangy **2** : provocative or charming —**pi·quan·cy** \-kənsē\ *n*

pique \'pēk\ *n* : resentment ~ *vb* **piqued; piqu·ing 1** : offend **2** : arouse by provocation

pi·qué, pi·que \pi'kā\ *n* : durable ribbed clothing fabric

pi·ra·cy \'pīrəsē\ *n, pl* **-cies 1** : robbery on the seas **2** : unauthorized use of another's production or invention

pi·ra·nha \pə'ranyə, -'ränə\ *n* : small So. American fish with sharp teeth

pi·rate \'pīrət\ *n* : one who commits piracy —**pirate** *vb* —**pi·rat·i·cal** \pə'ratikəl, pī-\ *adj*

pir·ou·ette \,pirə'wet\ *n* : ballet turn on the toe or ball of one foot —**pirouette** *vb*

pis *pl of* PI

pis·ta·chio \pə'stashē,ō, -'stäsh-\ *n, pl* **-chios** : small tree bearing a greenish edible seed or its seed

pis·til \'pistəl\ *n* : female reproductive organ in a flower —**pis·til·late** \'pistə,lāt\ *adj*

pis·tol \'pistəl\ *n* : firearm held with one hand

pis·ton \'pistən\ *n* : sliding piece that receives and transmits motion usu. inside a cylinder

¹pit \'pit\ *n* **1** : hole or shaft in the

ground 2 : sunken or enclosed place for a special purpose 3 : hell 4 : hollow or indentation ~ *vb* **-tt- 1** : form pits in 2 : become marred with pits

²pit *n* : stony seed of some fruits ~ *vb* **-tt-** : remove the pit from

pit bull *n* : powerful compact dog bred for fighting

¹pitch \'pich\ *n* : resin from conifers — **pitchy** *adj*

²pitch *vb* **1** : erect and fix firmly in place 2 : throw 3 : set at a particular tone level 4 : fall headlong ~ *n* **1** : action or manner of pitching 2 : degree of slope 3 : relative highness of a tone 4 : sales talk —**pitched** *adj*

¹pitch·er \'pichər\ *n* : container for liquids

²pitcher *n* : one that pitches (as in baseball)

pitch·fork *n* : long-handled fork for pitching hay

pit·e·ous \'pitēəs\ *adj* : arousing pity — **pit·e·ous·ly** *adv*

pit·fall \'pit,fȯl\ *n* : hidden danger

pith \'pith\ *n* **1** : spongy plant tissue 2 : essential or meaningful part —**pithy** *adj*

piti·able \'pitēəbəl\ *adj* : pitiful

piti·ful \'pitifəl\ *adj* **1** : arousing or deserving pity 2 : contemptible —**piti·ful·ly** *adv*

pit·tance \'pit°ns\ *n* : small portion or amount

pi·tu·itary \pə'tüə,terē, -'tyü-\ *adj* : relating to or being a small gland attached to the brain

pity \'pitē\ *n, pl* **pi·ties 1** : sympathetic sorrow 2 : something to be regretted ~ *vb* **pit·ied; pity·ing** : feel pity for —**piti·less** *adj* —**piti·less·ly** *adv*

piv·ot \'pivət\ *n* : fixed pin on which something turns ~ *vb* : turn on or as if on a pivot —**piv·ot·al** *adj*

pix·ie, pixy \'piksē\ *n, pl* **pix·ies** : mischievous sprite

piz·za \'pētsə\ *n* : thin pie of bread dough spread with a spiced mixture (as of tomatoes, cheese, and meat)

piz·zazz, pi·zazz \pə'zaz\ *n* : glamour

piz·ze·ria \,pētsə'rēə\ *n* : pizza restaurant

plac·ard \'plakərd, -,ärd\ *n* : poster ~ *vb* : display placards in or on

pla·cate \'plā,kāt, 'plak,āt\ *vb* **-cat·ed; -cat·ing** : appease —**pla·ca·ble** \'plakəbəl, 'plākə-\ *adj*

place \'plās\ *n* **1** : space or room 2 : indefinite area 3 : a particular building, locality, area, or part 4 : relative position in a scale or sequence 5 : seat 6 : job ~ *vb* **placed; plac·ing 1** : put in a place 2 : identify —**place·ment** *n*

pla·ce·bo \plə'sēbō\ *n, pl* **-bos** : something inactive prescribed as a remedy for its psychological effect

pla·cen·ta \plə'sentə\ *n, pl* **-tas** *or* **-tae** \-,ē\ : structure in a uterus by which a fetus is nourished —**pla·cen·tal** \-'sent°l\ *adj*

plac·id \'plasəd\ *adj* : undisturbed or peaceful —**pla·cid·i·ty** \pla'sidətē\ *n* —**plac·id·ly** *adv*

pla·gia·rize \'plājə,rīz\ *vb* **-rized; -riz·ing** : use (words or ideas) of another as if your own —**pla·gia·rism** \-,rizəm\ *n* —**pla·gia·rist** \-rist\ *n*

plague \'plāg\ *n* **1** : disastrous evil 2 : destructive contagious bacterial disease ~ *vb* **plagued; plagu·ing 1** : afflict with disease or disaster 2 : harass

plaid \'plad\ *n* : woolen fabric with a pattern of crossing stripes or the pattern itself —**plaid** *adj*

plain \'plān\ *n* : expanse of relatively level treeless country ~ *adj* **1** : lacking ornament 2 : not concealed or disguised 3 : easily understood 4 : frank 5 : not fancy or pretty —**plain·ly** *adv* —**plain·ness** \'plānnəs\ *n*

plain·tiff \'plāntəf\ *n* : complaining party in a lawsuit

plain·tive \'plāntiv\ *adj* : expressive of suffering or woe —**plain·tive·ly** *adv*

plait \'plāt, 'plat\ *n* **1** : pleat 2 : braid of hair or straw —**plait** *vb*

plan \'plan\ *n* **1** : drawing or diagram 2 : method for accomplishing something ~ *vb* **-nn- 1** : form a plan of 2 : intend —**plan·less** *adj* —**plan·ner** *n*

¹plane \'plān\ *vb* **planed; plan·ing** : smooth or level off with a plane ~ *n* : smoothing or shaping tool —**plan·er** *n*

²plane *n* **1** : level surface 2 : level of existence, consciousness, or development 3 : airplane ~ *adj* **1** : flat 2 : dealing with flat surfaces or figures

plan·et \'planət\ *n* : celestial body that revolves around the sun —**plan·e·tary** \-ə,terē\ *adj*

plan·e·tar·i·um \,planə'terēəm\ *n, pl* **-iums** *or* **-ia** \-ēə\ : building or room housing a device to project images of celestial bodies

plank \'plaŋk\ n 1 : heavy thick board 2 : article in the platform of a political party —**plank·ing** n

plank·ton \'plaŋktən\ n : tiny aquatic animal and plant life —**plank·ton·ic** \plaŋk'tänik\ adj

plant \'plant\ vb 1 : set in the ground to grow 2 : place firmly or forcibly ~ n 1 : living thing without sense organs that cannot move about 2 : land, buildings, and machinery used esp. in manufacture

¹plan·tain \'plantᵊn\ n : short-stemmed herb with tiny greenish flowers

²plantain n : banana plant with starchy greenish fruit

plan·ta·tion \plan'tāshən\ n : agricultural estate usu. worked by resident laborers

plant·er \'plantər\ n 1 : plantation owner 2 : plant container

plaque \'plak\ n 1 : commemorative tablet 2 : film layer on a tooth

plas·ma \'plazmə\ n : watery part of blood —**plas·mat·ic** \plaz'matik\ adj

plas·ter \'plastər\ n 1 : medicated dressing 2 : hardening paste for coating walls and ceilings~ vb : cover with plaster —**plas·ter·er** n

plas·tic \'plastik\ adj : capable of being molded ~ n : material that can be formed into rigid objects, films, or filaments —**plas·tic·i·ty** \plas'tisətē\ n

plate \'plāt\ n 1 : flat thin piece 2 : plated metalware 3 : shallow usu. circular dish 4 : denture or the part of it that fits to the mouth 5 : something printed from an engraving ~ vb **plat·ed**; **plat·ing** : overlay with metal —**plat·ing** n

pla·teau \pla'tō\ n, pl **-teaus** or **-teaux** \-'tōz\ : large level area of high land

plat·form \'plat,fȯrm\ n 1 : raised flooring or stage 2 : declaration of principles for a political party

plat·i·num \'platᵊnəm\ n : heavy grayish-white metallic chemical element

plat·i·tude \'platə,tüd, -,tyüd\ n : trite remark —**plat·i·tu·di·nous** \,platə-'tüdᵊnəs, -'tyüd-\ adj

pla·toon \plə'tün\ n : small military unit

platoon sergeant n : noncommissioned officer in the army ranking below a first sergeant

plat·ter \'platər\ n : large serving plate

platy·pus \'platipəs\ n : small aquatic egg-laying mammal

plau·dit \'plȯdət\ n : act of applause

plau·si·ble \'plȯzəbəl\ adj : reasonable or believable —**plau·si·bil·i·ty** \,plȯzə'bilətē\ n —**plau·si·bly** \-blē\ adv

play \'plā\ n 1 : action in a game 2 : recreational activity 3 : light or fitful movement 4 : free movement 5 : stage representation of a drama ~ vb 1 : engage in recreation 2 : move or toy with aimlessly 3 : perform music 4 : act in a drama —**play·act·ing** n —**play·er** n —**play·ful** \-fəl\ adj —**play·ful·ly** adv —**play·ful·ness** n —**play·pen** n —**play·suit** n —**play·thing** n

play·ground n : place for children to play

play·house n 1 : theater 2 : small house for children to play in

playing card n : one of a set of 24 to 78 cards marked to show its rank and suit and used to play a game of cards

play·mate n : companion in play

play–off n : contest or series of contests to determine a champion

play·wright \-,rīt\ n : writer of plays

pla·za \'plazə, 'pläz-\ n 1 : public square 2 : shopping mall

plea \'plē\ n 1 : defendant's answer to charges 2 : urgent request

plead \'plēd\ vb **plead·ed** \'plēdəd\ or **pled** \'pled\; **plead·ing** 1 : argue for or against in court 2 : answer to a charge or indictment 3 : appeal earnestly —**plead·er** n

pleas·ant \'plezᵊnt\ adj 1 : giving pleasure 2 : marked by pleasing behavior or appearance —**pleas·ant·ly** adv —**pleas·ant·ness** n

pleas·ant·ries \-ᵊntrēz\ n pl : pleasant and casual conversation

please \'plēz\ vb **pleased**; **pleas·ing** 1 : give pleasure or satisfaction to 2 : desire or intend

pleas·ing \'plēziŋ\ adj : giving pleasure —**pleas·ing·ly** adv

plea·sur·able \'plezhərəbəl\ adj : pleasant —**plea·sur·ably** \-blē\ adv

plea·sure \'plezhər\ n 1 : desire or inclination 2 : enjoyment 3 : source of delight

pleat \'plēt\ vb : arrange in pleats ~ n : fold in cloth

ple·be·ian \pli'bēən\ n : one of the common people ~ adj : ordinary

pledge \'plej\ n 1 : something given as security 2 : promise or vow ~ vb **pledged; pledg·ing** 1 : offer as or bind by a pledge 2 : promise

ple·na·ry \'plēnərē, 'plen-\ adj : full

pleni·po·ten·tia·ry \,plenəpə'tenchə- rē, -'tenchē,erē\ n : diplomatic agent having full authority —**plenipotenti- ary** adj

plen·i·tude \'plenə,tüd, -,tyüd\ n 1 : completeness 2 : abundance

plen·te·ous \'plentēəs\ adj : existing in plenty

plen·ty \'plentē\ n : more than adequate number or amount —**plen·ti·ful** \'plentifəl\ adj —**plen·ti·ful·ly** adv

pleth·o·ra \'plethərə\ n : excess

pleu·ri·sy \'plùrəsē\ n : inflammation of the chest membrane

pli·able \'plīəbəl\ adj : flexible

pli·ant \'plīənt\ adj : flexible —**pli·an- cy** \-ənsē\ n

pli·ers \'plīərz\ n pl : pinching or grip- ping tool

¹**plight** \'plīt\ vb : pledge

²**plight** n : bad state

plod \'pläd\ vb **-dd-** 1 : walk heavily or slowly 2 : work laboriously and mo- notonously —**plod·der** n —**plod- ding·ly** \-iŋlē\ adv

plot \'plät\ n 1 : small area of ground 2 : ground plan 3 : main story devel- opment (as of a book or movie) 4 : secret plan for doing something ~ vb **-tt-** 1 : make a plot or plan of 2 : plan or contrive —**plot·ter** n

plo·ver \'pləvər, 'plōvər\ n, pl **-ver** or **-vers** : shorebird related to the sand- piper

plow, plough \'plaů\ n 1 : tool used to turn soil 2 : device for pushing ma- terial aside ~ vb 1 : break up with a plow 2 : cleave or move through like a plow —**plow·man** \-mən, -,man\ n

plow·share \-,sher\ n : plow part that cuts the earth

ploy \'plói\ n : clever maneuver

pluck \'plək\ vb 1 : pull off or out 2 : tug or twitch ~ n 1 : act or instance of plucking 2 : spirit or courage

plucky \'pləkē\ adj **pluck·i·er; -est** : courageous or spirited

plug \'pləg\ n 1 : something for sealing an opening 2 : electrical connector at the end of a cord 3 : piece of favorable publicity ~ vb **-gg-** 1 : stop or make tight or secure by inserting a plug 2 : publicize

plum \'pləm\ n 1 : smooth-skinned juicy fruit 2 : fine reward

plum·age \'plümij\ n : feathers of a bird —**plum·aged** \-mijd\ adj

plumb \'pləm\ n : weight on the end of a line (**plumb line**) to show vertical direction ~ adv 1 : vertically 2 : completely ~ vb : sound or test with a plumb ~ adj : vertical

plumb·er \'pləmər\ n : one who repairs usu. water pipes and fixtures

plumb·ing \'pləmiŋ\ n : system of water pipes in a building

plume \'plüm\ n : large, conspicuous, or showy feather ~ vb **plumed; plum- ing** 1 : provide or deck with feathers 2 : indulge in pride —**plumed** \'plümd\ adj

plum·met \'pləmət\ vb : drop straight down

¹**plump** \'pləmp\ vb : drop suddenly or heavily ~ adv 1 : straight down 2 : in a direct manner

²**plump** adj : having a full rounded form —**plump·ness** n

plun·der \'pləndər\ vb : rob or take goods by force (as in war) ~ n : something taken in plundering —**plun·der·er** n

plunge \'plənj\ vb **plunged; plung·ing** 1 : thrust or drive with force 2 : leap or dive into water 3 : begin an action suddenly 4 : dip or move suddenly forward or down ~ n : act or instance of plunging —**plung·er** n

plu·ral \'plùrəl\ adj : relating to a word form denoting more than one —**plu- ral** n

plu·ral·i·ty \plù'ralətē\ n, pl **-ties** : greatest number of votes cast when not a majority

plu·ral·ize \'plùrə,līz\ vb **-ized; -iz·ing** : make plural —**plu·ral·i·za·tion** \,plùrələ'zāshən\ n

plus \'pləs\ prep : with the addition of ~ n 1 : sign + (**plus sign**) in mathe- matics to indicate addition 2 : added or positive quantity 3 : advantage ~ adj : being more or in addition ~ conj : and

plush \'pləsh\ n : fabric with a long pile ~ adj : luxurious —**plush·ly** adv — **plushy** adj —**plush·ness** n

plu·toc·ra·cy \plü'täkrəsē\ n, pl **-cies** 1 : government by the wealthy 2 : a controlling class of the wealthy — **plu·to·crat** \'plütə,krat\ n —**plu·to- crat·ic** \,plütə'kratik\ adj

plu·to·ni·um \plü'tōnēəm\ *n* : radio-active chemical element

¹ply \'plī\ *n, pl* **plies** : fold, thickness, or strand of which something is made

²ply *vb* **plied; ply·ing 1** : use or work at **2** : keep supplying something to **3** : travel regularly usu. by sea

ply·wood *n* : sheets of wood glued and pressed together

pneu·mat·ic \nú'matik, nyü-\ *adj* **1** : moved by air pressure **2** : filled with compressed air —**pneu·mat·i·cal·ly** *adv*

pneu·mo·nia \nú'mōnyə, nyü-\ *n* : inflammatory lung disease

¹poach \'pōch\ *vb* : cook in simmering liquid

²poach *vb* : hunt or fish illegally —**poach·er** *n*

pock \'päk\ *n* : small swelling on the skin or its scar —**pock·mark** *n* —**pock·marked** *adj*

pock·et \'päkət\ *n* **1** : small open bag sewn into a garment **2** : container or receptacle **3** : isolated area or group ~ *vb* : put in a pocket —**pock·et·ful** \-,fùl\ *n*

pock·et·book *n* **1** : purse **2** : financial resources

pock·et·knife *n* : knife with a folding blade carried in the pocket

pod \'päd\ *n* **1** : dry fruit that splits open when ripe **2** : compartment on a ship or craft

po·di·a·try \pə'dīətrē, pō-\ *n* : branch of medicine dealing with the foot —**po·di·a·trist** \pə'dīətrist, pō-\ *n*

po·di·um \'pōdēəm\ *n, pl* **-di·ums** or **-dia** \-ēə\ : dais

po·em \'pōəm\ *n* : composition in verse

po·et \'pōət\ *n* : writer of poetry

po·et·ry \'pōətrē\ *n* **1** : metrical writing **2** : poems —**po·et·ic** \pō'etik\, **po·et·i·cal** \-ikəl\ *adj*

po·grom \'pōgrəm, pə'gräm, 'pägrəm\ *n* : organized massacre

poi·gnant \'pòinyənt\ *adj* **1** : emotionally painful **2** : deeply moving —**poi·gnan·cy** \-nyənsē\ *n*

poin·set·tia \pòin'setēə, -'setə\ *n* : showy tropical American plant

point \'pòint\ *n* **1** : individual often essential detail **2** : purpose **3** : particular place, time, or stage **4** : sharp end **5** : projecting piece of land **6** : dot or period **7** : division of the compass **8** : unit of counting ~ *vb* **1** : sharpen **2** : indicate direction by extending a

finger **3** : direct attention to **4** : aim —**point·ed·ly** \-ədlē\ *adv* —**point·less** *adj*

point–blank *adj* **1** : so close to a target that a missile fired goes straight to it **2** : direct —**point–blank** *adv*

point·er \'pòintər\ *n* **1** : one that points out **2** : large short-haired hunting dog **3** : hint or tip

poise \'pòiz\ *vb* **poised; pois·ing** : balance ~ *n* : self-possessed calmness

poi·son \'pòiz²n\ *n* : chemical that can injure or kill ~ *vb* **1** : injure or kill with poison **2** : apply poison to **3** : affect destructively —**poi·son·er** *n* —**poi·son·ous** \'pòiz²nəs\ *adj*

poke \'pōk\ *vb* **poked; pok·ing 1** : prod **2** : dawdle ~ *n* : quick thrust

¹pok·er \'pōkər\ *n* : rod for stirring a fire

²pok·er *n* : card game for gambling

po·lar \'pōlər\ *adj* : relating to a geographical or magnetic pole

po·lar·ize \'pōlə,rīz\ *vb* **-ized; -iz·ing 1** : cause to have magnetic poles **2** : break up into opposing groups — **po·lar·i·za·tion** \,pōlərə'zāshən\ *n*

¹pole \'pōl\ *n* : long slender piece of wood or metal

²pole *n* **1** : either end of the earth's axis **2** : battery terminal **3** : either end of a magnet

pole·cat \'pōl,kat\ *n, pl* **polecats** or **polecat 1** : European carnivorous mammal **2** : skunk

po·lem·ics \pə'lemiks\ *n sing or pl* : practice of disputation —**po·lem·i·cal** \-ikəl\ *adj* —**po·lem·i·cist** \-əsist\ *n*

po·lice \pə'lēs\ *n, pl* **police 1** : department of government that keeps public order and enforces the laws **2** : members of the police ~ *vb* -**liced; -lic·ing** : regulate and keep in order —**po·lice·man** \-mən\ *n* —**police·wom·an** *n*

police officer *n* : member of the police

¹pol·i·cy \'päləsē\ *n, pl* **-cies** : course of action selected to guide decisions

²policy *n, pl* **-cies** : insurance contract —**pol·i·cy·hold·er** *n*

po·lio \'pōlē,ō\ *n* : poliomyelitis —**polio** *adj*

po·lio·my·eli·tis \-,mīə'lītəs\ *n* : acute virus disease of the spinal cord

pol·ish \'pälish\ *vb* **1** : make smooth and glossy **2** : develop or refine ~ *n* **1** : shiny surface **2** : refinement

po·lite \pə'līt\ adj **-lit·er; -est** : marked by courteous social conduct —**po·lite·ly** adv —**po·lite·ness** n

pol·i·tic \'pälə,tik\ adj : shrewdly tactful·

politically correct adj : seeking to avoid offending members of a different group

pol·i·tics \'pälə,tiks\ n sing or pl : practice of government and managing of public affairs —**po·lit·i·cal** \pə'litikəl\ adj —**po·lit·i·cal·ly** adv —**pol·i·ti·cian** \,pälə'tishən\ n

pol·ka \'pōlkə\ n : lively couple dance —**polka** vb

pol·ka dot \'pōkə,dät\ n : one of a series of regular dots in a pattern

poll \'pōl\ n 1 : head 2 : place where votes are cast —usu. pl. 3 : a sampling of opinion ~ vb 1 : cut off 2 : receive or record votes 3 : question in a poll —**poll·ster** \-stər\ n

pol·len \'pälən\ n : spores of a seed plant

pol·li·na·tion \,pälə'nāshən\ n : the carrying of pollen to fertilize the seed —**pol·li·nate** \'pälə,nāt\ vb —**pol·li·na·tor** \-ər\ n

pol·lute \pə'lüt\ vb **-lut·ed; -lut·ing** : contaminating with waste products —**pol·lut·ant** \-'lüt⁰nt\ n —**pol·lut·er** n —**pol·lu·tion** \-'lüshən\ n

pol·i·wog, pol·li·wog \'pälē,wäg\ n : tadpole

po·lo \'pōlō\ n : game played by 2 teams on horseback using long-handled mallets to drive a wooden ball

pol·ter·geist \'pōltər,gīst\ n : mischievous ghost

pol·troon \päl'trün\ n : coward

poly·es·ter \'pälē,estər\ n : synthetic fiber

po·lyg·a·my \pə'ligəmē\ n : marriage to several spouses at the same time —**po·lyg·a·mist** \-mist\ n —**po·lyg·a·mous** \-məs\ adj

poly·gon \'päli,gän\ n : closed plane figure with straight sides

poly·mer \'päləmər\ n : chemical compound of molecules joined in long strings —**po·lym·er·i·za·tion** \pə,limərə'zāshən\ n —**po·lym·er·ize** \pə'limə,rīz\ vb

poly·tech·nic \,päli'teknik\ adj : relating to many technical arts or applied sciences

poly·the·ism \'pälithē,izəm\ n : worship of many gods —**poly·the·ist** \-,thēist\ adj or n

poly·un·sat·u·rat·ed \,pälē,ən'sachə-,rātəd\ adj : having many double or triple bonds in a molecule

pome·gran·ate \'päm,granət, 'pämə-\ n : tropical reddish fruit with many seeds

pom·mel \'pəməl, 'päm-\ n 1 : knob on the hilt of a sword 2 : knob at the front of a saddle ~ \'pəməl\ vb **-meled** or **-melled; -mel·ing** or **-mel·ling** : pummel

pomp \'pämp\ n 1 : brilliant display 2 : ostentation

pomp·ous \'pämpəs\ adj : pretentiously dignified —**pom·pos·i·ty** \päm-'päsətē\ n —**pomp·ous·ly** adv

pon·cho \'pänchō\ n, pl **-chos** : blanketlike cloak

pond \'pänd\ n : small body of water

pon·der \'pändər\ vb : consider

pon·der·ous \'pändərəs\ adj 1 : very heavy 2 : clumsy 3 : oppressively dull

pon·tiff \'päntəf\ n : pope —**pon·tif·i·cal** \pän'tifikəl\ adj

pon·tif·i·cate \pän'tifə,kāt\ vb **-cat·ed; -cat·ing** : talk pompously

pon·toon \pän'tün\ n : flat-bottomed boat or float

po·ny \'pōnē\ n, pl **-nies** : small horse

po·ny·tail \-,tāl\ n : hair arrangement like the tail of a pony

poo·dle \'püd⁰l\ n : dog with a curly coat

¹pool \'pül\ n 1 : small body of water 2 : puddle

²pool n 1 : amount contributed by participants in a joint venture 2 : game of pocket billiards ~ vb : combine in a common fund

poor \'pur, 'pōr\ adj 1 : lacking material possessions 2 : less than adequate 3 : arousing pity 4 : unfavorable —, **poor·ly** adv

¹pop \'päp\ vb **-pp-** 1 : move suddenly 2 : burst with or make a sharp sound 3 : protrude ~ n 1 : sharp explosive sound 2 : flavored soft drink

²pop adj : popular

pop·corn \'päp,kórn\ n : corn whose kernels burst open into a light mass when heated

pope \'pōp\ n, often cap : head of the Roman Catholic Church

pop·lar \'päplər\ n : slender quick-growing tree

pop·lin \'päplən\ n : strong plain-woven fabric with crosswise ribs

pop·over \'päp,ōvər\ n : hollow muffin made from egg-rich batter

pop·py \'päpē\ *n, pl* **-pies** : herb with showy flowers

pop·u·lace \'päpyələs\ *n* **1** : common people **2** : population

pop·u·lar \'päpyələr\ *adj* **1** : relating to the general public **2** : widely accepted **3** : commonly liked —**pop·u·lar·i·ty** \,päpyə'larətē\ *n* —**pop·u·lar·ize** \'päpyələ,rīz\ *vb* —**pop·u·lar·ly** \-lərlē\ *adv*

pop·u·late \'päpyə,lāt\ *vb* **-lat·ed; -lat·ing** : inhabit or occupy

pop·u·la·tion \,päpyə'lāshən\ *n* : people or number of people in an area

pop·u·list \'päpyəlist\ *n* : advocate of the rights of the common people —**pop·u·lism** \-,lizəm\ *n*

pop·u·lous \'päpyələs\ *adj* : densely populated —**pop·u·lous·ness** *n*

por·ce·lain \'pōrsələn\ *n* : fine-grained ceramic ware

porch \'pōrch\ *n* : covered entrance

por·cu·pine \'pórkyə,pīn\ *n* : mammal with sharp quills

¹pore \'pōr\ *vb* **pored; por·ing** : read attentively

²pore *n* : tiny hole (as in the skin) —**pored** *adj*

pork \'pōrk\ *n* : pig meat

pork barrel *n* : government projects benefiting political patrons

por·nog·ra·phy \pór'nägrəfē\ *n* : depiction of erotic behavior intended to cause sexual excitement —**por·no·graph·ic** \,pórnə'grafik\ *adj*

po·rous \'pōrəs\ *adj* : permeable to fluids —**po·ros·i·ty** \pə'räsətē\ *n*

por·poise \'pórpəs\ *n* **1** : small whale with a blunt snout **2** : dolphin

por·ridge \'pórij\ *n* : soft boiled cereal

por·rin·ger \'pórənjər\ *n* : low one-handled metal bowl or cup

¹port \'pōrt\ *n* **1** : harbor **2** : city with a harbor

²port *n* **1** : inlet or outlet (as in an engine) for a fluid **2** : porthole

³port *n* : left side of a ship or airplane looking forward —**port** *adj*

⁴port *n* : sweet wine

por·ta·ble \'pōrtəbəl\ *adj* : capable of being carried —**portable** *n*

por·tage \'pōrtij, pór'täzh\ *n* : carrying of boats overland between navigable bodies of water or the route where this is done —**portage** *vb*

por·tal \'pōrtᵊl\ *n* : entrance

por·tend \pór'tend\ *vb* : give a warning of beforehand

por·tent \'pór,tent\ *n* : something that foreshadows a coming event —**por·ten·tous** \pór'tentəs\ *adj*

por·ter \'pōrtər\ *n* : baggage carrier

por·ter·house \-,haùs\ *n* : choice cut of steak

port·fo·lio \pōrt'fōlē,ō\ *n, pl* **-lios 1** : portable case for papers **2** : office or function of a diplomat **3** : investor's securities

port·hole \'pōrt,hōl\ *n* : window in the side of a ship or aircraft

por·ti·co \'pōrti,kō\ *n, pl* **-coes** or **-cos** : colonnade forming a porch

por·tion \'pōrshən\ *n* : part or share of a whole ~ *vb* : divide into or allot portions

port·ly \'pōrtlē\ *adj* **-li·er; -est** : somewhat stout

por·trait \'pōrtrət, -,trāt\ *n* : picture of a person —**por·trait·ist** \-ist\ *n* —**trai·ture** \'pōrtrə,chùr\ *n*

por·tray \pōr'trā\ *vb* **1** : make a picture of **2** : describe in words **3** : play the role of —**por·tray·al** *n*

por·tu·laca \,pōrchə'lakə\ *n* : tropical herb with showy flowers

pose \'pōz\ *vb* **posed; pos·ing 1** : assume a posture or attitude **2** : propose **3** : pretend to be what one is not ~ *n* **1** : sustained posture **2** : pretense —**pos·er** *n*

posh \'päsh\ *adj* : elegant

po·si·tion \pə'zishən\ *n* **1** : stand taken on a question **2** : place or location **3** : status **4** : job —**position** *vb*

pos·i·tive \'päzətiv\ *adj* **1** : definite **2** : confident **3** : relating to or being an adjective or adverb form that denotes no increase **4** : greater than zero **5** : having a deficiency of electrons **6** : affirmative —**pos·i·tive·ly** *adv* —**pos·i·tive·ness** *n*

pos·se \'päsē\ *n* : emergency assistants of a sheriff

pos·sess \pə'zes\ *vb* **1** : have as property or as a quality **2** : control —**pos·ses·sion** \-'zeshən\ *n* —**pos·ses·sor** \-'zesər\ *n*

pos·ses·sive \pə'zesiv\ *adj* **1** : relating to a grammatical case denoting ownership **2** : jealous —**possessive** *n* —**pos·ses·sive·ness** *n*

pos·si·ble \'päsəbəl\ *adj* **1** : that can be done **2** : potential —**pos·si·bil·i·ty** \,päsə'bilətē\ *n* —**pos·si·bly** *adv*

pos·sum \'päsəm\ *n* : opossum

¹**post** \'pōst\ *n* : upright stake serving to support or mark ~ *vb* : put up or announce by a notice

²**post** *vb* **1** : mail **2** : inform

³**post** *n* **1** : sentry's station **2** : assigned task **3** : army camp ~ *vb* : station

post- *prefix* : after or subsequent to

postadolescent	postinoculation
postattack	postmarital
postbaccalau-	postmenopausal
reate	postnatal
postbiblical	postnuptial
postcollege	postproduction
postcolonial	postpuberty
postelection	postrecession
postexercise	postretirement
postflight	postrevolu-
postgame	tionary
postgraduate	postseason
postgraduation	postsecondary
postharvest	postsurgical
posthospital	posttreatment
postimperial	posttrial
postinaugural	postvaccination
postindustrial	postwar

post-age \'pōstij\ *n* : fee for mail

post-al \'pōst²l\ *adj* : relating to the mail

post-card *n* : card for mailing a message

post-date \,pōst'dāt\ *vb* : assign a date to that is later than the actual date of execution

post-er \'pōstər\ *n* : large usu. printed notice

pos-te-ri-or \pō'stirēər, pä-\ *adj* **1** : later **2** : situated behind ~ *n* : buttocks

pos-ter-i-ty \pä'sterətē\ *n* : all future generations

post-haste \'pōst'hāst\ *adv* : speedily

post-hu-mous \'päschəməs\ *adj* : occurring after one's death —**post-hu-mous-ly** *adv*

post-man \'pōstmən, -,man\ *n* : mail carrier

post-mark *n* : official mark on mail —**postmark** *vb*

post-mas-ter *n* : chief of a post office

post me-ri-di-em \'pōstmə'ridēəm, -ē-,em\ *adj* : being after noon

post-mor-tem \,pōst'mórtəm\ *adj* : occurring or done after death ~ *n* **1** : medical examination of a corpse **2** : analysis after an event

post office *n* : agency or building for mail service

post-op-er-a-tive \,pōst'äpərətiv, -'äpə-,rāt-\ *adj* : following surgery

post-paid *adv* : with postage paid by the sender

post-par-tum \-'pärtəm\ *adj* : following childbirth —**postpartum** *adv*

post-pone \-'pōn\ *vb* **-poned; -pon-ing** : put off to a later time —**post-pone-ment** *n*

post-script \'pōst,skript\ *n* : added note

pos-tu-lant \'päschələnt\ *n* : candidate for a religious order

pos-tu-late \'päschə,lāt\ *vb* **-lat-ed; -lat-ing** : assume as true ~ *n* : assumption

pos-ture \'päschər\ *n* : bearing of the body ~ *vb* **-tured; -tur-ing** : strike a pose

po-sy \'pōzē\ *n, pl* **-sies** : flower or bunch of flowers

pot \'pät\ *n* : rounded container ~ *vb* **-tt-** : place in a pot —**pot-ful** *n*

po-ta-ble \'pōtəbəl\ *adj* : drinkable

pot-ash \'pät,ash\ *n* : white chemical salt of potassium used esp. in agriculture

po-tas-si-um \pə'tasēəm\ *n* : silver-white metallic chemical element

po-ta-to \pə'tātō\ *n, pl* **-toes** : edible plant tuber

pot-bel-ly *n* : paunch —**pot-bel-lied** *adj*

po-tent \'pōt²nt\ *adj* : powerful or effective —**po-ten-cy** \-²nsē\ *n*

po-ten-tate \'pōt²n,tāt\ *n* : powerful ruler

po-ten-tial \pə'tenchəl\ *adj* : capable of becoming actual ~ *n* **1** : something that can become actual **2** : degree of electrification with reference to a standard —**po-ten-ti-al-i-ty** \pə,ten-chē'alətē\ *n* —**po-ten-tial-ly** *adv*

poth-er \'päthər\ *n* : fuss

pot-hole \'pät,hōl\ *n* : large hole in a road surface

po-tion \'pōshən\ *n* : liquid medicine or poison

pot-luck *n* : whatever food is available

pot-pour-ri \,pōpu'rē\ *n* **1** : mix of flowers, herbs, and spices used for scent **2** : miscellaneous collection

pot-shot *n* **1** : casual or easy shot **2** : random critical remark

pot-ter \'pätər\ *n* : pottery maker

pot-tery \'pätərē\ *n, pl* **-ter-ies** : objects (as dishes) made from clay

pouch \'paùch\ *n* **1** : small bag **2** : bodily sac

poul-tice \'pōltəs\ *n* : warm medicated dressing —**poultice** *vb*

poul-try \'pōltrē\ *n* : domesticated fowl

pounce \'paùns\ *vb* **pounced; pounc-ing** : spring or swoop upon and seize

¹pound \'paund\ *n* **1** : unit of weight equal to 16 ounces **2** : monetary unit (as of the United Kingdom) **—poundage** \-ij\ *n*

²pound *n* : shelter for stray animals

³pound *vb* **1** : crush by beating **2** : strike heavily **3** : drill **4** : move along heavily

pour \'pŏr\ *vb* **1** : flow or supply esp. copiously **2** : rain hard

pout \'paut\ *vb* : look sullen **—pout** *n*

pov·er·ty \'pävərtē\ *n* **1** : lack of money or possessions **2** : poor quality

pow·der \'paudər\ *n* : dry material of fine particles ~ *vb* : sprinkle or cover with powder **—pow·dery** *adj*

pow·er \'pauər\ *n* **1** : position of authority **2** : ability to act **3** : one that has power **4** : physical might **5** : force or energy used to do work ~ *vb* : supply with power **—pow·er·ful** \-fəl\ *adj* **—pow·er·ful·ly** *adv* **—pow·er·less** *adj*

pow·er·house *n* : dynamic or energetic person

pow·wow \'pau,wau\ *n* : conference

pox \'päks\ *n, pl* **pox** *or* **pox·es** : disease marked by skin rash

prac·ti·ca·ble \'praktikəbəl\ *adj* : feasible **—prac·ti·ca·bil·i·ty** \,praktikə'bilətē\ *n*

prac·ti·cal \'praktikəl\ *adj* **1** : relating to practice **2** : virtual **3** : capable of being put to use **4** : inclined to action as opposed to speculation **—prac·ti·cal·i·ty** \,prakti'kalətē\ *n* **—prac·ti·cal·ly** \'praktiklē\ *adv*

prac·tice, prac·tise \'praktəs\ *vb* **-ticed** *or* **-tised; -tic·ing** *or* **-tis·ing** **1** : perform repeatedly to become proficient **2** : do or perform customarily **3** : be professionally engaged in ~ *n* **1** : actual performance **2** : habit **3** : exercise for proficiency **4** : exercise of a profession

prac·ti·tio·ner \prak'tishənər\ *n* : one who practices a profession

prag·ma·tism \'pragmə,tizəm\ *n* : practical approach to problems **—prag·mat·ic** \prag'matik\ *adj* **—prag·mat·i·cal·ly** *adv*

prai·rie \'prerē\ *n* : broad grassy rolling tract of land

praise \'prāz\ *vb* **praised; prais·ing** **1** : express approval of **2** : glorify **—praise** *n* **—praise·wor·thy** *adj*

prance \'prans\ *vb* **pranced; pranc·ing** **1** : spring from the hind legs **2** : swagger **—prance** *n* **—pranc·er** *n*

prank \'praŋk\ *n* : playful or mischievous act **—prank·ster** \-stər\ *n*

prate \'prāt\ *vb* **prat·ed; prat·ing** : talk long and foolishly

prat·fall \'prat,fól\ *n* : fall on the buttocks

prat·tle \'pratᵊl\ *vb* **-tled; -tling** : babble **—prattle** *n*

prawn \'prón\ *n* : shrimplike crustacean

pray \'prā\ *vb* **1** : entreat **2** : ask earnestly for something **3** : address God or a god

prayer \'prer\ *n* **1** : earnest request **2** : an addressing of God or a god **3** : words used in praying **—prayer·ful** *adj* **—prayer·ful·ly** *adv*

praying mantis *n* : mantis

pre- *prefix* : before, prior to, or in advance

preadmission	predrill
preadolescence	preelection
preadolescent	preelectric
preadult	preemployment
preanesthetic	preestablish
prearrange	preexist
prearrangement	preexistence
preassembled	preexistent
preassign	prefight
prebattle	preform
prebiblical	pregame
prebreakfast	preheat
precalculus	preinaugural
precancel	preindustrial
precancellation	preinterview
preclear	prejudge
preclearance	prekindergarten
precollege	prelaunch
precolonial	prelife
precombustion	premarital
precompute	premenopausal
preconceive	premenstrual
preconception	premix
preconcert	premodern
precondition	premodify
preconstructed	premoisten
preconvention	premold
precook	prenatal
precool	prenotification
precut	prenotify
predawn	prenuptial
predefine	preopening
predeparture	preoperational
predesignate	preoperative
predetermine	preordain
predischarge	prepackage

prepay
preplan
preprocess
preproduction
preprofessional
preprogram
prepubertal
prepublication
prepunch
prepurchase
prerecorded
preregister
preregistration
prerehearsal
prerelease
preretirement
prerevolution-
ary
prerinse
presale
preschool

preseason
preselect
preset
preshrink
preshrunk
presoak
presort
prestamp
presterilize
prestrike
presurgery
presweeten
pretape
pretelevision
pretournament
pretreat
pretreatment
pretrial
prewar
prewash
prewrap

preach \'prēch\ *vb* 1 : deliver a sermon 2 : advocate earnestly —**preach·er** *n* —**preach·ment** *n*

pre·am·ble \'prē,ambəl\ *n* : introduction

pre·can·cer·ous \,prē'kansərəs\ *adj* : likely to become cancerous

pre·car·i·ous \pri'karēəs\ *adj* : dangerously insecure —**pre·car·i·ous·ly** *adv* —**pre·car·i·ous·ness** *n*

pre·cau·tion \pri'kóshən\ *n* : care taken beforehand —**pre·cau·tion·ary** \-shə,nerē\ *adj*

pre·cede \pri'sēd\ *vb* -**ced·ed**; -**ced·ing** : be, go, or come ahead of —**prec·e·dence** \'presədəns, pri'sēd⁽əⁿ⁾s\ *n*

prec·e·dent \'presədənt\ *n* : something said or done earlier that serves as an example

pre·cept \'prē,sept\ *n* : rule of action or conduct

pre·cinct \'prē,siŋkt\ *n* 1 : district of a city 2 *pl* : vicinity

pre·cious \'preshəs\ *adj* 1 : of great value 2 : greatly cherished 3 : affected

prec·i·pice \'presəpəs\ *n* : steep cliff

pre·cip·i·tate \pri'sipə,tāt\ *vb* -**tat·ed**; -**tat·ing** 1 : cause to happen quickly or abruptly 2 : cause to separate out of a liquid 3 : fall as rain, snow, or hail ~ *n* : solid matter precipitated from a liquid ~ \-'sipətət, -ə,tāt\ *adj* : unduly hasty —**pre·cip·i·tate·ly** *adv* —**pre·cip·i·tate·ness** *n* —**pre·cip·i·tous** \pri'sipətəs\ *adj* —**pre·cip·i·tous·ly** *adv*

pre·cip·i·ta·tion \pri,sipə'tāshən\ *n* 1 : rash haste 2 : rain, snow, or hail

pré·cis \prā'sē\ *n, pl* **pré·cis** \-'sēz\ : concise summary of essentials

pre·cise \pri'sīs\ *adj* 1 : definite 2 : highly accurate —**pre·cise·ly** *adv* —**pre·cise·ness** *n*

pre·ci·sion \pri'sizhən\ *n* : quality or state of being precise

pre·clude \pri'klüd\ *vb* -**clud·ed**; -**clud·ing** : make impossible

pre·co·cious \pri'kōshəs\ *adj* : exceptionally advanced —**pre·co·cious·ly** *adv* —**pre·coc·i·ty** \pri'käsətē\ *n*

pre·cur·sor \pri'kərsər\ *n* : harbinger

pred·a·to·ry \'predə,tōrē\ *adj* : preying upon others —**pred·a·tor** \'predətər\ *n*

pre·de·ces·sor \'predə,sesər, 'prēd-\ *n* : a previous holder of a position

pre·des·tine \prē'destən\ *vb* : settle beforehand —**pre·des·ti·na·tion** \-,destə'nāshən\ *n*

pre·dic·a·ment \pri'dikəmənt\ *n* : difficult situation

pred·i·cate \'predikət\ *n* : part of a sentence that states something about the subject ~ \'predə,kāt\ *vb* -**cat·ed**; -**cat·ing** 1 : affirm 2 : establish —**pred·i·ca·tion** \,predə'kāshən\ *n*

pre·dict \pri'dikt\ *vb* : declare in advance —**pre·dict·abil·i·ty** \-,diktə'bilətē\ *n* —**pre·dict·able** \-'diktəbəl\ *adj* —**pre·dict·ably** \-blē\ *adv* —**pre·dic·tion** \-'dikshən\ *n*

pre·di·lec·tion \,predᵊl'ekshən, ,prēd-\ *n* : established preference

pre·dis·pose \,prēdis'pōz\ *vb* : cause to be favorable or susceptible to something beforehand —**pre·dis·po·si·tion** \,prē,dispə'zishən\ *n*

pre·dom·i·nate \pri'dämə,nāt\ *vb* : be superior —**pre·dom·i·nance** \-nəns\ *n* —**pre·dom·i·nant** \-nənt\ *adj* —**pre·dom·i·nant·ly** *adv*

pre·em·i·nent \prē'emənənt\ *adj* : having highest rank —**pre·em·i·nence** \-nəns\ *n* —**pre·em·i·nent·ly** *adv*

pre·empt \prē'empt\ *vb* 1 : seize for oneself 2 : take the place of —**pre·emp·tion** \-'empshən\ *n* —**pre·emp·tive** \-'emptiv\ *adj*

preen \'prēn\ *vb* : dress or smooth up (as feathers)

pre·fab·ri·cat·ed \'prē'fabrə,kātəd\ *adj* : manufactured for rapid assembly elsewhere —pre·fab·ri·ca·tion \,prē-,fabri'kāshən\ n

pref·ace \'prefəs\ n : introductory comments ~ vb -aced; -ac·ing : introduce with a preface —pref·a·to·ry \'prefe-,tōrē\ adj

pre·fect \'prē,fekt\ n : chief officer or judge —pre·fec·ture \-,fekchər\ n

pre·fer \pri'fər\ vb -rr- 1 : like better 2 : bring (as a charge) against a person —pref·er·a·ble \'prefərəbəl\ adj —pref·er·a·bly adv —pref·er·ence \-ərəns\ n —pref·er·en·tial \,prefə-'renchəl\ adj

pre·fer·ment \pri'fərmənt\ n : promotion

pre·fig·ure \prē'figyər\ vb : foreshadow

¹pre·fix \'prē,fiks, prē'fiks\ vb : place before

²pre·fix \'prē,fiks\ n : affix at the beginning of a word

preg·nant \'pregnənt\ adj 1 : containing unborn young 2 : meaningful —preg·nan·cy \-nənsē\ n

pre·hen·sile \prē'hensəl, -,sīl\ adj : adapted for grasping

pre·his·tor·ic \,prēhis'tōrik\, **pre·his·tor·i·cal** \-ikəl\ adj : relating to the period before written history

prej·u·dice \'prejədəs\ n 1 : damage esp. to one's rights 2 : unreasonable attitude for or against something ~ vb -diced; -dic·ing 1 : damage 2 : cause to have prejudice —prej·u·di·cial \,prejə'dishəl\ adj

prel·ate \'prelət\ n : clergy member of high rank —prel·a·cy \-əsē\ n

pre·lim·i·nary \pri'limə,nerē\ n, pl -nar·ies : something that precedes or introduces —**preliminary** adj

pre·lude \'prel,üd, -,yüd; 'prā,lüd\ n : introductory performance, event, or musical piece

pre·ma·ture \,prēmə'tùər, -'tyùr, -'chùr\ adj : coming before the usual or proper time —pre·ma·ture·ly adv

pre·med·i·tate \pri'medə,tāt\ vb : plan beforehand —pre·med·i·ta·tion \-,medə'tāshən\ n

pre·mier \pri'mir, -'myir; 'prēmēər\ adj : first in rank or importance ~ n : prime minister —pre·mier·ship n

pre·miere \pri'myer, -'mir\ n : 1st performance ~ vb -miered; -mier·ing : give a 1st performance of

prem·ise \'preməs\ n 1 : statement made or implied as a basis of argument 2 pl : piece of land with the structures on it

pre·mi·um \'prēmēəm\ n 1 : bonus 2 : sum over the stated value 3 : sum paid for insurance 4 : high value

pre·mo·ni·tion \,prēmə'nishən, ,premə-\ n : feeling that something is about to happen —pre·mon·i·to·ry \pri'mänə,tōrē\ adj

pre·oc·cu·pied \prē'äkyə,pīd\ adj : lost in thought

pre·oc·cu·py \-,pī\ vb : occupy the attention of —pre·oc·cu·pa·tion \prē-,äkyə'pāshən\ n

pre·pare \pri'par\ vb -pared; -par·ing 1 : make or get ready often beforehand 2 : put together or compound —prep·a·ra·tion \,prepə'rāshən\ n —pre·pa·ra·to·ry \pri'parə,tōrē\ adj —pre·pared·ness \-'parədnəs\ n

pre·pon·der·ant \pri'pändərənt\ adj : having great weight, power, importance, or numbers —pre·pon·der·ance \-rəns\ n —pre·pon·der·ant·ly adv

prep·o·si·tion \,prepə'zishən\ n : word that combines with a noun or pronoun to form a phrase —prep·o·si·tion·al \-'zishənəl\ adj

pre·pos·sess·ing \,prēpə'zesiŋ\ adj : tending to create a favorable impression

pre·pos·ter·ous \pri'pästərəs\ adj : absurd

pre·req·ui·site \prē'rekwəzət\ n : something required beforehand —**prerequisite** adj

pre·rog·a·tive \pri'rägətiv\ n : special right or power

pre·sage \'presij, pri'sāj\ vb -saged; -sag·ing 1 : give a warning of 2 : predict —pre·sage \'presij\ n

pres·by·ter \'prezbətər\ n : priest or minister

pre·science \'prēshəns, 'presh-\ n : foreknowledge of events —pre·scient \-ənt\ adj

pre·scribe \pri'skrīb\ vb -scribed; -scrib·ing 1 : lay down as a guide 2 : direct the use of as a remedy

pre·scrip·tion \pri'skripshən\ n : written direction for the preparation and use of a medicine or the medicine prescribed

pres·ence \'prez^əns\ n 1 : fact or condition of being present 2 : appearance or bearing

¹pres·ent \'prez²nt\ *n* : gift

²pre·sent \pri'zent\ *vb* **1** : introduce **2** : bring before the public **3** : make a gift to or of **4** : bring before a court-for inquiry —**pre·sent·able** *adj* —**pre·sen·ta·tion** \,prē,zen'tāshən, ,prez²n-\ *n* —**pre·sent·ment** \pri'zent-mənt\ *n*

³pres·ent \'prez²nt\ *adj* : now existing, in progress, or attending ~ *n* : present time

pre·sen·ti·ment \pri'zentəmənt\ *n* : premonition

pres·ent·ly \'prez²ntlē\ *adv* **1** : soon **2** : now

present participle *n* : participle that typically expresses present action

pre·serve \pri'zərv\ *vb* **-served; -serv·ing 1** : keep safe from danger or spoilage **2** : maintain ~ *n* **1** : preserved fruit —often in pl. **2** : area for protection of natural resources —**pres·er·va·tion** \,prezər'vāshən\ *n* —**pre·ser·va·tive** \pri'zərvətiv\ *adj or n* —**pre·serv·er** \-'zərvər\ *n*

pre·side \pri'zīd\ *vb* **-sid·ed; -sid·ing 1** : act as chairman **2** : exercise control

pres·i·dent \'prezədənt\ *n* **1** : one chosen to preside **2** : chief official (as of a company or nation) —**pres·i·den·cy** \-ənsē\ *n* —**pres·i·den·tial** \,prezə'denchəl\ *adj*

press \'pres\ *n* **1** : crowded condition **2** : machine or device for exerting pressure and esp. for printing **3** : pressure **4** : printing or publishing establishment **5** : news media and esp. newspapers ~ *vb* **1** : lie against and exert pressure on **2** : smooth with an iron or squeeze with something heavy **3** : urge **4** : crowd **5** : force one's way —**press·er** *n*

press·ing *adj* : urgent

pres·sure \'preshər\ *n* **1** : burden of distress or urgent business **2** : direct application of force —**pressure** *vb* —**pres·sur·i·za·tion** \,preshərə'zāshən\ *n* —**pres·sur·ize** \-,īz\ *vb*

pres·ti·dig·i·ta·tion \,prestə,dijə'tāshən\ *n* : sleight of hand

pres·tige \pres'tēzh, -'tēj\ *n* : estimation in the eyes of people —**pres·ti·gious** \-'tijəs\ *n*

pres·to \'prestō\ *adv or adj* : quickly

pre·sume \pri'züm\ *vb* **-sumed; -sum·ing 1** : assume authority without right to do so **2** : take for granted —**pre-**

sum·able \-'züməbəl\ *adj* —**pre·sum·ably** \-blē\ *adv*

pre·sump·tion \pri'zəmpshən\ *n* **1** : presumptuous attitude or conduct **2** : belief supported by probability —**pre·sump·tive** \-tiv\ *adj*

pre·sump·tu·ous \pri'zəmpchəwəs\ *adj* : too bold or forward —**pre·sump·tu·ous·ly** *adv*

pre·sup·pose \,prēsə'pōz\ *vb* : take for granted —**pre·sup·po·si·tion** \,prē-,səpə'zishən\ *n*

pre·tend \pri'tend\ *vb* **1** : act as if something is real or true when it is not **2** : act in a way that is false **3** : lay claim —**pre·tend·er** *n*

pre·tense, pre·tence \'prē,tens. pri'tens\ *n* **1** : insincere effort **2** : deception —**pre·ten·sion** \pri'tenchən\ *n*

pre·ten·tious \pri'tenchəs\ *adj* : overly showy or self-important —**pre·ten·tious·ly** *adv* —**pre·ten·tious·ness** *n*

pre·ter·nat·u·ral \,prētər'nachərəl\ *adj* **1** : exceeding what is natural **2** : inexplicable by ordinary means —**pre·ter·nat·u·ral·ly** *adv*

pre·text \'prē,tekst\ *n* : falsely stated purpose

pret·ty \'pritē. 'purt-\ *adj* **-ti·er; -est** : pleasing by delicacy or attractiveness ~ *adv* : in some degree ~ *vb* **-tied; -ty·ing** : make pretty —**pret·ti·ly** \'prit²lē\ *adv* —**pret·ti·ness** *n*

pret·zel \'pretsəl\ *n* : twisted thin bread that is glazed and salted

pre·vail \pri'vāl\ *vb* **1** : triumph **2** : urge successfully **3** : be frequent, widespread, or dominant

prev·a·lent \'prevələnt\ *adj* : widespread —**prev·a·lence** \-ləns\ *n*

pre·var·i·cate \pri'varə,kāt\ *vb* **-cat·ed; -cat·ing** : deviate from the truth —**pre·var·i·ca·tion** \-,varə'kāshən\ *n* —**pre·var·i·ca·tor** \-'varə,kātər\ *n*

pre·vent \pri'vent\ *vb* : keep from happening or acting —**pre·vent·able** *adj* —**pre·ven·tion** \-'venchən\ *n* —**pre·ven·tive** \-'ventiv\ *adj or n* —**pre·ven·ta·tive** \-'ventətiv\ *adj or n*

pre·view \'prē,vyü\ *vb* : view or show beforehand —**preview** *n*

pre·vi·ous \'prēvēəs\ *adj* : having gone, happened, or existed before —**pre·vi·ous·ly** *adv*

prey \'prā\ *n. pl* **preys 1** : animal taken for food by another **2** : victim ~ *vb* **1** : seize and devour animals as prey **2** : have a harmful effect on

price \'prīs\ *n* : cost ~ *vb* **priced; pricing** : set a price on

price·less \-ləs\ *adj* : too precious to have a price

pric·ey \'prīsē\ *adj* **pric·i·er; -est** : expensive

prick \'prik\ *n* **1** : tear or small wound made by a point **2** : something sharp or pointed ~ *vb* : pierce slightly with a sharp point —**prick·er** *n*

prick·le \'prikəl\ *n* **1** : small sharp spine or thorn **2** : slight stinging pain ~ *vb* **-led; -ling** : tingle —**prick·ly** \'priklē\ *adj*

pride \'prīd\ *n* : quality or state of being proud ~ *vb* **prid·ed; prid·ing** : indulge in pride —**pride·ful** *adj*

priest \'prēst\ *n* : person having authority to perform the sacred rites of a religion —**priest·hood** *n* —**priest·li·ness** \-lēnəs\ *n* —**priest·ly** *adj*

priest·ess \'prēstəs\ *n* : woman who is a priest

prig \'prig\ *n* : one who irritates by rigid or pointed observance of proprieties —**prig·gish** \-ish\ *adj* —**prig·gish·ly** *adv*

prim \'prim\ *adj* **-mm-** : stiffly formal and proper —**prim·ly** *adv* —**prim·ness** *n*

pri·mal \'prīməl\ *adj* **1** : original or primitive **2** : most important

pri·ma·ry \'prī,merē, 'prīmərē\ *adj* : first in order of time, rank, or importance ~ *n, pl* **-ries** : preliminary election —**pri·mar·i·ly** \prī'merəlē\ *adv*

primary school *n* : elementary school

pri·mate *n* **1** \'prī,māt, -mət\ : highest-ranking bishop **2** \-,māt\ : mammal of the group that includes humans and monkeys

prime \'prīm\ *n* : earliest or best part or period ~ *adj* : standing first (as in significance or quality) ~ *vb* **primed; prim·ing 1** : fill or load **2** : lay a preparatory coating on

prime minister *n* : chief executive of a parliamentary government

¹prim·er \'primər\ *n* : small introductory book

²prim·er \'prīmər\ *n* **1** : device for igniting an explosive **2** : material for priming a surface

pri·me·val \prī'mēvəl\ *adj* : relating to the earliest ages

prim·i·tive \'primətiv\ *adj* **1** : relating to or characteristic of an early stage of development **2** : of or relating to a tribal people or culture ~ *n* : one that is primitive —**prim·i·tive·ly** *adv* —**prim·i·tive·ness** *n*

pri·mor·di·al \prī'mórdēəl\ *adj* : primeval

primp \'primp\ *vb* : dress or groom in a finicky manner

prim·rose \'prim,rōz\ *n* : low herb with clusters of showy flowers

prince \'prins\ *n* **1** : ruler **2** : son of a king or queen —**prince·ly** *adj*

prin·cess \'prinsəs, -,ses\ *n* **1** : daughter of a king or queen **2** : wife of a prince

prin·ci·pal \'prinsəpəl\ *adj* : most important ~ *n* **1** : leading person **2** : head of a school **3** : sum lent at interest —**prin·ci·pal·ly** *adv*

prin·ci·pal·i·ty \,prinsə'palətē\ *n, pl* **-ties** : territory of a prince

prin·ci·ple \'prinsəpəl\ *n* **1** : general or fundamental law **2** : rule or code of conduct or devotion to such a code

print \'print\ *n* **1** : mark or impression made by pressure **2** : printed state or form **3** : printed matter **4** : copy made by printing **5** : cloth with a figure stamped on it ~ *vb* **1** : produce impressions of (as from type) **2** : write in letters like those of printer's type —**print·able** *adj* —**print·er** *n*

print·ing \'printiŋ\ *n* : art or business of a printer

print·out \'print,aut\ *n* : printed output produced by a computer —**print out** *vb*

¹pri·or \'prīər\ *n* : head of a religious house —**pri·o·ry** \'prīərē\ *n*

²prior *adj* : coming before in time, order, or importance —**pri·or·i·ty** \prī-'órətē\ *n*

pri·or·ess \'prīərəs\ *n* : nun who is head of a religious house

prism \'prizəm\ *n* : transparent 3-sided object that separates light into colors —**pris·mat·ic** \priz'matik\ *adj*

pris·on \'prizⁿn\ *n* : place where criminals are confined

pris·on·er \'prizⁿnər\ *n* : person on trial or in prison

pris·sy \'prisē\ *adj* **-si·er; -est** : overly prim —**pris·si·ness** *n*

pris·tine \'pris,tēn, pris'-\ *adj* : pure

pri·va·cy \'prīvəsē\ *n, pl* **-cies** : quality or state of being apart from others

pri·vate \'prīvət\ *adj* **1** : belonging to a particular individual or group **2** : carried on independently **3**

: withdrawn from company or observation ~ *n* : enlisted person of the lowest rank in the marine corps or of one of the two lowest ranks in the army —**pri·vate·ly** *adv*

pri·va·teer \,privə'tir\ *n* : private ship armed to attack enemy ships and commerce

private first class *n* : enlisted person ranking next below a corporal in the army and next below a lance corporal in the marine corps

pri·va·tion \prī'vāshən\ *n* : lack of what is needed for existence

priv·i·lege \'privəlij\ *n* : right granted as an advantage or favor —**priv·i·leged** *adj*

privy \'privē\ *adj* 1 : private or secret 2 : having access to private or secret information ~ *n, pl* **priv·ies** : outdoor toilet —**priv·i·ly** \'privəlē\ *adv*

¹prize \'prīz\ *n* 1 : something offered or striven for in competition or in contests of chance 2 : something very desirable —**prize** *adj* —**prize·win·ner** *n* —**prize·win·ning** *adj*

²prize *vb* **prized; priz·ing** : value highly

³prize *vb* **prized; priz·ing** : pry

prize·fight *n* : professional boxing match —**prize·fight·er** *n* —**prize·fight·ing** *n*

¹pro \'prō\ *n* : favorable argument or person ~ *adv* : in favor

²pro *n or adj* : professional

prob·a·ble \'präbəbəl\ *adj* : seeming true or real or to have a good chance of happening —**prob·a·bil·i·ty** \,präbə'bilətē\ *n* —**prob·a·bly** \'präbəblē\ *adv*

pro·bate \'prō,bāt\ *n* : judicial determination of the validity of a will ~ *vb* **-bat·ed; -bat·ing** : establish by probate

pro·ba·tion \prō'bāshən\ *n* 1 : period of testing and trial 2 : freedom for a convict during good behavior under supervision —**pro·ba·tion·ary** \-shə,nerē\ *adj* —**pro·ba·tion·er** *n*

probe \'prōb\ *n* 1 : slender instrument for examining a cavity 2 : investigation ~ *vb* **probed; prob·ing** 1 : examine with a probe 2 : investigate

pro·bi·ty \'prōbətē\ *n* : honest behavior

prob·lem \'präbləm\ *n* 1 : question to be solved 2 : source of perplexity or vex-

ation —**problem** *adj* —**prob·lem·at·ic** \,präblə'matik\ *adj* —**prob·lem·at·i·cal** \-ikəl\ *adj*

pro·bos·cis \prə'bäsəs\ *n, pl* **-cis·es** *also* **-ci·des** \-ə,dēz\ : long flexible snout

pro·ce·dure \prə'sējər\ *n* 1 : way of doing something 2 : series of steps in regular order —**pro·ce·dur·al** \-'sējərəl\ *adj*

pro·ceed \prō'sēd\ *vb* 1 : come forth 2 : go on in an orderly way 3 : begin and carry on an action 4 : advance

pro·ceed·ing *n* 1 : procedure 2 *pl* : something said or done or its official record

pro·ceeds \'prō,sēdz\ *n pl* : total money taken in

pro·cess \'präs,es, 'prōs-\ *n, pl* **-cess·es** \-,esəz, -əsəz, -ə,sēz\ 1 : something going on 2 : natural phenomenon marked by gradual changes 3 : series of actions or operations directed toward a result 4 : summons 5 : projecting part ~ *vb* : subject to a process —**pro·ces·sor** \-ər\ *n*

pro·ces·sion \prə'seshən\ *n* : group moving along in an orderly way

pro·ces·sion·al \-'seshənəl\ *n* : music for a procession

pro·claim \prō'klām\ *vb* : announce publicly or with conviction —**proc·la·ma·tion** \,präklə'māshən\ *n*

pro·cliv·i·ty \prō'klivətē\ *n, pl* **-ties** : inclination

pro·cras·ti·nate \prə'krastə,nāt\ *vb* **-nat·ed; -nat·ing** : put something off until later —**pro·cras·ti·na·tion** \-,krastə'nāshən\ *n* —**pro·cras·ti·na·tor** \-'krastə,nātər\ *n*

pro·cre·ate \'prōkrē,āt\ *vb* **-at·ed; -at·ing** : produce offspring —**pro·cre·ation** \,prōkrē'āshən\ *n* —**pro·cre·ative** \'prōkrē,ātiv\ *adj* —**pro·cre·ator** \-,ātər\ *n*

proc·tor \'präktər\ *n* : supervisor of students (as at an examination) —**proctor** *vb*

pro·cure \prə'kyûr\ *vb* **-cured; -cur·ing** : get possession of —**pro·cur·able** \-'kyûrəbəl\ *adj* —**pro·cure·ment** *n* —**pro·cur·er** *n*

prod \'präd\ *vb* **-dd-** : push with or as if with a pointed instrument —**prod** *n*

prod·i·gal \'prädigəl\ *adj* : recklessly extravagant or wasteful —**prodigal** *n* —**prod·i·gal·i·ty** \,prädə'galətē\ *n*

pro·di·gious \prə'dijəs\ *adj* : extraordinary in size or degree —**pro-di·gious·ly** adv

prod·i·gy \'prädəjē\ n, pl **-gies** : extraordinary person or thing

pro·duce \prə'düs, -'dyüs\ vb **-duced; -duc·ing 1** : present to view **2** : give birth to **3** : bring into existence ~ \'präd,üs, 'pröd-, -,yüs\ n **1** : product **2** : agricultural products —**pro·duc·er** \prə'düsər, -'dyü-\ n

prod·uct \'präd,əkt\ n **1** : number resulting from multiplication **2** : something produced

pro·duc·tion \prə'dəkshən\ n : act, process, or result of producing —**pro·duc·tive** \-'dəktiv\ adj —**pro·duc·tive·ness** n —**pro·duc·tiv·i·ty** \,prö-,dək'tivətē, ,prä-\ n

pro·fane \prö'fān\ vb **-faned; -fan·ing** : treat with irreverence ~ adj **1** : not concerned with religion **2** : serving to debase what is holy —**pro·fane·ly** adv —**pro·fane·ness** n —**pro·fan·i·ty** \prö'fanətē\ n

pro·fess \prə'fes\ vb **1** : declare openly **2** : confess one's faith in —**pro·fessed·ly** \-ədlē\ adv

pro·fes·sion \prə'feshən\ n **1** : open declaration of belief **2** : occupation requiring specialized knowledge and academic training

pro·fes·sion·al \prə'feshənəl\ adj **1** : of, relating to, or engaged in a profession **2** : playing sport for pay —**professional** n —**pro·fes·sion·al·ism** n —**pro·fes·sion·al·ize** vb —**pro·fes·sion·al·ly** adv

pro·fes·sor \prə'fesər\ n : university or college teacher —**pro·fes·so·ri·al** \,pröfə'sörēəl, ,präfə-\ adj —**pro·fes·sor·ship** n

prof·fer \'präfər\ vb **-fered; -fer·ing** : offer —**proffer** n

pro·fi·cient \prə'fishənt\ adj : very good at something —**pro·fi·cien·cy** \-ənsē\ n —**proficient** n —**pro·fi·cient·ly** adv

pro·file \'prö,fīl\ n : picture in outline —**profile** vb

prof·it \'präfət\ n **1** : valuable return **2** : excess of the selling price of goods over cost ~ vb **1** : gain a profit —**prof·it·able** \'präfətəbəl\ adj —**prof·it·ably** adv —**prof·it·less** adj

prof·i·teer \,präfə'tir\ n : one who makes an unreasonable profit —**profiteer** vb

prof·li·gate \'präfligət, -lə,gāt\ adj **1** : shamelessly immoral **2** : wildly extravagant —**prof·li·ga·cy** \-gəsē\ n —**profligate** n —**prof·li·gate·ly** adv

pro·found \prə'faúnd\ adj **1** : marked by intellectual depth or insight **2** : deeply felt —**pro·found·ly** adv —**pro·fun·di·ty** \-'fəndətē\ n

pro·fuse \prə'fyüs\ adj : pouring forth liberally —**pro·fuse·ly** adv —**pro·fu·sion** \-'fyüzhən\ n

pro·gen·i·tor \prö'jenətər\ n : direct ancestor

prog·e·ny \'präjənē\ n, pl **-nies** : offspring

pro·ges·ter·one \prö'jestə,rön\ n : female hormone

prog·no·sis \präg'nösəs\ n, pl **-no·ses** \-,sēz\ : prospect of recovery from disease

prog·nos·ti·cate \präg'nästə,kāt\ vb **-cat·ed; -cat·ing** : predict from signs or symptoms —**prog·nos·ti·ca·tion** \-,nästə'kāshən\ n —**prog·nos·ti·ca·tor** \-'nästə,kātər\ n

pro·gram \'prö,gram, -grəm\ n **1** : outline of the order to be pursued or the subjects included (as in a performance) **2** : plan of procedure **3** : coded instructions for a computer ~ vb **-grammed** or **-gramed; -gram·ming** or **-gram·ing 1** : enter in a program **2** : provide a computer with a program —**pro·gram·ma·bil·i·ty** \,prö,gramə'bilətē\ n —**pro·gram·ma·ble** \'prö,graməbəl\ adj —**pro·gram·mer** \'prö,gramər\ n

prog·ress \'prägrəs, -,res\ n : movement forward or to a better condition ~ \prə'gres\ vb **1** : move forward **2** : improve —**pro·gres·sive** \-'gresiv\ adj —**pro·gres·sive·ly** adv

pro·gres·sion \prə'greshən\ n **1** : act of progressing **2** : continuous connected series

pro·hib·it \prö'hibət\ vb : prevent by authority

pro·hi·bi·tion \,pröə'bishən\ n **1** : act of prohibiting **2** : legal restriction on sale or manufacture of alcoholic beverages —**pro·hi·bi·tion·ist** \-'bishənist\ n —**pro·hib·i·tive** \prö'hibətiv\ adj —**pro·hib·i·tive·ly** adv —**pro·hib·i·to·ry** \-'hibə,törē\ adj

proj·ect \'präj,ekt, -ikt\ n : planned undertaking ~ \prə'jekt\ vb **1** : design or plan **2** : protrude **3** : throw forward —**pro·jec·tion** \-'jekshən\ n

pro·jec·tile \prə'jekt³l\ n : missile hurled by external force

pro·jec·tor \-'jektər\ n : device for projecting pictures on a screen

pro·le·tar·i·an \,prōlə'terēən\ n : member of the proletariat —**proletarian** adj

pro·le·tar·i·at \-ēət\ n : laboring class

pro·lif·er·ate \prə'lifə,rāt\ vb -at·ed; -at·ing : grow or increase in number rapidly —**pro·lif·er·a·tion** \-,lifə'rāshən\ n

pro·lif·ic \prə'lifik\ adj : producing abundantly —**pro·lif·i·cal·ly** adv

pro·logue \'prō,lóg, -,läg\ n : preface

pro·long \prə'lón\ vb : lengthen in time or extent —**pro·lon·ga·tion** \,prō,lón'gāshən\ n

prom \'präm\ n : formal school dance

prom·e·nade \prämə'nād, -'näd\ n 1 : leisurely walk 2 : place for strolling —**promenade** vb

prom·i·nence \'prämənəns\ n 1 : quality, state, or fact of being readily noticeable or distinguished 2 : something that stands out —**prom·i·nent** \-nənt\ adj —**prom·i·nent·ly** adv

pro·mis·cu·ous \prə'miskyəwəs\ adj : having a number of sexual partners —**prom·is·cu·i·ty** \,prämis'kyüətē, ,prō,mis-\ n —**pro·mis·cu·ous·ly** adv —**pro·mis·cu·ous·ness** n

prom·ise \'präməs\ n 1 : statement that one will do or not do something 2 : basis for expectation —**promise** vb —**prom·is·so·ry** \-ə,sōrē\ adj

prom·is·ing \'präməsiŋ\ adj : likely to succeed —**prom·is·ing·ly** adv

prom·on·to·ry \'prämən,tōrē\ n, pl -ries : point of land jutting into the sea

pro·mote \prə'mōt\ vb -mot·ed; -mot·ing 1 : advance in rank 2 : contribute to the growth, development, or prosperity of —**pro·mot·er** n —**pro·mo·tion** \-'mōshən\ n —**pro·mo·tion·al** \-'mōshənəl\ adj

¹**prompt** \'prämpt\ vb 1 : incite 2 : give a cue to (an actor or singer) —**prompt·er** n

²**prompt** adj : ready and quick —**prompt·ly** adv —**prompt·ness** n

prone \'prōn\ adj 1 : having a tendency 2 : lying face downward —**prone·ness** \'prōnnəs\ n

prong \'prón\ n : sharp point of a fork —**pronged** \'prónd\ adj

pro·noun \'prō,naún\ n : word used as a substitute for a noun

pro·nounce \prə'naúns\ vb -nounced; -nounc·ing 1 : utter officially or as an opinion 2 : say or speak esp. correctly —**pro·nounce·able** adj —**pro·nounce·ment** n —**pro·nun·ci·a·tion** \-,nənsē'āshən\ n

pro·nounced \-'naúnst\ adj : decided

¹**proof** \'prüf\ n 1 : evidence of a truth or fact 2 : trial impression or print

²**proof** adj : designed·for or successful in resisting or repelling

proof·read vb : read and mark corrections in —**proof·read·er** n

prop \'präp\ vb -pp- 1 : support 2 : sustain —**prop** n

pro·pa·gan·da \,präpə'gandə, ,prōpə-\ n : the spreading of ideas or information to further or damage a cause —**pro·pa·gan·dist** \-dist\ n —**pro·pa·gan·dize** \-,dīz\ vb

prop·a·gate \'präpə,gāt\ vb -gat·ed; -gat·ing 1 : reproduce biologically 2 : cause to spread —**prop·a·ga·tion** \,präpə'gāshən\ n

pro·pane \'prō,pān\ n : heavy flammable gaseous fuel

pro·pel \prə'pel\ vb -ll- : drive forward —**pro·pel·lant, pro·pel·lent** n or adj

pro·pel·ler \prə'pelər\ n : hub with revolving blades that propels a craft

pro·pen·si·ty \prə'pensətē\ n, pl -ties : particular interest or inclination

prop·er \'präpər\ adj 1 : suitable or right 2 : limited to a specified thing 3 : correct 4 : strictly adhering to standards of social manners, dignity, or good taste —**prop·er·ly** adv

prop·er·ty \'präpərtē\ n, pl -ties 1 : quality peculiar to an individual 2 : something owned 3 : piece of real estate 4 : ownership

proph·e·cy \'präfəsē\ n, pl -cies : prediction

proph·e·sy \-,sī\ vb -sied; -sy·ing : predict —**proph·e·si·er** \-,sīər\ n

proph·et \'präfət\ n : one who utters revelations or predicts events —**proph·et·ess** \-əs\ n —**pro·phet·ic** \prə'fetik\, **pro·phet·i·cal** \-ikəl\ adj —**pro·phet·i·cal·ly** adv

pro·pin·qui·ty \prə'piŋkwətē\ n : nearness

pro·pi·ti·ate \prō'pishē,āt\ vb -at·ed; -at·ing : gain or regain the favor of —**pro·pi·ti·a·tion** \-,pishē'āshən\ n —**pro·pi·tia·to·ry** \-'pishēə,tōrē\ adj

pro·pi·tious \prə'pishəs\ *adj* : favorable

pro·po·nent \prə'pōnənt\ *n* : one who argues in favor of something

pro·por·tion \prə'pōrshən\ *n* 1 : relation of one part to another or to the whole with respect to magnitude, quantity, or degree 2 : symmetry 3 : share ~ *vb* : adjust in size in relation to others —**pro·por·tion·al** \-shənəl\ *adj* —**pro·por·tion·al·ly** *adv* —**pro·por·tion·ate** \-shənət\ *adj* —**pro·por·tion·ate·ly** *adv*

pro·pose \prə'pōz\ *vb* -**posed**; -**pos·ing** 1 : plan or intend 2 : make an offer of marriage 3 : present for consideration —**pro·pos·al** \-'pōzəl\ *n*

prop·o·si·tion \,präpə'zishən\ *n* : something proposed ~ *vb* : suggest sexual intercourse to

pro·pound \prə'paúnd\ *vb* : set forth for consideration

pro·pri·etor \prə'prīətər\ *n* : owner —**pro·pri·e·tary** \prə'prīə,terē\ *adj* —**pro·pri·etor·ship** *n* —**pro·pri·etress** \-'prīətrəs\ *n*

pro·pri·ety \prə'prīətē\ *n, pl* -**eties** : standard of acceptability in social conduct

pro·pul·sion \prə'pəlshən\ *n* 1 : action of propelling 2 : driving power —**pro·pul·sive** \-siv\ *adj*

pro·sa·ic \prō'zāik\ *adj* : dull

pro·scribe \prō'skrīb\ *vb* -**scribed**; -**scrib·ing** : prohibit —**pro·scrip·tion** \-'skripshən\ *n*

prose \'prōz\ *n* : ordinary language

pros·e·cute \'präsi,kyüt\ *vb* -**cut·ed**; -**cut·ing** 1 : follow to the end 2 : seek legal punishment of —**pros·e·cu·tion** \,präsi'kyüshən\ *n* —**pros·e·cu·tor** \'präsi,kyütər\ *n*

pros·e·lyte \'präsə,līt\ *n* : new convert —**pros·e·ly·tize** \'präsələ,tīz\ *vb*

pros·pect \'präs,pekt\ *n* 1 : extensive view 2 : something awaited 3 : potential buyer ~ *vb* : look for mineral deposits —**pro·spec·tive** \prə-'spektiv, 'präs,pek-\ *adj* —**pro·spec·tive·ly** *adv* —**pros·pec·tor** \-,pektər, -'pek-\ *n*

pro·spec·tus \prə'spektəs\ *n* : introductory description of an enterprise

pros·per \'präspər\ *vb* : thrive or succeed —**pros·per·ous** \-pərəs\ *adj*

pros·per·i·ty \präs'perətē\ *n* : economic well-being

pros·tate \'präs,tāt\ *n* : glandular body about the base of the male urethra — **prostate** *adj*

pros·the·sis \präs'thēsəs, 'prästhə-\ *n, pl* -**the·ses** \-,sēz\ : artificial replacement for a body part —**pros·thet·ic** \präs-'thetik\ *adj*

pros·ti·tute \'prästə,tüt, -,tyüt\ *vb* -**tut·ed**; -**tut·ing** 1 : offer sexual activity for money 2 : put to corrupt or unworthy purposes ~ *n* : one who engages in sexual activities for money —**pros·ti·tu·tion** \,prästə'tüshən, -'tyü-\ *n*

pros·trate \'präs,trāt\ *adj* : stretched out with face on the ground ~ *vb* -**trat·ed**; -**trat·ing** 1 : fall or throw (oneself) into a prostrate position 2 : reduce to helplessness —**pros·tra·tion** \präs'trāshən\ *n*

pro·tag·o·nist \prō'tagənist\ *n* : main character in a drama or story

pro·tect \prə'tekt\ *vb* : shield from injury —**pro·tec·tor** \-tər\ *n*

pro·tec·tion \prə'tekshən\ *n* 1 : act of protecting 2 : one that protects —**pro·tec·tive** \-'tektiv\ *adj*

pro·tec·tor·ate \-tərət\ *n* : state dependent upon the authority of another state

pro·té·gé \'prōtə,zhā\ *n* : one under the care and protection of an influential person

pro·tein \'prō,tēn\ *n* : complex combination of amino acids present in living matter

pro·test \'prō,test\ *n* 1 : organized public demonstration of disapproval 2 : strong objection ~ \prə'test\ *vb* 1 : assert positively 2 : object strongly —**pro·tes·ta·tion** \,prätəs'tāshən\ *n* —**pro·test·er, pro·tes·tor** \'prō-,testər\ *n*

Prot·es·tant \'prätəstənt\ *n* : Christian not of a Catholic or Orthodox church —**Prot·es·tant·ism** \'prätəstənt,izəm\ *n*

pro·to·col \'prōtə,kól\ *n* : diplomatic etiquette

pro·ton \'prō,tän\ *n* : positively charged atomic particle

pro·to·plasm \'prōtə,plazəm\ *n* : complex colloidal living substance of plant and animal cells —**pro·to·plas·mic** \,prōtə'plazmik\ *adj*

pro·to·type \'prōtə,tīp\ *n* : original model

pro·to·zo·an \,prōtə'zōən\ *n* : single-celled lower invertebrate animal

pro·tract \prō'trakt\ vb : prolong

pro·trac·tor \-'traktər\ n : instrument for drawing and measuring angles

pro·trude \prō'trüd\ vb -trud·ed; -trud·ing : stick out or cause to stick out — **pro·tru·sion** \-'trüzhən\ n

pro·tu·ber·ance \prō'tübərəns, -'tyü-\ n : something that protrudes — **pro·tu·ber·ant** adj

proud \praüd\ adj 1 : having or showing excessive self-esteem 2 : highly pleased 3 : having proper self-respect 4 : glorious — **proud·ly** adv

prove \prüv\ vb proved; proved or prov·en \'prüvən\; prov·ing 1 : test by experiment or by a standard 2 : establish the truth of by argument or evidence 3 : turn out esp. after trial or test — **prov·able** \'prüvəbəl\ adj

prov·en·der \'prävəndər\ n : dry food for domestic animals

prov·erb \'präv,ərb\ n : short meaningful popular saying — **pro·ver·bi·al** \prə'vərbēəl\ adj

pro·vide \prə'vīd\ vb -vid·ed; -vid·ing 1 : take measures beforehand 2 : make a stipulation 3 : supply what is needed — **pro·vid·er** n

pro·vid·ed conj : if

prov·i·dence \'prävədəns\ n 1 often cap : divine guidance 2 cap : God 3 : quality of being provident

prov·i·dent \-ədənt\ adj 1 : making provision for the future 2 : thrifty — **prov·i·dent·ly** adv

prov·i·den·tial \,prävə'denchəl\ adj 1 : relating to Providence 2 : opportune

pro·vid·ing conj : provided

prov·ince \'prävəns\ n 1 : administrative district 2 pl : all of a country outside the metropolis 3 : sphere

pro·vin·cial \prə'vinchəl\ adj 1 : relating to a province 2 : limited in outlook — **pro·vin·cial·ism** \-,izəm\ n

pro·vi·sion \prə'vizhən\ n 1 : act of providing 2 : stock of food —usu. in pl. 3 : stipulation ~ vb : supply with provisions

pro·vi·sion·al \-'vizhənəl\ adj : provided for a temporary need — **pro·vi·sion·al·ly** adv

pro·vi·so \prə'vīzō\ n, pl -sos or -soes : stipulation

pro·voke \prə'vōk\ vb -voked; -vok·ing 1 : incite to anger 2 : stir up on purpose — **prov·o·ca·tion** \,prävə-

'kāshən\ n — **pro·voc·a·tive** \prə-'väkətiv\ adj

prow \praü\ n : bow of a ship

prow·ess \'praüəs\ n 1 : valor 2 : extraordinary ability

prowl \'praül\ vb : roam about stealthily — **prowl** n — **prowl·er** n

prox·i·mate \'präksəmət\ adj : very near

prox·im·i·ty \präk'simətē\ n : nearness

proxy \'präksē\ n, pl prox·ies : authority to act for another — **proxy** adj

prude \'prüd\ n : one who shows extreme modesty — **prud·ery** \'prüdərē\ n — **prud·ish** \'prüdish\ adj

pru·dent \'prüd°nt\ adj 1 : shrewd 2 : cautious 3 : thrifty — **pru·dence** \-°ns\ n — **pru·den·tial** \prü'denchəl\ adj — **pru·dent·ly** adv

¹**prune** \'prün\ n : dried plum

²**prune** vb pruned; prun·ing : cut off unwanted parts

pru·ri·ent \'prürēənt\ adj : lewd — **pru·ri·ence** \-ēəns\ n

¹**pry** \'prī\ vb pried; pry·ing : look closely or inquisitively

²**pry** vb pried; pry·ing : raise, move, or pull apart with a lever

psalm \'säm, 'sälm\ n : sacred song or poem — **psalm·ist** n

pseu·do·nym \'süd°n,im\ n : fictitious name — **pseu·don·y·mous** \sü'dänəməs\ adj

pso·ri·a·sis \sə'rīəsəs\ n : chronic skin disease

psy·che \'sīkē\ n : soul or mind

psy·chi·a·try \sə'kīətrē, sī-\ n : branch of medicine dealing with mental, emotional, and behavioral disorders — **psy·chi·at·ric** \,sīkē'atrik\ adj — **psy·chi·a·trist** \sə'kīətrist, sī-\ n

psy·chic \'sīkik\ adj 1 : relating to the psyche 2 : sensitive to supernatural forces ~ n : person sensitive to supernatural forces — **psy·chi·cal·ly** adv

psy·cho·anal·y·sis \,sīkōə'naləsəs\ n : study of the normally hidden content of the mind esp. to resolve conflicts — **psy·cho·an·a·lyst** \-'an°list\ n — **psy·cho·an·a·lyt·ic** \-,an°l'itik\ adj — **psy·cho·an·a·lyze** \-'an°l,īz\ vb

psy·chol·o·gy \sī'käləjē\ n, pl -gies 1 : science of mind and behavior 2 : mental and behavioral aspect (as of an individual) — **psy·cho·log·i·cal** \,sīkə'läjikəl\ adj — **psy·cho·log·i·cal·ly** adv — **psy·chol·o·gist** \sī-'käləjist\ n

psy·cho·path \'sīkə,path\ n : mentally ill or unstable person —**psy·cho·path·ic** \,sīkə'pathik\ adj

psy·cho·sis \sī'kōsəs\ n, pl **-cho·ses** \-,sēz\ : mental derangement (as paranoia) —**psy·chot·ic** \-'kätik\ adj or n

psy·cho·so·mat·ic \,sīkōsə'matik\ adj : relating to bodily symptoms caused by mental or emotional disturbance

psy·cho·ther·a·py \,sīkō'therəpē\ n : treatment of mental disorder by psychological means —**psy·cho·ther·a·pist** \-pist\ n

pto·maine \'tō,mān\ n : bacterial decay product

pu·ber·ty \'pyübərtē\ n : time of sexual maturity

pu·bic \'pyübik\ adj : relating to the lower abdominal region

pub·lic \'pəblik\ adj 1 : relating to the people as a whole 2 : civic 3 : not private 4 : open to all 5 : well-known ~ n : people as a whole —**pub·lic·ly** adv

pub·li·ca·tion \,pəblə'kāshən\ n 1 : process of publishing 2 : published work

pub·lic·i·ty \pə'blisətē\ n 1 : news information given out to gain public attention 2 : public attention

pub·li·cize \'pəblə,sīz\ vb **-cized; -ciz·ing** : bring to public attention —**pub·li·cist** \-sist\ n

pub·lish \'pəblish\ vb 1 : announce publicly 2 : reproduce for sale esp. by printing —**pub·lish·er** n

puck·er \'pəkər\ vb : pull together into folds or wrinkles ~ n : wrinkle

pud·ding \'pudiŋ\ n : creamy dessert

pud·dle \'pədᵊl\ n : very small pool of water

pudgy \'pəjē\ adj **pudg·i·er; -est** : short and plump

pu·er·ile \'pyürəl\ adj : childish

puff \'pəf\ vb 1 : blow in short gusts 2 : pant 3 : enlarge ~ n 1 : short discharge (as of air) 2 : slight swelling 3 : something light and fluffy —**puffy** adj

pug \'pəg\ n : small stocky dog

pu·gi·lism \'pyüjə,lizəm\ n : boxing —**pu·gi·list** \-list\ n —**pu·gi·lis·tic** \,pyüjə'listik\ adj

pug·na·cious \,pəg'nāshəs\ adj : prone to fighting —**pug·nac·i·ty** \-'nasətē\ n

puke \'pyük\ vb **puked; puk·ing** : vomit —**puke** n

pul·chri·tude \'pəlkrə,tüd, -,tyüd\ n : beauty —**pul·chri·tu·di·nous** \,pəlkrə'tüdᵊnəs, -'tyüd-\ adj

pull \'pul\ vb 1 : exert force so as to draw (something) toward or out 2 : move 3 : stretch or tear ~ n 1 : act of pulling 2 : influence 3 : device for pulling something —**pull·er** n

pul·let \'pulət\ n : young hen

pul·ley \'pulē\ n, pl **-leys** : wheel with a grooved rim

Pull·man \'pulmən\ n : railroad car with berths

pull·over \'pul,ōvər\ adj : put on by being pulled over the head —**pullover** n

pul·mo·nary \'pulmə,nerē, 'pəl-\ adj : relating to the lungs

pulp \'pəlp\ n 1 : soft part of a fruit or vegetable 2 : soft moist mass (as of mashed wood) —**pulpy** adj

pul·pit \'pul,pit\ n : raised desk used in preaching

pul·sate \'pəl,sāt\ vb **-sat·ed; -sat·ing** : expand and contract rhythmically —**pul·sa·tion** \,pəl'sāshən\ n

pulse \'pəls\ n : arterial throbbing caused by heart contractions —**pulse** vb

pul·ver·ize \'pəlvə,rīz\ vb **-ized; -iz·ing** : beat or grind into a powder

pu·ma \'pümə, 'pyü-\ n : cougar

pum·ice \'pəməs\ n : light porous volcanic glass used in polishing

pum·mel \'pəməl\ vb **-meled; -mel·ing** : beat

¹**pump** \'pəmp\ n : device for moving or compressing fluids ~ vb 1 : raise (as water) with a pump 2 : fill by means of a pump —**with** up 3 : move like a pump —**pump·er** n

²**pump** n : woman's low shoe

pum·per·nick·el \'pəmpər,nikəl\ n : dark rye bread

pump·kin \'pəŋkən, 'pəmpkən\ n : large usu. orange fruit of a vine related to the gourd

pun \'pən\ n : humorous use of a word in a way that suggests two or more interpretations —**pun** vb

¹**punch** \'pənch\ vb 1 : strike with the fist 2 : perforate with a punch ~ n : quick blow with the fist —**punch·er** n

²**punch** n : tool for piercing or stamping

³**punch** n : mixed beverage often including fruit juice

punc·til·i·ous \pəŋk'tilēəs\ adj : marked by precise accordance with conventions

punc·tu·al \'pəŋkchəwəl\ adj : prompt —**punc·tu·al·i·ty** \,pəŋkchə'walətē\ n —**punc·tu·al·ly** adv

punc·tu·ate \'pəŋkchə,wāt\ vb -**at·ed**; -**at·ing** : mark with punctuation

punc·tu·a·tion \,pəŋkchə'wāshən\ n : standardized marks in written matter to clarify the meaning and separate parts

punc·ture \'pəŋkchər\ n : act or result of puncturing ~ vb -**tured**; -**tur·ing** : make a hole in

pun·dit \'pəndət\ n 1 : learned person 2 : expert or critic

pun·gent \'pənjənt\ adj : having a sharp or stinging odor or taste —**pun·gen·cy** \-jənsē\ n —**pun·gent·ly** adv

pun·ish \'pənish\ vb : impose a penalty on or for —**pun·ish·able** adj —**pun·ish·ment** n

pu·ni·tive \'pyünətiv\ adj : inflicting punishment

pun·kin var of PUMPKIN

¹**punt** \'pənt\ n : long narrow flat-bottomed boat ~ vb : propel (a boat) by pushing with a pole

²**punt** vb : kick a ball dropped from the hands ~ n : act of punting a ball

pu·ny \'pyünē\ adj -**ni·er**; -**est** : slight in power or size

pup \'pəp\ n : young dog

pu·pa \'pyüpə\ n, pl -**pae** \-,pē, -,pī\ or -**pas** : insect (as a moth) when it is in a cocoon —**pu·pal** \-pəl\ adj

¹**pu·pil** \'pyüpəl\ n : young person in school

²**pupil** n : dark central opening of the iris of the eye

pup·pet \'pəpət\ n : small doll moved by hand or by strings —**pup·pe·teer** \,pəpə'tir\ n

pup·py \'pəpē\ n, pl -**pies** : young dog

pur·chase \'pərchəs\ vb -**chased**; -**chas·ing** : obtain in exchange for money ~ n 1 : act of purchasing 2 : something purchased 3 : secure grasp —**pur·chas·er** n

pure \'pyür\ adj **pur·er**; **pur·est** : free of foreign matter, contamination, or corruption —**pure·ly** adv

pu·ree \pyü'rā, -'rē\ n : thick liquid mass of food —**puree** vb

pur·ga·to·ry \'pərgə,tōrē\ n, pl -**ries** : intermediate state after death for purification by expiating sins —**pur·ga·to·ri·al** \,pərgə'tōrēəl\ adj

purge \'pərj\ vb **purged**; **purg·ing** 1 : purify esp. from sin 2 : have or cause emptying of the bowels 3 : to get rid of ~ n 1 : act or result of purging 2 : something that purges —**pur·ga·tive** \'pərgətiv\ adj or n

pu·ri·fy \'pyürə,fī\ vb -**fied**; -**fy·ing** : make or become pure —**pu·ri·fi·ca·tion** \,pyürəfə'kāshən\ n —**pu·ri·fi·er** \-,fīər\ n

Pu·rim \'pürim\ n : Jewish holiday celebrated in February or March in commemoration of the deliverance of the Jews from the massacre plotted by Haman

pu·ri·tan \'pyürət⁰n\ n : one who practices or preaches a very strict moral code —**pu·ri·tan·i·cal** \,pyürə'tanikəl\ adj —**pu·ri·tan·i·cal·ly** adv

pu·ri·ty \'pyürətē\ n : quality or state of being pure

purl \'pərl\ n : stitch in knitting ~ vb : knit in purl stitch

pur·loin \pər'lȯin, 'pər,lȯin\ vb : steal

pur·ple \'pərpəl\ n : bluish red color —**pur·plish** \'pərpəlish\ adj

pur·port \pər'pȯrt\ vb : convey outwardly as the meaning ~ \'pər,pȯrt\ n : meaning —**pur·port·ed·ly** \-ədlē\ adv

pur·pose \'pərpəs\ n 1 : something (as a result) aimed at 2 : resolution ~ vb -**posed**; -**pos·ing** : intend —**pur·pose·ful** \-fəl\ adj —**pur·pose·ful·ly** adv —**pur·pose·less** adj —**pur·pose·ly** adv

purr \'pər\ n : low murmur typical of a contented cat —**purr** vb

¹**purse** \'pərs\ n 1 : bag or pouch for money and small objects 2 : financial resource 3 : prize money

²**purse** vb **pursed**; **purs·ing** : pucker

pur·su·ance \pər'süəns\ n : act of carrying out or into effect

pursuant to \-'süənt-\ prep : according to

pur·sue \pər'sü\ vb -**sued**; -**su·ing** 1 : follow in order to overtake 2 : seek to accomplish 3 : proceed along 4 : engage in —**pur·su·er** n

pur·suit \pər'süt\ n 1 : act of pursuing 2 : occupation

pur·vey \pər'vā\ *vb* **-veyed; -vey·ing** : supply (as provisions) usu. as a business —**pur·vey·or** \-ər\ *n*

pus \'pəs\ *n* : thick yellowish fluid (as in a boil)

push \'pùsh\ *vb* **1** : press against to move forward **2** : urge on or provoke ~ *n* **1** : vigorous effort **2** : act of pushing —**push·cart** *n* —**push·er** \'pùshər\ *n*

pushy \'pùshē\ *adj* **push·i·er; -est** : objectionably aggressive

pu·sil·lan·i·mous \,pyüsə'lanəməs\ *adj* : cowardly

pussy \'pùsē\ *n, pl* **puss·ies** : cat

pus·tule \'pəschül\ *n* : pus-filled pimple

put \'pùt\ *vb* **put; put·ting 1** : bring to a specified position or condition **2** : subject to pain, suffering, or death **3** : impose or cause to exist **4** : express **5** : cause to be used or employed —**put off** *vb* : postpone or delay —**put out** *vb* : bother or inconvenience —**put up** *vb* **1** : prepare for storage **2** : lodge **3** : contribute or pay —**put up with** : endure

pu·tre·fy \'pyütrə,fī\ *vb* **-fied; -fy·ing** : make or become putrid —**pu·tre·fac·tion** \,pyütrə'fakshən\ *n*

pu·trid \'pyütrəd\ *adj* : rotten —**pu·trid·i·ty** \pyü'tridətē\ *n*

put·ty \'pətē\ *n, pl* **-ties** : doughlike cement —**putty** *vb*

puz·zle \'pəzəl\ *vb* **-zled; -zling 1** : confuse **2** : attempt to solve —**with** *out* or *over* ~ *n* : something that confuses or tests ingenuity —**puz·zle·ment** *n* —**puz·zler** \-ələr\ *n*

pyg·my \'pigmē\ *n, pl* **-mies** : dwarf —**pygmy** *adj*

py·lon \'pī,län, -lən\ *n* : tower or tall post

pyr·a·mid \'pirə,mid\ *n* : structure with a square base and 4 triangular sides meeting at a point

pyre \'pīr\ *n* : material heaped for a funeral fire

py·ro·ma·nia \,pīrō'mānēə\ *n* : irresistible impulse to start fires —**py·ro·ma·ni·ac** \-nē,ak\ *n*

py·ro·tech·nics \,pīrə'tekniks\ *n pl* : spectacular display (as of fireworks) —**py·ro·tech·nic** \-nik\ *adj*

Pyr·rhic \'pirik\ *adj* : achieved at excessive cost

py·thon \'pī,thän, -thən\ *n* : very large constricting snake

Q

q \'kyü\ *n, pl* **q's** *or* **qs** \'kyüz\ : 17th letter of the alphabet

¹quack \'kwak\ *vb* : make a cry like that of a duck —**quack** *n*

²quack *n* : one who pretends to have medical or healing skill —**quack** *adj* —**quack·ery** \-ərē\ *n* —**quack·ish** *adj*

quad·ran·gle \'kwäd,raŋgəl\ *n* : rectangular courtyard

quad·rant \'kwädrənt\ *n* : 1/4 of a circle

quad·ri·lat·er·al \,kwädrə'latərəl\ *n* : 4-sided polygon

qua·drille \kwä'dril, kə-\ *n* : square dance for 4 couples

quad·ru·ped \'kwädrə,ped\ *n* : animal having 4 feet

quad·ru·ple \kwä'drüpəl, -'drəp-; 'kwädrəp-\ *vb* **-pled; -pling** \-pliŋ\ : multiply by 4 ~ *adj* : being 4 times as great or as many

qua·dru·plet \kwä'drəplət, -'drüp-; 'kwädrəp-\ *n* : one of 4 offspring born at one birth

quaff \'kwäf, 'kwaf\ *vb* : drink deeply or repeatedly —**quaff** *n*

quag·mire \'kwag,mīr, 'kwäg-\ *n* : soft land or bog

qua·hog \'kō,hòg, 'kwò-, 'kwō-, -,häg\ *n* : thick-shelled clam

¹quail \'kwāl\ *n, pl* **quail** *or* **quails** : short-winged plump game bird

²quail *vb* : cower in fear

quaint \'kwānt\ *adj* : pleasingly old-fashioned or odd —**quaint·ly** *adv* —**quaint·ness** *n*

quake \'kwāk\ *vb* **quaked; quak·ing** : shake or tremble ~ *n* : earthquake

qual·i·fi·ca·tion \,kwäləfə'kāshən\ *n* **1** : limitation or stipulation **2** : special skill or experience for a job

qual·i·fy \'kwälə,fī\ *vb* **-fied; -fy·ing 1**

: modify or limit **2** : fit by skill or training for some purpose **3** : become eligible —**qual·i·fied** adj —**qual·i·fi·er** \-,fīər\ n

qual·i·ty \'kwälətē\ n, pl **-ties 1** : peculiar and essential character, nature, or feature **2** : excellence or distinction

qualm \'kwäm, 'kwälm, 'kwóm\ n : sudden feeling of doubt or uneasiness

quan·da·ry \'kwändrē\ n, pl **-ries** : state of perplexity or doubt

quan·ti·ty \'kwäntətē\ n, pl **-ties 1** : something that can be measured or numbered **2** : considerable amount

quan·tum theory \'kwäntəm-\ n : theory in physics that radiant energy (as light) is composed of separate packets of energy

quar·an·tine \'kwórən,tēn\ n **1** : restraint on the movements of persons or goods to prevent the spread of pests or disease **2** : place or period of quarantine —**quarantine** vb

quar·rel \'kwórəl\ n : basis of conflict —**quarrel** vb —**quar·rel·some** \-səm\ adj

[1]**quar·ry** \'kwórē\ n, pl **quarries** : prey
[2]**quarry** n, pl **-ries** : excavation for obtaining stone —**quarry** vb

quart \'kwórt\ n : unit of liquid measure equal to .95 liter or of dry measure equal to 1.10 liters

quar·ter \'kwórtər\ n **1** : 1/4 part **2** : 1/4 of a dollar **3** : city district **4** pl : place to live esp. for a time **5** : mercy ~ vb : divide into 4 equal parts

quar·ter·ly \'kwórtərlē\ adv or adj : at 3-month intervals ~ n, pl **-lies** : periodical published 4 times a year

quar·ter·mas·ter n **1** : ship's helmsman **2** : army supply officer

quar·tet \kwór'tet\ n **1** : music for 4 performers **2** : group of 4

quar·to \'kwórtō\ n, pl **-tos** : book printed on pages cut 4 from a sheet

quartz \'kwórts\ n : transparent crystalline mineral

quash \'kwäsh, 'kwósh\ vb **1** : set aside by judicial action **2** : suppress summarily and completely

qua·si \'kwä,zī, -sī; 'kwäzē, 'kwäs-; 'kwäzē\ adj : similar or nearly identical

qua·train \'kwä,trān\ n : unit of 4 lines of verse

qua·ver \'kwävər\ vb : tremble or trill —**quaver** n

quay \'kē, 'kā, 'kwā\ n : wharf

quea·sy \'kwēzē\ adj **-si·er; -est** : nauseated —**quea·si·ly** \-zəlē\ adv —**quea·si·ness** \-zēnəs\ n

queen \'kwēn\ n **1** : wife or widow of a king **2** : female monarch **3** : woman of rank, power, or attractiveness **4** : fertile female of a social insect —**queen·ly** adj

queer \'kwir\ adj : differing from the usual or normal —**queer·ly** adv —**queer·ness** n

quell \'kwel\ vb : put down by force

quench \'kwench\ vb **1** : put out **2** : satisfy (a thirst) —**quench·able** adj —**quench·er** n

quer·u·lous \'kwerələs, -yələs\ adj : fretful or whining —**quer·u·lous·ly** adv —**quer·u·lous·ness** n

que·ry \'kwirē, 'kwer-\ n, pl **-ries** : question —**query** vb

quest \'kwest\ n or vb : search

ques·tion \'kweschən\ n **1** : something asked **2** : subject for debate **3** : dispute ~ vb **1** : ask questions **2** : doubt or dispute **3** : subject to analysis —**ques·tion·er** n

ques·tion·able \'kweschənəbəl\ adj **1** : not certain **2** : of doubtful truth or morality —**ques·tion·ably** \-blē\ adv

question mark n : a punctuation mark ? used esp. at the end of a sentence to indicate a direct question

ques·tion·naire \,kweschə'nar\ n : set of questions

queue \'kyü\ n **1** : braid of hair **2** : a waiting line ~ vb **queued; queu·ing** or **queue·ing** : line up

quib·ble \'kwibəl\ n : minor objection —**quibble** vb —**quib·bler** n

quick \'kwik\ adj **1** : rapid **2** : alert or perceptive ~ n : sensitive area of living flesh —**quick** adv —**quick·ly** adv —**quick·ness** n

quick·en \'kwikən\ vb **1** : come to life **2** : increase in speed

quick·sand n : deep mass of sand and water

quick·sil·ver n : mercury

qui·es·cent \kwī'esənt\ adj : being at rest —**qui·es·cence** \-əns\ n

qui·et \'kwīət\ adj **1** : marked by little motion or activity **2** : gentle **3** : free from noise **4** : not showy **5** : secluded ~ vb : pacify —**quiet** adv or n —**qui·et·ly** adv —**qui·et·ness** n

qui·etude \'kwīə,tüd, -,tyüd\ *n* : quietness or repose

quill \'kwil\ *n* 1 : a large stiff feather 2 : porcupine's spine

quilt \'kwilt\ *n* : padded bedspread ~ *vb* : stitch or sew in layers with padding in between

quince \'kwins\ *n* : hard yellow apple-like fruit

qui·nine \'kwī,nīn\ *n* : bitter drug used against malaria

quin·tes·sence \kwin'tes³ns\ *n* 1 : purest essence of something 2 : most typical example —**quint·es·sen·tial** \,kwintə'senchəl\ *adj* —**quin·tes·sen·tial·ly** *adv*

quin·tet \kwin'tet\ *n* 1 : music for 5 performers 2 : group of 5

quin·tu·ple \kwin'tüpəl, -'tyüp-, -'təp-; 'kwintəp-\ *adj* 1 : having 5 units or members 2 : being 5 times as great or as many —**quintuple** *n or vb*

quin·tu·plet \-plət\ *n* : one of 5 offspring at one birth

quip \'kwip\ *vb* -**pp**- : make a clever remark —**quip** *n*

quire \'kwīr\ *n* : 24 or 25 sheets of paper of the same size and quality

quirk \'kwərk\ *n* : peculiarity of action or behavior —**quirky** *adj*

quit \'kwit\ *vb* **quit**; **quit·ting** 1 : stop 2 : leave —**quit·ter** *n*

quite \'kwīt\ *adv* 1 : completely 2 : to a considerable extent

quits \'kwits\ *adj* : even or equal with another (as by repaying a debt)

¹quiv·er \'kwivər\ *n* : case for arrows

²quiver *vb* : shake or tremble —**quiver** *n*

quix·ot·ic \kwik'sätik\ *adj* : idealistic to an impractical degree —**quix·ot·i·cal·ly** \-tiklē\ *adv*

quiz \'kwiz\ *n, pl* **quiz·zes** : short test ~ *vb* -**zz**- : question closely

quiz·zi·cal \'kwizikəl\ *adj* 1 : teasing 2 : curious

quoit \'kóit, 'kwóit, 'kwät\ *n* : ring thrown at a peg in a game (**quoits**)

quon·dam \'kwändəm, -,dam\ *adj* : former

quo·rum \'kwōrəm\ *n* : required number of members present

quo·ta \'kwōtə\ *n* : proportional part or share

quotation mark *n* : one of a pair of punctuation marks '' '' or ' ' used esp. to indicate the beginning and the end of a quotation

quote \'kwōt\ *vb* **quot·ed**; **quot·ing** 1 : repeat (another's words) exactly 2 : state (a price) —**quot·able** *adj* —**quo·ta·tion** \kwō'tāshən\ *n* —**quote** *n*

quo·tient \'kwōshənt\ *n* : number obtained from division

R

r \'är\ *n, pl* **r's** *or* **rs** \'ärz\ : 18th letter of the alphabet

rab·bet \'rabət\ *n* : groove in a board

rab·bi \'rab,ī\ *n* : Jewish religious leader —**rab·bin·ic** \rə'binik\, **rab·bin·i·cal** \-ikəl\ *adj*

rab·bin·ate \'rabənət, -,nāt\ *n* : office of a rabbi

rab·bit \'rabət\ *n, pl* -**bit** *or* -**bits** : long-eared burrowing mammal

rab·ble \'rabəl\ *n* : mob

ra·bid \'rabəd\ *adj* 1 : violent 2 : fanatical 3 : affected with rabies —**ra·bid·ly** *adv*

ra·bies \'rābēz\ *n, pl* **rabies** : acute deadly virus disease

rac·coon \ra'kün\ *n, pl* -**coon** *or* -**coons** : tree-dwelling mammal with a black mask and a bushy ringed tail

¹race \'rās\ *n* 1 : strong current of water 2 : contest of speed 3 : election campaign ~ *vb* **raced**; **rac·ing** 1 : run in a race 2 : rush —**race·course** *n* —**rac·er** *n* —**race·track** *n*

²race *n* 1 : family, tribe, people, or nation of the same stock 2 : division of mankind based on hereditary traits —**ra·cial** \'rāshəl\ *adj* —**ra·cial·ly** *adv*

race·horse *n* : horse used for racing

rac·ism \'rās,izəm\ *n* : discrimination based on the belief that some races are by nature superior —**rac·ist** \-ist\ *n*

rack \'rak\ *n* 1 : framework for display or storage 2 : instrument that stretches the body for torture ~ *vb* : torture with or as if with a rack

¹rack·et \'rakət\ *n* : bat with a tight netting across an open frame

²racket *n* **1** : confused noise **2** : fraudulent scheme —**rack·e·teer** \,rakə'tir\ *n* —**rack·e·teer·ing** *n*

ra·con·teur \,rak,än'tər\ *n* : storyteller

racy \'räsē\ *adj* **rac·i·er; -est** : risqué — **rac·i·ly** *adv* —**rac·i·ness** *n*

ra·dar \'rā,där\ *n* : radio device for determining distance and direction of distant objects

ra·di·al \'rādēəl\ *adj* : having parts arranged like rays coming from a common center —**ra·di·al·ly** *adv*

ra·di·ant \'rādēənt\ *adj* **1** : glowing **2** : beaming with happiness **3** : transmitted by radiation —**ra·di·ance** \-əns\ *n* —**ra·di·ant·ly** *adv*

ra·di·ate \'rādē,āt\ *vb* **-at·ed; -at·ing 1** : issue rays or in rays **2** : spread from a center —**ra·di·a·tion** \,rādē'āshən\ *n*

ra·di·a·tor \'rādē,ātər\ *n* : cooling or heating device

rad·i·cal \'radikəl\ *adj* **1** : fundamental **2** : extreme ~ *n* : person favoring extreme changes —**rad·i·cal·ism** \-,izəm\ *n* —**rad·i·cal·ly** *adv*

radii *pl of* RADIUS

ra·dio \'rādē,ō\ *n, pl* **-di·os 1** : wireless transmission or reception of sound by means of electric waves **2** : radio receiving set ~ *vb* : send a message to by radio —**radio** *adj*

ra·dio·ac·tiv·i·ty \,rādēō,ak'tivətē\ *n* : property of an element that emits energy through nuclear disintegration —**ra·dio·ac·tive** \-'aktiv\ *adj*

ra·di·ol·o·gy \,rādē'äləjē\ *n* : medical use of radiation —**ra·di·ol·o·gist** \-jist\ *n*

rad·ish \'radish\ *n* : pungent fleshy root usu. eaten raw

ra·di·um \'rādēəm\ *n* : metallic radioactive chemical element

ra·di·us \'rādēəs\ *n, pl* **-dii** \-ē,ī\ **1** : line from the center of a circle or sphere to the circumference or surface **2** : area defined by a radius

ra·don \'rā,dän\ *n* : gaseous radioactive chemical element

raff·ish \'rafish\ *adj* : flashily vulgar — **raff·ish·ly** *adv* —**raff·ish·ness** *n*

raf·fle \'rafəl\ *n* : lottery among people who have bought tickets ~ *vb* **-fled; -fling** : offer in a raffle

¹raft \'raft\ *n* : flat floating platform ~ *vb* : travel or transport by raft

²raft *n* : large amount or number

raf·ter \'raftər\ *n* : beam supporting a roof

¹rag \'rag\ *n* : waste piece of cloth

²rag *n* : composition in ragtime

rag·a·muf·fin \'ragə,məfən\ *n* : ragged dirty person

rage \'rāj\ *n* **1** : violent anger **2** : vogue ~ *vb* **raged; rag·ing 1** : be extremely angry or violent **2** : be out of control

rag·ged \'ragəd\ *adj* : torn —**rag·ged·ly** *adv* —**rag·ged·ness** *n*

ra·gout \ra'gü\ *n* : meat stew

rag·time *n* : syncopated music

rag·weed *n* : coarse weedy herb with allergenic pollen

raid \'rād\ *n* : sudden usu. surprise attack —**raid** *vb* —**raid·er** *n*

¹rail \'rāl\ *n* **1** : bar serving as a guard or barrier **2** : bar forming a track for wheeled vehicles **3** : railroad

²rail *vb* : scold someone vehemently — **rail·er** *n*

rail·ing \'rāliŋ\ *n* : rail or a barrier of rails

rail·lery \'rālərē\ *n, pl* **-ler·ies** : good-natured ridicule

rail·road \'rāl,rōd\ *n* : road for a train laid with iron rails and wooden ties ~ *vb* : force something hastily —**rail·road·er** *n* —**rail·road·ing** *n*

rail·way \-,wā\ *n* : railroad

rai·ment \'rāmənt\ *n* : clothing

rain \'rān\ *n* **1** : water falling in drops from the clouds **2** : shower of objects ~ *vb* : fall as or like rain —**rain·coat** *n* — **rain·drop** *n* —**rain·fall** *n* —**rain·mak·er** *n* —**rain·mak·ing** *n* —**rain·storm** *n* —**rain·water** *n* —**rainy** *adj*

rain·bow \-,bō\ *n* : arc of colors formed by the sun shining through moisture

raise \'rāz\ *vb* **raised; rais·ing 1** : lift **2** : arouse **3** : erect **4** : collect **5** : breed, grow, or bring up **6** : increase **7** : make light ~ *n* : increase esp. in pay —**rais·er** *n*

rai·sin \'rāzªn\ *n* : dried grape

ra·ja, ra·jah \'räjə\ *n* : Indian prince

¹rake \'rāk\ *n* : garden tool for smoothing or sweeping ~ *vb* **raked; rak·ing 1** : gather, loosen, or smooth with or as if with a rake **2** : sweep with gunfire

²rake *n* : dissolute man

rak·ish \'rākish\ *adj* : smart or jaunty — **rak·ish·ly** *adv* —**rak·ish·ness** *n*

ral·ly \'ralē\ *vb* **-lied; -ly·ing 1** : bring or come together **2** : revive or recover

3 : make a comeback ~ *n, pl* **-lies 1**
: act of rallying **2** : mass meeting
ram \'ram\ *n* **1** : male sheep **2** : beam
used in battering down walls or doors
~ *vb* **-mm-** **1** : force or drive in or
through **2** : strike against violently
RAM \'ram\ *n* : main internal storage
area in a computer
ram•ble \'rambəl\ *vb* **-bled; -bling**
: wander —**ramble** *n* —**ram•bler**
\-blər\ *n*
ram•bunc•tious \ram'bəŋkshəs\ *adj*
: unruly
ram•i•fi•ca•tion \,raməfə'kāshən\ *n*
: consequence
ram•i•fy \'ramə,fī\ *vb* **-fied; -fy•ing**
: branch out
ramp \'ramp\ *n* : sloping passage or
connecting roadway
ram•page \'ram,pāj, ram'pāj\ *vb*
-paged; -pag•ing : rush about wildly
~ \'ram,-\ *n* : violent or riotous action
or behavior
ram•pant \'rampənt\ *adj* : widespread
—**ram•pant•ly** *adv*
ram•part \'ram,pärt\ *n* : embankment of
a fortification
ram•rod *n* : rod used to load or clean a
gun — *adj* : strict or inflexible
ram•shack•le \'ram,shakəl\ *adj* : shaky
ran *past of* RUN
ranch \'ranch\ *n* **1** : establishment for
the raising of cattle, sheep, or horses
2 : specialized farm ~ *vb* : operate a
ranch —**ranch•er** *n*
ran•cid \'ransəd\ *adj* : smelling or tast-
ing as if spoiled —**ran•cid•i•ty** \ran-
'sidətē\ *n*
ran•cor \'raŋkər\ *n* : bitter deep-seated
ill will —**ran•cor•ous** *adj*
ran•dom \'randəm\ *adj* : occurring by
chance —**ran•dom•ly** *adv* —**ran-
dom•ness** *n* —**at random** : without
definite aim or method
ran•dom•ize \'randə,mīz\ *vb* **-ized; -iz-
ing** : select, assign, or arrange in a
random way
rang *past of* RING
range \'rānj\ *n* **1** : series of things in a
row **2** : open land for grazing **3**
: cooking stove **4** : variation within
limits **5** : place for target practice **6**
: extent ~ *vb* **ranged; rang•ing 1**
: arrange **2** : roam at large, freely, or
over **3** : vary within limits
rang•er \'rānjər\ *n* : officer who manages and protects public lands

rangy \'rānjē\ *adj* **rang•i•er; -est** : being
slender with long limbs —**rang•i•ness**
n
¹**rank** \'raŋk\ *adj* **1** : vigorous in growth
2 : unpleasantly strong-smelling —
rank•ly *adv* —**rank•ness** *n*
²**rank** *n* **1** : line of soldiers **2** : orderly
arrangement **3** : grade of official
standing **4** : position within a group
~ *vb* **1** : arrange in formation or according to class **2** : take or have a relative position
rank and file *n* : general membership
ran•kle \'raŋkəl\ *vb* **-kled; -kling**
: cause anger, irritation, or bitterness
ran•sack \'ran,sak\ *vb* : search through
and rob
ran•som \'ransəm\ *n* : something demanded for the freedom of a captive
~ *vb* : gain the freedom of by paying
a price —**ran•som•er** *n*
rant \'rant\ *vb* : talk or scold violently
—**rant•er** *n* —**rant•ing•ly** *adv*
¹**rap** \'rap\ *n* : sharp blow or rebuke ~
vb **-pp-** : strike or criticize sharply
²**rap** *vb* **-pp-** : talk freely
ra•pa•cious \rə'pāshəs\ *adj* **1** : excessively greedy **2** : ravenous —**ra•pa-
cious•ly** *adv* —**ra•pa•cious•ness** *n* —
ra•pac•i•ty \-'pasətē\ *n*
¹**rape** \'rāp\ *n* : herb grown as a forage
crop and for its seeds (**rape•seed**)
²**rape** *vb* **raped; rap•ing** : force to have
sexual intercourse —**rape** *n* —**rap•er**
n —**rap•ist** \'rāpist\ *n*
rap•id \'rapəd\ *adj* : very fast —**ra•pid-
i•ty** \rə'pidətē\ *n* —**rap•id•ly** *adv*
rap•ids \-ədz\ *n pl* : place in a stream
where the current is swift
ra•pi•er \'rāpēər\ *n* : narrow 2-edged
sword
rap•ine \'rapən, -,īn\ *n* : plunder
rap•port \ra'pōr\ *n* : harmonious relationship
rapt \'rapt\ *adj* : engrossed —**rapt•ly**
adv —**rapt•ness** *n*
rap•ture \'rapchər\ *n* : spiritual or emotional ecstasy —**rap•tur•ous** \-chə-
rəs\ *adj* —**rap•tur•ous•ly** *adv*
¹**rare** \'rar\ *adj* **rar•er; rar•est** : having
a portion relatively uncooked
²**rare** *adj* **rar•er; rar•est 1** : not dense
2 : unusually fine **3** : seldom met with
—**rare•ly** *adv* —**rare•ness** *n* —**rar-
i•ty** \'rarətē\ *n*
rar•e•fy \'rarə,fī\ *vb* **-fied; -fy•ing**

: make or become rare, thin, or less dense —**rar·e·fac·tion** \,rarə'fak-shən\ n

rar·ing \'rarən, -iŋ\ adj : full of enthusiasm

ras·cal \'raskəl\ n : mean, dishonest, or mischievous person —**ras·cal·i·ty** \ras'kalətē\ n —**ras·cal·ly** \'raskəlē\ adj

¹**rash**\'rash\ adj : too hasty in decision or action —**rash·ly** adv —**rash·ness** n

²**rash** n : a breaking out of the skin with red spots

rasp \'rasp\ vb 1 : rub with or as if with a rough file 2 : to speak in a grating tone ~ n : coarse file

rasp·ber·ry \'raz,berē\ n : edible red or black berry

rat \'rat\ n : destructive rodent larger than the mouse ~ vb : betray or inform on

ratch·et \'rachət\ n : notched device for allowing motion in one direction

rate \'rāt\ n 1 : quantity, amount, or degree measured in relation to some other quantity 2 : rank ~ vb **rat·ed**; **rat·ing** 1 : estimate or determine the rank or quality of 2 : deserve

rath·er \'rathər, 'rath-, 'rāth-\ adv 1 : preferably 2 : on the other hand 3 : more properly 4 : somewhat

rat·i·fy \'ratə,fī\ vb **-fied**; **-fy·ing** : approve and accept formally —**rat·i·fi·ca·tion** \,ratəfə'kāshən\ n

rat·ing \'rātiŋ\ n : classification according to grade

ra·tio \'rāshēō\ n, pl **-tios** : relation in number, quantity, or degree between things

ra·tion \'rashən, 'rāshən\ n : share or allotment (as of food) ~ vb : use or allot sparingly

ra·tio·nal \'rashənəl\ adj 1 : having reason or sanity 2 : relating to reason —**ra·tio·nal·ly** adv

ra·tio·nale \,rashə'nal\ n 1 : explanation of principles of belief or practice 2 : underlying reason

ra·tio·nal·ize \'rashənə,līz\ vb **-ized**; **-iz·ing** : justify (as one's behavior or weaknesses) esp. to oneself —**ra·tio·nal·i·za·tion** \,rashənələ'zāshən\ n

rat·tan \ra'tan, rə-\ n : palm with long stems used esp. for canes and wickerwork

rat·tle \'rat⁰l\ vb **-tled**; **-tling** 1 : make a series of clattering sounds 2 : say

briskly 3 : confuse or upset ~ n 1 : series of clattering sounds 2 : something (as a toy) that rattles

rat·tler \'ratlər\ n : rattlesnake

rat·tle·snake n : American venomous snake with a rattle at the end of the tail

rat·ty \'ratē\ adj **rat·ti·er**; **-est** : shabby

rau·cous \'rókəs\ adj : harsh or boisterous —**rau·cous·ly** adv —**rau·cous·ness** n

rav·age \'ravij\ n : destructive effect ~ vb **-aged**; **-ag·ing** : lay waste —**rav·ag·er** n

rave \'rāv\ vb **raved**; **rav·ing** 1 : talk wildly in or as if in delirium 2 : talk with extreme enthusiasm ~ n 1 : act of raving 2 : enthusiastic praise

rav·el \'ravəl\ vb **-eled** or **-elled**; **-el·ing** or **-el·ling** 1 : unravel 2 : tangle ~ n 1 : something tangled 2 : loose thread

ra·ven \'rāvən\ n : large black bird ~ adj : black and shiny

rav·en·ous \'ravənəs\ adj : very hungry —**rav·en·ous·ly** adv —**rav·en·ous·ness** n

ra·vine \rə'vēn\ n : narrow steep-sided valley

rav·ish \'ravish\ vb 1 : seize and take away by violence 2 : overcome with joy or delight 3 : rape —**rav·ish·er** n —**rav·ish·ment** n

raw \'ró\ adj **raw·er** \'róər\; **raw·est** \'róəst\ 1 : not cooked 2 : not processed 3 : not trained 4 : having the surface rubbed off 5 : cold and damp 6 : vulgar —**raw·ness** n

raw·hide \'ró,hīd\ n : untanned skin of cattle

ray \'rā\ n 1 : thin beam of radiant energy (as light) 2 : tiny bit

ray·on \'rā,än\ n : fabric made from cellulose fiber

raze \'rāz\ vb **razed**; **raz·ing** : destroy or tear down

ra·zor \'rāzər\ n : sharp cutting instrument used to shave off hair

re- \rē, ,rē, 'rē\ prefix 1 : again or anew 2 : back or backward

reaccelerate	readdress
reaccept	readjust
reacclimatize	readjustment
reaccredit	readmit
reacquaint	readopt
reacquire	reaffirm
reactivate	realign
reactivation	realignment

reallocate
reanalysis
reanalyze
reappear
reappearance
reapply
reappoint
reapportion
reappraisal
reappraise
reapprove
reargue
rearrange
rearrest
reassemble
reassert
reassess
reassessment
reassign
reassignment
reattach
reattain
reawaken
rebalance
rebaptize
rebid
rebind
reborn
rebroadcast
rebuild
rebury
recalculate
recapture
recast
recertification
recertify
rechannel
recharge
rechargeable
recheck
rechristen
recirculate
recirculation
reclassification
reclassify
recolonize
recombine
recompute
reconceive
reconnect
reconquer
reconquest
reconsider
reconsideration
reconsolidate
reconstruct
recontaminate
reconvene

reconvict
recopy
re-create
recross
redecorate
rededicate
rededication
redefine
redeposit
redesign
redevelop
rediscover
rediscovery
redissolve
redistribute
redraft
redraw
reemerge
reemergence
reemphasize
reenergize
reengage
reenlist
reenlistment
reenroll
reenter
reequip
reestablish
reestablishment
reestimate
reevaluate
reevaluation
reexamination
reexamine
refinance
refire
refloat
refocus
refold
reformulate
refreeze
refuel
regain
regrow
regrowth
rehear
reheat
rehire
rehospitaliza-
   tion
rehospitalize
reidentify
reignite
reimplant
reimpose
reincorporate
reindict
reinfection

reinflate
reinject
reinjection
reinoculate
reinsert
reinsertion
reinspect
reinstall
reinstitute
reintegrate
reintegration
reinter
reintroduce
reinvent
reinvestigate
reinvestigation
reinvigorate
rejudge
rekindle
reknit
relabel
relandscape
relaunch
relearn
relight
reline
reload
remarriage
remarry
rematch
remelt
remobilize
remoisten
remold
remotivate
rename
renegotiate
reoccupy
reoccur
reoccurrence
reoperate
reorchestrate
reorganization
reorganize
reorient
repack
repave
rephotograph
replan
replaster
replay
replot
repolish
repopulate
repressurize
reprice
reprint
reprocess

reprogram
reread
rereading
rerecord
reregister
reroof
reroute
resalable
resale
reschedule
reseal
resegregate
resell
resentence
reset
resettle
resew
reshoot
reshow
resocialization
resod
resolidify
restage
restart
restate
restatement
restimulate
restock
restructure
restudy
restyle
resubmit
resupply
resurface
resurvey
resynthesis
resynthesize
retarget
reteach
retell
retest
rethink
retighten
retrain
retranslate
retransmit
retry
retune
retype
reupholster
reusable
reuse
reutilize
revaccinate
revaccination
revisit
rewash
reweave

rewind rewrap
rewire

reach \'rēch\ vb 1 : stretch out 2 : touch or try to touch or grasp 3 : extend to or arrive at 4 : communicate with ~ n 1 : act of reaching 2 : distance one can reach 3 : ability to reach —**reach·able** adj —**reach·er** n

re·act \rē'akt\ vb 1 : act in response to some influence or stimulus 2 : undergo chemical change —**re·active** \-'aktiv\ adj

re·ac·tion \rē'akshən\ n 1 : action or emotion caused by and directly related or counter to another action 2 : chemical change

re·ac·tion·ary \-shə,nerē\ adj : relating to or favoring return to an earlier political order or policy —**reactionary** n

re·ac·tor \rē'aktər\ n 1 : one that reacts 2 : device for the controlled release of nuclear energy

read \'rēd\ vb read \'red\; **read·ing** \'rēdiŋ\ 1 : understand written language 2 : utter aloud printed words 3 : interpret 4 : study 5 : indicate ~ adj \'red\ : informed by reading —**read·a·bil·i·ty** \,rēdə'bilətē\ n —**read·able** adj —**read·ably** adv —**read·er** n —**read·er·ship** n

read·ing \'rēdiŋ\ n 1 : something read or for reading 2 : particular version, interpretation, or performance 3 : data indicated by an instrument

ready \'redē\ adj **read·i·er; -est** 1 : prepared or available for use or action 2 : willing to do something ~ vb **read·ied; ready·ing** : make ready ~ n : state of being ready —**read·i·ly** adv —**read·i·ness** n

re·al \'rēl\ adj 1 : relating to fixed or immovable things (as land) 2 : genuine 3 : not imaginary ~ adv : very —**re·al·ness** n —**for real** 1 : in earnest 2 : genuine

real estate n : property in houses and land

re·al·ism \'rēə,lizəm\ n 1 : disposition to deal with facts practically 2 : faithful portrayal of reality —**re·al·ist** \-list\ adj or n —**re·al·is·tic** \,rēə'listik\ adj —**re·al·is·ti·cal·ly** \-ti-klē\ adv

re·al·i·ty \rē'alətē\ n, pl **-ties** 1 : quality or state of being real 2 : something real

re·al·ize \'rēə,līz\ vb **-ized; -iz·ing** 1 : make actual 2 : obtain 3 : be aware of —**re·al·iz·able** adj —**re·al·i·za·tion** \,rēələ'zāshən\ n

re·al·ly \'rēlē, 'ril-\ adv : in truth

realm \'relm\ n 1 : kingdom 2 : sphere

¹ream \'rēm\ n : quantity of paper that is 480, 500, or 516 sheets

²ream vb : enlarge, shape, or clean with a specially shaped tool (**reamer**)

reap \'rēp\ vb : cut or clear (as a crop) with a scythe or machine —**reap·er** n

¹rear \'rir\ vb 1 : raise upright 2 : breed or bring up 3 : rise on the hind legs

²rear n 1 : back 2 : position at the back of something ~ adj : being at the back —**rear·ward** \-wərd\ adj or adv

rear admiral n : commissioned officer in the navy or coast guard ranking next below a vice admiral

rea·son \'rēz⁰n\ n 1 : explanation or justification 2 : motive for action or belief 3 : power or process of thinking ~ vb 1 : use the faculty of reason 2 : try to persuade another —**rea·son·er** n —**rea·son·ing** \'rēz⁰niŋ\ n

rea·son·able \'rēz⁰nəbəl\ adj 1 : being within the bounds of reason 2 : inexpensive —**rea·son·able·ness** n —**rea·son·ably** \-blē\ adv

re·as·sure \,rēə'shúr\ vb : restore one's confidence —**re·as·sur·ance** \-'shúr-əns\ n —**re·as·sur·ing·ly** adv

re·bate \'rē,bāt\ n : return of part of a payment —**rebate** vb

reb·el \'rebəl\ n : one that resists authority ~ \ri'bel\ vb **-belled; -bel·ling** 1 : resist authority 2 : feel or exhibit anger —**rebel** \'rebəl\ adj

re·bel·lion \ri'belyən\ n : resistance to authority and esp. to one's government

re·bel·lious \-yəs\ adj 1 : engaged in rebellion 2 : inclined to resist authority —**re·bel·lious·ly** adv —**re·bel·lious·ness** n

re·birth \'rē'bərth\ n 1 : new or second birth 2 : revival

re·bound \'rē'baúnd, ri-\ vb 1 : spring back on striking something 2 : recover from a reverse ~ \'rē,-\ n 1 : action of rebounding 2 : reaction to a reverse

re·buff \ri'bəf\ vb : refuse or repulse rudely —**rebuff** n

re·buke \-'byük\ vb **-buked; -buk·ing** : reprimand sharply —**rebuke** n

re·bus \'rēbəs\ n : riddle representing syllables or words with pictures

re·but \ri'bət\ vb -but·ted; -but·ting : refute —**re·but·ter** n

re·but·tal \-ᵊl\ n : opposing argument

re·cal·ci·trant \ri'kalsətrənt\ adj 1 : stubbornly resisting authority 2 : resistant to handling or treatment —**re·cal·ci·trance** \-trəns\ n

re·call \ri'kȯl\ vb 1 : call back 2 : remember 3 : revoke ∼ \ri'-, 'rē,-\ 1 : a summons to return 2 : remembrance 3 : act of revoking

re·cant \ri'kant\ vb : take back (something said) publicly

re·ca·pit·u·late \,rēkə'pichə,lāt\ vb -lat·ed; -lat·ing : summarize —**re·ca·pit·u·la·tion** \-,picha'lāshən\ n

re·cede \ri'sēd\ vb -ced·ed; -ced·ing 1 : move back or away 2 : slant backward

re·ceipt \-'sēt\ n 1 : act of receiving 2 : something (as payment) received — usu. in pl. 3 : writing acknowledging something received

re·ceive \ri'sēv\ vb -ceived; -ceiv·ing 1 : take in or accept 2 : greet or entertain (visitors) 3 : pick up radio waves and convert into sounds or pictures —**re·ceiv·able** adj

re·ceiv·er \ri'sēvər\ n 1 : one that receives 2 : one having charge of property or money involved in a lawsuit 3 : apparatus for receiving radio waves —**re·ceiv·er·ship** n

re·cent \'rēsᵊnt\ adj 1 : having lately come into existence 2 : of the present time or time just past —**re·cent·ly** adv —**re·cent·ness** n

re·cep·ta·cle \ri'septikəl\ n : container

re·cep·tion \ri'sepshən\ n 1 : act of receiving 2 : social gathering at which guests are formally welcomed

re·cep·tion·ist \-shənist\ n : person employed to greet callers

re·cep·tive \ri'septiv\ adj : open and responsive to ideas, impressions, or suggestions —**re·cep·tive·ly** adv —**re·cep·tive·ness** n —**re·cep·tiv·i·ty** \,rē,sep'tivətē\ n

re·cess \'rē,ses, ri'ses\ n 1 : indentation in a line or surface 2 : suspension of a session for rest ∼ vb 1 : make a recess in or put into a recess 2 : interrupt a session for a recess

re·ces·sion \ri'seshən\ n 1 : departing procession 2 : period of reduced economic activity

rec·i·pe \'resə,pē\ n : instructions for making something

re·cip·i·ent \ri'sipēənt\ n : one that receives

re·cip·ro·cal \ri'siprəkəl\ adj 1 : affecting each in the same way 2 : so related that one is equivalent to the other —**re·cip·ro·cal·ly** adv —**re·ci·proc·i·ty** \,resə'präsətē\ n

re·cip·ro·cate \-,kāt\ vb -cat·ed; -cat·ing : make a return for something done or given —**re·cip·ro·ca·tion** \-,siprə'kāshən\ n

re·cit·al \ri'sītᵊl\ n 1 : public reading or recitation 2 : music or dance concert or exhibition by pupils —**re·cit·al·ist** \-ᵊlist\ n

rec·i·ta·tion \,resə'tāshən\ n : a reciting or recital

re·cite \ri'sīt\ vb -cit·ed; -cit·ing 1 : repeat verbatim 2 : recount —**re·cit·er** n

reck·less \'rekləs\ adj : lacking caution —**reck·less·ly** adv —**reck·less·ness** n

reck·on \'rekən\ vb 1 : count or calculate 2 : consider

reck·on·ing n 1 : act or instance of reckoning 2 : settling of accounts

re·claim \ri'klām\ vb 1 : change to a desirable condition 2 : obtain from a waste product or by-product 3 : demand or obtain the return of —**re·claim·able** adj —**rec·la·ma·tion** \,reklə'māshən\ n

re·cline \ri'klīn\ vb -clined; -clin·ing : lean backward or lie down

rec·luse \'rek,lüs, ri'klüs\ n : one who leads a secluded or solitary life

rec·og·ni·tion \,rekig'nishən\ n : act of recognizing or state of being recognized

re·cog·ni·zance \ri'känəzəns, -'käg-\ n : promise recorded before a court

rec·og·nize \'rekig,nīz\ vb -nized; -niz·ing 1 : identify as previously known 2 : take notice of 3 : acknowledge esp. with appreciation —**rec·og·niz·able** \'rekəg,nīzəbəl\ adj —**rec·og·niz·ably** \-blē\ adv

re·coil \ri'kȯil\ vb : draw or spring back ∼ \'rē,-, ri'-\ n : action of recoiling

rec·ol·lect \,rekə'lekt\ vb : remember

rec·ol·lec·tion \,rekə'lekshən\ n 1 : act or power of recollecting 2 : something recollected

rec·om·mend \,rekə'mend\ vb 1

: present as deserving of acceptance or trial **2** : advise —**rec·om·mend·able** \-'mendəbəl\ adj

rec·om·men·da·tion \‚rekəmən'dāshən\ n **1** : act of recommending **2** : something recommended or that recommends

rec·om·pense \'rekəm‚pens\ n : compensation —**recompense** vb

rec·on·cile \'rekən‚sīl\ vb **-ciled; -cil·ing 1** : cause to be friendly again **2** : adjust or settle **3** : bring to acceptance —**rec·on·cil·able** adj —**rec·on·cile·ment** n —**rec·on·cil·er** n —**rec·on·cil·i·a·tion** \‚rekən‚silē'āshən\ n

re·con·dite \'rekən‚dīt, ri'kän-\ adj **1** : hard to understand **2** : little known

re·con·di·tion \‚rēkən'dishən\ vb : restore to good condition

re·con·nais·sance \ri'känəzəns, -səns\ n : exploratory survey of enemy territory

re·con·noi·ter, re·con·noi·tre \‚rēkə-'nóitər, ‚rekə-\ vb **-tered** or **-tred; -ter·ing** or **-tring** : make a reconnaissance of

re·cord \ri'kórd\ vb **1** : set down in writing **2** : register permanently **3** : indicate **4** : preserve (as sound or images) for later reproduction ~ \'rekərd\ n **1** : something recorded **2** : best performance

re·cord·er \ri'kórdər\ n **1** : person or device that records **2** : wind instrument with finger holes

¹re·count \ri'kaùnt\ vb : relate in detail

²re·count \‚rē'-\ vb : count again —**re·count** \'rē‚-, ‚rē'-\ n

re·coup \ri'küp\ vb : make up for (an expense or loss)

re·course \'rē‚kórs, ri'-\ n : source of aid or a turning to such a source

re·cov·er \ri'kəvər\ vb **1** : regain position, poise, or health **2** : recoup —**re·cov·er·able** adj —**re·cov·ery** \-'kə-vərē\ n

rec·re·a·tion \‚rekrē'āshən\ n : a refreshing of strength or spirits as a change from work or study —**rec·re·a·tion·al** \-shənəl\ adj

re·crim·i·na·tion \ri‚krimə'nāshən\ n : retaliatory accusation —**re·crim·i·nate** vb

re·cruit \ri'krüt\ n : newly enlisted member ~ vb : enlist the membership or services of —**re·cruit·er** n —**re·cruit·ment** n

rect·an·gle \'rek‚taŋgəl\ n : 4-sided figure with 4 right angles —**rect·an·gu·lar** \rek'taŋgyələr\ adj

rec·ti·fy \'rektə‚fī\ vb **-fied; -fy·ing** : make or set right —**rec·ti·fi·ca·tion** \‚rektəfə'kāshən\ n

rec·ti·tude \'rektə‚tüd, -‚tyüd\ n : moral integrity

rec·tor \'rektər\ n : pastor

rec·to·ry \'rektərē\ n, pl **-ries** : rector's residence

rec·tum \'rektəm\ n, pl **-tums** or **-ta** \-tə\ : last part of the intestine joining the colon and anus —**rec·tal** \-t⁹l\ adj

re·cum·bent \ri'kəmbənt\ adj : lying down

re·cu·per·ate \ri'küpə‚rāt, -'kyü-\ vb **-at·ed; -at·ing** : recover (as from illness) —**re·cu·per·a·tion** \-‚küpə-'rāshən, -‚kyü-\ n —**re·cu·per·a·tive** \-'küpərātiv, -'kyü-\ adj

re·cur \ri'kər\ vb **-rr- 1** : return in thought or talk **2** : occur again —**re·cur·rence** \-'kərəns\ n —**re·cur·rent** \-ənt\ adj

re·cy·cle \rē'sīkəl\ vb : process (as glass or cans) in order to regain a material for human use —**re·cy·cla·ble** \-kələbəl\ adj

red \'red\ n **1** : color of blood or of the ruby **2** cap : communist —**red** adj —**red·dish** adj —**red·ness** n

red·den \'red⁹n\ vb : make or become red or reddish

re·deem \ri'dēm\ vb **1** : regain, free, or rescue by paying a price **2** : atone for **3** : free from sin **4** : convert into something of value —**re·deem·able** adj —**re·deem·er** n

re·demp·tion \-'dempshən\ n : act of redeeming —**re·demp·tive** \-tiv\ adj —**re·demp·to·ry** \-tərē\ adj

red·head \-‚hed\ n : one having red hair —**red·head·ed** \-'hedəd\ adj

red·o·lent \'red⁹lənt\ adj **1** : having a fragrance **2** : suggestive —**red·o·lence** \-əns\ n —**red·o·lent·ly** adv

re·dou·ble \rē'dəbəl\ vb **1** : make twice as great in size or amount **2** : intensify

re·doubt \ri'daùt\ n : small fortification

re·doubt·able \-əbəl\ adj : arousing dread

re·dound \ri'daùnd\ vb : have an effect

re·dress \ri'dres\ vb : set right ~ n **1** : relief or remedy **2** : compensation

red tape n : complex obstructive official routine

re·duce \ri'düs, -'dyüs\ vb **-duced; -duc·ing 1** : lessen **2** : put in a lower rank

3 : lose weight—**re·duc·er** n —**re·duc·ible** \-'düsəbəl, -'dyü-\ adj

re·duc·tion \ri'dəkshən\ n 1 : act of reducing 2 : amount lost in reducing 3 : something made by reducing

re·dun·dant \ri'dəndənt\ adj : using more words than necessary —**re·dun·dan·cy** \-dənsē\ n —**re·dun·dant·ly** adv

red·wood n : tall coniferous timber tree

reed \'rēd\ n 1 : tall slender grass of wet areas 2 : elastic strip that vibrates to produce tones in certain wind instruments —**reedy** adj

reef \'rēf\ n : ridge of rocks or sand at or near the surface of the water

reek \'rēk\ n : strong or disagreeable fume or odor ~ vb : give off a reek

¹reel \'rēl\ n : revolvable device on which something flexible is wound or a quantity of something wound on it ~ vb 1 : wind on a reel 2 : pull in by reeling —**reel·able** adj —**reel·er** n

²reel vb 1 : whirl or waver as from a blow 2 : walk or move unsteadily ~ n : reeling motion

³reel n : lively dance

re·fer \ri'fər\ vb -rr- 1 : direct or send to some person or place 2 : submit for consideration or action 3 : have connection 4 : mention or allude to something —**re·fer·able** \'refərəbəl, ri-'fərə-\ adj —**re·fer·ral** \ri'fərəl\ n

ref·er·ee \,refə'rē\ n 1 : one to whom an issue is referred for settlement 2 : sports official ~ vb -eed; -ee·ing : act as referee

ref·er·ence \'refərəns\ n 1 : act of referring 2 : a bearing on a matter 3 : consultation for information 4 : person who can speak for one's character or ability or a recommendation given by such a person

ref·er·en·dum \,refə'rendəm\ n, pl -da \-də\ or -dums : a submitting of legislative measures for voters' approval or rejection

re·fill \,rē'fil\ vb : fill again —**re·fill** \'rē-,-\ n —**re·fill·able** adj

re·fine \ri'fīn\ vb -fined; -fin·ing 1 : free from impurities or waste matter 2 : improve or perfect 3 : free or become free of what is coarse or uncouth —**re·fine·ment** \-mənt\ n —**re·fin·er** n

re·fin·ery \ri'fīnərē\ n, pl -er·ies : place for refining (as oil or sugar)

re·flect \ri'flekt\ vb 1 : bend or cast back

(as light or heat) 2 : bring as a result 3 : cast reproach or blame 4 : ponder —**re·flec·tion** \-'flekshən\ n —**re·flec·tive** \-tiv\ adj —**re·flec·tor** \ri-'flektər\ n

re·flex \'rē,fleks\ n : automatic response to a stimulus ~ adj 1 : bent back 2 : relating to a reflex —**re·flex·ly** adv

re·flex·ive \ri'fleksiv\ adj : of or relating to an action directed back upon the doer or the grammatical subject —**reflexive** n—**re·flex·ive·ly** adv —**re·flex·ive·ness** n

re·form \ri'fórm\ vb : make or become better esp. by correcting bad habits —**reform** n —**re·form·able** adj —**re·for·ma·tive** \-'fórmətiv\ adj —**re·form·er** n

re·for·ma·to·ry \ri'fórmə,tōrē\ n, pl -ries : penal institution for reforming young offenders

re·fract \ri'frakt\ vb : subject to refraction

re·frac·tion \-'frakshən\ n : the bending of a ray (as of light) when it passes from one medium into another —**re·frac·tive** \-tiv\ adj

re·frac·to·ry \ri'fraktərē\ adj : obstinate or unmanageable

re·frain \ri'frān\ vb : hold oneself back ~ n : verse recurring regularly in a song —**re·frain·ment** n

re·fresh \ri'fresh\ vb 1 : make or become fresh or fresher 2 : supply or take refreshment —**re·fresh·er** n —**re·fresh·ing·ly** adv

re·fresh·ment \-mənt\ n 1 : act of refreshing 2 pl : light meal

re·frig·er·ate \ri'frijə,rāt\ vb -at·ed; -at·ing : chill or freeze (food) for preservation —**re·frig·er·ant** \-ərənt\ adj or n —**re·frig·er·a·tion** \-,frijə'rāshən\ n —**re·frig·er·a·tor** \-'frijə,rātər\ n

ref·uge \'ref,yüj\ n 1 : protection from danger 2 : place that provides protection

ref·u·gee \,refyù'jē\ n : person who flees for safety

re·fund \ri'fənd, 'rē,fənd\ vb : give or put back (money) ~ \'rē,-\ n 1 : act of refunding 2 : sum refunded —**re·fund·able** adj

re·fur·bish \ri'fərbish\ vb : renovate

¹re·fuse \ri'fyüz\ vb -fused; -fus·ing : decline to accept, do, or give — **re·fus·al** \-'fyüzəl\ n

²ref·use \'ref,yüs, -,yüz\ *n* : worthless matter

re·fute \ri'fyüt\ *vb* -fut·ed; -fut·ing : prove to be false —ref·u·ta·tion \,refyü'tāshən\ *n* —refut·er \ri-'fyütər\ *n*

re·gal \'rēgəl\ *adj* 1 : befitting a king 2 : stately —re·gal·ly *adv*

re·gale \ri'gāl\ *vb* -galed; -gal·ing 1 : entertain richly or agreeably 2 : delight

re·ga·lia \ri'gālyə\ *n pl* 1 : symbols of royalty 2 : insignia of an office or order 3 : finery

re·gard \ri'gärd\ *n* 1 : consideration 2 : feeling of approval and liking 3 *pl* : friendly greetings 4 : relation ~ *vb* 1 : pay attention to 2 : show respect for 3 : have an opinion of 4 : look at 5 : relate to —re·gard·ful *adj* —re·gard·less *adj*

re·gard·ing *prep* : concerning

regardless of \ri'gärdləs-\ *prep* : in spite of

re·gen·er·ate \ri'jenərət\ *adj* 1 : formed or created again 2 : spiritually reborn ~ \-'jenə,rāt\ *vb* 1 : reform completely 2 : replace (a lost body part) by new tissue growth 3 : give new life to —re·gen·er·a·tion \-,jenə'rāshən\ *n* —re·gen·er·a·tive \-'jenə,rātiv\ *adj* —re·gen·er·a·tor \-,rātər\ *n*

re·gent \'rējənt\ *n* 1 : person who rules during the childhood, absence, or incapacity of the sovereign 2 : member of a governing board —re·gen·cy \-jənsē\ *n*

re·gime \rā'zhēm, ri-\ *n* : government in power

reg·i·men \'rejəmən\ *n* : systematic course of treatment or training

reg·i·ment \'rejəmənt\ *n* : military unit ~ \-,ment\ *vb* 1 : organize rigidly for control 2 : make orderly —reg·i·men·tal \,rejə'ment⁸l\ *adj* —reg·i·men·ta·tion \-mən'tāshən\ *n*

re·gion \'rējən\ *n* : indefinitely defined area —re·gion·al \'rejənəl\ *adj* —re·gion·al·ly *adv*

reg·is·ter \'rejəstər\ *n* 1 : record of items or details or a book for keeping such a record 2 : device to regulate ventilation 3 : counting or recording device 4 : range of a voice or instrument ~ *vb* 1 : enter in a register 2 : record automatically 3 : get special care for mail by paying more postage

reg·is·trar \-,strär\ *n* : official keeper of records

reg·is·tra·tion \,rejə'strāshən\ *n* 1 : act of registering 2 : entry in a register

reg·is·try \'rejəstrē\ *n, pl* -tries 1 : enrollment 2 : place of registration 3 : official record book

re·gress \ri'gres\ *vb* : go or cause to go back or to a lower level —re·gres·sion \-'greshən\ *n* —re·gres·sive *adj*

re·gret \ri'gret\ *vb* -tt- 1 : mourn the loss or death of 2 : be very sorry for ~ *n* 1 : sorrow or the expression of sorrow 2 *pl* : message declining an invitation —re·gret·ful \-fəl\ *adj* —re·gret·ful·ly *adv* —re·gret·ta·ble \-əbəl\ *adj* —re·gret·ta·bly \-blē\ *adv* —re·gret·ter *n*

reg·u·lar \'regyələr\ *adj* 1 : conforming to what is usual, normal, or average 2 : steady, uniform, or unvarying —regular *n* —reg·u·lar·i·ty \,regyə-'larətē\ *n* —reg·u·lar·ize \'regyələ-,rīz\ *vb* —reg·u·lar·ly *adv*

reg·u·late \'regyə,lāt\ *vb* -lat·ed; -lat·ing 1 : govern according to rule 2 : adjust to a standard —reg·u·la·tive \-,lātiv\ *adj* —reg·u·la·tor \-,lātər\ *n* —reg·u·la·to·ry \-lə,tōrē\ *adj*

reg·u·la·tion \,regyə'lāshən\ *n* 1 : act of regulating 2 : rule dealing with details of procedure

re·gur·gi·tate \rē'gərjə,tāt\ *vb* -tat·ed; -tat·ing : vomit —re·gur·gi·ta·tion \-,gərjə'tāshən\ *n*

re·ha·bil·i·tate \,rēhə'bilə,tāt\ *vb* -tat·ed; -tat·ing 1 : reinstate 2 : make good or usable again —re·ha·bil·i·ta·tion \-,bilə'tāshən\ *n*

re·hears·al \ri'hərsəl\ *n* : practice session or performance

re·hearse \-'hərs\ *vb* -hearsed; -hears·ing 1 : repeat or recount 2 : engage in a rehearsal of —re·hears·er *n*

reign \'rān\ *n* : sovereign's authority or rule ~ *vb* : rule as a sovereign

re·im·burse \,rēəm'bərs\ *vb* -bursed; -burs·ing : repay —re·im·burs·able *adj* —re·im·burse·ment *n*

rein \'rān\ *n* 1 : strap fastened to a bit to control an animal 2 : restraining influence ~ *vb* : direct by reins

re·in·car·na·tion \,rē,in,kär'nāshən\ *n* : rebirth of the soul —re·in·car·nate \,rēin'kär,nāt\ *vb*

rein·deer \'rān,dir\ *n* : caribou

re·in·force \,rēən'fōrs\ *vb* : strengthen

or support —**re·in·force·ment** *n* —**re·in·forc·er** *n*

re·in·state \,rēən'stāt\ *vb* : restore to a former position —**re·in·state·ment** *n*

re·it·er·ate \rē'itə,rāt\ *vb* : say again —**re·it·er·a·tion** \-,itə'rāshən\ *n*

re·ject \ri'jekt\ *vb* **1** : refuse to grant or consider **2** : refuse to admit, believe, or receive **3** : throw out as useless or unsatisfactory ~ \'rē,-\ *n* : rejected person or thing —**re·jec·tion** \-'jekshən\ *n*

re·joice \ri'jóis\ *vb* **-joiced; -joic·ing** : feel joy —**re·joic·er** *n*

re·join *vb* **1** \,rē'jóin\ : join again **2** \ri'-\ : say in answer

re·join·der \ri'jóindər\ *n* : answer

re·ju·ve·nate \ri'jüvə,nāt\ *vb* **-nat·ed; -nat·ing** : make young again —**re·ju·ve·na·tion** \-,jüvə'nāshən\ *n*

re·lapse \ri'laps, 'rē,laps\ *n* : recurrence of illness after a period of improvement ~ \ri'-\ *vb* : suffer a relapse

re·late \ri'lāt\ *vb* **-lat·ed; -lat·ing 1** : give a report of **2** : show a connection between **3** : have a relationship —**re·lat·able** *adj* —**re·lat·er, re·la·tor** *n*

re·la·tion \-'lāshən\ *n* **1** : account **2** : connection **3** : relationship **4** : reference **5** *pl* : dealings

re·la·tion·ship \-,ship\ *n* : the state of being related or interrelated

rel·a·tive \'relətiv\ *n* : person connected with another by blood or marriage ~ *adj* : considered in comparison with something else —**rel·a·tive·ly** *adv* —**rel·a·tive·ness** *n*

re·lax \ri'laks\ *vb* **1** : make or become less tense or rigid **2** : make less severe **3** : seek rest or recreation —**re·lax·er** *n*

re·lax·a·tion \,rē,lak'sāshən\ *n* **1** : lessening of tension **2** : recreation

re·lay \'rē,lā\ *n* : fresh supply (as of horses or people) arranged to relieve others ~ \'rē,-, ri'-\ *vb* **-layed; -lay·ing** : pass along in stages

re·lease \ri'lēs\ *vb* **-leased; -leas·ing 1** : free from confinement or oppression **2** : relinquish **3** : permit publication, performance, exhibition, or sale ~ *n* **1** : relief from trouble **2** : discharge from an obligation **3** : act of releasing or what is released

rel·e·gate \'relə,gāt\ *vb* **-gat·ed; -gat·ing 1** : remove to some less prominent position **2** : assign to a particular class

or sphere —**rel·e·ga·tion** \,relə'gāshən\ *n*

re·lent \ri'lent\ *vb* : become less severe

re·lent·less \-ləs\ *adj* : mercilessly severe or persistent —**re·lent·less·ly** *adv* —**re·lent·less·ness** *n*

rel·e·vance \'reləvəns\ *n* : relation to the matter at hand —**rel·e·vant** \-vənt\ *adj* —**rel·e·vant·ly** *adv*

re·li·able \ri'līəbəl\ *adj* : fit to be trusted —**re·li·abil·i·ty** \-,līə'bilətē\ *n* —**re·li·able·ness** *n* —**re·li·ably** \-'līəblē\ *adv*

re·li·ance \ri'līəns\ *n* : act or result of relying

re·li·ant \ri'līənt\ *adj* : dependent

rel·ic \'relik\ *n* **1** : object venerated because of its association with a saint or martyr **2** : remaining trace

re·lief \ri'lēf\ *n* **1** : lightening of something oppressive **2** : welfare

re·lieve \ri'lēv\ *vb* **-lieved; -liev·ing 1** : free from a burden or distress **2** : release from a post or duty **3** : break the monotony of —**re·liev·er** *n*

re·li·gion \ri'lijən\ *n* **1** : service and worship of God **2** : set or system of religious beliefs —**re·li·gion·ist** *n*

re·li·gious \-'lijəs\ *adj* **1** : relating or devoted to an ultimate reality or deity **2** : relating to religious beliefs or observances **3** : faithful, fervent, or zealous —**re·li·gious·ly** *adv*

re·lin·quish \ri'liŋkwish, -'lin-\ *vb* **1** : renounce **2** : let go of —**re·lin·quish·ment** *n*

rel·ish \'relish\ *n* **1** : keen enjoyment **2** : highly seasoned sauce (as of pickles) ~ *vb* : enjoy —**rel·ish·able** *adj*

re·live \,rē'liv\ *vb* : live over again (as in the imagination)

re·lo·cate \,rē'lō,kāt, ,rēlō'kāt\ *vb* : move to a new location —**re·lo·ca·tion** \,rēlō'kāshən\ *n*

re·luc·tant \ri'ləktənt\ *adj* : feeling or showing doubt or unwillingness —**re·luc·tance** \ri'ləktəns\ *n* —**re·luc·tant·ly** *adv*

re·ly \ri'lī\ *vb* **-lied; -ly·ing** : place faith or confidence—often with *on*

re·main \ri'mān\ *vb* **1** : be left after others have been removed **2** : be something yet to be done **3** : stay behind **4** : continue unchanged

re·main·der \-'māndər\ *n* : that which is left over

re·mains \-'mānz\ *n pl* **1** : remaining part or trace **2** : dead body re·mark \ri'märk\ vb : express as an observation ~ n : passing comment

re·mark·able \-'märkəbəl\ adj : extraordinary —re·mark·able·ness n —re·mark·ably \-blē\ adv

re·me·di·al \ri'mēdēəl\ adj : intended to remedy or improve

rem·e·dy \'remədē\ n, pl -dies 1 : medicine that cures 2 : something that corrects an evil or compensates for a loss ~ vb -died; -dy·ing : provide or serve as a remedy for

re·mem·ber \ri'membər\ vb 1 : think of again 2 : keep from forgetting 3 : convey greetings from

re·mem·brance \-brəns\ n 1 : act of remembering 2 : something that serves to bring to mind

re·mind \ri'mīnd\ vb : cause to remember —re·mind·er n

rem·i·nisce \,remə'nis\ vb -nisced; -nisc·ing : indulge in reminiscence

rem·i·nis·cence \-'nisˀns\ n 1 : recalling of a past experience 2 : account of a memorable experience

rem·i·nis·cent \-ˀnt\ adj 1 : relating to reminiscence 2 : serving to remind —rem·i·nis·cent·ly adv

re·miss \ri'mis\ adj : negligent or careless in performance of duty —re·miss·ly adv —re·miss·ness n

re·mis·sion \ri'mishən\ n 1 : act of forgiving 2 : a period of relief from or easing of symptoms of a disease

re·mit \ri'mit\ vb -tt- 1 : pardon 2 : send money in payment

re·mit·tance \ri'mitˀns\ n : sum of money remitted

rem·nant \'remnənt\ n : small part or trace remaining

re·mod·el \rē'mädˀl\ vb : alter the structure of

re·mon·strance \ri'mänstrəns\ n : act or instance of remonstrating

re·mon·strate \ri'män,strāt\ vb -strated; -strat·ing : speak in protest, reproof, or opposition —re·mon·stra·tion n \ri,män'strāshən, ,remən-\

re·morse \ri'mórs\ n : distress arising from a sense of guilt —re·morse·ful adj —re·morse·less adj

re·mote \ri'mōt\ adj -mot·er; -est 1 : far off in place or time 2 : hard to reach or find 3 : acting, acted on, or controlled indirectly or from afar 4 : slight 5 : distant in manner —re·mote·ly adv —re·mote·ness n

re·move \ri'müv\ vb -moved; -mov·ing

1 : move by lifting or taking off or away 2 : get rid of —re·mov·able adj —re·mov·al \-vəl\ n —re·mov·er n

re·mu·ner·ate \ri'myünə,rāt\ vb -at·ed; -at·ing : pay —re·mu·ner·a·tion n —re·mu·ner·a·tor \-,rātər\ n

re·mu·ner·a·tive \ri'myünərətiv, -,rāt-\ adj : gainful

re·nais·sance \,renə'säns, -'zäns\ n : rebirth or revival

re·nal \'rēnˀl\ adj : relating to the kidneys

rend \'rend\ vb rent \'rent\; rend·ing : tear apart forcibly

ren·der \'rendər\ vb 1 : extract by heating 2 : hand over or give up 3 : do (a service) for another 4 : cause to be or become

ren·dez·vous \'rändi,vü, -dā-\ n, pl ren·dez·vous \-,vüz\ 1 : place appointed for a meeting 2 : meeting at an appointed place ~ vb -voused; -vous·ing : meet at a rendezvous

ren·di·tion \ren'dishən\ n : version

ren·e·gade \'reni,gād\ n : deserter of one faith or cause for another

re·nege \ri'nig, -'neg, -'nēg, -'nāg\ vb -neged; -neg·ing : go back on a promise —re·neg·er n

re·new \ri'nü, -'nyü\ vb 1 : make or become new, fresh, or strong again 2 : begin again 3 : grant or obtain an extension of —re·new·able adj —re·new·al n —re·new·er n

re·nounce \ri'naüns\ vb -nounced; -nounc·ing : give up, refuse, or resign —re·nounce·ment n

ren·o·vate \'renə,vāt\ vb -vat·ed; -vat·ing : make like new again —ren·o·va·tion \,renə'vāshən\ n —ren·o·va·tor \'renə,vātər\ n

re·nown \ri'naün\ n : state of being widely known and honored —re·nowned \-'naünd\ adj

1rent \'rent\ n : money paid or due periodically for the use of another's property ~ vb : hold or give possession and use of for rent —rent·al n or adj — rent·er n

2rent n : a tear in cloth

re·nun·ci·a·tion \ri,nənsē'āshən\ n : act of renouncing

1re·pair \ri'par\ vb : go

2repair vb : restore to good condition ~ n 1 : act or instance of repairing 2 : condition —re·pair·er n —re·pair·man \-,man\ n

rep·a·ra·tion \,repə'rāshən\ n : money paid for redress—usu. pl.

rep·ar·tee \,repär'tē\ n : clever replies

re·past \ri'past, 'rē,past\ n : meal

re·pa·tri·ate \rē'pātrē,āt\ vb -at·ed; -at·ing : send back to one's own country —**re·pa·tri·ate** \-trēət, -trē,āt\ n —**re·pa·tri·a·tion** \-,pātrē'āshən\ n

re·pay \rē'pā\ vb -paid; -pay·ing : pay back —**re·pay·able** adj —**re·pay·ment** n

re·peal \ri'pēl\ vb : annul by legislative action —**repeal** n —**re·peal·er** n

re·peat \ri'pēt\ vb : say or do again ~ n 1 : act of repeating 2 : something repeated —**re·peat·able** adj —**re·peat·ed·ly** adv —**re·peat·er** n

re·pel \ri'pel\ vb -pelled; -pel·ling 1 : drive away 2 : disgust —**re·pel·lent** \-'pelənt\ adj or n

re·pent \ri'pent\ vb 1 : turn from sin 2 : regret —**re·pen·tance** \ri'pentⁿns\ n —**re·pen·tant** \-ⁿnt\ adj

re·per·cus·sion \,rēpər'kəshən, ,rep-\ n : effect of something done or said

rep·er·toire \'repər,twär\ n : pieces a company or performer can present

rep·er·to·ry \'repər,tōrē\ n, pl -ries 1 : repertoire 2 : theater with a resident company doing several plays

rep·e·ti·tion \,repə'tishən\ n : act or instance of repeating

rep·e·ti·tious \-'tishəs\ adj : tediously repeating —**rep·e·ti·tious·ly** adv —**rep·e·ti·tious·ness** n

re·pet·i·tive \ri'petətiv\ adj : repetitious —**re·pet·i·tive·ly** adv —**re·pet·i·tive·ness** n

re·pine \ri'pīn\ vb re·pined; re·pin·ing : feel or express discontent

re·place \ri'plās\ vb 1 : restore to a former position 2 : take the place of 3 : put something new in the place of —**re·place·able** adj —**re·place·ment** n —**re·plac·er** n

re·plen·ish \ri'plenish\ vb : stock or supply anew —**re·plen·ish·ment** n

re·plete \ri'plēt\ adj : full —**re·plete·ness** n —**re·ple·tion** \-'plēshən\ n

rep·li·ca \'replikə\ n : exact copy

rep·li·cate \'replə,kāt\ vb -cat·ed; -cat·ing : duplicate or repeat —**rep·li·cate** \-likət\ n —**rep·li·ca·tion** \-lə'kāshən\ n

re·ply \ri'plī\ vb -plied; -ply·ing : say or do in answer ~ n, pl -plies : answer

re·port \ri'pōrt\ n 1 : rumor 2 : statement of information (as events or causes) 3 : explosive noise ~ vb 1 : give an account of 2 : present an account of (an event) as news 3 : present oneself 4 : make known to authorities —**re·port·age** \ri'pōrtij, ,repər'tāzh, ,rep-,ȯr'-\ n —**re·port·ed·ly** adv —**re·port·er** n —**re·por·to·ri·al** \,repər'tōrēəl\ adj

re·pose \ri'pōz\ vb -posed; -pos·ing : lay or lie at rest ~ n 1 : state of resting 2 : calm or peace —**re·pose·ful** adj

re·pos·i·to·ry \ri'päzə,tōrē\ n, pl -ries : place where something is stored

re·pos·sess \,rēpə'zes\ vb : regain possession and legal ownership of —**re·pos·ses·sion** \-'zeshən\ n

rep·re·hend \,repri'hend\ vb : censure —**rep·re·hen·sion** \-'henchən\ n

rep·re·hen·si·ble \-'hensəbəl\ adj : deserving condemnation —**rep·re·hen·si·bly** adv

rep·re·sent \,repri'zent\ vb 1 : serve as a sign or symbol of 2 : act or speak for 3 : describe as having a specified quality or character —**rep·re·sen·ta·tion** \,repri,zen'tāshən\ n

rep·re·sen·ta·tive \,repri'zentətiv\ adj 1 : standing or acting for another 2 : carried on by elected representatives ~ n 1 : typical example 2 : one that represents another 3 : member of usu. the lower house of a legislature —**rep·re·sen·ta·tive·ly** adv —**rep·re·sen·ta·tive·ness** n

re·press \ri'pres\ vb : restrain or suppress —**re·pres·sion** \-'preshən\ n —**re·pres·sive** \-'presiv\ adj

re·prieve \ri'prēv\ n 1 : a delay in punishment 2 : temporary respite —**re·prieve** vb

rep·ri·mand \'reprə,mand\ n : formal or severe criticism —**reprimand** vb

re·pri·sal \ri'prīzəl\ n : act in retaliation

re·prise \ri'prēz\ n : musical repetition

re·proach \ri'prōch\ n 1 : disgrace 2 : rebuke ~ vb : express disapproval to —**re·proach·ful** adj —**re·proach·ful·ly** adv —**re·proach·ful·ness** n

rep·ro·bate \'reprə,bāt\ n : scoundrel —**reprobate** adj

rep·ro·ba·tion \,reprə'bāshən\ n : strong disapproval

re·pro·duce \,rēprə'düs, -'dyüs\ vb 1 : produce again or anew 2 : produce offspring —**re·pro·duc·ible** \-'düsəbəl, -'dyü-\ adj —**re·pro·duc-**

tion \-'dəkshən\ *n* —**re·pro·duc·tive** \-'dəktiv\ *adj*

re·proof \ri'prüf\ *n* : blame or censure for a fault

re·prove \ri'prüv\ *vb* **-proved; -prov·ing** : express disapproval to or of

rep·tile \'rept^əl, -,tīl\ *n* : air-breathing scaly vertebrate —**rep·til·ian** \rep-'tilēən\ *adj or n*

re·pub·lic \ri'pəblik\ *n* : country with representative government

re·pub·li·can \-likən\ *adj* **1** : relating to or resembling a republic **2** : supporting a republic —**republican** *n* —**re·pub·li·can·ism** *n*

re·pu·di·ate \ri'pyüdē,āt\ *vb* **-at·ed; -at·ing** : refuse to have anything to do with —**re·pu·di·a·tion** \-,pyüdē-'āshən\ *n*

re·pug·nant \ri'pəgnənt\ *adj* : contrary to one's tastes or principles —**re·pug·nance** \-nəns\ *n* —**re·pug·nant·ly** *adv*

re·pulse \ri'pəls\ *vb* **-pulsed; -puls·ing 1** : drive or beat back **2** : rebuff **3** : be repugnant to —**repulse** *n* —**re·pul·sion** \-'pəlshən\ *n*

re·pul·sive \-siv\ *adj* : arousing aversion or disgust —**re·pul·sive·ly** *adv* —**re·pul·sive·ness** *n*

rep·u·ta·ble \'repyətəbəl\ *adj* : having a good reputation —**rep·u·ta·bly** \-blē\ *adv*

rep·u·ta·tion \,repyə'tāshən\ *n* : one's character or public esteem

re·pute \ri'pyüt\ *vb* **-put·ed; -put·ing** : think of as being ~ *n* : reputation —**re·put·ed** *adj* —**re·put·ed·ly** *adv*

re·quest \ri'kwest\ *n* : act or instance of asking for something or a thing asked for ~ *vb* **1** : make a request of **2** : ask for —**re·quest·er** *n*

re·qui·em \'rekwēəm, 'rāk-\ *n* : Mass for a dead person or a musical setting for this

re·quire \ri'kwīr\ *vb* **-quired; -quir·ing 1** : insist on **2** : call for as essential —**re·quire·ment** *n*

req·ui·site \'rekwəzət\ *adj* : necessary —**requisite** *n*

req·ui·si·tion \,rekwə'zishən\ *n* : formal application or demand —**requisition** *vb*

re·quite \ri'kwīt\ *vb* **-quit·ed; -quit·ing** : make return for or to —**re·quit·al** \-'kwīt^əl\ *n*

re·scind \ri'sind\ *vb* : repeal or cancel —**re·scis·sion** \-'sizhən\ *n*

res·cue \'reskyü\ *vb* **-cued; -cu·ing** : set free from danger or confinement —**rescue** *n* —**res·cu·er** *n*

re·search \ri'sərch, 'rē,sərch\ *n* : careful or diligent search esp. for new knowledge —**research** *vb* —**re·search·er** *n*

re·sem·ble \ri'zembəl\ *vb* **-sem·bled; -sem·bling** : be like or similar to —**re·sem·blance** \-'zembləns\ *n*

re·sent \ri'zent\ *vb* : feel or show annoyance at —**re·sent·ful** *adj* —**re·sent·ful·ly** *adv* —**re·sent·ment** *n*

res·er·va·tion \,rezər'vāshən\ *n* **1** : act of reserving or something reserved **2** : limiting condition

re·serve \ri'zərv\ *vb* **-served; -serv·ing 1** : store for future use **2** : set aside for special use ~ *n* **1** : something reserved **2** : restraint in words or bearing **3** : military forces withheld from action or not part of the regular services —**re·served** *adj*

res·er·voir \'rezər,vwär, -,vwör, -,vör, -,vȯi\ *n* : place where something (as water) is kept in store

re·side \ri'zīd\ *vb* **-sid·ed; -sid·ing 1** : make one's home **2** : be present

res·i·dence \'rezədəns\ *n* **1** : act or fact of residing in a place **2** : place where one lives —**res·i·dent** \-ənt\ *adj or n* —**res·i·den·tial** \,rezə'denchəl\ *adj*

res·i·due \'rezə,dü, -,dyü\ *n* : part remaining —**re·sid·u·al** \ri'zijəwəl\ *adj*

re·sign \ri'zīn\ *vb* **1** : give up deliberately **2** : give (oneself) over without resistance —**res·ig·na·tion** \,rezig-'nāshən\ *n* —**re·signed·ly** \-'zīnədlē\ *adv*

re·sil·ience \ri'zilyəns\ *n* : ability to recover or adjust easily

re·sil·ien·cy \-yənsē\ *n* : resilience

re·sil·ient \-yənt\ *adj* : elastic

res·in \'rez^ən\ *n* : substance from the gum or sap of trees —**res·in·ous** *adj*

re·sist \ri'zist\ *vb* **1** : withstand the force or effect of **2** : fight against —**re·sist·ible** \-'zistəbəl\ *adj* —**re·sist·less** *adj*

re·sis·tance \ri'zistəns\ *n* **1** : act of resisting **2** : ability of an organism to resist disease **3** : opposition to electric current

re·sis·tant \-tənt\ *adj* : giving resistance

res·o·lute \'rezə,lüt\ *adj* : having a fixed purpose —**res·o·lute·ly** *adv* —**res·o·lute·ness** *n*

res·o·lu·tion \,rezə'lüshən\ *n* **1** : process of resolving **2** : firmness of purpose **3** : statement of the opinion, will, or intent of a body

re·solve \ri'zälv\ vb -solved; -solv·ing 1 : find an answer to 2 : make a formal resolution ~ n 1 : something resolved 2 : steadfast purpose —re·solv·able adj

res·o·nant \'rezᵊnənt\ adj 1 : continuing to sound 2 : relating to intensification or prolongation of sound (as by a vibrating body) —res·o·nance \-əns\ n —res·o·nant·ly adv

re·sort \ri'zórt\ n 1 : source of help 2 : place to go for vacation ~ vb 1 : go often or habitually 2 : have recourse

re·sound \ri'zaúnd\ vb : become filled with sound

re·sound·ing \-iŋ\ adj : impressive —re·sound·ing·ly adv

re·source \'rē,sórs, ri'sórs\ n 1 : new or reserve source 2 pl : available funds 3 : ability to handle situations —re·source·ful adj —re·source·ful·ness n

re·spect \ri'spekt\ n 1 : relation to something 2 : high or special regard 3 : detail ~ vb : consider deserving of high regard —re·spect·er n —re·spect·ful adj —re·spect·ful·ly adv —re·spect·ful·ness n

re·spect·able \ri'spektəbəl\ adj 1 : worthy of respect 2 : fair in size, quantity, or quality —re·spect·abil·i·ty \-,spektə'bilətē\ n —re·spect·ably \-'spektəblē\ adv

re·spec·tive \-tiv\ adj : individual and specific

re·spec·tive·ly \-lē\ adv 1 : as relating to each 2 : each in the order given

res·pi·ra·tion \,respə'rāshən\ n : act or process of breathing —re·spi·ra·to·ry \'respərə,tōrē, ri'spīrə-\ adj —re·spire \ri'spīr\ vb

res·pi·ra·tor \'respə,rātər\ n : device for artificial respiration

re·spite \'respət\ n : temporary delay or rest

re·splen·dent \ri'splendənt\ adj : shining brilliantly —re·splen·dence \-dəns\ n —re·splen·dent·ly adv

re·spond \ri'spänd\ vb 1 : answer 2 : react —re·spon·dent \-'spändənt\ n or adj —re·spond·er n

re·sponse \ri'späns\ n 1 : act of responding 2 : answer

re·spon·si·ble \ri'spänsəbəl\ adj 1 : answerable for acts or decisions 2 : able to fulfill obligations 3 : having important duties —re·spon·si·bil·i·ty \ri,spänsə'bilətē\ n —re·spon·si·ble·ness n —re·spon·si·bly \-blē\ adv

re·spon·sive \-siv\ adj : quick to respond —re·spon·sive·ly adv —re·spon·sive·ness n

¹rest \'rest\ n 1 : sleep 2 : freedom from work or activity 3 : state of inactivity 4 : something used as a support ~ vb 1 : get rest 2 : cease action or motion 3 : give rest to 4 : sit or lie fixed or supported 5 : depend —rest·ful adj —rest·ful·ly adv

²rest n : remainder

res·tau·rant \'restərənt, -tə,ränt\ n : public eating place

res·ti·tu·tion \,restə'tüshən, -'tyü-\ n : act or fact of restoring something or repaying someone

res·tive \'restiv\ adj : uneasy or fidgety —res·tive·ly adv —res·tive·ness n

rest·less \'restləs\ adj 1 : lacking or giving no rest 2 : always moving 3 : uneasy —rest·less·ly adv —rest·less·ness n

re·store \ri'stōr\ vb -stored; -stor·ing 1 : give back 2 : put back into use or into a former state —re·stor·able adj —res·to·ra·tion \,restə'rāshən\ n —re·stor·ative \ri'stōrətiv\ n or adj —re·stor·er n

re·strain \ri'strān\ vb : limit or keep under control —re·strain·able adj —re·strained \-'strānd\ adj —re·strain·ed·ly \-'strānədlē\ adv —re·strain·er n

restraining order n : legal order directing one person to stay away from another

re·straint \-'strānt\ n 1 : act of restraining 2 : restraining force 3 : control over feelings

re·strict \ri'strikt\ vb 1 : confine within bounds 2 : limit use of —re·stric·tion \-'strikshən\ n —re·stric·tive adj —re·stric·tive·ly adv

re·sult \ri'zəlt\ vb : come about because of something else ~ n 1 : thing that results 2 : something obtained by calculation or investigation —re·sul·tant \-'zəltᵊnt\ adj or n

re·sume \ri'züm\ vb -sumed; -sum·ing : return to or take up again after interruption —re·sump·tion \-'zəmpshən\ n

ré·su·mé, re·su·me, re·su·mé \'rezə,mā, ,rezə'-\ n : summary of one's career and qualifications

re·sur·gence \ri'sərjəns\ n : a rising again —re·sur·gent \-jənt\ adj

res·ur·rect \,rezə'rekt\ vb 1 : raise from

the dead **2** : bring to attention or use again —**res·ur·rec·tion** \-'rekshən\ *n*

re·sus·ci·tate \ri'səsə,tāt\ *vb* **-tat·ed; -tat·ing** : bring back from apparent death —**re·sus·ci·ta·tion** \ri,səsə-'tāshən, ,rē-\ *n* —**re·sus·ci·ta·tor** \-,tātər\ *n*

re·tail \'rē,tāl\ *vb* : sell in small quantities directly to the consumer ~ *n* : business of selling to consumers —**retail** *adj or adv* —**re·tail·er** *n*

re·tain \ri'tān\ *vb* **1** : keep or hold onto **2** : engage the services of

re·tain·er *n* **1** : household servant **2** : retaining fee

re·tal·i·ate \ri'talē,āt\ *vb* **-at·ed; -at·ing** : return (as an injury) in kind —**re·tal·i·a·tion** \-,talē'āshən\ *n* —**re·tal·ia·to·ry** \-'talyə,tōrē\ *adj*

re·tard \ri'tärd\ *vb* : hold back —**re·tar·da·tion** \,rē,tär'dāshən, ri-\ *n*

re·tard·ed \ri'tärdəd\ *adj* : slow or limited in intellectual development

retch \'rech\ *vb* : try to vomit

re·ten·tion \ri'tenchən\ *n* **1** : state of being retained **2** : ability to retain —**re·ten·tive** \-'tentiv\ *adj*

ret·i·cent \'retəsənt\ *adj* : tending not to talk —**ret·i·cence** \-səns\ *n* —**ret·i·cent·ly** *adv*

ret·i·na \'ret³nə\ *n, pl* **-nas** *or* **-nae** \-³n-,ē\ : sensory membrane lining the eye —**ret·i·nal** \'ret³nəl\ *adj*

ret·i·nue \'ret³n,ü, -,yü\ *n* : attendants or followers of a distinguished person

re·tire \ri'tīr\ *vb* **-tired; -tir·ing** **1** : withdraw for privacy **2** : end a career **3** : go to bed —**re·tir·ee** \ri,tī'rē\ *n* —**re·tire·ment** *n*

re·tir·ing \ri'tīriŋ\ *adj* : shy

re·tort \ri'tórt\ *vb* : say in reply ~ *n* : quick, witty, or cutting answer

re·trace \,rē'trās\ *vb* : go over again or in reverse

re·tract \ri'trakt\ *vb* **1** : draw back or in **2** : withdraw a charge or promise —**re·tract·able** *adj* —**re·trac·tion** \-'trakshən\ *n*

re·treat \ri'trēt\ *n* **1** : act of withdrawing **2** : place of privacy or safety or meditation and study ~ *vb* : make a retreat

re·trench \ri'trench\ *vb* : cut down (as expenses) —**re·trench·ment** *n*

ret·ri·bu·tion \,retrə'byushən\ *n* : retaliation —**re·trib·u·tive** \ri'tribyətiv\ *adj* —**re·trib·u·to·ry** \-yə,tōrē\ *adj*

re·trieve \ri'trēv\ *vb* **-trieved; -triev·ing** **1** : search for and bring in game **2**

: recover —**re·triev·able** *adj* —**re·triev·al** \-'trēvəl\ *n*

re·triev·er \-'trēvər\ *n* : dog for retrieving game

ret·ro·ac·tive \,retrō'aktiv\ *adj* : made effective as of a prior date —**ret·ro·ac·tive·ly** *adv*

ret·ro·grade \'retrə,grād\ *adj* **1** : moving backward **2** : becoming worse

ret·ro·gress \,retrə'gres\ *vb* : move backward —**ret·ro·gres·sion** \-'greshən\ *n*

ret·ro·spect \'retrə,spekt\ *n* : review of past events —**ret·ro·spec·tion** \,retrə'spekshən\ *n* —**ret·ro·spec·tive** \-'spektiv\ *adj* —**ret·ro·spec·tive·ly** *adv*

re·turn \ri'tərn\ *vb* **1** : go or come back **2** : pass, give, or send back to an earlier possessor **3** : answer **4** : bring in as a profit **5** : give or do in return ~ *n* **1** : act of returning or something returned **2** *pl* : report of balloting results **3** : statement of taxable income **4** : profit —**return** *adj* —**re·turn·able** *adj or n* —**re·turn·er** *n*

re·union \rē'yünyən\ *n* **1** : act of reuniting **2** : a meeting of persons after a separation

re·vamp \,rē'vamp\ *vb* : renovate or revise

re·veal \ri'vēl\ *vb* **1** : make known **2** : show plainly

rev·eil·le \'revəlē\ *n* : military signal sounded about sunrise

rev·el \'revəl\ *vb* **-eled** *or* **-elled; -el·ing** *or* **-el·ling** **1** : take part in a revel **2** : take great pleasure ~ *n* : wild party or celebration —**rev·el·er, rev·el·ler** \-ər\ *n* —**rev·el·ry** \-rē\ *n*

rev·e·la·tion \,revə'lāshən\ *n* **1** : act of revealing **2** : something enlightening or astonishing

re·venge \ri'venj\ *vb* **-venged; -veng·ing** : avenge ~ *n* **1** : desire for retaliation **2** : act of retaliation —**re·venge·ful** *adj* —**re·veng·er** *n*

rev·e·nue \'revə,nü, -,nyü\ *n* : money collected by a government

re·ver·ber·ate \ri'vərbə,rāt\ *vb* **-at·ed; -at·ing** : resound in a series of echoes —**re·ver·ber·a·tion** \-,vərbə'rāshən\ *n*

re·vere \ri'vir\ *vb* **-vered; -ver·ing** : show honor and devotion to —**rev·er·ence** \'revərəns\ *n* —**rev·er·ent** \-rənt\ *adj* —**rev·er·ent·ly** *adv*

rev·er·end \'revərənd\ adj : worthy of reverence ~ n : clergy member

rev·er·ie \'revərē\ n, pl **-er·ies** : daydream

re·verse \ri'vərs\ adj 1 : opposite to a previous or normal condition 2 : acting in an opposite way ~ vb **-versed; -vers·ing** 1 : turn upside down or completely around 2 : change to the contrary or in the opposite direction ~ n 1 : something contrary 2 : change for the worse 3 : back of something —**re·ver·sal** \-səl\ n —**re·verse·ly** adv —**re·vers·ible** \-'vərsəbəl\ adj

re·vert \ri'vərt\ vb : return to an original type or condition —**re·ver·sion** \-'vərzhən\ n

re·view \ri'vyü\ n 1 : formal inspection 2 : general survey 3 : critical evaluation 4 : second or repeated study or examination ~ vb 1 : examine or study again 2 : reexamine judicially 3 : look back over 4 : examine critically 5 : inspect —**re·view·er** n

re·vile \ri'vīl\ vb **-viled; -vil·ing** : abuse verbally —**re·vile·ment** n —**re·vil·er** n

re·vise \-'vīz\ vb **-vised; -vis·ing** 1 : look over something written to correct or improve 2 : make a new version of —**re·vis·able** adj —**revise** n —**re·vis·er, re·vi·sor** \-'vīzər\ n —**re·vi·sion** \-'vizhən\ n

re·viv·al \-'vīvəl\ n 1 : act of reviving or state of being revived 2 : evangelistic meeting

re·vive \-'vīv\ vb **-vived; -viv·ing** : bring back to life or consciousness or into use —**re·viv·er** n

re·vo·ca·tion \,revə'kāshən\ n : act or instance of revoking

re·voke \ri'vōk\ vb **-voked; -vok·ing** : annul by recalling —**re·vok·er** n

re·volt \-'vōlt\ vb 1 : throw off allegiance 2 : cause or experience disgust or shock ~ n : rebellion or revolution —**re·volt·er** n

re·volt·ing \-iŋ\ adj : extremely offensive —**re·volt·ing·ly** adv

rev·o·lu·tion \,revə'lüshən\ n 1 : rotation 2 : progress in an orbit 3 : sudden, radical, or complete change (as overthrow of a government) —**rev·o·lu·tion·ary** \-shə,nərē\ adj or n

rev·o·lu·tion·ize \-shə,nīz\ vb **-ized; -iz·ing** : change radically —**rev·o·lu·tion·iz·er** n

re·volve \ri'välv\ vb **-volved; -volv·ing** 1 : ponder 2 : move in an orbit 3 : rotate —**re·volv·able** adj

re·volv·er \ri'välvər\ n : pistol with a revolving cylinder

re·vue \ri'vyü\ n : theatrical production of brief numbers

re·vul·sion \ri'vəlshən\ n : complete dislike or repugnance

re·ward \ri'wôrd\ vb : give a reward to or for ~ n : something offered for service or achievement

re·write \rē'rīt\ vb **-wrote; -writ·ten; -writ·ing** : revise —**rewrite** n

rhap·so·dy \'rapsədē\ n, pl **-dies** 1 : expression of extravagant praise 2 : flowing free-form musical composition —**rhap·sod·ic** \rap'sädik\ adj —**rhap·sod·i·cal·ly** \-iklē\ adv —**rhap·so·dize** \'rapsə,dīz\ vb

rhet·o·ric \'retərik\ n : art of speaking or writing effectively —**rhe·tor·i·cal** \ri'tórikəl\ adj —**rhet·o·ri·cian** \,retə'rishən\ n

rheu·ma·tism \'rümə,tizəm, 'rüm-\ n : disorder marked by inflammation or pain in muscles or joints —**rheu·mat·ic** \rü'matik\ adj

rhine·stone \'rīn,stōn\ n : a colorless imitation gem

rhi·no \'rīnō\ n, pl **-no** or **-nos** : rhinoceros

rhi·noc·er·os \rī'näsərəs\ n, pl **-noc·er·os·es** or **-noc·er·os** or **-noc·eri** \-'näsə,rī\ : large thick-skinned mammal with 1 or 2 horns on the snout

rho·do·den·dron \,rōdə'dendrən\ n : flowering evergreen shrub

rhom·bus \'rämbəs\ n, pl **-bus·es** or **-bi** \-,bī\ : parallelogram with equal sides

rhu·barb \'rü,bärb\ n : garden plant with edible stalks

rhyme \'rīm\ n 1 : correspondence in terminal sounds 2 : verse that rhymes ~ vb **rhymed; rhym·ing** : make or have rhymes

rhythm \'rithəm\ n : regular succession of sounds or motions —**rhyth·mic** \'rithmik\, **rhyth·mi·cal** \-mikəl\ adj —**rhyth·mi·cal·ly** adv

rhythm and blues n : popular music based on blues and black folk music

rib \'rib\ n 1 : curved bone joined to the spine 2 : riblike thing ~ vb **-bb-** 1 : furnish or mark with ribs 2 : tease —**rib·ber** n

rib·ald \'ribəld\ adj : coarse or vulgar —**rib·ald·ry** \-əldrē\ n

rib·bon \'ribən\ *n* 1 : narrow strip of fabric used esp. for decoration 2 : strip of inked cloth (as in a typewriter)

ri·bo·fla·vin \,rībə'flāvən, 'rībə,-\ *n* : growth-promoting vitamin

rice \'rīs\ *n, pl* **rice** : starchy edible seeds of an annual cereal grass

rich \'rich\ *adj* 1 : having a lot of money or possessions 2 : valuable 3 : containing much sugar, fat, or seasoning 4 : abundant 5 : deep and pleasing in color or tone 6 : fertile — **rich·ly** *adv* —**rich·ness** *n*

rich·es \'richəz\ *n pl* : wealth

rick·ets \'rikəts\ *n* : childhood bone disease

rick·ety \'rikətē\ *adj* : shaky

rick·sha, rick·shaw \'rik,shô\ *n* : small covered 2-wheeled carriage pulled by one person

ric·o·chet \'rikə,shā, *Brit also* -,shet\ *vb* **-cheted** \-,shād\ *or* **-chet·ted** \-,shetəd\; **-chet·ing** \-,shāiŋ\ *or* **-chet·ting** \-,shetiŋ\ : bounce off at an angle —**ricochet** *n*

rid \'rid\ *vb* **rid; rid·ding** : make free of something unwanted —**rid·dance** \'ridⁿs\ *n*

rid·den \'ridⁿn\ *adj* : overburdened with—used in combination

¹rid·dle \'ridⁿl\ *n* : puzzling question ~ *vb* **-dled; -dling** : speak in riddles

²riddle *vb* **-dled; -dling** : fill full of holes

ride \'rīd\ *vb* **rode** \'rōd\; **rid·den** \'ridⁿn\; **rid·ing** \'rīdiŋ\ 1 : be carried along 2 : sit on and cause to move 3 : travel over a surface 4 : tease or nag ~ *n* 1 : trip on an animal or in a vehicle 2 : mechanical device ridden for amusement

rid·er *n* 1 : one that rides 2 : attached clause or document —**rid·er·less** *adj*

ridge \'rij\ *n* 1 : range of hills 2 : raised line or strip 3 : line of intersection of 2 sloping surfaces —**ridgy** *adj*

rid·i·cule \'ridə,kyül\ *vb* **-culed; -culing** : laugh at or make fun of —**ridicule** *n*

ri·dic·u·lous \rə'dikyələs\ *adj* : arousing ridicule —**ri·dic·u·lous·ly** *adv* —**ri·dic·u·lous·ness** *n*

rife \'rīf\ *adj* : abounding —**rife** *adv*

riff·raff \'rif,raf\ *n* : mob

¹ri·fle \'rīfəl\ *vb* **-fled; -fling** : ransack esp. with intent to steal —**ri·fler** \-flər\ *n*

²rifle *n* : long shoulder weapon with

spiral grooves in the bore —**ri·fle·man** \-mən\ *n* —**ri·fling** *n*

rift \'rift\ *n* : separation —**rift** *vb*

¹rig \'rig\ *vb* **-gg-** 1 : fit out with rigging 2 : set up esp. as a makeshift ~ *n* 1 : distinctive shape, number, and arrangement of sails and masts of a sailing ship 2 : equipment 3 : carriage with its horse

²rig *vb* **-gg-** : manipulate esp. by deceptive or dishonest means

rig·ging \'rigiŋ, -ən\ *n* : lines that hold and move the masts, sails, and spars of a sailing ship

right \'rīt\ *adj* 1 : meeting a standard of conduct 2 : correct 3 : genuine 4 : normal 5 : opposite of left ~ *n* 1 : something that is correct, just, proper, or honorable 2 : something to which one has a just claim 3 : something that is on the right side ~ *adv* 1 : according to what is right 2 : immediately 3 : completely 4 : on or to the right ~ *vb* 1 : restore to a proper state 2 : bring or become upright again —**right·er** *n* —**right·ness** *n* —**right·ward** \-wərd\ *adj*

right angle *n* : angle whose sides are perpendicular to each other —**right-an·gled** \'rīt'aŋgəld\ *or* **right-an·gle** \-gəl\ *adj*

righ·teous \'rīchəs\ *adj* : acting or being in accordance with what is just or moral —**righ·teous·ly** *adv* —**righ·teous·ness** *n*

right·ful \'rītfəl\ *adj* : lawful —**right·ful·ly** \-ē\ *adv* —**right·ful·ness** *n*

right·ly \'rītlē\ *adv* 1 : justly 2 : properly 3 : correctly

rig·id \'rijəd\ *adj* : lacking flexibility —**ri·gid·i·ty** \rə'jidətē\ *n* —**rig·id·ly** *adv*

rig·ma·role \'rigmə,rōl, 'rigə-\ *n* 1 : meaningless talk 2 : complicated often unnecessary procedure

rig·or \'rigər\ *n* : severity —**rig·or·ous** *adj* —**rig·or·ous·ly** *adv*

rig·or mor·tis \,rigər'mórtəs\ *n* : temporary stiffness of muscles occurring after death

rile \'rīl\ *vb* **riled; ril·ing** : anger

rill \'ril\ *n* : small brook

rim \'rim\ *n* : edge esp. of something curved ~ *vb* **-mm-** : border

¹rime \'rīm\ *n* : frost —**rimy** \'rīmē\ *adj*

²rime *var of* RHYME

rind \'rīnd\ *n* : usu. hard or tough outer layer

¹ring \'riŋ\ *n* 1 : circular band used as

an ornament or for holding or fastening 2 : something circular 3 : place for contest or display 4 : group with a selfish or dishonest aim ~ vb : surround —ringed \'riŋd\ adj — ring·like adj

²ring vb rang \'raŋ\; rung \'rəŋ\; ring·ing 1 : sound resonantly when struck 2 : cause to make a metallic sound by striking 3 : resound 4 : call esp. by a bell ~ n 1 : resonant sound or tone 2 : act or instance of ringing

ring·er \'riŋər\ n 1 : one that sounds by ringing 2 : illegal substitute 3 : one that closely resembles another

ring·lead·er \'riŋ‚lēdər\ n : leader esp. of troublemakers

ring·let n : long curl

ring·worm n : contagious skin disease caused by fungi

rink \'riŋk\ n : enclosed place for skating

rinse \'rins\ vb rinsed; rins·ing 1 : cleanse usu. with water only 2 : treat (hair) with a rinse ~ n : liquid used for rinsing —rins·er n

ri·ot \'rīət\ n 1 : violent public disorder 2 : random or disorderly profusion — riot vb —ri·ot·er n —ri·ot·ous adj

rip \'rip\ vb -pp- : cut or tear open ~ n : rent made by ripping —rip·per n

ripe \'rīp\ adj rip·er; rip·est : fully grown, developed, or prepared — ripe·ly adv —rip·en \'rīpən\ vb — ripe·ness n

rip-off n : theft —rip off vb

rip·ple \'ripəl\ vb -pled; -pling 1 : become lightly ruffled on the surface 2 : sound like rippling water —ripple n

rise \'rīz\ vb rose \'rōz\; ris·en \'rizən\; ris·ing \'rīziŋ\ 1 : get up from sitting, kneeling, or lying 2 : take arms 3 : appear above the horizon 4 : ascend 5 : gain a higher position or rank 6 : increase ~ n 1 : act of rising 2 : origin 3 : elevation 4 : increase 5 : upward slope 6 : area of high ground —ris·er \'rīzər\ n

risk \'risk\ n : exposure to loss or injury —risk vb —risk·i·ness n —risky adj

ris·qué \ris'kā\ adj : nearly indecent

rite \'rīt\ n 1 : set form for conducting a ceremony 2 : liturgy of a church 3 : ceremonial action

rit·u·al \'richəwəl\ n : rite —ritual adj —rit·u·al·ism \-‚izəm\ n —rit·u·al·is·tic \‚richəwəl'istik\ adj —rit·u·al·

is·ti·cal·ly \-tiklē\ adv —rit·u·al·ly \'richəwəlē\ adv

ri·val \'rīvəl\ n 1 : competitor 2 : peer ~ vb -valed or -valled; -val·ing or -val·ling 1 : be in competition with 2 : equal —rival adj —ri·val·ry \-rē\ n

riv·er \'rivər\ n : large natural stream of water —riv·er·bank n —riv·er·bed n —riv·er·boat n —riv·er·side n

riv·et \'rivət\ n : headed metal bolt ~ vb : fasten with a rivet —riv·et·er n

riv·u·let \'rivyələt\ n : small stream

roach \'rōch\ n : cockroach

road \'rōd\ n : open way for vehicles, persons, and animals —road·bed n —road·side n or adj —road·way n

road·block n : obstruction on a road

road·run·ner n : large fast-running bird

roam \'rōm\ vb : wander

roan \'rōn\ adj : of a dark color sprinkled with white ~ n : animal with a roan coat

roar \'rōr\ vb : utter a full loud prolonged sound —roar n —roar·er n

roast \'rōst\ vb 1 : cook by dry heat 2 : criticize severely ~ n : piece of meat suitable for roasting —roast adj — roast·er n

rob \'räb\ vb -bb- 1 : steal from 2 : commit robbery —rob·ber n

rob·bery \'räbərē\ n, pl -ber·ies : theft of something from a person by use of violence or threat

robe \'rōb\ n 1 : long flowing outer garment 2 : covering for the lower body ~ vb robed; rob·ing : clothe with or as if with a robe

rob·in \'räbən\ n : No. American thrush with a reddish breast

ro·bot \'rō‚bät, -bət\ n 1 : machine that looks and acts like a human being 2 : efficient but insensitive person — ro·bot·ic \rō'bätik\ adj

ro·bust \rō'bəst, 'rō‚bəst\ adj : strong and vigorously healthy — ro·bust·ly adv —ro·bust·ness n

¹rock \'räk\ vb : sway or cause to sway back and forth ~ n 1 : rocking movement 2 : popular music marked by repetition and a strong beat·

²rock n : mass of hard mineral material —rock adj —rocky adj

rock·er n 1 : curved piece on which a chair rocks 2 : chair that rocks

rock·et \'räkət\ n 1 : self-propelled firework or missile 2 : jet engine that carries its own oxygen ~ vb : rise abruptly and rapidly —**rock·et·ry** \-ətrē\ n

rod \'räd\ n 1 : straight slender stick 2 : unit of length equal to 5 yards

rode past of RIDE

ro·dent \'rōd⁰nt\ n : usu. small gnawing mammal

ro·deo \'rōdē,ō, rō'dāō\ n, pl **-de·os** : contest of cowboy skills

roe \'rō\ n : fish eggs

rogue \'rōg\ n : dishonest or mischievous person —**rogu·ery** \'rōgərē\ n —**rogu·ish** \'rōgish\ adj —**rogu·ish·ly** adv —**rogu·ish·ness** n

roil \'ròil\ vb 1 : make cloudy or muddy by stirring up 2 : make angry

role \'rōl\ n 1 : part to play 2 : function

roll \'rōl\ n 1 : official record or list of names 2 : something rolled up or rounded 3 : bread baked in a small rounded mass 4 : sound of rapid drum strokes 5 : heavy reverberating sound 6 : rolling movement ~ vb 1 : move by turning over 2 : move on wheels 3 : flow in a continuous stream 4 : swing from side to side 5 : shape or be shaped in rounded form 6 : press with a roller

roll·er n 1 : revolving cylinder 2 : rod on which something is rolled up 3 : long heavy ocean wave

roller skate n : a skate with wheels instead of a runner —**roller–skate** vb

rol·lick·ing \'rälikiŋ\ adj : full of good spirits

Ro·man Catholic \'rōmən-\ n : member of a Christian church led by a pope —**Roman Catholic** adj —**Roman Catholicism** n

ro·mance \rō'mans, 'rō,mans\ n 1 : medieval tale of knightly adventure 2 : love story 3 : love affair ~ vb **-manced; -manc·ing** 1 : have romantic fancies 2 : have a love affair with —**ro·manc·er** n

ro·man·tic \rō'mantik\ adj 1 : visionary or imaginative 2 : appealing to one's emotions —**ro·man·ti·cal·ly** \-iklē\ adv

romp \'rämp\ vb : play actively and noisily —**romp** n

roof \'rüf, 'ruf\ n, pl **roofs** \'rüfs, 'rufs: 'rüvz, 'ruvz\ : upper covering part of a building ~ vb : cover with a roof —**roofed** \'rüft, 'ruft\ adj —**roof·ing** n —**roof·less** adj —**roof·top** n

rook·ie \'rukē\ n : novice

room \'rüm, 'rum\ n 1 : sufficient space 2 : partitioned part of a building ~ vb : occupy lodgings —**room·er** n —**room·ful** n —**roomy** adj

room·mate n : one sharing the same lodgings

roost \'rüst\ n : support on which birds perch ~ vb : settle on a roost

roost·er \'rüstər, 'rus-\ n : adult male domestic chicken

¹**root** \'rüt, 'rut\ n 1 : leafless underground part of a seed plant 2 : rootlike thing or part 3 : source 4 : essential core ~ vb : form. fix. or become fixed by roots —**root·less** adj —**root·let** \-lət\ n —**root·like** adj

²**root** vb : turn up with the snout

³**root** \'rüt, 'rut\ vb : applaud or encourage noisily —**root·er** n

rope \'rōp\ n : large strong cord of strands of fiber —**roped; rop·ing** 1 : tie with a rope 2 : lasso

ro·sa·ry \'rōzərē\ n, pl **-ries** 1 : string of beads used in praying 2 : Roman Catholic devotion

¹**rose** past of RISE

²**rose** \'rōz\ n 1 : prickly shrub with bright flowers 2 : purplish red —**rose** adj —**rose·bud** n —**rose·bush** n

rose·mary \'rōz,merē\ n, pl **-mar·ies** : fragrant shrubby mint

ro·sette \rō'zet\ n : rose-shaped ornament

Rosh Ha·sha·nah \,räshhä'shänə, ,rōsh-\ n : Jewish New Year observed as a religious holiday in September or October

ros·in \'räz⁰n\ n : brittle resin

ros·ter \'rästər\ n : list of names

ros·trum \'rästrəm\ n, pl **-trums** or **-tra** \-trə\ : speaker's platform

rosy \'rōzē\ adj **ros·i·er; -est** 1 : of the color rose 2 : hopeful —**ros·i·ly** adv —**ros·i·ness** n

rot \'rät\ vb **-tt-** : undergo decomposition ~ n 1 : decay 2 : disease in which tissue breaks down

ro·ta·ry \'rōtərē\ adj 1 : turning on an axis 2 : having a rotating part

ro·tate \'rō,tāt\ vb **-tat·ed; -tat·ing** 1 : turn about an axis or a center 2 : alternate in a series —**ro·ta·tion** \rō-'tāshən\ n —**ro·ta·tor** \'rō,tātər\ n

rote \'rōt\ n : repetition from memory

ro·tor \'rōtər\ n 1 : part that rotates 2 : system of rotating horizontal blades for supporting a helicopter

rot·ten \'rät°n\ *adj* 1 : having rotted 2 : corrupt 3 : extremely unpleasant or inferior —**rot·ten·ness** *n*

ro·tund \rō'tənd\ *adj* : rounded —**ro·tun·di·ty** \-'təndətē\ *n*

ro·tun·da \rō'təndə\ *n* : building or room with a dome

roué \rú'ā\ *n* : man given to debauched living

rouge \'rüzh, 'rüj\ *n* : cosmetic for the cheeks —**rouge** *vb*

rough \'rəf\ *adj* 1 : not smooth 2 : not calm 3 : harsh, violent, or rugged 4 : crudely or hastily done ~ *n* : rough state or something in that state ~ *vb* 1 : roughen 2 : manhandle 3 : make roughly —**rough·ly** *adv* —**rough·ness** *n*

rough·age \'rəfij\ *n* : coarse bulky food

rough·en \'rəfən\ *vb* : make or become rough

rough·neck \'rəf,nek\ *n* : rowdy

rou·lette \rü'let\ *n* : gambling game using a whirling numbered wheel

¹**round** \'raùnd\ *adj* 1 : having every part the same distance from the center 2 : cylindrical 3 : complete 4 : approximate 5 : blunt 6 : moving in or forming a circle ~ *n* 1 : round or curved thing 2 : series of recurring actions or events 3 : period of time or a unit of action 4 : fired shot 5 : cut of beef ~ *vb* 1 : make or become round 2 : go around 3 : finish 4 : express as an approximation —**round·ish** *adj* —**round·ly** *adv* —**round·ness** *n*

²**round** *prep or adv* : around

round·about *adj* : indirect

round·up \'raùnd,əp\ *n* 1 : gathering together of range cattle 2 : summary —**round up** *vb*

rouse \'raùz\ *vb* **roused; rous·ing** 1 : wake from sleep 2 : stir up

rout \'raùt\ *n* 1 : state of wild confusion 2 : disastrous defeat ~ *vb* : defeat decisively

route \'rüt, 'raùt\ *n* : line of travel ~ *vb* **rout·ed; rout·ing** : send by a selected route

rou·tine \rü'tēn\ *n* 1 : regular course of procedure 2 : an often repeated speech, formula, or part —**routine** *adj* —**rou·tine·ly** *adv*

rove \'rōv\ *vb* **roved; rov·ing** : wander or roam —**rov·er** *n*

¹**row** \'rō\ *vb* 1 : propel a boat with oars 2 : carry in a rowboat ~ *n* : act of rowing —**row·boat** *n* —**row·er** \'rōər\ *n*

²**row** *n* : number of objects in a line

³**row** \'raù\ *n* : noisy quarrel —**row** *vb*

row·dy \'raùdē\ *adj* **-di·er; -est** : coarse or boisterous in behavior —**row·di·ness** *n* —**rowdy** *n*

roy·al \'roiəl\ *adj* : relating to or befitting a king ~ *n* : person of royal blood —**roy·al·ly** *adv*

roy·al·ty \'roiəltē\ *n, pl* **-ties** 1 : state of being royal 2 : royal persons 3 : payment for use of property

rub \'rəb\ *vb* **-bb-** 1 : use pressure and friction on a body 2 : scour, polish, erase, or smear by pressure and friction 3 : chafe with friction ~ *n* : difficulty

rub·ber \'rəbər\ *n* 1 : one that rubs 2 : waterproof elastic substance or something made of it —**rubber** *adj* —**rub·ber·ize** \-,īz\ *vb* —**rub·bery** *adj*

rub·bish \'rəbish\ *n* : waste or trash

rub·ble \'rəbəl\ *n* : broken fragments esp. of a destroyed building

ru·ble \'rübəl\ *n* : monetary unit of Russia

ru·by \'rübē\ *n, pl* **-bies** : precious red stone or its color —**ruby** *adj*

rud·der \'rədər\ *n* : steering device at the rear of a ship or aircraft

rud·dy \'rədē\ *adj* **-di·er; -est** : reddish —**rud·di·ness** *n*

rude \'rüd\ *adj* **rud·er; rud·est** 1 : roughly made 2 : impolite —**rude·ly** *adv* —**rude·ness** *n*

ru·di·ment \'rüdəmənt\ *n* 1 : something not fully developed 2 : elementary principle —**ru·di·men·ta·ry** \,rüdə'mentərē\ *adj*

rue \'rü\ *vb* **rued; ru·ing** : feel regret for ~ *n* : regret —**rue·ful** \-fəl\ *adj* —**rue·ful·ly** *adv* —**rue·ful·ness** *n*

ruf·fi·an \'rəfēən\ *n* : brutal person

ruf·fle \'rəfəl\ *vb* **-fled; -fling** 1 : draw into or provide with pleats 2 : roughen the surface of 3 : irritate ~ *n* : strip of fabric pleated on one edge —**ruf·fly** \'rəfəlē, -flē\ *adj*

rug \'rəg\ *n* : piece of heavy fabric used as a floor covering

rug·ged \'rəgəd\ *adj* 1 : having a rough uneven surface 2 : severe 3 : strong —**rug·ged·ly** *adv* —**rug·ged·ness** *n*

ru·in \'rüən\ *n* 1 : complete collapse or destruction 2 : remains of something

destroyed —usu. in pl. **3** : cause of destruction ~ *vb* **1** : destroy **2** : damage beyond repair **3** : bankrupt

ru·in·ous \'rüənəs\ *adj* : causing ruin — **ruin·ous·ly** *adv*

rule \'rül\ *n* **1** : guide or principle for governing action **2** : usual way of doing something **3** : government **4** : straight strip (as of wood or metal) marked off in units for measuring ~ *vb* **ruled; rul·ing 1** : govern **2** : give as a decision —**rul·er** *n*

rum \'rəm\ *n* : liquor made from molasses or sugarcane

rum·ble \'rəmbəl\ *vb* **-bled; -bling** : make a low heavy rolling sound — **rumble** *n*

ru·mi·nant \'rümənənt\ *n* : hoofed mammal (as a cow or deer) that chews the cud —**ruminant** *adj*

ru·mi·nate \'rümə,nāt\ *vb* **-nat·ed; -nat·ing** : contemplate —**ru·mi·na·tion** \,rümə'nāshən\ *n*

rum·mage \'rəmij\ *vb* **-maged; -mag·ing** : search thoroughly

rum·my \'rəmē\ *n* : card game

ru·mor \'rümər\ *n* **1** : common talk **2** : widespread statement not authenticated —**rumor** *vb*

rump \'rəmp\ *n* : rear part of an animal

rum·ple \'rəmpəl\ *vb* **-pled; -pling** : tousle or wrinkle —**rumple** *n*

rum·pus \'rəmpəs\ *n* : disturbance

run \'rən\ *vb* **ran** \'ran\; **run; run·ning 1** : go rapidly or hurriedly **2** : enter a race or election **3** : operate **4** : continue in force **5** : flow rapidly **6** : take a certain direction **7** : manage **8** : incur ~ *n* **1** : act of running **2** : brook **3** : continuous series **4** : usual kind **5** : freedom of movement **6** : lengthwise ravel

run·around *n* : evasive or delaying action esp. in response to a request

run·away \'rənə,wā\ *n* : fugitive ~ *adj* **1** : fugitive **2** : out of control

run–down *adj* : being in poor condition

¹**rung** *past part of* RING

²**rung** \'rən\ *n* : horizontal piece of a chair or ladder

run·ner \'rənər\ *n* **1** : one that runs **2** : thin piece or part on which something slides **3** : slender creeping branch of a plant

run·ner–up *n. pl* **run·ners–up** : competitor who finishes second

run·ning \'rəniŋ\ *adj* **1** : flowing **2** : continuous

runt \'rənt\ *n* : small person or animal —**runty** *adj*

run·way \'rən,wā\ *n* : strip on which aircraft land and take off

ru·pee \rü'pē, 'rü,-\ *n* : monetary unit (as of India)

rup·ture \'rəpchər\ *n* **1** : breaking or tearing apart **2** : hernia ~ *vb* **-tured; -tur·ing** : cause or undergo rupture

ru·ral \'rürəl\ *adj* : relating to the country or agriculture

ruse \'rüs, 'rüz\ *n* : trick

¹**rush** \'rəsh\ *n* : grasslike marsh plant

²**rush** *vb* **1** : move forward or act with too great haste **2** : perform in a short time ~ *n* : violent forward motion ~ *adj* : requiring speed —**rush·er** *n*

rus·set \'rəsət\ *n* **1** : reddish brown color **2** : a baking potato —**russet** *adj*

rust \'rəst\ *n* **1** : reddish coating on exposed iron **2** : reddish brown color — **rust** *vb* —**rusty** *adj*

rus·tic \'rəstik\ *adj* : relating to or suitable for the country or country dwellers ~ *n* : rustic person —**rus·ti·cal·ly** *adv*

rus·tle \'rəsəl\ *vb* **-tled; -tling 1** : make or cause a rustle **2** : forage food **3** : steal cattle from the range ~ *n* : series of small sounds —**rus·tler** \-ələr\ *n*

rut \'rət\ *n* **1** : track worn by wheels or feet **2** : set routine —**rut·ted** *adj*

ruth·less \'rüthləs\ *adj* : having no pity —**ruth·less·ly** *adv* —**ruth·less·ness** *n*

-ry \rē\ *n suffix* : -ery

rye \'rī\ *n* **1** : cereal grass grown for grain **2** : whiskey from rye

S

s \'es\ *n, pl* **s's** *or* **ss** \'esəz\ : 19th letter of the alphabet

¹**-s** \s *after sounds* f, k, k̲, p, t, th; əz *after sounds* ch, j, s, sh, z, zh; z *after*

other sounds —used to form the plural of most nouns

2-s \vb suffix\ —used to form the 3d person singular present of most verbs

Sab•bath \'sabəth\ n 1 : Saturday observed as a day of worship by Jews and some Christians 2 : Sunday observed as a day of worship by Christians

sa•ber, sa•bre \'sābər\ n : curved cavalry sword

sa•ble \'sābəl\ n 1 : black 2 : dark brown mammal or its fur

sab•o•tage \'sabə,täzh\ n : deliberate destruction or hampering ~ vb -taged; -tag•ing : wreck through sabotage

sab•o•teur \,sabə'tər\ n : person who sabotages

sac \'sak\ n : anatomical pouch

sac•cha•rin \'sakərən\ n : low-calorie artificial sweetener

sac•cha•rine \-ərən\ adj : nauseatingly sweet

sa•chet \sa'shā\ n : small bag with perfumed powder (**sachet powder**)

1sack \'sak\ n : bag ~ vb : fire

2sack vb : plunder a captured place

sack•cloth n : rough garment worn as a sign of penitence

sac•ra•ment \'sakrəmənt\ n : formal religious act or rite —**sac•ra•men•tal** \,sakrə'mentᵊl\ adj

sa•cred \'sākrəd\ adj 1 : set apart for or worthy of worship 2 : worthy of reverence 3 : relating to religion —**sa•cred•ly** adv —**sa•cred•ness** n

sac•ri•fice \'sakrə,fīs\ n 1 : the offering of something precious to a deity or the thing offered 2 : loss or deprivation ~ vb -ficed; -fic•ing : offer or give up as a sacrifice —**sac•ri•fi•cial** \,sakrə'fishəl\ adj

sac•ri•lege \'sakrəlij\ n : violation of something sacred —**sac•ri•le•gious** \,sakrə'lijəs, -'lējəs\ adj

sac•ro•sanct \'sakrō,saŋkt\ adj : sacred

sad \'sad\ adj -dd- 1 : affected with grief or sorrow 2 : causing sorrow —**sad•den** \'sadᵊn\ vb —**sad•ly** adv —**sad•ness** n

sad•dle \'sadᵊl\ n : seat for riding on horseback ~ vb -dled; -dling : put a saddle on

sa•dism \'sā,dizəm, 'sad,iz-\ n : delight in cruelty —**sa•dist** \'sādist, 'sad-\ n —**sa•dis•tic** \sə'distik\ adj —**sa•dis•ti•cal•ly** adv

sa•fa•ri \sə'färē, -'far-\ n : hunting expedition in Africa

safe \'sāf\ adj **saf•er; saf•est** 1 : free from harm 2 : providing safety ~ n : container to keep valuables safe —**safe•keep•ing** n —**safe•ly** adv

safe•guard n : measure or device for preventing accidents —**safeguard** vb

safe•ty \'sāftē\ n, pl -ties 1 : freedom from danger 2 : protective device

saf•flow•er \'saf,laȯər\ n : herb with seeds rich in edible oil

saf•fron \'safrən\ n : orange powder from a crocus flower used in cooking

sag \'sag\ vb -gg- : droop, sink, or settle —**sag** n

sa•ga \'sägə\ n : story of heroic deeds

sa•ga•cious \sə'gāshəs\ adj : shrewd —**sa•gac•i•ty** \-'gasətē\ n

1sage \'sāj\ adj : wise or prudent ~ n : wise man —**sage•ly** adv

2sage n : mint used in flavoring

sage•brush n : low shrub of the western U.S.

said past of SAY

sail \'sāl\ n 1 : fabric used to catch the wind and move a boat or ship 2 : trip on a sailboat ~ vb 1 : travel on a ship or sailboat 2 : move with ease or grace —**sail•boat** n —**sail•or** \'sālər\ n

sail•fish n : large fish with a very large dorsal fin

saint \'sānt, before a name ,sānt or sənt\ n : holy or godly person —**saint•ed** \-əd\ adj —**saint•hood** \-,hu̇d\ n —**saint•li•ness** n —**saint•ly** adj

1sake \'sāk\ n 1 : purpose or reason 2 : one's good or benefit

2sa•ke, sa•ki \'säkē\ n : Japanese rice wine

sa•la•cious \sə'lāshəs\ adj : sexually suggestive —**sa•la•cious•ly** adv

sal•ad \'saləd\ n : dish usu. of raw lettuce, vegetables, or fruit

sal•a•man•der \'salə,mandər\ n : lizardlike amphibian

sa•la•mi \sə'lämē\ n : highly seasoned dried sausage

sal•a•ry \'salərē\ n, pl -ries : regular payment for services

sale \'sāl\ n 1 : transfer of ownership of property for money 2 : selling at bargain prices 3 **sales** pl : activities involved in selling —**sal•able, sale•able** \'sāləbəl\ adj —**sales•man** \-mən\ n —**sales•per•son** n —**sales•wom•an** n

sa·lient \'sālyənt\ adj : standing out conspicuously

sa·line \'sā,lēn, -,līn\ adj : containing salt —**sa·lin·i·ty** \sā'linətē, sə-\ n

sa·li·va \sə'līvə\ n : liquid secreted into the mouth —**sal·i·vary** \'salə,verē\ adj —**sal·i·vate** \-,vāt\ vb —**sal·i·va·tion** \,salə'vāshən\ n

sal·low \'salō\ adj : of a yellowish sickly color

sal·ly \'salē\ n, pl **-lies 1** : quick attack on besiegers **2** : witty remark —**sally** vb

salm·on \'samən\ n, pl **salmon 1** : food fish with pink or red flesh **2** : deep yellowish pink color

sa·lon \sə'län, 'sal,än, sa'lōⁿ\ n : elegant room or shop

sa·loon \sə'lün\ n **1** : public cabin on a passenger ship **2** : barroom

sal·sa \'sólsə, 'säl-\ n : spicy sauce of tomatoes, onions, and hot peppers

salt \'sólt\ n **1** : white crystalline substance that consists of sodium and chlorine **2** : compound formed usu. from acid and metal —**salt** vb or adj —**salt·i·ness** n —**salty** adj

salt·wa·ter adj : relating to or living in salt water

sa·lu·bri·ous \sə'lübrēəs\ adj : good for health

sal·u·tary \'salyə,terē\ adj : health-giving or beneficial

sal·u·ta·tion \,salyə'tāshən\ n : greeting

sa·lute \sə'lüt\ vb **-lut·ed; -lut·ing** : honor by ceremony or formal movement —**salute** n

sal·vage \'salvij\ n : something saved from destruction ~ vb **-vaged; -vag·ing** : rescue or save

sal·va·tion \sal'vāshən\ n : saving of a person from sin or danger

salve \'sav, 'sáv\ n : medicinal ointment ~ vb **salved; salv·ing** : soothe

sal·ver \'salvər\ n : small tray

sal·vo \'salvō\ n, pl **-vos** or **-voes** : simultaneous discharge of guns

same \'sām\ adj : being the one referred to ~ pron : the same one or ones ~ adv : in the same manner —**same·ness** n

sam·ple \'sampəl\ n : piece or part that shows the quality of a whole ~ vb **-pled; -pling** : judge by a sample

sam·pler \'samplər\ n : piece of needlework testing skill in embroidering

san·a·to·ri·um \,sanə'tōrēəm\ n, pl **-riums** or **-ria** \-ēə\ : hospital for the chronically ill

sanc·ti·fy \'saŋktə,fī\ vb **-fied; -fy·ing** : make holy —**sanc·ti·fi·ca·tion** \,saŋktəfə'kāshən\ n

sanc·ti·mo·nious \,saŋktə'mōnēəs\ adj : hypocritically pious —**sanc·ti·mo·nious·ly** adv

sanc·tion \'saŋkshən\ n **1** : authoritative approval **2** : coercive measure —usu. pl ~ vb : approve

sanc·ti·ty \'saŋktətē\ n, pl **-ties** : quality or state of being holy or sacred

sanc·tu·ary \'saŋkchə,werē\ n, pl **-ar·ies 1** : consecrated place **2** : place of refuge

sand \'sand\ n : loose granular particles of rock ~ vb : smooth with an abrasive —**sand·bank** n —**sand·er** n —**sand·storm** n —**sandy** adj

san·dal \'sandᵊl\ n : shoe consisting of a sole strapped to the foot

sand·pa·per n : abrasive paper —**sandpaper** vb

sand·pip·er \-,pīpər\ n : long-billed shorebird

sand·stone n : rock made of naturally cemented sand

sand·wich \'sand,wich\ n : 2 or more slices of bread with a filling between them ~ vb : squeeze or crowd in

sane \'sān\ adj **san·er; san·est 1** : mentally healthy **2** : sensible —**sane·ly** adv

sang past of SING

san·gui·nary \'saŋgwə,nerē\ adj : bloody

san·guine \'saŋgwən\ adj **1** : reddish **2** : cheerful

san·i·tar·i·um \,sanə'terēəm\ n, pl **-i·ums** or **-ia** \-ēə\ : sanatorium

san·i·tary \'sanə,terē\ adj **1** : relating to health **2** : free from filth or infective matter

san·i·ta·tion \,sanə'tāshən\ n : protection of health by maintenance of sanitary conditions

san·i·ty \'sanətē\ n : soundness of mind

sank past of SINK

¹sap \'sap\ n **1** : fluid that circulates through a plant **2** : gullible person

²sap vb **-pp- 1** : undermine **2** : weaken or exhaust gradually

sa·pi·ent \'sāpēənt, 'sapē-\ adj : wise —**sa·pi·ence** \-əns\ n

sap·ling \'sapliŋ\ n : young tree

sap·phire \'saf,īr\ n : hard transparent blue gem

sap·py \'sapē\ *adj* **-pi·er; -est 1** : full of sap **2** : overly sentimental

sap·suck·er \'sap,səkər\ *n* : small No. American woodpecker

sar·casm \'sär,kazəm\ *n* **1** : cutting remark **2** : ironical criticism or reproach —**sar·cas·tic** \sär'kastik\ *adj* —**sar·cas·ti·cal·ly** *adv*

sar·coph·a·gus \sär'käfəgəs\ *n, pl* **-gi** \-,gī, -,jī\ : large stone coffin

sar·dine \sär'dēn\ *n* : small fish preserved for use as food

sar·don·ic \sär'dänik\ *adj* : disdainfully humorous —**sar·don·i·cal·ly** *adv*

sa·rong \sə'róŋ, -'räŋ\ *n* : loose garment worn esp. by Pacific islanders

sar·sa·pa·ril·la \,saspə'rilə, ,särs-\ *n* : dried roots of a tropical American plant used esp. for flavoring or a carbonated drink flavored with this

sar·to·ri·al \sär'tōrēəl\ *adj* : relating to a tailor or men's clothes

¹sash \'sash\ *n* : broad band worn around the waist or over the shoulder

²sash *n, pl* **sash 1** : frame for a pane of glass in a door or window **2** : movable part of a window

sas·sa·fras \'sasə,fras\ *n* : No. American tree or its dried root bark

sassy \'sasē\ *adj* **sass·i·er; -est** : saucy

sat *past of* SIT

Sa·tan \'sāt³n\ *n* : devil —**sa·tan·ic** \sə'tanik, sā-\ *adj* —**sa·tan·i·cal·ly** *adv*

satch·el \'sachəl\ *n* : small bag

sate \'sāt\ *vb* **sat·ed; sat·ing** : satisfy fully

sat·el·lite \'sat³l,īt\ *n* **1** : toady **2** : body or object that revolves around a larger celestial body

sa·ti·ate \'sāshē,āt\ *vb* **-at·ed; -at·ing** : sate —**sa·ti·e·ty** \sə'tīətē\ *n*

sat·in \'sat³n\ *n* : glossy fabric —**sat·iny** *adj*

sat·ire \'sa,tīr\ *n* : literary ridicule done with humor —**sa·tir·ic** \sə'tirik\, **sa·tir·i·cal** \-ikəl\ *adj* —**sa·tir·i·cal·ly** *adv* —**sat·i·rist** \'satərist\ *n* —**sat·i·rize** \-ə,rīz\ *vb*

sat·is·fac·tion \,satəs'fakshən\ *n* : state of being satisfied —**sat·is·fac·to·ri·ly** \-'faktərəlē\ *adv* —**sat·is·fac·to·ry** \-'faktərē\ *adj*

sat·is·fy \'satəs,fī\ *vb* **-fied; -fy·ing 1** : make happy **2** : pay what is due to or on —**sat·is·fy·ing·ly** *adv*

sat·u·rate \'sachə,rāt\ *vb* **-rat·ed; -rat·ing** : soak or charge thoroughly —**sat·u·ra·tion** \,sachə'rāshən\ *n*

Sat·ur·day \'satərdā, -dē\ *n* : 7th day of the week

sat·ur·nine \'satər,nīn\ *adj* : sullen

sa·tyr \'sātər, 'sat-\ *n* : pleasure-loving forest god of ancient Greece

sauce \'sós\ *n* : fluid dressing or topping for food —**sauce·pan** *n*

sau·cer \'sósər\ *n* : small shallow dish under a cup

saucy \'sasē, 'sósē\ *adj* **sauc·i·er; -est** : insolent —**sauc·i·ly** *adv* —**sauc·i·ness** *n*

sau·er·kraut \'saúər,kraút\ *n* : finely cut and fermented cabbage

sau·na \'saúnə\ *n* : steam or dry heat bath or a room or cabinet used for such a bath

saun·ter \'sóntər, 'sänt-\ *vb* : stroll

sau·sage \'sósij\ *n* : minced and highly seasoned meat

sau·té \so'tā, sō-\ *vb* **-téed** *or* **-téd; -té·ing** : fry in a little fat —**sauté** *n*

sav·age \'savij\ *adj* **1** : wild **2** : cruel ~ *n* : person belonging to a primitive society —**sav·age·ly** *adv* —**sav·age·ness** *n* —**sav·age·ry** *n*

¹save \'sāv\ *vb* **saved; sav·ing 1** : rescue from danger **2** : guard from destruction **3** : redeem from sin **4** : put aside as a reserve —**sav·er** *n*

²save *prep* : except

sav·ior, sav·iour \'sāvyər\ *n* **1** : one who saves **2** *cap* : Jesus Christ

sa·vor \'sāvər\ *n* : special flavor ~ *vb* : taste with pleasure —**sa·vory** *adj*

¹saw *past of* SEE

²saw \'só\ *n* : cutting tool with teeth ~ *vb* **sawed; sawed** *or* **sawn; saw·ing** : cut with a saw —**saw·dust** \-,dəst\ *n* —**saw·mill** *n* —**saw·yer** \-yər\ *n*

saw·horse *n* : support for wood being sawed

sax·o·phone \'saksə,fōn\ *n* : wind instrument with a reed mouthpiece and usu. a bent metal body

say \'sā\ *vb* **said** \'sed\; **say·ing** \'sāiŋ\; **says** \'sez\ **1** : express in words **2** : state positively ~ *n, pl* **says** \'sāz\ **1** : expression of opinion **2** : power of decision

say·ing \'sāiŋ\ *n* : commonly repeated statement

scab \'skab\ *n* **1** : protective crust over a sore or wound **2** : worker taking a striker's job ~ *vb* **-bb- 1** : become covered with a scab **2** : work as a scab —**scab·by** *adj*

scab·bard \'skabərd\ n : sheath for the blade of a weapon

scaf·fold \'skafəld, -ōld\ n 1 : raised platform for workmen 2 : platform on which a criminal is executed

scald \'skȯld\ vb 1 : burn with hot liquid or steam 2 : heat to the boiling point

¹scale \'skāl\ n : weighing device ~ vb **scaled; scal·ing** : weigh

²scale n 1 : thin plate esp. on the body of a fish or reptile 2 : thin coating or layer ~ vb **scaled; scal·ing** : strip of scales —**scaled** \'skāld\ adj —**scaleless** adj —**scaly** adj

³scale n 1 : graduated series 2 : size of a sample (as a model) in proportion to the size of the actual thing 3 : standard of estimation or judgment 4 : series of musical tones ~ vb **scaled; scal·ing** 1 : climb by a ladder 2 : arrange in a graded series

scal·lion \'skalyən\ n : bulbless onion

scal·lop \'skäləp, 'skal-\ n 1 : marine mollusk 2 : rounded projection on a border

scalp \'skalp\ n : skin and flesh of the head ~ vb 1 : remove the scalp from 2 : resell at a greatly increased price —**scalp·er** n

scal·pel \'skalpəl\ n : surgical knife

scamp \'skamp\ n : rascal

scam·per \'skampər\ vb : run nimbly — **scamper** n

scan \'skan\ vb **-nn-** 1 : read (verses) so as to show meter 2 : examine closely or hastily 3 : examine with a sensing device —**scan** n —**scan·ner** n

scan·dal \'skandᵊl\ n 1 : disgraceful situation 2 : malicious gossip —**scandal·ize** vb —**scan·dal·ous** adj

scant \'skant\ adj : barely sufficient ~ vb : stint —**scant·i·ly** adv —**scanty** adj

scape·goat \'skāp,gōt\ n : one that bears the blame for others

scap·u·la \'skapyələ\ n, pl **-lae** \-,lē\ or **-las** : shoulder blade

scar \'skär\ n : mark where a wound has healed —**scar** vb

scar·ab \'skarəb\ n : large dark beetle or an ornament representing one

scarce \'skers\ adj **scarc·er; scarc·est** : lacking in quantity or number — **scar·ci·ty** \'skersətē\ n

scarce·ly \'skerslē\ adv 1 : barely 2 : almost not

scare \'sker\ vb **scared; scar·ing** : frighten ~ n : fright —**scary** adj

scare·crow \'sker,krō\ n : figure for scaring birds from crops

scarf \'skärf\ n, pl **scarves** \'skärvz\ or **scarfs** : cloth worn about the shoulders or the neck

scar·let \'skärlət\ n : bright red color — **scarlet** adj

scarlet fever n : acute contagious disease marked by fever, sore throat, and red rash

scath·ing \'skāthiŋ\ adj : bitterly severe

scat·ter \'skatər\ vb 1 : spread about irregularly 2 : disperse

scav·en·ger \'skavənjər\ n 1 : person that collects refuse or waste 2 : animal that feeds on decayed matter —**scavenge** \'skavənj\ vb

sce·nar·io \sə'narē,ō, -'när-\ n, pl **-i·os** 1 : plot of a play or movie 2 : possible sequence of events

scene \'sēn\ n 1 : single situation in a play or movie 2 : stage setting 3 : view 4 : display of emotion —**scenic** \'sēnik\ adj

scen·ery \'sēnərē\ n, pl **-er·ies** 1 : painted setting for a stage 2 : picturesque view

scent \'sent\ vb 1 : smell 2 : fill with odor ~ n 1 : odor 2 : sense of smell 3 : perfume —**scent·ed** \'sentəd\ adj

scep·ter \'septər\ n : staff signifying authority

scep·tic \'skeptik\ var of SKEPTIC

sched·ule \'skejül, esp Brit 'shedyül\ n : list showing sequence of events ~ vb **-uled; -ul·ing** : make a schedule of

scheme \'skēm\ n 1 : crafty plot 2 : systematic design ~ vb **schemed; schem·ing** : form a plot —**sche·mat·ic** \ski'matik\ adj —**schem·er** n

schism \'sizəm, 'skiz-\ n : split —**schismat·ic** \siz'matik, skiz-\ n or adj

schizo·phre·nia \,skitsə'frēnēə\ n : severe mental illness —**schiz·oid** \'skit,sȯid\ adj or n —**schizo·phren·ic** \,skitsə'frenik\ adj or n

schol·ar \'skälər\ n : student or learned person —**schol·ar·ly** adj

schol·ar·ship \-,ship\ n 1 : qualities or learning of a scholar 2 : money given to a student to pay for education

scho·las·tic \skə'lastik\ adj : relating to schools, scholars, or scholarship

¹school \'skül\ n 1 : institution for learning 2 : pupils in a school 3 : group with shared beliefs ~ vb : teach — **school·boy** n —**school·girl** n —

school•house n —school•mate n —
school•room n —school•teach•er n

²school n : large number of fish swimming together

schoo•ner \'skünər\ n : sailing ship

sci•ence \'sīəns\ n : branch of systematic
study esp. of the physical world —
sci•en•tif•ic \,sīən'tifik\ adj —sci•en-
tif•i•cal•ly adv —sci•en•tist \'sīəntist\
n

scin•til•late \'sintᵊl,āt\ vb -lat•ed; -lat-
ing : flash —scin•til•la•tion \,sintᵊl-
'āshən\ n

scin•til•lat•ing adj : brilliantly lively or
witty

sci•on \'sīən\ n : descendant

scis•sors \'sizərz\ n pl : small shears

scoff \'skäf\ vb : mock —scoff•er n

scold \'skōld\ n : person who scolds ~
vb : criticize severely

scoop \'küp\ n : shovellike utensil ~ vb
1 : take out with a scoop 2 : dig out

scoot \'küt\ vb : move swiftly

scoot•er \'skütər\ n : child's foot-pro-
pelled vehicle

¹scope \'skōp\ n 1 : extent 2 : room for
development

²scope n : viewing device (as a micro-
scope)

scorch \'skórch\ vb : burn the surface of

score \'skōr\ n, pl scores 1 or pl score
: twenty 2 : cut 3 : record of points
made (as in a game) 4 : debt 5 : music
of a composition ~ vb scored; scoring 1 : record 2 : mark with lines 3
: gain in a game 4 : assign a grade to
5 : compose a score for —score•less
adj —scor•er n

scorn \'skórn\ n : emotion involving
both anger and disgust ~ vb : hold in
contempt —scorn•er n —scorn•ful
\-fəl\ adj —scorn•ful•ly adv

scor•pi•on \'skórpēən\ n : poisonous
long-tailed animal

scoun•drel \'skaúndrəl\ n : villain

¹scour \'skaúər\ vb : examine thoroughly

²scour vb : rub in order to clean

scourge \'skərj\ n 1 : whip 2 : punishment ~ vb scourged; scourg•ing 1
: lash 2 : punish severely

scout \'skaút\ vb : inspect or observe to
get information ~ n : person sent out
to get information

scow \'skaú\ n : large flat-bottomed boat
with square ends

scowl \'skaúl\ vb : make a frowning expression of displeasure —scowl n

scrag•gly \'skraglē\ adj : irregular or un-
kempt

scram \'skram\ vb -mm- : go away at
once

scram•ble \'skrambəl\ vb -bled; -bling
1 : clamber clumsily around 2
: struggle for possession of something
3 : mix together 4 : cook (eggs) by
stirring during frying —scramble n

¹scrap \'skrap\ n 1 : fragment 2
: discarded material ~ vb -pp- : get
rid of as useless

²scrap vb -pp- : fight —scrap n —
scrap•per n

scrap•book n : blank book in which mementos are kept

scrape \'skrāp\ vb scraped; scrap•ing 1
: remove by drawing a knife over 2
: clean or smooth by rubbing 3 : draw
across a surface with a grating sound
4 : damage by contact with a rough
surface 5 : gather or proceed with difficulty ~ n 1 : act of scraping 2
: predicament —scrap•er n

scratch \'skrach\ vb 1 : scrape or dig
with or as if with claws or nails 2
: cause to move gratingly 3 : delete
by or as if by drawing a line through
~ n : mark or sound made in scratch-
ing —scratchy adj

scrawl \'skról\ vb : write hastily and
carelessly —scrawl n

scraw•ny \'skrónē\ adj -ni•er; -est : very
thin

scream \'skrēm\ vb : cry out loudly and
shrilly ~ n : loud shrill cry

screech \'skrēch\ vb or n : shriek

screen \'skrēn\ n 1 : device or partition
used to protect or decorate 2 : surface
on which pictures appear (as in movies) ~ vb : shield or separate with or
as if with a screen

screw \'skrü\ n 1 : grooved fastening device 2 : propeller ~ vb 1 : fasten by
means of a screw 2 : move spirally

screw•driv•er \'skrü,drīvər\ n : tool for
turning screws

scrib•ble \'skribəl\ vb -bled; -bling
: write hastily or carelessly —scribble n —scrib•bler \-ələr\ n

scribe \'skrīb\ n : one who writes or copies writing

scrimp \'skrimp\ vb : economize greatly

scrip \'skrip\ n 1 : paper money for less
than a dollar 2 : certificate entitling
one to something (as stock)

script \'skript\ n : text (as of a play)

scrip·ture \'skripchər\ *n* : sacred writings of a religion —**scrip·tur·al** \'skripchərəl\ *adj*

scroll \'skrōl\ *n* **1** : roll of paper for writing a document **2** : spiral or coiled design

scro·tum \'skrōtəm\ *n, pl* **-ta** \-ə\ *or* **-tums** : pouch containing the testes

scrounge \'skraúnj\ *vb* **scrounged; scroung·ing** : collect by or as if by foraging

¹scrub \'skrəb\ *n* : stunted tree or shrub or a growth of these —**scrub** *adj* — **scrub·by** *adj*

²scrub *vb* **-bb-** : clean or wash by rubbing —**scrub** *n*

scruff \'skrəf\ *n* : loose skin of the back of the neck

scrump·tious \'skrəmpshəs\ *adj* : delicious

scru·ple \'skrüpəl\ *n* : reluctance due to ethical considerations —**scruple** *vb* —**scru·pu·lous** \-pyələs\ *adj* —**scru·pu·lous·ly** *adv*

scru·ti·ny \'skrüt³nē\ *n, pl* **-nies** : careful inspection —**scru·ti·nize** \-³n‚īz\ *vb*

scud \'skəd\ *vb* **-dd-** : move speedily

scuff \'skəf\ *vb* : scratch, scrape, or wear away —**scuff** *n*

scuf·fle \'skəfəl\ *vb* **-fled; -fling 1** : struggle at close quarters **2** : shuffle one's feet —**scuffle** *n*

scull \'skəl\ *n* **1** : oar **2** : racing shell propelled with sculls ~ *vb* : propel a boat by an oar over the stern

scul·lery \'skələrē\ *n, pl* **-ler·ies** : room for cleaning dishes and cookware

sculpt \'skəlpt\ *vb* : sculpture

sculp·ture \'skəlpchər\ *n* : work of art carved or molded ~ *vb* **-tured; -tur·ing** : form as sculpture —**sculp·tor** \-tər\ *n* —**sculp·tur·al** \-chərəl\ *adj*

scum \'skəm\ *n* : slimy film on a liquid

scur·ri·lous \'skərələs\ *adj* : vulgar or abusive

scur·ry \'skərē\ *vb* **-ried; -ry·ing** : scamper

scur·vy \'skərvē\ *n* : vitamin-deficiency disease

¹scut·tle \'skət³l\ *n* : pail for coal

²scuttle *vb* **-tled; -tling** : sink (a ship) by cutting holes in its bottom

³scuttle *vb* **-tled; -tling** : scamper

scythe \'sīth\ *n* : tool for mowing by hand —**scythe** *vb*

sea \'sē\ *n* **1** : large body of salt water **2**

: ocean **3** : rough water —**sea** *adj* — **sea·coast** *n* —**sea·food** *n* —**sea·port** *n* —**sea·shore** *n* —**sea·wa·ter** *n*

sea·bird *n* : bird frequenting the open ocean

sea·board *n* : country's seacoast

sea·far·er \-‚farər\ *n* : seaman —**sea·far·ing** \-‚fariŋ\ *adj or n*

sea horse *n* : small fish with a horselike head

¹seal \'sēl\ *n* : large sea mammal of cold regions —**seal·skin** *n*

²seal *n* **1** : device for stamping a design **2** : something that closes ~ *vb* **1** : affix a seal to **2** : close up securely **3** : determine finally —**seal·ant** \-ənt\ *n* —**seal·er** *n*

sea lion *n* : large Pacific seal with external ears

seam \'sēm\ *n* **1** : line of junction of 2 edges **2** : layer of a mineral ~ *vb* : join by sewing —**seam·less** *adj*

sea·man \'sēmən\ *n* **1** : one who helps to handle a ship **2** : naval enlisted man ranking next below a petty officer third class —**sea·man·ship** *n*

seaman apprentice *n* : naval enlisted man ranking next below a seaman

seaman recruit *n* : naval enlisted man of the lowest rank

seam·stress \'sēmstrəs\ *n* : woman who sews

seamy \'sēmē\ *adj* **seam·i·er; -est** : unpleasant or sordid

sé·ance \'sā‚äns\ *n* : meeting for communicating with spirits

sea·plane *n* : airplane that can take off from and land on the water

sear \'sir\ *vb* : scorch —**sear** *n*

search \'sərch\ *vb* **1** : look through **2** : seek —**search** *n* —**search·er** *n* — **search·light** *n*

sea·sick *adj* : nauseated by the motion of a ship —**sea·sick·ness** *n*

¹sea·son \'sēz³n\ *n* **1** : division of the year **2** : customary time for something —**sea·son·al** \'sēz³nəl\ *adj* —**sea·son·al·ly** *adv*

²season *vb* **1** : add spice to (food) **2** : make strong or fit for use —**sea·son·ing** \-niŋ\ *n*

sea·son·able \'sēznəbəl\ *adj* : occurring at a suitable time —**sea·son·ably** \-blē\ *adv*

seat \'sēt\ *n* **1** : place to sit **2** : chair, bench, or stool for sitting on **3** : place that serves as a capital or center ~ *vb*

1 : place in or on a seat 2 : provide seats for

sea·weed *n* : marine alga

sea·wor·thy *adj* : strong enough to hold up to a sea voyage

se·cede \si'sēd\ *vb* -ced·ed; -ced·ing : withdraw from a body (as a nation)

se·clude \si'klüd\ *vb* -clud·ed; -clud·ing : shut off alone —**se·clu·sion** \si-'klüzhən\ *n*

¹sec·ond \'sekənd\ *adj* : next after the 1st ~ *n* 1 : one that is second 2 : one who assists (as in a duel) —**second**, **se·cond·ly** *adv*

²second *n* 1 : 60th part of a minute 2 : moment

sec·ond·ary \'sekən,derē\ *adj* 1 : second in rank or importance 2 : coming after the primary or elementary

sec·ond·hand *adj* 1 : not original 2 : used before

second lieutenant *n* : lowest ranking commissioned officer of the army, air force, or marines

se·cret \'sēkrət\ *adj* 1 : hidden 2 : kept from general knowledge —**se·cre·cy** \-krəsē\ *n* —**secret** *n* —**se·cre·tive** \'sēkrətiv, si'krēt-\ *adj* —**se·cret·ly** *adv*

sec·re·tar·i·at \,sekrə'terēət\ *n* : administrative department

sec·re·tary \'sekrə,terē\ *n*, *pl* -tar·ies 1 : one hired to handle correspondence and other tasks for a superior 2 : official in charge of correspondence or records 3 : head of a government department —**sec·re·tar·i·al** \,sekrə-'terēəl\ *adj*

¹se·crete \si'krēt\ *vb* -cret·ed; -cret·ing : produce as a secretion

²se·crete \si'krēt, 'sēkrət\ *vb* -cret·ed; -cret·ing : hide

se·cre·tion \si'krēshən\ *n* 1 : process of secreting 2 : product of glandular activity

sect \'sekt\ *n* : religious group

sec·tar·i·an \sek'terēən\ *adj* 1 : relating to a sect 2 : limited in character or scope ~ *n* : member of a sect

sec·tion \'sekshən\ *n* : distinct part —**sec·tion·al** \-shənəl\ *adj*

sec·tor \'sektər\ *n* 1 : part of a circle between 2 radii 2 : distinctive part

sec·u·lar \'sekyələr\ *adj* 1 : not sacred 2 : not monastic

se·cure \si'kyür\ *adj* -cur·er; -est : free from danger or loss ~ *vb* 1 : fasten safely 2 : get —**se·cure·ly** *adv*

se·cu·ri·ty \si'kyürətē\ *n*, *pl* -ties 1 : safety 2 : something given to guarantee payment 3 *pl* : bond or stock certificates

se·dan \si'dan\ *n* 1 : chair carried by 2 men 2 : enclosed automobile

¹se·date \si'dāt\ *adj* : quiet and dignified —**se·date·ly** *adv*

²sedate *vb* -dat·ed; -dat·ing : dose with sedatives —**se·da·tion** \si'dāshən\ *n*

sed·a·tive \'sedətiv\ *adj* : serving to relieve tension ~ *n* : sedative drug

sed·en·tary \'sed³n,terē\ *adj* : characterized by much sitting

sedge \'sej\ *n* : grasslike marsh plant

sed·i·ment \'sedəmənt\ *n* : material that settles to the bottom of a liquid or is deposited by water or a glacier —**sed·i·men·ta·ry** \,sedə'mentərē\ *adj* —**sed·i·men·ta·tion** \-mən'tā-shən, -,men-\ *n*

se·di·tion \si'dishən\ *n* : revolution against a government —**se·di·tious** \-əs\ *adj*

se·duce \si'düs, -'dyüs\ *vb* -duced; -duc·ing 1 : lead astray 2 : entice to sexual intercourse —**se·duc·er** *n* —**se·duc·tion** \-'dəkshən\ *n* —**se·duc·tive** \-tiv\ *adj*

sed·u·lous \'sejələs\ *adj* : diligent

¹see \'sē\ *vb* saw \'sò\; seen \'sēn\; see·ing 1 : perceive by the eye 2 : have experience of 3 : understand 4 : make sure 5 : meet with or escort

²see *n* : jurisdiction of a bishop

seed \'sēd\ *n*, *pl* seed *or* seeds 1 : part by which a plant is propagated 2 : source ~ *vb* 1 : sow 2 : remove seeds from —**seed·less** *adj*

seed·ling \-liŋ\ *n* : young plant grown from seed

seedy \-ē\ *adj* seed·i·er; -est 1 : full of seeds 2 : shabby

seek \'sēk\ *vb* sought \'sòt\; seek·ing 1 : search for 2 : try to reach or obtain —**seek·er** *n*

seem \'sēm\ *vb* : give the impression of being —**seem·ing·ly** *adv*

seem·ly \-lē\ *adj* seem·li·er; -est : proper or fit

seep \'sēp\ *vb* : leak through fine pores or cracks —**seep·age** \'sēpij\ *n*

seer \'sēər\ *n* : one who foresees or predicts events

seer·suck·er \'sir,səkər\ *n* : light puckered fabric

see·saw \'sē,sò\ *n* : board balanced in the middle —**seesaw** *vb*

seethe \'sēth\ *vb* **seethed; seeth·ing**
: become violently agitated

seg·ment \'segmənt\ *n* : division of a
thing —**seg·ment·ed** \-,mentəd\ *adj*

seg·re·gate \'segri,gāt\ *vb* **-gat·ed; -gat·ing** 1 : cut off from others 2 : separate
by races —**seg·re·ga·tion** \,segri-
'gāshən\ *n*

seine \'sān\ *n* : large weighted fishing
net ~ *vb* : fish with a seine

seis·mic \'sīzmik, 'sīs-\ *adj* : relating to
an earthquake

seis·mo·graph \-mə,graf\ *n* : apparatus
for detecting earthquakes

seize \'sēz\ *vb* **seized; seiz·ing** : take by
force —**sei·zure** \'sēzhər\ *n*

sel·dom \'seldəm\ *adv* : not often

se·lect \sə'lekt\ *adj* 1 : favored 2
: discriminating ~ *vb* : take by preference —**se·lec·tive** \-'lektiv\ *adj*

se·lec·tion \sə'lekshən\ *n* : act of selecting or thing selected

se·lect·man \si'lekt,man, -mən\ *n* : New
England town official

self \'self\ *n, pl* **selves** \'selvz\ : essential
person distinct from others

self- *comb form* 1 : oneself or itself 2
: of oneself or itself 3 : by oneself or
automatic 4 : to, for, or toward oneself

self-addressed	self-defense
self-adminis-	self-denial
tered	self-denying
self-analysis	self-destruction
self-appointed	self-destructive
self-assertive	self-determina-
self-assurance	tion
self-assured	self-determined
self-awareness	self-discipline
self-cleaning	self-doubt
self-closing	self-educated
self-complacent	self-employed
self-conceit	self-employment
self-confessed	self-esteem
self-confidence	self-evident
self-confident	self-explanatory
self-contained	self-expression
self-contempt	self-fulfilling
self-contradic-	self-fulfillment
tion	self-governing
self-contradic-	self-government
tory	self-help
self-control	self-image
self-created	self-importance
self-criticism	self-important
self-defeating	self-imposed

self-improve-	self-reliance
ment	self-reliant
self-indulgence	self-respect
self-indulgent	self-respecting
self-inflicted	self-restraint
self-interest	self-sacrifice
self-love	self-satisfaction
self-operating	self-satisfied
self-pity	self-service
self-portrait	self-serving
self-possessed	self-starting
self-possession	self-styled
self-preserva-	self-sufficiency
tion	self-sufficient
self-proclaimed	self-supporting
self-propelled	self-taught
self-propelling	self-winding
self-protection	

self-cen·tered *adj* : concerned only
with one's own self

self-con·scious *adj* : uncomfortably
aware of oneself as an object of observation —**self-con·scious·ly** *adv* —
self-con·scious·ness *n*

self·ish \'selfish\ *adj* : excessively or ex-
clusively concerned with one's own
well-being —**self·ish·ly** *adv* —**self-
ish·ness** *n*

self·less \'selfləs\ *adj* : unselfish —**self-
less·ness** *n*

self-made *adj* : having succeeded by
one's own efforts

self-righ·teous *adj* : strongly convinced
of one's own righteousness

self·same \'self,sām\ *adj* : precisely the
same

sell \'sel\ *vb* **sold** \'sōld\; **sell·ing** 1
: transfer (property) esp. for money 2
: deal in as a business 3 : be sold —
sell·er *n*

selves *pl of* SELF

se·man·tic \si'mantik\ *adj* : relating to
meaning in language —**se·man·tics**
\-iks\ *n sing or pl*

sem·a·phore \'semə,fōr\ *n* 1 : visual signaling apparatus 2 : signaling by flags

sem·blance \'sembləns\ *n* : appearance

se·men \'sēmən\ *n* : male reproductive
fluid

se·mes·ter \sə'mestər\ *n* : half a school
year

semi- \-, semi, 'sem-, -,ī\ *prefix* 1 : half 2
: partial

semi·co·lon \'semi,kōlən\ *n* : punctuation mark ;

semi·con·duc·tor *n* : substance between

a conductor and a nonconductor in ability to conduct electricity —**semi·con·duct·ing** adj

semi·fi·nal adj : being next to the final —**semifinal** n

semi·for·mal adj : being or suitable for an occasion of moderate formality

sem·i·nal \'semən³l\ adj 1 : relating to seed or semen 2 : causing or influencing later development

sem·i·nar \'semə,när\ n : conference or conferencelike study

sem·i·nary \'semə,nerē\ n, pl **-nar·ies** : school and esp. a theological school —**sem·i·nar·i·an** \,semə'nerēən\ n

sen·ate \'senət\ n : upper branch of a legislature —**sen·a·tor** \-ər\ n —**sen·a·to·rial** \,senə'tōrēəl\ adj

send \'send\ vb **sent** \'sent\; **send·ing** 1 : cause to go 2 : propel —**send·er** n

se·nile \'sēn,īl, 'sen-\ adj : mentally deficient through old age —**se·nil·i·ty** \si'nilətē\ n

se·nior \'sēnyər\ adj : older or higher ranking —**senior** n —**se·nior·i·ty** \,sēn'yorətē\ n

senior chief petty officer n : petty officer in the navy or coast guard ranking next below a master chief petty officer

senior master sergeant n : noncommissioned officer in the air force ranking next below a chief master sergeant

sen·sa·tion \sen'sāshən\ n 1 : bodily feeling 2 : condition of excitement or the cause of it —**sen·sa·tion·al** \-shənəl\ adj

sense \'sens\ n 1 : meaning 2 : faculty of perceiving something physical 3 : sound mental capacity ~ vb **sensed**; **sens·ing** 1 : perceive by the senses 2 : detect automatically —**sense·less** adj —**sense·less·ly** adv

sen·si·bil·i·ty \,sensə'bilətē\ n, pl **-ties** : delicacy of feeling

sen·si·ble \'sensəbəl\ adj 1 : capable of sensing or being sensed 2 : aware or conscious 3 : reasonable —**sen·si·bly** \-blē\ adv

sen·si·tive \'sensətiv\ adj 1 : subject to excitation by or responsive to stimuli 2 : having power of feeling 3 : easily affected —**sen·si·tive·ness** n —**sen·si·tiv·i·ty** \,sensə'tivətē\ n

sen·si·tize \'sensə,tīz\ vb **-tized**; **-tiz·ing** : make or become sensitive

sen·sor \'sen,sor, -sər\ n : device that responds to a physical stimulus

sen·so·ry \'sensərē\ adj : relating to sensation or the senses

sen·su·al \'senchəwəl, -shəwəl\ adj 1 : pleasing the senses 2 : devoted to the pleasures of the senses —**sen·su·al·ist** n —**sen·su·al·i·ty** \,senchə'walətē\ n —**sen·su·al·ly** adv

sen·su·ous \'senchəwəs\ adj : having strong appeal to the senses

sent past of SEND

sen·tence \'sent³ns, -³nz\ n 1 : judgment of a court 2 : grammatically self-contained speech unit ~ vb **-tenced**; **-tenc·ing** : impose a sentence on

sen·ten·tious \sen'tenchəs\ adj : using pompous language

sen·tient \'senchēənt\ adj : capable of feeling

sen·ti·ment \'sentəmənt\ n 1 : belief 2 : feeling

sen·ti·men·tal \,sentə'ment³l\ adj : influenced by tender feelings —**sen·ti·men·tal·ism** n —**sen·ti·men·tal·ist** n —**sen·ti·men·tal·i·ty** \-,men'talətē, -mən-\ n —**sen·ti·men·tal·ize** \-'ment³l,īz\ vb —**sen·ti·men·tal·ly** adv

sen·ti·nel \'sent³nəl\ n : sentry

sen·try \'sentrē\ n, pl **-tries** : one who stands guard

se·pal \'sēpəl, 'sep-\ n : modified leaf in a flower calyx

sep·a·rate \'sepə,rāt\ vb **-rat·ed**; **-rat·ing** 1 : set or keep apart 2 : become divided or detached ~ \'seprət, 'sepə-\ adj 1 : not connected or shared 2 : distinct from each other —**sep·a·ra·ble** \'sepərəbəl\ adj —**sep·a·rate·ly** adv —**sep·a·ra·tion** \,sepə'rāshən\ n —**sep·a·ra·tor** \'sepə,rātər\ n

se·pia \'sēpēə\ n : brownish gray

Sep·tem·ber \sep'tembər\ n : 9th month of the year having 30 days

sep·ul·chre, **sep·ul·cher** \'sepəlkər\ n : burial vault —**se·pul·chral** \sə'pəlkrəl\ adj

se·quel \'sēkwəl\ n 1 : consequence or result 2 : continuation of a story

se·quence \'sēkwəns\ n : continuous or connected series —**se·quen·tial** \si'kwenchəl\ adj —**se·quen·tial·ly** adv

se·ques·ter \si'kwestər\ vb : segregate

se·quin \'sēkwən\ n : spangle

se·quoia \si'kwóiə\ n : huge California coniferous tree

sera pl of SERUM

ser·aph \'serəf\ n, pl **-a·phim** \-ə,fim\ or **-aphs** : angel —**se·raph·ic** \sə'rafik\ adj

sere \'sir\ adj : dried up or withered

ser·e·nade \,serə'nād\ n : music sung or played esp. to a woman being courted —**serenade** vb

ser·en·dip·i·ty \,serən'dipətē\ n : good luck in finding things not sought for —**ser·en·dip·i·tous** \-əs\ adj

se·rene \sə'rēn\ adj : tranquil —**se·rene·ly** adv —**se·ren·i·ty** \sə'renətē\ n

serf \'sərf\ n : peasant obligated to work the land —**serf·dom** \-dəm\ n

serge \'sərj\ n : twilled woolen cloth

ser·geant \'särjənt\ n : noncommissioned officer (as in the army) ranking next below a staff sergeant

sergeant first class n : noncommissioned officer in the army ranking next below a master sergeant

sergeant major n, pl **sergeants major** or **sergeant majors** 1 : noncommissioned officer serving as an enlisted adviser in a headquarters 2 : noncommissioned officer in the marine corps ranking above a first sergeant

se·ri·al \'sirēəl\ adj : being or relating to a series or sequence ~ n : story appearing in parts —**se·ri·al·ly** adv

se·ries \'sirēz\ n, pl series : number of things in order

se·ri·ous \'sirēəs\ adj 1 : subdued in appearance or manner 2 : sincere 3 : of great importance —**se·ri·ous·ly** adv —**se·ri·ous·ness** n

ser·mon \'sərmən\ n : lecture on religion or behavior

ser·pent \'sərpənt\ n : snake —**ser·pen·tine** \-pən,tēn, -,tīn\ adj

ser·rated \'ser,ātəd\ adj : saw-toothed

se·rum \'sirəm\ n, pl **-rums** or **-ra** \-ə\ : watery part of blood

ser·vant \'sərvənt\ n : person employed for domestic work

serve \'sərv\ vb served; serv·ing 1 : work through or perform a term of service 2 : be of use 3 : prove adequate 4 : hand out (food or drink) 5 : be of service to —**serv·er** n

ser·vice \'sərvəs\ n 1 : act or means of serving 2 : meeting for worship 3 : branch of public employment or the persons in it 4 : set of dishes or silverware 5 : benefit ~ vb **-viced; -vic·ing** : repair —**ser·vice·able** adj —

ser·vice·man \-,man, -mən\ n —**ser·vice·wom·an** n

ser·vile \'sərvəl, -,vīl\ adj : behaving like a slave —**ser·vil·i·ty** \,sər'vilətē\ n

serv·ing \'sərviŋ\ n : helping

ser·vi·tude \'sərvə,tüd, -,tyüd\ n : slavery

ses·a·me \'sesəmē\ n : annual herb or its seeds that are used in flavoring

ses·sion \'seshən\ n : meeting

set \'set\ vb set; set·ting 1 : cause to sit 2 : place 3 : settle, arrange, or adjust 4 : cause to be or do 5 : become fixed or solid 6 : sink below the horizon ~ adj : settled ~ n 1 : group classed together 2 : setting for the scene of a play or film 3 : electronic apparatus 4 : collection of mathematical elements —**set forth** : begin a trip —**set off** vb : set forth —**set out** vb : begin a trip or undertaking —**set up** vb 1 : assemble or erect 2 : cause

set·back n : reverse

set·tee \se'tē\ n : bench or sofa

set·ter \'setər\ n : large long-coated hunting dog

set·ting \'setiŋ\ n : the time, place, and circumstances in which something occurs

set·tle \'setªl\ vb **-tled; -tling** 1 : come to rest 2 : sink gradually 3 : establish in residence 4 : adjust or arrange 5 : calm 6 : dispose of (as by paying) 7 : decide or agree on —**set·tle·ment** \-mənt\ n —**set·tler** \'setªlər\ n

sev·en \'sevən\ n : one more than 6 —**seven** adj or pron —**sev·enth** \-ənth\ adj or adv or n

sev·en·teen \,sevən'tēn\ n : one more than 16 —**seventeen** adj or pron —**sev·en·teenth** \-'tēnth\ adj or n

sev·en·ty \'sevəntē\ n, pl **-ties** : 7 times 10 —**sev·en·ti·eth** \-tēəth\ adj or n —**seventy** adj or pron

sev·er \'sevər\ vb **-ered; -er·ing** : cut off or apart —**sev·er·ance** \'sevrəns, -vərəns\ n

sev·er·al \'sevrəl, 'sevə-\ adj 1 : distinct 2 : consisting of an indefinite but not large number —**sev·er·al·ly** adv

se·vere \sə'vir\ adj **-ver·er; -est** 1 : strict 2 : restrained or unadorned 3 : painful or distressing 4 : hard to endure —**se·vere·ly** adv —**se·ver·i·ty** \-'verətē\ n

sew \'sō\ vb sewed; sewn \'sōn\ or sewed; sew·ing : join or fasten by stitches —**sew·ing** n

sew•age \'süij\ *n* : liquid household waste

¹sew•er \'sōər\ *n* : one that sews

²sew•er \'süər\ *n* : pipe or channel to carry off waste matter

sex \'seks\ *n* **1** : either of 2 divisions into which organisms are grouped according to their reproductive roles or the qualities which differentiate them **2** : copulation —**sexed** \'sekst\ *adj* —**sex•less** *adj* —**sex•ual** \'sekshəwəl\ *adj* —**sex•u•al•i•ty** \,sekshə'walətē\ *n* —**sex•u•al•ly** *adv* —**sexy** *adj*

sex•ism \'sek,sizəm\ *n* : discrimination based on sex and esp. against women —**sex•ist** \'seksist\ *adj or n*

sex•tant \'sekstənt\ *n* : instrument for navigation

sex•tet \sek'stet\ *n* **1** : music for 6 performers **2** : group of 6

sex•ton \'sekstən\ *n* : church caretaker

shab•by \'shabē\ *adj* **-bi•er; -est 1** : worn and faded **2** : dressed in worn clothes **3** : not generous or fair —**shab•bi•ly** *adv* —**shab•bi•ness** *n*

shack \'shak\ *n* : hut

shack•le \'shakəl\ *n* : metal device to bind legs or arms ~ *vb* **-led; -ling** : bind or fasten with shackles

shad \'shad\ *n* : Atlantic food fish

shade \'shād\ *n* **1** : space sheltered from the light esp. of the sun **2** : gradation of color **3** : small difference **4** : something that shades ~ *vb* **shad•ed; shad•ing 1** : shelter from light and heat **2** : add shades of color to **3** : show slight differences esp. in color or meaning

shad•ow \'shadō\ *n* **1** : shade cast upon a surface by something blocking light **2** : trace **3** : gloomy influence ~ *vb* **1** : cast a shadow **2** : follow closely —**shad•owy** *adj*

shady \'shādē\ *adj* **shad•i•er; -est 1** : giving shade **2** : of dubious honesty

shaft \'shaft\ *n* **1** : long slender cylindrical part **2** : deep vertical opening (as of a mine)

shag \'shag\ *n* : shaggy tangled mat

shag•gy \'shagē\ *adj* **-gi•er; -est 1** : covered with long hair or wool **2** : not neat and combed

shake \'shāk\ *vb* **shook** \'shuk\; **shak•en** \'shākən\; **shak•ing 1** : move or cause to move quickly back and forth **2** : distress **3** : clasp (hands) as friendly gesture —**shake** *n* —**shak•er** \-ər\ *n*

shake–up *n* : reorganization

shaky \'shākē\ *adj* **shak•i•er; -est** : not sound, stable, or reliable —**shak•i•ly** *adv* —**shak•i•ness** *n*

shale \'shāl\ *n* : stratified rock

shall \'shal\ *vb, past* **should** \'shud\; *pres sing & pl* **shall** —used as an auxiliary to express a command, futurity, or determination

shal•low \'shalō\ *adj* **1** : not deep **2** : not intellectually profound

shal•lows \-ōz\ *n pl* : area of shallow water

sham \'sham\ *adj or n or vb* : fake

sham•ble \'shambəl\ *vb* **-bled; -bling** : shuffle along —**sham•ble** *n*

sham•bles \'shambəlz\ *n* : state of disorder

shame \'shām\ *n* **1** : distress over guilt or disgrace **2** : cause of shame or regret ~ *vb* **shamed; sham•ing 1** : make ashamed **2** : disgrace —**shame•ful** \-fəl\ *adj* —**shame•ful•ly** \-ē\ *adv* —**shame•less** *adj* —**shame•less•ly** *adv*

shame•faced \'shām'fāst\ *adj* : ashamed

sham•poo \sham'pü\ *vb* : wash one's hair ~ *n, pl* **-poos** : act of or preparation used in shampooing

sham•rock \'sham,räk\ *n* : plant of legend with 3-lobed leaves

shank \'shaŋk\ *n* : part of the leg between the knee and ankle

shan•ty \'shantē\ *n, pl* **-ties** : hut

shape \'shāp\ *vb* **shaped; shap•ing** : form esp. in a particular structure or appearance ~ *n* **1** : distinctive appearance or arrangement of parts **2** : condition —**shape•less** \-ləs\ *adj* —**shape•li•ness** *n* —**shape•ly** *adj*

shard \'shärd\ *n* : broken piece

share \'sher\ *n* **1** : portion belonging to one **2** : interest in a company's stock ~ *vb* **shared; shar•ing** : divide or use with others —**share•hold•er** *n* —**shar•er** *n*

share•crop•per \-,kräpər\ *n* : farmer who works another's land in return for a share of the crop —**share•crop** *vb*

shark \'shärk\ *n* : voracious sea fish

sharp \'shärp\ *adj* **1** : having a good point or cutting edge **2** : alert, clever, or sarcastic **3** : vigorous or fierce **4** : having prominent angles or a sudden change in direction **5** : distinct **6** : higher than the true pitch ~ *adv* : exactly ~ *n* : sharp note —**sharp•ly** *adv* —**sharp•ness** *n*

sharp·en \'shärpən\ *vb* : make sharp — **sharp·en·er** \-ənər\ *n*

sharp·shoot·er *n* : expert marksman — **sharp·shoot·ing** *n*

shat·ter \'shatər\ *vb* : smash or burst into fragments —**shat·ter·proof** \-,prüf\ *adj*

shave \'shāv\ *vb* **shaved; shaved** *or* **shav·en** \'shāvən\; **shav·ing 1** : cut off with a razor **2** : make bare by cutting the hair from **3** : slice very thin ~ *n* : act or instance of shaving — **shav·er** *n*

shawl \'shol\ *n* : loose covering for the head or shoulders

she \'shē\ *pron* : that female one

sheaf \'shēf\ *n, pl* **sheaves** \'shēvz\ : bundle esp. of grain stalks

shear \'shir\ *vb* **sheared; sheared** *or* **shorn** \'shōrn\; **shear·ing 1** : trim wool from **2** : cut off with scissorlike action

shears \'shirz\ *n pl* : cutting tool with 2 blades fastened so that the edges slide by each other

sheath \'shēth\ *n, pl* **sheaths** \'shēthz, 'shēths\ : covering (as for a blade)

sheathe \'shēth\ *vb* **sheathed; sheath·ing** : put into a sheath

shed \'shed\ *vb* **shed; shed·ding 1** : give off (as tears or hair) **2** : cause to flow or diffuse ~ *n* : small storage building

sheen \'shēn\ *n* : subdued luster

sheep \'shēp\ *n, pl* **sheep** : domesticated mammal covered with wool —**sheep·skin** *n*

sheep·ish \'shēpish\ *adj* : embarrassed by awareness of a fault

sheer \'shir\ *adj* **1** : pure **2** : very steep **3** : very thin or transparent —**sheer** *adv*

sheet \'shēt\ *n* : broad flat piece (as of cloth or paper)

sheikh, sheik \'shēk, 'shāk\ *n* : Arab chief —**sheikh·dom, sheik·dom** \-dəm\ *n*

shelf \'shelf\ *n, pl* **shelves** \'shelvz\ **1** : flat narrow structure used for storage or display **2** : sandbank or rock ledge

shell \'shel\ *n* **1** : hard or tough outer covering **2** : case holding explosive powder and projectile for a weapon **3** : light racing boat with oars ~ *vb* **1** : remove the shell of **2** : bombard — **shelled** \'sheld\ *adj* —**shell·er** *n*

shel·lac \shə'lak\ *n* : varnish ~ *vb* **-lacked; -lack·ing 1** : coat with shellac **2** : defeat —**shel·lack·ing** *n*

shell·fish *n* : water animal with a shell

shel·ter \'sheltər\ *n* : something that gives protection ~ *vb* : give refuge to

shelve \'shelv\ *vb* **shelved; shelv·ing 1** : place or store on shelves **2** : dismiss or put aside

she·nan·i·gans \shə'nanigənz\ *n pl* : mischievous or deceitful conduct

shep·herd \'shepərd\ *n* : one that tends sheep ~ *vb* : act as a shepherd or guardian

shep·herd·ess \'shepərdəs\ *n* : woman who tends sheep

sher·bet \'shərbət\, **sher·bert** \-bərt\ *n* : fruit-flavored frozen dessert

sher·iff \'sherəf\ *n* : county law officer

sher·ry \'sherē\ *n, pl* **-ries** : type of wine

shield \'shēld\ *n* **1** : broad piece of armor carried on the arm **2** : something that protects —**shield** *vb*

shier *comparative of* SHY

shiest *superlative of* SHY

shift \'shift\ *vb* **1** : change place, position, or direction **2** : get by ~ *n* **1** : loose-fitting dress **2** : an act or instance of shifting **3** : scheduled work period

shift·less \-ləs\ *adj* : lazy

shifty \'shiftē\ *adj* **shift·i·er; -est** : tricky or untrustworthy

shil·le·lagh \shə'lālē\ *n* : club or stick

shil·ling \'shiliŋ\ *n* : former British coin

shil·ly-shal·ly \'shilē,shalē\ *vb* **-shal·lied; -shally·ing 1** : hesitate **2** : dawdle

shim·mer \'shimər\ *vb or n* : glimmer

shin \'shin\ *n* : front part of the leg below the knee ~ *vb* **-nn-** : climb by sliding the body close along

shine \'shīn\ *vb* **shone** \-shōn\ *or* **shined; shin·ing 1** : give off or cause to give off light **2** : be outstanding **3** : polish ~ *n* : brilliance

shin·gle \'shiŋgəl\ *n* **1** : small thin piece used in covering roofs or exterior walls —**shingle** *vb*

shin·gles \'shiŋgəlz\ *n pl* : acute inflammation of spinal nerves

shin·ny \'shinē\ *vb* **-nied; -ny·ing** : shin

shiny \'shīnē\ *adj* **shin·i·er; -est** : bright or polished

ship \'ship\ *n* **1** : large oceangoing vessel **2** : aircraft or spacecraft ~ *vb* **-pp- 1** : put on a ship **2** : transport by carrier —**ship·board** *n* —**ship·build·er** *n* —**ship·per** *n* —**ship·wreck** *n or vb* — **ship·yard** *n*

-ship \,ship\ *n suffix* **1** : state, condition,

or quality **2** : rank or profession **3**
: skill **4** : something showing a state
or quality

ship·ment \-mənt\ *n* : an act of shipping
or the goods shipped

ship·ping \'shipiŋ\ *n* **1** : ships **2**
: transportation of goods

ship·shape *adj* : tidy

shire \'shīr, *in place-name compounds*
,shir, shər\ *n* : British county

shirk \'shərk\ *vb* : evade —**shirk·er** *n*

shirr \'shər\ *vb* **1** : gather (cloth) by
drawing up parallel lines of stitches **2**
: bake (eggs) in a dish

shirt \'shərt\ *n* : garment for covering
the torso —**shirt·less** *adj*

shiv·er \'shivər\ *vb* : tremble —**shiver** *n*
—**shiv·ery** *adj*

shoal \'shōl\ *n* : shallow place (as in a
river)

¹shock \'shäk\ *n* : pile of sheaves set up
in a field

²shock *n* **1** : forceful impact **2** : violent
mental or emotional disturbance **3**
: effect of a charge of electricity **4**
: depression of the vital bodily processes ~ *vb* **1** : strike with surprise,
horror, or disgust **2** : subject to an
electrical shock —**shock·proof** *adj*

³shock *n* : bushy mass (as of hair)

shod·dy \'shädē\ *adj* **-di·er; -est** : poorly
made or done —**shod·di·ly** \'shäd³lē\
adv —**shod·di·ness** *n*

shoe \'shü\ *n* **1** : covering for the human
foot **2** : horseshoe ~ *vb* **shod** \'shäd\:
shoe·ing : put horseshoes on —**shoe·**
lace *n* —**shoe·ma·ker** *n*

shone *past of* SHINE

shook *past of* SHAKE

shoot \'shüt\ *vb* **shot** \'shät\: **shoot·ing** **1**
: propel (as an arrow or bullet) **2**
: wound or kill with a missile **3**
: discharge (a weapon) **4** : drive (as a
ball) at a goal **5** : photograph **6** : move
swiftly ~ *n* : new plant growth —
shoot·er *n*

shop \'shäp\ *n* : place where things are
made or sold ~ *vb* **-pp-** : visit stores
—**shop·keep·er** *n* —**shop·per** *n*

shop·lift *vb* : steal goods from a store
—**shop·lift·er** \-,liftər\ *n*

¹shore \'shōr\ *n* : land along the edge of
water —**shore·line** *n*

²shore *vb* **shored; shor·ing** : prop up ~
n : something that props

shore·bird *n* : bird of the seashore

shorn *past part of* SHEAR

short \'short\ *adj* **1** : not long or tall or

extending far **2** : brief in time **3** : curt
4 : not having or being enough ~ *adv*
: curtly ~ *n* **1** *pl* : short drawers or
trousers **2** : short circuit —**short·en**
\-³n\ *vb* —**short·ly** *adv* —**short·ness**
n

short·age \'shortij\ *n* : deficiency

short·cake *n* : dessert of biscuit with
sweetened fruit

short·change *vb* : cheat esp. by giving
too little change

short circuit *n* : abnormal electric connection —**short–circuit** *vb*

short·com·ing *n* : fault or failing

short·cut \-,kət\ *n* **1** : more direct route
than that usu. taken **2** : quicker way
of doing something

short·hand *n* : method of speed writing

short–lived \'short'līvd, -,līvd\ *adj* : of
short life or duration

short·sight·ed *adj* : lacking foresight

shot \'shät\ *n* **1** : act of shooting **2**
: attempt (as at making a goal) **3**
: small pellets forming a charge **4**
: range or reach **5** : photograph **6**
: injection of medicine **7** : small serving of liquor —**shot·gun** *n*

should \'shüd\ *past of* SHALL —used as
an auxiliary to express condition, obligation, or probability

shoul·der \'shōldər\ *n* **1** : part of the
body where the arm joins the trunk **2**
: part that projects or lies to the side
~ *vb* : push with or bear on the shoulder

shoulder blade *n* : flat triangular bone
at the back of the shoulder

shout \'shaut\ *vb* : give voice loudly —
shout *n*

shove \'shəv\ *vb* **shoved; shov·ing**
: push along or away —**shove** *n*

shov·el \'shəvəl\ *n* : broad tool for digging or lifting ~ *vb* **-eled** *or* **-elled;**
-el·ing *or* **-el·ling** : take up or dig with
a shovel

show \'shō\ *vb* **showed** \'shōd\; **shown**
\'shōn\ *or* **showed; show·ing** **1**
: present to view **2** : reveal or demonstrate **3** : teach **4** : prove **5** : conduct
or escort **6** : appear or be noticeable
~ *n* **1** : demonstrative display **2**
: spectacle **3** : theatrical, radio, or
television program —**show·case** *n*

show off *vb* **1** : display proudly **2** : act
so as to attract attention —**show up**
vb : arrive

show·down *n* : decisive confrontation

show·er \'shauər\ *n* **1** : brief fall of rain

2 : bath in which water sprinkles down on the person or a facility for such a bath **3** : party at which someone gets gifts ~ *vb* **1** : rain or fall in a shower **2** : bathe in a shower — **show·ery** *adj*

showy \'shō\ *adj* **show·i·er; -est** : very noticeable or overly elaborate — **show·i·ly** *adv* —**show·i·ness** *n*

shrap·nel \'shrapnᵊl\ *n, pl* **shrapnel** : metal fragments of a bomb

shred \'shred\ *n* : narrow strip cut or torn off ~ *vb* **-dd-** : cut or tear into shreds

shrew \'shrü\ *n* **1** : scolding woman **2** : mouselike mammal —**shrew·ish** \-ish\ *adj*

shrewd \'shrüd\ *adj* : clever —**shrewd·ly** *adv* —**shrewd·ness** *n*

shriek \'shrēk\ *n* : shrill cry —**shriek** *vb*

shrill \'shril\ *adj* : piercing and high-pitched —**shril·ly** *adv*

shrimp \'shrimp\ *n* : small sea crustacean

shrine \'shrīn\ *n* **1** : tomb of a saint **2** : hallowed place

shrink \'shriŋk\ *vb* **shrank** \'shraŋk\; **shrunk** \'shrəŋk\ *or* **shrunk·en** \'shrəŋkən\: **shrink·ing 1** : draw back or away **2** : become smaller —**shrink·able** *adj*

shrink·age \'shriŋkij\ *n* : amount lost by shrinking

shriv·el \'shrivəl\ *vb* **-eled** *or* **-elled; -el·ing** *or* **-el·ling** : shrink or wither into wrinkles

shroud \'shraúd\ *n* **1** : cloth put over a corpse **2** : cover or screen ~ *vb* : veil or screen from view

shrub \'shrəb\ *n* : low woody plant — **shrub·by** *adj*

shrub·bery \'shrəbərē\ *n, pl* **-ber·ies** : growth of shrubs

shrug \'shrəg\ *vb* **-gg-** : hunch the shoulders up in doubt, indifference, or uncertainty —**shrug** *n*

shuck \'shək\ *vb* : strip off a shell or husk —**shuck** *n*

shud·der \'shədər\ *vb* : tremble —**shud·der** *n*

shuf·fle \'shəfəl\ *vb* **-fled; -fling 1** : mix together **2** : walk with a sliding movement —**shuffle** *n*

shuf·fle·board \'shəfəl,bōrd\ *n* : game of sliding disks into a scoring area

shun \'shən\ *vb* **-nn-** : keep away from

shunt \'shənt\ *vb* : turn off to one side

shut \'shət\ *vb* **shut; shut·ting 1** : bar passage into or through (as by moving a lid or door) **2** : suspend activity — **shut out** *vb* : exclude —**shut up** *vb* : stop or cause to stop talking

shut-in *n* : invalid

shut·ter \'shətər\ *n* **1** : movable cover for a window **2** : camera part that exposes film

shut·tle \'shətᵊl\ *n* **1** : part of a weaving machine that carries thread back and forth **2** : vehicle traveling back and forth over a short route ~ *vb* **-tled; -tling** : move back and forth frequently

shut·tle·cock \'shətᵊl,käk\ *n* : light conical object used in badminton

shy \'shī\ *adj* **shi·er** *or* **shy·er** \'shīər\; **shi·est** *or* **shy·est** \'shīəst\ **1** : sensitive and hesitant in dealing with others **2** : wary **3** : lacking ~ *vb* **shied; shy·ing** : draw back (as in fright) —**shy·ly** *adv* —**shy·ness** *n*

sib·i·lant \'sibələnt\ *adj* : having the sound of the *s* or the *sh* in *sash* — **sibilant** *n*

sib·ling \'sibliŋ\ *n* : brother or sister

sick \'sik\ *adj* **1** : not in good health **2** : nauseated **3** : relating to or meant for the sick —**sick·bed** *n* —**sick·en** \-ən\ *vb* —**sick·ly** *adj* —**sick·ness** *n*

sick·le \'sikəl\ *n* : curved short-handled blade

side \'sīd\ *n* **1** : part to left or right of an object or the torso **2** : edge or surface away from the center or at an angle to top and bottom or ends **3** : contrasting or opposing position or group —**sid·ed** *adj*

side·board *n* : piece of dining-room furniture for table service

side·burns \-,bərnz\ *n pl* : whiskers in front of the ears

side·long \'sīd,lóŋ\ *adv or adj* : to or along the side

side·show *n* : minor show at a circus

side·step *vb* **1** : step aside **2** : avoid

side·swipe \-,swīp\ *vb* : strike with a glancing blow —**sideswipe** *n*

side·track *vb* : lead aside or astray

side·walk *n* : paved walk at the side of a road

side·ways \-,wāz\ *adv or adj* **1** : to or from the side **2** : with one side to the front

sid·ing \'sīdiŋ\ *n* **1** : short railroad track **2** : material for covering the outside of a building

si·dle \'sīdᵊl\ *vb* **-dled; -dling** : move sideways or unobtrusively

siege \'sēj\ *n* : persistent attack (as on a fortified place)

si·es·ta \sē'estə\ *n* : midday nap

sieve \'siv\ *n* : utensil with holes to separate particles

sift \'sift\ *vb* 1 : pass through a sieve 2 : examine carefully —**sift·er** *n*

sigh \'sī\ *n* : audible release of the breath (as to express weariness) —**sigh** *vb*

sight \'sīt\ *n* 1 : something seen or worth seeing 2 : process, power, or range of seeing 3 : device used in aiming 4 : view or glimpse ~ *vb* : get sight of —**sight·ed** *adj* —**sight·less** *adj* —**sight–see·ing** *adj* —**sight·seer** \-,sēər\ *n*

sign \'sīn\ *n* 1 : symbol 2 : gesture expressing a command or thought 3 : public notice to advertise or warn 4 : trace ~ *vb* 1 : mark with or make a sign 2 : write one's name on —**sign·er** *n*

sig·nal \'signᵊl\ *n* 1 : sign of command or warning 2 : electronic transmission ~ *vb* -naled *or* -nalled; -nal·ing *or* -nal·ling : communicate or notify by signals ~ *adj* : distinguished

sig·na·to·ry \'signə,tōrē\ *n, pl* -ries : person or government that signs jointly with others

sig·na·ture \'signə,chùr\ *n* : one's name written by oneself

sig·net \'signət\ *n* : small seal

sig·nif·i·cance \sig'nifikəns\ *n* 1 : meaning 2 : importance —**sig·nif·i·cant** \-kənt\ *adj* —**sig·nif·i·cant·ly** *adv*

sig·ni·fy \'signə,fī\ *vb* -fied; -fy·ing 1 : show by a sign 2 : mean —**sig·ni·fi·ca·tion** \,signəfə'kāshən\ *n*

si·lence \'sīləns\ *n* : state of being without sound ~ *vb* -lenced; -lenc·ing : keep from making noise or sound —**si·lenc·er** *n*

si·lent \'sīlənt\ *adj* : having or producing no sound —**si·lent·ly** *adv*

sil·hou·ette \,silə'wet\ *n* : outline filled in usu. with black ~ *vb* -ett·ed; -ett·ing : represent by a silhouette

sil·i·ca \'silikə\ *n* : mineral found as quartz and opal

sil·i·con \'silikən, -,kän\ *n* : nonmetallic chemical element

silk \'silk\ *n* 1 : fine strong lustrous protein fiber from moth larvae (**silk·worms** \-,wərmz\) 2 : thread or cloth made from silk —**silk·en** \'silkən\ *adj* —**silky** *adj*

sill \'sil\ *n* : bottom part of a window frame or a doorway

sil·ly \'silē\ *adj* **sil·li·er; -est** : foolish or stupid —**sil·li·ness** *n*

si·lo \'sīlō\ *n, pl* -los : tall building for storing animal feed

silt \'silt\ *n* : fine earth carried by rivers ~ *vb* : obstruct or cover with silt

sil·ver \'silvər\ *n* 1 : white ductile metallic chemical element 2 : silverware ~ *adj* : having the color of silver —**sil·very** *adj*

sil·ver·ware \-,war\ *n* : eating and serving utensils esp. of silver

sim·i·lar \'simələr\ *adj* : resembling each other in some ways —**sim·i·lar·i·ty** \,simə'larətē\ *n* —**sim·i·lar·ly** \'simələrlē\ *adv*

sim·i·le \'simə,lē\ *n* : comparison of unlike things using *like* or *as*

sim·mer \'simər\ *vb* : stew gently

sim·per \'simpər\ *vb* : give a silly smile —**simper** *n*

sim·ple \'simpəl\ *adj* -pler; -plest 1 : free from dishonesty, vanity, or pretense 2 : of humble origin or modest position 3 : not complex 4 : lacking education, experience, or intelligence —**sim·ple·ness** *n* —**sim·ply** \-plē\ *adv*

sim·ple·ton \'simpəltən\ *n* : fool

sim·plic·i·ty \sim'plisətē\ *n* : state or fact of being simple

sim·pli·fy \'simplə,fī\ *vb* -fied; -fy·ing : make easier —**sim·pli·fi·ca·tion** \,simpləfə'kāshən\ *n*

sim·u·late \'simyə,lāt\ *vb* -lat·ed; -lat·ing : create the effect or appearance of —**sim·u·la·tion** \,simyə'lāshən\ *n* —**sim·u·la·tor** \'simyə,lātər\ *n*

si·mul·ta·ne·ous \,sīməl'tānēəs\ *adj* : occurring or operating at the same time —**si·mul·ta·ne·ous·ly** *adv* —**si·mul·ta·ne·ous·ness** *n*

sin \'sin\ *n* : offense against God ~ *vb* -nn- : commit a sin —**sin·ful** \-fəl\ *adj* —**sin·less** *adj* —**sin·ner** *n*

since \'sins\ *adv* 1 : from a past time until now 2 : backward in time ~ *prep* 1 : in the period after 2 : continuously from ~ *conj* 1 : from the time when 2 : because

sin·cere \sin'sir\ *adj* -cer·er; -cer·est : genuine or honest —**sin·cere·ly** *adv* —**sin·cer·i·ty** \-'serətē\ *n*

si·ne·cure \'sīni,kyùr, 'sini-\ *n* : well-paid job that requires little work

sin·ew \'sinyū\ *n* 1 : tendon 2 : physical strength —**sin·ewy** *adj*

sing \'siŋ\ *vb* **sang** \'saŋ\ *or* **sung** \'səŋ\; **sung**; **sing·ing** : produce musical tones with the voice —**sing·er** *n*

singe \'sinj\ *vb* **singed**; **singe·ing** : scorch lightly

sin·gle \'siŋgəl\ *adj* 1 : one only 2 : unmarried ~ *n* : separate one —**sin·gle·ness** *n* —**sin·gly** \-glē\ *adv* — **sin·gle out** *vb* : select or set aside

sin·gu·lar \'siŋgyələr\ *adj* 1 : relating to a word form denoting one 2 : outstanding or superior 3 : queer —**singular** *n* —**sin·gu·lar·i·ty** \,siŋgyə'larətē\ *n* —**sin·gu·lar·ly** \'siŋgyə-lərlē\ *adv*

sin·is·ter \'sinəstər\ *adj* : threatening evil

sink \'siŋk\ *vb* **sank** \'saŋk\ *or* **sunk** \'səŋk\; **sunk**; **sink·ing** 1 : submerge or descend 2 : grow worse 3 : make by digging or boring 4 : invest ~ *n* : basin with a drain

sink·er \'siŋkər\ *n* : weight to sink a fishing line

sin·u·ous \'sinyəwəs\ *adj* : winding in and out —**sin·u·os·i·ty** \,sinyə-'wäsətē\ *n* —**sin·u·ous·ly** *adv*

si·nus \'sīnəs\ *n* : skull cavity usu. connecting with the nostrils

sip \'sip\ *vb* **-pp-** : drink in small quantities —**sip** *n*

si·phon \'sīfən\ *n* : tube that draws liquid by suction —**siphon** *vb*

sir \'sər\ *n* 1 —used before the first name of a knight or baronet 2 —used as a respectful form of address

sire \'sīr\ *n* : father ~ *vb* **sired**; **sir·ing** : beget

si·ren \'sīrən\ *n* 1 : seductive woman 2 : wailing warning whistle

sir·loin \'sər,lóin\ *n* : cut of beef

sirup *var of* SYRUP

si·sal \'sīsəl, -zəl\ *n* : strong rope fiber

sis·sy \'sisē\ *n, pl* **-sies** : timid or effeminate boy

sis·ter \'sistər\ *n* : female sharing one or both parents with another person — **sis·ter·hood** \-,hud\ *n* —**sis·ter·ly** *adj*

sis·ter-in-law *n, pl* **sis·ters-in-law** : sister of one's spouse or wife of one's brother

sit \'sit\ *vb* **sat** \'sat\; **sit·ting** 1 : rest on the buttocks or haunches 2 : roost 3 : hold a session 4 : pose for a portrait 5 : have a location 6 : rest or fix in place —**sit·ter** *n*

site \'sīt\ *n* : place

sit·u·at·ed \'sichə,wātəd\ *adj* : located

sit·u·a·tion \,sichə'wāshən\ *n* 1 : location 2 : condition 3 : job

six \'siks\ *n* : one more than 5 —**six** *adj or pron* —**sixth** \'siksth\ *adj or adv or n*

six·teen \siks'tēn\ *n* : one more than 15 —**sixteen** *adj or pron* —**six·teenth** \-'tēnth\ *adj or n*

six·ty \'sikstē\ *n, pl* **-ties** : 6 times 10 —**six·ti·eth** \-əth\ *adj or n* —**sixty** *adj or pron*

siz·able, size·able \'sīzəbəl\ *adj* : quite large —**siz·ably** \-blē\ *adv*

size \'sīz\ *n* : measurement of the amount of space something takes up ~ *vb* : grade according to size

siz·zle \'sizəl\ *vb* **-zled**; **-zling** : fry with a hissing sound —**sizzle** *n*

skate \'skāt\ *n* 1 : metal runner on a shoe for gliding over ice 2 : roller skate —**skate** *vb* —**skat·er** *n*

skein \'skān\ *n* : loosely twisted quantity of yarn or thread

skel·e·ton \'skelət³n\ *n* : bony framework —**skel·e·tal** \-ət³l\ *adj*

skep·tic \'skeptik\ *n* : one who is critical or doubting —**skep·ti·cal** \-tikəl\ *adj* —**skep·ti·cism** \-tə,sizəm\ *n*

sketch \'skech\ *n* 1 : rough drawing 2 : short story or essay —**sketch** *vb* —**sketchy** *adj*

skew·er \'skyüər\ *n* : long pin for holding roasting meat —**skewer** *vb*

ski \'skē\ *n, pl* **skis** : long strip for gliding over snow or water —**ski** *vb* —**ski·er** *n*

skid \'skid\ *n* 1 : plank for supporting something or on which it slides 2 : act of skidding ~ *vb* **-dd-** : slide sideways

skiff \'skif\ *n* : small boat

skill \'skil\ *n* : developed or learned ability —**skilled** \'skild\ *adj* —**skill·ful** \-fəl\ *adj* —**skill·ful·ly** *adv*

skil·let \'skilət\ *n* : pan for frying

skim \'skim\ *vb* **-mm-** 1 : take off from the top of a liquid 2 : read or move over swiftly ~ *adj* : having the cream removed —**skim·mer** *n*

skimp \'skimp\ *vb* : give too little of something —**skimpy** *adj*

skin \'skin\ *n* 1 : outer layer of an animal body 2 : rind ~ *vb* **-nn-** : take the skin from —**skin·less** *adj* —**skinned** *adj* —**skin·tight** *adj*

skin diving *n* : sport of swimming under water with a face mask and flippers

skin·flint \'skin,flint\ *n* : stingy person

skin·ny \'skinē\ *adj* **-ni·er; -est** : very thin

skip \'skip\ *vb* **-pp- 1** : move with leaps **2** : read past or ignore —**skip** *n*

skip·per \'skipər\ *n* : ship's master — **skipper** *vb*

skir·mish \'skərmish\ *n* : minor combat —**skirmish** *vb*

skirt \'skərt\ *n* : garment or part of a garment that hangs below the waist ~ *vb* : pass around the edge of

skit \'skit\ *n* : brief usu. humorous play

skit·tish \'skitish\ *adj* : easily frightened

skulk \'skəlk\ *vb* : move furtively

skull \'skəl\ *n* : bony case that protects the brain

skunk \'skəŋk\ *n* : mammal that can forcibly eject an ill-smelling fluid

sky \'skī\ *n, pl* **skies 1** : upper air **2** : heaven —**sky·line** *n* —**sky·ward** \-wərd\ *adv or adj*

sky·lark \'skī,lärk\ *n* : European lark noted for its song

sky·light *n* : window in a roof or ceiling

sky·rock·et *n* : shooting firework ~ *vb* : rise suddenly

sky·scrap·er \-,skrāpər\ *n* : very tall building

slab \'slab\ *n* : thick slice

slack \'slak\ *adj* **1** : careless **2** : not taut **3** : not busy ~ *n* **1** : part hanging loose **2** *pl* : casual trousers —**slack·en** *vb* —**slack·ly** *adv* —**slack·ness** *n*

slag \'slag\ *n* : waste from melting of ores

slain *past part of* SLAY

slake \'slāk\ *vb* **slaked; slak·ing** : quench

slam \'slam\ *n* : heavy jarring impact ~ *vb* **-mm-** : shut, strike, or throw violently and loudly

slan·der \'slandər\ *n* : malicious gossip ~ *vb* : hurt (someone) with slander —**slan·der·er** *n* —**slan·der·ous** *adj*

slang \'slaŋ\ *n* : informal nonstandard vocabulary —**slangy** *adj*

slant \'slant\ *vb* **1** : slope **2** : present with a special viewpoint ~ *n* : sloping direction, line, or plane

slap \'slap\ *vb* **-pp-** : strike sharply with the open hand —**slap** *n*

slash \'slash\ *vb* **1** : cut with sweeping strokes **2** : reduce sharply ~ *n* : gash

slat \'slat\ *n* : thin narrow flat strip

slate \'slāt\ *n* **1** : dense fine-grained layered rock **2** : roofing tile or writing tablet of slate **3** : list of candidates ~ *vb* **slat·ed; slat·ing** : designate

slat·tern \'slatərn\ *n* : untidy woman — **slat·tern·ly** *adj*

slaugh·ter \'slotər\ *n* **1** : butchering of livestock for market **2** : great and cruel destruction of lives ~ *vb* : commit slaughter upon —**slaugh·ter·house** *n*

slave \'slāv\ *n* : one owned and forced into service by another ~ *vb* **slaved; slav·ing** : work as or like a slave — **slave** *adj* —**slav·ery** \'slāvərē\ *n*

sla·ver \'slavər, 'slāv-\ *vb or n* : slobber

slav·ish \'slāvish\ *adj* : of or like a slave —**slav·ish·ly** *adv*

slay \'slā\ *vb* **slew** \'slü\; **slain** \'slān\; **slay·ing** : kill —**slay·er** *n*

slea·zy \'slēzē, 'slā-\ *adj* **-zi·er; -est** : shabby or shoddy

sled \'sled\ *n* : vehicle on runners —**sled** *vb*

¹sledge \'slej\ *n* : sledgehammer

²sledge *n* : heavy sled

sledge·ham·mer *n* : heavy long-handled hammer —**sledgehammer** *adj or vb*

sleek \'slēk\ *adj* : smooth or glossy — **sleek** *vb*

sleep \'slēp\ *n* : natural suspension of consciousness ~ *vb* **slept** \'slept\; **sleep·ing** : rest in a state of sleep — **sleep·er** *n* —**sleep·less** *adj* —**sleep·walk·er** *n*

sleepy \'slēpē\ *adj* **sleep·i·er; -est 1** : ready for sleep **2** : quietly inactive —**sleep·i·ly** \'slēpəlē\ *adv* —**sleep·i·ness** \-pēnəs\ *n*

sleet \'slēt\ *n* : frozen rain —**sleet** *vb* — **sleety** *adj*

sleeve \'slēv\ *n* : part of a garment for the arm —**sleeve·less** *adj*

sleigh \'slā\ *n* : horse-drawn sled with seats ~ *vb* : drive or ride in a sleigh

sleight of hand \'slīt-\ *n* : skillful manual manipulation or a trick requiring it

slen·der \'slendər\ *adj* **1** : thin esp. in physique **2** : scanty

sleuth \'slüth\ *n* : detective

slew \'slü\ *past of* SLAY

slice \'slīs\ *n* : thin flat piece ~ *vb* **sliced; slic·ing** : cut a slice from

slick \'slik\ *adj* **1** : very smooth **2** : clever —**slick** *vb*

slick·er \'slikər\ *n* : raincoat

slide \'slīd\ *vb* **slid** \'slid\; **slid·ing** \'slīdiŋ\ : move smoothly along a surface ~ *n* **1** : act of sliding **2** : surface on which something slides **3** : transparent picture for projection

slier *comparative of* SLY

sliest *superlative of* SLY

slight \'slīt\ *adj* **1** : slender **2** : frail **3** : small in degree ~ *vb* **1** : ignore or treat as unimportant —**slight** *n* —**slight•ly** *adv*

slim \'slim\ *adj* **-mm- 1** : slender **2** : scanty ~ *vb* **-mm-** : make or become slender

slime \'slīm\ *n* : dirty slippery film (as on water) —**slimy** *adj*

sling \'sliŋ\ *vb* **slung** \'sləŋ\; **sling•ing** : hurl with or as if with a sling ~ *n* **1** : strap for swinging and hurling stones **2** : looped strap or bandage to lift or support

sling•shot *n* : forked stick with elastic bands for shooting pebbles

slink \'sliŋk\ *vb* **slunk** \'sləŋk\; **slink•ing** : move stealthily or sinuously — **slinky** *adj*

¹slip \'slip\ *vb* **-pp- 1** : escape quietly or secretly **2** : slide along smoothly **3** : make a mistake **4** : to pass without being noticed or done **5** : fall off from a standard ~ *n* **1** : ship's berth **2** : sudden mishap **3** : mistake **4** : woman's undergarment

²slip *n* **1** : plant shoot **2** : small strip (as of paper)

slip•per \'slipər\ *n* : shoe that slips on easily

slip•pery \'slipərē\ *adj* **-peri•er; -est 1** : slick enough to slide on **2** : tricky —**slip•peri•ness** *n*

slip•shod \'slip,shäd\ *adj* : careless

slit \'slit\ *vb* **slit; slit•ting** : make a slit in ~ *n* : long narrow cut

slith•er \'slithər\ *vb* : glide along like a snake —**slith•ery** *adj*

sliv•er \'slivər\ *n* : splinter

slob \'släb\ *n* : untidy person

slob•ber \'släbər\ *vb* : dribble saliva — **slobber** *n*

slo•gan \'slōgən\ *n* : word or phrase expressing the aim of a cause

sloop \'slüp\ *n* : one-masted sailboat

slop \'släp\ *n* : food waste for animal feed ~ *vb* **-pp-** : spill

slope \'slōp\ *vb* **sloped; slop•ing** : deviate from the vertical or horizontal ~ *n* : upward or downward slant

slop•py \'släpē\ *adj* **-pi•er; -est 1** : muddy **2** : untidy

slot \'slät\ *n* : narrow opening

sloth \'slóth, 'slōth\ *n, pl* **sloths** \with ths

or thz\ **1** : laziness **2** : slow-moving mammal —**sloth•ful** *adj*

slouch \'slaúch\ *n* **1** : drooping posture **2** : lazy or incompetent person ~ *vb* : walk or stand with a slouch

¹slough \'slü, 'slaú\ *n* : swamp

²slough \'sləf\, **sluff** *vb* : cast off (old skin)

slov•en•ly \'sləvənlē\ *adj* : untidy

slow \'slō\ *adj* **1** : sluggish or stupid **2** : moving, working, or happening at less than the usual speed ~ *vb* **1** : make slow **2** : go slower —**slow** *adv* —**slow•ly** *adv* —**slow•ness** *n*

sludge \'sləj\ *n* : slushy mass (as of treated sewage)

slug \'sləg\ *n* **1** : mollusk related to the snails **2** : bullet **3** : metal disk ~ *vb* **-gg-** : strike forcibly —**slug•ger** *n*

slug•gish \'sləgish\ *adj* : slow in movement or flow —**slug•gish•ly** *adv* — **slug•gish•ness** *n*

sluice \'slüs\ *n* : channel for water ~ *vb* **sluiced; sluic•ing** : wash in running water

slum \'sləm\ *n* : thickly populated area marked by poverty

slum•ber \'sləmbər\ *vb or n* : sleep

slump \'sləmp\ *vb* **1** : sink suddenly **2** : slouch —**slump** *n*

slung *past of* SLING

slunk *past of* SLINK

¹slur \'slər\ *vb* **-rr-** : run (words or notes) together —**slur** *n*

²slur *n* : malicious or insulting remark

slurp \'slərp\ *vb* : eat or drink noisily — **slurp** *n*

slush \'sləsh\ *n* : partly melted snow — **slushy** *adj*

slut \'slət\ *n* **1** : untidy woman **2** : lewd woman —**slut•tish** *adj*

sly \'slī\ *adj* **sli•er** \'slīər\; **sli•est** \'slīəst\ : given to or showing secrecy and deception —**sly•ly** *adv* —**sly•ness** *n*

¹smack \'smak\ *n* : characteristic flavor ~ *vb* : have a taste or hint

²smack *vb* **1** : move (the lips) so as to make a sharp noise **2** : kiss or slap with a loud noise ~ *n* **1** : sharp noise made by the lips **2** : noisy slap

³smack *adv* : squarely and sharply

⁴smack *n* : fishing boat

small \'smól\ *adj* **1** : little in size or amount **2** : few in number **3** : trivial —**small•ish** *adj* —**small•ness** *n*

small•pox \'smól,päks\ *n* : contagious virus disease

smart \'smärt\ *vb* **1** : cause or feel sting-

ing pain **2** : endure distress ~ *adj* **1**
: intelligent or resourceful **2** : stylish
—**smart** *n* —**smart·ly** *adv* —**smart·ness** *n*

smash \'smash\ *vb* : break or be broken
into pieces ~ *n* **1** : smashing blow **2**
: act or sound of smashing

smat·ter·ing \'smatəriŋ\ *n* **1** : superficial
knowledge **2** : small scattered number
or amount

smear \'smir\ *n* : greasy stain ~ *vb* **1**
: spread (something sticky) **2**
: smudge **3** : slander

smell \'smel\ *vb* **smelled** \'smeld\ *or*
smelt \'smelt\; **smell·ing 1** : perceive
the odor of **2** : have or give off an
odor ~ *n* **1** : sense by which one perceives odor **2** : odor —**smelly** *adj*

¹**smelt** \'smelt\ *n, pl* **smelts** *or* **smelt**
: small food fish

²**smelt** *vb* : melt or fuse (ore) in order
to separate the metal —**smelt·er** *n*

smile \'smīl\ *n* : facial expression with
the mouth turned up usu. to show
pleasure —**smile** *vb*

smirk \'smərk\ *vb* : wear a conceited
smile —**smirk** *n*

smite \'smīt\ *vb* **smote** \'smōt\; **smit·ten**
\'smit'n\ *or* **smote; smit·ing** \'smītiŋ\
1 : strike heavily or kill **2** : affect
strongly

smith \'smith\ *n* : worker in metals and
esp. a blacksmith

smithy \'smithē\ *n, pl* **smith·ies** : a
smith's workshop

smock \'smäk\ *n* : loose dress or protective coat

smog \'smäg, 'smóg\ *n* : fog and smoke
—**smog·gy** *adj*

smoke \'smōk\ *n* : sooty gas from burning ~ *vb* **smoked; smok·ing 1** : give
off smoke **2** : inhale the fumes of
burning tobacco **3** : cure (as meat)
with smoke —**smoke·less** *adj* —
smok·er *n* —**smoky** *adj*

smoke·stack *n* : chimney through which
smoke is discharged

smol·der, smoul·der \'smōldər\ *vb* **1**
: burn and smoke without flame **2** : be
suppressed but active —**smolder** *n*

smooth \'smüth\ *adj* **1** : having a surface
without irregularities **2** : not jarring or
jolting ~ *vb* : make smooth —
smooth·ly *adv* —**smooth·ness** *n*

smor·gas·bord \'smórgəs,bórd\ *n*
: buffet consisting of many foods

smoth·er \'sməthər\ *vb* **1** : kill by depriving of air **2** : cover thickly

smudge \'sməj\ *vb* **smudged; smudg-
ing** : soil or blur by rubbing ~ *n* **1**
: thick smoke **2** : dirty smoke

smug \'sməg\ *adj* **-gg-** : content in one's
own virtue or accomplishment —
smug·ly *adv* —**smug·ness** *n*

smug·gle \'sməgəl\ *vb* **-gled; -gling**
: import or export secretly or illegally
—**smug·gler** \'sməglər\ *n*

smut \'smət\ *n* **1** : something that soils
2 : indecent language or matter **3**
: disease of plants caused by fungi —
smut·ty *adj*

snack \'snak\ *n* : light meal

snag \'snag\ *n* : unexpected difficulty ~
vb **-gg-** : become caught on something that sticks out

snail \'snāl\ *n* : small mollusk with a spiral shell

snake \'snāk\ *n* : long-bodied limbless
reptile —**snake·bite** *n*

snap \'snap\ *vb* **-pp- 1** : bite at something **2** : utter angry words **3** : break
suddenly with a sharp sound ~ *n* **1**
: act or sound of snapping **2**
: fastening that closes with a click **3**
: something easy to do —**snap·per** *n*
—**snap·pish** *adj* —**snap·py** *adj*

snap·drag·on *n* : garden plant with
spikes of showy flowers

snap·shot \'snap,shät\ *n* : casual photograph

snare \'snar\ *n* : trap for catching game
~ *vb* : capture or hold with or as if
with a snare

¹**snarl** \'snärl\ *n* : tangle ~ *vb* : cause to
become knotted

²**snarl** *vb or n* : growl

snatch \'snach\ *vb* **1** : try to grab something suddenly **2** : seize or take away
suddenly ~ *n* **1** : act of snatching **2**
: something brief or fragmentary

sneak \'snēk\ *vb* : move or take in a furtive manner ~ *n* : one who acts in a
furtive manner —**sneak·i·ly** \'snē-
kəlē\ *adv* —**sneak·ing·ly** *adv* —
sneaky *adj*

sneak·er \'snēkər\ *n* : sports shoe

sneer \'snir\ *vb* : smile scornfully —
sneer *n*

sneeze \'snēz\ *vb* **sneezed; sneez·ing**
: force the breath out with sudden and
involuntary violence —**sneeze** *n*

snick·er \'snikər\ *n* : partly suppressed
laugh —**snicker** *vb*

snide \'snīd\ *adj* : subtly ridiculing

sniff \'snif\ *vb* **1** : draw air audibly up

the nose 2 : detect by smelling —**sniff** n

snip \'snip\ n : fragment snipped off ~ vb -**pp**- : cut off by bits

¹snipe \'snīp\ n, pl **snipes** or **snipe** : game bird of marshy areas

²snipe vb **sniped**; **snip·ing** : shoot at an enemy from a concealed position —**snip·er** n

snips \'snips\ n pl : scissorslike tool

sniv·el \'snivəl\ vb -**eled** or -**elled**; -**el·ing** or -**el·ling** 1 : have a running nose 2 : whine

snob \'snäb\ n : one who acts superior to others —**snob·bery** \-ərē\ n —**snob·bish** adj —**snob·bish·ly** adv —**snob·bish·ness** n

snoop \'snüp\ vb : pry in a furtive way ~ n : prying person

snooze \'snüz\ vb **snoozed**; **snooz·ing** : take a nap —**snooze** n

snore \'snōr\ vb **snored**; **snor·ing** : breathe with a hoarse noise while sleeping —**snore** n

snort \'snȯrt\ vb : force air noisily through the nose —**snort** n

snout \'snaut\ n : long projecting muzzle (as of a swine)

snow \'snō\ n : crystals formed from water vapor ~ vb : fall as snow —**snow·ball** n —**snow·bank** n —**snow·drift** n —**snow·fall** n —**snow·plow** n —**snow·storm** n —**snowy** adj

snow·shoe n : frame of wood strung with thongs for walking on snow

snub \'snəb\ vb -**bb**- : ignore or avoid through disdain —**snub** n

¹snuff \'snəf\ vb : put out (a candle) —**snuff·er** n

²snuff vb : draw forcibly into the nose ~ n : pulverized tobacco

snug \'snəg\ adj -**gg**- 1 : warm, secure, and comfortable 2 : fitting closely —**snug·ly** adv —**snug·ness** n

snug·gle \'snəgəl\ vb -**gled**; -**gling** : curl up comfortably

so \'sō\ adv 1 : in the manner or to the extent indicated 2 : in the same way 3 : therefore 4 : finally 5 : thus ~ conj : for that reason

soak \'sōk\ vb 1 : lie in a liquid 2 : absorb ~ n : act of soaking

soap \'sōp\ n : cleaning substance —**soap** vb —**soapy** adj

soar \'sōr\ vb : fly upward on or as if on wings

sob \'säb\ vb -**bb**- : weep with convulsive heavings of the chest —**sob** n

so·ber \'sōbər\ adj 1 : not drunk 2 : serious or solemn —**so·ber·ly** adv

so·bri·ety \sə'brīətē, sō-\ n : quality or state of being sober

soc·cer \'säkər\ n : game played by kicking a ball

so·cia·ble \'sōshəbəl\ adj : friendly —**so·cia·bil·i·ty** \,sōshə'bilətē\ n —**so·cia·bly** \'sōshəblē\ adv

so·cial \'sōshəl\ adj 1 : relating to pleasant companionship 2 : naturally living or growing in groups 3 : relating to human society ~ n : social gathering —**so·cial·ly** adv

so·cial·ism \'sōshə,lizəm\ n : social system based on government control of the production and distribution of goods —**so·cial·ist** \'sōshəlist\ n or adj —**so·cial·is·tic** \,sōshə'listik\ adj

so·cial·ize \'sōshə,līz\ vb -**ized**; -**iz·ing** 1 : regulate by socialism 2 : adapt to social needs 3 : participate in a social gathering —**so·cial·i·za·tion** \,sōshələ'zāshən\ n

social work n : services concerned with aiding the poor and socially maladjusted —**social worker** n

so·ci·ety \sə'sīətē\ n, pl -**et·ies** 1 : companionship 2 : community life 3 : rich or fashionable class 4 : voluntary group

so·ci·ol·o·gy \,sōsē'äləjē\ n : study of social relationships —**so·ci·o·log·i·cal** \-ə'läjikəl\ adj —**so·ci·ol·o·gist** \-'äləjist\ n

¹sock \'säk\ n, pl **socks** or **sox** : short stocking

²sock vb or n : punch

sock·et \'säkət\ n : hollow part that holds something

sod \'säd\ n : turf ~ vb -**dd**- : cover with sod

so·da \'sōdə\ n 1 : carbonated water or a soft drink 2 : ice cream drink made with soda

sod·den \'säd°n\ adj 1 : lacking spirit 2 : soaked or soggy

so·di·um \'sōdēəm\ n : soft waxy silver white metallic chemical element

so·fa \'sōfə\ n : wide padded chair

soft \'sȯft\ adj 1 : not hard, rough, or harsh 2 : nonalcoholic —**soft·en** \'sȯfən\ vb —**soft·en·er** \-ənər\ n —**soft·ly** adv —**soft·ness** n

soft·ball n : game like baseball

soft·ware \'sȯft,war\ n : computer programs

sog·gy \\'sägē\\ adj -gi·er; -est : heavy with moisture —**sog·gi·ness** \\-ēnəs\\ n

¹soil \\'sȯil\\ vb : make or become dirty ~ n : embedded dirt

²soil n : loose surface material of the earth

so·journ \\'sō,jərn, sō'jərn\\ n : temporary stay ~ vb : reside temporarily

so·lace \\'säləs\\ n or vb : comfort

so·lar \\'sōlər\\ adj : relating to the sun or the energy in sunlight

sold past of SELL

sol·der \\'sädər, 'sȯd-\\ n : metallic alloy melted to join metallic surfaces ~ vb : cement with solder

sol·dier \\'sōljər\\ n : person in military service ~ vb : serve as a soldier —**sol·dier·ly** adj or adv

¹sole \\'sōl\\ n : bottom of the foot or a shoe —**soled** adj

²sole n : flatfish caught for food

³sole adj : single or only —**sole·ly** adv

sol·emn \\'säləm\\ adj 1 : dignified and ceremonial 2 : highly serious —**sol·em·ni·ty** \\sə'lemnətē\\ n —**sol·emn·ly** adv

so·lic·it \\sə'lisət\\ vb : ask for —**so·lic·i·ta·tion** \\-,lisə'tāshən\\ n

so·lic·i·tor \\sə'lisətər\\ n 1 : one that solicits 2 : lawyer

so·lic·i·tous \\sə'lisətəs\\ adj : showing or expressing concern —**so·lic·i·tous·ly** adv —**so·lic·i·tude** \\sə'lisə,tüd, -,tyüd\\ n

sol·id \\'säləd\\ adj 1 : not hollow 2 : having 3 dimensions 3 : hard 4 : of good quality 5 : of one character ~ n 1 : 3-dimensional figure 2 : substance in solid form —**solid** adv —**so·lid·i·ty** \\sə'lidətē\\ n —**sol·id·ly** adv —**sol·id·ness** n

sol·i·dar·i·ty \\,sälə'darətē\\ n : unity of purpose

so·lid·i·fy \\sə'lidə,fī\\ vb -fied; -fy·ing : make or become solid —**so·lid·i·fi·ca·tion** \\-,lidəfə'kāshən\\ n

so·lil·o·quy \\sə'liləkwē\\ n, pl -quies : dramatic monologue —**so·lil·o·quize** \\-,kwīz\\ vb

sol·i·taire \\'sälə,tar\\ n 1 : solitary gem 2 : card game for one person

sol·i·tary \\-,terē\\ adj 1 : alone 2 : secluded 3 : single

sol·i·tude \\-,tüd, -,tyüd\\ n : state of being alone

so·lo \\'sōlō\\ n, pl -los : performance by only one person ~ adv : alone —**solo** adj or vb —**so·lo·ist** n

sol·stice \\'sälstəs\\ n : time of the year when the sun is farthest north or south of the equator

sol·u·ble \\'sälyəbəl\\ adj 1 : capable of being dissolved 2 : capable of being solved —**sol·u·bil·i·ty** \\,sälyə'bilətē\\ n

so·lu·tion \\sə'lüshən\\ n 1 : answer to a problem 2 : homogeneous liquid mixture

solve \\'sälv\\ vb solved; solv·ing : find a solution for —**solv·able** adj

sol·vent \\'sälvənt\\ adj 1 : able to pay all debts 2 : dissolving or able to dissolve ~ n : substance that dissolves or disperses another substance —**sol·ven·cy** \\-vənsē\\ n

som·ber, som·bre \\'sämbər\\ adj 1 : dark 2 : grave —**som·ber·ly** adv

som·bre·ro \\səm'brerō\\ n, pl -ros : broad-brimmed hat

some \\'səm\\ adj 1 : one unspecified 2 : unspecified or indefinite number of 3 : at least a few or a little ~ pron : a certain number or amount

-some \\səm\\ adj suffix : characterized by a thing, quality, state, or action

some·body \\'səmbədē, -,bäd-\\ pron : some person

some·day \\'səm,dā\\ adv : at some future time

some·how \\-,haú\\ adv : by some means

some·one \\-,wən\\ pron : some person

som·er·sault \\'səmər,sȯlt\\ n : body flip —**somersault** vb

some·thing \\'səmthiŋ\\ pron : some undetermined or unspecified thing

some·time \\'səm,tīm\\ adv : at a future, unknown, or unnamed time

some·times \\-,tīmz\\ adv : occasionally

some·what \\-,hwət, -,hwät\\ adv : in some degree

some·where \\-,hwer\\ adv : in, at, or to an unknown or unnamed place

som·no·lent \\'sämnələnt\\ adj : sleepy —**som·no·lence** \\-ləns\\ n

son \\'sən\\ n : male offspring

so·nar \\'sō,när\\ n : device that detects and locates underwater objects using sound waves

so·na·ta \\sə'nätə\\ n : instrumental composition

song \\'sȯŋ\\ n : music and words to be sung

song·bird n : bird with musical tones

son·ic \\'sänik\\ adj : relating to sound waves or the speed of sound

son–in–law *n, pl* **sons–in–law** : husband of one's daughter

son·net \'sänət\ *n* : poem of 14 lines

so·no·rous \sə'nōrəs, 'sänərəs\ *adj* 1 : loud, deep, or rich in sound 2 : impressive —**so·nor·i·ty** \sə'nórətē\ *n*

soon \'sün\ *adv* 1 : before long 2 : promptly 3 : early

soot \'sut, 'sət, 'süt\ *n* : fine black substance formed by combustion —**sooty** *adj*

soothe \'süth\ *vb* **soothed; sooth·ing** : calm or comfort —**sooth·er** *n*

sooth·say·er \'süth,sāər\ *n* : prophet —**sooth·say·ing** \-iŋ\ *n*

sop \'säp\ *n* : conciliatory bribe, gift, or concession ~ *vb* **-pp-** 1 : dip in a liquid 2 : soak 3 : mop up

so·phis·ti·cat·ed \sə'fistə,kātəd\ *adj* 1 : complex 2 : wise, cultured, or shrewd in human affairs —**so·phis·ti·ca·tion** \-,fistə'kāshən\ *n*

soph·ist·ry \'säfəstrē\ *n* : subtly fallacious reasoning or argument —**soph·ist** \'säfist\ *n*

soph·o·more \'säf²m,ōr, 'säf,mōr\ *n* : 2d-year student

so·po·rif·ic \,säpə'rifik, ,sōp-\ *adj* : causing sleep or drowsiness

so·pra·no \sə'pranō\ *n, pl* **-nos** : highest singing voice

sor·cery \'sórsərē\ *n* : witchcraft —**sor·cer·er** \-rər\ *n* —**sor·cer·ess** \-rəs\ *n*

sor·did \'sórdəd\ *adj* : filthy or vile —**sor·did·ly** *adv* —**sor·did·ness** *n*

sore \'sōr\ *adj* **sor·er; sor·est** 1 : causing pain or distress 2 : severe or intense 3 : angry ~ *n* : sore usu. infected spot on the body —**sore·ly** *adv* —**sore·ness** *n*

sor·ghum \'sórgəm\ *n* : forage grass

so·ror·i·ty \sə'rórətē\ *n, pl* **-ties** : women's student social group

¹**sor·rel** \'sórəl\ *n* : brownish orange to light brown color or an animal of this color

²**sorrel** *n* : herb with sour juice

sor·row \'särō\ *n* : deep distress, sadness, or regret or a cause of this —**sor·row·ful** \-fəl\ *adj* —**sor·row·ful·ly** *adv*

sor·ry \'särē\ *adj* **-ri·er; -est** 1 : feeling sorrow, regret, or penitence 2 : dismal

sort \'sórt\ *n* 1 : kind 2 : nature ~ *vb* : classify —**out of sorts** : grouchy

sor·tie \'sórtē, sór'tē\ *n* : military attack esp. against besiegers

SOS \,es,ō'es\ *n* : call for help

so–so \'sō'sō\ *adj or adv* : barely acceptable

sot \'sät\ *n* : drunkard —**sot·tish** *adj*

souf·flé \sü'flā\ *n* : baked dish made light with beaten egg whites

sought *past of* SEEK

soul \'sōl\ *n* 1 : immaterial essence of an individual life 2 : essential part 3 : person

soul·ful \'sōlfəl\ *adj* : full of or expressing deep feeling —**soul·ful·ly** *adv*

¹**sound** \'saund\ *adj* 1 : free from fault, error, or illness 2 : firm or hard 3 : showing good judgment —**sound·ly** *adv* —**sound·ness** *n*

²**sound** *n* 1 : sensation of hearing 2 : energy of vibration sensed in hearing 3 : something heard ~ *vb* 1 : make or cause to make a sound 2 : seem —**sound·less** *adj* —**sound·less·ly** *adv* —**sound·proof** *adj or vb*

³**sound** *n* : wide strait ~ *vb* 1 : measure the depth of (water) 2 : investigate

soup \'süp\ *n* : broth usu. containing pieces of solid food —**soupy** *adj*

sour \'sauər\ *adj* 1 : having an acid or tart taste 2 : disagreeable ~ *vb* : become or make sour —**sour·ish** *adj* —**sour·ly** *adv* —**sour·ness** *n*

source \'sōrs\ *n* 1 : point of origin 2 : one that provides something needed

souse \'saus\ *vb* **soused; sous·ing** 1 : pickle 2 : immerse 3 : intoxicate ~ *n* 1 : something pickled 2 : drunkard

south \'saúth\ *adv* : to or toward the south ~ *adj* : situated toward, at, or coming from the south ~ *n* 1 : direction to the right of sunrise 2 *cap* : regions to the south —**south·er·ly** \'səthərlē\ *adv or adj* —**south·ern** \'səthərn\ *adj* —**South·ern·er** *n* —**south·ern·most** \-,mōst\ *adj* —**south·ward** \'saúthwərd\ *adv or adj* —**south·wards** \-wərdz\ *adv*

south·east \saúth'ēst, *naut* saú'ēst\ *n* 1 : direction between south and east 2 *cap* : regions to the southeast —**southeast** *adj or adv* —**south·east·er·ly** *adv or adj* —**south·east·ern** \-ərn\ *adj*

south pole *n* : the southernmost point of the earth

south·west \saúth'west, *naut* saú'west\ *n* 1 : direction between south and west 2 *cap* : regions to the southwest —**southwest** *adj or adv* —**south·west-**

er·ly *adv or adj* —**south·west·ern** \-ərn\ *adj*

sou·ve·nir \'süvə,nir\ *n* : something that is a reminder of a place or event

sov·er·eign \'sävərən\ *n* 1 : supreme ruler 2 : gold coin of the United Kingdom ~ *adj* 1 : supreme 2 : independent —**sov·er·eign·ty** \-tē\ *n*

¹sow \'saü\ *n* : female swine

²sow \'sō\ *vb* **sowed; sown** \'sōn\ *or* **sowed, sow·ing** 1 : plant or strew with seed 2 : scatter abroad —**sow·er** \'sōər\ *n*

sox *pl of* SOCK

soy·bean \'sói,bēn\ *n* : legume with edible seeds

spa \'spä\ *n* : resort at a mineral spring

space \'spās\ *n* 1 : period of time 2 : area in, around, or between 3 : region beyond earth's atmosphere 4 : accommodations ~ *vb* **spaced; spac·ing** : place at intervals —**space·craft** *n* —**space·flight** *n* —**space·man** *n* —**space·ship** *n*

spa·cious \'spāshəs\ *adj* : large or roomy —**spa·cious·ly** *adv* —**spa·cious·ness** *n*

¹spade \'spād\ *n or vb* : shovel —**spade·ful** *n*

²spade *n* : playing card marked with a black figure like an inverted heart

spa·ghet·ti \spə'getē\ *n* : pasta strings

span \'span\ *n* 1 : amount of time 2 : distance between supports ~ *vb* **-nn-** : extend across

span·gle \'spaŋgəl\ *n* : small disk of shining metal or plastic —**spangle** *vb*

span·iel \'spanyəl\ *n* : small or medium-sized dog with drooping ears and long wavy hair

spank \'spaŋk\ *vb* : hit on the buttocks with an open hand

¹spar \'spär\ *n* : pole or boom

²spar *vb* **-rr-** : practice boxing

spare \'spar\ *adj* 1 : held in reserve 2 : thin or scanty ~ *vb* **spared; spar·ing** 1 : reserve or avoid using 2 : avoid punishing or killing —**spare** *n*

spar·ing \'spariŋ\ *adj* : thrifty —**spar·ing·ly** *adv*

spark \'spärk\ *n* 1 : tiny hot and glowing particle 2 : smallest beginning or germ 3 : visible electrical discharge ~ *vb* 1 : emit or produce sparks 2 : stir to activity

spar·kle \'spärkəl\ *vb* **-kled; -kling** 1 : flash 2 : effervesce ~ *n* : gleam —**spark·ler** \-klər\ *n*

spar·row \'sparō\ *n* : small singing bird

sparse \'spärs\ *adj* **spars·er; spars·est** : thinly scattered —**sparse·ly** *adv*

spasm \'spazəm\ *n* 1 : involuntary muscular contraction 2 : sudden, violent, and temporary effort or feeling —**spas·mod·ic** \spaz'mädik\ *adj* —**spas·mod·i·cal·ly** *adv*

spas·tic \'spastik\ *adj* : relating to, marked by, or affected with muscular spasm —**spastic** *n*

¹spat \'spat\ *past of* SPIT

²spat *n* : petty dispute

spa·tial \'spāshəl\ *adj* : relating to space —**spa·tial·ly** *adv*

spat·ter \'spatər\ *vb* : splash with drops of liquid —**spatter** *n*

spat·u·la \'spachələ\ *n* : flexible knife-like utensil

spawn \'spón\ *vb* 1 : produce eggs or offspring 2 : bring forth ~ *n* : egg cluster —**spawn·er** *n*

spay \'spā\ *vb* : remove the ovaries of (a female)

speak \'spēk\ *vb* **spoke** \'spōk\; **spo·ken** \'spōkən\; **speak·ing** 1 : utter words 2 : express orally 3 : address an audience 4 : use (a language) in talking —**speak·er** *n*

spear \'spir\ *n* : long pointed weapon ~ *vb* : strike or pierce with a spear

spear·head *n* : leading force, element, or influence —**spearhead** *vb*

spear·mint *n* : aromatic garden mint

spe·cial \'speshəl\ *adj* 1 : unusual or unique 2 : particularly favored 3 : set aside for a particular use —**special** *n* —**spe·cial·ly** *adv*

spe·cial·ist \'speshəlist\ *n* 1 : person who specializes in a particular branch of learning or activity 2 : any of four enlisted ranks in the army corresponding to the grades of corporal through sergeant first class

spe·cial·ize \'speshə,līz\ *vb* **-ized; -iz·ing** : concentrate one's efforts —**spe·cial·i·za·tion** \,speshələ'zāshən\ *n*

spe·cial·ty \'speshəltē\ *n, pl* **-ties** : area or field in which one specializes

spe·cie \'spēshē, -sē\ *n* : money in coin

spe·cies \'spēshēz, -sēz\ *n, pl* **spe·cies** : biological grouping of closely related organisms

spe·cif·ic \spi'sifik\ *adj* : definite or exact —**spe·cif·i·cal·ly** *adv*

spec·i·fi·ca·tion \,spesəfə'kāshən\ *n* **1** : act or process of specifying **2** : detailed description of work to be done —usu. pl.

spec·i·fy \'spesə,fī\ *vb* **-fied; -fy·ing** : mention precisely or by name

spec·i·men \-əmən\ *n* : typical example

spe·cious \'spēshəs\ *adj* : apparently but not really genuine or correct

speck \'spek\ *n* : tiny particle or blemish —**speck** *vb*

speck·led \'spekəld\ *adj* : marked with spots

spec·ta·cle \'spektikəl\ *n* **1** : impressive public display **2** *pl* : eyeglasses

spec·tac·u·lar \spek'takyələr\ *adj* : sensational or showy

spec·ta·tor \'spek,tātər\ *n* : person who looks on

spec·ter, spec·tre \'spektər\ *n* **1** : ghost **2** : haunting vision

spec·tral \'spektrəl\ *adj* : relating to or resembling a specter or spectrum

spec·trum \'spektrəm\ *n, pl* **-tra** \-trə\ *or* **-trums** : series of colors formed when white light is dispersed into its components

spec·u·late \'spekyə,lāt\ *vb* **-lat·ed; -lat·ing** **1** : think about things yet unknown **2** : risk money in a business deal in hope of high profit —**spec·u·la·tion** \,spekyə'lāshən\ *n* —**spec·u·la·tive** \'spekyə,lātiv\ *adj* —**spec·u·la·tor** \-,lātər\ *n*

speech \'spēch\ *n* **1** : power, act, or manner of speaking **2** : talk given to an audience —**speech·less** *adj*

speed \'spēd\ *n* **1** : quality of being fast **2** : rate of motion or performance ~ *vb* **sped** \'sped\ *or* **speed·ed; speed·ing** : go at a great or excessive rate of speed —**speed·boat** *n* —**speed·er** *n* —**speed·i·ly** \'spēd'lē\ *adv* —**speed·up** \-,əp\ *n* —**speedy** *adj*

speed·om·e·ter \spi'dämətər\ *n* : instrument for indicating speed

¹spell \'spel\ *n* : influence of or like magic

²spell *vb* **1** : name, write, or print the letters of **2** : mean —**spell·er** *n*

³spell *vb* : substitute for or relieve (someone) ~ *n* **1** : turn at work **2** : period of time

spell·bound *adj* : held by a spell

spend \'spend\ *vb* **spent** \'spent\; **spend·ing** **1** : pay out **2** : cause or allow to pass —**spend·er** *n*

spend·thrift \'spend,thrift\ *n* : wasteful person

sperm \'spərm\ *n, pl* **sperm** *or* **sperms** : semen or a germ cell in it

spew \'spyü\ *vb* : gush out in a stream

sphere \'sfir\ *n* **1** : figure with every point on its surface at an equal distance from the center **2** : round body **3** : range of action or influence —**spher·i·cal** \'sfirikəl, 'sfer-\ *adj*

spher·oid \'sfir-\ *n* : spherelike figure

spice \'spīs\ *n* **1** : aromatic plant product for seasoning food **2** : interesting quality —**spice** *vb* —**spicy** *adj*

spi·der \'spīdər\ *n* : small insectlike animal with 8 legs —**spi·dery** *adj*

spig·ot \'spigət, 'spikət\ *n* : faucet

spike \'spīk\ *n* : very large nail ~ *vb* **spiked; spik·ing** : fasten or pierce with a spike —**spiked** \'spīkt\ *adj*

spill \'spil\ *vb* **1** : fall, flow, or run out unintentionally **2** : divulge ~ *n* **1** : act of spilling **2** : something spilled —**spill·able** *adj*

spill·way *n* : passage for surplus water

spin \'spin\ *vb* **spun** \'spən\; **spin·ning** **1** : draw out fiber and twist into thread **2** : form thread from a sticky body fluid **3** : revolve or cause to revolve extremely fast ~ *n* : rapid rotating motion —**spin·ner** *n*

spin·ach \'spinich\ *n* : garden herb with edible leaves

spi·nal \'spīn'l\ *adj* : relating to the backbone —**spi·nal·ly** *adv*

spinal cord *n* : thick strand of nervous tissue that extends from the brain along the back within the backbone

spin·dle \'spind'l\ *n* **1** : stick used for spinning thread **2** : shaft around which something turns

spin·dly \'spindlē\ *adj* : tall and slender

spine \'spīn\ *n* **1** : backbone **2** : stiff sharp projection on a plant or animal —**spine·less** *adj* —**spiny** *adj*

spin·et \'spinət\ *n* : small piano

spin·ster \'spinstər\ *n* : woman who has never married

spi·ral \'spīrəl\ *adj* : circling or winding around a single point or line —**spiral** *n or adj vb* —**spi·ral·ly** *adv*

spire \'spīr\ *n* : steeple —**spiry** *adj*

spir·it \'spirət\ *n* **1** : life-giving force **2** *cap* : presence of God **3** : ghost **4** : mood **5** : vivacity or enthusiasm **6** *pl* : alcoholic liquor ~ *vb* : carry off secretly —**spir·it·ed** *adj* —**spir·it·less** *adj*

spir·i·tu·al \'spirichəwəl\ *adj* 1 : relating to the spirit or sacred matters 2 : deeply religious ~ *n* : religious folk song —**spir·i·tu·al·i·ty** \,spirichə'walətē\ *n* —**spir·i·tu·al·ly** *adv*

spir·i·tu·al·ism \'spirichəwə,lizəm\ *n* : belief that spirits communicate with the living —**spir·i·tu·al·ist** \-list\ *n or adj*

¹**spit** \'spit\ *n* 1 : rod for holding and turning meat over a fire 2 : point of land that runs into the water

²**spit** *vb* **spit** *or* **spat** \'spat\; **spit·ting** : eject saliva from the mouth ~ *n* 1 : saliva 2 : perfect likeness

spite \'spīt\ *n* : petty ill will ~ *vb* **spit·ed; spit·ing** : annoy or offend —**spite·ful** \-fəl\ *adj* —**spite·ful·ly** *adv* —**in spite of** : in defiance or contempt of

spit·tle \'spit^əl\ *n* : saliva

spit·toon \spi'tün\ *n* : receptacle for spit

splash \'splash\ *vb* : scatter a liquid on —**splash** *n*

splat·ter \'splatər\ *vb* : spatter —**splat·ter** *n*

splay \'splā\ *vb* : spread out or apart —**splay** *n or adj*

spleen \'splēn\ *n* 1 : organ for maintenance of the blood 2 : spite or anger

splen·did \'splendəd\ *adj* 1 : impressive in beauty or brilliance 2 : outstanding —**splen·did·ly** *adv*

splen·dor \'splendər\ *n* 1 : brilliance 2 : magnificence

splice \'splīs\ *vb* **spliced; splic·ing** : join (2 things) end to end —**splice** *n*

splint \'splint\ *n* 1 : thin strip of wood 2 : something that keeps an injured body part in place

splin·ter \'splintər\ *n* : thin needlelike piece ~ *vb* : break into splinters

split \'split\ *vb* **split; split·ting** : divide lengthwise or along a grain —**split** *n*

splotch \'splächᵊ\ *n* : blotch

splurge \'splərj\ *vb* **splurged; splurg·ing** : indulge oneself —**splurge** *n*

splut·ter \'splətər\ *n* : sputter —**splutter** *vb*

spoil \'spȯil\ *n* : plunder ~ *vb* **spoiled** \'spȯild, 'spȯilt\ *or* **spoilt** \'spȯilt\; **spoil·ing** 1 : pillage 2 : ruin 3 : rot —**spoil·age** \'spȯilij\ *n* —**spoil·er** *n*

¹**spoke** \'spōk\ *past of* SPEAK

²**spoke** *n* : rod from the hub to the rim of a wheel

spo·ken *past part of* SPEAK

spokes·man \spōksmən\ *n* : person who speaks for others

spokes·wom·an \-,wümən\ *n* : woman who speaks for others

sponge \'spənj\ *n* 1 : porous water-absorbing mass that forms the skeleton of some marine animals 2 : spongelike material used for wiping ~ *vb* **sponged; spong·ing** 1 : wipe with a sponge 2 : live at another's expense —**spongy** \'spənjē\ *adj*

spon·sor \'spänsər\ *n* : one who assumes responsibility for another or who provides financial support —**sponsor** *vb* —**spon·sor·ship** *n*

spon·ta·ne·ous \spän'tānēəs\ *adj* : done, produced, or occurring naturally or without planning — **spon·ta·ne·i·ty** \,späntən'ēətē\ *n* — **spon·ta·ne·ous·ly** \spän'tānēəslē\ *adv*

spoof \'spüf\ *vb* : make good-natured fun of —**spoof** *n*

spook \'spük\ *n* : ghost ~ *vb* : frighten —**spooky** *adj*

spool \'spül\ *n* : cylinder on which something is wound

spoon \'spün\ *n* : utensil consisting of a small shallow bowl with a handle —**spoon** *vb* —**spoon·ful** \-,fûl\ *n*

spoor \'spûr, 'spȯr\ *n* : track or trail esp. of a wild animal

spo·rad·ic \spə'radik\ *adj* : occasional —**spo·rad·i·cal·ly** *adv*

spore \'spȯr\ *n* : primitive usu. one-celled reproductive body

sport \'spȯrt\ *vb* 1 : frolic 2 : show off ~ *n* 1 : physical activity engaged in for pleasure 2 : jest 3 : person who shows good sportsmanship —**sport·ive** \-iv\ *adj* —**sporty** *adj*

sports·cast \'spȯrts,kast\ *n* : broadcast of a sports event —**sports·cast·er** \-,kastər\ *n*

sports·man \-mən\ *n* : one who enjoys hunting and fishing

sports·man·ship \-mən,ship\ *n* : ability to be gracious in winning or losing

spot \'spät\ *n* 1 : blemish 2 : distinctive small part 3 : location ~ *vb* **-tt-** 1 : mark with spots 2 : see or recognize ~ *adj* : made at random or in limited numbers —**spot·less** *adj* — **spot·less·ly** *adv*

spot·light *n* 1 : intense beam of light 2 : center of public interest —**spotlight** *vb*

spot·ty \'spätē\ *adj* **-ti·er; -est** : uneven in quality

spouse \'spaus\ *n* : one's husband or wife

spout \'spaut\ *vb* 1 : shoot forth in a stream 2 : say pompously ~ *n* 1 : opening through which liquid spouts 2 : jet of liquid

sprain \'sprān\ *n* : twisting injury to a joint ~ *vb* : injure with a sprain

sprat \'sprat\ *n* : small or young herring

sprawl \'sprol\ *vb* : lie or sit with limbs spread out —**sprawl** *n*

¹**spray** \'sprā\ *n* : branch or arrangement of flowers

²**spray** *n* 1 : mist 2 : device that discharges liquid as a mist —**spray** *vb* —**spray·er** *n*

spread \'spred\ *vb* **spread; spread·ing** 1 : open up or unfold 2 : scatter or smear over a surface 3 : cause to be known or to exist over a wide area ~ *n* 1 : extent to which something is spread 2 : cloth cover 3 : something intended to be spread —**spread·er** *n*

spread·sheet \'spred,shēt\ *n* : accounting program for a computer

spree \'sprē\ *n* : burst of indulging in something

sprig \'sprig\ *n* : small shoot or twig

spright·ly \'sprītlē\ *adj* **-li·er; -est** : lively —**spright·li·ness** *n*

spring \'spriŋ\ *vb* **sprang** \'spraŋ\ *or* **sprung** \'sprəŋ\; **sprung; spring·ing** 1 : move or grow quickly or by elastic force 2 : come from by descent 3 : make known suddenly ~ *n* 1 : source 2 : flow of water from underground 3 : season between winter and summer 4 : elastic body or device (as a coil of wire) 5 : leap 6 : elastic power —**springy** *adj*

sprin·kle \'spriŋkəl\ *vb* **-kled; -kling** : scatter in small drops or particles ~ *n* : light rainfall —**sprin·kler** *n*

sprint \'sprint\ *n* : short run at top speed —**sprint** *vb* —**sprint·er** *n*

sprite \'sprīt\ *n* : elf or elfish person

sprock·et \'spräkət\ *n* : toothed wheel whose teeth engage the links of a chain

sprout \'spraut\ *vb* : send out new growth ~ *n* : plant shoot

¹**spruce** \'sprüs\ *n* : conical evergreen tree

²**spruce** *adj* **spruc·er; spruc·est** : neat and stylish in appearance ~ *vb* **spruced; spruc·ing** : make or become neat

spry \'sprī\ *adj* **sprі·er** *or* **spry·er**

\'sprīər\; **spri·est** *or* **spry·est** \'sprīəst\ : agile and active

spume \'spyüm\ *n* : froth

spun *past of* SPIN

spunk \'spəŋk\ *n* : courage —**spunky** *adj*

spur \'spər\ *n* 1 : pointed device used to urge on a horse 2 : something that urges to action 3 : projecting part ~ *vb* **-rr-** : urge on —**spurred** *adj*

spu·ri·ous \'spyurēəs\ *adj* : not genuine

spurn \'spərn\ *vb* : reject

¹**spurt** \'spərt\ *n* : burst of effort, speed, or activity ~ *vb* : make a spurt

²**spurt** *vb* : gush out ~ *n* : sudden gush

sput·ter \'spətər\ *vb* 1 : talk hastily and indistinctly in excitement 2 : make popping sounds —**sputter** *n*

spy \'spī\ *vb* **spied; spy·ing** : watch or try to gather information secretly —**spy** *n*

squab \'skwäb\ *n, pl* **squabs** *or* **squab** : young pigeon

squab·ble \'skwäbəl\ *n or vb* : dispute

squad \'skwäd\ *n* : small group

squad·ron \'skwädrən\ *n* : small military unit

squal·id \'skwäləd\ *adj* : filthy or wretched

squall \'skwol\ *n* : sudden violent brief storm —**squally** *adj*

squa·lor \'skwälər\ *n* : quality or state of being squalid

squan·der \'skwändər\ *vb* : waste

square \'skwar\ *n* 1 : instrument for measuring right angles 2 : flat figure that has 4 equal sides and 4 right angles 3 : open area in a city 4 : product of number multiplied by itself ~ *adj* **squar·er; squar·est** 1 : being a square in form 2 : having sides meet at right angles 3 : multiplied by itself 4 : being a square unit of area 5 : honest ~ *vb* **squared; squar·ing** 1 : form into a square 2 : multiply (a number) by itself 3 : conform 4 : settle —**square·ly** *adv*

¹**squash** \'skwäsh, 'skwosh\ *vb* 1 : press flat 2 : suppress

²**squash** *n, pl* **squash·es** *or* **squash** : garden vegetable

squat \'skwät\ *vb* **-tt-** 1 : stoop or sit on one's heels 2 : settle on land one does not own ~ *n* : act or posture of squatting ~ *adj* **squat·ter; squat·test** : short and thick —**squat·ter** *n*

squaw \'skwo\ *n* : American Indian woman

squawk \'skwȯk\ *n* : harsh loud cry — **squawk** *vb*

squeak \'skwēk\ *vb* : make a thin high-pitched sound — **squeak** *n* — **squeaky** *adj*

squeal \'skwēl\ *vb* 1 : make a shrill sound or cry 2 : protest — **squeal** *n*

squea·mish \'skwēmish\ *adj* : easily nauseated or disgusted

squeeze \'skwēz\ *vb* **squeezed; squeez·ing** 1 : apply pressure to 2 : extract by pressure — **squeeze** *n* — **squeez·er** *n*

squelch \'skwelch\ *vb* : suppress (as with a retort) — **squelch** *n*

squid \'skwid\ *n*, *pl* **squid** *or* **squids** : 10-armed long-bodied sea mollusk

squint \'skwint\ *vb* : look with the eyes partly closed — **squint** *n or adj*

squire \'skwīr\ *n* 1 : knight's aide 2 : country landholder 3 : lady's devoted escort ~ *vb* **squired; squir·ing** : escort

squirm \'skwərm\ *vb* : wriggle

squir·rel \'skwərəl\ *n* : rodent with a long bushy tail

squirt \'skwərt\ *vb* : eject liquid in a spurt — **squirt** *n*

stab \'stab\ *n* 1 : wound made by a pointed weapon 2 : quick thrust 3 : attempt ~ *vb* **-bb-** : pierce or wound with or as if with a pointed weapon

¹sta·ble \'stābəl\ *n* : building for domestic animals ~ *vb* **-bled; -bling** : keep in a stable

²stable *adj* **sta·bler; sta·blest** 1 : firmly established 2 : mentally and emotionally healthy 3 : steady — **sta·bil·i·ty** \stə'bilətē\ *n* — **sta·bi·li·za·tion** \ˌstābələˈzāshən\ *n* — **sta·bi·lize** \'stābəˌlīz\ *vb* — **sta·bi·liz·er** *n*

stac·ca·to \stə'kätō\ *adj* : disconnected

stack \'stak\ *n* : large pile ~ *vb* : pile up

sta·di·um \'stādēəm\ *n* : outdoor sports arena

staff \'staf\ *n*, *pl* **staffs** \'stafs, stavz\ *or* **staves** \'stavz, 'stāvz\ 1 : rod or supporting cane 2 : people assisting a leader 3 : 5 horizontal lines on which music is written ~ *vb* : supply with workers — **staff·er** *n*

staff sergeant *n* : noncommissioned officer ranking next above a sergeant in the army, air force, or marine corps

stag \'stag\ *n*, *pl* **stags** *or* **stag** : male deer ~ *adj* : only for men ~ *adv* : without a date

stage \'stāj\ *n* 1 : raised platform for a speaker or performers 2 : theater 3 : step in a process ~ *vb* **staged; stag·ing** : produce (a play)

stage·coach *n* : passenger coach

stag·ger \'stagər\ *vb* 1 : reel or cause to reel from side to side 2 : overlap or alternate — **stagger** *n* — **stag·ger·ing·ly** *adv*

stag·nant \'stagnənt\ *adj* : not moving or active — **stag·nate** \-ˌnāt\ *vb* — **stag·na·tion** \stag'nāshən\ *n*

¹staid \'stād\ *adj* : sedate

²staid *past of* STAY

stain \'stān\ *vb* 1 : discolor 2 : dye (as wood) 3 : disgrace ~ *n* 1 : discolored area 2 : mark of guilt 3 : coloring preparation — **stain·less** *adj*

stair \'star\ *n* 1 : step in a series for going from one level to another 2 *pl* : flight of steps — **stair·way** *n*

stair·case *n* : series of steps with their framework

stake \'stāk\ *n* 1 : usu. small post driven into the ground 2 : bet 3 : prize in a contest ~ *vb* **staked; stak·ing** 1 : mark or secure with a stake 2 : bet

sta·lac·tite \stə'lakˌtīt\ *n* : icicle-shaped deposit hanging in a cavern

sta·lag·mite \stə'lagˌmīt\ *n* : icicle-shaped deposit on a cavern floor

stale \'stāl\ *adj* **stal·er; stal·est** 1 : having lost good taste and quality from age 2 : no longer new, strong, or effective — **stale·ness** *n*

stale·mate \'stālˌmāt\ *n* : deadlock — **stalemate** *vb*

¹stalk \'stȯk\ *vb* 1 : walk stiffly or proudly 2 : pursue stealthily

²stalk *n* : plant stem — **stalked** \'stȯkt\ *adj*

¹stall \'stȯl\ *n* 1 : compartment in a stable 2 : booth where articles are sold

²stall *vb* : bring or come to a standstill unintentionally

³stall *vb* : delay, evade, or keep a situation going to gain advantage or time

stal·lion \'stalyən\ *n* : male horse

stal·wart \'stȯlwərt\ *adj* : strong or brave

sta·men \'stāmən\ *n* : flower organ that produces pollen

stam·i·na \'stamənə\ *n* : endurance

stam·mer \'stamər\ *vb* : hesitate in speaking — **stammer** *n*

stamp \'stamp\ *vb* 1 : pound with the sole of the foot or a heavy implement 2 : impress or imprint 3 : cut out with a die 4 : attach a postage stamp to ~

n **1** : device for stamping **2** : act of stamping **3** : government seal showing a tax or fee has been paid

stam·pede \stam'pēd\ *n* : headlong rush of frightened animals ~ *vb* **-ped·ed; -ped·ing** : flee in panic

stance \'stans\ *n* : way of standing

¹**stanch** \'stȯnch, 'stänch\ *vb* : stop the flow of (as blood)

²**stanch** *var of* STAUNCH

stan·chion \'stanchən\ *n* : upright support

stand \'stand\ *vb* **stood** \'stu̇d\; **stand·ing 1** : be at rest in or assume an upright position **2** : remain unchanged **3** : be steadfast **4** : maintain a relative position or rank **5** : set upright **6** : undergo or endure ~ *n* **1** : act or place of standing, staying, or resisting **2** : sales booth **3** : structure for holding something upright **4** : group of plants growing together **5** *pl* : tiered seats **6** : opinion or viewpoint

stan·dard \'standərd\ *n* **1** : symbolic figure or flag **2** : model, rule, or guide **3** : upright support —**standard** *adj* —**stan·dard·i·za·tion** \,standərdə'zā-shən\ *n* —**stan·dard·ize** \'standərd,īz\ *vb*

standard time *n* : time established over a region or country

stand·ing \'standiŋ\ *n* **1** : relative position or rank **2** : duration

stand·still *n* : state of rest

stank *past of* STINK

stan·za \'stanzə\ *n* : division of a poem

¹**sta·ple** \'stāpəl\ *n* : U-shaped wire fastener —**staple** *vb* —**sta·pler** \-plər\ *n*

²**staple** *n* : chief commodity or item —**staple** *adj*

star \'stär\ *n* **1** : celestial body visible as a point of light **2** : 5- or 6-pointed figure representing a star **3** : leading performer ~ *vb* **-rr- 1** : mark with a star **2** : play the leading role —**star·dom** \'stärdəm\ *n* —**star·less** *adj* —**star·light** *n* —**star·ry** *adj*

star·board \'stärbərd\ *n* : right side of a ship or airplane looking forward —**starboard** *adj*

starch \'stärch\ *n* : nourishing carbohydrate from plants also used in adhesives and laundering ~ *vb* : stiffen with starch —**starchy** *adj*

stare \'star\ *vb* **stared; star·ing** : look intently with wide-open eyes —**stare** *n* —**star·er** *n*

stark \'stärk\ *adj* **1** : absolute **2** : severe

or bleak ~ *adv* : completely —**stark·ly** *adv*

star·ling \'stärliŋ\ *n* : bird related to the crows

start \'stärt\ *vb* **1** : twitch or jerk (as from surprise) **2** : perform or show performance of the first part of an action or process ~ *n* **1** : sudden involuntary motion **2** : beginning —**start·er** *n*

star·tle \'stärt⁵l\ *vb* **-tled; -tling** : frighten or surprise suddenly

starve \'stärv\ *vb* **starved; starv·ing 1** : suffer or die from hunger **2** : kill with hunger —**star·va·tion** \stär'vāshən\ *n*

stash \'stash\ *vb* : store in a secret place for future use —**stash** *n*

state \'stāt\ *n* **1** : condition of being **2** : condition of mind **3** : nation or a political unit within it ~ *vb* **stat·ed; stat·ing 1** : express in words **2** : establish —**state·hood** \-,hu̇d\ *n*

state·ly \'stātlē\ *adj* **-li·er; -est** : having impressive dignity —**state·li·ness** *n*

state·ment \'stātmənt\ *n* **1** : something stated **2** : financial summary

state·room *n* : private room on a ship

states·man \'stātsmən\ *n* : one skilled in government or diplomacy —**states·man·like** *adj* —**states·man·ship** *n*

stat·ic \'statik\ *adj* **1** : relating to bodies at rest or forces in equilibrium **2** : not moving **3** : relating to stationary charges of electricity ~ *n* : noise on radio or television from electrical disturbances

sta·tion \'stāshən\ *n* **1** : place of duty **2** : regular stop on a bus or train route **3** : social standing **4** : place where radio or television programs originate ~ *vb* : assign to a station

sta·tion·ary \'stāshə,nerē\ *adj* **1** : not moving or not movable **2** : not changing

sta·tio·nery \'stāshə,nerē\ *n* : letter paper with envelopes

sta·tis·tic \stə'tistik\ *n* : single item of statistics

sta·tis·tics \-tiks\ *n pl* : numerical facts collected for study —**sta·tis·ti·cal** \-tikəl\ *adj* —**sta·tis·ti·cal·ly** *adv* —**stat·is·ti·cian** \,statə'stishən\ *n*

stat·u·ary \'stachə,werē\ *n, pl* **-ar·ies** : collection of statues

stat·ue \'stachü\ *n* : solid 3-dimensional likeness —**stat·u·ette** \,stachə'wet\ *n*

stat·u·esque \,stachə'wesk\ *adj* : tall and shapely

stat·ure \'stachər\ n 1 : height 2 : status gained by achievement

sta·tus \'stātəs, 'stat-\ n : relative situation or condition

status quo \-'kwō\ n : existing state of affairs

stat·ute \'stachüt\ n : law —**stat·u·to·ry** \'stachə₁tōrē\ adj

staunch \'stònch\ adj : steadfast —**staunch·ly** adv

stave \'stāv\ n : narrow strip of wood ~ vb **staved** or **stove** \'stōv\: **stav·ing 1** : break a hole in 2 : drive away

staves pl of STAFF

¹stay \'stā\ n : support ~ vb **stayed**; **stay·ing** : prop up

²stay vb **stayed** \'stād\ or **staid** \'stād\: **stay·ing 1** : pause 2 : remain 3 : reside 4 : stop or postpone 5 : satisfy for a time ~ n : a staying

stead \'sted\ n : one's place, job, or function —**in good stead** : to advantage

stead·fast \-₁fast\ adj : faithful or determined —**stead·fast·ly** adv

steady \'stedē\ adj **stead·i·er; -est 1** : firm in position or sure in movement 2 : calm or reliable 3 : constant 4 : regular ~ vb **stead·ied; steady·ing** : make or become steady —**stead·i·ly** \'sted³lē\ adv —**steadi·ness** n —**steady** adv

steak \'stāk\ n : thick slice of meat

steal \'stēl\ vb **stole** \'stōl\: **sto·len** \'stōlən\: **steal·ing 1** : take and carry away wrongfully and with intent to keep 2 : move secretly or slowly

stealth \'stelth\ n : secret or unobtrusive procedure —**stealth·i·ly** \-thəlē\ adv —**stealthy** adj

steam \'stēm\ n : vapor of boiling water ~ vb : give off steam —**steam·boat** n —**steam·ship** n —**steamy** adj

steed \'stēd\ n : horse

steel \'stēl\ n : tough carbon-containing iron ~ vb : fill with courage —**steel** adj —**steely** adj

¹steep \'stēp\ adj : having a very sharp slope or great elevation —**steep·ly** adv —**steep·ness** n

²steep vb : soak in a liquid

stee·ple \'stēpəl\ n : usu. tapering church tower

stee·ple·chase n : race over hurdles

¹steer \'stir\ n : castrated ox

²steer vb 1 : direct the course of (as a ship or car) 2 : guide

steer·age \'stirij\ n : section in a ship for people paying the lowest fares

stein \'stīn\ n : mug

stel·lar \'stelər\ adj : relating to stars or resembling a star

¹stem \'stem\ n : main upright part of a plant ~ vb **-mm- 1** : derive 2 : make progress against —**stem·less** adj —**stemmed** adj

²stem vb **-mm-** : stop the flow of

stench \'stench\ n : stink

sten·cil \'stensəl\ n : printing sheet cut with letters to let ink pass through —**stencil** vb

ste·nog·ra·phy \stə'nägrəfē\ n : art or process of writing in shorthand —**ste·nog·ra·pher** \-fər\ n —**steno·graph·ic** \₁stenə'grafik\ adj

sten·to·ri·an \sten'tōrēən\ adj : extremely loud and powerful

step \'step\ n 1 : single action of a leg in walking or running 2 : rest for the foot in going up or down 3 : degree, rank, or stage 4 : way of walking ~ vb **-pp- 1** : move by steps 2 : press with the foot

step- \step-\ comb form : related by a remarriage and not by blood

step·lad·der n : light portable set of steps in a hinged frame

steppe \'step\ n : dry grassy treeless land esp. of Asia

-ster \stər\ n suffix 1 : one that does, makes, or uses 2 : one that is associated with or takes part in 3 : one that is

ste·reo \'sterē₁ō, 'stir-\ n, pl **-reos** : stereophonic sound system —**stereo** adj

ste·reo·phon·ic \₁sterēə'fänik, ₁stir-\ adj : relating to a 3-dimensional effect of reproduced sound

ste·reo·type \'sterēə₁tīp, 'stir-\ n : gross often mistaken generalization —**stereotype** vb —**ste·reo·typ·i·cal** \₁sterēə'tipikəl\ adj —**ste·reo·typi·cal·ly** adv

ste·reo·typed \'sterēə₁tīpt, 'stir-\ adj : lacking originality or individuality

ster·ile \'sterəl\ adj 1 : unable to bear fruit, crops, or offspring 2 : free from disease germs —**ste·ril·i·ty** \stə'rilətē\ n —**ster·il·iza·tion** \₁sterələ'zāshən\ n —**ster·il·ize** \-ə₁līz\ vb —**ster·il·iz·er** n

ster·ling \'stərliŋ\ adj 1 : being or made of an alloy of 925 parts of silver with 75 parts of copper 2 : excellent

¹stern \'stərn\ adj : severe —**stern·ly** adv —**stern·ness** n

²**stern** n : back end of a boat

ster·num \'stərnəm\ n, pl **-nums** or **-na** \-nə\ : long flat chest bone joining the 2 sets of ribs

stetho·scope \'stethə,skōp\ n : instrument used for listening to sounds in the chest

ste·ve·dore \'stēvə,dōr\ n : worker who loads and unloads ships

stew \'stü, 'styü\ n 1 : dish of boiled meat and vegetables 2 : state of worry or agitation —**stew** vb

stew·ard \'stüərd, 'styü-\ n 1 : manager of an estate or an organization 2 : person on a ship or airliner who looks after passenger comfort —**stew·ard·ship** n

stew·ard·ess \-əs\ n : woman who is a steward (as on an airplane)

¹**stick** \'stik\ n 1 : cut or broken branch 2 : long thin piece of wood or something resembling it

²**stick** vb **stuck** \'stək\; **stick·ing** 1 : stab 2 : thrust or project 3 : hold fast to something 4 : attach 5 : become jammed or fixed

stick·er \'stikər\ n : adhesive label

stick·ler \'stiklər\ n : one who insists on exactness or completeness

sticky \'stikē\ adj **stick·i·er**; **-est** 1 : adhesive or gluey 2 : muggy 3 : difficult

stiff \'stif\ adj 1 : not bending easily 2 : tense 3 : formal 4 : strong 5 : severe —**stiff·en** \'stifən\ vb —**stiff·en·er** \-ənər\ n —**stiff·ly** adv —**stiff·ness** n

sti·fle \'stīfəl\ vb **-fled**; **-fling** 1 : smother or suffocate 2 : suppress

stig·ma \'stigmə\ n, pl **-ma·ta** \stig-'mätə, 'stigmətə\ or **-mas** : mark of disgrace —**stig·ma·tize** \'stigmə,tīz\ vb

stile \'stīl\ n : steps for crossing a fence

sti·let·to \stə'letō\ n, pl **-tos** or **-toes** : slender dagger

¹**still** \'stil\ adj 1 : motionless 2 : silent ~ vb : make or become still ~ adv 1 : without motion 2 : up to and during this time 3 : in spite of that ~ n : silence —**still·ness** n

²**still** n : apparatus used in distillation

still·born adj : born dead —**still·birth** n

stilt \'stilt\ n : one of a pair of poles for walking

stilt·ed \'stiltəd\ adj : not easy and natural

stim·u·lant \'stimyələnt\ n : substance that temporarily increases the activity of an organism —**stimulant** adj

stim·u·late \-,lāt\ vb **-lat·ed**; **-lat·ing** : make active —**stim·u·la·tion** \,stim-yə'lāshən\ n

stim·u·lus \'stimyələs\ n, pl **-li** \-,lī\ : something that stimulates

sting \'stiŋ\ vb **stung** \'stəŋ\; **sting·ing** 1 : prick painfully 2 : cause to suffer acutely ~ n : act of stinging or a resulting wound —**sting·er** n

stin·gy \'stinjē\ adj **stin·gi·er**; **-est** : not generous —**stin·gi·ness** n

stink \'stiŋk\ vb **stank** \'staŋk\ or **stunk** \'stəŋk\; **stunk**; **stink·ing** : have a strong offensive odor —**stink** n —**stink·er** n

stint \'stint\ vb : be sparing or stingy ~ n 1 : restraint 2 : quantity or period of work

sti·pend \'stī,pend, -pənd\ n : money paid periodically

stip·ple \'stipəl\ vb **-pled**; **-pling** : engrave, paint, or draw with dots instead of lines —**stipple** n

stip·u·late \'stipyə,lāt\ vb **-lat·ed**; **-lat·ing** : demand as a condition —**stip·u·la·tion** \,stipyə'lāshən\ n

stir \'stər\ vb **-rr-** 1 : move slightly 2 : prod or push into activity 3 : mix by continued circular movement ~ n : act or result of stirring

stir·rup \'stərəp\ n : saddle loop for the foot

stitch \'stich\ n 1 : loop formed by a needle in sewing 2 : sudden sharp pain ~ vb 1 : fasten or decorate with stitches 2 : sew

stock \'stäk\ n 1 : block or part of wood 2 : original from which others derive 3 : farm animals 4 : supply of goods 5 : money invested in a large business 6 pl : instrument of punishment like a pillory with holes for the feet or feet and hands ~ vb : provide with stock

stock·ade \stä'kād\ n : defensive or confining enclosure

stock·ing \'stäkiŋ\ n : close-fitting covering for the foot and leg

stock·pile n : reserve supply —**stock·pile** vb

stocky \'stäkē\ adj **stock·i·er**; **-est** : short and relatively thick

stock·yard n : yard for livestock to be slaughtered or shipped

stodgy \'stäjē\ adj **stodg·i·er**; **-est** 1 : dull 2 : old-fashioned

sto·ic \'stōik\, **sto·i·cal** \-ikəl\ adj

: showing indifference to pain —**stoic** n —**sto·i·cal·ly** adv —**sto·i·cism** \'stōə,sizəm\ n

stoke \'stōk\ vb **stoked; stok·ing** : stir up a fire or supply fuel to a furnace —**stok·er** n

¹**stole** \'stōl\ past of STEAL

²**stole** n : long wide scarf

stolen past part of STEAL

stol·id \'stäləd\ adj : having or showing little or no emotion —**stol·id·ly** \'stälədlē\ adv

stom·ach \'stəmək, -ik\ n 1 : saclike digestive organ 2 : abdomen 3 : appetite or desire ~ vb : put up with —**stom·ach·ache** n

stomp \'stämp, 'stómp\ vb : stamp

stone \'stōn\ n 1 : hardened earth or mineral matter 2 : small piece of rock 3 : seed that is hard or has a hard covering ~ vb **stoned; ston·ing** : pelt or kill with stones —**stony** adj

stood past of STAND

stool \'stül\ n 1 : seat usu. without back or arms 2 : footstool 3 : discharge of feces

¹**stoop** \'stüp\ vb 1 : bend over 2 : lower oneself ~ n 1 : act of bending over 2 : bent position of shoulders

²**stoop** n : small porch at a house door

stop \'stäp\ vb **-pp-** 1 : block an opening 2 : end or cause to end 3 : pause for rest or a visit in a journey ~ n 1 : plug 2 : act or place of stopping 3 : delay in a journey —**stop·light** n —**stop·page** \-ij\ n —**stop·per** n

stop·gap n : temporary measure or thing

stor·age \'stórij\ n : safekeeping of goods (as in a warehouse)

store \'stōr\ vb **stored; stor·ing** : put aside for future use ~ n 1 : something stored 2 : retail business establishment —**store·house** n —**store·keep·er** n —**store·room** n

stork \'stórk\ n : large wading bird

storm \'stórm\ n 1 : heavy fall of rain or snow 2 : violent outbreak ~ vb 1 : rain or snow heavily 2 : rage 3 : make an attack against —**stormy** adj

¹**sto·ry** \'stōrē\ n, pl **-ries** 1 : narrative 2 : report —**sto·ry·tell·er** n

²**story** n, pl **-ries** : floor of a building

stout \'staút\ adj 1 : firm or strong 2 : thick or bulky —**stout·ly** adv —**stout·ness** n

¹**stove** \'stōv\ n : apparatus for providing heat (as for cooking or heating)

²**stove** past of STAVE

stow \'stō\ vb 1 : pack in a compact mass 2 : put or hide away

strad·dle \'strad°l\ vb **-dled; -dling** : stand over or sit on with legs on opposite sides —**straddle** n

strafe \'strāf\ vb **strafed; straf·ing** : fire upon with machine guns from a low-flying airplane

strag·gle \'stragəl\ vb **-gled; -gling** : wander or become separated from others —**strag·gler** \-ələr\ n

straight \'strāt\ adj 1 : having no bends, turns, or twists 2 : just, proper, or honest 3 : neat and orderly ~ adv : in a straight manner —**straight·en** \'strāt°n\ vb

straight·for·ward \strāt'fórwərd\ adj : frank or honest

straight·way adv : immediately

¹**strain** \'strān\ n 1 : lineage 2 : trace

²**strain** vb 1 : exert to the utmost 2 : filter or remove by filtering 3 : injure by improper use ~ n 1 : excessive tension or exertion 2 : bodily injury from excessive effort —**strain·er** n

strait \'strāt\ n 1 : narrow channel connecting 2 bodies of water 2 pl : distress

strait·en \'strāt°n\ vb 1 : hem in 2 : make distressing or difficult

¹**strand** \'strand\ vb 1 : drive or cast upon the shore 2 : leave helpless

²**strand** n 1 : twisted fiber of a rope 2 : length of something ropelike

strange \'strānj\ adj **strang·er; strang·est** 1 : unusual or queer 2 : new —**strange·ly** adv —**strange·ness** n

strang·er \'strānjər\ n : person with whom one is not acquainted

stran·gle \'strangəl\ vb **-gled; -gling** : choke to death —**stran·gler** \-glər\ n

stran·gu·la·tion \,strangyə'lāshən\ n : act or process of strangling

strap \'strap\ n : narrow strip of flexible material used esp. for fastening ~ vb 1 : secure with a strap 2 : beat with a strap —**strap·less** n

strap·ping \'strapiŋ\ adj : robust

strat·a·gem \'stratəjəm, -,jem\ n : deceptive scheme or maneuver

strat·e·gy \'stratəjē\ n, pl **-gies** : carefully worked out plan of action —**stra·te·gic** \strə'tējik\ adj —**strat·e·gist** \'stratəjist\ n

strat·i·fy \'stratə,fī\ vb **-fied; -fy·ing**

: form or arrange in layers —**strat·i·fi·ca·tion** \ˌstratəfəˈkāshən\ n

strato·sphere \ˈstratəˌsfir\ n : earth's atmosphere from about 7 to 31 miles above the surface

stra·tum \ˈstrātəm, ˈstrat-\ n, pl **-ta** \ˈstrātə, ˈstrat-\ : layer

straw \ˈstrȯ\ n 1 : grass stems after grain is removed 2 : tube for drinking ~ adj : made of straw

straw·ber·ry \ˈstrȯˌberē\ n : juicy red pulpy fruit

stray \ˈstrā\ vb : wander or deviate ~ n : person or animal that strays ~ adj : separated from or not related to anything close by

streak \ˈstrēk\ n 1 : mark of a different color 2 : narrow band of light 3 : trace 4 : run (as of luck) or series ~ vb 1 : form streaks in or on 2 : move fast

stream \ˈstrēm\ n 1 : flow of water on land 2 : steady flow (as of water or air) ~ vb 1 : flow in a stream 2 : pour out streams

stream·er \ˈstrēmər\ n : long ribbon or ribbonlike flag

stream·lined \-ˌlīnd, -ˈlīnd\ adj 1 : made with contours to reduce air or water resistance 2 : simplified 3 : modernized —**streamline** vb

street \ˈstrēt\ n : thoroughfare esp. in a city or town

street·car n : passenger vehicle running on rails in the streets

strength \ˈstreŋth\ n 1 : quality of being strong 2 : toughness 3 : intensity

strength·en \ˈstreŋthən\ vb : make, grow, or become stronger —**strength·en·er** \ˈstreŋthənər\ n

stren·u·ous \ˈstrenyəwəs\ adj 1 : vigorous 2 : requiring or showing energy —**stren·u·ous·ly** adv

stress \ˈstres\ n 1 : pressure or strain that tends to distort a body 2 : relative prominence given to one thing among others 3 : state of physical or mental tension or something inducing it ~ vb : put stress on —**stress·ful** \ˈstresfəl\ adj

stretch \ˈstrech\ vb 1 : spread or reach out 2 : draw out in length or breadth 3 : make taut 4 : exaggerate 5 : become extended without breaking ~ n : act of extending beyond normal limits

stretch·er \ˈstrechər\ n : device for carrying a sick or injured person

strew \ˈstrü\ vb **strewed**; **strewed** or **strewn** \ˈstrün\; **strew·ing** 1 : scatter 2 : cover by scattering something over

strick·en \ˈstrikən\ adj : afflicted with disease

strict \ˈstrikt\ adj 1 : allowing no escape or evasion 2 : precise —**strict·ly** adv —**strict·ness** n

stric·ture \ˈstrikchər\ n : hostile criticism

stride \ˈstrīd\ vb **strode** \ˈstrōd\; **strid·den** \ˈstridᵊn\; **strid·ing** : walk or run with long steps ~ n 1 : long step 2 : manner of striding

stri·dent \ˈstrīdᵊnt\ adj : loud and harsh

strife \ˈstrīf\ n : conflict

strike \ˈstrīk\ vb **struck** \ˈstrək\; **struck**; **strik·ing** \ˈstrīkiŋ\ 1 : hit sharply 2 : delete 3 : produce by impressing 4 : cause to sound 5 : afflict 6 : occur to or impress 7 : cause (a match) to ignite by rubbing 8 : refrain from working 9 : find 10 : take on (as a pose) ~ n 1 : act or instance of striking 2 : work stoppage 3 : military attack —**strik·er** n —**strike out** vb : start out vigorously —**strike up** vb : start

strik·ing \ˈstrīkiŋ\ adj : very noticeable —**strik·ing·ly** adv

string \ˈstriŋ\ n 1 : line usu. of twisted threads 2 : series 3 pl : stringed instruments ~ vb **strung** \ˈstrəŋ\; **string·ing** 1 : thread on or with a string 2 : hang or fasten by a string

stringed \ˈstriŋd\ adj : having strings

strin·gent \ˈstrinjənt\ adj : severe

stringy \ˈstriŋē\ adj **string·i·er; -est** : tough or fibrous

¹**strip** \ˈstrip\ vb **-pp-** 1 : take the covering or clothing from 2 : undress —**strip·per** n

²**strip** n : long narrow flat piece

stripe \ˈstrīp\ n : distinctive line or long narrow section ~ vb **striped** \ˈstrīpt\; **strip·ing** : make stripes on —**striped** \ˈstrīpt, ˈstrīpəd\ adj

strive \ˈstrīv\ vb **strove** \ˈstrōv\; **stri·ven** \ˈstrivən\ or **strived**; **striv·ing** \ˈstrīviŋ\ 1 : struggle 2 : try hard

strode past of STRIDE

stroke \ˈstrōk\ vb **stroked**; **strok·ing** : rub gently ~ n 1 : act of swinging or striking 2 : sudden action

stroll \ˈstrōl\ vb : walk leisurely —**stroll** n —**stroll·er** n

strong \ˈstrȯŋ\ adj 1 : capable of exerting great force or of withstanding stress or violence **2** : healthy **3** : zealous —**strong·ly** adv

strong·hold n : fortified place

struck past of STRIKE

struc·ture \'strəkchər\ n **1** : building **2** : arrangement of elements ~ vb **-tured; -tur·ing** : make into a structure —**struc·tur·al** \-chərəl\ adj

strug·gle \'strəgəl\ vb **-gled; -gling 1** : make strenuous efforts to overcome an adversary **2** : proceed with great effort ~ n **1** : strenuous effort **2** : intense competition for superiority

strum \'strəm\ vb **-mm-** : play (a musical instrument) by brushing the strings with the fingers

strum·pet \'strəmpət\ n : prostitute

strung past of STRING

strut \'strət\ vb **-tt-** : walk in a proud or showy manner ~ n **1** : proud walk **2** : supporting bar or rod

strych·nine \'strik,nīn, -nən, -,nēn\ n : bitter poisonous substance

stub \'stəb\ n : short end or section ~ vb **-bb-** : strike against something

stub·ble \'stəbəl\ n : short growth left after cutting —**stub·bly** adj

stub·born \'stəbərn\ adj **1** : determined not to yield **2** : hard to control —**stub·born·ly** adv —**stub·born·ness** n

stub·by \'stəbē\ adj : short, blunt, and thick

stuc·co \'stəkō\ n, pl **-cos** or **-coes** : plaster for coating outside walls —**stuc·coed** \'stəkōd\ adj

stuck past of STICK

stuck-up \'stək'əp\ adj : conceited

¹stud \'stəd\ n : male horse kept for breeding

²stud n **1** : upright beam for holding wall material **2** : projecting nail, pin, or rod ~ vb **-dd-** : supply or dot with studs

stu·dent \'stüdᵊnt, 'styü-\ n : one who studies

stud·ied \'stədēd\ adj : premeditated

stu·dio \'stüdē,ō, 'styü-\ n, pl **-dios 1** : artist's workroom **2** : place where movies are made or television or radio shows are broadcast

stu·di·ous \'stüdēəs, 'styü-\ adj : devoted to study —**stu·di·ous·ly** adv

study \'stədē\ n, pl **stud·ies 1** : act or process of learning about something **2** : branch of learning **3** : careful examination **4** : room for reading or studying ~ vb **stud·ied; study·ing**

: apply the attention and mind to a subject

stuff \'stəf\ n **1** : personal property **2** : raw or fundamental material **3** : unspecified material or things ~ vb n : fill by packing things in —**stuff·ing** n

stuffy \'stəfē\ adj **stuff·i·er; -est 1** : lacking fresh air **2** : unimaginative or pompous

stul·ti·fy \'stəltə,fī\ vb **-fied; -fy·ing 1** : cause to appear foolish **2** : impair or make ineffective **3** : have a dulling effect on

stum·ble \'stəmbəl\ vb **-bled; -bling 1** : lose one's balance or fall in walking or running **2** : speak or act clumsily **3** : happen by chance —**stumble** n

stump \'stəmp\ n : part left when something is cut off ~ vb : confuse —**stumpy** adj

stun \'stən\ vb **-nn- 1** : make senseless or dizzy by or as if by a blow **2** : bewilder

stung past of STING

stunk past of STINK

stun·ning \'stəniŋ\ adj **1** : astonishing or incredible **2** : strikingly beautiful —**stun·ning·ly** adv

¹stunt \'stənt\ vb : hinder the normal growth or progress of

²stunt n : spectacular feat

stu·pe·fy \'stüpə,fī, 'styü-\ vb **-fied; -fy·ing 1** : make insensible by or as if by drugs **2** : amaze

stu·pen·dous \stu'pendəs, styü-\ adj : very big or impressive —**stu·pen·dous·ly** adv

stu·pid \'stüpəd, 'styü-\ adj : not sensible or intelligent —**stu·pid·i·ty** \stü'pidətē, styü-\ n —**stu·pid·ly** adv

stu·por \'stüpər, 'styü-\ n : state of being conscious but not aware or sensible

stur·dy \'stərdē\ adj **-di·er; -est** : strong —**stur·di·ly** \'stərdᵊlē\ adv —**stur·di·ness** n

stur·geon \'stərjən\ n : fish whose roe is caviar

stut·ter \'stətər\ vb or n : stammer

¹sty \'stī\ n, pl **sties** : pig pen

²sty, stye \'stī\ n, pl **sties** or **styes** : inflamed swelling on the edge of an eyelid

style \'stīl\ n **1** : distinctive way of speaking, writing, or acting **2** : elegant or fashionable way of living ~ vb **styled; styl·ing 1** : name **2** : give a particular design or style to —**styl-**

ish \'stīlish\ adj —styl·ish·ly adv —styl·ish·ness n —styl·ist \-ist\ n —styl·ize \'stīl,īz\ vb

sty·lus \'stīləs\ n, pl -li \'stīl,ī\ 1 : pointed writing tool 2 : phonograph needle

sty·mie \'stīmē\ vb -mied; -mie·ing : block or frustrate

suave \'swäv\ adj : well-mannered and gracious —suave·ly adv

¹sub \'səb\ n or vb : substitute

²sub n : submarine

sub- \,səb, 'səb\ prefix 1 : under or beneath 2 : subordinate or secondary 3 : subordinate portion of 4 : with repetition of a process so as to form, stress, or deal with subordinate parts or relations 5 : somewhat 6 : nearly

subacute	subindustry
subagency	sublease
subagent	sublethal
subarctic	sublevel
subarea	subliterate
subatmospheric	subnetwork
subaverage	suboceanic
subbase	suborder
subbasement	subpar
subbranch	subpart
subcabinet	subplot
subcategory	subpolar
subclass	subprincipal
subclassification	subprocess
subclassify	subprogram
subcommission	subproject
subcommittee	subregion
subcommunity	subsea
subcomponent	subsection
subcontract	subsense
subcontractor	subspecialty
subculture	subspecies
subdean	substage
subdepartment	subsurface
subdistrict	subsystem
subentry	subtemperate
subfamily	subtheme
subfreezing	subtopic
subgroup	subtotal
subhead	subtreasury
subheading	subtype
subhuman	subunit
subindex	subvariety

sub·con·scious \,səb'känchəs\ adj : existing without conscious awareness ~ n : part of the mind concerned with subconscious activities —sub·con·scious·ly adv

sub·di·vide \,səbdə'vīd, 'səbdə,vīd\ vb 1 : divide into several parts 2 : divide (land) into building lots —sub·di·vi·sion \-'vizhən, -,vizh-\ n

sub·due \səb'dü, -'dyü\ vb -dued; -du·ing 1 : bring under control 2 : reduce the intensity of

sub·ject \'səbjikt\ n 1 : person under the authority of another 2 : something being discussed or studied 3 : word or word group about which something is said in a sentence ~ adj 1 : being under one's authority 2 : prone 3 : dependent on some condition or act ~ \səb'jekt\ vb 1 : bring under control 2 : cause to undergo —sub·jec·tion \-'jekshən\ n

sub·jec·tive \,səb'jektiv\ adj : deriving from an individual viewpoint or bias —sub·jec·tive·ly adv —sub·jec·tiv·i·ty \-,jek'tivətē\ n

sub·ju·gate \'səbji,gāt\ vb -gat·ed; -gat·ing : bring under one's control —sub·ju·ga·tion \,səbji'gāshən\ n

sub·junc·tive \səb'jəŋktiv\ adj : relating to a verb form which expresses possibility or contingency —subjunctive n

sub·let \'səb,let\ vb -let; -let·ting : rent (a property) from a lessee

sub·lime \sə'blīm\ adj : splendid —sub·lime·ly adv

sub·ma·rine \'səbmə,rēn, ,səbmə'-\ adj : existing, acting, or growing under the sea ~ n : underwater boat

sub·merge \səb'mərj\ vb -merged; -merg·ing : put or plunge under the surface of water —sub·mer·gence \-'mərjəns\ n —sub·mers·ible \səb-'mərsəbəl\ adj or n —sub·mer·sion \-'mərzhən\ n

sub·mit \səb'mit\ vb -tt- 1 : yield 2 : give or offer —sub·mis·sion \-'mi-shən\ n —sub·mis·sive \-'misiv\ adj

sub·nor·mal \,səb'nórməl\ adj : falling below what is normal

sub·or·di·nate \sə'bórd°nət\ adj : lower in rank ~ n : one that is subordinate ~ \sə'bórd°n,āt\ vb -nat·ed; -nat·ing : place in a lower rank or class —sub·or·di·na·tion \-,bórd°n'āshən\ n

sub·poe·na \sə'pēnə\ n : summons to appear in court ~ vb -naed; -na·ing : summon with a subpoena

sub·scribe \səb'skrīb\ vb -scribed; -scrib·ing 1 : give consent or approval 2 : agree to support or to receive and pay for —**sub·scrib·er** n

sub·scrip·tion \səb'skripshən\ n : order for regular receipt of a publication

sub·se·quent \'səbsikwənt, -sə,kwent\ adj : following after —**sub·sequent·ly** \-,kwentlē, -kwənt-\ adv

sub·ser·vi·ence \səb'sərvēəns\ n : obsequious submission —**sub·ser·vi·en·cy** \-ənsē\ n —**sub·ser·vi·ent** \-ənt\ adj

sub·side \səb'sīd\ vb -**sid·ed**; -**sid·ing** : die down in intensity

sub·sid·iary \səb'sidē,erē\ adj 1 : furnishing support 2 : of secondary importance ~ n : company controlled by another company

sub·si·dize \'səbsə,dīz\ vb -**dized**; -**diz·ing** : aid with a subsidy

sub·si·dy \'səbsədē\ n, pl -**dies** : gift of supporting funds

sub·sist \səb'sist\ vb : acquire the necessities of life —**sub·sis·tence** \-'sistəns\ n

sub·stance \'səbstəns\ n 1 : essence or essential part 2 : physical material 3 : wealth

sub·stan·dard \,səb'standərd\ adj : falling short of a standard or norm

sub·stan·tial \səb'stanchəl\ adj 1 : plentiful 2 : considerable —**sub·stan·tial·ly** adv

sub·stan·ti·ate \səb'stanchē,āt\ vb -**at·ed**; -**at·ing** : verify —**sub·stan·ti·a·tion** \-,stanchē'āshən\ n

sub·sti·tute \'səbstə,tüt, -,tyüt\ n : replacement ~ vb -**tut·ed**; -**tut·ing** : put or serve in place of another —**substitute** adj —**sub·sti·tu·tion** \,səbstə'tüshən, -'tyü-\ n

sub·ter·fuge \'səbtər,fyüj\ n : deceptive trick

sub·ter·ra·nean \,səbtə'rānēən\ adj : lying or being underground

sub·ti·tle \'səb,tīt°l\ n : movie caption

sub·tle \'sət°l\ adj -**tler** \-ər\; -**tlest** \-ist\ 1 : hardly noticeable 2 : clever —**subtle·ty** \-tē\ n —**subt·ly** \-°lē\ adv

sub·tract \səb'trakt\ vb : take away (as one number from another) —**sub·trac·tion** \-'trakshən\ n

sub·urb \'səb,ərb\ n : residential area adjacent to a city —**sub·ur·ban** \sə'bərbən\ adj or n —**sub·ur·ban·ite** \-bə,nīt\ n

sub·vert \səb'vərt\ vb : overthrow or ruin —**sub·ver·sion** \-'vərzhən\ n —**sub·ver·sive** \-'vərsiv\ adj

sub·way \'səb,wā\ n : underground electric railway

suc·ceed \sək'sēd\ vb 1 : follow (someone) in a job, role, or title 2 : attain a desired object or end

suc·cess \-'ses\ n 1 : favorable outcome 2 : gaining of wealth and fame 3 : one that succeeds —**suc·cess·ful** \-fəl\ adj —**suc·cess·ful·ly** adv

suc·ces·sion \sək'seshən\ n 1 : order, act, or right of succeeding 2 : series

suc·ces·sive \-'sesiv\ adj : following in order —**suc·ces·sive·ly** adv

suc·ces·sor \-'sesər\ n : one that succeeds another

suc·cinct \sək'siŋkt, sə'siŋkt\ adj : brief —**suc·cinct·ly** adv —**suc·cinct·ness** n

suc·cor \'səkər\ n or vb : help

suc·co·tash \'səkə,tash\ n : beans and corn cooked together

suc·cu·lent \'səkyələnt\ adj : juicy —**suc·cu·lence** \-ləns\ n —**succulent** n

suc·cumb \sə'kəm\ vb 1 : yield 2 : die

such \'səch\ adj 1 : of this or that kind 2 : having a specified quality —**such** pron or adv

suck \'sək\ vb 1 : draw in liquid with the mouth 2 : draw liquid from by or as if by mouth —**suck** n

suck·er \'səkər\ n 1 : one that sucks or clings 2 : easily deceived person

suck·le \'səkəl\ vb -**led**; -**ling** : give or draw milk from the breast or udder

suck·ling \'səkliŋ\ n : young unweaned mammal

su·crose \'sü,krōs, -,krōz\ n : cane or beet sugar

suc·tion \'səkshən\ n 1 : act of sucking 2 : act or process of drawing in by partially exhausting the air

sud·den \'səd°n\ adj 1 : happening unexpectedly 2 : steep 3 : hasty —**sud·den·ly** adv —**sud·den·ness** n

suds \'sədz\ n pl : soapy water esp. when frothy —**sudsy** \'sədzē\ adj

sue \'sü\ vb **sued**; **su·ing** 1 : petition 2 : bring legal action against

suede, suède \'swād\ n : leather with a napped surface

su·et \'süət\ n : hard beef fat

suf·fer \'səfər\ vb 1 : experience pain, loss, or hardship 2 : permit —**suf·fer·er** n

suf·fer·ing \-əriŋ\ n : pain or hardship

suf·fice \sə'fīs\ vb -**ficed**; -**fic·ing** : be sufficient

suf·fi·cient \sə'fishənt\ adj : adequate

—**suf·fi·cien·cy** \-ənsē\ n —**suf·fi·cient·ly** adv

suf·fix \'səf,iks\ n : letters added at the end of a word —**suffix** \,sə'fiks\ vb —**suf·fix·a·tion** \,səf·ik'sāshən\ n

suf·fo·cate \'səfə,kāt\ vb -**cat·ed; -cat·ing** : suffer or die or cause to die from lack of air —**suf·fo·cat·ing·ly** adv —**suf·fo·ca·tion** \,səfə'kāshən\ n

suf·frage \'səfrij\ n : right to vote

suf·fuse \sə'fyüz\ vb -**fused; -fus·ing** : spread over or through

sug·ar \'shủgər\ n : sweet substance ~ vb : mix, cover, or sprinkle with sugar —**sug·ar·cane** n —**sug·ary** adj

sug·gest \səg'jest, səg-\ vb 1 : put into someone's mind 2 : remind one by association of ideas —**sug·gest·ible** \-'jestəbəl\ adj —**sug·ges·tion** \-'jeschən\ n

sug·ges·tive \-'jestiv\ adj : suggesting something improper —**sug·ges·tive·ly** adv —**sug·ges·tive·ness** n

su·i·cide \'süə,sīd\ n 1 : act of killing oneself purposely 2 : one who commits suicide —**su·i·cid·al** \,süə'sīd^əl\ adj

suit \'süt\ n 1 : action in court to recover a right or claim 2 : number of things used or worn together 3 : one of the 4 sets of playing cards ~ vb 1 : be appropriate or becoming to 2 : meet the needs of —**suit·abil·i·ty** \,sütə'bilətē\ n —**suit·able** \'sütəbəl\ adj —**suit·ably** adv

suit·case n : case for a traveler's clothing

suite \'swēt, for 2 also 'süt\ n 1 : group of rooms 2 : set of matched furniture

suit·or \'sütər\ n : one who seeks to marry a woman

sul·fur \'səlfər\ n : nonmetallic yellow chemical element —**sul·fu·ric** \,səl'fyürik\ adj —**sul·fu·rous** \-'fyürəs, 'səlfərəs, 'səlfyə-\ adj

sulk \'səlk\ vb : be moodily silent or irritable —**sulk** n

sulky \'səlkē\ adj : inclined to sulk ~ n : light 2-wheeled horse-drawn cart —**sulk·i·ly** \'səlkəlē\ adv —**sulk·i·ness** \-kēnəs\ n

sul·len \'sələn\ adj 1 : gloomily silent 2 : dismal —**sul·len·ly** adv —**sul·len·ness** n

sul·ly \'səlē\ vb -**lied; -ly·ing** : cast doubt or disgrace on

sul·tan \'səlt^ən\ n : sovereign of a Muslim state —**sul·tan·ate** \-,āt\ n

sul·try \'səltrē\ adj -**tri·er; -est** 1 : very hot and moist 2 : sexually arousing

sum \'səm\ n 1 : amount 2 : gist 3 : result of addition ~ vb -**mm-** : find the sum of

su·mac \'shü,mak, 'sü-\ n : shrub with spikes of berries

sum·ma·ry \'səmərē\ adj 1 : concise 2 : done without delay or formality ~ n, pl -**ries** : concise statement —**sum·mar·i·ly** \sə'merəlē, 'səmərəlē\ adv —**sum·ma·rize** \'səmə,rīz\ vb

sum·ma·tion \sə'māshən\ n : a summing up esp. in court

sum·mer \'səmər\ n : season in which the sun shines most directly —**sum·mery** adj

sum·mit \'səmət\ n 1 : highest point 2 : high-level conference

sum·mon \'səmən\ vb 1 : send for or call together 2 : order to appear in court —**sum·mon·er** n

sum·mons \'səmənz\ n, pl **sum·mons·es** : an order to answer charges in court

sump·tu·ous \'səmpchəwəs\ adj : lavish

sun \'sən\ n 1 : shining celestial body around which the planets revolve 2 : light of the sun ~ vb -**nn-** : expose to the sun —**sun·beam** n —**sun·block** n —**sun·burn** n or vb —**sun·glass·es** n pl —**sun·light** n —**sun·ny** adj —**sun·rise** n —**sun·set** n —**sun·shine** n —**sun·tan** n

sun·dae \'səndē\ n : ice cream with topping

Sun·day \'səndā, -dē\ n : 1st day of the week

sun·di·al \-,dīəl\ n : device for showing time by the sun's shadow

sun·dries \'səndrēz\ n, pl : various small articles

sun·dry \-drē\ adj : several

sun·fish n : perchlike freshwater fish

sun·flow·er n : tall plant grown for its oil-rich seeds

sung past of SING

sunk past of SINK

sunk·en \'səŋkən\ adj 1 : submerged 2 : fallen in

sun·spot n : dark spot on the sun

sun·stroke n : heatstroke from the sun

sup \'səp\ vb -**pp-** : eat the evening meal

super \'süpər\ adj : very fine

super- \,süpər, 'sü-\ prefix 1 : higher in quantity, quality, or degree than 2 : in addition **3** : exceeding a norm **4** : in excessive degree or intensity **5** : surpassing others of its kind **6** : situated above, on, or at the top of **7** : more inclusive than **8** : superior in status or position

superabundance	superpatriotism
superabundant	superplane
superambitious	superpolite
superathlete	superport
superbomb	superpowerful
superclean	superrich
supercolossal	supersalesman
superconvenient	superscout
supercop	supersecrecy
superdense	supersecret
supereffective	supersensitive
superefficiency	supersize
superefficient	supersized
superfast	superslick
supergood	supersmooth
supergovern-ment	supersoft
	superspecial
supergroup	superspecialist
superhero	superspy
superheroine	superstar
superhuman	superstate
superintellec-tual	superstrength
	superstrong
superintellig-ence	supersystem
	supertanker
superintelligent	superthick
superman	superthin
supermodern	supertight
superpatriot	superweapon
superpatriotic	superwoman

su·perb \su̇'pərb\ adj : outstanding — su·perb·ly adv
su·per·cil·i·ous \ˌsüpər'silēəs\ adj : haughtily contemptuous
su·per·fi·cial \ˌsüpər'fishəl\ adj : relating to what is only apparent — su·per·fi·ci·al·i·ty \-ˌfishē'alətē\ n — su·per·fi·cial·ly adv
su·per·flu·ous \su̇'pərflōwəs\ adj : more than necessary — su·per·flu·i·ty \ˌsü-pər'flüətē\ n
su·per·im·pose \ˌsüpərim'pōz\ vb : lay over or above something
su·per·in·tend \ˌsüpərin'tend\ vb : have charge and oversight of — su·per·in·ten·dence \-'tendəns\ n — su·per·in·ten·den·cy \-dənsē\ n — su·per·in·ten·dent \-dənt\ n
su·pe·ri·or \su̇'pirēər\ adj 1 : higher, better, or more important 2 : haughty

—superior n —su·pe·ri·or·i·ty \-ˌpirē'órətē\ n
su·per·la·tive \su̇'pərlətiv\ adj 1 : relating to or being an adjective or adverb form that denotes an extreme level 2 : surpassing others —super·lative n —su·per·la·tive·ly adv
su·per·mar·ket \'süpər,märkət\ n : self-service grocery store
su·per·nat·u·ral \ˌsüpər'nachərəl\ adj : beyond the observable physical world —su·per·nat·u·ral·ly adv
su·per·pow·er \'süpər,pau̇ər\ n : politically and militarily dominant nation
su·per·sede \ˌsüpər'sēd\ vb -sed·ed; -sed·ing : take the place of
su·per·son·ic \-'sänik\ adj : faster than the speed of sound
su·per·sti·tion \ˌsüpər'stishən\ n : beliefs based on ignorance, fear of the unknown, or trust in magic —su·per·sti·tious \-əs\ adj
su·per·struc·ture \'süpər,strəkchər\ n : something built on a base or as a vertical extension
su·per·vise \'süpər,vīz\ vb -vised; -vis·ing : have charge of —su·per·vi·sion \ˌsüpər'vizhən\ n —su·per·vi·sor \'süpər,vīzər\ n —su·per·vi·so·ry \ˌsüpər'vīzərē\ adj
su·pine \su̇'pīn\ adj 1 : lying on the back 2 : indifferent or abject
sup·per \'səpər\ n : evening meal
sup·plant \sə'plant\ vb : take the place of
sup·ple \'səpəl\ adj -pler; -plest : able to bend easily
sup·ple·ment \'səpləmənt\ n : something that adds to or makes up for a lack —supplement vb —sup·ple·men·tal \ˌsəplə'mentᵊl\ adj —sup·ple·men·ta·ry \-'mentərē\ adj
sup·pli·ant \'səplēənt\ n : one who supplicates
sup·pli·cate \'səplə,kāt\ vb -cat·ed; -cat·ing 1 : pray to God 2 : ask earnestly and humbly —sup·pli·cant \-likənt\ n —sup·pli·ca·tion \ˌsə-plə'kāshən\ n
sup·ply \sə'plī\ vb -plied; -ply·ing : furnish ~ n, pl -plies 1 : amount needed or available 2 pl : provisions —sup·pli·er \-'plīər\ n
sup·port \sə'pōrt\ vb 1 : take sides with 2 : provide with food, clothing, and shelter 3 : hold up or serve as a foundation for —support n —sup·port·able adj —sup·port·er n

sup·pose \sə'pōz\ *vb* **-posed; -pos·ing 1** : assume to be true **2** : expect **3** : think probable —**sup·po·si·tion** \,səpə-'zishən\ *n*

sup·pos·i·to·ry \sə'päzə,tōrē\ *n, pl* **-ries** : medicated material for insertion (as into the rectum)

sup·press \sə'pres\ *vb* **1** : put an end to by authority **2** : keep from being known **3** : hold back —**sup·pres·sant** \sə'pres²nt\ *n* —**sup·pres·sion** \-'preshən\ *n*

su·prem·a·cy \sù'preməsē\ *n, pl* **-cies** : supreme power or authority

su·preme \sù'prēm\ *adj* **1** : highest in rank or authority **2** : greatest possible —**su·preme·ly** *adv*

Supreme Being *n* : God

sur·charge \'sər,chärj\ *n* **1** : excessive load or burden **2** : extra fee or cost

sure \'shùr\ *adj* **sur·er; sur·est 1** : confident **2** : reliable **3** : not to be disputed **4** : bound to happen ~ *adv* : surely —**sure·ness** *n*

sure·ly \'shùrlē\ *adv* **1** : in a sure manner **2** : without doubt **3** : indeed

sure·ty \'shùrətē\ *n, pl* **-ties 1** : guarantee **2** : one who gives a guarantee for another person

surf \'sərf\ *n* : waves that break on the shore ~ *vb* : ride the surf —**surf·board** *n* —**surf·er** *n* —**surf·ing** *n*

sur·face \'sərfəs\ *n* **1** : the outside of an object **2** : outward aspect ~ *vb* **-faced; -fac·ing** : rise to the surface

sur·feit \'sərfət\ *n* **1** : excess **2** : excessive indulgence (as in food or drink) **3** : disgust caused by excess ~ *vb* : feed, supply, or indulge to the point of surfeit

surge \'sərj\ *vb* **surged; surg·ing** : rise and fall in or as if in waves ~ *n* : sudden increase

sur·geon \'sərjən\ *n* : physician who specializes in surgery

sur·gery \'sərjərē\ *n, pl* **-ger·ies** : medical treatment involving cutting open the body

sur·gi·cal \'sərjikəl\ *adj* : relating to surgeons or surgery —**sur·gi·cal·ly** *adv*

sur·ly \'sərlē\ *adj* **-li·er; -est** : having a rude nature —**sur·li·ness** *n*

sur·mise \sər'mīz\ *vb* **-mised; -mis·ing** : guess —**surmise** *n*

sur·mount \-'maúnt\ *vb* **1** : prevail over **2** : get to or be the top of

sur·name \'sər,nām\ *n* : family name

sur·pass \sər'pas\ *vb* : go beyond or exceed —**sur·pass·ing·ly** *adv*

sur·plice \'sərpləs\ *n* : loose white outer ecclesiastical vestment

sur·plus \'sər,pləs\ *n* : quantity left over

sur·prise \sə'prīz, sər-\ *vb* **-prised; -pris·ing 1** : come upon or affect unexpectedly **2** : amaze —**surprise** *n* —**sur·pris·ing** *adj* —**sur·pris·ing·ly** *adv*

sur·ren·der \sə'rendər\ *vb* : give up oneself or a possession to another ~ *n* : act of surrendering

sur·rep·ti·tious \,sərəp'tishəs\ *adj* : done, made, or acquired by stealth —**sur·rep·ti·tious·ly** *adv*

sur·rey \'sərē\ *n, pl* **-reys** : horse-drawn carriage

sur·ro·gate \'sərəgāt, -gət\ *n* : substitute

sur·round \sə'raúnd\ *vb* : enclose on all sides

sur·round·ings \sə'raúndiŋz\ *n pl* : objects, conditions, or area around something

sur·veil·lance \sər'vāləns, -'vālyəns, -'vāəns\ *n* : careful watch

sur·vey \sər'vā\ *vb* **-veyed; -vey·ing 1** : look over and examine closely **2** : make a survey of (as a tract of land) ~ \'sər,-\ *n, pl* **-veys 1** : inspection **2** : process of measuring (as land) —**sur·vey·or** \-ər\ *n*

sur·vive \sər'vīv\ *vb* **-vived; -viv·ing 1** : remain alive or in existence **2** : outlive or outlast —**sur·viv·al** *n* —**sur·vi·vor** \-'vīvər\ *n*

sus·cep·ti·ble \sə'septəbəl\ *adj* : likely to allow or be affected by something —**sus·cep·ti·bil·i·ty** \-,septə'bilətē\ *n*

sus·pect \'səs,pekt, sə'spekt\ *adj* **1** : regarded with suspicion **2** : questionable ~ \'səs,pekt\ *n* : one who is suspected (as of a crime) ~ \sə'spekt\ *vb* **1** : have doubts of **2** : believe guilty without proof **3** : guess

sus·pend \sə'spend\ *vb* **1** : temporarily stop or keep from a function or job **2** : withhold (judgment) temporarily **3** : hang

sus·pend·er \sə'spendər\ *n* : one of 2 supporting straps holding up trousers and passing over the shoulders

sus·pense \sə'spens\ *n* : excitement and uncertainty as to outcome —**sus·pense·ful** *adj*

sus·pen·sion \sə'spenchən\ *n* : act of

suspending or the state or period of being suspended

sus·pi·cion \sə'spishən\ n 1 : act of suspecting something 2 : trace

sus·pi·cious \-əs\ adj 1 : arousing suspicion 2 : inclined to suspect —**sus·pi·cious·ly** adv

sus·tain \sə'stān\ vb 1 : provide with nourishment 2 : keep going 3 : hold up 4 : suffer 5 : support or prove

sus·te·nance \'səstənəns\ n 1 : nourishment 2 : something that sustains or supports

svelte \'sfelt\ adj : slender and graceful

swab \'swäb\ n 1 : mop 2 : wad of absorbent material for applying medicine ~ vb -bb- : use a swab on

swad·dle \'swäd⁰l\ vb -dled; -dling \'swäd⁰liŋ\ : bind (an infant) in bands of cloth

swag·ger \'swagər\ vb -gered; -ger·ing 1 : walk with a conceited swing 2 : boast —**swagger** n

¹**swal·low** \'swälō\ n : small migratory bird

²**swallow** vb 1 : take into the stomach through the throat 2 : envelop or take in 3 : accept too easily —**swallow** n

swam past of SWIM

swamp \'swämp\ n : wet spongy land ~ vb : deluge (as with water) —**swampy** adj

swan \'swän\ n : white long-necked swimming bird

swap \'swäp\ vb -pp- : trade —**swap** n

swarm \'swórm\ n 1 : mass of honeybees leaving a hive to start a new colony 2 : large crowd ~ vb : gather in a swarm

swar·thy \'swórthē, -thē\ adj -thi·er; -est : dark in complexion

swash·buck·ler \'swäsh,bəklər\ n : swaggering or daring soldier or adventurer —**swash·buck·ling** \-,bəkliŋ\ adj

swat \'swät\ vb -tt- : hit sharply —**swat** n —**swat·ter** n

swatch \'swäch\ n : sample piece (as of fabric)

swath \'swäth, 'swóth\, **swathe** \'swäth, 'swóth, 'swäth\ n : row or path cut (as through grass)

swathe \'swäth, 'swóth, 'swäth\ vb **swathed; swath·ing** : wrap with or as if with a bandage

sway \'swā\ vb 1 : swing gently from side to side 2 : influence ~ n 1 : gentle swinging from side to side 2 : controlling power or influence

swear \'swar\ vb **swore** \'swōr\; **sworn** \'sōrn\; **swear·ing** 1 : make or cause to make a solemn statement under oath 2 : use profane language —**swear·er** n —**swear·ing** n

sweat \'swet\ vb **sweat or sweat·ed; sweat·ing** 1 : excrete salty moisture from skin glands 2 : form drops of moisture on the surface 3 : work or cause to work hard —**sweat** n —**sweaty** adj

sweat·er \'swetər\ n : knitted jacket or pullover

sweat·shirt \'swet,shərt\ n : loose collarless heavy cotton jersey pullover

sweep \'swēp\ vb **swept** \'swept\; **sweep·ing** 1 : remove or clean by a brush or a single forceful wipe (as of the hand) 2 : move with speed and force (as of the hand) 3 : move or extend in a wide curve ~ n 1 : a clearing off or away 2 : single forceful wipe or swinging movement 3 : scope —**sweep·er** n —**sweep·ing** adj

sweep·stakes \'swēp,stāks\ n, pl **sweep·stakes** : contest in which the entire prize may go to the winner

sweet \'swēt\ adj 1 : being or causing the pleasing taste typical of sugar 2 : not stale or spoiled 3 : not salted 4 : pleasant 5 : much loved ~ n : something sweet —**sweet·en** \'swēt⁰n\ vb —**sweet·ly** adv —**sweet·ness** n —**sweet·en·er** \-⁰nər\ n

sweet·heart n : person one loves

sweet potato n : sweet yellow edible root of a tropical vine

swell \'swel\ vb **swelled; swelled or swol·len** \'swōlən\; **swell·ing** 1 : enlarge or bulge 3 : fill or be filled with emotion ~ n 1 : long rolling ocean wave 2 : condition of bulging —**swell·ing** n

swel·ter \'sweltər\ vb : be uncomfortable from excessive heat

swept past of SWEEP

swerve \'swərv\ vb **swerved; swerv·ing** : move abruptly aside from a course —**swerve** n

¹**swift** \'swift\ adj 1 : moving with great speed 2 : occurring suddenly —**swift·ly** adv —**swift·ness** n

²**swift** n : small insect-eating bird

swig \'swig\ vb -gg- : drink in gulps —**swig** n

swill \'swil\ vb : swallow greedily ~ n 1 : animal food of refuse and liquid 2 : garbage

swim \'swim\ vb **swam** \'swam\; **swum** \'swəm\; **swim·ming** 1 : propel oneself in water 2 : float in or be surrounded with a liquid 3 : be dizzy ~ n : act or period of swimming — **swim·mer** n

swin·dle \'swind°l\ vb **-dled**; **-dling** \-iŋ\ : cheat (someone) of money or property — **swindle** n — **swin·dler** \-ər\ n

swine \'swīn\ n, pl **swine** : short-legged hoofed mammal with a snout — **swin·ish** \'swīnish\ adj

swing \'swiŋ\ vb **swung** \'swəŋ\; **swing·ing** 1 : move or cause to move rapidly in an arc 2 : sway or cause to sway back and forth 3 : hang so as to sway or sag 4 : turn on a hinge or pivot 5 : manage or handle successfully ~ n 1 : act or instance of swinging 2 : swinging movement (as in trying to hit something) 3 : suspended seat for swinging — **swing** adj — **swing·er** n

swipe \'swīp\ n : strong sweeping blow ~ vb **swiped**; **swip·ing** 1 : strike or wipe with a sweeping motion 2 : steal esp. with a quick movement

swirl \'swərl\ vb : move or cause to move in a circle — **swirl** n

swish \'swish\ n : hissing, sweeping, or brushing sound — **swish** vb

switch \'swich\ n 1 : slender flexible whip or twig 2 : blow with a switch 3 : shift, change, or reversal 4 : device that opens or closes an electrical circuit ~ vb 1 : punish or urge on with a switch 2 : change or reverse roles, positions, or subjects 3 : operate a switch of

switch·board n : panel of switches to make and break telephone connections

swiv·el \'swivəl\ vb **-eled** or **-elled**; **-el·ing** or **-el·ling** : swing or turn on a pivot — **swivel** n

swollen past part of SWELL

swoon \'swün\ n : faint — **swoon** vb

swoop \'swüp\ vb : make a swift diving attack — **swoop** n

sword \'sȯrd\ n : thrusting or cutting weapon with a long blade

sword·fish n : large ocean fish with a long swordlike projection

swore past of SWEAR

sworn past part of SWEAR

swum past part of SWIM

swung past of SWING

syc·a·more \'sikə‚mōr\ n : shade tree

syc·o·phant \'sikəfənt\ n : servile flatterer — **syc·o·phan·tic** \‚sikə'fantik\ adj

syl·la·ble \'siləbəl\ n : unit of a spoken word — **syl·lab·ic** \sə'labik\ adj

syl·la·bus \'siləbəs\ n, pl **-bi** \-‚bī\ or **-bus·es** : summary of main topics (as of a course of study)

syl·van \'silvən\ adj 1 : living or located in a wooded area 2 : abounding in woods

sym·bol \'simbəl\ n : something that represents or suggests another thing — **sym·bol·ic** \sim'bälik\ adj — **sym·bol·i·cal·ly** adv

sym·bol·ism \'simbə‚lizəm\ n : representation of meanings with symbols

sym·bol·ize \'simbə‚līz\ vb **-ized**; **-iz·ing** : serve as a symbol of — **sym·bol·i·za·tion** \‚simbələ'zāshən\ n

sym·me·try \'simətrē\ n, pl **-tries** : regularity and balance in the arrangement of parts — **sym·met·ri·cal** \sə'metrikəl\ adj — **sym·met·ri·cal·ly** adv

sym·pa·thize \'simpə‚thīz\ vb **-thized**; **-thiz·ing** : feel or show sympathy — **sym·pa·thiz·er** n

sym·pa·thy \'simpəthē\ n, pl **-thies** 1 : ability to understand or share the feelings of another 2 : expression of sorrow for another's misfortune — **sym·pa·thet·ic** \‚simpə'thetik\ adj — **sym·pa·thet·i·cal·ly** adv

sym·pho·ny \'simfənē\ n, pl **-nies** : composition for an orchestra or the orchestra itself — **sym·phon·ic** \sim'fänik\ adj

sym·po·sium \sim'pōzēəm\ n, pl **-sia** \-zēə\ or **-siums** : conference at which a topic is discussed

symp·tom \'simptəm\ n : unusual feeling or reaction that is a sign of disease — **symp·tom·at·ic** \‚simptə'matik\ adj

syn·a·gogue, **syn·a·gog** \'sinə‚gäg, -‚gȯg\ n : Jewish house of worship

syn·chro·nize \'siŋkrə‚nīz, 'sin-\ vb **-nized**; **-niz·ing** 1 : occur or cause to occur at the same instant 2 : cause to agree in time —**syn·chro·ni·za·tion** \,siŋkrənə'zāshən, ,sin-\ n

syn·co·pa·tion \,siŋkə'pāshən, ,sin-\ n : shifting of the regular musical accent to the weak beat —**syn·co·pate** \'siŋkə,pāt, 'sin-\ vb

syn·di·cate \'sindikət\ n : business association ~ \-də,kāt\ vb -**cat·ed; -cat·ing** 1 : form a syndicate 2 : publish through a syndicate —**syn·di·ca·tion** \,sində'kā-shən\ n

syn·drome \'sin,drōm\ n : particular group of symptoms

syn·onym \'sinə,nim\ n : word with the same meaning as another —**syn·on·y·mous** \sə'nänəməs\ adj —**syn·on·y·my** \-mē\ n

syn·op·sis \sə'näpsəs\ n, pl -**op·ses** \-,sēz\ : condensed statement or outline

syn·tax \'sin,taks\ n : way in which words are put together —**syn·tac·tic**

\'sin'taktik\ or **syn·tac·ti·cal** \-tikəl\ adj

syn·the·sis \'sinthəsəs\ n, pl -**the·ses** \-,sēz\ : combination of parts or elements into a whole —**syn·the·size** \-,sīz\ vb

syn·thet·ic \sin'thetik\ adj : artificially made —**synthetic** n —**syn·thet·i·cal·ly** adv

syph·i·lis \'sifələs\ n : venereal disease

sy·ringe \sə'rinj, 'sirinj\ n : plunger device for injecting or withdrawing liquids

syr·up \'sərəp, 'sirəp\ n : thick sticky sweet liquid —**syr·upy** adj

sys·tem \'sistəm\ n 1 : arrangement of units that function together 2 : regular order —**sys·tem·at·ic** \,sistə'matik\ adj —**sys·tem·at·i·cal·ly** adv —**sys·tem·a·tize** \'sistəmə,tīz\ vb

sys·tem·ic \sis'temik\ adj : relating to the whole body

T

t \'tē\ n, pl **t's** or **ts** \'tēz\ : 20th letter of the alphabet

tab \'tab\ n 1 : short projecting flap 2 pl : careful watch

tab·by \'tabē\ n, pl -**bies** : domestic cat

tab·er·na·cle \'tabər,nakəl\ n : house of worship

ta·ble \'tābəl\ n 1 : piece of furniture having a smooth slab fixed on legs 2 : supply of food 3 : arrangement of data in columns 4 : short list —**ta·ble·cloth** —**ta·ble·top** —**ta·ble·ware** n —**tab·u·lar** \'tabyələr\ adj

tab·leau \'tab,lō\ n, pl -**leaux** \-,lōz\ 1 : graphic description 2 : depiction of a scene by people in costume

ta·ble·spoon n 1 : large serving spoon 2 : measuring spoon holding ½ fluid ounce —**ta·ble·spoon·ful** \-,fủl\ n

tab·let \'tablət\ n 1 : flat slab suited for an inscription 2 : collection of sheets of paper glued together at one edge 3 : disk-shaped pill

tab·loid \'tab,lòid\ n : newspaper of small page size

ta·boo \tə'bü, ta-\ adj : banned esp. as

immoral or dangerous —**taboo** n or vb

tab·u·late \'tabyə,lāt\ vb -**lat·ed; -lat·ing** : put in the form of a table —**tab·u·la·tion** \,tabyə'lāshən\ n —**tab·u·la·tor** \'tabyə,lātər\ n

tac·it \'tasət\ adj : implied but not expressed —**tac·it·ly** adv —**tac·it·ness** n

tac·i·turn \'tasə,tərn\ adj : not inclined to talk

tack \'tak\ n 1 : small sharp nail 2 : course of action ~ vb 1 : fasten with tacks 2 : add on

tack·le \'takəl, naut often 'tāk-\ n 1 : equipment 2 : arrangement of ropes and pulleys 3 : act of tackling ~ vb -**led; -ling** 1 : seize or throw down 2 : start dealing with

¹**tacky** \'takē\ adj **tack·i·er; -est** : sticky to the touch

²**tacky** adj **tack·i·er; -est** : cheap or gaudy

tact \'takt\ n : sense of the proper thing to say or do —**tact·ful** \-fəl\ adj —**tact·ful·ly** adv —**tact·less** adj —**tact·less·ly** adv

tac·tic \'taktik\ n : action as part of a plan

tac·tics \'taktiks\ n sing or pl 1 : science of maneuvering forces in combat 2 : skill of using available means to reach an end —**tac·ti·cal** \-tikəl\ adj —**tac·ti·cian** \tak'tishən\ n

tac·tile \'takt³l, -ˌtīl\ adj : relating to or perceptible through the sense of touch

tad·pole \'tad,pōl\ n : larval frog or toad with tail and gills

taf·fe·ta \'tafətə\ n : crisp lustrous fabric (as of silk)

taf·fy \'tafē\ n, pl **-fies** : candy stretched until porous

¹tag \'tag\ n : piece of hanging or attached material ~ vb **-gg-** 1 : provide or mark with a tag 2 : follow closely

²tag n : children's game of trying to catch one another ~ vb : touch a person in tag

tail \'tāl\ n 1 : rear end or a growth extending from the rear end of an animal 2 : back or last part 3 : the reverse of a coin ~ vb : follow —**tailed** \'tāld\ adj —**tail·less** adj

tail·gate \-ˌgāt\ n : hinged gate on the back of a vehicle that can be lowered for loading ~ vb **-gat·ed; -gat·ing** : drive too close behind another vehicle

tail·light n : red warning light at the back of a vehicle

tai·lor \'tālər\ n : one who makes or alters garments ~ vb 1 : fashion or alter (clothes) 2 : make or adapt for a special purpose

tail·spin n : spiral dive by an airplane

taint \'tānt\ vb : affect or become affected with something bad and esp. decay ~ n : trace of decay or corruption

take \'tāk\ vb **took** \'tůk\; **tak·en** \'tākən\; **tak·ing** 1 : get into one's possession 2 : become affected by 3 : receive into one's body (as by eating) 4 : pick out or remove 5 : use for transportation 6 : need or make use of 7 : lead, carry, or cause to go to another place 8 : undertake and do, make, or perform ~ n : amount taken —**take·over** n —**tak·er** n —**take ad·vantage of** : profit by —**take exception** : object —**take off** vb 1 : remove 2 : go away 3 : mimic 4 : begin flight —**take over** vb : assume control or possession of or responsibility for —**take place** : happen

take·off n : act or instance of taking off

talc \'talk\ n : soft mineral used in making toilet powder (**tal·cum powder** \'talkəm-\)

tale \'tāl\ n 1 : story or anecdote 2 : falsehood

tal·ent \'talənt\ n : natural mental or creative ability —**tal·ent·ed** adj

tal·is·man \'taləsmən, -əz-\ n, pl **-mans** : object thought to act as a charm

talk \'tók\ vb 1 : express one's thoughts in speech 2 : discuss 3 : influence to a position or course of action by talking ~ n 1 : act of talking 2 : formal discussion 3 : rumor 4 : informal lecture —**talk·a·tive** \-ətiv\ adj —**talk·er** n

tall \'tól\ adj : extending to a great or specified height —**tall·ness** n

tal·low \'talō\ n : hard white animal fat used esp. in candles

tal·ly \'talē\ n, pl **-lies** : recorded amount ~ vb **-lied; -ly·ing** 1 : add or count up 2 : match

tal·on \'talən\ n : bird's claw

tam \'tam\ n : tam-o'-shanter

tam·bou·rine \ˌtambə'rēn\ n : small drum with loose disks at the sides

tame \'tām\ adj **tam·er; tam·est** 1 : changed from being wild to being controllable by man 2 : docile 3 : dull ~ vb **tamed; tam·ing** : make or become tame —**tam·able, tame·able** adj —**tame·ly** adv —**tam·er** n

tam-o'-shan·ter \'tamə,shantər\ n : Scottish woolen cap with a wide flat circular crown

tamp \'tamp\ vb : drive down or in by a series of light blows

tam·per \'tampər\ vb : interfere so as to change for the worse

tan \'tan\ vb **-nn-** 1 : change (hide) into leather esp. by soaking in a liquid containing tannin 2 : make or become brown (as by exposure to the sun) ~ n 1 : brown skin color induced by the sun 2 : light yellowish brown —**tan·ner** n —**tan·nery** \'tanərē\ n

tan·dem \'tandəm\ adv : one behind another

tang \'taŋ\ n : sharp distinctive flavor —**tangy** adj

tan·gent \'tanjənt\ adj : touching a curve or surface at only one point ~ n 1 : tangent line, curve, or surface 2 : abrupt change of course —**tan·gen·tial** \tan'jenchəl\ adj

tan·ger·ine \'tanjə,rēn, ,tanjə'-\ n : deep orange citrus fruit

tan·gi·ble \'tanjəbəl\ adj 1 : able to be touched 2 : substantially real —**tan·gi·bly** adv

tan·gle \'taŋgəl\ vb -gled; -gling : unite in intricate confusion ~ n : tangled twisted mass

tan·go \'taŋgō\ n, pl -gos : dance of Latin-American origin —**tango** vb

tank \'taŋk\ n 1 : large artificial receptacle for liquids 2 : armored military vehicle —**tank·ful** n

tan·kard \'taŋkərd\ n : tall one-handled drinking vessel

tank·er \'taŋkər\ n : vehicle or vessel with tanks for transporting a liquid

tan·nin \'tanən\ n : substance of plant origin used in tanning and dyeing

tan·ta·lize \'tant°l,īz\ vb -lized; -liz·ing : tease or torment by keeping something desirable just out of reach —**tan·ta·liz·er** n —**tan·ta·liz·ing·ly** adv

tan·ta·mount \'tantə,maůnt\ adj : equivalent in value or meaning

tan·trum \'tantrəm\ n : fit of bad temper

¹**tap** \'tap\ n 1 : faucet 2 : act of tapping ~ vb -pp- 1 : pierce so as to draw off fluid 2 : connect into —**tap·per** n

²**tap** vb -pp- : rap lightly ~ n : light stroke or its sound

tape \'tāp\ n 1 : narrow flexible strip (as of cloth, plastic, or metal) 2 : tape measure ~ vb taped; tap·ing 1 : fasten with tape 2 : record on tape

tape measure n : strip of tape marked in units for use in measuring

ta·per \'tāpər\ n 1 : slender wax candle 2 : gradual lessening of width in a long object ~ vb : make or become smaller toward one end 2 : diminish gradually

tap·es·try \'tapəstrē\ n, pl -tries : heavy handwoven ruglike wall hanging

tape·worm n : long flat intestinal worm

tap·i·o·ca \,tapē'ōkə\ n : a granular starch used esp. in puddings

tar \'tär\ n : thick dark sticky liquid distilled (as from coal) ~ vb -rr- : treat or smear with tar

ta·ran·tu·la \tə'ranchələ. -'rant°lə\ n : large hairy usu. harmless spider

tar·dy \'tärdē\ adj -di·er; -est : late —**tar·di·ly** \'tärd°lē\ adv —**tar·di·ness** n

tar·get \'tärgət\ n 1 : mark to shoot at 2 : goal to be achieved ~ vb 1 : make a target of 2 : establish as a goal

tar·iff \'tarəf\ n 1 : duty or rate of duty imposed on imported goods 2 : schedule of tariffs, rates, or charges

tar·nish \'tärnish\ vb : make or become dull or discolored —**tarnish** n

tar·pau·lin \tär'pólən, 'tärpə-\ n : waterproof protective covering

¹**tar·ry** \'tarē\ vb -ried; -ry·ing : be slow in leaving

²**tar·ry** \'tärē\ adj : resembling or covered with tar

¹**tart** \'tärt\ adj 1 : pleasantly sharp to the taste 2 : caustic —**tart·ly** adv —**tart·ness** n

²**tart** n : small pie

tar·tan \'tärt°n\ n : woolen fabric with a plaid design

tar·tar \'tärtər\ n : hard crust on the teeth

task \'task\ n : assigned work

task·mas·ter n : one that burdens another with labor

tas·sel \'tasəl. 'täs-\ n : hanging ornament made of a bunch of cords fastened at one end

taste \'tāst\ vb tast·ed; tast·ing 1 : test or determine the flavor of 2 : eat or drink in small quantities 3 : have a specific flavor ~ n 1 : small amount tasted 2 : bit 3 : special sense that identifies sweet, sour, bitter, or salty qualities 4 : individual preference 5 : critical appreciation of quality —**taste·ful** \-fəl\ adj —**taste·ful·ly** adv —**taste·less** adj —**taste·less·ly** adv —**tast·er** n

tasty \'tāstē\ adj tast·i·er; -est : pleasing to the sense of taste —**tast·i·ness** n

tat·ter \'tatər\ n 1 : part torn and left hanging 2 pl : tattered clothing ~ vb : make or become ragged

tat·tle \'tat°l\ vb -tled; -tling : inform on someone —**tat·tler** n

tat·tle·tale n : one that tattles

tat·too \ta'tü\ vb : mark the skin with indelible designs or figures —**tattoo** n

taught past of TEACH

taunt \'tónt\ n : sarcastic challenge or insult —**taunt** vb —**taunt·er** n

taut \'tót\ adj : tightly drawn —**taut·ly** adv —**taut·ness** n

tav·ern \'tavərn\ n : establishment where liquors are sold to be drunk on the premises

taw·dry \'tódrē\ adj -dri·er; -est : cheap and gaudy —**taw·dri·ly** \'tódrəlē\ adv

taw·ny \'tȯnē\ *adj* **-ni·er; -est**
: brownish orange

tax \'taks\ *vb* **1** : impose a tax on **2**
: charge **3** : put under stress ~ *n* **1**
: charge by authority for public purposes **2** : strain **—tax·able** *adj* **—tax-
a·tion** \tak'sāshən\ *n* **—tax·pay·er** *n*
—tax·pay·ing *adj*

taxi \'taksē\ *n, pl* **tax·is** \-sēz\
: automobile transporting passengers
for a fare ~ *vb* **tax·ied; taxi·ing** *or*
taxy·ing; tax·is *or* **tax·ies 1**
: transport or go by taxi **2** : move
along the ground before takeoff or after landing

taxi·cab \'taksē,kab\ *n* : taxi

taxi·der·my \'taksə,dərmē\ *n* : skill or
job of stuffing and mounting animal
skins **—taxi·der·mist** \-mist\ *n*

tea \'tē\ *n* : cured leaves of an oriental
shrub or a drink made from these **—
tea·cup** *n* **—tea·pot** *n*

teach \'tēch\ *vb* **taught** \'tȯt\: **teaching**
1 : tell or show the fundamentals or
skills of something **2** : cause to know
the consequences **3** : impart knowledge of **—teach·able** *adj* **—teach·er**
n **—teach·ing** *n*

teak \'tēk\ *n* : East Indian timber tree or
its wood

tea·ket·tle \'tē,ket³l\ *n* : covered kettle
with a handle and spout for boiling
water

teal \'tēl\ *n, pl* **teal** *or* **teals** : small short-
necked wild duck

team \'tēm\ *n* **1** : draft animals har-
nessed together **2** : number of people
organized for a game or work ~ *vb*
: form or work together as a team **—
team** *adj* **—team·mate** *n* **—team-
work** *n*

team·ster \'tēmstər\ *n* **1** : one that drives
a team of animals **2** : one that drives
a truck

¹**tear** \'tir\ *n* : drop of salty liquid that
moistens the eye **—tear·ful** \-fəl\ *adj*
—tear·ful·ly *adv*

²**tear** \'tar\ *vb* **tore** \'tȯr\; **torn** \'tȯrn\;
tear·ing 1 : separate or pull apart by
force **2** : move or act with violence or
haste ~ *n* **1** : act or result of tearing

tease \'tēz\ *vb* **teased; teas·ing** : annoy
by goading, coaxing, or tantalizing ~
n **1** : act of teasing or state of being
teased **2** : one that teases

tea·spoon \'tē,spün\ *n* **1** : small spoon
for stirring or sipping **2** : measuring

spoon holding ⅓ fluid ounce **—tea-
spoon·ful** \-,fúl\ *n*

teat \'tēt\ *n* : protuberance through
which milk is drawn from an udder or
breast

tech·ni·cal \'teknikəl\ *adj* **1** : having or
relating to special mechanical or scientific knowledge **2** : by strict interpretation of rules **—tech·ni·cal·ly** *adv*

tech·ni·cal·i·ty \,teknə'kalətē\ *n, pl* **-ties**
: detail meaningful only to a specialist

technical sergeant *n* : noncommissioned officer in the air force
ranking next below a master sergeant

tech·ni·cian \tek'nishən\ *n* : person with
the technique of a specialized skill

tech·nique \tek'nēk\ *n* : manner of accomplishing something

tech·nol·o·gy \tek'näləjē\ *n, pl* **-gies**
: applied science **—tech·no·log·i·cal**
\,teknə'läjikəl\ *adj*

te·dious \'tēdēəs\ *adj* : wearisome from
length or dullness **—te·dious·ly** *adv*
—te·dious·ness *n*

te·di·um \'tēdēəm\ *n* : tedious state or
quality

tee \'tē\ *n* : mound or peg on which a
golf ball is placed before beginning
play **—tee** *vb*

teem \'tēm\ *vb* : become filled to overflowing

teen·age \'tēn,āj\, **teen·aged** \-,ājd\ *adj*
: relating to people in their teens **—
teen·ag·er** \-,ājər\ *n*

teens \'tēnz\ *n pl* : years 13 to 19 in a
person's life

tee·pee *var of* TEPEE

tee·ter \'tētər\ *vb* **1** : move unsteadily **2**
: seesaw **—teeter** *n*

teeth *pl of* TOOTH

teethe \'tēth\ *vb* **teethed; teeth·ing**
: grow teeth

tele·cast \'teli,kast\ *vb* **-cast; -cast·ing**
: broadcast by television **—telecast** *n*
—tele·cast·er *n*

tele·com·mu·ni·ca·tion \'teləkəmyü-
nə'kāshən\ *n* : communication at a
distance (as by radio or telephone)

tele·gram \'telə,gram\ *n* : message sent
by telegraph

tele·graph \-,graf\ *n* : system for communication by electrical transmission
of coded signals ~ *vb* : send by telegraph **—te·leg·ra·pher** \tə'legrəfər\ *n*
—tele·graph·ic \,telə'grafik\ *adj*

te·lep·a·thy \tə'lepəthē\ *n* : apparent
communication without known sen-

sory means —**tele·path·ic** \,tel-ə'pathik\ adj —**tele·path·i·cal·ly** adv

tele·phone \'telə,fōn\ n : instrument or system for electrical transmission of spoken words ~ vb -**phoned; -phon·ing** : communicate with by telephone —**tele·phon·er** n

tele·scope \-,skōp\ n : tube-shaped optical instrument for viewing distant objects ~ vb -**scoped; -scop·ing** : slide or cause to slide inside another similar section —**tele·scop·ic** \,telə'skäpik\ adj

tele·vise \'telə,vīz\ vb -**vised; -vis·ing** : broadcast by television

tele·vi·sion \-,vizhən\ n : transmission and reproduction of images by radio waves

tell \'tel\ vb told \'tōld\; **tell·ing 1** : count **2** : relate in detail **3** : reveal **4** : give information or an order to **5** : find out by observing

tell·er \'telər\ n **1** : one that relates or counts **2** : bank employee handling money

te·mer·i·ty \tə'merətē\ n, pl -**ties** : boldness

temp \'temp\ n **1** : temperature **2** : temporary worker

tem·per \'tempər\ vb **1** : dilute or soften **2** : toughen ~ n **1** : characteristic attitude or feeling **2** : toughness **3** : disposition or control over one's emotions

tem·per·a·ment \'tempərəmənt\ n : characteristic frame of mind —**tem·per·a·men·tal** \,temprə'ment^əl\ adj

tem·per·ance \'temprəns\ n : moderation in or abstinence from indulgence and esp. the use of intoxicating drink

tem·per·ate \'tempərət\ adj : moderate

tem·per·a·ture \'tempər,chúr, -prə-,chúr, -chər\ n **1** : degree of hotness or coldness **2** : fever

tem·pest \'tempəst\ n : violent storm —**tem·pes·tu·ous** \tem'peschəwəs\ adj

¹tem·ple \'tempəl\ n : place of worship

²temple n : flattened space on each side of the forehead

tem·po \'tempō\ n, pl -**pi** \-,pē\ or -**pos** : rate of speed

tem·po·ral \'tempərəl\ adj : relating to time or to secular concerns

tem·po·rary \'tempə,rerē\ adj : lasting for a short time only —**tem·po·rar·i·ly** \,tempə'rerəlē\ adv

tempt \'tempt\ vb **1** : coax or persuade to do wrong **2** : attract or provoke —**tempt·er** n —**tempt·ing·ly** adv —**tempt·ress** \'temptrəs\ n

temp·ta·tion \temp'tāshən\ n **1** : act of tempting **2** : something that tempts

ten \'ten\ n **1** : one more than 9 **2** : 10th in a set or series **3** : thing having 10 units —**ten** adj or pron —**tenth** \'tenth\ adj or adv or n

ten·a·ble \'tenəbəl\ adj : capable of being held or defended —**ten·a·bil·i·ty** \,tenə'bilətē\ n

te·na·cious \tə'nāshəs\ adj **1** : holding fast **2** : retentive —**te·na·cious·ly** adv —**te·nac·i·ty** \tə'nasətē\ n

ten·ant \'tenənt\ n : one who occupies a rented dwelling —**ten·an·cy** \-ənsē\ n

¹tend \'tend\ vb : take care of or supervise something

²tend vb **1** : move in a particular direction **2** : show a tendency

ten·den·cy \'tendənsē\ n, pl -**cies** : likelihood to move, think, or act in a particular way

¹ten·der \'tendər\ adj **1** : soft or delicate **2** : expressing or responsive to love or sympathy **3** : sensitive (as to touch) —**ten·der·ly** adv —**ten·der·ness** n

²ten·der \'tendər\ n **1** : one that tends **2** : boat providing transport to a larger ship **3** : vehicle attached to a steam locomotive for carrying fuel and water

³ten·der n **1** : offer of a bid for a contract **2** : something that may be offered in payment —**tender** vb

ten·der·ize \'tendə,rīz\ vb -**ized; -iz·ing** : make (meat) tender —**ten·der·iz·er** \'tendə,rīzər\ n

ten·der·loin \'tendər,lóin\ n : tender beef or pork strip from near the backbone

ten·don \'tendən\ n : cord of tissue attaching muscle to bone —**ten·di·nous** \-dənəs\ adj

ten·dril \'tendrəl\ n : slender coiling growth of some climbing plants

ten·e·ment \'tenəmənt\ n **1** : house divided into apartments **2** : shabby dwelling

te·net \'tenət\ n : principle of belief

ten·nis \'tenəs\ n : racket-and-ball game played across a net

ten·or \'tenər\ n **1** : general drift or meaning **2** : highest natural adult male voice

ten·pin \'ten,pin\ n : bottle-shaped pin bowled at in a game (**tenpins**)

¹**tense** \'tens\ *n* : distinct verb form that indicates time

²**tense** *adj* **tens•er; tens•est 1** : stretched tight **2** : marked by nervous tension —**tense** *vb* —**tense•ly** *adv* —**tense•ness** *n* —**ten•si•ty** \'tensətē\ *n*

ten•sile \'tensəl, -,sīl\ *adj* : relating to tension

ten•sion \'tenchən\ *n* **1** : tense condition **2** : state of mental unrest or of potential hostility or opposition

tent \'tent\ *n* : collapsible shelter

ten•ta•cle \'tentikəl\ *n* : long flexible projection of an insect or mollusk —**ten•ta•cled** \-kəld\ *adj* —**ten•tac•u•lar** \ten'takyələr\ *adj*

ten•ta•tive \'tentətiv\ *adj* : subject to change or discussion —**ten•ta•tive•ly** *adv*

ten•u•ous \'tenyəwəs\ *adj* **1** : not dense or thick **2** : flimsy or weak —**ten•u•ous•ly** *adv* —**ten•u•ous•ness** *n*

ten•ure \'tenyər\ *n* : act, right, manner, or period of holding something —**ten•ured** \-yərd\ *adj*

te•pee \'tē,pē\ *n* : conical tent

tep•id \'tepəd\ *adj* : moderately warm

term \'tərm\ *n* **1** : period of time **2** : mathematical expression **3** : special word or phrase **4** *pl* : conditions **5** *pl* : relations ~ *vb* : name

ter•mi•nal \'tərmənᵊl\ *n* **1** : end **2** : device for making an electrical connection **3** : station at end of a transportation line —**terminal** *adj*

ter•mi•nate \'tərmə,nāt\ *vb* **-nat•ed; -nat•ing** : bring or come to an end —**ter•mi•na•ble** \-nəbəl\ *adj* —**ter•mi•na•tion** \,tərmə'nāshən\ *n*

ter•mi•nol•o•gy \,tərmə'näləjē\ *n* : terms used in a particular subject

ter•mi•nus \'tərmənəs\ *n, pl* **-ni** \-,nī\ *or* **-nus•es 1** : end of a transportation line **2** : end of a transportation line

ter•mite \'tər,mīt\ *n* : wood-eating insect

tern \'tərn\ *n* : small sea bird

ter•race \'terəs\ *n* **1** : balcony or patio **2** : bank with a flat top ~ *vb* **-raced; -rac•ing** : landscape in a series of banks

ter•ra–cot•ta \,terə'kätə\ *n* : reddish brown earthenware

ter•rain \tə'rān\ *n* : features of the land

ter•ra•pin \'terəpən\ *n* : No. American turtle

ter•rar•i•um \tə'rareəm\ *n, pl* **-ia** \-ēə\ *or* **-i•ums** : container for keeping plants or animals

ter•res•tri•al \tə'restrēəl\ *adj* **1** : relating to the earth or its inhabitants **2** : living or growing on land

ter•ri•ble \'terəbəl\ *adj* **1** : exciting terror **2** : distressing **3** : intense **4** : of very poor quality —**ter•ri•bly** \-blē\ *adv*

ter•ri•er \'terēər\ *n* : small dog

ter•rif•ic \tə'rifik\ *adj* **1** : exciting terror **2** : extraordinary

ter•ri•fy \'terə,fī\ *vb* **-fied; -fy•ing** : fill with terror —**ter•ri•fy•ing•ly** *adv*

ter•ri•to•ry \'terə,tōrē\ *n, pl* **-ries** : particular geographical region —**ter•ri•to•ri•al** \,terə'tōrēəl\ *adj*

ter•ror \'terər\ *n* : intense fear and panic or a cause of it

ter•ror•ism \-,izəm\ *n* : systematic covert warfare to produce terror for political coercion —**ter•ror•ist** \-ist\ *adj or n*

ter•ror•ize \-,īz\ *vb* **-ized; -iz•ing 1** : fill with terror **2** : coerce by threat or violence

ter•ry \'terē\ *n, pl* **-ries** : absorbent fabric with a loose pile

terse \'tərs\ *adj* **ters•er; ters•est** : concise —**terse•ly** *adv* —**terse•ness** *n*

ter•tia•ry \'tərshē,erē\ *adj* : of 3d rank, importance, or value

test \'test\ *n* : examination or evaluation ~ *vb* : examine by a test —**test•er** *n*

tes•ta•ment \'testəmənt\ *n* **1** *cap* : division of the Bible **2** : will —**tes•ta•men•ta•ry** \,testə'mentərē\ *adj*

tes•ti•cle \'testikəl\ *n* : testis

tes•ti•fy \'testə,fī\ *vb* **-fied; -fy•ing 1** : give testimony **2** : serve as evidence

tes•ti•mo•ni•al \,testə'mōnēəl\ *n* **1** : favorable recommendation **2** : tribute —**testimonial** *adj*

tes•ti•mo•ny \'testə,mōnē\ *n, pl* **-nies** : statement given as evidence in court

tes•tis \'testəs\ *n, pl* **-tes** \-,tēz\ : male reproductive gland

tes•ty \'testē\ *adj* **-ti•er; -est** : easily annoyed

tet•a•nus \'tetᵊnəs\ *n* : bacterial disease producing violent spasms

tête–à–tête \,tātə'tāt\ *adv* : privately ~ *n* : private conversation ~ *adj* : private

teth•er \'tethər\ *n* : leash ~ *vb* : restrain with a leash

text \'tekst\ *n* **1** : author's words **2** : main body of printed or written matter on a page **3** : textbook **4** : scriptural passage used as the theme of a sermon **5** : topic —**tex·tu·al** \'tekstʃəwəl\ adj

text·book \-ˌbùk\ n : book on a school subject

tex·tile \'tek.stīl, 'tekstˀl\ n : fabric

tex·ture \'tekschər\ n **1** : feel and appearance of something **2** : structure

than \'than\ conj or prep —used in comparisons

thank \'thaŋk\ vb : express gratitude to

thank·ful \-fəl\ adj : giving thanks — **thank·ful·ly** adv —**thank·ful·ness** n

thank·less adj : not appreciated

thanks \'thaŋks\ n pl : expression of gratitude

Thanks·giv·ing \thaŋks'giviŋ\ n : 4th Thursday in November observed as a legal holiday for giving thanks for divine goodness

that \'that\ pron, pl **those** \thōz\ **1** : something indicated or understood **2** : the one farther away ~ adj, pl **those** : being the one mentioned or understood or farther away ~ conj or pron —used to introduce a clause ~ adv : to such an extent

thatch \'thach\ vb : cover with thatch ~ n : covering of matted straw

thaw \'thò\ vb : melt or cause to melt — **thaw** n

the \thə, before vowel sounds usu thē\ definite article : that particular one ~ adv —used before a comparative or superlative

the·ater, the·atre \'thēətər\ n **1** : building or room for viewing a play or movie **2** : dramatic arts

the·at·ri·cal \thē'atrikəl\ adj **1** : relating to the theater **2** : involving exaggerated emotion

thee \'thē\ pron, archaic objective case of THOU

theft \'theft\ n : act of stealing

their \'ther\ adj : relating to them

theirs \'therz\ pron : their one or ones

the·ism \'thē.izəm\ n : belief in the existence of a god or gods —**the·ist** \-ist\ n or adj —**the·is·tic** \thē'istik\ adj

them \'them\ pron, objective case of THEY

theme \'thēm\ n **1** : subject matter **2** : essay **3** : melody developed in a piece of music —**the·mat·ic** \thi-'matik\ adj

them·selves \thəm'selvz, them-\ pron pl

: they, them —used reflexively or for emphasis

then \'then\ adv **1** : at that time **2** : soon after that **3** : in addition **4** : in that case **5** : consequently ~ n : that time ~ adj : existing at that time

thence \'thens, 'thens\ adv : from that place or fact

the·oc·ra·cy \thē'äkrəsē\ n, pl **-cies** : government by officials regarded as divinely inspired —**the·o·crat·ic** \ˌthēə'kratik\ adj

the·ol·o·gy \thē'äləjē\ n, pl **-gies** : study of religion —**the·o·lo·gian** \ˌthēə-'lōjən\ n —**the·o·log·i·cal** \-'läjikəl\ adj

the·o·rem \'thēərəm, 'thirəm\ n : provable statement of truth

the·o·ret·i·cal \ˌthēə'retikəl\ adj : relating to or being theory —**the·o·ret·i·cal·ly** adv

the·o·rize \'thēəˌrīz\ vb **-rized; -riz·ing** : put forth theories —**the·o·rist** n

the·o·ry \'thēərē, 'thirē\ n, pl **-ries 1** : general principles of a subject **2** : plausible or scientifically acceptable explanation **3** : judgment, guess, or opinion

ther·a·peu·tic \ˌtherə'pyütik\ adj : offering or relating to remedy — **ther·a·peu·ti·cal·ly** adv

ther·a·py \'therəpē\ n, pl **-pies** : treatment for mental or physical disorder —**ther·a·pist** \-pist\ n

there \'thar\ adv **1** : in, at, or to that place **2** : in that respect ~ pron — used to introduce a sentence or clause ~ n : that place or point

there·abouts, there·about \ˌtharə-'baùts, 'tharə-,-,-'baùt\ adv : near that place, time, number, or quantity

there·af·ter \thar'aftər\ adv : after that

there·by \thar'bī, 'thar,bī\ adv **1** : by that **2** : connected with or with reference to that

there·fore \'thar,fōr\ adv : for that reason

there·in \thar'in\ adv **1** : in or into that place, time, or thing **2** : in that respect

there·of \-'əv, -'äv\ adv **1** : of that or it **2** : from that

there·upon \'tharə,pòn, -,pän; ˌtharə-'pòn, -'pän\ adv **1** : on that matter **2** : therefore **3** : immediately after that

there·with \thar'with, -'with\ adv : with that

ther·mal \'thərməl\ adj : relating to,

caused by, or conserving heat —**ther-mal-ly** adv

ther-mo-dy-nam-ics \,thərmədī'na-miks\ n : physics of heat

ther-mom-e-ter \thər'mämətər\ n : instrument for measuring temperature —**ther-mo-met-ric** \,thərmə-'metrik\ adj —**ther-mo-met-ri-cal-ly** adv

ther-mos \'thərməs\ n : double-walled bottle used to keep liquids hot or cold

ther-mo-stat \'thərmə,stat\ n : automatic temperature control —**ther-mo-stat-ic** \,thərmə'statik\ adj —**ther-mo-stat-i-cal-ly** adv

the-sau-rus \thi'sórəs\ n, pl -**sau-ri** \-'sór,ī\ or -**sau-rus-es** \-'sórəsəz\ : book of words and esp. synonyms

these pl of THIS

the-sis \'thēsəs\ n, pl **the-ses** \'thē,sēz\ 1 : proposition to be argued for 2 : essay embodying results of original research

thes-pi-an \'thespēən\ adj : dramatic ~ n : actor

they \'thā\ pron 1 : those ones 2 : people in general

thi-a-mine \'thīəmən, -,mēn\ n : essential vitamin

thick \'thik\ adj 1 : having relatively great mass from front to back or top to bottom 2 : viscous ~ n : most crowded or thickest part —**thick-ly** adv —**thick-ness** n

thick-en \'thikən\ vb : make or become thick —**thick-en-er** \-ənər\ n

thick-et \'thikət\ n : dense growth of bushes or small trees

thick-skinned \-'skind\ adj : insensitive to criticism

thief \'thēf\ n, pl **thieves** \'thēvz\ : one that steals

thieve \'thēv\ vb **thieved; thiev-ing** : steal —**thiev-ery** n

thigh \'thī\ n : upper part of the leg

thigh-bone \'thī,bōn\ n : femur

thim-ble \'thimbəl\ n : protective cap for the finger in sewing —**thim-ble-ful** n

thin \'thin\ adj **-nn-** 1 : having relatively little mass from front to back or top to bottom 2 : not closely set or placed 3 : relatively free flowing 4 : lacking substance, fullness, or strength ~ vb **-nn-** : make or become thin —**thin-ly** adv —**thin-ness** n

thing \'thiŋ\ n 1 : matter of concern 2 : event or act 3 : object 4 pl : possessions

think \'thiŋk\ vb **thought** \'thot\: **think-ing** 1 : form or have in the mind 2 : have as an opinion 3 : ponder 4 : devise by thinking 5 : imagine —**think-er** n

thin-skinned adj : extremely sensitive to criticism

third \'thərd\ adj : being number 3 in a countable series ~ n 1 : one that is third 2 : one of 3 equal parts —**third, third-ly** adv

third dimension n : thickness or depth —**third-dimensional** adj

third world n : less developed nations of the world

thirst \'thərst\ n 1 : dryness in mouth and throat 2 : intense desire ~ vb : feel thirst —**thirsty** adj

thir-teen \,thər'tēn\ n : one more than 12 —**thirteen** adj or pron —**thir-teenth** \-'tēnth\ adj or n

thir-ty \'thərtē\ n, pl **thirties** : 3 times 10 —**thir-ti-eth** \-ēəth\ adj or n —**thirty** adj or pron

this \'this\ pron, pl **these** \'thēz\ : something close or under immediate discussion ~ adj, pl **these** : being the one near, present, just mentioned, or more immediately under observation ~ adv : to such an extent or degree

this-tle \'thisəl\ n : tall prickly herb

thith-er \'thithər\ adv : to that place

thong \'thoŋ\ n : strip of leather or hide

tho-rax \'thor,aks\ n, pl -**rax-es** or -**ra-ces** \'thōrə,sēz\ 1 : part of the body between neck and abdomen 2 : middle of 3 divisions of an insect body —**tho-rac-ic** \thə'rasik\ adj

thorn \'thorn\ n : sharp spike on a plant or a plant bearing these —**thorny** adj

thor-ough \'thərō\ adj : omitting or overlooking nothing —**thor-ough-ly** adv —**thor-ough-ness** n

thor-ough-bred \'thərə,bred\ n 1 cap : light speedy racing horse 2 : one of excellent quality—**thoroughbred** adj

thor-ough-fare \'thərə,far\ n : public road

those pl of THAT

thou \'thau\ pron, archaic : you

though \'thō\ adv : however ~ conj 1 : despite the fact that 2 : granting that

thought \'thot\ past of THINK ~ n 1 : process of thinking 2 : serious consideration 3 : idea

thought-ful \-fəl\ adj 1 : absorbed in or

showing thought **2** : considerate of others **—thought·ful·ly** *adv* **—thought·ful·ness** *n*

thought·less \-ləs\ *adj* **1** : careless or reckless **2** : lacking concern for others **—thought·less·ly** *adv*

thou·sand \'thaúz°nd\ *n, pl* **-sands** or **-sand** : 10 times 100 **—thousand** *adj* **—thou·sandth** \-°nth\ *adj or n*

thrash \'thrash\ *vb* **1** : thresh **2** : beat **3** : move about violently **—thrash·er** *n*

thread \'thred\ *n* **1** : fine line of fibers **2** : train of thought **3** : ridge around a screw ~ *vb* **1** : pass thread through **2** : put together on a thread **3** : make one's way through or between

thread·bare *adj* **1** : worn so that the thread shows **2** : trite

threat \'thret\ *n* **1** : expression of intention to harm **2** : thing that threatens

threat·en \'thret°n\ *vb* **1** : utter threats **2** : show signs of being near or impending **—threat·en·ing·ly** *adv*

three \'thrē\ *n* **1** : one more than 2 **2** : 3d in a set or series **—three** *adj or pron*

three·fold \'thrē,fōld\ *adj* : triple **—three·fold** \-'fōld\ *adv*

three·score *adj* : being 3 times 20

thresh \'thresh, 'thrash\ *vb* : beat to separate grain **—thresh·er** *n*

thresh·old \'thresh,ōld\ *n* **1** : sill of a door **2** : beginning stage

threw *past of* THROW

thrice \'thrīs\ *adv* : 3 times

thrift \'thrift\ *n* : careful management or saving of money **—thrift·i·ly** \'thriftəlē\ *adv* **—thrift·less** *adj* **—thrifty** *adj*

thrill \'thril\ *vb* **1** : have or cause to have a sudden sharp feeling of excitement **2** : tremble **—thrill** *n* **—thrill·er** *n* **—thrill·ing·ly** *adv*

thrive \'thrīv\ *vb* **throve** \'thrōv\ or **thrived; thriv·en** \'thrivən\ **1** : grow vigorously **2** : prosper

throat \'thrōt\ *n* **1** : front part of the neck **2** : passage to the stomach **—throat·ed** *adj* **—throaty** *adj*

throb \'thräb\ *vb* **-bb-** : pulsate **—throb** *n*

throe \'thrō\ *n* **1** : pang or spasm **2** *pl* : hard or painful struggle

throne \'thrōn\ *n* : chair representing power or sovereignty

throng \'throŋ\ *n or vb* : crowd

throt·tle \'thrät°l\ *vb* **-tled; -tling** : choke ~ *n* : valve regulating volume

of fuel and air delivered to engine cylinders

through \'thrü\ *prep* **1** : into at one side and out at the other side of **2** : by way of **3** : among, between, or all around **4** : because of **5** : throughout the time of ~ \'thrü\ *adv* **1** : from one end or side to the other **2** : from beginning to end **3** : to the core **4** : into the open ~ *adj* **1** : going directly from origin to destination **2** : finished

through·out \thrü'aút\ *adv* **1** : everywhere **2** : from beginning to end ~ *prep* **1** : in or to every part of **2** : during the whole of

throve *past of* THRIVE

throw \'thrō\ *vb* **threw** \'thrü\; **thrown** \'thrōn\; **throw·ing 1** : propel through the air **2** : cause to fall or fall off **3** : put suddenly in a certain position or condition **4** : move quickly as if throwing **5** : put on or off hastily **— throw** *n* **—throw·er** \'thrōər\ *n* **— throw up** *vb* : vomit

thrush \'thrəsh\ *n* : songbird

thrust \'thrəst\ *vb* **thrust; thrust·ing 1** : shove forward **2** : stab or pierce **— thrust** *n*

thud \'thəd\ *n* : dull sound of something falling **—thud** *vb*

thug \'thəg\ *n* : ruffian or gangster

thumb \'thəm\ *n* **1** : short thick division of the hand opposing the fingers **2** : glove part for the thumb ~ *vb* : leaf through with the thumb **—thumb·nail** *n*

thump \'thəmp\ *vb* : strike with something thick or heavy causing a dull sound **—thump** *n*

thun·der \'thəndər\ *n* : sound following lightning **—thunder** *vb* **—thun·der·clap** *n* **—thun·der·ous** \'thəndərəs\ *adj* **—thun·der·ous·ly** *adv*

thun·der·bolt \-,bōlt\ *n* : discharge of lightning with thunder

thun·der·show·er \'thəndər,shaúər\ *n* : shower with thunder and lightning

thun·der·storm *n* : storm with thunder and lightning

Thurs·day \'thərzdā, -dē\ *n* : 5th day of the week

thus \'thəs\ *adv* **1** : in this or that way **2** : to this degree or extent **3** : because of this or that

thwart \'thwòrt\ *vb* : block or defeat

thy \'thī\ *adj, archaic* : your

thyme \'tīm, 'thīm\ *n* : cooking herb

thy·roid \'thī,rȯid\ *adj* : relating to a

large endocrine gland (**thyroid gland**)

thy·self \thī'self\ *pron, archaic* : yourself

ti·ara \tē'arə, -'är-\ *n* : decorative formal headband

tib·ia \'tibēə\ *n, pl* **-i·ae** \-ē,ē\ : bone between the knee and ankle

tic \'tik\ *n* : twitching of facial muscles

¹**tick** \'tik\ *n* : small 8-legged bloodsucking animal

²**tick** *n* 1 : light rhythmic tap or beat 2 : check mark ~ *vb* 1 : make ticks 2 : mark with a tick 3 : operate

tick·er \'tikər\ *n* 1 : something (as a watch) that ticks 2 : telegraph instrument that prints on paper tape

tick·et \'tikət\ *n* 1 : tag showing price, payment of a fee or fare, or a traffic offense 2 : list of candidates ~ *vb* : put a ticket on

tick·ing \'tikiŋ\ *n* : fabric covering of a mattress

tick·le \'tikəl\ *vb* **-led; -ling** 1 : please or amuse 2 : touch lightly causing uneasiness, laughter, or spasmodic movements —**tickle** *n*

tick·lish \'tiklish\ *adj* 1 : sensitive to tickling 2 : requiring delicate handling —**tick·lish·ly** *adv* —**tick·lish·ness** *n*

tid·al wave \'tīdᵊl-\ *n* : high sea wave following an earthquake

tid·bit \'tid,bit\ *n* : choice morsel

tide \'tīd\ *n* : alternate rising and falling of the sea ~ *vb* **tid·ed; tid·ing** : be enough to allow (one) to get by for a time —**tid·al** \'tīdᵊl\ *adj* —**tide·water** *n*

tid·ings \'tīdiŋz\ *n pl* : news or message

ti·dy \'tīdē\ *adj* **-di·er; -est** 1 : well ordered and cared for 2 : large or substantial —**ti·di·ness** *n* —**tidy** *vb*

tie \'tī\ *n* 1 : line or ribbon for fastening, uniting, or closing 2 : cross support to which railroad rails are fastened 3 : uniting force 4 : equality in score or tally or a deadlocked contest 5 : necktie ~ *vb* **tied; ty·ing** *or* **tie·ing** 1 : fasten or close by wrapping and knotting a tie 2 : form a knot in 3 : gain the same score or tally as an opponent

tier \'tir\ *n* : one of a steplike series of rows

tiff \'tif\ *n* : petty quarrel —**tiff** *vb*

ti·ger \'tīgər\ *n* : very large black-striped cat —**ti·ger·ish** \-gərish\ *adj* —**ti·gress** \-grəs\ *n*

tight \'tīt\ *adj* 1 : fitting close together esp. so as not to allow air or water in 2 : held very firmly 3 : taut 4 : fitting too snugly 5 : difficult 6 : stingy 7 : evenly contested 8 : low in supply —**tight** *adv* —**tight·en** \-ᵊn\ *vb* —**tight·ly** *adv* —**tight·ness** *n*

tights \'tīts\ *n pl* : skintight garments

tight·wad \'tīt,wäd\ *n* : stingy person

tile \'tīl\ *n* : thin piece of stone or fired clay used on roofs, floors, or walls ~ *vb* : cover with tiles

¹**till** \'til\ *prep or conj* : until

²**till** *vb* : cultivate (soil) —**till·able** *adj*

³**till** *n* : money drawer

¹**till·er** \'tilər\ *n* : one that cultivates soil

²**til·ler** \'tilər\ *n* : lever for turning a boat's rudder

tilt \'tilt\ *vb* : cause to incline ~ *n* : slant

tim·ber \'timbər\ *n* 1 : cut wood for building 2 : large squared piece of wood 3 : wooded land or trees for timber ~ *vb* : cover, frame, or support with timbers —**tim·bered** *adj* —**tim·ber·land** \-,land\ *n*

tim·bre \'tambər, 'tim-\ *n* : sound quality

time \'tīm\ *n* 1 : period during which something exists or continues or can be accomplished 2 : point at which something happens 3 : customary hour 4 : age 5 : tempo 6 : moment, hour, day, or year as indicated by a clock or calendar 7 : one's experience during a particular period ~ *vb* **timed; tim·ing** 1 : arrange or set the time of 2 : determine or record the time, duration, or rate of —**time·keeper** *n* —**time·less** *adj* —**time·less·ness** *n* —**time·li·ness** *n* —**time·ly** *adv* —**tim·er** *n*

time·piece *n* : device to show time

times \'tīmz\ *prep* : multiplied by

time·ta·ble \'tīm,tābəl\ *n* : table of departure and arrival times

tim·id \'timəd\ *adj* : lacking in courage or self-confidence —**ti·mid·i·ty** \tə'midətē\ *n* —**tim·id·ly** *adv*

tim·o·rous \'timərəs\ *adj* : fearful —**tim·o·rous·ly** *adv* —**tim·o·rous·ness** *n*

tim·pa·ni \'timpənē\ *n pl* : set of kettledrums —**tim·pa·nist** \-nist\ *n*

tin \'tin\ *n* 1 : soft white metallic chemical element 2 : metal food can

tinc·ture \'tiŋkchər\ n : alcoholic solution of a medicine

tin·der \'tindər\ n : substance used to kindle a fire

tine \'tīn\ n : one of the points of a fork

tin·foil \'tin,fȯil\ n : thin metal sheeting

tinge \'tinj\ vb tinged; tinge·ing or ting·ing \'tinjiŋ\ 1 : color slightly 2 : affect with a slight odor ~ n : slight coloring or flavor

tin·gle \'tiŋgəl\ vb -gled; -gling : feel a ringing, stinging, or thrilling sensation —tingle n

tin·ker \'tiŋkər\ vb : experiment in repairing something —tin·ker·er n

tin·kle \'tiŋkəl\ vb -kled; -kling : make or cause to make a high ringing sound —tinkle n

tin·sel \'tinsəl\ n : decorative thread or strip of glittering metal or paper

tint \'tint\ n 1 : slight or pale coloration 2 : color shade ~ vb : give a tint to

ti·ny \'tīnē\ adj -ni·er; -est : very small

¹tip \'tip\ vb -pp- 1 : overturn 2 : lean ~ n : act or state of tipping

²tip n : pointed end of something ~ vb -pp- 1 : furnish with a tip 2 : cover the tip of

³tip n : small sum given for a service performed ~ vb : give a tip to

⁴tip n : piece of confidential information ~ vb -pp- : give confidential information to

tip-off \'tip,ȯf\ n : indication

tip·ple \'tipəl\ vb -pled; -pling : drink intoxicating liquor esp. habitually or excessively —tip·pler n

tip·sy \'tipsē\ adj -si·er; -est : unsteady or foolish from alcohol

tip·toe \'tip,tō\ n : the toes of the feet ~ adv or adj : supported on tiptoe ~ vb -toed; -toe·ing : walk quietly or on tiptoe

tip–top n : highest point ~ adj : excellent

ti·rade \'tī,rād, 'tī,-\ n : prolonged speech of abuse

¹tire \'tīr\ vb tired; tir·ing 1 : make or become weary 2 : wear out the patience of —tire·less adj —tire·less·ly adv —tire·less·ness n —tire·some \-səm\ adj —tire·some·ly adv —tire·some·ness n

²tire n : rubber cushion encircling a car wheel

tired \'tīrd\ adj : weary

tis·sue \'tishü\ n 1 : soft absorbent paper 2 : layer of cells forming a basic struc-

tural element of an animal or plant body

ti·tan·ic \tī'tanik, tə-\ adj : gigantic

ti·ta·ni·um \tī'tānēəm, tə-\ n : gray light strong metallic chemical element

tithe \'tīth\ n : tenth part paid or given esp. for the support of a church —tithe vb —tith·er n

tit·il·late \'tit⁰l,āt\ vb -lat·ed; -lat·ing : excite pleasurably —tit·il·la·tion \,tit⁰l'āshən\ n

ti·tle \'tīt⁰l\ n 1 : legal ownership 2 : distinguishing name 3 : designation of honor, rank, or office 4 : championship —ti·tled adj

tit·ter \'titər\ n : nervous or affected laugh —titter vb

tit·u·lar \'tichələr\ adj 1 : existing in title only 2 : relating to or bearing a title

tiz·zy \'tizē\ n, pl tizzies : state of agitation or worry

TNT \,tē,en'tē\ n : high explosive

to \'tü\ prep 1 : in the direction of 2 : at, on, or near 3 : resulting in 4 : before or until 5 —used to show a relationship or object of a verb 6 —used with an infinitive ~ adv 1 : forward 2 : to a state of consciousness

toad \'tōd\ n : tailless leaping amphibian

toad·stool \-,stül\ n : mushroom esp. when inedible or poisonous

toady \'tōdē\ n, pl toad·ies : one who flatters to gain favors —toady vb

toast \'tōst\ vb 1 : make (as a slice of bread) crisp and brown 2 : drink in honor of someone or something 3 : warm ~ n 1 : toasted sliced bread 2 : act of drinking in honor of someone —toast·er n

to·bac·co \tə'bakō\ n, pl -cos : broad-leaved herb or its leaves prepared for smoking or chewing

to·bog·gan \tə'bägən\ n : long flat-bottomed light sled ~ vb : coast on a toboggan

to·day \tə'dā\ adv 1 : on or for this day 2 : at the present time ~ n : present day or time

tod·dle \'täd⁰l\ vb -dled; -dling : walk with tottering steps like a young child —toddle n —tod·dler \'täd⁰lər\ n

to-do \tə'dü\ n, pl to-dos \-'düz\ : disturbance or fuss

toe \'tō\ n : one of the 5 end divisions of the foot —toe·nail n

tof·fee, tof·fy \'tȯfē, 'tä-\ n, pl toffees or

toffies : candy made of boiled sugar and butter

to·ga \'tōgə\ *n* : loose outer garment of ancient Rome

to·geth·er \tə'gethər\ *adv* **1** : in or into one place or group **2** : in or into contact or association **3** : at one time **4** : as a group —**to·geth·er·ness** *n*

togs \'tägz, 'tȯgz\ *n pl* : clothing

toil \'tȯil\ *vb* : work hard and long —**toil** *n* —**toil·er** *n* —**toil·some** *adj*

toi·let \'tȯilət\ *n* **1** : dressing and grooming oneself **2** : bathroom **3** : water basin to urinate and defecate in

to·ken \'tōkən\ *n* **1** : outward sign or expression of something **2** : small part representing the whole **3** : piece resembling a coin

told *past of* TELL

tol·er·a·ble \'tälərəbəl\ *adj* **1** : capable of being endured **2** : moderately good —**tol·er·a·bly** \-blē\ *adv*

tol·er·ance \'tälərəns\ *n* **1** : lack of opposition for beliefs or practices differing from one's own **2** : capacity for enduring **3** : allowable deviation —**tol·er·ant** *adj* —**tol·er·ant·ly** *adv*

tol·er·ate \'tälə,rāt\ *vb* **-at·ed; -at·ing 1** : allow to be or to be done without opposition **2** : endure or resist the action of —**tol·er·a·tion** \,tälə'rāshən\ *n*

¹**toll** \'tōl\ *n* **1** : fee paid for a privilege or service **2** : cost of achievement in loss or suffering —**toll·booth** *n* —**toll·gate** *n*

²**toll** *vb* **1** : cause the sounding of (a bell) **2** : sound with slow measured strokes ~ *n* : sound of a tolling bell

tom·a·hawk \'tämə,hȯk\ *n* : light ax used as a weapon by American Indians

to·ma·to \tə'mātō, -'mät-\ *n, pl* **-toes** : tropical American herb or its fruit

tomb \'tüm\ *n* : house, vault, or grave for burial

tom·boy \'täm,bȯi\ *n* : girl who behaves in a manner usu. considered boyish

tomb·stone *n* : stone marking a grave

tom·cat \'täm,kat\ *n* : male cat

tome \'tōm\ *n* : large or weighty book

to·mor·row \tə'märō\ *adv* : on or for the day after today —**tomorrow** *n*

tom-tom \'täm,täm\ *n* : small-headed drum beaten with the hands

ton \'tən\ *n* : unit of weight equal to 2000 pounds

tone \'tōn\ *n* **1** : vocal or musical sound **2** : sound of definite pitch **3** : manner of speaking that expresses an emotion or attitude **4** : color quality **5** : healthy condition **6** : general character or quality ~ *vb* : soften or muffle —often used with *down* —**ton·al** \-ᵊl\ *adj* —**to·nal·i·ty** \tō'nalətē\ *n*

tongs \'täŋz, 'tȯŋz\ *n pl* : grasping device of 2 joined or hinged pieces

tongue \'təŋ\ *n* **1** : fleshy movable organ of the mouth **2** : language **3** : something long and flat and fastened at one end —**tongued** \'təŋd\ *adj* —**tongue·less** *adj*

ton·ic \'tänik\ *n* : something (as a drug) that invigorates or restores health —**tonic** *adj*

to·night \tə'nīt\ *adv* : on this night ~ *n* : present or coming night

ton·sil \'tänsəl\ *n* : either of a pair of oval masses in the throat —**ton·sil·lec·to·my** \,tänsə'lektəmē\ *n* —**ton·sil·li·tis** \-'lītəs\ *n*

too \'tü\ *adv* **1** : in addition **2** : excessively

took *past of* TAKE

tool \'tül\ *n* : device worked by hand ~ *vb* : shape or finish with a tool

toot \'tüt\ *vb* : sound or cause to sound esp. in short blasts —**toot** *n*

tooth \'tüth\ *n, pl* **teeth** \'tēth\ **1** : one of the hard structures in the jaws for chewing **2** : one of the projections on the edge of a gear wheel —**tooth·ache** *n* —**tooth·brush** *n* —**toothed** \'tütht\ *adj* —**tooth·less** *adj* —**tooth·paste** *n* —**tooth·pick** *n*

tooth·some \'tüthsəm\ *adj* **1** : delicious **2** : attractive

¹**top** \'täp\ *n* **1** : highest part or level of something **2** : lid or covering ~ *vb* **-pp- 1** : cover with a top **2** : surpass **3** : go over the top of ~ *adj* : being at the top —**topped** *adj*

²**top** *n* : spinning toy

to·paz \'tō,paz\ *n* : hard gem

top·coat *n* : lightweight overcoat

top·ic \'täpik\ *n* : subject for discussion or study

top·i·cal \-ikəl\ *adj* **1** : relating to or arranged by topics **2** : relating to current or local events —**top·i·cal·ly** *adv*

top·most \'täp,mōst\ *adj* : highest of all

top-notch \-'näch\ *adj* : of the highest quality

to·pog·ra·phy \tə'pägrəfē\ *n* **1** : art of mapping the physical features of a place **2** : outline of the form of a place

—to·pog·ra·pher \-fər\ *n* **—top·o·graph·ic** \,täpə'grafik\. **top·o·graph·i·cal** \-ikəl\ *adj*

top·ple \'täpəl\ *vb* **-pled; -pling** : fall or cause to fall

top·sy-tur·vy \,täpsē'tərvē\ *adv or adj* **1** : upside down **2** : in utter confusion

torch \'tȯrch\ *n* : flaming light **—torch·bear·er** *n* **—torch·light** *n*

tore *past of* TEAR

tor·ment \'tȯr,ment\ *n* : extreme pain or anguish or a source of this ~ *vb* **1** : cause severe anguish to **2** : harass **—tor·men·tor** \-ər\ *n*

torn *past part of* TEAR

tor·na·do \tȯr'nādō\ *n, pl* **-does** *or* **-dos** : violent destructive whirling wind

tor·pe·do \tȯr'pēdō\ *n, pl* **-does** : self-propelled explosive submarine missile ~ *vb* : hit with a torpedo

tor·pid \'tȯrpəd\ *adj* **1** : having lost motion or the power of exertion **2** : lacking vigor **—tor·pid·i·ty** \tȯr'pidətē\ *n*

tor·por \'tȯrpər\ *n* : extreme sluggishness or lethargy

torque \'tȯrk\ *n* : turning force

tor·rent \'tȯrənt\ *n* **1** : rushing stream **2** : tumultuous outburst **—tor·ren·tial** \tȯ'renchəl, tə-\ *adj*

tor·rid \'tȯrəd\ *adj* **1** : parched with heat **2** : impassioned

tor·sion \'tȯrshən\ *n* : a twisting or being twisted **—tor·sion·al** \'tȯrshənəl\ *adj* **—tor·sion·al·ly** *adv*

tor·so \'tȯrsō\ *n, pl* **-sos** *or* **-si** \-,sē\ : trunk of the human body

tor·til·la \tȯr'tēyə\ *n* : round flat cornmeal or wheat flour bread

tor·toise \'tȯrtəs\ *n* : land turtle

tor·tu·ous \'tȯrchəwəs\ *adj* **1** : winding **2** : tricky

tor·ture \'tȯrchər\ *n* **1** : use of pain to punish or force **2** : agony ~ *vb* **-tured; -tur·ing** : inflict torture on **—tor·tur·er** *n*

toss \'tȯs, 'täs\ *vb* **1** : move to and fro or up and down violently **2** : throw with a quick light motion **3** : move restlessly **—toss** *n*

toss-up *n* **1** : a deciding by flipping a coin **2** : even chance

tot \'tät\ *n* : small child

to·tal \'tōt°l\ *n* : entire amount ~ *vb* **-taled** *or* **-talled; -tal·ing** *or* **-tal·ling** **1** : add up **2** : amount to **—total** *adj* **—to·tal·ly** *adv*

to·tal·i·tar·i·an \tō,talə'terēən\ *adj* : relating to a political system in which the government has complete control over the people **—totalitarian** *n* **—to·tal·i·tar·i·an·ism** \-ē·ə-,nizəm\ *n*

to·tal·i·ty \tō'talətē\ *n, pl* **-ties** : whole amount or entirety

tote \'tōt\ *vb* **tot·ed; tot·ing** : carry

to·tem \'tōtəm\ *n* : often carved figure used as a family or tribe emblem

tot·ter \'tätər\ *vb* **1** : sway as if about to fall **2** : stagger

touch \'təch\ *vb* **1** : make contact with so as to feel **2** : be or cause to be in contact **3** : take into the hands or mouth **4** : treat or mention a subject **5** : relate or concern **6** : move to sympathetic feeling ~ *n* **1** : light stroke **2** : act or fact of touching or being touched **3** : sense of feeling **4** : trace **5** : state of being in contact **—touch up** *vb* : improve with minor changes

touch·down \'təch,daún\ *n* : scoring of 6 points in football

touch·stone *n* : test or criterion of genuineness or quality

touchy \'təchē\ *adj* **touch·i·er; -est** **1** : easily offended **2** : requiring tact

tough \'təf\ *adj* **1** : strong but elastic **2** : not easily chewed **3** : severe or disciplined **4** : stubborn ~ *n* : rowdy **—tough·ly** *adv* **—tough·ness** *n*

tough·en \'təfən\ *vb* : make or become tough

tou·pee \tü'pā\ *n* : small wig for a bald spot

tour \'túr\ *n* **1** : period of time spent at work or on an assignment **2** : journey with a return to the starting point ~ *vb* : travel over to see the sights **—tour·ist** \'túrist\ *n*

tour·na·ment \'túrnəmənt, 'tər-\ *n* **1** : medieval jousting competition **2** : championship series of games

tour·ney \-nē\ *n, pl* **-neys** : tournament

tour·ni·quet \'túrnikət, 'tər-\ *n* : tight bandage for stopping blood flow

tou·sle \'taúzəl\ *vb* **-sled; -sling** : dishevel (as someone's hair)

tout \'taút, 'tüt\ *vb* : praise or publicize loudly

tow \'tō\ *vb* : pull along behind **—tow** *n*

to·ward, to·wards \'tōrd, tə'wȯrd, 'tȯrdz, tə'wȯrdz\ *prep* **1** : in the direction of **2** : with respect to **3** : in part payment on

tow·el \'taúəl\ *n* : absorbent cloth or paper for wiping or drying

tow·er \'taúər\ *n* : tall structure ~ *vb* : rise to a great height —**tow·ered** \'taúərd\ *adj* —**tow·er·ing** *adj*

tow·head \'tō,hed\ *n* : person having whitish blond hair —**tow·head·ed** \-,hedəd\ *adj*

town \'taún\ *n* **1** : small residential area **2** : city —**towns·peo·ple** \'taúnz-,pēpəl\ *n pl*

town·ship \'taún,ship\ *n* **1** : unit of local government **2** : 36 square miles of U.S. public land

tox·ic \'täksik\ *adj* : poisonous —**tox·ic·i·ty** \täk'sisətē\ *n*

tox·in \'täksən\ *n* : poison produced by an organism

toy \'tói\ *n* : something for a child to play with ~ *vb* : amuse oneself or play with something ~ *adj* **1** : designed as a toy **2** : very small

¹trace \'trās\ *vb* **traced; trac·ing 1** : mark over the lines of (a drawing) **2** : follow the trail or the development of ~ *n* **1** : track **2** : tiny amount or residue —**trace·able** *adj* —**trac·er** *n*

²trace *n* : line of a harness

tra·chea \'trākēə\ *n, pl* **-che·ae** \-kē,ē\ : windpipe —**tra·che·al** \-kēəl\ *adj*

track \'trak\ *n* **1** : trail left by wheels or footprints **2** : racing course **3** : train rails **4** : awareness of a progression **5** : looped belts propelling a vehicle ~ *vb* **1** : follow the trail of **2** : make tracks on —**track·er** *n*

track–and–field *adj* : relating to athletic contests of running, jumping, and throwing events

¹tract \'trakt\ *n* **1** : stretch of land **2** : system of body organs

²tract *n* : pamphlet of propaganda

trac·ta·ble \'traktəbəl\ *adj* : easily controlled

trac·tion \'trakshən\ *n* : gripping power to permit movement —**trac·tion·al** \-shənəl\ *adj* —**trac·tive** \'traktiv\ *adj*

trac·tor \'traktər\ *n* **1** : farm vehicle used esp. for pulling **2** : truck for hauling a trailer

trade \'trād\ *n* **1** : one's regular business **2** : occupation requiring skill **3** : the buying and selling of goods **4** : act of trading ~ *vb* **trad·ed; trad·ing 1** : give in exchange for something **2** : buy and sell goods **3** : be a regular customer —**trades·peo·ple** \'trādz-,pēpəl\ *n pl*

trade–in \'trād,in\ *n* : an item traded to a merchant at the time of a purchase

trade·mark \'trād,märk\ *n* : word or mark identifying a manufacturer —**trademark** *vb*

trades·man \'trādzmən\ *n* : shopkeeper

fra·di·tion \trə'dishən\ *n* : belief or custom passed from generation to generation —**tra·di·tion·al** \-'dishənəl\ *adj* —**tra·di·tion·al·ly** *adv*

tra·duce \trə'düs, -'dyüs\ *vb* **-duced; -duc·ing** : lower the reputation of —**tra·duc·er** *n*

traf·fic \'trafik\ *n* **1** : business dealings **2** : movement along a route ~ *vb* : do business —**traf·fick·er** *n* —**traffic light** *n*

trag·e·dy \'trajədē\ *n, pl* **-dies 1** : serious drama describing a conflict and having a sad end **2** : disastrous event

trag·ic \'trajik\ *adj* : being a tragedy —**trag·i·cal·ly** *adv*

trail \'trāl\ *vb* **1** : hang down and drag along the ground **2** : draw along behind **3** : follow the track of **4** : dwindle ~ *n* **1** : something that trails **2** : path or evidence left by something

trail·er \'trālər\ *n* **1** : vehicle intended to be hauled **2** : dwelling designed to be towed to a site

train \'trān\ *n* **1** : trailing part of a gown **2** : retinue or procession **3** : connected series **4** : group of linked railroad cars ~ *vb* **1** : cause to grow as desired **2** : make or become prepared or skilled **3** : point —**train·ee** *n* —**train·er** *n* —**train·load** *n*

traipse \'trāps\ *vb* **traipsed; traips·ing** : walk

trait \'trāt\ *n* : distinguishing quality

trai·tor \'trātər\ *n* : one who betrays a trust or commits treason —**trai·tor·ous** *adj*

tra·jec·to·ry \trə'jektərē\ *n, pl* **-ries** : path of something moving through air or space

tram·mel \'traməl\ *vb* **-meled** *or* **-melled; -mel·ing** *or* **-mel·ling** : impede —**trammel** *n*

tramp \'tramp\ *vb* **1** : walk or hike **2** : tread on ~ *n* : beggar or vagrant

tram·ple \'trampəl\ *vb* **-pled; -pling** : walk or step on so as to bruise or crush —**trample** *n* —**tram·pler** \-plər\ *n*

tram·po·line \,trampə'lēn, 'trampə,-\ *n* : resilient sheet or web supported by springs and used for bouncing —**tram·po·lin·ist** \-ist\ *n*

trance \trans\ *n* **1** : sleeplike condition **2** : state of mystical absorption

tran·quil \traŋkwəl, 'tran-\ *adj* : quiet and undisturbed —**tran·quil·ize** \-kwə,līz\ *vb* —**tran·quil·iz·er** *n* —**tran·quil·i·ty** *or* **tran·quil·li·ty** \tran-'kwilətē, traŋ-\ *n* —**tran·quil·ly** *adv*

trans·act \trans'akt, tranz-\ *vb* : conduct (business)

trans·ac·tion \-'akshən\ *n* **1** : business deal **2** *pl* : records of proceedings

tran·scend \trans'end\ *vb* : rise above or surpass —**tran·scen·dent** \-'endənt\ *adj* —**tran·scen·den·tal** \,trans,en'dentəl, -ən-\ *adj*

tran·scribe \trans'krīb\ *vb* **-scribed**; **-scrib·ing** : make a copy, arrangement, or recording of —**tran·scrip·tion** \trans'kripshən\ *n*

tran·script \'trans,kript\ *n* : official copy

tran·sept \'trans,ept\ *n* : part of a church that crosses the nave at right angles

trans·fer \trans'fər, 'trans,fər\ *vb* **-rr-** **1** : move from one person, place, or situation to another **2** : convey ownership of **3** : print or copy by contact **4** : change to another vehicle or transportation line ~ \'trans,fər\ *n* **1** : act or process of transferring **2** : one that transfers or is transferred **3** : ticket permitting one to transfer —**trans·fer·able** \trans'fərəbəl\ *adj* —**trans·fer·al** \-əl\ *n* —**trans·fer·ence** \-əns\ *n*

trans·fig·ure \trans'figyər\ *vb* **-ured**; **-ur·ing** **1** : change the form or appearance of **2** : glorify —**trans·fig·u·ra·tion** \,trans,figyə'rāshən\ *n*

trans·fix \trans'fiks\ *vb* **1** : pierce through **2** : hold motionless

trans·form \-'fȯrm\ *vb* **1** : change in structure, appearance, or character **2** : change (an electric current) in potential or type —**trans·for·ma·tion** \,transfər'māshən\ *n* —**trans·form·er** \trans'fȯrmər\ *n*

trans·fuse \trans'fyüz\ *vb* **-fused**; **-fus·ing** **1** : diffuse into or through **2** : transfer (as blood) into a vein —**trans·fu·sion** \-'fyüzhən\ *n*

trans·gress \trans'gres, tranz-\ *vb* : sin —**trans·gres·sion** \-'greshən\ *n* —**trans·gres·sor** \-'gresər\ *n*

tran·sient \'tranchənt\ *adj* : not lasting or staying long —**transient** *n* —**tran·sient·ly** *adv*

tran·sis·tor \tranz'istər, trans-\ *n* : small electronic device used in electronic equipment —**tran·sis·tor·ize** \-tə,rīz\ *vb*

tran·sit \'transət, 'tranz-\ *n* **1** : movement over, across, or through **2** : local and esp. public transportation **3** : surveyor's instrument

tran·si·tion \trans'ishən, tranz-\ *n* : passage from one state, stage, or subject to another —**tran·si·tion·al** \-'ishənəl\ *adj*

tran·si·to·ry \'transə,tȯrē, 'tranz-\ *adj* : of brief duration

trans·late \trans'lāt, tranz-\ *vb* **-lat·ed**; **-lat·ing** : change into another language —**trans·lat·able** *adj* —**trans·la·tion** \-'lāshən\ *n* —**trans·la·tor** \-'lātər\ *n*

trans·lu·cent \trans'lüsənt, tranz-\ *adj* : not transparent but clear enough to allow light to pass through —**trans·lu·cence** \-əns\ *n* —**trans·lu·cen·cy** \-ənsē\ *n* —**trans·lu·cent·ly** *adv*

trans·mis·sion \-'mishən\ *n* **1** : act or process of transmitting **2** : system of gears between a car engine and drive wheels

trans·mit \-'mit\ *vb* **-tt-** **1** : transfer from one person or place to another **2** : pass on by inheritance **3** : broadcast —**trans·mis·si·ble** \-'misəbəl\ *adj* —**trans·mit·ta·ble** \-'mitəbəl\ *adj* —**trans·mit·tal** \-'mitəl\ *n* —**trans·mit·ter** *n*

tran·som \'transəm\ *n* : often hinged window above a door

trans·par·ent \trans'parənt\ *adj* **1** : clear enough to see through **2** : obvious —**trans·par·en·cy** \-ənsē\ *n* —**trans·par·ent·ly** *adv*

tran·spire \trans'pīr\ *vb* **-spired**; **-spir·ing** : take place —**tran·spi·ra·tion** \,transpə'rāshən\ *n*

trans·plant \trans'plant\ *vb* **1** : dig up and move to another place **2** : transfer from one body part or person to another —**transplant** \'trans,-\ *n* —**trans·plan·ta·tion** \,trans,plan'tāshən\ *n*

trans·port \trans'pȯrt\ *vb* **1** : carry or deliver to another place **2** : carry away by emotion ~ \'trans,-\ *n* **1** : act of transporting **2** : rapture **3** : ship or plane for carrying troops or supplies —**trans·por·ta·tion** \,transpȯr'tāshən\ *n* —**trans·port·er** *n*

trans·pose \trans'pōz\ *vb* **-posed**; **-pos·ing** : change the position, sequence, or key —**trans·po·si·tion** \,transpə-'zishən\ n

trans·ship \tran'ship, trans-\ vb : transfer from one mode of transportation to another —**trans·ship·ment** n

trans·verse \trans'vərs, tranz-\ adj : lying across —**trans·verse** \'trans,vərs, 'tranz-\ n —**trans·verse·ly** adv

trap \'trap\ n 1 : device for catching animals 2 : something by which one is caught unawares 3 : device to allow one thing to pass through while keeping other things out ~ vb -pp- : catch in a trap —**trap·per** n

trap·door n : door in a floor or roof

tra·peze \tra'pēz\ n : suspended bar used by acrobats

trap·e·zoid \'trapə,zȯid\ n : plane 4-sided figure with 2 parallel sides —**trap·e·zoi·dal** \,trapə'zȯid³l\ adj

trap·pings \'trapiŋz\ n pl 1 : ornamental covering 2 : outward decoration or dress

trash \'trash\ n : something that is no good —**trashy** adj

trau·ma \'traủmə, 'trȯ-\ n : bodily or mental injury —**trau·mat·ic** \trə-'matik, trȯ-, traủ-\ adj

tra·vail \trə'vāl, 'trav,āl\ n : painful work or exertion ~ vb : labor hard

trav·el \'travəl\ vb -eled or -elled; -el·ing or -el·ling 1 : take a trip or tour 2 : move or be carried from point to point ~ n : journey —often pl. —**trav·el·er, trav·el·ler** n

tra·verse \trə'vərs, tra'vərs, 'travərs\ vb -versed; -vers·ing : go or extend across —**tra·verse** \'travərs\ n

trav·es·ty \'travəstē\ n, pl -ties : imitation that makes crude fun of something —**travesty** vb

trawl \'trȯl\ vb : fish or catch with a trawl ~ n : large cone-shaped net —**trawl·er** n

tray \'trā\ n : shallow flat-bottomed receptacle for holding or carrying something

treach·er·ous \'trechərəs\ adj : disloyal or dangerous —**treach·er·ous·ly** adv

treach·ery \'trechərē\ n, pl -er·ies : betrayal of a trust

tread \'tred\ vb trod \'träd\; trod·den \'träd³n\ or trod; tread·ing 1 : step on or over 2 : walk 3 : press or crush with the feet ~ n 1 : way of walking 2 : sound made in walking 3 : part on which a thing runs

trea·dle \'tred³l\ n : foot pedal operating a machine —**treadle** vb

tread·mill n 1 : mill worked by walking persons or animals 2 : wearisome routine

trea·son \'trēz³n\ n : attempt to overthrow the government —**trea·son·able** \'trēz³nəbəl\ adj —**trea·son·ous** \-³nəs\ adj

trea·sure \'trezhər, 'trāzh-\ n 1 : wealth stored up 2 : something of great value ~ vb -sured; -sur·ing : keep as precious

trea·sur·er \'trezhərər, 'trāzh-\ n : officer who handles funds

trea·sury \'trezhərē, 'trāzh-\ n, pl -sur·ies : place or office for keeping and distributing funds

treat \'trēt\ vb 1 : have as a topic 2 : pay for the food or entertainment of 3 : act toward or regard in a certain way 4 : give medical care to ~ n 1 : food or entertainment paid for by another 2 : something special and enjoyable —**treat·ment** n

trea·tise \'trētəs\ n : systematic written exposition or argument

trea·ty \'trētē\ n, pl -ties : agreement between governments

tre·ble \'trebəl\ n 1 : highest part in music 2 : upper half of the musical range ~ adj : triple in number or amount ~ vb -bled; -bling : make triple —**tre·bly** adv

tree \'trē\ n : tall woody plant ~ vb treed; tree·ing : force up a tree —**tree·less** adj

trek \'trek\ n : difficult trip ~ vb -kk- : make a trek

trel·lis \'treləs\ n : structure of crossed strips

trem·ble \'trembəl\ vb -bled; -bling 1 : shake from fear or cold 2 : move or sound as if shaken

tre·men·dous \tri'mendəs\ adj : amazingly large, powerful, or excellent —**tre·men·dous·ly** adv

trem·or \'tremər\ n : a trembling

trem·u·lous \'tremyələs\ adj : trembling or quaking

trench \'trench\ n : long narrow cut in land

tren·chant \'trenchənt\ adj : sharply perceptive

trend \'trend\ n : prevailing tendency, direction, or style ~ vb : move in a particular direction —**trendy** \'trendē\ adj trep·i·da·tion \,trepə'dāshən\ n : nervous apprehension

tres·pass \'trespəs, -,pas\ n 1 : sin 2 : unauthorized entry onto someone's property ~ vb 1 : sin 2 : enter illegally —tres·pass·er n

tress \'tres\ n : long lock of hair

tres·tle \'tresəl\ n 1 : support with a horizontal piece and spreading legs 2 : framework bridge

tri·ad \'trī,ad, -əd\ n : union of 3

tri·age \trē'äzh, 'trē,äzh\ n : system of dealing with cases (as patients) according to priority guidelines intended to maximize success

tri·al \'trīəl\ n 1 : hearing and judgment of a matter in court 2 : source of great annoyance 3 : test use or experimental effort —trial adj

tri·an·gle \'trī,aŋgəl\ n : plane figure with 3 sides and 3 angles —tri·an·gu·lar \trī'aŋgyələr\ adj

tribe \'trīb\ n : social group of numerous families —trib·al \'trībəl\ adj —tribes·man \'trībzmən\ n

trib·u·la·tion \,tribyə'lāshən\ n : suffering from oppression

tri·bu·nal \trī'byūnᵊl, tri-\ n 1 : court 2 : something that decides

trib·u·tary \'tribyə,terē\ n, pl -tar·ies : stream that flows into a river or lake

trib·ute \'trib,yūt\ n 1 : payment to acknowledge submission 2 : tax 3 : gift or act showing respect

trick \'trik\ n 1 : scheme to deceive 2 : prank 3 : deceptive or ingenious feat 4 : mannerism 5 : knack 6 : tour of duty ~ vb : deceive by cunning —trick·ery \-ərē\ n —trick·ster \-stər\ n

trick·le \'trikəl\ vb -led; -ling : run in drops or a thin stream —trickle n

tricky \'trikē\ adj trick·i·er; -est 1 : inclined to trickery 2 : requiring skill or caution

tri·cy·cle \'trī,sikəl\ n : 3-wheeled bicycle

tri·dent \'trīdᵊnt\ n : 3-pronged spear

tri·en·ni·al \trī'enēəl\ adj : lasting, occurring, or done every 3 years —triennial n

tri·fle \'trīfəl\ n : something of little value or importance ~ vb -fled; -fling 1 : speak or act in a playful or flirting way 2 : toy —tri·fler n

tri·fling \'trīfliŋ\ adj : trivial

trig·ger \'trigər\ n : finger-piece of a firearm lock that fires the gun ~ vb : set into motion —trigger adj —trig·gered \-ərd\ adj

trig·o·nom·e·try \,trigə'nämətrē\ n : mathematics dealing with triangular measurement —trig·o·no·met·ric \-nə'metrik\ adj

trill \'tril\ n 1 : rapid alternation between 2 adjacent tones 2 : rapid vibration in speaking ~ vb : utter in or with a trill

tril·lion \'trilyən\ n : 1000 billions — trillion adj —tril·lionth \-yənth\ adj or n

tril·o·gy \'triləjē\ n, pl -gies : 3-part literary or musical composition

trim \'trim\ vb -mm- 1 : decorate 2 : make neat or reduce by cutting ~ adj -mm- : neat and compact ~ n 1 : state or condition 2 : ornaments —trim·ly adv —trim·mer n

trim·ming \'trimiŋ\ n : something that ornaments or completes

Trin·i·ty \'trinətē\ n : divine unity of Father, Son, and Holy Spirit

trin·ket \'triŋkət\ n : small ornament

trio \'trēō\ n, pl tri·os 1 : music for 3 performers 2 : group of 3

trip \'trip\ vb -pp- 1 : step lightly 2 : stumble or cause to stumble 3 : make or cause to make a mistake 4 : release (as a spring or switch) ~ n 1 : journey 2 : stumble 3 : drug-induced experience

tri·par·tite \trī'pär,tīt\ adj : having 3 parts or parties

tripe \'trīp\ n 1 : animal's stomach used as food 2 : trash

tri·ple \'tripəl\ vb -pled; -pling : make 3 times as great ~ n : group of 3 ~ adj 1 : having 3 units 2 : being 3 times as great or as many

trip·let \'triplət\ n 1 : group of 3 2 : one of 3 offspring born together

trip·li·cate \'triplikət\ adj : made in 3 identical copies ~ n : one of 3 copies

tri·pod \'trī,päd\ n : a stand with 3 legs —tripod, tri·po·dal \'tripədᵊl, 'trī,päd-\ adj

tri·sect \'trī,sekt, trī'-\ vb : divide into 3 usu. equal parts —tri·sec·tion \'trī,sekshən\ n

trite \'trīt\ adj trit·er; trit·est : commonplace

tri·umph \'trīəmf\ n, pl -umphs : victory or great success ~ vb : obtain or celebrate victory —tri·um·phal \trī'əmfəl\ adj —tri·um·phant \-fənt\ adj —tri·um·phant·ly adv

tri·um·vi·rate \trī'əmvərət\ *n* : ruling body of 3 persons

triv·et \'trivət\ *n* 1 : 3-legged stand 2 : stand to hold a hot dish

triv·ia \'trivēə\ *n sing or pl* : unimportant details

triv·i·al \'trivēəl\ *adj* : of little importance —**triv·i·al·i·ty** \,trivē'alətē\ *n*

trod *past of* TREAD

trodden *past part of* TREAD

troll \'trōl\ *n* : dwarf or giant of folklore inhabiting caves or hills

trol·ley \'trälē\ *n, pl* -leys : streetcar run by overhead electric wires

trol·lop \'träləp\ *n* : untidy or immoral woman

trom·bone \träm'bōn, 'träm-\ *n* : musical instrument with a long sliding tube —**trom·bon·ist** \-'bōnist, -,bō-\ *n*

troop \'trüp\ *n* 1 : cavalry unit 2 *pl* : soldiers 3 : collection of people or things ~ *vb* : move or gather in crowds

troop·er \'trüpər\ *n* 1 : cavalry soldier 2 : police officer on horseback or state police officer

tro·phy \'trōfē\ *n, pl* -phies : prize gained by a victory

trop·ic \'träpik\ *n* 1 : either of the 2 parallels of latitude one 23½ degrees north of the equator (**tropic of Can·cer** \-'kansər\) and one 23½ degrees south of the equator (**tropic of Cap·ri·corn** \-'kaprə,kórn\) 2 *pl* : region lying between the tropics —**trop·ic, trop·i·cal** \-ikəl\ *adj*

trot \'trät\ *n* : moderately fast gait esp. of a horse with diagonally paired legs moving together ~ *vb* -tt- : go at a trot —**trot·ter** *n*

troth \'träth, 'trōth, 'trȯth\ *n* 1 : pledged faithfulness 2 : betrothal

trou·ba·dour \'trübə,dōr\ *n* : medieval lyric poet

trou·ble \'trəbəl\ *vb* -bled; -bling 1 : disturb 2 : afflict 3 : make an effort ~ *n* 1 : cause of mental or physical distress 2 : effort —**trou·ble·mak·er** *n* —**trou·ble·some** *adj* —**trou·ble·some·ly** *adv*

trough \'trȯf\ *n, pl* **troughs** \'trȯfs, 'trȯvz\ 1 : narrow container for animal feed or water 2 : long channel or depression (as between waves)

trounce \'traủns\ *vb* **trounced; trounc·ing** : thrash, punish, or defeat severely

troupe \'trüp\ *n* : group of stage performers —**troup·er** *n*

trou·sers \'traủzərz\ *n pl* : long pants —**trouser** *adj*

trous·seau \'trüsō, trü'sō\ *n, pl* -seaux \-,sōz, -'sōz\ *or* -seaus : bride's collection of clothing and personal items

trout \'traủt\ *n, pl* **trout** : freshwater food and game fish

trow·el \'traủəl\ *n* 1 : tool for spreading or smoothing 2 : garden scoop —**trowel** *vb*

troy \'trȯi\ *n* : system of weights based on a pound of 12 ounces

tru·ant \'trüənt\ *n* : student absent from school without permission —**tru·an·cy** \-ənsē\ *n* —**truant** *adj*

truce \'trüs\ *n* : agreement to halt fighting

truck \'trək\ *n* 1 : wheeled frame for moving heavy objects 2 : automotive vehicle for transporting heavy loads ~ *vb* : transport on a truck —**truck·er** *n* —**truck·load** *n*

truck·le \'trəkəl\ *vb* -led; -ling : yield slavishly to another

tru·cu·lent \'trəkyələnt\ *adj* : aggressively self-assertive —**tru·cu·lence** \-ləns\ *n* —**tru·cu·len·cy** \-lənsē\ *n* —**tru·cu·lent·ly** *adv*

trudge \'trəj\ *vb* **trudged; trudg·ing** : walk or march steadily and with difficulty

true \'trü\ *adj* **tru·er; tru·est** 1 : loyal 2 : in agreement with fact or reality 3 : genuine ~ *adv* 1 : truthfully 2 : accurately ~ *vb* **trued; tru·ing** : make balanced or even —**tru·ly** *adv*

true–blue *adj* : loyal

truf·fle \'trəfəl\ *n* 1 : edible fruit of an underground fungus 2 : ball-shaped chocolate candy

tru·ism \'trü,izəm\ *n* : obvious truth

trump \'trəmp\ *n* : card of a designated suit any of whose cards will win over other cards ~ *vb* : take with a trump

trumped–up \'trəmpt'əp\ *adj* : made-up

trum·pet \'trəmpət\ *n* : tubular brass wind instrument with a flaring end ~ *vb* 1 : blow a trumpet 2 : proclaim loudly —**trum·pet·er** *n*

trun·cate \'trəŋ,kāt, 'trən-\ *vb* -cat·ed; -cat·ing : cut short —**trun·ca·tion** \,trəŋ'kāshən\ *n*

trun·dle \'trənd°l\ *vb* -dled; -dling : roll along

trunk \'trəŋk\ *n* 1 : main part (as of a

body or tree) **2** : long muscular nose of an elephant **3** : storage chest **4** : storage space in a car **5** *pl* : shorts

truss \'trəs\ *vb* : bind tightly ~ *n* **1** : set of structural parts forming a framework **2** : appliance worn to hold a hernia in place

trust \'trəst\ *n* **1** : reliance on another **2** : assured hope **3** : credit **4** : property held or managed in behalf of another **5** : combination of firms that reduces competition **6** : something entrusted to another's care **7** : custody ~ *vb* **1** : depend **2** : hope **3** : entrust **4** : have faith in —**trust·ful** \-fəl\ *adj* —**trust·ful·ly** *adv* —**trust·ful·ness** *n* —**trust·worthi·ness** *n* —**trust·wor·thy** *adj*

trust·ee \‚trəs'tē\ *n* : person holding property in trust —**trust·ee·ship** *n*

trusty \'trəstē\ *adj* **trust·i·er**; **-est** : dependable

truth \'trüth\ *n*, *pl* **truths** \'trüthz, 'trüths\ **1** : real state of things **2** : true or accepted statement **3** : agreement with fact or reality —**truth·ful** \-fəl\ *adj* —**truth·ful·ly** *adv* —**truth·ful·ness** *n*

try \'trī\ *vb* **tried**; **try·ing** **1** : conduct the trial of **2** : put to a test **3** : strain **4** : make an effort at ~ *n*, *pl* **tries** : act of trying

try·out *n* : competitive test of performance esp. for athletes or actors —**try out** *vb*

tryst \'trist, 'trīst\ *n* : secret rendezvous of lovers

tsar \'zär, 'tsär, 'sär\ *var of* CZAR

T-shirt \'tē‚shərt\ *n* : collarless pullover shirt with short sleeves

tub \'təb\ *n* **1** : wide bucketlike vessel **2** : bathtub

tu·ba \'tübə, 'tyü-\ *n* : large low-pitched brass wind instrument

tube \'tüb, 'tyüb\ *n* **1** : hollow cylinder **2** : round container from which a substance can be squeezed **3** : airtight circular tube of rubber inside a tire **4** : electronic device consisting of a sealed usu. glass container with electrodes inside —**tubed** \'tübd, 'tyübd\ *adj* —**tube·less** *adj*

tu·ber \'tübər, 'tyü-\ *n* : fleshy underground growth (as of a potato) —**tu·ber·ous** \-rəs\ *adj*

tu·ber·cu·lo·sis \tù‚bərkyə'lōsəs, tyù-\ *n*, *pl* **-lo·ses** \-‚sēz\ : bacterial disease esp. of the lungs —**tu·ber·cu·lar** \-'bərkyələr\ *adj* —**tu·ber·cu·lous** \-ləs\ *adj*

tub·ing \'tübiŋ, 'tyü-\ *n* : series or arrangement of tubes

tu·bu·lar \'tübyələr, 'tyü-\ *adj* : of or like a tube

tuck \'tək\ *vb* **1** : pull up into a fold **2** : put into a snug often concealing place **3** : make snug in bed —**with** *in* ~ *n* : fold in a cloth

tuck·er \'təkər\ *vb* : fatigue

Tues·day \'tüzdā, 'tyüz-, -dē\ *n* : 3d day of the week

tuft \'təft\ *n* : clump (as of hair or feathers) —**tuft·ed** \'təftəd\ *adj*

tug \'təg\ *vb* **-gg-** **1** : pull hard **2** : move by pulling ~ *n* **1** : act of tugging **2** : tugboat

tug·boat *n* : boat for towing or pushing ships through a harbor

tug-of–war \‚təgə'wór\ *n*, *pl* **tugs-of–war** : pulling contest between 2 teams

tu·ition \tù'ishən, 'tyü-\ *n* : cost of instruction

tu·lip \'tüləp, 'tyü-\ *n* : herb with cup-shaped flowers

tum·ble \'təmbəl\ *vb* **-bled**; **-bling** **1** : perform gymnastic feats of rolling and turning **2** : fall or cause to fall suddenly **3** : toss ~ *n* : act of tumbling

tum·bler \'təmblər\ *n* **1** : acrobat **2** : drinking glass **3** : obstruction in a lock that can be moved (as by a key)

tu·mid \'tüməd, 'tyü-\ *adj* : turgid

tum·my \'təmē\ *n*, *pl* **-mies** : belly

tu·mor \'tümər 'tyü-\ *n* : abnormal and useless growth of tissue —**tu·mor·ous** *adj*

tu·mult \'tü‚məlt 'tyü-\ *n* **1** : uproar **2** : violent agitation of mind or feelings —**tu·mul·tu·ous** \tù'məlchəwəs, tyü-\ *adj*

tun \'tən\ *n* : large cask

tu·na \'tünə 'tyü-\ *n*, *pl* **-na** or **-nas** : large sea food fish

tun·dra \'təndrə\ *n* : treeless arctic plain

tune \'tün, 'tyün\ *n* **1** : melody **2** : correct musical pitch **3** : harmonious relationship ~ *vb* **tuned**; **tun·ing** **1** : bring or come into harmony **2** : adjust in musical pitch **3** : adjust a receiver so as to receive a broadcast **4** : put in first-class working order —**tun·able** *adj* —**tune·ful** \-fəl\ *adj* —**tun·er** *n*

tung·sten \'təŋstən\ *n* : metallic element used for electrical purposes and in hardening alloys (as steel)

tu·nic \'tünik. 'tyü-\ *n* **1** : ancient knee-length garment **2** : hip-length blouse or jacket

tun·nel \'tən³l\ *n* : underground passageway ~ *vb* **-neled** *or* **-nelled; -nel·ing** *or* **-nel·ling** : make a tunnel through or under something

tur·ban \'tərbən\ *n* : wound headdress worn esp. by Muslims

tur·bid \'tərbəd\ *adj* **1** : dark with stirred-up sediment **2** : confused — **tur·bid·i·ty** \,tər'bidətē\ *n*

tur·bine \'tərbən. -,bīn\ *n* : engine turned by the force of gas or water on fan blades

tur·bo·jet \'tərbō,jet\ *n* : airplane powered by a jet engine having a turbine-driven air compressor or the engine itself

tur·bo·prop \'tərbō,präp\ *n* : airplane powered by a propeller turned by a jet engine-driven turbine

tur·bu·lent \'tərbyələnt\ *adj* **1** : causing violence or disturbance **2** : marked by agitation or tumult — **tur·bu·lence** \-ləns\ *n* — **tur·bu·lent·ly** *adv*

tu·reen \tə'rēn, tyü-\ *n* : deep bowl for serving soup

turf \'tərf\ *n* : upper layer of soil bound by grass and roots

tur·gid \'tərjəd\ *adj* **1** : swollen **2** : too highly embellished in style — **tur·gid·i·ty** \,tər'jidətē\ *n*

tur·key \'tərkē\ *n, pl* **-keys** : large American bird raised for food

tur·moil \'tər,mȯil\ *n* : extremely agitated condition

turn \'tərn\ *vb* **1** : move or cause to move around an axis **2** : twist (a mechanical part) to operate **3** : wrench **4** : cause to face or move in a different direction **5** : reverse the sides or surfaces of **6** : upset **7** : go around **8** : become or cause to become **9** : seek aid from a source ~ *n* **1** : act or instance of turning **2** : change **3** : place at which something turns **4** : place, time, or opportunity to do something in order — **turn·er** *n* — **turn down** *vb* : decline to accept — **turn in** *vb* **1** : deliver or report to authorities **2** : go to bed — **turn off** *vb* : stop the functioning of — **turn out** *vb* **1** : expel **2** : produce **3** : come together **4** : prove to be in the end — **turn over** *vb* : transfer — **turn up** *vb* **1** : discover or appear **2** : happen unexpectedly

turn·coat *n* : traitor

tur·nip \'tərnəp\ *n* : edible root of an herb

turn·out \'tərn,aȯt\ *n* **1** : gathering of people for a special purpose **2** : size of a gathering

turn·over *n* **1** : upset or reversal **2** : filled pastry **3** : volume of business **4** : movement (as of goods or people) into, through, and out of a place

turn·pike \'tərn,pīk\ *n* : expressway on which tolls are charged

turn·stile \-,stīl\ *n* : post with arms pivoted on the top that allows people to pass one by one

turn·ta·ble *n* : platform that turns a phonograph record

tur·pen·tine \'tərpən,tīn\ *n* : oil distilled from pine-tree resin and used as a solvent

tur·pi·tude \'tərpə,tüd, -,tyüd\ *n* : inherent baseness

tur·quoise \'tər,kȯiz, -,kwȯiz\ *n* : blue or greenish gray gemstone

tur·ret \'tərət\ *n* **1** : little tower on a building **2** : revolving tool holder or gun housing

tur·tle \'tərt³l\ *n* : reptile with the trunk enclosed in a bony shell

tur·tle·dove *n* : wild pigeon

tur·tle·neck *n* : high close-fitting collar that can be turned over or a sweater or shirt with this collar

tusk \'təsk\ *n* : long protruding tooth (as of an elephant) — **tusked** \'təskt\ *adj*

tus·sle \'təsəl\ *n or vb* : struggle

tu·te·lage \'tüt³lij, 'tyüt-\ *n* **1** : act of protecting **2** : instruction esp. of an individual

tu·tor \'tütər, 'tyü-\ *n* : private teacher ~ *vb* : teach usu. individually

tux·e·do \,tək'sēdō\ *n, pl* **-dos** *or* **-does** : semiformal evening clothes for a man

TV \,tē'vē, 'tē,vē\ *n* : television

twain \'twān\ *n* : two

twang \'twaŋ\ *n* **1** : harsh sound like that of a plucked bowstring **2** : nasal speech or resonance ~ *vb* : sound or speak with a twang

tweak \'twēk\ *vb* : pinch and pull playfully — **tweak** *n*

tweed \'twēd\ *n* **1** : rough woolen fabric **2** *pl* : tweed clothing — **tweedy** *adj*

tweet \'twēt\ *n* : chirping note — **tweet** *vb*

twee·zers \'twēzərz\ *n pl* : small pincer-like tool

twelve \'twelv\ *n* 1 : one more than 11 2 : 12th in a set or series 3 : something having 12 units —**twelfth** \'twelfth\ *adj or n* —**twelve** *adj or pron*

twen·ty \'twentē\ *n, pl* **-ties** : 2 times 10 —**twen·ti·eth** \-ēəth\ *adj or n* —**twenty** *adj or pron*

twen·ty–twen·ty, 20–20 *adj* : being vision of normal sharpness

twice \'twīs\ *adv* 1 : on 2 occasions 2 : 2 times

twig \'twig\ *n* : small branch —**twig·gy** *adj*

twi·light \'twī,līt\ *n* : light from the sky at dusk or dawn —**twilight** *adj*

twill \'twil\ *n* : fabric with a weave that gives an appearance of diagonal lines in the fabric

twilled \'twild\ *adj* : made with a twill weave

twin \'twin\ *n* : either of 2 offspring born together ~ *adj* 1 : born with one another or as a pair at one birth 2 : made up of 2 similar parts

twine \'twīn\ *n* : strong twisted thread ~ *vb* **twined; twin·ing** 1 : twist together 2 : coil about a support —**twin·er** *n* —**twiny** *adj*

twinge \'twinj\ *vb* **twinged; twing·ing** *or* **twinge·ing** : affect with or feel a sudden sharp pain ~ *n* : sudden sharp stab (as of pain)

twin·kle \'twiŋkəl\ *vb* **-kled; -kling** : shine with a flickering light ~ *n* 1 : wink 2 : intermittent shining —**twin·kler** \-klər\ *n*

twirl \'twərl\ *vb* : whirl round ~ *n* 1 : act of twirling 2 : coil —**twirl·er** *n*

twist \'twist\ *vb* 1 : unite by winding (threads) together 2 : wrench 3 : move in or have a spiral shape 4 : follow a winding course ~ *n* 1 : act or result of twisting 2 : unexpected development

twist·er \'twistər\ *n* : tornado

¹**twit** \'twit\ *n* : fool

²**twit** *vb* **-tt-** : taunt

twitch \'twich\ *vb* : move or pull with a sudden motion ~ *n* : act of twitching

twit·ter \'twitər\ *vb* : make chirping noises ~ *n* : small intermittent noise

two \'tü\ *n, pl* **twos** 1 : one more than one 2 : the 2d in a set or series 3 : something having 2 units —**two** *adj or pron*

two·fold \'tü,fōld\ *adj* : double —**two·fold** \-'fōld\ *adv*

two·some \'tüsəm\ *n* : couple

-ty *n suffix* : quality, condition, or degree

ty·coon \tī'kün\ *n* : powerful and successful businessman

tying *pres part of* TIE

tyke \'tīk\ *n* : small child

tym·pa·num \'timpənəm\ *n, pl* **-na** \-nə\ : eardrum or the cavity which it closes externally —**tym·pan·ic** \tim'panik\ *adj*

type \'tīp\ *n* 1 : class, kind, or group set apart by common characteristics 2 : special design of printed letters ~ *vb* **typed; typ·ing** 1 : write with a typewriter 2 : identify or classify as a particular type

type·writ·er *n* : keyboard machine that produces printed material by striking a ribbon with raised letters —**type·write** *vb*

ty·phoid \'tī,fȯid, tī'-\ *adj* : relating to or being a communicable bacterial disease (**typhoid fever**)

ty·phoon \tī'fün\ *n* : hurricane of the western Pacific ocean

ty·phus \'tīfəs\ *n* : severe disease with fever, delirium, and rash

typ·i·cal \'tipikəl\ *adj* : having the essential characteristics of a group —**typ·i·cal·i·ty** \,tipə'kalətē\ *n* —**typ·i·cal·ly** *adv* —**typ·i·cal·ness** *n*

typ·i·fy \'tipə,fī\ *vb* **-fied; -fy·ing** : be typical of

typ·ist \'tīpist\ *n* : one who operates a typewriter

ty·pog·ra·phy \tī'pägrəfē\ *n* 1 : art of printing with type 2 : style, arrangement, or appearance of printed matter —**ty·po·graph·ic** \,tīpə'grafik\, **ty·po·graph·i·cal** \-ikəl\ *adj* —**ty·po·graph·i·cal·ly** *adv*

ty·ran·ni·cal \tə'ranikəl, tī-\ *adj* : relating to a tyrant —**ty·ran·ni·cal·ly** *adv*

tyr·an·nize \'tirə,nīz\ *vb* **-nized; -niz·ing** : rule or deal with in the manner of a tyrant —**tyr·an·niz·er** *n*

tyr·an·ny \'tirənē\ *n, pl* **-nies** : unjust use of absolute governmental power

ty·rant \'tīrənt\ *n* : harsh ruler having absolute power

ty·ro \'tīrō\ *n, pl* **-ros** : beginner

tzar \'zär, 'tsär, 'sär\ *var of* CZAR

U

u \'yü\ *n, pl* **u's** *or* **us** \'yüz\ : 21st letter of the alphabet

ubiq·ui·tous \yü'bikwətəs\ *adj* : omnipresent —**ubiq·ui·tous·ly** *adv* —**ubiq·ui·ty** \-wətē\ *n*

ud·der \'ədər\ *n* : animal sac containing milk glands and nipples

ug·ly \'əglē\ *adj* **ug·li·er; -est 1** : offensive to look at **2** : mean or quarrelsome —**ug·li·ness** *n*

uku·le·le \,yükə'lālē\ *n* : small 4-string guitar

ul·cer \'əlsər\ *n* : eroded sore —**ul·cer·ous** *adj*

ul·cer·ate \'əlsə,rāt\ *vb* **-at·ed; -at·ing** : become affected with an ulcer —**ul·cer·a·tion** \,əlsə'rāshən\ *n* —**ul·cer·a·tive** \'əlsə,rātiv\ *adj*

ul·na \'əlnə\ *n* : bone of the forearm opposite the thumb

ul·te·ri·or \,əl'tirēər\ *adj* : not revealed

ul·ti·mate \'əltəmət\ *adj* : final, maximum, or extreme —**ultimate** *n* —**ul·ti·mate·ly** *adv*

ul·ti·ma·tum \,əltə'mātəm, -'mät-\ *n, pl* **-tums** *or* **-ta** \-ə\ : final proposition or demand carrying or implying a threat

ul·tra·vi·o·let \,əltrə'vīələt\ *adj* : having a wavelength shorter than visible light

um·bil·i·cus \,əmbə'līkəs, ,əm'bili-\ *n, pl* **-li·ci** \-bə'lī,kī, -,sī; -'bilə,kī, -,kē\ *or* **-li·cus·es** : small depression on the abdominal wall marking the site of the cord (**umbilical cord**) that joins the unborn fetus to its mother —**um·bil·i·cal** \,əm'bilikəl\ *adj*

um·brage \'əmbrij\ *n* : resentment

um·brel·la \,əm'brelə\ *n* : collapsible fabric device to protect from sun or rain

um·pire \'əm,pīr\ *n* **1** : arbitrator **2** : sport official —**umpire** *vb*

ump·teen \'əmp'tēn\ *adj* : very numerous —**ump·teenth** \-'tēnth\ *adj*

un- \,ən, 'ən\ *prefix* **1** : not **2** : opposite of

unable	unaccompanied
unabridged	unaccounted
unacceptable	unacquainted

unaddressed	unconventional
unadorned	unconvention-
unadulterated	ally
unafraid	unconverted
unaided	uncooked
unalike	uncooperative
unambiguous	uncoordinated
unambitious	uncovered
unannounced	uncultivated
unanswered	undamaged
unanticipated	undated
unappetizing	undecided
unappreciated	undeclared
unapproved	undefeated
unarguable	undemocratic
unarguably	undependable
unassisted	undeserving
unattended	undesirable
unattractive	undetected
unauthorized	undetermined
unavailable	undeveloped
unavoidable	undeviating
unbearable	undignified
unbiased	undisturbed
unbranded	undivided
unbreakable	undomesticated
uncensored	undrinkable
unchallenged	unearned
unchangeable	uneducated
unchanged	unemotional
unchanging	unending
uncharacteristic	unendurable
uncharged	unenforceable
unchaste	unenlightened
uncivilized	unethical
unclaimed	unexcitable
unclear	unexciting
uncleared	unexplainable
unclothed	unexplored
uncluttered	unfair
uncombed	unfairly
uncomfortable	unfairness
uncomfortably	unfavorable
uncomplimen-	unfavorably
tary	unfeigned
unconfirmed	unfilled
unconsummated	unfinished
uncontested	unflattering
uncontrolled	unforeseeable
uncontroversial	unforeseen

unforgivable
unforgiving
unfulfilled
unfurnished
ungenerous
ungentlemanly
ungraceful
ungrammatical
unharmed
unhealthful
unheated
unhurt
unidentified
unimaginable
unimaginative
unimportant
unimpressed
uninformed
uninhabited
uninjured
uninsured
unintelligent
unintelligible
unintelligibly
unintended
unintentional
unintentionally
uninterested
uninteresting
uninterrupted
uninvited
unjust
unjustifiable
unjustified
unjustly
unknowing
unknowingly
unknown
unleavened
unlicensed
unlikable
unlimited
unlovable
unmanageable
unmarked
unmarried
unmerciful
unmercifully
unmerited
unmolested
unmotivated
unmoving
unnamed
unnecessarily
unnecessary
unneeded
unnoticeable
unnoticed

unobjectionable
unobservable
unobservant
unobtainable
unobtrusive
unobtrusively
unofficial
unopened
unopposed
unorganized
unoriginal
unorthodox
unorthodoxy
unpaid
unpardonable
unpatriotic
unpaved
unpleasant
unpleasantly
unpleasantness
unpopular
unpopularity
unposed
unpredictability
unpredictable
unpredictably
unprejudiced
unprepared
unpretentious
unproductive
unprofitable
unprotected
unproved
unproven
unprovoked
unpunished
unqualified
unquenchable
unquestioning
unreachable
unreadable
unready
unrealistic
unreasonable
unreasonably
unrefined
unrelated
unreliable
unremembered
unrepentant
unrepresented
unrequited
unresolved
unresponsive
unrestrained
unrestricted
unrewarding
unripe

unsafe
unsalted
unsanitary
unsatisfactory
unsatisfied
unscented
unscheduled
unseasoned
unseen
unselfish
unselfishly
unselfishness
unshaped
unshaven
unskillful
unskillfully
unsolicited
unsolved
unsophisticated
unsound
unsoundly
unsoundness
unspecified
unspoiled
unsteadily
unsteadiness
unsteady
unstructured
unsubstantiated
unsuccessful
unsuitable
unsuitably
unsuited
unsupervised
unsupported
unsure

unsurprising
unsuspecting
unsweetened
unsympathetic
untamed
untanned
untidy
untouched
untrained
untreated
untrue
untrustworthy
untruthful
unusable
unusual
unvarying
unverified
unwanted
unwarranted
unwary
unwavering
unweaned
unwed
unwelcome
unwholesome
unwilling
unwillingly
unwillingness
unwise
unwisely
unworkable
unworthily
unworthiness
unworthy
unyielding

un·ac·cus·tomed *adj* **1** : not customary **2** : not accustomed

un·af·fect·ed *adj* **1** : not influenced or changed by something **2** : natural and sincere —**un·af·fect·ed·ly** *adv*

unan·i·mous \yu̇'nanəməs\ *adj* **1** : showing no disagreement **2** : formed with the agreement of all — **una·nim·i·ty** \ˌyünə'nimətē\ *n* — **unan·i·mous·ly** *adv*

un·armed *adj* : not armed or armored

un·as·sum·ing *adj* : not bold or arrogant

un·at·tached *adj* **1** : not attached **2** : not married or engaged

un·aware *adv* : unawares ~ *adj* : not aware

un·awares \ˌənə'warz\ *adv* **1** : without warning **2** : unintentionally

un·bal·anced *adj* **1** : not balanced **2** : mentally unstable

un·beat·en *adj* : not beaten

un·be·com·ing *adj* : not proper or suitable —un·be·com·ing·ly *adv*

un·be·liev·able *adj* 1 : improbable 2 : superlative —un·be·liev·ably *adv*

un·bend *vb* -bent; -bend·ing : make or become more relaxed and friendly

un·bend·ing *adj* : formal and inflexible

un·bind *vb* -bound; -bind·ing 1 : remove bindings from 2 : release

un·bolt *vb* : open or unfasten by withdrawing a bolt

un·born *adj* : not yet born

un·bo·som *vb* : disclose thoughts or feelings

un·bowed \,ən'baud\ *adj* : not defeated or subdued

un·bri·dled \,ən'brīd²ld\ *adj* : unrestrained

un·bro·ken *adj* 1 : not damaged 2 : not interrupted

un·buck·le *vb* : unfasten the buckle of

un·bur·den *vb* : relieve (oneself) of anxieties

un·but·ton *vb* : unfasten the buttons of

un·called-for *adj* : too harsh or rude for the occasion

un·can·ny \ən'kanē\ *adj* 1 : weird 2 : suggesting superhuman powers —un·can·ni·ly \-'kan²lē\ *adv*

un·ceas·ing *adj* : never ceasing —un·ceas·ing·ly *adv*

un·cer·e·mo·ni·ous *adj* : acting without ordinary courtesy —un·cer·e·mo·ni·ous·ly *adv*

un·cer·tain *adj* 1 : not determined, sure, or definitely known 2 : subject to chance or change —un·cer·tain·ly *adv* —un·cer·tain·ty *n*

un·chris·tian *adj* : not consistent with Christian teachings

un·cle \'əŋkəl\ *n* 1 : brother of one's father or mother 2 : husband of one's aunt

un·clean *adj* : not clean or pure —un·clean·ness *n*

un·clog *vb* : remove an obstruction from

un·coil *vb* : release or become released from a coiled state

un·com·mit·ted *adj* : not pledged to a particular allegiance or course of action

un·com·mon *adj* 1 : rare 2 : superior —un·com·mon·ly *adv*

un·com·pro·mis·ing *adj* : not making or accepting a compromise

un·con·cerned *adj* 1 : disinterested 2 : not anxious or upset —un·con·cerned·ly *adv*

un·con·di·tion·al *adj* : not limited in any way —un·con·di·tion·al·ly *adv*

un·con·scio·na·ble *adj* : shockingly unjust or unscrupulous —un·con·scio·na·bly *adv*

un·con·scious *adj* 1 : not awake or aware of one's surroundings 2 : not consciously done ~ *n* : part of one's mental life that one is not aware of —un·con·scious·ly *adv* —un·con·scious·ness *n*

un·con·sti·tu·tion·al *adj* : not according to or consistent with a constitution

un·con·trol·la·ble *adj* : incapable of being controlled —un·con·trol·la·bly *adv*

un·count·ed *adj* : countless

un·couth \,ən'küth\ *adj* : rude and vulgar

un·cov·er *vb* 1 : reveal 2 : expose by removing a covering

unc·tion \'əŋkshən\ *n* 1 : rite of anointing 2 : exaggerated or insincere earnestness

unc·tu·ous \'əŋkchəwəs\ *adj* 1 : oily 2 : insincerely smooth in speech or manner —unc·tu·ous·ly *adv*

un·cut *adj* 1 : not cut down, into, off, or apart 2 : not shaped by cutting 3 : not abridged

un·daunt·ed *adj* : not discouraged —un·daunt·ed·ly *adv*

un·de·ni·able *adj* : plainly true —un·de·ni·ably *adv*

un·der \'əndər\ *adv* : below or beneath something ~ *prep* 1 : lower than and sheltered by 2 : below the surface of 3 : covered or concealed by 4 : subject to the authority of 5 : less than ~ *adj* 1 : lying below or beneath 2 : subordinate 3 : less than usual, proper, or desired

un·der·age \,əndər'āj\ *adj* : of less than legal age

un·der·brush \'əndər,brəsh\ *n* : shrubs and small trees growing beneath large trees

un·der·clothes \'əndər,klōz, -,klōthz\ *n pl* : underwear

un·der·cloth·ing \-,klōthiŋ\ *n* : underwear

un·der·cov·er \,əndər'kəvər\ *adj* : employed or engaged in secret investigation

un·der·cur·rent \'əndər,kərənt\ *n* : hidden tendency or opinion

un·der·cut \,əndər'kət\ *vb* -cut; -cut-

ting : offer to sell or to work at a lower rate than

un·der·de·vel·oped \,əndərdi'veləpt\ *adj* : not normally or adequately developed esp. economically

un·der·dog \'əndər,dóg\ *n* : contestant given least chance of winning

un·der·done \,əndər'dən\ *adj* : not thoroughly done or cooked

un·der·es·ti·mate \,əndər'estə,māt\ *vb* : estimate too low

un·der·ex·pose \,əndərik'spōz\ *vb* : give less than normal exposure to —**un·der·ex·po·sure** *n*

un·der·feed \,əndər'fēd\ *vb* **-fed; -feed·ing** : feed inadequately

un·der·foot \,əndər'fút\ *adv* **1** : under the feet **2** : in the way of another

un·der·gar·ment \'əndər,gärmənt\ *n* : garment to be worn under another

un·der·go \,əndər'gō\ *vb* **-went** \-'went\; **-gone; -go·ing 1** : endure **2** : go through (as an experience)

un·der·grad·u·ate \,əndər'grajəwət\ *n* : university or college student

un·der·ground \,əndər'graúnd\ *adv* **1** : beneath the surface of the earth **2** : in secret ~ \'əndər,-\ *adj* **1** : being or growing under the surface of the ground **2** : secret ~ \'əndər,-\ *n* : secret political movement or group

un·der·growth \'əndər,grōth\ *n* : low growth on the floor of a forest

un·der·hand \'əndər,hand\ *adv or adj* **1** : with secrecy and deception **2** : with the hand kept below the waist

un·der·hand·ed \,əndər'handəd\ *adj or adv* : underhand —**un·der·hand·ed·ly** *adv* —**un·der·hand·ed·ness** *n*

un·der·line \'əndər,līn\ *vb* **1** : draw a line under **2** : stress —**underline** *n*

un·der·ling \'əndərliŋ\ *n* : inferior

un·der·ly·ing \,əndər,līiŋ\ *adj* : basic

un·der·mine \,əndər'mīn\ *vb* **1** : excavate beneath **2** : weaken or wear away secretly or gradually

un·der·neath \,əndər'nēth\ *prep* : directly under ~ *adv* **1** : below a surface or object **2** : on the lower side

un·der·nour·ished \,əndər'nərisht\ *adj* : insufficiently nourished —**un·der·nour·ish·ment** *n*

un·der·pants \'əndər,pants\ *n pl* : short undergarment for the lower trunk

un·der·pass \-,pas\ *n* : passageway crossing underneath another

un·der·pin·ning \'əndər,piniŋ\ *n* : support

un·der·priv·i·leged *adj* : poor

un·der·rate \,əndər'rāt\ *vb* : rate or value too low

un·der·score \'əndər,skōr\ *vb* **1** : underline **2** : emphasize —**underscore** *n*

un·der·sea \,əndər'sē\ *adj* : being, carried on, or used beneath the surface of the sea ~ \,əndər'sē\, **un·der·seas** \-'sēz\ *adv* : beneath the surface of the sea

un·der sec·re·tary *n* : deputy secretary

un·der·sell \,əndər'sel\ *vb* **-sold; -sell·ing** : sell articles cheaper than

un·der·shirt \'əndər,shərt\ *n* : shirt worn as underwear

un·der·shorts \'əndər,shórts\ *n pl* : short underpants

un·der·side \'əndər,sīd, ,əndər'sīd\ *n* : side or surface lying underneath

un·der·sized \,əndər'sīzd\ *adj* : unusually small

un·der·stand \,əndər'stand\ *vb* **-stood** \-'stúd\; **-stand·ing 1** : be aware of the meaning of **2** : deduce **3** : have a sympathetic attitude —**un·der·stand·able** \-'standəbəl\ *adj* —**un·der·stand·ably** \-blē\ *adv*

un·der·stand·ing \,əndər'standiŋ\ *n* **1** : intelligence **2** : ability to comprehend and judge **3** : mutual agreement ~ *adj* : sympathetic

un·der·state \,əndər'stāt\ *vb* **1** : represent as less than is the case **2** : state with restraint —**un·der·state·ment** *n*

un·der·stood \,əndər'stúd\ *adj* **1** : agreed upon **2** : implicit

un·der·study \'əndər,stədē, ,əndər'-\ *vb* : study another actor's part in order to substitute —**understudy** \'əndər,-\ *n*

un·der·take \,əndər'tāk\ *vb* **-took; -tak·en; -tak·ing 1** : attempt (a task) or assume (a responsibility) **2** : guarantee

un·der·tak·er \'əndər,tākər\ *n* : one in the funeral business

un·der·tak·ing \'əndər,tākiŋ, ,əndər'-\ *n* **1** : something (as work) that is undertaken **2** : promise

under–the–counter *adj* : illicit

un·der·tone \'əndər,tōn\ *n* : low or subdued tone or utterance

un·der·tow \-,tō\ *n* : current beneath the waves that flows seaward

un·der·val·ue \,əndər'valyü\ *vb* : value too low

un·der·wa·ter \-'wótər, -'wät-\ *adj*

: being or used below the surface of the water —**underwater** adv

under way adv : in motion or in progress

un·der·wear \'əndər,war\ n : clothing worn next to the skin and under ordinary clothes

un·der·world \'əndər,wərld\ n 1 : place of departed souls 2 : world of organized crime

un·der·write \'əndər,rīt, ,əndər,-\ vb -wrote; -writ·ten; -writ·ing 1 : provide insurance for 2 : guarantee financial support of —**un·der·writ·er** n

un·dies \'əndēz\ n pl : underwear

un·do vb -did; -done; -do·ing 1 : unfasten 2 : reverse 3 : ruin —**un·do·ing** n

un·doubt·ed adj : certain —**un·doubt·ed·ly** adv

un·dress vb : remove one's clothes ~ n : state of being naked

un·due adj : excessive —**un·du·ly** adv

un·du·late \'ənjə,lāt\ vb -lat·ed; -lat·ing : rise and fall regularly —**un·du·la·tion** \,ənjə'lāshən\ n

un·dy·ing adj : immortal or perpetual

un·earth vb : dig up or discover

un·earth·ly adj : supernatural

un·easy adj 1 : awkward or embarrassed 2 : disturbed or worried —**un·eas·i·ly** adv —**un·eas·i·ness** n

un·em·ployed adj : not having a job —**un·em·ploy·ment** n

un·equal adj : not equal or uniform —**un·equal·ly** adv

un·equaled, un·equalled adj : having no equal

un·equiv·o·cal adj : leaving no doubt —**un·equiv·o·cal·ly** adv

un·err·ing adj : infallible —**un·err·ing·ly** adv

un·even adj 1 : not smooth 2 : not regular or consistent —**un·even·ly** adv —**un·even·ness** n

un·event·ful adj : lacking interesting or noteworthy incidents —**un·event·ful·ly** adv

un·ex·pect·ed \ənik'spektəd\ adj : not expected —**un·ex·pect·ed·ly** adv

un·fail·ing adj : steadfast —**un·fail·ing·ly** adv

un·faith·ful adj : not loyal —**un·faith·ful·ly** adv —**un·faith·ful·ness** n

un·fa·mil·iar adj 1 : not well known 2 : not acquainted —**un·fa·mil·iar·i·ty** n

un·fas·ten vb : release a catch or lock

un·feel·ing adj : lacking feeling or compassion —**un·feel·ing·ly** adv

un·fit adj : not suitable —**un·fit·ness** n

un·flap·pa·ble \,ən'flapəbəl\ adj : not easily upset or panicked —**un·flap·pa·bly** adv

un·fold vb 1 : open the folds of 2 : reveal 3 : develop

un·for·get·ta·ble adj : memorable —**un·for·get·ta·bly** adv

un·for·tu·nate adj 1 : not lucky or successful 2 : deplorable —**unfortunate** n —**un·for·tu·nate·ly** adv

un·found·ed adj : lacking a sound basis

un·freeze vb -froze; -fro·zen; -freez·ing : thaw

un·friend·ly adj : not friendly or kind —**un·friend·li·ness** n

un·furl vb : unfold or unroll

un·gain·ly adj : clumsy —**un·gain·li·ness** n

un·god·ly adj : wicked —**un·god·li·ness** n

un·grate·ful adj : not thankful for favors —**un·grate·ful·ly** adv —**un·grate·ful·ness** n

un·guent \'əngwənt, 'ən-\ n : ointment

un·hand vb : let go

un·hap·py adj 1 : unfortunate 2 : sad —**un·hap·pi·ly** adv —**un·hap·pi·ness** n

un·healthy adj 1 : not wholesome 2 : not well

un·heard-of \,ən'hərdəv, -,äv\ adj : unprecedented

un·hinge \,ən'hinj\ vb 1 : take from the hinges 2 : make unstable esp. mentally

un·hitch vb : unfasten

un·ho·ly adj : sinister or shocking —**un·ho·li·ness** n

un·hook vb : release from a hook

uni·cel·lu·lar \,yüni'selyələr\ adj : having or consisting of a single cell

uni·corn \'yünə,kórn\ n : legendary animal with one horn in the middle of the forehead

uni·cy·cle \'yüni,sīkəl\ n : pedal-powered vehicle with only a single wheel

uni·di·rec·tion·al \,yünidə'rekshənəl, -dī-\ adj : working in only a single direction

uni·form \'yünə,fórm\ adj : not changing or showing any variation ~ n : distinctive dress worn by members of a particular group —**uni·for·mi·ty** \,yünə'fórmətē\ n —**u·ni·form·ly** adv

uni·fy \'yünə,fī\ vb -**fied**; -**fy·ing** : make into a coherent whole —**uni·fi·ca·tion** \,yünəfə'kāshən\ n

uni·lat·er·al \,yünə'latərəl\ adj : having, affecting, or done by one side only —**uni·lat·er·al·ly** adv

un·im·peach·able adj : blameless

un·in·hib·it·ed adj : free of restraint —**un·in·hib·it·ed·ly** adv

union \'yünyən\ n 1 : act or instance of joining 2 or more things into one or the state of being so joined 2 : confederation of nations or states 3 : organization of workers (**labor union**, **trade union**)

union·ize \'yünyə,nīz\ vb -**ized**; -**iz·ing** : form into a labor union —**union·i·za·tion** \,yünyənə'zāshən\ n

unique \yu̇'nēk\ adj 1 : being the only one of its kind 2 : very unusual —**unique·ly** adv —**unique·ness** n

uni·son \'yünəsən, -nəzən\ n 1 : sameness in pitch 2 : exact agreement

unit \'yünət\ n 1 : smallest whole number 2 : definite amount or quantity used as a standard of measurement 3 : single part of a whole —**unit** adj

unite \yu̇'nīt\ vb **unit·ed**; **unit·ing** : put or join together

uni·ty \'yünətē\ n, pl -**ties** 1 : quality or state of being united or a unit 2 : harmony

uni·ver·sal \,yünə'vərsəl\ adj 1 : relating to or affecting everyone or everything 2 : present or occurring everywhere —**uni·ver·sal·ly** adv

uni·verse \'yünə,vərs\ n : the complete system of all things that exist

uni·ver·si·ty \,yünə'vərsətē\ n, pl -**ties** : institution of higher learning

un·kempt \,ən'kempt\ adj : not neat or combed

un·kind adj : not kind or sympathetic —**un·kind·li·ness** n —**un·kind·ly** adv —**un·kind·ness** n

un·law·ful adj : illegal —**un·law·ful·ly** adv

un·leash vb : free from control or restraint

un·less \ən'les\ conj : except on condition that

un·like \ən'līk, 'ən,līk\ adj 1 : not similar 2 : not equal ∼ prep : different from —**un·like·ly** \ən'līklē\ adv —**un·like·ness** \-nəs\ n —**un·like·li·hood** \-lēhu̇d\ n

un·load vb 1 : take (cargo) from a ve-hicle, vessel, or plane 2 : take a load from 3 : discard

un·lock vb 1 : unfasten through release of a lock 2 : release or reveal

un·lucky adj 1 : experiencing bad luck 2 : likely to bring misfortune —**un·luck·i·ly** adv

un·mis·tak·able adj : not capable of being mistaken or misunderstood —**un·mis·tak·ably** adv

un·moved adj 1 : not emotionally affected 2 : remaining in the same place or position

un·nat·u·ral adj 1 : not natural or spontaneous 2 : abnormal —**un·nat·u·ral·ly** adv —**un·nat·u·ral·ness** n

un·nerve vb : deprive of courage, strength, or steadiness

un·oc·cu·pied adj 1 : not busy 2 : not occupied

un·pack vb 1 : remove (things packed) from a container 2 : remove the contents of (a package)

un·par·al·leled adj : having no equal

un·plug vb 1 : unclog 2 : disconnect from an electric circuit by removing a plug

un·prec·e·dent·ed adj : unlike or superior to anything known before

un·prin·ci·pled adj : unscrupulous

un·ques·tion·able adj : acknowledged as beyond doubt —**un·ques·tion·ably** adv

un·rav·el vb 1 : separate the threads of 2 : solve

un·re·al adj : not real or genuine —**un·re·al·i·ty** n

un·rea·son·ing adj : not using or being guided by reason

un·re·lent·ing adj : not yielding or easing —**un·re·lent·ing·ly** adv

un·rest n : turmoil

un·ri·valed, **un·ri·valled** adj : having no rival

un·roll vb 1 : unwind a roll of 2 : become unrolled

un·ruf·fled adj : not agitated or upset

un·ruly \,ən'rülē\ adj : not readily controlled or disciplined —**un·rul·i·ness** n

un·scathed \,ən'skāthd\ adj : unharmed

un·sci·en·tif·ic adj : not in accord with the principles and methods of science

un·screw vb : loosen or remove by withdrawing screws or by turning

un·scru·pu·lous adj : being or acting in total disregard of conscience, ethical principles, or rights of others —**un·**

scru·pu·lous·ly *adv* —un·scru·pu·lous·ness *n*

un·seal *vb* : break or remove the seal of

un·sea·son·able *adj* : not appropriate or usual for the season —un·sea·son·ably *adv*

un·seem·ly \ən'sēmlē\ *adj* : not polite or in good taste —un·seem·li·ness *n*

un·set·tle *vb* : disturb —un·set·tled *adj*

un·sight·ly \ən'sītlē\ *adj* : not attractive

un·skilled *adj* : not having or requiring a particular skill

un·snap *vb* : loosen by undoing a snap

un·speak·able \ən'spēkəbəl\ *adj* : extremely bad —un·speak·ably \-blē\ *adv*

un·sta·ble *adj* 1 : not mentally or physically balanced 2 : tending to change

un·stop *vb* 1 : unclog 2 : remove a stopper from

un·stop·pa·ble \ən'stäpəbəl\ *adj* : not capable of being stopped

un·strung \ən'strən\ *adj* : nervously tired or anxious

un·sung \ən'sən\ *adj* : not celebrated in song or verse

un·tan·gle *vb* 1 : free from a state of being tangled 2 : find a solution to

un·think·able \ən'thiŋkəbəl\ *adj* : not to be thought of or considered possible

un·think·ing *adj* : careless —un·think·ing·ly *adv*

un·tie *vb* -tied; -ty·ing *or* -tie·ing : open by releasing ties

un·til \ən'til\ *prep* : up to the time of ~ *conj* : to the time that

un·time·ly *adj* 1 : premature 2 : coming at an unfortunate time

un·to \ən'tü, 'ən,-\ *prep* : to

un·told *adj* 1 : not told 2 : too numerous to count

un·tow·ard \ən'tōrd\ *adj* 1 : difficult to manage 2 : inconvenient

un·truth *n* 1 : lack of truthfulness 2 : lie

un·used *adj* 1 \ən'yüst, -'yüzd\ : not accustomed 2 \-'yüzd\ : not used

un·well *adj* : sick

un·wieldy \ən'wēldē\ *adj* : too big or awkward to manage easily

un·wind *vb* -wound; -wind·ing 1 : undo something that is wound 2 : become unwound 3 : relax

un·wit·ting *adj* 1 : not knowing 2 : not intended —un·wit·ting·ly *adv*

un·wont·ed *adj* 1 : unusual 2 : not accustomed by experience

un·wrap *vb* : remove the wrappings from

un·writ·ten *adj* : made or passed on only in speech or through tradition

un·zip *vb* : zip open

up \'əp\ *adv* 1 : in or to a higher position or level 2 : from beneath a surface or level 3 : in or into an upright position 4 : out of bed 5 : to or with greater intensity 6 : into existence, evidence, or knowledge 7 : away 8 — used to indicate a degree of success, completion, or finality 9 : in or into parts ~ *adj* 1 : in the state of having risen 2 : raised to or at a higher level 3 : moving, inclining, or directed upward 4 : in a state of greater intensity 5 : at an end ~ *vb* upped *or in 1* up; upped; up·ping; ups *or in 1* up 1 : act abruptly 2 : move or cause to move upward ~ *prep* 1 : to, toward, or at a higher point of 2 : along or toward the beginning of

up·braid \əp'brād\ *vb* : criticize or scold

up·bring·ing \'əp,briŋiŋ\ *n* : process of bringing up and training

up·com·ing \əp'kəmiŋ\ *adj* : approaching

up·date \əp'dāt\ *vb* : bring up to date —update \'əp,dāt\ *n*

up·end \əp'end\ *vb* 1 : stand or rise on end 2 : overturn

up·grade \'əp,grād\ *n* 1 : upward slope 2 : increase ~ \'əp,-, ,əp'-\ *vb* : raise to a higher position

up·heav·al \əp'hēvəl\ *n* 1 : a heaving up (as of part of the earth's crust) 2 : violent change

up·hill \əp'hil\ *adv* : upward on a hill or incline ~ \'əp,-\ *adj* 1 : going up 2 : difficult

up·hold \əp'hōld\ *vb* -held; -hold·ing : support or defend —up·hold·er *n*

up·hol·ster \əp'hōlstər\ *vb* : cover (furniture) with padding and fabric (up·hol·stery \-stərē\) —up·hol·ster·er *n*

up·keep \'əp,kēp\ *n* : act or cost of keeping up or maintaining

up·land \'əplənd, -,land\ *n* : high land —upland *adj*

up·lift \əp'lift\ *vb* 1 : lift up 2 : improve the condition or spirits of —up·lift \'əp,-\ *n*

up·on \ə'pón, -'pän\ *prep* : on

up·per \'əpər\ *adj* : higher in position, rank, or order ~ *n* : top part of a shoe

upper·hand *n* : advantage

up·per·most \'əpər,mōst\ *adv* : in or into the highest or most prominent position —**uppermost** *adj*

up·pi·ty \'əpətē\ *adj* : acting with a manner of undue importance

up·right \'əp,rīt\ *adj* 1 : vertical 2 : erect in posture 3 : morally correct ~ *n* : something that stands upright —**up·right** *adv* —**up·right·ly** *adv* —**up·right·ness** *n*

up·ris·ing \'əp,rīziŋ\ *n* : revolt

up·roar \'əp,rōr\ *n* : state of commotion or violent disturbance

up·roar·i·ous \,əp'rōrēəs\ *adj* 1 : marked by uproar 2 : extremely funny —**up·roar·i·ous·ly** *adv*

up·root \,əp'rüt, -'rút\ *vb* : remove by or as if by pulling up by the roots

up·set \,əp'set\ *vb* -**set; -set·ting** 1 : force or be forced out of the usual position 2 : disturb emotionally or physically ~ \'əp,-\ *n* 1 : act of throwing into disorder 2 : minor physical disorder ~ *adj* : emotionally disturbed or agitated

up·shot \'əp,shät\ *n* : final result

up·side down \,əp,sīd'daún\ *adv* 1 : turned so that the upper and lower parts are reversed 2 : in or into confusion or disorder —**upside-down** *adj*

up·stairs \'əp,starz, ,əp'-\ *adv* : up the stairs or to the next floor ~ *adj* : situated on the floor above ~ *n sing or pl* : part of a building above the ground floor

up·stand·ing \,əp'standiŋ, 'əp,-\ *adj* : honest

up·start \'əp,stärt\ *n* : one who claims more personal importance than is warranted —**upstart** *adj*

up·swing \'əp,swiŋ\ *n* : marked increase (as in activity)

up·tight \,əp'tīt\ *adj* 1 : tense 2 : angry 3 : rigidly conventional

up-to-date *adj* : current —**up-to-date·ness** *n*

up·town \'əp,taún\ *n* : upper part of a town or city —**uptown** *adj or adv*

up·turn \'əp,tərn\ *n* : improvement or increase

up·ward \'əpwərd\, **up·wards** \-wərdz\ *adv* 1 : in a direction from lower to higher 2 : toward a higher or greater state or number ~ *adj* : directed toward or situated in a higher place —**up·ward·ly** *adv*

up·wind \,əp'wind\ *adv or adj* : in the direction from which the wind is blowing

ura·ni·um \yú'rānēəm\ *n* : metallic radioactive chemical element

ur·ban \'ərbən\ *adj* : characteristic of a city

ur·bane \,ər'bān\ *adj* : polished in manner —**ur·ban·i·ty** \,ər'banətē\ *n*

ur·ban·ite \'ərbə,nīt\ *n* : city dweller

ur·chin \'ərchən\ *n* : mischievous youngster

-ure *n suffix* : act or process

ure·thra \yú'rēthrə\ *n, pl* -**thras** or -**thrae** \-,thrē\ : canal that carries off urine from the bladder —**ure·thral** \-thrəl\ *adj*

urge \'ərj\ *vb* **urged; urging** 1 : earnestly plead for or insist on (an action) 2 : try to persuade 3 : impel to a course of activity ~ *n* : force or impulse that moves one to action

ur·gent \'ərjənt\ *adj* 1 : calling for immediate attention 2 : urging insistently —**ur·gen·cy** \-jənsē\ *n* —**ur·gent·ly** *adv*

uri·nal \'yúrən³l\ *n* : receptacle to urinate in

uri·nate \'yúrə,nāt\ *vb* -**nat·ed; -nat·ing** : discharge urine —**uri·na·tion** \,yúrə'nāshən\ *n*

urine \'yúrən\ *n* : liquid waste material from the kidneys —**uri·nary** \-ə,nerē\ *adj*

urn \'ərn\ *n* 1 : vaselike or cuplike vessel on a pedestal 2 : large coffee pot

us \'əs\ *pron, objective case of* WE

us·able \'yüzəbəl\ *adj* : suitable or fit for use —**us·abil·i·ty** \,yüzə'bilətē\ *n*

us·age \'yüsij, -zij\ *n* 1 : customary practice 2 : way of doing or of using something

use \'yüs\ *n* 1 : act or practice of putting something into action 2 : state of being used 3 : way of using 4 : privilege, ability, or power to use something 5 : utility or function 6 : occasion or need to use ~ \'yüz\ *vb* **used** \'yüzd; *"used to" usu* \'yüstə\; **us·ing** \'yüziŋ\ 1 ` : put into action or service 2 : consume 3 : behave toward 4 : to make use of 5 —used in the past tense with *to* to indicate a former practice —**use·ful** \'yüsfəl\ *adj* —**use·ful·ly** *adv* —**use·ful·ness** *n* —**use·less** \'yüsləs\ *adj* —**use·less·ly** *adv* —**use·less·ness** *n* —**us·er** *n*

used \'yüzd\ *adj* : not new

ush·er \'əshər\ *n* : one who escorts people to their seats ~ *vb* : conduct to a place

ush·er·ette \,əshə'ret\ *n* : woman or girl who is an usher

usu·al \'yüzhəwəl\ *adj* : being what is expected according to custom or habit —**usu·al·ly** \'yüzhəwəlē\ *adv*

usurp \yü'sərp, -'zərp\ *vb* : seize and hold by force or without right —**usur·pa·tion** \,yüsər'pāshən, -zər-\ *n* —**usurp·er** *n*

usu·ry \'yüzhərē\ *n, pl* -ries 1 : lending of money at excessive interest or the rate or amount of such interest —**usu·rer** \-zhərər\ *n* —**usu·ri·ous** \yü-'zhürēəs\ *adj*

uten·sil \yü'tensəl\ *n* 1 : eating or cooking tool 2 : useful tool

uter·us \'yütərəs\ *n, pl* uteri \-,rī\ : organ for containing and nourishing an unborn offspring —**uter·ine** \-,rīn, -rən\ *adj*

util·i·tar·i·an \yü,tilə'terēən\ *adj* : being or meant to be useful rather than beautiful

util·i·ty \yü'tilətē\ *n, pl* -ties 1 : usefulness 2 : regulated business providing a public service (as electricity)

uti·lize \'yüt³l,īz\ *vb* -lized; -liz·ing : make use of —**uti·li·za·tion** \,yüt³lə'zāshən\ *n*

ut·most \'ət,mōst\ *adj* 1 : most distant 2 : of the greatest or highest degree or amount —**utmost** *n*

uto·pia \yü'tōpēə\ *n* : place of ideal perfection —**uto·pi·an** \-pēən\ *adj or n*

ut·ter \'ətər\ *adj* : absolute ~ *vb* : express with the voice —**ut·ter·er** \-ərər\ *n* —**ut·ter·ly** *adv*

ut·ter·ance \'ətərəns\ *n* : what one says

V

v \'vē\ *n, pl* **v's** *or* **vs** \'vēz\ : 22d letter of the alphabet

va·can·cy \'vākənsē\ *n, pl* -cies 1 : state of being vacant 2 : unused or unoccupied place or office

va·cant \-kənt\ *adj* 1 : not occupied, filled, or in use 2 : devoid of thought or expression —**va·cant·ly** *adv*

va·cate \-,kāt\ *vb* -cat·ed; -cat·ing 1 : annul 2 : leave unfilled or unoccupied

va·ca·tion \vā'kāshən, və-\ *n* : period of rest from routine —**vacation** *vb* —**va·ca·tion·er** *n*

vac·ci·nate \'vaksə,nāt\ *vb* -nat·ed; -nat·ing : administer a vaccine usu. by injection

vac·ci·na·tion \,vaksə'nāshən\ *n* : act of or the scar left by vaccinating

vac·cine \vak'sēn, 'vak,-\ *n* : substance to induce immunity to a disease

vac·il·late \'vasə,lāt\ *vb* -lat·ed; -lat·ing : waver between courses or opinions —**vac·il·la·tion** \,vasə'lāshən\ *n*

vac·u·ous \'vakyəwəs\ *adj* 1 : empty 2 : dull or inane —**va·cu·ity** \va'kyüətē, və-\ *n* —**vac·u·ous·ly** *adv* —**vac·u·ous·ness** *n*

vac·u·um \'vak,yüm, -yəm\ *n, pl* **vac·u·ums** *or* **vac·ua** \-yəwə\ : empty space with no air ~ *vb* : clean with a vacuum cleaner

vacuum cleaner *n* : appliance that cleans by suction

vag·a·bond \'vagə,bänd\ *n* : wanderer with no home —**vagabond** *adj*

va·ga·ry \'vāgərē, və'gerē\ *n, pl* -ries : whim

va·gi·na \və'jīnə\ *n, pl* -nae \-,nē\ *or* -nas : canal that leads out from the uterus —**vag·i·nal** \'vajən³l\ *adj*

va·grant \'vāgrənt\ *n* : person with no home and no job —**va·gran·cy** \-grənsē\ *n* —**vagrant** *adj*

vague \'vāg\ *adj* **vagu·er; vagu·est** : not clear, definite, or distinct —**vague·ly** *adv* —**vague·ness** *n*

vain \'vān\ *adj* 1 : of no value 2 : unsuccessful 3 : conceited —**vain·ly** *adv*

va·lance \'valəns, 'vāl-\ *n* : border drapery

vale \'vāl\ *n* : valley

vale·dic·to·ri·an \,valə,dik'tōrēən\ *n* : student giving the farewell address at commencement

vale·dic·to·ry \-'diktərē\ adj : bidding farewell —**valedictory** n

va·lence \'vāləns\ n : degree of combining power of a chemical element

val·en·tine \'valən,tīn\ n : sweetheart or a card sent to a sweetheart or friend on St. Valentine's Day

va·let \'valət, 'val,ā, va'lā\ n : male personal servant

val·iant \'valyənt\ adj : brave or heroic —**val·iant·ly** adv

val·id \'valəd\ adj 1 : proper and legally binding 2 : founded on truth or fact —**va·lid·i·ty** \və'lidətē, va-\ n —**val·id·ly** adv

val·i·date \'valə,dāt\ vb -**dat·ed**; -**dat·ing** : establish as valid —**val·i·da·tion** \,valə'dāshən\ n

va·lise \və'lēs\ n : suitcase

val·ley \'valē\ n, pl -**leys** : long depression between ranges of hills

val·or \'valər\ n : bravery or heroism —**val·or·ous** \'valərəs\ adj

valu·able \'valyəwəbəl\ adj 1 : worth a lot of money 2 : being of great importance or use —**valuable** n

val·u·a·tion \,valyə'wāshən\ n 1 : act or process of valuing 2 : market value of a thing

val·ue \'valyü\ n 1 : fair return or equivalent for something exchanged 2 : how much something is worth 3 : distinctive quality (as of a color or sound) 4 : guiding principle or ideal—usu. pl. ~ vb **val·ued**; **val·u·ing** 1 : estimate the worth of 2 : appreciate the importance of —**val·ue·less** adj —**val·u·er** n

valve \'valv\ n : structure or device to control flow of a liquid or gas —**valved** \'valvd\ adj —**valve·less** adj

vam·pire \'vam,pīr\ n 1 : legendary night-wandering dead body that sucks human blood 2 : bat that feeds on the blood of animals

1van \'van\ n : vanguard

2van n : enclosed truck

va·na·di·um \və'nādēəm\ n : soft ductile metallic chemical element

van·dal \'vandᵊl\ n : person who willfully defaces or destroys property —**van·dal·ism** \-,izəm\ n —**van·dal·ize** \-,īz\ vb

vane \'vān\ n : bladelike device designed to be moved by force of the air or water

van·guard \'van,gärd\ n 1 : troops moving at the front of an army 2 : forefront of an action or movement

va·nil·la \və'nilə\ n : a flavoring made from the pods of a tropical orchid or this orchid

van·ish \'vanish\ vb : disappear suddenly

van·i·ty \'vanətē\ n, pl -**ties** 1 : futility or something that is futile 2 : undue pride in oneself 3 : makeup case or table

van·quish \'vankwish, 'van-\ vb 1 : overcome in battle or in a contest 2 : gain mastery over

van·tage \'vantij\ n : position of advantage or perspective

va·pid \'vapəd, 'vāpəd\ adj : lacking spirit, liveliness, or zest —**va·pid·i·ty** \va'pidətē\ n —**vap·id·ly** \'vapədlē\ adv —**vap·id·ness** n

va·por \'vāpər\ n 1 : fine separated particles floating in and clouding the air 2 : gaseous form of an ordinarily liquid substance —**va·por·ous** \-pərəs\ adj

va·por·ize \'vāpə,rīz\ vb -**ized**; -**iz·ing** : convert into vapor —**va·por·i·za·tion** \,vāpərə'zāshən\ n —**va·por·iz·er** n

vari·able \'verēəbəl\ adj : apt to vary —**vari·abil·i·ty** \,verēə'bilətē\ n —**vari·able** n —**vari·ably** adv

vari·ance \'verēəns\ n 1 : instance or degree of variation 2 : disagreement or dispute 3 : legal permission to build contrary to a zoning law

vari·ant \-ənt\ n : something that differs from others of its kind —**variant** adj

vari·a·tion \,verē'āshən\ n : instance or extent of varying

vari·cose \'varə,kōs\ adj : abnormally swollen and dilated

var·ied \'verēd\ adj : showing variety —**var·ied·ly** adv

var·ie·gat·ed \'verēə,gātəd\ adj : having patches, stripes, or marks of different colors —**var·ie·gate** \-,gāt\ vb —**var·ie·ga·tion** \,verēə'gāshən\ n

va·ri·ety \və'rīətē\ n, pl -**et·ies** 1 : state of being different 2 : collection of different things 3 : something that differs from others of its kind

var·i·ous \'verēəs\ adj : being many and unlike —**var·i·ous·ly** adv

var·nish \'värnish\ *n* : liquid that dries to a hard glossy protective coating ~ *vb* : cover with varnish

var·si·ty \'värsətē\ *n, pl* **-ties** : principal team representing a school

vary \'verē\ *vb* **var·ied; vary·ing 1** : alter **2** : make or be of different kinds

vas·cu·lar \'vaskyələr\ *adj* : relating to a channel for the conveyance of a body fluid (as blood or sap)

vase \'vās, 'vāz\ *n* : tall usu. ornamental container to hold flowers

vas·sal \'vasəl\ *n* **1** : one acknowledging another as feudal lord **2** : one in a dependent position —**vas·sal·age** \-əlij\ *n*

vast \'vast\ *adj* : very great in size, extent, or amount —**vast·ly** *adv* —**vast·ness** *n*

vat \'vat\ *n* : large tub- or barrel-shaped container

vaude·ville \'vódvəl, 'väd-, 'vōd-, -ˌvil, -əvəl, -ə,vil\ *n* : stage entertainment of unrelated acts

¹**vault** \'vólt\ *n* **1** : masonry arch **2** : usu. underground storage or burial room ~ *vb* : form or cover with a vault —**vault·ed** *adj* —**vaulty** *adj*

²**vault** *vb* : spring over esp. with the help of the hands or a pole ~ *n* : act of vaulting —**vault·er** *n*

vaunt \'vónt\ *vb* : boast —**vaunt** *n*

veal \'vēl\ *n* : flesh of a young calf

veer \'vir\ *vb* : change course esp. gradually —**veer** *n*

veg·e·ta·ble \'vejtəbəl, 'vejə-\ *adj* **1** : relating to or obtained from plants **2** : like that of a plant ~ *n* **1** : plant **2** : plant grown for food

veg·e·tar·i·an \ˌvejə'tereən\ *n* : person who eats no meat —**vegetarian** *adj* —**veg·e·tar·i·an·ism** \-ē,nizəm\ *n*

veg·e·tate \'vejə,tāt\ *vb* **-tat·ed; -tat·ing** : lead a dull inert life

veg·e·ta·tion \ˌvejə'tāshən\ *n* : plant life —**veg·e·ta·tion·al** \-shənəl\ *adj* —**veg·e·ta·tive** \'vejə,tātiv\ *adj*

ve·he·ment \'vēəmənt\ *adj* : showing strong esp. violent feeling —**ve·he·mence** \-məns\ *n* —**ve·he·ment·ly** *adv*

ve·hi·cle \'vē,hikəl, 'vēəkəl\ *n* **1** : medium through which something is expressed, applied, or administered **2** : structure for transporting something esp. on wheels —**ve·hic·u·lar** \vē-'hikyələr\ *adj*

veil \'vāl\ *n* **1** : sheer material to hide something or to cover the face and head **2** : something that hides ~ *vb* : cover with a veil

vein \'vān\ *n* **1** : rock fissure filled with deposited mineral matter **2** : vessel that carries blood toward the heart **3** : sap-carrying tube in a leaf **4** : distinctive element or style of expression —**veined** \'vānd\ *adj*

ve·loc·i·ty \və'läsətē\ *n, pl* **-ties** : speed

ve·lour, ve·lours \və'lúr\ *n, pl* **velours** \-'lúrz\ : fabric with a velvetlike pile

vel·vet \'velvət\ *n* : fabric with a short soft pile —**velvet** *adj* —**vel·vety** *adj*

ve·nal \'vēnˀl\ *adj* : capable of being corrupted esp. by money —**ve·nal·i·ty** \vi'nalətē\ *n* —**ve·nal·ly** *adv*

vend \'vend\ *vb* : sell —**vend·ible** *adj* —**ven·dor** \'vendər\ *n*

ven·det·ta \ven'detə\ *n* : feud marked by acts of revenge

ve·neer \və'nir\ *n* **1** : thin layer of fine wood glued over a cheaper wood **2** : superficial display ~ *vb* : overlay with a veneer

ven·er·a·ble \'venərəbəl\ *adj* : deserving of respect

ven·er·ate \'venə,rāt\ *vb* **-at·ed; -at·ing** : respect esp. with reverence —**ven·er·a·tion** \ˌvenə'rāshən\ *n*

venereal disease \və'nirēəl-\ *n* : contagious disease spread through copulation

ven·geance \'venjəns\ *n* : punishment in retaliation for an injury or offense

venge·ful \'venjfəl\ *adj* : filled with a desire for revenge —**venge·ful·ly** *adv*

ve·nial \'vēnēəl\ *adj* : capable of being forgiven

ven·i·son \'venəsən, -əzən\ *n* : deer meat

ven·om \'venəm\ *n* **1** : poison secreted by certain animals **2** : ill will —**ven·om·ous** \-əməs\ *adj*

vent \'vent\ *vb* **1** : provide with or let out at a vent **2** : give expression to ~ *n* : opening for passage or for relieving pressure

ven·ti·late \'ventˀl,āt\ *vb* **-lat·ed; -lat·ing** : allow fresh air to circulate through —**ven·ti·la·tion** \ˌventˀl-'āshən\ *n* —**ven·ti·la·tor** \'ventˀl-,ātər\ *n*

ven·tri·cle \'ventrikəl\ *n* : heart chamber that pumps blood into the arteries

ven·tril·o·quist \ven'trilə,kwist\ *n* : one who can make the voice appear to come from another source —**ven·tril·o·quism** \-,kwizəm\ *n* —**ven·tril·o·quy** \-kwē\ *n*

ven·ture \'venchər\ *vb* **-tured; -tur·ing** 1 : risk or take a chance on 2 : put forward (an opinion) ~ *n* : speculative business enterprise

ven·ture·some \-səm\ *adj* : brave or daring —**ven·ture·some·ly** *adv* —**ven·ture·some·ness** *n*

ven·ue \'venyü\ *n* : scene of an action or event

ve·rac·i·ty \və'rasətē\ *n, pl* **-ties** : truthfulness or accuracy —**ve·ra·cious** \və'rāshəs\ *adj*

ve·ran·da, ve·ran·dah \və'randə\ *n* : large open porch

verb \'vərb\ *n* : word that expresses action or existence

ver·bal \'vərbəl\ *adj* 1 : having to do with or expressed in words 2 : oral 3 : relating to or formed from a verb —**ver·bal·i·za·tion** \,vərbələ'zāshən\ *n* —**ver·bal·ize** \'vərbə,līz\ *vb* —**ver·bal·ly** \-ē\ *adv*

verbal auxiliary *n* : auxiliary verb

ver·ba·tim \vər'bātəm\ *adv or adj* : using the same words

ver·biage \'vərbēij\ *n* : excess of words

ver·bose \vər'bōs\ *adj* : using more words than are needed —**ver·bos·i·ty** \-'bäsətē\ *n*

ver·dant \'vərdᵊnt\ *adj* : green with growing plants —**ver·dant·ly** *adv*

ver·dict \'vərdikt\ *n* : decision of a jury

ver·dure \'vərjər\ *n* : green growing vegetation or its color

verge \'vərj\ *vb* **verged; verg·ing** : be almost on the point of happening or doing something ~ *n* 1 : edge 2 : threshold

ver·i·fy \'verə,fī\ *vb* **-fied; -fy·ing** : establish the truth, accuracy, or reality of —**ver·i·fi·able** *adj* —**ver·i·fi·ca·tion** \,verəfə'kāshən\ *n*

ver·i·ly \'verəlē\ *adv* : truly or confidently

ver·i·si·mil·i·tude \,verəsə'milə,tüd\ *n* : appearance of being true

ver·i·ta·ble \'verətəbəl\ *adj* : actual or true —**ver·i·ta·bly** *adv*

ver·i·ty \'verətē\ *n, pl* **-ties** : truth

ver·mi·cel·li \,vərmə'chelē, -'sel-\ *n* : thin spaghetti

ver·min \'vərmən\ *n, pl* **vermin** : small animal pest

ver·mouth \vər'müth\ *n* : dry or sweet wine flavored with herbs

ver·nac·u·lar \vər'nakyələr\ *adj* : relating to a native language or dialect and esp. its normal spoken form ~ *n* : vernacular language

ver·nal \'vərnᵊl\ *adj* : relating to spring

ver·sa·tile \'vərsətᵊl\ *adj* : having many abilities or uses —**ver·sa·til·i·ty** \,vərsə'tilətē\ *n*

¹verse \'vərs\ *n* 1 : line or stanza of poetry 2 : poetry 3 : short division of a chapter in the Bible

²verse *vb* **versed; vers·ing** : make familiar by experience, study, or practice

ver·sion \'vərzhən\ *n* 1 : translation of the Bible 2 : account or description from a particular point of view

ver·sus \'vərsəs\ *prep* : opposed to or against

ver·te·bra \'vərtəbrə\ *n, pl* **-brae** \-,brā, -,brē\ *or* **-bras** : segment of the backbone —**ver·te·bral** \vər'tēbrəl, 'vərtə-\ *adj*

ver·te·brate \'vərtəbrət, -,brāt\ *n* : animal with a backbone —**vertebrate** *adj*

ver·tex \'vər,teks\ *n, pl* **ver·ti·ces** \'vərtə,sēz\ 1 : point of intersection of lines or surfaces 2 : highest point

ver·ti·cal \'vərtikəl\ *adj* : rising straight up from a level surface —**vertical** *n* —**ver·ti·cal·i·ty** \,vərtə'kalətē\ *n* —**ver·ti·cal·ly** *adv*

ver·ti·go \'vərti,gō\ *n, pl* **-goes** *or* **-gos** : dizziness

verve \'vərv\ *n* : liveliness or vividness

very \'verē\ *adj* **veri·er; -est** 1 : exact 2 : exactly suitable 3 : mere or bare 4 : precisely the same ~ *adv* 1 : to a high degree 2 : in actual fact

ves·i·cle \'vesikəl\ *n* : membranous cavity —**ve·sic·u·lar** \və'sikyələr\ *adj*

ves·pers \'vespərz\ *n pl* : late afternoon or evening worship service

ves·sel \'vesəl\ *n* 1 : a container (as a barrel, bottle, bowl, or cup) for a liquid 2 : craft for navigation esp. on water 3 : tube in which a body fluid is circulated

¹vest \'vest\ *vb* 1 : give a particular authority, right, or property to 2 : clothe with or as if with a garment

²vest *n* : sleeveless garment usu. worn under a suit coat

ves·ti·bule \'vestə,byül\ *n* : enclosed entrance —**ves·tib·u·lar** \ve'stibyələr\ *adj*

ves·tige \'vestij\ *n* : visible trace or remains —**ves·ti·gial** \ve'stijēəl\ *adj* —**ves·ti·gial·ly** *adv*

vest·ment \'vestmənt\ *n* : clergy member's garment

ves·try \'vestrē\ *n, pl* **-tries** : church storage room for garments and articles

vet·er·an \'vetərən\ *n* 1 : former member of the armed forces 2 : person with long experience —**veteran** *adj*

Veterans Day *n* : 4th Monday in October or formerly November 11 observed as a legal holiday in commemoration of the end of war in 1918 and 1945

vet·er·i·nar·i·an \,vetərən'erēən\ *n* : doctor of animals —**vet·er·i·nary** \'vetərən,erē\ *adj*

ve·to \'vētō\ *n, pl* **-toes** 1 : power to forbid and esp. the power of a chief executive to prevent a bill from becoming law 2 : exercise of the veto ~ *vb* 1 : forbid 2 : reject a legislative bill

vex \'veks\ *vb* **vexed; vex·ing** : trouble, distress, or annoy —**vex·a·tion** \vek·'sāshən\ *n* —**vex·a·tious** \-shəs\ *adj*

via \'vīə, 'vēə\ *prep* : by way of

vi·a·ble \'vīəbəl\ *adj* 1 : capable of surviving or growing 2 : practical or workable —**vi·a·bil·i·ty** \,vīə'bilətē\ *n* —**vi·a·bly** \'vīəblē\ *adv*

via·duct \'vīə,dəkt\ *n* : elevated roadway or railway bridge

vi·al \'vīəl\ *n* : small bottle

vi·brant \'vībrənt\ *adj* 1 : vibrating 2 : pulsing with vigor or activity 3 : sounding from vibration —**vi·bran·cy** \-brənsē\ *n*

vi·brate \'vī,brāt\ *vb* **-brat·ed; -brat·ing** 1 : move or cause to move quickly back and forth or side to side 2 : respond sympathetically —**vi·bra·tion** \vī'brāshən\ *n* —**vi·bra·tor** \'vī,brātər\ *n* —**vi·bra·to·ry** \'vībrə,tórē\ *adj*

vic·ar \'vikər\ *n* : parish clergy member —**vi·car·i·ate** \-ēət\ *n*

vi·car·i·ous \vī'karēəs\ *adj* : sharing in someone else's experience through imagination or sympathetic feelings —**vi·car·i·ous·ly** *adv* —**vi·car·i·ous·ness** *n*

vice \'vīs\ *n* 1 : immoral habit 2 : depravity

vice- \,vīs\ *prefix* : one that takes the place of

vice-chancellor	vice president
vice-consul	vice presidential
vice presidency	vice-regent

vice admiral *n* : commissioned officer in the navy or coast guard ranking above a rear admiral

vice·roy \'vīs,rói\ *n* : provincial governor who represents the sovereign

vice ver·sa \,vīsi'vərsə, ,vīs'vər-\ *adv* : with the order reversed

vi·cin·i·ty \və'sinətē\ *n, pl* **-ties** : surrounding area

vi·cious \'vishəs\ *adj* 1 : wicked 2 : savage 3 : malicious —**vi·cious·ly** *adv* —**vi·cious·ness** *n*

vi·cis·si·tude \və'sisə,tüd, vī-, -,tyüd\ *n* : irregular, unexpected, or surprising change —usu. used in pl.

vic·tim \'viktəm\ *n* : person killed, hurt, or abused

vic·tim·ize \'viktə,mīz\ *vb* **-ized; -iz·ing** : make a victim of —**vic·tim·i·za·tion** \,viktəmə'zāshən\ *n* —**vic·tim·iz·er** \'viktə,mīzər\ *n*

vic·tor \'viktər\ *n* : winner

Vic·to·ri·an \vik'tōrēən\ *adj* : relating to the reign of Queen Victoria of England or the art, taste, or standards of her time ~ *n* : one of the Victorian period

vic·to·ri·ous \vik'tōrēəs\ *adj* : having won a victory —**vic·to·ri·ous·ly** *adv*

vic·to·ry \'viktərē\ *n, pl* **-ries** : success in defeating an enemy or opponent or in overcoming difficulties

vict·uals \'vit³lz\ *n pl* : food

vid·eo \'vidē,ō\ *adj* : relating to the television image

vid·eo·cas·sette \,vidē,ōkə'set\ *n* : cassette containing videotape

vid·eo·tape \'vidēō,tāp\ *vb* : make a recording of (a television production) on special tape —**videotape** *n*

vie \'vī\ *vb* **vied; vy·ing** : contend —**vi·er** \'vīər\ *n*

view \'vyü\ *n* 1 : process of seeing or examining 2 : opinion 3 : area of landscape that can be seen 4 : range of vision 5 : purpose or object ~ *vb* 1 : look at 2 : think about or consider —**view·er** *n*

view·point *n* : position from which something is considered

vigil \'vijəl\ *n* 1 : day of devotion before a religious feast 2 : act or time of keeping awake 3 : long period of keeping watch (as over a sick or dying person)

vig·i·lant \'vijələnt\ *adj* : alert esp. to avoid danger —**vig·i·lance** \-ləns\ *n* —**vig·i·lant·ly** *adv*

vig·i·lan·te \,vijə'lantē\ *n* : one of a group independent of the law working to suppress crime

vi·gnette \vin'yet\ *n* : short descriptive literary piece

vig·or \'vigər\ *n* 1 : energy or strength 2 : intensity or force —**vig·or·ous** \'vigərəs\ *adj* —**vig·or·ous·ly** *adv* —**vig·or·ous·ness** *n*

vile \'vīl\ *adj* **vil·er; vil·est** : thoroughly bad or contemptible —**vile·ly** *adv* —**vile·ness** *n*

vil·i·fy \'vilə,fī\ *vb* **-fied; -fy·ing** : speak evil of —**vil·i·fi·ca·tion** \,viləfə'kāshən\ *n* —**vil·i·fi·er** \-lə,fīər\ *n*

vil·la \'vilə\ *n* : country estate

vil·lage \'vilij\ *n* : small country town —**vil·lag·er** *n*

vil·lain \'vilən\ *n* : bad person —**vil·lain·ess** \-ənəs\ *n* —**vil·lainy** *n*

vil·lain·ous \-ənəs\ *adj* : evil or corrupt —**vil·lain·ous·ly** *adv* —**vil·lain·ous·ness** *n*

vim \'vim\ *n* : energy

vin·di·cate \'vində,kāt\ *vb* **-cat·ed; -cat·ing** 1 : avenge 2 : exonerate 3 : justify —**vin·di·ca·tion** \,vində'kāshən\ *n* —**vin·di·ca·tor** \'vində,kātər\ *n*

vin·dic·tive \vin'diktiv\ *adj* : seeking or meant for revenge —**vin·dic·tive·ly** *adv* —**vin·dic·tive·ness** *n*

vine \'vīn\ *n* : climbing or trailing plant

vin·e·gar \'vinigər\ *n* : acidic liquid obtained by fermentation —**vin·e·gary** \-gərē\ *adj*

vine·yard \'vinyərd\ *n* : plantation of grapevines

vin·tage \'vintij\ *n* 1 : season's yield of grapes or wine 2 : period of origin ~ *adj* : of enduring interest

vi·nyl \'vīnᵊl\ *n* : strong plastic

vi·o·la \vē'ōlə\ *n* : instrument of the violin family tuned lower than the violin —**vi·o·list** \-list\ *n*

vi·o·late \'vīə,lāt\ *vb* **-lat·ed; -lat·ing** 1 : act with disrespect or disregard of 2 : rape 3 : desecrate —**vi·o·la·tion** \,vīə'lāshən\ *n* —**vi·o·la·tor** \'vīə,lātər\ *n*

vi·o·lence \'vīələns\ *n* : intense physical force that causes or is intended to cause injury or destruction —**vi·o·lent** \-lənt\ *adj* —**vi·o·lent·ly** *adv*

vi·o·let \'vīələt\ *n* 1 : small flowering plant 2 : reddish blue

vi·o·lin \,vīə'lin\ *n* : bowed stringed instrument —**vi·o·lin·ist** \-nist\ *n*

VIP \,vē,ī'pē\ *n, pl* **VIPs** \-'pēz\ : very important person

vi·per \'vīpər\ *n* 1 : venomous snake 2 : treacherous or malignant person

vi·ra·go \və'rägō, -'rā-; 'virə,gō\ *n, pl* **-goes** *or* **-gos** : shrew

vi·ral \'vīrəl\ *adj* : relating to or caused by a virus

vir·gin \'vərjən\ *n* 1 : unmarried woman 2 : a person who has never had sexual intercourse ~ *adj* 1 : chaste 2 : natural and unspoiled —**vir·gin·al** \-əl\ *adj* —**vir·gin·al·ly** *adv* —**vir·gin·i·ty** \vər'jinətē\ *n*

vir·gule \'vərgyül\ *n* : mark / used esp. to denote "or" or "per"

vir·ile \'virəl\ *adj* : masculine —**vi·ril·i·ty** \və'rilətē\ *n*

vir·tu·al \'vərchəwəl\ *adj* : being in effect but not in fact or name —**vir·tu·al·ly** *adv*

vir·tue \'vərchü\ *n* 1 : moral excellence 2 : effective or commendable quality 3 : chastity

vir·tu·os·i·ty \,vərchə'wäsətē\ *n, pl* **-ties** : great skill (as in music)

vir·tu·o·so \,vərchə'wōsō, -zō\ *n, pl* **-sos** *or* **-si** \-,sē, -,zē\ : highly skilled performer esp. of music —**virtuoso** *adj*

vir·tu·ous \'vərchəwəs\ *adj* 1 : morally good 2 : chaste —**vir·tu·ous·ly** *adv*

vir·u·lent \'virələnt, -yələnt\ *adj* 1 : extremely severe or infectious 2 : full of malice —**vir·u·lence** \-ləns\ *n* —**vir·u·lent·ly** *adv*

vi·rus \'vīrəs\ *n* 1 : tiny disease-causing agent 2 : a computer program that performs a malicious action (as destroying data)

vi·sa \'vēzə, -sə\ *n* : authorization to enter a foreign country

vis·age \'vizij\ *n* : face

vis·cera \'visərə\ *n pl* : internal bodily organs esp. of the trunk

vis·cer·al \'visərəl\ *adj* 1 : bodily 2 : instinctive 3 : deeply or crudely emotional —**vis·cer·al·ly** *adv*

vis·cid \'visəd\ *adj* : viscous —**vis·cid·i·ty** \vis'idətē\ *n*

vis·count \'vī,kaůnt\ *n* : British nobleman ranking below an earl and above a baron

vis·count·ess \-əs\ *n* 1 : wife of a viscount 2 : woman with rank of a viscount

vis·cous \'viskəs\ *adj* : having a thick or sticky consistency —**vis·cos·i·ty** \vis-'käsətē\ *n*

vise \'vīs\ *n* : device for clamping something being worked on

vis·i·bil·i·ty \,vizə'bilətē\ *n, pl* -ties : degree or range to which something can be seen

vis·i·ble \'vizəbəl\ *adj* 1 : capable of being seen 2 : manifest or apparent —**vis·i·bly** *adv*

vi·sion \'vizhən\ *n* 1 : vivid picture seen in a dream or trance or in the imagination 2 : foresight 3 : power of seeing ~ *vb* : imagine

vi·sion·ary \'vizhə,nerē\ *adj* 1 : given to dreaming or imagining 2 : illusory 3 : not practical ~ *n* : one with great dreams or projects

vis·it \'vizət\ *vb* 1 : go or come to see 2 : stay with for a time as a guest 3 : cause or be a reward, affliction, or punishment ~ *n* : short stay as a guest —**vis·it·able** *adj* —**vis·i·tor** \-ər\ *n*

vis·i·ta·tion \,vizə'tāshən\ *n* 1 : official visit 2 : divine punishment or favor 3 : severe trial

vi·sor \'vīzər\ *n* 1 : front piece of a helmet 2 : part (as on a cap or car windshield) that shades the eyes

vis·ta \'vistə\ *n* : distant view

vi·su·al \'vizhəwəl\ *adj* 1 : relating to sight 2 : visible —**vi·su·al·ly** *adv*

vi·su·al·ize \'vizhəwə,līz\ *vb* -ized; -iz·ing : form a mental image of —**vi·su·al·i·za·tion** \,vizhəwələ'zāshən\ *n* —**vi·su·al·iz·er** \'vizhəwə,līzər\ *n*

vi·tal \'vīt³l\ *adj* 1 : relating to, necessary for, or characteristic of life 2 : full of life and vigor 3 : fatal 4 : very important —**vi·tal·ly** *adv*

vi·tal·i·ty \vī'talətē\ *n, pl* -ties 1 : life force 2 : energy

vital signs *n pl* : body's pulse rate, respiration, temperature, and usu. blood pressure

vi·ta·min \'vītəmən\ *n* : natural organic substance essential to health

vi·ti·ate \'vishē,āt\ *vb* -at·ed; -at·ing 1

: spoil or impair 2 : invalidate —**vi·ti·a·tion** \,vishē'āshən\ *n* —**vi·ti·a·tor** \'vishē,ātər\ *n*

vit·re·ous \'vitrēəs\ *adj* : relating to or resembling glass

vit·ri·ol \'vitrēəl\ *n* : something caustic, corrosive, or biting —**vit·ri·ol·ic** \,vitrē'älik\ *adj*

vi·tu·per·ate \vī'tüpə,rāt, və, -'tyü-\ *vb* -at·ed; -at·ing : abuse in words —**vi·tu·per·a·tion** \-,tüpə'rāshən, -,tyü-\ *n* —**vi·tu·per·a·tive** \-'tüpərətiv, -'tyü-, -pə,rāt-\ *adj* —**vi·tu·per·a·tive·ly** *adv*

vi·va·cious \və'vāshəs, vī-\ *adj* : lively —**vi·va·cious·ly** *adv* —**vi·va·cious·ness** *n* —**vi·vac·i·ty** \-'vasətē\ *n*

viv·id \'vivəd\ *adj* 1 : lively 2 : brilliant 3 : intense or sharp —**viv·id·ly** *adv* —**viv·id·ness** *n*

viv·i·fy \'vivə,fī\ *vb* -fied; -fy·ing : give life or vividness to

vivi·sec·tion \,vivə'sekshən, 'vivə,-\ *n* : experimental operation on a living animal

vix·en \'viksən\ *n* 1 : scolding woman 2 : female fox

vo·cab·u·lary \vō'kabyə,lerē\ *n, pl* -lar·ies 1 : list or collection of words 2 : stock of words used by a person or about a subject

vo·cal \'vōkəl\ *adj* 1 : relating to or produced by or for the voice 2 : speaking out freely and usu. emphatically

vocal cords *n pl* : membranous folds in the larynx that are important in making vocal sounds

vo·cal·ist \'vōkəlist\ *n* : singer

vo·cal·ize \-,līz\ *vb* -ized; -iz·ing : give vocal expression to

vo·ca·tion \vō'kāshən\ *n* : regular employment —**vo·ca·tion·al** \-shənəl\ *adj*

vo·cif·er·ous \vō'sifərəs\ *adj* : noisy and insistent —**vo·cif·er·ous·ly** *adv*

vod·ka \'vädkə\ *n* : colorless distilled grain liquor

vogue \'vōg\ *n* : brief but intense popularity —**vogu·ish** \'vōgish\ *adj*

voice \'vóis\ *n* 1 : sound produced through the mouth by humans and many animals 2 : power of speaking 3 : right of choice or opinion ~ *vb* voiced; voic·ing : express in words —**voiced** \'vóist\ *adj*

void \'vóid\ *adj* 1 : containing nothing

2 : lacking —with *of* 3 : not legally binding ~ *n* 1 : empty space 2 : feeling of hollowness ~ *vb* 1 : discharge (as body waste) 2 : make (as a contract) void —**void·able** *adj* —**void·er** *n*

vol·a·tile \'välət^əl\ *adj* 1 : readily vaporizing at a relatively low temperature 2 : likely to change suddenly — **vol·a·til·i·ty** \,välə'tilətē\ *n* —**vol·a·til·ize** \'välət^əl,īz\ *vb*

vol·ca·no \väl'kānō\ *n, pl* -noes *or* -nos : opening in the earth's crust from which molten rock and steam come out —**vol·ca·nic** \-'kanik\ *adj*

vo·li·tion \vō'lishən\ *n* : free will —**vo·li·tion·al** \-'lishənəl\ *adj*

vol·ley \'välē\ *n, pl* -leys 1 : flight of missiles (as arrows) 2 : simultaneous shooting of many weapons

vol·ley·ball *n* : game of batting a large ball over a net

volt \'vōlt\ *n* : unit for measuring the force that moves an electric current

volt·age \'vōltij\ *n* : quantity of volts

vol·u·ble \'välyəbəl\ *adj* : fluent and smooth in speech —**vol·u·bil·i·ty** \,välyə'bilətē\ *n* —**vol·u·bly** \'välyəblē\ *adv*

vol·ume \'välyəm\ *n* 1 : book 2 : space occupied as measured by cubic units 3 : amount 4 : loudness of a sound

vo·lu·mi·nous \və'lümənəs\ *adj* : large or bulky

vol·un·tary \'välən,terē\ *adj* 1 : done, made, or given freely and without expecting compensation 2 : relating to or controlled by the will —**vol·un·tar·i·ly** *adv*

vol·un·teer \,välən'tir\ *n* : person who offers to help or work without expecting payment or reward ~ *vb* 1 : offer or give voluntarily 2 : offer oneself as a volunteer

vo·lup·tuous \və'ləpchəwəs\ *adj* 1 : luxurious 2 : having a full and sexually attractive figure —**vo·lup·tuous·ly** *adv* —**vo·lup·tuous·ness** *n*

vom·it \'vämət\ *vb* : throw up the contents of the stomach —**vomit** *n*

voo·doo \'vüdü\ *n, pl* voodoos 1 : religion derived from African polytheism and involving sorcery 2 : one who practices voodoo 3 : charm or fetish used in voodoo —**voodoo** *adj* —**voo·doo·ism** \-,izəm\ *n*

vo·ra·cious \vȯ'rāshəs, və-\ *adj* : greedy or exceedingly hungry — **vo·ra·cious·ly** *adv* —**vo·ra·cious·ness** *n* —**vo·rac·i·ty** \-'rasətē\ *n*

vor·tex \'vȯr,teks\ *n, pl* **vor·ti·ces** \'vȯrtə,sēz\ : whirling liquid

vo·ta·ry \'vōtərē\ *n, pl* -ries 1 : devoted participant, adherent, admirer, or worshiper

vote \'vōt\ *n* 1 : individual expression of preference in choosing or reaching a decision 2 : right to indicate one's preference or the preference expressed ~ *vb* vot·ed; vot·ing 1 : cast a vote 2 : choose or defeat by vote — **vote·less** *adj* —**vot·er** *n*

vo·tive \'vōtiv\ *adj* : consisting of or expressing a vow, wish, or desire

vouch \'vaùch\ *vb* : give a guarantee or personal assurance

vouch·er \'vaùchər\ *n* : written record or receipt that serves as proof of a transaction

vouch·safe \vaùch'sāf\ *vb* -safed; -saf·ing : grant as a special favor

vow \vaù\ *n* : solemn promise to do something or to live or act a certain way —**vow** *vb*

vow·el \'vaùəl\ *n* 1 : speech sound produced without obstruction or friction in the mouth 2 : letter representing such a sound

voy·age \'vȯiij\ *n* : long journey esp. by water or through space ~ *vb* -aged; -ag·ing : make a voyage —**voy·ag·er** *n*

vul·ca·nize \'vəlkə,nīz\ *vb* -nized; -niz·ing : treat (as rubber) to make more elastic or stronger

vul·gar \'vəlgər\ *adj* 1 : relating to the common people 2 : lacking refinement 3 : offensive in manner or language —**vul·gar·ism** \-,rizəm\ *n* —**vul·gar·ize** \-,rīz\ *vb* —**vul·gar·ly** *adv*

vul·gar·i·ty \,vəl'garətē\ *n, pl* -ties 1 : state of being vulgar 2 : vulgar language or act

vul·ner·a·ble \'vəlnərəbəl\ *adj* : susceptible to attack or damage — **vul·ner·a·bil·i·ty** \,vəlnərə'bilətē\ *n* —**vul·ner·a·bly** *adv*

vul·ture \'vəlchər\ *n* : large flesh-eating bird

vul·va \'vəlvə\ *n, pl* -vae \-,vē, -,vī\ : external genital parts of the female

vying *pres part of* VIE

W

w \'dəbəl,yü\ *n. pl* **w's** *or* **ws** \-,yüz\ : 23d letter of the alphabet

wad \'wäd\ *n* **1** : little mass **2** : soft mass of fibrous material **3** : pliable plug to retain a powder charge **4** : considerable amount ~ *vb* **1** : form into a wad **2** : stuff with a wad

wad•dle \'wäd⁰l\ *vb* **-dled; -dling** : walk with short steps swaying from side to side —**waddle** *n*

wade \'wād\ *vb* **wad•ed; wad•ing** **1** : step in or through (as water) **2** : move with difficulty —**wade** *n* — **wad•er** *n*

wa•fer \'wāfər\ *n* **1** : thin crisp cake or cracker **2** : waferlike thing

waf•fle \'wäfəl\ *n* : crisped cake of batter cooked in a hinged utensil (**waffle iron**) ~ *vb* : vacillate

waft \'wäft, 'waft\ *vb* : cause to move lightly by wind or waves —**waft** *n*

¹wag \'wag\ *vb* **-gg-** : sway or swing from side to side or to and fro —**wag** *n*

²wag *n* : wit —**wag•gish** *adj*

wage \'wāj\ *vb* **waged; wag•ing** : engage in ~ *n* **1** : payment for labor or services **2** : compensation

wa•ger \'wājər\ *n or vb* : bet

wag•gle \'wagəl\ *vb* **-gled; -gling** : wag —**waggle** *n*

wag•on \'wagən\ *n* **1** : 4-wheeled vehicle drawn by animals **2** : child's 4-wheeled cart

waif \'wāf\ *n* : homeless child

wail \'wāl\ *vb* **1** : mourn **2** : make a sound like a mournful cry —**wail** *n*

wain•scot \'wānskət, -,skōt, -,skät\ *n* : usu. paneled wooden lining of an interior wall —**wainscot** *vb*

waist \'wāst\ *n* **1** : narrowed part of the body between chest and hips **2** : waistlike part —**waist•line** *n*

wait \'wāt\ *vb* **1** : remain in readiness or expectation **2** : delay **3** : attend as a waiter ~ *n* **1** : concealment **2** : act or period of waiting

wait•er \'wātər\ *n* : person who serves others at tables

wait•per•son \'wāt,pərsən\ *n* : a waiter or waitress

wait•ress \'wātrəs\ *n* : woman who serves others at tables

waive \'wāv\ *vb* **waived; waiv•ing** : give up claim to

waiv•er \'wāvər\ *n* : act of waiving right, claim, or privilege

¹wake \'wāk\ *vb* **woke** \'wōk\; **wo•ken** \'wōkən\; **wak•ing** **1** : keep watch **2** : bring or come back to consciousness after sleep ~ *n* **1** : state of being awake **2** : watch held over a dead body

²wake *n* : track left by a ship

wake•ful \'wākfəl\ *adj* : not sleeping or able to sleep —**wake•ful•ness** *n*

wak•en \'wākən\ *vb* : wake

wale \'wāl\ *n* : ridge on cloth

walk \'wök\ *vb* **1** : move or cause to move on foot **2** : pass over, through, or along by walking ~ *n* **1** : a going on foot **2** : place or path for walking **3** : distance to be walked **4** : way of living **5** : way of walking **6** : slow 4-beat gait of a horse —**walk•er** *n*

wall \'wöl\ *n* **1** : structure for defense or for enclosing something **2** : upright enclosing part of a building or room **3** : something like a wall ~ *vb* : provide, separate, surround, or close with a wall —**walled** \'wöld\ *adj*

wal•la•by \'wäləbē\ *n, pl* **-bies** : small or medium-sized kangaroo

wal•let \'wälət\ *n* : pocketbook with compartments

wall•flow•er *n* **1** : mustardlike plant with showy fragrant flowers **2** : one who remains on the sidelines of social activity

wal•lop \'wäləp\ *n* **1** : powerful blow **2** : ability to hit hard ~ *vb* **1** : beat soundly **2** : hit hard

wal•low \'wälō\ *vb* **1** : roll about in deep mud **2** : indulge oneself excessively ~ *n* : place for wallowing

wall•pa•per *n* : decorative paper for walls —**wallpaper** *vb*

wal•nut \'wöl,nət\ *n* **1** : nut with a furrowed shell and adherent husk 2 : tree on which this nut grows or its brown wood

wal·rus \'wòlrəs, 'wäl-\ *n, pl* **-rus** *or* **-rus·es** : large seallike mammal of northern seas having ivory tusks

waltz \'wòlts\ *n* : gliding dance to music having 3 beats to the measure or the music —**waltz** *vb*

wam·pum \'wämpəm\ *n* : strung shell beads used by No. American Indians as money

wan \'wän\ *adj* **-nn-** : sickly or pale — **wan·ly** *adv* —**wan·ness** *n*

wand \'wänd\ *n* : slender staff

wan·der \'wändər\ *vb* 1 : move about aimlessly 2 : stray 3 : become delirious —**wan·der·er** *n*

wan·der·lust \'wändər,ləst\ *n* : strong urge to wander

wane \'wän\ *vb* **waned; wan·ing** 1 : grow smaller or less 2 : lose power, prosperity, or influence —**wane** *n*

wan·gle \'waŋgəl\ *vb* **-gled; -gling** : obtain by sly or devious means

want \'wònt\ *vb* 1 : lack 2 : need 3 : desire earnestly ~ *n* 1 : deficiency 2 : dire need 3 : something wanted

want·ing \-iŋ\ *adj* 1 : not present or in evidence 2 : falling below standards 3 : lacking in ability ~ *prep* 1 : less or minus 2 : without

wan·ton \'wòntən\ *adj* 1 : lewd 2 : having no regard for justice or for others' feelings, rights, or safety ~ *n* : lewd or immoral person ~ *vb* : be wanton —**wan·ton·ly** *adv* —**wan·ton·ness** *n*

wa·pi·ti \'wäpətē\ *n, pl* **-ti** *or* **-tis** : elk

war \'wòr\ *n* 1 : armed fighting between nations 2 : state of hostility or conflict 3 : struggle between opposing forces or for a particular end ~ *vb* **-rr-** : engage in warfare —**war·less** \-ləs\ *adj* —**war·time** *n*

war·ble \'wòrbəl\ *n* 1 : melodious succession of low pleasing sounds 2 : musical trill ~ *vb* **-bled; -bling** : sing or utter in a trilling way

war·bler \'wòrblər\ *n* 1 : small thrushlike singing bird 2 : small bright-colored insect-eating bird

ward \'wòrd\ *n* 1 : a guarding or being under guard or guardianship 2 : division of a prison or hospital 3 : electoral or administrative division of a city 4 : person under protection of a guardian or a law court ~ *vb* : turn aside —**ward·ship** *n*

1-ward \wərd\ *adj suffix* 1 : that moves, tends, faces, or is directed toward 2 : that occurs or is situated in the direction of

2-ward, -wards *adv suffix* 1 : in a (specified) direction 2 : toward a (specified) point, position, or area

war·den \'wòrdən\ *n* 1 : guardian 2 : official charged with supervisory duties or enforcement of laws 3 : official in charge of a prison

ward·er \'wòrdər\ *n* : watchman or warden

ward·robe \'wòrd,rōb\ *n* 1 : clothes closet 2 : collection of wearing apparel

ware \'war\ *n* 1 : articles for sale —often *pl.* 2 : items of fired clay

ware·house \-,haús\ *n* : place for storage of merchandise —**warehouse** *vb* — **ware·house·man** \-mən\ *n* —**warehous·er** \-,haúzər, -sər\ *n*

war·fare \'wòr,far\ *n* 1 : military operations between enemies 2 : struggle

war·head \-,hed\ *n* : part of a missile holding the explosive material

war·like *adj* : fond of, relating to, or used in war

warm \'wòrm\ *adj* 1 : having or giving out moderate or adequate heat 2 : serving to retain heat 3 : showing strong feeling 4 : giving a pleasant impression of warmth, cheerfulness, or friendliness ~ *vb* 1 : make or become warm 2 : give warmth or energy to 3 : experience feelings of affection 4 : become increasingly ardent, interested, or competent —**warm·er** *n* — **warm·ly** *adv* —**warm up** *vb* : make ready by preliminary activity

war·mon·ger \'wòr,məŋgər, -,mäŋ-\ *n* : one who attempts to stir up war

warmth \'wòrmth\ *n* 1 : quality or state of being warm 2 : enthusiasm

warn \'wòrn\ *vb* 1 : put on guard 2 : notify in advance —**warn·ing** \-iŋ\ *n or adj*

warp \'wòrp\ *n* 1 : lengthwise threads in a woven fabric 2 : twist ~ *vb* 1 : twist out of shape 2 : lead astray 3 : distort

war·rant \'wòrənt, 'wär-\ *n* 1 : authorization 2 : legal writ authorizing action ~ *vb* 1 : declare or maintain positively 2 : guarantee 3 : approve 4 : justify

warrant officer *n* **1** : officer in the armed forces ranking next below a commissioned officer **2** : commissioned officer in the navy or coast guard ranking below an ensign

war·ran·ty \'wȯrəntē, 'wär-\ *n, pl* **-ties** : guarantee of the integrity of a product

war·ren \'wȯrən, 'wär-\ *n* : area where rabbits are bred and kept

war·rior \'wȯryər, 'wȯrēər; 'wärē-, 'wäryər\ *n* : man engaged or experienced in warfare

war·ship \'wȯr,ship\ *n* : naval vessel

wart \'wȯrt\ *n* **1** : small projection on the skin caused by a virus **2** : wartlike protuberance —**warty** *adj*

wary \'warē\ *adj* **war·i·er; -est** : careful in guarding against danger or deception

was *past 1st & 3d sing of* BE

wash \'wȯsh, 'wäsh\ *vb* **1** : cleanse with or as if with a liquid (as water) **2** : wet thoroughly with liquid **3** : flow along the border of **4** : flow in a stream **5** : move or remove by or as if by the action of water **6** : cover or daub lightly with a liquid **7** : undergo laundering ~ *n* **1** : act of washing or being washed **2** : articles to be washed **3** : surging action of water or disturbed air —**wash·able** \-əbəl\ *adj*

wash·board *n* : grooved board to scrub clothes on

wash·bowl *n* : large bowl for water for washing hands and face

wash·cloth *n* : cloth used for washing one's face and body

washed–up \'wȯsht'əp, 'wäsht-\ *adj* : no longer capable or usable

wash·er \'wȯshər, 'wäsh-\ *n* **1** : machine for washing **2** : ring used around a bolt or screw to ensure tightness and relieve friction

wash·ing \'wȯshiŋ, 'wäsh-\ *n* : articles to be washed

Washington's Birthday *n* : the 3d Monday in February or formerly February 22 observed as a legal holiday

wash·out *n* **1** : washing out or away of earth **2** : failure

wash·room *n* : bathroom

wasp \'wäsp, 'wȯsp\ *n* : slender-bodied winged insect related to the bees and having a formidable sting

wasp·ish \'wäspish, 'wȯs-\ *adj* : irritable

was·sail \'wäsəl, wä'sāl\ *n* **1** : toast to someone's health **2** : liquor drunk on festive occasions **3** : riotous drinking —**wassail** *vb*

waste \'wāst\ *n* **1** : sparsely settled or barren region **2** : act or an instance of wasting **3** : refuse (as garbage or rubbish) **4** : material (as feces) produced but not used by a living body ~ *vb* **wast·ed; wast·ing** **1** : ruin **2** : spend or use carelessly **3** : lose substance or energy ~ *adj* **1** : wild and uninhabited **2** : being of no further use —**wast·er** *n* —**waste·ful** \-fəl\ *adj* —**waste·ful·ly** *adv* —**waste·ful·ness** *n*

waste·bas·ket \-,baskət\ *n* : receptacle for refuse

waste·land \-,land, -lənd\ *n* : barren uncultivated land

was·trel \'wāstrəl, 'wästrəl\ *n* : one who wastes

watch \'wäch, 'wȯch\ *vb* **1** : be or stay awake intentionally **2** : be on the lookout for danger **3** : observe **4** : keep oneself informed about ~ *n* **1** : act of keeping awake to guard **2** : close observation **3** : one that watches **4** : period of duty on a ship or those on duty during this period **5** : timepiece carried on the person —**watch·er** *n*

watch·dog *n* **1** : dog kept to guard property **2** : one that protects

watch·ful \-fəl\ *adj* : steadily attentive —**watch·ful·ly** *adv* —**watch·ful·ness** *n*

watch·man \-mən\ *n* : person assigned to watch

watch·word *n* **1** : secret word used as a signal **2** : slogan

wa·ter \'wȯtər, 'wät-\ *n* **1** : liquid that descends as rain and forms rivers, lakes, and seas **2** : liquid containing or resembling water ~ *vb* **1** : supply with or get water **2** : dilute with or as if with water **3** : form or secrete watery matter

water buffalo *n* : common oxlike often domesticated Asian buffalo

wa·ter·col·or *n* **1** : paint whose liquid part is water **2** : picture made with watercolors

wa·ter·course *n* : stream of water

wa·ter·cress \-,kres\ *n* : perennial salad plant with white flowers

wa·ter·fall *n* : steep descent of the water of a stream

wa·ter·fowl *n* **1** : bird that frequents the water **2 waterfowl** *pl* : swimming game birds

wa·ter·front n : land fronting a body of water

water lily n : aquatic plant with floating leaves and showy flowers

wa·ter·logged \-,lógd, -,lägd\ adj : filled or soaked with water

wa·ter·mark n 1 : mark showing how high water has risen 2 : a marking in paper visible under light ~ vb : mark (paper) with a watermark

wa·ter·mel·on n : large fruit with sweet juicy usu. red pulp

water moccasin n : venomous snake of the southeastern U.S.

wa·ter·pow·er n : power of moving water used to run machinery

wa·ter·proof adj : not letting water through ~ vb : make waterproof — **wa·ter·proof·ing** n

wa·ter·shed \-,shed\ n : dividing ridge between two drainage areas or one of these areas

water ski n : ski used on water when the wearer is towed —**wa·ter-ski** vb —**wa·ter-ski·er** n

wa·ter·spout n 1 : pipe from which water is spouted 2 : tornado over a body of water

wa·ter·tight adj 1 : so tight as not to let water in 2 : allowing no possibility for doubt or uncertainty

wa·ter·way n : navigable body of water

wa·ter·works n pl : system by which water is supplied (as to a city)

wa·tery \'wótərē, 'wät-\ adj 1 : containing, full of, or giving out water 2 : being like water 3 : soft and soggy

watt \'wät\ n : unit of electric power — **watt·age** \'wätij\ n

wat·tle \'wätᵊl\ n 1 : framework of flexible branches used in building 2 : fleshy process hanging usu. about the head or neck (as of a bird) —**wat·tled** \-ᵊld\ adj

wave \'wāv\ vb **waved; wav·ing** 1 : flutter 2 : signal with the hands 3 : wave to and fro with the hand 4 : curve up and down like a wave ~ n 1 : moving swell on the surface of water 2 : wave-like shape 3 : waving motion 4 : surge 5 : disturbance that transfers energy from point to point — **wave·let** \-lət\ n —**wave·like** adj —**wavy** adj

wave·length \'wāv,leŋkth\ n 1 : distance from crest to crest in the line of advance of a wave 2 : line of thought that reveals a common understanding

wa·ver \'wāvər\ vb 1 : fluctuate in opinion, allegiance, or direction 2 : flicker 3 : falter —**waver** n —**wa·ver·er** n —**wa·ver·ing·ly** adv

¹wax \'waks\ n 1 : yellowish plastic substance secreted by bees 2 : substance like beeswax ~ vb : treat or rub with wax esp. for polishing

²wax vb 1 : grow larger 2 : become

wax·en \'waksən\ adj : made of or resembling wax

waxy \'waksē\ adj **wax·i·er; -est** : made of, full of, or resembling wax

way \'wā\ n 1 : thoroughfare for travel or passage 2 : route 3 : course of action 4 : method 5 : detail 6 : usual or characteristic state of affairs 7 : condition 8 : distance 9 : progress along a course —**by the way** : in a digression —**by way of** 1 : for the purpose of 2 : by the route through —**out of the way** : remote

way·bill n : paper that accompanies a shipment and gives details of goods, route, and charges

way·far·er \'wā,farər\ n : traveler esp. on foot —**way·far·ing** \-,fariŋ\ adj

way·lay \'wā,lā\ vb **-laid** \-,lād\; **-lay·ing** : lie in wait for

way·side n : side of a road

way·ward \'wāwərd\ adj 1 : following one's own capricious inclinations 2 : unpredictable

we \'wē\ pron —used of a group that includes the speaker or writer

weak \'wēk\ adj 1 : lacking strength or vigor 2 : deficient in vigor of mind or character 3 : of less than usual strength 4 : not having or exerting authority —**weak·en** \'wēkən\ vb — **weak·ly** adv

weak·ling \-liŋ\ n : person who is physically, mentally, or morally weak

weak·ly \'wēklē\ adj : feeble

weak·ness \-nəs\ n 1 : quality or state of being weak 2 : fault 3 : object of special liking

wealth \'welth\ n 1 : abundant possessions or resources 2 : profusion

wealthy \'welthē\ adj **wealth·i·er; -est** : having wealth

wean \'wēn\ vb 1 : accustom (a young mammal) to take food by means other than nursing 2 : free from dependence

weap·on \'wepən\ n 1 : something (as a gun) that may be used to fight with 2 : means by which one contends against another —**weap·on·less** adj

wear \'war\ *vb* **wore** \'wōr\; **worn** \'wōrn\; **wear·ing 1** : use as an article of clothing or adornment **2** : carry on the person **3** : show an appearance of **4** : decay by use or by scraping **5** : lessen the strength of **6** : endure use ~ *n* **1** : act of wearing **2** : clothing **3** : lasting quality **4** : result of use — **wear·able** \'warəbəl\ *adj* —**wear·er** *n* —**wear out** *vb* **1** : make or become useless by wear **2** : tire

wea·ri·some \'wērēsəm\ *adj* : causing weariness —**wea·ri·some·ly** *adv* — **wea·ri·some·ness** *n*

wea·ry \'wirē\ *adj* **-ri·er; -est 1** : worn out in strength, freshness, or patience **2** : expressing or characteristic of weariness ~ *vb* **-ried; -ry·ing** : make or become weary —**wea·ri·ly** *adv* — **wea·ri·ness** *n*

wea·sel \'wēzəl\ *n* : small slender flesh-eating mammal

weath·er \'wethər\ *n* : state of the atmosphere ~ *vb* **1** : expose to or endure the action of weather **2** : endure

weath·er-beat·en *adj* : worn or damaged by exposure to the weather

weath·er·man \-,man\ *n* : one who forecasts and reports the weather

weath·er·proof *adj* : able to withstand exposure to weather —**weatherproof** *vb*

weather vane *n* : movable device that shows the way the wind blows

weave \'wēv\ *vb* **wove** \'wōv\ *or* **weaved; wo·ven** \'wōvən\ *or* **weaved; weav·ing 1** : form by interlacing strands of material **2** : to make as if by weaving together parts **3** : follow a winding course ~ *n* : pattern or method of weaving —**weav·er** *n*

web \'web\ *n* **1** : cobweb **2** : animal or plant membrane **3** : network ~ *vb* **-bb-** : cover or provide with a web — **webbed** \'webd\ *adj*

web·bing \'webiŋ\ *n* : strong closely woven tape

wed \'wed\ *vb* **-dd- 1** : marry **2** : unite

wed·ding \'wediŋ\ *n* : marriage ceremony and celebration

wedge \'wej\ *n* : V-shaped object used for splitting, raising, forcing open, or tightening ~ *vb* **wedged; wedg·ing 1** : tighten or split with a wedge **2** : force into a narrow space

wed·lock \'wed,läk\ *n* : marriage

Wednes·day \'wenzdā, -dē\ *n* : 4th day of the week

wee \'wē\ *adj* : very small

weed \'wēd\ *n* : unwanted plant ~ *vb* **1** : remove weeds **2** : get rid of —**weed·er** *n* —**weedy** *adj*

weeds *n pl* : mourning clothes

week \'wēk\ *n* **1** : 7 successive days **2** : calendar period of 7 days beginning with Sunday and ending with Saturday **3** : the working or school days of the calendar week

week·day \'wēk,dā\ *n* : any day except Sunday and often Saturday

week·end \-,end\ *n* : Saturday and Sunday ~ *vb* : spend the weekend

week·ly \'wēklē\ *adj* : occurring, appearing, or done every week ~ *n, pl* **-lies** : weekly publication —**weekly** *adv*

weep \'wēp\ *vb* **wept** \'wept\; **weep·ing** : shed tears —**weep·er** *n* —**weepy** *adj*

wee·vil \'wēvəl\ *n* : small injurious beetle with a long head usu. curved into a snout —**wee·vily, wee·vil·ly** \'wēvəlē\ *adj*

weft \'weft\ *n* : crosswise threads or yarn in weaving

weigh \'wā\ *vb* **1** : determine the heaviness of **2** : have a specified weight **3** : consider carefully **4** : raise (an anchor) off the sea floor **5** : press down or burden

weight \'wāt\ *n* **1** : amount that something weighs **2** : relative heaviness **3** : heavy object **4** : burden or pressure **5** : importance ~ *vb* **1** : load with a weight **2** : oppress —**weight·less** \-ləs\ *adj* —**weight·less·ness** *n* — **weighty** \'wātē\ *adj*

weird \'wird\ *adj* **1** : unearthly or mysterious **2** : strange —**weird·ly** *adv* — **weird·ness** *n*

wel·come \'welkəm\ *vb* **-comed; -com·ing** : accept or greet cordially ~ *adj* : received or permitted gladly ~ *n* : cordial greeting or reception

weld \'weld\ *vb* : unite by heating, hammering, or pressing ~ *n* : union by welding —**weld·er** *n*

wel·fare \'wel,far\ *n* **1** : prosperity **2** : government aid for those in need

¹**well** \'wel\ *n* **1** : spring **2** : hole sunk in the earth to obtain a natural deposit (as of oil) **3** : source of supply **4** : open space extending vertically through floors ~ *vb* : flow forth

²**well** *adv* **bet·ter** \'betər\; **best** \'best\ **1** : in a good or proper manner **2** : satisfactorily **3** : fully **4** : intimately

5 : considerably ~ *adj* **1** : satisfactory **2** : prosperous **3** : desirable **4** : healthy

well–adjusted \,welə'jəstəd\ *adj* : well-balanced

well–ad·vised \,weləd'vīzd\ *adj* : prudent

well–balanced \'wel'baln̂st\ *adj* **1** : evenly balanced **2** : emotionally or psychologically sound

well–be·ing \'wel'bēiŋ\ *n* : state of being happy, healthy, or prosperous

well–bred \-'bred\ *adj* : having good manners

well–done *adj* **1** : properly performed **2** : cooked thoroughly

well–heeled \-'hēld\ *adj* : financially well-off

well–mean·ing *adj* : having good intentions

well–nigh *adv* : nearly

well–off *adj* : being in good condition esp. financially

well–read \-'red\ *adj* : well informed through reading

well–round·ed \-'raúndəd\ *adj* : broadly developed

well·spring *n* : source

well–to–do \,welt̄ə'dü\ *adj* : prosperous

welsh \'welsh, 'welch\ *vb* **1** : avoid payment **2** : break one's word

Welsh rabbit *n* : melted often seasoned cheese poured over toast or crackers

Welsh rare·bit \-'rarbət\ *n* : Welsh rabbit

welt \'welt\ *n* **1** : narrow strip of leather between a shoe upper and sole **2** : ridge raised on the skin usu. by a blow ~ *vb* : hit hard

wel·ter \'weltər\ *vb* **1** : toss about **2** : wallow ~ *n* : confused jumble

wen \'wen\ *n* : abnormal growth or cyst

wench \'wench\ *n* : young woman

wend \'wend\ *vb* : direct one's course

went *past of* GO

wept *past of* WEEP

were *past 2d sing, past pl,* or *past subjunctive of* BE

were·wolf \'wer,wúlf, 'wir-, 'wər-\ *n, pl* **-wolves** \-,wúlvz\ : person held to be able to change into a wolf

west \'west\ *adv* : to or toward the west ~ *adj* : situated toward or at or coming from the west ~ *n* **1** : direction of sunset **2** *cap* : regions to the west — **west·er·ly** \'westərlē\ *adv or adj* — **west·ward** \-wərd\ *adv or adj* — **west·wards** \-wərdz\ *adv*

west·ern \'westərn\ *adj* **1** *cap* : of a region designated West **2** : lying toward or coming from the west — **West·ern·er** *n*

wet \'wet\ *adj* **-tt-** **1** : consisting of or covered or soaked with liquid **2** : not dry ~ *n* : moisture ~ *vb* **-tt-** : make or become moist — **wet·ly** *adv* — **wet·ness** *n*

whack \'hwak\ *vb* : strike sharply ~ *n* **1** : sharp blow **2** : proper working order **3** : chance **4** : try

¹**whale** \'hwāl\ *n, pl* **whales** *or* **whale** : large marine mammal ~ *vb* **whaled**; **whal·ing** : hunt for whales — **whale·boat** *n* — **whal·er** *n*

²**whale** *vb* **whaled**; **whal·ing** : strike or hit vigorously

whale·bone *n* : horny substance attached to the upper jaw of some large whales (**whalebone whales**)

wharf \'hwórf\ *n, pl* **wharves** \'hwórvz\ : structure alongside which boats lie to load or unload

what \'hwät\ *pron* **1** —used to inquire the identity or nature of something **2** : that which **3** : whatever ~ *adv* : in what respect ~ *adj* **1** —used to inquire about the identity or nature of something **2** : how remarkable or surprising **3** : whatever

what·ev·er \hwät'evər\ *pron* **1** : anything or everything that **2** : no matter what ~ *adj* : of any kind at all

what·not \'hwät,nät\ *pron* : any of various other things that might be mentioned

what·so·ev·er \,hwätsō'evər\ *pron or adj* : whatever

wheal \'hwēl\ *n* : a welt on the skin

wheat \'hwēt\ *n* : cereal grain that yields flour — **wheat·en** *adj*

whee·dle \'hwēdəl\ *vb* **-dled; -dling** : coax or tempt by flattery

wheel \'hwēl\ *n* **1** : disk or circular frame capable of turning on a central axis **2** : device of which the main part is a wheel ~ *vb* **1** : convey or move on wheels or a wheeled vehicle **2** : rotate **3** : turn so as to change direction — **wheeled** *adj* — **wheel·er** *n* — **wheel·less** *adj*

wheel·bar·row \-,barō\ *n* : one-wheeled vehicle for carrying small loads

wheel·base *n* : distance in inches between the front and rear axles of an automotive vehicle

wheel·chair *n* : chair mounted on

wheels esp. for the use of disabled persons

wheeze \'hwēz\ *vb* **wheezed; wheez·ing** : breathe with difficulty and with a whistling sound —**wheeze** *n* — **wheezy** *adj*

whelk \'hwelk\ *n* : large sea snail

whelp \'hwelp\ *n* : one of the young of various carnivorous mammals (as a dog) ~ *vb* : bring forth whelps

when \'hwen\ *adv* —used to inquire about or designate a particular time ~ *conj* 1 : at or during the time that 2 : every time that 3 : if 4 : although ~ *pron* : what time

whence \'hwens\ *adv or conj* : from what place, source, or cause

when·ev·er \hwen'evər\ *conj or adv* : at whatever time

where \'hwer\ *adv* 1 : at, in, or to what place 2 : at, in, or to what situation, position, direction, circumstances, or respect ~ *conj* 1 : at, in, or to what place, position, or circumstance 2 : at, in, or to which place ~ *n* : place

where·abouts \-ə,baúts\ *adv* : about where ~ *n sing or pl* : place where a person or thing is

where·as \hwer'az\ *conj* 1 : while on the contrary 2 : since

where·by *conj* : by, through, or in accordance with which

where·fore \'hwer,fōr\ *adv* 1 : why 2 : therefore ~ *n* : reason

where·in \hwer'in\ *adv* : in what respect

where·of \-'əv, -äv\ *conj* : of what, which, or whom

where·up·on \'hwerə,pón, -,pän\ *conj* 1 : on which 2 : and then

wher·ev·er \hwer'evər\ *adv* : where ~ *conj* : at, in, or to whatever place or circumstance

where·with·al \'hwerwith,ól, -with-\ *n* : resources and esp. money

whet \'hwet\ *vb* **-tt-** 1 : sharpen by rubbing (as with a stone) 2 : stimulate — **whet·stone** *n*

whether \'hwethər\ *conj* 1 : if it is or was true that 2 : if it is or was better 3 : whichever is the case

whey \'hwā\ *n* : watery part of sour milk

which \'hwich\ *adj* 1 : being what one or ones out of a group 2 : whichever ~ *pron* 1 : which one or ones 2 : whichever

which·ev·er \hwich'evər\ *pron or adj* : no matter what one

whiff \'hwif\ *n* 1 : slight gust 2

: inhalation of odor, gas, or smoke 3 : slight trace ~ *vb* : inhale an odor

while \'hwīl\ *n* 1 : period of time 2 : time and effort used ~ *conj* 1 : during the time that 2 : as long as 3 : although ~ *vb* **whiled; whil·ing** : cause to pass esp. pleasantly

whim \'hwim\ *n* : sudden wish, desire, or change of mind

whim·per \'hwimpər\ *vb* : cry softly — **whimper** *n*

whim·si·cal \'hwimzikəl\ *adj* 1 : full of whims 2 : erratic —**whim·si·cal·i·ty** \,hwimzə'kalətē\ *n* —**whim·si·cal·ly** *adv*

whim·sy, whim·sey \'hwimzē\ *n, pl* **-sies** *or* **-seys** 1 : whim 2 : fanciful creation

whine \'hwīn\ *vb* **whined; whin·ing** 1 : utter a usu. high-pitched plaintive cry 2 : complain —**whine** *n* —**whin·er** *n* —**whiny** *adj*

whin·ny \'hwinē\ *vb* **-nied; -ny·ing** : neigh —**whinny** *n*

whip \'hwip\ *vb* **-pp-** 1 : move quickly 2 : strike with something slender and flexible 3 : defeat 4 : incite 5 : beat into a froth ~ *n* 1 : flexible device used for whipping 2 : party leader responsible for discipline 3 : thrashing motion —**whip·per** *n*

whip·cord *n* 1 : thin tough cord 2 : cloth made of hard-twisted yarns

whip·lash *n* : injury from a sudden sharp movement of the neck and head

whip·per·snap·per \'hwipər,snapər\ *n* : small, insignificant, or presumptuous person

whip·pet \'hwipət\ *n* : small swift dog often used for racing

whip·poor·will \'hwipər,wil\ *n* : American nocturnal bird

whir \'hwər\ *vb* **-rr-** : move, fly, or revolve with a whir ~ *n* : continuous fluttering or vibratory sound

whirl \'hwərl\ *vb* 1 : move or drive in a circle 2 : spin 3 : move or turn quickly 4 : reel ~ *n* 1 : rapid circular movement 2 : state of commotion or confusion 3 : try

whirl·pool *n* : whirling mass of water having a depression in the center

whirl·wind *n* : whirling wind storm

whisk \'hwisk\ *n* 1 : quick light sweeping or brushing motion 2 : usu. wire kitchen implement for beating ~ *vb* 1 : move or convey briskly 2 : beat 3 : brush lightly

whisk broom *n* : small broom

whis·ker \'hwiskər\ *n* **1** *pl* : beard **2** : long bristle or hair near an animal's mouth —**whis·kered** \-kərd\ *adj*

whis·key, whis·ky \'hwiskē\ *n, pl* **-keys** *or* **-kies** : liquor distilled from a fermented mash of grain

whis·per \'hwispər\ *vb* **1** : speak softly **2** : tell by whispering ~ *n* **1** : soft low sound **2** : rumor

whist \'hwist\ *n* : card game

whis·tle \'hwisəl\ *n* **1** : device by which a shrill sound is produced **2** : shrill clear sound made by a whistle or through the lips ~ *vb* **-tled; -tling 1** : make or utter a whistle **2** : signal or call by a whistle **3** : produce by whistling —**whis·tler** *n*

whis·tle–blow·er \'hwisəl,blōər\ *n* : informer

whis·tle–stop *n* : brief political appearance

whit \'hwit\ *n* : bit

white \'hwīt\ *adj* **whit·er; -est 1** : free from color **2** : of the color of new snow or milk **3** : having light skin ~ *n* **1** : color of maximum lightness **2** : white part or thing **3** : person who is light-skinned —**white·ness** *n* — **whit·ish** *adj*

white blood cell *n* : blood cell that does not contain hemoglobin

white·cap \'hwīt,kap\ *n* : wave crest breaking into white foam

white–col·lar *adj* : relating to salaried employees with duties not requiring protective or work clothing

white elephant *n* : something costly but of little use or value

white·fish \'hwīt,fish\ *n* : freshwater food fish

whit·en \'hwīt²n\ *vb* : make or become white —**whit·en·er** \'hwīt²nər\ *n*

white slave *n* : woman or girl held unwillingly for purposes of prostitution —**white slavery** *n*

white·tail \'hwīt,tāl\ *n* : No. American deer

white·wash *vb* **1** : whiten with a composition (as of lime and water) **2** : gloss over or cover up faults or wrongdoing —**whitewash** *n*

whith·er \'hwithər\ *adv* **1** : to what place **2** : to what situation, position, degree, or end

¹whit·ing \'hwītiŋ\ *n* : usu. light or silvery food fish

²whiting *n* : pulverized chalk or limestone

whit·tle \'hwit²l\ *vb* **-tled; -tling 1** : pare **2** : shape by paring **3** : reduce gradually

whiz, whizz \'hwiz\ *vb* **-zz-** : make a sound like a speeding object —**whiz, whizz** *n*

who \'hü\ *pron* **1** what or which person or persons **2** : person or persons that **3** : —used to introduce a relative clause

who·dun·it \hü'dənət\ *n* : detective or mystery story

who·ev·er \hü'evər\ *pron* : no matter who

whole \'hōl\ *adj* **1** : being in healthy or sound condition **2** : having all its parts or elements **3** : constituting the total sum of ~ *n* **1** : complete amount or sum **2** : something whole or entire — **on the whole 1** : considering all circumstances **2** : in general —**whole·ness** *n*

whole·heart·ed \'hōl'härtəd\ *adj* : sincere

whole number *n* : integer

whole·sale *n* : sale of goods in quantity usu. for resale by a retail merchant ~ *adj* **1** : of or relating to wholesaling **2** : performed on a large scale ~ *vb* **-saled; -sal·ing** : sell at wholesale — **wholesale** *adv* —**whole·sal·er** *n*

whole·some \-səm\ *adj* **1** : promoting mental, spiritual, or bodily health **2** : healthy —**whole·some·ness** *n*

whole wheat *adj* : made of ground entire wheat kernels

whol·ly \'hōlē\ *adv* **1** : totally **2** : solely

whom \'hüm\ *pron, objective case of* WHO

whom·ev·er \hüm'evər\ *pron, objective case of* WHOEVER

whoop \'hwüp, 'hwúp, 'hüp, 'húp\ *vb* : shout loudly ~ *n* : shout

whooping cough *n* : infectious disease marked by convulsive coughing fits

whop·per \'hwäpər\ *n* **1** : something unusually large or extreme of its kind **2** : monstrous lie

whop·ping \'hwäpiŋ\ *adj* : extremely large

whore \'hōr\ *n* : prostitute

whorl \'hwórl, 'hwərl\ *n* : spiral — **whorled** *adj*

whose \'hüz\ *adj* : of or relating to whom or which ~ *pron* : whose one or ones

who·so·ev·er \,hüsō'evər\ *pron* : whoever

why \'hwī\ *adv* : for what reason, cause, or purpose ~ *conj* 1 : reason for which 2 : for which ~ *n, pl* **whys** : reason ~ *interj* —used esp. to express surprise

wick \'wik\ *n* : cord that draws up oil, tallow, or wax to be burned

wick·ed \'wikəd\ *adj* 1 : morally bad 2 : harmful or troublesome 3 : very unpleasant 4 : very impressive —**wick·ed·ly** *adv* —**wick·ed·ness** *n*

wick·er \'wikər\ *n* 1 : small pliant branch 2 : wickerwork —**wicker** *adj*

wick·er·work *n* : work made of wickers

wick·et \'wikət\ *n* 1 : small gate, door, or window 2 : frame in cricket or arch in croquet

wide \'wīd\ *adj* **wid·er; wid·est** 1 : covering a vast area 2 : measured at right angles to the length 3 : having a great measure across 4 : opened fully 5 : far from the thing in question ~ *adv* **wid·er; wid·est** 1 : over a great distance 2 : so as to leave considerable space between 3 : fully —**wide·ly** *adv* —**wid·en** \'wīd'n\ *vb*

wide–awake *adj* : alert

wide–eyed *adj* 1 : having the eyes wide open 2 : amazed 3 : naive

wide·spread *adj* : widely extended

wid·ow \'widō\ *n* : woman who has lost her husband by death and has not married again ~ *vb* : cause to become a widow —**wid·ow·hood** *n*

wid·ow·er \'widəwər\ *n* : man who has lost his wife by death and has not married again

width \'width\ *n* 1 : distance from side to side 2 : largeness of extent 3 : measured and cut piece of material

wield \'wēld\ *vb* 1 : use or handle esp. effectively 2 : exert —**wield·er** *n*

wie·ner \'wēnər\ *n* : frankfurter

wife \'wīf\ *n, pl* **wives** \'wīvz\ : married woman —**wife·hood** *n* —**wife·less** *adj* —**wife·ly** *adj*

wig \'wig\ *n* : manufactured covering of hair for the head

wig·gle \'wigəl\ *vb* **-gled; -gling** 1 : move with quick jerky or shaking movements 2 : wriggle —**wiggle** *n* —**wig·gler** *n*

wig·gly \-əlē\ *adj* 1 : tending to wiggle 2 : wavy

wig·wag \'wig,wag\ *vb* : signal by a flag or light waved according to a code

wig·wam \'wig,wäm\ *n* : American Indian hut consisting of a framework of poles overlaid with bark, rush mats, or hides

wild \'wīld\ *adj* 1 : living or being in a state of nature and not domesticated or cultivated 2 : unrestrained 3 : turbulent 4 : crazy 5 : uncivilized 6 : erratic ~ *n* 1 : wilderness 2 : undomesticated state ~ *adv* : without control —**wild·ly** *adv* —**wild·ness** *n*

wild·cat \-,kat\ *n* : any of various undomesticated cats (as a lynx) ~ *adj* 1 : not sound or safe 2 : unauthorized

wil·der·ness \'wildərnəs\ *n* : uncultivated and uninhabited region

wild·fire \'wīld,fīr\ *n* : sweeping and destructive fire

wild·fowl *n* : game waterfowl

wild·life \'wīld,līf\ *n* : undomesticated animals

wile \'wīl\ *n* : trick to snare or deceive ~ *vb* **wiled; wil·ing** : lure

will \'wil\ *vb, past* **would** \'wúd\; *pres sing & pl* **will** 1 : wish 2 —used as an auxiliary verb to express (1) desire or willingness (2) customary action (3) simple future time (4) capability (5) determination (6) probability (7) inevitability or (8) a command 3 : dispose of by a will ~ *n* 1 : often determined wish 2 : act, process, or experience of willing 3 : power of controlling one's actions or emotions 4 : legal document disposing of property after death

will·ful, wil·ful \'wilfəl\ *adj* 1 : governed by will without regard to reason 2 : intentional —**will·ful·ly** *adv*

will·ing \'wiliŋ\ *adj* 1 : inclined or favorably disposed in mind 2 : prompt to act 3 : done, borne, or accepted voluntarily or without reluctance —**will·ing·ly** *adv* —**will·ing·ness** *n*

will–o'–the–wisp \,wiləthə'wisp\ *n* 1 : light that appears at night over marshy grounds 2 : misleading or elusive goal or hope

wil·low \'wilō\ *n* : quick-growing shrub or tree with flexible shoots

wil·lowy \'wiləwē\ *adj* : gracefully tall and slender

will·pow·er \'wil,paúər\ *n* : energetic determination

wil·ly–nil·ly \,wilē'nilē\ *adv or adj* : without regard for one's choice

wilt \'wilt\ *vb* **1** : lose or cause to lose freshness and become limp esp. from lack of water **2** : grow weak

wily \'wī-lē\ *adj* **wil·i·er;** **-est** : full of craftiness —**wil·i·ness** *n*

win \'win\ *vb* **won** \'wən\; **win·ning 1** : get possession of esp. by effort **2** : gain victory in battle or a contest **3** : make friendly or favorable ~ *n* : victory

wince \'wins\ *vb* **winced; winc·ing** : shrink back involuntarily —**wince** *n*

winch \'winch\ *n* : machine for hoisting or pulling with a drum around which rope is wound —**winch** *vb*

¹wind \'wind\ *n* **1** : movement of the air **2** : breath **3** : gas in the stomach or intestines **4** : air carrying a scent **5** : intimation ~ *vb* **1** : get a scent of **2** : cause to be out of breath

²wind \'wīnd\ *vb* **wound** \'waùnd\; **wind·ing 1** : have or follow a curving course **2** : move or lie to encircle **3** : encircle or cover with something pliable **4** : tighten the spring of ~ *n* : turn or coil —**wind·er** *n*

wind·break \-,brāk\ *n* : trees and shrubs to break the force of the wind

wind·break·er \-,brākər\ *n* : light wind-resistant jacket

wind·fall \'wind,fȯl\ *n* **1** : thing blown down by wind **2** : unexpected benefit

wind instrument *n* : musical instrument (as a flute or horn) sounded by wind and esp. by the breath

wind·lass \'windləs\ *n* : winch esp. for hoisting anchor

wind·mill \'wind,mil\ *n* : machine worked by the wind turning vanes

win·dow \'windō\ *n* **1** : opening in the wall of a building to let in light and air **2** : pane in a window **3** : span of time for something **4** : area of a computer display —**win·dow·less** *adj*

win·dow-shop *vb* : look at the displays in store windows —**win·dow-shop·per** *n*

wind·pipe \'wind,pīp\ *n* : passage for the breath from the larynx to the lungs

wind·shield \-,shēld\ *n* : transparent screen in front of the occupants of a vehicle

wind·up \'wīnd,əp\ *n* : end —**wind up** *vb*

wind·ward \'windwərd\ *adj* : being in or facing the direction from which the wind is blowing ~ *n* : direction from which the wind is blowing

windy \'windē\ *adj* **wind·i·er;** **-est 1** : having wind **2** : indulging in useless talk

wine \'wīn\ *n* **1** : fermented grape juice **2** : usu. fermented juice of a plant product (as fruit) used as a beverage ~ *vb* : treat to or drink wine

wing \'wiŋ\ *n* **1** : movable paired appendage for flying **2** : winglike thing **3** *pl* : area at the side of the stage out of sight **4** : faction ~ *vb* **1** : fly **2** : propel through the air —**winged** *adj* —**wing·less** *adj* —**on the wing** : in flight —**under one's wing** : in one's charge or care

wink \'wiŋk\ *vb* **1** : close and open the eyes quickly **2** : avoid seeing or noticing something **3** : twinkle **4** : close and open one eye quickly as a signal or hint ~ *n* **1** : brief sleep **2** : act of winking **3** : instant —**wink·er** *n*

win·ner \'winər\ *n* : one that wins

win·ning \-iŋ\ *n* **1** : victory **2** : money won at gambling ~ *adj* **1** : victorious **2** : charming

win·now \'winō\ *vb* **1** : remove (as chaff) by a current of air **2** : sort or separate something

win·some \'winsəm\ *adj* **1** : causing joy **2** : cheerful or gay —**win·some·ly** *adv* —**win·some·ness** *n*

win·ter \'wintər\ *n* : season between autumn and spring ~ *adj* : sown in autumn for harvest the next spring or summer —**win·ter·time** *n*

win·ter·green \'wintər,grēn\ *n* : low heathlike evergreen plant with red berries

win·try \'wintrē\ *adj* **win·tri·er;** **-est 1** : characteristic of winter **2** : cold in feeling

wipe \'wīp\ *vb* **wiped; wip·ing 1** : clean or dry by rubbing **2** : remove by rubbing **3** : erase completely **4** : destroy **5** : pass over a surface ~ *n* : act or instance of wiping —**wip·er** *n*

wire \'wīr\ *n* **1** : thread of metal **2** : work made of wire **3** : telegram or cablegram ~ *vb* **1** : provide with wire **2** : bind or mount with wire **3** : telegraph —**wire·less** *adj*

wire·less \-ləs\ *n, chiefly Brit* : radio

wire·tap *vb* : connect into a telephone or telegraph wire to get information —**wiretap** *n* —**wire·tap·per** *n*

wir·ing \'wiriŋ\ *n* : system of wires

wiry \'wīrē\ *adj* **wir·i·er** \'wīrēər\; **-est**

1 : resembling wire 2 : slender yet strong and sinewy —**wir·i·ness** n

wis·dom \'wizdəm\ n 1 : accumulated learning 2 : good sense

wisdom tooth n : last tooth on each half of each human jaw

1wise \'wīz\ n : manner

2wise adj **wis·er; wis·est** 1 : having or showing wisdom, good sense, or good judgment 2 : aware of what is going on —**wise·ly** adv

wise·crack n : clever, smart, or flippant remark ~ vb : make a wisecrack

wish \'wish\ vb 1 : have a desire 2 : express a wish concerning 3 : request ~ n 1 : a wishing or desire 2 : expressed will or desire

wish·bone n : forked bone in front of the breastbone in most birds

wish·ful \-fəl\ adj 1 : expressive of a wish 2 : according with wishes rather than fact

wishy–washy \'wishē,wóshē. -,wäsh-\ adj : weak or insipid

wisp \'wisp\ n 1 : small bunch of hay or straw 2 : thin strand, strip, fragment, or streak 3 : something frail, slight, or fleeting —**wispy** adj

wis·te·ria \wis'tirēə\ n : pealike woody vine with long clusters of flowers

wist·ful \'wistfəl\ adj : full of longing —**wist·ful·ly** adv —**wist·ful·ness** n

wit \'wit\ n 1 : reasoning power 2 : mental soundness —usu. pl. 3 : quickness and cleverness in handling words and ideas 4 : talent for clever remarks or one noted for witty remarks —**wit·less** adj —**wit·less·ly** adv —**wit·less·ness** n —**wit·ted** adj

witch \'wich\ n 1 : person believed to have magic power 2 : ugly old woman ~ vb : bewitch

witch·craft \'wich,kraft\ n : power or practices of a witch

witch·ery \'wichərē\ n, pl **-er·ies** 1 : witchcraft 2 : charm

witch ha·zel \'wich,hāzəl\ n 1 : shrub having small yellow flowers in fall 2 : alcoholic lotion made from witch hazel bark

witch–hunt n 1 : searching out and persecution of supposed witches 2 : harassment esp. of political opponents

with \'with, 'with\ prep 1 : against, to, or toward 2 : in support of 3 : because of 4 : in the company of 5 : having 6 : despite 7 : containing 8 : by means of

with·draw \with'dró, with-\ vb **-drew** \-'drü\; **-drawn** \-'drón\; **-draw·ing** \-'dróiŋ\ 1 : take back or away 2 : call back or retract 3 : go away 4 : terminate one's participation in or use of —**with·draw·al** \-'dróəl\ n

with·drawn \with'drón\ adj : socially detached and unresponsive

with·er \'wither\ vb 1 : shrivel 2 : lose or cause to lose energy, force, or freshness

with·ers \'withərz\ n pl : ridge between the shoulder bones of a horse

with·hold \with'hōld, with-\ vb **-held** \-'held\; **-hold·ing** 1 : hold back 2 : refrain from giving

with·in \with'in, with-\ adv 1 : in or into the interior 2 : inside oneself ~ prep 1 : in or to the inner part of 2 : in the limits or compass of

with·out \with'aút, with-\ prep 1 : outside 2 : lacking 3 : unaccompanied or unmarked by —**without** adv

with·stand \with'stand, with-\ vb **-stood** \-'stúd\; **-stand·ing** : oppose successfully

wit·ness \'witnəs\ n 1 : testimony 2 : one who testifies 3 : one present at a transaction to testify that it has taken place 4 : one who has personal knowledge or experience 5 : something serving as proof ~ vb 1 : bear witness 2 : act as legal witness of 3 : furnish proof of 4 : be a witness of 5 : be the scene of

wit·ti·cism \'witə,sizəm\ n : witty saying or phrase

wit·ting \'witiŋ\ adj : intentional —**wit·ting·ly** adv

wit·ty \'witē\ adj **-ti·er; -est** : marked by or full of wit —**wit·ti·ly** \'wit³lē\ adv —**wit·ti·ness** n

wives pl of WIFE

wiz·ard \'wizərd\ n 1 : magician 2 : very clever person —**wiz·ard·ry** \-ərdrē\ n

wiz·ened \'wiz³nd\ adj : dried up

wob·ble \'wäbəl\ vb **-bled; -bling** 1 : move or cause to move with an irregular rocking motion 2 : tremble 3 : waver —**wobble** n —**wob·bly** \'wäbəlē\ adj

woe \'wō\ n 1 : deep suffering 2 : misfortune

woe·be·gone \'wōbi,gón\ adj : exhibiting woe, sorrow, or misery

woe·ful \'wōfəl\ adj 1 : full of woe 2 : bringing woe —**woe·ful·ly** adv

woke past of WAKE

woken past part of WAKE

wolf \'wu̇lf\ n. pl **wolves** \'wu̇lvz\ : large doglike predatory mammal ~ vb : eat greedily —**wolf·ish** adj

wol·fram \'wu̇lfrəm\ n : tungsten

wol·ver·ine \,wu̇lvə'rēn\ n. pl **-ines** : flesh–eating mammal related to the weasels

wom·an \'wu̇mən\ n. pl **wom·en** \'wimən\ 1 : adult female person 2 : womankind 3 : feminine nature —**wom·an·hood** \-,hu̇d\ n —**wom·an·ish** adj

wom·an·kind \-,kīnd\ n : females of the human race

wom·an·ly \-lē\ adj : having qualities characteristic of a woman —**wom·an·li·ness** \-lēnəs\ n

womb \'wüm\ n : uterus

won past of WIN

won·der \'wəndər\ n 1 : cause of astonishment or surprise 2 : feeling (as of astonishment) aroused by something extraordinary ~ vb 1 : feel surprise 2 : feel curiosity or doubt

won·der·ful \'wəndərfəl\ adj 1 : exciting wonder 2 : unusually good —**won·der·ful·ly** adv —**won·der·ful·ness** n

won·der·land \-,land, -lənd\ n 1 : fairylike imaginary realm 2 : place that excites admiration or wonder

won·der·ment \-mənt\ n : wonder

won·drous \'wəndrəs\ adj : wonderful —**won·drous·ly** adv —**won·drous·ness** n

wont \'wȯnt, 'wōnt\ adj : accustomed ~ n : habit —**wont·ed** adj

woo \'wü\ vb : try to gain the love or favor of —**woo·er** n

wood \'wu̇d\ n 1 : dense growth of trees usu. smaller than a forest —often pl. 2 : hard fibrous substance of trees and shrubs beneath the bark 3 : wood prepared for some use (as burning) ~ adj 1 : wooden 2 : suitable for working with wood 3 or **woods** \'wu̇dz\ : living or growing in woods —**wood·chop·per** n —**wood·pile** n —**wood·shed** n

wood·bine \'wu̇d,bīn\ n : climbing vine

wood·chuck \-,chək\ n : thick-bodied grizzled animal of No. America

matters relating to the woods 2 : skill in making articles from wood

wood·cut \-,kət\ n 1 : relief printing surface engraved on wood 2 : print from a woodcut

wood·ed \'wu̇dəd\ adj : covered with woods

wood·en \'wu̇dᵊn\ adj 1 : made of wood 2 : lacking resilience 3 : lacking ease. liveliness or interest —**wood·en·ly** adv —**wood·en·ness** n

wood·land \-lənd. -,land\ n : land covered with trees

wood·peck·er \'wu̇d,pekər\ n : brightly marked bird with a hard bill for drilling into trees

woods·man \'wu̇dzmən\ n : person who works in the woods

wood·wind \'wu̇d,wind\ n : one of a group of wind instruments (as a flute or oboe)

wood·work n : work (as interior house fittings) made of wood

woody \'wu̇dē\ adj **wood·i·er; -est** 1 : abounding with woods 2 : of, containing. or like wood fibers —**wood·i·ness** n

woof \'wu̇f\ n : weft

wool \'wu̇l\ n 1 : soft hair of some mammals and esp. the sheep 2 : something (as a textile) made of wool —**wooled** \'wu̇ld\ adj

wool·en, wool·len \'wu̇lən\ adj 1 : made of wool 2 : relating to the manufacture of woolen products ~ n 1 : woolen fabric 2 : woolen garments —usu. pl.

wool·gath·er·ing n : idle daydreaming

wool·ly \'wu̇lē\ adj **-li·er; -est** 1 : of, relating to. or bearing wool 2 : consisting of or resembling wool 3 : confused or turbulent

woo·zy \'wüzē\ adj **-zi·er; -est** 1 : confused 2 : somewhat dizzy, nauseated, or weak —**woo·zi·ness** n

word \'wərd\ n 1 : brief remark 2 : speech sound or series of speech sounds that communicates a meaning 3 : written representation of a word 4 : order 5 : news 6 : promise 7 pl : dispute ~ vb : express in words —**word·less** adj

word·ing \'wərdiŋ\ n : verbal expression

word processing n : production of structured and printed documents through a computer program (**word processor**) —**word process** vb

wordy \'wərdē\ *adj* **word·i·er; -est**
: using many words —**word·i·ness** *n*
wore *past of* WEAR
work \'wərk\ *n* 1 : labor 2 : employment
3 : task 4 : something (as an artistic
production) produced by mental effort or physical labor 5 *pl* : place
where industrial labor is done 6 *pl*
: moving parts of a mechanism 7
: workmanship ~ *adj* 1 : suitable for
wear while working 2 : used for work
~ *vb* **worked** \'wərkt\ *or* **wrought**
\'rȯt\. **work·ing** 1 : bring to pass 2
: create by expending labor upon 3
: bring or get into a form or condition
4 : set or keep in operation 5 : solve
6 : cause to labor 7 : arrange 8 : excite
9 : labor 10 : perform work regularly
for wages 11 : function according to
plan or design 12 : produce a desired
effect —**work·bench** *n* —**work·man**
\-mən\ *n* —**work·room** *n* —**in the
works** : in preparation
work·able \'wərkəbəl\ *adj* 1 : capable
of being worked 2 : feasible —**work-
able·ness** *n*
work·a·day \'wərkə,dā\ *adj* 1 : relating
to or suited for working days 2
: ordinary
work·a·hol·ic \,wərkə'hȯlik, -'häl-\ *n*
: compulsive worker
work·day \'wərk,dā\ *n* 1 : day on which
work is done 2 : period of time during
which one is working
work·er \'wərkər\ *n* : person who works
esp. for wages
work·horse *n* 1 : horse used for hard
work 2 : person who does most of the
work of a group task
work·house *n* : place of confinement for
persons who have committed minor
offenses
work·ing \'wərkiŋ\ *adj* 1 : adequate to
allow work to be done 2 : adopted or
assumed to help further work or activity ~ *n* : operation —usu. used in
pl.
work·ing·man \'wərkiŋ,man\ *n*
: worker
work·man·like \-,līk\ *adj* : worthy of a
good workman
work·man·ship \-,ship\ *n* 1 : art or skill
of a workman 2 : quality of a piece of
work
work·out \'wərk,aȯt\ *n* : exercise to improve one's fitness
work out *vb* 1 : bring about by effort 2

: solve 3 : develop 4 : to be successful
5 : perform exercises
work·shop *n* 1 : small establishment for
manufacturing or handicrafts 2
: seminar emphasizing exchange of
ideas and practical methods
world \'wərld\ *n* 1 : universe 2 : earth
with its inhabitants and all things
upon it 3 : people in general 4 : great
number or quantity 5 : class of persons or their sphere of interest
world·ly \'wərldlē\ *adj* 1 : devoted to
this world and its pursuits rather than
to religion 2 : sophisticated —**world-
li·ness** *n*
world·ly·wise *adj* : possessing understanding of human affairs
world·wide *adj* : extended throughout
the entire world —**worldwide** *adv*
worm \'wərm\ *n* 1 : earthworm or a similar animal 2 *pl* : disorder caused by
parasitic worms ~ *vb* 1 : move or
cause to move in a slow and indirect
way 2 : to free from worms —**wormy**
adj
worm·wood \'wərm,wu̇d\ *n* 1 : aromatic
woody herb (as sagebrush) 2
: something bitter or grievous
worn *past part of* WEAR
worn-out \'wōrn'au̇t\ *adj* : exhausted or
used up by or as if by wear
wor·ri·some \'wərēsəm\ *adj* 1 : causing
worry 2 : inclined to worry
wor·ry \'wərē\ *vb* **-ried; -ry·ing** 1
: shake and mangle with the teeth 2
: disturb 3 : feel or express anxiety ~
n, pl **-ries** 1 : anxiety 2 : cause of
anxiety —**wor·ri·er** *n*
worse \'wərs\ *adj, comparative of* BAD
or of ILL 1 : bad or evil in a greater
degree 2 : more unwell ~ *n* 1 : one
that is worse 2 : greater degree of badness ~ *adv, comparative of* BAD *or of*
ILL : in a worse manner
wors·en \'wərsᵊn\ *vb* : make or become
worse
wor·ship \'wərshəp\ *n* 1 : reverence toward a divine being or supernatural
power 2 : expression of reverence 3
: extravagant respect or devotion ~
vb **-shiped** *or* **-shipped; -ship·ing** *or*
-ship·ping 1 : honor or reverence 2
: perform or take part in worship —
wor·ship·er *or* **wor·ship·per** *n*
worst \'wərst\ *adj, superlative of* BAD *or*
of ILL 1 : most bad, evil, ill, or corrupt
2 : most unfavorable, unpleasant, or
painful ~ *n* : one that is worst ~ *adv,*

superlative of ILL *or of* BAD *or* BADLY
: to the extreme degree of badness ~
vb : defeat

wor·sted \'wůstəd, 'wərstəd\ *n* : smooth compact wool yarn or fabric made from such yarn

worth \'wərth\ *prep* **1** : equal in value to **2** : deserving of ~ *n* **1** : monetary value **2** : value of something measured by its qualities **3** : moral or personal merit

worth·less \-ləs\ *adj* **1** : lacking worth **2** : useless —**worth·less·ness** *n*

worth·while \-'hwīl\ *adj* : being worth the time or effort spent

wor·thy \'wərthē\ *adj* **-thi·er; -est 1** : having worth or value **2** : having sufficient worth ~ *n, pl* **-thies** : worthy person —**wor·thi·ly** *adv* — **wor·thi·ness** *n*

would \'wůd\ *past of* WILL —used to express (1) preference (2) intent (3) habitual action (4) contingency (5) probability or (6) a request

would–be \'wůd'bē\ *adj* : desiring or pretending to be

1wound \'wünd\ *n* **1** : injury in which the skin is broken **2** : mental hurt ~ *vb* : inflict a wound to or in

2wound \'waůnd\ *past of* WIND

wove *past of* WEAVE

woven *past part of* WEAVE

wrack \'rak\ *n* : ruin

wraith \'rāth\ *n, pl* **wraiths** \'rāthz, 'rāths\ **1** : ghost **2** : insubstantial appearance

wran·gle \'raŋgəl\ *vb or n* : quarrel — **wran·gler** *n*

wrap \'rap\ *vb* **-pp- 1** : cover esp. by winding or folding **2** : envelop and secure for transportation or storage **3** : enclose, surround, or conceal wholly **4** : coil, fold, draw, or twine about something ~ *n* **1** : wrapper or wrapping **2** : outer garment (as a shawl)

wrap·per \'rapər\ *n* **1** : that in which something is wrapped **2** : one that wraps

wrap·ping *n* : something used to wrap an object

wrath \'rath\ *n* : violent anger —**wrath·ful** \-fəl\ *adj*

wreak \'rēk\ *vb* **1** : inflict **2** : bring about

wreath \'rēth\ *n, pl* **wreaths** \'rēthz, 'rēths\ : something (as boughs) intertwined into a circular shape

wreathe \'rēth\ *vb* **wreathed; wreath·ing 1** : shape into or take on the shape

of a wreath **2** : decorate or cover with a wreath

wreck \'rek\ *n* **1** : broken remains (as of a ship or vehicle) after heavy damage **2** : something disabled or in a state of ruin **3** : an individual who has become weak or infirm **4** : action of breaking up or destroying something ~ *vb* : ruin or damage by breaking up

wreck·age \'rekij\ *n* **1** : act of wrecking **2** : remains of a wreck

wreck·er \-ər\ *n* **1** : automotive vehicle for removing disabled cars **2** : one that wrecks or tears down and removes buildings

wren \'ren\ *n* : small mostly brown singing bird

wrench \'rench\ *vb* **1** : pull with violent twisting or force **2** : injure or disable by a violent twisting or straining ~ *n* **1** : forcible twisting **2** : tool for exerting a twisting force

wrest \'rest\ *vb* **1** : pull or move by a forcible twisting movement **2** : gain with difficulty ~ *n* : forcible twist

wres·tle \'resəl, 'ras-\ *vb* **-tled; -tling 1** : scuffle with and attempt to throw and pin an opponent **2** : compete against in wrestling **3** : struggle (as with a problem) ~ *n* : action or an instance of wrestling —**wres·tler** \'reslər, 'ras-\ *n*

wres·tling \'resliŋ\ *n* : sport in which 2 opponents try to throw and pin each other

wretch \'rech\ *n* **1** : miserable unhappy person **2** : vile person

wretch·ed \'rechəd\ *adj* **1** : deeply afflicted, dejected, or distressed **2** : grievous **3** : inferior —**wretch·ed·ly** *adv* —**wretch·ed·ness** *n*

wrig·gle \'rigəl\ *vb* **-gled; -gling 1** : twist and turn restlessly **2** : move along by twisting and turning —**wrig·gle** *n* —**wrig·gler** \'rigələr\ *n*

wring \'riŋ\ *vb* **wrung** \'rəŋ\; **wring·ing 1** : squeeze or twist out moisture **2** : get by or as if by twisting or pressing **3** : twist together in anguish **4** : pain —**wring·er** *n*

wrin·kle \'riŋkəl\ *n* : crease or small fold on a surface (as in the skin or in cloth) ~ *vb* **-kled; -kling** : develop or cause to develop wrinkles —**wrin·kly** \-kəlē\ *adj*

wrist \'rist\ *n* : joint or region between the hand and the arm

writ \'rit\ *n* **1** : something written **2** : legal order in writing

write \'rīt\ *vb* **wrote** \'rōt\; **writ·ten** \'rit⁹n\; **writ·ing** \'rītiŋ\ **1** : form letters or words on a surface **2** : form the letters or the words of (as on paper) **3** : make up and set down for others to read **4** : write a letter to —**write off** *vb* : cancel

writ·er \'rītər\ *n* : one that writes esp. as a business or occupation

writhe \'rīth\ *vb* **writhed; writh·ing** : twist and turn this way and that

writ·ing \'rītiŋ\ *n* **1** : act of one that writes **2** : handwriting **3** : something written or printed

wrong \'roŋ\ *n* **1** : unfair or unjust act **2** : something that is contrary to justice **3** : state of being or doing wrong ~ *adj* **wrong·er** \'roŋər\; **wrong·est** \'roŋəst\ **1** : sinful **2** : not right according to a standard **3** : unsuitable **4** : incorrect ~ *adv* **1** : in a wrong direction or manner **2** : incorrectly ~ *vb* **wronged; wrong·ing 1** : do wrong to **2** : treat unjustly —**wrong·ly** *adv*

wrong·do·er \-'düər\ *n* : one who does wrong —**wrong·do·ing** \-'düiŋ\ *n*

wrong·ful \-fəl\ *adj* **1** : wrong **2** : illegal —**wrong·ful·ly** *adv* —**wrong·ful·ness** *n*

wrong·head·ed \'roŋ'hedəd\ *adj* : stubborn in clinging to wrong opinion or principles —**wrong·head·ed·ly** *adv* —**wrong·head·ed·ness** *n*

wrote *past of* WRITE

wrought \'rot\ *adj* **1** : formed **2** : hammered into shape **3** : deeply stirred

wrung *past of* WRING

wry \'rī\ *adj* **wri·er** \'rīər\; **wri·est** \'rīəst\ **1** : turned abnormally to one side **2** : twisted **3** : cleverly and often ironically humorous —**wry·ly** *adv* —**wry·ness** *n*

X

x \'eks\ *n*, *pl* **x's** *or* **xs** \'eksəz\ **1** : 24th letter of the alphabet **2** : unknown quantity ~ *vb* **x-ed; x·ing** *or* **x'ing** : cancel with a series of *x*'s—usu. with *out*

xe·non \'zē,nän, 'zen,än\ *n* : heavy gaseous chemical element

xe·no·pho·bia \,zenə'fōbēə, ,zēn-\ *n* : fear and hatred of foreign people and things —**xe·no·phobe** \'zenə,fōb, 'zēn-\ *n*

Xmas \'krisməs\ *n* : Christmas

x–ra·di·a·tion *n* **1** : exposure to X rays **2** : radiation consisting of X rays

x-ray \'eks,rā\ *vb* : examine, treat, or photograph with X rays

X ray *n* **1** : radiation of short wavelength that is able to penetrate solids **2** : photograph taken with X rays —**X-ray** *adj*

xy·lo·phone \'zīlə,fōn\ *n* : musical instrument with wooden bars that are struck —**xy·lo·phon·ist** \-,fōnist\ *n*

Y

y \'wī\ *n*, *pl* **y's** *or* **ys** \'wīz\ : 25th letter of the alphabet

1-y \ē\ *adj suffix* **1** : composed or full of **2** : like **3** : performing or apt to perform an action

2-y \ē\ *n suffix*, *pl* **-ies 1** : state, condition, or quality **2** : activity, place of business, or goods dealt with **3** : whole group

yacht \'yät\ *n* : luxurious pleasure boat ~ *vb* : race or cruise in a yacht

ya·hoo \'yāhü, 'yä-\ *n*, *pl* **-hoos** : uncouth or stupid person

yak \'yak\ *n* : big hairy Asian ox

yam \'yam\ *n* **1** : edible root of a tropical vine **2** : deep orange sweet potato

yam·mer \'yamər\ *vb* **1** : whimper **2** : chatter —**yammer** *n*

yank \'yaŋk\ *n* : strong sudden pull —**yank** *vb*

Yank \'yaŋk\ *n* : Yankee

Yan·kee \'yaŋkē\ *n* : native or inhabitant of New England. the northern U.S.. or the U.S.

yap \'yap\ *vb* **-pp-** **1** : yelp **2** : chatter —**yap** *n*

¹yard \'yärd\ *n* **1** : 3 feet **2** : long spar for supporting and spreading a sail —**yard·age** \-ij\ *n*

²yard *n* **1** : enclosed roofless area **2** : grounds of a building **3** : work area

yard·arm \'yärd,ärm\ *n* : end of the yard of a square-rigged ship

yard·stick *n* **1** : measuring stick 3 feet long **2** : standard for judging

yar·mul·ke \'yäməkə. 'yär-. -məl-\ *n* : a small brimless cap worn by Jewish males in a synagogue

yarn \'yärn\ *n* **1** : spun fiber for weaving or knitting **2** : tale

yaw \'yó\ *vb* : deviate erratically from a course —**yaw** *n*

yawl \'yól\ *n* : sailboat with 2 masts

yawn \'yón\ *vb* : open the mouth wide ~ *n* : deep breath through a wide-open mouth —**yawn·er** *n*

ye \'yē\ *pron* : you

yea \'yā\ *adv* **1** : yes **2** : truly ~ *n* : affirmative vote

year \'yir\ *n* **1** : period of about 365 days **2** *pl* : age

year·book *n* : annual report of the year's events

year·ling \'yirliŋ. 'yərlən\ *n* : one that is or is rated as a year old

year·ly \'yirlē\ *adj* : annual —**yearly** *adv*

yearn \'yərn\ *vb* **1** : feel desire esp. for what one cannot have **2** : feel tenderness or compassion

yearn·ing \-iŋ\ *n* : tender or urgent desire

yeast \'yēst\ *n* : froth or sediment in sugary liquids containing a tiny fungus and used in making alcoholic liquors and as a leaven in baking —**yeasty** *adj*

yell \'yel\ *vb* : utter a loud cry —**yell** *n*

yel·low \'yelō\ *adj* **1** : of the color yellow **2** : sensational **3** : cowardly ~ *vb* : make or turn yellow ~ *n* **1** : color

of lemons **2** : yolk of an egg —**yellow·ish** \'yeləwish\ *adj*

yellow fever *n* : virus disease marked by prostration. jaundice. fever. and often hemorrhage

yellow jacket *n* : wasp with yellow stripes

yelp \'yelp\ *vb* : utter a sharp quick shrill cry —**yelp** *n*

yen \'yen\ *n* : strong desire

yeo·man \'yōmən\ *n* **1** : attendant or officer in a royal or noble household **2** : small farmer **3** : naval petty officer with clerical duties —**yeo·man·ry** \-rē\ *n*

-yer —see -ER

yes \'yes\ *adv* —used to express consent or agreement ~ *n* : affirmative answer

ye·shi·va, ye·shi·vah \yə'shēvə\ *n. pl* **yeshivas** *or* **ye·shi·voth** \-,shē'vōt, -'vōth\ : Jewish school

yes–man \'yes,man\ *n* : person who agrees with every opinion or suggestion of a boss

yes·ter·day \'yestərdē\ *adv* **1** : on the day preceding today **2** : only a short time ago ~ *n* **1** : day last past **2** : time not long past

yet \'yet\ *adv* **1** : in addition **2** : up to now **3** : so soon as now **4** : nevertheless ~ *conj* : but

yew \'yü\ *n* : evergreen tree or shrubs with dark stiff poisonous needles

yield \'yēld\ *vb* **1** : surrender **2** : grant **3** : bear as a crop **4** : produce **5** : cease opposition or resistance ~ *n* : quantity produced or returned

yo·del \'yōdᵊl\ *vb* **-deled** *or* **-delled; -del·ing** *or* **-del·ling** : sing by abruptly alternating between chest voice and falsetto —**yodel** *n* —**yo·del·er** \'yōdᵊlər\ *n*

yo·ga \'yōgə\ *n* : system of exercises for attaining bodily or mental control and well-being

yo·gi \'yōgē\ : person who practices yoga

yo·gurt \'yōgərt\ *n* : fermented slightly acid soft food made from milk

yoke \'yōk\ *n* **1** : neck frame for coupling draft animals or for carrying loads **2** : clamp **3** : slavery **4** : tie or link **5** : piece of a garment esp. at the shoulder ~ *vb* **yoked; yok·ing 1** : couple with a yoke **2** : join

yo·kel \'yōkəl\ *n* : naive and gullible country person

yolk \'yōk\ n : yellow part of an egg —
yolked \'yōkt\ adj

Yom Kip·pur \,yōmki'pur, ,yäm-,
-'kipər\ n : Jewish holiday observed
in September or October with fasting
and prayer as a day of atonement

yon \'yän\ adj or adv : YONDER

yon·der \'yändər\ adv : at or to that
place ~ adj : distant

yore \'yōr\ n : time long past

you \'yü\ pron 1 : person or persons addressed 2 : person in general

young \'yəŋ\ adj **young·er** \'yəŋgər\;
young·est \'yəŋgəst\ 1 : being in the
first or an early stage of life, growth,
or development 2 : recently come into
being 3 : youthful ~ n, pl **young**
: persons or animals that are young —
young·ish \-ish\ adj

young·ster \-stər\ n 1 : young person 2
: child

your \yər, 'yur, 'yōr\ adj : relating to
you or yourself

yours \'yurz, 'yōrz\ pron : the ones belonging to you

your·self \yər'self\ pron, pl **your·selves**
\-'selvz\ : you —used reflexively or
for emphasis

youth \'yüth\ n, pl **youths** \'yüthz,
'yüths\ 1 : period between childhood
and maturity 2 : young man 3 : young
persons 4 : state or quality of being
young, fresh, or vigorous

youth·ful \'yüthfəl\ adj 1 : relating to or
appropriate to youth 2 : young 3
: vigorous and fresh —**youth·ful·ly**
adv —**youth·ful·ness** n

yowl \'yaul\ vb : utter a loud long
mournful cry —**yowl** n

yo–yo \'yō,yō\ n, pl **-yos** : toy that falls
from or rises to the hand as it unwinds
and rewinds on a string

yuc·ca \'yəkə\ n : any of several plants
related to the lilies that grow in dry
regions

yule \'yül\ n : Christmas —**yule·tide**
\-,tīd\ n

yum·my \'yəmē\ adj **-mi·er; -est**
: highly attractive or pleasing

Z

z \'zē\ n, pl **z's** or **zs** : 26th letter of the
alphabet

za·ny \'zānē\ n, pl **-nies** 1 : clown 2
: silly person ~ adj **-ni·er; -est** : crazy
or foolish —**za·ni·ly** adv — **za·ni·
ness** n

zeal \'zēl\ n : enthusiasm

zeal·ot \'zelət\ n : fanatical partisan

zeal·ous \'zeləs\ adj : filled with zeal —
zeal·ous·ly adv —**zeal·ous·ness** n

ze·bra \'zēbrə\ n : horselike African
mammal marked with light and dark
stripes

zeit·geist \'tsīt,gīst, 'zīt-\ n : general
spirit of an era

ze·nith \'zēnəth\ n : highest point

zeph·yr \'zefər\ n : gentle breeze

zep·pe·lin \'zepələn\ n : rigid airship
like a blimp

ze·ro \'zērō\ n, pl **-ros** 1 : number represented by the symbol 0 or the sym-
bol itself 2 : starting point 3 : lowest
point ~ adj : having no size or quantity

zest \'zest\ n 1 : quality of enhancing

enjoyment 2 : keen enjoyment —
zest·ful \-fəl\ adj —**zest·ful·ly** adv —
zest·ful·ness n

zig·zag \'zig,zag\ n : one of a series of
short sharp turns or angles ~ adj
: having zigzags ~ adv : in or by a
zigzag path ~ vb **-gg-** : proceed along
a zigzag path

zil·lion \'zilyən\ n : large indeterminate
number

zinc \'ziŋk\ n : bluish white crystaline
metallic chemical element

zing \'ziŋ\ n 1 : shrill humming noise 2
: energy —**zing** vb

zin·nia \'zinēə, 'zēnyə\ n : American
herb widely grown for its showy
flowers

¹**zip** \'zip\ vb **-pp-** : move or act with
speed ~ n : energy

²**zip** vb **-pp-** : close or open with a zip-
per

zip code n : number that identifies a
U.S. postal delivery area

zip·per \'zipər\ n : fastener consisting of
2 rows of interlocking teeth

zip•py \'zipē\ *adj* **-pi•er; -est** : brisk

zir•con \'zər,kän\ *n* : zirconium-containing mineral sometimes used in jewelry

zir•co•ni•um \,zər'kōnēəm\ *n* : corrosion-resistant gray metallic element

zith•er \'zithər, 'zith-\ *n* : stringed musical instrument played by plucking

zi•ti \'zētē\ *n, pl* **ziti** : short tubular pasta

zo•di•ac \'zōdē,ak\ *n* : imaginary belt in the heavens encompassing the paths of the planets and divided into 12 signs used in astrology —**zo•di•a•cal** \zō'dīəkəl\ *adj*

zom•bie \'zämbē\ *n* : person thought to have died and been brought back to life without free will

zon•al \'zōnᵊl\ *adj* : of, relating to, or having the form of a zone —**zon•al•ly** *adv*

zone \'zōn\ *n* **1** : division of the earth's surface based on latitude and climate **2** : distinctive area ~ *vb* **zoned; zoning 1** : mark off into zones **2** : reserve for special purposes —**zo•na•tion** \zō'nāshən\ *n*

zoo \'zü\ *n, pl* **zoos** : collection of living animals usu. for public display —**zoo•keep•er** *n*

zo•ol•o•gy \zō'äləjē\ *n* : science of animals —**zo•o•log•i•cal** \,zōə'läjikəl\ *adj* —**zo•ol•o•gist** \zō'äləjist\ *n*

zoom \'züm\ *vb* **1** : move with a loud hum or buzz **2** : move or increase with great speed —**zoom** *n*

zuc•chi•ni \zu'kēnē\ *n, pl* **-ni** *or* **-nis** : summer squash with smooth cylindrical dark green fruits

zwie•back \'swēbak, 'swī-, 'zwē-, 'zwī-\ *n* : biscuit of baked, sliced, and toasted bread

zy•gote \'zī,gōt\ *n* : cell formed by the union of 2 sexual cells —**zy•got•ic** \zī'gätik\ *adj*

Abbreviations

Most of these abbreviations have been given in one form. Variation in use of periods, in type, and in capitalization is frequent and widespread (as *mph, MPH, m.p.h., Mph*).

abbr abbreviation
AC alternating current
acad academic, academy
AD in the year of our Lord
adj adjective
adv adverb, advertisement
advt advertisement
AF air force, audio frequency
agric agricultural, agriculture
AK Alaska
aka also known as
AL, Ala Alabama
alg algebra
Alta Alberta
a.m., AM before noon
Am, Amer America, American
amp ampere
amt amount
anc ancient
anon anonymous
ans answer
ant antonym
APO army post office
approx approximate, approximately
Apr April
apt apartment, aptitude
AR Arkansas
arith arithmetic
Ariz Arizona
Ark Arkansas
art article, artificial
assn association
assoc associate, associated, association
asst assistant
ATM automated teller machine
att attached, attention, attorney
attn attention
atty attorney
Aug August
auth authentic, author, authorized
aux, auxil auxiliary
av avoirdupois

AV audiovisual
ave avenue
avg average
AZ Arizona
BA bachelor of arts
bal balance
bar barometer, barrel
bbl barrel, barrels
BC before Christ, British Columbia
BCE before the Christian Era, before the Common Era
bet between
biog biographer, biographical, biography
biol biologic, biological, biologist, biology
bldg building
blvd boulevard
BO backorder, best offer, body odor, box office, branch office
Brit Britain, British
bro brother, brothers
bros brothers
BS bachelor of science
Btu British thermal unit
bu bureau, bushel
c carat, cent, centimeter, century, chapter, circa, cup
C Celsius, centigrade
ca circa
CA, Cal, Calif California
cal calendar, caliber, calorie
Can, Canad Canada, Canadian
cap capacity, capital, capitalize, capitalized
Capt captain
CB citizens band
CDT central daylight time
cen central
cert certificate, certification, certified, certify
cf compare
chap chapter

chem chemistry
cir circle, circuit, circular, circumference
civ civil, civilian
cm centimeter
co company, county
CO Colorado
c/o care of
COD cash on delivery, collect on delivery
col colonial, colony, color, colored, column, counsel
Col colonel, Colorado
Colo Colorado
comp comparative, compensation, compiled, compiler, composition, compound, comprehensive, comptroller
cong congress, congressional
conj conjunction
Conn Connecticut
cont continued
contr contract, contraction
corp corporal, corporation
corr corrected, correction
cp compare, coupon
CPR cardiopulmonary resuscitation
cr credit, creditor
CSA Confederate States of America
CST Central standard time
ct carat, cent, count, court
CT central time, certified teacher, Connecticut
cu cubic
cur currency, current
CZ Canal Zone
d penny
DA district attorney
dag dekagram
dal dekaliter
dam dekameter
dbl double
DC direct current, District of Columbia
DDS doctor of dental science, doctor of dental surgery
DE Delaware
dec deceased, decrease
Dec December
deg degree
Del Delaware
Dem Democrat, Democratic
dept department

det detached, detachment, detail, determine
dg decigram
dia, diam diameter
diag diagonal, diagram
dict dictionary
dif, diff difference
dim dimension, diminished
dir director
disc discount
dist distance, district
div divided, dividend, division, divorced
dl deciliter
dm decimeter
DMD doctor of dental medicine
DOB date of birth
doz dozen
DP data processing
dr dram, drive, drum
Dr doctor
DST daylight saving time
DUI driving under the influence
DWI driving while intoxicated
dz dozen
e east, eastern, excellent
ea each
ecol ecological, ecology
econ economics, economist, economy
EDT Eastern daylight time
e.g. for example
EKG electrocardiogram, electrocardiograph
elec electric, electrical, electricity
elem elementary
eng engine, engineer, engineering
Eng England, English
esp especially
EST Eastern standard time
ET eastern time
et al and others
etc et cetera
ex example, express, extra
exec executive
f false, female, feminine
F, Fah, Fahr Fahrenheit
Feb February
fed federal, federation
fem female, feminine
FL, Fla Florida
fl oz fluid ounce
FPO fleet post office
fr father, friar, from
Fri Friday

ft feet. foot. fort
fut future
FYI for your information
g gram
Ga, GA Georgia
gal gallery. gallon
gen general
geog geographic. geographical.
   geography
geol geologic. geological. geology
geom geometric. geometrical.
   geometry
gm gram
GMT Greenwich mean time
GOP Grand Old Party (Republican)
gov government, governor
govt government
GP general practice, general
   practitioner
gr grade, grain, gram
gram grammar, grammatical
gt great
GU Guam
hd head
hf half
hgt height
hgwy highway
HI Hawaii
hist historian, historical, history
hon honor, honorable, honorary
hr here, hour
HS high school
ht height
HT Hawaiian time
hwy highway
i intransitive, island, isle
Ia, IA Iowa
ICU intensive care unit
ID Idaho, identification
i.e. that is
IL, Ill Illinois
imp imperative, imperfect
in inch
IN Indiana
inc incomplete, incorporated
ind independent
Ind Indian, Indiana
inf infinitive
int interest
interj interjection
intl, intnl international
ital italic, italicized
Jan January
JD juvenile delinquent

jour journal, journeyman
JP justice of the peace
jr, jun junior
JV junior varsity
Kans Kansas
kg kilogram
km kilometer
KS Kansas
kW kilowatt
Ky, KY Kentucky
l late. left. liter. long
L large
La Louisiana
LA Los Angeles, Louisiana
lat latitude
lb pound
lg large, long
lib liberal, librarian, library
long longitude
m male, masculine, meter, mile
M medium
MA Massachusetts
Man Manitoba
Mar March
masc masculine
Mass Massachusetts
math mathematical, mathematician
max maximum
Md Maryland
MD doctor of medicine, Maryland
MDT mountain daylight time
Me, ME Maine
med medium
mg milligram
mgr manager
MI, Mich Michigan
mid middle
min minimum, minor, minute
Minn Minnesota
misc miscellaneous
Miss Mississippi
ml milliliter
mm millimeter
MN Minnesota
mo month
Mo, MO Missouri
Mon Monday
Mont Montana
mpg miles per gallon
mph miles per hour
MRI magnetic resonance imaging
MS Mississippi
MST Mountain standard time
mt mount, mountain

MT Montana, Mountain time
n neuter, noun
N north, northern
NA North America, not applicable
nat national, native, natural
natl national
naut nautical
NB New Brunswick
NC North Carolina
ND, N Dak North Dakota
NE, Neb, Nebr Nebraska
neg negative
neut neuter
Nev Nevada
Nfld Newfoundland
NH New Hampshire
NJ New Jersey
NM, N Mex New Mexico
no north, number
Nov November
NR not rated
NS Nova Scotia
NV Nevada
NWT Northwest Territories
NY New York
NYC New York City
O Ohio
obj object, objective
occas occasionally
Oct October
off office, officer, official
OH Ohio
OJ orange juice
OK, Okla Oklahoma
Ont Ontario
opp opposite
OR, Ore, Oreg Oregon
orig original, originally
oz ounce, ounces
p page
Pa Pennsylvania
PA Pennsylvania, public address
PAC political action committee
par paragraph, parallel
part participle, particular
pass passenger, passive
pat patent
PC percent, politically correct,
  postcard
pd paid
PD police department
PDT Pacific daylight time
PE physical education
PEI Prince Edward Island

Penn, Penna Pennsylvania
pg page
PIN personal identification
  number
pk park, peak, peck
pkg package
pl place, plural
p.m., PM afternoon
PMS premenstrual syndrome
PO post office
Port Portugal, Portuguese
pos position, positive
poss possessive
pp pages
PQ Province of Quebec
pr pair, price, printed
PR public relations, Puerto Rico
prep preposition
pres present, president
prob probable, probably, problem
prof professor
pron pronoun
prov province
PS postscript, public school
PST Pacific standard time
psych psychology
pt part, payment, pint, point
PT Pacific time, physical therapy
pvt private
qr quarter
qt quantity, quart
Que Quebec
quot quotation
r right, river
rd road, rod, round
RDA recommended daily
  allowance, recommended dietary
  allowance
recd received
reg region, register, registered,
  regular
rel relating, relative, religion
rep report, reporter, representative,
  republic
Rep Republican
res residence
rev reverse, review, revised,
  revision, revolution
Rev reverend
RFD rural free delivery
RI Rhode Island
rm room
rpm revolutions per minute
RR railroad, rural route

RSVP please reply
rt right
rte route
s small, south, southern
SA South America
SASE self-addressed stamped envelope
Sask Saskatchewan
Sat Saturday
SC South Carolina
sci science, scientific
SD, S Dak South Dakota
secy secretary
sen senate, senator, senior
Sept, Sep September
sing singular
sm small
so south, southern
soph sophomore
sp spelling
spec special, specifically
specif specific, specifically
SPF sun protection factor
sq square
sr senior
Sr sister
SSN Social Security number
SSR Soviet Socialist Republic
st street
St saint
std standard
subj subject
Sun Sunday
supt superintendent
SWAT Special Weapons and Tactics
syn synonym
t teaspoon, temperature, ton, transitive, troy, true
T tablespoon
tbs, tbsp tablespoon
TD touchdown
tech technical, technician, technology

Tenn Tennessee
terr territory
Tex Texas
Th, Thu, Thur, Thurs Thursday
TN Tennessee
trans translated, translation, translator
tsp teaspoon
Tu, Tue, Tues Tuesday
TX Texas
UK United Kingdom
UN United Nations
univ universal, university
US United States
USA United States of America
USSR Union of Soviet Socialist Republics
usu usual, usually
UT Utah
UV ultraviolet
v verb, versus
Va, VA Virginia
var variant, variety
vb verb
VG very good
VI Virgin Islands
vol volume, volunteer
VP vice-president
vs versus
Vt, VT Vermont
W west, western
WA, Wash Washington
Wed Wednesday
WI, Wis, Wisc Wisconsin
wk week, work
wt weight
WV, W Va West Virginia
WY, Wyo Wyoming
XL extra large, extra long
yd yard
yr year, younger, your
YT Yukon Territory

Handbook of Style

Punctuation

The English writing system uses punctuation marks to separate groups of words for meaning and emphasis; to convey an idea of the variations of pitch, volume, pauses, and intonations of speech; and to help avoid ambiguity. English punctuation marks, together with general rules and bracketed examples of their use, follow.

APOSTROPHE '

1. **indicates the possessive case of nouns and indefinite pronouns** ⟨the boy's mother⟩ ⟨the boys' mothers⟩ ⟨It is anyone's guess.⟩
2. **marks omissions in contracted words** ⟨didn't⟩ ⟨o'clock⟩
3. **often forms plurals of letters, figures, and words referred to as words** ⟨You should dot your *i*'s and cross your *t*'s.⟩ ⟨several 8's⟩ ⟨She has trouble pronouncing her *the*'s.⟩

BRACKETS [ ]

1. **set off extraneous data such as editorial additions esp. within quoted material** ⟨wrote that the author was "trying to dazzle his readers with phrases like *jeu de mots* [play on words]"⟩
2. **function as parentheses within parentheses** ⟨Bowman Act (22 Stat., ch. 4, § [or sec.] 4, p. 50)⟩

COLON :

1. **introduces word, clause, or phrase that explains, illustrates, amplifies, or restates what has gone before** ⟨The sentence was poorly constructed: it lacked both unity and coherence.⟩
2. **introduces a series** ⟨Three countries were represented: England, France, and Belgium.⟩
3. **introduces lengthy quoted material set off from the rest of a text by indentation but not by quotation marks** ⟨I quote from the text of Chapter One:⟩
4. **separates data in time-telling and data in bibliographic**

and biblical references ⟨8:30 a.m.⟩ ⟨New York: Smith Publishing Co.⟩ ⟨John 4:10⟩

5. **separates titles and subtitles (as of books)** ⟨*The Tragic Dynasty: A History of the Romanovs*⟩
6. **follows the salutation in formal correspondence** ⟨Dear Sir:⟩ ⟨Gentlemen:⟩

COMMA ,

1. **separates main clauses joined by a coordinating conjunction (as *and, but, or, nor,* or *for*) and very short clauses not so joined** ⟨She knew very little about him, and he volunteered nothing.⟩ ⟨I came, I saw, I conquered.⟩
2. **sets off an adverbial clause (or a long phrase) that precedes the main clause** ⟨When she found that her friends had deserted her, she sat down and cried.⟩
3. **sets off from the rest of the sentence transitional words and expressions (as *on the contrary, on the other hand*), conjunctive adverbs (as *consequently, furthermore, however*), and expressions that introduce an illustration or example (as *namely, for example*)** ⟨Your second question, on the other hand, remains open.⟩ ⟨The mystery, however, remains unsolved.⟩ ⟨She expects to travel through two countries, namely, France and England.⟩
4. **separates words, phrases, or clauses in series and coordinate adjectives modifying a noun** ⟨Men, women, and children crowded into the square.⟩ ⟨The harsh, cold wind was strong.⟩
5. **sets off from the rest of the sentence parenthetic elements (as nonrestrictive modifiers)** ⟨Our guide, who wore a blue beret, was an experienced traveler.⟩ ⟨We visited Gettysburg, the site of a famous battle.⟩
6. **introduces a direct quotation, terminates a direct quotation that is neither a question nor an exclamation, and encloses split quotations** ⟨John said, "I am leaving."⟩ ⟨"I am leaving," John said.⟩ ⟨"I am leaving," John said with determination, "even if you want me to stay."⟩
7. **sets off words in direct address, absolute phrases, and mild interjections** ⟨You may go, Mary, if you wish.⟩ ⟨I fear the encounter, his temper being what it is.⟩ ⟨Ah, that's my idea of an excellent dinner.⟩
8. **separates a question from the rest of the sentence which it ends** ⟨It's a fine day, isn't it?⟩
9. **indicates the omission of a word or words, and esp. a**

word or words used earlier in the sentence ⟨Common stocks are preferred by some investors; bonds, by others.⟩

10. **is used to avoid ambiguity** ⟨To Mary, Jane was someone special.⟩

11. **is used to group numbers into units of three in separating thousands, millions, etc.; however, it is generally not used in numbers of four figures, in page numbers, in dates, or in street numbers** ⟨Smithville, pop. 100,000⟩ *but* ⟨3600 rpm⟩ ⟨the year 1973⟩ ⟨page 1411⟩ ⟨4507 Smith Street⟩

12. **punctuates an inverted name** ⟨Smith, John W., Jr.⟩

13. **separates a proper name from a following academic, honorary, governmental, or military title** ⟨John Smith, M.D.⟩

14. **sets off geographical names (as state or country from city), items in dates, and addresses from the rest of a text** ⟨Shreveport, Louisiana, is the site of a large air base.⟩ ⟨On Sunday, June 23, 1940, he was wounded.⟩ ⟨Number 10 Downing Street, London, is a famous address.⟩

15. **follows the salutation in informal correspondence and follows the closing line of a formal or informal letter** ⟨Dear Mary,⟩ ⟨Affectionately,⟩ ⟨Very truly yours,⟩

DASH —

1. **usu. marks an abrupt change or break in the continuity of a sentence** ⟨When in 1960 the stockpile was sold off—indeed, dumped as surplus—natural-rubber sales were hard hit.—Barry Commoner⟩

2. **introduces a summary statement after a series** ⟨Oil, steel, and wheat—these are the sinews of industrialization.⟩

3. **often precedes the attribution of a quotation** ⟨My foot is on my native heath . . . . —Sir Walter Scott⟩

ELLIPSIS . . .   .

1. **indicates the omission of one or more words within a quoted passage** ⟨The head is not more native to the heart . . . than is the throne of Denmark to thy father.—Shakespeare⟩

2. **indicates halting speech or an unfinished sentence in dialogue** ⟨"I'd like to . . . that is . . . if you don't mind. . . ." He faltered and then stopped speaking.⟩

3. **indicates the omission of one or more sentences within**

a quoted passage or the omission of words at the end of a sentence by using four spaced dots the last of which represents the period ⟨That recovering the manuscripts would be worth almost any effort is without question. . . . The monetary value of a body of Shakespeare's manuscripts would be almost incalculable—Charlton Ogburn⟩

4. **usu. indicates omission of one or more lines of poetry when ellipsis is extended the length of the line**

⟨Thus driven
By the bright shadow of that lovely dream
. . . .
He fled.

—P. B. Shelley⟩

EXCLAMATION POINT !

1. **terminates an emphatic phrase or sentence** ⟨Get out of here!⟩
2. **terminates an emphatic interjection** ⟨Encore!⟩

HYPHEN

1. **marks separation or division of a word at the end of a line** ⟨mill-[end of line]stone⟩
2. **is used between some prefix and word combinations, as prefix + proper name;** ⟨pre-Renaissance⟩ **prefix ending with a vowel + word beginning often with the same vowel** ⟨co-opted⟩ ⟨re-ink⟩; **stressed prefix + word, esp. when this combination is similar to a different one** ⟨re-cover a sofa⟩ *but* ⟨recover from an illness⟩
3. **is used in some compounds, esp. those containing prepositions** ⟨president-elect⟩ ⟨sister-in-law⟩
4. **is often used between elements of a unit modifier in attributive position in order to avoid ambiguity** ⟨He is a small-business man.⟩ ⟨She has gray-green eyes.⟩
5. **suspends the first part of a hyphened compound when used with another hyphened compound** ⟨a six- or eight-cylinder engine⟩
6. **is used in writing out compound numbers between 21 and 99** ⟨thirty-four⟩ ⟨one hundred twenty-eight⟩
7. **is used between the numerator and the denominator in writing out fractions esp. when they are used as modifiers** ⟨a two-thirds majority of the vote⟩
8. **serves instead of the phrase "(up) to and including"**

> **between numbers and dates** ⟨pages 40-98⟩ ⟨the decade 1960-69⟩

HYPHEN, DOUBLE   =

is used in the end-of-line division of a hyphened compound to indicate that the compound is hyphened and not closed ⟨self=[end of line]seeker⟩ *but* ⟨self-[end of line]same⟩

PARENTHESES   ( )

1. **set off supplementary, parenthetic, or explanatory material when the interruption is more marked than that usu. indicated by commas** ⟨Three old destroyers (all now out of commission) will be scrapped.⟩ ⟨He is hoping (as we all are) that this time he will succeed.⟩
2. **enclose numerals which confirm a written number in a text** ⟨Delivery will be made in thirty (30) days.⟩
3. **enclose numbers or letters in a series** ⟨We must set forth (1) our long-term goals, (2) our immediate objectives, and (3) the means at our disposal.⟩

PERIOD

1. **terminates sentences or sentence fragments that are neither interrogatory nor exclamatory** ⟨Obey the law.⟩ ⟨He obeyed the law.⟩
2. **follows some abbreviations and contractions** ⟨Dr.⟩ ⟨Jr.⟩ ⟨etc.⟩ ⟨cont.⟩

QUESTION MARK   ?

1. **terminates a direct question** ⟨Who threw the bomb?⟩ ⟨"Who threw the bomb?" he asked.⟩ ⟨To ask the question Who threw the bomb? is unnecessary.⟩
2. **indicates the writer's ignorance or uncertainty** ⟨Omar Khayyém, Persian poet (?-?1123)⟩

QUOTATION MARKS, DOUBLE   " "

1. **enclose direct quotations in conventional usage** ⟨He said, "I am leaving."⟩
2. **enclose words or phrases borrowed from others, words used in a special way, and often slang when it is introduced into formal writing** ⟨He called himself "em-

peror,'' but he was really just a dictator.) ⟨He was arrested for smuggling ''smack.''⟩

3. **enclose titles of short poems, short stories, articles, lectures, chapters of books, songs, short musical compositions, and radio and TV programs** ⟨Robert Frost's ''Dust of Snow''⟩ ⟨Pushkin's ''Queen of Spades''⟩ ⟨The third chapter of *Treasure Island* is entitled ''The Black Spot.''⟩ ⟨''America the Beautiful''⟩ ⟨Ravel's ''Bolero''⟩ ⟨NBC's ''Today Show''⟩

4. **are used with other punctuation marks in the following ways: the period and the comma fall** *within* **the quotation marks** ⟨''I am leaving,'' he said.⟩ ⟨His camera was described as ''waterproof,'' but ''moisture-resistant'' would have been a better description.⟩ **the semicolon falls** *outside* **the quotation marks** ⟨He spoke of his ''little cottage in the country''; he might have called it a mansion.⟩ **the dash, the question mark, and the exclamation point fall** *within* **the quotation marks when they refer to the quoted matter only; they fall** *outside* **when they refer to the whole sentence** ⟨He asked, ''When did you leave?''⟩ ⟨What is the meaning of ''the open door''?⟩ ⟨The sergeant shouted, ''Halt!''⟩ ⟨Save us from his ''mercy''!⟩

QUOTATION MARKS, SINGLE ‘ ’

enclose a quotation within a quotation in conventional usage ⟨The witness said, ''I distinctly heard him say, 'Don't be late,' and then I heard the door close.''⟩

SEMICOLON ;

1. **links main clauses not joined by coordinating conjunctions** ⟨Some people have the ability to write well; others do not.⟩

2. **links main clauses joined by conjunctive adverbs (as** *consequently, furthermore, however* ⟨Speeding is illegal; furthermore, it is very dangerous.⟩

3. **links clauses which themselves contain commas even when such clauses are joined by coordinating conjunctions** ⟨Mr. King, whom you met yesterday, will be our representative on the committee; but you should follow the proceedings carefully yourself, because they are vitally important to us.⟩

VIRGULE   /

1. **separates alternatives** ⟨. . . designs intended for high-heat and/or high-speed applications—F. S. Badger, Jr.⟩
2. **separates successive divisions (as months or years) of an extended period of time** ⟨the fiscal year 1972/73⟩
3. **serves as a dividing line between run-in lines of poetry** ⟨Say, sages, what's the charm on earth/Can turn death's dart aside?—Robert Burns⟩
4. **often represents *per* in abbreviations** ⟨9 ft/sec⟩ ⟨20 km/hr⟩

Italicization

The following are usually italicized in print and underlined in manuscript:

1. **titles of books, magazines, newspapers, plays, movies, works of art, and longer musical compositions** ⟨Eliot's *The Waste Land*⟩ ⟨*Saturday Review*⟩ ⟨*Christian Science Monitor*⟩ ⟨Shakespeare's *Othello*⟩ ⟨the movie *Gone With the Wind*⟩ ⟨Gainsborough's *Blue Boy*⟩ ⟨Mozart's *Don Giovanni*⟩
2. **names of ships and aircraft, and often spacecraft** ⟨M.V. *West Star*⟩ ⟨Lindbergh's *Spirit of St. Louis*⟩ ⟨*Apollo 13*⟩
3. **words, letters, and figures when referred to as words, letters, and figures** ⟨The word *receive* is often misspelled.⟩ ⟨The *g* in *align* is silent.⟩ ⟨The first *2* and the last *0* in the address are barely legible.⟩
4. **foreign words and phrases that have not been naturalized in English** ⟨*che sarà, sarà*⟩ ⟨*ich dien*⟩
5. **New Latin scientific names of genera, species, subspecies, and varieties (but not groups of higher rank) in botanical and zoological names** ⟨a thick-shelled American clam (*Mercenaria mercenaria*)⟩

Capitalization

Capitals are used for two broad purposes in English: they mark a beginning (as of a sentence) and they signal a proper noun or adjective.

1. **The first word of a sentence or sentence fragment is capitalized.** ⟨The play lasted nearly three hours.⟩ ⟨How are you feeling?⟩ ⟨Bravo!⟩
2. **The first word of a direct quotation is capitalized.** ⟨And

God said, Let there be light.—Gen 1:3⟩ ⟨He replied, "We can stay only a few minutes."⟩

3. **The first word of a direct question within a sentence is capitalized.** ⟨That question is this: Is man an ape or an angel?—Benjamin Disraeli⟩

4. **The first word of a line of poetry is conventionally capitalized.**
⟨The best lack all conviction, while the worst
Are full of passionate intensity.—W. B. Yeats⟩

5. **Words in titles are capitalized with the exception of internal conjunctions, prepositions, and articles.** ⟨*The Way of the World*⟩ ⟨*Of Mice and Men*⟩

6. **The first word of the salutation of a letter and the first word of the closing line are capitalized.** ⟨Dear Mary⟩ ⟨My dear Mrs. Smith⟩ ⟨Sincerely yours⟩

7. **The names of persons and places, of organizations and their members, of congresses and councils, and of historical periods and events are capitalized.** ⟨Noah Webster⟩ ⟨Rome⟩ ⟨Texas⟩ ⟨England⟩ ⟨Rotary International⟩ ⟨Baptists⟩ ⟨the Atomic Energy Commission⟩ ⟨the Yalta Conference⟩ ⟨the Middle Ages⟩ ⟨World War II⟩

8. **The names of ships, aircraft, and spacecraft are capitalized.** ⟨Lindbergh's *Spirit of St. Louis*⟩

9. **Words designating peoples and languages are capitalized.** ⟨Canadians⟩ ⟨Iroquois⟩ ⟨Latin⟩

10. **Derivatives of proper names are capitalized when used in their primary sense.** ⟨Roman customs⟩ ⟨Shakespearean comedies⟩ ⟨the Edwardian era⟩

11. **Words of family relationship preceding the name of a person are capitalized.** ⟨Uncle George⟩

12. **Titles preceding the name of a person and epithets used instead of a name are capitalized.** ⟨President Roosevelt⟩ ⟨Professor Harris⟩ ⟨Pope Paul⟩ ⟨Old Hickory⟩ ⟨the Iron Chancellor⟩

13. **The pronoun *I* is capitalized.** ⟨only I know the real story⟩

14. **Words designating the Deity (and pronouns referring thereto) are often capitalized.** ⟨God⟩ ⟨Jehovah⟩ ⟨Allah⟩ ⟨the Supreme Being in His great wisdom⟩

15. **Personifications are capitalized.** ⟨She dwells with Beauty—John Keats⟩

16. **The days of the week, the months of the year, and holidays and holy days are capitalized.** ⟨Tuesday⟩ ⟨June⟩ ⟨Thanksgiving⟩ ⟨Yom Kippur⟩

17. **Names of specific courts of law are capitalized.** ⟨the United States Court of Appeals for the Second Circuit⟩
18. **Names of treaties are capitalized.** ⟨Treaty of Versailles⟩ ⟨Kellogg-Briand Pact⟩
19. **Registered trademarks and other registered marks are capitalized.** ⟨Orlon⟩ ⟨Air Express⟩
20. **Geological eras, periods, epochs, strata, and names of prehistoric divisions are capitalized.** ⟨Silurian period⟩ ⟨Age of Reptiles⟩ ⟨Neolithic age⟩
21. **Planets, constellations, asteroids, stars, and groups of stars are capitalized; however, sun, earth, and moon are not capitalized unless they are listed with other capitalized astronomical names.** ⟨Venus⟩ ⟨Big Dipper⟩ ⟨Sirius⟩
22. **Genera in scientific names in zoology and botany are capitalized; names of species are not.** ⟨a cabbage butterfly ⟨*Pieris rapae*⟩⟩

Plurals

The plurals of English words are regularly formed by the addition of the suffix -*s* **or** -*es* **to the singular, as**
⟨dog → dogs⟩ ⟨race → races⟩ ⟨guy → guys⟩ ⟨monarch → monarchs⟩ ⟨grass → grasses⟩ ⟨dish → dishes⟩ ⟨buzz → buzzes⟩ ⟨branch → branches⟩

The plurals of words that follow other patterns, as
⟨army → armies⟩ ⟨duo → duos⟩ ⟨ox → oxen⟩ ⟨foot → feet⟩ ⟨p. → pp.⟩ ⟨sheep → sheep⟩ ⟨phenomenon → phenomena *or* phenomenons⟩ ⟨libretto → librettos *or* libretti⟩ ⟨curriculum → curricula⟩ ⟨alga → algae⟩ ⟨corpus → corpora⟩ ⟨sergeant major → sergeants major *or* sergeant majors⟩ **are given at the appropriate entries in the main body of the dictionary.**

GUIDE TO SYNONYMS

Preface

The Guide to Synonyms section of this book is designed to be a concise handbook to the understanding and use of synonyms. Whereas a thesaurus usually simply lists words with similar meanings, a dictionary of synonyms discusses the fine distinctions between their meanings. It is intended for people who wish to appreciate the shades of difference among English words that have the same or nearly same essential meaning and who desire to choose the precisely suitable word for a particular purpose.

This section begins with an alphabetically arranged "Synonym List," containing the approximately 3,300 words discussed in the entries beginning on page 459. A word in boldface capitals (e.g., "**ABANDON**") indicates that an entry of synonym descriptions can be found under that word in the main text. Each word in lowercase letters is followed by a cross-reference to the headword under which it is discussed (e.g., "desert—see ABANDON").

When a word is discussed at more than one entry and is treated as the same part of speech at each entry, cross-references list all of the headwords at which that word is described (e.g., "casual—see ACCIDENTAL, RANDOM").

When a word is discussed at more than one entry and is treated as a different part of speech at each entry, it is entered once for each part of speech:

> humor *vb*—see INDULGE
>
> humor *n*—see WIT
>
> **MALIGN** *vb*
>
> malign *adj*—see SINISTER

The main text, beginning on page 459, is a collection of more than 700 entries in each of which distinctions are drawn among a group of synonyms. Each entry begins with a list of the words to be discussed and a concise statement of the element of meaning they share:

> **ABANDON, desert, forsake** mean to leave without intending to return.

A series of statements then describes the differences that distinguish the synonyms from one another. These are supplemented and clarified by examples, set in angle brackets, that illustrate typical ways in which the words may be used:

> **Abandon** suggests that the thing or person left may be helpless without protection <they *abandoned* their cat at summer's end>.
>
> **Desert** implies that the object left may be weakened but not destroyed by one's absence <a town *deserted* once the gold ran out>.
>
> **Forsake** suggests an action more likely to bring impoverishment or bereavement to that which is forsaken than its exposure to physical dangers <*forsook* his wife and family for a younger woman>.

Several abbreviations for parts of speech and frequently used words appear in this section, as follows:

adj	adjective	esp.	especially
adv	adverb	occas.	occasionally
n	noun	specif.	specifically
vb	verb	usu.	usually

SYNONYM LIST

Words in boldface capitals are discussed in alphabetical order in the synonym paragraphs beginning on page 49. Words in lowercase are discussed at the paragraphs indicated by "see."

ABANDON
ABASE
abash—see EMBARRASS
ABATE
abbreviate—see SHORTEN
ABDICATE
aberrant—see ABNORMAL
abet—see INCITE
abeyant—see LATENT
abhor—see HATE
abhorrent—see HATEFUL.
  REPUGNANT
abide—see BEAR.
  CONTINUE
abject—see MEAN
ABJURE
ABLE
ABNORMAL
abominable—see HATEFUL
abominate—see HATE
ABOMINATION
aboriginal—see NATIVE
abridge—see SHORTEN
ABRIDGMENT
abrogate—see NULLIFY
abrupt—see PRECIPITATE.
  STEEP
ABSOLUTE
absolve—see EXCULPATE
ABSORB
abstract—see ABRIDGMENT
abundant—see PLENTIFUL

ABUSE
accede—see ASSENT
acceptation—see MEANING
ACCIDENTAL
accommodate—see ADAPT.
  CONTAIN
ACCOMPANY
accomplish—see PERFORM
accomplishment—see
  ACQUIREMENT
accord *vb*—see GRANT
accord *n*—see HARMONY
accountable—see
  RESPONSIBLE
accoutre—see FURNISH
accredit—see APPROVE
accumulative—see
  CUMULATIVE
accurate—see CORRECT
ACCUSE
accustomed—see USUAL
acerbity—see ACRIMONY
achieve—see PERFORM
achievement—see FEAT
ACKNOWLEDGE
acme—see SUMMIT
acquaint—see INFORM
acquiesce—see ASSENT
acquire—see GET
ACQUIREMENT
acquisition—see
  ACQUIREMENT

acquisitive—see COVETOUS
acquit—see BEHAVE,
  EXCULPATE
acrid—see CAUSTIC
ACRIMONY
actuate—see MOVE
acumen—see DISCERNMENT
ACUTE
adamant—see INFLEXIBLE
ADAPT
adaptable—see PLASTIC
additive—see CUMULATIVE
address—see TACT
adept—see PROFICIENT
adequate—see SUFFICIENT
adhere—see STICK
adherent—see FOLLOWER
ADJACENT
adjoining—see ADJACENT
adjure—see BEG
adjust—see ADAPT
administer—see EXECUTE
admire—see REGARD
admission—see
  ADMITTANCE
admit—see ACKNOWLEDGE
ADMITTANCE
admonish—see REPROVE
ADOPT
adore—see REVERE
ADORN
adroit—see CLEVER,
  DEXTEROUS
ADULTERY
ADVANCE
advantageous—see
  BENEFICIAL
advent—see ARRIVAL
ADVENTUROUS

adversary—see OPPONENT
ADVERSE
adversity—see MISFORTUNE
ADVICE
advisable—see EXPEDIENT
advise—see CONFER
advocate—see SUPPORT
affable—see GRACIOUS
AFFECT
affectation—see POSE
affecting—see MOVING
affection—see FEELING
affinity—see ATTRACTION,
  LIKENESS
affirm—see ASSERT
affix—see FASTEN
AFFLICT
affluent—see RICH
afford—see GIVE
affront—see OFFEND
afraid—see FEARFUL
age—see PERIOD
aggravate—see INTENSIFY
AGGRESSIVE
aggrieve—see WRONG
AGILE
agitate—see DISCOMPOSE,
  SHAKE
agony—see DISTRESS
AGREE
aid—see HELP
aim—see INTENTION
air *vb*—see EXPRESS
air *n*—see POSE
airs—see POSE
alacrity—see CELERITY
alarm—see FEAR
alert—see INTELLIGENT,
  WATCHFUL

alibi—see APOLOGY
alien—see EXTRINSIC
alienate—see ESTRANGE
alive—see AWARE, LIVING
all—see WHOLE
allay—see RELIEVE
allegiance—see FIDELITY
alleviate—see RELIEVE
ALLIANCE
allocate—see ALLOT
ALLOT
allow—see LET
allure—see ATTRACT
ally—see CONFEDERATE
ALONE
aloof—see INDIFFERENT
alter—see CHANGE
altercation—see QUARREL
alternative—see CHOICE
altitude—see HEIGHT
amalgamate—see MIX
AMATEUR
amaze—see SURPRISE
AMBIGUITY
ambiguous—see OBSCURE
AMBITION
ameliorate—see IMPROVE
amenable—see OBEDIENT,
  RESPONSIBLE
amend—see CORRECT
AMIABLE
AMICABLE
ample—see PLENTIFUL,
  SPACIOUS
amplify—see EXPAND
AMUSE
analogous—see SIMILAR
analogy—see LIKENESS
ANALYZE

anathema—see
  ABOMINATION
anathematize—see
  EXECRATE
ancient—see OLD
ANGER
angle—see PHASE
anguish—see SORROW
animal—see CARNAL
animate *adj*—see LIVING
animate *vb*—see QUICKEN
animated—see LIVELY,
  LIVING
animosity—see ENMITY
animus—see ENMITY
announce—see DECLARE
ANNOY
annul—see NULLIFY
anomalous—see IRREGULAR
ANSWER
answerable—see
  RESPONSIBLE
antagonism—see ENMITY
antagonist—see OPPONENT
antagonistic—see ADVERSE
antagonize—see OPPOSE
antecedent *n*—see CAUSE
antecedent *adj*—see
  PRECEDING
anterior—see PRECEDING
anticipate—see FORESEE,
  PREVENT
anticipation—see PROSPECT
antipathy—see ENMITY
antiquated—see OLD
antique—see OLD
antithetical—see OPPOSITE
anxiety—see CARE
anxious—see EAGER

apathetic—see IMPASSIVE
ape—see COPY
aperçu—see COMPENDIUM
apex—see SUMMIT
aplomb—see CONFIDENCE
apocryphal—see FICTITIOUS
apologia—see APOLOGY
APOLOGY
appall—see DISMAY
APPARENT
appease—see PACIFY
appetizing—see PALATABLE
appliance—see IMPLEMENT
applicable—see RELEVANT
appoint—see FURNISH
apportion—see ALLOT
apposite—see RELEVANT
appraise—see ESTIMATE
appreciable—see
 PERCEPTIBLE
APPRECIATE
apprehend—see FORESEE
APPREHENSION
apprehensive—see FEARFUL
apprise—see INFORM
APPROPRIATE
appropriate *adj*—see FIT
APPROVE
apropos—see RELEVANT
apt—see FIT, QUICK
aptitude—see GIFT
arbitrary—see ABSOLUTE
archaic—see OLD
ardent—see IMPASSIONED
ardor—see PASSION
arduous—see HARD
argot—see DIALECT
argue—see DISCUSS
arise—see SPRING
ARISTOCRACY

arm—see FURNISH
aroma—see SMELL
aromatic—see ODOROUS
arrange—see ORDER
ARRIVAL
arrogant—see PROUD
arrogate—see APPROPRIATE
ART
artful—see SLY
artifice—see ART. TRICK
ARTIFICIAL
artless—see NATURAL
ascertain—see DISCOVER
ascetic—see SEVERE
ASCRIBE
asinine—see SIMPLE
ASK *vb*
ASK *vb*
aspect—see PHASE
asperity—see ACRIMONY
asperse—see MALIGN
aspiration—see AMBITION
assail—see ATTACK
assassinate—see KILL
assault—see ATTACK
assemble—see GATHER
ASSENT
ASSERT
assertive—see AGGRESSIVE
assess—see ESTIMATE
assiduous—see BUSY
assign—see ALLOT,
 ASCRIBE
assignment—see TASK
assimilate—see ABSORB
assist—see HELP
associate—see JOIN
assuage—see RELIEVE
assault—see ATTACK
ASSUME

assurance—see CERTAINTY, CONFIDENCE
assure—see ENSURE
astonish—see SURPRISE
astound—see SURPRISE
astute—see SHREWD
athirst—see EAGER
ATMOSPHERE
atrocious—see OUTRAGEOUS
attach—see FASTEN
ATTACK
attainment—see ACQUIREMENT
ATTEMPT
attend—see ACCOMPANY
attest—see CERTIFY
ATTRACT
ATTRACTION
attribute *vb*—see ASCRIBE
attribute *n*—see QUALITY
atypical—see ABNORMAL
audacity—see TEMERITY
augment—see INCREASE
aura—see ATMOSPHERE
auspicious—see FAVORABLE
austere—see SEVERE
AUTHENTIC
authenticate—see CONFIRM
authority—see INFLUENCE, POWER
autocratic—see ABSOLUTE
automatic—see SPONTANEOUS
autonomous—see FREE
avaricious—see COVETOUS
AVERAGE
averse—see DISINCLINED
avert—see PREVENT

avid—see EAGER
avoid—see ESCAPE
avow—see ACKNOWLEDGE, ASSERT
awake—see AWARE
award—see GRANT
AWARE
AWKWARD

baby—see INDULGE
back—see RECEDE, SUPPORT
BACKGROUND
BAD
badger—see BAIT
baffle—see FRUSTRATE
bag—see CATCH
BAIT
balance—see COMPENSATE
bald—see BARE
baleful—see SINISTER
balk—see FRUSTRATE
balky—see CONTRARY
banal—see INSIPID
baneful—see PERNICIOUS
BANISH
bankrupt—see DEPLETE
barbarous—see FIERCE
BARE
barren—see BARE
BASE
bashful—see SHY
batter—see MAIM
BEAR
BEARING
BEAUTIFUL
beautify—see ADORN
BEG
BEGIN

beguile—see DECEIVE
BEHAVE
BELIEF
belittle—see DECRY
bellicose—see
  BELLIGERENT
BELLIGERENT
bemoan—see DEPLORE
bend—see CURVE
BENEFICIAL
benign—see KIND
benignant—see KIND
bent—see GIFT
berate—see SCOLD
beseech—see BEG
bestial—see BRUTAL
bestow—see GIVE
bête noire—see
  ABOMINATION
betray—see REVEAL
better—see IMPROVE
bewail—see DEPLORE
bewilder—see PUZZLE
bias *vb*—see INCLINE
bias *n*—see PREDILECTION
bid—see COMMAND
billingsgate—see ABUSE
biting—see INCISIVE
bizarre—see FANTASTIC
blamable—see
  BLAMEWORTHY
blame—see CRITICIZE
BLAMEWORTHY
bland—see SUAVE
blandish—see COAX
blank—see EMPTY
blasé—see SOPHISTICATED
blatant—see VOCIFEROUS
bleak—see DISMAL
BLEMISH

blench—see RECOIL
blend—see MIX
blithe—see MERRY
block—see HINDER
BLOODY
blot out—see ERASE
BLUFF
blunder—see ERROR
blunt—see BLUFF, DULL
BOAST
BODILY
boisterous—see
  VOCIFEROUS
bombard—see ATTACK
bona fide—see AUTHENTIC
bon vivant—see EPICURE
BOORISH
boost—see LIFT
booty—see SPOIL
BORDER
bother—see ANNOY
bountiful—see LIBERAL
brag—see BOAST
brandish—see SWING
BREACH
break down—see ANALYZE
bridle—see RESTRAIN
BRIEF
BRIGHT
brilliant—see BRIGHT
brim—see BORDER
brink—see BORDER
brisk—see AGILE
brittle—see FRAGILE
broach—see EXPRESS
BROAD
browbeat—see INTIMIDATE
brusque—see BLUFF
BRUTAL
brutish—see BRUTAL

bucolic—see RURAL

bugbear—see
  ABOMINATION

bulge—see PROJECTION

BULK

bulldoze—see INTIMIDATE

bully—see INTIMIDATE

burdensome—see ONEROUS

burlesque—see
  CARICATURE

bury—see HIDE

BUSINESS

BUSY

butt in—see INTRUDE

cabal—see PLOT

cajole—see COAX

calamity—see DISASTER

CALCULATE

call—see SUMMON

calling—see WORK

CALM

calumniate—see MALIGN

cancel—see ERASE

candid—see FRANK

canon—see LAW

cant—see DIALECT

capable—see ABLE

capacious—see SPACIOUS

capitulate—see YIELD

CAPRICE

capricious—see
  INCONSTANT

captious—see CRITICAL

captivate—see ATTRACT

capture—see CATCH

cardinal—see ESSENTIAL

CARE

CAREFUL

CARICATURE

CARNAL

carping—see CRITICAL

carriage—see BEARING

CARRY

case—see INSTANCE

cast—see DISCARD, THROW

castigate—see PUNISH

casual—see ACCIDENTAL,
  RANDOM

cataclysm—see DISASTER

catastrophe—see DISASTER

CATCH

CAUSE

CAUSTIC

CAUTIOUS

cease—see STOP

celebrate—see KEEP

celebrated—see FAMOUS

CELERITY

censorious—see CRITICAL

censure—see CRITICIZE

CEREMONIAL

ceremonious—see
  CEREMONIAL

certain—see SURE

CERTAINTY

CERTIFY

certitude—see CERTAINTY

champion—see SUPPORT

CHANGE

character—see DISPOSITION,
  QUALITY, TYPE

CHARACTERISTIC

charge—see ACCUSE,
  COMMAND

charity—see MERCY

charm—see ATTRACT

charter—see HIRE

chary—see CAUTIOUS

CHASE
CHASTE
chasten—see PUNISH
chastise—see PUNISH
CHEAT
check—see RESTRAIN
cheek—see TEMERITY
cheerless—see DISMAL
cherish—see APPRECIATE
chide—see REPROVE
chimerical—see IMAGINARY
chivalrous—see CIVIL
chivy—see BAIT
CHOICE *n*
CHOICE *adj*
choleric—see IRASCIBLE
chore—see TASK
chronic—see INVETERATE
churlish—see BOORISH
chutzpah—see TEMERITY
circumscribe—see LIMIT
circumspect—see CAUTIOUS
circumstance—see
  OCCURRENCE
CIRCUMSTANTIAL
circumvent—see
  FRUSTRATE
citation—see ENCOMIUM
cite—see SUMMON
CITIZEN
CIVIL
claim—see DEMAND
clamorous—see
  VOCIFEROUS
clandestine—see SECRET
CLEAR *adj*
CLEAR *adj*
clear-cut—see INCISIVE
cleave—see STICK, TEAR
clemency—see MERCY

CLEVER
climax—see SUMMIT
cling—see STICK
cloak—see DISGUISE
clog—see HAMPER
CLOSE *vb*
CLOSE *adj*
clownish—see BOORISH
cloy—see SATIATE
clumsy—see AWKWARD
clutch—see TAKE
coalesce—see MIX
coalition—see ALLIANCE
COARSE
COAX
cocksure—see SURE
coerce—see FORCE
coeval—see
  CONTEMPORARY
cogent—see VALID
cogitate—see THINK
cognizant—see AWARE
cohere—see STICK
coincide—see AGREE
coincident—see
  CONTEMPORARY
collate—see COMPARE
colleague—see
  CONFEDERATE
collect—see GATHER
collected—see COOL
colossal—see ENORMOUS
combat—see OPPOSE
combine—see JOIN
comely—see BEAUTIFUL
COMFORT
COMFORTABLE
comic—see LAUGHABLE
comical—see LAUGHABLE
COMMAND *vb*

command *n*—see POWER
commemorate—see KEEP
commence—see BEGIN
commensurable—see
  PROPORTIONAL
commensurate—see
  PROPORTIONAL
commerce—see BUSINESS
commingle—see MIX
commisseration—see PITY
COMMIT
commodious—see SPACIOUS
COMMON
common sense—see SENSE
COMMOTION
compact—see CLOSE
COMPARE
compass—see RANGE
compassion—see PITY
compatible—see
  CONSONANT
compel—see FORCE
compendious—see CONCISE
COMPENDIUM
COMPENSATE
competent—see ABLE,
  SUFFICIENT
complaisant—see AMIABLE
complete—see CLOSE
complete—see FULL
COMPLEX
complicated—see COMPLEX
component—see ELEMENT
comport—see BEHAVE
composed—see COOL
composure—see
  EQUANIMITY
comprehend—see INCLUDE,
  UNDERSTAND
compress—see CONTRACT

compunction—see
  PENITENCE, QUALM
compute—see CALCULATE
conceal—see HIDE
concede—see GRANT
conceive—see THINK
concept—see IDEA
conception—see IDEA
concern—see CARE
conciliate—see PACIFY
CONCISE
conclude—see CLOSE,
  INFER
CONCLUSIVE
concord—see HARMONY
concur—see AGREE
condemn—see CRITICIZE
condense—see CONTRACT
condescend—see STOOP
condolence—see PITY
condone—see EXCUSE
CONDUCT
CONFEDERATE
confederation—see
  ALLIANCE
CONFER
confess—see
  ACKNOWLEDGE
confide—see COMMIT
CONFIDENCE
configuration—see FORM
confine—see LIMIT
CONFIRM
confirmed—see
  INVETERATE
confiscate—see
  APPROPRIATE
conflict—see DISCORD
conform—see ADAPT
conformation—see FORM

confound—see PUZZLE
confute—see DISPROVE
congenial—see CONSONANT
congenital—see INNATE
congregate—see GATHER
congruous—see
 CONSONANT
CONJECTURE
conjugal—see
 MATRIMONIAL
connect—see JOIN
connubial—see
 MATRIMONIAL
CONQUER
conscientious—see UPRIGHT
conscious—see AWARE
consecrate—see DEVOTE
consent—see ASSENT
consequence—see EFFECT,
 IMPORTANCE
CONSIDER
consign—see COMMIT
consistent—see CONSONANT
console—see COMFORT
CONSONANT
conspectus—see
 ABRIDGMENT
conspicuous—see
 NOTICEABLE
conspiracy—see PLOT
constant—see CONTINUAL,
 FAITHFUL
constituent—see ELEMENT
constrain—see FORCE
constrict—see CONTRACT
consult—see CONFER
CONTAIN
CONTAMINATE
contemn—see DESPISE

contemplate—see CONSIDER
contemporaneous—see
 CONTEMPORARY
CONTEMPORARY
CONTEMPTIBLE
contention—see DISCORD
contentious—see
 BELLIGERENT
contiguous—see ADJACENT
contingency—see JUNCTURE
contingent—see
 ACCIDENTAL
CONTINUAL
CONTINUE
continuous—see
 CONTINUAL
contort—see DEFORM
contour—see OUTLINE
CONTRACT
contradict—see DENY
contradictory—see OPPOSITE
CONTRARY
contrast—see COMPARE
contravene—see DENY
contrition—see PENITENCE
control vb—see CONDUCT
control n—see POWER
controvert—see DISPROVE
conundrum—see MYSTERY
convene—see SUMMON
conventional—see
 CEREMONIAL
convert—see TRANSFORM
convey—see CARRY
conviction—see CERTAINTY,
 OPINION
convincing—see VALID
convoke—see SUMMON
convulse—see SHAKE

convulsive—see FITFUL

COOL

copartner—see CONFEDERATE

copious—see PLENTIFUL

COPY *vb*

copy *n* —see REPRODUCTION

coquet—see TRIFLE

cordial—see GRACIOUS

corporal—see BODILY

corporeal—see BODILY, MATERIAL

CORRECT *vb*

CORRECT *adj*

corroborate—see CONFIRM

corrupt *vb*—see DEBASE

corrupt *adj*—see VICIOUS

COSTLY

counsel—see ADVICE

countenance—see FACE

counter—see ADVERSE

counteractive—see ADVERSE

counterfeit *vb*—see ASSUME

counterfeit *n*—see IMPOSTURE

countervail—see COMPENSATE

COURAGE

court—see INVITE

courteous—see CIVIL

covert—see SECRET

covet—see DESIRE

COVETOUS

cow—see INTIMIDATE

COWARDLY

cower—see FAWN

coy—see SHY

cozen—see CHEAT

cozy—see COMFORTABLE

crabbed—see SULLEN

craft—see ART

crafty—see SLY

cranky—see IRASCIBLE

crave—see DESIRE

craven—see COWARDLY

craze—see FASHION

create—see INVENT

credence—see BELIEF

credit *vb*—see ASCRIBE

credit *n*—see BELIEF, INFLUENCE

crime—see OFFENSE

cringe—see FAWN

cripple—see MAIM, WEAKEN

crisis—see JUNCTURE

crisp—see FRAGILE, INCISIVE

criterion—see STANDARD

CRITICAL

CRITICIZE

cross—see IRASCIBLE, STUPID

crotchet—see CAPRICE

crow—see BOAST

CROWD

crucial—see ACUTE

crude—see RUDE

cruel—see FIERCE

CRUSH *vb*

crush *n*—see CROWD

crusty—see BLUFF

cryptic—see OBSCURE

culmination—see SUMMIT

culpable—see BLAMEWORTHY

cumbersome—see HEAVY

cumbrous—see HEAVY
CUMULATIVE
cunning n—see ART
cunning adj—see CLEVER, SLY
curb—see RESTRAIN
CURE
CURIOUS
current adj—see PREVAILING
current n—see TENDENCY
curse—see EXECRATE
cursory—see SUPERFICIAL
curt—see BLUFF
curtail—see SHORTEN
CURVE
custom—see HABIT
customary—see USUAL
cutting—see INCISIVE
CYNICAL

dabbler—see AMATEUR
dainty—see CHOICE, NICE
dally—see DELAY, TRIFLE
damage—see INJURE
damn—see EXECRATE
damp—see WET
DANGEROUS
dank—see WET
daredevil—see ADVENTUROUS
daring—see ADVENTUROUS
DARK
dastardly—see COWARDLY
daunt—see DISMAY
dawdle—see DELAY
DEAD
DEADLY
deal—see DISTRIBUTE

dear—see COSTLY
debar—see EXCLUDE
DEBASE
debate—see DISCUSS
debauch—see DEBASE
debilitate—see WEAKEN
decadence—see DETERIORATION
DECAY
deceased—see DEAD
deceitful—see DISHONEST
DECEIVE
decency—see DECORUM
decent—see CHASTE
DECEPTION
DECIDE
DECLARE
decisive—see CONCLUSIVE
deck—see ADORN
DECLINE vb
decline n—see DETERIORATION
decompose—see DECAY
decorate—see ADORN
DECORUM
decoy—see LURE
DECREASE
decree—see DICTATE
decrepit—see WEAK
DECRY
dedicate—see DEVOTE
deduce—see INFER
deep—see BROAD
deep-rooted—see INVETERATE
deep-seated—see INVETERATE
defame—see MALIGN
defeat—see CONQUER
defect—see BLEMISH

DEFEND
DEFER
deference—see HONOR
defile—see CONTAMINATE
definite—see EXPLICIT
definitive—see CONCLUSIVE
deflate—see CONTRACT
DEFORM
defraud—see CHEAT
deft—see DEXTEROUS
defunct—see DEAD
degenerate—see VICIOUS
degeneration—see
  DETERIORATION
degrade—see ABASE
deign—see STOOP
dejected—see DOWNCAST
dejection—see SADNESS
DELAY *vb*
DELAY *vb*
delete—see ERASE
deleterious—see
  PERNICIOUS
deliberate *vb*—see THINK
deliberate *adj*—see
  VOLUNTARY
delicate—see CHOICE
deliver—see RESCUE
delude—see DECEIVE
DEMAND
demean—see ABASE
demeanor—see BEARING
demented—see INSANE
demonstrate—see SHOW
demur—see QUALM
denounce—see CRITICIZE
dense—see CLOSE, STUPID
DENY
depart—see SWERVE
departed—see DEAD

DEPLETE
DEPLORE
deport—see BANISH,
  BEHAVE
deportment—see BEARING
deprave—see DEBASE
depreciate—see DECRY
depreciatory—see
  DEROGATORY
depressed—see DOWNCAST
depression—see SADNESS
deranged—see INSANE
deride—see RIDICULE
derive—see SPRING
DEROGATORY
description—see TYPE
desert—see ABANDON
design—see INTENTION,
  PLAN
DESIRE
desist—see STOP
desolate—see ALONE,
  DISMAL
despairing—see
  DESPONDENT
desperate—see
  DESPONDENT
despicable—see
  CONTEMPTIBLE
DESPISE
despoil—see RAVAGE
DESPONDENT
despotic—see ABSOLUTE
destiny—see FATE
destitution—see POVERTY
desultory—see RANDOM
detached—see INDIFFERENT
detail—see ITEM
detailed—see
  CIRCUMSTANTIAL

detain—see DELAY, KEEP
DETERIORATION
determinant—see CAUSE
determinative—see
 CONCLUSIVE
determine—see DECIDE,
 DISCOVER
detest—see HATE
detestable—see HATEFUL
detrimental—see
 PERNICIOUS
devastate—see RAVAGE
deviate—see SWERVE
DEVOTE
devotion—see FIDELITY
DEVOUT
DEXTEROUS
DIALECT
DICTATE
DICTATORIAL
DIFFERENT
difficult—see HARD
diffident—see SHY
diffuse—see WORDY
digest—see COMPENDIUM
dignity—see DECORUM
digress—see SWERVE
dilate—see EXPAND
dilemma—see
 PREDICAMENT
dilettante—see AMATEUR
diligent—see BUSY
dim—see DARK
diminish—see DECREASE
diminutive—see SMALL
diplomatic—see SUAVE
direct—see COMMAND,
 CONDUCT
DIRTY
disable—see WEAKEN

disaffect—see ESTRANGE
disallow—see DISCLAIM
DISASTER
disavow—see DISCLAIM
DISCARD
DISCERNMENT
discharge—see PERFORM
disciple—see FOLLOWER
discipline—see PUNISH,
 TEACH
DISCLAIM
disclose—see REVEAL
discomfit—see EMBARRASS
DISCOMPOSE
disconcert—see EMBARRASS
disconsolate—see
 DOWNCAST
discontinue—see STOP
DISCORD
DISCOVER
discrete—see DISTINCT
discrimination—see
 DISCERNMENT
DISCUSS
disdain—see DESPISE
disdainful—see PROUD
disembarrass—see
 EXTRICATE
disencumber—see
 EXTRICATE
disentangle—see EXTRICATE
DISGRACE
DISGUISE
DISHONEST
dishonor—see DISGRACE
DISINCLINED
disinterested—see
 INDIFFERENT
disloyal—see FAITHLESS
DISMAL

DISMAY
dismiss—see EJECT
disown—see DISCLAIM
disparage—see DECRY
disparaging—see
  DEROGATORY
disparate—see DIFFERENT
dispassionate—see FAIR
dispatch *n*—see HASTE
dispatch *vb*—see KILL
dispel—see SCATTER
dispense—see DISTRIBUTE
disperse—see SCATTER
dispirited—see DOWNCAST
dispiriting—see DISMAL
displace—see REPLACE
display—see SHOW
dispose—see INCLINE
DISPOSITION
DISPROVE
dispute—see DISCUSS
disquiet—see DISCOMPOSE
disregard—see NEGLECT
disrepute—see DISGRACE
dissect—see ANALYZE
dissemble—see DISGUISE
dissension—see DISCORD
dissipate—see SCATTER
distasteful—see REPUGNANT
distend—see EXPAND
DISTINCT
distinctive—see
  CHARACTERISTIC
distinguished—see FAMOUS
distort—see DEFORM
distract—see PUZZLE
DISTRESS
DISTRIBUTE
disturb—see DISCOMPOSE
diverge—see SWERVE

divergent—see DIFFERENT
diverse—see DIFFERENT
divert—see AMUSE
divide—see DISTRIBUTE.
  SEPARATE
divine—see FORESEE
division—see PART
divorce—see SEPARATE
divulge—see REVEAL
docile—see OBEDIENT
doctrinaire—see
  DICTATORIAL
dogged—see OBSTINATE
dogmatic—see
  DICTATORIAL
dole—see DISTRIBUTE
DOMINANT
domineering—see
  MASTERFUL
dominion—see POWER
donate—see GIVE
doom—see FATE
dormant—see LATENT
double-dealing—see
  DECEPTION
double entendre—see
  AMBIGUITY
doubt—see UNCERTAINTY
DOUBTFUL
DOWNCAST
drag—see PULL
drain—see DEPLETE
DRAMATIC
draw—see PULL
dread—see FEAR
dreary—see DISMAL
drench—see SOAK
drift—see TENDENCY
drive—see MOVE
drudgery—see WORK

DRUNK
drunken—see DRUNK
dubiety—see UNCERTAINTY
dubious—see DOUBTFUL
ductile—see PLASTIC
dudgeon—see OFFENSE
DULL
dumb—see STUPID
dumbfound—see PUZZLE
DUPE
duplicate—see
  REPRODUCTION
durable—see LASTING
dusky—see DARK
duty—see FUNCTION. TASK
dwindle—see DECREASE

EAGER
earn—see GET
earnest—see SERIOUS
earsplitting—see LOUD
EARTHLY
EASY
ebb—see ABATE
eccentric—see STRANGE
economical—see SPARING
ECSTASY
edge—see BORDER
educate—see TEACH
EDUCE
eerie—see WEIRD
efface—see ERASE
EFFECT n
effect vb—see PERFORM
EFFECTIVE
effectual—see EFFECTIVE
efficacious—see EFFECTIVE
efficient—see EFFECTIVE
EFFORT

effortless—see EASY
effrontery—see TEMERITY
EJECT
ELASTIC
election—see CHOICE
elegant—see CHOICE
ELEMENT
elevate—see LIFT
elevation—see HEIGHT
elicit—see EDUCE
eliminate—see EXCLUDE
elucidate—see EXPLAIN
elude—see ESCAPE
emanate—see SPRING
emancipate—see FREE
emasculate—see UNNERVE
EMBARRASS
embellish—see ADORN
embolden—see ENCOURAGE
embrace—see ADOPT.
  INCLUDE
emend—see CORRECT
emergency—see JUNCTURE
eminent—see FAMOUS
emotion—see FEELING
employ—see USE
employment—see WORK
EMPTY
enchant—see ATTRACT
ENCOMIUM
ENCOURAGE
encroach—see TRESPASS
END n
end vb—see CLOSE
endeavor—see ATTEMPT
endemic—see NATIVE
ending—see END
endorse—see APPROVE
endure—see BEAR.
  CONTINUE

energetic—see VIGOROUS
energy—see POWER
enervate—see UNNERVE
enfeeble—see WEAKEN
engineer—see GUIDE
enhance—see INTENSIFY
enigma—see MYSTERY
enigmatic—see OBSCURE
enjoin—see COMMAND
enlarge—see INCREASE
enliven—see QUICKEN
ENMITY
ENORMOUS
enough—see SUFFICIENT
ensnare—see CATCH
ensue—see FOLLOW
ENSURE
ENTER
entertain—see AMUSE
enthusiasm—see PASSION
entice—see LURE
entire—see PERFECT,
  WHOLE
entrap—see CATCH
entreat—see BEG
entrench—see TRESPASS
entrust—see COMMIT
environment—see
  BACKGROUND
envisage—see THINK
envision—see THINK
ephemeral—see TRANSIENT
EPICURE
episode—see OCCURRENCE
epitome—see ABRIDGMENT
epoch—see PERIOD
equable—see STEADY
equal—see SAME
EQUANIMITY
equip—see FURNISH

equitable—see FAIR
equivalent—see SAME
equivocal—see OBSCURE
equivocate—see LIE
equivocation—see
  AMBIGUITY
era—see PERIOD
eradicate—see
  EXTERMINATE
ERASE
erratic—see STRANGE
ERROR
ersatz—see ARTIFICIAL
erudition—see KNOWLEDGE
ESCAPE
eschew—see ESCAPE
escort—see ACCOMPANY
especial—see SPECIAL
espouse—see ADOPT
essay—see ATTEMPT
ESSENTIAL
esteem—see REGARD
ESTIMATE
estimate—see CALCULATE
ESTRANGE
ethical—see MORAL
etiquette—see DECORUM
eulogy—see ENCOMIUM
evade—see ESCAPE
evaluate—see ESTIMATE
evanescent—see TRANSIENT
even—see LEVEL, STEADY
event—see OCCURRENCE
eventual—see LAST
evict—see EJECT
evidence—see SHOW
EVIDENT
evil—see BAD
evince—see SHOW
evoke—see EDUCE

exact *adj*—see CORRECT
exact *vb*—see DEMAND
exacting—see ONEROUS
examine—see SCRUTINIZE
example—see INSTANCE,
   MODEL
exasperate—see IRRITATE
EXCEED
excel—see EXCEED
EXCESSIVE
excite—see PROVOKE
EXCLUDE
EXCULPATE
EXCUSE *vb*
excuse *n*—see APOLOGY
EXECRATE
EXECUTE
exemplar—see MODEL
exertion—see EFFORT
exhaust—see DEPLETE, TIRE
exhibit—see SHOW
exigency—see JUNCTURE
exile—see BANISH
exonerate—see EXCULPATE
exorbitant—see EXCESSIVE
EXPAND
EXPECT
EXPEDIENT *adj*
expedient *n*—see RESOURCE
expedition—see HASTE
expeditious—see FAST
expel—see EJECT
expensive—see COSTLY
expert—see PROFICIENT
EXPLAIN
explicate—see EXPLAIN
EXPLICIT
exploit—see FEAT
expose—see SHOW
exposed—see LIABLE

expostulate—see OBJECT
expound—see EXPLAIN
EXPRESS *vb*
express *adj*—see EXPLICIT
expunge—see ERASE
exquisite—see CHOICE
EXTEMPORANEOUS
EXTEND
EXTERMINATE
extinguish—see CRUSH
extirpate—see
   EXTERMINATE
extort—see EDUCE
extract—see EDUCE
extraneous—see EXTRINSIC
extravagant—see EXCESSIVE
extreme—see EXCESSIVE
EXTRICATE
EXTRINSIC
exuberant—see PROFUSE

fabricate—see MAKE
fabulous—see FICTITIOUS
FACE
facet—see PHASE
facetious—see WITTY
facile—see EASY
facsimile—see
   REPRODUCTION
factitious—see ARTIFICIAL
factor—see ELEMENT
faculty—see GIFT
fad—see FASHION
fag—see TIRE
failing—see FAULT
FAIR
faith—see BELIEF
FAITHFUL
FAITHLESS

fake—see IMPOSTURE
false—see FAITHLESS
falter—see HESITATE
FAMILIAR
FAMOUS
fanciful—see IMAGINARY
fancy—see THINK
FANTASTIC
fascinate—see ATTRACT
FASHION *n*
fashion *vb*—see MAKE
FAST
FASTEN
fastidious—see NICE
fatal—see DEADLY
FATE
fateful—see OMINOUS
fatigue—see TIRE
fatuous—see SIMPLE
FAULT
faultfinding—see CRITICAL
FAVORABLE
FAWN
fealty—see FIDELITY
FEAR
FEARFUL
feasible—see POSSIBLE
FEAT
fecund—see FERTILE
federation—see ALLIANCE
feeble—see WEAK
FEELING
feign—see ASSUME
feint—see TRICK
felicitous—see FIT
feral—see BRUTAL
ferocious—see FIERCE
FERTILE
fervent—see IMPASSIONED
fervid—see IMPASSIONED

fervor—see PASSION
fetid—see MALODOROUS
fetter—see HAMPER
fib—see LIE
fickle—see INCONSTANT
FICTITIOUS
FIDELITY
FIERCE
figure—see FORM
filch—see STEAL
filthy—see DIRTY
final—see LAST
FINANCIAL
finicky—see NICE
finish—see CLOSE
FIRM
fiscal—see FINANCIAL
FIT
FITFUL
fitting—see FIT
fix *vb*—see FASTEN
fix *n*—see PREDICAMENT
flabbergast—see SURPRISE
FLAGRANT
FLASH
flashy—see GAUDY
flat—see INSIPID, LEVEL
flaunt—see SHOW
flaw—see BLEMISH
fleer—see SCOFF
fleet—see FAST
fleeting—see TRANSIENT
fleshly—see CARNAL
flexible—see ELASTIC
flightiness—see LIGHTNESS
flinch—see RECOIL
fling—see THROW
flippancy—see LIGHTNESS
flirt—see TRIFLE
flourish—see SWING

flout—see SCOFF
flow—see SPRING
fluctuate—see SWING
fluster—see DISCOMPOSE
foible—see FAULT
foil—see FRUSTRATE
FOLLOW
FOLLOWER
foment—see INCITE
foolhardy—see
 ADVENTUROUS
foolish—see SIMPLE
FORBEARING
FORBID
FORCE *vb*
force *n*—see POWER
foreboding—see
 APPREHENSION
forecast—see FORETELL
foregoing—see PRECEDING
foreign—see EXTRINSIC
foreknow—see FORESEE
FORERUNNER
FORESEE
forestall—see PREVENT
foretaste—see PROSPECT
FORETELL
forge—see MAKE
forget—see NEGLECT
FORGETFUL
forgive—see EXCUSE
forlorn—see ALONE
FORM *n*
form *vb*—see MAKE
formal—see CEREMONIAL
former—see PRECEDING
fornication—see ADULTERY
forsake—see ABANDON
forswear—see ABJURE

fortuitous—see
 ACCIDENTAL
fortunate—see LUCKY
forward—see ADVANCE
foul—see DIRTY
foxy—see SLY
FRAGILE
fragment—see PART
FRAGRANCE
fragrant—see ODOROUS
frail—see WEAK
frailty—see FAULT
frangible—see FRAGILE
FRANK
fraud—see DECEPTION,
 IMPOSTURE
FREE *adj*
FREE *vb*
FREEDOM
fresh—see NEW
friable—see FRAGILE
friendly—see AMICABLE
fright—see FEAR
frivolity—see LIGHTNESS
FROWN
frugal—see SPARING
fruitful—see FERTILE
fruitless—see FUTILE
FRUSTRATE
fugitive—see TRANSIENT
fulfill—see PERFORM
FULL
FULSOME
FUN
FUNCTION
fundamental—see
 ESSENTIAL
FURNISH
further—see ADVANCE

furtive—see SECRET
fury—see ANGER
fuse—see MIX
fusty—see MALODOROUS
FUTILE

gain—see GET
gainsay—see DENY
gall—see TEMERITY
gallant—see CIVIL
gallantry—see HEROISM
game—see FUN
gamut—see RANGE
gape—see GAZE
garish—see GAUDY
garnish—see ADORN
garrulous—see TALKATIVE
gastronome—see EPICURE
GATHER
gauche—see AWKWARD
GAUDY
gauge—see STANDARD
gaunt—see LEAN
gay—see LIVELY
GAZE
general—see UNIVERSAL
generic—see UNIVERSAL
generous—see LIBERAL
genial—see GRACIOUS
genius—see GIFT
gentry—see ARISTOCRACY
genuine—see AUTHENTIC
germane—see RELEVANT
GET
GHASTLY
gibe—see SCOFF
GIFT
gigantic—see ENORMOUS

GIVE
glance—see FLASH
glare—see GAZE
glaring—see FLAGRANT
gleam—see FLASH
glee—see MIRTH
glimmer—see FLASH
glint—see FLASH
glisten—see FLASH
glitter—see FLASH
gloom—see SADNESS
gloomy—see DARK, SULLEN
glorious—see SPLENDID
glossy—see SLEEK
glower—see FROWN
glum—see SULLEN
glut—see SATIATE
gluttonous—see VORACIOUS
goad—see MOTIVE
goal—see INTENTION
good-natured—see AMIABLE
gorge—see SATIATE
gorgeous—see SPLENDID
gory—see BLOODY
gourmet—see EPICURE
GOVERN
grab—see TAKE
grace—see MERCY
GRACIOUS
GRAND
grandiose—see GRAND
GRANT
GRAPHIC
grasp—see TAKE
grasping—see COVETOUS
gratuitous—see
  SUPEREROGATORY
grave—see SERIOUS
greedy—see COVETOUS

grief—see SORROW
grievance—see INJUSTICE
grill—see AFFLICT
grind—see WORK
grisly—see GHASTLY
gross—see COARSE.
  FLAGRANT
grotesque—see FANTASTIC
grudge—see MALICE
gruesome—see GHASTLY
gruff—see BLUFF
guard—see DEFEND
guess—see CONJECTURE
GUIDE
guilty—see BLAMEWORTHY
gull—see DUPE
gumption—see SENSE

HABIT
habitual—see USUAL
hackneyed—see TRITE
hale—see HEALTHY
hallow—see DEVOTE
HAMPER
HANDLE
handsome—see BEAUTIFUL
hanker—see LONG
haphazard—see RANDOM
happy—see FIT. LUCKY
harass—see WORRY
harbinger—see
  FORERUNNER
HARD
hardihood—see TEMERITY
harm—see INJURE
HARMONY
harry—see WORRY
harsh—see ROUGH
HASTE

hasty—see FAST
HATE
HATEFUL
haughty—see PROUD
haul—see PULL
HAVE
hazardous—see
  DANGEROUS
headlong—see
  PRECIPITATE
headstrong—see UNRULY
heal—see CURE
HEALTHFUL
HEALTHY
hearten—see ENCOURAGE
heartfelt—see SINCERE
hearty—see SINCERE
heave—see LIFT
HEAVY
heckle—see BAIT
hector—see BAIT
HEIGHT
heighten—see INTENSIFY
heinous—see OUTRAGEOUS
HELP
herald—see FORERUNNER
hereditary—see INNATE
HEROISM
hesitant—see DISINCLINED
HESITATE
HIDE
HIGH
hilarity—see MIRTH
HINDER
hint—see SUGGEST
HIRE
histrionic—see DRAMATIC
hoax—see DUPE
hoist—see LIFT
hold—see CONTAIN. HAVE

hollow—see VAIN
homage—see HONOR
honest—see UPRIGHT
HONESTY
HONOR
honorable—see UPRIGHT
hope—see EXPECT
hopeless—see DESPONDENT
horde—see CROWD
horrify—see DISMAY
hostility—see ENMITY
hound—see BAIT
huff—see OFFENSE
huge—see ENORMOUS
HUMBLE
humbug—see IMPOSTURE
humid—see WET
humiliate—see ABASE
humor *vb*—see INDULGE
humor *n*—see WIT
humorous—see WITTY
hunger—see LONG
hurl—see THROW
hurry—see HASTE
hurt—see INJURE
hypercritical—see CRITICAL
HYPOTHESIS

IDEA
ideal—see MODEL
identical—see SAME
idle—see INACTIVE. VAIN
ignoble—see MEAN
ignominy—see DISGRACE
IGNORANT
ignore—see NEGLECT
ill—see BAD
illiterate—see IGNORANT
illusory—see APPARENT

illustration—see INSTANCE
illustrious—see FAMOUS
ill will—see MALICE
IMAGINARY
imagine—see THINK
imbibe—see ABSORB
imbue—see INFUSE
imitate—see COPY
immense—see ENORMOUS
immoderate—see
  EXCESSIVE
impair—see INJURE
impartial—see FAIR
IMPASSIONED
IMPASSIVE
impeach—see ACCUSE
impede—see HINDER
impel—see MOVE
imperative—see
  MASTERFUL
imperious—see MASTERFUL
IMPERTINENT
imperturbable—see COOL
impetuous—see
  PRECIPITATE
IMPLANT
IMPLEMENT
implore—see BEG
imply—see SUGGEST
import—see MEANING
IMPORTANCE
importune—see BEG
impose—see DICTATE
imposing—see GRAND
IMPOSTURE
impoverish—see DEPLETE
impregnate—see SOAK
impress—see AFFECT
impression—see IDEA
impressive—see MOVING

impromptu—see
  EXTEMPORANEOUS
improper—see INDECOROUS
IMPROVE
improvised—see
  EXTEMPORANEOUS
impulse—see MOTIVE
impulsive—see
  SPONTANEOUS
impute—see ASCRIBE
INACTIVE
inane—see INSIPID
inaugurate—see BEGIN
inborn—see INNATE
inbred—see INNATE
incense—see FRAGRANCE
incentive—see MOTIVE
inception—see ORIGIN
incessant—see CONTINUAL
incest—see ADULTERY
incident—see OCCURRENCE
INCISIVE
INCITE
INCLINE
INCLUDE
INCONSTANT
INCREASE
inculcate—see IMPLANT
incurious—see INDIFFERENT
indecent—see INDECOROUS
INDECOROUS
INDEFATIGABLE
indelicate—see
  INDECOROUS
indemnify—see PAY
independent—see FREE
indict—see ACCUSE
INDIFFERENT
indigence—see POVERTY
indigenous—see NATIVE

indignation—see ANGER
individual—see
  CHARACTERISTIC, SPECIAL
indolent—see LAZY
inducement—see MOTIVE
INDULGE
indulgent—see FORBEARING
industrious—see BUSY
industry—see BUSINESS
inebriated—see DRUNK
inept—see AWKWARD
inerrable—see INFALLIBLE
inerrant—see INFALLIBLE
inert—see INACTIVE
inexorable—see INFLEXIBLE
INFALLIBLE
infamy—see DISGRACE
INFER
infirm—see WEAK
infix—see IMPLANT
inflate—see EXPAND
INFLEXIBLE
INFLUENCE *n*
influence *vb*—see AFFECT
INFORM
infraction—see BREACH
INFREQUENT
infringe—see TRESPASS
infringement—see BREACH
INFUSE
ingenious—see CLEVER
ingenuous—see NATURAL
ingrain—see INFUSE
ingredient—see ELEMENT
inhibit—see FORBID
iniquitous—see VICIOUS
initiate—see BEGIN
INJURE
injury—see INJUSTICE
INJUSTICE

INNATE
inoculate—see INFUSE
inordinate—see EXCESSIVE
inquire—see ASK
inquisitive—see CURIOUS
INSANE
inseminate—see IMPLANT
insert—see INTRODUCE
insight—see DISCERNMENT
insinuate—see INTRODUCE,
  SUGGEST
INSIPID
insolent—see PROUD
inspect—see SCRUTINIZE
inspirit—see ENCOURAGE
INSTANCE
instigate—see INCITE
instill—see IMPLANT
instinctive—see
  SPONTANEOUS
instruct—see COMMAND,
  TEACH
instrument—see IMPLEMENT
insult—see OFFEND
insure—see ENSURE
insurrection—see
  REBELLION
intact—see PERFECT
integrity—see HONESTY,
  UNITY
INTELLIGENT
INTENSIFY
intent—see INTENTION
INTENTION
intentional—see
  VOLUNTARY
intercalate—see INTRODUCE
intercede—see INTERPOSE
interdict—see FORBID
interfere—see INTERPOSE

interject—see INTRODUCE
interlope—see INTRUDE
interpolate—see INTRODUCE
INTERPOSE
interpret—see EXPLAIN
interrogate—see ASK
intervene—see INTERPOSE
intimate *adj*—see FAMILIAR
intimate *vb*—see SUGGEST
INTIMIDATE
intoxicated—see DRUNK
intractable—see UNRULY
intricate—see COMPLEX
intrigue—see PLOT
INTRODUCE
INTRUDE
intrusive—see IMPERTINENT
invade—see TRESPASS
invalidate—see NULLIFY
invaluable—see COSTLY
invective—see ABUSE
inveigle—see LURE
INVENT
invert—see TRANSPOSE
INVETERATE
invidious—see REPUGNANT
INVITE
involve—see INCLUDE
involved—see COMPLEX
IRASCIBLE
ire—see ANGER
irk—see ANNOY
ironic—see SARCASTIC
irony—see WIT
IRREGULAR
IRRITATE
isolation—see SOLITUDE
issue *n*—see EFFECT
issue *vb*—see SPRING
ITEM

jade—see TIRE
jam—see PREDICAMENT
jargon—see DIALECT
jeer—see SCOFF
jejune—see INSIPID
JEST
job—see TASK
jocose—see WITTY
jocular—see WITTY
jocund—see MERRY
JOIN
joke—see JEST
jollity—see MIRTH
jolly—see MERRY
jovial—see MERRY
judge—see INFER
judgment—see SENSE
judicious—see WISE
JUNCTURE
junk—see DISCARD
jurisdiction—see POWER
just—see FAIR, UPRIGHT
justify—see MAINTAIN
juxtaposed—see ADJACENT

keen—see EAGER, SHARP
KEEP *vb*
KEEP *vb*
kick—see OBJECT
KILL
KIND *adj*
kind *n*—see TYPE
kindly—see KIND
knack—see GIFT
knotty—see COMPLEX
KNOWLEDGE

labor—see WORK
laconic—see CONCISE

lag—see DELAY
lament—see DEPLORE
languor—see LETHARGY
lank—see LEAN
lanky—see LEAN
lapse—see ERROR
lassitude—see LETHARGY
LAST *adj*
last *vb*—see CONTINUE
LASTING
late—see DEAD
LATENT
LAUGHABLE
lavish—see PROFUSE
LAW
LAWFUL
lax—see NEGLIGENT
LAZY
lead—see GUIDE
league—see ALLIANCE
LEAN
LEANING
learn—see DISCOVER
learning—see KNOWLEDGE
lease—see HIRE
leaven—see INFUSE
leech—see PARASITE
legal—see LAWFUL
legendary—see FICTITIOUS
legitimate—see LAWFUL
lengthen—see EXTEND
lenient—see FORBEARING
lenity—see MERCY
lessen—see DECREASE
LET
lethal—see DEADLY
LETHARGY
LEVEL
levity—see LIGHTNESS
LIABLE

LIBERAL
liberate—see FREE
liberty—see FREEDOM
license—see FREEDOM
licit—see LAWFUL
LIE
LIFT
light—see EASY
lighten—see RELIEVE
LIGHTNESS
LIKENESS
LIMIT
limpid—see CLEAR
lingo—see DIALECT
link—see JOIN
little—see SMALL
LIVELY
LIVING
loath—see DISINCLINED
loathe—see HATE
lofty—see HIGH
loiter—see DELAY
lone—see ALONE
lonely—see ALONE
lonesome—see ALONE
LONG
look—see EXPECT
loot—see SPOIL
loquacious—see
  TALKATIVE
lordly—see PROUD
lot—see FATE
LOUD
loutish—see BOORISH
lovely—see BEAUTIFUL
low—see BASE
lower—see FROWN
lowly—see HUMBLE
loyal—see FAITHFUL
loyalty—see FIDELITY

lucid—see CLEAR
LUCKY
ludicrous—see LAUGHABLE
luminous—see BRIGHT
lunatic—see INSANE
LURE
lurid—see GHASTLY
LURK
lush—see PROFUSE
lustrous—see BRIGHT
lusty—see VIGOROUS
luxuriant—see PROFUSE
LUXURIOUS
lying—see DISHONEST

macabre—see GHASTLY
machination—see PLOT
mad—see INSANE
magisterial—see
  DICTATORIAL
magnificent—see GRAND
MAIM
MAINTAIN
majestic—see GRAND
MAKE
makeshift—see RESOURCE
maladroit—see AWKWARD
malevolence—see MALICE
MALICE
MALIGN *vb*
malign *adj*—see SINISTER
malignity—see MALICE
malleable—see PLASTIC
MALODOROUS
mammoth—see ENORMOUS
manacle—see HAMPER
manage—see CONDUCT
maneuver—see TRICK
mangle—see MAIM

maniac—see INSANE
manifest *adj*—see EVIDENT
manifest *vb*—see SHOW
manipulate—see HANDLE
manner—see BEARING,
  METHOD
mannerism—see POSE
manufacture—see MAKE
manumit—see FREE
mar—see INJURE
margin—see BORDER
marital—see MATRIMONIAL
mark—see SIGN
marshal—see ORDER
mask—see DISGUISE
mass—see BULK
MASTERFUL
MATERIAL
MATRIMONIAL
MEAGER
MEAN *adj*
mean *n*—see AVERAGE
meander—see WANDER
MEANING
mechanical—see
  SPONTANEOUS
meddlesome—see
  IMPERTINENT
median—see AVERAGE
mediate—see INTERPOSE
meditate—see PONDER
meek—see HUMBLE
meet—see FIT
melancholia—see SADNESS
melancholy—see SADNESS
melodramatic—see
  DRAMATIC
member—see PART
MEMORY

MEND
mendacious—see
  DISHONEST
mercurial—see INCONSTANT
MERCY
meretricious—see GAUDY
merge—see MIX
MERRY
metamorphose—see
  TRANSFORM
METHOD
methodize—see ORDER
meticulous—see CAREFUL
métier—see WORK
mettle—see COURAGE
mien—see BEARING
might—see POWER
milieu—see BACKGROUND
militant—see AGGRESSIVE
mimic—see COPY
mingle—see MIX
miniature—see SMALL
minimize—see DECRY
minute—see
  CIRCUMSTANTIAL, SMALL
MIRTH
misanthropic—see CYNICAL
mischance—see
  MISFORTUNE
mise-en-scène—see
  BACKGROUND
miserly—see STINGY
misery—see DISTRESS
MISFORTUNE
misgiving—see
  APPREHENSION
mishap—see MISFORTUNE
mislead—see DECEIVE
misogynistic—see CYNICAL

mistake—see ERROR
mistrust—see UNCERTAINTY
mitigate—see RELIEVE
MIX
mob—see CROWD
mock—see COPY, RIDICULE
mode—see FASHION,
 METHOD
MODEL
modern—see NEW
modest—see CHASTE,
 HUMBLE, SHY
modify—see CHANGE
moist—see WET
mollify—see PACIFY
mollycoddle—see INDULGE
moment—see IMPORTANCE
momentary—see TRANSIENT
monetary—see FINANCIAL
MONSTROUS
MORAL
mordant—see CAUSTIC
morose—see SULLEN
mortal—see DEADLY
MOTIVE
MOVE
MOVING
mulish—see OBSTINATE
multiply—see INCREASE
mundane—see EARTHLY
munificent—see LIBERAL
murder—see KILL
murky—see DARK
muse—see PONDER
muster—see SUMMON
musty—see MALODOROUS
mutilate—see MAIM
mutiny—see REBELLION
mutual—see RECIPROCAL

MYSTERY
mythical—see FICTITIOUS

naive—see NATURAL
naked—see BARE
nasty—see DIRTY
national—see CITIZEN
NATIVE
NATURAL
nature—see TYPE
naughty—see BAD
nefarious—see VICIOUS
negate—see NULLIFY
NEGLECT
neglectful—see NEGLIGENT
NEGLIGENT
neighborly—see AMICABLE
nerve—see TEMERITY
nervous—see VIGOROUS
nettle—see IRRITATE
NEW
NICE
niggardly—see STINGY
nimble—see AGILE
nobility—see ARISTOCRACY
noble—see MORAL
noisome—see
 MALODOROUS
nonchalant—see COOL
nonplus—see PUZZLE
norm—see AVERAGE
normal—see REGULAR
note—see SIGN
noted—see FAMOUS
NOTICEABLE
notify—see INFORM
notion—see IDEA
notorious—see FAMOUS

novel—see NEW

noxious—see PERNICIOUS

nude—see BARE

nugatory—see VAIN

NULLIFY

nuptial—see MATRIMONIAL

obdurate—see INFLEXIBLE

OBEDIENT

OBJECT *adj*

object *n*—see INTENTION

objective *adj*—see FAIR,
    MATERIAL

objective *n*—see INTENTION

oblige—see FORCE

obliging—see AMIABLE

obliterate—see ERASE

oblivious—see FORGETFUL

obloquy—see ABUSE

obnoxious—see
    REPUGNANT

obscene—see COARSE

OBSCURE

obsequious—see
    SUBSERVIENT

observe—see KEEP

obsolete—see OLD

OBSTINATE

obstreperous—see
    VOCIFEROUS

obstruct—see HINDER

obtain—see GET

obtrude—see INTRUDE

obtrusive—see
    IMPERTINENT

obtuse—see DULL

obviate—see PREVENT

obvious—see EVIDENT

occasion—see CAUSE

occupation—see WORK

OCCURRENCE

odd—see STRANGE

odious—see HATEFUL

odor—see SMELL

ODOROUS

OFFEND

OFFENSE *n*

OFFENSE *n*

offhand—see
    EXTEMPORANEOUS

office—see FUNCTION

officious—see IMPERTINENT

offset—see COMPENSATE

oily—see FULSOME

OLD

oleaginous—see FULSOME

OMINOUS

omit—see NEGLECT

OMNIPRESENT

ONEROUS

open—see FRANK, LIABLE

OPINION

OPPONENT

OPPOSE.

OPPOSITE

oppress—see WRONG

oppressive—see ONEROUS

option—see CHOICE

opulent—see LUXURIOUS,
    RICH

oracular—see DICTATORIAL

orbit—see RANGE

ordain—see DICTATE

ORDER

ordinance—see LAW

ordinary—see COMMON

organize—see ORDER

ORIGIN

original—see NEW

originate—see SPRING
ornament—see ADORN
oscillate—see SWING
ostensible—see APPARENT
ostentatious—see SHOWY
otiose—see VAIN
oust—see EJECT
outcome—see EFFECT
outdo—see EXCEED
outfit—see FURNISH
outlandish—see STRANGE
OUTLINE
outlook—see PROSPECT
outrage—see OFFEND
OUTRAGEOUS
outstanding—see
NOTICEABLE
outstrip—see EXCEED
outwit—see FRUSTRATE
overbearing—see PROUD
overcome—see CONQUER
overlook—see NEGLECT
overthrow—see CONQUER
own—see ACKNOWLEDGE.
HAVE

PACIFY
pains—see EFFORT
PALATABLE
pall—see SATIATE
palpable—see PERCEPTIBLE
palter—see LIE
pamper—see INDULGE
panegyric—see ENCOMIUM
panic—see FEAR
parade—see SHOW
parallel—see SIMILAR
paramount—see DOMINANT
PARASITE

pardon—see EXCUSE
parley—see CONFER
parody—see CARICATURE
parsimonious—see STINGY
PART *n*
part *vb*—see SEPARATE
partake—see SHARE
participate—see SHARE
particular *adj*—see
CIRCUMSTANTIAL. NICE.
SINGLE. SPECIAL
particular *n*—see ITEM
partisan—see FOLLOWER
partner—see CONFEDERATE
pass—see JUNCTURE
PASSION
passionate—see
IMPASSIONED
passive—see INACTIVE
pastoral—see RURAL
patch—see MEND
patent—see EVIDENT
pathetic—see MOVING
pattern—see MODEL
PAY
peaceful—see CALM
peak—see SUMMIT
peculiar—see
CHARACTERISTIC.
STRANGE
pecuniary—see FINANCIAL
peer—see GAZE
peeve—see IRRITATE
pejorative—see
DEROGATORY
penchant—see LEANING
penetrate—see ENTER
penetration—see
DISCERNMENT
PENITENCE

penurious—see STINGY
penury—see POVERTY
PERCEPTIBLE
perception—see
 DISCERNMENT
peremptory—see
 MASTERFUL
perennial—see CONTINUAL
PERFECT
perfervid—see
 IMPASSIONED
perfidious—see FAITHLESS
PERFORM
perfume—see FRAGRANCE
perilous—see DANGEROUS
PERIOD
permanent—see LASTING
permit—see LET
PERNICIOUS
perpendicular—see
 VERTICAL
perpetual—see CONTINUAL
perplex—see PUZZLE
persecute—see WRONG
persist—see CONTINUE
personality—see
 DISPOSITION
perspicacious—see SHREWD
perspicuous—see CLEAR
persuasion—see OPINION
pertinacious—see
 OBSTINATE
pertinent—see RELEVANT
perturb—see DISCOMPOSE
perverse—see CONTRARY
pervert—see DEBASE
pessimistic—see CYNICAL
pester—see WORRY
PHASE
phenomenal—see MATERIAL

phlegm—see EQUANIMITY
phlegmatic—see IMPASSIVE
physical—see BODILY.
 MATERIAL
physiognomy—see FACE
pickle—see PREDICAMENT
pictorial—see GRAPHIC
picturesque—see GRAPHIC
piece—see PART
pierce—see ENTER
pietistic—see DEVOUT
piety—see FIDELITY
pilfer—see STEAL
pillage vb—see RAVAGE
pillage n—see SPOIL
pilot—see GUIDE
pinch—see JUNCTURE
pine—see LONG
pinnacle—see SUMMIT
pious—see DEVOUT
piquant—see PUNGENT
pique n—see OFFENSE
pique vb—see PROVOKE
pitch—see THROW
pithy—see CONCISE
pitiable—see
 CONTEMPTIBLE
PITY
placate—see PACIFY
placid—see CALM
plague—see WORRY
plain—see COMMON.
 EVIDENT. FRANK
PLAN
plane—see LEVEL
PLASTIC
play—see FUN
plea—see APOLOGY
plenary—see FULL
PLENTIFUL

pliable—see PLASTIC
pliant—see PLASTIC
plight—see PREDICAMENT
PLOT
plumb—see VERTICAL
plunder—see SPOIL
poignant—see MOVING,
 PUNGENT
poise—see TACT
polite—see CIVIL
politic—see EXPEDIENT,
 SUAVE
pollute—see CONTAMINATE
PONDER
ponderable—see
 PERCEPTIBLE
ponderous—see HEAVY
popular—see COMMON
portentous—see OMINOUS
portion—see FATE, PART
POSE
positive—see SURE
possess—see HAVE
POSSIBLE
postpone—see DEFER
potential—see LATENT
POVERTY
POWER *n*
POWER *n*
PRACTICABLE
practical—see PRACTICABLE
practice—see HABIT
precarious—see
 DANGEROUS
PRECEDING
precept—see LAW
precious—see COSTLY
PRECIPITATE
precipitous—see STEEP
précis—see COMPENDIUM

precise—see CORRECT
preclude—see PREVENT
precursor—see
 FORERUNNER
PREDICAMENT
predict—see FORETELL
PREDILECTION
predispose—see INCLINE
predominant—see
 DOMINANT
preempt—see APPROPRIATE
preference—see CHOICE
prejudice—see
 PREDILECTION
preponderant—see
 DOMINANT
prepossession—see
 PREDILECTION
prescribe—see DICTATE
present—see GIVE
presentiment—see
 APPREHENSION
prestige—see INFLUENCE
pretend—see ASSUME
pretension—see AMBITION
pretentious—see SHOWY
pretext—see APOLOGY
pretty—see BEAUTIFUL
PREVAILING
prevalent—see PREVAILING
prevaricate—see LIE
PREVENT *vb*
PREVENT *vb*
previous—see PRECEDING
priceless—see COSTLY
prior—see PRECEDING
prize *vb*—see APPRECIATE
prize *n*—see SPOIL
probe—see ENTER
probity—see HONESTY

problem—see MYSTERY
problematic—see DOUBTFUL
proceed—see SPRING
proclaim—see DECLARE
proclivity—see LEANING
procrastinate—see DELAY
procure—see GET
prodigal—see PROFUSE
prodigious—see
  MONSTROUS
PROFICIENT
profile—see OUTLINE
profitable—see BENEFICIAL
PROFUSE
prognosticate—see
  FORETELL
prohibit—see FORBID
project—see PLAN
PROJECTION
prolific—see FERTILE
prolix—see WORDY
prolong—see EXTEND
prominent—see
  NOTICEABLE
promote—see ADVANCE
prompt—see QUICK
promulgate—see DECLARE
PRONE
propel—see PUSH
propensity—see LEANING
proper—see FIT
property—see QUALITY
prophesy—see FORETELL
propitiate—see PACIFY
propitious—see FAVORABLE
PROPORTIONAL
proportionate—see
  PROPORTIONAL
propriety—see DECORUM
PROSPECT

prostrate—see PRONE
protect—see DEFEND
protest—see ASSERT,
  OBJECT
protract—see EXTEND
protrusion—see PROJECTION
protuberance—see
  PROJECTION
PROUD
providential—see LUCKY
province—see FUNCTION
PROVOKE
prowess—see HEROISM
prudent—see WISE
prying—see CURIOUS
publish—see DECLARE
pugnacious—see
  BELLIGERENT
PULL
punctilious—see CAREFUL
PUNGENT
PUNISH
pure—see CHASTE
purloin—see STEAL
purpose—see INTENTION
pursue—see CHASE
pursuit—see WORK
PUSH
pushing—see AGGRESSIVE
pusillanimous—see
  COWARDLY
putrefy—see DECAY
putrid—see MALODOROUS
PUZZLE vb
puzzle n—see MYSTERY

quail—see RECOIL
quaint—see STRANGE
qualified—see ABLE

QUALITY
QUALM
quandary—see
 PREDICAMENT
QUARREL
quarrelsome—see
 BELLIGERENT
quash—see CRUSH
queer—see STRANGE
quell—see CRUSH
query—see ASK
question—see ASK
questionable—see
 DOUBTFUL
QUICK
QUICKEN
quick-witted—see
 INTELLIGENT
quiescent—see LATENT
quip—see JEST
quit—see STOP
quixotic—see IMAGINARY

rack—see AFFLICT
racy—see PUNGENT
radiant—see BRIGHT
rage—see ANGER, FASHION
rail—see SCOLD
raise—see LIFT
ramble—see WANDER
rancor—see ENMITY
RANDOM
RANGE
rank—see FLAGRANT,
 MALODOROUS
ransom—see RESCUE
rapacious—see VORACIOUS
rapid—see FAST
rapture—see ECSTASY

rare—see CHOICE,
 INFREQUENT
rash—see ADVENTUROUS
rate—see ESTIMATE
rattle—see EMBARRASS
raucous—see LOUD
RAVAGE
ravenous—see VORACIOUS
raw—see RUDE
rawboned—see LEAN
ready—see QUICK
realize—see THINK
rear—see LIFT
reason *n*—see CAUSE
reason *vb*—see THINK
REBELLION
rebuild—see MEND
rebuke—see REPROVE
rebut—see DISPROVE
recalcitrant—see UNRULY
recall—see REMEMBER
recant—see ABJURE
RECEDE
RECIPROCAL
RECIPROCATE
reckless—see
 ADVENTUROUS
reckon—see CALCULATE
reclaim—see RESCUE
RECOIL
recollect—see REMEMBER
recollection—see MEMORY
recompense—see PAY
reconcile—see ADAPT
rectify—see CORRECT
recumbent—see PRONE
redeem—see RESCUE
redolence—see FRAGRANCE
redolent—see ODOROUS
redress—see CORRECT

reduce—see CONQUER, DECREASE
reflect—see THINK
reform—see CORRECT
refractory—see UNRULY
refresh—see RENEW
refuse—see DECLINE
refute—see DISPROVE
REGARD
regret—see SORROW
REGULAR
regulation—see LAW
reimburse—see PAY
reject—see DECLINE
rejoin—see ANSWER
rejuvenate—see RENEW
relate—see JOIN
release—see FREE
relegate—see COMMIT
relent—see YIELD
RELEVANT
RELIEVE
religious—see DEVOUT
RELINQUISH
reluctant—see DISINCLINED
remarkable—see NOTICEABLE
remedy—see CORRECT, CURE
REMEMBER
remembrance—see MEMORY
remind—see REMEMBER
reminisce—see REMEMBER
reminiscence—see MEMORY
remiss—see NEGLIGENT
remonstrate—see OBJECT
remorse—see PENITENCE
remunerate—see PAY
rend—see TEAR
RENEW

renounce—see ABDICATE, ABJURE
renovate—see RENEW
renowned—see FAMOUS
rent—see HIRE
repair—see MEND
repartee—see WIT
repay—see PAY
repellent—see REPUGNANT
repentance—see PENITENCE
REPLACE
replete—see FULL
replica—see REPRODUCTION
reply—see ANSWER
reprehend—see CRITICIZE
reprimand—see REPROVE
reproach—see REPROVE
reprobate—see CRITICIZE
REPRODUCTION
REPROVE
repudiate—see DECLINE, DISCLAIM
REPUGNANT
request—see ASK
require—see DEMAND
requite—see RECIPROCATE
RESCUE
resemblance—see LIKENESS
resentment—see OFFENSE
reserve—see KEEP
reserved—see SILENT
resign—see ABDICATE, RELINQUISH
resilient—see ELASTIC
resist—see OPPOSE
resolute—see FAITHFUL
resolution—see COURAGE
resolve—see DECIDE
resort—see RESOURCE

RESOURCE
respect—see REGARD
resplendent—see SPLENDID
respond—see ANSWER
RESPONSIBLE
restful—see COMFORTABLE
restive—see CONTRARY
restore—see RENEW
RESTRAIN
restrict—see LIMIT
result—see EFFECT
retain—see KEEP
retaliate—see RECIPROCATE
retard—see DELAY
reticent—see SILENT
retort—see ANSWER
retract—see ABJURE.
  RECEDE
retreat—see RECEDE
retrench—see SHORTEN
retrograde—see RECEDE
return—see RECIPROCATE
REVEAL
REVERE
reverence n—see HONOR
reverence vb—see REVERE
REVERSE
revile—see SCOLD
revise—see CORRECT
revolt—see REBELLION
revolution—see REBELLION
ribald—see COARSE
RICH
riddle—see MYSTERY
RIDICULE
ridiculous—see LAUGHABLE
rife—see PREVAILING
right—see CORRECT
righteous—see MORAL
RIGID

rigorous—see RIGID
rile—see IRRITATE
rim—see BORDER
rip—see TEAR
rise—see SPRING
risky—see DANGEROUS
rive—see TEAR
roam—see WANDER
robust—see HEALTHY
rock—see SHAKE
root—see ORIGIN
rot—see DECAY
ROUGH
rove—see WANDER
RUDE
rugged—see ROUGH
rule vb—see DECIDE.
  GOVERN
rule n—see LAW
ruminate—see PONDER
RURAL
ruse—see TRICK
rustic—see RURAL
ruth—see PITY

sack—see RAVAGE
SADNESS
safeguard—see DEFEND
sagacious—see SHREWD
sage—see WISE
salient—see NOTICEABLE
salubrious—see HEALTHFUL
salutary—see HEALTHFUL
SAME
sample—see INSTANCE
sanctimonious—see DEVOUT
sanction—see APPROVE
sane—see WISE
sangfroid—see EQUANIMITY

sanguinary—see BLOODY
sanguine—see BLOODY
sap—see WEAKEN
sapient—see WISE
sarcasm—see WIT
SARCASTIC
sardonic—see SARCASTIC
sate—see SATIATE
SATIATE
satire—see WIT
satiric—see SARCASTIC
satisfy—see PAY
saturate—see SOAK
saturnine—see SULLEN
savage—see FIERCE
save—see RESCUE
savoir faire—see TACT
savory—see PALATABLE
scabrous—see ROUGH
scan—see SCRUTINIZE
scandal—see OFFENSE
scant—see MEAGER
scanty—see MEAGER
scarce—see INFREQUENT
scathing—see CAUSTIC
SCATTER
scent—see FRAGRANCE.
  SMELL
scheme—see PLAN
scholarship—see
  KNOWLEDGE
school!—see TEACH
SCOFF
SCOLD
scope—see RANGE
scorn—see DESPISE
scowl—see FROWN
scrap—see DISCARD
scrawny—see LEAN
screen—see HIDE

scruple—see QUALM
scrupulous—see CAREFUL.
  UPRIGHT
SCRUTINIZE
scurrility—see ABUSE
scurvy—see CONTEMPTIBLE
seclusion—see SOLITUDE
SECRET
secrete—see HIDE
secretive—see SILENT
section—see PART
secure—see ENSURE. GET
sedate—see SERIOUS
seduce—see LURE
sedulous—see BUSY
seeming—see APPARENT
segment—see PART
seize—see TAKE
selection—see CHOICE
self-assertive—see
  AGGRESSIVE
self-possession—see
  CONFIDENCE
selfsame—see SAME
SENSE
sensible—see AWARE.
  MATERIAL. PERCEPTIBLE.
  WISE
sensitive—see LIABLE
sensual—see CARNAL.
  SENSUOUS
SENSUOUS
sentiment—see FEELING.
  OPINION
SEPARATE *vb*
separate *adj*—see DISTINCT.
  SINGLE
serene—see CALM
SERIOUS
servile—see SUBSERVIENT

setting—see BACKGROUND
settle—see DECIDE
sever—see SEPARATE
several—see DISTINCT
SEVERE
shackle—see HAMPER
SHAKE
shallow—see SUPERFICIAL
sham *vb*—see ASSUME
sham *n*—see IMPOSTURE
shape *n*—see FORM
shape *vb*—see MAKE
SHARE
SHARP
shed—see DISCARD
sheer—see STEEP
shield—see DEFEND
shift—see RESOURCE
shimmer—see FLASH
short—see BRIEF
SHORTEN
shove—see PUSH
SHOW *vb*
SHOW *vb*
SHOWY
SHREWD
shrink—see CONTRACT,
  RECOIL
shun—see ESCAPE
SHY
side—see PHASE
SIGN
significance—see
  IMPORTANCE, MEANING
signification—see MEANING
SILENT
silhouette—see OUTLINE
silken—see SLEEK
silly—see SIMPLE
SIMILAR

similarity—see LIKENESS
similitude—see LIKENESS
SIMPLE
simulate—see ASSUME
simultaneous—see
  CONTEMPORARY
sin—see OFFENSE
SINCERE
SINGLE
singular—see STRANGE
SINISTER
skepticism—see
  UNCERTAINTY
sketch—see COMPENDIUM
skill—see ART
skilled—see PROFICIENT
skillful—see PROFICIENT
skimpy—see MEAGER
skinny—see LEAN
skulk—see LURK
slack—see NEGLIGENT
slacken—see DELAY
slander—see MALIGN
slang—see DIALECT
slavish—see SUBSERVIENT
slay—see KILL
SLEEK
slender—see THIN
slick—see SLEEK
slight *vb*—see NEGLECT
slight *adj*—see THIN
slighting—see
  DEROGATORY
slim—see THIN
sling—see THROW
slink—see LURK
slip—see ERROR
slothful—see LAZY
slough—see DISCARD
slow—see DELAY

SLY
SMALL
SMELL
smooth—see EASY. LEVEL.
  SUAVE
snare—see CATCH
snatch—see TAKE
sneak—see LURK
sneer—see SCOFF
snug—see COMFORTABLE
SOAK
sober—see SERIOUS
sociable—see GRACIOUS
society—see ARISTOCRACY
solace—see COMFORT
sole—see SINGLE
solemn—see SERIOUS
solicit—see ASK. INVITE
solicitude—see CARE
solid—see FIRM
solidarity—see UNITY
solitary—see ALONE.
  SINGLE
SOLITUDE
somatic—see BODILY
SOPHISTICATED
sordid—see MEAN
SORROW
sorry—see CONTEMPTIBLE
sort—see TYPE
sound—see HEALTHY.
  VALID
source—see ORIGIN
sovereign—see DOMINANT.
  FREE
SPACIOUS
spare—see LEAN, MEAGER
SPARING
sparkle—see FLASH
sparse—see MEAGER

spasmodic—see FITFUL
spat—see QUARREL
SPECIAL
specific—see EXPLICIT.
  SPECIAL
specimen—see INSTANCE
speculate—see THINK
speed—see HASTE
speedy—see FAST
spirit—see COURAGE
spite—see MALICE
spleen—see MALICE
SPLENDID
splenetic—see IRASCIBLE
split—see TEAR
SPOIL *n*
spoil *vb*—see DECAY.
  INDULGE
sponge—see PARASITE
SPONTANEOUS
sporadic—see INFREQUENT
sport—see FUN
sprightly—see LIVELY
SPRING
springy—see ELASTIC
spry—see AGILE
spur—see MOTIVE
spurn—see DECLINE
squabble—see QUARREL
squalid—see DIRTY
squeamish—see NICE
stable—see LASTING
staid—see SERIOUS
stalwart—see STRONG
stand—see BEAR
STANDARD
stare—see GAZE
start—see BEGIN
stately—see GRAND
statute—see LAW

staunch—see FAITHFUL
stay—see DEFER
steadfast—see FAITHFUL
STEADY
STEAL
stealthy—see SECRET
STEEP *adj*
steep *vb*—see SOAK
steer—see GUIDE
stem—see SPRING
stentorian—see LOUD
stereotyped—see TRITE
stern—see SEVERE
STICK
STIFF
stimulate—see PROVOKE
STINGY
stinking—see MALODOROUS
stint—see TASK
stoic—see IMPASSIVE
stolid—see IMPASSIVE
STOOP
STOP
stopgap—see RESOURCE
storm—see ATTACK
stout—see STRONG
straits—see JUNCTURE
STRANGE
stratagem—see TRICK
strength—see POWER
strenuous—see VIGOROUS
strict—see RIGID
strident—see LOUD,
  VOCIFEROUS
strife—see DISCORD
strike—see AFFECT
striking—see NOTICEABLE
stringent—see RIGID
strive—see ATTEMPT
STRONG

stubborn—see OBSTINATE
study—see CONSIDER
stupendous—see
  MONSTROUS
STUPID
stupor—see LETHARGY
sturdy—see STRONG
style—see FASHION
SUAVE
subdue—see CONQUER
subject *n*—see CITIZEN
subject *adj*—see LIABLE
sublime—see SPLENDID
submit—see YIELD
subscribe—see ASSENT
SUBSERVIENT
subside—see ABATE
substantiate—see CONFIRM
subterfuge—see DECEPTION
succeed—see FOLLOW
succinct—see CONCISE
succumb—see YIELD
sudden—see PRECIPITATE
suffer—see BEAR
suffering—see DISTRESS
SUFFICIENT
suffuse—see INFUSE
SUGGEST
suitable—see FIT
sulky—see SULLEN
SULLEN
summary—see CONCISE
summative—see
  CUMULATIVE
SUMMIT
SUMMON
sumptuous—see LUXURIOUS
sunder—see SEPARATE
superb—see SPLENDID
supercilious—see PROUD

SUPEREROGATORY
SUPERFICIAL
supersede—see REPLACE
supervene—see FOLLOW
supine—see INACTIVE.
  PRONE
supplant—see REPLACE
supple—see ELASTIC
supplicate—see BEG
SUPPORT
suppress—see CRUSH
SURE
surfeit—see SATIATE
surly—see SULLEN
surmise—see CONJECTURE
surpass—see EXCEED
SURPRISE
surrender—see RELINQUISH
surreptitious—see SECRET
survey—see COMPENDIUM
susceptible—see LIABLE
suspend—see DEFER.
  EXCLUDE
suspicion—see
  UNCERTAINTY
sway *vb*—see AFFECT.
  SWING
sway *n*—see POWER
sweep—see RANGE
swell—see EXPAND
SWERVE
swift—see FAST
swindle—see CHEAT
SWING *vb*
SWING *vb*
sycophant—see PARASITE
syllabus—see COMPENDIUM
sympathetic—see
  CONSONANT

sympathy—see
  ATTRACTION. PITY
symptom—see SIGN
synchronous—see
  CONTEMPORARY
synopsis—see ABRIDGMENT
synthetic—see ARTIFICIAL
system—see METHOD
systematize—see ORDER

taciturn—see SILENT
TACT
taint—see CONTAMINATE
TAKE
talent—see GIFT
TALKATIVE
tall—see HIGH
tangible—see PERCEPTIBLE
TASK
tasty—see PALATABLE
taunt—see RIDICULE
tawdry—see GAUDY
TEACH
TEAR
tease—see WORRY
tell—see REVEAL
telling—see VALID
TEMERITY
temper—see DISPOSITION
temperament—see
  DISPOSITION
tempt—see LURE
tenacious—see STRONG
tenacity—see COURAGE
TENDENCY
tenor—see TENDENCY
tenuous—see THIN
tergiversation—see
  AMBIGUITY

terminal—see LAST
terminate—see CLOSE
termination—see END
terminus—see END
terror—see FEAR
terse—see CONCISE
testy—see IRASCIBLE
theatrical—see DRAMATIC
theory—see HYPOTHESIS
thick—see CLOSE
THIN
THINK *vb*
THINK *vb*
thirst—see LONG
thought—see IDEA
thrash—see SWING
threadbare—see TRITE
thrifty—see SPARING
throng—see CROWD
THROW
thrust—see PUSH
thwart—see FRUSTRATE
tiff—see QUARREL
tight—see DRUNK
tiny—see SMALL
tipsy—see DRUNK
TIRE
tireless—see
  INDEFATIGABLE
toady *vb*—see FAWN
toady *n*—see PARASITE
toil—see WORK
token—see SIGN
tolerant—see FORBEARING
tolerate—see BEAR
tool—see IMPLEMENT
toothsome—see PALATABLE
torment—see AFFLICT
torpor—see LETHARGY
torture—see AFFLICT

toss—see THROW
total—see WHOLE
touch—see AFFECT
touching—see MOVING
touchstone—see STANDARD
touchy—see IRASCIBLE
tough—see STRONG
toy—see TRIFLE
TRACE
track—see TRACE
tractable—see OBEDIENT
trade—see BUSINESS
traduce—see MALIGN
traffic—see BUSINESS
trail—see CHASE
train—see TEACH
traipse—see WANDER
traitorous—see FAITHLESS
trammel—see HAMPER
tranquil—see CALM
transcend—see EXCEED
transfigure—see
  TRANSFORM
TRANSFORM
TRANSIENT
transitory—see TRANSIENT
translucent—see CLEAR
transmogrify—see
  TRANSFORM
transmute—see TRANSFORM
transparent—see CLEAR
transport *vb*—see BANISH.
  CARRY
transport *n*—see ECSTASY
transpose—see REVERSE
trap—see CATCH
travail—see WORK
travesty—see CARICATURE
treacherous—see FAITHLESS
treasure—see APPRECIATE

tremendous—see
  MONSTROUS
trenchant—see INCISIVE
trend—see TENDENCY
trepidation—see FEAR
TRESPASS *vb*
trespass *n*—see BREACH
tribute—see ENCOMIUM
TRICK *n*
trick *vb*—see DUPE
trickery—see DECEPTION
tricky—see SLY
TRIFLE
TRITE
trouble—see EFFORT
truckle—see FAWN
TRUTH
try—see AFFLICT, ATTEMPT
tug—see PULL
tumult—see COMMOTION
turmoil—see COMMOTION
turn—see CURVE
twist—see CURVE
twit—see RIDICULE
TYPE
typical—see REGULAR
tyrannical—see ABSOLUTE
tyro—see AMATEUR

ubiquitous—see
  OMNIPRESENT
ultimate—see LAST
umbrage—see OFFENSE
unbecoming—see
  INDECOROUS
unbiased—see FAIR
uncalled-for—see
  SUPEREROGATORY

uncanny—see WEIRD
UNCERTAINTY
uncommon—see
  INFREQUENT
unconcerned—see
  INDIFFERENT
unctuous—see FULSOME
underhanded—see SECRET
undermine—see WEAKEN
UNDERSTAND
undulate—see SWING
unearth—see DISCOVER
unerring—see INFALLIBLE
uneven—see ROUGH
unfeigned—see SINCERE
unflagging—see
  INDEFATIGABLE
ungovernable—see UNRULY
union—see UNITY
unique—see SINGLE,
  STRANGE
unite—see JOIN
UNITY
UNIVERSAL
unlearned—see IGNORANT
unlettered—see IGNORANT
unman—see UNNERVE
unmindful—see FORGETFUL
unnatural—see IRREGULAR
UNNERVE
unpremeditated—see
  EXTEMPORANEOUS
unruffled—see COOL
UNRULY
unseemly—see
  INDECOROUS
unsophisticated—see
  NATURAL
unstable—see INCONSTANT

untangle—see EXTRICATE

untiring—see INDEFATIGABLE

untruthful—see DISHONEST

untutored—see IGNORANT

unwearied—see INDEFATIGABLE

upbraid—see SCOLD

upheaval—see COMMOTION

uphold—see SUPPORT

UPRIGHT

uprising—see REBELLION

uproot—see EXTERMINATE

upset—see DISCOMPOSE

urbane—see SUAVE

usage—see HABIT

USE

USUAL

usurp—see APPROPRIATE

utensil—see IMPLEMENT

utilize—see USE

utter—see EXPRESS

vacant—see EMPTY

vacillate—see HESITATE

vacuous—see EMPTY

vagary—see CAPRICE

vague—see OBSCURE

VAIN

VALID

validate—see CONFIRM

valor—see HEROISM

valuable—see COSTLY

value—see APPRECIATE, ESTIMATE

vanquish—see CONQUER

vapid—see INSIPID

variance—see DISCORD

various—see DIFFERENT

vary—see CHANGE

vast—see ENORMOUS

vaunt—see BOAST

veer—see SWERVE

venerable—see OLD

venerate—see REVERE

vent—see EXPRESS

venturesome—see ADVENTUROUS

veracity—see TRUTH

verbose—see WORDY

verge—see BORDER

verify—see CONFIRM

verisimilitude—see TRUTH

veritable—see AUTHENTIC

verity—see TRUTH

vernacular—see DIALECT

VERTICAL

very—see SAME

vestige—see TRACE

vex—see ANNOY

vibrate—see SWING

vice—see FAULT, OFFENSE

VICIOUS

view—see OPINION

vigilant—see WATCHFUL

VIGOROUS

vile—see BASE

vilify—see MALIGN

villainous—see VICIOUS

vindicate—see EXCULPATE, MAINTAIN

violation—see BREACH

virtuous—see MORAL

visage—see FACE

visionary—see IMAGINARY

vital—see ESSENTIAL, LIVING

vitiate—see DEBASE
vituperate—see SCOLD
vituperation—see ABUSE
vivacious—see LIVELY
vivid—see GRAPHIC
vivify—see QUICKEN
VOCIFEROUS
vogue—see FASHION
voice—see EXPRESS
void—see EMPTY
volatility—see LIGHTNESS
voluble—see TALKATIVE
volume—see BULK
VOLUNTARY
voluptuous—see SENSUOUS
VORACIOUS
vouch—see CERTIFY
vouchsafe—see GRANT
vulgar—see COARSE,
  COMMON

waive—see RELINQUISH
WANDER
wane—see ABATE
want *vb*—see DESIRE
want *n*—see POVERTY
wanton—see
  SUPEREROGATORY
ward off—see PREVENT
warp—see DEFORM
wary—see CAUTIOUS
waste—see RAVAGE
WATCHFUL
wave—see SWING
waver—see HESITATE,
  SWING
way—see METHOD
wayward—see CONTRARY
WEAK

WEAKEN
wealthy—see RICH
wean—see ESTRANGE
weary—see TIRE
weigh—see CONSIDER
weight—see IMPORTANCE,
  INFLUENCE
weighty—see HEAVY
WEIRD
well—see HEALTHY
WET
wheedle—see COAX
whim—see CAPRICE
WHOLE
wholehearted—see SINCERE
wholesome—see
  HEALTHFUL, HEALTHY
wicked—see BAD
wide—see BROAD
wide-awake—see
  WATCHFUL
wield—see HANDLE
wile—see TRICK
willful—see UNRULY
willing—see VOLUNTARY
win—see GET
wince—see RECOIL
wisdom—see SENSE
WISE
wisecrack—see JEST
wish—see DESIRE
WIT
withhold—see KEEP
withstand—see OPPOSE
witness—see CERTIFY
witticism—see JEST
WITTY
woe—see SORROW
woebegone—see
  DOWNCAST

wont—see HABIT
wonted—see USUAL
WORDY
WORK *n*
WORK *n*
worldly—see EARTHLY
worldly-wise—see
  SOPHISTICATED
WORRY *vb*
worry *n*—see CARE
worship—see REVERE
wrangle—see QUARREL

wrath—see ANGER
WRONG *vb*
wrong *n*—see INJUSTICE

yardstick—see STANDARD
yearn—see LONG
YIELD

zeal—see PASSION

A

ABANDON, desert, forsake mean to leave without intending to return.

Abandon suggests that the thing or person left may be helpless without protection ⟨they *abandoned* their cat at summer's end⟩.

Desert implies that the object left may be weakened but not destroyed by one's absence ⟨a town *deserted* once the gold ran out⟩.

Forsake suggests an action more likely to bring impoverishment or bereavement to that which is forsaken than its exposure to physical dangers ⟨*forsook* his wife and family for a younger woman⟩.

See in addition RELINQUISH.

ABASE, demean, debase, degrade, humiliate mean to lower in one's own estimation or in that of others.

Abase suggests losing or voluntarily yielding up dignity or prestige ⟨a fine stage actor who *abased* himself by turning to television⟩.

Demean implies losing or injuring social standing by an unsuitable act or association ⟨commercial endorsements *demean* the Olympics⟩.

Debase implies a deterioration of moral standards or character ⟨drunkenness has *debased* the Mardi Gras⟩.

Degrade suggests the taking of a step downward sometimes in rank but more often on the road to moral degeneration ⟨the public altercation *degraded* both candidates⟩.

Humiliate implies the severe wounding of one's pride and the causing of deep shame ⟨*humiliated* by his suggestive remarks⟩.

ABATE, subside, wane, ebb mean to die down in force or intensity.

Abate stresses the idea of progressive diminishing ⟨waited until the storm *abated*⟩.

Subside implies the ceasing of turbulence or agitation 〈the protests *subsided* after a few days〉.

Wane suggests the fading or weakening of something good or impressive 〈the public's *waning* interest in space flight〉.

Ebb suggests the receding of something (as the tide) that commonly comes and goes 〈the *ebbing* of daylight〉.

See in addition DECREASE.

ABDICATE, renounce, resign mean to give up a position with no possibility of resuming it.

Abdicate implies a giving up of sovereign power or sometimes an evading of responsibility such as that of a parent 〈by walking out he *abdicated* his rights as a father〉.

Renounce may replace it but often implies additionally a sacrifice for a greater end 〈by this marriage she *renounces* any hope of an inheritance〉.

Resign applies to the giving up of an unexpired office or trust 〈forced to *resign* from office〉.

ABJURE, renounce, forswear, recant, retract mean to withdraw one's word or professed belief.

Abjure implies a firm and final rejecting or abandoning often made under oath 〈candidates for citizenship must *abjure* allegiance to any foreign power〉.

Renounce often equals *abjure* but may carry the meaning of disclaim or disown 〈willing to *renounce* his lifelong friends〉.

Forswear may add to *abjure* an implication of perjury or betrayal 〈I cannot *forswear* my principles to win votes〉.

Recant stresses the withdrawing or denying of something professed or taught 〈the suspect *recanted* his confession and professed his innocence〉.

Retract applies to the withdrawing of a promise, an offer, or an accusation 〈under threat of lawsuit the paper *retracted* the statement〉.

ABLE, capable, competent, qualified mean having power or fitness for work.

Able suggests ability above the average as revealed in actual performance ⟨proved that she is an *able* Shakespearean actress⟩.

Capable stresses the having of qualities fitting one for work but does not imply outstanding ability ⟨*capable* of doing simple tasks under supervision⟩.

Competent and **qualified** imply having the experience or training for adequate performance ⟨a leap that any *competent* ballet dancer can execute⟩ ⟨seek help from a *qualified* medical professional⟩.

ABNORMAL, atypical, aberrant mean deviating markedly from the rule or standard of its kind.

Abnormal frequently suggests strangeness and sometimes deformity or monstrosity ⟨a classic study of *abnormal* personalities⟩.

Atypical stresses divergence upward or downward from some established norm ⟨a markedly *atypical* reaction to a drug⟩.

Aberrant implies a departure from the usual or natural type ⟨that joyriding incident must be regarded as an *aberrant* episode in his life⟩.

ABOMINATION, anathema, bugbear, bête noire mean a person or thing that arouses intense dislike.

Abomination suggests the arousal of loathing, disgust, and extreme displeasure ⟨in her opinion all of modern art is an *abomination*⟩.

Anathema suggests that something is so odious that it is dismissed or rejected out of hand ⟨anything that was Yankee was *anathema* to my Southern aunt⟩.

Bugbear suggests something so dreaded that one seeks continually to avoid it ⟨the deficit issue became an annual congressional *bugbear*⟩.

Bête noire suggests a pet aversion that one habitually or especially avoids ⟨his mooching brother-in-law was the *bête noire* of his life⟩.

ABRIDGMENT, abstract, synopsis, conspectus, epitome
mean a condensed treatment.
   Abridgment suggests reduction in compass with retention
of relative completeness ⟨a desk-size dictionary that is an
abridgment of a larger work⟩.
   Abstract applies to a summary of points of a treatise, document, or proposed treatment and usu. has no independent
worth ⟨a published *abstract* of a medical paper⟩.
   Synopsis implies a skeletal presentation of an argument or a
narrative suitable for rapid examination ⟨read a *synopsis* of
the screenplay⟩.
   Conspectus implies a quick overall view of a large detailed
subject ⟨the book is a *conspectus* of modern European
history⟩.
   Epitome suggests the briefest possible presentation of a
complex whole that still has independent value ⟨"know thy-
self" was the *epitome* of Greek philosophy⟩.

ABSOLUTE, autocratic, arbitrary, despotic, tyrannical
mean exercising power or authority without restraint.
   Absolute implies that one is not bound by legal constraints
or the control of another ⟨King Louis XIV was an *absolute*
monarch⟩.
   Autocratic suggests the egotistical, self-conscious use of
power or the haughty imposition of one's own will ⟨the flam-
boyant, *autocratic* director of the ballet company⟩.
   Arbitrary implies the exercise and usu. the abuse of power
according to one's momentary inclination ⟨his high-handed,
arbitrary way of running his department⟩.
   Despotic implies the arbitrary and imperious exercise of absolute power or control ⟨the most decadent and *despotic* of
the Roman emperors⟩.
   Tyrannical implies the abuse of absolute power and harsh
or oppressive rule ⟨a new regime as *tyrannical* as the one it
had deposed⟩.

ABSORB, imbibe, assimilate mean to take something in so as to become imbued with it.

Absorb may connote a loss of identity in what is taken in or an enrichment of what takes in ⟨can quickly *absorb* highly technical reports⟩.

Imbibe implies a drinking in which may be unconscious but whose effect may be significant or profound ⟨children *imbibe* the values of their parents⟩.

Assimilate stresses an incorporation into the substance of the body or mind ⟨asked to *assimilate* a mass of material in a brief time⟩.

ABUSE, vituperation, invective, obloquy, scurrility, billingsgate mean vehemently expressed condemnation or disapproval.

Abuse, the most general term, implies the anger of the speaker and stresses the harshness of the language ⟨charged her husband with verbal *abuse*⟩.

Vituperation implies fluent and sustained abuse ⟨subjected his aide to a torrent of *vituperation*⟩.

Invective implies a comparable vehemence but suggests greater verbal and rhetorical skill and may apply to a public denunciation ⟨a politician known for his blistering *invective*⟩.

Obloquy suggests defamation and consequent shame and disgrace ⟨silently endured the *obloquy* of his former friend⟩.

Scurrility implies viciousness of attack and coarseness or foulness of language ⟨a debate that was not an exchange of ideas but an exercise in *scurrility*⟩.

Billingsgate implies practiced fluency and variety of profane or obscene abuse ⟨a *billingsgate* that would make a drunken sailor blush⟩.

ACCIDENTAL, fortuitous, casual, contingent mean not amenable to planning or prediction.

Accidental stresses chance ⟨any resemblance to actual persons is entirely *accidental*⟩.

Fortuitous so strongly suggests chance that it often connotes entire absence of cause (believes that life is more than a series of *fortuitous* events).

Casual stresses lack of real or apparent premeditation or intent (a *casual* encounter between two acquaintances).

Contingent suggests possibility of happening but stresses uncertainty and dependence on other future events for existence or occurrence (the *contingent* effects of a proposed amendment to the constitution).

ACCOMPANY, attend, escort mean to go along with.

When referring to persons, **accompany** usu. implies equality of status (*accompanied* his wife to the theater).

Attend implies a waiting upon in order to serve usu. as a subordinate (will *attend* the President at the summit meeting).

Escort adds to *accompany* implications of protection, ceremony, or courtesy (a motorcade *escorted* the visiting queen).

ACCUSE, charge, indict, impeach mean to declare a person guilty of a fault or offense.

Accuse implies a direct, personal declaration (*accused* him of trying to steal his wallet).

Charge usu. implies a formal declaration of a serious offense (an athlete *charged* with taking illegal drugs before the race).

Indict is usu. used in a legal context and implies a formal consideration of evidence prior to a trial (*indicted* by a grand jury for first-degree murder).

Impeach technically refers to a formal charge of malfeasance in office on the part of a public official (the House of Representatives *impeached* President Andrew Johnson of high crimes and misdemeanors).

ACKNOWLEDGE, admit, own, avow, confess mean to disclose against one's will or inclination.

Acknowledge implies the disclosing of something that has been or might be concealed (*acknowledged* an early short-lived marriage).

Admit implies reluctance to disclose, grant, or concede and refers usu. to facts rather than their implications (*admitted* that the project was over budget).

Own implies acknowledging something in close relation to oneself (must *own* that I know little about computers).

Avow implies boldly declaring, often in the face of hostility, what one might be expected to be silent about (*avowed* that he was homosexual).

Confess may apply to an admission of a weakness, failure, omission, or guilt (*confessed* that she had a weakness for sweets).

ACQUIREMENT, acquisition, attainment, accomplishment mean a power or skill won through deliberate effort.

Acquirement suggests the result of constant endeavor to cultivate oneself (an appreciation of good music was not one of his *acquirements*).

Acquisition stresses the effort involved and the inherent value of what is gained (the ability to concentrate is a valuable *acquisition*).

Attainment suggests a distinguished achievement (honored as woman of the year for her many *attainments*).

Accomplishment implies a socially useful skill (wittiness in conversation is an *accomplishment* to be cherished).

ACRIMONY, acerbity, asperity mean temper or language marked by angry irritation.

Acrimony implies feelings of bitterness and a stinging verbal attack (a campaign marked by verbal exchanges of intense *acrimony*).

Acerbity suggests a morose, embittered, or crabbed temperament (an inbred *acerbity* that pervades even his personal letters).

Asperity suggests harshness or roughness of expression rather than feelings of bitterness (a certain *asperity* of expression was part of her style).

ACUTE, critical, crucial mean of uncertain outcome.

Acute stresses intensification of conditions leading to a culmination or breaking point ⟨the housing shortage is becoming *acute*⟩.

Critical adds to **acute** implications of imminent change, of attendant suspense, and of decisiveness in the outcome ⟨the war has entered a *critical* phase⟩.

Crucial suggests a dividing of the ways and often a test or trial involving the determination of a future course or direction ⟨for the campaign, the coming weeks will be *crucial*⟩. See in addition SHARP.

ADAPT, adjust, accommodate, conform, reconcile mean to bring one thing into correspondence with another.

Adapt implies a modification according to changing circumstances ⟨they *adapted* themselves to the warmer climate⟩.

Adjust suggests bringing into a close and exact correspondence or harmony as exists between the parts of a mechanism ⟨*adjusted* the budget to allow for inflation⟩.

Accommodate may suggest yielding or compromising in order to effect a correspondence ⟨*accommodated* his political beliefs in order to win⟩.

Conform applies to bringing into harmony or accordance with a pattern, example, or principle ⟨refused to *conform* to society's idea of morality⟩.

Reconcile implies the demonstration of the underlying consistency or congruity of things that seem to be incompatible ⟨tried to *reconcile* what they said with what I knew⟩.

ADJACENT, adjoining, contiguous, juxtaposed mean being in close proximity.

Adjacent may or may not imply contact but always implies absence of anything of the same kind in between ⟨the price of the house and the *adjacent* garage⟩.

Adjoining definitely implies meeting and touching at some point or line ⟨assigned *adjoining* rooms at the hotel⟩.

Contiguous implies having contact on all or most of one side ⟨offices in all 48 *contiguous* states⟩.

Juxtaposed means placed side by side esp. so as to permit comparison and contrast ⟨an ultramodern office building *juxtaposed* to a Gothic church⟩.

ADMITTANCE, admission mean permitted entrance.

Admittance is usu. applied to mere physical entrance to a locality or a building ⟨members must show their cards upon *admittance* to the club⟩.

Admission applies to entrance or formal acceptance (as into a club) that carries with it rights, privileges, standing, or membership ⟨candidates for *admission* must submit recommendations from two club members⟩.

ADOPT, embrace, espouse mean to take an opinion, policy, or practice as one's own.

Adopt implies accepting something created by another or foreign to one's nature ⟨forced to *adopt* the procedures of the new parent company⟩.

Embrace implies a ready or happy acceptance ⟨eagerly *embraced* the ways and customs of their new homeland⟩.

Espouse adds an implication of close attachment to a cause and a sharing of its fortunes ⟨spent her lifetime *espousing* equal rights for women⟩.

ADORN, decorate, ornament, embellish, beautify, deck, garnish mean to enhance the appearance of something by adding something unessential.

Adorn implies an enhancing by something beautiful in itself ⟨a diamond necklace *adorned* her neck⟩.

Decorate suggests relieving plainness or monotony by adding beauty of color or design ⟨*decorate* a birthday cake with colored frosting⟩.

Ornament and **embellish** imply the adding of something extraneous, *ornament* stressing the heightening or setting off of the original ⟨a white house *ornamented* with green shutters⟩, *embellish* often stressing the adding of superfluous or adventitious ornament ⟨*embellish* a page with floral borders⟩.

Beautify adds to *embellish* a suggestion of counterbalancing plainnesss or ugliness ⟨will *beautify* the park with flower beds⟩.

Deck implies the addition of something that contributes to gaiety, splendor, or showiness ⟨a house all *decked* out for Christmas⟩.

Garnish suggests decorating with a small final touch and is used esp. in referring to the serving of food ⟨airline food is invariably *garnished* with parsley⟩.

ADULTERY, fornication, incest designate forms of illicit sexual intercourse that are clearly distinguished in legal use.

Adultery can be applied only to sexual intercourse between a married person and a partner other than his or her wife or husband ⟨listed *adultery* as grounds for divorce⟩.

Fornication designates sexual intercourse on the part of an unmarried person ⟨religious laws strictly forbidding *fornication*⟩.

Incest refers to sexual intercourse between persons proscribed from marrying on the basis of kinship ties ⟨*incest* involving father and daughter is the most common⟩.

ADVANCE, promote, forward, further mean to help (someone or something) to move ahead.

Advance stresses effective assisting in hastening a process or bringing about a desired end ⟨a gesture intended to *advance* the cause of peace⟩.

Promote suggests an encouraging or fostering and may denote an increase in status or rank ⟨a company trying to *promote* better health among employees⟩.

Forward implies an impetus forcing something ahead ⟨a wage increase would *forward* productivity⟩.

Further suggests a removing of obstacles in the way of a desired advance ⟨used the marriage to *further* his career⟩.

ADVENTUROUS, venturesome, daring, daredevil, rash, reckless, foolhardy mean exposing oneself to danger more than required by good sense.

Adventurous implies a willingness to accept risks but not necessarily imprudence ⟨*adventurous* pioneers opened the West⟩.

Venturesome implies a jaunty eagerness for perilous undertakings ⟨*venturesome* pilots became popular heroes⟩.

Daring heightens the implication of fearlessness in courting danger ⟨mountain climbing attracts the *daring* types⟩.

Daredevil stresses ostentation in daring ⟨*daredevil* motorcyclists performing stunts⟩.

Rash suggests imprudence and lack of forethought ⟨a *rash* decision that you will regret later⟩.

Reckless implies heedlessness of probable consequences ⟨a *reckless* driver who was drunk⟩.

Foolhardy suggests a recklessness that is inconsistent with good sense ⟨only a *foolhardy* sailor would venture into this storm⟩.

ADVERSE, antagonistic, counter, counteractive mean so opposed as to cause often harmful interference.

Adverse applies to what is unfavorable, harmful, or detrimental ⟨very sensitive to *adverse* criticism⟩.

Antagonistic usu. implies mutual opposition and either hostility or incompatibility ⟨neighboring countries were *antagonistic* to the new nation⟩.

Counter applies to forces coming from opposite directions with resulting conflict or tension ⟨the *counter* demands of family and career⟩.

Counteractive implies an opposition between two things that nullifies the effect of one or both ⟨poor eating habits will have a *counteractive* effect on any gains from exercise⟩.

ADVICE, counsel denote recommendation as to a decision or a course of conduct.

Advice implies real or pretended knowledge or experience, often professional or technical, on the part of the one who advises ⟨a book of *advice* for would-be entrepreneurs⟩.

Counsel often stresses the fruit of wisdom or deliberation and may presuppose a weightier occasion, or more authority,

or more personal concern on the part of the one giving counsel ⟨Father would often give me the benefit of his *counsel*⟩.

AFFECT, influence, touch, impress, strike, sway mean to
produce or have an effect upon.

Affect implies the action of a stimulus that can produce a
response or reaction ⟨the sight *affected* her to tears⟩.

Influence implies a force that brings about a change (as in
nature or behavior) ⟨our beliefs are *influenced* by our up-
bringing⟩ ⟨a drug that *influences* growth rates⟩.

Touch may carry a vivid suggestion of close contact and may
connote stirring, arousing, or harming ⟨plants *touched* by
frost⟩ ⟨his emotions were *touched* by her distress⟩.

Impress stresses the depth and persistence of the effect ⟨only
one of the plans *impressed* him⟩.

Strike, similar to but weaker than *impress*, may convey the
notion of sudden sharp perception or appreciation ⟨*struck* by
the solemnity of the occasion⟩.

Sway implies the acting of influences that are not resisted or
are irresistible, with resulting change in character or course
of action ⟨politicians who are *swayed* by popular opinion⟩.
See in addition ASSUME.

AFFLICT, try, torment, torture, rack, grill mean to inflict
on a person something that is hard to bear.

Afflict is a general term and applies to the causing of pain
or suffering or of acute annoyance, embarrassment, or any
distress ⟨many elderly persons who are *afflicted* with
blindness⟩.

Try suggests imposing something that strains the powers of
endurance or of self-control ⟨young children often *try* their
parents' patience⟩.

Torment suggests persecution or the repeated inflicting of
suffering or annoyance ⟨the horses are *tormented* by flies⟩.

Torture adds the implication of causing unbearable pain or
suffering ⟨*tortured* by a sense of guilt⟩.

Rack stresses straining or wrenching ⟨a mind *racked* by guilt⟩.

Grill suggests causing acute discomfort as by long and relentless questioning ⟨they *grilled* the prisoner for hours on end⟩.

AGGRESSIVE, militant, assertive, self-assertive, pushing mean obtrusively energetic esp. in pursuing particular goals.

Aggressive implies a disposition to dominate often in disregard of others' rights or in determined and energetic pursuit of one's ends ⟨books on how to be *aggressive* in the business world⟩.

Militant also implies a fighting disposition but suggests not self-seeking but devotion to a cause, movement, or principle ⟨*militant* environmentalists staged a protest⟩.

Assertive suggests bold self-confidence in expression of opinion ⟨*assertive* speakers dominated the open forum⟩.

Self-assertive connotes forwardness or brash self-confidence ⟨a *self-assertive* young executive climbing the corporate ladder⟩.

Pushing may apply to ambition or enterprise or to snobbish and crude intrusiveness or officiousness ⟨*pushing* salespeople using high-pressure tactics⟩.

AGILE, nimble, brisk, spry mean acting or moving with easy quickness.

Agile implies dexterity and ease in physical or mental actions ⟨very *agile* about distancing himself from unpopular issues⟩.

Nimble stresses lightness and swiftness of action or thought ⟨a *nimble* tennis player⟩.

Brisk suggests liveliness, animation, or vigor of movement sometimes with a suggestion of hurry ⟨a *brisk* cleaning-up before the relatives arrived⟩.

Spry stresses an ability for quick action that is unexpected because of age or known infirmity ⟨*spry* older runners sometimes beat out younger competitors⟩.

AGREE, concur, coincide mean to come into or be in harmony regarding a matter of opinion.

Agree implies complete accord usually attained by discussion and adjustment of differences ⟨on some points we all can *agree*⟩.

Concur tends to suggest cooperative thinking or acting toward an end but sometimes implies no more than approval (as of a decision reached by others) ⟨if my wife *concurs*, then it's a deal⟩.

Coincide, used more often of opinions, judgments, wishes, or interests than of people, implies an agreement amounting to identity ⟨their wishes *coincide* exactly with my desire⟩. See in addition ASSENT.

ALLIANCE, league, coalition, confederation, federation mean an association to further the common interests of its members.

Alliance applies to an association formed for the mutual benefit of its members ⟨an *alliance* between feminist and religious groups against pornography⟩.

League applies to a more formal compact often with a definite goal ⟨the *League* of Nations⟩.

Coalition applies to a temporary association of parties often of opposing interests ⟨formed a *coalition* government with two other parties⟩.

Confederation applies to a union of independent states under a central government having powers dealing with common external relations ⟨the *confederation* formed by the American colonies following the revolution⟩.

Federation specif. applies to a sovereign power formed by a union of states and having a central government and several state and local governments ⟨the United States of America constitutes a *federation*⟩.

ALLOT, assign, apportion, allocate mean to give as a share, portion, role, or lot.

Allot may imply haphazard or arbitrary distribution ⟨each student is *alloted* an hour of computer time⟩.

Assign stresses an authoritative and fixed allotting but carries no clear implication of an even division ⟨each employee is *assigned* a parking space⟩.

Apportion implies a dividing according to some principle ⟨profits were *apportioned* according to a predetermined ratio⟩.

Allocate suggests a fixed appropriation usu. of money to a person or group for a particular use ⟨*allocated* $50,000 for park improvements⟩.

ALONE, solitary, lonely, lonesome, lone, forlorn, desolate mean isolated from others.

Alone suggests the objective fact of being by oneself with slighter notion of emotional involvement than most of the remaining terms ⟨everyone needs to be *alone* sometimes⟩.

Solitary may indicate isolation as a chosen course ⟨glorying in the calm of her *solitary* life⟩ but more often it suggests sadness and a sense of loss ⟨left *solitary* by the death of his wife⟩.

Lonely adds to *solitary* a suggestion of longing for companionship ⟨felt *lonely* and forsaken⟩.

Lonesome heightens the suggestion of sadness and poignancy ⟨an only child sometimes leads a *lonesome* life⟩.

Lone may replace *lonely* or *lonesome* but typically is as objective as *alone* ⟨a *lone* robin pecking at the lawn⟩.

Forlorn stresses dejection, woe, and listlessness at separation from one held dear ⟨a *forlorn* lost child⟩.

Desolate implies inconsolable grief at loss or bereavement ⟨her brother's death now left her totally *desolate*⟩.

AMATEUR, dilettante, dabbler, tyro mean a person who follows a pursuit without attaining proficiency or professional status.

Amateur often applies to one practicing an art without mastery of its essentials ⟨a painting obviously done by an *amateur*⟩, and in sports it may also suggest not so much lack of skill but avoidance of direct remuneration ⟨must remain an *amateur* in order to qualify for the Olympics⟩.

Dilettante may apply to the lover of an art rather than its skilled practitioner but usu. implies elegant trifling in the arts and an absence of serious commitment ⟨a serious art teacher with no patience for *dilettantes*⟩.

Dabbler suggests desultory habits of work and lack of persistence ⟨a *dabbler* who never finished a single novel⟩.

Tyro implies inexperience often combined with audacity with resulting crudeness or blundering ⟨a *tyro* who has yet to master the basics of playwriting⟩.

AMBIGUITY, equivocation, tergiversation, double entendre mean an expression capable of more than one interpretation.

Ambiguity usu. refers to the use of a word or phrase in such a way that it may be taken in either of two senses ⟨the *ambiguity* in the directive's wording caused much confusion⟩.

Equivocation suggests that the ambiguity is intentional and the intent is to mislead ⟨the government's report on the nuclear accident is filled with *equivocations*⟩.

Tergiversation stresses the shifting of senses during the course of one's argument and usu. suggests intentional subterfuge ⟨a thesis that resorts to several *tergiversations* of the word "society"⟩.

Double entendre refers to a word or expression allowing two interpretations, one of them being risqué ⟨the *double entendres* that are de rigueur in any bedroom farce⟩.

AMBITION, aspiration, pretension mean strong desire for advancement.

Ambition applies to the desire for personal advancement or preferment and may suggest equally a praiseworthy or an inordinate desire ⟨driven by the *ambition* to be very rich⟩.

Aspiration implies a striving after something higher than oneself and usu. implies that the striver is thereby ennobled ⟨an *aspiration* to become President someday⟩.

Pretension suggests ardent desire for recognition of accomplishment without actual possession of the necessary ability and therefore implies presumption ⟨several people with literary *pretensions* frequent her salon⟩.

AMIABLE, good-natured, obliging, complaisant mean having the desire or disposition to please.

Amiable implies having qualities that make one liked and easy to deal with ⟨a travel club that attracts *amiable* types⟩.

Good-natured implies cheerfulness or helpfulness and sometimes a willingness to be imposed upon ⟨a *good-natured* boy who was always willing to pitch in⟩.

Obliging stresses a friendly readiness to be helpful ⟨our *obliging* innkeeper accommodated our request⟩.

Complaisant often implies passivity or a yielding to others because of weakness ⟨*complaisant* people who only say what others want to hear⟩.

AMICABLE, neighborly, friendly mean exhibiting goodwill and an absence of antagonism.

Amicable implies a state of peace and a desire on the part of the parties not to quarrel ⟨maintained *amicable* relations even after the divorce⟩.

Neighborly implies a disposition to live on good terms with others and to be helpful on principle ⟨a *neighborly* concern prompted the inquiry about her health⟩.

Friendly stresses cordiality and often warmth or intimacy of personal relations ⟨sought his *friendly* advice on this important matter⟩.

AMUSE, divert, entertain mean to pass or cause to pass the time pleasantly.

Amuse suggests that one's attention is engaged lightly or frivolously ⟨*amuse* yourselves while I prepare dinner⟩.

Divert implies the distracting of the attention from worry or routine occupation esp. by something funny ⟨tired businessmen looking for a light comedy to *divert* them⟩.

Entertain suggests supplying amusement or diversion by specially prepared or contrived methods ⟨comedians and pretty girls *entertained* the troops⟩.

ANALYZE, dissect, break down mean to divide a complex whole into its parts or elements.

Analyze suggests separating or distinguishing the component parts of something (as a substance, a process, a situation) so as to discover its true nature or inner relationships ⟨*analyzed* the basis for the current problem of trade imbalances⟩.

Dissect suggests a searching analysis by laying bare parts or pieces for individual scrutiny ⟨commentators *dissected* every word of the President's statement⟩.

Break down implies a reducing to simpler parts or divisions ⟨*break down* the budget to see where the money is going⟩.

ANGER, ire, rage, fury, indignation, wrath mean an intense emotional state induced by displeasure.

Anger, the most general term, names the reaction but in itself conveys nothing about intensity or justification or manifestation of the emotional state ⟨tried to hide his *anger*⟩.

Ire, more frequent in literary contexts, may suggest greater intensity than *anger,* often with an evident display of feeling ⟨cheeks flushed dark with *ire*⟩.

Rage suggests loss of self-control from violence of emotion ⟨screaming with *rage*⟩.

Fury is overmastering destructive rage verging on madness ⟨in her *fury* she started to accuse everyone around her⟩.

Indignation stresses righteous anger at what one considers unfair, mean, or shameful ⟨behavior that caused general *indignation*⟩.

Wrath is likely to suggest a desire or intent to revenge or punish ⟨rose in his *wrath* and struck his tormentor to the floor⟩.

ANNOY, vex, irk, bother mean to upset a person's composure.

Annoy implies a wearing on the nerves by persistent petty unpleasantness ⟨their constant complaining *annoys* us⟩.

Vex implies greater provocation and stronger disturbance and usu. connotes anger but sometimes perplexity or anxiety ⟨a problem that *vexes* cancer researchers⟩.

Irk stresses difficulty in enduring and the resulting weariness or impatience of spirit ⟨chronic tardiness *irks* the boss⟩.

Bother suggests interference with comfort or peace of mind ⟨that discrepancy *bothers* me⟩.

See in addition WORRY.

ANSWER, respond, reply, rejoin, retort mean to say, write, or do something in return.

Answer implies the satisfying of a question, demand, call, or need ⟨*answered* all the questions on the form⟩.

Respond may suggest an immediate or quick reaction ⟨chose not to *respond* to that comment⟩.

Reply implies making a return commensurate with the original question or demand ⟨an invitation that requires you to *reply* at once⟩.

Rejoin often implies sharpness or quickness in answering ⟨"who asked you?" she *rejoined*⟩.

Retort suggests responding to an explicit charge or criticism by way of retaliation ⟨he *retorted* to her every charge with biting sarcasm⟩.

APOLOGY, apologia, excuse, plea, pretext, alibi mean matter offered in explanation or defense.

Apology usu. applies to an expression of regret for a mistake or wrong with implied admission of guilt or fault and with or without reference to palliating circumstances ⟨said by way of *apology* that he would have met them if he could⟩.

Sometimes *apology*, like **apologia**, implies not admission of guilt or regret but a desire to make clear the grounds for some course, belief, or position ⟨the speech was an effective *apologia* for his foreign policy⟩.

Excuse implies an intent to avoid or remove blame or censure ⟨used his illness as an *excuse* for missing the meeting⟩.

Plea stresses argument or appeal for understanding or sympathy or mercy ⟨her usual *plea* that she was nearsighted⟩.

Pretext suggests subterfuge and the offering of false reasons or motives in excuse or explanation ⟨used any *pretext* to get out of work⟩.

Alibi implies a desire to shift blame or evade punishment and imputes plausibility rather than truth to the explanation offered ⟨his *alibi* failed to stand scrutiny⟩.

APPARENT, illusory, seeming, ostensible mean not actually being what appearance indicates.

Apparent suggests appearance to unaided senses that is not or may not be borne out by more rigorous examination or greater knowledge ⟨the *apparent* cause of the train wreck⟩.

Illusory implies a false impression based on deceptive resemblance or faulty observation, or influenced by emotions that prevent a clear view ⟨vertical stripes will give an *illusory* height to her figure⟩.

Seeming implies a character in the thing observed that gives it the appearance, sometimes through intent, of something else ⟨the *seeming* simplicity of the story⟩.

Ostensible suggests a discrepancy between an openly declared or naturally implied aim or reason and the true one ⟨business was the *ostensible* reason for their visit⟩.

See in addition EVIDENT.

APPRECIATE, value, prize, treasure, cherish mean to hold in high estimation.

Appreciate often connotes sufficient understanding to enjoy or admire a thing's excellence ⟨*appreciates* fine wine⟩.

Value implies rating a thing highly for its intrinsic worth ⟨*values* our friendship⟩.

Prize implies taking a deep pride in something one possesses ⟨Americans *prize* their freedom⟩.

Treasure emphasizes jealously safeguarding something considered precious ⟨she *treasures* every memento of her youth⟩.

Cherish implies a special love and care for something ⟨*cherishes* her children above all⟩.

See in addition UNDERSTAND.

APPREHENSION, foreboding, misgiving, presentiment mean a feeling that something undesirable will or is about to happen.

Apprehension implies a mind preoccupied with fear and anxiety ⟨approached the dangerous undertaking with great *apprehension*⟩.

Foreboding suggests fear that is oppressive, unreasoning, or indefinable ⟨the deserted streets filled me with strange *forebodings*⟩.

Misgiving suggests uneasiness and mistrust ⟨had my *misgivings* about her from the start⟩.

Presentiment implies a vague or uncanny sense that something is bound to happen ⟨a *presentiment* that some of our group would not survive⟩.

APPROPRIATE *vb* **Appropriate, preempt, arrogate, usurp, confiscate** mean to seize high-handedly.

Appropriate suggests making something one's own or converting to one's own use without authority or with questionable right ⟨just *appropriated* the tools meant to be shared by all⟩.

Preempt implies beforehandedness in taking something desired or needed by others ⟨TV *preempted* much of the programming once broadcast by radio⟩.

Arrogate implies insolence, presumption, and exclusion of others in seizing rights, powers, or functions ⟨White House staffers *arrogated* powers belonging to cabinet members⟩.

Usurp implies unlawful or unwarranted intrusion into the place of another and seizure of what is his by custom, right, or law ⟨her new stepmother had *usurped* her status in the household⟩.

Confiscate always implies seizure through exercise of authority ⟨customs officers *confiscate* all contraband⟩.

APPROVE, endorse, sanction, accredit, certify mean to have or express a favorable opinion of.

Approve often implies no more than this but may suggest considerable esteem or admiration ⟨the parents *approve* of the marriage⟩.

Endorse suggests an explicit statement of support ⟨publicly *endorsed* her for Senator⟩.

Sanction implies both approval and authorization ⟨the President *sanctioned* covert operations⟩.

Accredit and **certify** usu. imply official endorsement attesting to conformity to set standards ⟨the board voted to *accredit* the college⟩ ⟨must be *certified* to teach⟩.

ARISTOCRACY, nobility, gentry, society mean a body of people constituting a socially superior caste.

Aristocracy usu. refers to those persons of superior birth, breeding, and social station ⟨plantation families constituted the *aristocracy* of the antebellum South⟩.

Nobility refers to persons of a privileged and titled class that ranks just below royalty ⟨the duke ranks highest in British *nobility*⟩.

Gentry refers to a class of leisured, well-bred persons who are considered gentlefolk but are without hereditary titles ⟨a private school favored by generations of the *gentry*⟩.

Society refers to that class of people who are celebrated for their active social life, conspicuous leisure, and fashionable clothes ⟨Newport *society* was famous for its lavish balls⟩.

ARRIVAL, advent mean the reaching of a destination.

Arrival emphasizes the preceding travel or movement ⟨a traffic jam greatly delayed their *arrival*⟩.

Advent applies to a momentous or conspicuous arrival, an appearance upon a scene esp. for the first time, or a beginning ⟨the *advent* of a new age in space travel⟩.

ART, skill, cunning, artifice, craft mean the faculty of executing well what one has devised.

Art distinctively implies a personal, unanalyzable creative power ⟨an *art* for saying the right thing⟩.

Skill stresses technical knowledge and proficiency ⟨the *skills* required of a surgeon⟩.

Cunning suggests ingenuity and subtlety in devising, inventing, or executing ⟨a mystery thriller written with great *cunning*⟩.

Artifice suggests mechanical skill esp. in imitating things in nature ⟨a painter with much of the *artifice* of Rubens and none of the art⟩.

Craft may imply expertness in workmanship ⟨a saltcellar wrought with *craft* worthy of Cellini⟩.

ARTIFICIAL, factitious, synthetic, ersatz mean brought into being not by nature but by art or effort.

Artificial is applicable to anything that is not the result of natural processes or conditions ⟨the state is an *artificial* society⟩ but esp. to something that has a counterpart in nature ⟨*artificial* teeth⟩.

Factitious applies chiefly to emotions or states of mind not naturally caused or spontaneously aroused ⟨created a *factitious* demand for the product⟩.

Synthetic applies esp. to a manufactured substance or to a natural substance so treated that it acquires the appearance or qualities of another and may substitute for it ⟨*synthetic* furs⟩.

Ersatz often implies the use of an inferior substitute for a natural product ⟨served *ersatz* cream with the coffee⟩.

ASCRIBE, attribute, assign, impute, credit mean to lay something to the account of a person or thing.

Ascribe suggests an inferring or conjecturing of cause, quality. authorship ⟨none of the frivolity commonly *ascribed* to teenagers⟩.

Attribute suggests less tentativeness than *ascribe*. less definiteness than *assign* ⟨*attribute* the project's failure to poor planning⟩.

Assign implies ascribing with certainty or after deliberation ⟨an investigatory panel *assigned* blame to top officials⟩.

Impute suggests ascribing something that brings discredit by way of accusation or blame ⟨tried to *impute* sinister motives to my actions⟩.

Credit implies ascribing a thing or esp. an action to a person or other thing as its agent, source, or explanation ⟨*credited* his insecurities to an unhappy childhood⟩.

ASK *vb* **Ask, question, interrogate, query, inquire** mean to address a person in order to gain information.

Ask implies no more than the putting of a question ⟨*ask* for directions⟩.

Question usu. suggests the asking of series of questions ⟨*questioned* them about every detail of the trip⟩.

Interrogate suggests formal or official systematic questioning ⟨the prosecutor *interrogated* the witness all day⟩.

Query implies a desire for authoritative information or confirmation ⟨*queried* the reference librarian about the book⟩.

Inquire implies a searching for facts or for truth often specifically by asking questions ⟨began to *inquire* into the charges of espionage⟩.

ASK *vb* **Ask, request, solicit** mean to seek to obtain by making one's wants known.

Ask implies no more than the statement of the desire ⟨*ask* a favor of a friend⟩.

Request implies greater formality and courtesy ⟨*requests* the pleasure of your company at the ball⟩.

Solicit suggests a calling attention to one's wants or desires by public announcement or advertisement ⟨a classified ad that *solicits* a situation as a babysitter⟩.

ASSENT, consent, accede, acquiesce, agree, subscribe mean to concur with what has been proposed.

Assent implies an act involving the understanding or judgment and applies to propositions or opinions ⟨potential members must *assent* to the organization's credo⟩.

Consent involves the will or feelings and indicates compliance with what is requested or desired ⟨*consented* to their daughter's going on the trip⟩.

Accede implies a yielding, often under pressure, of assent or consent ⟨officials *acceded* to every prisoner demand⟩.

Acquiesce implies tacit acceptance or forbearance of opposition ⟨usually *acquiesces* to his wife's wishes⟩.

Agree sometimes implies previous difference of opinion or attempts at persuasion ⟨finally *agreed* to give him a raise⟩.

Subscribe implies not only consent or assent but hearty approval and active support ⟨totally *subscribed* to the free enterprise system⟩.

ASSERT, declare, affirm, protest, avow mean to state positively usu. in anticipation of denial or objection.

Assert implies stating confidently without need for proof or regard for evidence ⟨*asserted* that modern music is just noise⟩.

Declare stresses open or public statement ⟨the jury *declared* the defendant guilty⟩.

Affirm implies conviction based on evidence, experience, or faith ⟨*affirmed* the existence of an afterlife⟩.

Protest emphasizes affirming in the face of denial or doubt ⟨*protested* that he had never had a more splendid meal⟩.

Avow stresses frank declaration and acknowledgment of personal responsibility for what is declared ⟨*avowed* that all investors would be repaid in full⟩.

See in addition MAINTAIN.

ASSUME, affect, pretend, simulate, feign, counterfeit, sham mean to put on a false or deceptive appearance.

Assume often implies a justifiable motive rather than an intent to deceive ⟨*assumed* an air of cheerfulness for the sake of the patient⟩.

Affect implies making a false show of possessing, using, or feeling ⟨willing to *affect* an interest in art in order to impress her⟩.

Pretend implies an overt and sustained false appearance ⟨*pretended* that nothing had happened⟩.

Simulate suggests a close imitation of the appearance of something ⟨the training chamber *simulates* a weightless atmosphere⟩.

Feign implies more artful invention than *pretend*, less specific mimicry than *simulate* ⟨*feigned* sickness in order to stay home from school⟩.

Counterfeit implies achieving the highest degree of verisimilitude of any of these words ⟨*counterfeited* drunkenness so perfectly that many forgot he was acting⟩.

Sham implies an obvious falseness that fools only the gullible ⟨*shammed* a most unconvincing limp⟩.

ATMOSPHERE, feeling, aura mean an intangible quality that gives something an individual and distinctly recognizable character.

Atmosphere implies a quality that accrues to something or that pervades it as a whole and that determines the impression given by that thing ⟨a country inn with a warm and friendly *atmosphere*⟩.

Feeling implies that something has distinctive qualities that create a definite if unanalyzable impression ⟨a grand hotel resort with an old-world *feeling*⟩.

Aura suggests an ethereal or mysterious quality that seems to emanate from a person or thing ⟨a movie queen with an unmistakable *aura* of glamour⟩.

ATTACK, assail, assault, bombard, storm mean to make an onslaught upon.

Attack implies taking the initiative in a struggle ⟨plan to *attack* at dawn⟩.

Assail implies attempting to break down resistance by repeated blows or shots ⟨*assailed* the enemy with artillery fire⟩.
Assault suggests a direct attempt to overpower by suddenness and violence of onslaught ⟨commando troops *assaulted* the building from all sides⟩.
Bombard applies to attacking with bombs or shells ⟨*bombarded* the city nightly⟩.
Storm implies attempting to break into a defended position ⟨a fortress that has never been successfully *stormed*⟩.

ATTEMPT, try, endeavor, essay, strive mean to make an effort to accomplish an end.
Attempt stresses the initiation or beginning of an effort ⟨will *attempt* to photograph the rare bird⟩.
Try stresses effort or experiment made in the hope of testing or proving something ⟨*tried* several times to find a solution⟩.
Endeavor heightens the implications of exertion and difficulty ⟨*endeavored* to find survivors of the crash⟩.
Essay implies difficulty but also suggests tentative trying or experimenting ⟨had *essayed* dramatic roles on two earlier occasions⟩.
Strive implies great exertion against great difficulty and specif. suggests persistent effort ⟨continues to *strive* for a lasting peaceful solution⟩.

ATTRACT, allure, charm, captivate, fascinate, enchant mean to draw another by exerting a powerful influence.
Attract applies to any degree or kind of ability to exert influence over another ⟨a university that *attracts* students from around the world⟩.
Allure implies an enticing by what is fair, pleasing, or seductive ⟨the excitement of the big city *allures* young people⟩.
Charm implies the power of casting a spell over the person or thing affected and so compelling a response ⟨*charmed* by the beauty of that scene isle⟩, but it may, like **captivate**, suggest no more than evoking delight or admiration ⟨her grace and beauty *captivated* us all⟩.

Fascinate suggests a magical influence and tends to stress the ineffectiveness of attempts to resist ⟨a story that continues to *fascinate* children⟩.

Enchant is perhaps the strongest of these terms in stressing the appeal of the agent and the degree of delight evoked in the subject ⟨hopelessly *enchanted* by his dashing looks and deep voice⟩.

ATTRACTION, affinity, sympathy mean the relationship existing between things or persons that are naturally or involuntarily drawn together.

Attraction implies the possession by one thing of a quality that pulls another to it ⟨a curious *attraction* between people of opposite temperaments⟩.

Affinity implies a susceptibility or predisposition on the part of the one drawn ⟨a student with an *affinity* for mathematics⟩.

Sympathy implies a reciprocal or natural relation between two things that are both susceptible to the same influence ⟨there is close *sympathy* between the heart and the lungs⟩.

AUTHENTIC, genuine, veritable, bona fide mean being actually and exactly what is claimed.

Authentic implies being fully trustworthy as according with fact or actuality ⟨the *authentic* story⟩.

Genuine implies accordance with an original or a type without counterfeiting, admixture, or adulteration ⟨*genuine* maple syrup⟩ or it may stress sincerity ⟨*genuine* piety⟩.

Veritable may stress true existence or actual identity ⟨*veritable* offspring⟩ but more commonly merely asserts the suitability of a metaphor ⟨*veritable* hail of questions⟩.

Bona fide can apply when sincerity of intention is in question ⟨*bona fide* sale of securities⟩.

AVERAGE, mean, median, norm mean something that represents a middle point.

Average is exactly or approximately the quotient obtained by dividing the sum total of a set of figures by the number

of figures ⟨scōred an *average* of 85 in a series of five tests⟩.
Mean may be the simple average or it may represent value midway between two extremes ⟨a high of 70° and a low of 50° give a *mean* of 60°⟩.

Median applies to the value that represents the point at which there are as many instances above as there are below ⟨*average* of a group of persons earning 3, 4, 5, 8, and 10 dollars a day is 6 dollars, whereas the *median* is 5 dollars⟩.

Norm means the computed or estimated average of performance of a significantly large group, class, or grade ⟨scores about the *norm* for 5th grade arithmetic⟩

AWARE, cognizant, conscious, sensible, alive, awake mean having knowledge of something.

Aware implies vigilance in observing or alertness in drawing inferences from what one experiences ⟨*aware* of a greater number of police officers out and about⟩.

Cognizant implies having special or certain knowledge as from firsthand sources ⟨as yet, not fully *cognizant* of all the facts⟩.

Conscious implies that one is focusing one's attention on something or is even preoccupied by it ⟨*conscious* that my heart was pounding away⟩.

Sensible implies direct or intuitive perceiving esp. of intangibles or of emotional states or qualities ⟨a doctor who was *sensible* of the woman's deep depression⟩.

Alive adds to *sensible* the implication of acute sensitivity to something ⟨we were fully *alive* to the momentousness of the occasion⟩.

Awake implies that one has become alive to something and is on the alert ⟨a country not *awake* to the dangers of persistent inflation⟩.

AWKWARD, clumsy, maladroit, inept, gauche mean not marked by ease (as of performance or movement).

Awkward is widely applicable and may suggest unhandiness, inconvenience, lack of muscular control, embarrassment, or lack of tact 〈a dinner party marked by periods of *awkward* silence〉.

Clumsy implies stiffness and heaviness and so may connote inflexibility, unwieldiness, or lack of ordinary skill 〈a writer with a persistently *clumsy* style〉.

Maladroit suggests a tendency to create awkward situations 〈a *maladroit* handling of a delicate situation〉.

Inept often implies complete failure or inadequacy 〈blamed the conviction on his *inept* defense attorney〉.

Gauche implies the effects of shyness, inexperience, or ill breeding 〈always felt *gauche* and unsophisticated at formal parties〉.

B

BACKGROUND, setting, environment, milieu, mise-en-scène mean the place, time, and circumstances in which something occurs.

Background often refers to the circumstances or events that precede a phenomenon or development 〈a *background* that prepared her well for the task〉.

Setting suggests looking at real-life situations as though they were dramatic or literary representations 〈a social reformer who was born into the most unlikely social *setting*〉.

Environment applies to all the external factors that have a formative influence on one's physical, mental, or moral development 〈the kind of *environment* that produces juvenile delinquents〉.

Milieu applies esp. to the physical and social surroundings of a person or group of persons 〈an intellectual *milieu* conducive to bold experimentation in the arts〉.

Mise-en-scène strongly suggests the use of properties to achieve a particular atmosphere or theatrical effect 〈a tale of the occult having a carefully crafted *mise-en-scène*〉.

BAD, evil, ill, wicked, naughty mean not morally good.

Bad may apply to any degree of reprehensibility (the *bad* guys in a Western).

Evil is a stronger term than *bad* and usu. carries a baleful or sinister connotation (*evil* men who would commit murder).

Ill is a less emphatic synonym of *evil* and may imply malevolence or vice (paid dearly for his *ill* deeds).

Wicked usu. connotes malice and malevolence (a *wicked* person who delighted in the suffering of others).

Naughty applies either to trivial misdeeds or to matters impolite or amusingly risqué (looked up all the *naughty* words in the dictionary).

BAIT, badger, heckle, hector, chivy, hound mean to harass by efforts to break down.

Bait implies wanton cruelty or delight in persecuting a helpless victim (teenagers *baited* the chained dog).

Badger implies pestering so as to drive a person to confusion or frenzy (*badgered* her father for a raise in her allowance).

Heckle implies persistent interruptive questioning of a speaker in order to confuse or discomfit him (drunks *heckled* the stand-up comic).

Hector carries an implication of bullying and domineering that breaks the spirit (as a child he had been *hectored* by his father).

Chivy suggests persecution by teasing or nagging (*chivied* the new student mercilessly).

Hound implies unrelenting pursuit and harassing (*hounded* on all sides by creditors).

BANISH, exile, deport, transport mean to remove by authority from a state or country.

Banish implies compulsory removal from a country not necessarily one's own (a country that once *banished* the Jesuits).

Exile may imply compulsory removal or an enforced or voluntary absence from one's own country (a writer who *exiled* himself for political reasons).

Deport implies sending out of the country an alien who has illegally entered or whose presence is judged inimical to the public welfare ⟨illegal aliens will be *deported*⟩.

Transport implies sending a convicted criminal to an overseas penal colony ⟨a convict who was *transported* to Australia⟩.

BARE, naked, nude, bald, barren mean deprived of naturally or conventionally appropriate covering.

Bare implies the removal of what is additional, superfluous, ornamental, or dispensable ⟨a bleak apartment with *bare* walls⟩.

Naked suggests absence of protective or ornamental covering but may imply a state of nature, of destitution, of defenselessness, of simple beauty ⟨poor, half-*naked* children shivering in the cold⟩.

Nude applies esp. to the unclothed human figure ⟨a *nude* model posing for art students⟩.

Bald implies actual or seeming absence of natural covering and may suggest a conspicuous bareness ⟨a *bald* mountain peak⟩.

Barren often suggests aridity or impoverishment or sterility ⟨*barren* plains with few shrubs and no trees⟩.

BASE, low, vile mean deserving of contempt because of the absence of higher values.

Base stresses the ignoble and may suggest cruelty, treachery, greed, or grossness ⟨real estate developers with *base* motives⟩.

Low may connote crafty cunning, vulgarity, or immorality and regularly implies an outraging of one's sense of decency or propriety ⟨refused to listen to such *low* talk⟩.

Vile, the strongest of these words, tends to suggest disgusting depravity or filth ⟨a *vile* remark⟩.

BEAR, suffer, endure, abide, tolerate, stand mean to put up with something trying or painful.

Bear usu. implies the power to sustain without flinching or breaking ⟨forced to *bear* one personal tragedy after another⟩.

Suffer often suggests acceptance or passivity rather than courage or patience in bearing ⟨never *suffered* a single insult to go unchallenged⟩.

Endure implies continuing firm or resolute through trials and difficulties ⟨*endured* years of rejection and neglect⟩.

Abide suggests acceptance without resistance or protest ⟨I cannot *abide* their chronic rudeness⟩.

Tolerate suggests overcoming or successfully controlling an impulse to resist, avoid, or resent something injurious or distasteful ⟨*tolerated* his affairs for the sake of the children⟩.

Stand emphasizes even more strongly the ability to bear without discomposure or flinching ⟨she cannot *stand* teasing⟩.

See in addition CARRY.

BEARING, deportment, demeanor, mien, manner, carriage mean the outward manifestation of personality or attitude.

Bearing is the most general of these words but now usu. implies characteristic posture ⟨a woman of regal *bearing*⟩.

Deportment suggests actions or behavior as formed by breeding or training ⟨a child with atrocious *deportment*⟩.

Demeanor suggests one's attitude toward others as expressed in outward behavior ⟨the haughty *demeanor* of a headwaiter⟩.

Mien is a literary term referring both to bearing and demeanor ⟨a *mien* of supreme self-satisfaction⟩.

Manner implies characteristic or customary way of moving and gesturing and addressing others ⟨the imperious *manner* of a man used to giving orders⟩.

Carriage applies chiefly to habitual posture in standing or walking ⟨the kind of *carriage* learned at boarding school⟩.

BEAUTIFUL, lovely, handsome, pretty, comely, fair mean exciting sensuous or aesthetic pleasure.

Beautiful applies to whatever excites the keenest of pleasure to the senses and stirs emotion through the senses ⟨*beautiful* mountain scenery⟩.

Lovely is close to *beautiful* but applies to a narrower range of emotional excitation in suggesting the graceful, delicate, or exquisite ⟨a *lovely* melody⟩.

Handsome suggests aesthetic pleasure due to proportion, symmetry, or elegance ⟨a *handsome* Georgian mansion⟩.

Pretty applies to superficial or insubstantial attractiveness ⟨a painter of conventionally *pretty* scenes⟩.

Comely is like *handsome* in suggesting what is coolly approved rather than emotionally responded to ⟨the *comely* grace of a dancer⟩.

Fair suggests beauty because of purity, flawlessness, or freshness ⟨looking for fashion models with *fair* faces⟩.

BEG, entreat, beseech, implore, supplicate, adjure, importune mean to ask urgently.

Beg suggests earnestness or insistence esp. in asking for a favor ⟨children *begging* to stay up late⟩.

Entreat implies an effort to persuade or to overcome resistance ⟨*entreated* him to change his mind⟩.

Beseech implies great eagerness or anxiety ⟨I *beseech* you to have mercy⟩.

Implore adds to *beseech* a suggestion of greater urgency or anguished appeal ⟨*implored* her not to leave him⟩.

Supplicate suggests a posture of humility ⟨with bowed heads they *supplicated* their Lord⟩.

Adjure implies advising as well as pleading and suggests the involving of something sacred ⟨in God's name I *adjure* you to cease⟩.

Importune suggests an annoying persistence in trying to break down resistance to a request ⟨*importuned* his mother nearly every day to buy him a new bike⟩.

BEGIN, commence, start, initiate, inaugurate mean to take the first step in a course, process, or operation.

Begin and **commence** are practically identical in meaning but the latter suggests greater formality ⟨*began* taking dancing lessons⟩ ⟨let the games *commence*⟩.

Start, opposed to *stop*, suggests a getting or setting into motion or setting out on a journey ⟨the procession *started* out slowly⟩.

Initiate implies the taking of a first step of a process or series that is to continue ⟨*initiated* the custom of annual gift giving⟩.

Inaugurate implies a ceremonious beginning ⟨the discovery of penicillin *inaugurated* a new medical age⟩.

BEHAVE, conduct, deport, comport, acquit mean to act or to cause oneself to do something in a certain way.

Behave may apply to the meeting of a standard of what is proper or decorous ⟨*behaved* very badly throughout the affair⟩.

Conduct implies action or behavior that shows the extent of one's power to control or direct oneself ⟨*conducted* herself with unfailing good humor⟩.

Deport implies behaving so as to show how far one conforms to conventional rules of discipline or propriety ⟨an ingenue who *deports* herself in the best musical tradition⟩.

Comport suggests conduct measured by what is expected or required of one in a certain class or position ⟨*comported* themselves as the gentlemen they were⟩.

Acquit applies to action under stress that deserves praise or meets expectations ⟨*acquitted* himself well in his first battle⟩.

BELIEF, faith, credence, credit mean to assent to the truth of something offered for acceptance.

Belief may or may not imply certitude in the believer ⟨my *belief* that I had caught all the errors⟩.

Faith always does even where there is no evidence or proof ⟨an unshakable *faith* in God⟩.

Credence suggests intellectual assent without implying anything about grounds for assent ⟨a theory given little *credence* by scientists⟩.

Credit implies assent on grounds other than direct proof ⟨give no *credit* to idle rumors⟩.

See in addition OPINION.

BELLIGERENT, bellicose, pugnacious, quarrelsome, contentious mean having an aggressive or fighting attitude.

Belligerent implies being actually at war or engaged in hostilities ⟨*belligerent* nations respected the country's neutrality⟩.

Bellicose suggests a disposition to fight ⟨an intoxicated man in a *bellicose* mood⟩.

Pugnacious suggests a disposition that takes pleasure in personal combat ⟨a *pugnacious* student always getting into scraps⟩.

Quarrelsome stresses an ill-natured readiness to fight without good cause ⟨the stifling heat made us all *quarrelsome*⟩.

Contentious implies perverse and irritating fondness for arguing and quarreling ⟨wearied by her *contentious* disposition⟩.

BENEFICIAL, advantageous, profitable mean bringing good or gain.

Beneficial implies esp. promoting health or well-being ⟨legislation that would be *beneficial* to the elderly⟩.

Advantageous stresses a choice or preference that brings superiority or greater success in attaining an end ⟨a famous surname proved to be *advantageous* in business⟩.

Profitable implies the yielding of useful or lucrative returns ⟨study of the explanatory notes might be *profitable*⟩.

BLAMEWORTHY, blamable, guilty, culpable mean deserving reproach or punishment.

Blameworthy and **blamable** apply to any degree of reprehensibility ⟨conduct adjudged *blameworthy* by a military court⟩ ⟨an accident for which no one is *blamable*⟩.

Guilty implies responsibility for or consciousness of crime, sin, or, at the least, grave error or misdoing ⟨the defendant was found *guilty*⟩.

Culpable is weaker than *guilty* and is likely to connote malfeasance or errors of ignorance, omission, or negligence ⟨a clear case of *culpable* neglect on the part of the landlord⟩.

BLEMISH, defect, flaw mean an imperfection that mars or damages.

Blemish suggests something that affects only the surface or appearance ⟨fair skin completely devoid of *blemishes*⟩.

Defect implies a lack, often hidden, of something that is essential to completeness or perfect functioning ⟨the smoke-detector failed because of a mechanical *defect*⟩.

Flaw suggests a small defect in continuity or cohesion that is likely to cause failure under stress ⟨a *flaw* in a glass⟩.

BLOODY, sanguinary, sanguine, gory mean affected by or involving the shedding of blood.

Bloody is applied esp. to things that are actually covered with blood or are made up of blood ⟨*bloody* hands⟩.

Sanguinary applies esp. to something attended by, or someone inclined to, bloodshed ⟨the Civil War was America's most *sanguinary* conflict⟩.

Sanguine is applied specif. to bleeding, bloodthirstiness, or the color of blood ⟨one of the most *sanguine* of the Jacobean revenge tragedies⟩.

Gory suggests a profusion of blood and slaughter ⟨exceptionally *gory*, even for a horror movie⟩.

BLUFF, blunt, brusque, curt, crusty, gruff mean abrupt and unceremonious in speech and manner.

Bluff connotes good-natured outspokenness and unconventionality ⟨a bartender with a *bluff* manner⟩.

Blunt suggests directness of expression in disregard of others' feelings ⟨a *blunt* appraisal of the performance⟩.

Brusque applies to a sharpness or ungraciousness ⟨a *brusque* response to a civil question⟩.

Curt implies disconcerting shortness or rude conciseness ⟨a *curt* comment about the cause of the foul-up⟩.

Crusty suggests a harsh or surly manner sometimes concealing an inner kindliness ⟨a *crusty* exterior that conceals a heart of gold⟩.

Gruff suggests a hoarse or husky speech which may imply

bad temper but more often implies embarrassment or shyness ⟨puts on a *gruff* pose in front of strangers⟩.

BOAST, brag, vaunt, crow mean to express pride in oneself or one's accomplishments.

Boast often suggests ostentation and exaggeration ⟨ready to *boast* of every trivial success⟩, but it may imply acclaiming with proper and justifiable pride ⟨the town *boasts* one of the best hospitals in the area⟩.

Brag suggests crudity and artlessness in glorifying oneself ⟨boys *bragging* to each other⟩.

Vaunt usu. connotes more pomp and bombast than *boast* and less crudity or naivete than *brag* ⟨used the occasion to *vaunt* the country's military might⟩.

Crow usu. implies exultant boasting or bragging ⟨loved to *crow* about his triumphs⟩.

BODILY, physical, corporeal, corporal, somatic mean of or relating to the human body.

Bodily suggests contrasts with *mental* or *spiritual* ⟨an intellectual who also had *bodily* needs⟩.

Physical suggests more vaguely or less explicitly an organic structure ⟨their ordeal left them at the point of *physical* exhaustion⟩.

Corporeal suggests the substance of which the body is composed ⟨a divinity who assumed *corporeal* existence⟩.

Corporal applies chiefly to things that affect or involve the body ⟨a teacher who still used *corporal* punishment⟩.

Somatic implies contrast with *psychical* and is useful as being free of theological and poetic connotations ⟨*somatic* reactions to the drug⟩.

BOORISH, churlish, loutish, clownish mean uncouth in manners or appearance.

Boorish implies rudeness of manner due to insensitiveness to others' feelings and unwillingness to be agreeable ⟨your *boorish* behavior at the wedding reception⟩.

Churlish suggests surliness, unresponsiveness, and ungraciousness ⟨*churlish* remarks made during a television interview⟩.

Loutish implies bodily awkwardness together with stupidity ⟨her *loutish* boyfriend spoiled the cocktail party⟩.

Clownish suggests ill-bred awkwardness, ignorance or stupidity, ungainliness, and often a propensity for absurd antics ⟨*clownish* conduct that was out of keeping with the solemn occasion⟩.

BORDER, margin, verge, edge, rim, brim, brink mean a line or outer part that marks the limit of something.

Border denotes the part of a surface that marks its boundary line ⟨the magazine cover's red *border*⟩.

Margin denotes a border of definite width or distinguishing character ⟨a *margin* of one inch on the page's left side⟩.

Verge applies to the line marking an extreme limit or termination of something ⟨an empire that extended to the *verge* of the known world⟩.

Edge denotes the termination line made by two converging surfaces as of a blade or a box ⟨the *edge* of a table⟩.

Rim applies to an edge of something circular or curving ⟨the *rim* of a wagon wheel⟩.

Brim applies to the upper inner rim of something hollow ⟨fill the cup to the *brim*⟩.

Brink denotes the abrupt edge of something that falls away steeply ⟨walked to the *brink* of the cliff⟩.

BREACH, infraction, violation, trespass, infringement mean the breaking of a law, duty, or obligation.

Breach implies failure to keep a promise ⟨sued for *breech* of contract⟩.

Infraction usu. implies the breaking of a law or promise ⟨an *infraction* of the school rules⟩.

Violation implies the flagrant disregard of the law or the rights of others and often suggests the exercise of force or violence ⟨the police interference was a *violation* of the right to free assembly⟩.

Trespass implies an encroachment upon the rights, the comfort, or the property of others ⟨a would-be burglar who was arrested for *trespass*⟩.

Infringement implies an encroachment upon a legally protected right or privilege ⟨any unauthorized reproduction constitutes an *infringement* of the book's copyright⟩.

BRIEF, short mean lacking length.

Brief applies primarily to duration and may imply condensation, conciseness, or occas. intensity ⟨a *brief* speech⟩.

Short may imply sudden stoppage or incompleteness ⟨the interview was rather *short*⟩.

BRIGHT, brilliant, radiant, luminous, lustrous mean shining or glowing with light.

Bright implies emitting or reflecting a high degree of light ⟨one of the *brightest* stars in the sky⟩.

Brilliant implies intense often sparkling brightness ⟨*brilliant* diamonds⟩.

Radiant stresses the emission or seeming emission of rays of light ⟨an imposing figure in *radiant* armor⟩.

Luminous implies emission of steady, suffused, glowing light by reflection or in surrounding darkness ⟨*luminous* white houses dot the shore⟩.

Lustrous stresses an even, rich light from a surface that reflects brightly without sparkling or glittering ⟨the *lustrous* sheen of fine satin⟩.

BROAD, wide, deep mean having horizontal extent.

Broad and **wide** apply to a surface measured or viewed from side to side ⟨a *broad* avenue⟩.

Wide is more common when units of measurement are mentioned ⟨rugs eight feet *wide*⟩ or applied to unfilled space between limits ⟨*wide* doorway⟩.

Broad is preferred when full horizontal extent is considered ⟨*broad* shoulders⟩.

Deep may indicate horizontal extent away from the observer or from a front or peripheral point ⟨a *deep* cupboard⟩ ⟨*deep* woods⟩.

BRUTAL, brutish, bestial, feral mean characteristic of an animal in nature, action, or instinct.

Brutal applies to people, their acts, or their words and suggests a lack of intelligence, feeling, or humanity ⟨a senseless and *brutal* war⟩.

Brutish stresses likeness to an animal in low intelligence, in base appetites, and in behavior based on instinct ⟨*brutish* stupidity⟩.

Bestial suggests a depravity or state of degradation unworthy of man and fit only for beasts ⟨decadent Rome carried sexual indulgence to a *bestial* level⟩.

Feral suggests the savagery or ferocity of wild animals ⟨war had unleashed his *feral* impulses⟩.

BULK, mass, volume mean the aggregate that forms a body or unit.

Bulk implies an aggregate that is impressively large, heavy, or numerous ⟨the darkened *bulks* of skyscrapers towered over him⟩.

Mass suggests an aggregate made by piling together things of the same kind ⟨the cave held a *mass* of weapons⟩.

Volume applies to an aggregate without shape or outline and capable of flowing or fluctuating ⟨a tremendous *volume* of water⟩.

BUSINESS, commerce, trade, industry, traffic mean activity concerned with the supplying and distribution of commodities.

Business may be an inclusive term but specif. designates the activities of those engaged in the purchase or sale of commodities or in related financial transactions ⟨the *business* section of the newspaper⟩.

Commerce and **trade** imply the exchange and transportation of commodities ⟨full power to regulate interstate *commerce*⟩ ⟨seek ways to increase foreign *trade*⟩.

Industry applies to the producing of commodities, esp. by manufacturing or processing, usu. on a large scale ⟨*industry* has overtaken agriculture in the South⟩.

Traffic applies to the operation and functioning of public carriers of goods and persons ⟨*traffic* managers have rediscovered the railroads⟩.

See in addition WORK.

BUSY, industrious, diligent, assiduous, sedulous mean actively engaged or occupied.

Busy chiefly stresses activity as opposed to idleness or leisure ⟨too *busy* to spend time with the children⟩.

Industrious implies characteristic or habitual devotion to work ⟨they are by nature an *industrious* people⟩.

Diligent suggests earnest application to some specific object or pursuit ⟨very *diligent* in her pursuit of a degree⟩.

Assiduous stresses careful and unremitting application ⟨mastered the piano only after *assiduous* practice⟩.

Sedulous implies painstaking and persevering application ⟨a *sedulous* reconstruction of the events of that night⟩.

C

CALCULATE, compute, estimate, reckon mean to determine something mathematically.

Calculate is usu. preferred in reference to highly intricate processes and problematical rather than exact or definite results ⟨*calculated* when the comet would next appear⟩.

Compute is the simpler term for reaching an exact result by simpler arithmetic processes ⟨*computed* the interest at a quarterly rate⟩.

Estimate applies chiefly to the forecasting of costs or trends and suggests a seeking of usable but tentative and approximate results ⟨the mechanic *estimated* the cost of repairs⟩.

Reckon usu. suggests the simpler arithmetical processes or rough-and-ready methods ⟨*reckoned* the number of yards of fabric needed⟩.

CALM, tranquil, serene, placid, peaceful mean quiet and free from disturbance.

Calm often implies a contrast with a foregoing or nearby state of agitation or violence ⟨the protests ended, and the streets were *calm* again⟩.

Tranquil suggests a very deep quietude or composure ⟨the *tranquil* beauty of a formal garden⟩.

Serene stresses an unclouded and lofty tranquility ⟨a woman of *serene* beauty⟩.

Placid suggests an undisturbed appearance and often implies a degree of complacency ⟨led a very *placid* existence⟩.

Peaceful implies a state of repose in contrast with or following strife or turmoil ⟨a former firebrand grown *peaceful* in his old age⟩.

CAPRICE, whim, vagary, crotchet mean an irrational or unpredictable idea or desire.

Caprice stresses lack of apparent motivation and suggests willfulness ⟨by sheer *caprice* she quit her job⟩.

Whim implies a fantastic, capricious turn of mind or inclination ⟨an odd antique that was bought on a *whim*⟩.

Vagary stresses the erratic, irresponsible character of the notion or desire ⟨recently he had been prone to strange *vagaries*⟩.

Crochet implies an eccentric opinion or preference ⟨a serious scientist equally known for his bizarre *crotchets*⟩.

CARE, concern, solicitude, anxiety, worry mean a troubled or engrossed state of mind or the thing that causes this.

Care implies oppression of the mind weighed down by responsibility or disquieted by apprehension ⟨a face worn by a host of *cares*⟩.

Concern implies a troubled state of mind because of personal interest, relation, or affection ⟨your happiness is my only *concern*⟩.

Solicitude implies great concern and connotes either

thoughtful or hovering attentiveness toward another ⟨behaved with typical maternal *solicitude*⟩.

Anxiety stresses anguished uncertainty or fear of misfortune or failure ⟨plagued by *anxiety* and self-doubt⟩.

Worry suggests fretting over matters that may or may not be real cause for anxiety ⟨coping with an endless list of *worries*⟩.

CAREFUL, meticulous, scrupulous, punctilious mean showing close attention to detail.

Careful implies attentiveness and cautiousness in avoiding mistakes ⟨a *careful* worker⟩.

Meticulous may imply either commendable extreme carefulness or a hampering finicky caution over small points ⟨*meticulous* scholarship⟩.

Scrupulous applies to what is proper or fitting or ethical ⟨*scrupulous* honesty⟩.

Punctilious implies minute, even excessive attention to fine points ⟨*punctilious* observance of ritual⟩.

CARICATURE, burlesque, parody, travesty mean a comic or grotesque imitation.

Caricature implies ludicrous exaggeration of the characteristic features of a subject ⟨the movie is a *caricature* of the novel⟩.

Burlesque implies mockery either through treating a trivial subject in a mock-heroic style or through giving a serious or lofty subject a frivolous treatment ⟨a *burlesque* that treats a petty quarrel as a great battle⟩.

Parody applies esp. to treatment of a trivial or ludicrous subject in the exactly imitated style of a well-known author or work ⟨a witty *parody* of a popular soap opera⟩.

Travesty implies that the subject remains unchanged but that the style is extravagant or absurd ⟨this production is a *travesty* of a classic opera⟩.

CARNAL, fleshly, sensual, animal mean having a relation to the body.

Carnal may mean only this but more often connotes derogatorily an action or manifestation of man's lower nature ⟨a slave to *carnal* desires⟩.

Fleshly is somewhat less derogatory than *carnal* ⟨a saint who wrote at length on his *fleshly* temptations⟩.

Sensual may apply to any gratification of a bodily desire or pleasure but commonly implies sexual appetite with absence of the spiritual or intellectual ⟨a place infamous for providing *sensual* delight⟩.

Animal stresses the physical as distinguished from the rational nature of a person ⟨led a mindless, *animal* existence⟩.

CARRY, bear, convey, transport mean to move something from one place to another.

Carry tends to emphasize the means by which something is moved or the fact of supporting off the ground while moving ⟨*carried* the basket on her head⟩.

Bear stresses the effort of sustaining or the importance of what is carried ⟨*bear* the banner aloft⟩.

Convey suggests the continuous movement of something in the mass ⟨the pipeline *conveys* oil for more than a thousand miles⟩.

Transport implies the moving of something to its destination ⟨trucks *transporting* farm produce to market⟩.

CATCH, capture, trap, snare, entrap, ensnare, bag mean to come to possess or control by or as if by seizing.

Catch implies the seizing of something in motion or in flight or in hiding ⟨*caught* the dog as it ran by⟩.

Capture suggests taking by overcoming resistance or difficulty ⟨*capture* a stronghold of the enemy⟩.

Trap, snare, entrap, ensnare imply seizing by some device that holds the one caught at the mercy of the captor. *Trap* and *snare* apply more commonly to physical seizing ⟨*trap* animals⟩ ⟨*snared* butterflies with a net⟩. *Entrap* and *ensnare* more often are figurative ⟨*entrapped* the witness with a trick question⟩ ⟨a sting operation that *ensnared* burglars⟩.

Bag implies shooting down a fleeing or distant prey ⟨*bagged* a brace of pheasants⟩.

CAUSE, determinant, antecedent, reason, occasion mean something that produces an effect.

Cause applies to any event, circumstance, or condition that brings about or helps bring about a result ⟨an icy road was the *cause* of the accident⟩.

Determinant applies to a cause that fixes the nature of what results ⟨heredity may be a *determinant* of heart disease⟩.

Antecedent applies to that which has preceded and may therefore be in some degree responsible for what follows ⟨the *antecedents* of the famine⟩.

Reason applies to a traceable or explainable cause of a known effect ⟨the *reason* I was late was that my car would not start⟩.

Occasion applies to a particular time or situation at which underlying causes become effective ⟨the assassination was the *occasion* of the war⟩.

CAUSTIC, mordant, acrid, scathing mean stingingly incisive.

Caustic suggests a biting wit ⟨*caustic* comments about her singing ability⟩.

Mordant suggests a wit that is used with deadly effectiveness ⟨*mordant* reviews put the play out of its misery⟩.

Acrid implies bitterness and often malevolence ⟨a speech marked by *acrid* invective⟩.

Scathing implies indignant attacks delivered with fierce severity ⟨a *scathing* satire of corporate life⟩.

CAUTIOUS, circumspect, wary, chary mean prudently watchful and discreet in the face of danger or risk.

Cautious implies the exercise of forethought usu. prompted by fear of danger ⟨a *cautious* driver⟩.

Circumspect suggests less fear and stresses the surveying of all possible consequences before acting or deciding ⟨the panel must be *circumspect* in assigning blame⟩.

Wary emphasizes suspiciousness and alertness in watching for danger and cunning in escaping it ⟨be *wary* of those claiming to have all the answers⟩.

Chary implies a cautious reluctance to give, act, or speak freely ⟨I am *chary* of signing papers I have not read⟩.

CELERITY, alacrity mean quickness in movement or action.

Celerity implies speed in accomplishing work ⟨got dinner ready with remarkable *celerity*⟩.

Alacrity stresses promptness in response to suggestion or command ⟨the students volunteered with surprising *alacrity*⟩.

CEREMONIAL, ceremonious, formal, conventional mean marked by attention to or adhering strictly to prescribed forms.

Ceremonial and **ceremonious** both imply strict attention to what is prescribed by custom or by ritual, but *ceremonial* applies to things that are associated with ceremonies ⟨a *ceremonial* offering⟩, *ceremonious* to persons given to ceremony or to acts attended by ceremony ⟨a *ceremonious* old man⟩.

Formal applies both to things prescribed by and to persons obedient to custom and may suggest stiff, restrained, or old-fashioned behavior ⟨a *formal* report on the summit meeting⟩ ⟨a *formal* manner⟩.

Conventional implies accord with general custom and usage and may suggest a stodgy lack of originality or independence ⟨*conventional* courtesy⟩ ⟨*conventional* standards of beauty⟩.

CERTAINTY, certitude, assurance, conviction mean a state of being free from doubt.

Certainty and **certitude** are very close: *certainty* may stress the existence of objective proof ⟨claims that cannot be confirmed with any scientific *certainty*⟩, while **certitude** may emphasize a faith in something not needing or not capable of proof ⟨believes with all *certitude* in an afterlife⟩.

Assurance implies confidence rather than intellectual certainty ⟨as much *assurance* as is ever possible where hurricanes are concerned⟩.

Conviction applies esp. to belief strongly held by an individual (holds firm *convictions* about everything).

CERTIFY, attest, witness, vouch mean to testify to the truth or genuineness of something.

Certify usu. applies to a written statement, esp. one carrying a signature or seal (*certified* that the candidate had met all requirements).

Attest applies to oral or written testimony usu. from experts or witnesses (*attested* to the authenticity of the document).

Witness applies to the subscribing of one's own name to a document as evidence of its genuineness (two persons who *witnessed* the signing of the will).

Vouch applies to one who testifies as a competent authority or a reliable person and who will defend his affirmation (willing to *vouch* for the woman's integrity).

See in addition APPROVE.

CHANGE, alter, vary, modify mean to make or become different.

Change implies making either an essential difference often amounting to a loss of original identity or a substitution of one thing for another (*changed* the shirt for a larger size).

Alter implies a difference in some particular respect without suggesting loss of identity (slightly *altered* the original design).

Vary stresses a breaking away from sameness, duplication, or exact repetition (you can *vary* the speed of the conveyor belt).

Modify suggests a difference that limits, restricts, or adapts to a new purpose (*modified* the building for use by the handicapped).

CHARACTERISTIC, individual, peculiar, distinctive mean indicating a special quality or identity.

Characteristic applies to something that distinguishes or identifies a person or thing or class (responded with his *characteristic* wit).

Individual stresses qualities that distinguish one from all other members of the same kind or class ⟨a highly *individual* writing style⟩.

Peculiar applies to qualities possessed only by a particular individual or class or kind and stresses rarity or uniqueness ⟨an eccentricity that is *peculiar* to the British⟩.

Distinctive indicates qualities distinguishing and uncommon and often superior or praiseworthy ⟨her *distinctive* aura of grace and elegance⟩.

CHASE, pursue, follow, trail mean to go after or on the track of something or someone.

Chase implies going swiftly after and trying to overtake something fleeing or running ⟨a dog *chasing* a cat⟩.

Pursue suggests a continuing effort to overtake, reach, attain ⟨*pursued* the criminal through the narrow streets⟩.

Follow puts less emphasis upon speed or intent to overtake ⟨a stray dog *followed* me home⟩.

Trail may stress a following of tracks or traces rather than a visible object ⟨*trail* deer through deep snow⟩.

CHASTE, pure, modest, decent mean free from all taint of what is lewd or salacious.

Chaste primarily implies a refraining from acts or even thoughts or desires that are not virginal or not sanctioned by marriage vows ⟨maintained *chaste* relations until marriage⟩.

Pure differs from *chaste* in implying innocence and absence of temptation rather than control of one's impulses and actions ⟨the *pure* of heart⟩.

Modest and **decent** apply esp. to deportment and dress as outward signs of inward chastity or purity ⟨her dress was always *modest*⟩ ⟨*decent* people didn't go to such movies⟩.

CHEAT, cozen, defraud, swindle mean to get something by dishonesty or deception.

Cheat suggests using trickery that escapes observation ⟨*cheated* in the written examination⟩.

Cozen implies artful persuading or flattering to attain a thing or a purpose ⟨always able to *cozen* her doting grandfather out of a few dollars⟩.

Defraud stresses depriving one of his rights and usu. connotes deliberate perversion of the truth ⟨her own lawyer *defrauded* her of her inheritance⟩.

Swindle implies large-scale cheating by means of misrepresentation or abuse of confidence ⟨they were *swindled* of their savings by con artists⟩.

CHOICE *n* Choice, option, alternative, preference, selection, election mean the act or opportunity of choosing or the thing chosen.

Choice suggests the opportunity or privilege of choosing freely ⟨total freedom of *choice* in the matter⟩.

Option implies a power to choose that is specif. granted or guaranteed ⟨the *option* of paying now or later⟩.

Alternative implies a necessity to choose one and reject another possibility ⟨the *alternatives* were peace with dishonor or war⟩.

Preference suggests the guidance of choice by one's judgment or predilections ⟨stated a *preference* for red-haired women⟩.

Selection implies a wide range of choice ⟨a store offering a varied *selection* of furniture⟩.

Election implies an end or purpose which requires exercise of judgment ⟨the careful *election* of college courses⟩.

CHOICE *adj* Choice, exquisite, elegant, rare, delicate, dainty mean having qualities that appeal to a cultivated taste.

Choice stresses preeminence in quality or kind ⟨a *choice* bit of gossip⟩.

Exquisite implies a perfection in workmanship or design that appeals only to very sensitive taste ⟨an *exquisite* slender gold bracelet⟩.

Elegant applies to what is rich and luxurious but restrained by good taste ⟨the *elegant* dining room boasts genuine French antiques⟩.

Rare suggests an uncommon excellence ⟨refuses to drink any but the *rarest* of wines⟩.

Delicate implies exquisiteness, subtlety, fragility ⟨the play's *delicate* charm was lost onscreen⟩.

Dainty sometimes also suggests smallness and appeal to the eye or palate ⟨precious, *dainty* food that leaves you hungry⟩.

CIRCUMSTANTIAL, minute, particular, detailed mean dealing with a matter fully and usu. point by point.

Circumstantial implies fullness of detail that fixes something described in time and space ⟨a *circumstantial* account of our visit⟩.

Minute implies close and searching attention to the smallest details ⟨a *minute* examination of a fossil⟩.

Particular implies a precise attention to every detail ⟨a *particular* description of the scene of the crime⟩.

Detailed stresses abundance or completeness of detail ⟨a *detailed* analysis of the event⟩.

CITIZEN, subject, national mean a person owing allegiance to and entitled to the protection of a sovereign state.

Citizen is preferred for one owing allegiance to a state in which sovereign power is retained by the people and sharing in the political rights of those people ⟨the inalienable rights of a free *citizen*⟩.

Subject implies allegiance to a personal sovereign such as a monarch ⟨the king enjoys the loyalty of his *subjects*⟩.

National designates one who may claim the protection of a state and applies esp. to one living or traveling outside that state ⟨American *nationals* currently in Libya⟩.

CIVIL, polite, courteous, gallant, chivalrous mean observant of the forms required by good breeding.

Civil often suggests little more than the avoidance of overt rudeness ⟨a *civil* reply that showed a lack of real enthusiasm⟩.

Polite commonly implies polish of speech and manners and sometimes suggests an absence of cordiality ⟨if you can't be pleasant, at least be *polite*⟩.

Courteous implies more actively considerate or dignified politeness ⟨clerks who were unfailingly *courteous* to customers⟩.

Gallant and **chivalrous** imply courteous attentiveness esp. to women. *Gallant* suggests spirited and dashing behavior and ornate expressions of courtesy ⟨a *gallant* suitor of the old school⟩. *Chivalrous* suggests high-minded and self-sacrificing behavior ⟨a *chivalrous* display of duty⟩.

CLEAR *adj* **Clear, transparent, translucent, limpid** mean capable of being seen through.

Clear implies absence of cloudiness, haziness, or muddiness ⟨*clear* water⟩.

Transparent implies being so clear that objects can be seen distinctly ⟨a *transparent* sheet of film⟩.

Translucent implies the passage of light but not a clear view of what lies beyond ⟨*translucent* frosted glass⟩.

Limpid suggests the soft clearness of pure water ⟨pale *limpid* blue eyes⟩.

CLEAR *adj* **Clear, perspicuous, lucid** mean quickly and easily understood.

Clear implies freedom from obscurity, ambiguity, or undue complexity ⟨the instructions were perfectly *clear*⟩.

Perspicuous applies to a style that is simple and elegant as well as clear ⟨the *perspicuous* beauty of Shakespeare's sonnets⟩.

Lucid suggests a clear logical coherence and evident order of arrangement ⟨an amazingly *lucid* description of nuclear physics⟩.

See in addition EVIDENT.

CLEVER, adroit, cunning, ingenious mean having or showing practical wit or skill in contriving.

Clever stresses physical or mental quickness, deftness, or great aptitude ⟨a person *clever* with horses⟩.

Adroit often implies a skillful use of expedients to achieve one's purpose in spite of difficulties (an *adroit* negotiator of business deals).

Cunning implies great skill in constructing or creating (a writer who is *cunning* in his manipulation of the reader).

Ingenious suggests the power of inventing or discovering a new way of accomplishing something (an *ingenious* computer engineer keeping pace with ever-changing technology). See in addition INTELLIGENT.

CLOSE *vb* Close, end, conclude, finish, complete, terminate mean to bring or come to a stopping point or limit.

Close usu. implies that something has been in some way open as well as unfinished (*close* a debate).

End conveys a strong sense of finality (*ended* his life).

Conclude may imply a formal closing (as of a meeting) (the service *concluded* with a blessing).

Finish may stress completion of a final step in a process (after it is painted, the house will be *finished*).

Complete implies the removal of all deficiencies or a successful finishing of what has been undertaken (the resolving of this last issue *completes* the agreement).

Terminate implies the setting of a limit in time or space (your employment *terminates* after three months).

CLOSE *adj* Close, dense, compact, thick mean massed tightly together.

Close implies the least possible space or interval between elements without actual pressure or loss of individual identity (the paintings are hung *close* together).

Dense implies compression of parts or elements so great as to be almost impenetrable (the *dense* growth in a tropical rain forest).

Compact suggests a firm union or consolidation of parts within a small compass (a lithe, *compact*, muscular body).

Thick implies a concentrated abundance of parts or units (a *thick* head of hair).

See in addition STINGY.

COARSE, vulgar, gross, obscene, ribald mean offensive to good taste or morals.

Coarse implies roughness, rudeness, or crudeness of spirit, behavior, or language (found the *coarse* humor of her co-workers offensive).

Vulgar often implies boorishness or ill-breeding (a loud *vulgar* laugh).

Gross implies extreme coarseness and insensitiveness (*gross* eating habits make others lose their appetites).

Obscene applies to anything strongly repulsive to the sense of decency and propriety esp. in sexual matters (*obscene* language that violated the broadcasters' code).

Ribald applies to what is amusingly or picturesquely vulgar or irreverent or mildly indecent (entertained the campers with *ribald* folk songs).

COAX, cajole, wheedle, blandish mean to influence or gently urge by caressing or flattering.

Coax suggests an artful pleading or teasing in an attempt to gain one's ends (*coaxed* their friends into staying for dinner).

Cajole usu. suggests an ingratiating artfulness in attempting to persuade (*cajoled* by his wife into trying the exotic dish).

Wheedle stresses the use of soft words, artful flattery, or seductive appeal (a pretty young thing *wheedled* the old man out of his money).

Blandish suggests open flattery and the obvious use of charm in an effort to win over (a salesclerk not above shameless *blandishing* in order to make a sale).

COMFORT, console, solace mean to offer help in relieving suffering or sorrow.

Comfort implies imparting cheer, strength, or encouragement as well as lessening pain (a message intended to *comfort* the grieving family).

Console emphasizes the alleviating of grief or mitigating the sense of loss rather than distinct or full relief ⟨*consoled* herself by remembering the good times⟩.

Solace suggests a lifting of spirits often from loneliness or boredom as well as from pain or grief ⟨*solaced* himself by reading books and writing poetry⟩.

COMFORTABLE, cozy, snug, easy, restful mean enjoying or providing a position of contentment and security.

Comfortable applies to anything that encourages serenity, well-being, or complacency as well as physical ease ⟨began to feel *comfortable* in her new surroundings⟩.

Cozy suggests warmth, shelter, assured ease, and friendliness ⟨a *cozy* neighborhood coffee shop⟩.

Snug suggests having just enough space for comfort and safety but no more ⟨a *snug* little cottage⟩.

Easy implies relief from or absence of anything likely to cause physical or mental discomfort or constraint ⟨our host had a warm, *easy* manner⟩.

Restful applies to whatever induces or contributes to rest or relaxation ⟨a quiet *restful* inn where indolence is encouraged⟩.

COMMAND *vb* **Command, order, bid, enjoin, direct, instruct, charge** mean to issue orders.

Command and **order** imply authority and usu. some degree of formality and impersonality. *Command* stresses official exercise of authority ⟨when his superior *commands,* a soldier obeys⟩. *Order* may suggest peremptory or arbitrary exercise ⟨*ordered* his men about like slaves⟩.

Bid suggests giving orders peremptorily (as to children or servants) ⟨*bade* her fix a drink for him⟩.

Enjoin implies giving an order or direction authoritatively and urgently and often with admonition or solicitude ⟨our guide *enjoined* us to be quiet in the cathedral⟩.

Direct and **instruct** both connote expectation of obedience and usu. concern specific points of procedure or method, *in-*

struct sometimes implying greater explicitness or formality ⟨*directed* her assistant to hold all calls⟩ ⟨the judge *instructed* the jury to ignore the remark⟩.

Charge adds to *enjoin* an implication of imposing as a duty or responsibility ⟨*charged* by the President with a covert mission⟩.

COMMIT, entrust, confide, consign, relegate mean to assign to a person or place esp. for safekeeping.

Commit may express the general idea of delivering into another's charge or the special sense of transferring to a superior power or to a special place of custody ⟨*committed* the person to prison⟩.

Entrust implies committing with trust and confidence ⟨the president is *entrusted* with broad powers⟩.

Confide implies entrusting with assurance or reliance ⟨*confided* all power over my financial affairs to an attorney⟩.

Consign suggests transferring to remove from one's control with formality or finality ⟨*consigned* my paintings to a gallery for sale⟩.

Relegate implies a consigning to a particular class or sphere often with a suggestion of getting rid of ⟨*relegated* to an obscure position in the company⟩.

COMMON, ordinary, plain, familiar, popular, vulgar mean generally met with and not in any way special, strange, or unusual.

Common implies usual everyday quality or frequency of occurrence ⟨a *common* error⟩ ⟨lacked *common* honesty⟩ and may additionally suggest inferiority or coarseness ⟨his *common* manners shocked her family⟩.

Ordinary stresses conformance in quality or kind with the regular order of things ⟨an *ordinary* pleasant summer day⟩ ⟨a very *ordinary* sort of man⟩.

Plain is likely to suggest homely simplicity ⟨she comes from *plain*, hard-working stock⟩.

Familiar stresses the fact of being generally known and easily recognized ⟨a *familiar* melody⟩.

Popular applies to what is accepted by or prevalent among people in general sometimes in contrast to upper classes or special groups ⟨a hero typically found in *popular* fiction⟩.

Vulgar, otherwise similar to *popular,* is likely to carry derogatory connotations (as of inferiority or coarseness) ⟨goods designed to appeal to the *vulgar* taste⟩.

See in addition RECIPROCAL.

COMMOTION, tumult, turmoil, upheaval mean great physical, mental, or emotional excitement.

Commotion suggests disturbing sometimes violent bustle or hubbub ⟨the unexpected dinner guests caused quite a *commotion*⟩.

Tumult suggests a shaking up or stirring up that is accompanied by uproar, din, or great disorder ⟨the town was in a *tumult* over the war news⟩.

Turmoil suggests a state devoid of calm and seething with excitement ⟨a well-ordered life that was suddenly thrown into great *turmoil*⟩.

Upheaval suggests a violent and forceful thrusting that results in a heaving up or an overthrowing ⟨a nation in need of peace after years of *upheaval*⟩.

COMPARE, contrast, collate mean to set side by side in order to show differences and likenesses.

Compare implies an aim of showing relative values or excellences by bringing out characteristic qualities whether similar or divergent ⟨wanted to *compare* the convention facilities of the two cities⟩.

Contrast implies an emphasis on differences ⟨*contrasted* the computerized system with the old filing cards⟩.

Collate implies minute and critical inspection in order to note points of agreement or divergence ⟨data from police districts across the country will be *collated*⟩.

COMPENDIUM, syllabus, digest, survey, sketch, précis, aperçu mean a brief treatment of a subject.

A **compendium** gathers together and presents in concise or in outline form all the essential facts and details of a subject ⟨a *compendium* of computer technology to date⟩.

A **syllabus** gives the material necessary for a comprehensive view of a whole subject often in the form of a series of heads or propositions ⟨a *syllabus* for a college history course⟩.

A **digest** presents material gathered from many sources and arranged for ready reference ⟨a *digest* of world opinion on foreign policy questions⟩.

A **survey** is a brief but comprehensive treatment presented often as a preliminary to further study or discussion ⟨a *survey* of current trends in higher education⟩.

A **sketch** is a similar but slighter and more tentative treatment ⟨a *sketch* of the president's first year in office⟩.

A **précis** is a concise statement of essential facts or points ⟨a *précis* precedes the full medical report⟩.

An **aperçu** ignores details and gives a quick impression of the whole ⟨the magazine article is an *aperçu* of current cancer research⟩.

COMPENSATE, countervail, balance, offset mean to make up for what is excessive or deficient, helpful or harmful in another.

Compensate implies making up a lack or making amends for loss or injury ⟨*compensated* for an injury on the job⟩.

Countervail suggests counteracting a bad or harmful influence or the damage suffered through it ⟨a compassionate heart *countervails* his short temper⟩.

Balance implies the equalizing or adjusting of two or more things that are contrary or opposed so that no one outweighs the other or others in effect ⟨in sentencing prisoners, the judge *balanced* justice and mercy⟩.

Offset implies neutralizing one thing's good or evil effect by something that exerts a contrary effect ⟨overeating will *offset* the benefits of exercise⟩.

See in addition PAY.

COMPLEX, complicated, intricate, involved, knotty mean having confusingly interrelated parts.

Complex suggests the unavoidable result of a necessary combining and does not imply a fault or failure ⟨a *complex* problem that calls for a *complex* solution⟩.

Complicated applies to what offers great difficulty in understanding, solving, or explaining ⟨baffled by the *complicated* budgetary procedures⟩.

Intricate suggests such interlacing of parts as to make it nearly impossible to follow or grasp them separately ⟨the *intricate* balance of power among nations⟩.

Involved implies extreme complication and often disorder ⟨an *involved* explanation that clarified nothing⟩.

Knotty suggests complication and entanglement that make solution or understanding improbable ⟨*knotty* questions concerning free expression and censorship⟩.

CONCISE, terse, succinct, laconic, summary, pithy, compendious mean very brief in statement or expression.

Concise suggests the removal of all that is superfluous or elaborative ⟨a *concise* study of the situation⟩.

Terse implies pointed conciseness ⟨a *terse* reply that ended the conversation⟩.

Succinct implies the greatest possible compression ⟨a *succinct* letter of resignation⟩.

Laconic implies brevity to the point of seeming rude, indifferent, or mysterious ⟨a *laconic* people who are cold to strangers⟩.

Summary suggests the statement of main points with no elaboration or explanation ⟨a *summary* listing of the year's main events⟩.

Pithy adds to *succinct* or *terse* the implication of richness of meaning or substance ⟨the play's dialogue is studded with *pithy* one-liners⟩.

Compendious applies to a treatment at once full in scope and brief and concise in treatment ⟨a *compendious* report giving all that is known about the disease⟩.

CONCLUSIVE, decisive, determinative, definitive mean bringing to an end.

Conclusive applies to reasoning or logical proof that puts an end to debate or questioning ⟨*conclusive* evidence of criminal guilt⟩.

Decisive may apply to something that ends a controversy, a contest, or any uncertainty ⟨the *decisive* battle of the war⟩.

Determinative adds an implication of giving a fixed course or direction ⟨the *determinative* influence in her life⟩.

Definitive applies to what is put forth as final and permanent ⟨the *definitive* biography of Jefferson⟩.

CONDUCT, manage, control, direct mean to use one's powers to lead, guide, or dominate.

Conduct implies taking responsibility for the acts and achievements of a group ⟨in charge of *conducting* the negotiations⟩.

Manage implies direct handling and manipulating or maneuvering toward a desired result ⟨*manages* the financial affairs of the company⟩.

Control implies a regulating or restraining in order to keep within bounds or on a course ⟨try to *control* the number of people using the park⟩.

Direct implies constant guiding and regulating so as to achieve smooth operation ⟨*directs* the day-to-day running of the store⟩. See in addition BEHAVE.

CONFEDERATE, partner, copartner, colleague, ally mean one who acts in association with another.

Confederate implies an entering into a close or permanent union esp. for solidarity ⟨*confederates* in crime⟩.

Partner implies a business association or an association of two ⟨looking for a woman to be his lifelong *partner*⟩.

Copartner may stress the equality of the partnership ⟨management and labor are *copartners* in this endeavor⟩.

Colleague implies a professional association ⟨admired by her *colleagues* in the dance world⟩.

Ally implies an often temporary association in a common cause or in affairs of policy or statecraft ⟨a joint statement by the *allies* condemning the raid⟩.

CONFER *vb* **Confer, consult, advise, parley** mean to engage in discussion in order to reach a decision or settlement.

Confer implies comparison of views or opinions and usu. an equality between participants ⟨the executives *confer* weekly about current business problems⟩.

Consult adds to *confer* the implication of seeking or taking counsel ⟨before acting, the president *consulted* with his aides⟩.

Advise applies esp. to the seeking of opinions regarding personal matters ⟨before deciding to run, he *advised* with friends⟩.

Parley implies a conference for the sake of settling differences ⟨the government refusing to *parley* with the rebels⟩.
See in addition GIVE.

CONFIDENCE, assurance, self-possession, aplomb mean a state of mind or a manner marked by easy coolness and freedom from uncertainty, diffidence, or embarrassment.

Confidence stresses faith in oneself and one's powers without any suggestion of conceit or arrogance ⟨had the *confidence* that comes only from long experience⟩.

Assurance carries a stronger implication of certainty and may suggest arrogance or lack of objectivity in assessing one's own powers ⟨had an exaggerated *assurance* of his own worth⟩.

Self-possession implies an ease or coolness under stress that reflects perfect self-control and command of one's powers ⟨she answered the insolent question with complete *self-possession*⟩.

Aplomb implies a manifest self-possession in trying or challenging situations ⟨handled the horde of reporters with great *aplomb*⟩.

CONFIRM, corroborate, substantiate, verify, authenticate, validate mean to attest to the truth or validity of something.

Confirm implies the removing of doubts by an authoritative statement or indisputable fact ⟨*confirmed* reports of troop movments⟩.

Corroborate suggests the strengthening of what is already partly established ⟨witnesses *corroborated* his story⟩.

Substantiate implies the offering of evidence that sustains the contention ⟨claims that have yet to be *substantiated*⟩.

Verify implies the establishing of correspondence of actual facts or details with those proposed or guessed at ⟨all statements of fact in the article have been *verified*⟩.

Authenticate implies establishing genuineness by adducing legal or official documents or expert opinion ⟨handwriting experts *authenticated* the diaries⟩.

Validate implies establishing validity by authoritative affirmation or by factual proof ⟨*validate* a passport⟩.

CONJECTURE, surmise, guess mean to draw an inference from slight evidence.

Conjecture implies forming an opinion or judgment upon evidence insufficient for definite knowledge ⟨scientists could only *conjecture* about the animal's breeding cycle⟩.

Surmise implies even slighter evidence and suggests the influence of imagination or suspicion ⟨*surmised* the real reason for the generous gift⟩.

Guess stresses a hitting upon a conclusion either wholly at random or from very uncertain evidence ⟨you would never *guess* that they were wealthy⟩.

CONQUER, vanquish, defeat, subdue, reduce, overcome, overthrow mean to get the better of by force or strategy.

Conquer implies gaining mastery of ⟨*conquer* your fear of flying⟩.

Vanquish implies a complete overpowering ⟨*vanquished* the rebels in a decisive battle⟩.

Defeat does not imply the finality or completeness of *vanquish* which it otherwise equals ⟨have *defeated* the Miami team on several occasions⟩.

Subdue implies a defeating and suppression ⟨*subdued* the native tribes after years of fighting⟩.

Reduce implies a forcing to capitulate or surrender ⟨the city was *reduced* after a month-long siege⟩.

Overcome suggests getting the better of with difficulty or after hard struggle ⟨*overcame* a host of legal and bureaucratic troubles⟩.

Overthrow stresses the bringing down or destruction of enemy power ⟨violently *overthrew* the established government⟩.

CONSIDER, study, contemplate, weigh mean to think about in order to arrive at a judgment or decision.

Consider may suggest giving thought to in order to reach a suitable conclusion, opinion, or decision ⟨refused to even *consider* my proposal⟩.

Study implies sustained purposeful concentration and attention to details and minutiae ⟨*study* the budget before making sweeping cuts⟩.

Contemplate stresses focusing one's thoughts on something but does not imply coming to a conclusion or decision ⟨*contemplate* the consequences of such a decision⟩.

Weigh implies attempting to reach the truth or arrive at a decision by balancing conflicting claims or evidence ⟨*weigh* the pros and cons of the case⟩.

CONSONANT, consistent, compatible, congruous, conge-

nial, sympathetic mean being in agreement one with another or agreeable one to another.

Consonant implies the absence of elements making for discord or difficulty ⟨a spokesperson *consonant* with the company's philosophy⟩.

Consistent may also imply this or it may stress absence of contradiction between things or between details of the same thing ⟨behavior that is not *consistent* with her general character⟩.

Compatible suggests having a capacity for existing or functioning together without disagreement, discord, or mutual interference ⟨looking for a *compatible* roommate⟩.

Congruous is more positive in suggesting a pleasing effect resulting from fitness or appropriateness of component elements ⟨modern furniture is not *congruous* with a colonial house⟩.

Congenial implies a generally satisfying harmony between personalities or a fitness to one's personal taste ⟨did not find the atmosphere of the bar *congenial*⟩.

Sympathetic suggests a more subtle or quieter kind of harmony than *congenial* ⟨a music critic not very *sympathetic* to rock⟩.

CONTAIN, hold, accommodate mean to have or be capable of having within.

Contain implies the actual presence of a specified substance or quantity within something ⟨the can *contains* about a quart of oil⟩.

Hold implies the capacity of containing or the usual or permanent function of containing or keeping ⟨the container will *hold* a gallon of liquid⟩.

Accommodate stresses holding without crowding or inconvenience ⟨the banquet hall can *accommodate* 500 diners⟩.

CONTAMINATE, taint, pollute, defile mean to make impure or unclean.

Contaminate implies intrusion of or contact with dirt or foulness from an outside source ⟨water *contaminated* by industrial wastes⟩.

Taint stresses the loss of purity or cleanliness that follows contamination ⟨*tainted* meat⟩ ⟨the scandal *tainted* the rest of his political career⟩.

Pollute, sometimes interchangeable with *contaminate,* distinctively may imply that the process which begins with contamination is complete and that what was pure or clean has been made foul, poisoned, or filthy ⟨the *polluted* waters of the lake, in parts no better than an open cesspool⟩.

Defile implies befouling of what could or should have been kept clean and pure or held sacred and commonly suggests violation or desecration ⟨*defile* a hero's memory with slanderous innuendo⟩.

CONTEMPORARY, contemporaneous, coeval, synchronous, simultaneous, coincident mean existing or occurring at the same time.

Contemporary is likely to apply to people and what relates to them ⟨Abraham Lincoln was *contemporary* with Charles Darwin⟩.

Contemporaneous applies to events ⟨Victoria's reign was *contemporaneous* with British hegemony⟩.

Coeval refers usu. to periods, ages, eras, eons ⟨the rise of the leisure class was *coeval* with the flowering of the arts⟩.

Synchronous implies exact correspondence in time and esp. in periodic intervals ⟨the movements of the two pendulums are *synchronous*⟩.

Simultaneous implies correspondence in a moment of time ⟨a *simultaneous* ringing of church bells miles apart⟩.

Coincident is applied to events and may be used in order to avoid implication of causal relationship ⟨the end of World War II was *coincident* with a great vintage year⟩.

CONTEMPTIBLE, despicable, pitiable, sorry, scurvy mean arousing or deserving scorn.

Contemptible may imply any quality provoking scorn or a

low standing in any scale of values 〈a *contemptible* bigot and liar〉.

Despicable may imply utter worthlessness and usu. suggests arousing an attitude of moral indignation 〈the *despicable* crime of child abuse〉.

Pitiable applies to what inspires mixed contempt and pity 〈the play is his *pitiable* attempt at tragedy〉.

Sorry may stress pitiable inadequacy or may suggest wretchedness or sordidness 〈the orphanage was the *sorriest* of places〉.

Scurvy adds to *despicable* an implication of arousing disgust 〈the offer of help turned out to be a *scurvy* trick〉.

CONTINUAL, continuous, constant, incessant, perpetual, perennial mean characterized by continued occurrence or recurrence.

Continual implies a close prolonged succession or recurrence 〈*continual* showers the whole weekend〉.

Continuous usu. implies an uninterrupted flow or spatial extension 〈the *continuous* roar of the falls〉.

Constant implies uniform or persistent occurrence or recurrence 〈lived in *constant* pain〉.

Incessant implies ceaseless or uninterrupted activity 〈the *incessant* quarreling frayed her nerves〉.

Perpetual suggests unfailing repetition or lasting duration 〈the fear of *perpetual* torment after death〉.

Perennial implies enduring existence often through constant renewal 〈a *perennial* source of controversy〉.

CONTINUE, last, endure, abide, persist mean to exist over a period of time or indefinitely.

Continue applies to a process going on without ending 〈the stock market will *continue* to rise〉.

Last, esp. when unqualified, may stress existing beyond what is normal or expected 〈buy shoes that will *last*〉.

Endure adds an implication of resisting destructive forces or agencies 〈in spite of everything, her faith *endured*〉.

Abide implies stable and constant existing esp. as opposed to mutability ⟨through 40 years of marriage, their love *abided*⟩.

Persist suggests outlasting the normal or appointed time and often connotes obstinacy or doggedness ⟨the sense of guilt *persisted*⟩.

CONTRACT, shrink, condense, compress, constrict, deflate mean to decrease in bulk or volume.

Contract applies to a drawing together of surfaces or particles or a reduction of area or length ⟨caused his muscles to *contract*⟩.

Shrink implies a contracting or a loss of material and stresses a falling short of original dimensions ⟨the sweater will *shrink* if washed improperly⟩.

Condense implies a reducing of something homogeneous to greater compactness without significant loss of content ⟨*condense* the report to five pages⟩.

Compress implies a pressing into a small compass and definite shape usu. against resistance ⟨*compressed* the comforter to fit the box⟩.

Constrict implies a tightening that reduces diameter ⟨the throat is *constricted* by too tight a collar⟩.

Deflate implies a contracting by reducing the internal pressure of contained air or gas ⟨*deflate* the balloon⟩.

CONTRARY, perverse, restive, balky, wayward mean inclined to resist authority or control.

Contrary implies a temperamental unwillingness to accept orders or advice ⟨the most *contrary* child in my class⟩.

Perverse may imply wrongheaded, determined, or cranky opposition to what is reasonable or normal ⟨offered the most *perverse* argument for declaring war⟩.

Restive suggests unwillingness or inability to submit to discipline or follow orders ⟨*restive* individuals who had no place in the army⟩.

Balky suggests a refusing to proceed in a desired direction or course of action ⟨workers became *balky* when asked to accept pay cuts⟩.

Wayward suggests strong-willed capriciousness and irregularity in behavior ⟨*wayward* inmates are isolated from the others⟩.

See in addition OPPOSITE.

COOL, composed, collected, unruffled, imperturbable, nonchalant mean free from agitation or excitement.

Cool may imply calmness. deliberateness. or dispassionateness ⟨kept a *cool* head during the emergency⟩.

Composed implies freedom from agitation as a result of self-discipline or a sedate disposition ⟨the *composed* pianist gave a flawless concert⟩.

Collected implies a concentration of mind that eliminates distractions esp. in moments of crisis ⟨even in heated debate she remains very *collected*⟩.

Unruffled suggests apparent serenity and poise in the face of setbacks or in the midst of excitement ⟨his mother remained *unruffled* during the wedding⟩.

Imperturbable implies coolness or assurance even under severe provocation ⟨a guest speaker who maintained an air of *imperturbable* civility⟩.

Nonchalant stresses an easy coolness of manner or casualness that suggests indifference or unconcern ⟨*nonchalant* as ever. she was oblivious to the crying baby⟩.

COPY *vb* **Copy, imitate, mimic, ape, mock** mean to make something so that it resembles an existing thing.

Copy suggests duplicating an original as nearly as possible ⟨*copied* the painting and sold the fake as an original⟩.

Imitate suggests following a model or a pattern but may allow for some variation ⟨*imitate* a poet's style⟩.

Mimic implies a close copying (as of voice or mannerism) often for fun. ridicule. or lifelike imitation ⟨pupils *mimicking* their teacher⟩.

Ape may suggest presumptuous. slavish. or inept imitating of a superior original ⟨American fashion designers *aped* their European colleagues⟩.

Mock usu. implies imitation with derision ⟨*mocking* a vain man's manner⟩.

CORRECT *vb* **Correct, rectify, emend, remedy, redress, amend, reform, revise** mean to make right what is wrong.

Correct implies taking action to remove errors, faults, deviations, defects ⟨*corrected* all her spelling errors⟩.

Rectify implies a more essential changing to make something right, just, or properly controlled or directed ⟨a major error in judgment that should be *rectified* at once⟩.

Emend specif. implies correction of a text or manuscript ⟨*emend* the text to match the first edition⟩.

Remedy implies removing or making harmless a cause of trouble, harm, or evil ⟨set out to *remedy* the evils of the world⟩.

Redress implies making compensation or reparation for an unfairness, injustice, or imbalance ⟨we must *redress* past social injustices⟩.

Amend, reform, revise imply an improving by making corrective changes. *amend* usu. suggesting slight changes ⟨a law that needs to be *amended*⟩. *reform* implying drastic change ⟨plans to *reform* the entire court system⟩. and *revise* suggesting a careful examination of something and the making of necessary changes ⟨forced to *revise* the production schedule⟩.

See in addition PUNISH.

CORRECT *adj* **Correct, accurate, exact, precise, nice, right** mean conforming to fact, standard, or truth.

Correct usu. implies freedom from fault or error ⟨*correct* answers⟩ ⟨socially *correct* dress⟩.

Accurate implies fidelity to fact or truth attained by exercise of care ⟨an *accurate* description of the whole situation⟩.

Exact stresses a very strict agreement with fact, standard, or truth ⟨a suit tailored to *exact* measurements⟩.

Precise adds to *exact* an emphasis on sharpness of definition or delimitation ⟨the *precise* terms of the contract⟩.

Nice stresses great precision and delicacy of adjustment or discrimination ⟨makes *nice* distinctions between freedom and license⟩.

Right is close to *correct* but has a stronger positive emphasis on conformity to fact or truth rather than mere absence of error or fault ⟨the *right* thing to do⟩.

COSTLY, expensive, dear, valuable, precious, invaluable, priceless mean having a high esp. monetary value.

Costly implies high price and may suggest sumptuousness, luxury, or rarity ⟨the *costliest* of delicacies grace her table⟩.

Expensive may further imply a price beyond the thing's value or the buyer's means ⟨the resort's shops seemed rather *expensive*⟩.

Dear implies a relatively high or exorbitant price usu. due to factors other than the thing's intrinsic value ⟨coffee was *dear* during the war⟩.

Valuable may suggest worth measured in usefulness as well as in market value ⟨iron ore was a *valuable* commodity⟩.

Precious applies to what is of great or even incalculable value because scarce or irreplaceable ⟨our *precious* natural resources⟩.

Invaluable and **priceless** imply such great worth as to make valuation nearly impossible ⟨a good education is *invaluable*⟩ ⟨a bon mot that was *priceless*⟩.

COURAGE, mettle, spirit, resolution, tenacity mean mental or moral strength to resist opposition, danger, or hardship.

Courage implies firmness of mind and will in the face of danger or extreme difficulty ⟨the *courage* to support unpopular causes⟩.

Mettle suggests an ingrained capacity for meeting strain or difficulty with fortitude and resilience ⟨a challenge that will test your *mettle*⟩.

Spirit also suggests a quality of temperament enabling one to hold one's own or keep up one's morale when opposed or threatened ⟨too many failures had broken the *spirit* of the man⟩.

Resolution stresses firm determination to achieve one's ends ⟨the strong *resolution* of the pioneer women⟩.

Tenacity adds to *resolution* implications of stubborn persistence and unwillingness to admit defeat ⟨the *tenacity* to continue when all others doubted⟩.

COVETOUS, greedy, acquisitive, grasping, avaricious mean having or showing a strong desire for material possessions.

Covetous implies inordinate desire often for another's possessions ⟨*covetous* of his brother's success⟩.

Greedy stresses lack of restraint and often of discrimination in desire ⟨soldiers *greedy* for glory⟩.

Acquisitive implies both eagerness to possess and ability to acquire and keep ⟨mansions that were the pride of the *acquisitive* class⟩.

Grasping adds to *covetous* and *greedy* an implication of selfishness and often suggests unfair or ruthless means ⟨*grasping* developers defrauded the homesteaders⟩.

Avaricious implies obsessive acquisitiveness esp. of money and strongly suggests stinginess ⟨*avaricious* capitalists detested the social programs⟩.

COWARDLY, pusillanimous, craven, dastardly mean having or showing a lack of courage.

Cowardly implies a weak or ignoble lack of courage ⟨the *cowardly* retreat of the army⟩.

Pusillanimous suggests a contemptible lack of courage ⟨*pusillanimous* politicians feared crossing him⟩.

Craven suggests extreme defeatism and complete lack of resistance ⟨secretly despised the *craven* toadies around her⟩.

Dastardly implies behavior that is both cowardly and treach-

erous or skulking or outrageous ⟨a *dastardly* attack on un-
armed civilians⟩.

**CRITICAL, hypercritical, faultfinding, captious, carping,
censorious** mean inclined to look for and point out faults and
defects.

Critical may also imply an effort to see a thing clearly and
truly in order to judge it fairly ⟨a *critical* essay on modern
drama⟩.

Hypercritical suggests a tendency to judge by unreasonably
strict standards ⟨petty, *hypercritical* disparagement of other
people's success⟩.

Faultfinding implies a querulous or exacting temperament
⟨a *faultfinding* theater reviewer⟩.

Captious suggests a readiness to detect trivial faults or raise
objections on trivial grounds ⟨no point is too minute for this
captious critic to overlook⟩.

Carping implies an ill-natured or perverse picking of flaws
⟨the *carping* editorial writer soon wearied readers⟩.

Censorious implies a disposition to be severely critical and
condemnatory ⟨the *censorious* tone of the papal encyclical⟩.
See in addition ACUTE.

**CRITICIZE, reprehend, blame, censure, reprobate, con-
demn, denounce** mean to find fault with openly.

Criticize implies finding fault esp. with methods or policies
or intentions ⟨*criticized* the police for using violence⟩.

Reprehend implies both criticism and severe rebuking ⟨*rep-
rehends* the self-centeredness of today's students⟩.

Blame may imply simply the opposite of *praise* but more
often suggests the placing of responsibility for something bad
or unfortunate ⟨*blames* herself for the accident⟩.

Censure carries a stronger suggestion of authority and of
reprimanding than *blame* ⟨a Senator formally *censured* by
his peers⟩.

Reprobate implies strong disapproval or firm refusal to sanction ⟨*reprobated* his son's adulterous adventures⟩.

Condemn usu. suggests an unqualified and final unfavorable judgment ⟨*condemn* the government's racial policies⟩.
Denounce adds to *condemn* the implication of a public declaration ⟨bishops have *denounced* abortion⟩.

CROWD, throng, crush, mob, horde mean an assembled multitude usu. of people
Crowd implies a close gathering and pressing together ⟨a small *crowd* greeted the returning athletes⟩.
Throng strongly suggests movement and pushing ⟨a *throng* of reporters followed the President⟩.
Crush emphasizes the compactness of the group, the difficulty of individual movement, and the attendant discomfort ⟨a *crush* of fans waited outside the theater⟩.
Mob implies a disorderly crowd with the potential for violence ⟨heard an angry *mob* outside the jail⟩.
Horde suggests a rushing or tumultuous crowd ⟨a *horde* of shoppers looking for bargains⟩.

CRUSH *vb* **Crush, quell, extinguish, suppress, quash** mean to bring to an end by destroying or defeating.
Crush implies a force that destroys all opposition or brings an operation to a halt ⟨a rebellion that was brutally *crushed*⟩.
Quell means to overwhelm completely and to reduce to submission, inactivity, or passivity ⟨statements intended to *quell* the fears of the people⟩.
Extinguish suggests ending something as abruptly and completely as putting out a flame ⟨a promising life *extinguished* by a single bullet⟩.
Suppress implies a conscious determination to subdue ⟨the government *suppressed* all opposition newspapers⟩.
Quash implies a sudden and summary extinction ⟨the rejection *quashed* all their hopes for a better life⟩.

CUMULATIVE, accumulative, additive, summative mean increasing or produced by the addition of new material of the same kind.
Cumulative implies a constant increase (as in amount or

power) by a series of additions, accretions, or repetitions ⟨the *cumulative* effect of taking a drug for many months⟩.

Accumulative may distinctively imply that something has reached its maximum or greatest magnitude through many additions ⟨the *accumulative* impact of a well-ordered sales presentation⟩.

Additive implies that something is capable of assimilating or incorporating new material ⟨as new art forms arise, we develop an *additive* notion of what is art⟩.

Summative implies that something is capable of association or combination with others so as to create a total effect ⟨the *summative* effect of the show's music, dancing, and staging⟩.

CURE, heal, remedy mean to rectify an unhealthy or undesirable condition.

Cure implies restoration to health after disease ⟨no *cure* for a disease that inevitably results in death⟩ .

Heal may also apply to this but commonly suggests restoring to soundness after a wound or sore ⟨his wounds were slow to *heal*⟩.

Remedy suggests correction or relief of a morbid or evil condition ⟨vainly searched for something to *remedy* her arthritis⟩.

CURIOUS, inquisitive, prying mean interested in what is not one's personal or proper concern.

Curious, a neutral term, basically connotes an active desire to learn or to know ⟨children are *curious* about everything⟩.

Inquisitive suggests impertinent and habitual curiosity and persistent quizzing ⟨dreaded the visits of their *inquisitive* relatives⟩.

Prying implies busy meddling and officiousness ⟨*prying* neighbors who refuse to mind their own business⟩.

CURVE, bend, turn, twist mean to swerve or cause to swerve from a straight line.

Curve implies following or producing a line suggesting the arc of a circle or ellipse ⟨the road *curves* sharply to the left⟩.

Bend suggests a yielding to force and usu. implies a distortion from normal or desirable straightness ⟨metal rods *bending* under the immense weight⟩.

Turn implies change of direction essentially by rotation and not usu. as a result of force ⟨the comet will *turn* closer towards the earth⟩.

Twist implies the influence of irresistible force having a spiral effect throughout the object or course involved ⟨the *twisted* wreckage of the spacecraft⟩.

CYNICAL, misanthropic, pessimistic, misogynistic mean deeply distrustful.

Cynical implies having a sneering disbelief in sincerity or integrity ⟨always *cynical* about other people's motives⟩.

Misanthropic suggests a rooted distrust and dislike of human beings and their society ⟨an artist who had grown *misanthropic* in recent years⟩.

Pessimistic implies having a gloomy, distrustful view of life ⟨a philosopher *pessimistic* about the future of the human race⟩.

Misogynistic applies to a man having a deep-seated distrust of and aversion to women ⟨a *misogynistic* scientist more at home in his laboratory⟩.

D

DANGEROUS, hazardous, precarious, perilous, risky mean bringing or involving the chance of loss or injury.

Dangerous applies to something that may cause harm or loss unless dealt with carefully ⟨soldiers on a *dangerous* mission⟩.

Hazardous implies great and continuous risk of harm or failure and small chance of successfully avoiding disaster ⟨claims that smoking is *hazardous* to your health⟩.

Precarious suggests both insecurity and uncertainty ⟨has only a *precarious* hold on reality⟩.

Perilous strongly implies the immediacy of danger ⟨the situation at the foreign embassy has grown *perilous*⟩.

Risky often applies to a known and accepted danger ⟨shy away from *risky* investments⟩.

DARK, dim, dusky, murky, gloomy mean more or less deficient in light.

Dark, the general term, implies utter or virtual lack of illumination ⟨a *dark* cave⟩.

Dim suggests too weak a light for things to be seen clearly or distinctly ⟨a clandestine meeting in a *dim* bar⟩.

Dusky suggests deep twilight and close approach to darkness ⟨trudging through *dusky* woods at day's end⟩.

Murky implies a heavy darkness such as that caused by smoke, fog, or dust in air or mud in water ⟨fish cannot live in the river's *murky* waters⟩.

Gloomy implies serious interference with normal light and connotes cheerlessness and pessimism ⟨a *gloomy* room in the basement of the house⟩.

See in addition OBSCURE.

DEAD, defunct, deceased, departed, late mean devoid of life.

Dead applies literally to what is deprived of vital force but is used figuratively of anything that has lost any attribute (as energy, activity, radiance) suggesting life ⟨a *dead* engine⟩.

Defunct stresses cessation of active existence or operation ⟨a *defunct* television series⟩.

Deceased, departed, and **late** apply to persons who have died recently, *deceased* occurring esp. in legal use ⟨the rights of the *deceased* must be acknowledged⟩, *departed* usu. as a euphemism ⟨pray for our *departed* mother⟩, and *late* esp. with reference to a person in a specific relation or status ⟨the *late* president of the company⟩.

DEADLY, mortal, fatal, lethal mean causing or capable of causing death.

Deadly applies to an established or very likely cause of death ⟨a *deadly* disease⟩.

Mortal implies that death has occurred or is inevitable ⟨a *mortal* wound⟩.

Fatal stresses the inevitability of what has in fact resulted in death or destruction ⟨*fatal* consequences⟩.

Lethal applies only to something that is bound to cause death or exists for the destruction of life ⟨*lethal* gas⟩.

DEBASE, vitiate, deprave, corrupt, debauch, pervert mean to cause deterioration or lowering in quality or character.

Debase implies a loss of position, worth, value, or dignity ⟨commercialism has *debased* the holiday⟩.

Vitiate implies a destruction of purity, validity, or effectiveness by allowing entrance of a fault or defect ⟨partisanship and factionalism *vitiated* our foreign policy⟩.

Deprave implies moral deterioration by evil thoughts or influences ⟨accused of *depraving* the children⟩.

Corrupt implies loss of soundness, purity, or integrity ⟨believes that bureaucratese *corrupts* the language⟩.

Debauch implies a debasing through sensual indulgence ⟨led a *debauched* life after the divorce⟩.

Pervert implies a twisting or distorting from what is natural or normal ⟨*perverted* the original goals of the institute⟩.

See in addition ABASE.

DECAY, decompose, rot, putrefy, spoil mean to undergo destructive dissolution.

Decay implies a slow change from a state of soundness or perfection ⟨a *decaying* Southern mansion⟩.

Decompose stresses a breaking down by chemical·change and when applied to organic matter a corruption ⟨the body was badly *decomposed*⟩.

Rot is a close synonym of *decompose* and often connotes foulness ⟨grain was left to *rot* in warehouses⟩.

Putrefy implies the rotting of animal matter and offensiveness to sight and smell ⟨corpses *putrefying* on the battlefield⟩.

Spoil applies chiefly to the decomposition of foods ⟨be on guard against *spoiled* mayonnaise⟩.

DECEIVE, mislead, delude, beguile mean to lead astray or frustrate usu. by underhandedness.

Deceive implies imposing a false idea or belief that causes ignorance, bewilderment, or helplessness ⟨the salesman tried to *deceive* me about the car⟩.

Mislead implies a leading astray that may or may not be intentional ⟨I was *mislead* by the confusing sign⟩.

Delude implies deceiving so thoroughly as to obscure the truth ⟨we were *deluded* into thinking we were safe⟩.

Beguile stresses the use of charm and persuasion in deceiving ⟨his ingratiating ways *beguiled* us all⟩.

DECEPTION, fraud, double-dealing, subterfuge, trickery mean the acts or practices of one who deliberately deceives.

Deception may or may not imply blameworthiness, since it may suggest cheating or merely tactical resource ⟨magicians are masters of *deception*⟩.

Fraud always implies guilt and often criminality in act or practice ⟨indicted for *fraud*⟩.

Double-dealing suggests treachery or at least action contrary to a professed attitude ⟨the guerillas accused the go-between of *double-dealing*⟩.

Subterfuge suggests the adoption of a stratagem or the telling of a lie in order to escape guilt or to gain an end ⟨obtained the papers by *subterfuge*⟩.

Trickery implies ingenious acts intended to dupe or cheat ⟨will resort to any *trickery* to gain her ends⟩.

DECIDE, determine, settle, rule, resolve mean to come or cause to come to a conclusion.

Decide implies previous consideration of a matter causing doubt, wavering, debate, or controversy ⟨will *decide* tonight where to build the school⟩.

Determine implies fixing the identity, character, scope, or direction of something ⟨*determined* the cause of the problem⟩.

Settle implies a decision reached by someone with power to end all dispute or uncertainty ⟨the court's decision *settles* the matter⟩.

Rule implies a determination by judicial or administrative authority (the judge *ruled* that the evidence was inadmissible).

Resolve implies an expressed or clear decision or determination to do or refrain from doing something (both nations *resolved* to stop terrorism).

DECLARE, announce, publish, proclaim, promulgate mean to make known publicly.

Declare implies explicitness and usu. formality in making known (the referee *declared* the contest a draw).

Announce implies the declaration for the first time of something that is of interest or has created speculation (*announced* their engagement at a party).

Publish implies making public through print (*published* the list of winners in the paper).

Proclaim implies declaring clearly, forcefully, and authoritatively (the president *proclaimed* a national day of mourning).

Promulgate implies the proclaiming of a dogma, doctrine, or law (*promulgated* an edict of religious toleration).

See in addition ASSERT.

DECLINE *vb* **Decline, refuse, reject, repudiate, spurn** mean to turn away by not accepting, receiving, or considering.

Decline often implies courteous refusal esp. of offers or invitations (*declined* the invitation to dinner).

Refuse suggests more positiveness or ungraciousness and often implies the denial of something asked for (*refused* them the loan they needed).

Reject implies a peremptory refusal by sending away or discarding (*rejected* the plan as unworkable).

Repudiate implies a casting off or disowning as untrue, unauthorized, or unworthy of acceptance (*repudiated* the values of their parents).

Spurn stresses contempt or disdain in rejection or repudiation (*spurned* his amorous advances).

DECORUM, decency, propriety, dignity, etiquette mean observance of the rules governing proper conduct.

Decorum suggests conduct according with good taste, often formally prescribed ⟨had violated the *decorum* expected of an army officer⟩.

Decency implies behavior according with normal self-respect or humane feeling for others, or with what is fitting to a particular profession or condition in life ⟨maintained a strict *decency* in dress⟩.

Propriety suggests an artificial standard of what is correct in conduct or speech ⟨regarded the *propriety* expected of a society matron as stifling⟩.

Dignity implies reserve or restraint in conduct prompted less by obedience to a code than by a sense of personal integrity or of social importance ⟨conveyed a quiet *dignity* and sincerity that won him respect⟩.

Etiquette is the usual term for the detailed rules governing manners and conduct and for the observance of these rules ⟨the *etiquette* peculiar to the U.S. Senate⟩.

DECREASE, lessen, diminish, reduce, abate, dwindle mean to grow or make less.

Decrease suggests a progressive decline in size, amount, numbers, or intensity ⟨slowly *decreased* the amount of pressure⟩.

Lessen suggests a decline in amount rather than in number ⟨has been unable to *lessen* her debt at all⟩.

Diminish emphasizes a perceptible loss and implies its subtraction from a total ⟨his muscular strength has *diminished* with age⟩.

Reduce implies a bringing down or lowering ⟨*reduce* your caloric intake⟩.

Abate implies a reducing of something excessive or oppressive in force or amount ⟨the storm *abated* in the afternoon⟩.

Dwindle implies progressive lessening and is applied to

things growing visibly smaller ⟨their provisions *dwindled* slowly but surely⟩.

DECRY, depreciate, disparage, belittle, minimize mean to express a low opinion of.

Decry implies open condemnation with intent to discredit ⟨*decried* their do-nothing attitude⟩.

Depreciate implies a representing as being of less value than commonly believed ⟨critics *depreciate* his plays for being unabashedly sentimental⟩.

Disparage implies depreciation by indirect means such as slighting or invidious comparison ⟨*disparaged* golf as recreation for the middle-aged⟩.

Belittle and **minimize** imply depreciation, *belittle* suggesting usu. a contemptuous or envious attitude ⟨inclined to *belittle* the achievements of others⟩, *minimize* connoting less personal animus ⟨do not try to *minimize* the danger involved⟩.

DEFEND, protect, shield, guard, safeguard mean to keep secure from danger or against attack.

Defend denotes warding off actual or threatened attack ⟨a large army needed to *defend* the country⟩.

Protect implies the use of something (as a covering) as a bar to the admission or impact of what may attack or injure ⟨*protect* one's eyes from the sun with dark glasses⟩.

Shield suggests protective intervention in imminent danger or actual attack ⟨tried to *shield* her child from the real world⟩.

Guard implies protecting with vigilance and force against expected danger ⟨all White House entrances are well *guarded*⟩.

Safeguard implies taking precautionary protective measures against merely possible danger ⟨individual rights must be *safeguarded* whatever the cost⟩.

See in addition MAINTAIN.

DEFER, postpone, suspend, stay mean to delay an action or proceeding.

Defer implies a deliberate putting off to a later time ⟨*deferred* buying a car until next spring⟩.

Postpone implies an intentional deferring usu. to a definite time ⟨the game was *postponed* until Saturday⟩.

Suspend implies temporary stoppage with an added suggestion of waiting until some condition is satisfied ⟨all business has been *suspended* while repairs are being made⟩.

Stay suggests the stopping or checking by an intervening agency or authority ⟨measures intended to *stay* the soaring rate of inflation⟩.

See in addition YIELD.

DEFORM, distort, contort, warp mean to mar or spoil by or as if by twisting.

Deform may imply a change of shape through stress, injury, or some accident of growth ⟨relentless winds *deformed* the pines into bizarre shapes⟩.

Distort and **contort** both imply a wrenching from the natural, normal or justly proportioned, but *contort* suggests a more involved twisting and a more grotesque and painful result ⟨the odd camera angle *distorts* his face in the photograph⟩ ⟨a degenerative bone disease had painfully *contorted* her body⟩.

Warp indicates physically an uneven shrinking that bends or twists out of a flat plane ⟨*warped* floorboards⟩.

DELAY *vb* **Delay, retard, slow, slacken, detain** mean to cause to be late or behind in movement or progress.

Delay implies a holding back, usu. by interference, from completion or arrival ⟨bad weather *delayed* our arrival⟩.

Retard applies chiefly to motion and suggests reduction of speed without actual stopping ⟨language barriers *retarded* their rate of learning⟩.

Slow and **slacken** both imply also a reduction of speed, *slow* often suggesting deliberate intention ⟨the engineer *slowed* the train⟩, *slacken* an easing up or relaxing of power or effort ⟨he needs to *slacken* his pace if he intends to finish the race⟩.

Detain implies a holding back beyond a reasonable or appointed time ⟨unexpected business had *detained* her⟩.

DELAY *vb* **Delay, procrastinate, lag, loiter, dawdle, dally** mean to move or act slowly so as to fall behind.

Delay usu. implies a putting off (as a beginning or departure) ⟨a tight schedule means we cannot *delay* any longer⟩.

Procrastinate implies blameworthy delay esp. through laziness or apathy ⟨*procrastinates* about making every decision⟩.

Lag implies failure to maintain a speed set by others ⟨we *lag* behind other countries in shoe production⟩.

Loiter and **dawdle** imply delay while in progress, esp. in walking, but *dawdle* more clearly suggests an aimless wasting of time ⟨*loitered* at several store windows before going to church⟩ ⟨children *dawdling* on their way home from school⟩.

Dally suggests delay through trifling or vacillation when promptness is necessary ⟨stop *dallying* and get to work⟩.

DEMAND, claim, require, exact mean to ask or call for something as due or as necessary.

Demand implies peremptoriness and insistence and often the right to make requests that are to be regarded as commands ⟨the physician *demanded* payment of her bill⟩.

Claim implies a demand for the delivery or concession of something due as one's own or one's right ⟨*claimed* to be the first to describe the disease⟩.

Require suggests the imperativeness that arises from inner necessity, compulsion of law or regulation, or the exigencies of the situation ⟨the patient *requires* constant attention⟩.

Exact implies not only demanding but getting what one demands ⟨the president *exacts* absolute loyalty from his aides⟩.

DENY, gainsay, contradict, contravene mean to refuse to accept as true or valid.

Deny implies a firm refusal to accept as true, to grant or concede, or to acknowledge the existence or claims of ⟨tried to *deny* the charges⟩.

Gainsay implies disputing the truth of what another has said ⟨no one can *gainsay* that everything I've said is a fact⟩.

Contradict implies an open or flat denial ⟨her report *contradicts* every point of his statement to the police⟩.

Contravene implies not so much an intentional opposition as some inherent incompatibility ⟨laws against whaling that *contravene* Eskimo tradition⟩.

DEPLETE, drain, exhaust, impoverish, bankrupt mean to deprive of something essential to existence or potency.

Deplete implies a reduction in number or quantity so as to endanger the ability to function ⟨we cannot afford to *deplete* our natural resources⟩.

Drain implies a gradual withdrawal and ultimate deprivation of what is necessary to a thing's existence ⟨a series of personal tragedies *drained* him of hope⟩.

Exhaust stresses a complete emptying or evacuation ⟨a theme that can never be *exhausted*⟩.

Impoverish suggests a deprivation of something essential to vigorous well-being ⟨without the arts we would lead an *impoverished* existence⟩.

Bankrupt suggests impoverishment to the point of imminent collapse ⟨war had *bankrupted* the nation of manpower and resources⟩.

DEPLORE, lament, bewail, bemoan mean to express grief or sorrow for something.

Deplore implies regret for the loss or impairment of something of value ⟨*deplores* the bad manners of today's young people⟩.

Lament implies a profound or demonstrative expression of sorrow ⟨never stopped *lamenting* the loss of their only son⟩.

Bewail and **bemoan** imply sorrow, disappointment, or protest finding outlet in words or cries, *bewail* commonly suggesting loudness, and *bemoan* lugubriousness, in uttering complaints or expressing regret ⟨fans *bewailed* the thunderous defeat of the home team⟩ ⟨purists continually *bemoan* the corruption of the language⟩.

DEROGATORY, depreciatory, disparaging, slighting, pejorative mean designed or tending to belittle.

Derogatory often applies to expressions or modes of expression that are intended to detract or belittle ⟨does not consider the word "politician" a *derogatory* term⟩.

Depreciatory is often applied to writing or speech that tends to lower a thing in value or status ⟨her habit of referring to the human body in the most *depreciatory* of ways⟩.

Disparaging implies an intent to depreciate by the use of oblique or indirect methods ⟨a *disparaging* look at some popular heroes⟩.

Slighting may imply mild disparagement, indifference, or even scorn ⟨made brief but *slighting* references to the other candidates in the race⟩.

Pejorative is applied esp. to words whose basic meaning is depreciated either by a suffix or by semantic application or association ⟨"egghead" is a *pejorative* term for an intellectual⟩.

DESIRE, wish, want, crave, covet mean to have a longing for.

Desire stresses the strength of feeling and often implies strong intention or aim ⟨*desires* to start a new life in another state⟩.

Wish sometimes implies a general or transient longing esp. for the unattainable ⟨she *wished* that there were some way she could help⟩.

Want specif. suggests a felt need or lack ⟨*want* to have a family⟩.

Crave stresses the force of physical appetite or emotional need ⟨*crave* constantly for sweets⟩.

Covet implies strong envious desire ⟨one of the most *coveted* honors in the sports world⟩.

DESPISE, contemn, scorn, disdain mean to regard as unworthy of one's notice or consideration.

Despise may suggest an emotional response ranging from strong dislike to loathing ⟨*despises* those who show any sign of weakness⟩.

Contemn implies a vehement condemnation of a person or thing as low, vile, feeble, or ignominious ⟨*contemns* the image of women promoted by advertisers⟩.

Scorn implies a ready or indignant contempt ⟨*scorns* the very thought of retirement⟩.

Disdain implies an arrogant or supercilious aversion to what is regarded as unworthy ⟨*disdained* all manner of popular music⟩.

DESPONDENT, despairing, desperate, hopeless mean having lost all or nearly all hope.

Despondent implies a deep dejection arising from a conviction of the uselessness of further effort ⟨*despondent* over the death of her father⟩.

Despairing suggests the slipping away of all hope and often despondency ⟨*despairing* appeals for the return of the kidnapped boy⟩.

Desperate implies despair that prompts reckless action or violence in the face of defeat or frustration ⟨one last *desperate* attempt to turn the tide of the war⟩.

Hopeless suggests despair and the cessation of effort or resistance and often implies acceptance or resignation ⟨the situation of the trapped miners is *hopeless*⟩.

DETERIORATION, degeneration, decadence, decline mean the falling from a higher to a lower level in quality, character, or vitality.

Deterioration implies impairment of vigor, resilience, or usefulness ⟨the *deterioration* of her memory in recent years⟩.

Degeneration stresses physical, intellectual, or esp. moral retrogression ⟨the *degeneration* of his youthful idealism to cynicism⟩.

Decadence presupposes a reaching and passing the peak of development and implies a turn downward with a consequent loss in vitality or energy ⟨cited rock music as a sign of cultural *decadence*⟩.

Decline differs from *decadence* in suggesting a more markedly downward direction and greater momentum as well as more obvious evidence of deterioration ⟨the meteoric rise and *decline* of his career⟩.

DEVOTE, dedicate, consecrate, hallow mean to set apart for a special and often higher end.

Devote is likely to imply compelling motives and often attachment to an objective ⟨*devoted* his evenings to study⟩.

Dedicate implies solemn and exclusive devotion to a sacred or serious use or purpose ⟨*dedicated* her life to medical research⟩.

Consecrate stresses investment with a solemn or sacred quality ⟨*consecrate* a church to the worship of God⟩.

Hallow, often differing little from *dedicate* or *consecrate*, may distinctively imply an attribution of intrinsic sanctity ⟨battleground *hallowed* by the blood of patriots⟩.

DEVOUT, pious, religious, pietistic, sanctimonious mean showing fervor in the practice of religion.

Devout stresses a mental attitude that leads to frequent and sincere though not always outwardly evident prayer and worship ⟨a pilgrimage that is the goal of *devout* Christians⟩.

Pious applies to the faithful performance of religious duties and maintenance of outwardly religious attitudes ⟨a *pious* family that faithfully observes the Sabbath⟩.

Religious may imply devoutness and piety but it emphasizes faith in a deity and adherence to a way of life in keeping with that faith ⟨a basically *religious* man, although not a regular churchgoer⟩.

Pietistic implies an insistence on the emotional as opposed to the intellectual aspects of religion ⟨regarded religious articles as *pietistic* excess⟩.

Sanctimonious implies pretensions to holiness or smug appearance of piety ⟨a *sanctimonious* preacher without mercy or human kindness⟩.

DEXTEROUS, adroit, deft mean ready and skilled in physical movement.

Dexterous implies expertness with consequent facility and quickness in manipulation ⟨a *dexterous* handling of a volatile situation⟩.

Adroit implies dexterity but may also stress resourcefulness or artfulness or inventiveness ⟨the *adroit* host of a radio call-in show⟩.

Deft emphasizes lightness, neatness, and sureness of touch or handling ⟨a *deft* interweaving of the novel's several subplots⟩.

DIALECT, vernacular, lingo, jargon, cant, argot, slang mean a form of language that is not recognized as standard.

Dialect applies commonly to a form of language found regionally or among the uneducated ⟨the *dialect* of the Cajuns in Louisiana⟩.

Vernacular applies to the everyday speech of the people in contrast to that of the learned ⟨the doctor used the *vernacular* in describing the disease⟩.

Lingo is a mildly contemptuous term for any language not readily understood ⟨foreign tourists speaking some strange *lingo*⟩.

Jargon applies to a technical or esoteric language used by a profession, trade, or cult ⟨educationese is the *jargon* of educational theorists⟩.

Cant is applied derogatorily to language that is both peculiar to a group or class and marked by hackneyed expressions ⟨the *cant* of TV sportscasters⟩.

Argot is applied to a peculiar language of a clique or other closely knit group ⟨the *argot* of narcotics smugglers⟩.

Slang designates a class of mostly recently coined and frequently short-lived terms or usages informally preferred to standard language as being forceful, novel, or voguish ⟨the ever-changing *slang* of college students⟩.

DICTATE, prescribe, ordain, decree, impose mean to issue something to be followed, observed, obeyed, or accepted.

Dictate implies an authoritative directive given orally or as if orally ⟨in matters of love, do as the heart *dictates*⟩.

Prescribe implies an authoritative pronouncement that is clear and definite ⟨the *prescribed* procedure for requesting new supplies⟩.

Ordain implies institution, establishment, or enactment by a supreme or unquestioned authority ⟨nature has *ordained* that we humans either swelter or shiver⟩.

Decree implies a formal pronouncement esp. by one of great or absolute authority ⟨the Pope *decreed* that next year will be a Holy Year⟩.

Impose implies a subjecting to what must be borne, endured, or submitted to ⟨morality cannot be *imposed* by law⟩.

DICTATORIAL, magisterial, dogmatic, doctrinaire, oracular mean imposing one's will or opinions on others.

Dictatorial stresses autocratic, high-handed methods and a domineering manner ⟨a *dictatorial* manner that alienates her colleagues⟩.

Magisterial stresses assumption or use of prerogatives appropriate to a magistrate or schoolmaster in forcing acceptance of one's opinions ⟨the *magisterial* tone of his arguments imply that only a fool would disagree⟩.

Dogmatic implies being unduly and offensively positive in laying down principles and expressing opinions ⟨very *dogmatic* about deciding what is art and what is not⟩.

Doctrinaire implies a disposition to follow abstract theories in framing laws or policies affecting people ⟨a *doctrinaire* conservative unable to deal with complex realities⟩.

Oracular implies the manner of one who delivers opinions in cryptic phrases or with pompous dogmatism ⟨for three decades she was the *oracular* voice of fashion⟩.

DIFFERENT, diverse, divergent, disparate, various mean unlike in kind or character.

Different may imply little more than separateness but it may also imply contrast or contrariness ⟨*different* foods⟩.

Diverse implies both distinctness and marked contrast ⟨such *diverse* interests as dancing and football⟩.

Divergent implies movement away from each other and unlikelihood of ultimate meeting or reconciliation ⟨went on to pursue two very *divergent* careers⟩.

Disparate emphasizes incongruity or incompatibility ⟨*disparate* notions of freedom⟩.

Various stresses the number of sorts or kinds ⟨*various* methods have been tried⟩.

DIRTY, filthy, foul, nasty, squalid mean conspicuously unclean or impure.

Dirty emphasizes the presence of dirt more than an emotional reaction to it ⟨children *dirty* from play⟩ ⟨a *dirty* littered street⟩.

Filthy carries a strong suggestion of offensiveness and typically of gradually accumulated dirt that begrimes and besmears ⟨a stained greasy floor, utterly *filthy*⟩.

Foul implies extreme offensiveness and an accumulation of what is rotten or stinking ⟨a *foul*-smelling open sewer⟩.

Nasty applies to what is actually foul or is repugnant to one used to or expecting freshness, cleanliness, or sweetness ⟨it's a *nasty* job to clean up after a sick cat⟩. In practice, *nasty* is often weakened to the point of being no more than a synonym of *unpleasant* or *disagreeable* ⟨had a *nasty* fall⟩ ⟨his answer gave her a *nasty* shock⟩.

Squalid adds to the idea of dirtiness and filth that of slovenly neglect ⟨living in *squalid* poverty⟩ ⟨*squalid* slums⟩.

All these terms are applicable to moral uncleanness or baseness or obscenity. **Dirty** then stresses meanness or despicableness ⟨don't ask me to do your *dirty* work⟩, while **filthy** and **foul** describe disgusting obscenity or loathsome behavior ⟨*filthy* language⟩ ⟨a *foul* story of lust and greed⟩, and **nasty** implies a peculiarly offensive unpleasantness ⟨his comedy always has a *nasty* ring to it⟩. Distinctively **squalid** implies sordidness as well as baseness and dirtiness ⟨her life was a series of *squalid* affairs⟩.

DISASTER, catastrophe, calamity, cataclysm mean an event or situation that is a terrible misfortune.
Disaster is an unforeseen, ruinous, and often sudden misfortune that happens either through lack of foresight or through some hostile external agency ⟨the war proved to be a *disaster* for the country⟩.
Catastrophe implies a disastrous conclusion emphasizing finality ⟨speculation about the *catastrophe* that befell Atlantis⟩.
Calamity stresses a great personal or public loss ⟨the father's sudden death was a *calamity* for the family⟩.
Cataclysm, orig. a deluge or geological convulsion, applies to an event or situation that produces an upheaval or complete reversal ⟨the French Revolution ranks as one of the *cataclysms* of the modern era⟩.

DISCARD, cast, shed, slough, scrap, junk mean to get rid of.
Discard implies the letting go or throwing away of something that has become useless or superfluous though often not intrinsically valueless ⟨*discard* any clothes you are unlikely to wear again⟩.
Cast, esp. when used with *off, away,* and *out* implies a forceful rejection or repudiation ⟨*cast* off her friends when they grew tiresome⟩.
Shed and **slough** imply a throwing off of something both useless and encumbering and often suggest a consequent renewal of vitality or luster ⟨the willpower needed to *shed* a bad habit⟩ ⟨finally *sloughed* her air of jaded worldliness⟩.
Scrap and **junk** imply throwing away or breaking up as

worthless inexistent form ⟨all the old ideas of warfare had to be *scrapped*⟩ ⟨those who would *junk* our entire educational system⟩.

DISCERNMENT, discrimination, perception, penetration, insight, acumen mean a power to see what is not evident to the average mind.

Discernment stresses accuracy (as in reading character or motives or appreciating art) ⟨had not the *discernment* to know who her friends really were⟩.

Discrimination stresses the power to distinguish and select what is true or appropriate or excellent ⟨acquire *discrimination* by looking at a lot of art⟩.

Perception implies quick and often sympathetic discernment (as of shades of feeling) ⟨a novelist of keen *perception*⟩.

Penetration implies a searching mind that goes beyond what is obvious or superficial ⟨has not the *penetration* to see beneath their deceptive facade⟩.

Insight suggests depth of discernment coupled with understanding sympathy ⟨a documentary providing *insight* into the plight of the homeless⟩.

Acumen implies characteristic penetration combined with keen practical judgment ⟨a theater director of reliable critical *acumen*⟩.

DISCLAIM, disavow, repudiate, disown, disallow mean to refuse to admit, accept, or approve.

Disclaim implies a refusal to accept either a rightful claim or an imputation made by another ⟨*disclaimed* in equal measure the virtues and vices attributed to her⟩.

Disavow implies a vigorous denial of personal responsibility, acceptance, or approval ⟨the radical group *disavowed* any responsibility for the bombing⟩.

Repudiate implies a rejection or denial of something that had been previously acknowledged, recognized, or accepted ⟨*repudiated* the socialist views of his college days⟩.

Disown implies a vigorous rejection or denial of something with which one formerly had a close relationship ⟨*disowned* his allegiance to the country of his birth⟩.

Disallow implies the withholding of sanction or approval and sometimes suggests complete rejection or condemnation ⟨IRS auditors *disallowed* that deduction⟩.

DISCOMPOSE, disquiet, disturb, perturb, agitate, upset, fluster mean to destroy capacity for collected thought or decisive action.

Discompose implies some degree of loss of self-control or self-confidence esp. through emotional stress ⟨*discomposed* by the loss of his beloved wife⟩.

Disquiet suggests loss of sense of security or peace of mind ⟨the *disquieting* news of a tragic accident⟩.

Disturb implies interference with one's mental processes caused by worry, perplexity, or interruption ⟨the puzzling discrepancy *disturbed* me⟩.

Perturb implies deep disturbance of mind and emotions ⟨*perturbed* by her husband's strange behavior⟩.

Agitate suggests obvious external signs of nervous or emotional excitement ⟨in his *agitated* state he was unfit to go to work⟩.

Upset implies the disturbance of normal or habitual functioning by disappointment, distress, or grief ⟨constant bickering that greatly *upsets* their son⟩.

Fluster suggests bewildered agitation ⟨his amorous advances completely *flustered* her⟩.

DISCORD, strife, conflict, contention, dissension, variance mean a state or condition marked by a lack of agreement or harmony.

Discord implies an intrinsic or essential lack of harmony producing quarreling, factiousness, or antagonism ⟨years of *discord* had left its mark on the political party⟩.

Strife emphasizes a struggle for superiority rather than the incongruity or incompatibility of the persons or things involved ⟨during his reign the empire was free of *strife*⟩.

Conflict usu. stresses the action of forces in opposition but in static applications implies an irreconcilability as of duties or desires ⟨a *conflict* of professional interests⟩.

Contention applies to strife or competition that shows itself in quarreling, disputing, or controversy ⟨several points of *contention* between the two sides⟩.

Dissension implies strife or discord and stresses a division into factions ⟨religious *dissensions* threatened to split the colony⟩.

Variance implies a clash between persons or things owing to a difference in nature, opinion, or interest ⟨cultural *variances* delayed the process of national unification⟩.

DISCOVER, ascertain, determine, unearth, learn mean to find out what one did not previously know.

Discover may apply to something requiring exploration or investigation or to a chance encounter ⟨*discovered* the source of the river⟩.

Ascertain implies effort to find the facts or the truth proceeding from awareness of ignorance or uncertainty ⟨will try to *ascertain* the population of the region⟩.

Determine emphasizes the intent to establish the facts definitely or precisely ⟨unable to *determine* the exact etiology of the disease⟩.

Unearth implies bringing to light something forgotten or hidden ⟨*unearth* old records⟩.

Learn may imply acquiring knowledge with little effort or conscious intention (as by simply being told) or it may imply study and practice ⟨I *learned* her name only today⟩ ⟨spent years *learning* Greek⟩.

See in addition INVENT, REVEAL.

DISCUSS, argue, debate, dispute mean to discourse about in order to reach conclusions or to convince.

Discuss implies a sifting of possibilities esp. by presenting considerations pro and con ⟨*discussed* the need for widening the expressway⟩.

Argue implies the offering of reasons or evidence in support of convictions already held (*argued* that the project would be too costly).

Debate suggests formal or public argument between opposing parties (*debated* the merits of the proposed constitutional amendment); it may also apply to deliberation with oneself (I'm *debating* whether I should go).

Dispute implies contentious or heated argument (scientists *dispute* the reasons for the extinction of the dinosaurs).

DISGRACE, dishonor, disrepute, infamy, ignominy mean the state or condition of suffering loss of esteem and of enduring reproach.

Disgrace often implies complete humiliation and sometimes ostracism (his conviction for bribery brought *disgrace* upon his family).

Dishonor emphasizes the loss of honor that one has enjoyed or the loss of self-esteem (prefer death to life with *dishonor*).

Disrepute stresses loss of one's good name or the acquiring of a bad reputation (a once-proud name now fallen into *disrepute*).

Infamy usu. implies notoriety as well as exceeding shame (a gangster whose name retains an enduring *infamy*).

Ignominy stresses the almost unendurable contemptibility or despicableness of the disgrace (suffered the *ignominy* of being brought back in irons).

DISGUISE, cloak, mask, dissemble mean to alter the dress or appearance so as to conceal the identity or true nature.

Disguise implies a change in appearance or behavior that misleads by presenting a different apparent identity (*disguised* himself as a peasant to escape detection).

Cloak suggests a means of hiding a movement or an intention completely (*cloaks* her greed and self-interest in the rhetoric of philosophy).

Mask suggests some usu. obvious means of preventing recognition and does not always imply deception or pretense (a smiling front that *masks* a will of iron⟩.

Dissemble stresses simulation for the purpose of deceiving ⟨*dissembled* madness to survive the intrigues at court⟩.

DISHONEST, deceitful, mendacious, lying, untruthful mean unworthy of trust or belief.

Dishonest implies a willful perversion of truth in order to deceive, cheat, or defraud ⟨a swindle usually involves two *dishonest* people⟩.

Deceitful usu. implies an intent to mislead and commonly suggests a false appearance or double-dealing ⟨the secret affairs of the *deceitful* spouse⟩.

Mendacious is less forthright than *lying*, may suggest bland or even harmlessly mischievous deceit, and used of people often suggests a habit of telling untruths ⟨his sea stories became increasingly *mendacious*⟩.

Lying implies a specific act or instance rather than a habit or tendency ⟨a conviction based upon testimony of a *lying* witness⟩.

Untruthful is a less brutal term than *lying* and in application to accounts or description stresses a discrepancy between what is said and fact or reality rather than an intent to deceive ⟨an *untruthful* account of their actions⟩.

DISINCLINED, hesitant, reluctant, loath, averse mean lacking the will or desire to do something indicated.

Disinclined implies lack of taste for or inclination toward and often active disapproval of the thing suggested ⟨*disinclined* to believe their story⟩.

Hesitant implies a holding back through fear, uncertainty, or disinclination ⟨*hesitant* about asking her for a date⟩.

Reluctant implies a holding back through unwillingness ⟨I'm *reluctant* to blame anyone just now⟩.

Loath implies hesitancy because of conflict with one's opinions, predilections, or liking ⟨*loath* to believe that he could do anything right⟩.

Averse implies a holding back from or avoiding because of distaste or repugnance ⟨seems *averse* to anything requiring work⟩.

DISMAL, dreary, cheerless, dispiriting, bleak, desolate mean devoid of all that is cheerful and comfortable.

Dismal may imply extreme gloominess or somberness that is utterly depressing ⟨a *dismal* day of unrelenting rain⟩.

Dreary implies a sustained gloom, dullness, or tiresomeness that discourages or enervates ⟨spent her days alone in a *dreary* apartment⟩.

Cheerless stresses a pervasive, disheartening joylessness or hopelessness ⟨faced a *cheerless* life as a drudge⟩.

Dispiriting implies a lessening of morale or determination ⟨problems that made for a *dispiriting* start for their new venture⟩.

Bleak implies a chilly, dull barrenness ⟨a *bleak*, windswept landscape offering no refuge for the wayward traveler⟩.

Desolate implies that something disheartens by being utterly barren, lifeless, uninhabitable, or abandoned ⟨the long trek into the country's *desolate* interior⟩.

DISMAY, appall, horrify, daunt mean to unnerve or deter by arousing fear, apprehension, or aversion.

Dismay implies that one is balked and perplexed or at a loss as to how to deal with something ⟨*dismayed* to find herself the center of attention⟩.

Appall implies that one is faced with that which perturbs, confounds, or shocks ⟨*appalled* by your utter lack of concern⟩.

Horrify stresses a reaction of horror or revulsion ⟨the scope of the famine is quite *horrifying*⟩.

Daunt suggests a cowing, subduing, disheartening, or frightening in a venture requiring courage ⟨problems that would *daunt* even the most intrepid of reformers⟩.

DISPOSITION, temperament, temper, character, personality mean the dominant quality or qualities distinguishing a person or group.

Disposition implies customary moods and attitude toward the life around one ⟨a boy of cheerful *disposition*⟩.

Temperament implies a pattern of innate characteristics associated with one's specific physical and nervous organization ⟨an artistic *temperament* inherited from his mother⟩.

Temper implies the qualities acquired through experience that determine how a person or group meets difficulties or handles situations ⟨the national *temper* has always been one of optimism⟩.

Character applies to the aggregate of moral qualities by which a person is judged apart from his intelligence, competence, or special talents ⟨a woman of iron-willed *character*⟩.

Personality applies to an aggregate of qualities that distinguish one as a person ⟨a somber *personality* not to everyone's liking⟩.

DISPROVE, refute, confute, rebut, controvert mean to show or try to show by presenting evidence that something is not true.

Disprove implies the demonstration by any method of the falseness or invalidity of a claim or argument ⟨the view that one can neither prove nor *disprove* the existence of God⟩.

Refute stresses a logical method of disproving ⟨*refuted* every piece of his argument⟩.

Confute implies reducing an opponent to silence by an overwhelming argument ⟨a triumphal flight that *confuted* all of the doubters⟩.

Rebut suggests formality in the act of answering an argument and does not necessarily imply success in disproving ⟨give the opposing side time to *rebut*⟩.

Controvert stresses the act of opposing with denial or an answering argument ⟨a thesis that withstood every attempt to *controvert* it⟩.

DISTINCT, separate, several, discrete mean not being each and every one the same.

Distinct indicates that something is distinguished by the mind or eye as being apart or different from others ⟨each and every bowl is hand-decorated and *distinct*⟩.

Separate often stresses lack of connection or a difference in identity between two things ⟨the two schools are *separate* and unequal⟩.

Several indicates distinctness, difference, or separation from similar items ⟨a survey of the *several* opinions of the new building⟩.

Discrete strongly emphasizes individuality and lack of physical connection despite apparent similarity or seeming continuity ⟨two *discrete* issues are being confused here⟩.

See in addition EVIDENT.

DISTRESS, suffering, misery, agony mean the state of being in great trouble.

Distress implies an external and usu. temporary cause of great physical or mental strain and stress ⟨news of the hurricane put everyone in great *distress*⟩.

Suffering implies conscious endurance of pain or distress ⟨the *suffering* of earthquake victims⟩.

Misery stresses the unhappiness attending esp. sickness, poverty, or loss ⟨the poor live with *misery* every day⟩.

Agony suggests pain too intense to be borne ⟨in *agony* over their daughter's suicide⟩.

DISTRIBUTE, dispense, divide, deal, dole mean to give out, usu. in shares, to each member of a group.

Distribute implies an apportioning by separation of something into parts, units, or amounts ⟨*distributed* the work to all employees⟩.

Dispense suggests the giving of a carefully weighed or measured portion to each of a group according to due or need ⟨*dispensed* medicine during the epidemic⟩.

Divide stresses the separation of a whole into parts and implies that the parts are equal ⟨three charitable groups *divided* the proceeds⟩.

Deal emphasizes the allotment of something piece by piece ⟨*deal* out equipment and supplies to each soldier⟩.

Dole implies a carefully measured portion that is often scant or niggardly ⟨*doled* out the little food there was⟩.

DOMINANT, predominant, paramount, preponderant, sovereign mean superior to all others in power, influence, or importance.

Dominant applies to something that is uppermost because ruling or controlling ⟨a *dominant* social class⟩.

Predominant applies to something that exerts, often temporarily, the most marked influence ⟨at the time fear was my *predominant* emotion⟩.

Paramount implies supremacy in importance, rank, or jurisdiction ⟨inflation was the *paramount* issue in the campaign⟩.

Preponderant applies to an element or factor that outweighs all others in influence or effect ⟨*preponderant* evidence in his favor⟩.

Sovereign indicates quality or rank to which everything else is clearly subordinate or inferior ⟨the *sovereign* power resides in the people⟩.

DOUBTFUL, dubious, problematic, questionable mean not affording assurance of the worth, soundness, or certainty of something.

Doubtful implies little more than a lack of conviction or certainty ⟨still *doubtful* about the cause of the explosion⟩.

Dubious stresses suspicion, mistrust, or hesitation ⟨*dubious* about the practicality of the scheme⟩.

Problematic applies esp. to things whose existence, meaning, fulfillment, or realization is highly uncertain ⟨whether the project will ever be finished is *problematic*⟩.

Questionable may imply no more than the existence of doubt but usu. suggests that the suspicions are well-grounded ⟨a real estate agent of *questionable* honesty⟩.

DOWNCAST, dispirited, dejected, depressed, disconso-

late, woebegone mean affected by or showing very low spirits.

Downcast implies an overwhelming shame, mortification, or loss of confidence (negative reviews left all of the actors feeling *downcast*).

Dispirited implies extreme low-spiritedness resulting from failure (*dispirited*, the doomed explorers resigned themselves to failure).

Dejected implies a sudden but often temporary loss of hope, courage, or vigor (a crushing defeat that left the team in a *dejected* mood).

Depressed may imply either a temporary or a chronic low-spiritedness (*depressed* by his failures to the point of suicide).

Disconsolate implies being inconsolable or very uncomfortable (*disconsolate* motorists leaning against their disabled car).

Woebegone suggests a defeated, spiritless condition (a run-down, *woebegone* motel on an empty backroad).

DRAMATIC, theatrical, histrionic, melodramatic mean having a character or an effect like that of acted plays.

Dramatic applies to situations in life and literature that stir the imagination and emotions deeply (a *dramatic* meeting of world leaders).

Theatrical implies a crude appeal through artificiality or exaggeration in gesture or vocal expression (a *theatrical* oration).

Histrionic applies to tones, gestures, and motions and suggests a deliberate affectation or staginess (a *histrionic* show of grief).

Melodramatic suggests an exaggerated emotionalism or an inappropriate theatricalism (making a *melodramatic* scene in public).

DRUNK, drunken, intoxicated, inebriated, tipsy, tight mean considerably affected by alcohol.

Drunk and **drunken** are the plainspoken, direct, and inclusive terms ⟨arrived at the party already *drunk*⟩ ⟨a *drunken* man stumbled out of the bar⟩.

Intoxicated is a more formal term and likely to be used in legal or medical contexts ⟨arrested for driving while *intoxicated*⟩.

Inebriated stresses the hilarious or noisy aspects of drunkenness ⟨the *inebriated* revelers bellowed out songs⟩.

Tipsy may imply only slight drunkenness ⟨a *tipsy* patron began making unwelcome amorous advances⟩.

Tight usu. suggests partial but obvious drunkenness ⟨worried that some of her guests were getting *tight* before dinner⟩.

DULL, blunt, obtuse mean not sharp, keen, or acute.

Dull suggests a lack or loss of keenness, zest, or pungency ⟨a *dull* pain⟩ ⟨a *dull* mind⟩.

Blunt suggests an inherent lack of sharpness or quickness of feeling or perception ⟨even a person of his *blunt* sensibility was moved⟩.

Obtuse implies such bluntness as makes one insensitive in perception or imagination ⟨too *obtuse* to realize that she had deeply hurt us⟩.

See in addition STUPID.

DUPE, gull, trick, hoax mean to deceive by underhanded means.

Dupe suggests unwariness in the person deluded ⟨*duped* us into buying a lemon of a car⟩.

Gull stresses credulousness or readiness to be imposed on (as through greed) on the part of the victim ⟨are you so easily *gulled* by these contest promoters⟩.

Trick implies an intent to delude by means of a ruse or fraud but does not always imply a vicious intent ⟨special effects can *trick* moviegoers into believing anything⟩.

Hoax implies the contriving of an elaborate or adroit imposture in order to deceive ⟨*hoaxed* the public by broadcasting news of a Martian invasion⟩.

E

EAGER, avid, keen, anxious, athirst mean moved by a strong and urgent desire or interest.

Eager implies ardor and enthusiasm and sometimes impatience at delay or restraint (*eager* to get started on the trip).

Avid adds to *eager* the implication of insatiability or greed (young pleasure-seekers *avid* for the next thrill).

Keen suggests intensity of interest and quick responsiveness in action (very *keen* on the latest styles and fashions).

Anxious emphasizes fear of frustration or failure or disappointment (*anxious* to know that they got home safely).

Athirst stresses yearning but not necessarily readiness for action (*athirst* for adventure on her first trip to India).

EARTHLY, worldly, mundane mean belonging to or characteristic of the earth.

Earthly often implies a contrast with what is heavenly or spiritual (abandoned *earthly* concerns and entered a convent).

Worldly and **mundane** both imply a relation to the immediate concerns and activities of human beings, *worldly* suggesting tangible personal gain or gratification (a philosopher with no interest in *worldly* goods), and *mundane* suggesting reference to the immediate and practical (a *mundane* discussion of finances).

EASY, facile, simple, light, effortless, smooth mean not demanding effort or involving difficulty.

Easy is applicable either to persons or things imposing tasks or to activity required by such tasks (an *easy* college course requiring little work).

Facile often adds to *easy* the connotation of undue haste or shallowness (offers only *facile* solutions to complex problems).

Simple stresses ease in understanding or dealing with because complication is absent ⟨a *simple* problem in arithmetic⟩.

Light stresses freedom from what is burdensome, and often suggests quickness of movement ⟨her novels are pretty *light* stuff⟩.

Effortless stresses the appearance of ease and usu. implies the prior attainment of artistry or expertness ⟨a champion figure skater moving with *effortless* grace⟩.

Smooth stresses the absence or removal of all difficulties, hardships, or obstacles ⟨a *smooth* transition to the new administration⟩.

See in addition COMFORTABLE.

ECSTASY, rapture, transport mean intense exaltation of mind and feelings.

Ecstasy may apply to any strong emotion (as joy, fear, rage, adoration) ⟨the sculptor was in *ecstasy* when his work was unveiled⟩.

Rapture usu. implies in tense bliss or beatitude ⟨in speechless *rapture* during the entire wedding⟩.

Transport applies to any powerful emotion that lifts one out of oneself and usu. provokes vehement expression or frenzied action ⟨in a *transport* of rage after reading the article⟩.

EDUCE, evoke, elicit, extract, extort mean to draw out something hidden, latent, or reserved.

Educe implies the bringing out of something potential or latent ⟨a teacher who can *educe* the best in her students⟩.

Evoke implies a strong stimulus that arouses an emotion or an interest or recalls an image or memory ⟨a song that *evokes* many memories⟩.

Elicit usu. implies some effort or skill in drawing forth a response ⟨unable to *elicit* a straight answer from the candidate⟩.

Extract implies the use of force or pressure in obtaining answers or information ⟨*extract* testimony from a hostile witness⟩.

Extort suggests a wringing or wresting from one who resists strongly ⟨*extorted* the money from his father-in-law⟩.

EFFECT *n* **Effect, consequence, result, issue, outcome** mean a condition or occurrence traceable to a cause.

Effect designates something that necessarily and directly follows or occurs by reason of a cause ⟨the *effects* of radiation on the body⟩.

Consequence implies a looser or remoter connection with a cause and usu. implies that the cause is no longer operating ⟨a single act that had far-reaching *consequences*⟩.

Result applies often to the last in a series of effects ⟨the end *result* was a growth in business⟩.

Issue applies to a result that ends or solves a difficulty ⟨a successful *issue* that rendered all the controversy moot⟩.

Outcome suggests the final result of complex or conflicting causes or forces ⟨the *outcome* of generations of controlled breeding⟩.

EFFECTIVE, effectual, efficient, efficacious mean producing or capable of producing a result.

Effective stresses the actual production of or the power to produce an effect ⟨an *effective* rebuttal⟩.

Effectual suggests the accomplishment of a desired result esp. as viewed after the fact ⟨the measures to halt crime proved *effectual*⟩.

Efficient suggests an acting or a potential for action or use in such a way as to avoid loss or waste of energy in effecting, producing, or functioning ⟨an *efficient* small car⟩.

Efficacious suggests possession of a special quality or virtue that gives effective power ⟨a detergent that is *efficacious* in removing grease⟩.

EFFORT, exertion, pains, trouble mean the active use of energy in producing a result.

Effort often suggests a single action or attempt and implies the calling up or directing of energy by the conscious will ⟨made the supreme *effort* and crossed the finish line first⟩.

Exertion may describe the bringing into effect of any power of mind or body or it may suggest laborious and exhausting effort ⟨a job not requiring much physical *exertion*⟩.

Pains implies toilsome or solicitous effort ⟨take *pains* to do the job well⟩.

Trouble implies effort that inconveniences or slows down ⟨went through a lot of *trouble* to get the right equipment⟩.

EJECT, expel, oust, evict, dismiss mean to drive or force out.

Eject carries an esp. strong implication of throwing or thrusting out from within as a physical action ⟨*ejected* the obnoxious patron from the bar⟩.

Expel stresses a thrusting out or driving away esp. permanently which need not be physical ⟨a student *expelled* from college⟩.

Oust implies removal or dispossession by power of the law or by compulsion of necessity ⟨issued a general order *ousting* all foreigners⟩.

Evict chiefly applies to turning out of house and home ⟨they were *evicted* for nonpayment of rent⟩.

Dismiss implies a getting rid of something unpleasant or troublesome simply by refusing to consider it further ⟨simply *dismissed* the quarrel from her mind⟩.

ELASTIC, resilient, springy, flexible, supple mean able to endure strain without being permanently injured.

Elastic implies the property of resisting deformation by stretching ⟨slacks that come with an *elastic* waistband⟩.

Resilient implies the ability to recover shape quickly when the deforming force or pressure is removed ⟨a good running shoe has a *resilient* innersole⟩.

Springy stresses both the ease with which something yields to pressure and the quickness of its return to original shape ⟨the cake is done when the top is *springy*⟩.

Flexible applies to something which may or may not be resilient or elastic but which can be bent or folded without breaking ⟨*flexible* plastic tubing⟩.

Supple applies to something that can be readily bent, twisted, or folded without any sign of injury ⟨shoes made of luxurious, *supple* leather⟩.

ELEMENT, component, constituent, ingredient, factor mean one of the parts of a compound or complex whole.

Element applies to any such part and often connotes irreducible simplicity ⟨the basic *elements* of the gothic novel⟩.

Component and **constituent** may designate any of the substances (whether elements or compounds) or the qualities that enter into the makeup of a complex product; *component* stresses its separate entity or distinguishable character ⟨able to identify every *component* of his firearm⟩; *constituent* stresses its essential and formative character ⟨analyzed the *constituents* of the compound⟩.

Ingredient applies to any of the substances which when combined form a particular mixture (as a medicine or alloy) ⟨the *ingredients* of a cocktail⟩.

Factor applies to any constituent or element whose presence helps actively to perform a certain kind of work or produce a definite result ⟨price was a *factor* in her decision to buy⟩.

EMBARRASS, discomfit, abash, disconcert, rattle mean to distress by confusing or confounding.

Embarrass implies some influence that impedes thought, speech, or action ⟨*embarrassed* to admit that she liked the movie⟩.

Discomfit implies a hampering or frustrating accompanied by confusion ⟨persistent heckling *discomfited* the speaker⟩.

Abash presupposes some initial self-confidence that receives a sudden check by something that produces shyness, shame, or a conviction of inferiority ⟨completely *abashed* by her swift and cutting retort⟩.

Disconcert implies an upsetting of equanimity or assurance producing uncertainty or hesitancy ⟨*disconcerted* by the sight of the large audience⟩.

Rattle implies an agitation that impairs thought and judgment ⟨a tennis player not at all *rattled* by television cameras⟩.

EMPTY, vacant, blank, void, vacuous mean lacking contents which could or should be present.

Empty suggests a complete absence of contents ⟨an *empty* bucket⟩.

Vacant suggests an absence of appropriate contents or occupants ⟨a *vacant* apartment⟩.

Blank stresses the absence of any significant, relieving, or intelligible features on a surface ⟨a *blank* wall⟩.

Void suggests absolute emptiness as far as the mind or senses can determine ⟨a statement *void* of meaning⟩.

Vacuous suggests the emptiness of a vacuum and esp. the lack of intelligence or significance ⟨a *vacuous* facial expression⟩.

See in addition VAIN.

ENCOMIUM, eulogy, panegyric, tribute, citation mean a formal expression of praise.

Encomium implies enthusiasm and warmth in praising a person or a thing ⟨the subject of several spirited *encomiums* at the banquet⟩.

Eulogy applies to a prepared speech or writing extolling the virtues and services of a person ⟨delivered the *eulogy* at the funeral⟩.

Panegyric suggests an elaborate often poetic compliment ⟨coronations once inspired *panegyrics*⟩.

Tribute implies deeply felt praise conveyed either through words or through a significant act ⟨a page of *tributes* marking his fifty years of service⟩.

Citation applies to the formal praise accompanying the mention of a person in a military dispatch or in awarding an honorary degree ⟨a *citation* noting her lasting contribution to biology⟩.

ENCOURAGE, inspirit, hearten, embolden mean to fill with courage or strength of purpose.

Encourage suggests the raising of one's confidence esp. by an external agency ⟨the teacher's praise *encouraged* the student to try even harder⟩.

Inspirit implies instilling life, energy, courage, or vigor into something ⟨pioneers *inspirited* by the stirring accounts of the explorers⟩.

Hearten implies a dispiritedness or despondency that is lifted by an infusion of fresh courage or zeal ⟨a hospital patient *heartened* by the display of moral support⟩.

Embolden implies the giving of courage sufficient to overcome timidity or reluctance ⟨a successful climb *emboldened* her to try more difficult ones⟩.

END *n* **End, termination, ending, terminus** mean the point or line beyond which something does not or cannot go.

End is the inclusive term, implying the final limit in time or space, in extent of influence, or range of possibility ⟨the report put an *end* to all speculation⟩.

Termination and **ending** apply to the end of something having predetermined limits or being complete or finished ⟨the *termination* of a lease⟩ ⟨the *ending* of a search⟩. *Ending* often includes the portion leading to the actual final point ⟨a film marred by a contrived *ending*⟩.

Terminus applies commonly to the point to which one moves or progresses ⟨Chicago is the *terminus* for many air routes⟩.

See in addition INTENTION.

ENMITY, hostility, antipathy, antagonism, animosity, rancor, animus mean deep-seated dislike or ill will.

Enmity suggests positive hatred which may be open or concealed ⟨an unspoken *enmity* seethed between the two⟩.

Hostility suggests an enmity showing itself in attacks or aggression ⟨a history of *hostility* between the two nations⟩.

Antipathy and **antagonism** imply a natural or logical basis for one's hatred or dislike, *antipathy* suggesting repugnance, a desire to avoid or reject, and *antagonism* suggesting a clash of temperaments leading readily to hostility ⟨a natural *antipathy* for self-important upstarts⟩ ⟨a long-standing *antagonism* between the banker and his prodigal son⟩.

Animosity suggests intense ill will and vindictiveness that threaten to kindle hostility ⟨*animosity* that eventually led to revenge⟩.

Rancor esp. is applied to bitter brooding over a wrong ⟨*rancor* filled every line of his letters⟩.

Animus implies strong prejudice ⟨my objections are devoid of any personal *animus*⟩.

ENORMOUS, immense, huge, vast, gigantic, colossal, mammoth mean exceedingly large.

Enormous and **immense** both suggest an exceeding of all ordinary bounds in size or amount or degree, but *enormous* often adds an implication of abnormality or monstrousness ⟨the *enormous* expense of the program⟩ ⟨the *immense* size of the new shopping mall⟩.

Huge commonly suggests an immensity of bulk or amount ⟨quickly incurred a *huge* debt⟩.

Vast usu. suggests immensity of extent ⟨the *vast* Russian steppes⟩.

Gigantic stresses the contrast with the size of others of the same kind ⟨a *gigantic* sports stadium⟩.

Colossal applies esp. to a human creation of stupendous or incredible dimensions ⟨a *colossal* statue of Lincoln⟩.

Mammoth suggests both hugeness and ponderousness of bulk ⟨a *mammoth* boulder⟩.

ENSURE, insure, assure, secure mean to make a thing or person sure.

Ensure implies a virtual guarantee ⟨the government has *ensured* the safety of the foreign minister⟩.

Insure sometimes stresses the taking of necessary measures beforehand ⟨careful planning should *insure* the success of the party⟩.

Assure distinctively implies the removal of doubt and suspense from a person's mind ⟨I *assure* you that no one will be harmed⟩.

Secure implies action taken to guard against attack or loss ⟨made a reservation in order to *secure* a table⟩.

ENTER, penetrate, pierce, probe mean to make way into something.

Enter is the most general of these and may imply either going in or forcing a way in ⟨*entered* the city in triumph⟩.

Penetrate carries a strong implication of an impelling force or compelling power that achieves entrance ⟨no bullet has ever *penetrated* a vest of that material⟩.

Pierce adds to *penetrate* a clear implication of an entering point ⟨a fracture in which the bone *pierces* the skin⟩.

Probe implies penetration to investigate or explore something hidden from sight or knowledge ⟨*probed* the depths of the sea⟩.

EPICURE, gourmet, gastronome, bon vivant mean one who takes pleasure in eating and drinking.

Epicure implies fastidiousness and voluptuousness of taste ⟨a delicacy that only an *epicure* would appreciate⟩.

Gourmet implies being a connoisseur in food and drink and the discriminating enjoyment of them ⟨*gourmets* rate the restaurant highly⟩.

Gastronome implies that one has studied extensively the history and rituals of haute cuisine ⟨an annual banquet that attracts *gastronomes* from all over⟩.

Bon vivant stresses the enjoyment of fine food and drink in company ⟨*bon vivants* rang in the New Year in style⟩.

EQUANIMITY, composure, sangfroid, phlegm mean evenness of mind under stress.

Equanimity suggests a habit of mind that is only rarely disturbed under great strain ⟨accepted fortune's slings and arrows with resigned *equanimity*⟩.

Composure implies the controlling of emotional or mental agitation by an effort of will or as a matter of habit ⟨maintained his *composure* even under hostile questioning⟩.

Sangfroid implies great coolness and steadiness under strain ⟨an Olympian diver of remarkable *sangfroid*⟩.

Phlegm implies insensitiveness and suggests apathy rather than self-control ⟨good news and bad news alike had no effect on her *phlegm*⟩.

ERASE, expunge, cancel, efface, obliterate, blot out, delete mean to remove something so that it no longer has any effect or existence.

Erase implies the act of rubbing or wiping out (letters or impressions) often in preparation for correction or new matter ⟨*erase* what you wrote and start over⟩.

Expunge stresses a removal or destruction that leaves no trace ⟨*expunged* all references to the deposed leader⟩.

Cancel implies an action (as marking, revoking, or neutralizing) that makes a thing no longer effective or usable ⟨a crime that *cancelled* out all her good deeds⟩.

Efface implies the removal of an impression by damage to or wearing off of the surface ⟨the subway sign had been badly *effaced*⟩.

Obliterate and **blot out** both imply a covering up or smearing over that removes all traces of a thing's existence ⟨an outdoor mural almost *obliterated* by graffiti⟩ ⟨*blotted out* the offensive passage with black ink⟩.

Delete implies a deliberate exclusion, or a marking to direct exclusion, of written matter ⟨his editor *deleted* all unflattering references to others⟩.

ERROR, mistake, blunder, slip, lapse mean a departure from what is true, right, or proper.

Error suggests the existence of a standard or guide and a straying from the right course through failure to make effective use of this ⟨one *error* in judgment lost the battle⟩.

Mistake implies misconception or inadvertence and usu. expresses less criticism than *error* ⟨dialed the wrong number by *mistake*⟩.

Blunder regularly imputes stupidity or ignorance as a cause and connotes some degree of blame ⟨a political campaign noted mostly for its series of *blunders*⟩.

Slip stresses inadvertence or accident and applies esp. to trivial but embarrassing mistakes ⟨during the speech I made several *slips*⟩.

Lapse stresses forgetfulness, weakness, or inattention as a cause ⟨apart from a few grammatical *lapses*, the paper is good⟩.

ESCAPE, avoid, evade, elude, shun, eschew mean to get away or keep away from something.

Escape stresses the fact of getting away or being passed by not necessarily through effort or by conscious intent ⟨nothing *escapes* her sharp eyes⟩.

Avoid stresses forethought and caution in keeping clear of danger or difficulty ⟨with careful planning we can *avoid* the fate of previous attempts⟩.

Evade implies adroitness, ingenuity, or lack of scruple in escaping or avoiding ⟨*evaded* the question by changing the subject⟩.

Elude implies a slippery or baffling quality in the person or thing that escapes ⟨what she sees in him *eludes* me⟩.

Shun often implies an avoiding as a matter of habitual practice or policy and may imply repugnance or abhorrence ⟨you have *shunned* your responsibilities⟩.

Eschew implies an avoiding or abstaining from as unwise or distasteful ⟨a playwright who *eschews* melodrama and claptrap⟩.

ESSENTIAL, fundamental, vital, cardinal mean so important as to be indispensable.

Essential implies belonging to the very nature of a thing and therefore being incapable of removal without destroying the thing itself or its character ⟨conflict is an *essential* element in drama⟩.

Fundamental applies to something that is a foundation without which an entire system or complex whole would collapse ⟨the *fundamental* principles of democracy⟩.

Vital suggests something that is necessary to a thing's continued existence or operation ⟨air bases that are *vital* to our national security⟩.

Cardinal suggests something on which an outcome turns or depends ⟨one of the *cardinal* events of the Civil War⟩.

ESTIMATE, appraise, evaluate, value, rate, assess mean to judge something with respect to its worth or significance.

Estimate implies a judgment, considered or casual, that precedes or takes the place of actual measuring or counting or testing out ⟨*estimated* that there were a hundred people there⟩.

Appraise commonly implies the fixing by an expert of the monetary worth of a thing, but it may be used of any critical judgment ⟨a real estate agent *appraised* the house⟩.

Evaluate suggests an attempt to determine either the relative or intrinsic worth of something in terms other than monetary ⟨instructors will *evaluate* all students' work⟩.

Value equals *appraise* but without implying expertness of judgment ⟨a watercolor *valued* by the donor at $500⟩.

Rate adds to *estimate* the notion of placing a thing according to a scale of values ⟨an actress who is *rated* highly by her peers⟩.

Assess implies a critical appraisal for the purpose of understanding or interpreting, or as a guide in taking action ⟨officials are still trying to *assess* the damage⟩.

ESTRANGE, alienate, disaffect, wean mean to cause one to break a bond of affection or loyalty.

Estrange implies the development of indifference or hostility with consequent separation or divorcement ⟨a chance meeting with his *estranged* wife⟩.

Alienate may or may not suggest separation but always implies loss of affection or interest ⟨managed to *alienate* all her coworkers with her arrogance⟩.

Disaffect refers esp. to those from whom loyalty is expected and stresses the effects (as rebellion or discontent) of alienation without actual separation ⟨overly strict parents who *disaffect* their children⟩.

Wean implies separation from something having a strong hold on one ⟨willpower is needed to *wean* yourself from a bad habit⟩.

EVIDENT, manifest, patent, distinct, obvious, apparent, plain, clear mean readily perceived or apprehended.

Evident implies presence of visible signs that lead one to a definite conclusion ⟨an *evident* fondness for the company of beautiful women⟩.

Manifest implies an external display so evident that little or no inference is required ⟨her *manifest* joy upon receiving the award⟩.

Patent applies to a cause, effect, or significant feature that is clear and unmistakable once attention has been directed to it ⟨*patent* defects in the item when sold⟩.

Distinct implies such sharpness of outline or definition that no unusual effort to see or hear or comprehend is required ⟨my offer met with a *distinct* refusal⟩.

Obvious implies such ease in discovering or accounting for that it often suggests conspicuousness or little need for perspicacity in the observer ⟨the motives are *obvious* to all but the most obtuse⟩.

Apparent is very close to *evident* except that it may imply more conscious exercise of inference ⟨the absurdity of the charge is *apparent* to all who know him⟩.

Plain implies lack of intricacy, complexity, or elaboration ⟨her feelings about him are quite *plain*⟩.

Clear implies an absence of anything that confuses the mind or obscures the pattern ⟨it's *clear* now what's been going on⟩.

EXCEED surpass, transcend, excel, outdo, outstrip mean to go or be beyond a stated or implied limit, measure, or degree.

Exceed implies going beyond a limit set by authority or established by custom or by prior achievement ⟨*exceed* the speed limit⟩.

Surpass suggests superiority in quality, merit, or skill ⟨the book *surpassed* our expectations⟩.

Transcend implies a rising or extending notably above or beyond ordinary limits ⟨*transcended* the values of their culture⟩.

Excel implies preeminence in achievement or quality and may suggest superiority to all others ⟨*excels* in mathematics⟩.

Outdo applies to a bettering or exceeding what has been done before ⟨*outdid* herself this time⟩.

Outstrip suggests surpassing in a race or competition ⟨*outstripped* other firms in selling the new plastic⟩.

EXCESSIVE, immoderate, inordinate, extravagant, exorbitant, extreme mean going beyond a normal limit.

Excessive implies an amount or degree too great to be reasonable or acceptable ⟨punishment that was deemed *excessive*⟩.

Immoderate implies lack of desirable or necessary restraint ⟨an *immoderate* amount of time spent on grooming⟩.

Inordinate implies an exceeding of the limits dictated by reason or good judgment ⟨an *inordinate* portion of their budget goes to entertainment⟩.

Extravagant implies an indifference to restraints imposed by truth, prudence, or good taste ⟨*extravagant* claims for the product⟩.

Exorbitant implies a departure from accepted standards

regarding amount or degree ⟨a menu with *exorbitant* prices⟩.

Extreme may imply an approach to the farthest limit possible or conceivable but commonly means only to a notably high degree ⟨views concerning marriage that are a bit *extreme*⟩.

EXCLUDE, debar, eliminate, suspend mean to shut or put out.

Exclude implies keeping out what is already outside ⟨children under 17 are *excluded* from seeing the movie⟩.

Debar implies setting up a barrier that is effectual in excluding a person or class from what is open or accessible to others ⟨arbitrary standards that effectively *debar* most female candidates⟩.

Eliminate implies the getting rid of what is already within esp. as a constituent part or element ⟨a company's plans to *eliminate* a fourth of its workforce⟩.

Suspend implies temporary and commonly disciplinary removal from membership in a school or organization ⟨a student *suspended* for possession of drugs⟩.

EXCULPATE, absolve, exonerate, acquit, vindicate mean to free from a charge.

Exculpate implies a clearing from blame or fault often in a matter of small importance ⟨I cannot *exculpate* myself of the charge of overenthusiasm⟩.

Absolve implies a release either from an obligation that binds the conscience or from the consequences of disobeying the law or committing a sin ⟨*absolved* the subject from his oath of allegiance⟩.

Exonerate implies a complete clearance from an accusation or charge and from any attendant suspicion of blame or guilt ⟨a committee *exonerated* the governor of bribery⟩.

Acquit implies a formal decision in one's favor with respect to a definite charge ⟨*acquitted* by a jury of murder⟩.

Vindicate may refer to things as well as persons that have been subjected to critical attack or imputation of guilt. weakness. or folly. and implies a clearing effected by proving the unfairness of such criticism or blame ⟨an investigation *vindicated* the senator on all counts⟩.

EXCUSE *vb* **Excuse, condone, pardon, forgive** mean to exact neither punishment nor redress.

Excuse may refer to specific acts esp. in social or conventional situations or to the person responsible for these ⟨*excuse* an interruption⟩ ⟨*excused* her for interrupting⟩. Often the term implies extenuating circumstances ⟨injustice *excuses* strong responses⟩.

Condone implies that one overlooks without censure behavior (as dishonesty or violence) that involves a serious breach of a moral. ethical. or legal code. and the term may refer to the behavior or to the agent responsible for it ⟨a society that *condones* alcohol but not narcotics⟩.

Pardon implies that one remits a penalty due for an admitted or established offense ⟨*pardon* a criminal⟩ ⟨*pardon* the noisy enthusiasm of a child⟩.

Forgive implies that one gives up all claim to requital and to resentment or vengeful feelings ⟨could not *forgive* their rudeness⟩.

EXECRATE, curse, damn, anathematize mean to denounce violently.

Execrate implies intense loathing and usu. passionate fury ⟨*execrated* the men who had molested his family⟩.

Curse and **damn** imply angry denunciation by blasphemous oaths or profane imprecations ⟨a drunken wino *cursing* passersby⟩ ⟨*damns* the city council for not anticipating the problem⟩.

Anathematize implies solemn denunciation of an evil or an injustice ⟨preachers *anathematizing* pornography⟩.

EXECUTE, administer mean to carry out the declared intent of another.

Execute stresses the enforcing of the specific provisions of a law, will, commission, or a command ⟨charged with failing to *execute* the order⟩.

Administer implies the continuing exercise of delegated authority in pursuance of only generally indicated goals rather than specif. prescribed means of attaining them ⟨the agency in charge of *administering* Indian affairs⟩.

See in addition KILL, PERFORM.

EXPAND, amplify, swell, distend, inflate, dilate mean to increase in size or volume.

Expand may apply whether the increase comes from within or without and regardless of manner (as growth, unfolding, addition of parts) ⟨our business has *expanded* with every passing year⟩.

Amplify implies the extension or enlargement of something inadequate ⟨*amplify* the statement with some details⟩.

Swell implies gradual expansion beyond a thing's original or normal limits ⟨the bureaucracy *swelled* to unmanageable proportions⟩.

Distend implies outward extension caused by pressure from within ⟨a stomach *distended* by gas⟩.

Inflate implies expanding by introduction of air or something insubstantial and suggests a resulting vulnerability and liability to sudden collapse ⟨*inflate* a balloon⟩ ⟨an *inflated* ego⟩.

Dilate applies esp. to expansion of circumference ⟨dim light causes the pupils of the eyes to *dilate*⟩.

EXPECT, hope, look mean to await some occurrence or outcome.

Expect implies a high degree of certainty and usu. involves the idea of preparing or envisioning ⟨I *expect* to be finished by Tuesday⟩.

Hope implies little certainty but suggests confidence or assurance in the possibility that what one desires or longs for will happen ⟨she *hopes* to find a job soon⟩.

Look suggests a degree of expectancy and watchfulness rather than confidence or certainty ⟨we *look* to the day when peace will be universal⟩.

EXPEDIENT *adj* **Expedient, politic, advisable** mean dictated by practical or prudent motives.

Expedient usu. implies what is immediately advantageous without regard for ethics or consistent principles ⟨a truce was the *expedient* answer⟩.

Politic stresses judiciousness and tactical value but usu. implies some lack of candor or sincerity ⟨converted to Catholicism when it was *politic* to do so⟩.

Advisable applies to what is practical, prudent, or advantageous but lacks the derogatory implication of *expedient* and *politic* ⟨it's *advisable* to say nothing at all⟩.

EXPLAIN, expound, explicate, elucidate, interpret mean to make something clear or understandable.

Explain implies a making plain or intelligible what is not immediately obvious or entirely known ⟨the doctor *explained* what the operation would entail⟩.

Expound implies a careful often elaborate explanation ⟨a professor *expounding* the theory of relativity⟩.

Explicate adds the idea of a developed or detailed analysis ⟨a passage that critics have been inspired to *explicate* at length⟩.

Elucidate stresses the throwing of light upon as by offering details or motives previously obscure or only implicit ⟨a newspaper report that tries to *elucidate* the reasons for the crime⟩.

Interpret adds to *explain* the need for imagination or sympathy or special knowledge in dealing with something ⟨*interprets* the play as an allegory about good and evil⟩.

EXPLICIT, definite, express, specific mean perfectly clear in meaning.

Explicit implies such verbal plainness and distinctness that there is no need for inference and no room for difficulty in understanding 〈the dress code is very *explicit*〉.

Definite stresses precise, clear statement or arrangement that leaves no doubt or indecision 〈the law is *definite* regarding such cases〉.

Express implies both explicitness and direct and positive utterance 〈her *express* wish was to be cremated〉.

Specific applies to what is precisely and fully treated in detail or particular 〈two *specific* criticisms of the proposal〉.

EXPRESS *vb* **Express, vent, utter, voice, broach, air** mean to make known what one thinks or feels.

Express suggests an impulse to reveal in words, gestures, or actions, or through what one creates or produces 〈paintings that *express* the artist's loneliness〉.

Vent stresses a strong inner compulsion to express esp. in words 〈her stories *vent* the frustrations of black women〉.

Utter implies the use of the voice not necessarily in articulate speech 〈would occasionally *utter* words of encouragement〉.

Voice does not necessarily imply vocal utterance but does imply expression or formulation in words 〈an editorial *voicing* the concerns of many〉.

Broach adds the·implication of disclosing for the first time something long thought over or reserved for a suitable occasion 〈*broached* the subject of a divorce〉.

Air implies an exposing or parading of one's views often in order to gain relief or sympathy or attention 〈cabinet members publicly *airing* their differences〉.

EXTEMPORANEOUS, improvised, impromptu, offhand, unpremeditated mean done or devised on the spur of the moment and not beforehand.

Extemporaneous stresses the demands imposed by the occasion or situation and may imply a certain sketchiness or roughness 〈an *extemporaneous* shelter prompted by the sudden storm〉.

Improvised implies the constructing or devising of something without advance knowledge, thought, or preparation and often without the proper equipment ⟨*improvised* a barbecue pit at the campground⟩.

Impromptu stresses the immediacy and the spontaneity of the thing composed or devised ⟨an *impromptu* speech at an awards ceremony⟩.

Offhand strongly implies casualness, carelessness, or indifference ⟨his *offhand* remarks often got him into trouble⟩.

Unpremeditated suggests some strong often suddenly provoked emotion that impels one to action ⟨*unpremeditated* murder⟩.

EXTEND, lengthen, prolong, protract mean to draw out or add to so as to increase in length.

Extend and **lengthen** imply a drawing out in space or time but *extend* may also imply increase in width, scope, area, or range ⟨*extend* a vacation⟩ ⟨*extend* welfare services⟩ ⟨*lengthen* a skirt⟩ ⟨*lengthen* the workweek⟩.

Prolong suggests chiefly increase in duration esp. beyond usual limits ⟨*prolonged* illness⟩.

Protract adds to *prolong* implications of needlessness, vexation, or indefiniteness ⟨*protracted* litigation⟩.

EXTERMINATE, extirpate, eradicate, uproot mean to effect the destruction or abolition of something.

Exterminate implies complete and immediate extinction by killing off all individuals ⟨failed attempts to *exterminate* the mosquitoes⟩.

Extirpate implies extinction of a race, family, species, or sometimes an idea or doctrine by destruction or removal of its means of propagation ⟨many species have been *extirpated* from the area⟩.

Eradicate implies the driving out or elimination of something that has established itself ⟨polio had virtually been *eradicated*⟩.

Uproot implies a forcible or violent removal and stresses displacement or dislodgment rather than immediate destruction ⟨the war had *uprooted* thousands⟩.

EXTRICATE, disentangle, untangle, disencumber, disembarrass mean to free from what binds or holds back.

Extricate implies the use of care or ingenuity in freeing from a difficult position or situation ⟨a knack for *extricating* himself from damaging political rows⟩.

Disentangle and **untangle** suggest painstaking separation of a thing from other things ⟨a biography that *disentangles* the myth from the man⟩ ⟨*untangled* a web of deceit⟩.

Disencumber implies a release from something that clogs or weighs down ⟨a science article *disencumbered* of scientific jargon⟩.

Disembarrass suggests a release from something that impedes or hinders ⟨*disembarrassed* herself of her frivolous companions⟩.

EXTRINSIC, extraneous, foreign, alien mean external to a thing, its essential nature, or its original character.

Extrinsic applies to what is distinctly outside the thing in question or is not contained in or derived from its essential nature ⟨sentimental attachment that is *extrinsic* to the house's market value⟩.

Extraneous applies to what is on or comes from the outside and may or may not be capable of becoming an essential part ⟨*extraneous* arguments that obscure the real issue⟩.

Foreign applies to what is so different as to be rejected or repelled or, if admitted, to be incapable of becoming identified or assimilated by the thing in question ⟨inflammation resulting from a *foreign* body in the eye⟩.

Alien is stronger than *foreign* in suggesting opposition, repugnance, or irreconcilability ⟨a practice that is totally *alien* to our democratic principles⟩.

F

FACE, countenance, visage, physiognomy mean the front part of the head from forehead to chin.

Face is the simple, direct, and also the inclusive term ⟨a strikingly handsome *face*⟩.

Countenance applies to a face as seen and as revealing a mood or attitude ⟨the benign *countenance* of my grandmother⟩.

Visage suggests attention to shape and proportions and sometimes expression ⟨a penetrating gaze and an aquiline nose gave him a birdlike *visage*⟩.

Physiognomy suggests attention to the contours and characteristic expression as indicative of race, temperament, or qualities of mind or character ⟨a youth with the *physiognomy* of a warrior⟩.

FAIR, just, equitable, impartial, unbiased, dispassionate, objective mean free from favor toward either or any side.

Fair implies an elimination of one's own feelings, prejudices, and desires so as to achieve a proper balance of conflicting interests ⟨a *fair* decision by a judge⟩.

Just implies an exact following of a standard of what is right and proper ⟨a *just* settlement of territorial claims⟩.

Equitable implies a less rigorous standard than *just* and usu. suggests equal treatment of all concerned ⟨provides for the *equitable* distribution of his property⟩.

Impartial stresses an absence of favor or prejudice ⟨arbitration by an *impartial* third party⟩.

Unbiased implies even more strongly an absence of all prejudice ⟨your *unbiased* opinion of the whole affair⟩.

Dispassionate suggests freedom from the influence of strong feeling and often implies cool or even cold judgment ⟨a *dispassionate* summation of the facts⟩.

Objective stresses a tendency to view events or persons as

apart from oneself and one's own interest or feelings ⟨it's impossible for me to be *objective* about my own child⟩.
See in addition BEAUTIFUL.

FAITHFUL, loyal, constant, staunch, steadfast, resolute mean firm in adherence to whatever one owes allegiance.
  Faithful implies unswerving adherence to a person or thing or to the oath or promise by which a tie was contracted ⟨*faithful* to her promise⟩.
  Loyal implies a firm resistance to any temptation to desert or betray ⟨the army remained *loyal* to the czar⟩.
  Constant stresses continuing firmness of emotional attachment without necessarily implying strict obedience to promises or vows ⟨*constant* lovers⟩.
  Staunch suggests fortitude and resolution in adherence and imperviousness to influences that would weaken it ⟨a *staunch* defender of free speech⟩.
  Steadfast implies a steady and unwavering course in love, allegiance, or conviction ⟨*steadfast* in their support of democratic principles⟩.
  Resolute implies firm determination to adhere to a cause or purpose ⟨*resolute* in his determination to see justice done⟩.

FAITHLESS, false, disloyal, traitorous, treacherous, perfidious mean untrue to what should command one's fidelity or allegiance.
  Faithless applies to any failure to keep a promise or pledge or any breach of allegiance or loyalty ⟨*faithless* allies refused to support the sanctions⟩.
  False stresses the fact of failing to be true in any manner ranging from fickleness to cold treachery ⟨betrayed by *false* friends⟩.
  Disloyal implies a lack of complete faithfulness in thought or words or actions to a friend, cause, leader, or country ⟨accused the hostages of being *disloyal* to their country⟩.
  Traitorous implies either actual treason or a serious betrayal of trust ⟨*traitorous* acts punishable by death⟩.

Treacherous implies readiness to betray trust or confidence ⟨the victim of *treacherous* allies⟩.

Perfidious adds to *faithless* the implication of an incapacity for fidelity or reliability ⟨repeated and *perfidious* violations of the treaty⟩.

FAMILIAR, intimate mean closely acquainted.

Familiar suggests the ease, informality, absence of reserve or constraint natural among members of a family or acquaintances of long standing ⟨resent being addressed by strangers in a *familiar* tone⟩.

Intimate stresses the closeness and intensity rather than the mere frequency of personal association and suggests either deep mutual understanding or the sharing of deeply personal thoughts and feelings ⟨their love letters became increasingly *intimate*⟩.

See in addition COMMON.

FAMOUS, renowned, celebrated, noted, notorious, distinguished, eminent, illustrious mean known far and wide.

Famous implies little more than the fact of being, sometimes briefly, widely and popularly known ⟨a *famous* television actress⟩.

Renowned implies more glory and acclamation ⟨one of the most *renowned* figures in sports history⟩.

Celebrated implies notice and attention esp. in print ⟨the most *celebrated* beauty of her day⟩.

Noted suggests well-deserved public attention ⟨the *noted* mystery writer⟩.

Notorious frequently adds to *famous* an implication of questionableness or evil ⟨a *notorious* gangster⟩.

Distinguished implies acknowledged excellence or superiority ⟨a *distinguished* scientist who recently won the Nobel Prize⟩.

Eminent implies even greater conspicuousness for outstanding quality or character ⟨a conference of the country's most *eminent* writers⟩.

Illustrious stresses enduring honor and glory attached to a deed or person ⟨the *illustrious* deeds of national heroes⟩.

FANTASTIC, bizarre, grotesque mean conceived, made, or carried out without adherence to truth or reality.

Fantastic may connote unrestrained extravagance in conception or merely ingenuity of decorative invention ⟨*fantastic* theories about the origins of life⟩.

Bizarre applies to the sensationally queer or strange and implies violence of contrast or incongruity of combination ⟨a *bizarre* pseudo-medieval castle⟩.

Grotesque may apply to what is conventionally ugly but artistically effective or it may connote ludicrous awkwardness or incongruity often with sinister or tragic overtones ⟨*grotesque* statues adorn the cathedral⟩ ⟨*grotesque* attempts at operatic roles⟩.

See in addition IMAGINARY.

FASHION *n* Fashion, style, mode, vogue, fad, rage, craze mean the usage accepted by those who want to be up-to-date.

Fashion is the most general term and applies to any way of dressing, behaving, writing, or performing that is favored at any one time or place ⟨the current *fashion* for Russian ballet dancers⟩.

Style often implies a distinctive fashion adopted by people of wealth or taste ⟨a media mogul used to traveling in *style*⟩.

Mode suggests the fashion of the moment among those anxious to appear elegant and sophisticated ⟨sleek, tanned bodies are the *mode* at such resorts⟩.

Vogue stresses the wide acceptance of a fashion ⟨a novelist who is no longer much in *vogue*⟩.

Fad suggests caprice in taking up or in dropping a fashion ⟨nothing is more dated than last year's *fad*⟩.

Rage and **craze** stress intense enthusiasm in adopting a fad ⟨Cajun food was quite the *rage*⟩ ⟨a sport that is more than a passing *craze*⟩.

See in addition METHOD.

FAST, rapid, swift, fleet, quick, speedy, hasty, expeditious mean moving, proceeding, or acting with celerity.

Fast and **rapid** are very close in meaning, but *fast* applies particularly to the thing that moves ⟨*fast* horse⟩ and *rapid* to the movement itself ⟨*rapid* current⟩.

Swift suggests great rapidity coupled with ease of movement ⟨returned the ball with one *swift* stroke⟩.

Fleet adds the implication of lightness and nimbleness ⟨*fleet* runners⟩.

Quick suggests promptness and the taking of little time ⟨a *quick* wit⟩.

Speedy implies quickness of successful accomplishment ⟨*speedy* delivery of the mail⟩ and may also suggest unusual velocity.

Hasty suggests hurry and precipitousness and often connotes carelessness ⟨a *hasty* inspection⟩.

Expeditious suggests efficiency together with rapidity of accomplishment ⟨an *expeditious* processing of a merchandise order⟩.

FASTEN, fix, attach, affix mean to make something stay firmly in place.

Fasten implies an action such as tying, buttoning, nailing, locking, or otherwise securing ⟨*fastened* the horse to a post⟩.

Fix usu. implies a driving in, implanting, or embedding ⟨*fix* the stake so that it remains upright⟩.

Attach suggests a connecting or uniting by a bond, link, or tie in order to keep things together ⟨*attach* the W-2 form here⟩.

Affix implies an imposing of one thing on another by gluing, impressing, or nailing ⟨*affix* your address label here⟩.

FATE, destiny, lot, portion, doom mean a predetermined state or end.

Fate implies an inevitable and usu. an adverse outcome ⟨the *fate* of the mariners remains unknown⟩.

Destiny implies something foreordained and often suggests a great or noble course or end ⟨our country's *destiny*⟩.

Lot and **portion** imply a distribution by fate or destiny, *lot* suggesting blind chance ⟨it was her *lot* to die childless⟩, and *portion* implying the apportioning of good and evil ⟨the *portion* that has been meted out to me⟩.

Doom distinctly implies a grim or calamitous fate ⟨if the rebellion fails, our *doom* is certain⟩.

FAULT, failing, frailty, foible, vice mean an imperfection or weakness of character.

Fault implies a failure, not necessarily culpable, to reach some standard of perfection in disposition, action, or habit ⟨a woman of many virtues and few *faults*⟩.

Failing suggests a minor shortcoming in character ⟨procrastination is one of my *failings*⟩.

Frailty implies a general or chronic proneness to yield to temptation ⟨a fondness for chocolate is the most human of *frailties*⟩.

Foible applies to a harmless or endearing weakness or idiosyncrasy ⟨*foibles* that make him all the more lovable⟩.

Vice can be a general term for any imperfection or weakness, but it often suggests violation of a moral code or the giving of offense to the moral sensibilities of others ⟨gambling and drunkenness were the least of his *vices*⟩.

FAVORABLE, auspicious, propitious mean pointing toward a happy outcome.

Favorable implies that the persons involved are approving or helpful or that the circumstances are advantageous ⟨*favorable* weather conditions for a rocket launch⟩.

Auspicious applies to something taken as a sign or omen promising success before or at the beginning of an event ⟨an *auspicious* beginning for a great partnership⟩.

Propitious may also apply to beginnings but often implies a continuing favorable condition ⟨the time was not *propitious* for starting a new business⟩.

FAWN, toady, truckle, cringe, cower mean to behave abjectly before a superior.

Fawn implies seeking favor by servile flattery or exaggerated attention ⟨waiters *fawning* over a celebrity⟩.

Toady suggests the attempt to ingratiate oneself by an abjectly menial or subservient attitude ⟨never misses an opportunity to *toady* to his boss⟩.

Truckle implies the subordination of oneself and one's desires or judgment to those of a superior ⟨the rich are used to seeing others *truckle*⟩.

Cringe suggests a bowing or shrinking in fear or servility ⟨*cringing* before every supposed superior⟩.

Cower suggests a display of abject fear in the company of threatening or domineering people ⟨as an adult he still *cowered* before his father⟩.

FEAR, dread, fright, alarm, panic, terror, trepidation mean painful agitation in the presence or anticipation of danger.

Fear is the most general term and implies anxiety and usu. loss of courage ⟨*fear* of the unknown⟩.

Dread usu. adds the idea of intense reluctance to face or meet a person or situation and suggests aversion as well as anxiety ⟨the *dread* of having to face her mother⟩.

Fright implies the shock of sudden, startling fear ⟨imagine our *fright* at being awakened by screams⟩.

Alarm suggests a sudden and intense awareness of immediate danger ⟨view the situation with *alarm*⟩.

Panic implies unreasoning and overmastering fear causing hysterical activity ⟨news of the invasion caused great *panic*⟩.

Terror implies the most extreme degree of fear ⟨immobilized with *terror*⟩.

Trepidation adds to *dread* the implications of timidity, trembling, and hesitation ⟨raised the subject of marriage with some *trepidation*⟩.

FEARFUL, apprehensive, afraid mean disturbed by fear.

Fearful implies often a timorous or worrying temperament ⟨the child is *fearful* of loud noises⟩.

Apprehensive suggests a state of mind and implies a premonition of evil or danger ⟨*apprehensive* that war would break out⟩.

Afraid often suggests weakness or cowardice and regularly implies inhibition of action or utterance ⟨*afraid* to speak the truth⟩.

FEAT, exploit, achievement mean a remarkable deed.

Feat implies strength or dexterity or daring ⟨the *feat* of crossing the Atlantic in a balloon⟩.

Exploit suggests an adventurous or heroic act ⟨his celebrated *exploits* as a spy⟩.

Achievement implies hard-won success in the face of difficulty or opposition ⟨honored for her *achievements* as a chemist⟩.

FEELING, emotion, affection, sentiment, passion mean a subjective response to a person, thing, or situation.

Feeling denotes any partly mental, partly physical response marked by pleasure, pain, attraction, or repulsion; it may suggest the mere existence of a response but imply nothing about the nature or intensity of it ⟨whatever *feelings* I had for her are gone⟩.

Emotion carries a strong implication of excitement or agitation but, like *feeling*, encompasses both positive and negative responses ⟨a play in which the *emotions* are real⟩.

Affection applies to feelings that are also inclinations or likings ⟨memoirs filled with *affection* and understanding⟩.

Sentiment implies an emotion inspired by an idea ⟨her feminist *sentiments* are well known⟩.

Passion suggests a powerful or controlling emotion ⟨revenge became his ruling passion⟩.

See in addition ATMOSPHERE.

FERTILE, fecund, fruitful, prolific mean producing or capable of producing offspring or fruit.

Fertile implies the power to reproduce in kind or to assist in reproduction and growth ⟨*fertile* soil⟩; applied figuratively, it suggests readiness of invention and development ⟨a most *fertile* imagination⟩.

Fecund emphasizes abundance or rapidity in bearing fruit or offspring ⟨came from a remarkably *fecund* family⟩.

Fruitful adds to *fertile* and *fecund* the implication of desirable or useful results ⟨undertook *fruitful* research in virology⟩.

Prolific stresses rapidity of spreading or multiplying by or as if by natural reproduction ⟨one of the most *prolific* writers of science fiction⟩.

FICTITIOUS, fabulous, legendary, mythical, apocryphal mean having the nature of something imagined or invented.

Fictitious implies fabrication and suggests artificiality or contrivance more than deliberate falsification or deception ⟨all names used in the broadcast are *fictitious*⟩.

Fabulous stresses the marvelous or incredible character of something without necessarily implying impossibility or actual nonexistence ⟨a land of *fabulous* riches⟩.

Legendary suggests the elaboration of invented details and distortion of historical facts produced by popular tradition ⟨the *legendary* courtship of Miles Standish⟩.

Mythical implies a purely fanciful explanation of facts or the creation of beings and events out of the imagination ⟨*mythical* creatures such as centaurs⟩.

Apocryphal implies an unknown or dubious source or origin or may imply that the thing itself is dubious or inaccurate ⟨a book that repeats many *apocryphal* stories⟩.

FIDELITY, allegiance, fealty, loyalty, devotion, piety mean faithfulness to something to which one is bound by pledge or duty.

Fidelity implies strict and continuing faithfulness to an obligation, trust, or duty ⟨*fidelity* in the performance of one's duties⟩.

Allegiance suggests an adherence like that of a citizen to his country ⟨a politician who owes *allegiance* to no special interest⟩.

Fealty implies a fidelity acknowledged by the individual and as compelling as a sworn vow ⟨a critic's only *fealty* is to truth⟩.

Loyalty implies a faithfulness that is steadfast in the face of any temptation to renounce, desert, or betray ⟨valued the *loyalty* of his friends⟩.

Devotion stresses zeal and service amounting to self-dedication ⟨a painter's *devotion* to her artistic vision⟩.

Piety stresses fidelity to obligations regarded as natural and fundamental ⟨filial *piety* demands that I visit my parents⟩.

FIERCE, ferocious, barbarous, savage, cruel mean showing fury or malignity in looks or actions.

Fierce applies to humans and animals that inspire terror because of their wild and menacing aspect or fury in attack ⟨*fierce* tribes still inhabit the rain forest⟩.

Ferocious implies extreme fierceness and unrestrained violence and brutality ⟨signs warned of a *ferocious* dog⟩.

Barbarous implies a ferocity or mercilessness regarded as unworthy of civilized people ⟨the *barbarous* treatment of prisoners⟩.

Savage implies the absence of inhibitions restraining civilized people filled with rage, lust, or other violent passion ⟨*savage* reviews of the new play⟩.

Cruel implies indifference to suffering and even positive pleasure in inflicting it ⟨the *cruel* jokes of schoolboys⟩.

FINANCIAL, monetary, pecuniary, fiscal mean of or relating to money.

Financial implies money matters conducted on a large scale or involving some degree of complexity ⟨a business deal secured through a complex *financial* arrangement⟩.

Monetary refers to money as coined, distributed, or circulating ⟨the country's basic *monetary* unit is the peso⟩.

Pecuniary implies reference to money matters affecting the individual ⟨a struggling single mother constantly in *pecuniary* difficulties⟩.

Fiscal refers to money as providing revenue for the state or to the financial affairs of an institution or corporation ⟨the *fiscal* year ends on June 30⟩.

FIRM, hard, solid mean having a texture or consistency that resists deformation.

Firm implies such compactness and coherence and often elasticity of substance as to resist pulling, distorting, or pressing ⟨a *firm* mattress with good back support⟩.

Hard implies impenetrability and nearly complete but inelastic resistance to pressure or tension ⟨a diamond is one of the *hardest* substances known⟩.

Solid implies a texture of uniform density so as to be not only firm but heavy ⟨*solid* furniture that will last⟩.

FIT, suitable, meet, proper, appropriate, fitting, apt, happy, felicitous mean right with respect to some end, need, use, or circumstance.

Fit stresses adaptability and sometimes special readiness for use or action ⟨the vessel is now *fit* for service⟩.

Suitable implies an answering to requirements or demands ⟨shopped for clothes *suitable* for camping⟩.

Meet suggests a just proportioning ⟨a tip that was *meet* for the services rendered⟩.

Proper suggests a suitability through essential nature or accordance with custom ⟨the *proper* role of the First Lady⟩.

Appropriate implies eminent or distinctive fitness ⟨a golf bag is an *appropriate* gift for a golfer⟩.

Fitting implies harmony of mood or tone ⟨ *fitting* subjects for dinner table conversation⟩.

Apt connotes a fitness marked by nicety and discrimination ⟨a speech laced with some *apt* quotations⟩.

Happy suggests what is effectively or successfully appropriate ⟨a *happy* choice of words⟩.

Felicitous suggests an aptness that is opportune, telling, or graceful ⟨a *felicitous* note of apology⟩.

FITFUL, spasmodic, convulsive mean lacking steadiness or regularity in movement.

Fitful implies intermittence, a succession of starts and stops or risings and fallings ⟨the *fitful* beginnings of a new enterprise⟩.

Spasmodic adds to *fitful* the implication of violent activity alternating with inactivity ⟨*spasmodic* trading on the stock exchange⟩.

Convulsive suggests the breaking of regularity or quiet by uncontrolled movement ⟨the *convulsive* shocks of the earthquake⟩.

FLAGRANT, glaring, gross, rank mean conspicuously bad or objectionable.

Flagrant applies usu. to offenses or errors so bad that they can neither escape notice nor be condoned ⟨*flagrant* abuse of the office of president⟩.

Glaring implies painful or damaging obtrusiveness of something that is conspicuously wrong, faulty, or improper ⟨*glaring* errors in judgment⟩.

Gross implies the exceeding of reasonable or excusable limits ⟨*gross* carelessness on your part⟩.

Rank applies to what is openly and extremely objectionable and utterly condemned ⟨it's *rank* heresy to say that⟩.

FLASH, gleam, glance, glint, sparkle, glitter, glisten, glimmer, shimmer mean to send forth light.

Flash implies a sudden and transient outburst of bright light ⟨lightning *flashed*⟩.

Gleam suggests a steady light seen through an obscuring medium or against a dark background ⟨the lights of the town *gleamed* in the valley below⟩.

Glance suggests a bright darting light reflected from a quickly moving surface ⟨sunlight *glanced* off the hull of the boat⟩.

Glint implies a cold glancing light ⟨steel bars *glinted* in the moonlight⟩.

Sparkle suggests innumerable moving points of bright light ⟨the *sparkling* waters of the gulf⟩.

Glitter connotes a brilliant sparkling or gleaming ⟨*glittering* diamonds⟩.

Glisten applies to the soft sparkle from a wet or oily surface ⟨rain-drenched sidewalks *glistened* under the streetlights⟩.

Glimmer suggests a faint or wavering gleam ⟨a lone light *glimmered* in the distance⟩.

Shimmer implies a soft tremulous gleaming or a blurred reflection ⟨a *shimmering* satin dress⟩.

FOLLOW, succeed, ensue, supervene mean to come after something or someone.

Follow may apply to a coming after in time, position, or logical sequence ⟨speeches *followed* the dinner⟩.

Succeed implies a coming after immediately in a sequence determined by natural order, inheritance, election, or laws of rank ⟨she *succeeded* her father as head of the business⟩.

Ensue commonly suggests a logical consequence or naturally expected development ⟨after the lecture, a general discussion *ensued*⟩.

Supervene suggests the following or beginning of something unforeseen or unpredictable ⟨events *supervened* that brought tragedy into his life⟩.

See in addition CHASE.

FOLLOWER, adherent, disciple, partisan mean one who attaches himself to another.

Follower may apply to a person who attaches himself either to the person or beliefs of another ⟨an evangelist and his *followers*⟩.

Adherent suggests a close and persistent attachment ⟨*adherents* to Communism⟩.

Disciple implies a devoted allegiance to the teachings of one chosen as a master ⟨*disciples* of Gandhi⟩.

Partisan suggests a zealous often prejudiced attachment ⟨*partisans* of the President⟩.

FORBEARING, tolerant, lenient, indulgent mean not inclined to be severe or rigorous.

Forbearing implies patience under provocation and deliberate abstention from harsh judgment, punishment, or vengeance ⟨the most *forbearing* of music teachers⟩.

Tolerant implies a freedom from bias or dogmatism and a reluctance to judge others esp. harshly ⟨a very *tolerant* attitude towards dissenters⟩.

Lenient implies softness of temperament and a relaxation of discipline ⟨*lenient* parents pay for it later⟩.

Indulgent implies compliancy, mercifulness, and a willingness to make concessions ⟨a wife *indulgent* of her husband's shortcomings⟩.

FORBID, prohibit, interdict, inhibit mean to debar one from doing something or to order that something not be done.

Forbid implies that the order is from one in authority and that obedience is expected ⟨smoking is *forbidden* in the building⟩.

Prohibit suggests the issuing of laws, statutes, or regulations ⟨*prohibited* the manufacture and sale of unapproved drugs⟩.

Interdict implies prohibition by civil or ecclesiastical authority usu. for a given time or a declared purpose ⟨practices *interdicted* by the church⟩.

Inhibit implies the imposition of restraints or restrictions that amount to prohibitions, not only by authority but also by the exigencies of the time or situation ⟨laws that *inhibit* the growth of free trade⟩.

FORCE *vb* **Force, compel, coerce, constrain, oblige** mean to make someone or something yield.

Force is the general term and implies the overcoming of resistance by the exertion of strength, power, weight, stress, or duress ⟨*forced* the prisoner to sign the confession⟩.

Compel typically requires a personal object and suggests the working of an irresistible force ⟨all workers are *compelled* to pay taxes⟩.

Coerce suggests overcoming resistance or unwillingness by actual or threatened violence or pressure ⟨*coerced* by gangsters into selling his business⟩.

Constrain suggests the effect of a force or circumstance that limits freedom of action or choice ⟨*constrained* by my conscience to see that justice was done⟩.

Oblige implies the constraint of necessity, law, or duty ⟨I am *obliged* to inform you of your rights⟩.

FORERUNNER, precursor, harbinger, herald mean one who goes before or announces the coming of another.

Forerunner is applicable to anything that serves as a sign or presage ⟨the international incident was a *forerunner* to war⟩.

Precursor applies to a person or thing paving the way for the success or accomplishment of another ⟨18th century poets who were *precursors* of the Romantics⟩.

Harbinger and **herald** both apply, chiefly figuratively, to one that proclaims or announces the coming or arrival of a notable event ⟨an early victory that was the *harbinger* of a winning season⟩ ⟨the *herald* of a new age in medical science⟩.

FORESEE, foreknow, divine, apprehend, anticipate mean to know beforehand.

Foresee implies nothing about how the knowledge is derived and may apply to ordinary reasoning and experience ⟨no one could *foresee* the economic crisis⟩.

Foreknow usu. implies supernatural assistance, as through revelation ⟨if only we could *foreknow* our own destinies⟩.

Divine adds to *foresee* the suggestion of exceptional wisdom or discernment ⟨a European traveler who *divined* the course of American destiny⟩.

Apprehend implies foresight mingled with uncertainty, anxiety, or dread ⟨*apprehended* that his odd behavior was a sign of a troubled soul⟩.

Anticipate implies taking action about or responding emotionally to something before it happens ⟨the servants *anticipated* our every need⟩.

FORETELL, predict, forecast, prophesy, prognosticate mean to tell beforehand.

Foretell applies to the telling of the coming of a future event by any procedure or any source of information ⟨seers *foretold* of calamitous events⟩.

Predict commonly implies inference from facts or accepted laws of nature ⟨astronomers *predicted* the return of the comet⟩.

Forecast adds the implication of anticipating eventualities and differs from *predict* in being usu. concerned with probabilities rather than certainties ⟨*forecasted* a snowfall of six inches⟩.

Prophesy connotes inspired or mystic knowledge of the future esp. as the fulfilling of divine threats or promises ⟨preachers *prophesying* a day of divine retribution⟩.

Prognosticate suggests the learned or skilled interpretation of signs or symptoms ⟨economists are *prognosticating* a slow recovery⟩.

FORGETFUL, oblivious, unmindful mean losing one's memory or knowledge of something.

Forgetful usu. implies a heedless or negligent habit of failing to keep in mind ⟨I had been *forgetful* of my duties as host⟩.

Oblivious suggests a failure to notice or remember due to external causes or conditions or to a determination to ignore ⟨lost in thought, *oblivious* to the rushing crowd around her⟩.

Unmindful may suggest inattention and heedlessness or a deliberate ignoring ⟨a crusading reformer who was *unmindful* of his family's needs⟩.

FORM *n* **Form, figure, shape, conformation, configuration** mean outward appearance.

Form usu. suggests reference to both internal structure and external outline and often the principle that gives unity to the whole ⟨an architect who appreciates the interplay of *forms*⟩.

Figure applies chiefly to the form as determined by bounding or enclosing lines ⟨cutting doll *figures* out of paper⟩.

Shape like *figure*, suggests an outline but carries a stronger implication of the enclosed body or mass ⟨the *shape* of the monument was pyramidal⟩.

Conformation implies structure composed of related parts ⟨a body *conformation* that is well-proportioned and symmetrical⟩.

Configuration refers to the disposition and arrangement of component parts ⟨modular furniture allows for a number of *configurations*⟩.

FRAGILE, frangible, brittle, crisp, friable mean breaking easily.

Fragile implies extreme delicacy of material or construction and need for careful handling ⟨a *fragile* antique chair⟩.

Frangible implies susceptibility to being broken without implying weakness or delicacy ⟨*frangible* stone used as paving material⟩.

Brittle implies hardness together with lack of elasticity or flexibility or toughness ⟨elderly patients with *brittle* bones⟩.

Crisp implies a firmness and brittleness desirable esp. in some foods ⟨*crisp* lettuce⟩.

Friable applies to substances that are easily crumbled or pulverized ⟨*friable* soil⟩.

See in addition WEAK.

FRAGRANCE, perfume, scent, incense, redolence mean a sweet or pleasant odor.

Fragrance suggests the odors of flowers or other growing things ⟨household cleansers with the *fragrance* of pine⟩.

Perfume may suggest a stronger or heavier odor and applies esp. to a prepared or synthetic liquid ⟨the *perfume* of lilacs filled the room⟩.

Scent is very close to *perfume* but of wider application because more neutral in connotation ⟨furniture polish with a fresh lemon *scent*⟩.

Incense applies to the smoke from burning spices and gums and suggests an esp. pleasing odor ⟨the odor of *incense* permeated the temple⟩.

Redolence implies a mixture of fragrant or pungent odors ⟨the *redolence* of a forest after a rain⟩.

FRANK, candid, open, plain mean showing willingness to tell what one feels or thinks.

Frank stresses lack of shyness or secretiveness or of evasiveness from considerations of tact or expedience ⟨*frank* discussions on arms control⟩.

Candid suggests expression marked by sincerity and honesty esp. in offering unwelcome criticism or opinion ⟨a *candid* appraisal of her singing ability⟩.

Open implies frankness but suggests more indiscretion than *frank* and less earnestness than *candid* ⟨young children are *open* and artless in saying what they think⟩.

Plain suggests outspokenness and freedom from affectation or subtlety in expression ⟨was very *plain* about telling them to leave⟩.

FREE *adj* **Free, independent, sovereign, autonomous** mean not subject to the rule or control of another.

Free stresses the complete absence of external rule and the full right to make all of one's own decisions ⟨you're *free* to do as you like⟩.

Independent implies a standing alone; applied to a state it implies lack of connection with any other having power to interfere with its citizens, laws, or policies ⟨the struggle for Ireland to become *independent*⟩.

Sovereign stresses the absence of a superior power and implies supremacy within a thing's own domain or sphere ⟨a *sovereign* nation not subject to the laws of another⟩.

Autonomous stresses independence in matters pertaining to self-government ⟨a credible investigating committee must be *autonomous*⟩.

FREE *vb* **Free, release, liberate, emancipate, manumit** mean to set loose from restraint or constraint.

Free implies a usu. permanent removal from whatever binds, confines, entangles, or oppresses ⟨*freed* the animals from their cages⟩.

Release suggests a setting loose from confinement, restraint, or a state of pressure or tension, often without implication of permanent liberation ⟨*released* his anger by exercising⟩.

Liberate stresses particularly the resulting state of liberty ⟨*liberated* the novel from Victorian inhibitions⟩.

Emancipate implies the liberation of a person from subjection or domination ⟨labor-saving devices that *emancipated* women from housework⟩.

Manumit implies emancipation from slavery ⟨the proclamation *manumitted* the slaves⟩.

FREEDOM, liberty, license mean the power or condition of acting without compulsion.

Freedom has a broad range of application from total absence of restraint to merely a sense of not being unduly hampered or frustrated ⟨*freedom* of the press⟩.

Liberty suggests release from former restraint or compulsion ⟨the prisoners were willing to fight for their *liberty*⟩.

License implies freedom specially granted or conceded and may connote an abuse of freedom ⟨the editorial takes considerable *license* with the facts⟩.

FROWN, scowl, glower, lower mean to put on a dark or threatening face or appearance.

Frown implies conveying disapproval or displeasure by contracting the brows ⟨teachers *frowned* on boyish pranks⟩.

Scowl suggests a similar facial expression but conveying rather a bad humor, sullenness, or resentful puzzlement ⟨a grumpy old man who *scowled* habitually⟩.

Glower implies direct staring or glaring as in contempt or defiance ⟨the natives *glowered* at the invading tourists⟩.

Lower suggests a menacing blackness or gloomy anger ⟨*lowered* as he went about his work, never uttering a word⟩.

FRUSTRATE, thwart, foil, baffle, balk, circumvent, outwit mean to check or defeat another's plan or goal.

Frustrate implies making vain or ineffectual all efforts however vigorous or persistent ⟨*frustrated* all attempts at government reform⟩.

Thwart suggests frustration or checking by deliberately crossing or opposing ⟨the park department is *thwarted* by public indifference to littering⟩.

Foil implies checking or defeating so as to discourage further effort ⟨her parents *foiled* my efforts to see her⟩.

Baffle implies frustration by confusing or puzzling ⟨*baffled* by the maze of rules and regulations⟩.

Balk suggests the interposing of obstacles or hindrances ⟨legal restrictions *balked* police efforts to control crime⟩.

Circumvent implies frustration by a particular stratagem ⟨*circumvented* the law by finding loopholes⟩.

Outwit suggests craft and cunning ⟨the rebels *outwitted* the army repeatedly⟩.

FULL, complete, plenary, replete mean containing all that is wanted or needed or possible.

Full implies the presence or inclusion of everything that is wanted or required by something or that can be held, contained, or attained by it ⟨a *full* schedule of appointments⟩.

Complete applies when all that is needed is present ⟨the report does not give a *complete* picture of the situation⟩.

Plenary adds to *complete* the implication of fullness without qualification ⟨given *plenary* power as commander in chief⟩.

Replete implies being filled to the brim or to satiety ⟨a speech *replete* with innuendos and half-truths⟩.

FULSOME, oily, unctuous, oleaginous mean too obviously extravagant to be genuine or sincere.

Fulsome implies that something which is essentially good has been carried to an excessive and tasteless degree ⟨the *fulsome* flattery of a celebrity interviewer⟩.

Oily implies an offensively ingratiating quality and sometimes suggests a suavity or benevolence that masks a sinister intent ⟨*oily* developers trying to persuade residents to sell⟩.

Unctuous implies the hypocritical adoption of a grave, devout, or spiritual manner ⟨the *unctuous* pleading of the First Amendment by pornographers⟩.

Oleaginous may be used in place of *oily* to suggest even greater pomposity ⟨an *oleaginous* maître d' fawning over the female diners⟩.

FUN, jest, sport, game, play mean action or speech that provides amusement or arouses laughter.

Fun usu. implies laughter or gaiety but may imply merely a lack of serious or ulterior purpose ⟨played cards just for *fun*⟩.

Jest implies lack of earnestness in what is said or done and may suggest a hoaxing or teasing ⟨took seriously remarks said only in *jest*⟩.

Sport applies esp. to the arousing of laughter against someone ⟨teasing begun in *sport* ended in an ugly brawl⟩.

Game is close to *sport*, and often stresses mischievous or malicious fun ⟨habitually made *game* of their poor relations⟩.

Play stresses the opposition to *earnest* without implying any element of malice or mischief ⟨pretended to strangle his brother in *play*⟩.

FUNCTION, office, duty, province mean the acts or operations expected of a person or thing.

Function implies a definite end or purpose that the one in question serves or a particular kind of work it is intended to perform ⟨the *function* of the stomach is to digest food⟩.

Office is typically applied to the function or service expected of a person by reason of his trade or profession or his special relationship to others ⟨exercised the *offices* of both attorney and friend⟩.

Duty applies to a task or responsibility imposed by one's occupation, rank, status, or calling ⟨the lieutenant governor had few official *duties*⟩.

Province applies to a function, office, or duty that naturally or logically falls to one ⟨it is not the governor's *province* to set foreign policy⟩.

FURNISH, equip, outfit, appoint, accoutre, arm mean to supply one with what is needed.

Furnish implies the provision of any or all essentials for performing a function ⟨a sparsely *furnished* apartment⟩.

Equip suggests the provision of something making for efficiency in action or use ⟨a fully *equipped* kitchen with every modern appliance⟩.

Outfit implies provision of a complete list or set of articles as for a journey, an expedition, or a special occupation ⟨*outfitted* the whole family for a ski trip⟩.

Appoint implies provision of complete and usu. elegant or elaborate equipment or furnishings ⟨a lavishly *appointed* penthouse apartment⟩.

Accoutre suggests the supplying of personal dress or equipment for a special activity ⟨the fully *accoutred* members of a polar expedition⟩.

Arm implies provision for effective action or operation esp. in war ⟨*armed* to the teeth⟩.

FUTILE, vain, fruitless mean producing no result.

Futile may connote completeness of failure or unwisdom of undertaking ⟨a *futile* search for survivors of the crash⟩.

Vain usu. implies simple failure to achieve a desired result ⟨a *vain* attempt to get the car started⟩.

Fruitless comes close to *vain* but often suggests long and arduous effort or severe disappointment ⟨*fruitless* efforts to obtain a lasting peace⟩.

G

GATHER, collect, assemble, congregate mean to come or bring together into a group, mass, or unit.

Gather is the most general term for bringing or coming together from a spread-out or scattered state ⟨a crowd *gathers* whenever there is excitement⟩.

Collect often implies careful selection or orderly arrangement ⟨*collected* books on gardening⟩.

Assemble implies an ordered union or organization of persons or things often for a definite purpose ⟨the country's leading experts on aeronautics *assembled* under one roof⟩.

Congregate implies a spontaneous flocking together into a crowd or huddle ⟨persons were forbidden to *congregate* under martial law⟩.

See in addition INFER.

GAUDY, tawdry, garish, flashy, meretricious mean vulgarly or cheaply showy.

Gaudy implies a tasteless use of overly bright, often clashing colors or excessive ornamentation ⟨circus performers in *gaudy* costumes⟩.

Tawdry applies to what is at once gaudy and cheap and sleazy ⟨*tawdry* saloons along the waterfront⟩.

Garish describes what is distressingly or offensively bright ⟨*garish* signs along the commercial strip⟩.

Flashy implies an effect of brilliance quickly and easily seen to be shallow or vulgar ⟨a *flashy* nightclub act with leggy chorus girls⟩.

Meretricious stresses falsity and may describe a tawdry show that beckons with a false allure or promise ⟨a *meretricious* wasteland of casinos and bars⟩.

GAZE, gape, stare, glare, peer mean to look (at) long and attentively.

Gaze implies fixed and prolonged attention (as in wonder, admiration, or abstractedness) ⟨*gazing* at the waves breaking along the shore⟩.

Gape suggests an open mouthed often stupid wonder ⟨a crowd *gaped* at the man threatening to jump⟩.

Stare implies a direct open-eyed gazing denoting curiosity, disbelief. or insolence ⟨kept *staring* at them as they tried to eat⟩.

Glare is a fierce or angry staring ⟨silently *glared* back at her accusers⟩.

Peer suggests a looking narrowly and curiously as if through a small opening ⟨*peered* at the bird through his binoculars⟩.

GET, obtain, procure, secure, acquire, gain, win, earn mean to come into possession of.

Get is a very general term and may or may not imply effort or initiative ⟨*got* a car for my birthday⟩.

Obtain suggests the attainment of something sought for with some expenditure of time and effort ⟨*obtained* statements from all of the witnesses⟩.

Procure implies effort in obtaining something for oneself or for another ⟨in charge of *procuring* supplies for the office⟩.

Secure implies difficulty in obtaining and keeping in possession or under one's control ⟨an ad agency that *secured* many top accounts⟩.

Acquire often suggests an addition to what is already possessed ⟨*acquired* a greater appreciation of music⟩.

Gain suggests struggle and usu. value in the thing obtained ⟨gradually *gained* a reputation as a skilled musician⟩.

Win suggests favoring qualities or circumstances playing a part in the gaining ⟨*won* the admiration of his fellow actors⟩.

Earn implies a correspondence between the effort and what one gets by effort ⟨a compelling performance that *earned* her many awards⟩.

GHASTLY, grisly, gruesome, macabre, lurid mean horrifying and repellent in appearance or aspect.

Ghastly suggests the terrifying aspects of corpses and ghosts ⟨a *ghastly* portrait of life after a nuclear war⟩.

Grisly and **gruesome** suggest additionally the results of extreme violence or cruelty ⟨the case of an unusually *grisly* murder⟩ ⟨the *gruesome* history of the Nazi death camps⟩.

Macabre implies a morbid preoccupation with the physical aspects of death ⟨a *macabre* tale of premature burial⟩.

Lurid adds to *gruesome* the suggestion of shuddering fascination with violent death and esp. with murder ⟨the tabloids wallowed in the crime's *lurid* details⟩.

GIFT, faculty, aptitude, bent, talent, genius, knack mean a special ability for doing something.

Gift often implies special favor by God or nature ⟨the *gift* of a beautiful singing voice⟩.

Faculty applies to an innate or less often acquired ability for a particular accomplishment or function ⟨a rare *faculty* for remembering people's names⟩.

Aptitude implies a natural liking for some activity and the likelihood of success in it ⟨a definite mechanical *aptitude*⟩.

Bent is nearly equal to *aptitude* but it stresses inclination perhaps more than specific ability ⟨a family that has always had an artistic *bent*⟩.

Talent suggests a marked natural ability that needs to be developed ⟨allowed her dancing *talent* to go to waste⟩.

Genius suggests impressive inborn creative ability ⟨the *genius* of Mozart⟩.

Knack implies a comparatively minor but special ability making for ease and dexterity in performance ⟨has the *knack* for making swift, cutting retorts⟩.

GIVE, present, donate, bestow, confer, afford mean to convey to another as his possession.

Give, the general term, is applicable to any passing over of anything by any means ⟨*give* alms⟩ ⟨*give* a boy a ride on a pony⟩ ⟨*give* my love to your mother⟩.

Present carries a note of formality and ceremony ⟨*present* an award⟩ ⟨*presented* him the keys to the city⟩.

Donate is likely to imply a publicized giving (as to charity) ⟨*donate* a piano to the orphanage⟩.

Bestow implies the conveying of something as a gift and may suggest condescension on the part of the giver ⟨*bestow* unwanted advice⟩.

Confer implies a gracious giving (as of a favor or honor) ⟨the Pope *conferred* the rank of cardinal on three bishops⟩.

Afford implies a giving or bestowing usu. as a natural or legitimate consequence of the character of the giver ⟨the trees *afforded* us a welcome shade⟩ ⟨a development that *affords* us some hope⟩.

GOVERN, rule mean to exercise power or authority in controlling others.

Govern implies the aim of keeping in a straight course or smooth operation for the good of the individual and the whole ⟨the British monarch reigns, but the prime minister *governs*⟩.

Rule may imply no more than laying down laws or issuing commands that must be obeyed but often suggests the exercise of despotic or arbitrary power ⟨the emperor *ruled* with an iron hand⟩.

GRACIOUS, cordial, affable, genial, sociable mean markedly pleasant and easy in social intercourse.

Gracious implies courtesy and kindly consideration ⟨her *gracious* acceptance of the award⟩.

Cordial stresses warmth and heartiness ⟨our *cordial* host greeted us at the door⟩.

Affable implies easy approachability and readiness to respond pleasantly to conversation or requests or proposals ⟨the dean of students was surprisingly *affable*⟩.

Genial stresses cheerfulness and even joviality ⟨the emcee must be a *genial* extrovert⟩.

Sociable suggests a genuine liking for the companionship of others ⟨*sociable* people enjoying an ocean cruise⟩.

GRAND, magnificent, imposing, stately, majestic, grandiose mean large and impressive.

Grand adds to greatness of size the implications of handsomeness and dignity ⟨a mansion with a *grand* staircase⟩.

Magnificent implies an impressive largeness proportionate to scale without sacrifice of dignity or good taste ⟨*magnificent* paintings and tapestries⟩.

Imposing implies great size and dignity but esp. stresses impressiveness ⟨large, *imposing* buildings line the avenue⟩.

Stately may suggest poised dignity, erectness of bearing, handsomeness of proportions, ceremonious deliberation of movement ⟨the *stately* procession proceeded into the cathedral⟩.

Majestic combines the implications of *imposing* and *stately* and usu. adds a suggestion of solemn grandeur ⟨a *majestic* waterfall⟩.

Grandiose implies a size or scope exceeding ordinary experience but is most commonly applied derogatorily to inflated pretension or absurd exaggeration ⟨*grandiose* schemes of world conquest⟩.

GRANT, concede, vouchsafe, accord, award mean to give as a favor or a right.

Grant implies giving to a claimant or petitioner something that could be withheld ⟨*granted* them another month to finish the work⟩.

Concede implies yielding something reluctantly in response to a rightful or compelling claim ⟨even her critics *concede* she can be charming⟩.

Vouchsafe implies granting something as a courtesy or an act of gracious condescension ⟨the star refused to *vouchsafe* an interview⟩.

Accord implies giving to another what is due or proper ⟨*accorded* all the honors befitting a head of state⟩.

Award implies giving what is deserved or merited usu. after a careful weighing of pertinent factors ⟨*awarded* the company a huge defense contract⟩.

GRAPHIC, vivid, picturesque, pictorial mean giving a clear visual impression in words.

Graphic stresses the evoking of a clear lifelike picture ⟨a *graphic* account of his combat experiences⟩.

Vivid suggests an impressing on the mind the vigorous aliveness of something ⟨a *vivid* re-creation of an exciting period in history⟩.

Picturesque suggests the presentation of a striking or effective picture composed of features notable for their distinctness and charm ⟨Dickens is famous for his *picturesque* characters⟩.

Pictorial implies representation in the manner of painting with emphasis upon colors, shapes, and spatial relations ⟨a *pictorial* style of poetry marked by precise, developed imagery⟩.

GUIDE, lead, steer, pilot, engineer mean to direct in a course or show the way to be followed.

Guide implies intimate knowledge of the way and of all its difficulties and dangers ⟨*guided* the other scouts through the darkened cave⟩.

Lead implies a going ahead to show the way and often to keep those that follow under control and in order ⟨the flagship *led* the fleet⟩.

Steer implies an ability to keep to a chosen course and stresses the capacity of maneuvering correctly ⟨*steered* the ship through the narrow channel⟩.

Pilot suggests guidance over a dangerous, intricate, or complicated course ⟨successfully *piloted* the bill through the Senate⟩.

Engineer implies guidance by one who finds ways to avoid or overcome difficulties in achieving an end or carrying out a plan ⟨*engineered* his son's election to the governorship⟩.

H

HABIT, practice, usage, custom, wont mean a way of acting fixed through repetition.

Habit implies a doing unconsciously and often compulsively ⟨the *habit* of constantly tapping his fingers⟩.

Practice suggests an act or method followed with regularity and usu. through choice 〈our *practice* is to honor all major credit cards〉.

Usage suggests a customary action so generally followed that it has become a social norm 〈western-style dress is now common *usage* in international business〉.

Custom applies to a practice or usage so steadily associated with an individual or group as to have almost the force of unwritten law 〈the *custom* of mourners wearing black at funerals〉.

Wont usu. applies to an habitual manner, method, or practice distinguishing an individual or group 〈as was her *wont*, she slept until noon〉.

HAMPER, trammel, clog, fetter, shackle, manacle mean to hinder or impede in moving, progressing, or acting.

Hamper may imply the effect of any impeding or restraining influence 〈*hampered* the investigation by refusing to cooperate〉.

Trammel suggests entangling by or confining within a net 〈rules that serve only to *trammel* the artist's creativity〉.

Clog usu. implies a slowing by something extraneous or encumbering 〈feels that free enterprise is *clogged* by government regulation〉.

Fetter suggests a restraining so severe that freedom to move or progress is almost lost 〈a nation that is *fettered* by an antiquated class system〉.

Shackle and **manacle** are stronger than *fetter* and suggest total loss of freedom 〈a mind *shackled* by stubborn pride and prejudice〉 〈hatred can *manacle* the soul〉.

HANDLE, manipulate, wield mean to manage dexterously or efficiently.

Handle implies directing an acquired skill to the accomplishment of immediate ends 〈*handled* the crisis with cool efficiency〉.

Manipulate implies adroit handling and in extended use often suggests the use of craft or of fraud 〈brutally *manipulates* other people for his own selfish ends〉.

Wield implies mastery and vigor in handling a tool or a weapon or in exerting influence, authority, or power ⟨the news media *wield* a tremendous influence on the electorate⟩.

HARD, difficult, arduous mean demanding great exertion or effort.

Hard implies the opposite of all that is easy ⟨farming is *hard* work⟩.

Difficult implies the presence of obstacles to be surmounted or puzzles to be resolved and suggests the need of skill, patience, or courage ⟨a *difficult* decision requiring much thought and courage⟩.

Arduous stresses the need of laborious and persevering exertion ⟨the *arduous* task of rebuilding the town⟩.

See in addition FIRM.

HARMONY, accord, concord mean the state resulting when different things come together without clashing or disagreement.

Harmony implies a beautiful effect achieved by the agreeable blending or arrangement of parts ⟨a resort in splendid *harmony* with its natural setting⟩.

Accord may imply personal agreement or goodwill or the absence of friction ⟨parents and teachers are in *accord* on this issue⟩.

Concord adds to *accord* additional implications of peace and amity ⟨a planned utopian community in which all would live in *concord*⟩.

HASTE, hurry, speed, expedition, dispatch mean quickness in movement or action.

Haste applies to personal action and implies urgency and precipitancy and often rashness ⟨why this headlong *haste* to get married?⟩.

Hurry often has a strong suggestion of agitated bustle or confusion ⟨in the *hurry* of departure she forgot her toothbrush⟩.

Speed suggests swift efficiency in movement or action ⟨exercises to increase your reading *speed*⟩.

Expedition and **dispatch** both imply speed and efficiency in handling affairs but *expedition* stresses ease or efficiency of performance and *dispatch* carries a stronger suggestion of promptness in bringing matters to a conclusion 〈with surprising *expedition* the case came to trial〉 〈regularly paid her bills with the greatest possible *dispatch*〉.

HATE, detest, abhor, abominate, loathe mean to feel strong aversion or intense dislike for.

Hate implies an emotional aversion often coupled with enmity or malice 〈*hated* his former friend with a passion〉.

Detest suggests violent antipathy 〈I *detest* moral cowards〉.

Abhor implies a deep often shuddering repugnance 〈child abuse is a crime *abhorred* by all〉.

Abominate suggests strong detestation and often moral condemnation 〈virtually every society *abominates* incest〉.

Loathe implies utter disgust and intolerance 〈*loathed* self-appointed moral guardians〉.

HATEFUL, odious, abhorrent, detestable, abominable mean deserving of or arousing intense dislike.

Hateful applies to something or someone that arouses active hatred and hostility 〈the *hateful* crime of child abuse〉.

Odious applies to that which arouses offense or repugnance 〈you apparently find the plain truth *odious*〉.

Abhorrent characterizes that which outrages a sense of what is right, decent, just, or honorable 〈the *abhorrent* practice of stereotyping minority groups〉.

Detestable suggests something deserving extreme contempt 〈his *detestable* habit of passing the blame to subordinates〉.

Abominable suggests something fiercely condemned as vile or unnatural 〈the *abominable* living conditions of the plantation slaves〉.

HAVE, hold, own, possess mean to keep, control, retain, or experience as one's own.

Have is a general term carrying no specific implication 〈they *have* plenty of money〉.

Hold suggests stronger control, grasp, or retention ⟨*held* absolute power over the whole country⟩.

Own implies a natural or legal right to hold as one's property and under one's full control ⟨*own* property in several states⟩.

Possess is often the preferred term when referring to an intangible (as a characteristic, a power, or a quality) ⟨*possesses* a first-rate intellect⟩.

HEALTHFUL, wholesome, salubrious, salutary mean favorable to the health of mind or body.

Healthful implies a positive contribution to a healthy condition ⟨a *healthful* diet will provide more energy⟩.

Wholesome applies to what benefits, builds up, or sustains physically, mentally, or spiritually ⟨*wholesome* foods⟩ ⟨the movie is *wholesome* family entertainment⟩.

Salubrious applies chiefly to the helpful effects of climate or air ⟨the *salubrious* climate of the American Southwest⟩.

Salutary describes something corrective or beneficially effective, even though it may in itself be unpleasant ⟨a *salutary* warning that resulted in increased production⟩.

HEALTHY, sound, wholesome, robust, hale, well mean enjoying or indicative of good health.

Healthy implies full strength and vigor as well as freedom from signs of disease ⟨the doctor pronounced the whole family *healthy*⟩.

Sound emphasizes the absence of disease, weakness, or malfunction ⟨an examination showed his heart to be *sound*⟩.

Wholesome implies appearance and behavior indicating soundness and balance ⟨she looks especially *wholesome* in her tennis togs⟩.

Robust implies the opposite of all that is delicate or sickly ⟨a lively, *robust* little boy⟩.

Hale applies particularly to robustness in old age ⟨still *hale* at the age of eighty⟩.

Well implies merely freedom from disease or illness ⟨she has never been a *well* person⟩.

HEAVY, weighty, ponderous, cumbrous, cumbersome mean having great weight.

Heavy implies that something has greater density or thickness than the average of its kind or class ⟨a *heavy* child for his age⟩.

Weighty suggests having actual and not just relative weight ⟨really *weighty* parcels are shipped by freight⟩.

Ponderous implies having great weight because of size and massiveness with resulting great inertia ⟨*ponderous* galleons were outmaneuvered by smaller vessels⟩.

Cumbrous and **cumbersome** imply heaviness and bulkiness that make for difficulty in grasping, moving, carrying, or manipulating ⟨abandoned the *cumbrous* furniture rather than move it⟩ ⟨the old cameras were *cumbersome* and inconvenient⟩.

HEIGHT, altitude, elevation mean vertical distance either between the top and bottom of something or between a base and something above it.

Height refers to something measured vertically whether high or low ⟨a wall two meters in *height*⟩.

Altitude and **elevation** apply to height as measured by angular measurement or atmospheric pressure; *altitude* is preferable when referring to vertical distance above the surface of the earth or above sea level; *elevation* is used esp. in reference to vertical height on land ⟨fly at an *altitude* of 10,000 meters⟩ ⟨Denver is a city with a high *elevation*⟩.

HELP *vb* **Help, aid, assist** mean to supply what is needed to accomplish an end.

Help carries a strong implication of advance toward an objective ⟨*helped* to find a cure for the disease⟩.

Aid suggests the evident need of help or relief and so imputes weakness to the one aided and strength to the one aiding ⟨an army of volunteers *aided* the flood victims⟩.

Assist suggests a secondary role in the assistant or a subordinate character in the assistance ⟨*assisted* the chief surgeon during the operation⟩.

See in addition IMPROVE.

HEROISM, valor, prowess, gallantry mean courageous behavior esp. in conflict.

Heroism implies superlative courage esp. in fulfilling a high purpose against odds ⟨the boy's outstanding act of *heroism* during the fire⟩.

Valor implies illustrious bravery and audacity in fighting ⟨awarded the army's highest honor for *valor* in battle⟩.

Prowess stresses skill as well as bravery ⟨demonstrated his *prowess* in hunting⟩.

Gallantry implies dash and spirit as well as courage and indifference to danger or hardship ⟨special forces with a proud tradition of *gallantry*⟩.

HESITATE, waver, vacillate, falter mean to show irresolution or uncertainty.

Hesitate implies a pause before deciding or acting or choosing ⟨*hesitated* before answering the question⟩.

Waver implies hesitation after seeming to decide and so connotes weakness or a retreat ⟨*wavered* in his support of the rebels⟩.

Vacillate implies prolonged hesitation from inability to reach a firm decision ⟨*vacillated* until it was too late and events were out of control⟩.

Falter implies a wavering or stumbling and often nervousness, lack of courage, or outright fear ⟨never once *faltered* during her testimony⟩.

HIDE, conceal, screen, secrete, bury mean to withhold or withdraw from sight.

Hide may or may not suggest intent ⟨*hide* in a closet⟩ ⟨a house *hidden* by trees⟩.

Conceal usu. does imply intent and often specif. implies a refusal to divulge ⟨*concealed* the weapon in his jacket⟩.

Screen implies an interposing of something that prevents discovery ⟨*screened* her true identity from her colleagues⟩.

Secrete suggests a depositing in a place unknown to others ⟨*secreted* the cocaine in the hold of the ship⟩.

Bury implies covering up so as to hide completely ⟨*buried* the note in a pile of papers⟩.

HIGH, tall, lofty mean above the average in height.

High implies marked extension upward and is applied chiefly to things which rise from a base or foundation or are placed at a conspicuous height above a lower level ⟨a *high* hill⟩ ⟨a *high* ceiling⟩.

Tall applies to what grows or rises high by comparison with others of its kind and usu. implies relative narrowness ⟨a *tall* thin man⟩.

Lofty suggests great or imposing altitude ⟨*lofty* mountain peaks⟩.

HINDER, impede, obstruct, block mean to interfere with the activity or progress of.

Hinder stresses causing harmful or annoying delay or interference with progress ⟨the rain *hindered* our climbing⟩.

Impede implies making forward progress difficult by clogging, hampering, or fettering ⟨too-tight clothing *impeded* my movement⟩.

Obstruct implies interfering with something in motion or in progress by the sometimes intentional placing of obstacles in the way ⟨the view was *obstructed* by billboards⟩.

Block implies complete obstruction to passage or progress ⟨boulders *blocked* the road⟩.

HIRE, let, lease, rent, charter mean to engage or grant for use at a price.

Hire and **let,** strictly speaking, are complementary terms. *hire* implying the act of engaging or taking for use and *let* the granting of use ⟨we *hired* a car for the summer⟩ ⟨decided to *let* the cottage to a young couple⟩.

Lease strictly implies a letting under the terms of a contract but is often applied to hiring on a lease (the diplomat *leased* an apartment for a year).

Rent stresses the payment of money for the full use of property and may imply either hiring or letting (instead of buying a house, they decided to *rent*) (will not *rent* to families with children).

Charter applies to the hiring or letting of a vehicle usu. for exclusive use (*charter* a bus to go to the game).

HONESTY, honor, integrity, probity mean uprightness of character or action.

Honesty implies a refusal to lie, steal, or deceive in any way (a politician of scrupulous *honesty*).

Honor suggests an active or anxious regard for the standards of one's profession, calling, or position (a keen sense of *honor* in business matters).

Integrity implies trustworthiness and incorruptibility to a degree that one is incapable of being false to a trust, responsibility, or pledge (her unimpeachable *integrity* as a journalist).

Probity implies tried and proven honesty or integrity (a judge with a reputation for *probity*).

HONOR, homage, reverence, deference mean respect and esteem shown to another.

Honor may apply to the recognition of one's right to great respect or to any expression of such recognition (an *honor* just to be nominated).

Homage adds the implication of accompanying praise (for centuries dramatists have paid *homage* to Shakespeare).

Reverence implies profound respect mingled with love, devotion, or awe (have the greatest *reverence* for my father).

Deference implies a yielding or submitting to another's judgment or preference out of respect or reverence (refused to show any *deference* to senior staffers).

See in addition HONESTY.

HUMBLE, meek, modest, lowly mean lacking all signs of pride, aggressiveness, or self-assertiveness.

Humble may suggest a virtuous absence of pride or vanity or it may suggest undue self-depreciation or humiliation ⟨a quiet life as a simple, *humble* parish priest⟩.

Meek may suggest mildness or gentleness of temper or it may connote undue submissiveness ⟨the refugees were *meek* and grateful for whatever they got⟩.

Modest implies a lack of boastfulness or conceit, without any implication of abjectness ⟨sincerely *modest* about her singing talents⟩.

Lowly may stress lack of pretentiousness ⟨a volunteer willing to accept the *lowliest* hospital duties⟩.

HYPOTHESIS, theory, law mean a formula derived by inference from scientific data that explains a principle operating in nature.

Hypothesis implies insufficient evidence to provide more than a tentative explanation ⟨a *hypothesis* regarding the extinction of the dinosaurs⟩.

Theory implies a greater range of evidence and greater likelihood of truth ⟨the *theory* of evolution⟩.

Law implies a statement of order and relation in nature that has been found to be invariable under the same conditions ⟨the *law* of gravitation⟩.

I

IDEA, concept, conception, thought, notion, impression mean what exists in the mind as a representation (as of something comprehended) or as a formulation (as of a plan).

Idea may apply to a mental image or formulation of something seen or known or imagined, to a pure abstraction, or to something assumed or vaguely sensed ⟨a mind filled with innovative *ideas*⟩ ⟨my *idea* of paradise⟩.

Concept may apply to the idea formed by consideration of instances of a species or genus or, more broadly, to any idea of what a thing ought to be ⟨a society with no *concept* of private property⟩.

Conception is often interchangeable with *concept;* it may stress the process of imagining or formulating rather than the result ⟨our changing *conception* of what constitutes art⟩.

Thought is likely to suggest the result of reflecting, reasoning, or meditating rather than of imagining ⟨commit your *thoughts* to paper⟩.

Notion suggests an idea not much resolved by analysis or reflection and may suggest the capricious or accidental ⟨the oddest *notions* fly in and out of her head⟩.

Impression applies to an idea or notion resulting immediately from some stimulation of the senses ⟨the first *impression* is of soaring height⟩.

IGNORANT, illiterate, unlettered, untutored, unlearned mean not having knowledge.

Ignorant may imply a general condition or it may apply to lack of knowledge or awareness of a particular thing ⟨an *ignorant* fool⟩ ⟨he's *ignorant* of nuclear physics⟩.

Illiterate applies to either an absolute or a relative inability to read and write ⟨much of that country's population is still *illiterate*⟩.

Unlettered implies ignorance of the knowledge gained by reading ⟨a literary reference that is meaningless to the *unlettered*⟩.

Untutored may imply lack of schooling in the arts and ways of civilization ⟨strange monuments left by an *untutored* people⟩.

Unlearned suggests ignorance of advanced subjects ⟨a poet who speaks to the *unlearned*, common man⟩.

IMAGINARY, fanciful, visionary, fantastic, chimerical, quixotic mean unreal or unbelievable.

Imaginary applies to something which is fictitious and purely the product of one's imagination ⟨a chronic sufferer of several *imaginary* illnesses⟩.

Fanciful suggests the free play of the imagination ⟨the *fanciful* characters created by Lewis Carroll⟩.

Visionary stresses impracticality or incapability of realization ⟨*visionary* schemes for creating a rural utopia⟩.

Fantastic implies incredibility or strangeness beyond belief ⟨a *fantastic* world inhabited by prehistoric monsters⟩.

Chimerical combines the implication of *visionary* and *fantastic* ⟨*chimerical* plans for restoring the British Empire⟩.

Quixotic implies a devotion to romantic or chivalrous ideals unrestrained by ordinary prudence and common sense ⟨the *quixotic* notion that absolute equality is attainable⟩.

IMPASSIONED, passionate, ardent, fervent, fervid, perfervid mean showing intense feeling.

Impassioned implies warmth and intensity without violence and suggests fluent verbal expression ⟨an *impassioned* plea for international understanding⟩.

Passionate implies great vehemence and often violence and wasteful diffusion of emotion ⟨*passionate* denunciations of American arrogance⟩.

Ardent implies an intense degree of zeal, devotion, or enthusiasm ⟨an *ardent* admirer of the novels of Jane Austen⟩.

Fervent stresses sincerity and steadiness of emotional warmth or zeal ⟨*fervent* Christians on a pilgrimage⟩.

Fervid suggests warmly and spontaneously and often feverishly expressed emotion ⟨*fervid* love letters that suggested mental unbalance⟩.

Perfervid implies the expression of exaggerated or overwrought feelings ⟨wary of such *perfervid* expressions of selfless patriotism⟩.

IMPASSIVE, stoic, phlegmatic, apathetic, stolid mean unresponsive to something that might normally excite interest or emotion.

Impassive stresses the absence of any external sign of emotion in action or facial expression 〈just sat there with an *impassive* look〉.

Stoic implies an apparent indifference to pleasure or esp. to pain often as a matter of principle or self-discipline 〈remained resolutely *stoic* even in the face of adversity〉.

Phlegmatic implies a temperament or constitution hard to arouse 〈a *phlegmatic* man immune to amorous advances〉.

Apathetic may imply a puzzling or deplorable indifference or inertness 〈charitable appeals met an *apathetic* response〉.

Stolid implies an habitual absence of interest, responsiveness, or curiosity 〈*stolid* workers, wedded to routine〉.

IMPERTINENT, officious, meddlesome, intrusive, obtrusive mean given to thrusting oneself into the affairs of others.

Impertinent implies exceeding the bounds of propriety in showing interest or curiosity or in offering advice 〈resented their *impertinent* questions〉.

Officious implies the offering of services or attentions that are unwelcome or annoying 〈an *officious* salesman followed me outside〉.

Meddlesome stresses an annoying and usu. prying interference in others' affairs 〈*meddlesome* old gossips with nothing to do〉.

Intrusive implies a tactless or otherwise objectionable thrusting into others' affairs 〈an *intrusive* waiter interrupted our conversation〉.

Obtrusive stresses improper or offensive conspicuousness of interfering actions 〈*obtrusive* relatives dictated the wedding arrangements〉.

IMPLANT, inculcate, instill, inseminate, infix mean to introduce into the mind.

Implant implies teaching that makes for permanence of what is taught 〈*implanted* an enthusiasm for reading in her students〉.

Inculcate implies persistent or repeated efforts to impress on the mind 〈*inculcated* in him high moral standards〉.

Instill stresses gradual, gentle imparting of knowledge over a long period of time 〈*instill* traditional values in your children〉.

Inseminate applies to a sowing of ideas in many minds so that they spread through a class or nation 〈*inseminated* an unquestioning faith in technology〉.

Infix stresses firmly inculcating a habit of thought 〈*infixed* a chronic cynicism〉.

IMPLEMENT, tool, instrument, appliance, utensil mean a relatively simple device for performing work.

Implement may apply to anything necessary to perform a task 〈lawn and gardening *implements*〉.

Tool suggests an implement adapted to facilitate a definite kind or stage of work and suggests the need of skill more strongly than *implement* 〈a carpenter's *tools*〉.

Instrument suggests a device capable of delicate or precise work 〈the surgeon's *instruments*〉.

Appliance refers to a tool or instrument utilizing a power source and suggests portability or temporary attachment 〈modern *appliances* that take the drudgery out of housework〉.

Utensil applies to a device used in domestic work or some routine unskilled activity 〈knives, graters, and other kitchen *utensils*〉.

IMPORTANCE, consequence, moment, weight, significance mean a quality or aspect having great worth or significance.

Importance implies a value judgment of the superior worth or influence of something or someone 〈there are no cities of *importance* in this area〉.

Consequence may imply importance in social rank but more generally implies importance because of probable or possible effects 〈whatever style you choose is of little *consequence*〉.

Moment implies conspicuous or self-evident consequence ⟨a decision of very great *moment*⟩.

Weight implies a judgment of the immediate relative importance of something ⟨idle chitchat of no particular *weight*⟩.

Significance implies a quality or character that should mark a thing as important but that is not self-evident and may or may not be recognized ⟨time would reveal the *significance* of that casual act⟩.

IMPOSTURE, fraud, sham, fake, humbug, counterfeit mean a thing made to seem other than it is.

Imposture applies to any situation in which a spurious object or performance is passed off as genuine ⟨the movie's claim of social concern is an *imposture*⟩.

Fraud usu. implies a deliberate perversion of the truth ⟨a diary that was exposed as a *fraud*⟩.

Sham applies to fraudulent imitation of a real thing or action ⟨condemned the election as a *sham* and a travesty of democracy⟩.

Fake implies an imitation of or substitution for the genuine but does not necessarily imply dishonesty ⟨these are *fakes*, the real jewels being in the vault⟩.

Humbug suggests elaborate pretense usu. so flagrant as to be transparent ⟨the diet business is populated with *humbugs*⟩.

Counterfeit applies esp. to the close imitation of something valuable ⟨20-dollar bills that were *counterfeits*⟩.

IMPROVE, better, help, ameliorate mean to make more acceptable or bring nearer some standard.

Improve and **better** are general and interchangeable and apply to what is capable of being made better whether it is good or bad ⟨measures to *improve* the quality of medical care⟩ ⟨immigrants hoping to *better* their lot in life⟩.

Help implies a bettering that still leaves room for improvement ⟨a coat of paint would *help* that house⟩.

Ameliorate implies making more tolerable or acceptable

conditions that are hard to endure ⟨a cancerous condition that cannot be *ameliorated* by chemotherapy⟩.

INACTIVE, idle, inert, passive, supine mean not engaged in work or activity.

Inactive applies to anyone or anything not in action or in operation or at work ⟨a playwright who's been *inactive* for several years⟩.

Idle applies to persons that are not busy or occupied or to their powers or their implements ⟨tractors were *idle* in the fields⟩.

Inert as applied to things implies powerlessness to move or to affect other things; as applied to persons it suggests an inherent or habitual indisposition to activity ⟨*inert* ingredients in drugs⟩ ⟨an *inert* citizenry uninterested in social change⟩.

Passive implies immobility or lack of normally expected response to an external force or influence and often suggests deliberate submissiveness or self-control ⟨*passive* obedience⟩ ⟨a *passive* individual incapable of strong emotion⟩.

Supine applies only to persons and commonly implies abjectness or indolence ⟨remained *supine* in the face of his boss's verbal abuse⟩.

INCISIVE, trenchant, clear-cut, cutting, biting, crisp mean having or showing a keen mind.

Incisive implies a power to impress the mind by directness and decisiveness ⟨an *incisive* command that left no room for doubt⟩.

Trenchant implies an energetic cutting or probing deeply into a matter so as to reveal distinctions or to reach the center ⟨a *trenchant* critic of political pretensions⟩.

Clear-cut suggests the absence of any blurring, ambiguity, or uncertainty of statement or analysis ⟨made a *clear-cut* distinction between the two military actions⟩.

Cutting implies a ruthless accuracy or directness wounding to the feelings ⟨makes the most *cutting* remarks with that quiet voice⟩.

Biting adds a greater implication of harsh vehemence or ironic force ⟨a *biting* commentary on the election⟩.

Crisp suggests both incisiveness and vigorous terseness ⟨jurors were impressed by the witness's *crisp* answers⟩.

INCITE, instigate, abet, foment mean to spur to action.

Incite stresses a stirring up and urging on, and may or may not imply initiating ⟨charged with *inciting* a riot⟩.

Instigate definitely implies responsibility for initiating another's action and often connotes underhandedness or evil intention ⟨*instigated* a conspiracy against the commander⟩.

Abet implies both assisting and encouraging ⟨accused of aiding and *abetting* the enemy⟩.

Foment implies persistence in goading ⟨years of *fomenting* kept the flame of rebellion burning⟩.

INCLINE, bias, dispose, predispose mean to influence one to have or take an attitude toward something.

Incline implies a tendency to favor one of two or more actions or conclusions ⟨*inclined* to do nothing for the moment⟩.

Bias suggests a settled and predictable leaning in one direction and connotes unfair prejudice ⟨*biased* against young urban professionals⟩.

Dispose suggests an affecting of one's mood or temper so as to incline one toward something ⟨a naive nature *disposes* her to trust others too much⟩.

Predispose implies the operation of a disposing influence well in advance of the opportunity to manifest itself ⟨fictional violence *predisposes* them to accept violence in real life⟩.

INCLUDE, comprehend, embrace, involve mean to contain within as part of the whole.

Include suggests the containment of something as a constituent, component, or subordinate part of a larger whole ⟨the price of dinner *includes* dessert⟩.

Comprehend implies that something comes within the scope of a statement or definition ⟨his notion of manners *comprehends* more than just table etiquette⟩.

Embrace implies a gathering of separate items within a whole ⟨her faith *embraces* both Christian and non-Christian beliefs⟩.

Involve suggests inclusion by virtue of the nature of the whole, whether by being its natural or inevitable consequence ⟨a procedural change that will *involve* more work for everyone⟩.

INCONSTANT, fickle, capricious, mercurial, unstable mean lacking firmness or steadiness (as in purpose or devotion).

Inconstant implies an incapacity for steadiness and an inherent tendency to change ⟨the supply of materials was too *inconstant* to depend on⟩.

Fickle suggests unreliability because of perverse changeability and incapacity for steadfastness ⟨performers discover how *fickle* the public can be⟩.

Capricious suggests motivation by sudden whim or fancy and stresses unpredictability ⟨an utterly *capricious* manner of selecting candidates⟩.

Mercurial implies a rapid changeability in mood ⟨so *mercurial* in temperament that one never knew what to expect⟩.

Unstable implies an incapacity for remaining in a fixed position or steady course and applies esp. to a lack of emotional balance ⟨in love she was impulsive and *unstable*⟩.

INCREASE, enlarge, augment, multiply mean to make or become greater.

Increase used intransitively implies progressive growth in size, amount, intensity; used transitively it may imply simple not necessarily progressive addition ⟨his waistline *increased* with age⟩ ⟨*increased* her landholdings⟩.

Enlarge implies expansion or extension that makes greater in size or capacity ⟨*enlarged* the restaurant to its present capacity⟩.

Augment implies addition to what is already well grown or developed ⟨an inheritance that *augmented* his fortune⟩.

Multiply implies increase in number by natural generation or by indefinite repetition of a process ⟨with each tampering the problems *multiplied*⟩.

INDECOROUS, improper, unseemly, indecent, unbecoming, indelicate mean not conforming to what is accepted as right, fitting, or in good taste.

Indecorous suggests a violation of accepted standards of good manners ⟨your *indecorous* manners marred the wedding reception⟩.

Improper applies to a broader range of transgressions of rules not only of social behavior but of ethical practice or logical procedure or prescribed method ⟨the *improper* use of campaign contributions⟩.

Unseemly adds a suggestion of special inappropriateness to a situation or an offensiveness to good taste ⟨married again with *unseemly* haste⟩.

Indecent implies great unseemliness or gross offensiveness esp. in referring to sexual matters ⟨a scene judged by the censors as *indecent*⟩.

Unbecoming suggests behavior or language that does not suit one's character or. status ⟨conduct *unbecoming* an officer⟩.

Indelicate implies a lack of modesty or of tact or of refined perception of feeling ⟨*indelicate* expressions for bodily functions⟩.

INDEFATIGABLE, tireless, untiring, unwearied, unflagging mean capable of prolonged and strenuous effort.

Indefatigable implies persistent and unremitting activity or effort ⟨an *indefatigable* champion of women's rights⟩.

Tireless implies a remarkable energy or stamina ⟨honored as a teacher of *tireless* industry and limitless patience⟩.

Untiring implies the extraordinary ability to go on continuously and without interruption ⟨*untiring* researchers in the fight against the disease⟩.

Unwearied stresses the apparent absence of any sign of fatigue ⟨detectives remain *unwearied* in their search for the killer⟩.

Unflagging stresses the absence of any relaxation in one's efforts ⟨an *unflagging* attention to detail⟩.

INDIFFERENT, unconcerned, incurious, aloof, detached, disinterested mean not showing or feeling interest.

Indifferent implies neutrality of attitude from lack of inclination, preference, or prejudice ⟨*indifferent* to the dictates of fashion⟩.

Unconcerned suggests a lack of sensitivity or regard for others' needs or troubles ⟨*unconcerned* about the problems of the homeless⟩.

Incurious implies an inability to take a normal interest due to dullness of mind or to self-centeredness ⟨*incurious* about the world beyond their village⟩.

Aloof suggests a cool reserve arising from a sense of superiority or disdain for inferiors or from shyness ⟨remained *aloof* from the other club members⟩.

Detached implies an objective attitude achieved through absence of prejudice or selfishness ⟨observed family gatherings with *detached* amusement⟩.

Disinterested implies a circumstantial freedom from concern for personal or esp. financial advantage that enables one to judge or advise without bias ⟨a panel of *disinterested* observers to act as judges⟩.

INDULGE, pamper, humor, spoil, baby, mollycoddle mean to show undue favor to a person's desires and feelings.

Indulge implies excessive compliance and weakness in gratifying another's or one's own desires ⟨*indulged* herself with food at the slightest excuse⟩.

Pamper implies inordinate gratification of desire for luxury and comfort with consequent enervating effect ⟨*pampered* by the conveniences of modern living⟩.

Humor stresses a yielding to a person's moods or whims ⟨*humored* him by letting him tell the story⟩.

Spoil stresses the injurious effects on character by indulging or pampering ⟨fond but foolish parents *spoil* their children⟩.
Baby suggests excessive care, attention, or solicitude ⟨*babying* students by not holding them accountable⟩.
Mollycoddle suggests an excessive degree of care and attention to another's health or welfare ⟨refused to *mollycoddle* her teenaged patients⟩.

INFALLIBLE, inerrable, inerrant, unerring mean having or showing the inability to make errors.
Infallible may imply that one's freedom from error is divinely bestowed ⟨fundamentalists believe in an *infallible* Bible⟩.
Inerrable may be preferable when one wishes to avoid any association with religious or papal infallibility ⟨no reference source should be considered *inerrable*⟩.
Inerrant stresses the fact that no mistakes were made ⟨an *inerrant* interpretation of the most demanding role in drama⟩.
Unerring stresses reliability, sureness, exactness, or accuracy ⟨a photographer with an *unerring* eye for beauty⟩.

INFER, deduce, conclude, judge, gather mean to arrive at a mental conclusion.
Infer implies arriving at a conclusion by reasoning from evidence; if the evidence is slight, the term comes close to *surmise* ⟨from that remark, I *inferred* that they knew each other⟩.
Deduce adds to *infer* the special implication of drawing a particular inference from a generalization ⟨from that we can *deduce* that man is a mammal⟩.
Conclude implies arriving at a logically necessary inference at the end of a chain of reasoning ⟨*concluded* that only he could have committed the crime⟩.
Judge stresses critical examination of the evidence on which a conclusion is based ⟨*judge* people by their actions, not words⟩.
Gather suggests a direct or intuitive forming of a conclusion

from hints or implications ⟨*gathered* that the couple wanted to be alone⟩.

INFLEXIBLE, inexorable, obdurate, adamant mean unwilling to alter a predetermined course or purpose.

Inflexible implies rigid adherence or even slavish conformity to principle ⟨*inflexible* in her demands⟩.

Inexorable implies relentlessness of purpose or, esp. when applied to things, inevitableness ⟨the *inexorable* path of progress⟩.

Obdurate stresses hardness of heart and insensitivity to appeals for mercy or the influence of divine grace ⟨an *obdurate* governor who refused to grant clemency⟩.

Adamant implies utter immovability in the face of all temptation or entreaty ⟨was *adamant* that the project be completed on time⟩.

See in addition STIFF.

INFLUENCE *n* **Influence, authority, prestige, weight, credit** mean power exerted over the minds or behavior of others.

Influence may apply to a force exercised and received consciously or unconsciously ⟨used all of her *influence* to get the bill passed⟩.

Authority implies the power of winning devotion or allegiance or of compelling acceptance and belief ⟨a policy that has the *authority* of the school board behind it⟩.

Prestige implies the ascendancy given by conspicuous excellence or reputation for superiority ⟨the *prestige* of the newspaper⟩.

Weight implies measurable or decisive influence in determining acts or choices ⟨the wishes of the President obviously had much *weight*⟩.

Credit suggests influence that arises from proven merit or favorable reputation ⟨the *credit* that he had built up in the town⟩.

INFORM, acquaint, apprise, notify mean to make one aware of something.

Inform implies the imparting of knowledge esp. of facts or occurrences ⟨*informed* us of the crisis⟩.

Acquaint lays stress on introducing to or familiarizing with ⟨*acquainted* myself with the basics of the game⟩.

Apprise implies communicating something of special interest or importance ⟨*apprise* me of rallies in the stock market⟩.

Notify implies sending notice of something requiring attention or demanding action ⟨*notified* them that their mortgage payment was due⟩.

INFREQUENT, uncommon, scarce, rare, sporadic mean not common or abundant.

Infrequent implies occurrence at wide intervals in space or time ⟨family visits that were *infrequent* and brief⟩.

Uncommon suggests a frequency below normal expectation ⟨smallpox is now *uncommon* in many countries⟩.

Scarce implies falling short of a standard or required abundance ⟨jobs were *scarce* during the Depression⟩.

Rare suggests extreme scarcity or infrequency and often implies consequent high value ⟨*rare* first editions of classics fetch high prices⟩.

Sporadic implies occurrence in scattered instances or isolated outbursts ⟨*sporadic* cases of the genetic disorder⟩.

INFUSE, suffuse, imbue, ingrain, inoculate, leaven mean to introduce one thing into another so as to affect it throughout.

Infuse implies a pouring in of something that gives new life or significance ⟨new members *infused* enthusiasm into the club⟩.

Suffuse implies a spreading through of something that gives an unusual color or quality ⟨a room *suffused* with light and cheerfulness⟩.

Imbue implies the introduction of a quality that fills and permeates the whole being ⟨*imbued* her students with intellectual curiosity⟩.

Ingrain suggests the indelible stamping or deep implanting of a quality or trait ⟨clung to *ingrained* habits and beliefs⟩.

Inoculate implies an imbuing or implanting with a germinal idea and often suggests surreptitiousness or subtlety ⟨tried to *inoculate* the child with a taste for opera⟩.

Leaven implies introducing something that enlivens, tempers, or markedly alters the total quality ⟨a serious play *leavened* with comic moments⟩.

INJURE, harm, hurt, damage, impair, mar mean to affect injuriously.

Injure implies the inflicting of anything detrimental to one's looks, comfort, health, or success ⟨an accident that *injured* him physically and emotionally⟩.

Harm often stresses the inflicting of pain, suffering, or loss ⟨careful not to *harm* the animals⟩.

Hurt implies inflicting a wound to the body or to the feelings ⟨*hurt* by her callous remarks⟩.

Damage suggests injury that lowers value or impairs usefulness ⟨a table that was *damaged* in shipping⟩.

Impair suggests a making less complete or efficient by deterioration or diminution ⟨years of smoking had *impaired* his health⟩.

Mar applies to injury that spoils perfection (as of a surface) or causes disfigurement ⟨the text is *marred* by numerous typos⟩.

INJUSTICE, injury, wrong, grievance mean an act that inflicts undeserved hurt.

Injustice applies to any act that involves unfairness to another or violation of his rights ⟨the *injustices* suffered by the lower classes⟩.

Injury applies in law specif. to an injustice for which one may sue to recover compensation ⟨a libeled reputation is legally considered an *injury*⟩.

Wrong applies also in law to any act punishable according to the criminal code; it may apply more generally to any flagrant injustice ⟨a crusading reporter determined to right society's *wrongs*⟩.

Grievance applies to any circumstance or condition that constitutes an injustice to the sufferer and gives him just ground for complaint ⟨a committee for investigating employee *grievances*⟩.

INNATE, inborn, inbred, congenital, hereditary mean not acquired after birth.

Innate applies to qualities or characteristics that are part of one's inner essential nature ⟨a person with an *innate* sense of his own superiority⟩.

Inborn suggests a quality or tendency either actually present at birth or so marked and deep-seated as to seem so ⟨her *inborn* love of the rugged, outdoorsy life⟩.

Inbred suggests something acquired from parents either by heredity or early nurture but in any case deeply rooted and ingrained ⟨a person with *inbred* extremist political views⟩.

Congenital and **hereditary** refer to something acquired before or at birth, *congenital* applying to things acquired during fetal development and *hereditary* applying to things transmitted from one's ancestors ⟨a *congenital* heart condition⟩ ⟨eye color is *hereditary*⟩.

INSANE, mad, demented, deranged, lunatic, maniac mean having or showing an unsound mind.

Insane implies that one is unable to function safely and competently in everyday life and is not responsible for one's actions ⟨adjudged *insane* after a period of observation⟩.

Mad strongly suggests wildness, rabidness, raving, or complete loss of self-control ⟨drove her *mad* with jealousy⟩.

Demented suggests a clear deterioration into mental unsoundness that manifests itself by an incoherence in thought, speech, or action ⟨years of solitary confinement had left him *demented*⟩.

Deranged stresses a clear loss of control resulting in erratic behavior ⟨assassinated by a *deranged* anarchist⟩.

Lunatic may imply no more than extreme folly ⟨invested in one *lunatic* scheme after another⟩.

Maniac is close to *mad* and often suggests violence, fury, or raving ⟨once behind the wheel, she turns into a *maniac* driver⟩.

INSIPID, vapid, flat, jejune, banal, inane mean devoid of qualities that make for spirit and character.

Insipid implies a lack of sufficient taste or savor to please or interest ⟨*insipid* art and dull prose⟩.

Vapid suggests a lack of liveliness, force, or spirit ⟨a potentially exciting story given a *vapid* treatment⟩.

Flat applies to things that have lost their sparkle or zest ⟨although well-regarded in its day, this novel now seems *flat*⟩.

Jejune suggests a lack of rewarding or satisfying substance ⟨on close reading the poem comes across as *jejune*⟩.

Banal stresses the complete absence of freshness, novelty, or immediacy ⟨a *banal* tale of unrequited love⟩.

Inane implies a lack of any significant or convincing quality ⟨an *inane* interpretation of the play⟩.

INSTANCE, case, illustration, example, sample, specimen mean something that exhibits distinguishing characteristics in its category.

Instance applies to any individual person, act, or thing that may be offered to illustrate or explain ⟨an *instance* of history repeating itself⟩.

Case is used to direct attention to a real or assumed occurrence or situation that is to be considered, studied, or dealt with ⟨a *case* of mistaken identity⟩.

Illustration applies to an instance offered as a means of clarifying or illuminating a general statement ⟨an *illustration* of Murphy's law⟩.

Example applies to a typical, representative, or illustrative instance or case ⟨a typical *example* of bureaucratic waste⟩.

Sample implies a part or unit taken at random from a larger whole and so presumed to be typical of its qualities ⟨show us a *sample* of your work⟩.

Specimen applies to any example or sample whether representative or merely existent and available ⟨one of the finest *specimens* of the jeweler's art⟩.

INTELLIGENT, clever, alert, quick-witted mean mentally keen or quick.

Intelligent stresses success in coping with new situations and solving problems ⟨an *intelligent* person could assemble it in 10 minutes⟩.

Clever implies native ability or aptness and sometimes suggests a lack of more substantial qualities ⟨a hack writer who was somewhat *clever* with words⟩.

Alert stresses quickness in perceiving and understanding ⟨*alert* to new developments in technology⟩.

Quick-witted implies promptness in finding answers in debate or in devising expedients in moments of danger or challenge ⟨no match for her *quick-witted* opponent⟩.

INTENSIFY, aggravate, heighten, enhance mean to increase markedly in measure or degree.

Intensify implies a deepening or strengthening of a thing or of its characteristic quality ⟨police *intensified* their investigation⟩.

Aggravate implies an increasing in gravity or seriousness, esp. the worsening of something already bad or undesirable ⟨the problem has been *aggravated* by neglect⟩.

Heighten suggests a lifting above the ordinary or accustomed ⟨special effects *heightened* the sense of terror⟩.

Enhance implies a raising or strengthening above the normal in desirability, value, or attractiveness ⟨shrubbery *enhanced* the grounds of the estate⟩.

INTENTION, intent, purpose, design, aim, end, object, objective, goal mean what one purposes to accomplish or attain.

Intention implies little more than what one has in mind to do or bring about ⟨announced his *intention* to marry⟩.

Intent suggests clearer formulation or greater deliberateness ⟨the clear *intent* of the law⟩.

Purpose suggests a more settled determination ⟨she stopped for a *purpose*, not an idle chat⟩.

Design implies a more carefully calculated plan ⟨the order of events was by accident, not *design*⟩.

Aim adds to these implications of effort directed toward attaining or accomplishing ⟨pursued her *aims* with great courage⟩.

End stresses the intended effect of action often in distinction or contrast to the action or means as such ⟨will use any means to achieve his *end*⟩.

Object may equal *end* but more often applies to a more individually determined wish or need ⟨the *object* of the research study⟩.

Objective implies something tangible and immediately attainable ⟨their *objective* is to seize the oil fields⟩.

Goal suggests something attained only by prolonged effort and hardship ⟨worked years to achieve her *goal*⟩.

INTERPOSE, interfere, intervene, mediate, intercede mean to come or go between.

Interpose implies no more than this ⟨a road *interposed* between the house and the beach⟩.

Interfere implies a getting in the way or otherwise hindering ⟨noise *interfered* with my concentration⟩.

Intervene may imply an occurring in space or time between two things or a stepping in to halt or settle a quarrel or conflict ⟨family duties *intervened*, and the work came to a halt⟩.

Mediate implies intervening between hostile factions ⟨chosen to *mediate* between union and management⟩.

Intercede implies acting in behalf of an offender in begging mercy or forgiveness ⟨asked to *intercede* on our behalf⟩.
See in addition INTRODUCE.

INTIMIDATE, cow, bulldoze, bully, browbeat mean to frighten into submission.

Intimidate implies inducing fear or a sense of inferiority into another (*intimidated* by all the other bright young freshmen).
Cow implies reduction to a state where the spirit is broken or all courage is lost (not at all *cowed* by the odds against making it in show business).
Bulldoze implies an intimidating or an overcoming of resistance usu. by urgings, demands, or threats (*bulldozed* the city council into approving the plan).
Bully implies intimidation through swaggering threats or insults (tourists being *bullied* by taxi drivers).
Browbeat implies a cowing through arrogant, scornful, contemptuous, or insolent treatment (inmates were routinely *browbeaten* by the staff).

INTRODUCE, insert, insinuate, interpolate, intercalate, interpose, interject mean to put between or among others.
Introduce is a general term for bringing or placing a thing or person into a group or body already in existence (*introduced* a new topic into the conversation).
Insert implies putting into a fixed or open space between or among (*insert* a clause in the contract).
Insinuate implies introducing gradually or by gentle pressure (slyly *insinuated* himself into their confidence).
Interpolate applies to the inserting of something extraneous or spurious (*interpolated* her own comments into the report).
Intercalate suggests an intrusive inserting of something in an existing series or sequence (a book in which new material is *intercalated* with the old).
Interpose suggests inserting an obstruction or cause of delay (rules that *interpose* barriers between children and creativity).
Interject implies an abrupt or forced introduction (quickly *interjected* a question).

INTRUDE, obtrude, interlope, butt in mean to thrust oneself or something in without invitation or authorization.

Intrude suggests rudeness or officiousness in invading another's property. time. or privacy ⟨didn't mean to *intrude*
upon the family's private gathering⟩.

Obtrude stresses the impropriety or offensiveness of the intrusion ⟨never hesitant about *obtruding* her opinions even
when they were least welcome⟩.

Interlope implies placing oneself in a position leading to
adverse consequences ⟨wanted to avoid being seen as an *in-
terloping* social climber⟩.

Butt in implies an abrupt or offensive intrusion lacking in
propriety or decent restraint ⟨in-laws who *butt in* and tell
newlyweds what to do⟩.

INVENT, create, discover mean to bring something new into
existence.

Invent implies fabricating something useful usu. as a result
of ingenious thinking or experiment ⟨*invented* numerous en-
ergy-saving devices⟩.

Create implies an evoking of life out of nothing or producing
a thing for the sake of its existence rather than its function
or use ⟨*created* few lasting works of art⟩.

Discover presupposes preexistence of something and implies
a finding rather than a making ⟨attempts to *discover* the
source of the Nile⟩.

**INVETERATE, confirmed, chronic, deep-seated, deep-
rooted** mean firmly established.

Inveterate applies to a habit, attitude, feeling of such long
existence as to be practically ineradicable or unalterable ⟨an
inveterate smoker⟩.

Confirmed implies a growing stronger and firmer with time
so as to resist change or reform ⟨a *confirmed* bachelor⟩.

Chronic suggests what is persistent or endlessly recurrent
and troublesome ⟨sick and tired of his *chronic* complaining⟩.

Deep-seated and **deep-rooted** apply to qualities or attitudes
so deeply embedded as to become part of the core of char-

acter or of lasting endurance ⟨a *deep-seated* fear of heights⟩ ⟨the causes of the problem are *deep-rooted* and cannot be eliminated overnight⟩.

INVITE, solicit, court mean to request or encourage to respond or act.

Invite commonly implies a formal or courteous requesting of one's presence or participation, but may also apply to a tacit or unintended attracting or tempting ⟨a movie remake that *invites* comparison with the original⟩.

Solicit suggests urgency rather than courtesy in encouraging or asking ⟨continually *solicited* our advice⟩.

Court suggests an endeavoring to win favor or gain love by suitable acts or words ⟨a candidate *courting* the votes of young urban professionals⟩.

IRASCIBLE, choleric, splenetic, testy, touchy, cranky, cross mean easily angered.

Irascible implies a tendency to be angered on slight provocation ⟨teenagers got a rise out of the *irascible* old man⟩.

Choleric may suggest impatient excitability and unreasonableness in addition to hot temper ⟨a *choleric* invalid who sorely tried the nurses' patience⟩.

Splenetic suggests moroseness, and bad rather than hot temper ⟨the *splenetic* type that habored a grudge⟩.

Testy suggests irascibility over small annoyances ⟨everyone grew *testy* under the emotional strain⟩.

Touchy implies undue sensitiveness as from jealousy or bad conscience ⟨*touchy* about references to her weight⟩.

Cranky suggests an habitual fretful irritability ⟨*cranky* neighbors much given to complaining⟩.

Cross suggests a snappishness or grumpy irritability as from disappointment or discomfort ⟨a squabble that left her feeling *cross* all day⟩.

IRREGULAR, anomalous, unnatural mean not conforming to rule, law, or custom.

Irregular implies not conforming to a law or regulation imposed for the sake of uniformity in methods, practice, or conduct ⟨concerned about her *irregular* behavior⟩.

Anomalous implies not conforming to what might be expected because of the class or type to which it belongs or the laws that govern its existence ⟨an *anomalous* position of favoring better schools but not wanting to pay for them⟩.

Unnatural suggests what is contrary to nature or to principles or standards felt to be essential to the well-being of civilized society ⟨treated their prisoners of war with *unnatural* cruelty⟩.

IRRITATE, exasperate, nettle, provoke, rile, peeve mean to excite a feeling of anger or annoyance.

Irritate implies an often gradual arousing of angry feelings that may range from impatience to rage ⟨her constant nagging *irritated* him to no end⟩.

Exasperate suggests galling annoyance or vexation and the arousing of extreme impatience ⟨his *exasperating* habit of putting off every decision⟩.

Nettle suggests a light stinging or piquing ⟨your high-handed attitude *nettled* several people⟩.

Provoke implies an arousing of strong annoyance or vexation that may excite to action ⟨remarks that were made solely to *provoke* him⟩.

Rile implies inducing an angry or resentful agitation ⟨the new rules *riled* up the employees⟩.

Peeve suggests arousing fretful often petty or querulous irritation ⟨she is easily *peeved* after a sleepless night⟩.

ITEM, detail, particular mean one of the distinct parts of a whole.

Item applies to each thing specified separately in a list or in a group of things that might be listed or enumerated ⟨ordered every *item* on the list⟩.

Detail applies to one of the small component parts of a larger

whole such as a task. building. painting. narration. or process
〈leave the petty *details* to others〉.

Particular stresses the smallness. singleness. and esp. the
concreteness of a detail or item 〈a verbal attack that included
few *particulars*〉.

J

JEST, joke, quip, witticism, wisecrack mean something said
for the purpose of evoking laughter.

Jest is chiefly literary and applies to any utterance not seriously intended whether sarcastic. ironic. witty. or merely
playful 〈literary *jests* that were lost on her unsophisticated
friends〉.

Joke may apply to an act as well as an utterance and suggests
no intent to hurt feelings 〈he's very good at taking a *joke*〉.

Quip implies lightness and neatness of phrase more definitely than *jest* 〈whatever the topic. she's ready with a quick
quip〉.

Witticism and **wisecrack** both stress cleverness of phrasing
and both may suggest flippancy or unfeelingness 〈many felt
the sting of his *witticisms*〉 〈a comic known for abrasive
wisecracks〉.

See in addition FUN.

JOIN, combine, unite, connect, link, associate, relate mean
to bring or come together into some manner of union.

Join implies a bringing into contact or conjunction of any
degree of closeness 〈*joined* forces in an effort to win〉.

Combine implies some merging or mingling with corresponding loss of identity of each unit 〈*combine* the ingredients for a cake〉.

Unite implies somewhat greater loss of separate identity 〈the
colonies *united* to form a republic〉.

Connect suggests a loose or external attachment with little or no loss of identity ⟨a bridge *connects* the island to the mainland⟩.

Link may imply strong connection or inseparability of elements still retaining identity ⟨a name forever *linked* with liberty⟩.

Associate stresses the mere fact of frequent occurrence or existence together in space or in logical relation ⟨opera is popularly *associated* with high society⟩.

Relate suggests the existence of a real or presumed logical connection ⟨the two events were not *related*⟩.

JUNCTURE, pass, exigency, emergency, contingency, pinch, straits, crisis mean a critical or crucial time or state of affairs.

Juncture stresses the significant concurrence or convergence of events ⟨at an important *juncture* in our country's history⟩.

Pass implies a bad or distressing state or situation brought about by a combination of causes ⟨things have come to a sorry *pass* when it's not safe to be on the streets⟩.

Exigency stresses the pressure of restrictions or urgency of demands created by a special situation ⟨made no effort to provide for *exigencies*⟩.

Emergency applies to a sudden unforeseen situation requiring prompt action to avoid disaster ⟨the presence of mind needed to deal with *emergencies*⟩.

Contingency implies an emergency or exigency that is regarded as possible but uncertain of occurrence ⟨*contingency* plans prepared by the Pentagon⟩.

Pinch implies urgency or pressure for action to a less intense degree than *exigency* or *emergency* ⟨this will do in a *pinch*⟩.

Straits applies to a troublesome situation from which escape is extremely difficult ⟨in dire *straits* since the death of her husband⟩.

Crisis applies to a juncture whose outcome will make a decisive difference ⟨the fever broke and the *crisis* passed⟩.

K

KEEP *vb* **Keep, observe, celebrate, commemorate** mean to notice or honor a day, occasion, or deed.

Keep stresses the idea of not neglecting or violating (*keep* the Sabbath).

Observe suggests marking the occasion by ceremonious performance (not all holidays are *observed* nationally).

Celebrate suggests acknowledging an occasion by festivity (traditionally *celebrates* Thanksgiving with a huge dinner).

Commemorate suggests that an occasion is marked by observances that remind one of the origin and significance of the day (*commemorate* Memorial Day with the laying of wreaths).

KEEP *vb* **Keep, retain, detain, withhold, reserve** mean to hold in one's possession or under one's control.

Keep may suggest a holding securely in one's possession, custody, or control (*keep* this while I'm gone).

Retain implies continued keeping, esp. against threatened seizure or forced loss (managed to *retain* their dignity even in poverty).

Detain suggests a delay in letting go (*detained* them for questioning).

Withhold implies restraint in letting go or a refusal to let go (*withheld* information from the authorities).

Reserve suggests a keeping in store for future use (*reserve* some of your energy for the last mile).

KILL, slay, murder, assassinate, dispatch, execute mean to deprive of life.

Kill merely states the fact of death caused by an agency in any manner (routinely *killed* little bugs) (frost *killed* the plants).

Slay is a chiefly literary term implying deliberateness and violence but not necessarily motive (*slew* thousands of the Philistines).

Murder specif. implies stealth and motive and premeditation and therefore full moral responsibility ⟨convicted of *murdering* his parents⟩.

Assassinate applies to deliberate killing openly or secretly often for political motives ⟨terrorists *assassinated* the Senator⟩.

Dispatch stresses quickness and directness in putting to death ⟨*dispatched* the sentry with a single stab⟩.

Execute stresses putting to death as a legal penalty ⟨to be *executed* by firing squad at dawn⟩.

KIND *adj* **Kind, kindly, benign, benignant** mean showing a gentle, considerate nature.

Kind stresses a disposition to be helpful ⟨a *kind* heart beneath a gruff exterior⟩.

Kindly stresses more the expression of a sympathetic nature or impulse ⟨take a *kindly* interest in the poor of the community⟩.

Benign and **benignant** stress mildness and mercifulness and apply more often to gracious or patronizing acts or utterances of a superior rather than an equal ⟨the belief that a *benign* supreme being controls destiny⟩ ⟨cultural exchange programs have a *benignant* influence in world affairs⟩.

KNOWLEDGE, learning, erudition, scholarship mean what is or can be known by an individual or by mankind.

Knowledge applies to facts or ideas acquired by study, investigation, observation, or experience ⟨rich in the *knowledge* gained from life⟩.

Learning applies to knowledge acquired esp. through formal, often advanced, schooling ⟨a book that is evidence of the author's vast *learning*⟩.

Erudition strongly implies the acquiring of profound, recondite, or bookish learning ⟨an *erudition* unusual even for a classicist⟩.

Scholarship implies the possession of learning characteristic of the advanced scholar in a specialized field of study or investigation ⟨a work of first-rate literary *scholarship*⟩.

L

LAST *adj* **Last, final, terminal, eventual, ultimate** mean following all others (as in time, order, or importance).

Last applies to something that comes at the end of a series but does not always imply that the series is completed or stopped ⟨the *last* page of a book⟩ ⟨the *last* news we had of him⟩.

Final applies to that which definitely closes a series, process, or progress ⟨the *final* day of school⟩.

Terminal may indicate a limit of extension, growth, or development ⟨the *terminal* phase of a disease⟩.

Eventual applies to something that is bound to follow sooner or later as the final effect of causes already operating ⟨the *eventual* defeat of the enemy⟩.

Ultimate implies the last degree or stage of a long process beyond which further progress or change is impossible ⟨the *ultimate* collapse of civilization⟩.

LASTING, permanent, durable, stable mean enduring for so long as to seem fixed or established.

Lasting implies a capacity to continue indefinitely ⟨a book that left a *lasting* impression on me⟩.

Permanent adds usu. the implication of being designed or planned to stand or continue indefinitely ⟨a *permanent* living arrangement⟩.

Durable implies power to resist destructive agencies ⟨*durable* fabrics⟩.

Stable implies lastingness because of resistance to being overturned or displaced ⟨a *stable* government⟩.

LATENT, dormant, quiescent, potential, abeyant mean not now showing signs of activity or existence.

Latent applies to a power or quality that has not yet come forth but may emerge and develop ⟨a *latent* sadism that emerged during the war⟩.

Dormant suggests the inactivity of something (as a feeling or power) as though sleeping ⟨a *dormant* passion existed between them⟩.

Quiescent suggests a usu. temporary cessation of activity ⟨racial tensions were *quiescent* for the moment⟩.

Potential applies to what does not yet have existence or effect but is likely soon to have ⟨a toxic waste dump that is a *potential* disaster⟩.

Abeyant applies to what is for the time being held off or suppressed ⟨an *abeyant* distrust of the neighbors⟩.

LAUGHABLE, ludicrous, ridiculous, comic, comical mean provoking laughter or mirth.

Laughable applies to anything occasioning laughter intentionally or unintentionally ⟨her attempts at roller-skating were *laughable*⟩.

Ludicrous suggests absurdity or preposterousness that excites both laughter and scorn or sometimes pity ⟨a spy thriller with a *ludicrous* plot⟩.

Ridiculous suggests extreme absurdity, foolishness, or contemptibility ⟨a *ridiculous* portrayal of wartime combat⟩.

Comic applies esp. to that which arouses thoughtful amusement ⟨Falstaff is one of Shakespeare's great *comic* characters⟩.

Comical applies to that which arouses unrestrained spontaneous hilarity ⟨his *comical* appearance would have tested a saint⟩.

LAW, rule, regulation, precept, statute, ordinance, canon mean a principle governing action or procedure.

Law implies imposition by a sovereign authority and the obligation of obedience on the part of all subject to that authority ⟨obey the *law*⟩.

Rule applies to more restricted or specific situations ⟨the *rules* of a game⟩.

Regulation implies prescription by authority in order to control an organization or system ⟨*regulations* affecting nuclear power plants⟩.

Precept commonly suggests something advisory and not obligatory communicated typically through teaching ⟨the *precepts* of effective writing⟩.

Statute implies a law enacted by a legislative body ⟨a *statute* requiring the use of seatbelts⟩.

Ordinance applies to an order governing some detail of procedure or conduct enforced by a limited authority such as a municipality ⟨a city *ordinance*⟩.

Canon suggests in nonreligious use a principle or rule of behavior or procedure commonly accepted as a valid guide ⟨a house that violates all the *canons* of good taste⟩.

See in addition HYPOTHESIS.

LAWFUL, legal, legitimate, licit mean being in accordance with law.

Lawful may apply to conformity with law of any sort (as natural, divine, common, or canon) ⟨the *lawful* sovereign⟩.

Legal applies to what is sanctioned by law or in conformity with the law, esp. as it is written or administered by the courts ⟨*legal* residents of the state⟩.

Legitimate may apply to a legal right or status but also, in extended use, to a right or status supported by tradition, custom, or accepted standards ⟨a perfectly *legitimate* question about finances⟩.

Licit applies to a strict conformity to the provisions of the law and applies esp. to what is regulated by law ⟨the *licit* use of the drug by hospitals⟩.

LAZY, indolent, slothful mean not easily aroused to activity.

Lazy suggests a disinclination to work or to take trouble ⟨his habitually *lazy* son⟩.

Indolent suggests a love of ease and a settled dislike of movement or activity ⟨the summer's heat made us all *indolent*⟩.

Slothful implies a temperamental inability to act promptly or speedily when action or speed is called for ⟨the agency is usually *slothful* about fulfilling requests⟩.

LEAN, spare, lank, lanky, gaunt, rawboned, scrawny, skinny mean thin because of an absence of excess flesh.

Lean stresses lack of fat and of curving contours ⟨a *lean* racehorse⟩.

Spare suggests leanness from abstemious living or constant exercise ⟨the *spare* form of a long-distance runner⟩.

Lank implies tallness as well as leanness ⟨the pale, *lank* limbs of a prisoner of war⟩.

Lanky suggests awkwardness and loose-jointedness as well as thinness ⟨a *lanky* youth, all arms and legs⟩.

Gaunt implies marked thinness or emaciation as from overwork or suffering ⟨her *gaunt* face showed the strain of poverty⟩.

Rawboned suggests a large ungainly build without implying undernourishment ⟨*rawboned* lumberjacks squeezed into the booth⟩.

Scrawny and **skinny** imply an extreme leanness that suggests deficient strength and vitality ⟨*scrawny* village children⟩ ⟨*skinny* fashion models⟩.

LEANING, propensity, proclivity, penchant mean a strong instinct or liking for something.

Leaning suggests a liking or attraction not strong enough to be decisive or uncontrollable ⟨accused of having socialist *leanings*⟩.

Propensity implies a deeply ingrained and usu. irresistible longing ⟨the natural *propensity* of in-laws to offer advice⟩.

Proclivity suggests a strong natural proneness usu. to something objectionable or evil ⟨movies that reinforce viewers' *proclivities* for violence⟩.

Penchant implies a strongly marked taste in the person or an irresistible attraction in the object ⟨has a *penchant* for overdramatizing his troubles⟩.

LET, allow, permit mean not to forbid or prevent.

Let may imply a positive giving of permission but more often implies failure to prevent either through inadvertence and negligence or through lack of power or effective authority ⟨the goalie *let* the puck get by him⟩.

Allow implies little more than a forbearing to prohibit ⟨a teacher who *allows* her pupils to do as they like⟩.

Permit implies willingness or acquiescence ⟨the park *permits* powerboats on the lake⟩.

See in addition HIRE.

LETHARGY, languor, lassitude, stupor, torpor mean physical or mental inertness.

Lethargy implies such drowsiness or aversion to activity as is induced by disease, injury, drugs ⟨months of *lethargy* followed my skiing accident⟩.

Languor suggests inertia induced by an enervating climate or illness or love ⟨*languor* induced by a tropical vacation⟩.

Lassitude stresses listlessness or indifference resulting from fatigue or poor health ⟨a deepening depression marked by *lassitude*⟩.

Stupor implies a deadening of the mind and senses by shock, narcotics, or intoxicants ⟨lapsed into a *stupor* following a night of drinking⟩.

Torpor implies a state of suspended animation as of hibernating animals but may suggest merely extreme sluggishness ⟨a once-alert mind now in a state of *torpor*⟩.

LEVEL, flat, plane, even, smooth mean having a surface without bends, curves, or irregularities.

Level applies to a horizontal surface that lies on a line parallel with the horizon ⟨the vast prairies are nearly *level*⟩.

Flat applies to a surface devoid of noticeable curvatures, prominences, or depressions ⟨the work surface must be totally *flat*⟩.

Plane applies to any real or imaginary flat surface in which

a straight line between any two points on it lies wholly within
that surface ⟨the *plane* sides of a crystal⟩.

Even applies to a surface that is noticeably flat or level or to
a line that is observably straight ⟨trim the hedge so that it is
even⟩.

Smooth applies esp. to a polished surface free of irregularities ⟨a *smooth* dance floor⟩.

**LIABLE, open, exposed, subject, prone, susceptible, sen-
sitive** mean being by nature or through circumstances likely
to experience something adverse.

Liable implies a possibility or probability of incurring something because of position, nature, or particular situation ⟨un-
less you're careful, you're *liable* to fall⟩.

Open stresses a lack of barriers preventing incurrence ⟨a
claim that is *open* to question⟩.

Exposed suggests lack of protection or powers of resistance
against something actually present or threatening ⟨the town's
exposed position makes it impossible to defend⟩.

Subject implies an openness for any reason to something that
must be suffered or undergone ⟨all reports are *subject* to editorial revision⟩.

Prone stresses natural tendency or propensity to incur something ⟨a person who is *prone* to procrastination⟩.

Susceptible implies conditions existing in one's nature or
individual constitution that make incurrence probable ⟨young
children are *susceptible* to colds⟩.

Sensitive implies a readiness to respond to or be influenced
by forces or stimuli ⟨her eyes are *sensitive* to light⟩.

See in addition RESPONSIBLE.

LIBERAL, generous, bountiful, munificent mean giving
freely and unstintingly.

Liberal suggests openhandedness in the giver and largeness
in the thing or amount given ⟨a teacher *liberal* in bestowing
praise⟩.

Generous stresses warmhearted readiness to give more than size or importance of the gift ⟨a friend's *generous* offer of assistance⟩.

Bountiful suggests lavish, unremitting giving or providing ⟨*bountiful* grandparents spoiling the children⟩.

Munificent suggests a scale of giving appropriate to lords or princes ⟨the Queen was especially *munificent* to her favorite⟩.

LIE, prevaricate, equivocate, palter, fib mean to tell an untruth.

Lie is the blunt term, imputing dishonesty ⟨to *lie* under oath is a serious crime⟩.

Prevaricate softens the bluntness of *lie* by implying quibbling or confusing the issue ⟨during the hearings the witness did his best to *prevaricate*⟩.

Equivocate implies using words having more than one sense so as to seem to say one thing but intend another ⟨*equivocated*, dodged questions, and misled her inquisitors⟩.

Palter implies making unreliable statements of fact or intention or insincere promises ⟨a cad *paltering* with a naive, young girl⟩.

Fib applies to a telling of a trivial untruth ⟨*fibbed* about the price of the suit⟩. ·

LIFT, raise, rear, elevate, hoist, heave, boost mean to move from a lower to a higher place or position.

Lift usu. implies exerting effort to overcome resistance of weight ⟨*lift* the chair while I vacuum⟩.

Raise carries a stronger implication of bringing up to the vertical or to a high position ⟨soldiers *raising* a flagpole⟩.

Rear may add an element of suddenness to *raise* ⟨suddenly a flag of truce was *reared*⟩.

Elevate may replace *lift* or *raise* esp. when exalting or enhancing is implied ⟨*elevated* the musical tastes of the public⟩.

Hoist implies lifting something heavy esp. by mechanical means ⟨*hoisted* the cargo on board⟩.

Heave implies lifting with great effort or strain ⟨struggled to *heave* the heavy crate⟩.

Boost suggests assisting to climb or advance by a push ⟨*boosted* his brother over the fence⟩.

LIGHTNESS, levity, frivolity, flippancy, volatility, flightiness mean gaiety or indifference when seriousness is expected.

Lightness implies a lack of weight and seriousness in character, mood, or conduct ⟨the only bit of *lightness* in a dreary, ponderous drama⟩.

Levity suggests trifling or unseasonable gaiety ⟨injected a moment of *levity* in the solemn proceedings⟩.

Frivolity suggests irresponsible indulgence in gaieties or in idle speech or conduct ⟨a playgirl living a life of uninterrupted *frivolity*⟩.

Flippancy implies an unbecoming levity esp. in speaking of grave or sacred matters ⟨spoke of the bombing with annoying *flippancy*⟩.

Volatility implies such fickleness of disposition as prevents long attention to any one thing ⟨the *volatility* of the public interest in foreign aid⟩.

Flightiness implies extreme volatility that may approach loss of mental balance ⟨the *flightiness* of my grandmother in her old age⟩.

LIKENESS, similarity, resemblance, similitude, analogy, affinity mean agreement or correspondence in details.

Likeness implies a closer correspondence than **similarity** which often implies that things are merely somewhat alike ⟨a remarkable *likeness* to his late father⟩ ⟨some *similarity* between the two cases⟩.

Resemblance implies similarity chiefly in appearance or external qualities ⟨statements that bear no *resemblance* to the truth⟩.

Similitude applies chiefly to correspondence between abstractions ⟨the *similitude* of environments was rigidly maintained⟩.

Analogy implies likeness or parallelism in relations rather than in appearance or qualities (pointed out the *analogies* to past wars).

Affinity suggests a cause such as kinship or experiences or influences in common which is accountable for the similarity (a writer with a striking *affinity* for American Indian culture).

LIMIT, restrict, circumscribe, confine mean to set bounds for.

Limit implies setting a point or line (as in time, space, speed, or degree) beyond which something cannot or is not permitted to go (visits are *limited* to 30 minutes).

Restrict suggests a narrowing or tightening or restraining within or as if within an encircling boundary (laws intended to *restrict* the freedom of the press).

Circumscribe stresses a restriction on all sides and by clearly defined boundaries (the work of the investigating committee was carefully *circumscribed*).

Confine suggests severe restraint and a resulting cramping, fettering, or hampering (our freedom of choice was *confined* by finances).

LIVELY, animated, vivacious, sprightly, gay mean keenly alive and spirited.

Lively suggests briskness, alertness, or energy (a *lively* hour of news and information).

Animated applies to what is spirited, active, and sparkling (an *animated* discussion of current events).

Vivacious suggests an activeness of gesture and wit, often playful or alluring (a *vivacious* party hostess).

Sprightly suggests lightness and spirited vigor of manner or of wit (a tuneful, *sprightly* musical revue).

Gay stresses complete freedom from care and overflowing spirits (the *gay* spirit of Paris in the 1920s).

LIVING, alive, animate, animated, vital mean having or showing life.

Living and **alive** apply to organic bodies having life as opposed to those from which life has gone (*living* artists) (toss the lobster into the pot while it's still *alive*).

Animate is used chiefly in direct opposition to *inanimate* to denote things capable of life (a child seemingly afraid of every *animate* object).

Animated is applied to that which comes alive and active or is given motion simulating life (an *animated* cartoon).

Vital often suggests the opposite of *mechanical* in implying the energy and esp. the power to grow and reproduce characteristic of life (all of his *vital* functions seemed normal).

LONG, yearn, hanker, pine, hunger, thirst mean to have a strong desire for something.

Long implies a wishing with one's whole heart and often a striving to attain (*longed* for some peace and quiet).

Yearn suggests an eager, restless, or painful longing (*yearned* for a career on the stage).

Hanker suggests the uneasy promptings of unsatisfied appetite or desire (always *hankering* for more money).

Pine implies a languishing or a fruitless longing for what is impossible (*pined* for long-lost love).

Hunger and **thirst** imply an insistent or impatient craving or a compelling need (*hungered* for a business of his own) (*thirsted* for absolute power).

LOUD, stentorian, earsplitting, raucous, strident mean marked by intensity or volume of sound.

Loud applies to any volume above normal and may suggest undue vehemence or obtrusiveness (a *loud* obnoxious person).

Stentorian implies great power and range (an actor with a *stentorian* voice).

Earsplitting implies loudness that is physically discomforting (the *earsplitting* sound of a siren).

Raucous implies a loud harsh grating tone, esp. of voice, and may suggest rowdiness (a barroom filled with the *raucous* shouts of drunken revelers).

Strident implies a rasping discordant but insistent quality, esp. of voice ⟨the *strident* voices of hecklers⟩.

LUCKY, fortunate, happy, providential mean meeting with unforeseen success.

Lucky stresses the agency of chance in bringing about a favorable result ⟨the *lucky* day I met my future wife⟩.

Fortunate suggests being rewarded beyond one's deserts ⟨have been *fortunate* in my business investments⟩.

Happy combines the implications of *lucky* and *fortunate* with stress on being blessed ⟨a life that has been a series of *happy* accidents⟩.

Providential more definitely implies the help or intervention of a higher power ⟨it was *providential* that rescuers arrived in the nick of time⟩.

LURE, entice, inveigle, decoy, tempt, seduce mean to lead astray from one's true course.

Lure implies a drawing into danger, evil, or difficulty through attracting and deceiving ⟨*lured* naive investors with get-rich-quick schemes⟩.

Entice suggests drawing by artful or adroit means ⟨advertising designed to *entice* new customers⟩.

Inveigle implies enticing by cajoling or flattering ⟨*inveigled* her suitor into proposing marriage⟩.

Decoy implies a luring away or into entrapment by artifice ⟨the female bird attempted to *decoy* us away from her nest⟩.

Tempt implies the presenting of an attraction so strong that it overcomes the restraints of conscience or better judgment ⟨*tempted* by the offer of money⟩.

Seduce implies a leading astray by persuasion or false promises ⟨*seduced* young runaways into the criminal life⟩.

LURK, skulk, slink, sneak mean to behave so as to escape attention.

Lurk implies a lying in wait in a place of concealment and often suggests an evil intent ⟨suspicious men *lurking* in alleyways⟩.

Skulk suggests more strongly cowardice or fear or sinister intent ⟨spied something *skulking* in the shadows⟩.

Slink implies moving stealthily often merely to escape attention ⟨during the festivities. I *slunk* away⟩.

Sneak may add an implication of entering or leaving a place or evading a difficulty by furtive, indirect, or underhanded methods ⟨he *sneaked* out after the others had fallen asleep⟩.

LUXURIOUS, sumptuous, opulent mean ostentatiously rich or magnificent.

Luxurious applies to what is choice and costly and suggests gratification of the senses and desire for comfort ⟨a millionaire's *luxurious* penthouse apartment⟩.

Sumptuous applies to what is extravagantly rich, splendid, or luxurious ⟨an old-fashioned grand hotel with a *sumptuous* lobby⟩.

Opulent suggests a flaunting of luxuriousness, luxuriance, or costliness ⟨an *opulent* wedding intended to impress the guests⟩.

See in addition SENSUOUS.

M

MAIM, cripple, mutilate, batter, mangle mean to injure so severely as to cause lasting damage.

Maim implies the loss or injury of a bodily member through violence ⟨a swimmer *maimed* by a shark⟩.

Cripple implies the loss or serious impairment of an arm or leg ⟨the fall *crippled* her for life⟩.

Mutilate implies the cutting off or removal of an essential part of a person or thing thereby impairing its completeness, beauty, or function ⟨a poignant drama *mutilated* by inept acting⟩.

Batter implies a series of blows that bruise deeply, deform, or mutilate ⟨a ship *battered* by fierce storms at sea⟩.

Mangle implies a tearing or crushing that leaves deep extensive wounds 〈thousands are *mangled* every year by auto accidents〉.

MAINTAIN, assert, defend, vindicate, justify mean to uphold as true, right, just, or reasonable.

Maintain stresses firmness of conviction 〈steadfastly *maintained* his client's innocence〉.

Assert suggests determination to make others accept one's claim 〈fiercely *asserted* that credit for the discovery belonged to her〉.

Defend implies maintaining in the face of attack or criticism 〈I need not *defend* my wartime record〉.

Vindicate implies successfully defending 〈his success *vindicated* our faith in him〉.

Justify implies showing to be true, just, or valid by appeal to a standard or to precedent 〈threats to public safety *justified* such drastic steps〉.

MAKE, form, shape, fashion, fabricate, manufacture, forge mean to cause to come into being.

Make applies to producing or creating whether by an intelligent agency or blind forces and to either material or immaterial existence 〈*make* a wish〉 〈the factory *makes* furniture〉.

Form implies a definite outline, structure, or design in the thing produced 〈*form* a plan〉 〈*form* a line outside the door〉.

Shape suggests impressing a form upon some material 〈*shaped* shrubbery into animal figures〉.

Fashion suggests the use of inventive power or ingenuity 〈*fashioned* a bicycle out of spare parts〉.

Fabricate suggests a uniting of many parts into a whole and often implies an ingenious inventing of something false 〈*fabricated* an exotic background for her studio biography〉.

Manufacture implies making repeatedly by a fixed process and usu. by machinery 〈*manufacture* shoes〉.

Forge implies a making or effecting by great physical or mental effort ⟨*forged* an agreement after months of negotiating⟩.

MALICE, malevolence, ill will, spite, malignity, spleen, grudge mean the desire to see another experience pain, injury, or distress.

Malice implies a deep-seated often unexplainable desire to see another suffer ⟨felt no *malice* for their former enemies⟩.

Malevolence suggests a bitter persistent hatred that is likely to be expressed in malicious conduct ⟨deep *malevolence* governed his every act⟩.

Ill will implies a feeling of antipathy of limited duration ⟨a directive that provoked *ill will* among the employees⟩.

Spite implies petty feelings of envy and resentment that are often expressed in small harassments ⟨petty insults inspired only by *spite*⟩.

Malignity implies deep passion and relentlessness ⟨never viewed her daughter-in-law with anything but *malignity*⟩.

Spleen suggests the wrathful release of latent spite or persistent malice ⟨quick to vent his *spleen* at incompetent subordinates⟩.

Grudge implies a harbored feeling of resentment or ill will that seeks satisfaction ⟨never one to harbor a *grudge*⟩.

MALIGN *vb* **Malign, traduce, asperse, vilify, calumniate, defame, slander** mean to injure by speaking ill of.

Malign suggests specific and often subtle misrepresentation but may not always imply deliberate lying ⟨the most *maligned* monarch in British history⟩.

Traduce stresses the resulting ignominy and distress to the victim ⟨so *traduced* the governor that he was driven from office⟩.

Asperse implies continued attack on a reputation often by indirect or insinuated detraction ⟨both candidates *aspersed* the other's motives⟩.

Vilify implies attempting to destroy a reputation by open and direct abuse ⟨no President was more *vilified* in the press⟩.

Calumniate imputes malice to the speaker and falsity to his assertion ⟨threatened with a lawsuit for publicly *calumniating* the company⟩.

Defame stresses the actual loss of or injury to one's good name ⟨forced to pay a substantial sum for *defaming* her reputation⟩.

Slander stresses the suffering of the victim ⟨town gossips carelessly *slandered* their good name⟩.

MALODOROUS, stinking, fetid, noisome, putrid, rank, fusty, musty mean bad-smelling.

Malodorous may range from the unpleasant to the strongly offensive ⟨*malodorous* unidentifiable substances in the refrigerator⟩.

Stinking and **fetid** suggest the foul or disgusting ⟨prisoners were held in *stinking* cells⟩ ⟨skunk cabbage is a *fetid* weed⟩.

Noisome adds a suggestion of being harmful or unwholesome as well as offensive ⟨a *noisome* toxic waste dump⟩.

Putrid implies particularly the sickening odor of decaying organic matter ⟨the typically *putrid* smell of a fish pier⟩.

Rank suggests a strong unpleasant smell ⟨rooms filled with the smoke of *rank* cigars⟩.

Fusty and **musty** suggest lack of fresh air and sunlight, *fusty* also implying prolonged uncleanliness, *musty* stressing the effects of dampness, mildew, or age ⟨the *fusty* rooms of a boarded-up mansion⟩ ⟨the *musty* odor of a damp cellar⟩.

MASTERFUL, domineering, imperious, peremptory, imperative mean tending to impose one's will on others.

Masterful implies a strong personality and ability to act authoritatively ⟨her *masterful* personality soon dominated the movement⟩.

Domineering suggests an overbearing or arbitrary manner and an obstinate determination to enforce one's will ⟨children controlled by *domineering* parents⟩.

Imperious implies a commanding nature or manner and often suggests arrogant assurance ⟨an *imperious* executive used to getting his own way⟩.

Peremptory implies an abrupt dictatorial manner coupled with an unwillingness to brook disobedience or dissent ⟨his *peremptory* style does not allow for consultation or compromise⟩.

Imperative implies peremptoriness arising more from the urgency of the situation than from an inherent will to dominate ⟨an *imperative* appeal for assistance⟩.

MATERIAL, physical, corporeal, phenomenal, sensible, objective mean of or belonging to actuality.

Material implies formation out of tangible matter; used in contrast with *spiritual* or *ideal* it may connote the mundane, crass, or grasping ⟨*material* possessions⟩.

Physical applies to what is perceived directly by the senses and may contrast with *mental, spiritual,* or *imaginary* ⟨the *physical* benefits of exercise⟩.

Corporeal implies having the tangible qualities of a body such as shape, size, or resistance to force ⟨artists have portrayed angels as *corporeal* beings⟩.

Phenomenal applies to what is known or perceived through the senses rather than by intuition or rational deduction ⟨scientists concerned only with the *phenomenal* world⟩.

Sensible stresses the capability of readily or forcibly impressing the senses ⟨the earth's rotation is not *sensible* to us⟩.

Objective may stress material or independent existence apart from a subject perceiving it ⟨tears are the *objective* manifestation of grief⟩.

See in addition RELEVANT.

MATRIMONIAL, marital, conjugal, connubial, nuptial mean of, relating to, or characteristic of marriage.

Matrimonial and **marital** apply to whatever has to do with marriage and the married state ⟨enjoyed 40 years of *matri-*

monial bliss⟩ ⟨a *marital* relationship built upon mutual trust and understanding⟩.

Conjugal specif. applies to married persons and their rights ⟨inmates of the prison now have *conjugal* rights⟩.

Connubial may refer to the married state itself ⟨a *connubial* contract of no legal standing⟩.

Nuptial usu. refers to the marriage ceremony ⟨busy all week with the *nuptial* preparations⟩.

MEAGER, scanty, scant, skimpy, spare, sparse mean falling short of what is normal, necessary, or desirable.

Meager implies the absence of elements, qualities, or numbers necessary to a thing's richness, substance, or potency ⟨a *meager* portion of meat⟩.

Scanty stresses insufficiency in amount, quantity, or extent ⟨supplies too *scanty* to last the winter⟩.

Scant suggests a falling short of what is desired or desirable rather than of what is essential ⟨in January the daylight hours are *scant*⟩.

Skimpy usu. suggests niggardliness or penury as the cause of the deficiency ⟨tacky housing developments on *skimpy* lots⟩.

Spare may suggest a slight falling short of adequacy or merely an absence of superfluity ⟨a *spare*, concise style of writing⟩.

Sparse implies a thin scattering of units ⟨a *sparse* population⟩.

MEAN *adj* **Mean, ignoble, abject, sordid** mean below the normal standards of human decency and dignity.

Mean suggests having repellent characteristics (as small-mindedness, ill temper, or cupidity) ⟨*mean* and petty characterizations of former colleagues⟩.

Ignoble suggests a loss or lack of some essential high quality of mind or spirit ⟨*ignoble* collectors who view artworks merely as investments⟩.

Abject may imply degradation, debasement, or servility ⟨the *abject* poverty of her youth⟩.

Sordid is stronger than all of these in stressing physical or spiritual degradation and abjectness ⟨a *sordid* story of murder and revenge⟩.

MEANING, sense, acceptation, signification, significance, import denote the idea conveyed to the mind.

Meaning is the general term used of anything (as a word, sign, poem, or action) requiring or allowing of interpretation ⟨the poem's *meaning* has been fiercely debated⟩.

Sense denotes the meaning or more often a particular meaning of a word or phrase ⟨used ''nighthawk'' in its figurative *sense*⟩.

Acceptation is used of a sense of a word or phrase as regularly understood by a large number of speakers and writers ⟨the writer isn't using ''sane'' in its common *acceptation*⟩.

Signification denotes the established meaning of a term, symbol, or character ⟨any Christian would immediately know the *signification* of ''INRI''⟩.

Significance applies specif. to a covert as distinguished from the ostensible meaning of an utterance, act, or work of art ⟨an agreement that seemed to have little *significance* at the time⟩.

Import suggests the meaning a speaker tries to convey esp. through language ⟨failed at first to appreciate the *import* of the news⟩.

MEMORY, remembrance, recollection, reminiscence mean the capacity for or the act of remembering, or the thing remembered.

Memory applies both to the power of remembering and to what is remembered ⟨gifted with a remarkable *memory*⟩ ⟨no *memory* of that incident⟩.

Remembrance applies to the act of remembering or the fact of being remembered ⟨any *remembrance* of his deceased wife was painful⟩.

Recollection adds an implication of consciously bringing back to mind often with some effort ⟨after a moment's *recollection* he produced the name⟩.

Reminiscence suggests the recalling of incidents. experience. or feelings from a remote past ⟨recorded my grandmother's *reminiscences* of her Iowa girlhood⟩.

MEND, repair, patch, rebuild mean to put into good order something that has been injured. damaged. or defective.

Mend implies making whole or sound something broken. torn. or injured ⟨the wound *mended* slowly⟩.

Repair applies to the mending of more extensive damage or dilapidation ⟨the car needs to be *repaired* by a mechanic⟩.

Patch implies an often temporary mending of a rent or breach with new material ⟨*patch* potholes with asphalt⟩.

Rebuild suggests making like new without completely replacing ⟨a *rebuilt* telephone is cheaper than a brand-new one⟩.

MERCY, charity, clemency, grace, lenity mean a disposition to show kindness or compassion.

Mercy implies compassion that forbears punishing even when justice demands it ⟨admitted his guilt and then begged for *mercy*⟩.

Charity stresses benevolence and goodwill shown in broad understanding and tolerance of others ⟨show a little *charity* for the weak-willed⟩.

Clemency implies a mild or merciful disposition in one having the power or duty of punishing ⟨a judge little inclined to show *clemency*⟩.

Grace implies a benign attitude and a willingness to grant favors or make concessions ⟨the victor's *grace* in treating the vanquished⟩.

Lenity implies lack of severity in punishing ⟨criticized the courts for excessive *lenity*⟩.

MERRY, blithe, jocund, jovial, jolly mean showing high spirits or lightheartedness.

Merry suggests cheerful, joyous, uninhibited enjoyment of frolic or festivity ⟨a *merry* group of holiday revelers⟩.

Blithe suggests carefree, innocent, or even heedless gaiety ⟨arrived late in her usual *blithe* way⟩.

Jocund stresses elation and exhilaration of spirits ⟨good news had left him in a *jocund* mood⟩.

Jovial suggests the stimulation of conviviality and good fellowship ⟨grew increasingly *jovial* with every drink⟩.

Jolly suggests high spirits expressed in laughing, bantering, and jesting ⟨our *jolly* host enlivened the party⟩.

METHOD, mode, manner, way, fashion, system mean the means taken or procedure followed in achieving an end.

Method implies an orderly logical effective arrangement usu. in steps ⟨effective teaching *methods*⟩.

Mode implies an order or course followed by custom, tradition, or personal preference ⟨the preferred *mode* of transportation⟩.

Manner is close to *mode* but may imply a procedure or method that is individual or distinctive ⟨a highly distinctive *manner* of conducting⟩.

Way is very general and may be used for any of the preceding words ⟨her own *way* of doing things⟩.

Fashion may suggest a peculiar or characteristic way of doing something ⟨rushing about, in typical New Yorker *fashion*⟩.

System suggests a fully developed or carefully formulated method often emphasizing the idea of rational orderliness ⟨follows no *system* in playing the horses⟩.

MIRTH, glee, jollity, hilarity mean a feeling of high spirits that is expressed in laughter, play, or merrymaking.

Mirth implies generally lightness of heart and love of gaiety ⟨family gatherings that were the occasions of much *mirth*⟩.

Glee stresses exultation shown in laughter, cries of joy, or sometimes malicious delight ⟨cackled with *glee* at their misfortune⟩.

Jollity suggests exuberance or lack of restraint in mirth or glee ⟨his endless flow of jokes added to the *jollity*⟩.

Hilarity suggests loud or irrepressible laughter or high-spirited boisterousness ⟨a dull comedy not likely to inspire much *hilarity*⟩.

MISFORTUNE, mischance, adversity, mishap mean adverse fortune or an instance of this.

Misfortune may apply to either the incident or conjunction of events that is the cause of an unhappy change of fortune or to the ensuing state of distress ⟨never lost hope even in the depths of *misfortune*⟩.

Mischance applies esp. to a situation involving no more than slight inconvenience or minor annoyance ⟨took the wrong road by *mischance*⟩.

Adversity applies to a state of grave or persistent misfortune ⟨had never experienced much *adversity* in life⟩.

Mishap applies to a trivial instance of bad luck ⟨the usual *mishaps* that are part of a family vacation⟩.

MIX, mingle, commingle, blend, merge, coalesce, amalgamate, fuse mean to combine into a more or less uniform whole.

Mix may or may not imply loss of each element's identity ⟨*mix* the salad greens⟩.

Mingle usu. suggests that the elements are still somewhat distinguishable or separately active ⟨fear *mingled* with anticipation in my mind⟩.

Commingle implies a closer or more thorough mingling ⟨a sense of duty *commingled* with a fierce pride⟩.

Blend implies that the elements as such disappear in the resulting mixture ⟨*blended* several teas to create a balanced brew⟩.

Merge suggests a combining in which one or more elements are lost in the whole ⟨in her mind reality and fantasy *merged*⟩.

Coalesce implies an affinity in the merging elements and usu.

a resulting organic unity ⟨telling details that *coalesce* into a striking portrait⟩.

Amalgamate implies the forming of a close union without complete loss of individual identities ⟨immigrants that were readily *amalgamated* into the population⟩.

Fuse stresses oneness and indissolubility of the resulting product ⟨a building in which modernism and classicism are *fused*⟩.

MODEL, example, pattern, exemplar, ideal mean someone or something set before one for guidance or imitation.

Model applies to something taken or proposed as worthy of imitation ⟨a performance that is a *model* of charm and intelligence⟩.

Example applies to a person to be imitated or in some contexts on no account to be imitated but to be regarded as a warning ⟨for better or worse, children follow the *example* of their parents⟩.

Pattern suggests a clear and detailed archetype or prototype ⟨American industry set a *pattern* for others to follow⟩.

Exemplar suggests either a faultless example to be emulated or a perfect typification ⟨cited Hitler as the *exemplar* of power-mad egomania⟩.

Ideal implies the best possible exemplification either in reality or in conception ⟨never found a suitor who matched her *ideal*⟩.

MONSTROUS, prodigious, tremendous, stupendous mean extremely impressive.

Monstrous implies a departure from the normal (as in size, form, or character) and often carries suggestions of deformity, ugliness, or fabulousness ⟨the *monstrous* waste of the project⟩.

Prodigious suggests a marvelousness exceeding belief, usu. in something felt as going far beyond a previous maximum (as of goodness, greatness, intensity, or size) ⟨made a *prodigious* effort and rolled the stone aside⟩.

Tremendous may imply a power to terrify or inspire awe ⟨the *tremendous* roar of the cataract⟩, but in more general and much weakened use it means little more than very large or great or intense ⟨success gave him *tremendous* satisfaction⟩.

Stupendous implies a power to stun or astound, usu. because of size, numbers, complexity, or greatness beyond one's power to describe ⟨a *stupendous* volcanic eruption that destroyed the city⟩.

See in addition OUTRAGEOUS.

MORAL, ethical, virtuous, righteous, noble mean conforming to a standard of what is right and good.

Moral implies conformity to established sanctioned codes or accepted notions of right and wrong ⟨the basic *moral* values of a community⟩.

Ethical may suggest the involvement of more difficult or subtle questions of rightness, fairness, or equity ⟨his strict *ethical* code would not tolerate it⟩.

Virtuous implies the possession or manifestation of moral excellence in character ⟨a person not conventionally religious, but *virtuous* in all other respects⟩.

Righteous stresses guiltlessness or blamelessness and often suggests the sanctimonious ⟨responded to the charge with *righteous* indignation⟩.

Noble implies moral eminence and freedom from anything petty, mean, or dubious in conduct and character ⟨had only the *noblest* of reasons for pursuing the case⟩.

MOTIVE, impulse, incentive, inducement, spur, goad mean a stimulus to action.

Motive implies an emotion or desire operating on the will and causing it to act ⟨a crime without apparent *motive*⟩.

Impulse suggests a driving power arising from personal temperament or constitution ⟨my first *impulse* was to hit him⟩.

Incentive applies to an external influence (as an expected reward) inciting to action ⟨a bonus was offered as an *incentive* for meeting the deadline⟩.

Inducement suggests a motive prompted by the deliberate enticements or allurements of another ⟨offered a watch as an *inducement* to subscribe⟩.

Spur applies to a motive that stimulates the faculties or increases energy or ardor ⟨fear was the *spur* that kept me going⟩.

Goad suggests a motive that keeps one going against one's will or desire ⟨the need to earn a living is the daily *goad*⟩.

MOVE, actuate, drive, impel mean to set or keep in motion. **Move** is very general and implies no more than the fact of changing position ⟨the force that *moves* the moon around the earth⟩.

Actuate stresses transmission of power so as to work or set in motion ⟨turbines are *actuated* by the force of a current of water⟩.

Drive implies imparting forward and continuous motion and often stresses the effect rather than the impetus ⟨a ship *driven* aground by hurricane winds⟩.

Impel suggests a greater impetus producing more headlong action ⟨burning ambition *impelled* her to the seat of power⟩.

MOVING, impressive, poignant, affecting, touching, pathetic mean having the power to produce deep emotion. **Moving** may apply to any strong emotional effect including thrilling, agitating, saddening, or calling forth pity or sympathy ⟨a *moving* appeal for charitable contributions⟩.

Impressive implies compelling attention, admiration, wonder, or conviction ⟨an *impressive* list of achievements⟩.

Poignant applies to what keenly or sharply affects one's sensitivities ⟨a *poignant* documentary on the plight of the homeless⟩.

Affecting is close to *moving* but most often suggests pathos ⟨an *affecting* reunion of a mother and her child⟩.

Touching implies arousing tenderness or compassion ⟨the *touching* innocence in a child's eyes⟩.

Pathetic implies moving to pity or sometimes contempt ⟨*pathetic* attempts to justify gross negligence⟩.

MYSTERY, problem, enigma, riddle, puzzle, conundrum mean something which baffles or perplexes.

Mystery applies to what cannot be fully understood by human reason or less strictly to whatever resists or defies explanation ⟨the *mystery* of the stone monoliths on Easter Island⟩.

Problem applies to any question or difficulty calling for a solution or causing concern ⟨the *problems* created by high technology⟩.

Enigma applies to utterance or behavior that is very difficult to interpret ⟨his suicide was an *enigma* his family never solved⟩.

Riddle suggests an enigma or problem involving paradox or apparent contradiction ⟨the *riddle* of the reclusive billionaire⟩.

Puzzle applies to an enigma or problem that challenges ingenuity for its solution ⟨the mechanisms of heredity were long a *puzzle* for scientists⟩.

Conundrum applies to a question whose answer involves a pun or less often to a problem whose solution can only be speculative ⟨posed *conundrums* to which there are no practical solutions⟩.

N

NATIVE, indigenous, endemic, aboriginal mean belonging to a locality.

Native implies birth or origin in a place or region and may suggest compatibility with it ⟨*native* tribal customs⟩ ⟨a *native* New Yorker⟩.

Indigenous applies to species or races and adds to *native* the implication of not having been introduced from elsewhere ⟨maize is *indigenous* to America⟩.

Endemic implies being peculiar to a region ⟨edelweiss is *endemic* in the Alps⟩.

Aboriginal implies having no known race preceding in occupancy of the region ⟨the *aboriginal* peoples of Australia⟩.

NATURAL, ingenuous, naive, unsophisticated, artless mean free from pretension or calculation.

Natural implies lacking artificiality and self-consciousness and having a spontaneousness suggesting the natural rather than the man-made world ⟨her unaffected, *natural* quality comes across on film⟩.

Ingenuous implies inability to disguise or conceal one's feelings or intentions ⟨the *ingenuous,* spontaneous utterances of children⟩.

Naive suggests lack of worldly wisdom often connoting credulousness and unchecked innocence ⟨in money matters she was distressingly *naive*⟩.

Unsophisticated implies a lack of experience and training necessary for social ease and adroitness ⟨the store intimidates *unsophisticated* customers⟩.

Artless suggests a naturalness resulting from unawareness of the effect one is producing on others ⟨gave an *artless* impromptu speech at the dinner⟩.

See in addition REGULAR.

NEGLECT, omit, disregard, ignore, overlook, slight, forget mean to pass over without giving due attention.

Neglect implies giving insufficient attention to something that has a claim to one's attention ⟨habitually *neglected* his studies⟩.

Omit implies absence of all attention ⟨*omitted* to remove the telltale fingerprints⟩.

Disregard suggests voluntary inattention ⟨*disregarded* the wishes of the other members⟩.

Ignore implies a failure to regard something obvious ⟨*ignored* the snide remarks of passersby⟩.

Overlook suggests disregarding or ignoring through haste or lack of care ⟨in my rush I *overlooked* some relevant examples⟩.

Slight implies contemptuous or disdainful disregarding or omitting ⟨*slighted* several worthy authors in her survey⟩.

Forget may suggest either a willful ignoring or a failure to impress something on one's mind ⟨*forget* what others say and listen to your conscience⟩.

NEGLIGENT, neglectful, lax, slack, remiss mean culpably careless or indicative of such carelessness.

Negligent implies inattention to one's duty or business ⟨I had been *negligent* in my letter-writing⟩.

Neglectful adds a more disapproving implication of laziness or deliberate inattention ⟨a society callously *neglectful* of the poor⟩.

Lax implies a blameworthy lack of strictness, severity, or precision ⟨a reporter who is *lax* about getting the facts straight⟩.

Slack implies want of due or necessary diligence or care ⟨the *slack* workmanship and slipshod construction⟩.

Remiss implies blameworthy carelessness shown in slackness, forgetfulness, or neglect ⟨had been *remiss* in her familial duties⟩.

NEW, novel, modern, original, fresh mean having recently come into existence or use.

New may apply to what is freshly made and unused ⟨*new* brick⟩ or has not been known before ⟨*new* designs⟩ or not experienced before ⟨starts his *new* job⟩.

Novel applies to what is not only new but strange or unprecedented ⟨a *novel* approach to the problem⟩.

Modern applies to what belongs to or is characteristic of the present time or the present era ⟨the lifestyle of the *modern* woman⟩.

Original applies to what is the first of its kind to exist ⟨a man without one *original* idea⟩.

Fresh applies to what has not lost its qualities of newness such as liveliness, energy, brightness ⟨*fresh* towels⟩ ⟨a *fresh* start⟩.

NICE, dainty, fastidious, finicky, particular, squeamish mean having or showing exacting standards.

Nice implies fine discrimination in perception and evaluation ⟨makes a *nice* distinction between an artist and a craftsman⟩.

Dainty suggests a tendency to reject what does not satisfy one's delicate taste or sensibility ⟨when camping, one cannot afford to be *dainty* about food⟩.

Fastidious implies having very high and often capricious ethical, artistic, or social standards ⟨a woman too *fastidious* to tolerate messy little boys⟩.

Finicky implies an affected often exasperating fastidiousness ⟨small children are usually *finicky* eaters⟩.

Particular implies an insistence that one's exacting standards be met ⟨a customer who is very *particular* about his fried eggs⟩.

Squeamish suggests an oversensitive or prudish readiness to be nauseated, disgusted, or offended ⟨*squeamish* about erotic art⟩.

See in addition CORRECT.

NOTICEABLE, remarkable, prominent, outstanding, conspicuous, salient, striking mean attracting notice or attention.

Noticeable applies to something unlikely to escape observation ⟨a piano recital with no *noticeable* errors⟩.

Remarkable applies to something so extraordinary or exceptional as to invite comment ⟨a film of *remarkable* intelligence and wit⟩.

Prominent applies to something commanding notice by standing out from its surroundings or background ⟨a doctor who occupies a *prominent* position in the town⟩.

Outstanding applies to something that rises above and excels others of the same kind ⟨honored for her *outstanding* contributions to science⟩.

Conspicuous applies to something that is obvious and unavoidable to the sight or mind ⟨the *conspicuous* waste of the corrupt regime⟩.

Salient applies to something of significance that merits the attention given it ⟨list the *salient* points of the speech⟩.

Striking applies to something that impresses itself powerfully and deeply upon the observer's mind or vision ⟨the backwardness of the area is *striking* to even casual observers⟩.

NULLIFY, negate, annul, abrogate, invalidate mean to deprive of effective or continued existence.

Nullify implies counteracting completely the force, effectiveness, or value of something ⟨his critical insights are *nullified* by tiresome puns⟩.

Negate implies the destruction or canceling out of each of two things by the other ⟨a relationship *negated* by petty jealousies⟩.

Annul suggests making ineffective or nonexistent often by legal or official action ⟨the treaty *annuls* all previous agreements⟩.

Abrogate is like *annul* but more definitely implies a legal or official purposeful act ⟨a law that would *abrogate* certain diplomatic privileges⟩.

Invalidate implies making something powerless or unacceptable by declaration of its logical or moral or legal unsoundness ⟨the absence of witnesses *invalidates* the will⟩.

O

OBEDIENT, docile, tractable, amenable mean submissive to the will of another.

Obedient implies compliance with the demands or requests of one in authority ⟨cadets must be *obedient* to the honor code⟩.

Docile implies a predisposition to submit readily to control or guidance ⟨a *docile* child who never caused trouble⟩.

Tractable suggests having a character that permits easy handling or managing ⟨Indian elephants are more *tractable* than their African cousins⟩.

Amenable suggests a willingness to yield or to cooperate either because of a desire to be agreeable or because of a natural open-mindedness ⟨he's usually *amenable* to suggestions and new ideas⟩.

OBJECT *vb* **Object, protest, remonstrate, expostulate, kick** mean to oppose by arguing against.

Object stresses dislike or aversions ⟨*objected* to his sweeping generalizations⟩.

Protest suggests an orderly presentation of objections in speech or writing ⟨an open letter *protesting* the government's foreign policy⟩.

Remonstrate implies an attempt to convince by warning or reproving ⟨*remonstrated* on his son's free-spending ways at college⟩.

Expostulate suggests an earnest explanation of one's objection and firm insistence on change ⟨mother *expostulated*, but my room remained a mess⟩.

Kick suggests more informally a strenuous protesting or complaining ⟨everybody *kicks* when taxes are raised⟩.

OBSCURE, dark, vague, enigmatic, cryptic, ambiguous, equivocal mean not clearly understandable.

Obscure implies a hiding or veiling of meaning through some inadequacy of expression or withholding of full knowledge ⟨the poem is *obscure* to those unlearned in the classics⟩.

Dark implies an imperfect or clouded revelation often with ominous or sinister suggestion ⟨muttered *dark* hints of revenge⟩.

Vague implies a lack of clear formulation due to inadequate conception or consideration ⟨*vague* promises of reimbursement were made⟩.

Enigmatic stresses a puzzling, mystifying quality ⟨left behind *enigmatic* works on alchemy⟩.

Cryptic implies a purposely concealed meaning ⟨a *cryptic* message only a spy could decode⟩.

Ambiguous applies to a difficulty of understanding arising

from the use of a word or words of multiple meanings ⟨an *ambiguous* directive that could be taken either way⟩.
Equivocal applies to the deliberate use of language open to differing interpretations with the intention of deceiving or evading ⟨the prisoner would give only *equivocal* answers⟩.

OBSTINATE, dogged, stubborn, pertinacious, mulish mean fixed and unyielding in course or purpose.
Obstinate implies usu. a perverse or unreasonable persistence ⟨a President who was resolute but never *obstinate*⟩.
Dogged suggests a tenacious unwavering persistence ⟨pursued the story with *dogged* perseverance⟩.
Stubborn implies sturdiness in resisting attempts to change or abandon a course or opinion ⟨swallow your *stubborn* pride and admit that you are wrong⟩.
Pertinacious suggests an annoying or irksome persistence ⟨a *pertinacious* salesman who wouldn't take no for an answer⟩.
Mulish implies a thoroughly unreasonable obstinacy ⟨a *mulish* determination to stick with a lost cause⟩.

OCCURRENCE, event, incident, episode, circumstance mean something that happens or takes place.
Occurrence may apply to a happening without intent, volition, or plan ⟨a meeting that was a chance *occurrence*⟩.
Event usu. implies an occurrence of some importance and frequently one having antecedent cause ⟨the sequence of *events* following the assassination⟩.
Incident suggests an occurrence of brief duration or secondary importance ⟨one of the minor *incidents* of the war⟩.
Episode stresses the distinctiveness or apartness of an incident ⟨recounted some amusing *episodes* from his youth⟩.
Circumstance implies a specific detail attending an action or event as part of its setting or background ⟨couldn't remember the exact *circumstances*⟩.

ODOROUS, fragrant, redolent, aromatic mean emitting and diffusing scent.
Odorous applies to whatever has a strong distinctive smell

whether pleasant or unpleasant ⟨*odorous* cheeses should be tightly wrapped⟩.

Fragrant applies to things (as flowers or spices) with sweet or agreeable odors ⟨roses that were especially *fragrant*⟩.

Redolent applies usu. to a place or thing impregnated with odors ⟨the kitchen was often *redolent* of garlic and tomatoes⟩.

Aromatic applies to things emitting pungent often fresh odors ⟨an *aromatic* blend of rare tobaccos⟩.

OFFEND, outrage, affront, insult mean to cause hurt feelings or deep resentment.

Offend need not imply an intentional hurting but it may indicate merely a violation of the victim's sense of what is proper or fitting ⟨hoped that my remarks had not *offended* her⟩.

Outrage implies offending beyond endurance and calling forth extreme feelings ⟨corruption that *outrages* every citizen⟩.

Affront implies treating with deliberate rudeness or contemptuous indifference to courtesy ⟨a movie that *affronts* your intelligence⟩.

Insult suggests deliberately causing humiliation, hurt pride, or shame ⟨managed to *insult* every guest at the party⟩.

OFFENSE *n* **Offense, resentment, umbrage, pique, dudgeon, huff** mean an emotional response to a slight or indignity.

Offense implies hurt displeasure ⟨takes deep *offense* at racial slurs⟩.

Resentment suggests a longer lasting indignation or smoldering ill will ⟨harbored a lifelong *resentment* of his brother⟩.

Umbrage implies a feeling of being snubbed or ignored ⟨took *umbrage* at a lecturer who debunked American legends⟩.

Pique applies to a transient feeling of wounded vanity ⟨in a *pique* she foolishly declined the invitation⟩.

Dudgeon suggests an angry fit of indignation ⟨walked out of the meeting in high *dudgeon*⟩.

Huff implies a peevish short-lived spell of anger usu. at a petty cause ⟨in a *huff* he slammed the door⟩.

OFFENSE *n* **Offense, sin, vice, crime, scandal** mean a transgression of law.

Offense applies to the infraction of any law, rule, or code ⟨at that school no *offense* went unpunished⟩.

Sin implies an offense against the moral law ⟨the *sin* of blasphemy⟩.

Vice applies to a habit or practice that degrades or corrupts ⟨gambling was traditionally the gentleman's *vice*⟩.

Crime implies a serious offense punishable by the law of the state ⟨the *crime* of murder⟩.

Scandal applies to an offense that outrages the public conscience ⟨a career ruined by a sex *scandal*⟩.

OLD, ancient, venerable, antique, antiquated, archaic, obsolete mean having come into existence or use in the more or less distant past.

Old may apply to either actual or merely relative length of existence ⟨*old* houses⟩ ⟨an *old* sweater of mine⟩.

Ancient applies to occurrence, existence, or use in or survival from the distant past ⟨*ancient* accounts of dragons⟩.

Venerable stresses the impressiveness and dignity of great age ⟨the family's *venerable* patriarch⟩.

Antique applies to what has come down from a former or ancient time ⟨collected *antique* Chippendale furniture⟩.

Antiquated implies being discredited or outmoded or otherwise inappropriate to the present time ⟨*antiquated* teaching methods⟩.

Archaic implies having the character or characteristics of a much earlier time ⟨the play used *archaic* language to convey a sense of period⟩.

Obsolete implies having gone out of currency or habitual practice ⟨a computer that makes earlier models *obsolete*⟩.

OMINOUS, portentous, fateful mean having a menacing or threatening aspect.

Ominous implies a menacing, alarming character foreshadowing evil or disaster ⟨*ominous* rumblings from a dormant volcano⟩.

Portentous suggests being frighteningly big or impressive but now seldom definitely connotes forwarning of calamity ⟨the *portentous* voice of the host of a mystery series⟩.

Fateful suggests being of momentous or decisive importance ⟨the *fateful* conference that led to war⟩.

OMNIPRESENT, ubiquitous mean present or existent everywhere.

Omnipresent in its strict sense is a divine attribute equivalent to *immanent;* more commonly it implies never being absent ⟨residents in that neighborhood have an *omnipresent* sense of fear⟩.

Ubiquitous implies being so active or so numerous as to seem to be found everywhere ⟨*ubiquitous* tourists toting their *omnipresent* cameras⟩.

ONEROUS, burdensome, oppressive, exacting mean imposing hardship.

Onerous stresses being laborious and heavy esp. because distasteful ⟨the *onerous* task of informing the family of his death⟩.

Burdensome suggests causing mental as well as physical strain ⟨*burdensome* government regulations⟩.

Oppressive implies extreme harshness or severity in what is imposed ⟨found the pressure to conform socially *oppressive*⟩.

Exacting implies rigor or sternness rather than tyranny or injustice in the demands made or in the one demanding ⟨an *exacting* employer⟩.

OPINION, view, belief, conviction, persuasion, sentiment mean a judgment one holds as true.

Opinion implies a conclusion thought out yet open to dispute ⟨each expert seemed to be of a different *opinion*⟩.

View suggests a subjective opinion ⟨very assertive in stating his *views*⟩.

Belief implies often deliberate acceptance and intellectual assent ⟨a firm *belief* in a supreme being⟩.

Conviction applies to a firmly and seriously held belief ⟨a *conviction* that animal life is as sacred as human⟩.

Persuasion suggests a belief grounded on assurance (as by evidence) of its truth ⟨was of the *persuasion* that Republicans were better for business⟩.

Sentiment suggests a settled opinion reflective of one's feelings ⟨her feminist *sentiments* were well-known⟩.

OPPONENT, antagonist, adversary mean one that takes an opposite position.

Opponent implies little more than position on the other side as in a debate, election, contest, or conflict ⟨*opponents* of the project cite cost as a factor⟩.

Antagonist implies sharper opposition in a struggle for supremacy ⟨a formidable *antagonist* in the struggle for corporate control⟩.

Adversary may carry an additional implication of active hostility ⟨two peoples that have been bitter *adversaries* for centuries⟩.

OPPOSE, combat, resist, withstand, antagonize mean to set oneself against someone or something.

Oppose can apply to any conflict, from mere objection to bitter hostility or warfare ⟨*opposed* the plan to build a nuclear power plant⟩.

Combat stresses the forceful or urgent countering of something ⟨*combat* the disease by educating the public⟩.

Resist implies an overt recognition of a hostile or threatening force and a positive effort to counteract or repel it ⟨struggled valiantly to *resist* the temptation⟩.

Withstand suggests a more passive resistance ⟨unable to *withstand* peer pressure⟩.

Antagonize implies an arousing of resistance or hostility in another ⟨statements that *antagonized* even his own supporters⟩.

OPPOSITE, contradictory, contrary, antithetical mean being so far apart as to be or seem irreconcilable.

Opposite applies to things in sharp contrast or in conflict ⟨they held *opposite* views on foreign aid⟩.

Contradictory applies to two things that completely negate each other so that if one is true or valid the other must be untrue or invalid ⟨made *contradictory* predictions about the stock market⟩.

Contrary implies extreme divergence or diametrical opposition ⟨*contrary* accounts of the late president's character⟩.

Antithetical stresses clear and unequivocal diametrical opposition ⟨a law that is *antithetical* to the basic idea of democracy⟩.

ORDER, arrange, marshal, organize, systematize, methodize mean to put persons or things into their proper places in relation to each other.

Order suggests a straightening out so as to eliminate confusion ⟨*ordered* her business affairs before going on extended leave⟩.

Arrange implies a setting in sequence, relationship, or adjustment ⟨a bouquet of elaborately *arranged* flowers⟩.

Marshal suggests gathering and arranging in preparation for a particular operation or effective use ⟨an argument won by carefully *marshalled* facts⟩.

Organize implies arranging so that the whole aggregate works as a unit with each element having a proper function ⟨*organized* the volunteers into teams⟩.

Systematize implies arranging according to a predetermined scheme ⟨billing procedures that have yet to be *systematized*⟩.

Methodize suggests imposing an orderly procedure rather than a fixed scheme ⟨*methodizes* every aspect of her daily living⟩.

See in addition COMMAND.

ORIGIN, source, inception, root mean the point at which something begins its course or existence.

Origin applies to the things or persons from which something is ultimately derived and often to the causes operating before the thing itself comes into being ⟨an investigation into the *origins* of baseball⟩.

Source applies more often to the point where something springs into being ⟨the *source* of the Nile⟩ ⟨the *source* of recurrent trouble⟩.

Inception stresses the beginning of something without implying causes ⟨the business has been a success since its *inception*⟩.

Root suggests a first, ultimate, or fundamental source often not easily discerned ⟨a need to find the real *root* of the violence⟩.

OUTLINE, contour, profile, silhouette mean the line that bounds and gives form to something.

Outline applies to a line marking the outer limits or edges of a body or mass ⟨chalk *outlines* of the bodies on the sidewalk⟩.

Contour stresses the quality of an outline or a bounding surface as being smooth, jagged, curving, or sharply angled ⟨a car with smoothly flowing *contours*⟩.

Profile suggests a varied and sharply defined outline against a lighter background ⟨her face in *profile* accentuates her patrician beauty⟩.

Silhouette suggests a shape esp. of a head or figure with all detail blacked out in shadow leaving only the outline clearly defined ⟨a photograph of two figures in *silhouette* on a mountain ridge⟩.

OUTRAGEOUS, monstrous, heinous, atrocious mean enormously bad or horrible.

Outrageous implies exceeding the limits of what is bearable or endurable ⟨*outrageous* terrorist acts against civilians⟩.

Monstrous applies to what is abnormally or fantastically wrong, absurd, or horrible ⟨a *monstrous* waste of the taxpayers' money⟩.

Heinous implies being so flagrantly evil as to excite hatred or horror ⟨*heinous* crimes that exceeded normal wartime actions⟩.

Atrocious implies merciless cruelty, savagery, or contempt of ordinary values ⟨decent people cannot condone such *atrocious* treatment of prisoners⟩.

P

PACIFY, appease, placate, mollify, propitiate, conciliate mean to ease the anger or disturbance of.

Pacify suggests a smoothing or calming ⟨a sincere apology seemed to *pacify* him⟩.

Appease implies quieting insistent demands by making concessions ⟨nothing seemed to *appease* their appetite for territorial expansion⟩.

Placate suggests changing resentment or bitterness to goodwill ⟨bought flowers to *placate* his irate wife⟩.

Mollify implies soothing hurt feelings or rising anger ⟨a promise of a hearing *mollified* the demonstrators⟩.

Propitiate implies averting anger or malevolence esp. of a superior being ⟨*propitiated* his parents by wearing a tie⟩.

Conciliate suggests ending an estrangement by persuasion, concession, or settling of differences ⟨America's role in *conciliating* the nations of the Middle East⟩.

PALATABLE, appetizing, savory, tasty, toothsome mean agreeable or pleasant esp. to the sense of taste.

Palatable often applies to something that is unexpectedly found to be agreeable ⟨surprised to find Indian food quite *palatable*⟩.

Appetizing suggests a whetting of the appetite and applies to aroma and appearance as well as taste ⟨select from a cart filled with *appetizing* desserts⟩.

Savory applies to both taste and aroma and suggests piquancy and often spiciness ⟨egg rolls with various *savory* fillings⟩.

Tasty implies a pronounced taste ⟨stale shrimp that were far from *tasty*⟩.

Toothsome stresses the notion of agreeableness and sometimes implies tenderness or daintiness ⟨a dazzling array of *toothsome* hors d'oeuvres⟩.

PARASITE, sycophant, toady, leech, sponge mean an obsequious flatterer or self-seeker.

Parasite applies to one who clings to a person of wealth, power, or influence or is useless to society ⟨a jet-setter with the usual entourage of *parasites*⟩.

Sycophant adds to this a strong suggestion of fawning, flattery, or adulation ⟨a religious cult leader surrounded by *sycophants*⟩.

Toady emphasizes the servility and snobbery of the self-seeker ⟨the president's own *toady* made others grovel⟩.

Leech stresses persistence in clinging to or bleeding another for one's own advantage ⟨*leeches* who abandoned her when the money ran out⟩.

Sponge stresses the parasitic laziness, dependence, and opportunism of the cadger ⟨her brother, a shiftless *sponge*, often came by for a free meal⟩.

PART *n* **Part, portion, piece, member, division, section, segment, fragment** mean something less than the whole.

Part is a general term appropriate when indefiniteness is required ⟨they ran only *part* of the way⟩.

Portion implies an assigned or allotted part ⟨cut the pie into six *portions*⟩.

Piece applies to a separate or detached part of a whole ⟨a puzzle with 500 *pieces*⟩.

Member suggests one of the functional units composing a body ⟨an arm is a bodily *member*⟩.

Division applies to a large or diversified part ⟨the manufacturing *division* of the company⟩.

Section applies to a relatively small or uniform part ⟨the entertainment *section* of the newspaper⟩.

Segment applies to a part separated or marked out by or as if by natural lines of cleavage ⟨the retired *segment* of the population⟩.

Fragment applies to a part produced by or as if by breaking off or shattering ⟨only a *fragment* of the play still exists⟩.

PASSION, fervor, ardor, enthusiasm, zeal mean intense emotion compelling action.

Passion applies to an emotion that is deeply stirring or ungovernable ⟨developed a *passion* for reading⟩.

Fervor implies a warm and steady emotion ⟨read the poem aloud with great *fervor*⟩.

Ardor suggests warm and excited feeling likely to be fitful or short-lived ⟨the *ardor* of their honeymoon soon faded⟩.

Enthusiasm applies to lively or eager interest in or admiration for a proposal or cause or activity ⟨never showed much *enthusiasm* for sports⟩.

Zeal implies energetic and unflagging pursuit of an aim or devotion to a cause ⟨preaches with the *zeal* of the converted⟩. See in addition FEELING.

PAY, compensate, remunerate, satisfy, reimburse, indemnify, repay, recompense mean to give money or its equivalent in return for something.

Pay implies the discharge of an obligation incurred ⟨we *pay* taxes in exchange for government services⟩.

Compensate implies a making up for services rendered or help given ⟨an attorney well *compensated* for her services⟩.

Remunerate more clearly suggests paying for services rendered and may extend to payment that is generous or not contracted for ⟨promised to *remunerate* the searchers handsomely⟩.

Satisfy implies paying a person what is demanded or required by law ⟨all creditors will be *satisfied* in full⟩.

Reimburse implies a return of money that has been expended for another's benefit ⟨the company will *reimburse* employees for expenses incurred⟩.

Indemnify implies making good a loss suffered through accident, disaster, warfare (the government cannot *indemnify* the families of military casualties).

Repay stresses paying back an equivalent in kind or amount (*repay* a loan).

Recompense suggests due return in amends, friendly repayment, or reward (the hotel *recompensed* us with a free bottle of champagne).

PENITENCE, repentance, contrition, compunction, remorse mean regret for sin or wrongdoing.

Penitence implies sad and humble realization of and regret for one's misdeeds (absolution is dependent upon sincere *penitence*).

Repentance adds the implication of a resolve to change (a complete change of character accompanied his *repentance*).

Contrition stresses the sorrowful regret that constitutes true penitence (the beatings were usually followed by tearful expressions of *contrition*).

Compunction implies a painful sting of conscience esp. for contemplated wrongdoing (have no *compunctions* about taking back what is mine).

Remorse suggests prolonged and insistent self-reproach and mental anguish for past wrongs and esp. for those whose consequences cannot be remedied (swindlers are not usually plagued by feelings of *remorse*).

PERCEPTIBLE, sensible, palpable, tangible, appreciable, ponderable mean apprehensible as real or existent.

Perceptible applies to what can be discerned by the senses often to a minimal extent (a *perceptible* difference in sound).

Sensible applies to whatever is clearly apprehended through the senses or impresses itself strongly on the mind (a *sensible* change in the weather).

Palpable applies either to what has physical substance or to what is obvious and unmistakable (the tension in the air was almost *palpable*).

Tangible suggests what is capable of being handled or grasped both physically and mentally ⟨submitted the gun as *tangible* evidence⟩.

Appreciable applies to what is distinctly discernible by the senses c. definitely measurable ⟨an *appreciable* increase in temperature⟩.

Ponderable suggests having definitely measurable weight or importance esp. as distinguished from eluding such determination ⟨exerted a *ponderable* influence on world events⟩.

PERFECT, whole, entire, intact mean not lacking or faulty in any particular.

Perfect implies the soundness and the excellence of every part. element. or quality of a thing frequently as an unattainable or theoretical state ⟨a *perfect* set of teeth⟩ ⟨the *perfect* woman⟩.

Whole suggests a completeness or perfection that can be sought. gained. or regained ⟨an experience that made him feel a *whole* man again⟩.

Entire implies perfection deriving from integrity. soundness. or completeness of a thing ⟨recorded the *entire* Beethoven corpus⟩.

Intact implies retention of perfection of a thing in its natural or original state ⟨somehow the building survived the storm *intact*⟩.

PERFORM, execute, discharge, accomplish, achieve, effect, fulfill mean to carry out or into effect.

Perform implies action that follows established patterns or procedures or fulfills agreed-upon requirements and often connotes special skill ⟨*performed* gymnastics on the parallel bars⟩.

Execute stresses the carrying out of what exists in plan or in intent ⟨*executed* the heist exactly as planned⟩.

Discharge implies execution and completion of appointed duties or tasks ⟨*discharged* his duties promptly and effectively⟩.

Accomplish stresses the successful completion of a process rather than the means of carrying it out ⟨*accomplished* in a year what had taken others a lifetime⟩.

Achieve adds to *accomplish* the implication of conquered difficulties ⟨a nation struggling to *achieve* greatness⟩.

Effect adds to *achieve* an emphasis on the inherent force in the agent capable of surmounting obstacles ⟨a dynamic personality who *effected* sweeping reforms⟩.

Fulfill implies a complete realization of ends or possibilities ⟨the rare epic that *fulfills* its ambitions⟩.

PERIOD, epoch, era, age mean a division of time.

Period may designate an extent of time of any length ⟨*periods* of economic prosperity⟩.

Epoch applies to a period begun or set off by some significant or striking quality, change, or series of events ⟨the steam engine marked a new *epoch* in industry⟩.

Era suggests a period of history marked by a new or distinct order of things ⟨the *era* of global communications⟩.

Age is used frequently of a fairly definite period dominated by a prominent figure or feature ⟨the *age* of Samuel Johnson⟩.

PERNICIOUS, baneful, noxious, deleterious, detrimental mean exceedingly harmful.

Pernicious implies irreparable harm done through evil or insidious corrupting or undermining ⟨the claim that pornography has a *pernicious* effect on society⟩.

Baneful implies injury through poisoning or destroying ⟨the *baneful* notion that discipline destroys creativity⟩.

Noxious applies to what is both offensive and injurious to the health of a body or mind ⟨*noxious* fumes emanating from a chemical plant⟩.

Deleterious applies to what has an often unsuspected harmful effect ⟨megadoses of vitamins can have *deleterious* effects⟩.

Detrimental implies obvious harmfulness to something specified ⟨the *detrimental* effects of prolonged fasting⟩.

PHASE, aspect, side, facet, angle mean one of the possible ways of viewing or being presented to view.

Phase implies a change in appearance often without clear reference to an observer ⟨the second *phase* of the investigation⟩.

Aspect may stress the point of view of an observer and its limitation of what is seen or considered ⟨an article that considers the financial *aspect* of divorce⟩.

Side stresses one of several aspects from which something may be viewed ⟨a broadcast that told only one *side* of the story⟩.

Facet implies one of a multiplicity of sides each of which manifests the central quality of the whole ⟨explores the many *facets* of life in New York City⟩.

Angle suggests an aspect seen from a very restricted or specific point of view ⟨find a fresh *angle* for covering the political convention⟩.

PITY, compassion, commiseration, ruth, condolence, sympathy mean the act or capacity for sharing the interests of another.

Pity implies tender or sometimes slightly contemptuous sorrow for one in misery or distress ⟨no *pity* was shown to the captives⟩.

Compassion implies pity coupled with an urgent desire to aid or to spare ⟨treats alcoholics with great *compassion*⟩.

Commiseration suggests pity expressed outwardly in exclamations, tears, words of comfort ⟨murmurs of *commiseration* filled the loser's headquarters⟩.

Ruth implies pity coming from a change of heart or a relenting ⟨not a trace of *ruth* in the judge's sentencing⟩.

Condolence applies chiefly to formal expression of grief to one who has suffered loss ⟨expressed their *condolences* to the widow⟩.

Sympathy implies a power to enter into another's emotional experience of any sort ⟨my *sympathies* are with the rebels' cause⟩.

PLAN, design, plot, scheme, project mean a method devised for making or doing something or achieving an end.

Plan always implies mental formulation and sometimes graphic representation ⟨studied the *plans* for the proposed industrial park⟩.

Design often suggests a particular pattern and some degree of achieved order or harmony ⟨*designs* for three new gowns⟩.

Plot implies a laying out in clearly distinguished sections with attention to their relations and proportions ⟨outlined the *plot* of the new play⟩.

Scheme stresses calculation of the end in view and may apply to a plan motivated by craftiness and self-interest ⟨a *scheme* to swindle senior citizens of their savings⟩.

Project often stresses imaginative scope and vision ⟨a *project* to develop the waterfront⟩.

PLASTIC, pliable, pliant, ductile, malleable, adaptable mean susceptible of being modified in form or nature.

Plastic applies to substances soft enough to be molded yet capable of hardening into the desired fixed form ⟨*plastic* materials allow the sculptor greater freedom⟩.

Pliable suggests something easily bent, folded, twisted, or manipulated ⟨headphones that are *pliable* and can be bent to fit⟩.

Pliant may stress flexibility and sometimes connote springiness ⟨select an athletic shoe with a *pliant* sole⟩.

Ductile applies to what can be drawn out or extended with ease ⟨copper is one of the most *ductile* of metals⟩.

Malleable applies to what may be pressed or beaten into shape ⟨the *malleable* properties of gold enhance its value⟩.

Adaptable implies the capability of being easily modified to suit other conditions, needs, or uses ⟨computer hardware that is *adaptable*⟩.

PLENTIFUL, ample, abundant, copious mean more than sufficient without being excessive.

Plentiful implies a great or rich supply ⟨peaches are *plentiful* this summer⟩.

Ample implies a generous sufficiency to satisfy a particular requirement ⟨an *ample* amount of food to last the winter⟩.

Abundant suggests an even greater or richer supply than does *plentiful* ⟨has surprisingly *abundant* energy for a woman her age⟩.

Copious stresses largeness of supply rather than fullness or richness ⟨*copious* examples of bureaucratic waste⟩.

PLOT, intrigue, machination, conspiracy, cabal mean a plan secretly devised to accomplish an evil or treacherous end.

Plot implies careful foresight in planning a complex scheme ⟨foiled an assassination *plot*⟩.

Intrigue suggests secret underhanded maneuvering in an atmosphere of duplicity ⟨finagled the nomination by means of backroom *intrigues*⟩.

Machination implies a contriving of annoyances, injuries, or evils by indirect means ⟨through *machinations* she pieced together a publishing empire⟩.

Conspiracy implies a secret agreement among several people usu. involving treason or great treachery ⟨a *conspiracy* of oil companies to set prices⟩.

Cabal typically applies to political intrigue involving persons of some eminence ⟨the infamous *cabal* against General Washington⟩.

See in addition PLAN.

PONDER, meditate, muse, ruminate mean to consider or examine attentively or deliberately.

Ponder implies a careful weighing of a problem or, often, prolonged inconclusive thinking about a matter ⟨*pondered* at length the various recourses open to him⟩.

Meditate implies a definite focusing of one's thoughts on something so as to understand it deeply ⟨the sight of ruins prompted her to *meditate* upon human vanity⟩.

Muse suggests a more or less focused daydreaming as in remembrance ⟨*mused* upon the adventures had by heroines of gothic novels⟩.

Ruminate implies going over the same matter in one's thoughts again and again but suggests little of either purposive thinking or rapt absorption ⟨the product of fifty years of *ruminating* on the meaning of life⟩.

POSE, air, airs, affectation, mannerism mean an adopted way of speaking or behaving.

Pose implies an attitude deliberately assumed in order to impress others ⟨her shyness was just a *pose*⟩.

Air may suggest natural acquirement through environment or way of life ⟨years of living in Europe had given him a sophisticated *air*⟩.

Airs always implies artificiality and pretentiousness ⟨a snobby couple much given to putting on *airs*⟩.

Affectation applies to a trick of speech or behavior that strikes the observer as insincere ⟨his foreign accent is an *affectation*⟩.

Mannerism applies to an acquired eccentricity that has become a habit ⟨gesturing with a cigarette was her most noticeable *mannerism*⟩.

POSSIBLE, practicable, feasible mean capable of being realized.

Possible implies that a thing may certainly exist or occur given the proper conditions ⟨contends that life on other planets is *possible*⟩.

Practicable implies that something may be easily or readily effected by available means or under current conditions ⟨when television became *practicable*⟩.

Feasible applies to what is likely to work or be useful in attaining the end desired ⟨commercially *feasible* for mass production⟩.

POVERTY, indigence, penury, want, destitution mean the state of one with insufficient resources.

Poverty may cover a range from extreme want of necessities to an absence of material comforts ⟨the extreme *poverty* of the slum dwellers⟩.

Indigence implies seriously straitened circumstances ⟨the *indigence*,of her years as a graduate student⟩.

Penury suggests a cramping or oppressive lack of money ⟨given the *penury* of their lifestyle, few suspected their wealth⟩.

Want and **destitution** imply extreme poverty that threatens life itself through starvation or exposure ⟨lived in a perpetual state of *want*⟩ ⟨the widespread *destitution* in countries beset by famine⟩.

POWER *n* **Power, authority, jurisdiction, control, command, sway, dominion** mean the right to govern or rule or determine.

Power implies possession of ability to wield force, permissive authority, or substantial influence ⟨the *power* of the President to mold public opinion⟩.

Authority implies the granting of power for a specific purpose within specified limits ⟨gave her attorney the *authority* to manage her estate⟩.

Jurisdiction applies to official power exercised within prescribed limits ⟨the bureau that has *jurisdiction* over Indian affairs⟩.

Control stresses the power to direct and restrain ⟨you are responsible for students under your *control*⟩.

Command implies the power to make arbitrary decisions and compel obedience ⟨the respect of the men under his *command*⟩.

Sway suggests the extent or scope of exercised power or influence ⟨an empire that extended its *sway* over the known world⟩.

Dominion stresses sovereign power or supreme authority ⟨a world government that would have *dominion* over all nations).

POWER *n* **Power, force, energy, strength, might** mean the ability to exert effort.

Power may imply latent or exerted physical, mental, or spiritual ability to act or be acted upon ⟨the incredible *power* of flowing water⟩.

Force implies the actual effective exercise of power ⟨used enough *force* to push the door open⟩.

Energy applies to power expended or capable of being transformed into work ⟨a social reformer of untiring *energy*⟩.

Strength applies to the quality or property of a person or thing that makes possible the exertion of force or the withstanding of strain, pressure, or attack ⟨use weight training to build your *strength*⟩.

Might implies great or overwhelming power or strength ⟨all of his *might* was needed to budge the boulder⟩.

PRACTICABLE, practical mean capable of being put to use or put into practice.

Practicable applies to what has been proposed and seems feasible but has not been actually tested in use ⟨the question of whether colonies in space are *practicable*⟩.

Practical applies to things and to persons and implies proven success in meeting the demands made by actual living or use ⟨the copier is the most *practical* machine in the office⟩.

See in addition POSSIBLE.

PRECEDING, antecedent, foregoing, previous, prior, former, anterior mean being before.

Preceding usu. implies being immediately before in time or in place ⟨the last sentence of the *preceding* paragraph⟩.

Antecedent applies to order in time and may suggest a causal relation ⟨study the revolution and its *antecedent* economic conditions⟩.

Foregoing applies chiefly to statements ⟨a restatement of the *foregoing* paragraph⟩.

Previous and **prior** imply existing or occurring earlier, but *prior* often adds an implication of greater importance ⟨a child from a *previous* marriage⟩ ⟨the prices in this catalogue supersede all *prior* prices⟩.

Former implies always a definite comparison or contrast with something that is latter ⟨the *former* name of the company⟩.

Anterior applies to position before or ahead of usu. in space, sometimes in time or order ⟨the *anterior* lobe of the brain⟩.

PRECIPITATE, headlong, abrupt, impetuous, sudden mean showing undue haste or unexpectedness.

Precipitate stresses lack of due deliberation and implies prematureness of action ⟨the army's *precipitate* withdrawal⟩.

Headlong stresses rashness and lack of forethought ⟨a *headlong* flight from arrest⟩.

Abrupt stresses curtness and a lack of warning or ceremony ⟨an *abrupt* refusal⟩.

Impetuous stresses extreme impatience or impulsiveness ⟨it's a bit *impetuous* to propose on the third date⟩.

Sudden stresses unexpectedness and sharpness or violence of action ⟨flew into a *sudden* rage⟩.

PREDICAMENT, dilemma, quandary, plight, fix, jam, pickle mean a situation from which escape is difficult.

Predicament suggests a difficult situation usu. offering no satisfactory solution ⟨the *predicament* posed by increasing automation⟩.

Dilemma implies a predicament presenting a choice between equally bad alternatives ⟨faced with the *dilemma* of putting him in a nursing home or caring for him ourselves⟩.

Quandary stresses puzzlement and perplexity ⟨in a *quandary* about how to repair it⟩.

Plight suggests an unfortunate or trying situation ⟨a study on the *plight* of the homeless⟩.

Fix and **jam** are informal equivalents of *plight* but are more likely to suggest involvement through some fault or wrongdoing ⟨constantly getting their son out of some *fix*⟩ ⟨in a real financial *jam* now that she's lost her job⟩.

Pickle implies a distressing or embarrassing situation ⟨conflicting commitments that left me in a sorry *pickle*⟩.

PREDILECTION, prepossession, prejudice, bias mean an attitude of mind that predisposes one to favor something.

Predilection implies a strong liking deriving from one's temperament or experience ⟨teenagers with a *predilection* for gory horror movies⟩.

Prepossession suggests a fixed conception likely to preclude objective judgment of anything counter to it ⟨a slave to his *prepossessions*⟩.

Prejudice usu. implies an unfavorable prepossession and connotes a feeling rooted in suspicion, fear, or intolerance ⟨strong *prejudices* that are based upon neither reason nor experience⟩.

Bias implies an unreasoned and unfair distortion of judgment in favor of or against a person or thing ⟨society shows a *bias* against overweight people⟩.

PREVAILING, prevalent, rife, current mean generally circulated, accepted, or used in a certain time or place.

Prevailing stresses predominance ⟨the *prevailing* medical opinion regarding smoking⟩.

Prevalent implies only frequency ⟨dairy farms were once *prevalent* in the area⟩.

Rife implies a growing prevalence or rapid spread ⟨during the epidemic rumors were *rife*⟩.

Current applies to what is subject to change and stresses prevalence at the present time ⟨the *current* migration towards the Sunbelt⟩.

PREVENT *vb* **Prevent, anticipate, forestall** mean to deal with beforehand.

Prevent implies taking advance measures against something possible or probable ⟨measures taken to *prevent* an epidemic⟩.

Anticipate may imply merely getting ahead of another by being a precursor or forerunner or it may imply checking another's intention by acting first ⟨*anticipated* the firing so she decided to quit first⟩.

Forestall implies a getting ahead so as to stop or interrupt something in its course ⟨a government order that effectively *forestalled* a free election⟩.

PREVENT *vb* Prevent, preclude, obviate, avert, ward off mean to stop something from coming or occurring.

Prevent implies the existence of or the placing of an insurmountable obstacle ⟨the blizzard *prevented* us from going⟩.

Preclude implies the shutting out of every possibility of a thing's happening or taking effect ⟨an accident that *precluded* a career in football⟩.

Obviate suggests the use of forethought to avoid the necessity for unwelcome or disagreeable actions or measures ⟨her quitting *obviated* the task of firing her⟩.

Avert and **ward off** imply taking immediate and effective measures to avoid, repel, or counteract threatening evil ⟨deftly *averted* a hostile corporate takeover⟩ ⟨a hot drink to *ward off* a chill⟩.

PROFICIENT, adept, skilled, skillful, expert mean having great knowledge and experience in a trade or profession.

Proficient implies a thorough competence derived from training and practice ⟨a translator *proficient* in Russian⟩.

Adept implies special aptitude as well as proficiency ⟨*adept* at handling large numbers in his head⟩.

Skilled stresses mastery of technique ⟨a delicate operation requiring a *skilled* surgeon⟩.

Skillful implies individual dexterity in execution or performance ⟨a shrewd and *skillful* manipulation of public opinion⟩.

Expert implies extraordinary proficiency and often connotes knowledge as well as technical skill ⟨*expert* in the identification and evaluation of wines⟩.

PROFUSE, lavish, prodigal, luxuriant, lush, exuberant

mean giving or given out in great abundance.

Profuse implies pouring forth without restraint ⟨uttered *profuse* apologies⟩.

Lavish suggests an unstinted or unmeasured profusion ⟨a *lavish* wedding reception of obvious expense⟩.

Prodigal implies reckless or wasteful lavishness threatening to lead to early exhaustion of resources ⟨*prodigal* spending exhausted the fortune⟩.

Luxuriant suggests a rich and splendid abundance ⟨the *luxuriant* vegetation of a tropical rain forest⟩.

Lush suggests rich, soft luxuriance ⟨nude portraits that have a *lush*, sensual quality⟩.

Exuberant implies marked vitality or vigor in what produces abundantly ⟨a fantasy writer with an *exuberant* imagination⟩.

PROJECTION, protrusion, protuberance, bulge mean an extension beyond the normal line or surface.

Projection implies a jutting out esp. at a sharp angle ⟨those *projections* along the wall are safety hazards⟩.

Protrusion suggests a thrusting out so that the extension seems a deformity ⟨the bizarre *protrusions* of a coral reef⟩.

Protuberance implies a growing or swelling out in rounded form ⟨a skin disease marked by warty *protuberances*⟩.

Bulge suggests an expansion caused by internal pressure ⟨*bulges* soon appeared in the tile floor⟩.

PRONE, supine, prostrate, recumbent mean lying down.

Prone implies a position with the front of the body turned toward the supporting surface ⟨push-ups require the body to be in a *prone* position⟩.

Supine implies lying on one's back and suggests inertness or abjectness ⟨lying *supine* upon a couch⟩.

Prostrate implies lying full-length as in submission, defeat, or physical collapse ⟨a runner fell *prostrate* at the finish line⟩.

Recumbent implies the posture of one sleeping or resting ⟨he was *recumbent* and relaxed in his hospital bed⟩.

See in addition LIABLE.

PROPORTIONAL, proportionate, commensurate, commensurable mean duly proportioned to something else.

Proportional may apply to several closely related things that change without altering their relations ⟨medical fees are *proportional* to one's income⟩.

Proportionate applies to one thing that bears a reciprocal relationship to another ⟨a punishment not at all *proportionate* to the offense⟩.

Commensurate stresses an equality between things different from but in some way dependent on each other ⟨the salary will be *commensurate* with experience⟩.

Commensurable more strongly implies a common scale by which two quite different things can be shown to be significantly equal or proportionate ⟨equal pay for jobs that are *commensurable* in worth⟩.

PROSPECT, outlook, anticipation, foretaste mean an advance realization of something to come.

Prospect implies expectation of a particular event, condition, or development of definite interest or concern ⟨the appealing *prospect* of a quiet weekend⟩.

Outlook suggests a forecasting of the future ⟨a favorable *outlook* for the state's economy⟩.

Anticipation implies a prospect or outlook that involves advance suffering or enjoyment of what is foreseen ⟨the *anticipation* of the meeting was the worst of it⟩.

Foretaste implies an actual though brief or partial experience of something forthcoming ⟨the frost was a *foretaste* of winter⟩.

PROUD, arrogant, haughty, lordly, insolent, overbearing, supercilious, disdainful mean showing scorn for inferiors.

Proud may suggest an assumed superiority or loftiness ⟨a *proud* man, unwilling to admit failure⟩.

Arrogant implies a claiming for oneself of more consideration or importance than is warranted ⟨an *arrogant* business executive used to being kowtowed to⟩.

Haughty suggests a consciousness of superior birth or position ⟨a *haughty* manner that barely concealed his scorn⟩.

Lordly implies pomposity or an arrogant display of power ⟨a *lordly* indifference to the consequences of their carelessness⟩.

Insolent implies contemptuous haughtiness ⟨suffered the stares of *insolent* waiters⟩.

Overbearing suggests a tyrannical manner or an intolerable insolence ⟨an *overbearing* society hostess⟩.

Supercilious implies a cool, patronizing haughtiness ⟨*supercilious* parvenus asserting their position⟩.

Disdainful suggests a more active and openly scornful superciliousness ⟨*disdainful* of their social inferiors⟩.

PROVOKE, excite, stimulate, pique, quicken mean to arouse as if by pricking.

Provoke directs attention to the response called forth ⟨my stories usually *provoke* laughter⟩.

Excite implies a stirring up or moving profoundly ⟨news that *excited* anger and frustration⟩.

Stimulate suggests a rousing out of lethargy, quiescence, or indifference ⟨*stimulating* conversation⟩.

Pique suggests stimulating by mild irritation or challenge ⟨that remark *piqued* my interest⟩.

Quicken implies beneficially stimulating and making active or lively ⟨the high salary *quickened* her desire to have the job⟩.

See in addition IRRITATE.

PULL, draw, drag, haul, tug mean to cause to move in the direction determined by an applied force.

Pull is the general term but may emphasize the force exerted rather than resulting motion ⟨to open the drawer, *pull* hard⟩.

Draw implies a smoother, steadier motion and generally a lighter force than *pull* ⟨*drawing* his sled across the snow⟩.

Drag suggests great effort overcoming resistance or friction ⟨*dragged* the dead body across the room⟩.

Haul implies sustained pulling or dragging of heavy or bulky objects ⟨a team of horses *hauling* supplies⟩.

Tug applies to strenuous often spasmodic efforts to move ⟨the little girl *tugged* at her mother's hand⟩.

PUNGENT, piquant, poignant, racy mean sharp and stimulating to the mind or the senses.

Pungent implies a sharp, stinging, or biting quality esp. of odors ⟨a cheese with a *pungent* odor⟩.

Piquant suggests a power to whet the appetite or interest through tartness or mild pungency ⟨grapefruit juice gave the punch its *piquant* taste⟩.

Poignant suggests something is sharply or piercingly effective in stirring one's consciousness or emotions ⟨upon her departure he felt a *poignant* sense of loss⟩.

Racy implies having a strongly characteristic natural quality fresh and unimpaired ⟨the spontaneous, *racy* prose of the untutored writer⟩.

PUNISH, chastise, castigate, chasten, discipline, correct mean to inflict a penalty on in requital for wrongdoing.

Punish implies subjecting to a penalty for wrongdoing ⟨*punished* for stealing⟩.

Chastise may apply to either the infliction of corporal punishment or to verbal censure or denunciation ⟨*chastised* his son for neglecting his studies⟩.

Castigate usu. implies a severe, typically public censure ⟨an editorial *castigating* the entire city council⟩.

Chasten suggests any affliction or trial that leaves one humbled or subdued ⟨a stunning election defeat that left him *chastened*⟩.

Discipline implies a punishing or chastening in order to bring under control ⟨parents *discipline* their children⟩.

Correct implies punishing aimed at reforming an offender ⟨the function of prison is to *correct* the wrongdoer⟩.

PUSH, shove, thrust, propel mean to cause to move ahead or aside by force.

Push implies application of force by a body already in contact with the body to be moved ⟨*push* the door open⟩.

Shove implies a fast or rough pushing of something usu. along a surface ⟨*shoved* the man out of my way⟩.

Thrust suggests less steadiness and greater violence than *push* ⟨*thrust* the money in my hand and ran away⟩.

Propel suggests rapidly driving forward or onward by force applied in any manner ⟨ships *propelled* by steam⟩.

PUZZLE *vb* **Puzzle, perplex, bewilder, distract, nonplus, confound, dumbfound** mean to baffle and disturb mentally.

Puzzle implies existence of a problem difficult to solve ⟨a persistent fever which *puzzled* the doctor⟩.

Perplex adds a suggestion of worry and uncertainty esp. about making a necessary decision ⟨an odd change of personality that *perplexed* her friends⟩.

Bewilder stresses a confusion of mind that hampers clear and decisive thinking ⟨the number of videotapes available *bewilders* consumers⟩.

Distract implies agitation or uncertainty induced by conflicting preoccupations or interests ⟨a political scandal that *distracted* the country for two years⟩.

Nonplus implies a bafflement that makes orderly planning or deciding impossible ⟨she was utterly *nonplussed* by the abrupt change in plans⟩.

Confound implies temporary mental paralysis caused by astonishment or profound abasement ⟨tragic news that *confounded* us all⟩.

Dumbfound suggests intense but momentary confounding; often the idea of astonishment is so stressed that it becomes a near synonym of *astound* ⟨*dumbfounded* by her rejection of his marriage proposal⟩.

Q

QUALITY, property, character, attribute mean an intelligible feature by which a thing may be identified.

Quality is a general term applicable to any trait or characteristic whether individual or generic ⟨a star whose acting had a persistently amateurish *quality*⟩.

Property implies a characteristic that belongs to a thing's essential nature and may be used to describe a type or species ⟨name the basic *properties* of mammals⟩.

Character applies to a peculiar and distinctive quality of a thing or a class ⟨each of the island's villages has a distinctive *character*⟩.

Attribute implies a quality ascribed to a thing or a being ⟨a man with none of the traditional *attributes* of a popular hero⟩.

QUALM, scruple, compunction, demur mean a misgiving about what one is doing or going to do.

Qualm implies an uneasy fear that one is not following one's conscience or better judgment ⟨no *qualms* about traveling in the Middle East⟩.

Scruple implies doubt of the rightness of an act on grounds of principle ⟨a lawyer totally devoid of *scruples*⟩.

Compunction implies a spontaneous feeling of responsibility or compassion for a potential victim ⟨not likely to have *compunctions* about knocking out his opponent⟩.

Demur implies hesitation caused by objection to an outside suggestion or influence ⟨accepted her resignation without *demur*⟩.

QUARREL, wrangle, altercation, squabble, spat, tiff mean an angry dispute.

Quarrel implies a verbal clash followed by strained or severed relations ⟨a bitter *quarrel* that ended their friendship⟩.

Wrangle suggests a noisy, insistent dispute ⟨an ongoing *wrangle* over the town's finances⟩.

Altercation suggests determined verbal quarreling often with blows ⟨a violent *altercation* between pro- and anti-abortion groups⟩.

Squabble implies childish and unseemly wrangling ⟨the children constantly *squabble* over toys⟩.

Spat implies a lively but brief dispute over a trifle ⟨the couple averages a *spat* a week⟩.

Tiff suggests a trivial dispute without serious consequence ⟨a *tiff* that was forgotten by dinnertime⟩.

QUICK, prompt, ready, apt mean able to respond without delay or hesitation or indicative of such ability.

Quick stresses instancy of response and is likely to connote native rather than acquired power ⟨very *quick* in his reflexes⟩ ⟨a keen *quick* mind⟩.

Prompt is more likely to connote training and discipline that fits one for instant response ⟨the *prompt* response of emergency medical technicians⟩.

Ready suggests facility or fluency in response ⟨backed by a pair of *ready* assistants⟩.

Apt stresses the possession of qualities (as intelligence, a particular talent, or a strong bent) that makes quick effective response possible ⟨an *apt* student⟩ ⟨her answer was *apt* and to the point⟩.

See in addition FAST.

QUICKEN, animate, enliven, vivify mean to make alive or lively.

Quicken stresses a sudden renewal of life or activity esp. in something inert ⟨the arrival of spring *quickens* the earth⟩.

Animate emphasizes the imparting of motion or vitality to what is mechanical or artificial ⟨telling details that *animate* the familiar story⟩.

Enliven suggests a stimulus that arouses from dullness or torpidity ⟨*enlivened* his lecture with humorous anecdotes⟩.

Vivify implies a freshening or energizing through renewal of vitality ⟨her appearance *vivifies* a dreary drama⟩.

See in addition PROVOKE.

R

RANDOM, haphazard, casual, desultory mean determined by accident rather than design.

Random stresses lack of definite aim, fixed goal, or regular procedure ⟨a *random* sampling of public opinion⟩.

Haphazard applies to what is done without regard for regularity or fitness or ultimate consequence ⟨his selection of college courses was entirely *haphazard*⟩.

Casual suggests working or acting without deliberation, intention, or purpose ⟨a *casual* tour of the sights⟩.

Desultory implies a jumping or skipping from one thing to another without method or system ⟨a *desultory* discussion of current events⟩.

RANGE, gamut, compass, sweep, scope, orbit mean the extent that lies within the powers of something (as to cover or control).

Range is a general term indicating the extent of one's perception or the extent of powers, capacities, or possibilities ⟨the entire *range* of human experience⟩.

Gamut suggests a graduated series running from one possible extreme to another ⟨a performance that included a *gamut* of emotions⟩.

Compass implies a sometimes limited extent of perception, knowledge, or activity ⟨your concerns lie beyond the narrow *compass* of this study⟩.

Sweep suggests extent, often circular or arc-shaped, of motion or activity ⟨the book covers the entire *sweep* of criminal activity⟩.

Scope is applicable to an area of activity, predetermined and limited, but somewhat flexible ⟨as time went on, the *scope* of the investigation widened⟩.

Orbit suggests an often circumscribed range of activity or influence within which forces work toward accommodation ⟨within that restricted *orbit* they tried to effect social change⟩.

RAVAGE, devastate, waste, sack, pillage, despoil mean to lay waste by plundering or destroying.

Ravage implies violent often cumulative depredation and destruction ⟨a hurricane that *ravaged* the Gulf Coast⟩.

Devastate implies the complete ruin and desolation of a wide area ⟨the atomic bomb that *devastated* Hiroshima⟩.

Waste may imply producing the same result by a slow process rather than sudden and violent action ⟨years of drought had *wasted* the area⟩.

Sack implies carrying off all valuable possessions from a place ⟨barbarians *sacked* ancient Rome⟩.

Pillage implies ruthless plundering at will but without the completeness suggested by *sack* ⟨settlements *pillaged* by Vikings⟩.

Despoil applies to looting or robbing of a place or person without suggesting accompanying destruction ⟨the Nazis *despoiled* the art museums of Europe⟩.

REBELLION, revolution, uprising, revolt, insurrection, mutiny mean an armed outbreak against authority.

Rebellion implies an open formidable resistance that is often unsuccessful ⟨the *rebellion* failed for lack of popular support⟩.

Revolution applies to a successful rebellion resulting in a major change (as in government) ⟨the American *Revolution*⟩.

Uprising implies a brief, limited and often immediately ineffective rebellion ⟨quickly put down the *uprising*⟩.

Revolt and **insurrection** imply an armed uprising that quickly fails or succeeds ⟨a *revolt* by the Young Turks that surprised party leaders⟩ ⟨Nat Turner's unsuccessful slave *insurrection*⟩.

Mutiny applies to group insubordination or insurrection esp. against naval authority ⟨the famous *mutiny* aboard the Bounty⟩.

RECEDE, retreat, retrograde, retract, back mean to move backward.

Recede implies a gradual withdrawing from a forward or high fixed point in time or space ⟨the flood waters gradually *receded*⟩.

Retreat implies withdrawal from a point or position reached ⟨under cross-examination he *retreated* from that statement⟩.

Retrograde implies movement contrary to a normally progressive direction ⟨the position of women in some areas seems to be *retrograding* instead of advancing⟩.

Retract implies drawing back from an extended position ⟨a cat *retracting* its claws⟩.

Back is used with *up, down, out,* or *off,* to refer to any retrograde motion ⟨*backed* off when her claim was challenged⟩.

RECIPROCAL, mutual, common mean shared or experienced by each.

Reciprocal implies an equal return or counteraction by each of two sides toward or against or in relation to the other ⟨allies with a *reciprocal* defense agreement⟩.

Mutual applies to feelings or effects shared by two jointly ⟨two people with a *mutual* physical attraction⟩.

Common does not suggest reciprocity but merely a sharing with others ⟨a couple with many *common* interests⟩.

RECIPROCATE, retaliate, requite, return mean to give back usu. in kind or in quantity.

Reciprocate implies a mutual or equivalent exchange or a paying back of what one has received ⟨*reciprocated* their hospitality by inviting them for a visit⟩.

Retaliate usu. implies a paying back of injury in exact kind, often vengefully ⟨the enemy *retaliated* by executing their prisoners⟩.

Requite implies a paying back according to one's preference and often not equivalently ⟨*requited* her love with cold indifference⟩.

Return implies a paying back of something usu. in kind but sometimes by way of contrast ⟨*returned* their kindness with ingratitude⟩.

RECOIL, shrink, flinch, wince, blench, quail mean to draw back in fear or distaste.

Recoil implies a start or movement away through shock, fear, or disgust ⟨*recoils* at the sight of blood⟩.

Shrink suggests an instinctive recoil through sensitiveness, scrupulousness, or cowardice ⟨refused to *shrink* from family responsibilities⟩.

Flinch implies a failure to endure pain or face something dangerous or frightening with resolution ⟨faced her accusers without *flinching*⟩.

Wince suggests a slight involuntary physical reaction (as a start or recoiling) ⟨*winced* in pain⟩.

Blench implies fainthearted flinching ⟨never *blenched* even as his head was lowered on the guillotine⟩.

Quail suggests shrinking and cowering in fear ⟨*quailed* before the apparition⟩.

REGARD, respect, esteem, admire mean to recognize the worth of a person or thing.

Regard is a general term that is usu. qualified ⟨he is not highly *regarded* in the profession⟩.

Respect implies a considered evaluation or estimation ⟨after many years they came to *respect* her views⟩.

Esteem implies greater warmth of feeling accompanying a high valuation ⟨no citizen of the town was more highly *esteemed*⟩.

Admire suggests usu. enthusiastic appreciation and often deep affection ⟨a friend that I truly *admire*⟩.

REGULAR, normal, typical, natural mean being of the sort or kind that is expected as usual, ordinary, or average.

Regular stresses conformity to a rule, standard, or pattern ⟨the *regular* monthly meeting of the organization⟩.

Normal implies lack of deviation from what has been discovered or established as the most usual or expected ⟨*normal* behavior for a two-year-old⟩.

Typical implies showing all important traits of a type, class, or group and may suggest lack of strong individuality ⟨a *typical* small town in America⟩.

Natural applies to what conforms to a thing's essential nature, function, or mode of being ⟨the *natural* love of a mother for her child⟩.

RELEVANT, germane, material, pertinent, apposite, applicable, apropos mean relating to or bearing upon the matter in hand.

Relevant implies a traceable, significant, logical connection ⟨use any *relevant* evidence to support your argument⟩.

Germane may additionally imply a fitness for or appropriateness to the situation or occasion ⟨a topic not *germane* to our discussion⟩.

Material implies so close a relationship that it cannot be dispensed with without serious alteration of the case ⟨the scene is *material* to the rest of the play⟩.

Pertinent stresses a clear and decisive relevance ⟨a *pertinent* observation that cut to the heart of the matter⟩.

Apposite suggests a felicitous relevance ⟨the anecdotes in his sermons are always *apposite*⟩.

Applicable suggests the fitness of bringing a general rule or principle to bear upon a particular case ⟨a precedent that is not *applicable* in this case⟩.

Apropos suggests being both relevant and opportune ⟨for your term paper use only *apropos* quotations⟩.

RELIEVE, alleviate, lighten, assuage, mitigate, allay mean to make something less grievous.

Relieve implies a lifting of enough of a burden to make it tolerable ⟨took drugs to *relieve* the pain⟩.

Alleviate implies temporary or partial lessening of pain or distress ⟨new buildings that will help to *alleviate* the housing shortage⟩.

Lighten implies reducing a burdensome or depressing weight ⟨good news that *lightened* his worries⟩.

Assuage implies softening or sweetening what is harsh or disagreeable ⟨hoped that a vacation would *assuage* the pain of the divorce⟩.

Mitigate suggests a moderating or countering of the effect of something violent or painful ⟨ocean breezes *mitigated* the intense heat⟩.

Allay implies an effective calming or soothing of fears or alarms ⟨the encouraging report *allayed* their fears⟩.

RELINQUISH, yield, resign, surrender, abandon, waive mean to give up completely.

Relinquish usu. does not imply strong feeling but may suggest some regret, reluctance, or weakness ⟨*relinquished* her crown with bittersweet feelings⟩.

Yield implies concession or compliance or submission to force ⟨I *yield* to your greater expertise in this matter⟩.

Resign emphasizes voluntary relinquishment or sacrifice without struggle ⟨the model *resigned* all her rights to the photographs⟩.

Surrender implies a giving up after a struggle to retain or resist ⟨forced to sign a document *surrendering* all claims to the land⟩.

Abandon stresses finality and completeness in giving up ⟨*abandon* all hope⟩.

Waive implies conceding or forgoing with little or no compulsion ⟨*waived* the right to a trial by jury⟩.

REMEMBER, recollect, recall, remind, reminisce mean to bring an image or idea from the past into the mind.

Remember implies a keeping in memory that may be effortless or unwilled ⟨*remembers* that day as though it were yesterday⟩.

Recollect implies a bringing back to mind what is lost or scattered ⟨as near as I can *recollect*⟩.

Recall suggests an effort to bring back to mind and often to re-create in speech ⟨can't *recall* the words of the song⟩.

Remind suggests a jogging of one's memory by an association or similarity ⟨that *reminds* me of a story⟩.

Reminisce implies a casual often nostalgic recalling of experiences long past and gone ⟨old college friends like to *reminisce*⟩.

RENEW, restore, refresh, renovate, rejuvenate mean to make like new.

Renew implies so extensive a remaking that what had become faded or disintegrated now seems like new ⟨efforts to *renew* a failing marriage⟩.

Restore implies a return to an original state after depletion or loss ⟨*restored* a fine piece of furniture⟩.

Refresh implies the supplying of something necessary to restore lost strength, animation, or power ⟨lunch *refreshed* my energy⟩.

Renovate suggests a renewing by cleansing, repairing, or rebuilding ⟨the apartment has been entirely *renovated*⟩.

Rejuvenate suggests the restoration of youthful vigor, powers, and appearance ⟨the change in jobs *rejuvenated* her spirits⟩.

REPLACE, displace, supplant, supersede mean to put out of a usual or proper place or into the place of another.

Replace implies a filling of a place once occupied by something lost, destroyed, or no longer usable or adequate ⟨the broken window will have to be *replaced*⟩.

Displace implies an ousting or dislodging preceding a replacing ⟨thousands had been *displaced* by the floods⟩.

Supplant implies either a dispossessing or usurping of another's place, possessions, or privileges or an uprooting of something and its replacement with something else ⟨discovered that he had been *supplanted* in her affections by another⟩.

Supersede implies replacing a person or thing that has become superannuated, obsolete, or otherwise inferior ⟨the new edition *supersedes* all previous ones⟩.

REPRODUCTION, duplicate, copy, facsimile, replica mean a thing made to closely resemble another.

Reproduction implies an exact or close imitation of an existing thing ⟨*reproductions* from the museum's furniture collection⟩.

Duplicate implies a double or counterpart exactly corresponding to another thing ⟨make a *duplicate* of the key⟩.

Copy applies esp. to one of a number of things reproduced mechanically ⟨*copies* of the report were issued to all⟩.

Facsimile suggests a close reproduction in the same materials that may differ in scale ⟨a *facsimile* of an illuminated medieval manuscript⟩.

Replica implies the exact reproduction of something in all respects ⟨*replicas* of the ships used by Columbus⟩.

REPROVE, rebuke, reprimand, admonish, reproach, chide mean to criticize adversely.

Reprove implies an often kindly intent to correct a fault ⟨gently *reproved* her table manners⟩.

Rebuke suggests a sharp or stern reproof ⟨the papal letter *rebuked* dissenting church officials⟩.

Reprimand implies a severe, formal, often public or official rebuke ⟨a general officially *reprimanded* for speaking out of turn⟩.

Admonish suggests earnest or friendly warning and counsel ⟨*admonished* by my parents to control expenses⟩.

Reproach and **chide** suggest displeasure or disappointment expressed in mild reproof or scolding ⟨*reproached* him for tardiness⟩ ⟨*chided* by their mother for not keeping their room clean⟩.

REPUGNANT, repellent, abhorrent, distasteful, obnoxious, invidious mean so unlikable as to arouse antagonism or aversion.

Repugnant implies being alien to one's ideas, principles, or tastes and arousing resistance or loathing ⟨regards boxing as a *repugnant* sport⟩.

Repellent suggests a generally forbidding or unpleasant quality that causes one to back away ⟨the public display of grief was *repellent* to her⟩.

Abhorrent implies a repugnance causing active antagonism ⟨practices that are *abhorrent* to the American system⟩.

Distasteful implies a contrariness to one's tastes or inclinations ⟨a family to whom displays of affection are *distasteful*⟩.

Obnoxious suggests an objectionableness too great to tolerate ⟨the colonists found the tea tax especially *obnoxious*⟩.

Invidious applies to what cannot be used or performed without creating ill will, odium, or envy ⟨the *invidious* task of deciding custody of the child⟩.

RESCUE, deliver, redeem, ransom, reclaim, save mean to set free from confinement or danger.

Rescue implies freeing from imminent danger by prompt or vigorous action ⟨*rescue* the crew of a sinking ship⟩.

Deliver implies release usu. of a person from confinement, temptation, slavery, or suffering ⟨*delivered* his people from bondage⟩.

Redeem implies releasing from bondage or penalties by giving what is demanded or necessary ⟨*redeemed* her from a life of boredom⟩.

Ransom specif. applies to buying out of captivity ⟨subjects forced to *ransom* their king⟩.

Reclaim suggests a bringing back to a former state or condition of someone or something abandoned or debased ⟨*reclaimed* long-abandoned farms⟩.

Save may replace any of the foregoing terms; it may further imply a preserving or maintaining for usefulness or continued existence ⟨a social worker who *saved* youths from life as criminals⟩.

RESOURCE, resort, expedient, shift, makeshift, stopgap mean something one turns to in the absence of the usual means or source of supply.

Resource and **resort** apply to anything one falls back upon ⟨haven't exhausted all of my *resources* yet⟩ ⟨favor a sales tax only as a last *resort*⟩.

Expedient may apply to any device or contrivance used when the usual one is not at hand or not possible ⟨the flimsiest of *expedients* ends the tale⟩.

Shift implies a tentative or temporary imperfect expedient ⟨her desperate *shifts* satisfied no one⟩.

Makeshift implies an inferior expedient adopted because of urgent need or countenanced through indifference ⟨the space heater was supposed to be only a *makeshift*⟩.

Stopgap applies to something used temporarily as an emergency measure ⟨the farm aid bill is no more than a *stopgap*⟩.

RESPONSIBLE, answerable, accountable, amenable, liable mean subject to being held to account.

Responsible implies holding a specific office, duty, or trust ⟨the bureau *responsible* for revenue collection⟩.

Answerable suggests a relation between one having a moral or legal obligation and a court or other authority charged with oversight of its observance ⟨a fact-finding committee *answerable* only to the President⟩.

Accountable suggests imminence of retribution for unfulfilled trust or violated obligation ⟨in a democracy the politicians are *accountable* to the voters⟩.

Amenable and **liable** stress the fact of subjection to review, censure, or control by a designated authority under certain conditions ⟨laws are *amenable* to judicial review⟩ ⟨will not be *liable* for his ex-wife's debts⟩.

RESTRAIN, check, curb, bridle mean to hold back from or control in doing something.

Restrain suggests holding back by force or persuasion from acting or from going to extremes ⟨*restrained* themselves from trading insults⟩.

Check implies restraining or impeding a progress, activity, or impetus ⟨deep mud *checked* our progress⟩.

Curb suggests an abrupt or drastic checking ⟨learn to *curb* your appetite⟩.

Bridle implies keeping under control by subduing or holding in ⟨they could no longer *bridle* their passion⟩.

REVEAL, discover, disclose, divulge, tell, betray mean to make known what has been or should be concealed.

Reveal may apply to supernatural or inspired revelation of truths beyond the range of ordinary human vision or reason ⟨the belief that divine will is *revealed* in sacred writings⟩.

Discover implies an uncovering of matters kept secret and not previously known ⟨a step-by-step comparison that *discovered* a clear case of plagiarism⟩.

Disclose may also imply a discovering but more often an imparting of information previously kept secret ⟨candidates must *disclose* their financial assets⟩.

Divulge implies a disclosure involving some impropriety or breach of confidence ⟨refused to *divulge* confidential information⟩.

Tell implies an imparting of necessary or useful information ⟨*told* them what he had overheard⟩.

Betray implies a divulging that represents a breach of faith or an involuntary or unconscious disclosure ⟨a blush that *betrayed* her embarrassment⟩.

REVERE, reverence, venerate, worship, adore mean to honor and admire profoundly and respectfully.

Revere stresses deference and tenderness of feeling ⟨a retiring professor *revered* by generations of students⟩.

Reverence presupposes an intrinsic merit and inviolability in the one honored and a corresponding depth of feeling in the one honoring ⟨the general *reverenced* the army's code of honor⟩.

Venerate implies a holding as holy or sacrosanct because of character, association, or age ⟨national heroes who are still *venerated*⟩.

Worship implies homage usu. expressed in words or ceremony ⟨*worships* the memory of her husband⟩.

Adore implies love and stresses the notion of an individual and personal attachment ⟨a doctor who is practically *adored* by her patients⟩.

REVERSE, transpose, invert mean to change to the opposite position.

Reverse is the most general term and may imply change in order, side, direction, meaning ⟨*reversed* his position on the arms agreement⟩.

Transpose implies a change in order or relative position of units often through exchange of position ⟨anagrams are formed by *transposing* the letters of a word or phrase⟩.

Invert applies chiefly to turning upside down or inside out ⟨a typo consisting of a whole line of *inverted* type⟩.

RICH, wealthy, affluent, opulent mean having goods, property, and money in abundance.

Rich implies having more than enough to gratify normal needs or desires ⟨became *rich* through shrewd investments⟩.

Wealthy stresses the possession of property and intrinsically valuable things ⟨retired from politics a *wealthy* man⟩.

Affluent suggests prosperity and an increasing wealth ⟨an *affluent* society⟩.

Opulent suggests lavish expenditure and display of great wealth ⟨*opulent* mansions⟩.

RIDICULE, deride, mock, taunt, twit mean to make an object of laughter of.

Ridicule implies a deliberate often malicious belittling ⟨consistently *ridiculed* everything she said⟩.

Deride suggests contemptuous and often bitter ridicule ⟨*derided* their efforts to start their own business⟩.

Mock implies scorn often ironically expressed as by mimicry or sham deference ⟨youngsters began to *mock* the helpless old man⟩.

Taunt suggests jeeringly provoking insult or challenge ⟨terrorists *taunted* the hostages⟩.

Twit usu. suggests mild or good-humored teasing ⟨students *twitted* their teacher about his tardiness⟩.

RIGID, rigorous, strict, stringent mean extremely severe or stern.

Rigid implies uncompromising inflexibility ⟨the school's admission standards are *rigid*⟩.

Rigorous implies the imposition of hardship and difficulty ⟨the *rigorous* training of recruits⟩.

Strict emphasizes undeviating conformity to rules, standards, or requirements ⟨her doctor put her on a *strict* diet⟩.

Stringent suggests restrictions or limitations that curb or coerce ⟨the judge's ruling is a *stringent* interpretation of the law⟩.

See in addition STIFF.

ROUGH, harsh, uneven, rugged, scabrous mean not smooth or even.

Rough implies points, bristles, ridges, or projections on the surface ⟨a *rough* wooden board⟩.

Harsh implies a surface or texture distinctly unpleasant to the touch ⟨the *harsh* fabric chafed his skin⟩.

Uneven implies a lack of uniformity in height, breadth, or quality ⟨an old house with *uneven* floors⟩.

Rugged implies irregularity or roughness of land surface and connotes difficulty of travel ⟨follow the *rugged* road up the mountain⟩.

Scabrous implies scaliness or prickliness of surface ⟨an allergic condition that results in *scabrous* hands⟩.

See in addition RUDE.

RUDE, rough, crude, raw mean lacking in social refinement.

Rude implies ignorance of or indifference to good form; it may suggest intentional discourtesy ⟨consistently *rude* behavior toward her in-laws⟩.

Rough is likely to stress lack of polish and gentleness ⟨the *rough* manners of a man used to living in the outback⟩.

Crude may apply to thought or behavior limited to the gross, the obvious, or the primitive and ignorant of civilized amenities ⟨the *crude* antics of college students on spring break⟩.

Raw suggests being untested, inexperienced, or unfinished ⟨charged with turning *raw* youths into young men⟩.

RURAL, rustic, pastoral, bucolic mean relating to or characteristic of the country.

Rural suggests open country and farming ⟨a diminishing portion of the island remains *rural*⟩.

Rustic suggests more clearly a contrast with city life and connotes rudeness and lack of polish ⟨a hunting lodge filled with *rustic* furniture and decoration⟩.

Pastoral implies an idealized simplicity and peacefulness and apartness from the world ⟨the *pastoral* setting of an exclusive health resort⟩.

Bucolic may refer to either the desirable or undesirable aspects of country life ⟨fed-up city dwellers imagining a *bucolic* bliss⟩.

S

SADNESS, depression, melancholy, melancholia, dejection, gloom mean the state of mind of one who is unhappy.

Sadness is a general term that carries no suggestion of the cause, extent, or exact nature of low spirits ⟨a feeling of *sadness* marked the farewell dinner⟩.

Depression suggests a condition in which one feels let down, disheartened, or enervated ⟨under a doctor's care for severe *depression*⟩.

Melancholy suggests a mood of sad and serious but not wholly unpleasant pensiveness ⟨old love letters that gave her cause for *melancholy*⟩.

Melancholia applies to a settled deep depression verging on insanity ⟨fell into a state of *melancholia* after her husband's death⟩.

Dejection implies a usu. passing mood of being downcast or dispirited from a natural or logical cause ⟨a struggling actor used to periods of *dejection*⟩.

Gloom applies to the atmosphere or the effect on others created by one afflicted with any of these moods or conditions ⟨a universal *gloom* engulfed the devastated town⟩.

SAME, selfsame, very, identical, equivalent, equal mean not different or not differing from one another.

Same may imply and **selfsame** always implies that the things under consideration are one thing and not two or more things ⟨we both took the *same* route⟩ ⟨it was the *selfsame* ring I had lost years ago⟩.

Very, like *selfsame.* may imply identity. or. like *same.* may imply likeness in kind ⟨you're the *very* person I've been looking for⟩.

Identical may imply selfsameness or suggest absolute agreement in all details ⟨their test answers were *identical*⟩.

Equivalent implies amounting to the same thing in worth or significance ⟨two houses *equivalent* in market value⟩.

Equal implies being identical in value. magnitude. or some specified quality ⟨divided it into *equal* shares⟩.

SARCASTIC, satiric, ironic, sardonic mean marked by bitterness and a power or will to cut or sting.

Sarcastic implies an intentional inflicting of pain by deriding. taunting. or ridiculing ⟨a critic famous mainly for his *sarcastic* remarks⟩.

Satiric implies that the intent of the ridiculing is censure and reprobation ⟨a *satiric* look at contemporary sexual mores⟩.

Ironic implies an attempt to be amusing or provocative by saying usu. the opposite of what is meant ⟨made the *ironic* observation that the government could always be trusted⟩.

Sardonic implies scorn. mockery. or derision that is manifested by either verbal or facial expression ⟨surveyed the scene with a *sardonic* smile⟩.

SATIATE, sate, surfeit, cloy, pall, glut, gorge mean to fill to repletion.

Satiate and **sate** may sometimes imply only complete satisfaction but more often suggest repletion that has destroyed interest or desire ⟨movies that *satiated* their interest in sex⟩ ⟨audiences were *sated* with dizzying visual effects⟩.

Surfeit implies a nauseating repletion ⟨*surfeited* themselves with junk food⟩.

Cloy stresses the disgust or boredom resulting from such surfeiting ⟨sentimental pictures that *cloy* after a while⟩.

Pall emphasizes the loss of ability to stimulate interest or appetite ⟨even a tropical paradise begins to *pall* after ten trips⟩.

Glut implies excess in feeding or supplying ⟨bookstores *glutted* with diet books⟩.

Gorge suggests glutting to the point of bursting or choking ⟨*gorged* themselves with chocolate⟩.

SCATTER, disperse, dissipate, dispel mean to cause to separate or break up.

Scatter implies a force that drives parts or units irregularly in many directions ⟨the bowling ball *scattered* the pins⟩.

Disperse implies a wider separation and a complete breaking up of a mass or group ⟨police *dispersed* the crowd⟩.

Dissipate stresses complete disintegration or dissolution and final disappearance ⟨the fog was *dissipated* by the morning sun⟩.

Dispel stresses a driving away or getting rid of as if by scattering ⟨an authoritative statement that *dispelled* all doubt⟩.

SCOFF, jeer, gibe, fleer, sneer, flout mean to show one's contempt in derision or mockery.

Scoff stresses insolence, disrespect, or incredulity as motivating the derision ⟨*scoffed* at the religious faith of others⟩.

Jeer suggests a coarser more undiscriminating derision ⟨the crowd *jeered* the visiting team⟩.

Gibe implies taunting either good-naturedly or in sarcastic derision ⟨*gibed* at him for repeatedly missing the ball⟩.

Fleer suggests grinning or grimacing derisively ⟨some freshmen were greeted by *fleering* seniors⟩.

Sneer stresses insulting by contemptuous facial expression, phrasing, or tone of voice ⟨*sneered* at anything even remotely romantic⟩.

Flout stresses contempt shown by refusal to heed ⟨*flouted* the conventions of polite society⟩.

SCOLD, upbraid, berate, rail, revile, vituperate mean to reproach angrily and abusively.

Scold implies rebuking in irritation or ill temper justly or unjustly ⟨relieved her frustrations by *scolding* the children⟩.

Upbraid implies censuring on definite and usu. justifiable grounds ⟨the governor *upbraided* his aides for poor research⟩.

Berate suggests prolonged and often abusive scolding ⟨*berated* continually by a violent, abusive father⟩.

Rail (*at* or *against*) stresses an unrestrained berating ⟨*railed* loudly at the insolent bureaucrat⟩.

Revile implies a scurrilous, abusive attack prompted by anger or hatred ⟨a President vehemently *reviled* in the press⟩.

Vituperate suggests a violent reviling ⟨a preacher more given to *vituperating* than to inspiring⟩.

SCRUTINIZE, scan, inspect, examine mean to look at or over carefully and usu. critically.

Scrutinize stresses close attention to minute detail ⟨closely *scrutinized* the bill from the hospital⟩.

Scan implies a surveying from point to point often suggesting a cursory overall observation ⟨quickly *scanned* the wine list⟩.

Inspect implies scrutinizing for errors or defects ⟨*inspected* the restaurant for health-code violations⟩.

Examine suggests a scrutiny in order to determine the nature, condition, or quality of a thing ⟨*examined* the gems to see whether they were genuine⟩.

SECRET, covert, stealthy, furtive, clandestine, surreptitious, underhanded mean done without attracting observation.

Secret implies concealment on any grounds for any motive ⟨a *secret* meeting between lovers⟩.

Covert stresses the fact of not being open or declared ⟨*covert* operations against guerrilla forces⟩.

Stealthy suggests taking pains to avoid being seen or heard esp. in some misdoing ⟨the *stealthy* movements of a cat burglar⟩.

Furtive implies a sly or cautious stealthiness ⟨exchanged *furtive* smiles across the room⟩.

Clandestine implies secrecy usu. for an evil or illicit purpose ⟨a *clandestine* drug deal in a back alley⟩.

Surreptitious applies to action or behavior done secretly often with skillful avoidance of detection and in violation of custom, law, or authority ⟨the *surreptitious* stockpiling of weapons⟩.

Underhanded stresses fraud or deception ⟨a car dealership guilty of *underhanded* practices⟩.

SENSE, common sense, gumption, judgment, wisdom mean ability to reach intelligent conclusions.

Sense implies a reliable ability to judge and decide with soundness, prudence, and intelligence ⟨hasn't the *sense* to come in out of the rain⟩.

Common sense suggests an average degree of such ability without sophistication or special knowledge ⟨*common sense* tells me it's wrong⟩.

Gumption suggests a readiness to use or apply common sense ⟨a shrewd businessman known for his *gumption*⟩.

Judgment implies sense tempered and refined by experience, training, and maturity ⟨*judgment* is required of a camp counselor⟩.

Wisdom implies sense and judgment far above average ⟨the *wisdom* that comes from years of living⟩.

See in addition MEANING.

SENSUOUS, sensual, luxurious, voluptuous mean relating to or providing pleasure through gratification of the senses.

Sensuous implies gratification of the senses for the sake of aesthetic pleasure ⟨the *sensuous* delights of a Rubens painting⟩.

Sensual tends to imply the gratification of the senses or the indulgence of the physical appetites as ends in themselves ⟨a man who indulged his *sensual* appetites⟩.

Luxurious suggests the providing of or indulgence of sensuous pleasure inducing bodily ease and languor ⟨a vacation devoted to *luxurious* self-indulgence⟩.

Voluptuous implies more strongly an abandonment esp. to sensual pleasure ⟨promised a variety of *voluptuous* pleasures⟩.

SEPARATE *vb* **Separate, part, divide, sever, sunder, divorce** mean to become or cause to become disunited or disjointed.

Separate may imply any of several causes such as dispersion, removal of one from others, or presence of an intervening thing ⟨*separated* her personal life from her career⟩.

Part implies the separating of things or persons in close union or association ⟨an argument that *parted* the friends permanently⟩.

Divide implies separating into pieces or sections by cutting or breaking ⟨civil war *divided* the nation⟩.

Sever implies violence esp. in the removal of a part or member ⟨his arm had been *severed* by a chainsaw⟩.

Sunder suggests violent rending or wrenching apart ⟨a province *sundered* by two languages⟩.

Divorce implies separating two things that commonly interact and belong together ⟨would *divorce* scientific research from moral responsibility⟩.

SERIOUS, grave, solemn, sedate, staid, sober, earnest mean not light or frivolous.

Serious implies a concern for what really matters ⟨prefers gothic romances to *serious* fiction⟩.

Grave implies both seriousness and dignity in expression or attitude ⟨read the pronouncement in a *grave* voice⟩.

Solemn suggests an impressive gravity utterly free from levity ⟨the *solemn* occasion of a coronation⟩.

Sedate implies a composed and decorous seriousness ⟨amidst the frenzy of activity the bride remained *sedate*⟩.

Staid suggests a settled, accustomed sedateness and prim self-restraint ⟨her dinner parties were *staid* affairs⟩.

Sober stresses seriousness of purpose and absence of levity or frivolity ⟨an objective and *sober* look at the situation⟩.

Earnest suggests sincerity or often zealousness of purpose ⟨an *earnest* attempt at dramatizing the Bible⟩.

SEVERE, stern, austere, ascetic mean given to or marked by strict discipline and firm restraint.

Severe implies standards enforced without indulgence or laxity and may suggest harshness ⟨the *severe* dress of the Puritans⟩.

Stern stresses inflexibility and inexorability of temper or character ⟨a *stern* judge who seemed immune to pleas for mercy⟩.

Austere stresses absence of warmth, color, or feeling and may apply to rigorous restraint, simplicity, or self-denial ⟨the view that modern architecture is *austere*, brutal, and inhuman⟩.

Ascetic implies abstention from pleasure and comfort or self-indulgence as spiritual discipline ⟨the *ascetic* life of the monastic orders⟩.

SHAKE, agitate, rock, convulse mean to move up and down or to and fro with some violence.

Shake often carries a further implication of a particular purpose ⟨*shake* well before using⟩.

Agitate suggests a violent and prolonged tossing or stirring ⟨strong winds *agitated* the ship for hours⟩.

Rock suggests a swinging or swaying motion resulting from violent impact or upheaval ⟨the entire city was *rocked* by the explosion⟩.

Convulse suggests a violent pulling or wrenching as of a body in a paroxysm ⟨we were *convulsed* with laughter⟩.

SHARE, participate, partake mean to have, get, or use in common with another or others.

Share implies that one as the original holder grants to another the partial use, enjoyment, or possession of a thing though it may merely imply a mutual use or possession 〈*shared* my tools with the others〉.

Participate implies a having or taking part in an undertaking, activity, or discussion 〈students are encouraged to *participate* in outside activities〉.

Partake implies accepting or acquiring a share esp. of food or drink 〈invited everyone to *partake* freely in the refreshments〉.

SHARP, keen, acute mean having or showing alert competence and clear understanding.

Sharp implies quick perception, clever resourcefulness, or sometimes questionable trickiness 〈*sharp* enough to know a con job when he saw one〉.

Keen suggests quickness, enthusiasm, and a penetrating mind 〈a *keen* observer of the political scene〉.

Acute implies a power to penetrate and may suggest subtlety and sharpness of discrimination 〈an *acute* sense of what is linguistically effective〉.

SHORTEN, curtail, abbreviate, abridge, retrench mean to reduce in extent.

Shorten implies reduction in length or duration 〈*shorten* the speech to fit the allotted time〉.

Curtail adds an implication of cutting that in some way deprives of completeness or adequacy 〈the ceremonies were *curtailed* because of the rain〉.

Abbreviate implies a making shorter usu. by omitting some part 〈hostile questioning had the effect of *abbreviating* the interview〉.

Abridge implies a reduction in compass or scope with retention of essential elements and a relative completeness in the result 〈the *abridged* version of the novel〉.

Retrench suggests a reduction in extent or costs of something felt to be excessive 〈falling prices forced the company to *retrench*〉.

SHOW *vb* **Show, exhibit, display, expose, parade, flaunt**
mean to present so as to invite notice or attention.

Show implies no more than enabling another to see or examine ⟨*showed* her snapshots to the whole group⟩.

Exhibit stresses putting forward prominently or openly ⟨*exhibit* paintings at a gallery⟩.

Display emphasizes putting in a position where others may
see to advantage ⟨*display* sale items⟩.

Expose suggests bringing forth from concealment and displaying ⟨sought to *expose* the hypocrisy of the town fathers⟩.

Parade implies an ostentatious or arrogant displaying ⟨*parading* their piety for all to see⟩.

Flaunt suggests a shameless, boastful, often offensive parading ⟨nouveaux riches *flaunting* their wealth⟩.

SHOW *vb* **Show, manifest, evidence, evince, demonstrate**
mean to reveal outwardly or make apparent.

Show is the general term but sometimes implies that what is
revealed must be gained by inference from acts, looks, or
words ⟨careful not to *show* what he feels⟩.

Manifest implies a plainer, more immediate revelation ⟨*manifested* musical ability at an early age⟩.

Evidence suggests serving as proof of the actuality or existence of something ⟨her deep enmity is *evidenced* by her
silent glaring⟩.

Evince implies a showing by outward marks or signs
⟨*evinced* not the slightest grief at the funeral⟩.

Demonstrate implies showing by action or by display of
feeling ⟨*demonstrated* her appreciation in her own way⟩.

SHOWY, pretentious, ostentatious mean given to excessive
outward display.

Showy implies an imposing or striking appearance but usu.
suggests cheapness or poor taste ⟨the *showy* costumes of the
circus performers⟩.

Pretentious implies an appearance of importance not justified by the thing's value or the person's standing ⟨for a family-style restaurant, the menu was far too *pretentious*⟩.

Ostentatious stresses vainglorious display or parade ⟨very *ostentatious*, even for a debutante party⟩.

SHREWD, sagacious, perspicacious, astute mean acute in perception and sound in judgment.

Shrewd stresses practical, hardheaded cleverness and judgment ⟨a *shrewd* judge of character⟩.

Sagacious suggests wisdom, penetration, and farsightedness ⟨a series of *sagacious* investments tripled her wealth⟩.

Perspicacious implies unusual power to see through and understand what is puzzling or hidden ⟨a *perspicacious* counselor saw through his facade⟩.

Astute suggests shrewdness, perspicacity, and diplomatic skill ⟨an *astute* player of party politics⟩.

SHY, bashful, diffident, modest, coy mean not inclined to be forward.

Shy implies a timid reserve and a shrinking from familiarity or contact with others ⟨*shy* in front of total strangers⟩.

Bashful implies a frightened or hesitant shyness characteristic of childhood and adolescence ⟨the *bashful* boy rarely told us how he felt about anything⟩.

Diffident stresses a distrust of one's own ability or opinion that causes hesitation in acting or speaking ⟨felt *diffident* about raising an objection⟩.

Modest suggests absence of undue confidence or conceit ⟨very *modest* about reciting his achievements⟩.

Coy implies an assumed or affected shyness ⟨don't be misled by her *coy* demeanor⟩.

SIGN, mark, token, note, symptom mean a discernible indication of what is not itself directly perceptible.

Sign applies to any indication to be perceived by the senses or the reason ⟨interpreted her smile as a good *sign*⟩.

Mark suggests something impressed on or inherently characteristic of a thing often in contrast to general outward appearance ⟨integrity is the *mark* of a gentleman⟩.

Token applies to something that serves as a proof of something intangible ⟨this gift is a *token* of our esteem⟩.

Note suggests a distinguishing mark or characteristic ⟨a *note* of despair pervades her poetry⟩.

Symptom suggests an outward indication of an internal change or condition ⟨rampant violence is a *symptom* of that country's decline⟩.

SILENT, taciturn, reticent, reserved, secretive mean showing restraint in speaking.

Silent implies a habit of saying no more than is needed ⟨her husband was the *silent* type, not given to idle chatter⟩.

Taciturn implies a temperamental disinclination to speech and usu. connotes unsociability ⟨the locals are *taciturn* and not receptive to outsiders⟩.

Reticent implies a reluctance to speak out or at length, esp. about one's own affairs ⟨our guest was strangely *reticent* about his plans⟩.

Reserved implies reticence and suggests the restraining influence of caution or formality in checking easy informal conversational exchange ⟨greetings were brief, formal, and *reserved*⟩.

Secretive, too, implies reticence but usu. carries a suggestion of deviousness and lack of frankness or of an often ostentatious will to conceal ⟨a *secretive* public official usually stingy with news stories⟩.

SIMILAR, analogous, parallel mean closely resembling each other.

Similar implies the possibility of being mistaken for each other ⟨all the houses in the development are *similar*⟩.

Analogous applies to things belonging in essentially different categories but nevertheless having many similarities ⟨*analogous* political systems⟩.

Parallel suggests a marked likeness in the development of two things ⟨the *parallel* careers of two movie stars⟩.

SIMPLE, foolish, silly, fatuous, asinine mean actually or apparently deficient in intelligence.

Simple implies a degree of intelligence inadequate to cope with anything complex or involving mental effort ⟨*simple* peasants afraid of revolutionary ideas⟩.

Foolish implies the character of being or seeming unable to use judgment. discretion. or good sense ⟨*foolish* people believed the ghost story⟩.

Silly suggests failure to act as a rational being esp. by ridiculous behavior ⟨the *silly* stunts of vacationing college students⟩.

Fatuous implies foolishness. inanity. and disregard of reality ⟨the *fatuous* conspiracy theories of these extremists⟩.

Asinine suggests utter and contemptible failure to use normal rationality or perception ⟨a soap opera with an especially *asinine* plot⟩.

See in addition EASY.

SINCERE, wholehearted, heartfelt, hearty, unfeigned mean genuine in feeling.

Sincere stresses absence of hypocrisy. feigning. or any falsifying embellishment or exaggeration ⟨offered a *sincere* apology⟩.

Wholehearted suggests sincerity and earnest devotion without reservation or misgiving ⟨promised our *wholehearted* support to the cause⟩.

Heartfelt suggests depth of genuine feeling outwardly expressed ⟨a gift that expresses our *heartfelt* gratitude⟩.

Hearty suggests honesty. warmth. and exuberance in displaying feeling ⟨received a *hearty* welcome at the door⟩.

Unfeigned stresses spontaneity and absence of pretense ⟨her *unfeigned* delight at receiving the award⟩.

SINGLE, sole, unique, separate, solitary, particular mean one as distinguished from two or more or all others.

Single implies being unaccompanied by or unsupported by any other ⟨a *single* example will suffice⟩.

Sole applies to the one of its kind or character in existence ⟨my *sole* reason for moving there⟩.

Unique applies to the only one of its kind or character in existence ⟨the medal is *unique*, for no duplicates were made⟩.

Separate stresses discreteness and disconnection from every other one ⟨a country with a *separate* set of problems⟩.

Solitary implies being both single and isolated ⟨the television was her *solitary* link to the outside world⟩.

Particular implies numerical distinctness from other instances, examples, or members of a class ⟨a *particular* kind of wine⟩.

SINISTER, baleful, malign mean seriously threatening evil or disaster.

Sinister suggests a general or vague feeling of fear or apprehension on the part of the observer ⟨a *sinister* aura surrounded the place⟩.

Baleful imputes perniciousness or destructiveness to something whether working openly or covertly ⟨the *baleful* influence of recreational drugs on our society⟩.

Malign applies to what is inherently evil or harmful ⟨smoking's *malign* effects on one's health⟩.

SLEEK, slick, glossy, silken mean having a smooth bright surface or appearance.

Sleek suggests a smoothness or brightness resulting from attentive grooming or physical conditioning ⟨a *sleek* racehorse⟩.

Slick suggests extreme smoothness that results in a slippery surface ⟨slipped and fell on the *slick* floor⟩.

Glossy suggests a surface that is smooth and highly polished ⟨photographs having a *glossy* finish⟩.

Silken implies the smoothness and luster as well as the softness of silk ⟨*silken* hair⟩.

SLY, cunning, crafty, tricky, foxy, artful mean attaining or seeking to attain one's ends by devious means.

Sly implies furtiveness, lack of candor, and skill in concealing one's aims and methods ⟨a *sly* corporate-takeover scheme⟩.

Cunning suggests the inventive use of sometimes limited intelligence in overreaching or circumventing ⟨the *cunning* animal avoided the trap⟩.

Crafty implies cleverness and subtlety of method ⟨a *crafty* trial lawyer⟩.

Tricky is more likely to suggest shiftiness and unreliability than skill in deception and maneuvering ⟨a *tricky* interviewer who usually got what she wanted from her subject⟩.

Foxy implies a shrewd and wary craftiness usu. involving devious dealing ⟨a *foxy* thief got away with her jewels⟩.

Artful implies alluring indirectness in dealing and often connotes sophistication or coquetry or cleverness ⟨an *artful* matchmaker⟩.

SMALL, little, diminutive, minute, tiny, miniature mean noticeably below average in size.

Small and **little** are often interchangeable, but *small* applies more to relative size determined by capacity, value, number; *little* is more absolute in implication often carrying the idea of petiteness, pettiness, insignificance, or immaturity ⟨the theater was relatively *small*⟩ ⟨your pathetic *little* smile⟩.

Diminutive implies abnormal smallness ⟨the *diminutive* gymnast outshone her larger competitors⟩.

Minute implies extreme smallness ⟨a beverage with only a *minute* amount of caffeine⟩.

Tiny is an informal equivalent to *minute* ⟨*tiny* cracks have formed in the painting⟩.

Miniature applies to an exactly proportioned reproduction on a very small scale ⟨a doll house complete with *miniature* furnishings⟩.

SMELL, scent, odor, aroma mean the quality that makes a thing perceptible to the olfactory sense.

 Smell implies solely the sensation without suggestion of quality or character ⟨an odd *smell* permeated the room⟩.

 Scent applies to the characteristic smell given off by a substance, an animal, or a plant ⟨dogs trained to detect the *scent* of narcotics⟩.

 Odor may imply a stronger or more readily distinguished scent or it may be equivalent to *smell* ⟨a type of cheese with a very pronounced *odor*⟩.

 Aroma suggests a somewhat penetrating usu. pleasant odor ⟨the *aroma* of freshly ground coffee⟩.

SOAK, saturate, drench, steep, impregnate mean to permeate or be permeated with a liquid.

 Soak implies usu. prolonged immersion as for softening or cleansing ⟨*soak* the clothes in bleach and water to remove the stains⟩.

 Saturate implies a resulting effect of complete absorption until no more liquid can be held ⟨gym clothes *saturated* with sweat⟩.

 Drench implies a thorough wetting by something that pours down or is poured ⟨the cloudburst *drenched* us to the skin⟩.

 Steep suggests either the extraction of an essence (as of tea leaves) by the liquid or the imparting of a quality (as a color) to the thing immersed ⟨*steep* the tea leaves for exactly five minutes⟩.

 Impregnate implies a thorough interpenetration of one thing by another ⟨a cake strongly *impregnated* with brandy⟩.

SOLITUDE, isolation, seclusion mean the state of one who is alone.

 Solitude may imply a condition of being apart from all human beings or of being cut off by wish or compulsion from one's usual associates ⟨the *solitude* enjoyed by the long-distance trucker⟩.

Isolation stresses detachment from others often involuntarily ⟨the oppressive *isolation* of the village during winter⟩.

Seclusion suggests a shutting away or keeping apart from others often connoting deliberate withdrawal from the world or retirement to a quiet life ⟨lived in bucolic *seclusion* surrounded by his art collection⟩.

SOPHISTICATED, worldly-wise, blasé mean experienced in the ways of the world.

Sophisticated often implies refinement, urbanity, cleverness, and cultivation ⟨guests at her salon were usually rich and *sophisticated*⟩.

Worldly-wise suggests a close and practical knowledge of the affairs and manners of society and an inclination toward materialism ⟨a *worldly-wise* woman with a philosophy of personal independence⟩.

Blasé implies a lack of responsiveness to common joys as a result of a real or affected surfeit of experience and cultivation ⟨*blasé* travelers who claimed to have been everywhere⟩.

SORROW, grief, anguish, woe, regret mean distress of mind.

Sorrow implies a sense of loss or a sense of guilt and remorse ⟨a nation united in *sorrow* upon the death of the President⟩.

Grief implies poignant sorrow for an immediate cause ⟨gave his father much *grief*⟩.

Anguish suggests torturing grief or dread ⟨the *anguish* felt by the hostages⟩.

Woe is deep or inconsolable grief or misery ⟨cries of *woe* echoed throughout the bombed city⟩.

Regret implies pain caused by deep disappointment, fruitless longing, or unavailing remorse ⟨never felt a moment of *regret* following the divorce⟩.

SPACIOUS, commodious, capacious, ample mean larger in extent or capacity than the average.

Spacious implies great length and breadth ⟨a mansion with a *spacious* front lawn⟩.

Commodious stresses roominess and comfortableness ⟨a *commodious* and airy penthouse apartment⟩.

Capacious stresses the ability to hold, contain, or retain more than the average ⟨a *capacious* suitcase⟩.

Ample implies having a greater size, expanse, or amount than that deemed adequate ⟨we have *ample* means to buy the house⟩.

SPARING, frugal, thrifty, economical mean careful in the use of one's money or resources.

Sparing stresses abstention and restraint ⟨*sparing* in the offering of advice⟩.

Frugal implies absence of luxury and simplicity of lifestyle ⟨carried on in the *frugal* tradition of the Yankees⟩.

Thrifty stresses good management and industry ⟨the store prospered under his *thrifty* management⟩.

Economical stresses prudent management, lack of wastefulness, and use of things to their best advantage ⟨trucking remains an *economical* means of transport⟩.

SPECIAL, especial, specific, particular, individual mean of or relating to one thing or class.

Special stresses having a quality, character, identity, or use of its own ⟨airline passengers who require *special* meals⟩.

Especial may add implications of preeminence or preference ⟨a matter of *especial* importance⟩.

Specific implies a quality or character distinguishing a kind or a species ⟨children with *specific* nutritional needs⟩.

Particular stresses the distinctness of something as an individual ⟨an Alpine scene of *particular* beauty⟩.

Individual implies unequivocal reference to one of a class or group ⟨valued each *individual* opinion⟩.

SPLENDID, resplendent, gorgeous, glorious, sublime, superb mean extraordinarily or transcendently impressive.

Splendid implies outshining the usual or customary ⟨the wedding was a *splendid* occasion⟩.

Resplendent suggests a glowing or blazing splendor 〈the church was *resplendent* in its Easter decorations〉.

Gorgeous implies a rich splendor esp. in display of color 〈a *gorgeous* red dress〉.

Glorious suggests radiance that heightens beauty or distinction 〈a *glorious* sunset over the ocean〉.

Sublime implies an exaltation or elevation almost beyond human comprehension 〈the *sublime* grandeur of the thunderous falls〉.

Superb suggests a magnificence or excellence reaching the highest conceivable degree 〈a three-star restaurant offering *superb* cuisine〉.

SPOIL *n* **Spoil, pillage, plunder, booty, prize, loot** mean something taken from another by force or craft.

Spoil, more commonly **spoils,** applies to what belongs by right or custom to the victor in war or political contest 〈a governor who relished doling out the *spoils* of office〉.

Pillage stresses more open violence or lawlessness 〈filled his capital city with the *pillage* of Europe〉.

Plunder applies to what is taken not only in war but in robbery, banditry, grafting, or swindling 〈a fortune that was the *plunder* of years of political corruption〉.

Booty implies plunder to be shared among confederates 〈the thieves planned to divide their *booty* later〉.

Prize applies to spoils captured on the high seas or territorial waters of the enemy 〈a pirate ship ruthlessly seizing *prizes*〉.

Loot applies esp. to what is taken from victims of a catastrophe 〈prowlers searched the storm-damaged cottages for *loot*〉.

SPONTANEOUS, impulsive, instinctive, automatic, mechanical mean acting or activated without deliberation.

Spontaneous implies lack of prompting and connotes naturalness 〈a *spontaneous* burst of applause〉.

Impulsive implies acting under stress of emotion or spirit of the moment 〈*impulsive* acts of violence〉.

Instinctive stresses spontaneous action involving neither judgment nor will ⟨blinking is an *instinctive* reaction⟩.

Automatic implies action engaging neither the mind nor the emotions and connotes a predictable response ⟨his denial was *automatic*⟩.

Mechanical stresses the lifeless, often perfunctory character of the response ⟨over the years her style of teaching became *mechanical*⟩.

SPRING, arise, rise, originate, derive, flow, issue, emanate, proceed, stem mean to come up or out of something into existence.

Spring implies rapid or sudden emerging ⟨a brilliant idea that had *sprung* out of nowhere⟩.

Arise and **rise** may both convey the fact of coming into existence or notice but *rise* often stresses gradual growth or ascent ⟨a dispute *arose* over the property⟩ ⟨as time passed legends about the house *rose*⟩.

Originate implies a definite source or starting point ⟨the theory did not *originate* with Darwin⟩.

Derive implies a prior existence in another form ⟨their system of justice *derives* from British colonial law⟩.

Flow adds to *spring* a suggestion of abundance or ease of inception ⟨the belief that all good *flows* from God⟩.

Issue suggests emerging from confinement through an outlet ⟨shouts of joy *issued* from the team's locker room⟩.

Emanate applies to the coming of something immaterial (as a principle or thought) from a source ⟨serenity *emanated* from her⟩.

Proceed stresses place of origin, derivation, parentage, or logical cause ⟨bitterness that *proceeded* from an unhappy marriage⟩.

Stem implies originating by dividing or branching off from something as an outgrowth or subordinate development ⟨a whole new industry *stemmed* from the discovery⟩.

STANDARD, criterion, gauge, yardstick, touchstone mean a means of determining what a thing should be.

Standard applies to any definite rule, principle, or measure established by authority 〈the book is a classic by any *standard*〉.

Criterion may apply to anything used as a test of quality whether formulated as a rule or principle or not 〈in art there are no hard-and-fast *criteria*〉.

Gauge applies to a means of testing a particular dimension (as thickness, depth, diameter) or figuratively a particular quality or aspect 〈congressional mail is not always an accurate *gauge* of public opinion〉.

Yardstick is an informal substitute for *criterion* that suggests quantity more often than quality 〈the movie was a flop by most *yardsticks*〉.

Touchstone suggests a simple test of the authenticity or value of something intangible 〈fine service is one *touchstone* of a first-class restaurant〉.

STEADY, even, equable mean not varying throughout a course or extent.

Steady implies lack of fluctuation or interruption of movement 〈ran the race at a *steady* pace〉.

Even suggests a lack of variation in quality or character 〈read the statement in an *even* voice〉.

Equable implies lack of extremes or of sudden sharp changes 〈during exercise keep your pulse as *equable* as possible〉.

STEAL, pilfer, filch, purloin mean to take from another without right or without detection.

Steal may apply to any surreptitious taking of something and differs from the other terms by commonly applying to intangibles as well as material things 〈*steal* jewels〉 〈*stole* a look at her〉.

Pilfer implies stealing repeatedly in small amounts 〈dismissed for *pilfering* from the company〉.

Filch adds a suggestion of snatching quickly and surreptitiously ⟨*filched* an apple when the man looked away⟩.

Purloin stresses removing or carrying off for one's own use or purposes ⟨had *purloined* a typewriter and other office equipment⟩.

STEEP *adj* **Steep, abrupt, precipitous, sheer** mean having an incline approaching the perpendicular.

Steep implies such sharpness of pitch that ascent or descent is very difficult ⟨a *steep* staircase leading to the attic⟩.

Abrupt implies a sharper pitch and a sudden break in the level ⟨a beach with an *abrupt* drop-off⟩.

Precipitous applies to an incline approaching the vertical ⟨the airplane went into a *precipitous* nosedive⟩.

Sheer suggests an unbroken perpendicular expanse ⟨climbers able to ascend *sheer* cliffs⟩.

STICK, adhere, cohere, cling, cleave mean to become closely attached.

Stick implies attachment by affixing or by being glued together ⟨the gummed label will *stick* just by pressing⟩.

Adhere is often interchangeable with *stick* but sometimes implies a growing together ⟨muscle fibers will *adhere* following surgery⟩.

Cohere suggests a sticking together of parts so that they form a unified mass ⟨eggs will make the mixture *cohere*⟩.

Cling implies attachment by hanging on with arms or tendrils ⟨always *cling* to a capsized boat⟩.

Cleave stresses strength of attachment ⟨barnacles *cleaving* to the hull of a boat⟩.

STIFF, rigid, inflexible mean difficult to bend.

Stiff may apply to any degree of this condition ⟨muscles will become *stiff* if they are not stretched⟩.

Rigid applies to something so stiff that it cannot be bent without breaking ⟨a *rigid* surfboard⟩.

Inflexible stresses lack of suppleness or pliability ⟨for adequate support, rock-climbers wear shoes with *inflexible* soles⟩.

STINGY, close, niggardly, parsimonious, penurious, miserly mean being unwilling or showing unwillingness to share with others.

Stingy implies a marked lack of generosity ⟨a *stingy* child, not given to sharing⟩.

Close suggests keeping a tight grip on one's money and possessions ⟨folks who are very *close* when charity calls⟩.

Niggardly implies giving or spending the very smallest amount possible ⟨the *niggardly* amount budgeted for the library⟩.

Parsimonious suggests a frugality so extreme as to lead to stinginess ⟨a *parsimonious* lifestyle with no room for luxuries⟩.

Penurious implies niggardliness that gives an appearance of actual poverty ⟨the *penurious* eccentric left behind a fortune⟩.

Miserly suggests a sordid avariciousness and a morbid pleasure in hoarding ⟨a *miserly* man indifferent to the cries of the needy⟩.

STOOP, condescend, deign mean to descend from one's level to do something.

Stoop may imply a descent in dignity or from a relatively high moral plane to a much lower one ⟨how can you *stoop* to such childish name-calling⟩.

Condescend implies a stooping by one of high rank or position to socialize with social inferiors ⟨the boss's wife *condescending* to mingle with the employees⟩.

Deign suggests a reluctant condescension of one in a haughty mood ⟨scarcely *deigned* to speak with her poor relations⟩.

STOP, cease, quit, discontinue, desist mean to suspend or cause to suspend activity.

Stop applies to action or progress or to what is operating or progressing and may imply suddenness or definiteness ⟨*stopped* at the red light⟩.

Cease applies to states, conditions, or existence and may add a suggestion of gradualness and a degree of finality ⟨by nightfall the fighting had *ceased*⟩.

Quit may stress either finality or abruptness in stopping or ceasing ⟨the engine faltered, sputtered, then *quit* altogether⟩.

Discontinue applies to the stopping of an accustomed activity or practice ⟨we have *discontinued* the manufacture of that item⟩.

Desist implies forbearance or restraint as a motive for stopping or ceasing ⟨*desisted* from further efforts to persuade them⟩.

STRANGE, singular, unique, peculiar, eccentric, erratic, odd, queer, quaint, outlandish mean departing from what is ordinary, usual, or to be expected.

Strange stresses unfamiliarity and may apply to the foreign, the unnatural, the unaccountable ⟨a journey filled with *strange* sights⟩.

Singular suggests individuality or puzzling strangeness ⟨a *singular* feeling of impending disaster⟩.

Unique implies singularity and the fact of being without a known parallel ⟨a career that is *unique* in the annals of science⟩.

Peculiar implies a marked distinctiveness ⟨problems *peculiar* to inner-city areas⟩.

Eccentric suggests a wide divergence from the usual or normal esp. in behavior ⟨the *eccentric* eating habits of young children⟩.

Erratic stresses a capricious and unpredictable wandering or deviating ⟨disturbed by his friend's *erratic* behavior⟩.

Odd applies to a departure from the regular or expected ⟨an *odd* sense of humor⟩.

Queer suggests a dubious sometimes sinister oddness ⟨puzzled by the *queer* happenings since her arrival⟩.

Quaint suggests an old-fashioned but pleasant oddness ⟨a *quaint* and remote village in the mountains⟩.

Outlandish applies to what is uncouth, bizarre, or barbaric ⟨islanders having *outlandish* customs and superstitions⟩.

STRONG, stout, sturdy, stalwart, tough, tenacious mean showing power to resist or to endure.

Strong may imply power derived from muscular vigor, large size, structural soundness, intellectual or spiritual resources ⟨*strong* arms⟩ ⟨a *strong* desire to succeed⟩.

Stout suggests an ability to endure stress, pain, or hard use without giving way ⟨wear *stout* boots when hiking⟩.

Sturdy implies strength derived from vigorous growth, determination of spirit, solidity of construction ⟨a *sturdy* table⟩ ⟨people of *sturdy* independence⟩.

Stalwart suggests an unshakable dependability and connotes great physical strength ⟨*stalwart* supporters of the environmental movement⟩.

Tough implies great firmness and resiliency ⟨a *tough* political opponent⟩.

Tenacious suggests strength in seizing, retaining, clinging to, or holding together ⟨*tenacious* of their right to privacy⟩.

STUPID, dull, dense, crass, dumb mean lacking in power to absorb ideas or impressions.

Stupid implies a slow-witted or dazed state of mind that may be either congenital or temporary ⟨you're too *stupid* to know what's good for you⟩.

Dull suggests a slow or sluggish mind such as results from disease, depression, or shock ⟨monotonous work that left his mind *dull*⟩.

Dense implies a thickheaded imperviousness to ideas ⟨was too *dense* to take a hint⟩.

Crass suggests a grossness of mind precluding discrimination or delicacy ⟨a *crass*, materialistic people⟩.

Dumb applies to an exasperating obtuseness or lack of comprehension ⟨too *dumb* to figure out what's going on⟩.

SUAVE, urbane, diplomatic, bland, smooth, politic mean pleasantly tactful and well-mannered.

Suave suggests a specific ability to deal with others easily and without friction ⟨a luxury restaurant with an army of *suave* waiters⟩.

Urbane implies high cultivation and poise coming from wide social experience ⟨the *urbane* host of a television series⟩.

Diplomatic stresses an ability to deal with ticklish situations tactfully ⟨be *diplomatic* in asking them to leave⟩.

Bland emphasizes mildness of manner and absence of irritating qualities ⟨a *bland* manner suitable for early morning radio⟩.

Smooth suggests often a deliberately assumed suavity ⟨the *smooth* sales pitch of a car dealer⟩.

Politic implies shrewd as well as tactful and suave handling of people ⟨an ambassador's wife must be *politic* and discreet⟩.

SUBSERVIENT, servile, slavish, obsequious mean showing or characterized by extreme compliance or abject obedience.

Subservient implies the cringing manner of one very conscious of a subordinate position ⟨domestic help was expected to be properly *subservient*⟩.

Servile suggests the mean or fawning behavior of a slave ⟨a political boss and his entourage of *servile* hangers-on⟩.

Slavish suggests abject or debased servility ⟨the *slavish* status of migrant farm workers⟩.

Obsequious implies fawning or sycophantic compliance and exaggerated deference of manner ⟨waiters who are *obsequious* in the presence of celebrities⟩.

SUFFICIENT, enough, adequate, competent mean being what is necessary or desirable.

Sufficient suggests a close meeting of a need ⟨had supplies *sufficient* to last a month⟩.

Enough is less exact in suggestion than *sufficient* ⟨do you have *enough* food?⟩.

Adequate may imply barely meeting a requirement ⟨the room was *adequate*, no more⟩.

Competent suggests measuring up to all requirements without question or being adequately adapted to an end ⟨a *competent* income for their lifestyle⟩.

SUGGEST, imply, hint, intimate, insinuate mean to convey an idea indirectly.

Suggest may stress putting into the mind by association of ideas, awakening of a desire, or initiating a train of thought ⟨an actress who can *suggest* a whole character with one gesture⟩.

Imply is close to *suggest* but may indicate a more definite or logical relation of the unexpressed idea to the expressed ⟨pronouncements that *imply* he has lost touch with reality⟩.

Hint implies the use of slight or remote suggestion with a minimum of overt statement ⟨*hinted* that she might have a job lined up⟩.

Intimate stresses delicacy of suggestion without connoting any lack of candor ⟨*intimated* that he was ready to pop the question⟩.

Insinuate applies to the conveying of a usu. unpleasant idea in a sly underhanded manner ⟨*insinuated* that the neighbors were not what they appeared to be⟩.

SULLEN, glum, morose, surly, sulky, crabbed, saturnine, gloomy mean showing a forbidding or disagreeable mood.

Sullen implies a silent ill humor and a refusal to be sociable ⟨remained *sullen* throughout the party⟩.

Glum suggests a silent dispiritedness ⟨the whole team was *glum* following the defeat⟩.

Morose adds to *glum* an element of bitterness or misanthropy ⟨became *morose* after the death of his wife⟩.

Surly implies gruffness and sullenness of speech or manner ⟨a *surly* teenage boy⟩.

Sulky suggests childish resentment expressed in peevish sullenness ⟨*sulky* behavior followed every argument⟩.

Crabbed applies to a forbidding morose harshness of manner ⟨his *crabbed* exterior was only a pose⟩.

Saturnine describes a heavy forbidding aspect or suggests a bitter disposition ⟨a *saturnine* cynic always finding fault⟩.

Gloomy implies a depression in mood making for seeming sullenness or glumness ⟨bad news that put everyone in a *gloomy* mood⟩.

SUMMIT, peak, pinnacle, climax, apex, acme, culmination mean the highest point attained or attainable.

Summit implies the topmost level attainable ⟨a singer at the *summit* of his career⟩.

Peak suggests the highest among other high points ⟨an artist working at the *peak* of his powers⟩.

Pinnacle suggests a dizzying and often insecure height ⟨the *pinnacle* of success in the entertainment world⟩.

Climax implies the highest point in an ascending series ⟨the moon landing marked the *climax* of the program⟩.

Apex implies the point where all ascending lines converge ⟨Dutch culture reached its *apex* in the 17th century⟩.

Acme implies a level of quality representing the perfection of a thing ⟨a statue that was once the *acme* of beauty⟩.

Culmination suggests the outcome of a growth or development representing an attained objective ⟨the bill marked the *culmination* of the civil rights movement⟩.

SUMMON, call, cite, convoke, convene, muster mean to demand the presence of.

Summon implies the exercise of authority ⟨*summoned* by the court to appear as a witness⟩.

Call may be used less formally for *summon* ⟨the President *called* Congress for a special session⟩.

Cite implies a summoning to court usu. to answer a charge ⟨*cited* to answer the charge of drunken driving⟩.

Convoke implies a summons to assemble for deliberative or legislative purposes ⟨*convoked* an assembly of the world's leading scientists⟩.

Convene is somewhat less formal than *convoke* ⟨*convened* the students in the school auditorium⟩.

Muster suggests a calling up of a number of things that form a group in order that they may be exhibited, displayed, or utilized as a whole ⟨*muster* the troops for an inspection⟩.

SUPEREROGATORY, gratuitous, uncalled-for, wanton mean done without need or compulsion or warrant.

Supererogatory implies a giving above what is required by rule and may suggest adding something not needed or not wanted ⟨an abrupt man who regarded the usual pleasantries as *supererogatory*⟩.

Gratuitous usu. applies to something offensive or unpleasant given or done without provocation ⟨my civil question received a *gratuitous* insult⟩.

Uncalled-for implies impertinence or logical absurdity ⟨resented her *uncalled-for* advice⟩.

Wanton implies not only a lack of provocation but a malicious or sportive motive ⟨the *wanton* destruction of property by vandals⟩.

SUPERFICIAL, shallow, cursory mean lacking in depth or solidity.

Superficial implies a concern only with surface aspects ⟨a *superficial* examination of the wound⟩.

Shallow is more generally derogatory in implying lack of depth in knowledge, reasoning, emotions, or character ⟨a *shallow* interpretation of the character Hamlet⟩.

Cursory suggests a lack of thoroughness or a neglect of details ⟨even a *cursory* reading of the work will reveal that⟩.

SUPPORT, uphold, advocate, back, champion mean to favor actively one that meets opposition.

Support is least explicit about the nature of the assistance given ⟨people who *support* the development of the area⟩.

Uphold implies extended support given to something attacked ⟨*upheld* the legitimacy of the military action⟩.

Advocate stresses urging or pleading ⟨*advocated* a return to basics in public school education⟩.

Back suggests supporting by lending assistance to one failing or falling ⟨allies refused to *back* the call for sanctions⟩.

Champion suggests publicly defending one unjustly attacked or too weak to advocate his own cause ⟨*championed* the rights of pregnant women⟩.

SURE, certain, positive, cocksure mean having no doubt or uncertainty.

Sure usu. stresses the subjective or intuitive feeling of assurance ⟨felt *sure* that he had forgotten something⟩.

Certain may apply to a basing of a conclusion or conviction on definite grounds or indubitable evidence ⟨scientists are now *certain* what caused the explosion⟩.

Positive intensifies sureness or certainty and may imply opinionated conviction or forceful expression of it ⟨she is *positive* that he is the killer⟩.

Cocksure implies presumptuous or careless positiveness ⟨you're always so *cocksure* about everything⟩.

SURPRISE, astonish, astound, amaze, flabbergast mean to impress forcibly through unexpectedness.

Surprise stresses causing an effect through being unexpected at a particular time or place rather than by being essentially unusual or novel ⟨*surprised* to find his mother in a bar⟩.

Astonish implies surprising so greatly as to seem incredible ⟨the young player *astonished* the chess masters⟩.

Astound stresses the shock of astonishment ⟨news of the atomic bomb *astounded* everyone⟩.

Amaze suggests an effect of bewilderment ⟨*amazed* by the immense size of the place⟩.

Flabbergast may suggest thorough astonishment and bewilderment or dismay ⟨*flabbergasted* by his daughter's precocious comments⟩.

SWERVE, veer, deviate, depart, digress, diverge mean to turn aside from a straight course.

Swerve may suggest a physical, mental, or moral turning away from a given course, often with abruptness ⟨suddenly *swerved* to avoid hitting an animal⟩.

Veer implies a major change in direction ⟨at that point the road *veers* to the right⟩.

Deviate implies a turning from a customary or prescribed course 〈the witness never *deviated* from her story〉.

Depart suggests a deviation from a traditional or conventional course or type 〈a book that *departs* from the usual memoirs of a film star〉.

Digress applies to a departing from the subject of one's discourse 〈frequently *digressed* during his lecture〉.

Diverge may equal *depart* but usu. suggests a branching of a main path into two or more leading in different directions 〈after medical school their paths *diverged*〉.

SWING *vb* **Swing, wave, flourish, brandish, thrash** mean to wield or cause to move to and fro or up and down.

Swing implies regular or uniform movement 〈*swing* the rope back and forth〉.

Wave usu. implies smooth or continuous motion 〈a flag *waving* in the breeze〉.

Flourish suggests vigorous, ostentatious, or graceful movement 〈*flourishing* her racket, she challenged me to a match〉.

Brandish implies threatening or menacing motion 〈*brandishing* his fist, he vowed vengeance〉.

Thrash suggests vigorous, abrupt, violent movement 〈a child *thrashing* his arms about in a tantrum〉.

SWING *vb* **Swing, sway, oscillate, vibrate, fluctuate, waver, undulate** mean to move from one direction to its opposite.

Swing implies a movement of something attached at one end or one side 〈the door suddenly *swung* open〉.

Sway implies a slow swinging or teetering movement 〈the drunk *swayed* a little and then fell〉.

Oscillate stresses a usu. rapid alternation of direction 〈a fan that *oscillates* will cool more effectively〉.

Vibrate suggests the rapid oscillation of an elastic body under stress or impact 〈the *vibrating* strings of a piano〉.

Fluctuate suggests constant irregular changes of level, intensity, or value ⟨monetary exchange rates *fluctuate* constantly⟩.

Waver stresses irregular motion suggestive of reeling or tottering ⟨his whole body *wavered* as he crossed the finish line⟩.

Undulate suggests a gentle wave-like motion ⟨an *undulating* sea of grass⟩.

T

TACT, address, poise, savoir faire mean skill and grace in dealing with others.

Tact implies delicate and considerate perception of what is appropriate ⟨use *tact* when inquiring about the divorce⟩.

Address stresses dexterity and grace in dealing with new and trying situations and may imply success in attaining one's ends ⟨brought off the dinner party with remarkable *address*⟩.

Poise may imply both tact and address but stresses self-possession and ease in meeting difficult situations ⟨the *poise* of one who has been officiating all his life⟩.

Savoir faire is likely to stress worldly experience and a sure awareness of what is proper or expedient ⟨the *savoir faire* of a seasoned traveler⟩.

TAKE, seize, grasp, clutch, snatch, grab mean to get hold of by or as if by catching up with the hand.

Take is a general term applicable to any manner of getting something into one's possession or control ⟨*take* some salad from the bowl⟩ ⟨*took* control of the company⟩.

Seize implies a sudden and forcible movement in getting hold of something tangible or an apprehending of something fleeting or elusive when intangible ⟨*seized* the crook as he tried to escape⟩.

Grasp stresses a laying hold so as to have firmly in possession ⟨firmly *grasp* the handle and pull⟩.

Clutch suggests avidity or anxiety in seizing or grasping and may imply less success in holding ⟨frantically *clutching* the bush at the edge of the cliff⟩.

Snatch suggests more suddenness or quickness but less force than *seize* ⟨*snatched* a doughnut before running out the door⟩. **Grab** implies more roughness or rudeness than *snatch* ⟨roughly *grabbed* her by the arm⟩.

TALKATIVE, loquacious, garrulous, voluble mean given to talk or talking.

Talkative may imply a readiness to engage in talk or a disposition to enjoy conversation ⟨not the *talkative* type who would enjoy a party⟩.

Loquacious suggests the power of expressing oneself articulately, fluently, or glibly ⟨the corporation needs a spokesperson who is *loquacious* and telegenic⟩.

Garrulous implies prosy, rambling, or tedious loquacity ⟨forced to endure a *garrulous* companion the whole trip⟩.

Voluble suggests a free, easy, and unending loquacity ⟨the Italians are a *voluble* people⟩.

TASK, duty, job, chore, stint, assignment mean a piece of work to be done.

Task implies work imposed by a person in authority or an employer or by circumstance ⟨performed a variety of *tasks* for the company⟩.

Duty implies an obligation to perform or responsibility for performance ⟨the *duties* of a lifeguard⟩.

Job applies to a piece of work voluntarily performed; it may sometimes suggest difficulty or importance ⟨took on the *job* of turning the company around⟩.

Chore implies a minor routine activity necessary for maintaining a household or farm ⟨every child had a list of *chores* to do⟩.

Stint implies a carefully allotted or measured quantity of assigned work or service ⟨during his *stint* as governor⟩.

Assignment implies a definite limited task assigned by one in authority ⟨your *assignment* did not include interfering with others⟩.

TEACH, instruct, educate, train, discipline, school mean to cause to acquire knowledge or skill.

Teach applies to any manner of imparting information or skill so that others may learn ⟨*teach* French⟩ ⟨*taught* them how to ski⟩.

Instruct suggests methodical or formal teaching ⟨*instruct* the recruits in calisthenics at boot camp⟩.

Educate implies attempting to bring out latent capabilities ⟨*educate* students so that they are prepared for the future⟩.

Train stresses instruction and drill with a specific end in view ⟨*trained* foreign pilots to operate the new aircraft⟩.

Discipline implies subordinating to a master for the sake of controlling ⟨*disciplined* herself to exercise daily⟩.

School implies training or disciplining esp. in what is hard to master or to bear ⟨*schooled* myself not to flinch at the sight of blood⟩.

TEAR, rip, rend, split, cleave, rive mean to separate forcibly.

Tear implies a pulling apart by force and leaving jagged edges ⟨*tear* up lettuce for a salad⟩.

Rip implies a pulling apart in one rapid uninterrupted motion often along a seam or joint ⟨*ripped* the jacket along the side seams⟩.

Rend implies very violent or ruthless severing or sundering ⟨an angry mob *rent* his clothes⟩.

Split implies a cutting or breaking apart in a continuous, straight, and usu. lengthwise direction or in the direction of grain or layers ⟨*split* logs for firewood⟩.

Cleave implies very forceful splitting or cutting with a blow ⟨a bolt of lightning *cleaved* the giant oak⟩.

Rive suggests action rougher and more violent than *split* or *cleave* ⟨a friendship *riven* by jealousy⟩.

TEMERITY, audacity, hardihood, effrontery, nerve, cheek, gall, chutzpah mean conspicuous or flagrant boldness.

Temerity suggests boldness arising from rashness and contempt of danger ⟨had the *temerity* to ask for a favor after that insult⟩.

Audacity implies a disregard of restraints commonly imposed by convention or prudence ⟨an entrepreneur with *audacity* and vision⟩.

Hardihood suggests firmness in daring and defiance ⟨no serious scientist has the *hardihood* to claim that⟩.

Effrontery implies shameless, insolent disregard of propriety or courtesy ⟨had the *effrontery* to tell me how to do my job⟩.

Nerve, cheek, gall, and **chutzpah** are informal equivalents for *effrontery* ⟨the *nerve* of that guy⟩ ⟨has the *cheek* to bill herself as a singer⟩ ⟨had the *gall* to demand some evidence⟩ ⟨her *chutzpah* got her into the exclusive party⟩.

TENDENCY, trend, drift, tenor, current mean movement in a particular direction.

Tendency implies an inclination sometimes amounting to an impelling force ⟨the *tendency* to expand the limits of what is art⟩.

Trend applies to the general direction maintained by a winding or irregular course ⟨the long-term *trend* of the stock market is upward⟩.

Drift may apply to a tendency determined by external forces ⟨the *drift* of the population away from large cities⟩ or it may apply to an underlying or obscure trend of meaning or discourse ⟨a racist *drift* runs through all of his works⟩.

Tenor stresses a clearly perceptible direction and a continuous, undeviating course ⟨a suburb seeking to maintain its *tenor* of tranquility⟩.

Current implies a clearly defined but not necessarily unalterable course ⟨an encounter that altered forever the *current* of my life⟩.

THIN, slender, slim, slight, tenuous mean not thick, broad, abundant, or dense.

Thin implies comparatively little extension between surfaces or in diameter. or it may imply lack of substance. richness. or abundance ⟨*thin* wire⟩ ⟨soup that was *thin* and tasteless⟩.

Slender implies leanness or spareness often with grace and good proportion ⟨the *slender* legs of a Sheraton chair⟩.

Slim applies to slenderness that suggests fragility or scantiness ⟨a *slim* volume of poetry⟩ ⟨a *slim* chance of success⟩.

Slight implies smallness as well as thinness ⟨the *slight* build of a professional jockey⟩.

Tenuous implies extreme thinness. sheerness. or lack of substance and firmness ⟨the sword hung by a *tenuous* thread⟩.

THINK *vb* **Think, conceive, imagine, fancy, realize, envisage, envision** mean to form an idea of.

Think implies the entrance of an idea into one's mind with or without deliberate consideration or reflection ⟨I just *thought* of a good story⟩.

Conceive suggests the forming and bringing forth and usu. developing of an idea. plan. or design ⟨*conceive* of a plan to rescue the hostages⟩.

Imagine stresses a visualization ⟨*imagine* a permanently operating space station⟩.

Fancy suggests an imagining often unrestrained by reality but spurred by desires ⟨*fancied* himself a super athlete⟩.

Realize stresses a grasping of the significance of what is conceived or imagined ⟨*realized* the enormity of the task ahead⟩.

Envisage and **envision** imply a conceiving or imagining that is esp. clear or detailed ⟨*envisaged* a totally computerized operation⟩ ⟨*envisioned* a world free from hunger and want⟩.

THINK *vb* **Think, cogitate, reflect, reason, speculate, deliberate** mean to use one's powers of conception. judgment. or inference.

Think is general and may apply to any mental activity. but used alone often suggests attainment of clear ideas or conclusions ⟨a course that really teaches you to *think*⟩.

Cogitate implies deep or intent thinking ⟨quietly sitting and *cogitating* on the mysteries of nature⟩.

Reflect suggests unhurried consideration of something recalled to the mind ⟨*reflected* on fifty years of married life⟩.

Reason stresses consecutive logical thinking ⟨*reasoned* that the murderer and victim knew each other⟩.

Speculate implies reasoning about things theoretical or problematic ⟨historians have *speculated* about the fate of the Lost Colony⟩.

Deliberate suggests slow or careful reasoning before forming an opinion or reaching a conclusion or decision ⟨the jury *deliberated* for five hours⟩.

THROW, cast, toss, fling, hurl, pitch, sling mean to cause to move swiftly through space by a propulsive movement or a propelling force.

Throw is general and interchangeable with the other terms but may specif. imply a distinctive motion with bent arm ⟨*throws* the ball with great accuracy⟩.

Cast usu. implies lightness in the thing thrown and sometimes a scattering ⟨*cast* bread crumbs to the birds⟩.

Toss suggests a light or careless or aimless throwing and may imply an upward motion ⟨*tossed* her racket on the bed⟩.

Fling stresses a violent throwing ⟨*flung* the ring back in his face⟩.

Hurl implies power as in throwing a massive weight ⟨*hurled* the intruder out the window⟩.

Pitch suggests throwing carefully at a target ⟨*pitch* horseshoes⟩.

Sling suggests propelling with a sweeping or swinging motion, usu. with force and suddenness ⟨*slung* the bag over his shoulder⟩.

TIRE, weary, fatigue, exhaust, jade, fag mean to make or become unable or unwilling to continue.

Tire implies a draining of one's strength or patience ⟨the long ride *tired* us out⟩.

Weary stresses tiring until one is unable to endure more of the same thing ⟨*wearied* of the constant arguing⟩.

Fatigue suggests causing great lassitude through excessive strain or undue effort ⟨*fatigued* by the long, hard climb⟩.

Exhaust implies complete draining of strength by hard exertion ⟨shoveling snow *exhausted* him⟩.

Jade suggests the loss of all freshness and eagerness ⟨*jaded* with the endless round of society parties⟩.

Fag implies a drooping with fatigue ⟨arrived home, all *fagged* out by a day's shopping⟩.

TRACE, vestige, track mean a perceptible sign made by something that has passed.

Trace may suggest any line, mark, or discernible effect ⟨an animal species believed to have vanished without a *trace*⟩.

Vestige applies to a tangible reminder such as a fragment or remnant of what is past and gone ⟨boulders that are *vestiges* of the last ice age⟩.

Track implies a continuous line that can be followed ⟨the fossilized *tracks* of dinosaurs⟩.

TRANSFORM, metamorphose, transmute, convert, transmogrify, transfigure mean to change a thing into a different thing.

Transform implies a major change in form, nature, or function ⟨*transformed* a small company into a corporate giant⟩.

Metamorphose suggests an abrupt or startling change induced by or as if by magic or a supernatural power ⟨*metamorphosed* awkward girls into graceful ballerinas⟩.

Transmute implies transforming into a higher element or thing ⟨*transmuted* a shopworn tale into a psychological masterpiece⟩.

Convert implies a change fitting something for a new or different use or function ⟨*converted* the boys' room into a guest bedroom⟩.

Transmogrify suggests a grotesque or preposterous metamorphosis ⟨the prince was *transmogrified* into a frog⟩.

Transfigure implies a change that exalts or glorifies ⟨ecstasy *transfigured* her face⟩.

TRANSIENT, transitory, ephemeral, momentary, fugitive, fleeting, evanescent mean lasting or staying only a short time.

Transient applies to what is actually short in its duration or stay ⟨a hotel catering primarily to *transient* guests⟩.

Transitory applies to what is by its nature or essence bound to change, pass, or come to an end ⟨fame in the movies is *transitory*⟩.

Ephemeral implies striking brevity of life or duration ⟨many slang words are *ephemeral*⟩.

Momentary suggests coming and going quickly and therefore being merely a brief interruption of a more enduring state ⟨my feelings of guilt were only *momentary*⟩.

Fugitive and **fleeting** imply passing so quickly as to make apprehending difficult ⟨in winter the days are short and sunshine is *fugitive*⟩ ⟨a life with only *fleeting* moments of joy⟩.

Evanescent suggests a quick vanishing and an airy or fragile quality ⟨the story has an *evanescent* touch of whimsy that is lost on stage⟩.

TRESPASS *vb* **Trespass, encroach, entrench, infringe, invade** mean to make inroads upon the property, territory, or rights of another.

Trespass implies an unwarranted, unlawful, or offensive intrusion ⟨warned people about *trespassing* on their land⟩.

Encroach suggests gradual or stealthy entrance upon another's territory or usurpation of his rights or possessions ⟨on guard against laws that *encroach* upon our civil rights⟩.

Entrench suggests establishing and maintaining oneself in a position of advantage or profit at the expense of others ⟨opposed to regulations that *entrench* upon free enterprise⟩.

Infringe implies an encroachment clearly violating a right or prerogative ⟨a product that *infringes* upon another's patent⟩.

Invade implies a hostile and injurious entry into the territory or sphere of another ⟨practices that *invade* our right to privacy⟩.

TRICK *n* **Trick, ruse, stratagem, maneuver, artifice, wile, feint** mean an indirect means to gain an end.

Trick may imply deception, roguishness, illusion, and either an evil or harmless end ⟨used every *trick* to get the teacher's attention⟩.

Ruse stresses an attempt to mislead by a false impression ⟨the *ruses* of smugglers⟩.

Stratagem implies a ruse used to entrap, outwit, circumvent, or surprise an opponent or enemy ⟨a series of *stratagems* that convinced both sides he was their agent⟩.

Maneuver suggests adroit and skillful avoidance of difficulty ⟨a bold *maneuver* that won him the nomination⟩.

Artifice implies ingenious contrivance or invention ⟨his fawning smile was just an *artifice*⟩.

Wile suggests an attempt to entrap or deceive with false allurements ⟨used all of his *wiles* to win his uncle's favor⟩.

Feint implies a diversion or distraction of attention away from one's real intent ⟨ballcarriers use *feints* to draw defensemen out of position⟩.

TRIFLE, toy, dally, flirt, coquet mean to deal with or act toward without serious purpose.

Trifle may imply playfulness, unconcern, indulgent contempt ⟨*trifled* with her boyfriend's feelings⟩.

Toy implies acting without full attention or serious exertion of one's powers ⟨*toying* with the idea of taking a cruise⟩.

Dally suggests indulging in thoughts or plans merely as an amusement ⟨likes to *dally* with the idea of writing a book someday⟩.

Flirt implies an interest or attention that soon passes to another object ⟨*flirted* with one college major after another⟩.

Coquet implies attracting interest or admiration without serious intention ⟨brazenly *coquetted* with the husbands of her friends⟩.

TRITE, hackneyed, stereotyped, threadbare mean lacking the freshness that evokes attention or interest.

Trite applies to a once effective phrase or idea spoiled from long familiarity ⟨"you win some, you lose some" is a *trite* expression⟩.

Hackneyed stresses being worn out by overuse so as to become dull and meaningless ⟨all of the metaphors and images in the poem are *hackneyed*⟩.

Stereotyped implies falling invariably into the same pattern or form ⟨views of American Indians that are *stereotyped* and out-of-date⟩.

Threadbare applies to what has been used until its possibilities of interest have been totally exhausted ⟨a mystery novel with a *threadbare* plot⟩.

TRUTH, veracity, verity, verisimilitude mean the quality of keeping close to fact or reality.

Truth may apply to an ideal abstraction conforming to a universal or generalized reality or it may represent a quality of statements, acts, or feelings of adhering to reality and avoiding error or falsehood ⟨swore to the *truth* of the statement he had made⟩.

Veracity implies rigid and unfailing observance of truth ⟨a politician not known for his *veracity*⟩.

Verity refers to things of lasting, ultimate, or transcendent value ⟨a teacher still believing in the old *verities* of school pride and loyalty⟩.

Verisimilitude implies the quality of an artistic or literary representation that causes one to accept it as true to life or to human experience ⟨a novel about contemporary marriage that was praised for its *verisimilitude*⟩.

TYPE, kind, sort, nature, description, character mean a number of individuals thought of as a group because of a common quality or qualities.

Type may suggest strong and clearly marked similarity

throughout the items included so that each is typical of the group ⟨one of three basic body *types*⟩.

Kind may suggest natural grouping ⟨a zoo with animals of every *kind*⟩.

Sort often suggests some disparagement ⟨the *sort* of newspaper dealing in sensational stories⟩.

Nature may imply inherent, essential resemblance rather than obvious or superficial likenesses ⟨two problems of a similar *nature*⟩.

Description implies a group marked by agreement in all details belonging to a type as described or defined ⟨not all individuals of that *description* are truly psychotic⟩.

Character implies a group marked by distinctive likenesses peculiar to the type ⟨a society with little of the *character* of an advanced culture⟩.

U

UNCERTAINTY, doubt, dubiety, skepticism, suspicion, mistrust mean lack of sureness about someone or something.

Uncertainty may range from a falling short of certainty to an almost complete lack of definite knowledge esp. about an outcome or result ⟨general *uncertainty* about the program's future⟩.

Doubt suggests both uncertainty and inability to make a decision ⟨plagued by *doubts* about his upcoming marriage⟩.

Dubiety stresses a wavering between conclusions ⟨in times of crisis a leader must be free of all *dubiety*⟩.

Skepticism implies unwillingness to believe without conclusive evidence ⟨an economic forecast that was met with *skepticism*⟩.

Suspicion stresses lack of faith in the truth, reality, fairness, or reliability of something or someone ⟨viewed the new neighbors with *suspicion*⟩.

Mistrust implies a genuine doubt based upon suspicion ⟨had a great *mistrust* of all doctors⟩.

UNDERSTAND, comprehend, appreciate mean to have a clear or complete idea of.

Understand may differ from **comprehend** in implying a result whereas *comprehend* stresses the mental process of arriving at a result ⟨*understood* the instructions without *comprehending* their purpose⟩.

Appreciate implies a just estimation of a thing's value ⟨failed to *appreciate* the risks involved⟩.

UNITY, solidarity, integrity, union mean the quality of a whole made up of closely associated parts.

Unity implies oneness esp. of what is varied and diverse in its elements or parts ⟨a multiplicity of styles effectively combined into a *unity* of architectural design⟩.

Solidarity implies a unity in a group or class that enables it to manifest its strength and exert its influence as one ⟨an ethnic minority with a strong sense of *solidarity*⟩.

Integrity implies unity that indicates interdependence of the parts and completeness and perfection of the whole ⟨a farcical scene that destroys the play's *integrity*⟩.

Union implies a thorough integration and harmonious cooperation of the parts ⟨the *union* of 13 diverse colonies into one nation⟩.

UNIVERSAL, general, generic mean of or relating to all or the whole.

Universal implies reference to every one without exception in the class, category, or genus considered; **general** implies reference to all or nearly all ⟨the theory has met *general* but not *universal* acceptance⟩.

Generic implies reference to every member of a genus ⟨*generic* likenesses among all dogs⟩.

UNNERVE, enervate, unman, emasculate mean to deprive of strength or vigor and the capacity for effective action.

Unnerve implies marked often temporary loss of courage, self-control, or power to act ⟨*unnerved* by the near midair collision⟩.

Enervate suggests a gradual physical or moral weakening (as through luxury or indolence) until one is too feeble to make an effort ⟨totally *enervated* after a week's vacation⟩.

Unman implies a loss of manly vigor, fortitude, or spirit ⟨the sight of blood usually *unmanned* him⟩.

Emasculate stresses a depriving of characteristic force by removing something essential ⟨an amendment that *emasculates* existing gun-control laws⟩.

UNRULY, ungovernable, intractable, refractory, recalcitrant, willful, headstrong mean not submissive to government or control.

Unruly implies lack of discipline or incapacity for discipline and often connotes waywardness or turbulence of behavior ⟨*unruly* children⟩.

Ungovernable implies either an escape from control or guidance or a state of being unsubdued and incapable of controlling oneself or being controlled by others ⟨*ungovernable* rage⟩.

Intractable suggests stubborn resistance to guidance or control ⟨the farmers were *intractable* in their opposition to the hazardous-waste dump⟩.

Refractory stresses resistance to attempts to manage or to mold ⟨special schools for *refractory* children⟩.

Recalcitrant suggests determined resistance to or defiance of authority ⟨acts of sabotage by a *recalcitrant* populace⟩.

Willful implies an obstinate determination to have one's own way ⟨a *willful* disregard for the rights of others⟩.

Headstrong suggests self-will impatient of restraint, advice, or suggestion ⟨a *headstrong* young cavalry officer⟩.

UPRIGHT, honest, just, conscientious, scrupulous, honorable mean having or showing a strict regard for what is morally right.

Upright implies a strict adherence to moral principles ⟨ministers of the church must be *upright* and unimpeachable⟩.

Honest stresses adherence to such virtues as truthfulness, candor, fairness ⟨doctors must be *honest* with the terminally ill⟩.

Just stresses conscious choice and regular practice of what is right or equitable ⟨a reputation for being entirely *just* in business dealings⟩.

Conscientious and **scrupulous** imply an active moral sense governing all one's actions and painstaking efforts to follow one's conscience ⟨*conscientious* in doing all of her chores⟩ ⟨*scrupulous* in carrying out the terms of the will⟩.

Honorable suggests a firm holding to codes of right behavior and the guidance of a high sense of honor and duty ⟨the *honorable* thing would be to resign my position⟩.

USE, employ, utilize mean to put into service esp. to attain an end.

Use implies availing oneself of something as a means or instrument to an end ⟨willing to *use* any means to achieve her ends⟩.

Employ suggests the use of a person or thing that is available but idle, inactive, or disengaged ⟨your time might have been better *employed* by reading⟩.

Utilize may suggest the discovery of a new, profitable, or practical use for something ⟨meat processors *utilize* every part of the animal⟩.

USUAL, customary, habitual, wonted, accustomed mean familiar through frequent or regular repetition.

Usual stresses the absence of strangeness or unexpectedness ⟨my *usual* order for lunch⟩.

Customary applies to what accords with the practices, conventions, or usages of an individual or community ⟨a *customary* waiting period before the application is approved⟩.

Habitual suggests a practice settled or established by much repetition ⟨an *habitual* exercise regime that served her well⟩.

Wonted stresses habituation but usu. applies to what is favored, sought, or purposefully cultivated ⟨his *wonted* determination⟩.

Accustomed is less emphatic than *wonted* or *habitual* in suggesting fixed habit or invariable custom ⟨accepted the compliment with her *accustomed* modesty⟩.

V

VAIN, nugatory, otiose, idle, empty, hollow mean being without worth or significance.

Vain implies either absolute or relative absence of value ⟨it is *vain* to think that we can alter destiny⟩.

Nugatory suggests triviality or insignificance ⟨a monarch with *nugatory* powers⟩.

Otiose suggests that something serves no purpose and is either an encumbrance or a superfluity ⟨not a single scene in the film is *otiose*⟩.

Idle suggests being incapable of worthwhile use or effect ⟨it is *idle* to speculate on what might have been⟩.

Empty and **hollow** suggest a deceiving lack of real substance or soundness or genuineness ⟨an *empty* attempt at reconciliation⟩ ⟨a *hollow* victory that benefited no one⟩.

See in addition FUTILE.

VALID, sound, cogent, convincing, telling mean having such force as to compel serious attention and usu. acceptance.

Valid implies being supported by objective truth or generally accepted authority ⟨absences will be excused for *valid* reasons⟩.

Sound implies a basis of flawless reasoning or of solid grounds ⟨a *sound* proposal for combatting terrorism⟩.

Cogent may stress either weight of sound argument and evidence or lucidity of presentation ⟨the prosecutor's *cogent* summation won over the jury⟩.

Convincing suggests a power to overcome doubt, opposition, or reluctance to accept ⟨a documentary that makes a *convincing* case for court reform⟩.

Telling stresses an immediate and crucial effect striking at the heart of a matter ⟨a *telling* example of the bureaucratic mentality⟩.

VERTICAL, perpendicular, plumb mean being at right angles to a baseline.

Vertical suggests a line or direction rising straight upward toward a zenith ⟨the side of the cliff is almost *vertical*⟩.

Perpendicular may stress the straightness of a line making a right angle with any other line, not necessarily a horizontal one ⟨the parallel bars are *perpendicular* to the support posts⟩.

Plumb stresses an exact verticality determined (as with a plumb line) by earth's gravity ⟨make sure that the wall is *plumb*⟩.

VICIOUS, villainous, iniquitous, nefarious, corrupt, degenerate mean highly reprehensible or offensive in character. nature, or conduct.

Vicious may directly oppose *virtuous* in implying moral depravity, or may connote malignancy, cruelty, or destructive violence ⟨a *vicious* gangster wanted for murder⟩.

Villainous applies to any evil, depraved, or vile conduct or characteristic ⟨*villainous* behavior that must be punished⟩.

Iniquitous implies absence of all signs of justice or fairness ⟨an *iniquitous* tyrant, ruling by fear and intimidation⟩.

Nefarious suggests flagrant breaching of time-honored laws and traditions of conduct ⟨pornography, prostitution, and organized crime's other *nefarious* activities⟩.

Corrupt stresses a loss of moral integrity or probity causing betrayal of principle or sworn obligations ⟨city hall was filled with *corrupt* politicians⟩.

Degenerate suggests having sunk to an esp. vicious or enervated condition ⟨a *degenerate* regime propped up by foreign support⟩.

VIGOROUS, energetic, strenuous, lusty, nervous mean having great vitality and force.

Vigorous further implies showing no signs of depletion or diminishing of freshness or robustness ⟨still *vigorous* and sharp in her eightieth year⟩.

Energetic suggests a capacity for intense activity ⟨an *energetic* wife, mother, and career woman⟩.

Strenuous suggests a preference for coping with the arduous or the challenging ⟨moved to Alaska in search of the *strenuous* life⟩.

Lusty implies exuberant energy and capacity for enjoyment ⟨a huge meal to satisfy their *lusty* appetites⟩.

Nervous suggests esp. the forcibleness and sustained effectiveness resulting from mental vigor ⟨a *nervous* energy informs his sculptures⟩.

VOCIFEROUS, clamorous, blatant, strident, boisterous, obstreperous mean so loud or insistent as to compel attention.

Vociferous implies a vehement deafening shouting or calling out ⟨*vociferous* cries of protest and outrage⟩.

Clamorous may imply insistency as well as vociferousness in demanding or protesting ⟨*clamorous* demands for prison reforms⟩.

Blatant implies an offensive bellowing or insensitive loudness ⟨a *blatant* and abusive drunkard⟩.

Strident suggests harsh and discordant noise ⟨heard the *strident* cry of the crow⟩.

Boisterous suggests a noisiness and turbulence due to high spirits ⟨a *boisterous* crowd of partygoers⟩.

Obstreperous suggests unruly and aggressive noisiness and resistance to restraint ⟨the *obstreperous* demonstrators were removed from the hall⟩.

VOLUNTARY, intentional, deliberate, willing mean done or brought about of one's own will.

Voluntary implies freedom and spontaneity of choice or action without external compulsion ⟨*voluntary* enlistment in the armed services⟩.

Intentional stresses an awareness of an end to be achieved ⟨the *intentional* concealment of vital information⟩.

Deliberate implies full consciousness of the nature of one's act and its consequences ⟨the *deliberate* sabotaging of a nuclear power plant⟩.

Willing implies a readiness and eagerness to accede to or anticipate the wishes of another ⟨a *willing* accomplice in a bank robbery⟩.

VORACIOUS, gluttonous, ravenous, rapacious mean excessively greedy.

Voracious applies esp. to habitual gorging with food or drink ⟨teenagers are often *voracious* eaters⟩.

Gluttonous applies to one who delights in eating or acquiring things esp. beyond the point of necessity or satiety ⟨an admiral who was *gluttonous* for glory⟩.

Ravenous implies excessive hunger and suggests violent or grasping methods of dealing with food or with whatever satisfies an appetite ⟨football practice usually gives them *ravenous* appetites⟩.

Rapacious often suggests excessive and utterly selfish acquisitiveness or avarice ⟨*rapacious* land developers indifferent to the ruination of the environment⟩.

W

WANDER, roam, ramble, rove, traipse, meander mean to move about more or less aimlessly.

Wander implies an absence of or an indifference to a fixed course ⟨found her *wandering* about the square⟩.

Roam suggests wandering about freely and often far afield ⟨liked to *roam* through the woods⟩.

Ramble stresses carelessness and indifference to one's course or objective ⟨the speaker *rambled* on without ever coming to the point⟩.

Rove suggests vigorous and sometimes purposeful roaming ⟨armed brigands *roved* over the countryside⟩.

Traipse implies an erratic if purposeful course ⟨*traipsed* all over town looking for the right dress⟩.

Meander implies a winding or intricate course suggestive of aimless or listless wandering ⟨the river *meanders* for miles through rich farmland⟩.

WATCHFUL, vigilant, wide-awake, alert mean being on the lookout esp. for danger or opportunity.

Watchful is the least explicit term ⟨played under the *watchful* eyes of their mothers⟩.

Vigilant suggests intense, unremitting, wary watchfulness ⟨*vigilant* taxpayers forestalled all attempts to raise taxes⟩.

Wide-awake applies to watchfulness for opportunities and developments more often than dangers ⟨*wide-awake* observers will recall other summit meetings⟩.

Alert stresses readiness or promptness in meeting danger or in seizing opportunity ⟨*alert* traders anticipated the stock market's slide⟩.

WEAK, feeble, frail, fragile, infirm, decrepit mean not strong enough to endure strain, pressure, or strenuous effort.

Weak applies to deficiency or inferiority in strength or power of any sort ⟨a *weak* government likely to topple soon⟩.

Feeble suggests extreme weakness inviting pity or contempt ⟨a *feeble* attempt to resist the enemy attack⟩.

Frail implies delicacy and slightness of constitution or structure ⟨a once-robust man now *frail* with disease⟩.

Fragile suggest frailty and brittleness unable to resist rough usage ⟨a *fragile* beauty that the camera cannot convey⟩.

Infirm suggests instability, unsoundness, and insecurity due to old age or crippling illness ⟨an *infirm* old woman confined to her home⟩.

Decrepit implies being worn-out or broken-down from long use or old age ⟨the *decrepit* butler had been with the family for years⟩.

WEAKEN, enfeeble, debilitate, undermine, sap, cripple, disable mean to lose or cause to lose strength or vigor.

Weaken may imply loss of physical strength, health, soundness, or stability or of quality, intensity, or effective power ⟨a disease that *weakens* the body's defenses⟩.

Enfeeble implies an obvious and pitiable condition of weakness and helplessness ⟨so *enfeebled* by arthritis that he requires constant care⟩.

Debilitate suggests a less marked or more temporary impairment of strength or vitality ⟨the operation has a temporary *debilitating* effect⟩.

Undermine and **sap** suggest a weakening by something working surreptitiously and insidiously ⟨a poor diet *undermines* your health⟩ ⟨drugs had *sapped* his ability to think⟩.

Cripple implies causing a serious loss of functioning power through damaging or removing an essential part or element ⟨inflation had *crippled* the economy⟩.

Disable suggests a usu. sudden crippling or enfeebling ⟨*disabled* soldiers received an immediate discharge⟩.

WEIRD, eerie, uncanny mean mysteriously strange or fantastic.

Weird may imply an unearthly or supernatural strangeness or it may stress queerness or oddness ⟨*weird* creatures from another world⟩.

Eerie suggests an uneasy or fearful consciousness that mysterious and malign powers are at work ⟨an *eerie* calm preceded the bombing raid⟩.

Uncanny implies disquieting strangeness or mysteriousness ⟨bore an *uncanny* resemblance to his dead wife⟩.

WET, damp, dank, moist, humid mean covered or more or less soaked with liquid.

Wet usu. implies saturation but may suggest a covering of a surface with water or something (as paint) not yet dry ⟨slipped on the *wet* pavement⟩.

Damp implies a slight or moderate absorption and often connotes an unpleasant degree of moisture ⟨clothes will mildew if stored in a *damp* place⟩.

Dank implies a more distinctly disagreeable or unwholesome dampness ⟨a prisoner in a cold, *dank* cell⟩.

Moist applies to what is slightly damp or not felt as dry ⟨treat the injury with *moist* heat⟩.

Humid applies to the presence of much water vapor in the air ⟨the hot, *humid* conditions brought on heatstroke⟩.

WHOLE, entire, total, all mean including everything or everyone without exception.

Whole implies that nothing has been omitted, ignored, abated, or taken away ⟨read the *whole* book⟩.

Entire may suggest a state of completeness or perfection to which nothing can be added ⟨the *entire* population was wiped out⟩.

Total implies that everything has been counted, weighed, measured, or considered ⟨the *total* number of people present⟩.

All may equal *whole, entire,* or *total* ⟨*all* their money went to pay the rent⟩.

See in addition PERFECT.

WISE, sage, sapient, judicious, prudent, sensible, sane mean having or showing sound judgment.

Wise suggests great understanding of people and of situations and unusual discernment and judgment in dealing with them ⟨*wise* enough to know what really mattered in life⟩.

Sage suggests wide experience, great learning, and wisdom ⟨sought the *sage* advice of her father in times of crisis⟩.

Sapient suggests great sagacity and discernment ⟨the *sapient* observations of a veteran foreign correspondent⟩.

Judicious stresses a capacity for reaching wise decisions or just conclusions ⟨*judicious* parents using kindness and discipline in equal measure⟩.

Prudent suggests exercise of the restraint of sound practical wisdom and discretion ⟨a *prudent* decision to wait out the storm⟩.

Sensible applies to action guided and restrained by good sense and rationality ⟨a *sensible* woman who was not fooled by flattery⟩.

Sane stresses mental soundness, rationality, and levelheadedness ⟨remained *sane* even as the war raged around him⟩.

WIT, humor, irony, sarcasm, satire, repartee mean a mode of expression intended to arouse amusement.

Wit suggests the power to evoke laughter by remarks showing verbal felicity or ingenuity and swift perception esp. of the incongruous ⟨appreciate the *wit* of Wilde and Shaw⟩.

Humor implies an ability to perceive the ludicrous, the comical, and the absurd in human life and to express these usu. without bitterness ⟨a person with a finely honed sense of *humor*⟩.

Irony applies to a manner of expression in which the intended meaning is the opposite of what is seemingly expressed ⟨with wry *irony*, he said to the priest, "Thank God I'm an atheist!"⟩.

Sarcasm applies to expression frequently in the form of irony that is intended to cut or wound ⟨a cynic much given to heartless *sarcasm*⟩.

Satire applies to writing that exposes or ridicules conduct, doctrines, or institutions either by direct criticism or more often through irony, parody, or caricature ⟨the play is a *satire* on contemporary living arrangements⟩.

Repartee implies the power of answering quickly, pointedly, or wittily ⟨a dinner guest noted for *repartee*⟩.

WITTY, humorous, facetious, jocular, jocose mean provoking or intended to provoke laughter.

Witty suggests cleverness and quickness of mind and often a caustic tongue ⟨a film critic remembered for his *witty* reviews⟩.

Humorous applies broadly to anything that evokes usu. genial laughter and may contrast with *witty* in suggesting whimsicality or eccentricity ⟨laced her lectures with *humorous* anecdotes⟩.

Facetious stresses a desire to produce laughter and may be derogatory in implying dubious or ill-timed attempts at wit or humor ⟨*facetious* comments that were unappreciated⟩.

Jocular implies a usu. habitual fondness for jesting and joking ⟨a *jocular* fellow whose humor often brightened spirits⟩.

Jocose is somewhat less derogatory than *facetious* in suggesting habitual waggishness or playfulness ⟨the dim-witted took his *jocose* proposals seriously⟩.

WORDY, verbose, prolix, diffuse mean using more words than necessary to express thought.

Wordy may also imply loquaciousness or garrulity ⟨a *wordy* speech that said nothing⟩.

Verbose suggests a resulting dullness, obscurity, or lack of incisiveness or precision ⟨*verbose* position papers that no one reads⟩.

Prolix suggests unreasonable and tedious dwelling on details ⟨habitually transformed brief anecdotes into *prolix* sagas⟩.

Diffuse stresses lack of compactness and pointedness of style ⟨*diffuse* memoirs that are so many shaggy-dog stories⟩.

WORK *n* **Work, labor, travail, toil, drudgery, grind** mean activity involving effort or exertion.

Work may imply activity of body, of mind, of a machine, or of a natural force ⟨too tired to do any *work*⟩.

Labor applies to physical or intellectual work involving great and often strenuous exertion ⟨believes that farmers are poorly paid for their *labor*⟩.

Travail is bookish for labor involving pain or suffering ⟨years of *travail* were lost when the building burned⟩.

Toil implies prolonged and fatiguing labor ⟨his lot would be years of backbreaking *toil*⟩.

Drudgery suggests dull and irksome labor ⟨a job with a good deal of *drudgery*⟩.

Grind implies labor exhausting to mind or body ⟨the *grind* of performing the play eight times a week⟩.

WORK *n* Work, employment, occupation, calling, pursuit, métier, business mean a specific sustained activity engaged in esp. in earning one's living.

Work may apply to any purposeful activity whether remunerative or not ⟨her *work* as a hospital volunteer⟩.

Employment implies work for which one has been engaged and is being paid by an employer ⟨*employment* will be terminated in cases of chronic tardiness⟩.

Occupation implies work in which one engages regularly esp. as a result of training ⟨his *occupation* as a trained auto mechanic⟩.

Calling applies to an occupation viewed as a vocation or profession ⟨I feel the ministry is my true *calling*⟩.

Pursuit suggests a trade, profession, or avocation followed with zeal or steady interest ⟨her family considered medicine the only proper *pursuit*⟩.

Métier implies a calling or pursuit for which one believes oneself to be esp. fitted ⟨from childhood I considered acting my *métier*⟩.

Business suggests activity in commerce or the management of money and affairs ⟨the *business* of managing a hotel⟩.

WORRY *vb* Worry, annoy, harass, harry, plague, pester, tease mean to disturb or irritate by persistent acts.

Worry implies an incessant goading or attacking that drives one to desperation ⟨pursued a policy of *worrying* the enemy⟩.

Annoy implies disturbing one's composure or peace of mind by intrusion, interference, or petty attacks ⟨you're doing that just to *annoy* me⟩.

Harass implies petty persecutions or burdensome demands that exhaust one's nervous or mental power ⟨*harassed* on all sides by creditors⟩.

Harry may imply heavy oppression or maltreatment ⟨*harried* mothers trying to cope with small children⟩.

Plague implies a painful and persistent affliction 〈*plagued* all her life by poverty〉.

Pester stresses the repetition of petty attacks 〈the bureau was constantly *pestered* with trivial complaints〉.

Tease suggests an attempt to break down one's resistance or rouse to wrath 〈malicious children *teased* the dog〉.

WRONG *vb* **Wrong, oppress, persecute, aggrieve** mean to injure unjustly or outrageously.

Wrong implies inflicting injury either unmerited or out of proportion to what one deserves 〈a penal system that had *wronged* him〉.

Oppress suggests inhumane imposing of burdens one cannot endure or exacting more than one can perform 〈a people *oppressed* by a warmongering tyrant〉.

Persecute implies a relentless and unremitting subjection to annoyance or suffering 〈a child *persecuted* by constant criticism〉.

Aggrieve implies suffering caused by an infringement or denial of rights 〈a legal aid society representing *aggrieved* minority groups〉.

Y

YIELD, submit, capitulate, succumb, relent, defer mean to give way to someone or something that one can no longer resist.

Yield may apply to any sort or degree of giving way before force, argument, persuasion, or entreaty 〈*yields* too easily in any argument〉.

Submit suggests full surrendering after resistance or conflict to the will or control of another 〈voluntarily *submitted* to an inspection of the premises〉.

Capitulate stresses the fact of ending all resistance and may imply either a coming to terms (as with an adversary) or hopelessness in the face of an irresistible opposing force 〈the college president *capitulated* to the protesters' demands〉.

Succumb implies weakness and helplessness to the one that gives way or an overwhelming power to the opposing force ⟨a stage actor *succumbing* to the lure of Hollywood⟩.

Relent implies a yielding through pity or mercy by one who holds the upper hand ⟨finally *relented* and let the children stay up late⟩.

Defer implies a voluntary yielding or submitting out of respect or reverence for or deference and affection toward another ⟨I *defer* to your superior expertise in these matters⟩.

See in addition RELINQUISH.